PHYSICS for Tomorrow's World

Revised Second Edition

E. L. McFarland
A. J. Hirsch

NELSON EDUCATION

NELSON EDUCATION

Printed and bound in Canada
1 2 3 4 14 13 12 11

For more information contact Nelson Education Ltd., 1120 Birchmount Road, Toronto, Ontario, M1K 5G4. Or you can visit our Internet site at http://www.nelson.com

This textbook is a Nelson custom publication. Because your instructor has chosen to produce a custom publication, you pay only for material that you will use in your course.

ISBN-13: 978-0-17-663725-5
ISBN-10: 0-17-663725-7

Cover Credit:
Juli/Shutterstock

PROLOGUE

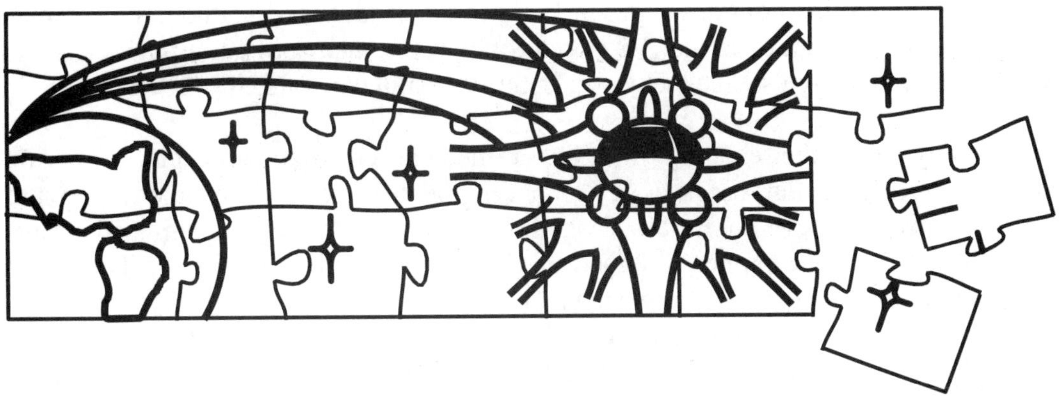

Imagine the year is 2044. The crew of astronauts consists of a mission commander, a flight engineer, a biochemist, and a paleontologist/geologist. They are safely strapped into the inclined control chairs containing sensors that will continually monitor their stress levels, reaction times, memory lapses, and other factors sure to affect the world's first human mission to Mars. Medicines developed to counteract the perils of extreme acceleration have taken effect, and countdown begins. Blastoff — an initial acceleration over 30 times as great as gravity, larger than any human has ever experienced except in test facilities. Such acceleration has been possible only recently as the technology of building a successful matter-antimatter (M-AM) propulsion system for space travel finally caught up with the theory. In the M-AM system, matter and antimatter annihilate each other in a controlled way, producing vast amounts of energy.

The astronauts begin to relax as Earth is left behind; now they must put into action all the years of innovating, planning, practising, and perfecting achieved by thousands of scientists and engineers from around the world who have worked on the project. If you had been on the team responsible for choosing the crew, what criteria would you have suggested? Among other factors, the crew was chosen based on their interdisciplinary knowledge and experience (in fields such as biology, chemistry, physics, mathematics, and computer science), their health, and their physical and mental conditioning. Would these criteria be put to the test soon?

The spacecraft en route to Mars is a marvel of futuristic design and technology. If you had been a member of its design team, what features would you have chosen to provide the safest and most efficient spacecraft? One important feature is the weight of the spacecraft: every component is made of the lightest possible material developed as an application of nanotechnology. The craft's thin outer layer consists of an organic compound that can absorb solar energy and transform it into electrical energy with high efficiency, or, when needed, completely reflect solar energy. Inside the craft, special containers with predetermined quantities of chemical elements feed molecules into machines that use lasers to create substances through chemical reactions. Thus, for example, whenever water is needed, lasers blast hydrogen and oxygen molecules together in the correct proportion.

Lasers, too, are used to recycle all waste material aboard the craft so that absolutely nothing is wasted. Communication devices, although miniaturized, are extremely high-speed and have huge memory capacities. All systems are computer-controlled, with backup systems on the spacecraft as well as at the control centre on Earth. These advanced features help to make the space mission a success, but even more importantly, they are also applied in practical ways here on Earth to improve energy use, reduce waste, improve health care, and sustain the environment.

Just two days into the exciting mission, a medical emergency occurs. The mission commander uses a multi-purpose scanner to check the afflicted astronaut and forwards the images to the medical crew on Earth. Together they analyze the problem and propose an operation using tiny robotic probes designed in Canada that will eliminate it. The astronauts' undersea training involving mock surgical procedures as well as all the experience of using communication systems to aid in medical emergencies around the world in the past half-century have led to efficiency in dealing with the emergency on the spacecraft, and the problem is soon rectified.

The first human mission to Mars is just one possible application of the diverse knowledge gained in the scientific world. In order for today's university students to become tomorrow's innovators, they must be part of that diversity. As such, they will be able to tackle future problems and try to make life better on Earth and, perhaps, in outer space.

It is the hope of the authors of this textbook that you will realize how important it is to have the subject of physics as part of your experience, and that you will enjoy learning how physics can be applied in other disciplines, such as biology, chemistry, and engineering.

This book is dedicated to our two wonderful wives, Mary and Judy, without whose patience, understanding, and support our work would have little meaning.

Acknowledgements: We wish to express sincere gratitude to the following members of the University of Guelph community:

- Carol Croft for her skills and expertise in inputting and formatting the text.
- Jennifer Rock for creating the digitized versions of the diagrams throughout the text.
- Dr. Joanne O'Meara of the Physics Department for her critical analysis and suggestions for improvement.
- The students, teaching assistants, and professors who have used previous editions of the text and offered valuable feedback.

We also wish to thank Rosalind Wright, Paul Fam, and Pamela Duprey at Nelson Education for their support, guidance and assistance.

PHYSICS FOR TOMORROW'S WORLD

Features of the Text

The textbook, *Physics for Tomorrow's World*, has many positive features that assist students in learning about physics and its numerous applications. Those features also assist teachers as they share their knowledge and enthusiasm with their students.

Following is a list of the main features of *Physics for Tomorrow's World.*

- Many helpful hints are provided in boxes with titles such as "Math Tip," "Notation Tip," "Units Tip," and "Problem-Solving Tip."

- "Did You Know?" boxes are used to introduce interesting historical and scientific facts.

- Awareness of common misconceptions held by students has led to a careful explanation of many concepts. For example, the introduction of centripetal force in many textbooks leads to the incorrect impression that centripetal force is a separate force of nature that produces circular motion. In *Physics for Tomorrow's World*, many examples are given to illustrate that centripetal force is just the name given to the resultant force directed toward the centre of the circle. As well, there are word questions in which the students are asked to identify the force(s) that constitute(s) the centripetal force in various situations.

- To aid student understanding, there are many clear drawings, photographs, etc. (on average, 31 per chapter), and many worked sample problems (8 per chapter, on average).

- There is a large selection of questions and problems to choose from – an average of 82 per chapter, including four or more multiple choice questions.

- Consistency in the use of symbols is found throughout the text (e.g., variables, such as d and v, are denoted using italics, and vectors, such as $\boldsymbol{R}$ and $\boldsymbol{g}$ are denoted using boldface italics).

- The answer to each numerical problem is given at the end of the problem. The answers to several narrative and multiple-choice questions are given at the end of each chapter. The latter questions are denoted using underlining (e.g., **<u>1-15</u>** and **<u>2-53</u>**).

- A number of questions, called *Fermi questions* after the famous physicist Enrico Fermi, give students practice in making real-life assumptions and calculations involving physics principles and applications.

- Extreme care has been taken to ensure that the number of significant digits is correct in answers to numerical problems.

- The SI metric system of measurement is used throughout the textbook.

- Since free-body diagrams are very important in analyzing many situations in mechanics, free-body diagrams are introduced painstakingly. There are many introductory questions in which students are asked only to draw free-body diagrams for objects in various circumstances. After students have received a solid foundation in drawing free-body diagrams, Newton's laws of motion are introduced, and more complex problems involving free-body diagrams and Newton's laws are handled.

- Much more attention has been paid to wording than in many textbooks. As an example, consider the use of the term "acceleration." Many books are careful in the chapters on kinematics to ensure that acceleration is considered (correctly) as a vector, with both magnitude and direction, but in the chapters on force, the term "acceleration" is often (incorrectly) used, particularly in problems, to indicate only the magnitude of the acceleration. This can lead to confusion on the part of the students. In *Physics for Tomorrow's World*, if the students are to calculate the magnitude of the acceleration only, this is clearly indicated.

- To add interest, real-life examples are included, not only in the narrative sections but also in the problems. Many of the examples are taken from the biological sciences. For example, the medical application involving positron emission tomography (PET) is featured in the topic of momentum in Chapter 9.

- Student understanding of many of the concepts are explored by word questions as well as numerical problems. For example, in the section on conservation of momentum, students are given word descriptions of various collisions and asked to choose those in which momentum of a particular pair of objects is conserved.

- Each chapter has several useful end-of-chapter features: Chapter Focus (a summary of the chapter), Vocabulary Review, Chapter Review (questions and problems), Applying Your Knowledge (more difficult problems, often integrating material from more than one chapter), Key Objectives, and Answers to Selected Questions. The Key Objectives are important: students use them to determine how well they understand the most important concepts in the chapter; teachers use them as a guideline to set up tests and examinations.

- The end of the textbook features an extensive set of Appendices, in some cases containing details not found in most texts, such as the origins of the metric prefixes in Appendix 3. Also provided is a comprehensive index.

- This textbook has had extensive class testing and revision over several years.

CONTENTS IN BRIEF

CHAPTER	TITLE
1	Measurement and Types of Quantities
2	One-Dimensional Kinematics
3	Vectors
4	Two-Dimensional Kinematics
5	Newton's Laws of Motion
6	Applying Newton's Laws
7	Work, Energy, and Power
8	Momentum and Collisions
9	Gravitation
10	Electric Charge and Electric Field
11	Electric Potential Energy, Potential, and Current
12	Electric Resistance and Circuits
13	Vibrations and Waves
14	Wave Optics
15	Wave-Particle Duality
16	The Quantum Nature of Atoms

The end of each chapter features the following:

- Chapter Focus
- Vocabulary Review
- Chapter Review
- Applying Your Knowledge
- Key Objectives
- Answers to Selected Questions

APPENDICES

1	SI Base Units
2	Some SI Derived Units
3	SI Prefixes
4	Numerical Constants
5	Trigonometric Relations
6	Data for the Sun, Moon, and Planets

TABLE OF CONTENTS

CHAPTER 1
MEASUREMENT AND TYPES OF QUANTITIES

		Page
1.1	The Importance of Measurement	1-1
1.2	Metric Units, Prefixes, and Conversions	1-4
1.3	Dimensional Analysis	1-11
1.4	Significant Digits	1-13
1.5	Types of Quantities	1-19
	End-of-Chapter Features	1-20

CHAPTER 2
ONE-DIMENSIONAL KINEMATICS

		Page
2.1	Distance and Speed	2-1
2.2	Position, Displacement, and Velocity	2-4
2.3	Acceleration	2-13
2.4	Solving Constant-Acceleration Problems	2-20
2.5	Acceleration Due to Gravity	2-28
	End-of-Chapter Features	2-38

CHAPTER 3
VECTORS

		Page
3.1	General Properties of Vectors	3-1
3.2	Addition and Subtraction of Vectors Using Scale Diagrams	3-3
3.3	Addition and Subtraction of Vectors Using Components	3-5
	End-of-Chapter Features	3-10

CHAPTER 4
TWO-DIMENSIONAL KINEMATICS

		Page
4.1	Displacement and Velocity in Two Dimensions	4-1
4.2	Acceleration in Two Dimensions	4-8
4.3	Projectile Motion	4-11
4.4	More Projectile Motion	4-18
4.5	Uniform Circular Motion	4-24
	End-of-Chapter Features	4-30

CHAPTER 5
NEWTON'S LAWS OF MOTION

		Page
5.1	Gravity, Normal Force, Friction, and Tension	5-1
5.2	Adding Forces	5-5
5.3	Newton's Second Law of Motion	5-8
5.4	Newton's First Law of Motion	5-12
5.5	Solving Problems Using Newton's First and Second Laws	5-15
5.6	More Problem-Solving	5-25
5.7	Newton's Third Law of Motion	5-31
5.8	The Fundamental Forces	5-38
	End-of-Chapter Features	5-39

CHAPTER 6
APPLYING NEWTON'S LAWS

		Page
6.1	Static and Kinetic Friction	6-1
6.2	Centripetal Force	6-9
6.3	Centrifugal "Force"	6-17
	End-of-Chapter Features	6-22

CHAPTER 7
WORK, ENERGY, AND POWER

		Page
7.1	Work Done by a Constant Force	7-1
7.2	Kinetic Energy and the Work-Energy Theorem	7-9
7.3	Gravitational Potential Energy	7-13
7.4	Law of Conservation of Energy	7-17
7.5	Work Done by Friction	7-21
7.6	Other Types of Energy	7-25
7.7	Efficiency of Energy Conversions	7-28
7.8	Power	7-32
	End-of-Chapter Features	7-37

CHAPTER 8
MOMENTUM AND COLLISIONS

		Page
8.1	Momentum	8-1
8.2	Conservation of Momentum in One Dimension	8-7
8.3	Elastic and Inelastic Collisions	8-15
8.4	Conservation of Momentum in Two Dimensions	8-22
	End-of-Chapter Features	8-29

CHAPTER 9
GRAVITATION

		Page
9.1	Law of Universal Gravitation	9-1
9.2	Gravity Due to Planets, Stars, etc.	9-7
9.3	Gravitational Field	9-12
9.4	Orbits and Weightlessness	9-16
9.5	Gravitational Potential Energy in General	9-21
	End-of-Chapter Features	9-31

CHAPTER 10
ELECTRIC CHARGE AND ELECTRIC FIELD

		Page
10.1	Electric Charge and Atoms	10-1
10.2	Transfer of Electric Charge	10-2
10.3	Conductors and Insulators	10-6
10.4	Coulomb's Law	10-10
10.5	Electric Field	10-15
10.6	Electric Field Lines	10-19
	End-of-Chapter Features	10-25

CHAPTER 11
ELECTRIC POTENTIAL ENERGY, POTENTIAL, AND CURRENT

		Page
11.1	Electric Potential Energy in a Uniform Electric Field	11-1
11.2	Electric Potential Energy of Point Charges	11-6
11.3	Electric Potential	11-9
11.4	Electric Potential in Various Situations	11-15
11.5	Electric Current	11-20
	End-of-Chapter Features	11-26

CHAPTER 12
ELECTRIC RESISTANCE AND CIRCUITS

		Page
12.1	Electric Resistance and Ohm's Law	12-1
12.2	Batteries and Electric Circuits	12-7
12.3	Resistors in Series and Parallel	12-11
12.4	Electric Energy and power	12-22
12.5	AC Circuits	12-27
	End-of-Chapter Features	12-32

CHAPTER 13
VIBRATIONS AND WAVES

		Page
13.1	Introducing Vibrations and Waves	13-1
13.2	Periodic Waves	13-7
13.3	Interference of Waves	13-19
13.4	Diffraction of Waves	13-30
	End-of-Chapter Features	13-32

CHAPTER 14
WAVE OPTICS

		Page
14.1	Diffraction of Light and Huygens' Principle	14-1
14.2	Double-Slit Interference of Light	14-4
14.3	Single-Slit Diffraction and Resolution	14-11
14.4	Diffraction Gratings and Spectroscopy	14-18
14.5	Refraction of Light	14-24
14.6	Thin-Film Interference	14-31
14.7	Light Theories and the Electromagnetic Spectrum	14-38
14.8	Polarization of Light	14-41
	End-of-Chapter Features	14-51

CHAPTER 15
WAVE-PARTICLE DUALITY

		Page
15.1	The Photoelectric Effect	15-1
15.2	The Compton Effect	15-15
15.3	Matter Waves	15-22
	End-of-Chapter Features	15-27

CHAPTER 16
THE QUANTUM NATURE OF ATOMS

		Page
16.1	Models of Atoms	16-1
16.2	The Bohr Model in Detail	16-7
16.3	De Broglie Electron Waves in Atoms	16-17
16.4	The Quantum-Mechanical (Electron "Cloud") Model of Atoms	16-20
16.5	Lasers	16-24
	End-of-Chapter Features	16-30

APPENDICES

		Page
1	SI Base Units	A-1
2	Some SI Derived Units	A-2
3	SI Prefixes	A-3
4	Numerical Constants	A-4
5	Trigonometric Relations	A-5
6	Data for the Sun, Moon, and Planets	A-9

INDEX

Page
Index-1

CHAPTER 1

MEASUREMENT AND TYPES OF QUANTITIES

Numerous measurements are made daily throughout the world. Some are very important – in the practice of medicine, for example, an error in measurement could endanger the health or even the life of a patient. Countless other measurements, most of which are less critical, are made each day, and many of these affect our personal lives.

We begin this text with topics related to measurement and other mathematical concepts. You may have studied some of these topics before, but just as in sports where you learn the rules of the sport and practise the skills before you begin to play the game, in physics, you learn to use measurement and other mathematical skills before getting into the physics concepts in Chapter 2.

1.1 THE IMPORTANCE OF MEASUREMENT

We use a great variety of ways of describing things: a necklace is beautiful; a new song sounds great; their efforts are boundless, and so on. These statements are called **qualitative descriptions** because they indicate the quality of some object, event, or idea. Such descriptions are subjective; in other words, their meanings depend on a person's previous experience and values, so they differ from one person to another. Thus, these descriptions do not have much value where comparisons must be made or communication must be exact.

Now consider these descriptions: the mass of phosphorus in a vitamin pill is 0.125 g; the air temperature is 32°C; a lecture room can accommodate 600 people; the ratio of the value of a quarter to a dollar is 1:4. These statements are called **quantitative descriptions** because they indicate a quantity. They have the same meaning to everyone who understands them, thus they are objective and they form the basis of comparing and communicating about objects, events, and ideas. Many quantitative descriptions involve counting (600 people), some involve ratios with no units (1:4), while others involve measurements (32°C).

Figure 1-1 *This sign shows poor communication because the measurement does not have a unit. The reader could argue that it means 40 km/h, 40 mi/h, or something else.*

A **measurement** is a numerical quantity found by measuring with a device or an instrument[1]. A measurement is expressed by a number followed by a unit. In the air temperature example, 32 is the number and °C (degrees Celsius) is the unit. To see how important the unit is, compare an air temperature of 32 in

[1]The word "measurement" can also mean the act of measuring.

the Celsius scale with 32 in the Fahrenheit scale. The numbers are the same, but the measurements are not! Another example of the importance of units is shown in Figure 1-1.

Measurement in Our Daily Lives

How do measured quantities affect our daily lives? Measurement of time is important to us: an alarm signals wake-up time; classes begin and end at scheduled times; a part-time job involves salary per unit of time. Length is also relevant: the pant length of a pair of slacks must be your size; the distance you walk, jog, or run each day affects your state of physical fitness. Mass, too, must be considered: groceries are often priced according to their mass in grams or kilograms (or pounds or ounces if the British measurement system is used); a common headache tablet contains 325 mg of acetylsalicylic acid. No doubt you can think of other examples of time, length, and mass, as well as measurements of other quantities that affect your life.

Measurement in the Past

In ancient civilizations, such as those of China, Egypt, Greece, and Rome, measured quantities helped in trading and bartering, in building structures such as temples, pyramids, roads, and irrigation systems, and in judging times for festivities, agricultural endeavours, and other events. Measurements at that time were very crude by today's standards. Consider, for example, the measurement of time. Large time intervals were measured using celestial bodies such as the sun, moon, and stars (Figure 1-2). Shorter time intervals could be measured approximately with dripping water or sand flowing through a narrow opening into a graduated container. More accurate timing devices began to appear during the Renaissance in Europe, especially after Galileo Galilei (1564-1642) of Italy discovered the principle of the pendulum clock.

Figure 1-2 *It is believed that these structures at Stonehenge in England were used to predict eclipses and the changing of the seasons over 3500 years ago.*

Did You Know? *In 1602, Sanctorius, a medical friend of Galileo, invented the pulsologium (a simple pendulum) to measure human pulse rates. The pendulum's length was adjusted until it matched the pulse rate, then the rate was recorded as the length of the pendulum.*

Along with improvements in measurement came developments in scientific experimentation. From about the late 1500s onward, science has continually advanced, in many ways due to the progress in measurement techniques. Evidence of this, as well as other examples of measurement in the past, will be presented later in the text.

Measurement in Physics

An important goal in physics is to analyze whatever can be observed. A physicist might perform an experiment involving measurements, then try to express the measurements in a mathematical equation. In some cases, an equation might lead to a theory explaining whatever was first observed. Often the theory will lead to a new question, which the physicist will try to answer by performing more experiments and measurements. Thus, measurement is an important step in the process of physics (Figure 1-3).

The research and theoretical aspects of physics may lead to practical applications, including biomedical engineering. Here, measurement plays a key role as theory is put into practice in the design and construction of everything from artificial heart valves and pacemakers to contact lenses, tooth braces, and artificial limbs.

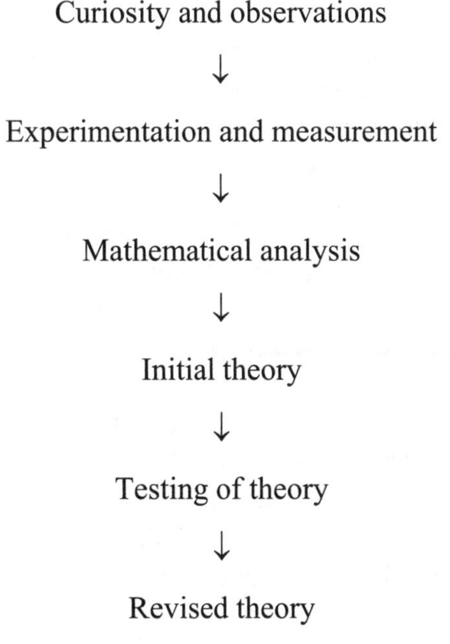

Figure 1-3 *Some basic steps in the development of physics theories.*

Another example involving measurement that is rapidly gaining importance is **nanotechnology**, the application of the study of the properties of extremely tiny particles, some as small as an atom. ("Nano" stems from nanometer, nm, which is 10^{-9} m or one-billionth of a metre. To get an idea of how small this is, a human hair is approximately 40 000 to 80 000 nm in diameter!) Nanoparticles can be used in a large variety of applications, such as treating cancerous tumours, creating efficient solar cells, making fire-resistant glass, and increasing computer memory and speed.

Since measurement is important in understanding physics and solving physics problems, it is the focus of the next three sections.

Practice

1-1 Give three examples of qualitative descriptions involving your sense of (a) taste and (b) smell.

1-2 State three qualitative and three quantitative descriptions of yourself and/or a friend.

1-3 Classify each of the following as a qualitative description or quantitative description:
(a) a dozen roses (b) a deafening noise (c) the fastest runner on the team
(d) a 100-m dash (e) a pulse rate of 56 min^{-1} (f) a blood pressure of 120/80 mm Hg

1-4 For each of the following, cite two examples of measurements that affect your daily lives: time, length, mass, and volume. Use examples other than those given in the text.

1-5 Name and give examples of quantities other than time, length, mass, and volume that you encounter from time to time.

1-6 List disadvantages of using celestial bodies as reference objects to measure time.

1-7 Describe, with examples, the difference(s) between theoretical aspects of physics and practical applications of physics research.

1.2 METRIC UNITS, PREFIXES, AND CONVERSIONS

In order for measurements to be useful in science, industry, and commerce, they must be stated using a set of standard units. A **standard unit** is one that can be reproduced according to its definition and does not change; thus it means the same for everyone using it. An inch and a centimetre are examples of standard units. The most common set of standard units in the world is the metric system. The other standard system is the British (Imperial) system, which is used in about 10% of the countries in the world, including the United States. This book will use the metric system almost exclusively. Science books throughout North America use the metric system, even though industries are slow in making this change. Furthermore, measurements associated with physics are easier to understand and manipulate using the metric system.

Did You Know? *The word "mile" in the British system of measurement originated from the Latin word "mille," which means one thousand. The original "millum" or mile, used during the time of the Roman Empire, was equal to 1000 double paces.*

International standard units are a relatively recent development in human history. Consider, for example, various ways of measuring length in the past. Human anatomy was often used as a reference for length. An English king would decree that the yard was the distance from the tip of his nose to the middle finger of his outstretched arm, and the inch was the width of his thumb. Other units included the fathom, span, palm, and digit. The size of each of these units varied with the size of the king, so the "standard" unit varied from one country to another. As trade and commerce grew, the need for an international standard set of units became obvious.

Base Units in the Metric System

A **base unit** is a standard unit of measurement from which other units may be derived. (Base units are also called *fundamental units.*) Although there are seven base units in the metric system, only the three used to measure length, mass, and time will be considered here. (Appendix 1 includes a complete summary of the metric base units.)

The metric system has several possible units for each measured quantity. However, by international agreement beginning in 1960, the system that has become standard is the *Système International d'Unités*, or simply the **SI**. SI units are used often in physics.

The *metre* (m) is the SI base unit of length.[2] It was originally defined in Paris in 1790, during the French Revolution, by the French Academy of Sciences as one ten-millionth (10^{-7}) of the assumed distance from the equator to the North Pole. Almost 100 years later, in 1889, the metre was redefined as the distance between two fine lines engraved near the ends of a metal bar. This standard metre was stored under controlled conditions near Paris, and copies were sent to countries around the world.

Did You Know? *The word "metre" was chosen from the Greek word "metron," which means "to measure."*

By 1960, there were sufficient improvements in measuring techniques to result in a new definition of the metre: 1 650 763.73 wavelengths of a particular orange-red light emitted by krypton-86 atoms in a vacuum. In an effort to improve precision, the metre was again redefined in 1983, this time in terms of the speed of light in a vacuum, 299 792 458 m/s. The standard metre is currently defined as the distance light travels in a vacuum in 1/(299 792 458) of a second. This quantity is believed to be constant and is reproducible anywhere, so it is an excellent standard.

The SI base unit of time is the *second* (s). Originally it was defined as 1/(86 400) of a mean solar day (1 day = 24 h = 1440 min = 86 400 s). A mean solar day is the length of a day from one high noon to the next, averaged over a period of one year. A tiny error was apparent with this definition because the length of a day depends on Earth's rotation, and that rotation is slowing down very gradually. Thus, an atomic standard was adopted for the second in 1967. One second is the time for 9 192 631 770 vibrations of light of a certain wavelength emitted from a cesium-133 atom, which is believed to be another constant quantity. It is estimated that cesium clocks will not gain or lose more than one second in 30 000 years. Physicists are doing research on a type of hydrogen laser that may be able to keep time to a precision of one second in 3 million years.

Did You Know? *Time standards can be heard on "speaking telephones" by calling certain telephone numbers in North America. A voice regularly states the time every 10 s, and a click is broadcast every second. The Canadian number is 613-745-1576.*

The SI base unit of mass is the *kilogram* (kg). The kilogram is the only base unit with a prefix (kilo), but it is a more convenient size than a gram. As well, the kilogram is the only standard unit not now defined in terms of natural events. Originally the kilogram was defined as the mass of a litre of water at 4°C at sea level, and a metal cylinder with the same mass was built as a standard and kept in France. Later, a small discrepancy was discovered in the measurement of the mass of the water, and the metal cylinder became the standard kilogram. Copies of this standard kilogram mass are kept in major centres around the world.

---

[2]The international spelling of metre will be used throughout this text. This also applies to the unit of liquid volume, the litre. Alternative spellings are meter and liter.

In summary, the standard SI base units for length, time, and mass are, respectively, the metre, second, and kilogram.

Scientific Notation

Very small or very large numbers are awkward to write in long form or key into a calculator. This problem is solved by using powers of ten and expressing the numbers in **scientific notation**. Using scientific notation, also called "standard form," a non-zero digit is placed before the decimal point with other digits after it, then the number is multiplied by the appropriate power of 10. Huge ranges of large to small measurements, listed in Table 1.1, illustrate why scientific notation is more convenient than long form.

When manipulating numbers containing exponents, remember to apply the exponent laws where appropriate:

$$x^{m} \cdot x^{n} = x^{m+n}$$

$$x^{m} \div x^{n} = x^{m-n}$$

$$\left(x^{m}\right)^{n} = x^{mn}$$

$$(xy)^{n} = x^{n} y^{n}$$

$$\left[\frac{x}{y}\right]^{n} = \frac{x^{n}}{y^{n}}$$

Sample Problem 1-1

What is the ratio of the mass of the sun to the mass of a uranium atom?

Solution: From Table 1.1, the ratio is $\dfrac{2\times10^{30}\ \text{kg}}{4\times10^{-25}\ \text{kg}} = 5\times10^{54}$

Thus the ratio of the masses is $5\times10^{54}:1$.

Notice that the units cancel out. Algebraically, units behave just like numbers.

Math Tip: *Use your calculator to perform the calculation in Sample Problem 1-1 to be sure you are using the EE or EXP key correctly. Avoid the error made by some students who try to enter a number like* 10^{24} *and get* 10^{25} *instead because they enter 10 EE 24 instead of the correct entry, 1 EE 24.*

Table 1.1 Ranges of Measurements (All values are approximate.)

Lengths:	Distance to most remote quasar	2×10^{26} m
	Distance to Andromeda Galaxy	2×10^{22} m
	Distance from sun to nearest star	4×10^{16} m
	Radius of Earth's orbit about sun	1.5×10^{11} m
	Diameter of Earth	1.3×10^{7} m
	Diameter of red blood cell	8×10^{-6} m
	Diameter of typical poliovirus	3×10^{-8} m
	Diameter of hydrogen atom	1×10^{-10} m
	Diameter of proton	1×10^{-15} m
Times:	Estimated age of universe	5×10^{17} s
	Age of solar system	1.5×10^{17} s
	Time since start of human existence	1×10^{13} s
	Age of Egyptian pyramids	1.4×10^{11} s
	One year	3.2×10^{7} s
	Time interval between heartbeats	1 s
	Duration of nerve impulse	1×10^{-3} s
	Period of typical radio waves	1×10^{-6} s
	Shortest pulse of light in laboratory	1×10^{-15} s
	Lifetime of a W particle (a boson)	3×10^{-25} s
Masses:	Known universe (estimated)	1×10^{53} kg
	Milky Way Galaxy	8×10^{41} kg
	Sun	2×10^{30} kg
	Earth	6×10^{24} kg
	Small mountain	1×10^{12} kg
	Ocean liner	8×10^{7} kg
	Car	1×10^{3} kg
	Mosquito	1×10^{-5} kg
	Speck of dust	7×10^{-10} kg
	Bacterium	1×10^{-15} kg
	Uranium atom	4×10^{-25} kg
	Electron	9×10^{-31} kg

Derived Units

The square metre (m^2) is a unit that denotes surface area. It is an example of a **derived unit**, a measurement unit that can be stated in terms of one or more of the base (SI) units. In this case, the unit is derived by multiplying length × length. Other examples of derived units are:

- the cubic metre (m^3) for volume
- the metre per second (m/s) for speed
- the kilogram per cubic metre (kg/m^3) for density.

Other derived units will be introduced throughout the text. Appendix 2 lists many of these units. Notice that several derived units are named after famous scientists.

Metric Prefixes

Although all lengths could be stated using the base unit of the metre, it is sometimes more convenient to state lengths in larger or smaller units, such as the kilometre, the centimetre, or the very tiny nanometre. The metric prefixes, such as "centi" and "kilo," are based on multiples of 10, a feature of the metric system that is a great advantage. Appendix 3 lists the 20 metric prefixes as well as their symbols, meanings, and origins.

Conversions Within the Metric System

Measurements to be added or subtracted must have a common unit. For example, you cannot add centimetres to metres without first converting to a common unit. Skill in converting one metric unit to another will assist you in solving physics problems.

In general, when converting from one metric unit to another, multiply by a conversion ratio such as 100 cm/1 m in which the numerator and denominator are equivalent. Such a ratio equals, effectively, one; multiplying by one does not change the quantity. To determine the ratio, either rely on your memory, which will improve with practice, or refer to the list of metric prefixes in Appendix 3.

Sample Problem 1-2

Convert 47.5 mm to metres.

Solution: The conversion ratio is either 1 m/1000 mm or 10^{-3} m/1 mm. The "mm" must be in the denominator to cancel the "mm" in 47.5 mm.

$$47.5 \text{ mm} = 47.5 \text{ mm} \times \frac{1 \text{ m}}{1000 \text{ mm}}$$

$$= 0.0475 \text{ m}$$

Thus, the length is 0.0475 m.

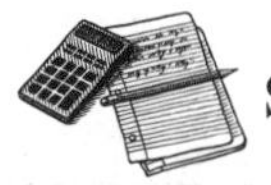

Sample Problem 1-3

Add 34 cm and 4.20 m.

Solution: Before adding, the measurements must be expressed in the same units. In this case, we will use metres.

$$\begin{aligned} 34\ \text{cm} + 4.20\ \text{m} &= 0.34\ \text{m} + 4.20\ \text{m} \\ &= 4.54\ \text{m} \end{aligned}$$

Thus, the sum is 4.54 m (or 454 cm).

Sample Problem 1-4

Convert 3.07×10^{12} ps to megaseconds.

Solution: From Appendix 3, pico = 10^{-12} and mega = 10^6. To avoid errors, the best way to perform this conversion is to proceed in two steps, first converting picoseconds to seconds, and then seconds to megaseconds. Both these steps can be carried out in one line:

$$\begin{aligned} 3.07 \times 10^{12}\ \text{ps} &= 3.07 \times 10^{12}\ \text{ps} \times \frac{10^{-12}\ \text{s}}{1\ \text{ps}} \times \frac{1\ \text{Ms}}{10^{6}\ \text{s}} \\ &= 3.07 \times 10^{-6}\ \text{Ms} \end{aligned}$$

Thus, the time is 3.07×10^{-6} Ms. Notice how the ratios were arranged so that "ps" cancelled "ps," and "s" cancelled "s," leaving Ms.

Sample Problem 1-5

Convert 5.3 kg/cm^3 to kilograms per cubic metre.

Solution: The conversion relating centimetres and metres is 100 cm = 1 m. Since the denominator contains cm^3, which represents cm·cm·cm, we must apply the factor three times, that is, we must cube it: $(100\ \text{cm})^3 = (1\ \text{m})^3$. Hence, we have:

$$\begin{aligned} 5.3\,\frac{\text{kg}}{\text{cm}^3} &= 5.3\,\frac{\text{kg}}{\text{cm}^3} \times \frac{(100\ \text{cm})^3}{1\ \text{m}^3} \\ &= 5.3 \times 10^{6}\ \text{kg/m}^3 \end{aligned}$$

Thus, the answer is 5.3×10^6 kg/m^3.

Practice

1-8 List reasons why the original definitions of the metre and second were unsatisfactory.

1-9 Use Table 1.1 to calculate these ratios:
(a) largest length to smallest length
(b) longest time to shortest time
(c) greatest mass to least mass
Which quantity has by far the greatest range of values?
[Ans. (a) 2×10^{41} (b) $(5/3) \times 10^{42}$ (c) 1×10^{83}]

Did You Know? *The world's smallest ruler used for measuring lengths in an electron microscope was developed in Canada for the National Research Council. Its divisions are only 18 atoms apart.*

1-10 If you could count one dollar each second, how long would it take to count to one billion (10^9) dollars? Express your answer in seconds and years (reference: Table 1.1).
[Ans. 10^9 s or 31 years]

1-11 Determine an estimate for the number of stars in our Milky Way Galaxy by assuming that the mass of the average star is the same as the sun's mass and the masses of other bodies, such as planets, are insignificant (reference: Table 1.1). [Ans. 4×10^{11} stars]

1-12 The mass of a hydrogen atom is about 1.7×10^{-27} kg. If the sun consists only of hydrogen atoms (actually, it is about 95% hydrogen), how many such atoms are in the sun? (Use Table 1.1 as reference.) [Ans. 1×10^{57} atoms]

1-13 Simplify:
(a) (2.1×10^{-24}) (4.0×10^9) (b) (2×10^{19}) (2×10^{-43}) (2×10^{-12})
(c) $(6.4 \times 10^{21}) \div (8.0 \times 10^{12})$ (d) $(3.88 \times 10^{-2}$ m$) \div (2.00 \times 10^{-7}$ s$)$
[Ans. (a) 8.4×10^{-15} (b) 8×10^{-36} (c) 8.0×10^8 (d) 1.94×10^5 m/s]

1-14 State and give examples of the difference between a derived unit and a base unit.

<u>**1-15**</u>[3] Many derived units are named after famous scientists. Name four of these and, in each case, state what the unit equals in terms of SI base units. (Reference: Appendix 2.)

<u>**1-16**</u> Describe what patterns can be seen in the list of metric prefixes in Appendix 3.

1-17 Write these measurements without using prefixes:
(a) The longest cells in the human body are motor neurons at a length of 1.3×10^{-1} dam.
(b) Each bristle of a carbon nanotube is 30 nm in diameter.
(c) At 1.23×10^4 km, the Hudson Bay shoreline is the longest bay shoreline in the world.

---

[3]Answers to questions with this underlining are found at the end of the chapter.

(d) Each day, *Voyageur 1* spacecraft travels another 1.486×10^{-3} Tm away from Earth.
[Ans. (a) 1.3 m (b) 3×10^{-8} m (c) 1.23×10^{7} m (d) 1.486×10^{9} m]

1-18 Perform the following unit conversions, showing your work. Express the final answer in scientific notation.
(a) 20 ms to seconds (b) 8.6 cm to micrometres (c) 3.28 g to megagrams
(d) 105 MHz to kilohertz (e) 2.4×10^{-3} MW/m^2 to milliwatts per square metre
(f) 9.8 m/s^2 to metres per square microsecond (g) 4.7 g/cm^3 to kilograms per cubic metre
(h) 53 people/km^2 to people per hectare (ha) (note: 1 ha = 10^4 m^2)
[Ans. (a) 2×10^{-2} s (b) 8.6×10^{4} μm (c) 3.28×10^{-6} Mg (d) 1.05×10^{5} kHz
(e) 2.4×10^{6} mW/m^2 (f) 9.8×10^{-12} m/μs^2 (g) 4.7×10^{3} kg/m^3 (h) 0.53 people/ha]

1-19 Simplify:
(a) 280 mm + 37 cm (b) 9850 mm – 1.68 m [Ans. (a) 65 cm (b) 8.17 m]

1-20 An American tourist driving in Canada decides to convert the speed limit of 100 km/h to miles per hour, with which she is more familiar. She knows that there are 5270 ft in 1 mi, that 1 ft contains 12 in, and that 1 in = 2.54 cm. Using this information and your knowledge of SI prefixes, determine the speed limit in miles per hour. [Ans. 62.1 mi/h]

1.3 DIMENSIONAL ANALYSIS

From earlier science courses, you are familiar with the definition of density as mass/volume or, using symbols, $\rho = m/V$. Rearranging this equation to solve for mass, we have mass = density × volume or $m = \rho V$. If this equation is used to solve a problem, the unit resulting from the product of density and volume must equal the unit of mass. The equals sign dictates that the units as well as the numbers are equal on both sides of the equation. An example will illustrate this. Let us find the mass of 0.20 m^3 of pure aluminum, which has a density of 2.7×10^3 kg/m^3.

$$\begin{aligned} m &= \rho V \\ &= 2.7 \times 10^3 \ \frac{\text{kg}}{\text{m}^3} \times 0.20 \ \text{m}^3 \\ &= 5.4 \times 10^2 \ \text{kg} \end{aligned}$$

Thus, the mass is 5.4×10^2 kg.

In this example, both sides of the equation have dimensions of mass. The symbols for the most important dimensions in mechanics – length, mass, and time – are written L, M, and T, respectively. We use square brackets to indicate the dimensions of a quantity; for instance, $[V]$ means the dimensions of volume V, and since volume is length × length × length, we have $[V] = \text{L}^3$.

The process of using dimensions to analyze a problem or an equation is called **dimensional analysis**. In this process, the quantities are expressed in terms of dimensions, such as length, mass, and time, and then the expressions are simplified algebraically. If you develop an equation during the solution of a physics problem, dimensional analysis is a useful tool to ensure that both the left-hand and right-hand sides of your equation have the same dimensions. If they do not, you must have made an error in developing the equation.

As an example, the dimensional analysis of the density equation, $m = \rho V$, involves determining the dimensions of both sides of the equation to ensure that they are equivalent:

$$\text{Dimensions of left-hand side (L.H.S.)} = [m] = \text{M}$$

$$\begin{aligned}\text{Dimensions of right-hand side (R.H.S.)} = [\rho][V] &= \frac{\text{M}}{\text{L}^3} \times \text{L}^3 \\ &= \text{M}\end{aligned}$$

Obviously, the L.H.S. and R.H.S. of the equation $m = \rho V$ have the same dimensions.

Sample Problem 1-6

A student reads a test question which asks for a distance d, given a time t of 2.2 s and a constant acceleration a of 4.0 m/s^2. Being unaware of the equation to use, the student decides to try dimensional analysis and comes up with the equation $d = at^2$. Is the equation dimensionally correct?

Solution: The dimensions involved are L for distance, T for time, and, based on the units m/s^2, L/T^2 for acceleration. Now,

$$\text{Dimensions of L.H.S.} = [d] = \text{L}$$

$$\begin{aligned}\text{Dimensions of R.H.S.} = [a][t^2] &= \frac{\text{L}}{\text{T}^2} \times \text{T}^2 \\ &= \text{L}\end{aligned}$$

Thus, the dimensions are equal on both sides of the equation, and the equation is dimensionally correct. Unfortunately for this student, the equation is not correct from the point of view of physics. The correct equation is $d = \frac{1}{2} at^2$, but since the "½" has no dimensions, it does not change the dimensions of the R.H.S. This illustrates a limitation of dimensional analysis, that is, it cannot detect errors involving multiplication or division by dimensionless constants.

Practice

1-21 Write the dimensions of the following measurements:
(a) a speed of 6.8 m/s (b) a speed of 100 km/h
(c) an acceleration of 9.8 m/s^2 (d) a density of 1.2 g/cm^3
[Ans. (a) L/T (b) L/T (c) L/T^2 (d) M/L^3]

1-22 Determine the final type of quantity produced (e.g., length, speed, etc.) in the following dimensional operations:
(a) $L \times T^{-1}$ (b) $(L/T^2) \times T \times T$ (c) $M \times L^{-3}$ (d) $(L/T^3) \times T$
[Ans. (a) speed (b) length (c) density (d) acceleration]

1-23 Use the information in Appendix 2 to write the dimensions of these derived units:
(a) newton (b) watt (c) hertz [Ans. (a) $M{\cdot}L/T^2$ (b) $M{\cdot}L^2/T^3$ (c) T^{-1}]

1-24 When a person is jogging at a constant speed, the distance travelled equals the product of speed and time, or $d = vt$. Show that the dimensions on both sides of this equation are equal.

1-25 Assume that for a certain type of motion, the distance travelled is related to time according to the equation: $d = kt^3$, where k is a constant. Determine the dimensions of k.
[Ans. L/T^3]

1-26 Prove that the equation $d = v_0 t + \frac{1}{2}at^2$ is dimensionally correct. (d is a distance, v_0 is initial velocity, t is time, and a is acceleration.)

1.4 SIGNIFICANT DIGITS

Quantities that are counted are exact, and there is no uncertainty about them. Two examples are found in these statements:

> There are 22 people in the room.
> Ten dimes have the same value as one dollar.

Measured quantities are much different because they are never exact. Suppose you are finding the mass of a friend in kilograms. You might try a bathroom scale and get 56 kg, then a scale in a physician's office and get 55.8 kg, and finally a sensitive electronic scale in a scientific laboratory and get 55.778 kg. Not one of these measurements is exact; even the most precise measurement, the last one, has an uncertainty.

Uncertainty is an estimate of the amount by which a measurement is off the "true" value; in other words, it is the possible error in the measurement. For the bathroom scale, the reading of 56 kg could mean that the mass is closer to 56 kg than either 55 kg or 57 kg, and the measurement could be written as 56 kg ± 1 kg. However, you may believe that you can read the scale to the closest 0.5 kg, in which case you would record the measurement as 56 kg ± 0.5 kg. In many instruments, the uncertainty is stated either on the scale or in the owner's manual. For example, the scale in the physician's office could have an uncertainty of ± 0.2 kg, so the measurement would be recorded as 55.8 kg ± 0.2 kg, and if the uncertainty of the electronic scale is ± 0.001 kg, the measurement is recorded as 55.778 kg ± 0.001 kg.

In any measurement, the digits that are reliably known are called **significant digits**. These include the digits known for certain and the single last digit that is estimated. Thus, the mass of 56 kg ± 1 kg has two significant digits, and 55.778 kg ± 0.001 kg has five significant digits.

When zeroes are included in a measurement, the number of significant digits can be determined by applying these rules:

(a) Zeroes placed before other digits are not significant: 0.089 kg has 2 significant digits.

(b) Zeroes placed between other digits are always significant: 4006 cm has 4 significant digits.

(c) Zeroes placed after other digits behind a decimal are significant: both 5.800 km and 703.0 N have 4 significant digits.

(d) Zeroes at the end of a number are significant only if they are indicated to be so using scientific notation. For example, 5 800 000 km may have anywhere from 2 to 7 significant digits. By using scientific notation, we can judge which digit is the estimated one, so we can determine the number of significant digits.

5.8×10^6 km has 2 significant digits

5.800×10^6 km has 4 significant digits

$5.800\,000 \times 10^6$ km has 7 significant digits

If the accepted value of a measurement is known, the **percent error** of an experimental measurement can be found using

$$\text{percent error} = \frac{|\text{measured value} - \text{accepted value}|}{\text{accepted value}} \times 100\%$$

Calculations Based on Measurements

Measurements made in experiments or given in problems are often used in calculations. For example, you might be asked to find the average speed of a cyclist given the measurement of the time it takes to travel a certain distance. The final answer of the problem should take into consideration the number of significant digits of each measurement, and it may have to be rounded off.

When adding or subtracting measured quantities, the final answer should have no more than one estimated digit.

Sample Problem 1-7

Add 123 cm + 12.4 cm + 5.38 cm

Solution:	123 cm	(the "3" is estimated)
	12.4 cm	(the "4" is estimated)
	+ 5.38 cm	(the "8" is estimated)
	140.78 cm	(the "0," the "7," and the "8" are estimated)

Thus, the answer should be rounded off to one estimated digit, or 141 cm.

When multiplying or dividing measured quantities, the final answer should have the same number of significant digits as the original measurement with the least number of significant digits.

Sample Problem 1-8

A cyclist travels 4.00×10^3 m on a racetrack in 292.4 s. Calculate the average speed of the cyclist.

Solution: Average speed (v) is distance (d) divided by time (t):

$$v = \frac{d}{t} = \frac{4.00 \times 10^3 \text{ m}}{2.924 \times 10^2 \text{ s}}$$
$$= 1.368.. \times 10^1 \text{ m/s}$$

This answer should be rounded off to three significant digits. Hence, we obtain an average speed of 1.37×10^1 m/s or 13.7 m/s.

In the sample problems above, the calculations were done first, then the answer was rounded off. When calculated answers are rounded off to the appropriate number of significant digits, the following rules apply.

(a) If the first digit to be dropped is 4 or less, the preceding digit is not changed; e.g., 3.814 becomes 3.81.

(b) If the first digit to be dropped is 6 or more, the preceding digit is raised by 1; e.g., 5.476 becomes 5.48.

(c) If the digits to be dropped are a 5 followed by digits other than zeroes, the preceding digit is raised by 1; e.g., 9.265 221 becomes 9.27.

(d) If the digit to be dropped is a 5 alone, or a 5 followed by zeroes, the preceding digit is raised by 1; e.g., 1.265 becomes 1.27.[4]

Most quantities written in this book have either two or three significant digits, although some quantities require more significant digits. The answers to the numerical problems have been written to the correct number of significant digits after rounding off following the rules given in this section. You will be able to practise the rules of significant digits with every numerical problem.

Round-off Error

Try the following exercise with your calculator:

1. Multiply 9.06 times 8.99.

2. Round off your answer from the first step to three significant digits, and then enter this three-digit number into your calculator in preparation for the next step.

3. Divide the three-digit number from step 2 by 8.99, and round off the answer to three significant digits. Your final answer should be 9.05.

Let us recap what was done: 9.06 and 8.99 were multiplied together, and the product (after rounding) was divided by 8.99. Summarizing this mathematically, we have

$$(9.06 \times 8.99) \div 8.99$$

You can see from the above expression that we could divide out each 8.99, leaving 9.06 as the answer. But the final answer that was determined was 9.05. To see how this happened, let us follow our steps. The product 9.06 × 8.99 in step 1 is equal to 81.4494. In rounding this off in step 2 to three significant digits, we discarded 0.0494, leaving only 81.4 This was divided by 8.99 in step 3, giving 9.05. This is less than the correct answer, 9.06, because we eliminated the 0.0494. You can see that, to obtain a final answer valid to three significant digits, it is necessary to keep *more* than three significant digits in intermediate answers. Rounding off too early introduces error, which is referred to a *round-off error*.

---

[4]In some specialized cases in statistical calculations, the digit preceding a 5 is not changed if it is even, but it is raised by 1 if it is odd; e.g., 1.265 becomes 1.26 and 1.275 becomes 1.28. This rule exists to avoid the accumulated error that would occur if the 5 were always rounded up.

Hence, when doing calculations, remember to *keep all the digits in your calculator until the final answer is determined*, and then round off this answer to the correct number of significant digits. (If it is necessary to write down an intermediate answer, use the correct number of significant digits, but keep the intermediate answer with all its digits in your calculator.)

Here is another calculator exercise to try:

1. Enter this number into your calculator: 1.000 000 1.

2. Press the squaring key (probably "x^2") 27 times. (This is equivalent to raising 1.000 000 1 to the power 2^{27}.)

The correct answer, to eight significant digits, is 674 530.47. Your answer probably differs from this somewhat, and if you try different brands and models of calculators, you will discover that you will obtain different answers. What is going on here? The reason for the discrepancies is related to round-off error. At each step, the calculator either rounds off or truncates[5] the answer to a fixed number of digits, usually one or two digits more than are shown on the display. Different calculators round off or truncate to different numbers of digits. As well, there are different procedures (algorithms) used by calculators for multiplication, and different methods for storing numbers, which affect the final result. In the particular example that we used above, many calculators produce four-digit accuracy in the final answer, after a calculation that involves only 27 operations. So beware when using a calculator for a lengthy calculation – the answer might not be as accurate as you think.

Order-of-Magnitude Estimations

When solving numerical problems in physics as well as in everyday experiences, it is good to be able to estimate the value of a quantity. This applies particularly when checking that a calculated answer makes sense.

An **order-of-magnitude estimation** is a calculation based on reasonable assumptions to obtain a value expressed to a power of 10. Often there is only one significant digit in the calculated value.

Consider, for example, an estimation of the volume of air in litres inhaled by a person in one year. We begin with two assumptions. First, a person would inhale about one litre (1 L) of air with each breath. (You might find a more accurate value by devising a water-displacement experiment.) Second, the number of breaths a person would take per minute would likely be between 10 and 20, let's say 15. Now we are ready for the calculation. Notice the cancellation of units in this calculation.

$$\begin{aligned}\text{volume of air} &= \frac{1\ \text{L}}{\text{breath}} \times \frac{15\ \text{breaths}}{\text{min}} \times \frac{60\ \text{min}}{\text{h}} \times \frac{24\ \text{h}}{\text{day}} \times \frac{365\ \text{d}}{\text{year}} \\ &= 8 \times 10^{6}\ \text{L/year} \quad \text{(one significant digit)}\end{aligned}$$

---

[5]To truncate a number means to eliminate all digits that appear after a particular digit, without rounding. For example, if the number 1.34957 is truncated to two decimal places, the result is 1.34.

Thus the volume of air inhaled by a person is approximately 8×10^6 L/year. Order-of-magnitude estimations are often rounded off to the nearest power of ten. In this example, we would then obtain 10^7 L/year.

This type of question will be asked from time to time in this text. Such a problem is called a **Fermi question**, named after Enrico Fermi (1901-1954), a famous physicist and professor who often asked his students to estimate quantities impossible to measure directly.

Practice

1-27 Three different scales are for sale at three different prices. A potential buyer measures the mass of a box on the scales and obtains these values:

42.40 kg ± 0.005 kg   42.4 kg ± 0.05 kg   42.4 kg ± 100 g

Which scale do you think would be the most expensive? least expensive? Why?

1-28 State the number of significant digits in each measurement:
(a) 0.04 Tm (b) 400.20 pm (c) 8.10×10^6 kg (d) 0.008 200 μs
[Ans. (a) 1 (b) 5 (c) 3 (d) 4]

1-29 Round off each quantity to three significant digits, and write the answer in scientific notation.
(a) 38 510 Gm (b) 0.000 940 488 MW (c) 55.055 dam
(d) 876.50 kL (e) 0.076 550 μg
[Ans. (a) 3.85×10^4 Gm (b) 9.40×10^{-4} MW (c) 5.51×10^1 dam
(d) 8.76×10^2 kL (e) 7.66×10^{-2} μg]

1-30 A student performs measurements to determine the density of pure water at 4°C, and obtains an average result of 1.08×10^3 kg/m^3. The accepted value is 1.00×10^3 kg/m^3. What is the percent error in the experimental measurement? [Ans. 8%]

1-31 A rectangular mirror measures 1.18 m by 0.378 m. Find the perimeter and the surface area of the mirror, expressing your answers to the appropriate number of significant digits.
[Ans. 3.12 m, 0.446 m^2]

1-32 Use the data in Appendix 4 to determine the difference in masses between:
(a) a neutron and a proton (b) a proton and an electron
[Ans. (a) 2.306×10^{-30} kg (b) $1.671\,710 \times 10^{-27}$ kg]

1-33 Assume that the Earth-sun distance has a constant value of $1.495\,988 \times 10^{11}$ m and the Earth-moon distance is constant at 3.844×10^8 m. Determine the greatest and least moon-sun distances, taking into consideration significant digits.
[Ans. $1.499\,832 \times 10^{11}$ m, $1.492\,144 \times 10^{11}$ m]

1-34 Find the time it takes light, travelling at 3.00×10^8 m/s, to travel from the sun to Earth. (Use the distance given in question 1-33, and remember significant digits.) [Ans. 499 s]

1-35 *Fermi Question*: Determine a reasonable order-of-magnitude estimation in each case. Show your reasoning.
(a) Assume that the mass of an average cell in your body is 1×10^{-12} kg. Calculate the number of cells in your body.
(b) What is the mass in kilograms of all the hamburger patties consumed in North America in one year?
(c) Assume that a Ferris wheel at the amusement park nearest to your home were to fall off its support and become a gigantic wheel. How many rotations, travelling in a straight line, would it have to make to reach the capital city of your country?
[Ans. (a) about 5×10^{13} to 1×10^{14} cells (b) 10^9 to 10^{11}]

Did You Know?
The Ferris wheel is named after G.W.G. Ferris (1859-1896), an American engineer and inventor.

1.5 TYPES OF QUANTITIES

A tourist, trying to find a museum in an unfamiliar city, asks how to get there and is told: "All you have to do is walk one-and-a-half kilometres from here." This information is obviously not very useful without a direction. A measurement of 1.5 km is an example of a **scalar quantity**, one with magnitude but no direction. (Magnitude means size.) A measurement such as 1.5 km west is an example of a **vector quantity**, one with both magnitude and direction.

Some common scalar quantities and typical examples are:

length or distance – A race track is 100 m long.

mass – The mass of a newborn baby is approximately 3 kg.

time – The time interval between heartbeats is about 1.0 s.

Vector quantities are common in physics. The ones used most frequently in the study of mechanics are:

displacement – A crane is used to lift a steel beam 40 m upward.

velocity – A military jet was travelling at 1600 km/h east.

acceleration – The acceleration due to gravity on the moon is 1.6 m/s^2 downward (toward the centre of the moon).

force – The force used to accelerate a proton in a particle-accelerator laboratory is measured to be 2.0×10^{-22} N forward.

Did You Know?
Scalar is derived from the Latin word scala, which means "ladder" or "steps" and implies magnitude. Vector is a copy of the Latin word vector, which means "carrier" and implies something being carried from one place to another in a certain direction. In biology, a vector can be an organism that carries disease or an agent that transfers genetic material.

Scalar quantities, also called scalars, are easy to manipulate algebraically. The ordinary rules of addition, subtraction, multiplication, and division apply. Vector quantities, or vectors, are more complex. They require special symbols and rules of addition, subtraction, and so on. The general nature of scalars and vectors will be considered as you proceed through Chapter 2. However, details regarding vectors are reserved for the chapter that prepares you for vector analysis in two-dimensional motion, namely Chapter 3.

Practice

1-36 List three scalar quantities other than those already given, and give an example of each.

1-37 For motion that you have experienced today, write two specific examples of displacement and two of velocity.

CHAPTER FOCUS

This chapter has emphasized the importance of measurement and basic mathematical skills in physics. Details of the SI units been presented; this system will be used throughout the text. A review was presented of scientific notation, units, uncertainties, significant digits, and order-of-magnitude estimations. Scalar and vector quantities were introduced and compared.

In the remainder of the text, you will apply and extend your knowledge of measurement and skills in mathematical operations. The next chapter deals with motion in one dimension. Then Chapter 3 describes mathematical details of vectors required for the study of motion in two dimensions in Chapter 4. Displacement, velocity, and acceleration vectors are important there.

VOCABULARY REVIEW

You should now be able to define or explain each of the following words or phrases.

qualitative description
quantitative description
measurement
nanotechnology
standard unit
base unit
SI
scientific notation
derived unit
dimensional analysis
uncertainty
significant digits
percent error
order-of-magnitude estimations
Fermi question
scalar quantity or scalar
vector quantity or vector

CHAPTER REVIEW

Note: The answers to underlined questions are found at the end of the chapter.

<u>**1-38**</u> The mass of a heavyweight male wrestler, in grams, is closest to:
(a) 10^3 (b) 10^4 (c) 10^5 (d) 10^6 (e) 10^7

<u>**1-39**</u> Which length is the smallest?
(a) 10^6 cm (b) 10^8 mm (c) 10^{10} μm (d) 10^{12} nm (e) 10^{14} pm

<u>**1-40**</u> Given these four masses: A: 10^{-4} Mg; B: 10^7 kg; C: 10^{-15} Yg; D: 10^2 Gg. These are ordered in descending size as:
(a) D, B, C, A (b) A, C, B, D (c) B, C, D, A (d) B, D, A, C (e) none of these

<u>**1-41**</u> How many significant digits are there in the sum 460.299 + 390.0008 + 6.123 + 5.07?
(a) 7 (b) 6 (c) 5 (d) 4 (e) 3

<u>**1-42**</u> How many significant digits are there in the product 8.005 00 × 0.005 380 1?
(a) 7 (b) 6 (c) 5 (d) 4 (e) 3

1-43 List reasons why measurement is important for use in (a) society and (b) physics.

1-44 List the SI base units of length, time, and mass.

1-45 Why is it not necessary to have a base unit for area in the SI?

1-46 A highrise apartment building is 30 stories high. Estimate the height of the building in metres and decametres, showing your reasoning.

1-47 Convert each measurement to the units indicated in parentheses. State the answers in scientific notation.
(a) Mt. Everest is 8.85 km high. (metres, decimetres, centimetres)
(b) The biggest animal known was a blue whale with a mass of 1.90×10^2 Mg. (kilograms, grams, centigrams)
(c) A "cosmic year" is the time our solar system takes to complete one revolution around the centre of the Milky Way Galaxy. It is about 2.2×10^8 years. (seconds, microseconds, and exaseconds)
[Ans. (a) 8.85×10^3 m, 8.85×10^4 dm, 8.85×10^5 cm (b) 1.90×10^5 kg, 1.90×10^8 g, 1.90×10^{10} cg (c) 7.0×10^{15} s, 7.0×10^{21} μs, 7.0×10^{-3} Es]

1-48 Determine the ratio of each of the following masses to your own mass:
(a) The world's largest erratic boulder (that is, one moved by a glacier), located in Alberta, has a mass of 16 Mg.
(b) The lightest human birth on record is 0.26 kg.
(c) The heaviest mass supported by a person's shoulders is 5.2×10^2 kg.
(d) A prize winning pumpkin had a mass of 6.7×10^6 dg.

1-49 The larva of a certain moth consumes 86 000 times its own mass at birth within its first 48 h. How much would a human with a mass at birth of 3.0 kg have to consume in the first 48 h to complete with this phenomenal eater? Express your answer in kilograms, then in a unit that requires a number between 1 and 1000. [Ans. 2.6×10^5 kg, 2.6×10^2 Mg]

1-50 Simplify:
(a) 2.00×10^2 km – 3.0×10^3 m
(b) $(4.4 \times 10^3 \text{ m}) \div (2.0 \times 10^5 \text{ s}^2)$
(c) $(4.4 \times 10^3 \text{ m}) \div (2.0 \times 10^5 \text{ s})^2$
[Ans. (a) 1.97×10^2 km (b) 2.2×10^{-2} m/s^2 (c) 1.1×10^{-7} m/s^2]

1-51 The equation for the area of a circle is $A = \pi r^2$ and the equation for the area of a right-angled triangle is $A = bh/2$.
(a) What do the symbols r, b, and h represent?
(b) Determine the dimensions of the right side of each equation. What do you conclude?

1-52 The list below shows the symbols and dimensions of some quantities used in physics.

force (F)	$[F] = \text{M}\cdot\text{L}/\text{T}^2$
energy (E)	$[E] = \text{M}\cdot\text{L}^2/\text{T}^2$
power (P)	$[P] = [E]/\text{T}$
pressure (p)	$[p] = [F]/\text{L}^2$

(a) What do the symbols M, L, and T mean?
(b) Make a similar list for these quantities: speed (v), acceleration (a), and area (A).
(c) Express the dimensions of power and pressure in terms of M, L, and T.
(d) How can the dimensions of energy be expressed in terms of mass and speed?
(e) How can the dimensions of power be expressed in terms of mass, speed, and acceleration?
[Ans. (c) $[P] = \text{M}\cdot\text{L}^2/\text{T}^3$, $[p] = \text{M}\cdot\text{L}^{-1}/\text{T}^{-2}$ (d) $[E] = \text{M}\cdot[v]^2$ (e) $[P] = \text{M}\cdot[v]\cdot[a]$]

1-53 If two measurements have different dimensions, can they be added? multiplied? Give an example to illustrate each answer.

1-54 Before a wooden metre stick is imprinted with millimetre and centimetre markings, it is important that the wood be cured (i.e., properly dried). Explain why.

1-55 An experiment is used to determine the speed of light in a transparent material. The measured value is 1.82×10^8 m/s and the accepted value is 1.86×10^8 m/s. What is the percent error in the measurement? [Ans. 2%]

1-56 A customer buys three 120-cm pieces of rope from a new roll that is 500 m long. Assume both measurements have three significant digits. What length of rope is left on the roll? (Don't forget significant digits.) [Ans. 496 m]

1-57 The equation for the volume of a cylinder is $V = \pi r^2 h$ where r is the radius and h is the height. Find the volume in cubic centimetres of a solid cylinder of gold that is 8.4 cm in diameter and 22.8 cm in height. Write your answer in scientific notation with the appropriate number of significant digits. [Ans. 1.3×10^3 cm^3]

1-58 *Fermi question*: Determine an order-of-magnitude estimation for each quantity. (Show your reasoning.)

(a) the number of your normal paces it would take to walk 1.6 km
(b) the number of kernels of corn in a container that holds 1.0 L (It may help you to know that a cube 1.0 dm (= 10 cm) on a side has a capacity of 1.0 L.)
(c) volume of water (in litres) in a typical above-ground backyard swimming pool (See the hint in (b) above.)
(d) the total mass gained by the entire live population of Canada in one year
(e) the number of times your heart has beat in your lifetime to date
[Ans. (a) approx. 2×10^3 to 3×10^3 (b) approx. 10^4 (c) approx. 10^4 L to 10^5 L)
(d) approx. 2×10^7 kg (e) approx. 7×10^8 beats]

1-59 Determine the approximate time it takes a fingernail to grow 1 nm. State your assumptions and show your calculations. (Note: Your answer indicates how quickly layers of atoms are assembled in the process of protein synthesis.) [Ans. approx. 2 to 3 s]

1-60 Classify each of the following as either scalar or vector.
(a) the force exerted by your biceps on your forearm as you hold a weight in your hand
(b) the number of cars in a parking lot
(c) the reading on a car's odometer
(d) the reading on a car's speedometer
(e) the gravitational force of the moon on Earth
(f) the age of the universe

APPLYING YOUR KNOWLEDGE

1-61 Do the prefixes *kilo*, *mega*, and *giga* (as used in connection with computers, e,g., kilobyte) have the same meaning as in the SI? Explain your answer.

1-62 At one time, Enrico Fermi stated that his 50 min lecture lasted one microcentury. Determine how close his estimate was.

1-63 If volume were a base dimension (V) in the SI, what would be the dimensions of length? of area? [Ans. $V^{1/3}$, $V^{2/3}$]

1-64 (a) In Canada, the speed limit on many highways is 100 km/h. Convert this measurement to metres per second.
(b) The fastest measured speed of any animal is 97 m/s, recorded as a peregrine falcon was diving. Convert the measurement to kilometres per hour.
(c) Suggest a convenient way of changing metres per second to kilometres per hour and vice versa.

1-65 Recent measurements have caused scientists to state that the length of a mean solar day increases by 1 ms each century.
(a) How much longer would a day be 3000 years from now?
(b) How long will it take from now for the day to be one minute longer?
[Ans. (a) 30 ms (b) 6×10^6 years]

KEY OBJECTIVES

Having completed this chapter, you should now be able to do the following:

1. Distinguish between qualitative and quantitative descriptions and give examples of each.
2. Define measurement and appreciate its importance in our day-to-day lives as well as in physics and applications such as nanotechnology.
3. Recognize that measuring techniques have improved significantly from ancient times and these improvements have influenced scientific development.
4. Define standard unit and be familiar with standard units in the metric system.
5. Recognize that the Système International (SI) is a special part of the metric system.
6. State the SI base units of length, mass, and time.
7. State the meaning of derived unit and give examples of such units.
8. Identify the meanings of common metric prefixes.
9. Convert from one metric unit to another.
10. Write numbers using scientific notation.
11. Apply the exponent laws, especially for multiplication and division involving powers.
12. Verify that the dimensions of an equation are correct by using dimensional analysis.
13. Define and give examples of uncertainty in measurement.
14. Write measurements to the appropriate number of significant digits.
15. Calculate the percent error of a measured value knowing the accepted value.
16. Perform calculations (+, −, ×, and ÷) involving measured quantities and round off the answer to the appropriate number of significant digits.
17. Develop skill in estimating quantities and calculate order-of-magnitude estimations.
18. State the difference between scalars and vectors and give examples of each.

ANSWERS TO SELECTED QUESTIONS

1-15 Four examples are: watt ($W = kg{\cdot}m^2{\cdot}s^{-3}$); pascal ($Pa = kg{\cdot}s^{-2}$); volt ($V = kg{\cdot}m^2{\cdot}s^{-3}A$); becquerel ($Bq = kg{\cdot}m^2{\cdot}s^{-3}$)

1-16 Some of the patterns are: the prefixes from 10^3 to 10^3 change by a factor 10^1; the remaining prefixes change by a factor of 10^3; the symbols for the large numbers (from mega upward) are capital letters, and all the other symbols are lower case; the origins of the prefixes are all non-English words; some original meanings relate to the power of 10 (e.g., *femten*, or 15, is used for 10^{-15}), while some others relate to a power of 10^3 (e.g., *zeta* or 7 is $(10^3)^7$ or 10^{21}).

1-38 (c) 1-39 (e) 1-40 (a) 1-41 (c) 1-42 (c)

1-53 It is possible for the measurements to be multiplied (e.g., area × length = volume or $L^2 \times L = L^3$), but it is not possible to add them (e.g., you can't add area and length).

1-54 Wood contracts as it dries, so it must be fully dried (cured) and totally contracted before marked to ensure accurate scale divisions.

1-61 The meanings are not the same. The SI is based on multiples of 10 whereas computers and data storage are based on powers of 2. For example, in the SI, kilo means 10^3 or 1000, and mega means 10^6, but a kilobyte is 2^{10} bytes, or 1024 bytes, and a megabyte is 2^{20} bytes.

CHAPTER 2

ONE-DIMENSIONAL KINEMATICS

Humans have always been concerned with motion. In prehistoric times, hunters tossed spears at moving animals, nomads crossed rivers in search of hospitable living areas, and everyone was influenced by the apparent motion of the sun, moon, and stars in the sky. Our current way of life involves obvious examples of motion, such as athletics, our vast networks of transportation, etc. It also involves less obvious motion, such as a satellite tracking weather systems to warn us of hurricanes and other disasters, a radioactive tracer as it passes through a patient's circulatory system, or motion of subatomic particles studied by scientific researchers and nanotechnologists.

The study of motion is called **kinematics**, which stems from the Greek word for motion, *kinema*. Kinematics involves descriptions of motion using both words and mathematical equations. We will not study the causes of the motion (that is, forces) until Chapter 5, at which point you will have a thorough understanding of kinematics.

Did You Know? *A quick check of the dictionary reveals several words with the prefix "kine." For example, kinesiology is the study of muscles, especially the mechanics of human body motion.*

In this chapter, kinematics is restricted to motion in a straight line, in other words, motion in one dimension. The concepts studied here can be applied to more complex motions, some of which will be seen in later chapters.

2.1 DISTANCE AND SPEED

A person begins jogging and covers the first 30 m in 10 s. This means that, during each second, the distance travelled is, on the average, 3.0 m; we say that the average speed is 3.0 m/s. **Speed** is the time rate of change of distance. The quantities distance, speed, and time are scalar quantities, which means they involve magnitude but not direction.

In physics we try to keep the descriptions as simple as possible. Thus, in the case of the jogger, when we consider average speed we don't consider that the person travels less than 3 m in the first second and perhaps more than 3 m in the last second. Also, we are not concerned about the motion of the person's arms or legs. We simply treat the moving body as if it were a single particle. Furthermore, we do not consider whether the path of motion is straight or curved or otherwise; rather we consider the total distance travelled in a certain amount of time.

The equation for the **average speed** of a moving object is:

$$\text{average speed} = \frac{\text{total distance travelled}}{\text{elapsed time}}$$

or, using symbols:

$$\text{speed}_{\text{av}} = \frac{d}{\Delta t} \qquad \textbf{(2-1)}$$

where the subscript "av" indicates "average" and the Greek letter Δ is used to denote the change in a quantity, in this case a change in time, that is, a time interval. Normally, "t" represents the time at which a single event occurs, whereas Δt represents the time between two events, that is, the elapsed time. (Δt is *not* the product of Δ and t.)

The units of average speed can be any length unit divided by any time unit. Typical units are metres per second (m/s) and kilometres per hour (km/h). In Chapter 1 you learned how to convert from metres per second to kilometres per hour, and vice versa. Table 2.1 shows examples of typical speeds in various units.

Table 2.1 Some Typical Speeds

Motion	Speed (in m/s)	Speed in Alternate Unit
continental drift	9.5×10^{-10} m/s	30 mm/yr
growth of hair on human head	5×10^{-9} m/s	5 nm/s
slow moving glacier	6×10^{-7} m/s	2 m/yr
growth of grass in spring	1×10^{-7} m/s	25 cm/month
running athlete	10 m/s	1.0 dam/s
highway speed limit	25 m/s	90 km/h
hockey puck after hard slapshot	50 m/s	180 km/h
electrical pulse along an axon	100 m/s	360 km/h
sound in air	340 m/s	0.34 km/s
supersonic jet	750 m/s	2.7 Mm/h
Earth in orbit around sun	3×10^{4} m/s	30 km/s
electron in hydrogen atom	2.2×10^{6} m/s	2.2 Mm/s
lightning upward return stroke	1.4×10^{8} m/s	140 Mm/s
light in a vacuum	3.0×10^{8} m/s	300 Mm/s

Sample Problem 2-1

A swimmer crosses a circular swimming pool of diameter 18 m in 22 s.
(a) Calculate the swimmer's average speed.
(b) At that same average speed, how long would the swimmer take to swim around the edge of the pool?

Solution: (a) We use Eqn. 2-1:

$$\text{speed}_{av} = \frac{d}{\Delta t} = \frac{18\text{ m}}{22\text{ s}}$$

$$= 0.82\text{ m/s (rounded off to two significant digits)}$$

Thus, the average speed is 0.82 m/s.

(b) Eqn. 2-1 for average speed can be re-arranged to solve for time. Thus:

$$\Delta t = \frac{d}{\text{speed}_{\text{av}}}$$

In this case, the distance travelled is the circumference of the pool, which is π times the diameter. Hence,

$$\Delta t = \frac{\pi \cdot \text{diameter}}{\text{speed}_{\text{av}}} = \frac{\pi(18\text{ m})}{0.82\text{ m/s}}$$
$$= 69\text{ s (rounded off to two significant digits)}$$

Thus, the time taken is 69 s.

Note: Significant digits and rounding of numbers were discussed in Section 1.4.

Instantaneous Speed

If you are travelling by car to a destination 100 km away and you have one hour to get there, your required average speed is 100 km/h. To achieve this average, parts of the trip would have to be at speeds greater than 100 km/h to make up for the starting and stopping times and other times when the speed is less than 100 km/h. There are two different types of speeds considered here — the average speed for the entire time elapsed, and the speed at any given instant, called the **instantaneous speed**. In a car the value indicated by the speedometer is the instantaneous speed.

From now on in the text whenever the word speed is used it will be assumed to be the instantaneous speed. If the average speed is required, it will be called, simply, average speed.

Uniform Motion

The simplest type of motion to study is called **uniform motion**, which is motion at a constant speed in a straight line (one dimension). A common example is a car travelling at constant speed along a straight, smooth highway. It should be obvious that with uniform motion the average speed and the instantaneous speed have the same value.

Practice

2-1 Determine the average speed in metres per second in each case. Express the final answer in scientific notation using the correct number of significant digits.
(a) A rack star runs a race of 4.00×10^2 m in 43.9 s.
(b) Sound travels 18.8 cm through a human muscle in 0.119 ms.
(c) The moon takes 27.3 days to complete one orbit around Earth. The average Earth-moon distance is 3.84×10^5 km. [Ans. (a) 9.11 m/s (b) 1.58×10^3 m/s (c) 1.02×10^3 m/s]

2-2 In empty space, light travels at 3.00×10^8 m/s. Determine the time in seconds for each of the following:
(a) Light travels from the sun to Earth. The average radius of Earth's orbit around the sun is 1.50×10^{11} m.
(b) Laser light is sent from Earth, reflects off a mirror on the moon, and returns to Earth. (See #2-1(c) above.) [Ans. (a) 5.00×10^2 s (b) 2.56 s]

2-3 (a) Write an equation for distance travelled in terms of average speed and time.
(b) Prove that your equation in (a) is dimensionally correct. (Dimensional analysis was discussed in Section 1.3.)

2-4 Determine the total distance travelled in each case.
(a) Sound travelling at 344 m/s crosses a room in 0.0350 s.
(b) Thirty-two scuba divers ride an underwater tricycle for 60.0 h at an average speed of 1.74 km/h. Express this answer in kilometres and metres.
(c) The women's world-record 6-day (144 h) long-distance race was set at an average speed of 6.14 km/h. [Ans. (a) 12.0 m (b) 104 km; 1.04×10^5 m (c) 884 km]

2-5 Under what conditions can each of the following situations occur?
(a) instantaneous speed equals average speed
(b) instantaneous speed is greater than average speed
(c) instantaneous speed is less than average speed

2.2 POSITION, DISPLACEMENT, AND VELOCITY

A tourist travelling by car through the Italian Alps enters a mountain pass. The road winds back and forth as it climbs to the top of the pass and back down. The tourist takes 90 min to travel 45 km, but the views are spectacular. Meanwhile a local driver, who has seen the views often, chooses to pay a toll and drive through a tunnel at the base of the mountain to get to the same destination as the tourist. It takes only 9.0 min to travel 15 km straight east through the tunnel. The two *distances* are different (15 km compared with 45 km), but the vehicles have the same displacement (15 km east) from the start of the motion to the end (Figure 2-1). **Displacement** is the change of position from the initial point to the final point.

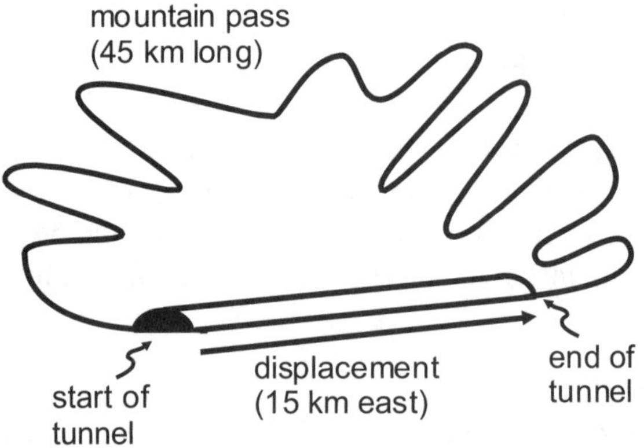

Figure 2-1 *Whether a car travels through the tunnel or across the mountain pass, the displacement for the trip is the same.*

The direction of a displacement can be specified as east, west, north, up, down, and so on. However, at this stage in mechanics it is also convenient to use a simple reference line to define direction, because we are using mainly motion in one dimension. We will call this reference line the x-axis. This axis can be horizontal or any other direction, depending on the situation. Consider Figure 2-2 (a), which shows a car in two different positions, initial and final, along the x-axis. The same situation is shown in (b) with the initial position labelled x_1 and the final position labelled x_2, relative to a reference point called the origin (labelled 0). Then, the displacement is defined as the change in position:

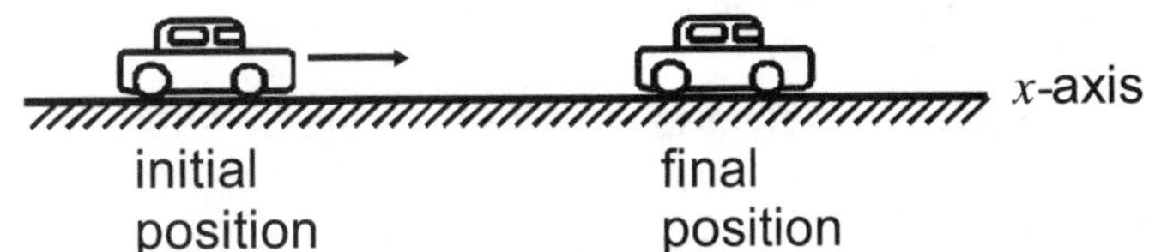

(a) *A car is travelling to the right along an x-axis.*

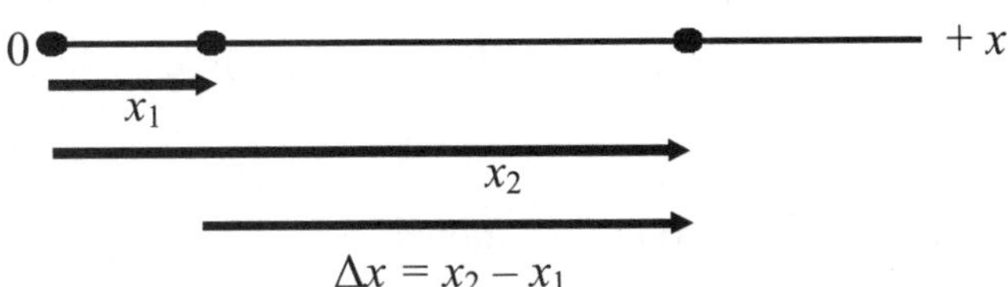

(b) *Using points to represent the positions shown in (a)*

Figure 2-2 *Illustrating displacement* $\Delta x = x_2 - x_1$.

$$\text{displacement} = \Delta x = x_2 - x_1 \quad \textbf{(2-2)}$$

Strictly speaking, displacement is a vector quantity, but we will not concern ourselves with details of its vector nature until Chapter 4 (Two-Dimensional Kinematics).

Average Velocity

Velocity is the vector counterpart of speed. Thus, **velocity** is the time rate of change of *position.* (Recall that speed is the time rate of change of *distance.*) To determine the **average velocity** over a period of time, we use the definition:

$$\text{average velocity} = \frac{\text{change of position}}{\text{elapsed time}} = \frac{\text{displacement}}{\text{elapsed time}}$$

To define average velocity in terms of symbols, we consider the one-dimensional motion of an object such as a car that is at position x_1 at time t_1, and at position x_2 at time t_2. The change of position, i.e., the displacement, is $\Delta x = x_2 - x_1$, and the elapsed time is $\Delta t = t_2 - t_1$. Hence, the average velocity (symbol v_{av}) is

$$v_{av} = \frac{\Delta x}{\Delta t} = \frac{x_2 - x_1}{t_2 - t_1} \quad \textbf{(2-3)}$$

Again, strictly speaking, average velocity is a vector, but its vector nature will not be described in detail until Chapter 4.

Sample Problem 2-2

Compare the average velocities for the two cars travelling in the Italian Alps (page 2-4).

Solution: In kinematics problems, it is very useful to begin by defining the positive direction of our co-ordinate system. Since both cars end up travelling east, it is convenient to define the $+x$ direction as east. In writing up a problem solution, you can make this definition in words, or by a small drawing: $\rightarrow +x$ (east). For both cars, the displacement is Δx = 15 km. (Note that this a positive quantity, meaning that the displacement is eastward. A displacement of Δx = –15 km would be westward.)

(a) For the car that went through the tunnel:

$$v_{av} = \frac{\Delta x}{\Delta t} \quad \text{where } \Delta t = 9.0\text{ min} = 0.15\text{ h}$$
$$= \frac{15\text{ km}}{0.15\text{ h}}$$
$$\therefore \quad v_{av} = 1.0 \times 10^2\text{ km/h}$$

Since the average velocity of this car is positive, the average velocity is eastward. Hence, the average velocity is 1.0×10^2 km/h eastward.

(b) For the car that went over the mountain pass:

$$v_{av} = \frac{\Delta x}{\Delta t} \quad \text{where } \Delta t = 90\text{ min} = 1.5\text{ h}$$
$$= \frac{15\text{ km}}{1.5\text{ h}}$$
$$= 10\text{ km/h}$$

> ***Notation Tip**: Notice how we deal with directions by use of positive and negative signs. We defined the +x direction as east, and since (in this problem) the displacement is eastward, we represent it as a positive quantity (+15 km). The average velocities of both cars turned out to be positive, indicating that they are eastward.*
>
> *Notice also that we do not use boldface type for the symbols Δx and v_{av}. The reason for this will be more obvious in Chapter 4.*

Since this average velocity is positive, it too is eastward. Hence, the average velocity of this car is 10 km/h eastward. The two average velocities are obviously very different even though the displacement is the same for both cars.

Instantaneous Velocity

Average velocity is defined for a particular period of elapsed time. However, we can also consider the velocity at particular instant of time, that is, the **instantaneous velocity**, represented by the symbol v. We will give a formal definition of instantaneous velocity a little later, but for now, you can think of it as being the same as instantaneous speed (Section 2.1), with the important addition that instantaneous velocity (being a vector) has a direction as well as a magnitude. Instantaneous speed is the magnitude of the instantaneous velocity. For example, if a car has an instantaneous velocity of 100 km/h west, its instantaneous speed is 100 km/h.

In the remainder of the text, the term velocity will indicate instantaneous velocity; when we are discussing average velocity, it will be clearly indicated.

Graphing Uniform Motion

Graphing provides a useful way of studying motion. We will begin by studying graphs of uniform motion, which is motion with a constant velocity. (How does this definition compare with the definition for uniform motion given in Section 2.1?)

Assume that a commuter train is travelling at a constant velocity of 20 m/s south for 3.0 min along a straight stretch of track. (In other words, the velocity at any instant — the instantaneous velocity — is 20 m/s south.) If we define the $+x$ direction as south, and choose the origin of our co-ordinate system (i.e., $x = 0$) to correspond to the train's position at some initial time $t = 0$, then the position-time data are as shown below and the corresponding graph of the motion is shown in Figure 2-3.

time t (s):	0	60	120	180
position x (m):	0	1.2×10^3	2.4×10^3	3.6×10^3

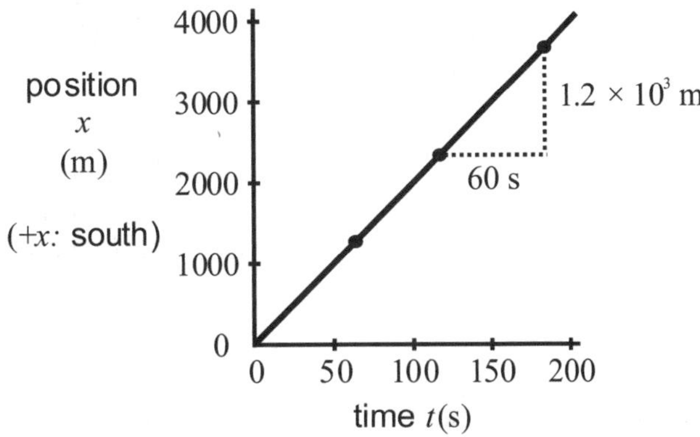

Figure 2-3 *Position vs. time graph for the commuter train.*

An important quantity to calculate on such a graph is the slope of the line. The equation to find the slope of a straight line on a graph is:

$$\text{slope} = \frac{\text{change in quantity plotted on vertical axis}}{\text{corresponding change in quantity plotted on horizontal axis}}$$

or in this case,

$$\text{slope} = \frac{\text{change in position}}{\text{change in time}}$$

In symbols: $$m = \frac{\Delta x}{\Delta t}$$

Notice that the right-hand-side of this expression, $\Delta x/\Delta t$, is the average velocity defined in Eqn. 2-3. Hence, the slope of a position-time graph gives the average velocity during the time interval Δt.

For example, let us calculate the slope between $t = 120$ s and $t = 180$ s.

$$m = \frac{\Delta x}{\Delta t} = \frac{\left(3.6 \times 10^3 - 2.4 \times 10^3\right)\text{m}}{\left(180 - 120\right)\text{s}}$$

$$\therefore \quad m = \frac{1.2 \times 10^3 \text{ m}}{60 \text{ s}} = 20 \text{ m/s}$$

Thus, the slope is 20 m/s. Since this is a positive quantity, and the $+x$ direction is south, we can state that the average velocity of the train is 2.0×10^1 m/s south (assuming two significant digits) between the times 120 s and 180 s. The slope is constant, so the average velocity would be the same no matter where we calculated it along the line. It should be apparent that for uniform motion, the average velocity during any time interval is equal to the instantaneous velocity at any specific time.

Sample Problem 2-3

Describe the motion represented by each position-time graph shown in Figure 2-4.

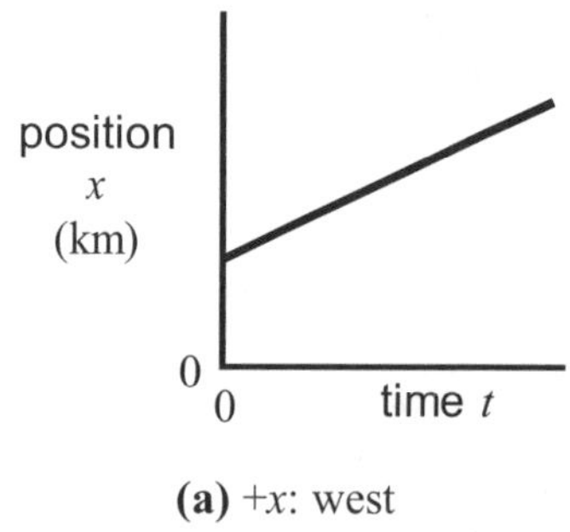

(a) $+x$: west

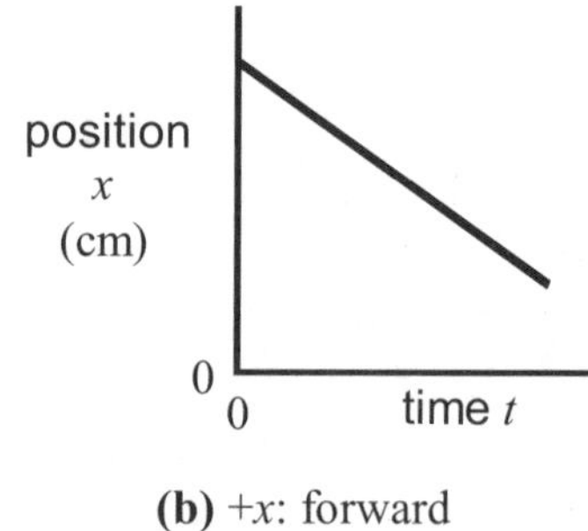

(b) $+x$: forward

Figure 2-4 *Sample Problem 2-3.*

Solution: (a) Since the line has a constant slope, the velocity is constant. The slope is positive, and since $+x$ is toward the west, the velocity is in the westerly direction. The initial position is not at the origin, and the object is moving away from the origin.

(b) Again the slope of the line is constant, however its value is negative. The $+x$ direction in this case is forward, and hence the velocity is constant in the backward direction. The initial position is not at the origin, and the moving object is travelling back toward the origin.

For uniform motion, the velocity is constant, and the velocity-time graph is very simple, being just a straight line parallel to the time axis (Figure 2-5). The area under the line (down to the time axis) on this graph can be calculated. In this case it is the area of a rectangle, $v \times \Delta t$. It is left as an exercise in the practice questions to prove that this area gives the displacement, Δx, during the time interval for which the area is found.

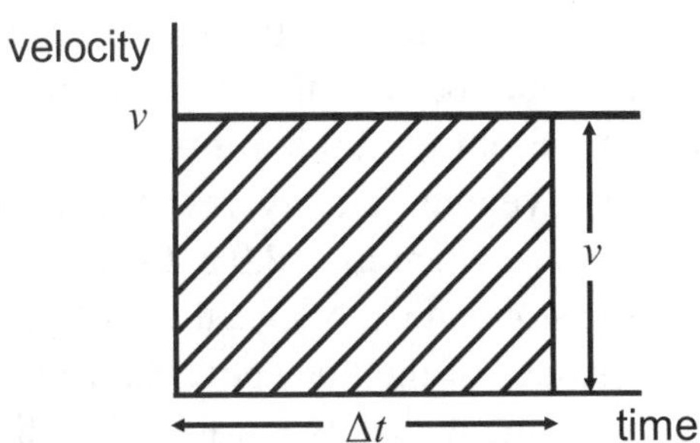

Figure 2-5 *For uniform motion, the velocity-time graph is a straight line parallel to the time axis. The area of the rectangle, $v\Delta t$, is the displacement, Δx.*

Graphing Non-Uniform Motion

Although uniform motion is easy to study, it is not common. **Non-uniform motion**, in which the velocity changes, occurs for most examples of motion. Non-uniform motion involves a change in speed (the magnitude of velocity), a change in direction, or both. In other words, the instantaneous velocity is changing.

Consider, for example, a car starting from rest and slowly speeding up. A possible set of position-time data for this motion is given below and the corresponding graph of the motion is shown in Figure 2-6. The $+x$ direction in this case is simply "forward."

time t (s):	0	2.0	4.0	6.0	8.0
position x (m):	0	4.0	16	36	64

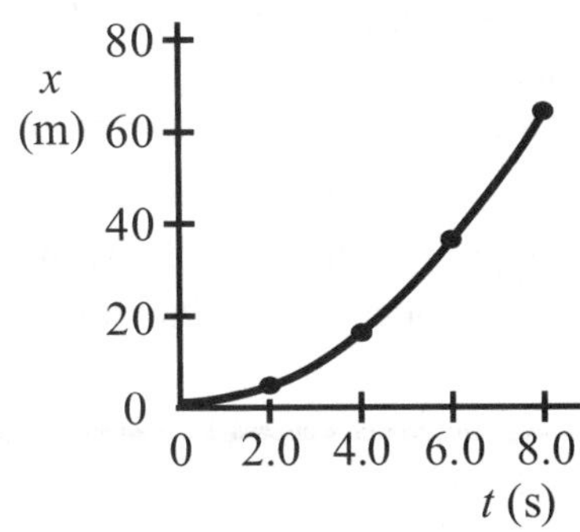

Figure 2-6 *Position vs. time graph for an example of non-uniform motion.*

Since the position-time graph shown in Figure 2-6 is not a straight line, the velocity is obviously not constant. How can we determine the velocity at any instant? Recall that for uniform motion the slope of the line on a position-time graph indicates the velocity. In this case, the slope of the curve continually changes, which means that the instantaneous velocity continually changes. To find the slope of a curved line at a particular instant, we draw a straight line parallel to the curve at that instant. This straight line is called a **tangent** to the curve. *The slope of the tangent to a curve on a position-time graph gives the instantaneous velocity.*

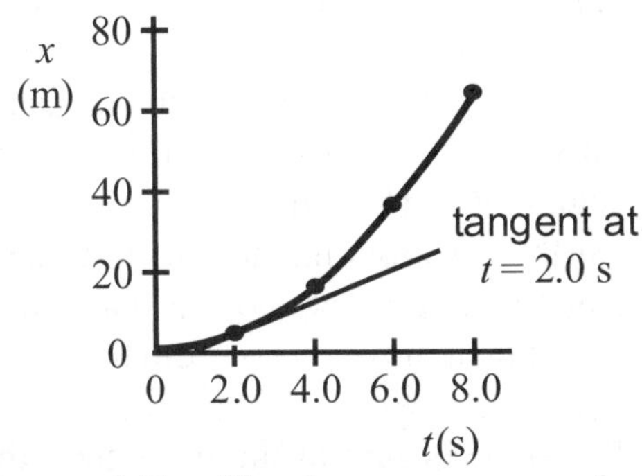

Figure 2-7 *The instantaneous velocity equals the slope of the tangent at a particular time, in this case at $t = 2.0$ s.*

Figure 2-7 shows the tangent drawn at $t = 2.0$ s for the same motion shown in the previous graph. In Figure 2-8 we compare this tangent with the average velocities between t = 2.0 s and later times. From t = 2.0 s to t = 8.0 s, the Δt is 6.0 s and the average velocity is the slope of line A in Figure 2-8. From t = 2.0 s to t = 6.0 s, Δt is 4.0 s and the average velocity is the slope of line B. Similarly, when Δt = 2.0 s, the average velocity is the slope of C. Notice that as Δt gets smaller, the slopes of the lines get nearer to the slope of the tangent that we want. In other words, as Δt becomes smaller, the average velocity ($\Delta x/\Delta t$) gets closer to the instantaneous velocity (v):

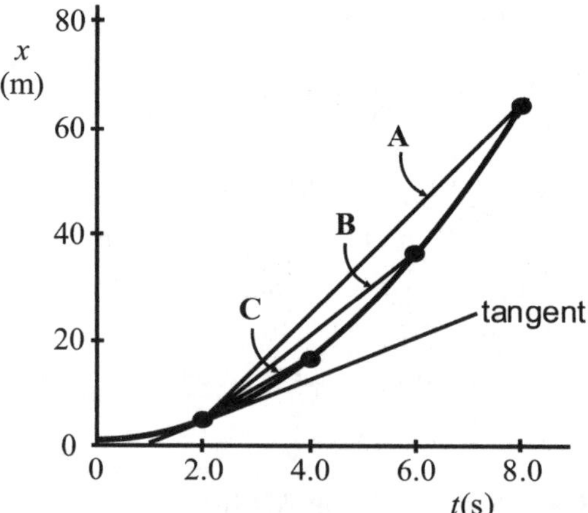

Figure 2-8 *Comparing the slope of the tangent at t = 2.0 s with the average velocities represented by the slopes of lines A, B, and C. Notice that the slope of C is almost the same as the slope of the tangent.*

$$v = \lim_{\Delta t \to 0} \frac{\Delta x}{\Delta t} \qquad \textbf{(2-4)}$$

This is read as: "The instantaneous velocity v equals the limit, as Δt approaches zero, of Δx divided by Δt." (In the notation of calculus the Δ symbols are replaced by d symbols to represent very small quantities. Thus, the instantaneous velocity is $v = dx/dt$.)

To summarize, the *instantaneous velocity* is the velocity at a particular instant, and it equals the slope of the tangent on the position-time graph at that instant. The *instantaneous speed* of a moving object equals the magnitude of its instantaneous velocity.

Sample Problem 2-4

Describe the motion represented by the curves in the position-time graphs of Figure 2-9. For both graphs, the $+x$ direction is east.

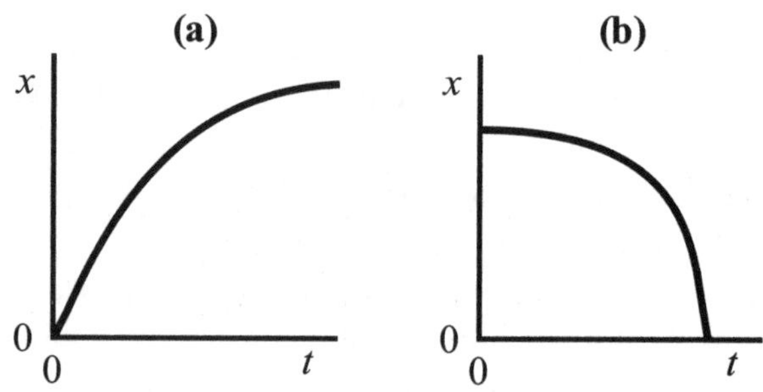

Figure 2-9 *Position-time graphs for Sample Problem 2-4.*

Solution: (a) The slope of the (tangent to the) curve is positive and is relatively steep at the beginning. Thus, the velocity starts off high in the easterly direction, then gradually reduces to zero. The object starts at the origin and then moves away from the origin.

(b) The slope is zero at the beginning, then it becomes negative. Thus, the velocity starts off at zero, then gradually increases in magnitude in the westerly direction. The object starts at a position east of the origin, then moves westward until it reaches the origin.

Sample Problem 2-5

Figure 2-10 shows a graph of position vs. time for a woman who is walking back and forth on a sidewalk, waiting for a friend. The $+x$ direction is west. At time $t = 25$ s, what is her instantaneous velocity?

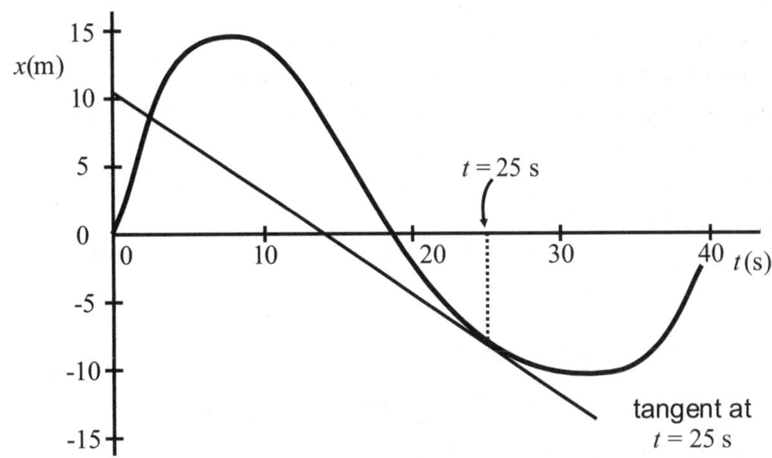

Figure 2-10 *Sample Problem 2-5.*

Solution: Since we are asked for the instantaneous velocity at $t = 25$ s, we draw a tangent to the curve at this point, and then calculate the slope of this tangent line. We can use the position and time co-ordinates of *any* two points on this line to calculate the slope. It is easiest if we extrapolate the line back to intersect both the x-axis and the t-axis, giving us these two points on the line: $(t_1, x_1) = (0\text{ s}, 10.5\text{ m})$ and $(t_2, x_2) = (14\text{ s}, 0\text{ m})$.

Calculating the slope:

$$\begin{aligned} m &= \frac{\Delta x}{\Delta t} = \frac{x_2 - x_1}{t_2 - t_1} \\ &= \frac{(0 - 10.5)\text{ m}}{(14 - 0)\text{ s}} \\ &= -0.75\text{ m/s} \end{aligned}$$

The negative sign indicates that the velocity is in the $-x$ direction, that is, eastward. Thus, the instantaneous velocity is approximately 0.75 m/s east. (We say "approximately" because of the large uncertainty in our hand-drawing of the tangent).

Math Tip: *When calculating velocity by determining the slope of a line, it is important to "match up" the x- and t-values in the numerator and denominator. In the solution to the sample problem above, the position value (x_2) that appears first in the numerator corresponds to the time value (t_2) appearing first in the denominator. Similarly, the position x_1 corresponds to the time t_1.*

Practice

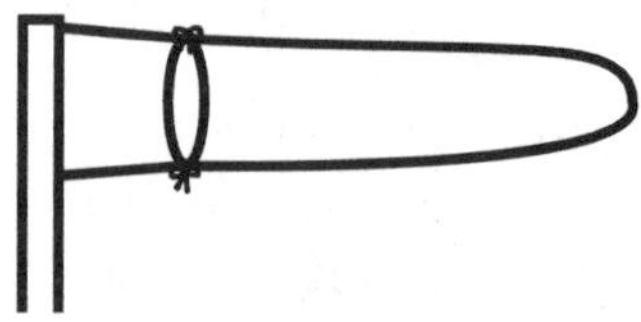

Figure 2-11 *Question 2-6.*

2-6 The windsock shown in Figure 2-11 is used at a small airport. Does this device indicate a scalar quantity or a vector quantity? What is that quantity?

2-7 (a) Under what conditions could the total distance travelled equal the magnitude of the displacement?
(b) Is it possible for the distance travelled to exceed the magnitude of the displacement? Explain, using an example.
(c) Is it possible for the magnitude of the displacement to exceed the distance travelled? Explain, using an example.

2-8 (a) State the difference between instantaneous speed and instantaneous velocity.
(b) Under what condition(s) could the average speed equal the magnitude of the average velocity?

2-9 A city bus travels a straight route that is 12 km from one end to the other. The bus takes 48 min to complete the route, including all stops *and the return* to the initial position.
(a) Calculate the average speed of the bus over the entire route.
(b) Calculate the average velocity of the bus over the entire route.
(c) Why are these answers different? [Ans. (a) 3.0×10^1 km/h (b) 0.0 km/h]

2-10 A billiard ball travels 0.46 m in the $+x$ direction, having started at the origin ($x = 0$), bounces off another ball to travel 0.84 m in the opposite direction, then bounces from the edge of the billiard table finally coming to rest 0.12 m from that edge. The entire motion is one-dimensional and takes 2.5 s. Determine the billiard ball's: (a) average speed
(b) final position (c) average velocity.
[Ans. (a) 0.57 m/s (b) –0.26 m (c) –0.10 m/s]

2-11 The graph in Figure 2-12 represents the position-time graph[1] of an automobile westward, i.e., the $+x$ direction is west. Determine the
(a) average speed between 0.0 s and 4.0 s; between 0.0 s and 8.0 s
(b) average velocity between 8.0 s and 10 s; between 12 s and 16 s; and between 0.0 s and 16 s
(c) instantaneous speed at 6.0 s; at 10 s
(d) instantaneous velocity at 14 s
[Ans. (a) 10 m/s, 5.0 m/s (b) 2.5 m/s west, 13 m/s east, 0 m/s (c) 0 m/s, 2.5 m/s (d) 13 m/s east]

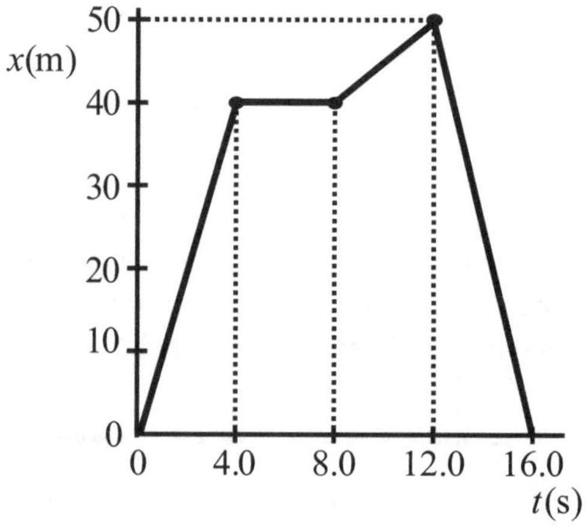

Figure 2-12 *Question 2-11.*

[1]The abrupt changes in the slopes of the lines in such graphs are idealized. The speed of an automobile cannot instantly change from 10 m/s to 0 m/s, for example; the sharp corners shown in graphs such as Figure 2-12 would be rounded for the motion of an actual automobile. However, the sharp corners make it easier for you to answer the questions.

2-12 A car driver sees an emergency and reacts to put on the brakes. During the 0.20 s reaction time, the car maintains its uniform velocity of 28 m/s forward. What is the car's displacement during the time it takes the driver to react? [Ans. 5.6 m forward]

2-13 At an average velocity of 8.5 m/s straight down, how long does it take a parachutist to descend from an altitude of 2.4×10^3 m above sea level to 7.2×10^2 m above sea level? [Ans. 2.0×10^2 s]

2-14 Describe the motion represented by each position-time graph in Figure 2-13.

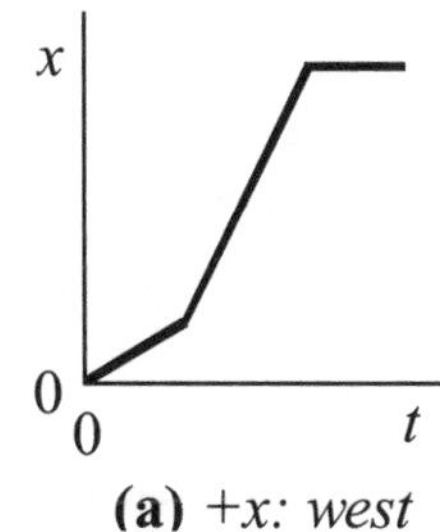

(a) *+x: west*

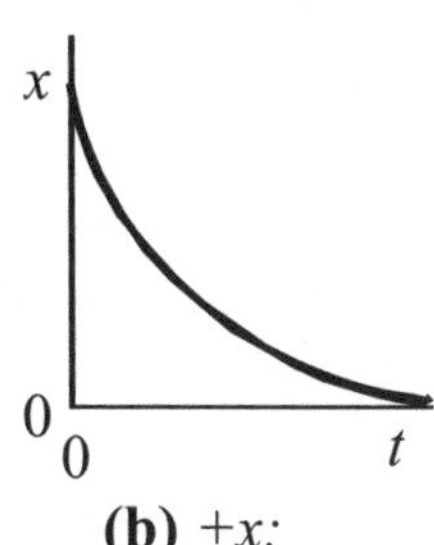

(b) *+x:*

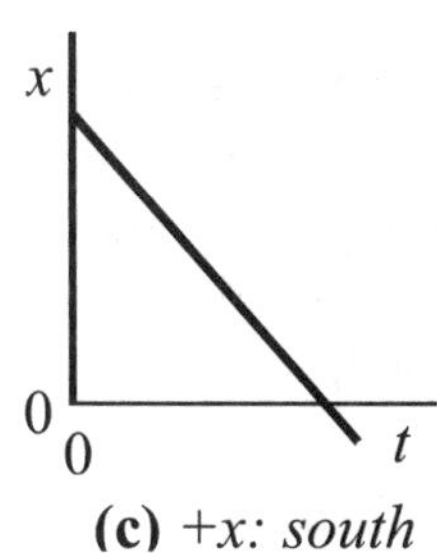

(c) *+x: south*

Figure 2-13 *Question 2-14.*

2-15 Determine the area between the line and the horizontal axis on the velocity-time graph in Figure 2-14. (The velocity is northward.) What does this area represent? (Hint: Be sure to include units in your calculation of area.) [Ans. 7.5 m (northward) = displacement]

2-16 Determine the instantaneous velocity at 2.5 s, 4.5 s, and 6.0 s from the graph in Figure 2-15. The $+x$ direction is south.
[Ans. approx. 8.3 cm/s south, approx. 13 cm/s south, 0 cm/s]

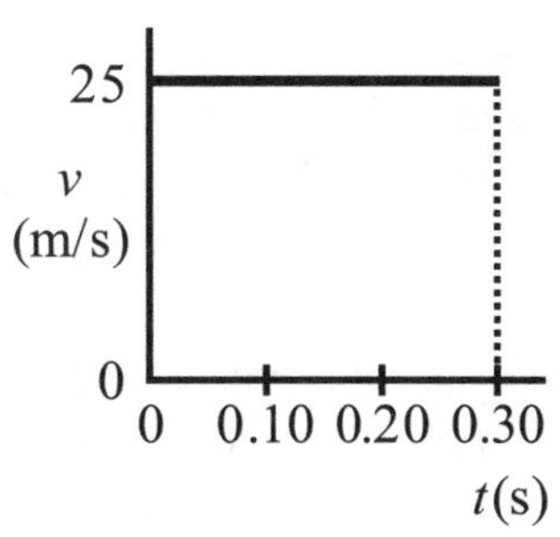

Figure 2-14 *Question 2-15.*

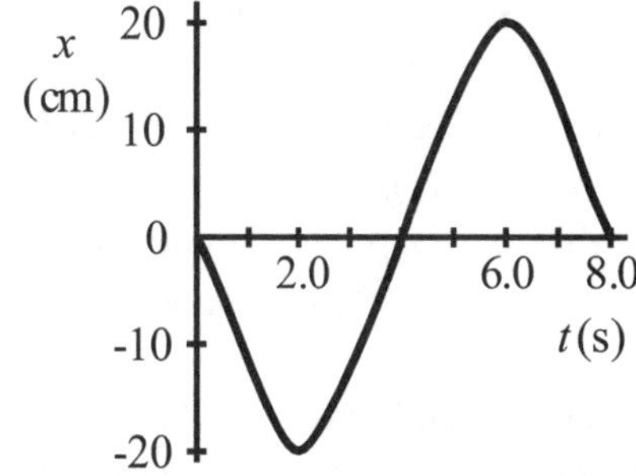

Figure 2-15 *Question 2-16.*

2.3 ACCELERATION

In this chapter you have encountered both uniform motion and non-uniform motion. The latter, in which there is a change in the magnitude of the velocity, the direction of the velocity, or both, is known formally as accelerated motion.

Acceleration is common in our daily lives, and some scientists devote their studies entirely to analyzing acceleration and its effects. One type of acceleration that we cannot escape is caused by the force of gravity pulling objects toward Earth. (We will study this acceleration in Section 2.5.) Acceleration occurs in all types of transportation — automobiles, aircraft, bicycles, even walking. Emergency escape systems in military aircraft produce a high acceleration for a brief period of time to eject the pilot out of the craft. Studies are made to improve these systems to reduce the injuries that may occur during this high acceleration. Astronauts must be placed in a lay-back position to prevent loss of blood to the head during upward acceleration. Acceleration in sports is also important. A sprinter with a greater acceleration has a better chance of winning a short race.

Acceleration that corresponds to decrease in speed is also of great concern to the average person. When a vehicle has a collision or must stop quickly, the driver and passengers tend to keep going, at least temporarily. Research is carried out to try to improve safety devices to prevent human injury during these emergencies. Headrests, seat belts, and air bags help reduce injury and deaths caused in automobile accidents.

To analyze accelerated motion we begin by stating the formal definition of **acceleration**: it is the time rate of change of velocity. In many cases in this text we will be concerned with **average acceleration**, which is:

$$\text{average acceleration} = \frac{\text{change in velocity}}{\text{elapsed time}}$$

In symbols:

$$a_{\text{av}} = \frac{\Delta v}{\Delta t} = \frac{v_2 - v_1}{t_2 - t_1} \qquad \textbf{(2-5)}$$

where v_1 is the velocity at time t_1, and v_2 is the velocity at time t_2.

Since velocity is a vector quantity, acceleration is also a vector quantity. Again because the motion studied in this chapter is in one dimension, details about the vector nature of acceleration are left for Chapter 4. The important thing to remember here is that vector quantities have a direction and their magnitudes can be positive or negative.

Various units can be used to denote acceleration, as long as they derive from a velocity unit divided by a time unit. Examples of units are found in the next two sample problems.

Sample Problem 2-6

A powerful racing car accelerates from rest to 96 km/h west in 4.1 s. Determine the average acceleration of this motion.

Solution: Define the $+x$ direction to be west. We use Eqn. 2-5:

$$a_{\text{av}} = \frac{\Delta v}{\Delta t}$$

In this problem, $\Delta v = v_2 - v_1 = (96 - 0)$ km/h, and $\Delta t = 4.1$ s.

Hence, $$a_{av} = \frac{96\text{ km/h}}{4.1\text{ s}} = 23\left(\text{km/h}\right)/\text{s}$$

Since the result of our calculation is a positive quantity, the average acceleration is in the $+x$ direction, that is, west. Thus, the average acceleration is 23 (km/h)/s west. This means that for every second that the acceleration occurs, the velocity increases by 23 km/h (west). Hence, the velocity is 23 km/h west after 1.0 s, then 46 km/h west after 2.0 s, and so on.

Sample Problem 2-7

A motorcyclist is travelling at 23 m/s in the $+x$ direction. Suddenly the cyclist brakes to prevent an accident and comes to a stop in 3.2 s.
(a) Determine the magnitude of the cyclist's average acceleration.
(b) Use the units found in (a) to show that acceleration has the dimensions L/T^2.

Solution: (a) Again we use Eqn. 2-5:

$$a_{av} = \frac{\Delta v}{\Delta t}$$

In this particular problem, $\Delta v = v_2 - v_1 = (0 - 23)$ m/s, and $\Delta t = 3.2$ s.

Notice that Δv is negative. It is important to remember that a change (Δ) in a quantity must always be calculated as the *final* value of the quantity minus the *initial* value.

Calculating a_{av}: $$a_{av} = \frac{-23\text{ m/s}}{3.2\text{ s}} = -7.2\text{ (m/s)/s} = -7.2\text{ m/s}^2$$

Thus, the average acceleration is -7.2 m/s^2, or 7.2 m/s^2 in the negative-x direction.

(b) The units of average acceleration determined in part (a) are m/s^2. Since metre is a unit of length, and second is a unit of time, the dimensions of acceleration are L/T^2.

Notice in Sample Problem 2-7 that the acceleration is negative. If a moving object has an initial velocity that is positive, then negative acceleration means that the object slows down, as is the case in the above problem. However, if an object is already moving in the negative direction, then a negative acceleration means that the object is speeding up. For example, if the $+x$ direction is east and a car is heading west, thus having a negative velocity, then a westward acceleration (which is also negative) would indicate that the car is speeding up in the westward direction.[2]

[2] Slowing down is sometimes called deceleration, but this term will not be used in this book.

Graphing Constant-Acceleration Motion

A skier, starting from rest at the top of a ski slope, experiences an acceleration of 3.0 m/s^2 down the slope. The acceleration remains constant for the first 6.0 s. A table of data for this example is shown below and the corresponding velocity-time graph is shown in Figure 2-16. The $+x$ direction is along the slope, downward.

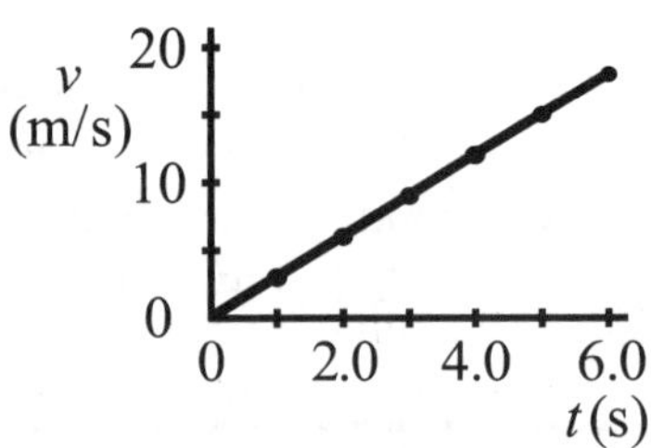

Figure 2-16 *Velocity-time graph for the constant-acceleration example.*

time t (s)	0.0	1.0	2.0	3.0	4.0	5.0	6.0
velocity v (m/s)	0.0	3.0	6.0	9.0	12	15	18

The slope of the line on the velocity-time graph in Figure 2-16 is:

$$\text{slope} = \frac{\Delta v}{\Delta t}$$

However, $\Delta v/\Delta t$ is just average acceleration. In this example, the slope is constant, and thus the average acceleration is constant. In addition, the acceleration at any instant — the instantaneous acceleration (symbol a) — is also constant. (We will define instantaneous acceleration mathematically shortly.) The acceleration-time graph for the above example is shown in Figure 2-17.

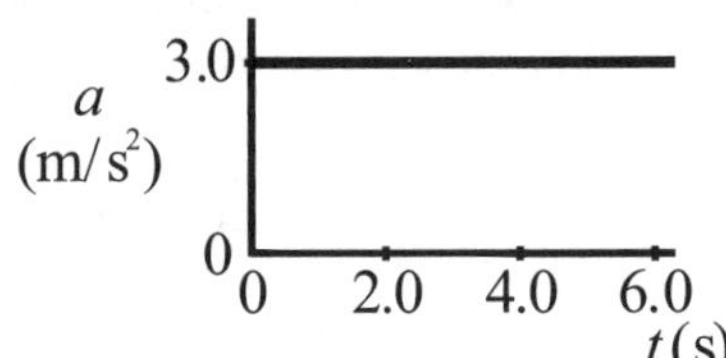

Figure 2-17 *Acceleration-time graph for the constant-acceleration example.*

What additional information can be found from the acceleration-time graph? Recall from the graphing of uniform motion that the area under the line on a velocity-time graph indicates the displacement, i.e., the change in position. Similarly, the area under the line on an acceleration-time graph indicates the change in velocity. This is verified in the next sample problem.

Sample Problem 2-8

A car, with a standard transmission, reaches 30 km/h in first gear, after which it undergoes acceleration for 10 s in second and third gears. The acceleration for this ten-second interval is indicated in Figure 2-18. (The $+x$ direction is "forward.") Determine the magnitude of the velocity at the end of 4.0 s of this acceleration and at the end of 10 s. Then draw a velocity-time graph corresponding to the acceleration-time graph.

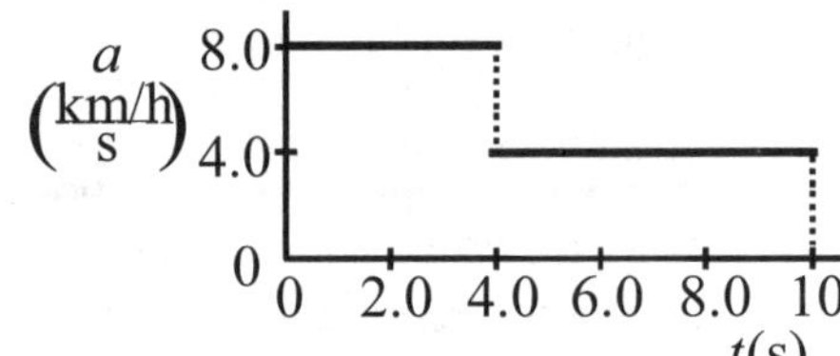

Figure 2-18 *Sample Problem 2-8.*

Solution: We consider the first 4.0 s. The definition of average acceleration, $a_{av} = \Delta v/\Delta t$, can be easily re-arranged to give the change in velocity, Δv: $\Delta v = a_{av}\Delta t$.

The average acceleration is 8.0 (km/h)/s, and $\Delta t = 4.0$ s. Hence,

$$\Delta v = 8.0\,\frac{\text{km/h}}{\text{s}} \times 4.0\text{ s} = 32\text{ km/h}$$

Thus, the velocity increases by 32 km/h during the first 4.0 s. Since the velocity at the beginning of this time interval was 30 km/h, the velocity at the end of 4.0 s is: (30 + 32) km/h = 62 km/h, in the forward direction.

Notice that the *increase* in velocity equals the area under the line on the acceleration-time graph between $t = 0$ and $t = 4.0$ s. This region has a height of 8.0 (km/h)/s and a width of 4.0 s, and hence an area (height × width) of 32 km/h.

To determine the increase in velocity from $t = 4.0$ s to $t = 10$ s, we will find the area under the line:

$$\begin{aligned}\text{area under line} &= \text{height} \times \text{width}\\ &= 4.0\,\frac{\text{km/h}}{\text{s}} \times 6.0\text{ s}\\ &= 24\text{ km/h}\end{aligned}$$

Therefore, at $t = 10$ s, the velocity is:

$$v = 62\text{ km/h} + 24\text{ km/h} = 86\text{ km/h, forward}$$

The corresponding velocity-time graph is shown in Figure 2-19. Notice again that during each period of constant acceleration, the velocity changes linearly with time.

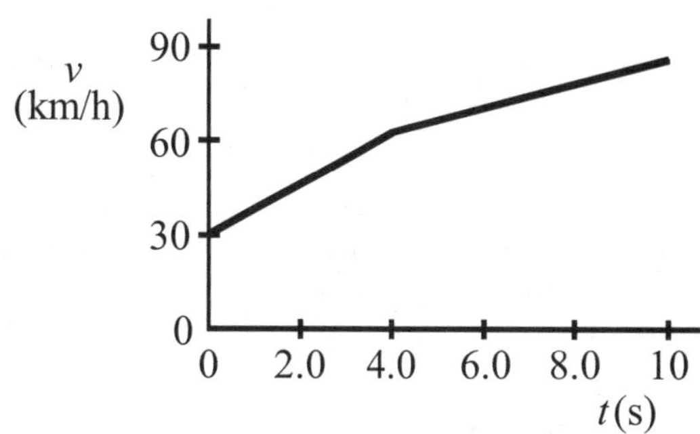

Figure 2-19 *Sample Problem 2-8 (solution).*

Let us summarize the concepts associated with graphs related to motion.

- The three graphs commonly drawn are position vs. time (or perhaps displacement vs. time), velocity vs. time, and acceleration vs. time.
- Two important quantities found from graphs are slope and area under the line (or, more generally, area under the curve).
- The slope of a position-time graph gives velocity.
- The slope of a velocity-time graph gives acceleration.
- The area under the line (curve) on an acceleration-time graph indicates the change in velocity.
- The area under the line (curve) on a velocity-time graph indicates the change in position, that is, the displacement.

Variable (Non-Constant) Acceleration

The velocity-time graph for an object undergoing constant acceleration is a straight line. For non-constant acceleration, however, the velocity-time graph is curved — the slope changes as the acceleration changes. An example of a velocity-time graph showing increasing acceleration is shown in Figure 2-20. The acceleration at any instant, called the **instantaneous acceleration**, is the slope of the tangent to the curve at that instant. In the figure, a tangent is drawn at $t = 4$ s. Just as instantaneous velocity is defined as the limit, as $\Delta t \to 0$, of $\Delta x/\Delta t$, instantaneous acceleration (symbol a) is defined as the limit, as $\Delta t \to 0$, of $\Delta v/\Delta t$:

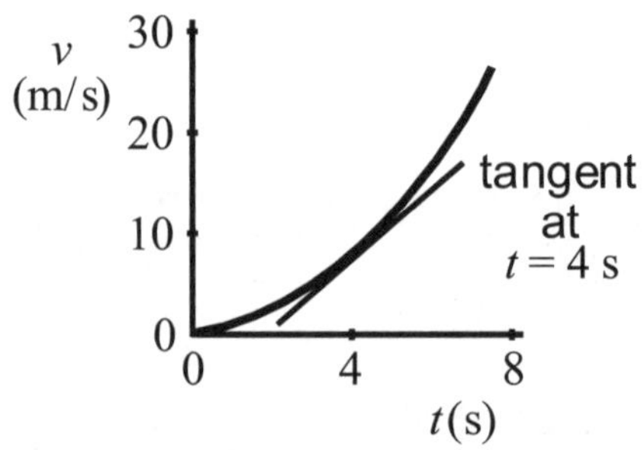

Figure 2-20 *A velocity-time graph showing non-constant acceleration. The acceleration at time t = 4 s equals the slope of the tangent to the curve at this time.*

$$a = \lim_{\Delta t \to 0} \frac{\Delta v}{\Delta t} \qquad \textbf{(2-6)}$$

In other words, as Δt approaches zero, the average acceleration ($\Delta v/\Delta t$) approaches the instantaneous acceleration. (Using the notation of calculus, instantaneous acceleration $a = dv/dt$.)

From now on, whenever the word acceleration is used it will be assumed to be the instantaneous acceleration. If average acceleration is required, it will be called average acceleration (symbol a_{av}).

Sample Problem 2-9

Describe the motion represented by the graph in Figure 2-21. The $+x$ direction is "forward."

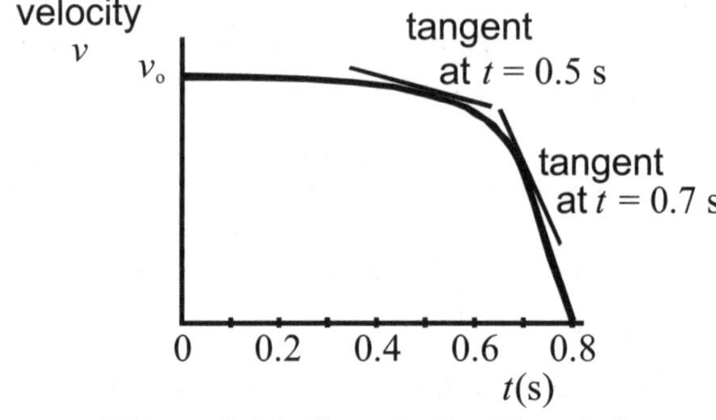

Figure 2-21 *Sample Problem 2-9.*

Solution: The motion begins with an initial velocity, v_0, and undergoes a slight slowing down or negative acceleration followed by a negative acceleration with increasing magnitude. (Tangents are drawn at 0.5 s and 0.7 s. Their slopes are negative, and the magnitude of the slope at 0.7 s is larger than that at 0.5 s.) The object, while always heading in the forward direction, slows down from a speed of v_0 at time $t = 0.0$ s, and comes to rest at $t = 0.8$ s.

Practice

2-17 Which of the following could be units of acceleration?
(a) km/min^2 (b) cm·s^{-2} (c) (Mm/h)·h (d) (dam/s)/h

2-18 A flock of geese is travelling south during the fall migration. The $+x$ direction is south. Describe the flock's motion when its acceleration is: (a) zero (b) positive (c) negative.

2-19 Is it possible to have westward velocity with eastward acceleration? Explain, with an example.

2-20 A track runner starts from rest and reaches a speed of 9.2 m/s in 3.8 s. Calculate the magnitude of the runner's average acceleration. [Ans. 2.4 m/s^2]

2-21 In an archery tournament an arrow, travelling at 42.8 m/s east, strikes a target and comes to a stop in 3.12×10^{-2} s. Determine the magnitude and direction of the arrow's average acceleration during this short period of time. [Ans. 1.37×10^3 m/s^2 west]

2-22 A supersonic jet travelling from New York City to London reduces its velocity from 1.65×10^3 km/h east to 1.12×10^3 km/h east before reaching the western shores of England.
(a) If this change of velocity takes 345 s, determine the jet's average acceleration in kilometres per hour per second ((km/h)/s).
(b) Determine this acceleration in metres per second squared.
[Ans. (a) 1.54 (km/h)/s west (b) 0.427 m/s^2 west]

2-23 Figure 2-22 shows a graph of velocity vs. time for a cat walking along a fallen tree. The $+x$ direction is north. Draw the corresponding acceleration-time graph.

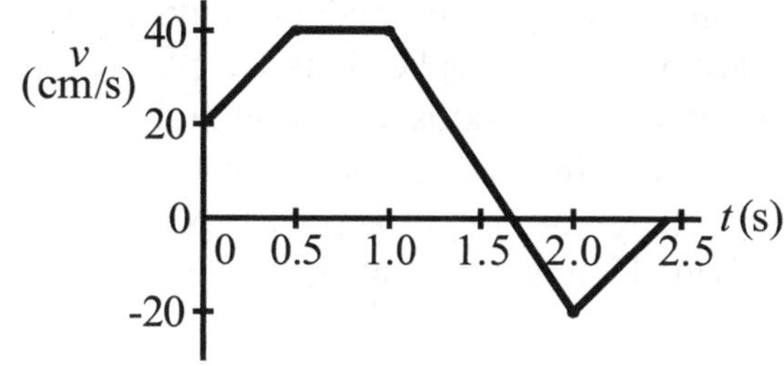

Figure 2-22 *Question 2-23.*

2-24 The data shown in the table below were recorded during an experiment involving measurements of the velocity of a baby crawling on a floor. The $+x$ direction is "forward."

time (s):	0.0	2.0	4.0	6.0	8.0	10	12
velocity (cm/s):	10	15	20	15	10	5.0	0.0

(a) Plot a velocity-time graph for this motion.
(b) Determine the slopes of the different line segments on the graph.
(c) Use the values found in (b) to plot an acceleration-time graph for this motion.

2-25 The acceleration-time graph of a football lineman being pushed by other players is illustrated in Figure 2-23. The $+x$ direction is west. Plot the corresponding velocity-time graph, assuming the initial velocity is zero.

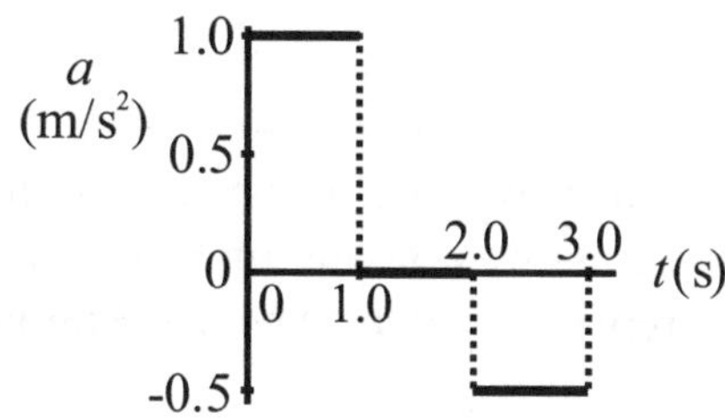

Figure 2-23 *Question 2-25.*

2-26 Under what conditions would average acceleration and instantaneous acceleration be equal?

2-27 Describe the motion represented in each graph in Figure 2-24. Be sure to consider the axes of each graph.

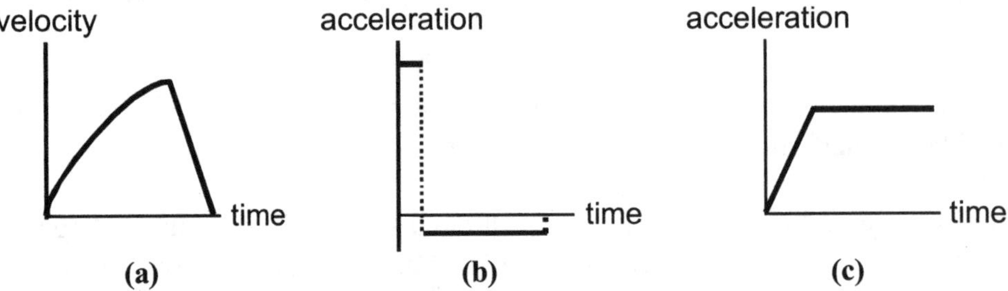

Figure 2-24 *Question 2-27.*

2.4 SOLVING CONSTANT-ACCELERATION PROBLEMS

Some of the joys of studying physics relate to understanding things that go on around us and learning about applications of physics principles. But studying physics also involves the development of skills in solving problems. To experience success in this aspect of physics requires practice. In this section, probably more than in most other parts of the text, you will gain knowledge in how to approach problem-solving in physics, and you will experience practice in solving kinematics problems logically.

We begin this section by deriving several equations that will be useful in a variety of circumstances, and then apply those equations in solving problems.

Equations of Kinematics for Constant Acceleration

A number of new and very useful equations can be derived by using substitution in equations already known. We start with the definition of average acceleration (Eqn. 2-5):

$$a_{av} = \frac{\Delta v}{\Delta t} = \frac{v_2 - v_1}{t_2 - t_1}$$

Since we are considering only constant acceleration in this section, the instantaneous acceleration, a, at any time equals the average acceleration, a_{av}, during any time interval, and we can replace a_{av} in the above equation with a. Hence, we can write:

$$a = \frac{v_2 - v_1}{t_2 - t_1}$$

In dealing with constant-acceleration situations, it is usually convenient to set the initial time t_1 equal to zero, and to write the final time t_2 simply as t. In addition, the initial velocity (at $t = 0$) is normally written as v_0, and the final velocity (at time t) is written just as v. Making these changes:

$$a = \frac{v - v_0}{t - 0}$$

Re-arranging this equation to solve for v:

$$v = v_0 + at \quad \text{(for constant acceleration)} \qquad \textbf{(2-7)}$$

Equation 2-7 will be used many times in solving physics problems involving constant acceleration. In words, it states that "final velocity equals the sum of initial velocity and acceleration times time."

We now develop further equations, starting with the definition of average velocity from Eqn. 2-3:

$$v_{\text{av}} = \frac{\Delta x}{\Delta t} = \frac{x_2 - x_1}{t_2 - t_1}$$

Since the acceleration is constant, the velocity is changing at a uniform rate (that is, linearly), and therefore the average velocity is midway between the initial and final velocities:

$$v_{\text{av}} = \frac{v_0 + v}{2}$$

Substituting this expression for v_{av} into the previous equation:

$$\frac{v_0 + v}{2} = \frac{x_2 - x_1}{t_2 - t_1}$$

As we did before, we now write the final time t_2 as t, and set the initial time t_1 to be zero. In addition, we write the initial position x_1 as x_0 (at time $t = 0$), and the final position x_2 simply as x (at time t):

$$\frac{v_0 + v}{2} = \frac{x - x_0}{t - 0}$$

Solving for $x - x_0$ gives: $$x - x_0 = \tfrac{1}{2}(v_0 + v)\,t$$

Re-arranging to solve for final position x:

$$x = x_0 + \tfrac{1}{2}(v_0 + v)\,t \quad \text{(for constant acceleration)} \qquad \textbf{(2-8)}$$

To obtain an equation for final position in terms of initial position, initial velocity, acceleration, and time, we substitute the expression for v from Eqn. 2-7 ($v = v_0 + at$) into Eqn. 2-8 to eliminate the final velocity:

$$x = x_0 + \tfrac{1}{2}\left(v_0 + \left(v_0 + at\right)\right)t$$

Simplifying: $$x = x_0 + v_0 t + \tfrac{1}{2} at^2 \quad \text{(for constant acceleration)} \qquad \textbf{(2-9)}$$

Finally, we derive an equation involving initial and final velocities, displacement, and acceleration. We begin with Eqn. 2-8:

$$x = x_0 + \tfrac{1}{2}\left(v_0 + v\right)t$$

From Eqn. 2-7, we can readily obtain the following expression for the time, t:

$$t = \frac{v - v_0}{a}$$

Substituting this expression for t into Eqn. 2-8:

$$x = x_0 + \tfrac{1}{2}\left(v_0 + v\right)\frac{\left(v - v_0\right)}{a}$$

Simplifying the right-hand-side: $$x = x_0 + \frac{v^2 - v_0^2}{2a}$$

Re-arranging: $$v^2 - v_0^2 = 2a\left(x - x_0\right) \quad \text{(for constant acceleration)} \qquad \textbf{(2-10)}$$

With equations 2-7, 2-8, 2-9, and 2-10, we are now in a position to solve any problem involving *constant acceleration* in one dimension. We list these equations below for handy reference:

$$v = v_0 + at \qquad \textbf{(2-7)}$$

$$x = x_0 + \tfrac{1}{2}\left(v_0 + v\right)t \qquad \textbf{(2-8)}$$

$$x = x_0 + v_0 t + \tfrac{1}{2} at^2 \qquad \textbf{(2-9)}$$

$$v^2 - v_0^2 = 2a\left(x - x_0\right) \qquad \textbf{(2-10)}$$

where a = acceleration (must be constant to use the above equations)

x_0 = (initial) position at time $t = 0$ $\quad$ x = (final) position at time t

v_0 = (initial) velocity at time $t = 0$ $\quad$ v = (final) velocity at time t

Notice that each of these equations does not involve all the variables. Equation 2-7 does not contain the position variables x and x_0; equation 2-8 does not contain acceleration, a; equation 2-9 does not have final velocity v; and equation 2-10 does not involve time t. Noting which variables are eliminated in the various equations makes problem solving easier.

When solving problems in kinematics, it is often handy to choose the initial position, x_0, to be zero. This produces obvious simplifications in Eqns. 2-8 to 2-10.

Learning how and when to use these kinematics equations takes practice. Before proceeding to solve some sample problems, we list in Table 2.2 the important quantities we have encountered so far in kinematics.

Table 2.2 Important Quantities in Kinematics

Quantity	*Type of Quantity*
distance	scalar
average speed	scalar
speed	scalar
time	scalar
initial position	vector
final position	vector
displacement (change in position)	vector
initial velocity	vector
final velocity	vector
average acceleration	vector
acceleration	vector

Applying the Kinematics Equations

To develop skill in solving problems that may involve up to five or even six variables, it is wise to follow a logical set of steps. Some basic problem-solving steps are listed below.

Problem-Solving Tips:

1. Read the problem then draw a sketch to help you understand the problem better.

2. Define a positive direction to use in that particular problem, and then be consistent with your signs for the various quantities. (For example, if you decide that the positive direction is east, then the velocity of a westward-moving bicycle is negative.)

3. Write down what is given, including words that translate into quantities, using the proper symbols and consistent units. (For example, if an object "starts from rest," its initial velocity is zero, or $v_0 = 0$, and if acceleration is given in metres per second squared and time is given in minutes, change the time to seconds.)

4. Determine which equations involve the quantities in the problem, and plan an attack involving these equations. Sometimes only one equation is needed.

5. When using an individual equation, re-arrange it to solve for the unknown quantity before

substituting the numerical values into the equation.

6. Write the answer with the correct units, the appropriate number of significant digits, and a direction if the answer is a vector.

7. Check to be sure the answer makes sense. If it seems too large or too small, check your steps and arithmetic.

These steps will be illustrated in the sample problems that follow.

Sample Problem 2-10

A motorcyclist shifts from second to third gear when travelling at 15 m/s. She then speeds up for 3.6 s with a constant acceleration of magnitude 5.2 m/s^2. How far did she travel during the acceleration?

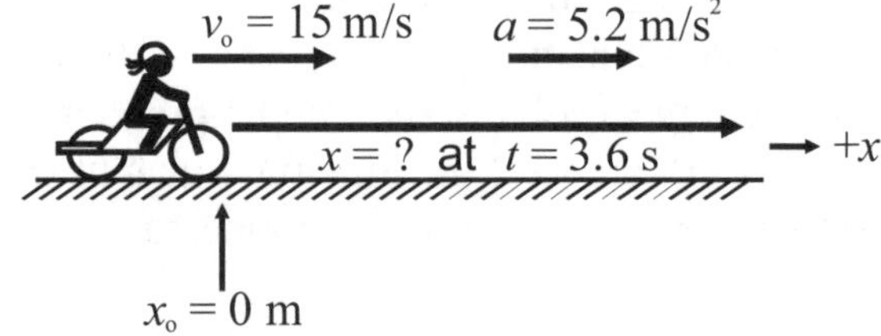

Figure 2-25 *Sample Problem 2-10.*

Solution: Define the $+x$ direction to be forward, and choose the initial position to be $x_0 = 0$ m (Figure 2-25).

The known quantities are:

$$v_0 = 15 \text{ m/s}$$
$$t = 3.6 \text{ s}$$
$$a = 5.2 \text{ m/s}^2$$
$$x_0 = 0 \text{ m}$$

The quantity required is x, and we note that the final velocity, v, is not provided.

We can use Eqn. 2-9 directly: $x = x_0 + v_0 t + \frac{1}{2} a t^2$

$$\therefore \quad x = (0 \text{ m}) + (15 \text{ m/s})(3.6 \text{ s}) + \tfrac{1}{2}(5.2 \text{ m/s}^2)(3.6 \text{ s})^2$$
$$= 54 \text{ m} + 34 \text{ m}$$
$$= 88 \text{ m} \quad \text{(to two significant digits)}$$

Thus, the cyclist travelled 88 m.

Sample Problem 2-11

A rocket is launched vertically from rest, and when it reaches an altitude of 4.7 km above the launch pad, its speed is 630 m/s. What is the magnitude of the rocket's acceleration (assumed constant)?

Solution: Choose the $+x$ direction to be up, and choose the initial position (the launch pad) to be $x_0 = 0$ m (Figure 2-26).

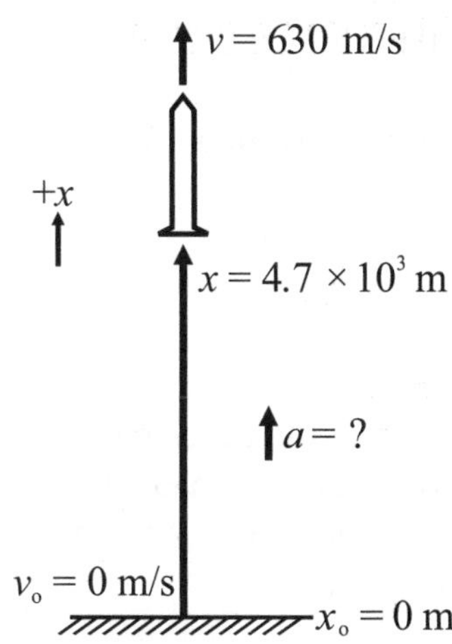

Figure 2-26 *Sample Problem 2-11.*

The known quantities are:

$v_0 = 0$ m/s ("launched vertically *from rest*")
$x = 4.7$ km $= 4.7 \times 10^3$ m
$v = 630$ m/s
$x_0 = 0$ m

The required quantity is the magnitude of the acceleration, a, and we note that the time, t, is not provided. We can use Eqn. 2-10, which does not involve time, to determine the acceleration:

$$v^2 - v_0^2 = 2a\left(x - x_0\right)$$

We first simplify this equation by noting that both v_0 and x_0 are zero.

Hence, $$v^2 = 2ax$$

We now re-arrange this equation to solve for the required acceleration, a:

$$a = \frac{v^2}{2x}$$

Substituting values: $$a = \frac{\left(630 \text{ m/s}\right)^2}{2\left(4.7 \times 10^3 \text{ m}\right)}$$

$$\therefore \quad a = 42 \text{ m/s}^2$$

Thus, the rocket's acceleration is 42 m/s^2 in magnitude.

Sample Problem 2-12

In a game of curling, a rock is sent along the ice where it experiences a constant acceleration of 4.8 cm/s^2 in a direction opposite to the initial velocity. The rock travels 28 m from release before coming to rest. Determine the rock's (a) initial velocity and (b) travel time.

Solution: We select the $+x$ direction to be in the direction of the rock's motion, and choose the point of release to be at $x_0 = 0$ m (Figure 2-27).

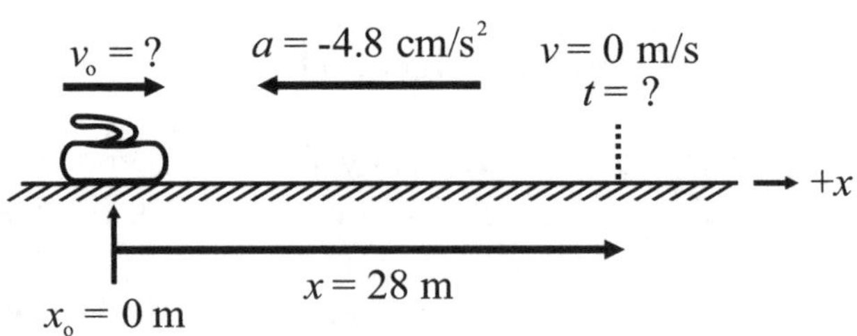

Figure 2-27 *Sample Problem 2-12.*

The given quantities are:

$x = 28$ m

$v = 0$ m/s

$a = -4.8 \text{ cm/s}^2 = -0.048 \text{ m/s}^2$

$x_0 = 0$ m

Notice that the acceleration is negative because its direction is opposite to the $+x$ direction (rock's motion). If we had chosen the positive direction to be opposite to the rock's motion, the acceleration would have been positive, but the initial velocity and the final position would have been negative.

(a) The required quantity is v_0, and the time is not provided.

We can use Eqn. 2-10: $v^2 - v_0^2 = 2a(x - x_0)$

Immediately substituting $v = 0$ m/s and $x_0 = 0$ m, and then solving for v_0^2:

$$v_0^2 = -2ax$$

Taking the square root: $v_0 = \pm\sqrt{-2ax}$

Substituting values:

$$v_0 = \pm\sqrt{-2(-0.048 \text{ m/s}^2)(28 \text{ m})}$$
$$= \pm 1.6 \text{ m/s}$$

Since the initial velocity is positive, we use only the positive square root. Thus, the initial velocity is 1.6 m/s forward.

(b) The required quantity is t. Since we know x, x_0, v, v_0, and a, we could use any of Eqns. 2-7, 2-8, or 2-9 to find t. The easiest is Eqn. 2-7: $v = v_0 + at$.

Re-arranging to solve for t: $t = \dfrac{v - v_0}{a}$

> ***Math Tip:*** *Beware of round-off error! In part (b) of this problem, we are using the answer (v_0) from part (a). To obtain the correct answer in (b) to two significant digits, we need to carry at least three digits in the value for v_0. Try it and see! When working on a problem, it is very useful to keep intermediate answers (such as v_0 in this case) in your calculator for possible later use. (Reference: Section 1.4)*

Substituting values:

$$t = \frac{(0 - 1.64)\ \text{m/s}}{-0.048\ \text{m/s}^2}$$

$$= 34\ \text{s} \quad \text{(to two significant digits)}$$

Hence, the time taken for the curling rock to slow down to a stop is 34 s.

Practice

2-28 You are asked to find the constant acceleration needed by an object, having a known initial velocity, to travel a known distance in a known time. Which equation (2-7, 2-8, 2-9, or 2-10) is appropriate for this situation?

2-29 Prove that Eqn. 2-10 is dimensionally correct.

2-30 Re-arrange Eqn. 2-8 to solve for the time, *t*.

2-31 The equations derived in this section could have been derived by starting with a velocity-time graph showing constant acceleration. An example of such a graph is shown in Figure 2-28. Use the fact that the area under the line on a velocity-time graph indicates the displacement ($x - x_0$) to derive Eqn. 2-8.

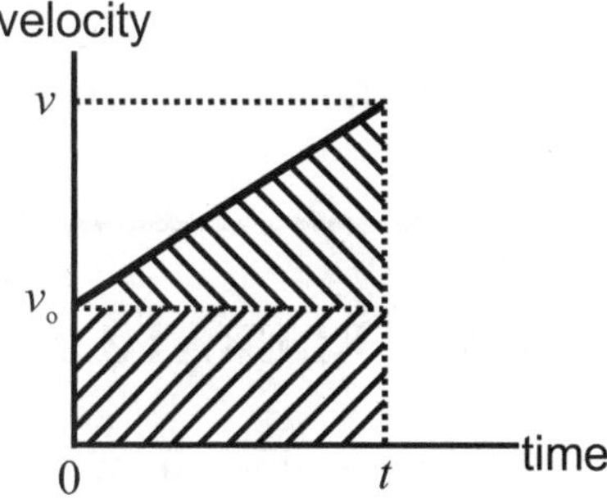

Figure 2-28 *Question 2-31.*

2-32 In a badminton game a "bird" is struck so that its horizontal velocity is +12.3 m/s. Assuming that air resistance causes its acceleration to be -2.6 m/s^2, what is the magnitude of its horizontal velocity after 1.5 s? We are neglecting its vertical motion. [Ans. 8.4 m/s]

2-33 A baseball, travelling horizontally with a speed of 40 m/s (about 140 km/h), is hit by a bat and has its velocity changed to 45 m/s in the opposite direction. The ball is in contact with the bat for 2.0 ms. What is the average acceleration experienced by the ball while being hit by the bat? [Ans. 4.2×10^4 m/s^2, in opposite direction to ball's initial velocity]

2-34 A sprinter leaves the starting block and, for a time of 3.3 s, undergoes a constant acceleration of magnitude 2.4 m/s^2.
(a) How far has the sprinter run in this time?
(b) How fast is the sprinter running at the end of this time? [Ans. (a) 13 m (b) 7.9 m/s]

2-35 A car travelling at 40 km/h on the entrance ramp of an expressway accelerates uniformly to 100 km/h in 36 s.
(a) Express 36 s in hours.
(b) How far (in km) does the car travel in this time?
(c) What is the car's average acceleration during this time?
[Ans. (a) 1.0×10^{-2} h (b) 0.70 km (c) 1.7 (km/h)/s forward]

2-36 A rocket begins its third stage of launch at a velocity of 2.28×10^2 m/s forward. It undergoes a constant acceleration of 62.5 m/s^2 while travelling 1.86 km, all in the same direction. What is the rocket's speed at the end of this motion? [Ans. 533 m/s]

2-37 Find the magnitude of constant acceleration required by a bullet to reach a muzzle speed of 4.0×10^2 m/s if the muzzle is 0.80 m long. [Ans. 1.0×10^5 m/s^2]

2-38 A train accelerates as it enters a valley from the top of a hill. It accelerates uniformly at 0.040 m/s^2 for 225 s and during this time travels 4.0 km. What was the magnitude of the velocity at the start of the acceleration? [Ans. 13 m/s]

2-39 An electron travelling at 6.74×10^7 m/s west enters a force field which reduces its velocity to 2.38×10^7 m/s west. While this (constant) acceleration is occurring, the electron experiences a displacement of 0.485 m in the same direction.
(a) How long did the force field take to cause this velocity change?
(b) What was the electron's acceleration during this time?
[Ans. (a) 1.06×10^{-8} s (b) 4.10×10^{15} m/s^2 east]

2.5 ACCELERATION DUE TO GRAVITY

A person who dives from a 10-m high board enters the water at a speed of about 50 km/h. Had the diver started from a lower height, the speed would have been less; and, of course, if the height had been larger, the speed would have been greater. The farther an object falls toward Earth, the faster is its speed (neglecting air resistance). The rate of increase of a falling object's velocity with time, or acceleration, is called the **acceleration due to gravity**.

Do all objects accelerate at the same rate near Earth's surface? If you drop an unfolded piece of paper and a pencil at the same instant, the paper will flutter downward and will land much later than the pencil. However, if you crumple the paper into a tight ball and try the experiment again, you will notice that the two objects land at about the same time. In this second case, the effect of air resistance has been reduced, and the accelerations are the same. Thus, we observe that if air resistance is negligible, the acceleration due to gravity of objects at the same location is constant. Any object falling with negligible air resistance is said to be undergoing "**free fall**."

Figure 2-29
Aristotle, depicted on a Greek postage stamp.

People have not always believed this observation. In fact, even great scientists of the past, such as the Greek philosopher Aristotle (384 B.C. to 322 B.C., Figure 2-29) thought that heavier objects fell faster than lighter objects. He and his followers based this belief on the observation that a stone falls to Earth more quickly than a feather. To explain this observation, the ancient Greeks stated that all matter on Earth was composed of four elements or pure substances — earth, water, air, and fire. All objects tend to reach their natural level, depending on their composition. For example, a stone is composed mainly of earth, so it falls rapidly toward its natural level, Earth. A feather is composed of more air than earth, so it tends to fall more slowly. Smoke from a fire rises because it is composed mainly of fire, which has a natural level above air, water, and earth.

Aristotle's theory of falling objects, as well as others of his theories, were accepted for nearly two thousand years. Finally, during the Renaissance era in Europe, scientists began to realize that experimentation was needed to test and verify theories. In a famous book titled *The Advancement of Learning*, published in 1605, an English philosopher and statesman, Francis Bacon, proposed that theories should be based on experimental facts. However, he did not perform experiments involving gravity. It was the renowned scientist from Italy, Galileo Galilei (1564-1642) who truly revolutionized science. He realized the importance of controlled experiments, which involve changing only one variable at a time to determine the effects on other variables. In performing motion experiments, for example, Galileo eliminated the effect of air resistance by dropping heavy and light objects of the same size, and demonstrated that both objects fell at the same rate toward Earth.

Did You Know? *Aristotle and other Greek philosophers believed that objects beyond Earth, namely the stars, were composed of a fifth element which they called quintessence. This word stems from "quinte," meaning fifth, and "essentia," meaning essence.*

Figure 2-30 *Galileo Galilei, shown on an Italian postage stamp. (Stamp courtesy of J.L. Hunt.)*

Galileo (Figure 2-30) was also the first person to prove that objects undergo acceleration as they fall toward Earth. As you know from the experience of dropping objects, they fall so quickly that it is hard to judge if they are accelerating or simply travelling really fast. Aristotle believed that a falling stone maintained a constant, high speed. He had no way of measuring short time intervals to prove otherwise. Galileo, however, devised ingenious ways of measuring time and was able to verify that acceleration does indeed occur. With today's technological advancements, we have many ways of observing this acceleration. One way is to use stroboscopic photography, with light flashing at regular intervals to reveal the motion of the falling object.

PROFILE: Galileo Galilei (1564-1642)

> "I, Galileo Galilei, son of the late Vincenzio Galilei, of Florence, aged 70 years, being brought to judgment . . . abandon the false opinion that the sun is the centre and immovable, and I will not hold, defend, or teach this false doctrine in any manner."

Galileo Galilei was a great and daring leader in the scientific world of the Renaissance. He was born in Pisa, Italy, in 1564, just 42 years after the first ship sailed around the world (proving that

Earth is round). That same year the great Italian artist, Michelangelo, died and the famous English playwright, William Shakespeare, was born. When just 17, Galileo entered the University of Pisa to study medicine, but he soon became more interested in the physical sciences and mathematics. By the age of 26 he was appointed professor of mathematics at the University of Pisa, but three years later he moved to the University of Padua.

Even early in his career he performed numerous experiments, made many important discoveries, and wrote valuable scientific reports and books. He discovered that a pendulum of fixed length always swings with the same period of time for each vibration. This discovery led to the invention of pendulum clocks, which were valuable in scientific investigations. He used rolling balls on inclined planes to discover that the acceleration due to gravity does not depend on mass and that it remains constant. One legend, not necessarily true, is that he dropped two balls of different mass from the Leaning Tower of Pisa (Figure 2-31) to verify that heavy and light objects fall at the same rate. He learned of the discovery that two lenses aligned properly could magnify distant objects, and he applied this breakthrough to the invention of the astronomical telescope. (In Figure 2-30, Galileo is shown holding such a telescope.) In 1609, with his newly made telescope, he made a number of significant findings, including the fact that the moon has craters, the planet Venus goes through a full set of phases, the sun has dark regions, now called sunspots, the Milky Way Galaxy is composed of individual stars, and the planet Jupiter has moons that revolve around it. The astronomical discoveries helped persuade Galileo that, contrary to the belief of Aristotle and the teachings of the Catholic Church, Earth was not the centre of the universe, with the sun revolving around it. Rather Earth and other planets revolve around the sun, a theory proposed earlier by a Polish astronomer, Nicholas Copernicus (1473-1543).

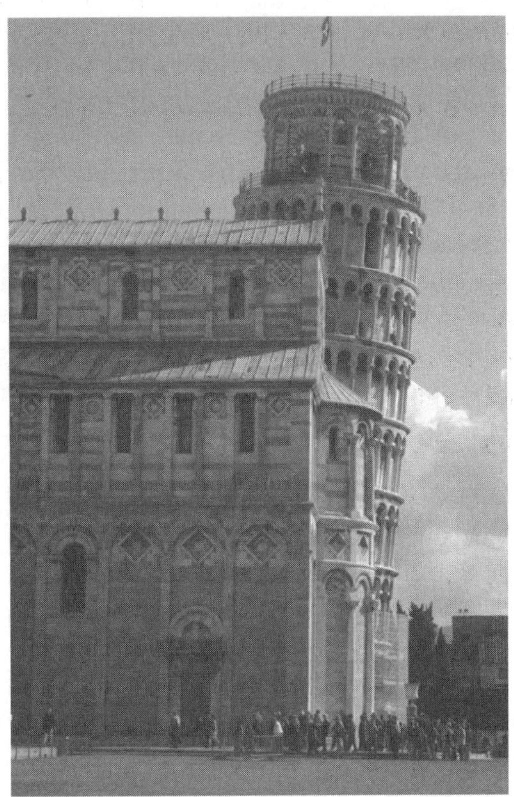

Figure 2-31 *The Leaning Tower of Pisa, Italy.*

Galileo described many of his discoveries and theories in the Italian language rather than the traditional Latin for scientific documents. Thus, a larger number of people could read his works. His publications caused controversy with the Roman Catholic Church, and in 1616 the Inquisition, a sort of religious police force, required Galileo to stop teaching and writing about the sun-centred theory.

However, Galileo continued writing and in 1632, when he was 68, he published a work entitled *Dialogue Concerning the Great World Systems,* in which he compared the Earth-centred and sun-centred theories. His belief in the latter theory was obvious, and in his book he scorned the theories of the Pope and other leaders. The Roman Catholic Inquisition found him guilty of teaching false theories, and forced him to deny his own beliefs. (See the quotation at the beginning of this profile.) Rather than sending the aging and unhealthy man to jail, the Inquisition put him under house arrest and tried to control him for the rest of his life.

Despite his persecution, Galileo continued to write in secrecy. In 1636 a book, *Dialogues of Two New Sciences*, was published in Holland after being smuggled out of Italy. This was his greatest work, dealing with his studies of motion.

In 1637 Galileo went blind but continued to write until he died in 1642. This was the same year that another great scientist, Isaac Newton, was born. Many of Galileo's discoveries and ideas helped Newton and other scientists develop new theories. The age of true science had begun.

Measuring the Acceleration Due to Gravity

Various methods can be used to measure the acceleration of a falling object experimentally. For example, a stroboscopic photograph that shows the position of a falling object at regular time intervals can be used. Such a photograph can be analysed to find the distance the object has fallen at the end of each known time interval. Then the kinematics equation $x = x_0 + v_0 t + \frac{1}{2}at^2$ can be reduced to $x = \frac{1}{2}at^2$ because $v_0 = 0$ (and x_0 can be chosen to be zero), and the acceleration can be determined by re-arrangement to find $a = 2x/t^2$.

With methods such as this, the acceleration of a falling object is found to be constant. Near Earth's surface, the acceleration, to two significant digits, is 9.8 m/s^2 downward. This value is used so often that it is given a special symbol, ***g***, the acceleration due to gravity. The magnitude of this acceleration is g = 9.8 m/s^2. (Do not confuse this g with the symbol g used for "gram.") The value of g = 9.8 m/s^2 applies to objects undergoing free fall; that is, objects that are not affected appreciably by air resistance.

> ***Did You Know?*** *Knowing the acceleration due to gravity to seven or more significant digits is of great interest to certain groups of people. Geologists and geophysicists can use the information to determine the structure of Earth's interior and help locate areas having high concentrations of mineral deposits. Military experts are concerned with variations in the acceleration due to gravity in the operation of such devises as cruise missiles. Space scientists use the data to help calculate the paths of artificial satellites. And cosmologists are interested in knowing whether g varies over the long term. If it does vary even slightly, their theories of the origin of the universe will require rethinking.*

Scientists throughout the world use more sophisticated techniques to measure the acceleration due to gravity at different locations. For example, at the International Bureau of Weights and Measures in France, investigations have been performed in a vacuum chamber in which an object is propelled upward using a special elastic band. At the top and bottom of the object are mirrors that reflect laser beams used to determine the time of flight. Using this technique, g at the Bureau is found to be 9.809 260 m/s^2.

The acceleration due to gravity varies slightly from one location to another. In general, the value is greater near Earth's north and south poles than near the equator, and it is greater at lower altitudes than at higher altitudes. Table 2.3 lists "*g*" at several locations. Notice that the average value, to two significant digits, is 9.8 m/s^2. Reasons for the variations in these values are discussed in Chapter 9. (Note that if you require three significant digits for g when solving a problem in this textbook, use $g = 9.80$ m/s^2.)

Table 2.3 Magnitude of the Acceleration Due to Gravity (*g*) at Various Locations on Earth

Location	*Latitude*	*Altitude (m)*	*g (m/s^2)*
Equator	0°	0	9.780
North Pole	90° north	0	9.832
Java	6° south	7	9.782
Toronto	44° north	162	9.805
London	51° north	30	9.823
Brussels	51° north	102	9.811
Washington, D.C.	39° north	8	9.801
Denver	40° north	1638	9.796

Calculations Involving Free Fall

Because free fall involves constant acceleration, the kinematics equations developed in Section 2.4 can be applied. However, we will make one important change when writing these equations — we will write y rather than x for position (Table 2.4). This will prevent confusion in the following chapters where x is used for horizontal motion and y for vertical motion.

Table 2.4 Equations of Kinematics Written for Vertical Motion

Variables Involved	*Variable(s) Eliminated*	*Equation*	
v, v_0, t	y, y_0	$v = v_0 + at$	**(2-7b)**
y, y_0, v_0, v, t	a	$y = y_0 + \frac{1}{2}(v_0 + v)t$	**(2-8b)**
y, y_0, v_0, a, t	v	$y = y_0 + v_0 t + \frac{1}{2}at^2$	**(2-9b)**
y, y_0, v_0, v, a	t	$v^2 - v_0^2 = 2a(y - y_0)$	**(2-10b)**

When applying these equations, remember that positive and negative signs are important. Begin each solution to a problem by choosing which direction is positive, then use that direction throughout the entire solution. For example, if upward is positive, then the acceleration is: $a = -g = -9.8$ m/s^2. However, if downward is positive, $a = g = 9.8$ m/s^2.

Sample Problem 2-13

A ball is thrown vertically with an initial velocity of 8.5 m/s upward. What maximum height will the ball reach above its starting point?

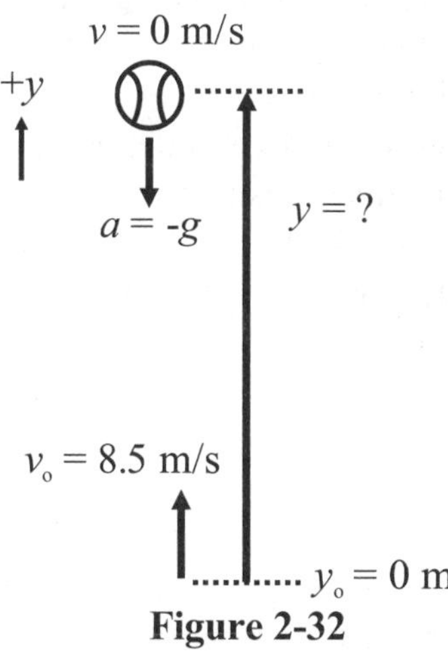

Figure 2-32
Sample problem 2-13.

Solution: Let us define upward as positive. We also choose $y_0 = 0$ m as the starting position (Figure 2-32).

The given quantities are:

$$v_0 = +8.5 \text{ m/s}$$
$$a = -g = -9.8 \text{ m/s}^2$$
$$v = 0 \text{ m/s}$$
$$y_0 = 0 \text{ m}$$

We are able to state that v = 0 m/s because at the top of its flight, the ball comes to rest instantaneously (then reverses its direction of motion). The required quantity is y, and the appropriate equation is:

$$v^2 - v_0^2 = 2a(y - y_0)$$

> ***Notation Tip:***
> *Some students write g = –9.8 m/s², but this is incorrect. The symbol "g" represents the magnitude of the vector **g**, and the magnitude of a non-zero vector is always a positive quantity.*

Substituting $v = 0$ m/s, $y_0 = 0$ m, and $a = -g$:

$$-v_0^2 = 2(-g)y$$

Re-arranging to solve for y: $$y = \frac{v_0^2}{2g}$$

Substituting numerical values:

$$y = \frac{(8.5 \text{ m/s})^2}{2(9.8 \text{ m/s}^2)}$$
$$= +3.7 \text{ m} \quad \text{(to two significant digits)}$$

Thus, the ball rises to a height of 3.7 m above its original position.

Sample Problem 2-14

An arrow is shot straight upward beside a building that is 51 m high. The arrow's initial speed is 36 m/s. Neglecting air resistance, find:

(a) the time(s) when the arrow passes the top of the building
(b) the total time of flight

Solution: Let us define upward as positive, and choose the initial position to be $y_0 = 0$ m (Figure 2-33).

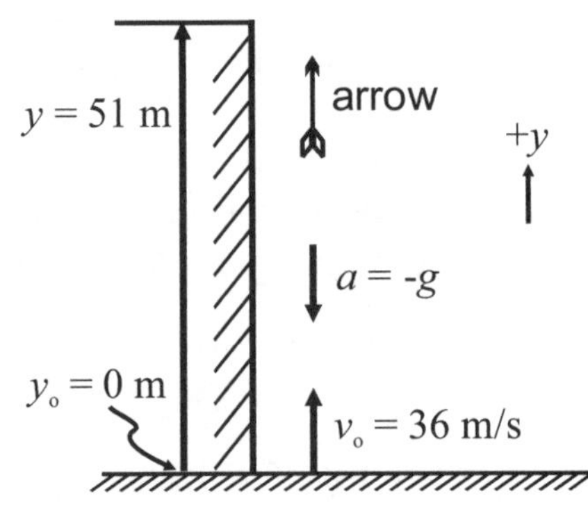

Figure 2-33 *Sample Problem 2-14.*

(a) The given quantities are:

$$v_0 = +36 \text{ m/s}$$
$$a = -g = -9.8 \text{ m/s}^2$$
$$y = 51 \text{ m}$$
$$y_0 = 0 \text{ m}$$

The required quantity is t, and the appropriate equation is:

$$y = y_0 + v_0 t + \tfrac{1}{2} a t^2$$

Taking care to use consistent units, we substitute the given quantities into the equation, but we omit the units for convenience: Thus,

$$51 = 0 + 36\,t - 4.9\,t^2$$

Re-arranging this equation so that it has the standard form of a quadratic equation:

$$4.9\,t^2 - 36\,t + 51 = 0$$

Using the quadratic formula:

$$t = \frac{-b \pm \sqrt{b^2 - 4ac}}{2a}$$

where $a = 4.9$, $b = -36$, and $c = 51$.

Thus, $$t = \frac{-(-36) \pm \sqrt{(-36)^2 - 4(4.9)(51)}}{2(4.9)}$$
$$= \frac{36 \pm 17.2}{9.8}$$
$$= 1.9 \text{ s and } 5.4 \text{ s}$$

Math Tip: *The quadratic formula is useful for finding the roots of a quadratic equation, i.e., an equation involving a square function (quadratic is Latin for "square"). If the quadratic equation is written in this form:*

$$ax^2 + bx + c = 0, \text{ where } a \neq 0,$$

then its roots are:

$$x = \frac{-b \pm \sqrt{b^2 - 4\,ac}}{2a}$$

Thus, there are two positive roots of this equation. This means that the arrow passes the top of the building at $t = 1.9$ s on the way up, and again at 5.4 s on the way down.

(b) There are various ways of finding the total time of flight. The given quantities are:

$$v_0 = +36 \text{ m/s}$$
$$a = -g = -9.8 \text{ m/s}^2$$
$$y_0 = 0 \text{ m}$$
$$y = 0 \text{ m} \quad \text{(assuming the arrow returns to its initial position)}$$

The required quantity is t, and the appropriate equation is:

$$y = y_0 + v_0 t + \tfrac{1}{2} a t^2$$

Immediately substituting $y_0 = y = 0$ m, and $a = -g$:

$$0 = v_0 t - \tfrac{1}{2} g t^2$$

Factoring out a "t":

$$0 = t\left(v_0 - \tfrac{1}{2} g t\right)$$

Hence, either $t = 0$, or $v_0 - \frac{1}{2} g t = 0$. The first solution ($t = 0$) corresponds to the initial condition — at time $t = 0$, the arrow is at position $y = 0$. The second solution is the one we want; solving for t gives:

$$t = \frac{2v_0}{g} = \frac{2(36 \text{ m/s})}{9.8 \text{ m/s}^2} = 7.3 \text{ s}$$

Thus, the total time of flight is 7.3 s.

A much faster solution would have been to realize that if the arrow took 1.9 s to rise to the top of the building, from (a) above, it would also take 1.9 s to travel from the top of the building down to the initial position. Add this to the 5.4 s it took to arrive at the top of the building on the way down to obtain the total time of 7.3 s.

A third technique in this case is to find the time for the arrow to rise to the top of its flight (where $v = 0$), then multiply that time by 2. The equation to use is $v = v_0 + at$, which can be solved for t when $v = 0$.

In solving problems involving uniform acceleration, remember that there is often more than one way to find the solution, especially in problems with more than one part.

Terminal Speed

A skydiver jumps out of an aircraft and experiences free fall for a short period of time. The diver's speed increases rapidly, and the air resistance to the diver's motion is soon strong. Eventually this resistance becomes so high that it prevents any more increase in speed. At this stage, the diver has reached **terminal speed,**[3] which is the maximum speed reached by an object falling in a gas or liquid. At terminal speed, the object's speed (and velocity) is constant, and its acceleration has become zero. A graphical representation of the speed of a falling object as a function of time is shown in Figure 2-34.

Did You Know? *Red blood cells in a human blood sample in a test tube reaches terminal speed almost instantaneously. The settling rate for an average male is about 3 mm/h, for an average female it is about 4 mm/h, but in diseased conditions, it can become as high as 100 mm/h.*

In general there are two situations in which an object can reach terminal speed in air:

(1) an object has a large surface area relative to its mass — examples include a parachute and a table-tennis ball;

(2) an object is falling with a high speed.

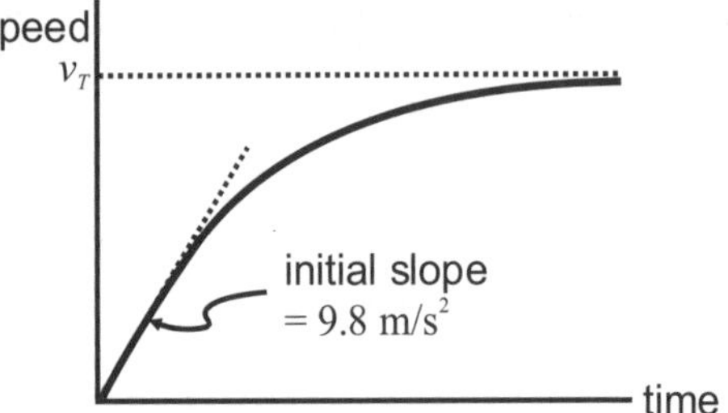

Figure 2-34 *The general shape of a speed-time graph for a falling object that reaches terminal speed, v_T.*

The terminal speeds of various falling objects in air are listed in Table 2.5. Terminal speeds are also important in liquids and in gases other than air.

Table 2.5
Approximate Terminal Speeds of Objects Falling in Air

Object	Terminal Speed (m/s)	Terminal Speed (km/h)
human	53	190
human with open parachute	5 to 10	18 to 36
dandelion seeds	0.5	1.8
dust particle (typical)	0.02	0.07

[3]Sometimes this is called terminal velocity, but since velocity is a vector and we are interested here only in the magnitude of the velocity (that is, the speed), terminal speed is a better term.

Practice

Note: Unless otherwise stated, assume that the falling object is undergoing free fall and its acceleration, to two significant digits, is 9.8 m/s^2 down.

2-40 You throw a ball vertically upward and catch it at the same position where it left your hand.
(a) How does its final velocity compare with its initial velocity?
(b) How does the rise time compare with the fall time?
(c) What is the ball's velocity at the top of its flight?
(d) What is the acceleration of the ball as it is rising? at the top of its flight? as it is falling?

2-41 Calculate the maximum speed in metres per second of each object just at the landing time. In each case assume the object starts from rest.
(a) A steel ball is dropped from the top of the Leaning Tower of Pisa, a distance of 55 m.
(b) To entertain tourists, divers in Acapulco, Mexico, dive from a cliff that is 36 m above the water level.
(c) A stone is dropped from a bridge and lands in the water 2.4 s later.
[Ans. (a) 33 m/s (b) 27 m/s (c) 24 m/s]

2-42 Prove that a free-falling ball dropped vertically from rest travels 3 times as far in the second second as in the first second.

2-43 A baseball pitcher throws a ball vertically straight upward and catches the ball 4.2 s later.
(a) With what velocity did the ball leave the pitcher's hand?
(b) What was the maximum height reached by the ball? [Ans. (a) 21 m/s upward (b) 22 m]

2-44 A sailing balloon is moving at a velocity of 2.1 m/s upward when the balloonist drops a ballast (a heavy mass used for control) over the edge. The ballast takes 3.8 s to land on the ground below. (a) How high was the balloon when the ballast was dropped?
(b) With what speed did the ballast strike the ground? [Ans. (a) 63 m (b) 35 m/s]

2-45 Assume that a high jumper has a vertical velocity of 5.112 m/s upward when jumping. Use the data in Table 2.3 to calculate and compare the maximum increase in height achieved by the jumper in London and Denver. Remember to use the correct number of significant digits.
[Ans. London: 1.330 m, Denver: 1.334 m]

2-46 An astronaut drops a camera from rest while exiting from a spacecraft on the moon. The camera takes 1.7 s to fall 2.3 m.
(a) Determine the magnitude of the acceleration due to gravity on the moon.
(b) What is the ratio of the magnitude of the acceleration due to gravity on Earth to that on the moon? [Ans. (a) 1.6 m/s^2 (b) 6.1:1]

2-47 During the first minute of blastoff, a space shuttle has an average acceleration of magnitude 5 *g*'s, i.e., 5 times the acceleration due to gravity on the surface of Earth. Calculate the shuttle's speed in metres per second and kilometres per hour after the first minute. (These values are approximate because the shuttle does not experience uniform acceleration in a straight line.) [Ans. 2.9×10^3 m/s = 1.1×10^4 km/h]

2-48 A person throws a golf ball vertically upward on Earth and the ball remains in flight a total time of 2.6 s. (a) How long did the ball rise?
(b) What was its initial velocity?
(c) With the same initial speed on Mars, how long would the ball remain in flight there? (Refer to Appendix 6 which lists data for the planets.) [Ans. (a) 1.3 s (b) 13 m/s upward (c) 6.8 s]

2-49 In a laboratory experiment a motion detector interfaced to a computer is used to determine that the time for a falling steel ball to travel the final 0.80 m before striking the floor is 0.087 s. With what speed does the ball strike the floor? [Ans. 9.6 m/s]

2-50 A stone is thrown vertically from a bridge with a velocity of 14 m/s downward. At what time will the stone reach the water 21 m below the bridge? (Hint: Apply the quadratic formula to solve this problem. Explain the meaning of both roots of the solution.) [Ans. 1.1 s]

2-51 *Fermi question:* Determine a reasonable estimate for the speed with which a raindrop would strike the ground from a high cloud if it did not experience any air resistance. [Ans. approx. 2×10^2 m/s]

2-52 Sketch a speed-time graph for a skydiver who jumps from an aircraft, reaches terminal speed some time later, then opens the parachute and reaches another terminal speed.

CHAPTER FOCUS

In this chapter several concepts from Chapter 1 have been extended and applied, including measurement, metric units, dimensional analysis, and scalar and vector quantities. The focus has been on the kinematics (motion) variables of speed, velocity, and acceleration, in each case distinguishing average and instantaneous values. A great emphasis was placed on solving problems related to motion, mostly using equations, but also by analysing graphs. The acceleration due to gravity provided the most common example of constant acceleration.

The motion studied in this chapter was one-dimensional. The concepts here will be applied to the study of two-dimensional motion in Chapter 4, then to the forces causing motion in Chapters 5 and 6.

VOCABULARY REVIEW

You should now be able to define each of the following words or phrases.

kinematics
speed
average speed (defining equation)
non-uniform motion
tangent to a curve
acceleration

instantaneous speed
uniform motion
displacement
velocity
average velocity (defining equation)
instantaneous velocity
average acceleration (defining equation)
instantaneous acceleration
acceleration due to gravity
free fall
g
terminal speed

CHAPTER REVIEW

Note: Unless otherwise stated, assume that the falling object is undergoing free fall and its acceleration, to two significant digits, is 9.8 m/s^2 down.

Note: The answers to underlined questions are found at the end of the chapter.

<u>**2-53**</u> During the time interval that an object undergoes uniform motion:
(a) the instantaneous velocity and the average velocity are equal
(b) the direction of motion must remain constant
(c) the displacement is directly proportional to the time interval
(d) all of the above are true
(e) only (a) and (b) above are true

<u>**2-54**</u> For any given object, which of the following pairs of quantities cannot be both constant and nonzero during the same time interval?
(a) the acceleration and the velocity
(b) the magnitude of the acceleration and the acceleration
(c) the distance and the displacement
(d) the speed and the velocity
(e) none of these

<u>**2-55**</u> A cyclist, moving westward on a level, straight path, coasts to a stop. During this motion, the directions of the acceleration, instantaneous velocity, and displacement are, respectively:
(a) west, west, west
(b) east, west, west
(c) east, east, west
(d) east, east, east
(e) west, east, east

<u>**2-56**</u> In a coin toss with upward defined as the positive direction, a quarter rises vertically upward (motion A), reached maximum height (condition B), and then falls vertically downward (motion C). During A, B, and C, the quarter's acceleration, in m/s^2, is respectively:
(a) +9.8; 0; –9.8 (b) +9.8; +9.8; +9.8 (c) –9.8; 0; –9.8
(d) –9.8; –9.8; –9.8 (e) –9.8, 0, +9.8

<u>**2-57**</u> You step off a high diving board (height Δd above the water) with an initial velocity of zero. The magnitude of the velocity with which you hit the water is proportional to:
(a) g and Δd (b) $\sqrt{g}$ and $\sqrt{\Delta d}$ (c) g and $\sqrt{\Delta d}$ (d) $\sqrt{g}$ and Δd (e) $g(\Delta d)^2$

2-58 In the Canadian Grand Prix auto race, the drivers travel a total distance of 304.29 km in 69 laps around the track. The fastest lap time is 84.118 s. Determine the average speed for this lap. [Ans. 52.426 m/s]

2-59 The driver's handbook in Ontario states that for any specific speed, the safe distance separating your car from the car ahead is the distance you would travel in 2.0 s at that speed.
(a) Determine this distance if the speed of your car is 25 m/s (90 km/h).
(b) About how many car lengths is this distance?
[Ans. (a) 5.0×10^1 m (b) approx. 12 car lengths]

2-60 An impatient driver, wanting to save time, drives along a city bypass at an average speed of 115 km/h where the speed limit is 90 km/h. If the bypass is 18 km long, how much time (in seconds) does the driver save by breaking the speed limit? (By the way, the driver consumes about 20% more fuel at the higher speed.) [Ans. 1.6×10^2 s]

<u>**2-61**</u> Two cars, 1 and 2, move at constant speeds in the same direction in adjacent lanes on a highway, as shown in Figure 2-35. The cars' positions at the same time are indicated by identical letters. Starting positions are not shown. Do the cars ever have the same instantaneous speeds? If so, at which position(s)? If not, explain how you know.

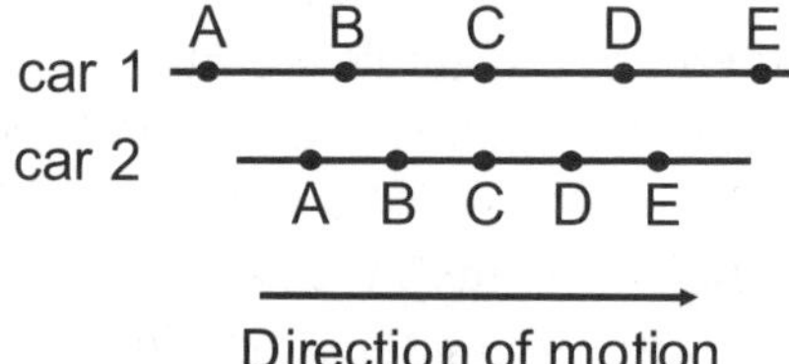

Figure 2-35 *Question 2-61.*

2-62 A truck travels at 80 km/h for 30 min, then at 60 km/h for 1.5 h. Assuming two significant digits in the given numbers, calculate the truck's (a) total distance travelled, and (b) average speed. [Ans. (a) 1.30×10^2 km (b) 65 km/h]

2-63 An eagle flies at 24 m/s for 1.2×10^3 m then glides at 18 m/s for 1.2×10^3 m.
(a) How long (in seconds) does this motion take?
(b) What is the eagle's average speed for this motion? [Ans. (a) 1.2×10^2 s (b) 21 m/s]

2-64 An electromagnetic (e.m.) signal, which travels at the speed of light, is sent from Earth to a satellite located 4.8×10^7 m away. The satellite receives the signal and after a delay of 0.55 s sends a return e.m. signal to Earth, still the same distance away. What total time elapses between sending the signal and receiving the return signal on Earth? [Ans. 0.87 s]

2-65 One person can run 100 m in 10 s and another person in 12 s, both at a constant speed. If the two runners pass by a reference position at the same instant, by what distance is the faster runner ahead of the slower runner after 100 m? [Ans. 17 m]

2-66 The planet Venus takes 2.1×10^7 s to complete its orbit around the sun. The radius of its orbit is 1.1×10^{11} m.
(a) Determine its average speed in metres per second and kilometres per hour.
(b) Find the magnitude of its average velocity after it has completed half a revolution around the sun. [Ans. (a) 3.3×10^4 m/s = 1.2×10^5 km/h (b) 2.1×10^4 m/s]

2-67 For uniform motion, compare:
(a) instantaneous speed with average speed
(b) instantaneous velocity with average velocity
(c) instantaneous speed with instantaneous velocity

2-68 Copenhagen lies 1100 km straight east of Glasgow and 1700 km straight west of Moscow. An airplane flies from Copenhagen to Glasgow in 2.2 h, stays there for 1.0 h, then flies to Moscow in 3.1 h. Determine the plane's:
(a) average speed for the entire trip
(b) average speed while in the air
(c) average velocity for the entire trip
[Ans. (a) 1.2×10^2 m/s (b) 1.5×10^2 m/s (c) 75 m/s east]

2-69 A professional baseball pitcher throws a fastball with a speed of 42 m/s, and 0.44 s later a batter bats the ball straight over the pitcher's head. The ball travels at 48 m/s until it is stopped by a fielder 1.9 s after the hit. (We are neglecting the vertical motion.)
(a) What is the distance from the pitcher's mound to home plate?
(b) Determine the baseball's average speed for the entire motion.
(c) Calculate the magnitude of its average velocity for the entire motion. [Ans. (a) 18 m (b) 47 m/s (c) 31 m/s]

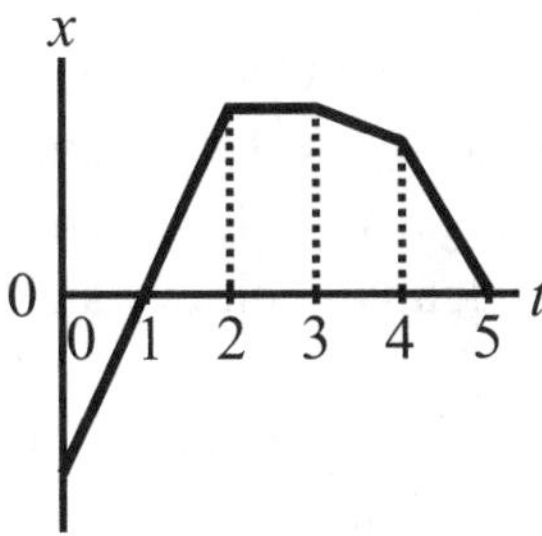

Figure 2-36 *Question 2-70.*

2-70 Describe the motion in each time segment of the position-time graph shown in Figure 2-36.

2-71 What quantity can be calculated from a position-time graph to indicate the velocity of an object? How can that quantity be found if the line on the graph is curved?

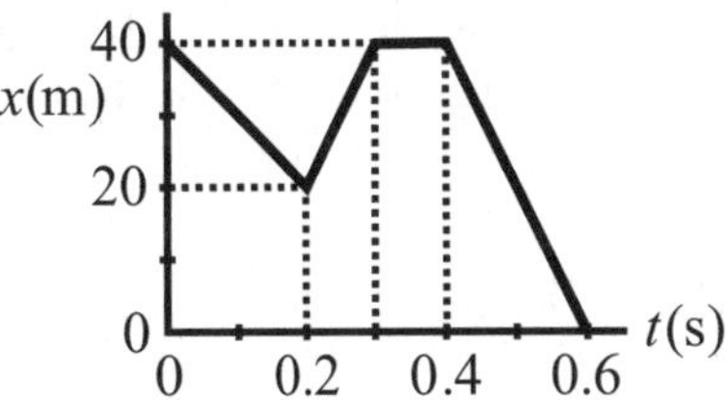

Figure 2-37 *Question 2-73.*

2-72 How can a velocity-time graph be used to determine (a) displacement, and (b) acceleration?

2-73 Sketch the velocity-time graph that corresponds to the position-time graph shown in Figure 2-37.

2-74 State the difference between uniform motion and uniform acceleration. Sketch displacement-time, velocity-time, and acceleration-time graphs of both types of motion.

2-75 Figure 2-38 shows the position of a child along a reference axis for 120 s.

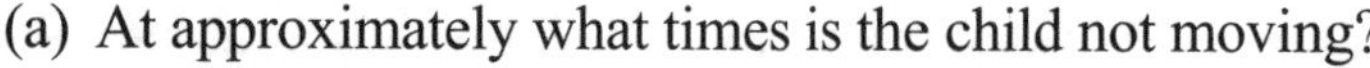

(a) At approximately what times is the child not moving?
(b) During which time intervals is the child's velocity positive? negative?
(c) Find the child's approximate velocity at 20 s, and at 40 s.

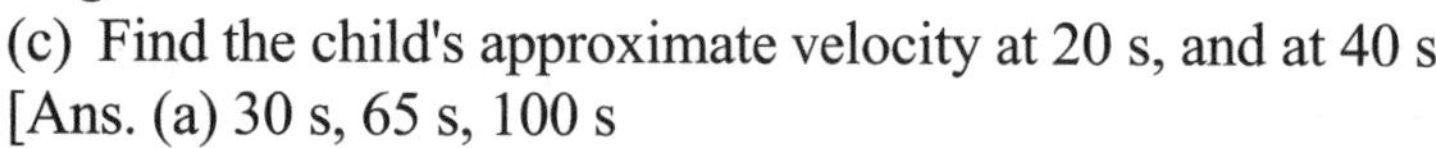

[Ans. (a) 30 s, 65 s, 100 s

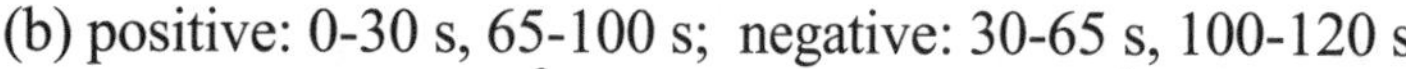

(b) positive: 0-30 s, 65-100 s; negative: 30-65 s, 100-120 s
(c) approx. $+6.7 \times 10^{-2}$ m/s, approx. -1.2×10^{-1} m/s]

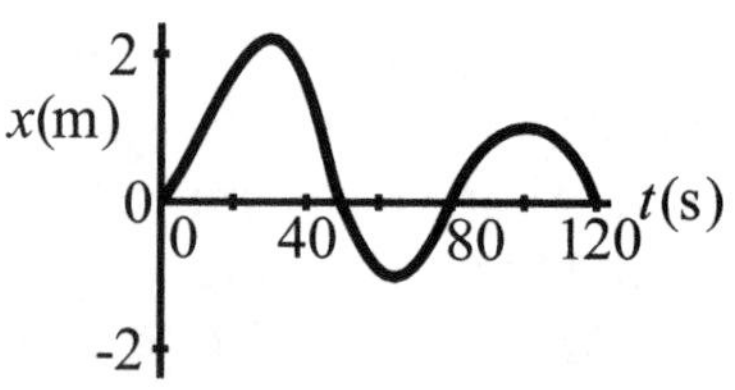

Figure 2-38 *Question 2-75.*

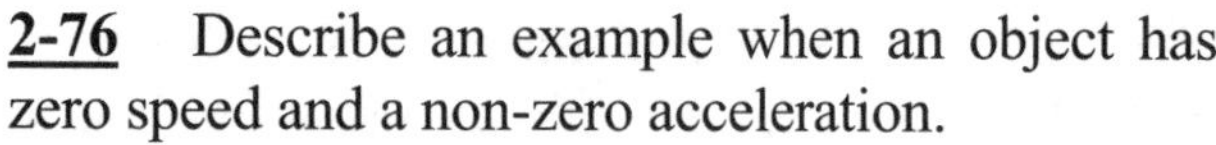

2-76 Describe an example when an object has zero speed and a non-zero acceleration.

2-77 A car is travelling east with an initial speed, v_0. Its acceleration, a, is in the westerly direction. Which diagram in Figure 2-39 best represents the position of the car (the dots) and its velocity and acceleration vectors (the arrows)? Explain.

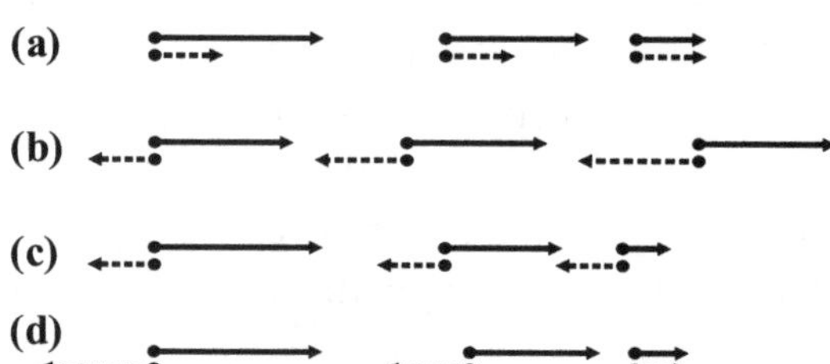

Figure 2-39 *Question 2-77. The solid lines are velocity vectors and the dashed lines are acceleration vectors. East is toward the right.*

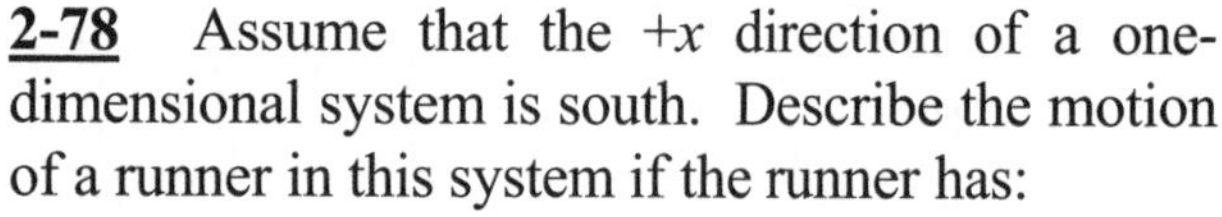

2-78 Assume that the $+x$ direction of a one-dimensional system is south. Describe the motion of a runner in this system if the runner has:
(a) a positive velocity and a positive acceleration
(b) a positive velocity and a negative acceleration
(c) a negative velocity and a positive acceleration
(d) a negative velocity and a negative acceleration.

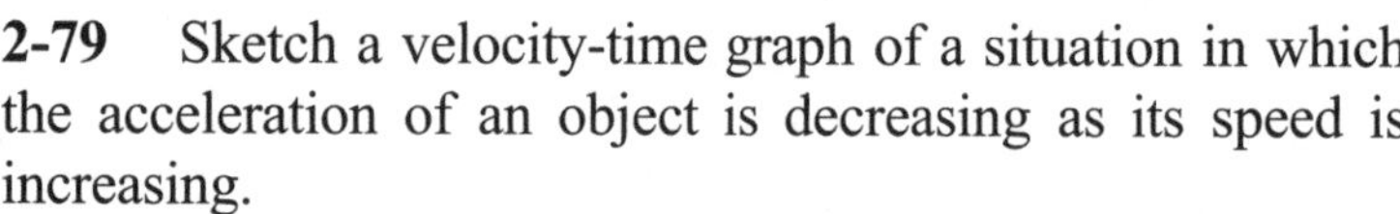

2-79 Sketch a velocity-time graph of a situation in which the acceleration of an object is decreasing as its speed is increasing.

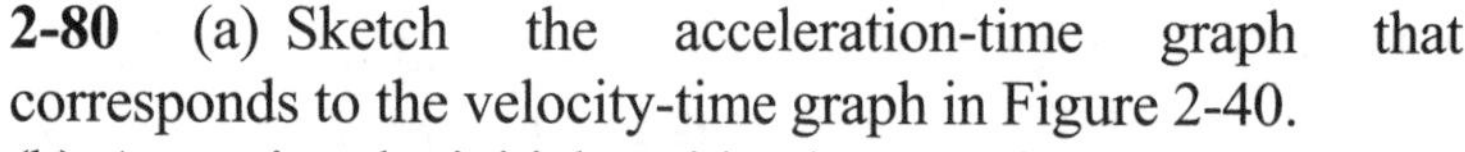

2-80 (a) Sketch the acceleration-time graph that corresponds to the velocity-time graph in Figure 2-40.
(b) Assuming the initial position is zero, sketch the position-time graph of the same motion.

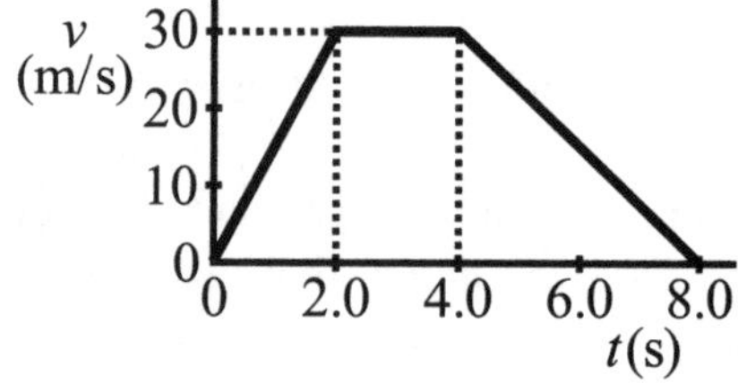

Figure 2-40 *Question 2-80.*

2-81 The table below gives the velocity-time data of the winning car in a drag race.

time (s)	0.00	1.00	2.00	3.00	4.00
velocity (m/s, forward)	0.0	14.4	38.8	59.1	74.2

(a) Plot a velocity-time graph of the motion.

(b) During which second was the car's average acceleration the greatest? the least? Determine the car's average acceleration for each of these seconds.
(c) Find the magnitude of the car's average acceleration for the entire motion.
[Ans. (b) 1.00-2.00 s, 0.00-1.00 s, 24.4 m/s^2 forward, 14.4 m/s^2 forward (c) 18.6 m/s^2]

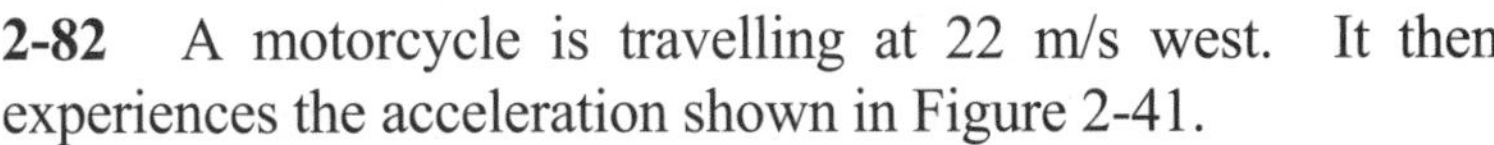

2-82 A motorcycle is travelling at 22 m/s west. It then experiences the acceleration shown in Figure 2-41.
(a) Plot a velocity-time graph of the motion from time $t = 0.0$ s to $t = 10$ s.
(b) Determine the displacement of the cycle during the 10 s interval. [Ans. 1.6 × 10^2 m west]

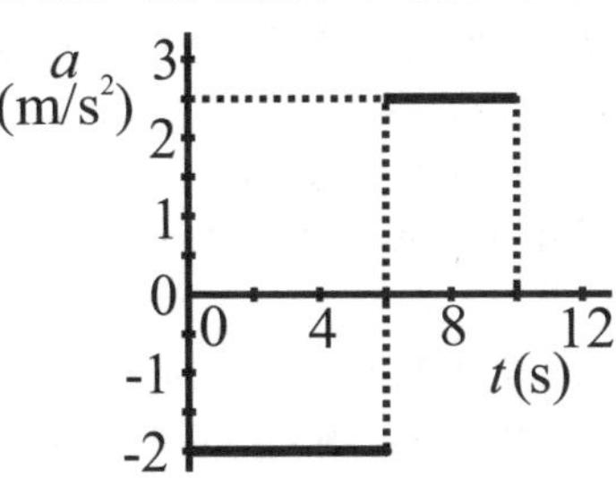

Figure 2-41 *Question 2-82. The positive direction is west.*

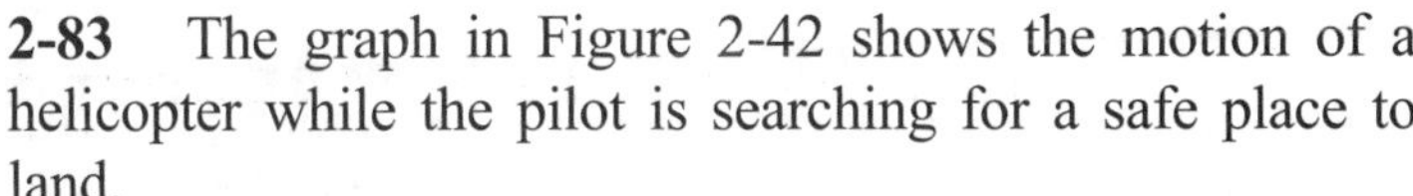

2-83 The graph in Figure 2-42 shows the motion of a helicopter while the pilot is searching for a safe place to land.
(a) At what times is the helicopter stopped?
(b) When is the helicopter's acceleration zero?
(c) During which time intervals is the helicopter accelerating northward?
(d) Calculate the approximate instantaneous acceleration at $t = 6.0$ s and $t = 12$ s.
[Ans. (a) 0.0 s, 6.0 s, 12 s (b) 4.0 s, 8.0 s, 14 s
(c) 4.0-8.0 s, 14-16 s (d) approx. 2.9 m/s^2 north, approx. 14 m/s^2 south]

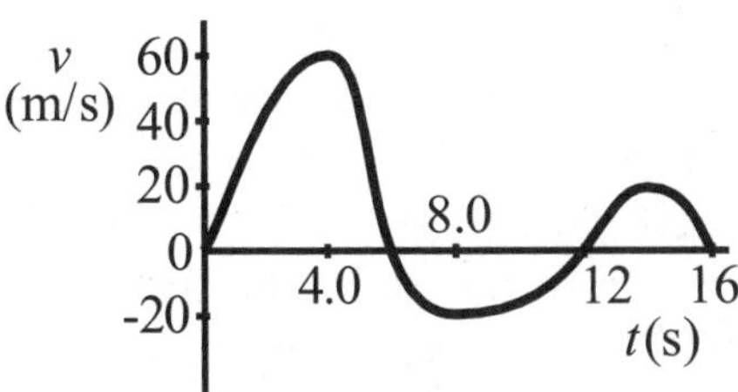

Figure 2-42 *Question 2-83. The positive direction is south.*

2-84 In a thrill ride at an amusement park the cars start from rest and accelerate rapidly forward, covering the first 15 m in 1.2 s.

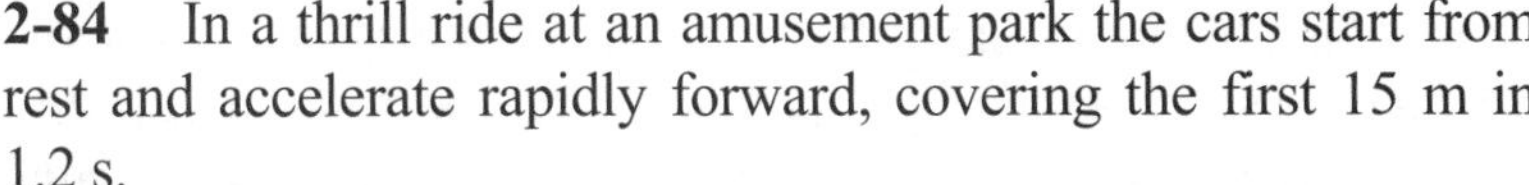

(a) What is the magnitude of the average acceleration of the cars?
(b) What is the speed of the cars at 1.2 s?
(c) Express the magnitude of the average acceleration in terms of the number of *g*'s.
[Ans. (a) 21 m/s^2 (b) 25 m/s (c) 2.1 *g*'s]

2-85 Give an example to show that an object's velocity can reverse direction when the acceleration is constant.

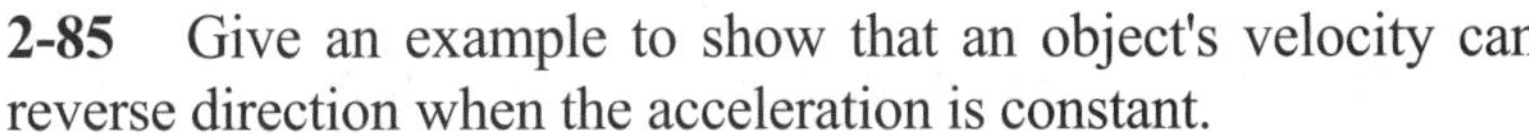

2-86 A bicyclist, travelling at 4.0 km/h at the top of a hill, coasts downhill with constant acceleration, reaching a speed of 33 km/h in 33 s. What distance, in metres, does the cyclist travel in that time? [Ans. 1.7 × 10^2 m]

2-87 Describe the motion represented by each graph shown in Figure 2-43.

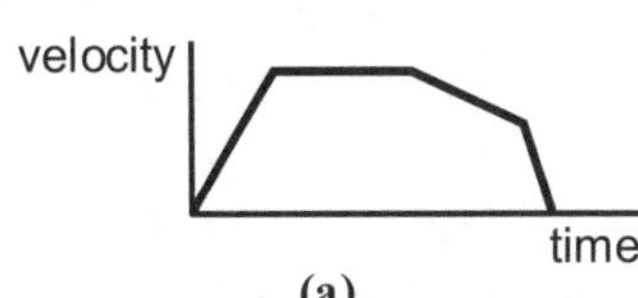

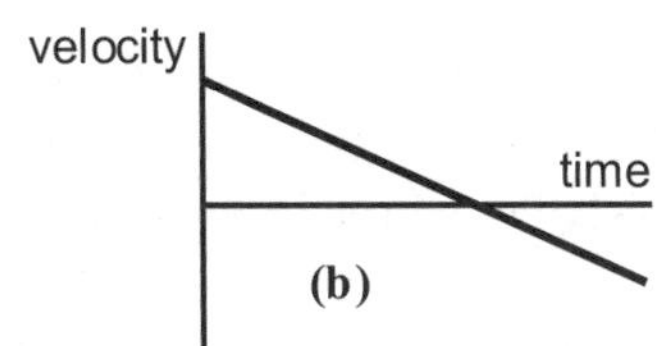

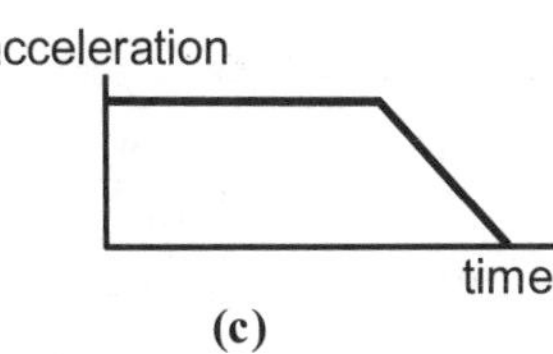

Figure 2-43 *Question 2-87.*

2-88 The heart's left ventricle accelerates blood from rest to a velocity of 25 cm/s forward during a displacement of 2.0 cm forward. Determine: (a) the blood's acceleration
(b) the time needed for the blood to reach its maximum velocity
[Ans. (a) 1.6×10^2 m/s^2 forward (b) 0.16 s]

2-89 (a) With a constant acceleration of magnitude 1.6 m/s^2, how long will it take a bus to travel 2.0×10^2 m, if the bus starts from rest?
(b) Repeat (a) if the bus starts with a speed of 8.0 m/s. (Hint: Use the quadratic formula.)
[Ans. (a) 16 s (b) 12 s]

2-90 In its final trip upstream to its spawning territory, a salmon must jump to the top of a waterfall that is 1.9 m high. With what minimum initial vertical velocity must the salmon jump to get to the top of the waterfall? [Ans. 6.1 m/s upward]

2-91 Some scientists are speculating that in the distant future one of the more powerful propulsion systems for space travel will be an matter-antimatter system. Assuming this system could provide an acceleration with a magnitude of 30 *g*'s, how long would it take a rocket, starting from rest, to reach a maximum speed that is 10% of the speed of light? (We are neglecting the effects of special relativity, which would begin to play a role at such a high speed.)
[Ans. 1.0×10^5 s]

2-92 A boy throws a stone downward from a bridge with an initial speed v_0, and a girl throws a stone upward from the same bridge with the same initial speed, v_0. Compare the velocities of their stones upon reaching the water below.

2-93 A steel ball, S, and a table tennis ball, T, are dropped from the top of a building. Assume that S experiences free fall, and T experiences air resistance and eventually reaches terminal speed.
(a) On a single set of axes, draw a velocity-time graph comparing the motions of the two balls. Assume downward is positive.
(b) Repeat, assuming upward is positive.

2-94 A boy standing on a third floor balcony of an apartment building sees a ball rising at a speed v_1 past the top of the railing. A short while later he sees the same ball falling at a speed v_2, past the same position. Choose which of the following statements is true, and explain your answer.

(A) $v_1 < v_2$ (B) $v_1 > v_2$ (C) $v_1 = v_2$ (D) the speeds cannot be compared with the information given

2-95 A camera is set up to take photographs of a ball undergoing vertical motion. The camera is 5.2 m above the ball launcher, which can launch the ball with an initial velocity of 17 m/s upward. Assuming that the ball goes straight up and straight down past the camera, at what times will the ball pass the camera? [Ans. 0.34 s, 3.1 s]

2-96 A camp employee applies some physics knowledge to determine the level of water in a well. She drops a stone from rest into the well and measures the time between the release and the

sound of the splash. The measured time is 1.4 s.
(a) Assuming that the time for the sound to travel from the water surface to the top of the well is negligible, calculate how far the water is from the top of the well.
(b) At a constant speed of 3.4×10^2 m/s, how long would it take sound to travel the distance found in (a) above? Is the answer in (a) valid? Explain. [Ans. (a) 9.6 m (b) 2.8×10^{-2} s]

APPLYING YOUR KNOWLEDGE

2-97 On a highway two posts are set up 1.0 km apart to help motorists judge the accuracy of their speedometers. An information sign tells the motorists to drive at exactly 90 km/h between the posts and to measure the time to travel the 1.0 km. For a motorist who follows this procedure and requires a time of 38 s, determine the actual speed of the car. [Ans. 95 km/h]

2-98 A helicopter is travelling horizontally, straight toward a cliff. When 700 m from the cliff, it sends a sonar signal and 3.4 s later receives the reflected signal. Assuming the signal travels at 350 m/s, determine the speed of the helicopter. [Ans. 62 m/s]

2-99 Two cars, A and B, are stopped for a red light beside each other at an intersection. The light turns green and the cars accelerate. Their velocity-time graphs are shown in Figure 2-44. The positive direction is "forward."
(a) At what time(s) do A and B have the same velocity?
(b) When does B overtake A? (Hint: Their displacements must be equal at that time and displacement can be found from a velocity-time graph.)
(c) How far have the cars travelled when B overtakes A?
[Ans. (a) 45 s (b) 75 s (c) 9.0×10^2 m]

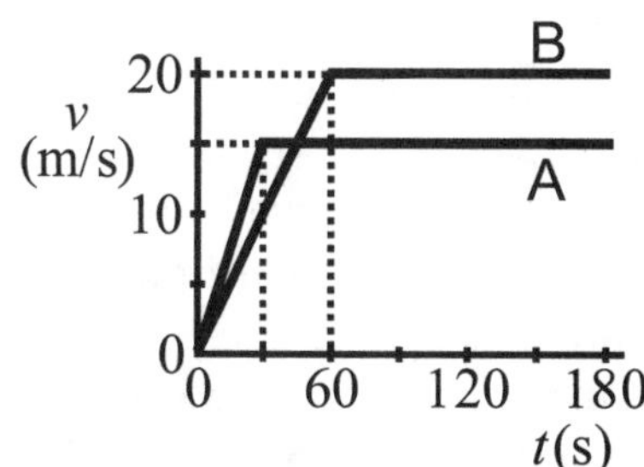

Figure 2-44 *Question 2-99.*

2-100 Assume that in a track-and-field competition the fastest time for the woman's 100-m dash is 11.0 s, and the time for the women's 400-m relay is 42.6 s. It appears as if each of the four women in the relay can run 100 m in less than 11.0 s. Explain this apparent discrepancy. (Hint: Consider acceleration.)

2-101 A car with one headlight burned out is travelling at a constant speed of 18 m/s and passes a stopped police car. The car is pursued immediately by the police cruiser, which has a constant acceleration of magnitude 2.2 m/s^2.
(a) How far does the police cruiser travel before catching the other car?
(b) At what time will this occur? (Hint: Graphing may help you visualize this problem.)
[Ans. (a) 2.9×10^2 m (b) 16 s after the car passes the cruiser]

2-102 The world record for the men's pole vault is about 6.0 m.
(a) How long does the vaulter take to fall the first 50 cm on the way down?
(b) Repeat (a) for the last 50 cm, assuming the vaulter comes down to ground level.
(c) Explain why the vaulter appears to be in "slow motion" near the top of the jump.
[Ans. (a) 0.32 s (b) 4.9×10^{-2} s]

2-103 *Fermi Question:* A patient with a detached retina is warned by an eye specialist that if she slows down with an acceleration greater than 2 *g*'s in magnitude, the retina could pull away entirely from the sclera. Help the patient decide whether or not a vigorous game of tennis would be acceptable. Estimate values of running speeds and stopping times to determine your answer.

2-104 Scientists use specially designed helmets with embedded electronic sensors to study the effects of impacts on hockey players' heads during a game. The sensors transmit data to a computer, which records the data. In one test of 14-year-old players, the impacts ranged from an acceleration of magnitude 77 m/s^2 (an impact on the chin) to 2.2×10^2 m/s^2 (an impact to the upper head).
(a) Express the range of accelerations in terms of *g*.
(b) If the impact to the upper head lasts 12 ms, determine the stopping distance during the collision. What assumption is required to perform this calculation?
(c) Some major league football players experience head impacts resulting in 100 *g*'s of acceleration, yet the concussions of the teen players may be more damaging. Give a reason for this apparent discrepancy. [Ans. (a) 7.9 to 22 *g*'s (b) 1.6 cm]

2-105 Research has shown that the average driver requires about 0.8 s to engage a car's brakes after seeing an emergency. However, this reaction time applies to people who have not been drinking alcoholic beverages. Approximate reaction times for beer consumers are shown in Figure 2-45. Use the data from this graph to determine the distance travelled while reacting (reaction distance) to complete the table below. [Ans. for 120 km/h and 5 bottles: 99 m]

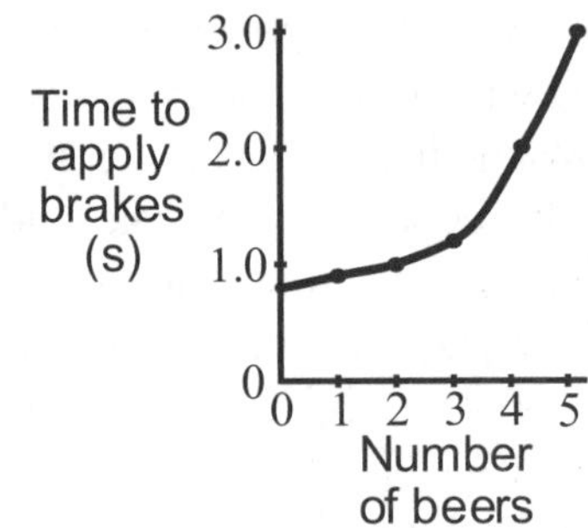

Figure 2-45 *Question 2-105. Reaction times for beer-drinking drivers.*

Speed	Reaction distance		
	no alcohol	3 bottles	5 bottles
50 km/h (14 m/s)	?	?	?
90 km/h (25 m/s)	?	?	?
120 km/h (33 m/s)	?	?	?

2-106 Use a 30-cm ruler or a metre stick to determine the reaction times of you and your friends. One person holds the top of the ruler and lets it hang lengthwise vertically. The person whose reaction time is being determined places a thumb and forefinger almost together just below the bottom of the ruler, so that when the ruler is released by the other person, it will fall between the thumb and forefinger. The person holding the ruler drops it without warning. The person being tested tries to grasp the ruler as soon as possible after it starts to fall freely. Find the average distance of several falls, then use a kinematics equation to determine reaction time.

KEY OBJECTIVES

Having completed this chapter you should now be able to do the following:

1. Define kinematics.
2. Define speed and calculate the average speed of a moving object.
3. Distinguish between instantaneous speed and average speed.
4. Recognize the conditions required for uniform motion.
5. Determine an object's displacement given its initial and final positions.
6. Define velocity and calculate the average velocity of a moving object.
7. Distinguish between instantaneous velocity and average velocity.
8. Plot position-time, velocity-time, and acceleration-time graphs involving uniform and non-uniform motion, and use slopes and areas on those graphs to determine unknown quantities.
9. Describe the motion portrayed in the types of graphs named in #8 above.
10. Define acceleration and calculate average acceleration.
11. Distinguish instantaneous acceleration and average acceleration.
12. Derive the kinematics equations for constant acceleration involving initial and final positions, time, initial and final velocities, and acceleration.
13. Apply the constant-acceleration equations to solve for any one of the variables, given at least three of the other variables.
14. Know the average acceleration due to gravity for free-falling objects near the surface of Earth.
15. Apply the constant-acceleration equations to situations involving the acceleration due to gravity.
16. Recognize the advantage of using a logical procedure in problem solving.
17. Describe the meaning and cause of terminal speed in air.

ANSWERS TO SELECTED QUESTIONS

2-5 (a) uniform motion (b) The object is speeding up. (c) The object is slowing down.

2-6 vector quantity; the velocity (both the speed and the direction) of the wind

2-7 (a) if motion is in one direction with no reversals of direction of motion
(b) yes, if an object reverses its direction of motion
(c) no, at most, the displacement's magnitude equals the distance (as in a)

2-8 (a) Speed (instantaneous) indicates how fast an object is moving; it is a scalar quantity. Velocity is a vector quantity; it is similar to speed in that at any time the magnitude of velocity equals the speed, but velocity also includes direction.
(b) if motion is in one direction with no reversals of direction of motion

2-14 (a) object is moving west away from the origin ($x = 0$) with constant velocity, then the velocity increases during a very short time interval and the object continues west with a larger constant velocity; finally the velocity is reduced to zero (during a very short time interval) and the object stays at one position, westward of the initial starting position
(b) object begins at a position that is east of the origin ($x = 0$), and travels toward the origin (i.e., westward) with a velocity that has a continually decreasing magnitude; the object eventually reaches the origin
(c) object begins at a position south of the origin ($x = 0$) and travels northward at a constant velocity, eventually passing and going beyond the origin

2-17 (a), (b), and (d)

2-18 (a) constant southward velocity (b) increasing southward velocity (c) decreasing southward velocity

2-19 Yes, a car that is travelling west and slowing down has a westward velocity but an eastward acceleration.

2-26 during constant or uniform acceleration

2-27 (a) object speeds up from rest with a continually decreasing acceleration; after reaching a maximum velocity, the object slows down with constant acceleration until it comes to rest
(b) object undergoes constant positive acceleration, followed by constant negative acceleration (of smaller magnitude but for a greater time period than the positive acceleration)
(c) object undergoes uniformly increasing acceleration followed by constant acceleration for a longer period of time

2-40 (a) same magnitude, opposite direction (b) same (c) zero (d) 9.8 m/s^2 down at all points

2-53 (d) 2-54 (a) 2-55 (b) 2-56 (d) 2-57 (b)

2-61 no, car 1 is travelling at a constant speed that is larger than the (constant) speed of car 2

2-67 (a) They are equal. (b) They are equal.
(c) The magnitude of the instantaneous velocity equals the instantaneous speed.

2-76 At the top of the path of a ball thrown vertically upward, the ball is instantaneously at rest (i.e., has zero speed), but it has non-zero acceleration (9.8 m/s^2 downward).

2-77 (c) The acceleration is shown as westerly, and the eastward velocity vectors are becoming smaller as the car moves toward the east.

2-78 (a) runner is moving south and is speeding up
(b) runner is moving south and is slowing down
(c) runner is moving north and is slowing down
(d) runner is moving north and is speeding up

2-92 The final velocities of the stones are equal.

2-94 (c) Neglecting air resistance, the motion of a ball going up and then down under the influence of gravity is symmetric.

2-96 expanded answer for part (b): The answer to (a) is not valid. Using a corrected time of 1.4 – 0.028 seconds gives a distance of 9.2 m, which is significantly different from the value determined without this correction in part (a). (This new distance of 9.2 m in turn gives a new answer of 0.027 seconds for the time taken by sound to travel from the water to the top of the well. This gives a new corrected time of 1.4 – 0.027 seconds, for the time for the stone to drop, and then a distance (unchanged to 2 significant figures) of 9.2 m.)

CHAPTER 3

VECTORS

Vectors have been dealt with briefly in Chapters 1 and 2, but many more details about vectors are required to understand motion in two dimensions in Chapter 4. If you have studied vectors in a mathematics course, some of the material in this chapter may be a review. If the mathematical details of vectors are new to you, this chapter is an important preliminary introduction to Chapter 4.

3.1 GENERAL PROPERTIES OF VECTORS

In this section, we look at some general properties of vectors. Scale diagrams with distance and angular measurements are important here, so you are advised to have a metric ruler and a protractor handy as you read this section.

Vector Symbols

A vector can be represented in a diagram by using a directed line segment or arrow. The length of the line segment is proportional to the magnitude of the vector, and the direction is the same as the direction of the vector. The line segment has an initial point (the tail of the arrow) and a terminal point (the head of the arrow). If a vector is drawn using a scale, such as 1.0 cm = 100 km, the scale should be indicated on the diagram. Figure 3-1 shows typical vectors drawn to scale.

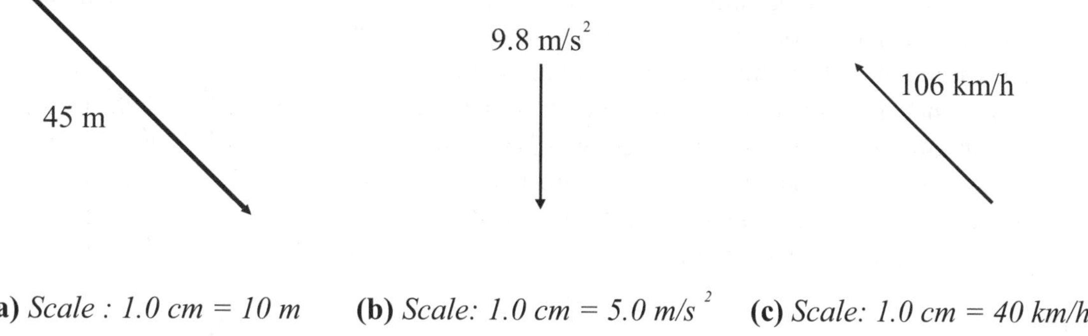

(a) *Scale : 1.0 cm = 10 m* **(b)** *Scale: 1.0 cm = 5.0 m/s^2* **(c)** *Scale: 1.0 cm = 40 km/h*

Figure 3-1 *Examples of vector quantities.*

Vector quantities in this book will be written in **boldface type**, for example, $\boldsymbol{A}$. The magnitude of a vector (such as $\boldsymbol{A}$) will be shown either as $|\boldsymbol{A}|$, or just A (note: not bold). This magnitude is always a positive quantity (unless zero), regardless of the direction of the vector. When reading this book, it is important to distinguish between boldface type and regular type, since they indicate different quantities. In hand-writing, a vector quantity is usually indicated by a short arrow (→) above the letter representing the vector: $\vec{A}$.

Directions of Vectors

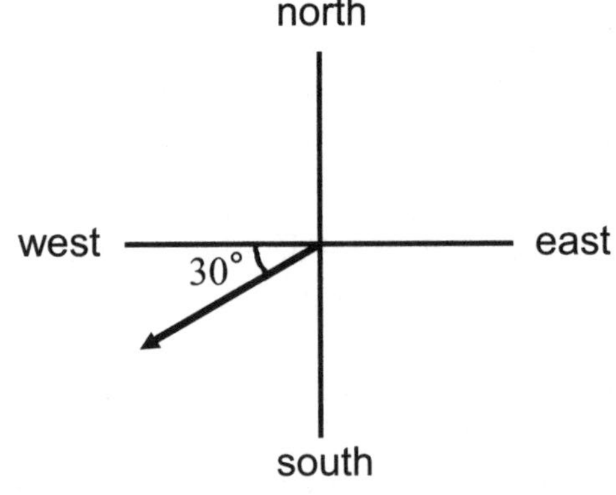

Figure 3-2 *A vector having a direction 30° south of west.*

Various ways can be used to denote vector directions. In this book directions are usually written after the magnitude and units of the measurement. For example, a velocity might be given as 100 km/h west. Typical examples of directions are listed below:

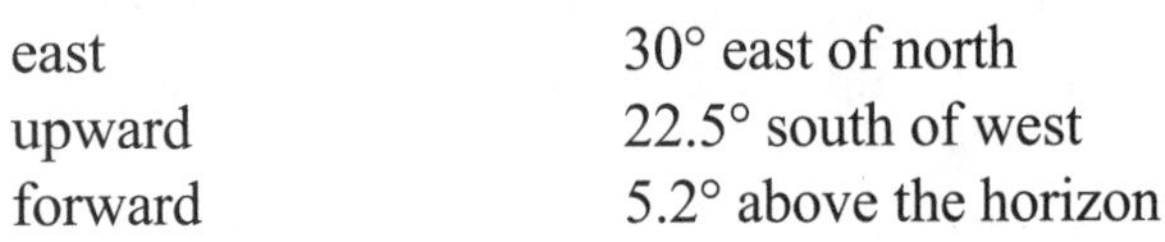

east	30° east of north
upward	22.5° south of west
forward	5.2° above the horizon

Figure 3-2 shows a vector having a direction 30° south of west, which is the same as 60° west of south. (This direction is sometimes written [W 30° S] or [S 60° W]). Notice that Figure 3-2 follows the convention used on maps, that is, north is toward the top of the page, east toward the right, etc.

> ***Math Tip:*** *Directions used in calculators and computers are measured counter-clockwise from the +x axis of an x-y co-ordinate system.*

Multiplying a Vector by a Scalar

A vector can be multiplied by a scalar, producing a vector with the same direction as the original vector but a different magnitude (unless the scalar happens to be "1," in which case the multiplication produces no change). Thus, 3***A*** is a vector 3 times as long as ***A*** and in the same direction. Multiplication of a vector by a scalar quantity that is negative produces a vector in the opposite direction. For example, the vector –2***A*** is twice as long as ***A*** and points in the opposite direction; if ***A*** points east, then –2***A*** points west. Multiplication of a vector by a scalar is illustrated in Figure 3-3.

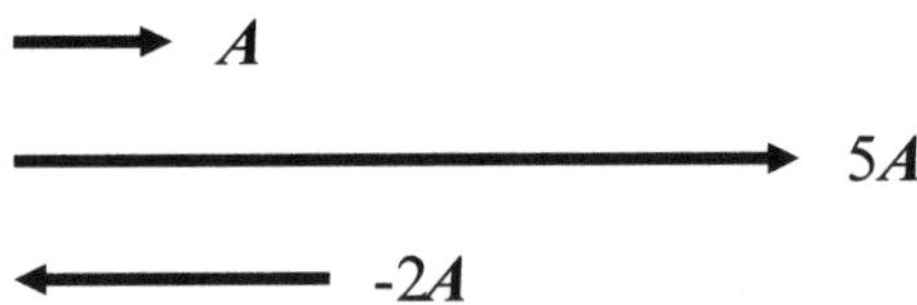

Figure 3-3 *Multiplying a vector by a scalar.*

 **Practice**

3-1 A velocity vector ***v*** is 22 m/s west.
What are (a) |***v***|? (b) *v*? [Ans. (a) & (b) 22 m/s]

3-2 Use a ruler and a protractor to determine the magnitude (with units) and direction of each vector shown in Figure 3-4.
[Ans. ***A*** = 21 m/s 35° west of north, ***B*** = 35 m/s 45° south of east]

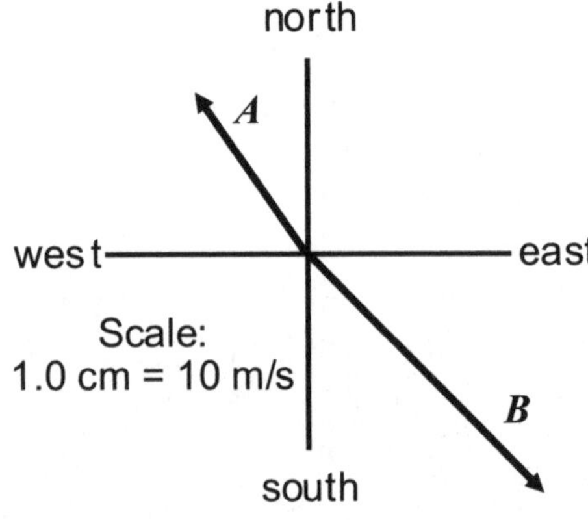

Figure 3-4 *Vectors for Question 3-2*

3-3 Draw a vector diagram to indicate each of the following vectors. In each case indicate the scale used to draw the diagram.

(a) 5.0×10^3 km 50° north of west
(b) 0.040 m/s 10° south of east
(c) 38 N at 25° above the horizontal
(d) 5***C***, where ***C*** is the vector given in (c) above
(e) −3***C***, where ***C*** is the vector given in (c) above

3-4 An acceleration vector ***a*** is 1.5 m/s^2 downward. What is −2***a***? [Ans. 3.0 m/s^2 upward]

3.2 ADDITION AND SUBTRACTION OF VECTORS USING SCALE DIAGRAMS

If a person walks 6.0 m west, then turns and walks 8.0 m south, the total *distance* travelled is 14.0 m (a scalar quantity). However, the *displacement*, which is a vector that points in a straight line from the initial position directly to the final position, has a magnitude less than 14.0 m and a specific direction. One way to find this displacement is to add the vectors using a scale diagram. If we let ***A*** = 6.0 m west and ***B*** = 8.0 m south, these vectors can be added as shown in Figure 3-5. The result of this addition is the total displacement, which is called the resultant displacement. If we use ***R*** as the symbol for the resultant displacement, then ***R*** = ***A*** + ***B***, where the "+" sign here means a *vector* addition. (The result of a vector addition has a variety of names including the general terms net vector, vector sum, resultant, and **resultant vector**. The word resultant will be used in this text, including specific cases such as resultant displacement, resultant force, and so on.)

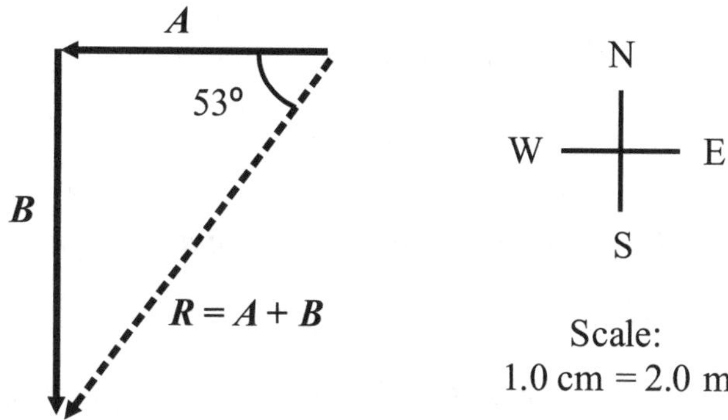

Figure 3-5 *Adding vectors using a scale diagram.*

In Figure 3-5, the resultant displacement, ***R*** = ***A*** + ***B***, can be found by using the scale to determine the magnitude and a protractor for the angle. In this example, ***R*** = 10.0 m 53° south of west. (Because the vectors ***A*** and ***B*** are perpendicular to each other, the magnitude in this particular base could also be found using the Pythagorean relation $R = (A^2 + B^2)^{1/2}$.) Using a scale diagram to determine the sum of vectors clearly has limited accuracy. In Section 3.3 we will introduce a more accurate way to add (and subtract) vectors using quantities called components of vectors.

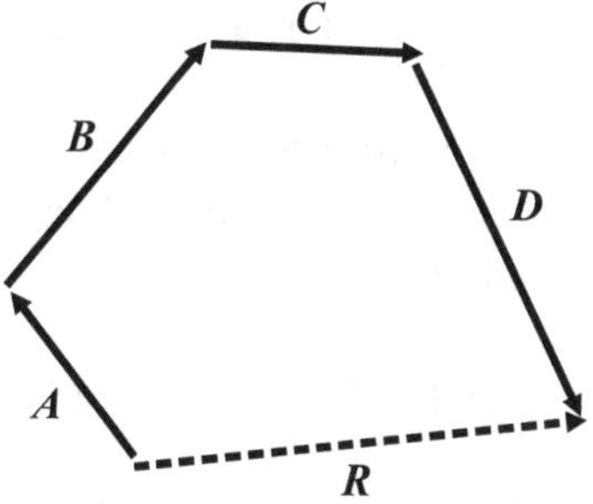

Figure 3-6 *Placing four vectors head-to-tail to obtain the resultant vector* ***R***. ***R*** = ***A*** + ***B*** + ***C*** + ***D***.

Notice in Figure 3-5 that the two vectors, ***A*** and ***B***, are placed so that the tail of ***B*** touches the head of ***A***, and the resultant vector ***R*** is drawn from the start (tail) of ***A*** to the finish (head) of ***B***. The process of adding vectors by placing them tail to head to find the resultant vector can be extended to any number of vectors having the same units (Figure 3-6). Notice that the resultant vector ***R*** points from the *tail* of the *first* vector ***A*** to the *head* of the *last* vector ***D***.

In the previous two examples, the vectors were already placed conveniently tail to head, so the resultant vector was simply drawn in from the tail of the first vector to the head of the last one. If, however, the vectors are not already placed tail to head in the diagram, they can be moved around so they become tail to head. This process is shown in Figure 3-7. When moving a vector on a diagram it is important that the redrawn vector has the same magnitude and direction as the initial vector. Otherwise it is not the same vector.

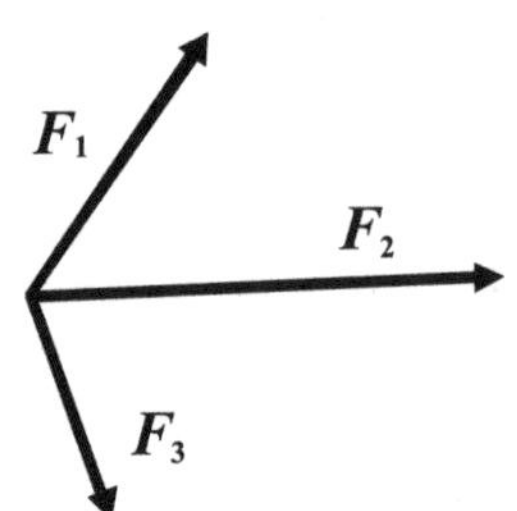

(a) *Three forces act at a single point.*

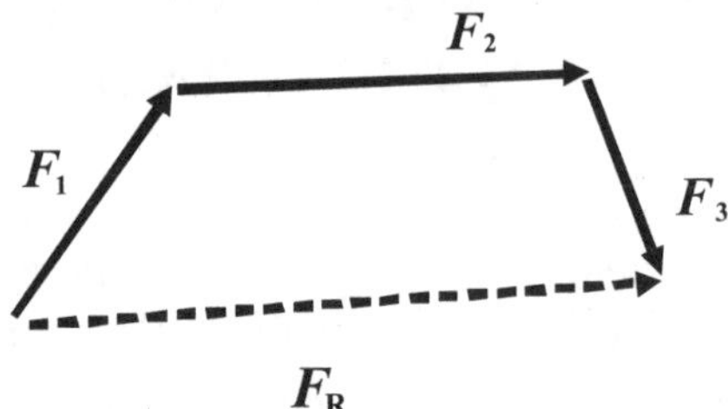

(b) $\boldsymbol{F_2}$ *and* $\boldsymbol{F_3}$ *are moved so that the net force* $\boldsymbol{F_R}$ *can be found* .

Figure 3-7 *Adding vectors by moving them parallel to themselves.*

Properties of Vector Addition

In mathematics courses you have learned of the commutative and associative laws. These laws can be applied to vector addition.

1. Vector addition is commutative; in other words, the order of addition does not matter.

$$\boldsymbol{A} + \boldsymbol{B} = \boldsymbol{B} + \boldsymbol{A}$$

2. Vector addition is associative; that is, if more than two vectors are added it does not matter how we group them.

$$(\boldsymbol{A} + \boldsymbol{B}) + \boldsymbol{C} = \boldsymbol{A} + (\boldsymbol{B} + \boldsymbol{C})$$

We will not present formal proofs of these laws in this text. However, Figure 3-8 illustrates the commutative law for vector addition. Notice in this Figure that ***A*** + ***B*** has the same magnitude and direction as ***B*** + ***A***.

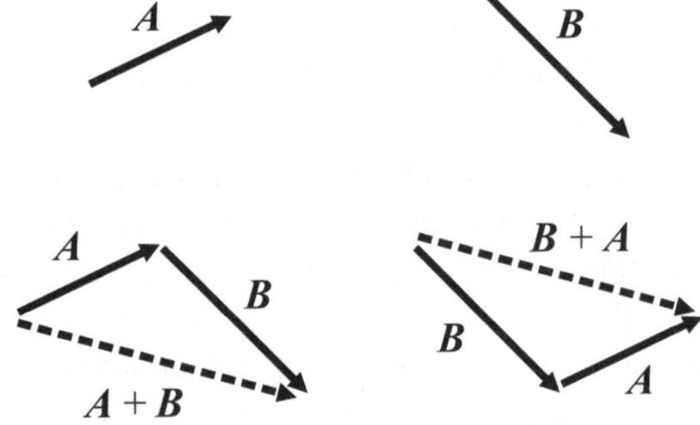

Figure 3-8 *Illustrating the commutative law for vector addition:* ***A*** + ***B*** = ***B*** + ***A***.

Vector Subtraction

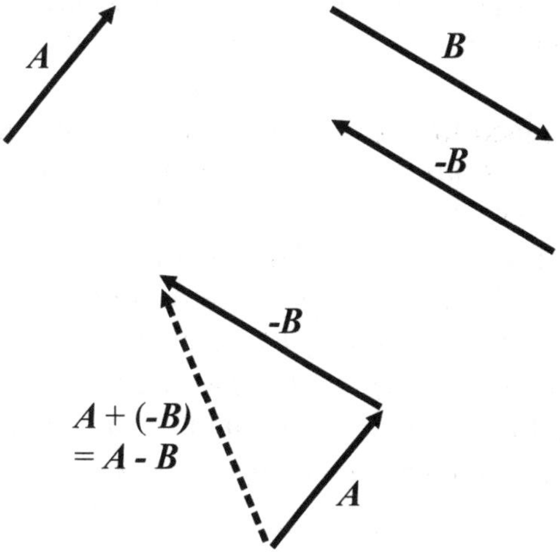

Vector subtraction occurs often in physics. We define the subtraction $\boldsymbol{A} - \boldsymbol{B}$ to be the sum of $\boldsymbol{A}$ and $-\boldsymbol{B}$, where $-\boldsymbol{B}$ has the same magnitude as $\boldsymbol{B}$ but is opposite in direction. Thus:

$$\boldsymbol{A} - \boldsymbol{B} = \boldsymbol{A} + (-\boldsymbol{B})$$

In other words, to subtract $\boldsymbol{B}$ from $\boldsymbol{A}$, add the opposite of $\boldsymbol{B}$ to $\boldsymbol{A}$. This is shown in Figure 3-9. It is left as an exercise (question 3-6) for you to prove, using a diagram, that $\boldsymbol{A} - \boldsymbol{B}$ does not equal $\boldsymbol{B} - \boldsymbol{A}$.

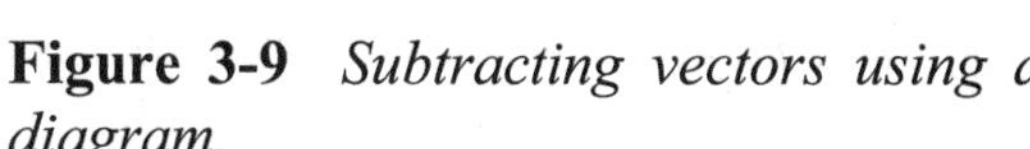

Figure 3-9 *Subtracting vectors using a diagram.*

Practice

3-5 Add each set of vectors by using a scale diagram.

(a) $\boldsymbol{C}$ = 28 km 20° north of east; $\boldsymbol{D}$ = 34 km 30° west of north

(b) $\boldsymbol{E}$ = 300 N east; $\boldsymbol{F}$ = 250 N 55° south of east; $\boldsymbol{G}$ = 600 N 15° south of west

[Ans. (a) 40 km 77° north of east (b) 3.9×10^2 N 17° west of south]

3-6 Assume $\boldsymbol{X}$ = 5.5 units 30° west of north and $\boldsymbol{Y}$ = 4.5 units 45° west of south. Use a scale diagram to find (a) $\boldsymbol{X} - \boldsymbol{Y}$ (b) $\boldsymbol{Y} - \boldsymbol{X}$.

(c) How does $(\boldsymbol{X} - \boldsymbol{Y})$ compare to $(\boldsymbol{Y} - \boldsymbol{X})$? What conclusion can be made?

(d) Does your conclusion in (c) apply if $\boldsymbol{X}$ and $\boldsymbol{Y}$ are equal?

[Ans. (a) 8.0 units 87° north of east (b) 8.0 units 87° south of west]

3-7 Find $\boldsymbol{A} + \boldsymbol{B} - \boldsymbol{C}$ diagrammatically, given $\boldsymbol{A}$ = 80 m 50° west of north, $\boldsymbol{B}$ = 60 m south, and $\boldsymbol{C}$ = 90 m 30° south of west. [Ans. 40 m 65° north of east]

3.3 ADDITION AND SUBTRACTION OF VECTORS USING COMPONENTS

Adding and subtracting vectors with diagrams, as shown in Section 3.2, is useful and instructive because the process helps to visualize the physical situation. However, the amount of uncertainty that the technique produces in the resultant vector is rather large. To reduce the uncertainty, vectors can be added by a mathematical technique using the components of vectors. This technique is especially useful when adding three or more vectors.

The **component of a vector** is a projection of a vector along an axis, usually of a rectangular coordinate system. Any vector can be completely described by its rectangular components. In this book we will use two rectangular components because we will consider two-dimensional situations only. (In three dimensions, three components are needed.)

> ***Did You Know?*** *Rectangular components, by definition, are perpendicular to each other. They are also known as orthogonal components. "Orthogonal" stems from the Greek "orthos" which means "right," and "gonia" which means "angle".*

Consider vector $\boldsymbol{A}$ in a rectangular co-ordinate system with x- and y-axes, as seen in Figure 3-10. The projection of $\boldsymbol{A}$ along the x-axis is the x-component and has the symbol A_x. The projection of $\boldsymbol{A}$ along the y-axis is the y-component and has the symbol A_y. In this textbook, we will show components with dashed (broken) lines. Notice that $\boldsymbol{A}$ is a vector, but the components A_x and A_y are not vectors; rather they are positive or negative numbers, having the same units as $\boldsymbol{A}$.

> ***Notation Tip:*** *Because components of vectors are not themselves vectors, you should not place an arrow over the hand-written letters (such as A_x and A_y) representing the components.*

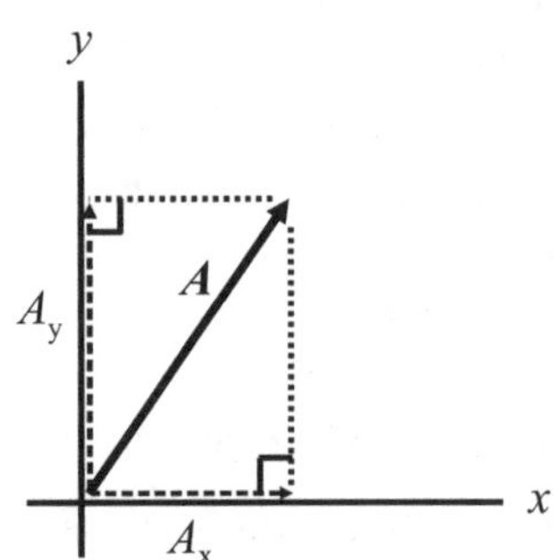

Figure 3-10 *The components of a vector.*

To calculate the components of a vector, the trigonometric ratios of sine, cosine, and tangent can be applied. (Components can also be found by using a scale diagram, but we are aiming for higher accuracy here.) Appendix 5 reviews the definitions of these three ratios and gives examples of how to apply them. If you find the next sample problem challenging to understand, you are advised to study Appendix 5 in detail.

Sample Problem 3-1

Determine the x- and y-components of the vectors shown in Figure 3-11.

Solution: Notice that $+x$ is to the right and $+y$ is upward. Hence, if the x-component of a vector is directed toward the right, it is positive, and if directed toward the left, it is negative. Similarly, an upward y-component is positive, and a downward y-component is negative.

$$A_x = +10 \cos 30° \qquad A_y = +10 \sin 30°$$
$$= 8.7 \qquad\qquad = 5.0$$

$$B_x = +15 \cos 70° \qquad B_y = -15 \sin 70°$$
$$= 5.1 \qquad\qquad = -14.1$$

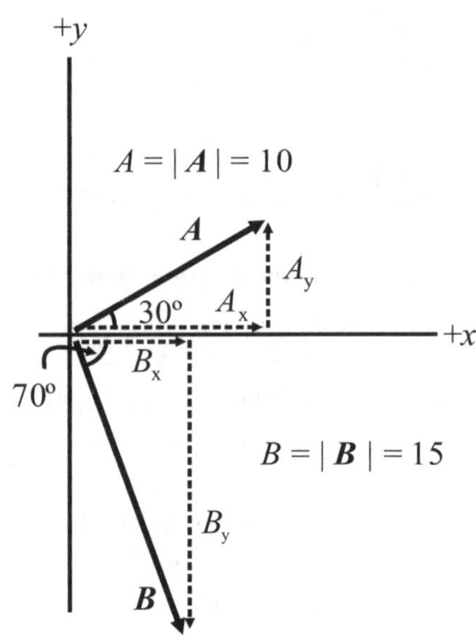

Figure 3-11 *Sample Problem 3-1.*

Addition of Vectors

When two vectors are added to give a resultant vector, the x-components of the original vectors add to give the x-component of the resultant, and the y-components of the original vectors add to give the resultant y-component. In symbols, for the addition $\boldsymbol{R} = \boldsymbol{A} + \boldsymbol{B}$:

$$R_x = A_x + B_x$$

$$R_y = A_y + B_y$$

This addition of components is illustrated in Figure 3-12.

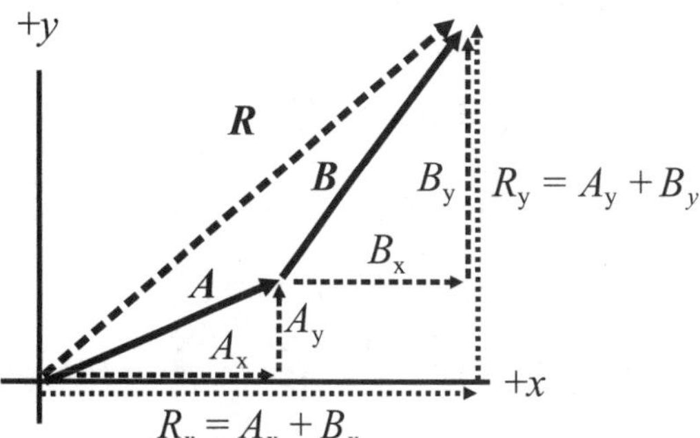

Figure 3-12 *Adding components of vectors* ***A*** *and* ***B*** *to give the components of the resultant vector* ***R****.*

To add any number of vectors by components, the steps listed below are used. These steps are applied in Sample Problem 3-2 below.

1. Define an x-y co-ordinate system, indicating which directions are positive.

2. Determine the x- and y-components of all the vectors.

3. Add all the x-components to find the resultant x-component.

4. Add all the y-components to find the resultant y-component.

5. Find the magnitude and direction of the resultant vector. (For this step, the Pythagorean relation, $R = (A^2 + B^2)^{1/2}$, and/or trigonometric ratios can be used.)

Sample Problem 3-2

A person walks 50 m 30° north of east, then 60 m east, and finally 80 m 40° south of west. Use components to find the person's final displacement, ***R***.

Solution: 1. The x-y co-ordinate system will be the regular east-west, north-south system. We will call the displacement vectors ***A***, ***B***, and ***C*** respectively, as shown in Figure 3-13 (a).

2. The x- and y-components of the vectors are shown in Figure 3-13 (b). They are:

$$A_x = (50\text{ m})\cos 30° = 43\text{ m}$$
$$A_y = (50\text{ m})\sin 30° = 25\text{ m}$$
$$B_x = 60\text{ m}$$
$$B_y = 0\text{ m}$$
$$C_x = -(80\text{ m})\cos 40° = -61\text{ m}$$
$$C_y = -(80\text{ m})\sin 40° = -51\text{ m}$$

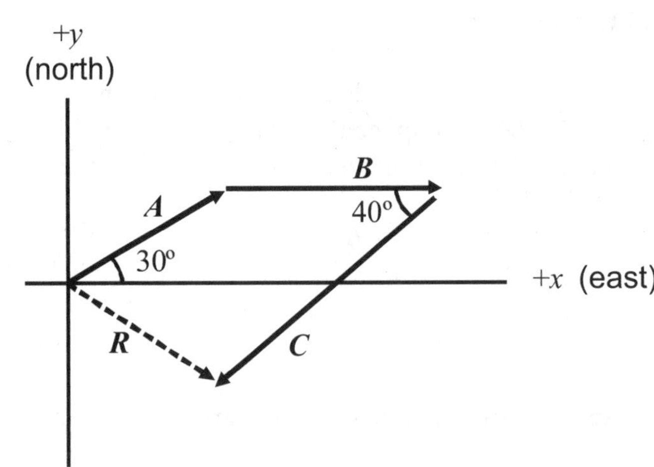

(a) *Showing the various displacement vectors.*

Notice that since **B** points east, B_y = 0 m. Note also that the components of **C** are both negative, indicating that **C** has components that are southward and westward.

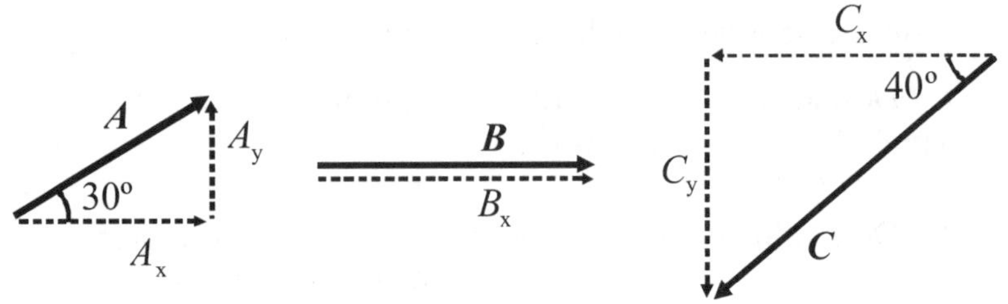

(b) *Showing the components of the vectors.*

3. The resultant x-component is:

$$R_x = A_x + B_x + C_x$$
$$= (43 + 60 - 61)\text{m}$$
$$\therefore\ R_x = 42\text{ m}$$

4. The resultant y-component is:

$$R_y = A_y + B_y + C_y$$
$$= (25 + 0 - 51)\text{m}$$
$$R_y = -26\text{ m}$$

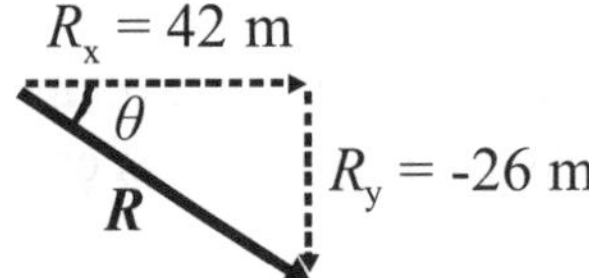

(c) *The resultant vector.*

Figure 3-13 *Sample Problem 3-2.*

5. The resultant components and the resultant displacement are shown in Figure 3-13 (c). $|\boldsymbol{R}|$ (or R) can be found using the Pythagorean relation:

$$R = \sqrt{(42\text{ m})^2 + (26\text{ m})^2}$$
$$= 49\text{ m}$$

The direction of ***R*** can be found from $\tan\theta = \dfrac{26\text{ m}}{42\text{ m}}$, hence, $\theta = \tan^{-1}(26/42) = 32°$.

Thus, the resultant displacement is 49 m 32° south of east.

> ***Math Tips:*** *Although a calculator gives answers almost instantaneously, do not rely on the answers without thinking about them. Inverse trig functions, such as* $\tan^{-1}$*, provide an example of the limitations of calculators. In the range of* $0°$ *to* $360°$ *there are always two angles with the same tangent. However, your calculator will give you only one angle, namely the smaller of the two possible angles. For example,* $\tan 20° = \tan 200° = 0.364$*, but when you find* $\tan^{-1} 0.364$ *on your calculator, you get only* $20°$*. Thus, you must decide on the appropriate way to interpret answers given by your calculator.*
>
> *Another warning about calculator use — scientific calculators can express angles in two or three different units. When cleared or first turned on, the calculator usually indicates angles in degrees (DEG). Pushing the appropriate key (e.g., DGR) will change the units to radians (RAD) or grads (GRA, where* $90° = 100$ *grads). For now, only degrees will be used in this book.*

Subtraction of Vectors

Components can also be used to perform subtraction of vectors. If we wish to subtract vector $\boldsymbol{B}$ from $\boldsymbol{A}$ to give $\boldsymbol{C}$ (that is, $\boldsymbol{C} = \boldsymbol{A} - \boldsymbol{B}$), the components of $\boldsymbol{C}$ can each be determined by subtraction using the components of $\boldsymbol{A}$ and $\boldsymbol{B}$:

$$C_x = A_x - B_x$$

$$C_y = A_y - B_y$$

 **Practice**

3-8 Determine the x- and y-components of each vector shown in Figure 3-14. In each case, the $+x$ axis is to the right and the $+y$ axis is toward the top of the page.
[Ans. (a) x: 5.3 cm, y: 1.5 cm (b) x: –37 km, y: 24 km (c) x: –32 cm/s, y: –28 cm/s]

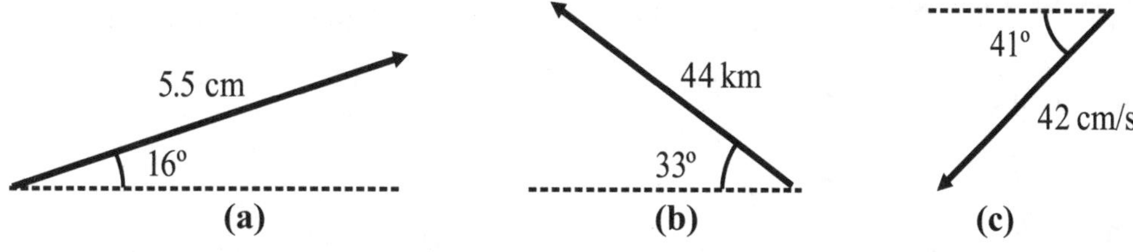

Figure 3-14 *Question 3-8.*

3-9 Find the magnitude and direction of the sum of vectors $\boldsymbol{A} + \boldsymbol{B} + \boldsymbol{C}$ using the component technique. Assume two significant digits. Show your steps clearly.

A = 20 km north *B* = 30 km east *C* = 50 km 55° west of north

[Ans. 50 km 77° north of west]

3-10 With the vectors ***A***, ***B***, and ***C*** from the previous question, use the component technique to determine the magnitude and direction of (a) ***A*** - ***B*** and (b) ***A*** - ***B*** - ***C***.
[Ans. (a) 36 km 56° west of north (b) 14 km 38° south of east]

3-11 Three people on a seaside dock are pulling on ropes attached to a yacht. The forces, ***D***, ***E***, and ***F***, are measured in newtons, N, and are shown in Figure 3-15. The magnitudes of the forces are: *D* = 281 N, *E* = 192 N, and *F* = 255 N. Their directions are indicated in the figure. Find the magnitude and direction of the resultant of these three forces.
[Ans. 5.7×10^2 N, at an angle of 256° measured counterclockwise from the +*x* axis]

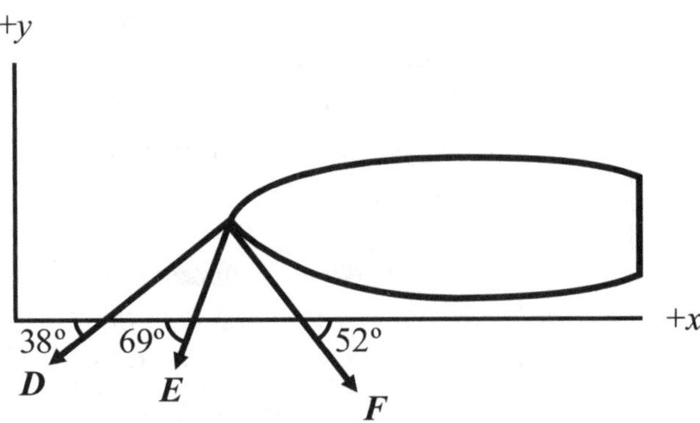

Figure 3-15 *Question 3-11.*

CHAPTER FOCUS

This chapter was devoted to vector terminology and properties, and the addition and subtraction of vectors. The very important concept of components of vectors was presented. These concepts will be applied to two-dimensional kinematics in Chapter 4.

VOCABULARY REVIEW

You should now be able to define or explain each of the following words or phrases.

resultant vector component of a vector

CHAPTER REVIEW

3-12 When does ***A*** – ***B*** = ***B*** – ***A***?
(a) never
(b) always
(c) only when ***A*** = ***B***
(d) more information is needed to answer the question

3-13 If vector ***A*** is 10 m 45° south of west and vector ***B*** is 24 m 45° south of east, then ***A*** + ***B*** has a magnitude of:
(a) 26 m (b) 34 m (c) 14 m (d) 0 m (e) none of these

3-14 Vectors ***A*** and ***B*** face west, and vector ***C*** faces east. All three vectors are equal in magnitude. The resultant of 2*A* – (2***B*** – 2*C*) is equal to:
(a) 2*A* (b) ***A*** (c) 2*C* (d) – ***A*** (e) 2*A* – 2*C*

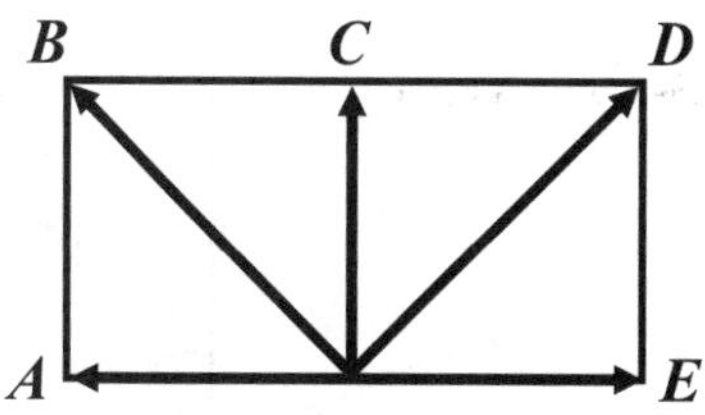

Figure 3-16 *Question 3-15*

3-15 In Figure 3-16, vector ***A*** is equal to:
(a) ***B*** – ***D***
(b) ***D*** – ***B***
(c) ***C*** + ***E*** – ***D***
(d) ***C*** – ***D***
(e) ***D*** – ***C***

3-16 In Figure 3-17, the component of vector ***A*** along the inclined plane is:
(a) *A* sinβ (b) *A* sinα (c) *A* (d) zero (e) none of these

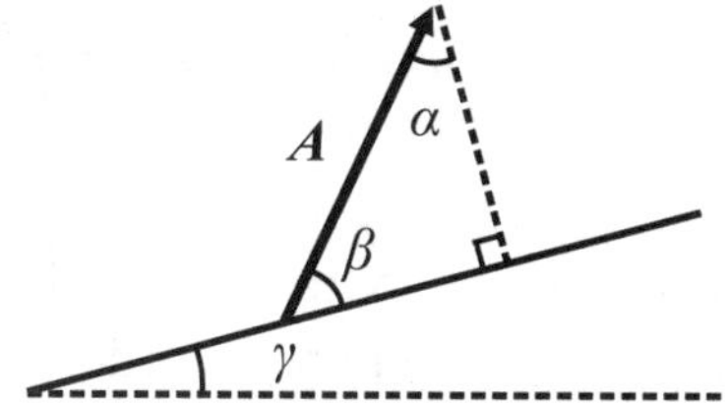

Figure 3-17 *Question 3-16*

3-17 Can a component of a vector have a magnitude greater than the vector's magnitude? Explain.

3-18 If vector ***A*** is perpendicular to vector ***B***, write an expression for the magnitude of ***A*** + ***B*** in terms of the magnitudes of ***A*** and ***B***. [Ans. $(A^2 + B^2)^{1/2}$]

3-19 Can a vector have zero magnitude if one of its components is different from zero? Justify your answer.

3-20 (a) Can two vectors having the same magnitude be combined to give a zero resultant vector? If so, how?
(b) Can two vectors having different magnitudes be combined to give a zero resultant vector? What about three vectors? Explain.

3-21 If ***A*** = 36 km east and ***B*** = 53 km west, find:
A + ***B***, ***B*** + ***A***, ***A*** – ***B***, and ***B*** – ***A***. [Ans. 17 km west, 17 km west, 89 km east, 89 km west]

3-22 Two muscles at the back of your leg, called the lateral and medial heads of the gastrocnemius muscle, exert forces on the Achilles tendon (Figure 3-18). The forces are measured in newtons, N. Use components to determine the resultant force on the tendon. [Ans. 4.4 × 10^2 N vertically upward]

3-23 A golfer drives a ball 214 m due east of the tee, then hits it 96 m 30° north of east, and finally putts the ball 12 m 40° south of east. The ball sinks into the hole. Determine the magnitude and direction of the displacement needed from the tee to yield a hole-in-one. Use (a) a scale diagram, and (b) components. Compare the two answers.
[Ans. 3.1 × 10^2 m 7.5° north of east]

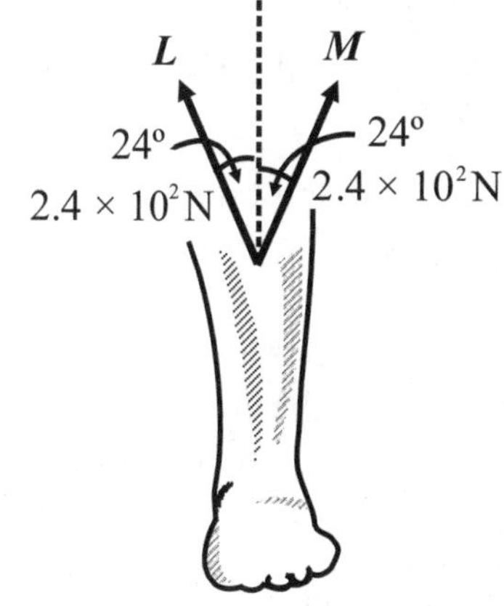

Figure 3-18 Question 3-22

3-24 Use components to find $\boldsymbol{C} + \boldsymbol{D} - \boldsymbol{E}$ in Figure 3-19.
[Ans. 1.2×10^2 m 83° counterclockwise from the $+x$ axis]

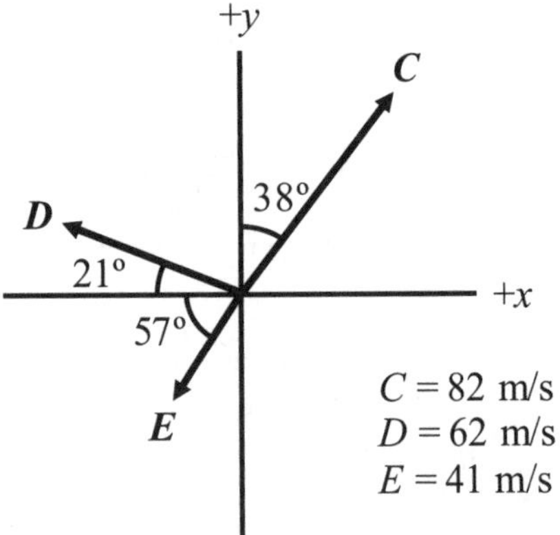

Figure 3-19 *Question 3-24.*

north
B
52°
A = 5.1 km
B = 6.8 km
east
71°
A

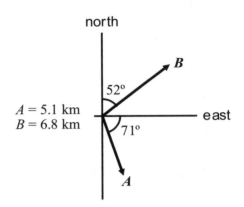

Figure 3-20 *Question 3-25.*

3-25 Determine the vector that must be added to the sum of $\boldsymbol{A}$ and $\boldsymbol{B}$ in Figure 3-20 to give a net displacement of (a) zero, and (b) 4.0 km W.
[Ans. (a) 7.0 km 5.1° north of west (b) 11 km 3.3° north of west]

3-26 *Fermi question:* Assume that a displacement vector can be drawn from a person's nose to his or her toes. For a city of one million people, estimate the resultant displacement vector of all the nose-to-toes vectors at (a) 5 p.m., and (b) 5 a.m. Explain your reasoning.
[Ans. (a) approx. 10^6 m downward (b) approx. 0 m]

3-27 Miami is 2050 km due south from Ottawa, and Chicago is 1780 km 30° west of north from Miami. Using components, determine the magnitude and direction of the displacement of an airline flight that goes directly from Ottawa to Chicago.
[Ans. 1.0×10^3 km 30° south of west]

APPLYING YOUR KNOWLEDGE

3-28 If the component of vector $\boldsymbol{B}$ along vector $\boldsymbol{A}$ is zero, what conclusion(s) can be stated?

3-29 Figure 3-21 shows a ski hill inclined at an angle of 20° to the horizontal. The x-y coordinate system is defined as shown, with the x-axis along the hill and the y-axis perpendicular to the hill. The acceleration due to gravity is the vector $\boldsymbol{g}$, which is 9.8 m/s^2 vertically downward, as illustrated. Determine the components of $\boldsymbol{g}$ along the axes shown.
[Ans. $g_x = 3.4$ m/s^2, $g_y = 9.2$ m/s^2]

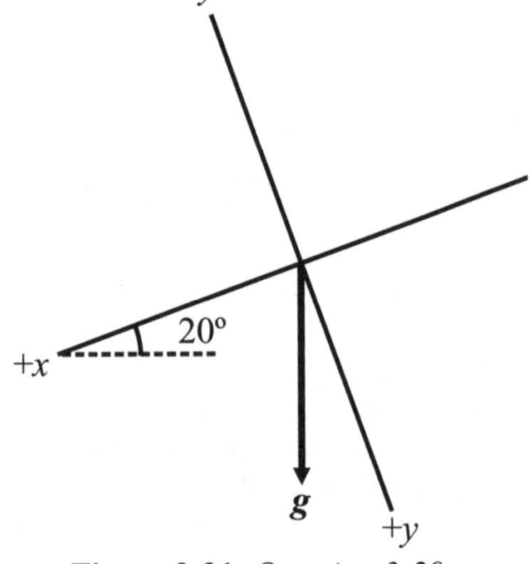

Figure 3-21 *Question 3-29.*

KEY OBJECTIVES

Having completed this chapter you should now be able to do the following:

1. Determine the magnitude and direction of a vector in a scale diagram.
2. Recognize the terminology and symbols associated with vectors.
3. Use a scale diagram to find the resultant vector when vectors are added or subtracted.
4. Define component of a vector.
5. Calculate the rectangular components of a vector using trigonometric ratios.
6. Perform vector addition or subtraction using components.
7. Use a scientific calculator to perform mathematical operations efficiently.
8. Appreciate the limitations of calculators.

ANSWERS TO SELECTED QUESTIONS

3-12 (c) 3-13 (a) 3-14 (c) 3-15 (d) 3-16 (b)

3-17 No. The component of a vector is its projection along an axis, so the component's magnitude may equal the vector's magnitude if the vector and axis are parallel, but the component's magnitude is less than the vector's magnitude in other situations.

3-19 No, the magnitude of the vector must be at least as large as one of its components.

3-20 (a) Yes, if the vectors are in opposite directions.
(b) Two vectors of different magnitude cannot be combined to give a zero resultant vector, but three vectors can. In the latter case, the three vectors must have magnitudes and directions such that when they are added head-to-tail, the resultant is zero.

3-28 Either vector ***B*** is perpendicular to vector ***A***, or ***B*** and/or ***A*** has a magnitude of zero.

CHAPTER 4

TWO-DIMENSIONAL KINEMATICS

In Chapter 2, you studied motion in a straight line, in other words, in one dimension. However, most motion we experience occurs in either two or three dimensions. Fortunately, much of the information you learned in one-dimensional kinematics applies to two-dimensional kinematics, so only part of this chapter will appear new.

Two-dimensional motion occurs in many situations, such as the movement of cars racing around tracks or travelling around corners. It applies to huge objects such as planets that travel in elliptical paths around the sun, and to tiny objects such as electrons that travel in regions around the nucleus of an atom. This type of motion is also common in sports where, for example, a ball travels in a curved path through the air. There are many examples of motion that, while being actually three-dimensional, can be treated as effectively two-dimensional; an example is the almost planar motion of a roller coaster around a loop-the-loop (Figure 4-1). Two-dimensional motion will be analysed in this chapter using some basic definitions and equations.

Figure 4-1 *The motion of a roller coaster around an almost planar loop can be treated as essentially two-dimensional.*

The concepts of kinematics in two dimensions can be applied to more complex motions in three dimensions, a task beyond the scope of this book.

4.1 DISPLACEMENT AND VELOCITY IN TWO DIMENSIONS

In Chapter 1, you learned the distinction between scalar and vector quantities, and in Chapter 3, you studied some properties of the addition and subtraction of vectors. Chapter 2 began with a description of distance and speed in one dimension. These scalar quantities have the same definitions and equations in two dimensions, so they will not be described here, although you will be asked to solve problems involving them. The majority of Chapter 2 was devoted to the vector quantities of displacement, velocity, and acceleration in one-dimensional motion. In this section, we will combine displacement and velocity with the mathematics of vectors from Chapter 3. One major difference between Chapter 2 and this chapter is that we omitted the vector notation in Chapter 2 because we were dealing with only one direction. Here, however, the vector notation will be used in most situations — directions are important in two-dimensional motion.

Displacement in Two Dimensions

Recall from Section 2.2 that displacement is the change of position, and has a direction from the initial position to the final position of a moving object. In one dimension, we used Δx as the symbol for displacement because the motion was constrained to be along only one reference axis. In two dimensions, we consider motion in a reference *x-y* plane, and use $\boldsymbol{r}$ as the symbol for position, and $\Delta \boldsymbol{r}$ for displacement. (Notice that the $\boldsymbol{r}$'s are in boldface type, indicating vectors.) Figure 4-2 shows how the defining equation for displacement,

$$\Delta \boldsymbol{r} = \boldsymbol{r}_2 - \boldsymbol{r}_1 \qquad \textbf{(4-1)}$$

applies to two dimensions just as $\Delta x = x_2 - x_1$ applies to one dimension.

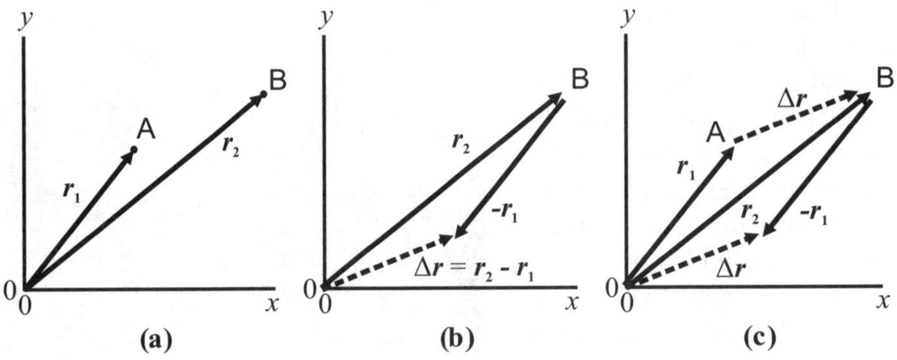

Figure 4-2 **(a)** *An object moves from point A to point B. Its position vector, relative to an origin, (0, 0), changes from* $\boldsymbol{r}_1$ *to* $\boldsymbol{r}_2$.
(b) *The displacement of the object is defined as* $\Delta \boldsymbol{r} = \boldsymbol{r}_2 - \boldsymbol{r}_1$. *It is shown here as the vector subtraction* $\boldsymbol{r}_2 - \boldsymbol{r}_1$.
(c) *The displacement can also be drawn as the vector from the initial point, A, to the final point, B. Notice that this displacement has the same magnitude and direction as the displacement drawn in (b); hence, these two displacement vectors are in fact the same vector.*

As a moving object goes from an initial position $\boldsymbol{r}_1$, having components x_1 and y_1 (Figure 4-3), to a final position $\boldsymbol{r}_2$ with components x_2 and y_2, the components of the displacement vector $\Delta \boldsymbol{r}$ are

$$\Delta x = x_2 - x_1 \qquad \text{and} \qquad \Delta y = y_2 - y_1 \qquad \textbf{(4-2)}$$

Notice in Figure 4-3 that the object moves from point A, having position co-ordinates (x_1,y_1), to point B, with co-ordinates (x_2,y_2).

The displacement, $\Delta \boldsymbol{r}$, defined by Eqn. 4-1 is sometimes called the **resultant displacement**. It is the vector addition of any individual displacement that an object might have undergone, as in Figure 4-4 (a). Notice that the resultant displacement depends only on the initial and final positions, not on the path taken. Figure 4-4 shows two distinctly different paths that have the same resultant displacement.

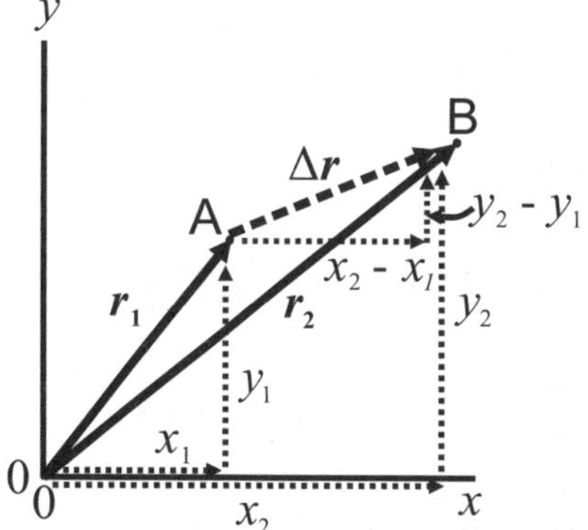

Figure 4-3 *The components of the displacement vector, Δr, are:* $\Delta x = x_2 - x_1$ *and* $\Delta y = y_2 - y_1$.

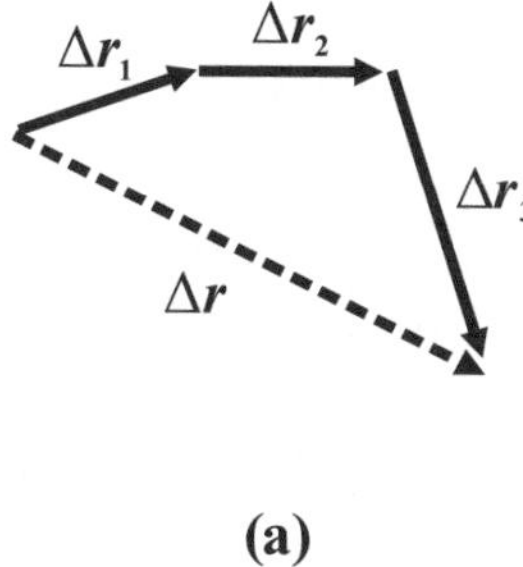

(a)

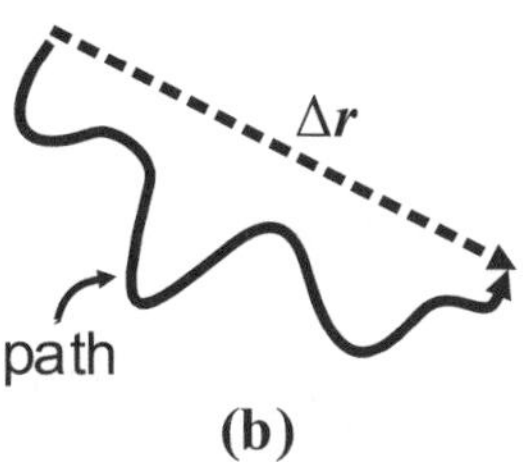

(b)

Figure 4-4 *The resultant displacement, Δr, is the same in both (a) and (b), although the paths taken are different. Notice in (a) that the resultant displacement is the vector addition of the individual displacements.*

Sample Problem 4-1

A duck on a pond follows the path shown in Figure 4-5. Determine the duck's:

(a) total distance travelled

(b) (resultant) displacement.

Solution: (a) The total distance travelled, being a scalar quantity, is: 22 m + 34 m = 56 m.

(b) If we did not care about accuracy, a scale diagram could be used to find the displacement. We will use components to give a more accurate answer. Let us call the two displacements $\boldsymbol{A}$ and $\boldsymbol{B}$, and define the $+x$ and $+y$ directions to be east and north, respectively (Figure 4-6 (a)). The components of $\boldsymbol{A}$ and $\boldsymbol{B}$ are:

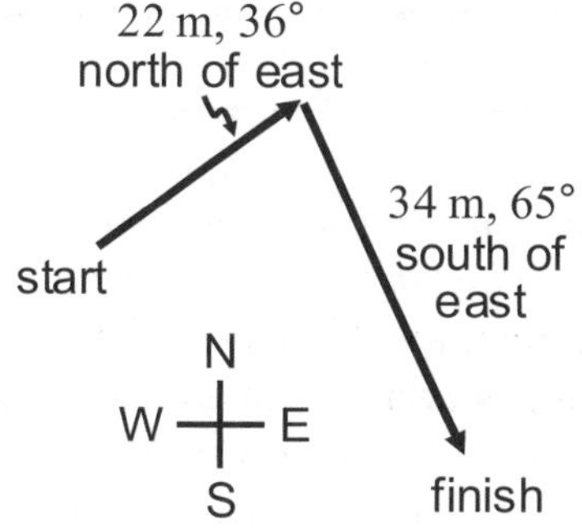

Figure 4-5 *Sample Problem 4-1.*

$$A_x = A\cos 36° = (22\text{ m})\cos 36° = 18\text{ m} \qquad A_y = A\sin 36° = (22\text{ m})\sin 36° = 13\text{ m}$$

$$B_x = B\cos 65° = (34\text{ m})\cos 65° = 14\text{ m} \qquad B_y = -B\sin 65° = -(34\text{ m})\sin 65° = -31\text{ m}$$

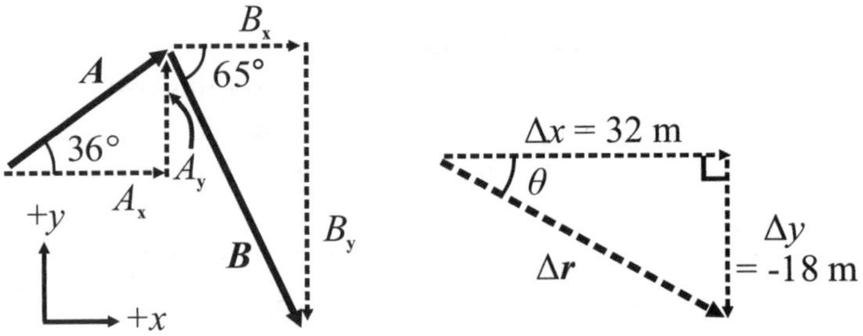

(a) (b)

Figure 4-6 (a) *Components of **A** and **B**.*
(b) *The resultant displacement **Δr**.*

The x-component of the resultant displacement is

$$\Delta x = A_x + B_x = (18 + 14)\text{ m} = 32\text{ m}$$

The y-component of the resultant displacement is

$$\Delta y = A_y + B_y = (13 - 31)\text{ m} = -18\text{ m}$$

Thus, the magnitude of the resultant displacement (Figure 4-6 (b)) is:

$$\Delta r = \sqrt{(32\text{ m})^2 + (-18\text{ m})^2} = 37\text{ m}$$

The direction (angle θ in Figure 4-6 (b)) of the resultant displacement can be found using:

$$\tan\theta = \frac{18\text{ m}}{32\text{ m}}$$

Hence, $\theta = \tan^{-1}(18/32) = 29°$.

Thus, the resultant displacement is 37 m 29° south of east.

Math Tip: *In Chapter 3, you have seen how to add vectors using either components or a scale diagram. An alternate technique uses the laws of sines and cosines from trigonometry. These laws, which are given in Appendix 5, are especially convenient in problems involving two vectors that are not perpendicular to each other. They become less useful when more than two vectors are involved. If you have expertise in using these laws, you might wish to try them out on some vector-addition problems. However, be sure that you have a thorough knowledge of how to use components, since many topics in later chapters involve this concept.*

Velocity in Two Dimensions

In Chapter 2, we found that the average velocity is given by

$$\text{average velocity} = \frac{\text{displacement}}{\text{elapsed time}} \quad \text{or} \quad v_{\text{av}} = \frac{\Delta x}{\Delta t}$$

Using symbols appropriate for two dimensions, this equation becomes

$$\boldsymbol{v}_{\text{av}} = \frac{\Delta \boldsymbol{r}}{\Delta t} \qquad \textbf{(4-3)}$$

The x- and y-components of this average velocity vector are given by

$$v_{\text{av,x}} = \frac{\Delta x}{\Delta t} \quad \text{and} \quad v_{\text{av,y}} = \frac{\Delta y}{\Delta t} \qquad \textbf{(4-4)}$$

One type of problem in which you are asked to find average velocity is shown in the next sample problem. Other types of questions will be introduced later in the chapter.

Sample Problem 4-2

If the time for the duck's motion in Sample Problem 4-1 took 2.0 min, what was the duck's (a) average speed, and (b) average velocity?

Solution: (a)

$$\text{speed}_{\text{av}} = \frac{d}{\Delta t} = \frac{56\ \text{m}}{120\ \text{s}} = 0.47\ \text{m/s}$$

(b)

$$\begin{aligned}\boldsymbol{v}_{\text{av}} &= \frac{\Delta \boldsymbol{r}}{\Delta t} \\ &= \frac{37\ \text{m}\ 29^\circ\ \text{south of east}}{120\ \text{s}} \\ &= 0.31\ \text{m/s}\ 29^\circ\ \text{south of east}\end{aligned}$$

Thus, the duck's average speed is 0.47 m/s, and its average velocity is 0.31 m/s 29° south of east. Notice that the magnitude of the average velocity does not equal the average speed in this case.

Instantaneous Velocity

Instantaneous velocity can also be found for two-dimensional motion. The defining equation in this case is:

$$\boldsymbol{v} = \lim_{\Delta t \to 0} \frac{\Delta \boldsymbol{r}}{\Delta t} \qquad \textbf{(4-5)}$$

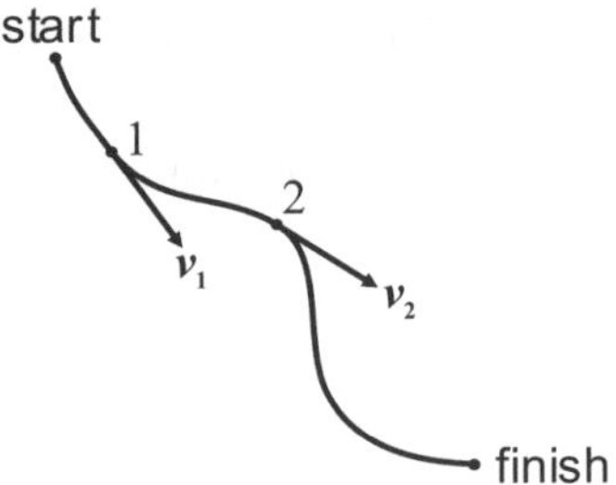

Figure 4-7 *The direction of the instantaneous velocity for an object travelling on a curved path is tangent to the curve.*

Remember that the symbol $\boldsymbol{v}$ with no subscript means instantaneous velocity. The *magnitude* of the instantaneous velocity equals the instantaneous speed of a moving object. Furthermore, for an object travelling in a curved path, the instantaneous velocity has a direction that is tangent to the curve at the instant involved (Figure 4-7).

The *x*- and *y*-components of the instantaneous velocity are

$$v_x = \lim_{\Delta t \to 0} \frac{\Delta x}{\Delta t} \quad \text{and} \quad v_y = \lim_{\Delta t \to 0} \frac{\Delta y}{\Delta t} \qquad \textbf{(4-6)}$$

Sample Problem 4-3

Figure 4-8 shows a circular track of radius 1.5×10^2 m. A runner takes 2.8×10^2 s to run around the track. Assuming that the runner's speed is constant, and that the runner is running clockwise around the track, determine the instantaneous velocity at A and at B.

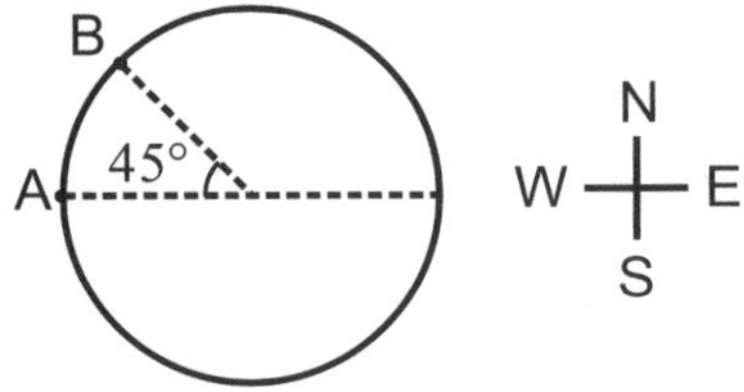

Figure 4-8 *Sample Problem 4-3.*

Solution: The runner's average speed is

$$\begin{aligned} \text{speed}_{av} &= \frac{d}{\Delta t} \\ &= \frac{2\pi r}{\Delta t} \\ &= \frac{2\pi\left(1.5 \times 10^2 \text{ m}\right)}{2.8 \times 10^2 \text{ s}} \\ &= 3.4 \text{ m/s} \end{aligned}$$

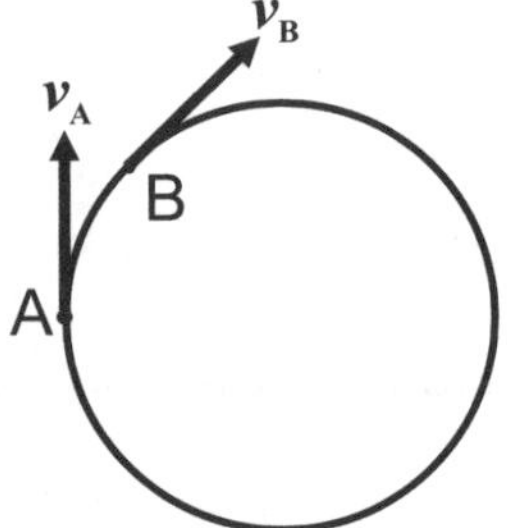

Figure 4-9 *Sample Problem 4-3 (solution).*

Since the speed is constant, the instantaneous speed is 3.4 m/s at any time, and the magnitude of the instantaneous velocity is also 3.4 m/s at any time. Since the direction of the instantaneous velocity is always tangent to the curve, the velocity at position A is 3.4 m/s north, and at B, it is 3.4 m/s 45° east of north. These velocities are shown in Figure 4-9.

Practice

4-1 Determine the displacement in each case.
(a) A person walks 38 m north, then 68 m west.
(b) A glider travels (horizontally) 550 m north, then 750 m east, and then 930 m south. (Assume two significant digits.)
(c) A boat on a lake follows the path shown on Figure 4-10, where the scale used to draw the diagram is 1.0 cm = 1.0 km.
[Ans. (a) 78 m 61° west of north (b) 8.4×10^2 m 27° south of east (c) 3.3 km 41° north of east]

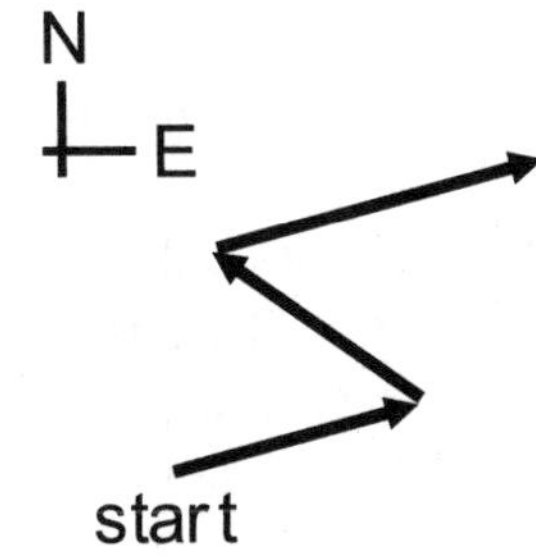

Figure 4-10 *Question 4-1.*

4-2 A car travels 12 km north, then 30 km west, then 21 km south, and finally 14 km east. The time for the entire trip is 1 h and 15 min. Determine the car's
(a) total distance travelled.
(b) resultant displacement.
(c) average speed in kilometres per hour for the entire trip.
(d) average velocity for the entire trip.
[Ans. (a) 77 km (b) 18 km 29° south of west (c) 62 km/h (d) 15 km/h 29° south of west]

4-3 A clock mounted on a vertical wall has a sweep second hand with a tip that is 14 cm from the centre of the clock.
(a) What is the average speed of the tip of the second hand?
(b) Determine the instantaneous velocity of the tip when it passes the 6:00 o'clock position; the 10:00 o'clock position.
(c) Find the tip's average velocity between the 1:00 o'clock position and the 5:00 o'clock position.
[Ans. (a) 1.5 cm/s (b) 1.5 cm/s horizontally to the left; 1.5 cm/s up and to the right, 60° above horizontal (c) 1.2 cm/s vertically downward]

4-4 A skater on Ottawa's Rideau Canal travels in a straight line 8.5×10^2 m 25° north of east, then 5.6×10^2 m in a straight line 21° east of north.
(a) Find the skater's resultant displacement.
(b) If the motion took 4.2 min, determine the skater's average speed and average velocity.
[Ans. (a) 1.3×10^3 m 42° north of east (b) 5.6 m/s; 5.2 m/s 42° north of east]

4-5 State in words (such as "up and to the right") the direction of the instantaneous velocity at each labelled position in the diagrams of curved motion illustrated in Figure 4-11. In Figure 4-11 (a), the object is moving counterclockwise around the circle.

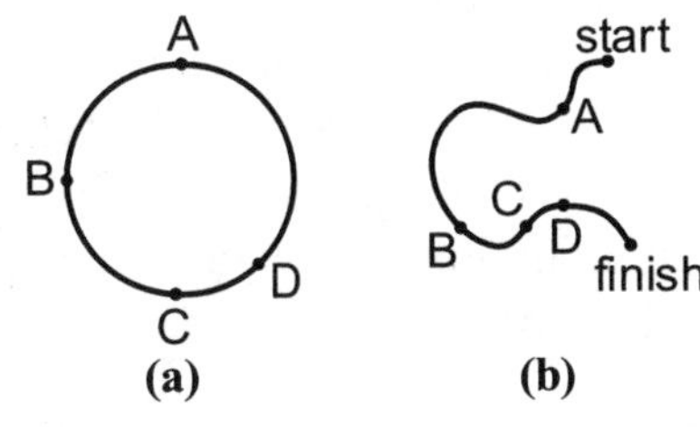

Figure 4-11 *Question 4-5.*

4-6 The average velocity of a car during a 14-min drive is 72 km/h 32° west of south.
(a) What is the car's displacement from its starting position?
(b) If the $+x$ and $+y$ directions are east and north, respectively, what are the x- and y-components of the average velocity? [Ans. (a) 17 km 32° west of south (b) $v_{av,x} = -38$ km/h , $v_{av,y} = -61$ km/h]

4.2 ACCELERATION IN TWO DIMENSIONS

A race car is travelling around a circular track at a constant speed of 150 km/h. Is the car accelerating? The answer is yes, because the velocity of the car is changing in direction even though its magnitude is constant. Acceleration in two dimensions occurs when an object's velocity undergoes a change in magnitude, or direction, or both.

To analyze acceleration in two dimensions, recall from Chapter 2 that acceleration is the time rate of change of velocity. The equation introduced there for average acceleration also applies to two-dimensional motion. Thus:

$$\boldsymbol{a}_{av} = \frac{\Delta \boldsymbol{v}}{\Delta t} = \frac{\boldsymbol{v}_2 - \boldsymbol{v}_1}{t_2 - t_1} \qquad \textbf{(4-7)}$$

where $\boldsymbol{v}_1$ and $\boldsymbol{v}_2$ are the velocities at times t_1 and t_2, respectively. Notice that since acceleration and velocity are vector quantities, the symbols "$\boldsymbol{a}$" and "$\boldsymbol{v}$" are in boldface type, and the subtraction indicated in $\boldsymbol{v}_2 - \boldsymbol{v}_1$ is a *vector* subtraction.

The components of the average acceleration are

$$a_{av,x} = \frac{\Delta v_x}{\Delta t} = \frac{v_{2x} - v_{1x}}{t_2 - t_1} \quad \text{and} \quad a_{av,y} = \frac{\Delta v_y}{\Delta t} = \frac{v_{2y} - v_{1y}}{t_2 - t_1} \qquad \textbf{(4-8)}$$

where, for example, v_{2x} represents the x-component of velocity $\boldsymbol{v}_2$.

Sample Problem 4-4

The straight stretches of a horse racing track are 250 m long and 160 m apart. The ends of the track are semicircles, as shown in Figure 4-12. A horse is galloping at a constant speed of 14 m/s in the direction shown. Determine the horse's average acceleration from (a) C to D, then (b) C to E.

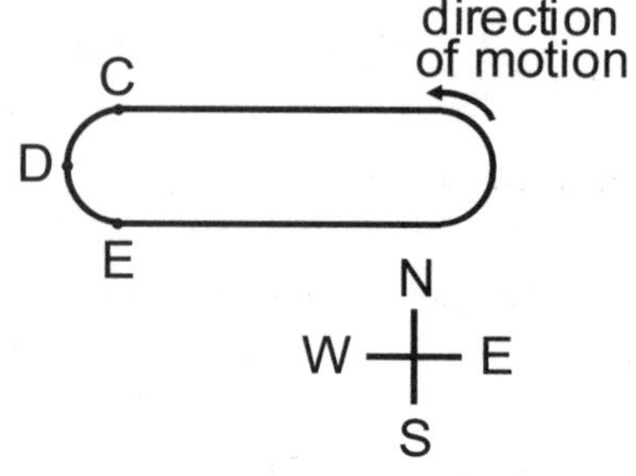

Figure 4-12 *Sample Problem 4-4.*

Solution: (a) The distance around the semi-circle from C to E is $\pi r = \pi$ (80 m) = 251 m. Hence, the distance from C to D is (251 m)/2 = 126 m. The time to gallop from C to D is:

$$\Delta t = \frac{d}{v_{\text{av}}} = \frac{126\text{ m}}{14\text{ m/s}} = 9.0\text{ s}$$

Point C is at the beginning of the semicircle, so the horse's velocity there is $\boldsymbol{v}_{\text{C}}$ = 14 m/s west. At D its velocity is $\boldsymbol{v}_{\text{D}}$ = 14 m/s south. The vector subtraction of $\Delta\boldsymbol{v} = \boldsymbol{v}_{\text{D}} - \boldsymbol{v}_{\text{C}}$ is shown in Figure 4-13 (a). The magnitude of $\Delta\boldsymbol{v}$ is given by the Pythagorean relation:

$$\Delta v = \sqrt{v_{\text{D}}^2 + v_{\text{C}}^2} = \sqrt{(14\text{ m/s})^2 + (14\text{ m/s})^2} = 20\text{ m/s}$$

The direction of $\Delta\boldsymbol{v}$ (angle θ in Figure 4-13 (a)) is simply 45° east of south, since $|\boldsymbol{v}_{\text{D}}| = |\boldsymbol{v}_{\text{C}}|$.

$\boldsymbol{v}_{\text{D}}$ θ $\Delta\boldsymbol{v} = \boldsymbol{v}_{\text{D}} - \boldsymbol{v}_{\text{C}}$

$-\boldsymbol{v}_{\text{C}}$

(a)

$\boldsymbol{v}_{\text{E}}$ $-\boldsymbol{v}_{\text{C}}$

$\Delta\boldsymbol{v} = \boldsymbol{v}_{\text{E}} - \boldsymbol{v}_{\text{C}}$

(b)

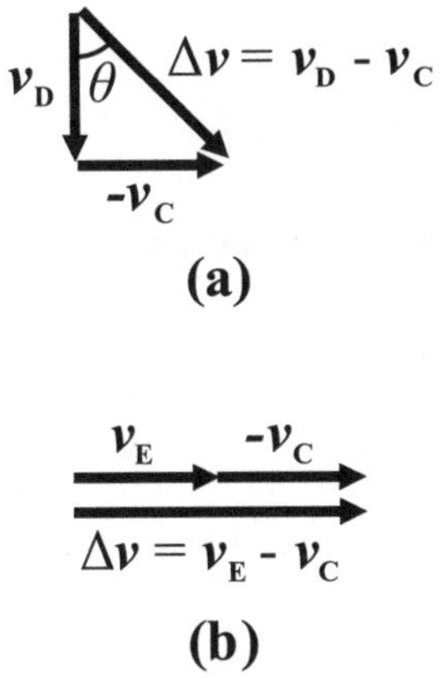

Figure 4-13 *Sample Problem 4-4 (solution).*

The average acceleration is therefore:

$$\begin{aligned} \boldsymbol{a}_{\text{av}} &= \frac{\Delta\boldsymbol{v}}{\Delta t} \\ &= \frac{20\text{ m/s }45°\text{ east of south}}{9.0\text{ s}} \\ &= 2.2\text{ m/s}^2\ 45°\text{ east of south} \end{aligned}$$

Thus, the average acceleration is 2.2 m/s^2 45° east of south.

(b) The time for the horse to gallop from C to E is double that in (a) above, or 18 s. The vector subtraction of $\Delta\boldsymbol{v} = \boldsymbol{v}_{\text{E}} - \boldsymbol{v}_{\text{C}}$ is shown in Figure 4-13 (b), giving $\Delta\boldsymbol{v}$ = 28 m/s east. Thus:

$$\begin{aligned} \boldsymbol{a}_{\text{av}} &= \frac{\Delta\boldsymbol{v}}{\Delta t} \\ \therefore\ \mathbf{a}_{\text{av}} &= \frac{28\text{ m/s east}}{18\text{ s}} \\ &= 1.6\text{ m/s}^2\text{ east} \end{aligned}$$

Thus, the average acceleration is 1.6 m/s^2 east.

Instantaneous Acceleration

The definition of instantaneous acceleration in two dimensions is the same as in one dimension. Thus:

$$\boldsymbol{a} = \lim_{\Delta t \to 0} \frac{\Delta\boldsymbol{v}}{\Delta t} \qquad \textbf{(4-9)}$$

Again, when no subscript accompanies the symbol "$\boldsymbol{a}$," the acceleration is assumed to be the instantaneous acceleration.

If the acceleration is constant, the constant-acceleration equations from Chapter 2 can also be used in two dimensions. For example, the expressions for $\mathbf{v}$ and $\mathbf{v}_0$ are:

$$\boldsymbol{v} = \boldsymbol{v}_0 + \boldsymbol{a}t \qquad \text{and} \qquad \boldsymbol{v}_0 = \boldsymbol{v} - \boldsymbol{a}t$$

The equation to find $\boldsymbol{v}$ involves a vector addition (see Question 4-10) and the equation to find $\boldsymbol{v}_0$ involves a vector subtraction (see Question 4-11).

Practice

4-7 An automobile has a velocity of 25 m/s east, and 15 s later its velocity is 25 m/s south. (a) Estimate the direction of the automobile's average acceleration during the 15 s time interval. (b) Calculate the magnitude and direction of the average acceleration.
[Ans. (b) 2.4 m/s^2 45° west of south]

4-8 Determine the average acceleration for the object shown in Figure 4-14 as it travels from A to B in 8.5 s.
[Ans. 0.85 m/s^2 50° south of west]

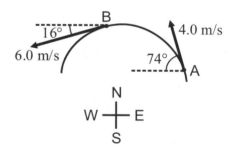

Figure 4-14 *Question 4-8.*

4-9 Determine the magnitude of the average acceleration during the time interval it takes each object described below to complete half a revolution around the central object.
(a) Planet Mercury travels once around the sun in 7.60 × 10^6 s at an average speed of 47.8 km/s.
(b) Mars takes 687 (Earth) days to travel once around the sun in its orbit of average radius 2.28 × 10^7 m.
(c) A military satellite takes 80.0 min to travel once around Earth in an orbit having a diameter of 1.29 × 10^7 m. [Ans. (a) 2.52 × 10^{-2} m/s^2 (b) 1.63 × 10^{-7} m/s^2 (c) 7.03 m/s^2]

4-10 A boat sailing east at 6.4 m/s undergoes an average acceleration of 2.0 m/s^2 south for 2.5 s. Determine the final velocity of the boat after this short time interval.
[Ans. 8.1 m/s 38° south of east]

4-11 A ball is thrown from a balloon with an initial unknown velocity. The ball accelerates at 9.8 m/s^2 downward for 2.0 s, at which time its instantaneous velocity is 24 m/s at an angle of 45° below the horizontal. Determine the magnitude and direction of the initial velocity.
[Ans. 17 m/s at an angle of 8.8° above the horizontal]

4-12 A car is travelling along a winding highway at a constant speed of 82 km/h. At 3:00 p.m.,

the car is heading 38.2° east of north, and at 3:15 p.m. it is heading 12.7° south of east. Define the $+x$ and $+y$ directions to be east and north, respectively. Use Eqn. 4-8 to determine the x- and y-components of the average acceleration during this time interval.
[Ans. $a_{av,x} = 9.0 \times 10^{-3}$ m/s^2; $a_{av,y} = -2.5 \times 10^{-2}$ m/s^2]

4.3 PROJECTILE MOTION

The following motions all have some common characteristics:

- a javelin is thrown through the air
- a squirrel jumps from one branch of a tree to another
- a skateboarder skates at top speed off the top end of a ramp
- a baseball is thrown from the outfield to the infield.

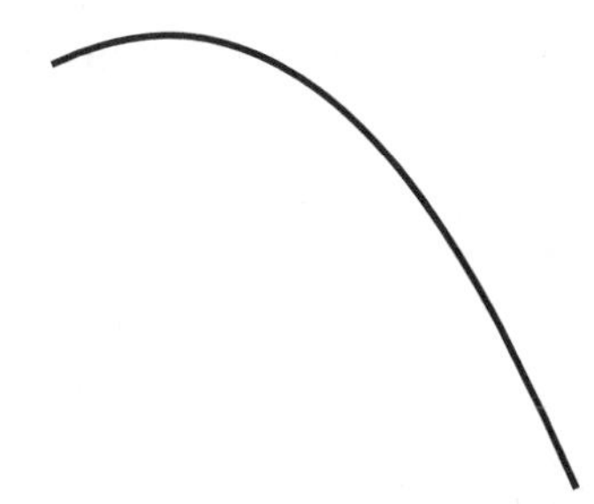

Figure 4-15 *A typical path followed by a projectile.*

Each motion involves an object moving through the air without any propulsion system, and following a curved path, such as illustrated in Figure 4-15. An object moving through the air in this way is called a **projectile**, and the motion of such an object is called projectile motion. (A more specific definition of this type of motion will be given soon.)

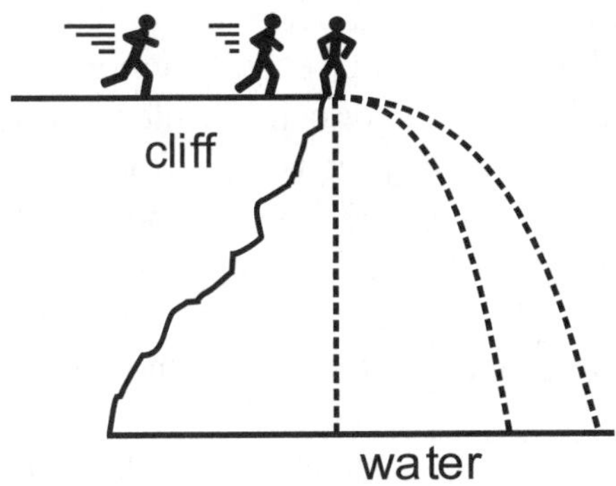

Figure 4-16 *When three people leave the edge of a cliff at the same instant, one dropping straight down and two running with different speeds, which will land in the water first?*

To begin the study of projectile motion, consider the situation illustrated in Figure 4-16. Three daring individuals are leaving the edge of a cliff above water. One person is going to drop straight down into the water, while the other two are running, one faster than the other. If all three leave the edge of the cliff at the same instant, following the paths shown in the diagram, which one will land first? By experimentation and close observation, we learn that all three land at the same time. This observation greatly affects our method of analyzing projectile motion.

Other experiments or demonstrations can be used to verify that this observation is true. Figure 4-17 shows a graph of the positions of two balls dropped simultaneously from a special device that projects one ball horizontally while releasing the other straight down from rest. The successive positions of the balls are indicated by two different symbols, one for each ball. The time between flashes remains constant. Although one ball falls straight down and the other also moves horizontally, both balls fall through the same vertical distance with each flash. Notice that the horizontal distance moved between flashes remains constant, but the vertical distance fallen increases during each succeeding time interval.

Based on the observation of the motion of the balls in Figure 4-17, we can make the following important conclusions about projectile motion:

- The horizontal velocity of a projectile is constant.
- In the vertical direction, the projectile undergoes constant acceleration downward, i.e., the acceleration due to gravity.
- For a projectile, the horizontal and vertical motions are independent of each other except that they have a common time.

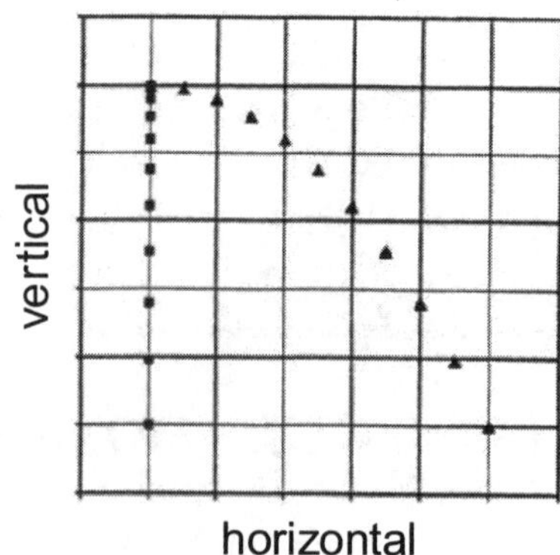

Figure 4-17 *The positions of two falling balls at equal time intervals.*

These conclusions are based on the assumption that air resistance can be neglected, an assumption also made when we analyzed motion in Chapter 2.

Using these facts, we can now write a formal definition of this type of motion. **Projectile motion** is motion with a constant horizontal velocity combined with constant vertical acceleration caused by gravity. The path of an object undergoing this type of motion is a *parabola.* Because the horizontal and vertical motions do not depend on each other, we can use separate sets of equations to analyse projectile motion. The uniform velocity equations from Section 2.2 apply to the horizontal motion and the constant-acceleration equations from Sections 2.4 and 2.5, using $g = 9.8\ m/s^2$ (or $9.80\ m/s^2$, if needed), apply to the vertical motion.

Table 4.1 summarizes the kinematics equations for both the horizontal and vertical portions of projectile motion. The symbols are not in boldface type, since they do not represent vectors. For example, v_{0x} represents the initial velocity's x-component (not a vector), and "t" represents time (a scalar quantity). See also Figure 4-18 for an explanation of the symbols v_{0x}, v_{0y}, and v_y.

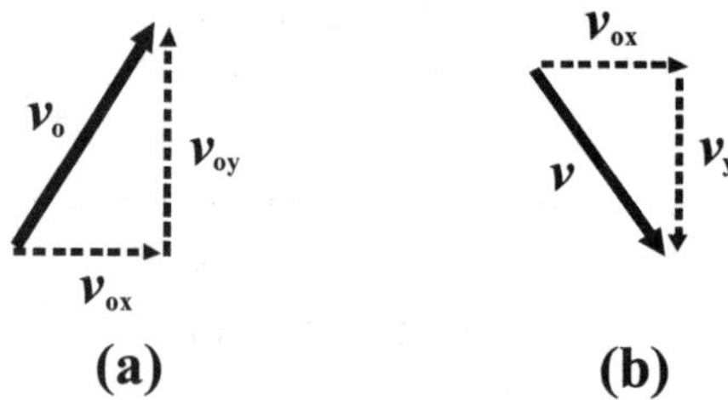

Figure 4-18 (a) *At time $t = 0$, the velocity $\mathbf{v}_0$ of a projectile has a horizontal component, v_{0x}, and a vertical component, v_{0y}.* **(b)** *At some time t later, the projectile's velocity* **v** *has the same horizontal component (neglecting air resistance), and a different vertical component, v_y.*

The equations in Table 4.1 can be used to solve a large variety of problems involving projectile motion. When solving these problems, remember that time is the common variable between the horizontal motion and the vertical motion.

Table 4.1 Kinematics Equations for Projectile Motion

Horizontal (x) Motion — constant-velocity (zero acceleration); only one equation (Eqn. 2-3) applies, but we will change the notation slightly from that used in Chapter 2. We start with Eqn. 2-3:

$$v_{\text{av,x}} = \frac{\Delta x}{\Delta t}$$

where we have explicitly indicated that this is the *x-component* of the average velocity. Since there is constant velocity in the x-direction, $v_{\text{av,x}}$ always equals the initial x-component of velocity, which we write as $v_{0\text{x}}$. We write Δt as t - t_0, and since we will always choose the initial time t_0 to be zero, we are left simply with "t." For the horizontal displacement, which is called the **horizontal range** of the projectile, symbol Δx, we write $x - x_0$. Hence, we have

$$v_{0\text{x}} = \frac{x - x_0}{t} \qquad \textbf{(4-10)}$$

This equation can easily be written in other forms to be used in particular types of problems:

$$x = x_0 + v_{0\text{x}}t \qquad \text{and} \qquad t = \frac{x - x_0}{v_{0\text{x}}} \qquad \textbf{(4-10b)}$$

Vertical (y) Motion — downward constant acceleration of magnitude g. The four kinematics equations for free fall, given in Table 2-4, apply here. We rewrite them below, including y-subscripts to indicate clearly the components of vectors:

$$v_{\text{y}} = v_{0\text{y}} + a_{\text{y}}t \qquad \textbf{(4-11)}$$

$$y = y_0 + \tfrac{1}{2}\left(v_{0\text{y}} + v_{\text{y}}\right)t \qquad \textbf{(4-12)}$$

$$y = y_0 + v_{0\text{y}}t + \tfrac{1}{2}a_{\text{y}}t^2 \qquad \textbf{(4-13)}$$

$$v_{\text{y}}^2 - v_{0\text{y}}^2 = 2a_{\text{y}}\left(y - y_0\right) \qquad \textbf{(4-14)}$$

Did You Know? *Military engineers in medieval times thought that a projectile travelled in a straight line to its maximum height, then fell straight downward toward Earth. This is shown in the drawing in Figure 4-19. Even with this misconception, the engineers probably realized that the maximum range of a projectile occurs when the projection angle is 45° above the horizontal.*

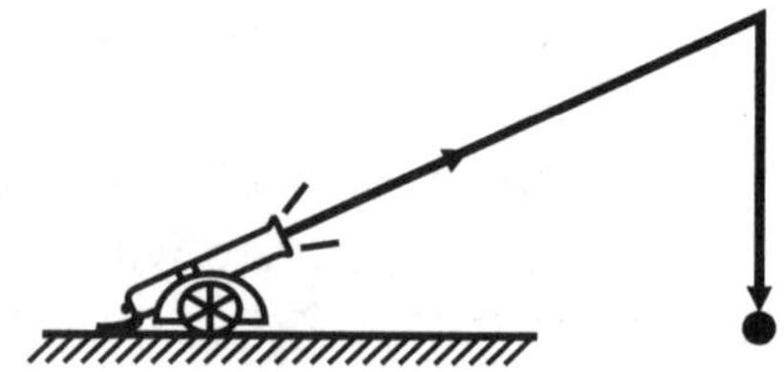

Figure 4-19 *This diagram shows the medieval misconception of projectile motion.*

Sample Problem 4-5

A ball is thrown off a balcony with an initial velocity of 20 m/s horizontally.
(a) Determine the location of the ball at later times of 1.0 s, 2.0 s, 3.0 s, and 4.0 s.
(b) Show these positions in a diagram.
(c) Name the shape of the resulting curved path.

Solution: (a) We choose the $+x$ direction to be the horizontal direction in which the ball is thrown, and the $+y$ direction to be downward (Figure 4-20). Let the position as the ball leaves the balcony be $(x_0, y_0) = (0\text{ m}, 0\text{ m})$.

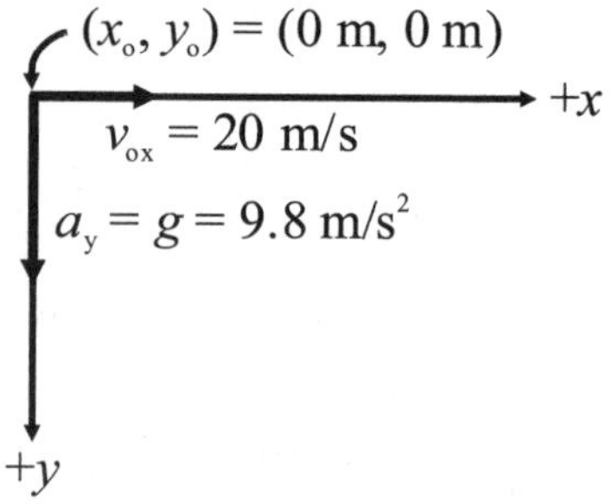

$(x_o, y_o) = (0\text{ m}, 0\text{ m})$
$+x$
$v_{ox} = 20\text{ m/s}$
$a_y = g = 9.8\text{ m/s}^2$
$+y$

Figure 4-20 *Sample Problem 4-5.*

The horizontal component of the initial velocity, v_{0x}, is given as 20 m/s. This component remains constant; thus, during each second the ball moves 20 m horizontally. Hence, after the first second, it has moved 20 m; after the second, 40 m, etc. The horizontal positions for the first four seconds are shown in the table below. More formally, these positions can be determined from Eqn. 4-10b: $x = x_0 + v_{0x}t$.

In the vertical direction, the y-component of acceleration is $a_y = g = 9.8\text{ m/s}^2$ (a positive quantity, since downward is positive). The vertical position can be found at the end of each second using Eqn. 4-13: $y = y_0 + v_{0y}t + \frac{1}{2}gt^2$, where $y_0 = 0\text{ m}$, and $v_{0y} = 0\text{ m/s}$. Thus, $y = \frac{1}{2}gt^2$. Results of using this equation are presented in the table below.

Time, t (s):	0.0	1.0	2.0	3.0	4.0
x-component of position, x (m):	0.0	20	40	60	80
y-component of position, y (m):	0.0	4.9	20	44	78

(b) Figure 4-21 shows a diagram of the position of the ball at the required times. The positions are joined with a smooth curve.
(c) The curved path shown in Figure 4-21 is a parabola.

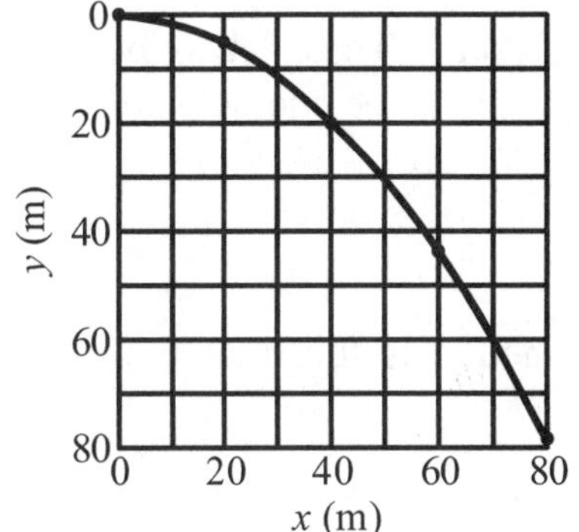

Figure 4-21 *Sample Problem 4-5 (solution).*

Sample Problem 4-6

A child travels down a slide, leaving it with a velocity having only a horizontal component of 4.6 m/s. The child then undergoes projectile motion and lands in a swimming pool, as illustrated in Figure 4-22. The slide is 3.5 m above the pool. Determine
(a) the time the child remains airborne
(b) the horizontal distance that the child travels while in the air
(c) the velocity with which the child enters the water.

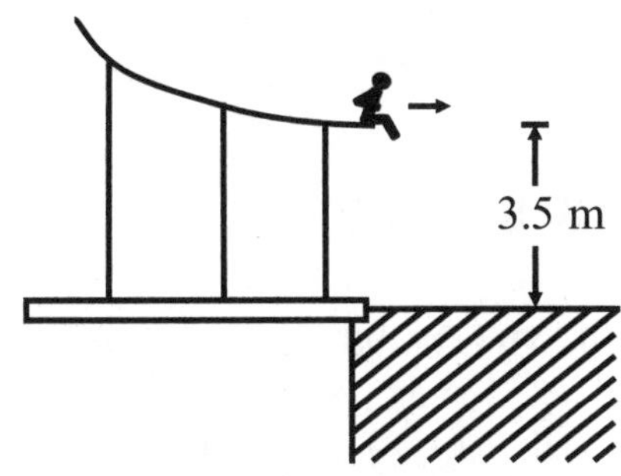

Figure 4-22 *Sample Problem 4-6.*

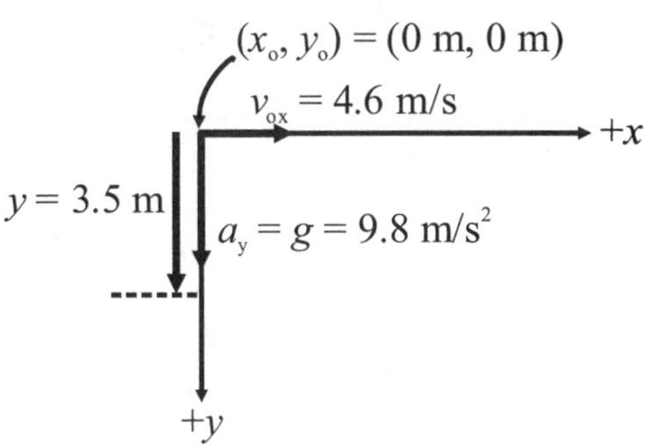

Figure 4-23 *Given quantities.*

Solution: (a) We define the $+y$ direction to be downward, and the $+x$ direction to be the horizontal direction that the child leaves the slide (Figure 4-23). We choose the position as the child leaves the slide to be $(x_0, y_0) = (0 \text{ m}, 0 \text{ m})$.

It is useful in projectile-motion problems to list the various quantities such as velocity, position, etc., in two columns, one for horizontal motion and one for vertical motion:

horizontal (constant velocity)	*vertical (constant acceleration)*
$x_0 = 0$ m	$y_0 = 0$ m
$x = ?$ (required to find in (b))	$y = 3.5$ m
$v_{0x} = 4.6$ m/s	$v_{0y} = 0$ m/s
$t = ?$ (required to find in (a))	$v_y = ?$ (needed in (c))
	$a_y = g = 9.8$ m/s^2
	$t = ?$ (required to find in (a))

The horizontal motion has two unknowns, so they cannot be determined until the vertical motion is analyzed. Thus, let us begin by using the vertical motion to find the time. The appropriate equation is the one with no v_y, i.e., Eqn. 4-13:

$$y = y_0 + v_{0y}t + \tfrac{1}{2}a_y t^2$$

Immediately substituting $y_0 = 0$ m, $v_{0y} = 0$ m/s, and $a_y = g$:

$$y = \tfrac{1}{2}gt^2$$

Hence,

$$t^2 = \frac{2y}{g}$$

$$\therefore \quad t = \pm\sqrt{\frac{2y}{g}} = \pm\sqrt{\frac{2(3.5\text{ m})}{9.8\text{ m/s}^2}} = \pm\, 0.85\text{ s}$$

Only the positive root applies, so the time for the fall is 0.85 s.

(b) We now use this time to find the horizontal displacement, x.

$$x = x_0 + v_{0x}t = 0\text{ m} + (4.6\text{ m/s}) \times (0.85\text{ s}) = 3.9\text{ m}$$

Thus, the child hits the water 3.9 m horizontally from the end of the slide. In other words, the horizontal range of the child's projectile motion is 3.9 m.

(c) To determine the magnitude and direction of the velocity as the child enters the water, we first find its x- and y-components. The x-component, v_{0x}, is constant at 4.6 m/s. The y-component can be found by using Eqn. 4-11, 4-12, or 4-14. We will use Eqn. 4-11:

$$v_y = v_{0y} + a_y t = 0\text{ m/s} + (9.8\text{ m/s}^2) \times (0.85\text{ s}) = 8.3\text{ m/s}$$

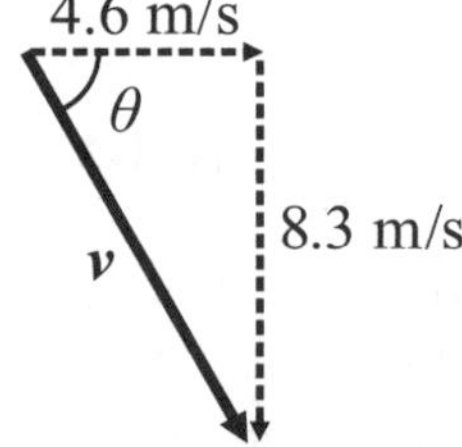

Figure 4-24 *The velocity as the child enters the water. $v = 9.5$ m/s; $\theta = 61°$.*

Knowing the x- and y-components, it is straightforward to determine the magnitude and direction (Figure 4-24) using the Pythagorean relation and trigonometry. Hence, the velocity is 9.5 m/s at an angle of 61° below the horizontal.

In some projectile-motion problems the initial velocity is unknown, but it can be found if enough information is provided, as seen in the next sample problem.

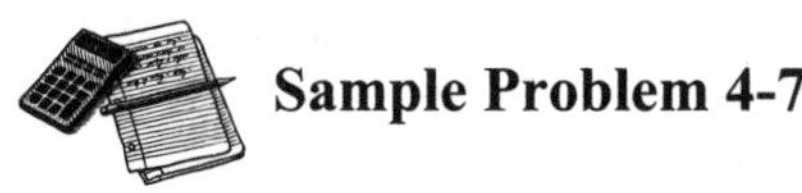

Sample Problem 4-7

A helicopter pilot is about to release a relief package which will land on the ground 100 m horizontally ahead. The helicopter, travelling horizontally, is 80 m above the ground and the package will leave the helicopter horizontally with the same velocity as the helicopter. What is that velocity? (Assume two significant digits throughout.)

Solution: We select the $+x$ direction to be the horizontal direction that the helicopter is travelling, and the $+y$ direction to be downward (Figure 4-25). We choose the point from which the package is released to be at $(x_0, y_0) = (0\text{ m}, 0\text{ m})$. The quantities involved are:

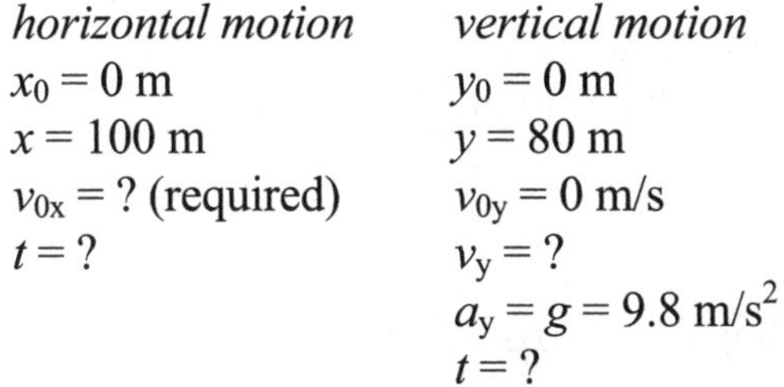

horizontal motion	*vertical motion*
$x_0 = 0$ m	$y_0 = 0$ m
$x = 100$ m	$y = 80$ m
$v_{0x} = ?$ (required)	$v_{0y} = 0$ m/s
$t = ?$	$v_y = ?$
	$a_y = g = 9.8\text{ m/s}^2$
	$t = ?$

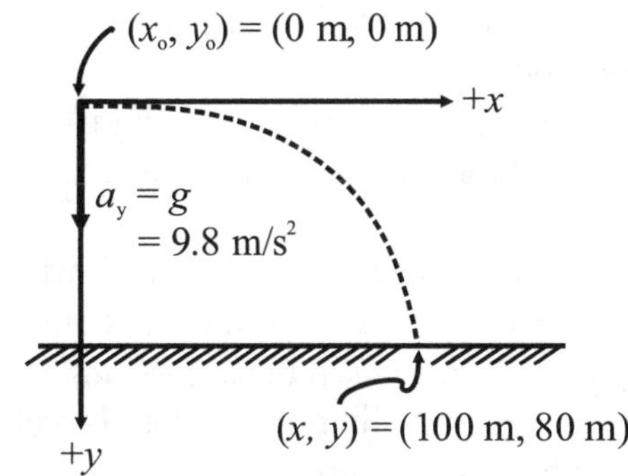

Figure 4-25 *Given quantities in Sample Problem 4-7.*

The common variable, time, can be found by considering the vertical motion. We use Eqn. 4-13:

$$y = y_0 + v_{0y}t + \tfrac{1}{2}a_y t^2$$

Substituting $y_0 = 0$ m, $v_{0y} = 0$ m/s, and $a_y = g$, we get

$$y = \tfrac{1}{2}gt^2 \quad \text{and} \quad t^2 = \frac{2y}{g}$$

$$\therefore \quad t = \pm\sqrt{\frac{2y}{g}} = \pm\sqrt{\frac{2\,(80\text{ m})}{9.8\text{ m/s}^2}} = \pm 4.0\text{ s}$$

Only the positive root applies, so the time is 4.0 s. Using this time in Eqn. 4-10 for the horizontal motion:

$$v_{0x} = \frac{x - x_0}{t} = \frac{(100 - 0)\text{m}}{4.0\text{ s}} = 25\text{ m/s}$$

Thus, the initial velocity of the package is 25 m/s horizontally.

Practice

Note: In all questions related to projectile motion, assume that air resistance is negligible.

4-13 A ball is thrown horizontally and moves freely though the air. What is its vertical acceleration? horizontal acceleration?

4-14 Why is an airplane flying through the air not an example of projectile motion?

4-15 A marble is rolled off a table at a horizontal velocity of 1.7 m/s. If the table top is 0.86 m above the floor:
(a) how long will the marble be in flight?
(b) where will the marble land? [Ans. (a) 0.42 s (b) 0.71 m from the edge of the table]

4-16 A tennis player serves a ball horizontally, giving it a speed of 24 m/s from a height of 2.5 m. The player is 12 m from the net and the top of the net is 0.90 m above the court surface.
(a) How long is the ball in the air, assuming it clears the net and lands in the other court?
(b) How far horizontally does the ball travel?
(c) With what velocity does the ball strike the court surface?
(d) By how much distance does the ball clear the net?
[Ans. (a) 0.71 s (b) 17 m (c) 25 m/s at an angle of 16° below the horizontal (d) 0.38 m]

4-17 A stone is thrown horizontally from a high cliff with a speed of 5.0 m/s. Determine the stone's position and velocity at t = 0.0 s, 0.50 s, 1.0 s, 1.5 s, and 2.0 s. Then draw a diagram showing the path of the projectile and the velocity at the times indicated.

4-18 With what horizontal speed must a pitcher throw a baseball so that it falls 90 cm (two significant digits) as it travels 18.4 m to the home plate? [Ans. 43 m/s]

4.4 MORE PROJECTILE MOTION

The previous sample problems concerning projectile motion have all had an initial velocity that was horizontal. The same kinematics equations apply if the initial velocity is at some angle to the horizontal, which means that v_{0y} is different from zero. When dealing with such situations, we need to be careful with the signs of the various quantities involved in the problem. As an example, suppose that the initial velocity has a vertical component that is upward, such as when a fly ball is hit in baseball. If the $+y$ direction is chosen to be upward, then v_{0y} will be positive, and the vertical position, y, will also be positive as the ball flies through the air (Figure 4-26 (a)). However, a_y will be negative, since the gravitational acceleration is downward. If, instead, we choose the $+y$ direction to be downward, then v_{0y} and y will be negative, and a_y will be positive (Figure 4-26 (b)). Of course, whether we choose the $+y$ direction to be up or down has no effect on the physics of the problem, that is, on how far the ball will travel, what its maximum height will be, how long it will be in the air, etc.

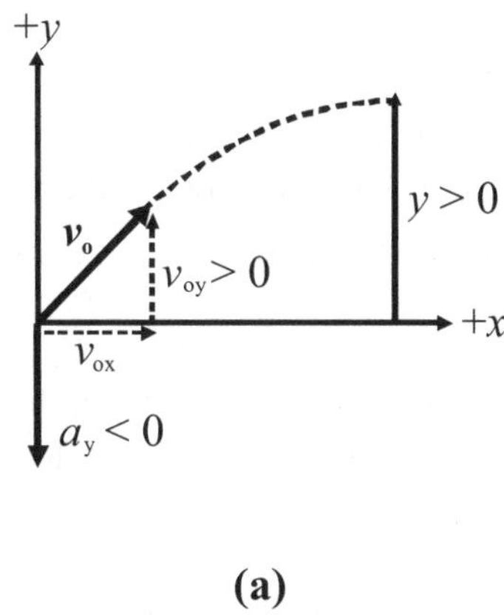

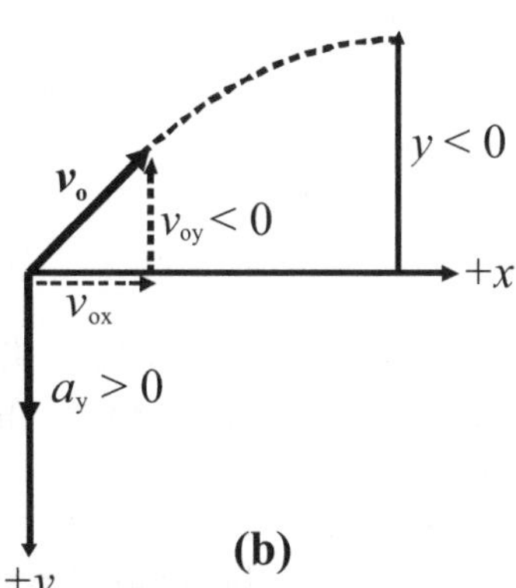

Figure 4-26 *Choosing the +y direction to be* **(a)** *upward, or* **(b)** *downward, affects the signs of y, v_{0y}, and a_y.*

Sample Problem 4-8

A woman strikes a golf ball, which leaves the ground with an initial velocity of 42 m/s at an angle of 32° above the horizontal. Determine the ball's
(a) horizontal range of travel
(b) maximum height
(c) horizontal distance travelled when it is 15 m above the ground.

Solution: (a) We choose the +*x* direction to be the horizontal direction toward which the ball is hit, and the +*y* direction to be vertically upward (Figure 4-27). We select the point where the ball is hit be at $(x_0, y_0) = (0\text{ m}, 0\text{ m})$.

We begin by finding the horizontal and vertical components of the initial velocity (Figure 4-27):

$$v_{0x} = (42\text{ m/s})(\cos 32°) = 36\text{ m/s}$$
$$v_{0y} = (42\text{ m/s})(\sin 32°) = 22\text{ m/s}$$

(To review trigonometric functions such as sine and cosine, refer to Appendix 5 at the back of the text.)

Next, we list the quantities of the horizontal and vertical motions separately.

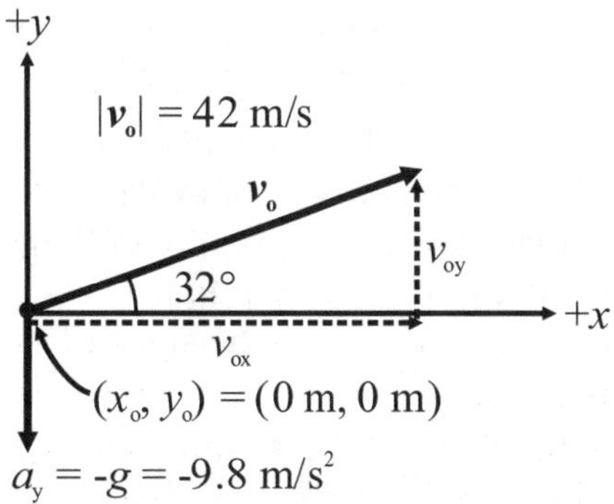

Figure 4-27 *Set-up for Sample Problem 4-8.*

horizontal (constant velocity)
$x_0 = 0$ m
$x = ?$ (required to find in (a))
$v_{0x} = 36$ m/s
$t = ?$

vertical (constant acceleration)
$y_0 = 0$ m
$y = 0$ m for (a)
$v_{0y} = 22$ m/s
$v_y = -22$ m/s for (a), by symmetry
$a_y = -g = -9.8$ m/s^2
$t = ?$

Notice in the above list that as the ball hits the ground (assumed level), it returns to the position $y = 0$ m, and its y-component of velocity is reversed from its initial value (just as for a ball going straight up and down).

In order to determine the horizontal range, we will first use the vertical data to find the time, and then use the time in calculating the range. There is more than one way to calculate the time. We will use Eqn. 4-13:

$$y = y_0 + v_{0y}t + \tfrac{1}{2}a_y t^2$$

Substituting numerical values (without units for convenience):

$$0 = 0 + 22t - 4.9t^2$$

Factoring out a "t":

$$0 = t(22 - 4.9t)$$

Hence, either $t = 0$ (when the ball is struck), or $22 - 4.9t = 0$ (when the ball lands). Solving this latter equation for t gives $t = 4.5$ s.

Now, the horizontal range can be found from Eqn. 4-10b:

$$x - x_0 = v_{0x}t = 36 \text{ m/s} \times 4.5 \text{ s} = 1.6 \times 10^2 \text{ m}$$

Thus, the horizontal range is 1.6×10^2 m.

(b) In order to find the ball's maximum height, we need to recognize that at the peak of the trajectory, the ball's y-component of instantaneous velocity is zero, i.e., $v_y = 0$ m/s. (This statement is similar to that for a ball travelling vertically straight up and down.) Knowing this, we can use Eqn. 4-14 to find the height:

$$v_y^2 - v_{0y}^2 = 2a_y(y - y_0)$$

Substituting immediately that $v_y = 0 \text{ m/s}, a_y = -g, \textit{and } y_0 = 0 \text{ m}$, gives

$$v_{0y}^2 = 2gy$$

Hence, $$y = \frac{v_{0y}^2}{2g} = \frac{(22\ \text{m/s})^2}{2(9.8\ \text{m/s}^2)} = 25\ \text{m}$$

Thus, the ball rises to a height of 25 m above the ground.

(c) We are required to find the horizontal distance travelled when the ball is 15 m above the ground. In other words, we are asked to determine "x," given that y = 15 m. We first use vertical information to find the time, and then use the time to determine "x." Equation 4-13 will give us the time:

$$y = y_0 + v_{0y}t + \tfrac{1}{2}a_y t^2$$

Substituting known quantities (without units):

$$15 = 0 + 22t - 4.9t^2$$

This is a quadratic equation, which we re-arrange into the standard form:

$$4.9t^2 - 22t + 15 = 0$$

Using the quadratic formula:

$$\begin{aligned} t &= \frac{-b \pm \sqrt{b^2 - 4ac}}{2a} \qquad \text{where } a = 4.9,\ b = -22, \text{ and } c = 15 \\ &= \frac{-(-22) \pm \sqrt{(-22)^2 - 4(4.9)(15)}}{2(4.9)} \\ &= 0.84\ \text{s or } 3.7\ \text{s} \end{aligned}$$

Thus, the ball is 15 m above the ground twice during the flight, once on the way up and again on the way down. We can now use Eqn. 4-9b to determine the horizontal position, x, for each time:

$$x_1 = x_0 + v_{0x}t_1 = 0\ \text{m} + (36\ \text{m/s}) \times (0.84\ \text{s}) = 3.0 \times 10^1\ \text{m}$$

and $$x_2 = x_0 + v_{0x}t_2 = 0\ \text{m} + (36\ \text{m/s}) \times (3.7\ \text{s}) = 1.3 \times 10^2\ \text{m}$$

Thus, when the ball has an elevation of 15 m, the horizontal distance that it has travelled is either 3.0×10^1 m or 1.3×10^2 m.

Maximum Range

As you learned in the previous sample problem, the range of a projectile can be found by applying the kinematics equations one step at a time. However, it is possible to derive an equation to find the range of a projectile given its initial speed, v_0, and angle of projection, θ (Figure 4-28). This derivation is given here for the special case in which the projectile lands at the same elevation from which it began.

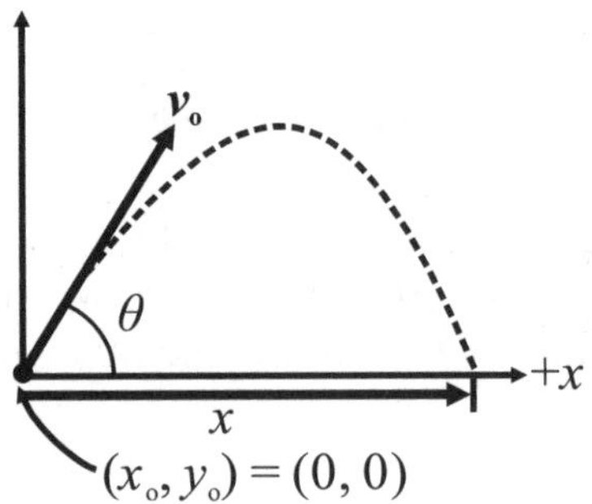

Figure 4-28 *The horizontal range, x, of a projectile.*

The horizontal range of a projectile is the displacement, Δx, or $x - x_0$. It is convenient to choose the initial x-component of position, x_0, to be zero. Hence, we can write the range simply as the x-position, x, which is equal to the product $v_{0x}t$ (from Eqn. 4-10b). The time, t, is the same as the time for the projectile to rise and fall back to its original vertical position, so we can determine this time using the vertical motion equations. Thus, for the vertical motion, using Eqn. 4-13:

$$y = y_0 + v_{0y}t + \tfrac{1}{2}a_y t^2$$

Substituting $y = 0$ (for landing),

$$y_0 = 0,\ v_{0y} = v_0 \sin\theta, \text{ and } a_y = -g:$$

$$0 = 0 + (v_0 \sin\theta)t - \tfrac{1}{2}gt^2$$

Thus, $$0 = t\left(v_0 \sin\theta - \tfrac{1}{2}gt\right)$$

Therefore, either $t = 0$ (takeoff), or $v_0 \sin\theta - \frac{1}{2}gt = 0$ (landing). Solving the latter equation for t gives:

$$t = \frac{2v_0 \sin\theta}{g}$$

Did You Know?
It was Galileo who brought the study of projectile motion out of the incorrect medieval views into the more realistic view. He realized that the motion of a projectile not influenced by air resistance is a parabola, and he proved that the maximum horizontal range occurs when the angle of projection is 45°.

Going back to the horizontal motion,

$$x = v_{0x}t = (v_0 \cos\theta)(t) = v_0 \cos\theta \times \frac{2v_0 \sin\theta}{g} = \frac{v_0^2}{g} 2\sin\theta\cos\theta$$

However, as shown in Appendix 5, $2\sin\theta\cos\theta = \sin 2\theta$. Hence, the horizontal range is given by

$$x = \frac{v_0^2}{g}\sin 2\theta$$

where v_0 is the magnitude of the initial velocity of the projectile at an angle θ above the horizontal. This applies only if the projectile lands at the same level from which it started. Do not use the equation for any other circumstance. (A general equation for range could be derived, but it is somewhat more complex.)

We can use the equation for range to determine the maximum range of a projectile. The maximum value of $\sin 2\theta$ is 1, and it occurs when $2\theta = 90°$ or $\theta = 45°$. Thus, the **maximum range** occurs when the projection angle is 45°, and the equation for range becomes

$$x_{\text{MAX}} = \frac{v_0^2}{g} \quad (\text{for } \theta = 45°)$$

The actual horizontal range would be somewhat less if air resistance were taken into consideration.

Practice

Note: In all questions related to projectile motion, assume that air resistance is negligible.

4-19 A soccer ball is kicked and it undergoes projectile motion.
(a) How does its rise time compare to its fall time?
(b) What is the ball's acceleration at the top of its flight?

4-20 A cannon is set at an angle of 45° above the horizontal. It gives a cannonball a muzzle speed of 2.2×10^2 m/s. Determine the cannonball's:
(a) maximum height
(b) time of flight
(c) horizontal range (to the same vertical level).
[Ans. (a) 1.2×10^3 m (b) 32 s (c) 4.9×10^3 m]

4-21 A football is placed on a line 25 m from the goalpost. The placement kicker kicks the ball directly toward the goalpost, giving it a velocity of 21 m/s at an angle of 47° above the horizontal. The horizontal bar of the goalpost is 3.0 m above the field. How far above or below the horizontal bar of the goalpost will the ball travel? [Ans. 8.9 m above]

4-22 A medieval prince trapped in a castle wraps a message around a rock and throws it from the top of the castle wall with an initial velocity of 12 m/s at an angle of 42° above the horizontal. The rock lands just beyond the castle's moat at a level 9.5 m beneath the initial height. See Figure 4-29.
(a) How long does the rock remain airborne?
(b) How wide is the moat?
(c) Determine the rock's velocity just before landing.
[Ans. (a) 2.4 s (b) 22 m (c) 18 m/s at an angle of 60° below the horizontal]

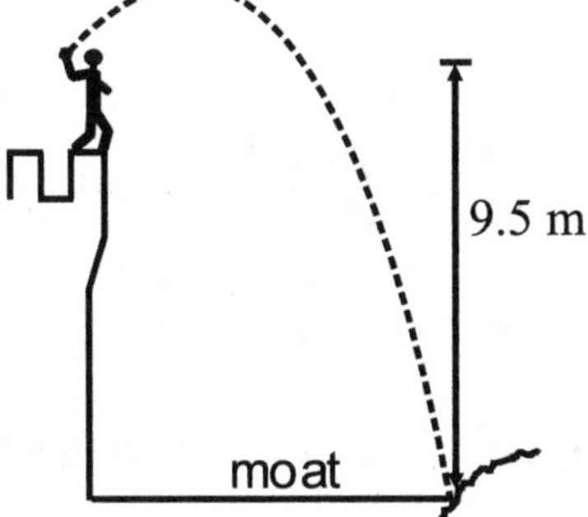

Figure 4-29 *Question 4-22.*

4-23 A girl throws a ball onto the roof of a house, as illustrated in Figure 4-30, and prepares to catch the ball with a baseball glove held 1.0 m above the ground. The ball rolls off the roof with a speed of 3.2 m/s.
(a) After leaving the roof, how long will the ball take to land in her glove?
(b) How far from the horizontal edge of the roof should she hold her glove?
(c) What is the ball's velocity as it reaches her glove?
[Ans. (a) 0.87 s (b) 2.3 m (c) 11 m/s at an angle of 75° below the horizontal]

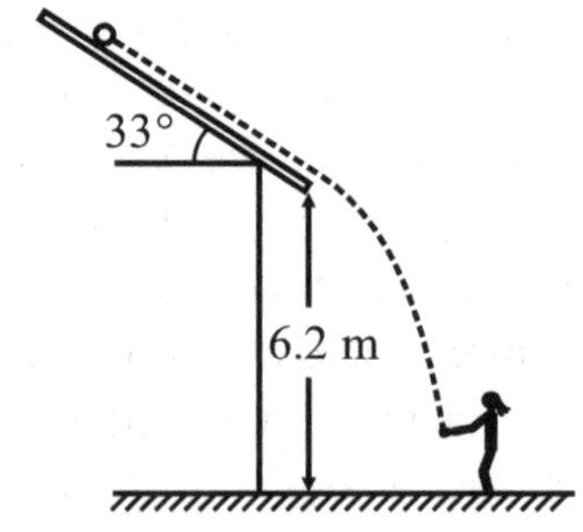

Figure 4-30 *Question 4-23.*

4-24 An arrow leaves a bow with an initial speed of 85 m/s.
(a) Assuming the arrow lands at the same elevation as its starting position, determine its horizontal range for these angles of projection above the horizontal: 20°; 70°; 40°; 50°; and 45°.
(b) Write conclusions based on your answers in (a) above.

4-25 Determine the maximum range of a projectile if its initial speed is (a) 2.2×10^2 m/s (b) 5.0×10^2 m/s. [Ans. (a) 4.9×10^3 m (b) 2.6×10^4 m]

4.5 UNIFORM CIRCULAR MOTION

Imagine that you have attached a rubber stopper to the end of a string and you are whirling the stopper around your head in a horizontal circle. If the radius of the path remains the same and the speed of the stopper remains constant, the type of motion is called **uniform circular motion**. Figure 4-31 shows the velocity and position vectors of the stopper's motion. Uniform circular motion also occurs if only part of a circle is covered.

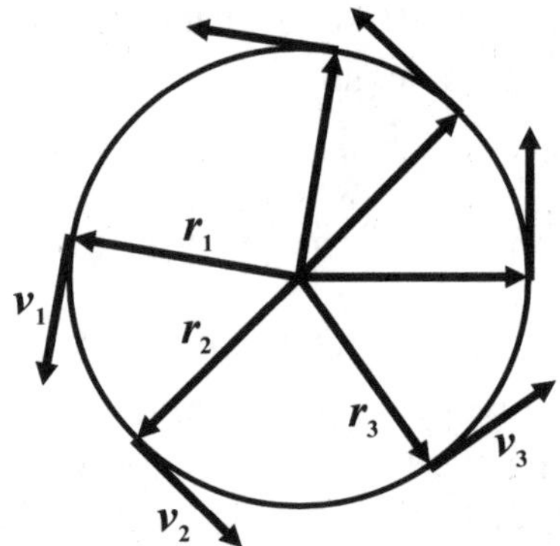

Figure 4-31 *In uniform circular motion, the speed of the object remains constant but the velocity vector changes because its direction changes. Notice that at any instant the position vector (sometimes called the radius vector) is perpendicular to the velocity vector and the velocity vectors are always tangent to the circle.*

Uniform circular motion occurs for the individual "particles" of any object spinning at a constant rate. Examples of such objects are electric fans and motors, lawn mower blades, wheels (from the point of view of the centre of the wheel), and rotating rides at amusement parks. Circular, or almost circular, motion occurs also for objects or particles in orbits around other objects. For example, we often make the assumption that the motion of a planet around the sun, or a satellite around Earth, or an electron around a nucleus is uniform circular motion.

As you learned in Section 4.2, an object travelling at constant speed is undergoing acceleration if the direction of the velocity is changing. This is certainly true for uniform circular motion. The type of acceleration that occurs in uniform circular motion is called **centripetal acceleration** for reasons that will be clear shortly. Centripetal acceleration is an instantaneous acceleration. We will study centripetal acceleration in two stages: first we will consider its direction, and then we will determine its magnitude.

Did You Know? *The word centripetal was coined by Sir Isaac Newton. It stems from the Latin words "centrum" which means centre and "petere" which means seek. Therefore, centripetal means seeking the centre or toward the centre. Don't confuse centripetal with centrifugal. "Fugal" stems from the Latin "fugere" which means flee, so centrifugal means fleeing away from centre the. This is described further in Chapter 6.*

The Direction of Centripetal Acceleration

Recall that the defining equation for instantaneous acceleration is Eqn. 4-9:

$$a = \lim_{\Delta t \to 0} \frac{\Delta v}{\Delta t}$$

To apply this definition to uniform circular motion, we will draw vector diagrams and perform vector subtractions. This is done in four stages in Figure 4-32. In each succeeding diagram, the time interval Δt between the initial velocity $\boldsymbol{v}_0$ and the final velocity $\boldsymbol{v}$ becomes smaller. In the final diagram it is clear that as the time interval approaches zero, the direction of the change of velocity, $\Delta \boldsymbol{v}$, is close to being toward the centre of the circle. From Eqn. 4-9 above, the acceleration is in the same direction as the change of velocity, since division of $\Delta \boldsymbol{v}$ by the scalar Δt has no effect on direction. We conclude that *the direction of the centripetal acceleration is toward the centre of the circle.* Notice that the centripetal acceleration and the velocity are perpendicular to each other, a fact that is commonly misunderstood.

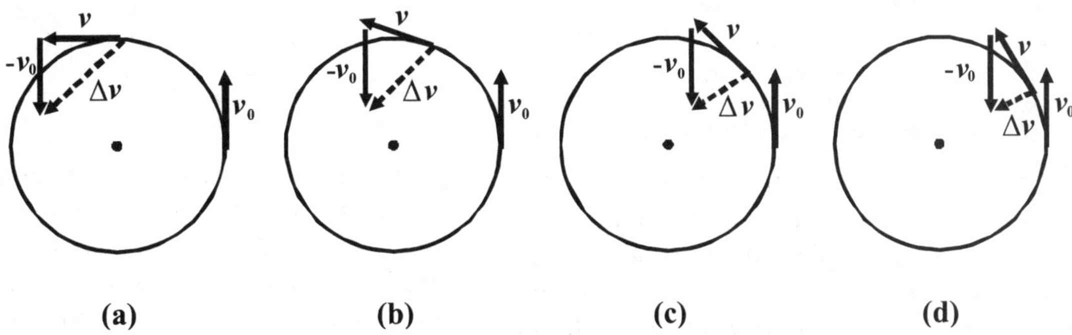

Figure 4-32 *As the time interval between* $\boldsymbol{v}_0$ *and* $\boldsymbol{v}$ *decreases, the direction of* $\Delta \boldsymbol{v}$ *becomes closer and closer to facing the centre of the circle. In (d),* Δt *is small and the* $\Delta \boldsymbol{v}$ *vector is nearly perpendicular to the instantaneous velocity vector* $\boldsymbol{v}$.

The Magnitude of Centripetal Acceleration

To derive an equation for the magnitude of the centripetal acceleration in terms of the instantaneous speed and the radius of the circle, consider the diagram in Figure 4-33 (a). It shows a particle in uniform circular motion as it moves from an initial position, $\boldsymbol{r}_0$, to a subsequent position, $\boldsymbol{r}$. Its corresponding velocities are $\boldsymbol{v}_0$ and $\boldsymbol{v}$. (Since we have *uniform* circular motion, $|\boldsymbol{v}_0| = |\boldsymbol{v}|$.) The change in position is $\Delta\boldsymbol{r}$ and the change in velocity is $\Delta\boldsymbol{v}$. Both of these quantities involve a vector subtraction, as shown in Figure 4-33 (b). In this figure, both triangles are isosceles because $|\boldsymbol{r}_0| = |\boldsymbol{r}|$, and $|\boldsymbol{v}_0| = |\boldsymbol{v}|$. Since $\boldsymbol{v}_0 \perp \boldsymbol{r}_0$ and $\boldsymbol{v} \perp \boldsymbol{r}$, the two triangles can easily be shown to be similar. Therefore, the following equation can be written:

$$\frac{|\Delta\boldsymbol{v}|}{|\boldsymbol{v}|} = \frac{|\Delta\boldsymbol{r}|}{|\boldsymbol{r}|} \quad \text{or} \quad |\Delta\boldsymbol{v}| = \frac{|\boldsymbol{v}| \times |\Delta\boldsymbol{r}|}{|\boldsymbol{r}|}$$

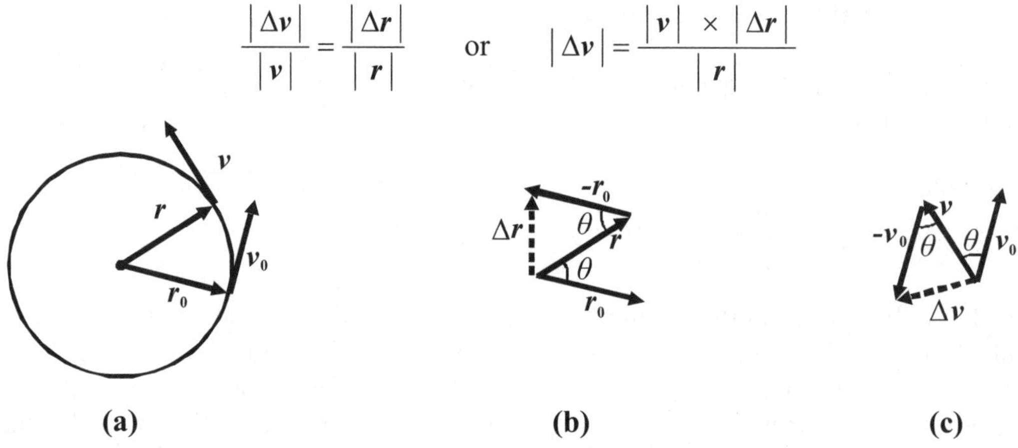

Figure 4-33 *Diagrams for uniform circular motion used to derive the magnitude of centripetal acceleration.*

Now, the magnitude of the acceleration is

$$|\mathbf{a}_{\mathrm{c}}| = \lim_{\Delta t \to 0} \frac{|\Delta\boldsymbol{v}|}{\Delta t}$$

where we have used $\boldsymbol{a}_{\mathrm{c}}$ for centripetal acceleration. We divide both sides of the equation for $|\Delta\boldsymbol{v}|$ by Δt to obtain:

$$\frac{|\Delta\boldsymbol{v}|}{\Delta t} = \frac{|\boldsymbol{v}|}{|\boldsymbol{r}|} \times \frac{|\Delta\boldsymbol{r}|}{\Delta t}$$

$$\therefore \quad |\boldsymbol{a}_{\mathrm{c}}| = \lim_{\Delta t \to 0} \frac{|\boldsymbol{v}|}{|\boldsymbol{r}|} \times \frac{|\Delta\boldsymbol{r}|}{\Delta t}$$

Now, $$\lim_{\Delta t \to 0} \frac{|\Delta \boldsymbol{r}|}{\Delta t} = |\boldsymbol{v}| \text{ (magnitude of the instantaneous velocity)}$$

$$\therefore \quad |\boldsymbol{a}_\text{c}| = \frac{|\boldsymbol{v}|}{|\boldsymbol{r}|} \times |\boldsymbol{v}|$$

Hence, the magnitude of the centripetal acceleration is:

$$a_\text{c} = \frac{v^2}{r} \qquad \textbf{(4-15)}$$

where v is the speed of the object undergoing uniform circular motion, and r is the radius of the circle or arc. Equation 4-15 will be used frequently in problem-solving.

The equation $a_\text{c} = v^2 / r$ makes sense, because as the speed of the object in circular motion increases the direction of the velocity changes more quickly, requiring a larger acceleration; as the radius becomes larger, the direction changes more slowly, meaning a smaller acceleration.

For objects undergoing uniform circular motion, it is often the case that the speed is not known, but the radius and the period of time for one complete trip around the circle are known. To find the centripetal acceleration with this information we use the fact that the speed is constant and equals the distance travelled in one complete revolution ($2\pi r$) divided by the **period of revolution**, T, which is the time for one revolution. Thus,

$$v = \frac{2\pi r}{T}$$

Substituting this expression for v into $a_\text{c} = v^2 / r$, we obtain

$$a_\text{c} = \frac{4\pi^2 r}{T^2} \qquad \textbf{(4-16)}$$

where a_c is measured in metres per second squared when r is measured in metres and T in seconds.

Finally, the **frequency of revolution,** f, is the number of revolutions per second. Frequency is the reciprocal of period and is measured in cycles per second, or s^{-1}. This unit is given a special SI name and symbol: hertz (Hz). Since $f = 1/T$, the equation for centripetal acceleration can also be written:

$$a_\text{c} = 4\pi^2 r f^2 \qquad \textbf{(4-17)}$$

Solving Centripetal Acceleration Problems

The following facts will be applied in solving centripetal acceleration problems.

- The speed of an object in uniform circular motion is constant and can often be found by using $v = 2\pi r/T$, where T is the period of one revolution of radius r.
- The centripetal acceleration is directed toward the centre of the circle and can be found using one or more of these equations:

$$a_c = \frac{v^2}{r} = \frac{4\pi^2 r}{T^2} = 4\pi^2 r f^2$$

Sample Problem 4-9

A child on a merry-go-round is 4.4 m from the centre of the ride and is travelling at a constant speed of 1.8 m/s. What is the magnitude of the child's centripetal acceleration?

Solution:

Using Eqn. 4-15, $$a_c = \frac{v^2}{r} = \frac{(1.8\text{ m/s})^2}{4.4\text{ m}} = 0.74\text{ m/s}^2$$

Thus, the magnitude of the centripetal acceleration is 0.74 m/s^2.

Sample Problem 4-10

Find the magnitude and direction of the centripetal acceleration of a dust particle that is sitting on the outside edge of an old "45" record that is 17.2 cm across. The record is being played on a turntable, and at the instant in question, the dust particle is moving northward.

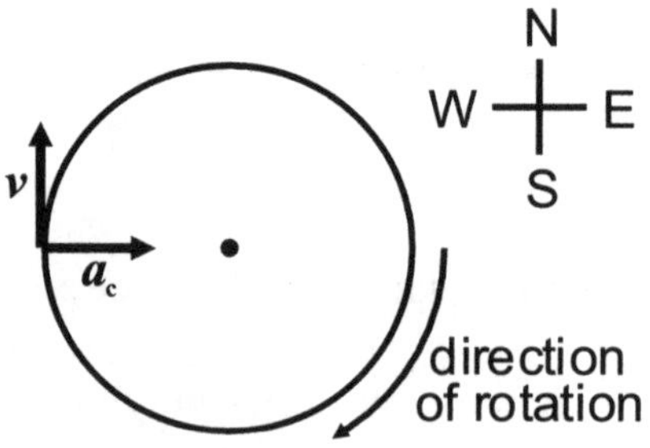

Figure 4-34 *Sample Problem 4-10.*

Solution: The "45" means the record revolves at a frequency of 45 rev/min, or 45/60 = 0.75 rev/s. Thus, f = 0.75 Hz or 0.75 s^{-1} and $r = \frac{1}{2}(17.2\text{ cm}) = 8.6\text{ cm}$. Using Eqn. 4-17:

$$\begin{aligned} a_c &= 4\pi^2 r f^2 \\ &= 4\pi^2(8.6\text{ cm})(0.75\text{ Hz})^2 \\ &= 1.9 \times 10^2\text{ cm/s}^2 \\ &= 1.9\text{ m/s}^2 \end{aligned}$$

Since a record moves clockwise around the turntable, the direction of the acceleration must be toward the east when the particle is travelling northward, as seen in Figure 4-34. Thus, the centripetal acceleration is 1.9 m/s^2 east.

Sample Problem 4-11

Determine the frequency and period of rotation of an ice skater spinning such that the centripetal acceleration of her nose has a magnitude of 1.2 × 10^2 m/s^2. Assume the distance from her nose to the axis of rotation is 12 cm.

Solution:

From $a_c = 4\pi^2 r f^2$, we have $f^2 = \dfrac{a_c}{4\pi^2 r}$

$$\therefore \quad f = \pm\sqrt{\frac{a_c}{4\pi^2 r}} = \pm\sqrt{\frac{1.2\times10^2\ \text{m/s}^2}{4\pi^2\,(0.12\ \text{m})}} = \pm 5.0\ \text{Hz}$$

A negative frequency has no meaning, so the required frequency is 5.0 Hz.

$$T = \frac{1}{f} = \frac{1}{5.0\ \text{Hz}} = 0.20\ \text{s}$$

Thus, the period of rotation is 0.20 s.

Practice

4-26 In the expression "uniform circular motion," what does the word "uniform" mean?

4-27 The motion of a particle undergoing uniform circular motion with a speed of 4.0 m/s is illustrated in Figure 4-35. For this motion:
(a) state the direction of the velocity vector, the acceleration vector, and the radius vector at the instant shown
(b) calculate the magnitude of the centripetal acceleration.
[Ans. (b) 2.0 × 10^1 m/s^2]

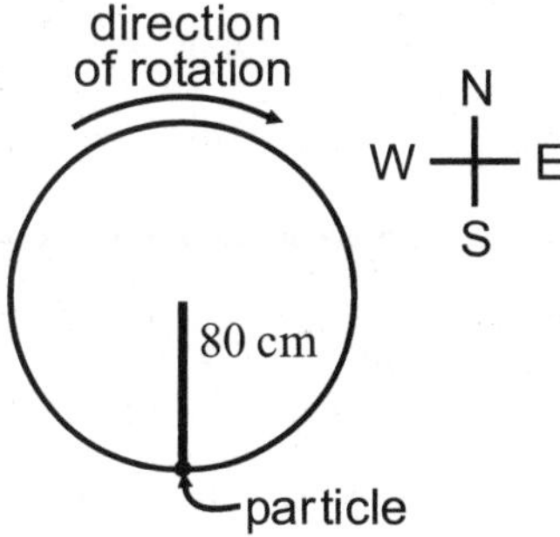

Figure 4-35 *Question 4-27.*

4-28 Determine the magnitude of the centripetal acceleration for each of the following motions, assuming that they involve uniform circular motion.
(a) A satellite travels around Earth at a speed of 7.77×10^3 m/s in an orbit of radius 6.57×10^6 m from Earth's centre.
(b) An electron travels around a nucleus with a speed of 2.18×10^6 m/s. The diameter of the electron's orbit is 1.06×10^{-10} m.
(c) A motorcycle travels at 25 m/s around a curve that has a radius of curvature of 1.2×10^2 m.
(d) In the death spiral in pairs figure skating, the speed of the woman's shoulder, which is 1.1 m from the axis of rotation, is 6.4 m/s.
[Ans. (a) 9.19 m/s^2 (b) 8.97×10^{22} m/s^2 (c) 5.2 m/s^2 (d) 37 m/s^2]

4-29 If the direction of an object moving with uniform circular motion is reversed, what happens to the direction of the centripetal acceleration?

4-30 A child is twirling a ball on the end of a string in a horizontal circle around her head. What is the effect on the magnitude of the centripetal acceleration of the ball if:
(a) the speed of the ball remains constant but the radius of the circle doubles?
(b) the radius of the circle remains constant but the speed doubles?

4-31 At a distance of 25 km from the "eye" of a hurricane, the wind is moving at 180 km/h in a circle around the eye. What is the magnitude of the centripetal acceleration, in metres per second squared, of the air particles that make up the wind? [Ans. 0.10 m/s^2]

4-32 A cowhand is about to lasso a calf with a rope that is undergoing uniform circular motion. The time for one complete revolution of the rope is 1.2 s and the end of the rope is 4.3 m from the centre of the circle. Calculate the magnitude of the centripetal acceleration of the end of the rope. [Ans. 1.2×10^2 m/s^2]

4-33 Using an ultracentrifuge, which is a centrifuge operating at a very high rate of rotation, greatly reduces the sedimentation time of blood cells or other materials. (Chapter 6 explains the physics of centrifuges.)
(a) Calculate the magnitude of the centripetal acceleration of a point 7.4 cm from the axis of an ultracentrifuge rotating at 1.3 MHz.
(b) Compare your answer in (a) to the magnitude of the acceleration due to gravity on Earth.
[Ans. (a) 4.9×10^{12} m/s^2 (b) 5.0×10^{11}]

CHAPTER FOCUS

The quantities of distance, displacement, speed, velocity, and acceleration studied in one-dimensional motion in Chapter 2 have been extended to two dimensions in this chapter. The skills of adding and subtracting vectors, introduced in Chapter 3, have been reviewed. Distinctions between average and instantaneous velocities, and average and instantaneous accelerations, have been made for two-dimensional motion. Projectile motion was analyzed by separating the motion into horizontal and vertical components and applying the kinematics equations from Chapter 2.

Finally, uniform circular motion was analyzed using equations for centripetal acceleration in terms of speed, radius, period, and frequency.

This completes the study of kinematics, but the way is now clear to study the forces that cause the motion presented in Chapters 2 and 4. Thus, Chapters 5 and 6 and parts of later chapters will apply the knowledge of kinematics in more detail.

VOCABULARY REVIEW

You should be able to define or explain each of the following words or phrases for two-dimensional motion. (In some cases, the original definition is found in Chapter 2 where one-dimensional motion was studied.)

resultant displacement
average velocity
instantaneous velocity
average acceleration
instantaneous acceleration
projectile
projectile motion
(horizontal) range
maximum range
uniform circular motion
centripetal acceleration
period (of revolution or rotation)
frequency (of revolution or rotation)

CHAPTER REVIEW

Note: In all questions related to projectile motion, assume that air resistance is negligible.

4-34 Assume that $\boldsymbol{A}$ is the shortest displacement vector between your eyes and the top of the front wall of your lecture hall, and $\boldsymbol{B}$ is the shortest displacement vector between your eyes and the bottom of the same wall. These vectors make an angle of θ (above) and β (below) the horizontal. The height of the wall is:

(a) $A\sin\theta - B\sin\beta$
(b) $A\sin\theta + B\sin\beta$
(c) $(A+B)\sin(\theta+\beta)$
(d) $\sqrt{|A|^2+|B|^2}$
(e) $A\tan\theta + B\tan\beta$

4-35 Two balls, C and D, are thrown horizontally from the roof of a building at the same instant, with the initial speed of C double that of D. Assuming air resistance can be neglected:

(a) C and D hit the ground at the same time and at the same speed.
(b) C reaches the ground first.
(c) D reaches the ground first.
(d) C and D hit the ground at the same time, but C's final speed is double D's final speed.
(e) none of the above

4-36 A bottle-nosed dolphin launches itself from the water through the air and follows a parabolic path. At the highest point in the path in the air:

(a) neither the velocity nor the acceleration is zero
(b) the velocity is not zero but the acceleration is zero
(c) both the velocity and the acceleration are zero
(d) the velocity is zero but the acceleration is not zero

4-37 An Olympic athlete launches a shot, and the shot follows a parabolic path. Point E is a position along the path as the shot is still rising, and point F is the highest position in the path. The relationships between the speed and the magnitudes of the accelerations of the shot at E and F are:

(a) $v_E < v_F$ and $a_E < a_F$
(b) $v_E < v_F$ and $a_E = a_F$
(c) $v_E > v_F$ and $a_E = a_F$
(d) $v_E = v_F$ and $a_E \neq a_F$
(e) $v_E > v_F$ and $a_E < a_F$

4-38 The minute hand of a 12-hour clock rotates clockwise (as expected) around the centre of the clock, C. During the time the tip of the hand moves from the 12:00 o'clock position to the 6:00 o'clock position, the directions of the average acceleration and the centripetal acceleration are, respectively:

(a) horizontally to the right; horizontally to the left
(b) toward C; toward C
(c) horizontally to the right; toward C
(d) horizontally to the left; toward C
(e) vertically upward; vertically downward

4-39 A boy throws a ball into the air at a steep angle to the horizontal, then runs and catches the ball. Compare the displacement of the boy with the displacement of the ball at the end of the motion.

4-40 A resultant displacement, $\Delta \boldsymbol{r}$, is the sum of displacements $\boldsymbol{A}$ and $\boldsymbol{B}$. Is $|\Delta \boldsymbol{r}|$ necessarily as large as $|\boldsymbol{A}| + |\boldsymbol{B}|$? Explain.

4-41 The magnitudes of two displacements are 25 m and 42 m. What are the maximum and minimum values of the magnitude of their vector sum? [Ans. 67 m, 17 m]

4-42 A square is inscribed in a circle of radius 12 m, as shown in Figure 4-36. One person walks from A to B along the edges of the square, and a second person walks along the circumference. Each person reaches B after 48 s. Calculate each person's:
(a) average speed (b) average velocity.
[Ans. (a) 0.71 m/s; 0.79 m/s (b) for each: 0.50 m/s at an angle of 45° up from bottom edge of square]

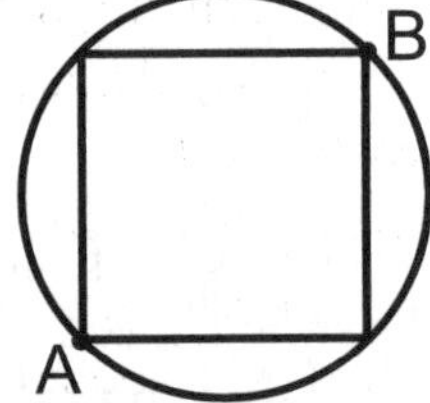

Figure 4-36 *Question 4-42.*

4-43 In 5.0 s, a fire fighter slides 4.5 m down a pole and runs 6.8 m straight to a fire truck. Determine the fire fighter's:

(a) total distance moved (b) average speed
(c) resultant displacement (d) average velocity
[Ans. (a) 11.3 m (b) 2.3 m/s (c) 8.2 m 33° below the horizontal (d) 1.6 m/s 33° below the horizontal]

4-44 A field hockey player runs 16 m 35° south of west, then 22 m 15° south of east, all in 6.4 s.
(a) Determine the magnitude and direction of the resultant displacement.
(b) Find the average velocity of the player.
[Ans. (a) 17 m 27° east of south (b) 2.7 m/s 27° east of south]

4-45 The cheetah, probably the world's fastest land animal, can run up to 100 km/h over short distances. The motion of a cheetah chasing its prey at top speed is illustrated in Figure 4-37, with north facing toward the top of the diagram. State the cheetah's instantaneous velocity, including the approximate direction, at positions A, B, and C.

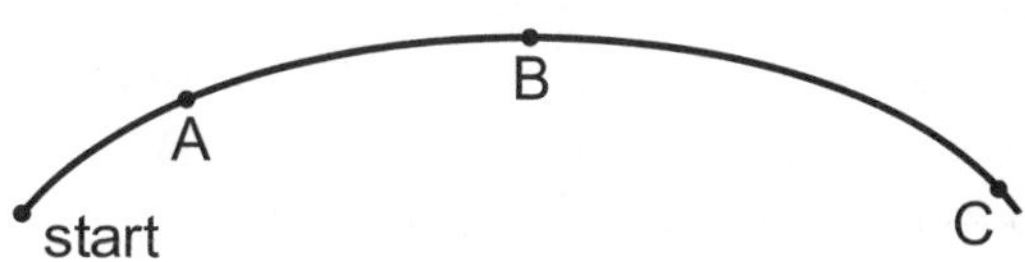

Figure 4-37 *Question 4-45.*

4-46 A bug is crawling along a checkered tablecloth on a picnic table. It starts at a position given by (x_0, y_0) = (42 cm, 28 cm), moves to position (x_1, y_1) = (29 cm, 36 cm), then moves to position (x_2, y_2) = (11 cm, 12 cm). Determine the magnitude and direction of the bug's displacement. [Ans. 35 cm 207° counterclockwise from the $+x$ axis]

4-47 The driver of a car has three different controls for producing acceleration. What are they?

4-48 An airplane is travelling at 240 m/s 28° south of east, then 35 s later at 220 m/s 28° east of south. Determine the airplane's average acceleration during this time.
[Ans. 3.9 m/s^2 53° west of south]

4-49 A horse is running at constant speed around a circular track, as shown in Figure 4-38. The diameter of the track is 1.2×10^2 m and the horse takes 28 s to complete one revolution. Determine the horse's:
(a) speed
(b) instantaneous velocity at positions A, B, and C
(c) average velocity between positions A and D
(d) average acceleration between positions B and D, then between A and D.
[Ans. (a) 13 m/s (b) 13 m/s east, 13 m/s north, 13 m/s 45° north of west (c) 8.6 m/s north
(d) 2.6 m/s^2 45° south of west; 1.9 m/s^2 west]

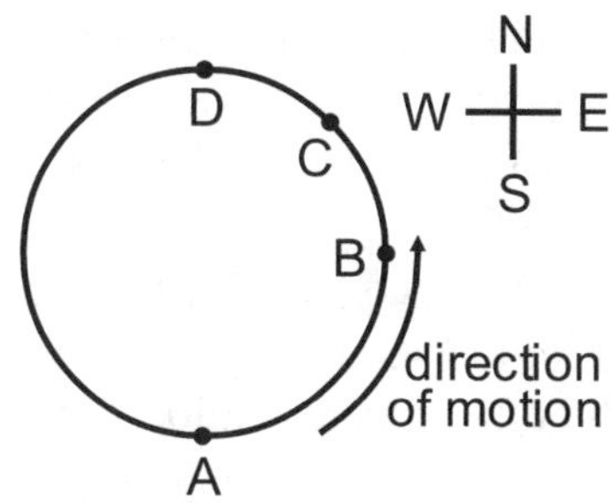

Figure 4-38 *Question 4-49.*

4-50 A train is travelling east at 23 m/s when it enters a curved portion of the track and experiences an average acceleration of 0.15 m/s^2 south for 95 s. What is the train's velocity at the end of this acceleration? [Ans. 27 m/s 32° south of east]

4-51 A race car driver wants to leave a curve in the track with a velocity of 54 m/s north. With what velocity should the car enter the curve if the average acceleration in the curve is 19 m/s^2 45° north of west for 4.0 s? [Ans. 54 m/s east]

4-52 A projectile lands at the same elevation from which it starts. At what position(s) in its path is the speed of the projectile the least? the greatest?

4-53 What are the horizontal and vertical accelerations of a projectile?

4-54 A child throws a snowball straight toward a tree with a horizontal velocity of 18 m/s. The tree is 9.0 m away and the snowball starts from a height of 1.5 m above the ground.
(a) How long will the snowball take to reach the tree?
(b) At what height above the ground will the snowball hit the tree?
(c) What is the snowball's velocity as it hits the tree?
[Ans. (a) 0.50 s (b) 0.3 m (c) 19 m/s 15° down from the horizontal]

4-55 A ball projected horizontally falls 1.5 m while it moves 16 m horizontally. What was its initial velocity? [Ans. 29 m/s horizontally]

4-56 During World War I, the German army used a huge gun to bombard Paris with shells from a large distance away. (The gun was named "Big Bertha" by the Allied forces.) The gun fired shells with an initial speed of 1.1×10^3 m/s. The gun was set at an angle of 45° above the horizontal.
(a) How long would each shell stay in the air?
(b) What was the maximum horizontal distance the gun could be from Paris to try to hit it?
(c) What maximum height did the shells reach?
[Ans. (a) 1.6×10^2 s (b) 1.2×10^2 km (c) 31 km]

4-57 An astronaut strikes a golf ball on the moon where the magnitude of the acceleration due to gravity is 1.6 m/s^2. The ball takes off with a velocity of 32 m/s at an angle 35° above the horizontal (the *moon's* horizontal) and lands in a valley 15 m below the level where it started. Determine the golf ball's: (a) maximum height (b) time of flight (c) horizontal distance travelled.
[Ans. (a) 1.1×10^2 m (b) 24 s (c) 6.2×10^2 m]

4-58 Neglecting air resistance, state another angle of projection above the horizontal that would result in the same range of a projectile fired at an angle of 38°; 15°; 44.5°. (Assume the projectile lands at the same elevation from which it starts.)

4-59 Is centripetal acceleration an average acceleration, an instantaneous acceleration, both, or neither?

4-60 Do all points along the second hand of a dial clock have the same centripetal acceleration? Explain your answer.

4-61 An engineer has calculated that the maximum centripetal acceleration of a car on a certain curve is 4.4 m/s^2 in magnitude. For a car travelling at 25 m/s, what is the minimum radius of curvature of this curve? [Ans. 1.4×10^2 m]

4-62 An astronaut in training is spinning around in a device that rotates at 21 revolutions per minute. (a) If the astronaut is 15 m from the centre of the device, what is the magnitude of the centripetal acceleration? (b) Express the answer in terms of "*g*," the magnitude of the acceleration due to gravity. (Note: Humans may lose consciousness if exposed to accelerations of more than about 7 *g*'s.) [Ans. (a) 72 m/s^2 (b) 7.4 *g*]

4-63 Determine the magnitude of the centripetal acceleration of the tip of the second hand, the minute hand, and the hour hand on the clock shown in Figure 4-39.
[Ans. 0.11 cm/s^2; 8.8×10^{-2} cm/s^2; 5.5×10^{-3} cm/s^2]

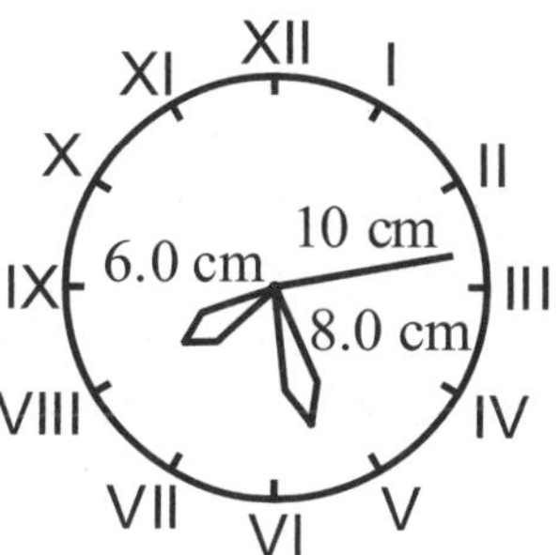

Figure 4-39 *Question 4-63.*

4-64 A turkey is centred on a rotating turntable in a microwave oven. The end of the drumstick, 16 cm from the centre of rotation, experiences a centripetal acceleration of magnitude 0.22 m/s^2. What is the period of rotation of the plate? [Ans. 5.4 s]

APPLYING YOUR KNOWLEDGE

4-65 On a detailed map of Mount Everest, the following data are observed. The elevation of the top of the mountain (which is the world's highest) is 8848 m. At a horizontal distance of 1500 m due north of the peak, in Tibet, the elevation has fallen to 7600 m. To the southwest, at a horizontal distance of 1800 m in Nepal, the elevation is 6800 m. Determine the average slope of each mountain side, and compare the slopes. (Note: A detailed map of Mount Everest came with the November 1988 edition of the *National Geographic* magazine.) [Ans. 40°; 49°]

4-66 A car, travelling at 80 km/h east, experiences an acceleration for a certain time and reaches a velocity of 100 km/h 45° south of east. The magnitude of the acceleration is 5.0 (km/h)/s. Determine the: (a) direction of the acceleration (b) time for the acceleration. (Assume two significant digits.) [Ans. (a) 82° south of east (b) 14 s]

<u>4-67</u> A baseball player wants to determine the speed given to a ball by a bat when the ball has its maximum range. How could this be done using only a measuring tape or metre stick and an equation?

4-68 *Fermi Question:* The women's world record for the hammer throw is about 77 m. Stating any assumptions and approximations, determine values for:
(a) the magnitude of the initial velocity of the throw
(b) the time of flight
(c) the maximum height reached by the hammer [Ans. (a) 27 m/s (b) 4.0 s (c) 39 m]

<u>4-69</u> If the speed of a particle in circular motion is increasing, is the acceleration still toward the centre of the circle? Use a diagram to prove your answer.

4-70 In a basketball game, a ball leaves a player's hand 6.1 m downrange from the basket from a height of 1.2 m below the level of the basket. If the initial velocity of the ball is 7.8 m/s at an angle of 55° above the horizontal and line with the basket, will the player score a basket? If not, by how much will the ball miss the basket? [Ans. No, short by 1.1 m]

4-71 In real life situations, projectile motion is often more complex than that presented in Sections 4.3 and 4.4. For example, to calculate the range, Δx, of a shot put, the following equation is used:

$$\Delta x = \Delta x_1 + \Delta x_2 + \Delta x_3$$

$$= 0.30\text{ m} + \frac{2\,v_0^2 \sin\theta\cos\theta}{g} + \frac{v_0 \sin\theta\sqrt{v_0^2 \sin^2\theta + 2g\Delta y}}{g}$$

where the 0.30 m is the average distance the athlete's hand goes beyond the starting line, v_0 is the initial speed, θ is the projection angle above the horizontal, Δy is the height above the ground where the shot leaves the hand, and g is the magnitude of the acceleration due to gravity. These quantities are illustrated in Figure 4-40.

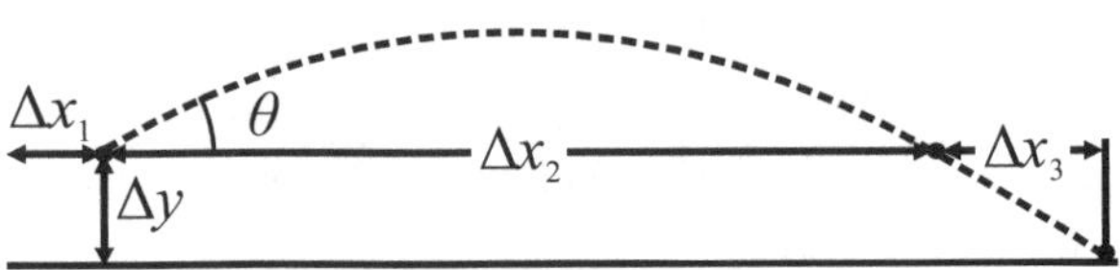

Figure 4-40 *Question 4-71.*

(a) If an athlete releases the shot at a height of 2.2 m above the ground with an initial velocity of 13 m/s 42° above the horizontal, determine the range of the shot.
(b) Compare your answer in (a) with the world record for the shot put (23.1 m at the time of the writing of this book). [Ans. (a) 2.0×10^1 m]

4-72 To produce artificial gravity on a space colony, it is proposed that the colony should rotate. Suppose that the acceleration required is equal in magnitude to the acceleration due to gravity on Earth. For a colony that is 1.0 km in diameter, determine the frequency of rotation, the period of rotation, as well as the speed of a person at the edge of the colony (relative to the centre of the colony). [Ans. 2.2×10^{-2} Hz; 45 s; 7.0×10^1 m/s]

KEY OBJECTIVES

Having completed this chapter you should now be able to do the following for two-dimensional motion:

1. Calculate the total distance travelled and the average speed using the equations learned in Chapter 2.
2. Determine the resultant displacement of an object.
3. Use the relationship involving average velocity, displacement, and time to determine one of these quantities, given the other two.
4. Determine the instantaneous velocity of an object travelling in any path, including a curved path if the instantaneous speed is known.
5. Use the vector subtraction of velocities to find the average acceleration of an object.
6. Determine the unknown quantity in the following list, given the other quantities: average

acceleration, time, initial velocity, and final velocity.
7. Define and give examples of projectile motion.
8. Recognize that the horizontal and vertical motions of a projectile can be treated independently.
9. Analyze projectile motion problems by applying the kinematics equations for constant velocity (horizontal component) and constant acceleration (vertical component).
10. Solve problems related to the range of a projectile.
11. Define and give examples of uniform circular motion.
12. Define centripetal acceleration and use a vector diagram to prove that the direction of the centripetal acceleration is toward the centre of the circle.
13. Recognize that the centripetal acceleration is an instantaneous acceleration.
14. Solve centripetal acceleration problems involving any or all of these variables: radius, speed, period of revolution, frequency of revolution.

ANSWERS TO SELECTED QUESTIONS

4-5 (a) A to the left, B toward the bottom of the page, C to the right, D up and to the right
(b) A down and to the left, B down and to the right, C up and to the right, D to the right (perhaps slightly downward)

4-13 $a_V = 9.8$ m/s^2 downward; $a_H = 0$

4-14 The airplane does not have a vertical downward acceleration.

4:19 (a) $t_{RISE} = t_{FALL}$ (b) $\boldsymbol{a} = \boldsymbol{g} = 9.8$ m/s^2 downward

4-24 The horizontal ranges for any two angles equidistant from 45° are equal, and the maximum horizontal range occurs when the launch angle is 45°.

4-26 The speed of an object in uniform circular motion remains constant.

4-27 (a) west; north; south

4-29 There is no change.

4-30 (a) a_c decreases by a factor of 2 (b) a_c increases by a factor of 4

4-34 (b) 4-35 (e) 4-36 (a) 4-37 (c) 4-38 (d)

4-39 They are equal.

4-40 No, it is only as large if $\boldsymbol{A}$ and $\boldsymbol{B}$ are parallel.

4-45 A: 100 km/h 24° north of east B: 100 km/h east C: 100 km/h 46° south of east

4-47 gas pedal; brake pedal; steering wheel

4-52 at the top of the curved path; twice: just after being released and just prior to landing

4-53 zero and 9.8 m/s^2 downward

4-58 The angles are 52°, 75°, and 0.5°, respectively.

4-59 instantaneous acceleration

4-60 No. Hint: Apply the equation $a_c = \dfrac{4\pi^2 r}{T^2}$.

4-67 Hint: The equation to apply involves x_{MAX}, v_o^2, and g.

4-69 No, as can be shown by the vector subtraction of two velocity vectors, where the final velocity is greater than the initial velocity for a particle moving in a circle of constant radius.

CHAPTER 5

NEWTON'S LAWS OF MOTION

In Chapters 2 to 4, we discussed kinematics (the study of motion) using concepts such as displacement, velocity, and acceleration. However, we did not consider the forces that cause objects to move the way they do. The motions of objects as large as stars or as small as red blood cells are determined by the forces acting on them. A knowledge of forces is essential for an understanding of motions as diverse as the graceful movements of a ballet dancer, the takeoff of an airplane, or the biting action of an animal's jaw. The three basic laws of motion, known as Newton's laws, are used in solving a wide variety of real-world problems in biomechanics, engineering, space science, and a host of other fields. Newton's laws also explain why the lines painted across the road shown in Figure 5-1 are not straight. The study of forces and their effects on the motion of objects is called **dynamics**.

Figure 5-1 *Why aren't the lines straight on this road? (For an explanation, see Section 5.7.)*

5.1 GRAVITY, NORMAL FORCE, FRICTION, AND TENSION

You know intuitively that forces are pushes and pulls, and there are a number of forces that are important to you in your everyday activities. Perhaps the most important is the force of **gravity**, which is a force of attraction between all objects. For an object close to Earth, gravity pulls *vertically downward* toward the centre of Earth. Indeed, the direction of the force of gravity *defines* what we mean by "vertically downward." (Force is a vector quantity, having a magnitude and a direction.) The force of gravity is represented by the symbol $\boldsymbol{F}_G$.[1]

The downward force of gravity is acting on this book right now. However, the book does not actually move downward (unless you drop it). If the book is sitting, say on a table, the table exerts an upward support force that prevents the book from moving downward. This force is called the **normal force**, symbolized as $\boldsymbol{F}_N$. In this context, the word "normal" means "perpendicular" (check it out in your dictionary). The essential feature of the normal force is

---

[1] Recall that in this book a vector will be indicated in boldface type (for example, $\boldsymbol{F}$ for force). The magnitude of a vector is indicated in normal (not boldface) type, such as F for the magnitude of the force vector $\boldsymbol{F}$. The magnitude of a vector can only be positive or zero, never negative. When you are writing the symbol for a vector by hand, it is customary to draw an arrow above the letter; for instance, a force vector would be written as $\vec{F}$.

that it is *perpendicular to the surfaces in contact* with each other, such as the lower surface of the book and the upper surface of the table. Its direction is not necessarily vertical, as shown in Figure 5-2 for a person standing on sloping ground.

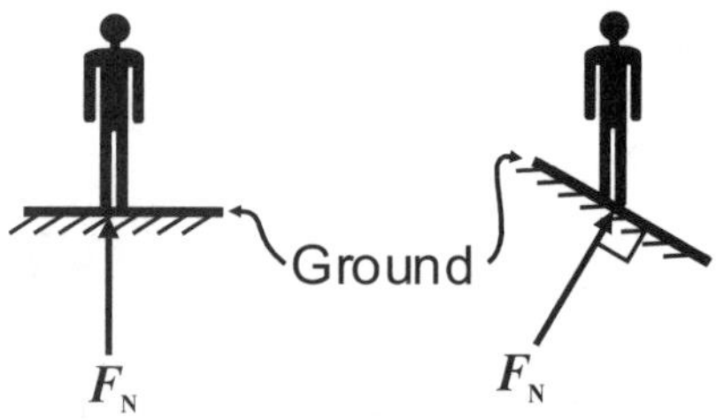

Figure 5-2 *The normal force, F_N, is perpendicular to the surfaces in contact.*

If you push this book across the table, and then stop pushing, the book stops moving fairly quickly. There is a force that opposes the book's motion, namely the **force of friction**, F_f, exerted on the book by the table. Friction is *parallel* to the surfaces in contact. At the molecular level, this force is due to attractive electrical forces between molecules in the book and molecules in the table.

Objects do not have to be moving in order for friction to act. If you push the book, but not hard enough to set it in motion, friction acts in the opposite direction to your push and prevents the book from moving. If an object is stationary and friction is acting, it acts in the opposite direction to the motion that would occur if friction were absent. If an object is moving, friction always acts in the opposite direction to the motion (that is, in the opposite direction to the velocity vector).

In most situations described in this book, we will be discussing the friction between solid objects sliding over one another. However, there is also friction when an object moves through a fluid, such as air or water. This is usually referred to as viscous friction, or air resistance (if the fluid is air). Viscous friction depends on the shape and speed of the object, and on the type of fluid. We will not be discussing this type of friction in detail, but it will be mentioned occasionally.

Often objects are pulled or supported by ropes, strings, or cables. The force exerted by ropes, etc., is called **tension**, represented as $\boldsymbol{T}$. Figure 5-3 shows two people pulling on a rope. From the point of view of person A, the rope is pulling to the right, that is, the tension is to the right. But from the point of view of person B, the tension is to the left. A rope, string or cable always has a tension that pulls *away* from the object that we are considering. The magnitude of the tension is usually the same at each end. Since the tensions exerted on the people in Figure 5-3 have the same magnitude but opposite directions, one tension is shown as $\boldsymbol{T}$ and the other as $-\boldsymbol{T}$.

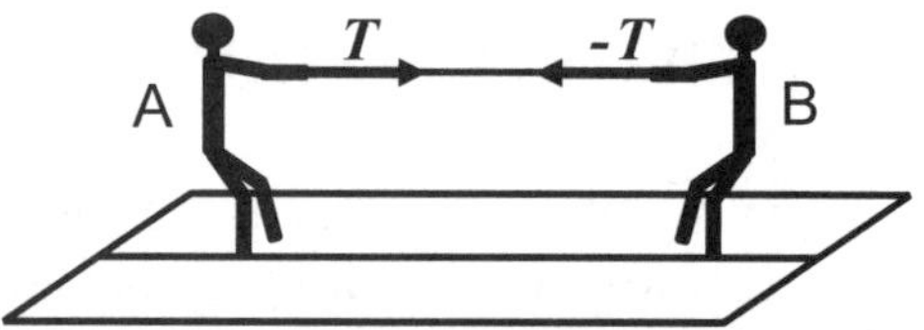

Figure 5-3 *Tension pulls away from the object being considered.*

Notice that in order for an object to experience a normal, friction, or tension force, it must be in direct *contact* with something (floor, rope, etc.) that exerts this force. Pushes and pulls exerted by people also are the result of direct contact. Such forces are often referred to as **contact forces**. However, in order for the force

Did You Know? *There is an old saying in engineering: "You can't push a rope." In other words, ropes can only pull objects — they cannot be used to push things.*

of gravity to act, contact is not required. Can you think of other forces that do not require contact?

Four forces have now been introduced in this section of the book: gravity, normal force, friction, and tension. Table 5-1 lists the symbols used for these forces.

Table 5.1
Symbols Used for Common Forces In This Book

F_G	gravity
F_N	normal force
F_f	friction
T	tension

Free-Body Diagrams

In order to analyze problems involving forces, it is handy to draw a diagram in which only the forces acting on a particular object are shown. Not shown are the object itself nor other objects that are exerting the forces. The object itself is just represented by a large dot. Such a diagram is called a **free-body diagram** or a **force diagram**. Usually the magnitudes of the forces are drawn roughly to scale if the magnitudes of the forces are known. Often the words "free-body diagram" are abbreviated as "**FBD**." Free-body diagrams are illustrated in the following two sample problems.

Sample Problem 5-1

Draw a free-body diagram (FBD) for a crate that is being dragged across the floor by a person pulling on a horizontal rope.

Solution: Before drawing the FBD, it is often useful to make a sketch such as Figure 5-4 (a) to illustrate the situation being described, and to help in identifying the forces involved. We can see in the sketch that the crate is being pulled by the horizontal rope, which means that there is a horizontal tension, T, acting on the crate. This tension is directed away from the crate. Notice that the person pulls on the rope, but does not touch the crate directly. Thus, the person does not exert a force on the crate. (The rope does.)

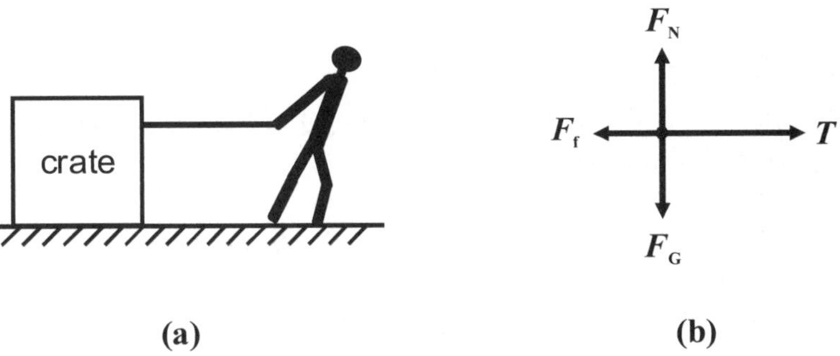

Figure 5-4 (a) *A sketch for Sample Problem 5-1, showing the crate being pulled.*
(b) *The FBD for the crate.*

The crate is also in contact with the floor. The floor exerts a normal force F_N upward on the crate, and a friction force F_f horizontally, in the direction opposite to the tension in the rope.

The final force acting on the crate is the force of gravity $\boldsymbol{F}_G$, acting vertically downward. The four forces acting on the crate are shown on the FBD in Figure 5-4 (b).

Sample Problem 5-2

Draw a FBD for a woman who is standing in an elevator that is moving upward.

Solution: A sketch is shown in Figure 5-5 (a), and the FBD in Figure 5-5 (b). The downward force of gravity $\boldsymbol{F}_G$ is acting on the woman, and the only object that is in contact with the woman is the floor of the elevator, which exerts an upward normal force $\boldsymbol{F}_N$. Since there is nothing in this situation to imply that the woman is being pushed horizontally, there is no friction force exerted by the floor on the woman. Notice that the upward motion of the elevator is not important in determining which forces are acting. Whether the elevator is moving up, standing still, or moving down, the FBD is the same.

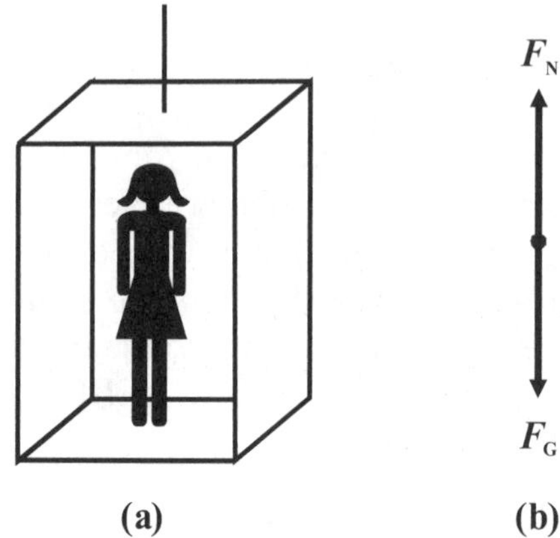

Figure 5-5 **(a)** *A sketch for Sample Problem 5-2.* **(b)** *The FBD for the woman.*

Practice

In questions 5-1 to 5-9 below, make a sketch of the situation, and draw a free-body diagram (FBD) for object A.

5-1 A ball (A) hangs at the end of a vertical string.
5-2 A cheeseburger (A) sits on a table.
5-3 A man (A) is standing in an elevator that is moving downward.
5-4 A red blood cell (A), or erythrocyte, is settling downward in blood plasma. (In addition to the force of gravity, there is an upward buoyant force and an upward fluid friction force.)
5-5 A metal girder (A) is being lifted upward by a cable connected to a crane.
5-6 A hockey puck (A) is sliding on ice.
5-7 A pen (A) is falling, having been knocked off a table. Neglect air resistance.
5-8 A box (A) full of car parts is being hauled across a floor by a person who is pulling on a rope that makes an angle of 30° upward from the horizontal.
5-9 A stove (A) is being pulled up a ramp into a truck by a cable that is parallel to the ramp. The ramp makes an angle of 20° with the horizontal.

5.2 ADDING FORCES

In order to analyze how forces affect the motion of objects, we first need to review how to add vectors. Since forces are vectors, they must be added as vectors. If one child pulls east on a wagon with a force of five newtons, and another child pulls west with a force of five newtons, then the total force is not ten newtons, but rather zero newtons. The SI unit of force is the Newton (N); it will be defined formally in Section 5.3.

The addition of vectors in one dimension, such as the forces on the wagon mentioned above, is straightforward. For vectors in two dimensions, we need to use more complex methods. One technique of adding vectors — discussed in Chapter 3 — is to use a scale diagram in which the vectors are placed head-to-tail in sequence, as shown in Figure 5-6. The tail of force $\boldsymbol{F}_2$ is placed at the head of $\boldsymbol{F}_1$, the tail of force $\boldsymbol{F}_3$ at the head of $\boldsymbol{F}_2$, etc. The total force is a vector drawn from the tail of the first force $\boldsymbol{F}_1$ to the head of the last force $\boldsymbol{F}_4$ in the sequence.

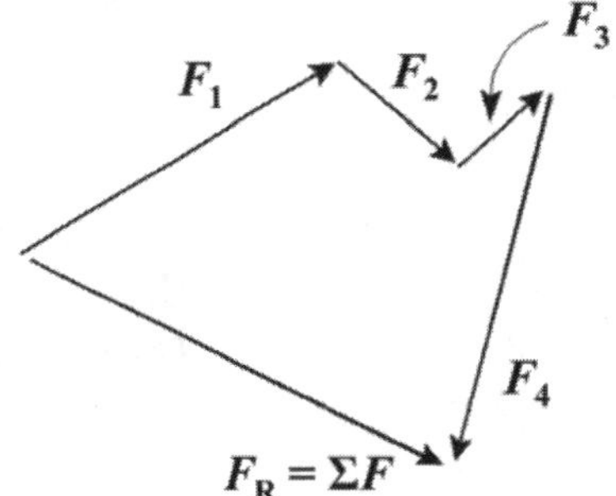

Figure 5-6 *Using a diagram to add forces.*

The total of the forces is given a variety of names: *resultant force, net force, total force, or sum of the forces*. In this book, we will use the term **resultant force**, and will symbolize it as $\boldsymbol{F}_R$ or $\Sigma \boldsymbol{F}$. The Greek capital letter sigma, Σ, means "sum of;" thus, $\Sigma \boldsymbol{F}$ means "sum of the forces."

Although a scale diagram is easy to draw, it does not give particularly accurate results, and components are usually used to add forces accurately. You might wish to review the addition of vectors before proceeding. A reminder: components of a vector are not themselves vectors, but rather are positive or negative numbers with units.

Sample Problem 5-3

At the instant shown in Figure 5-7 (a), two forces are being exerted on a baseball: the force of gravity ($\boldsymbol{F}_G$ = 1.5 N downward), and the force of air resistance ($\boldsymbol{F}_A$ = 0.50 N at an angle of 58° from the vertical). Determine the magnitude and direction of the resultant force on the ball.

Solution: We will use components to find the resultant force. We define the $+x$ axis to be to the left and the $+y$ axis to be downward, as shown in Figure 5-7 (b). Hence, $\boldsymbol{F}_G$ has only a y-component. The x- and y-components of $\boldsymbol{F}_A$ are

$$F_{Ax} = (0.50\text{ N})\sin 58° = 0.42\text{ N}$$
$$F_{Ay} = -(0.50\text{ N})\cos 58° = -0.26\text{ N}$$

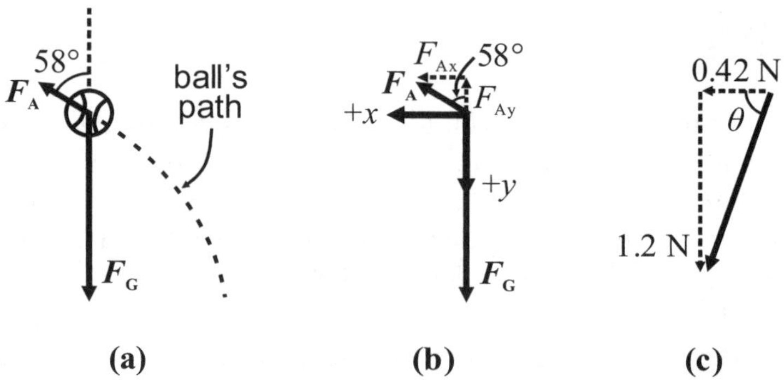

Figure 5-7 (a) *Forces acting on the baseball in Sample Problem 5-3.*
(b) *Components of the forces.*
(c) *The resultant force.*

Since $\boldsymbol{F}_\mathrm{G}$ has no x-component, the x-component of the resultant force, F_{Rx}, is just F_{Ax}:

$$F_{\mathrm{Rx}} = \Sigma F_\mathrm{x} = F_{\mathrm{Ax}} = 0.42\ \mathrm{N}$$

The y-component of the resultant force is

$$F_{\mathrm{Ry}} = \Sigma F_\mathrm{y} = F_\mathrm{G} + F_{\mathrm{Ay}} = (1.5 - 0.26)\,\mathrm{N} = 1.2\ \mathrm{N}$$

Figure 5-7 (c) shows the components of the resultant force, which has a magnitude of

$$F_\mathrm{R} = \sqrt{(0.42\ \mathrm{N})^2 + (1.2\ \mathrm{N})^2} = 1.3\ \mathrm{N}$$

> ***Notation tip:*** *Since $\boldsymbol{F}_\mathrm{G}$ does not have an x-component, the y-component equals the magnitude of the entire force. Hence, in writing the symbol for the y-component of $\boldsymbol{F}_\mathrm{G}$, we have not used F_{Gy}, but rather F_G.*

The direction of $\boldsymbol{F}_\mathrm{R}$ is given by angle θ in Figure 5-7 (c): $\theta = \tan^{-1}(1.2/0.42) = 71°$

Thus, the resultant force is 1.3 N at an angle of 71° from the horizontal.

Practice

<u>5-10</u> The force of gravity on a book is 19 N downward. When the book is being held stationary by a person's hand, the hand is providing a force of 19 N upward on the book.
(a) What is the magnitude of the resultant force on the book?
(b) If the hand is suddenly removed, what are the magnitude and direction of the resultant force on the book? (Neglect air resistance.)

In questions 5-11 to 5-15, determine the magnitude and direction of the resultant force on object A.

5-11 A skydiver (A) in free-fall experiences:
(a) a downward force of gravity of 586 N, and an upward force of air resistance of 492 N
(b) a force of gravity of 586 N downward, and air resistance of 586 N upward.
[Ans. (a) 94 N downward (b) 0 N]

5-12 A toboggan (A) is being pulled along a horizontal snow-covered field by a person exerting a force of 72 N horizontally. In the opposite direction, there is a horizontal friction force on the toboggan of magnitude 69 N. The force of gravity on the toboggan is 153 N in magnitude, and the normal force exerted by the snow on the toboggan has a magnitude of 153 N. [Ans. 3 N horizontally forward]

5-13 A soaring bird (A) is subject to three forces at a particular moment: the downward force of gravity (3.27 N), a horizontal air resistance drag force (0.354 N), and an upward lift force (3.74 N). [Ans. 0.59 N at 53° up from horizontal]

5-14 A long-jumper (A) at landing (Figure 5-8) experiences two forces: the force of gravity (F_G = 538 N), and the force exerted by the ground on her feet (F_{FEET} = 6382 N). Air resistance is negligible in comparison with these forces. (Note that the actual force exerted by the ground on the feet of a world-class jumper would be several times the value used in this problem.) [Ans. 6.15×10^3 N at 23.9° above horizontal]

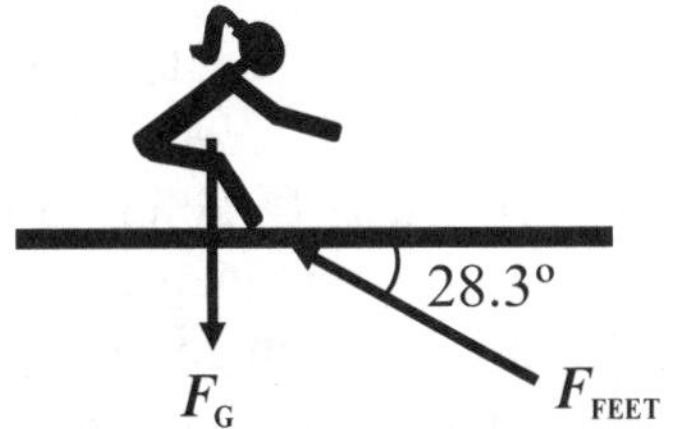

Figure 5-8 *Question 5-14. (Forces not to scale.)*

5-15 A quarterback (A) is hit simultaneously by two linebackers. The forces exerted by each linebacker are: horizontal, 412 N, 27.0° west of north; and horizontal, 478 N, 54.0° east of north. The force of gravity and the normal force exerted on the quarterback are equal in magnitude. Neglect friction.
[Ans. 678 N at 17.1° east of north]

5-16 A refrigerator is being moved along a horizontal floor by one person pulling on a rope that exerts a force of 252 N east, and by another person pushing east with a force of unknown magnitude. There is a friction force of 412 N west, and the force of gravity on the refrigerator and the normal force each have a magnitude of 1127 N. If the resultant force on the refrigerator is 2 N east, what is the magnitude of the unknown force? [Ans. 162 N]

5-17 A large crate is pulled across an icy sidewalk by two people pulling horizontally on ropes (Figure 5-9). The tension $\boldsymbol{T}_1$ in one of the ropes is 27 N east, and the resultant horizontal force on the crate due to the two rope tensions is 56 N at 16° south of east. Neglect friction. Determine the magnitude and direction of the tension $\boldsymbol{T}_2$ in the other rope. [Ans. 31 N at 30° south of east]

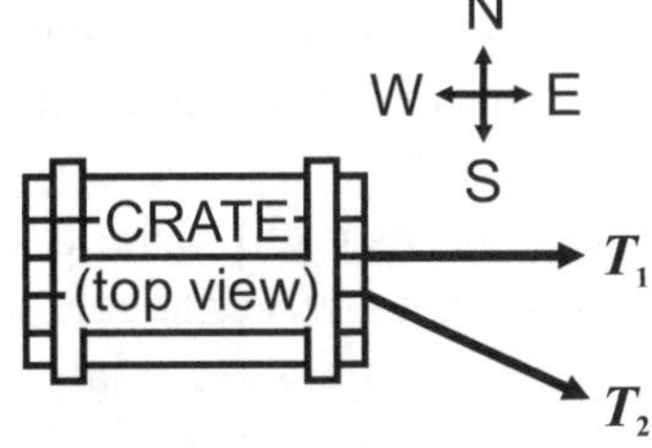

Figure 5-9 *Question 5-17.*

5-18 Figure 5-10 shows the three main forces acting on a horizontal forearm. The force of gravity, $\boldsymbol{F}_G$, has a magnitude of 12.0 N. The force exerted by the biceps muscle, $\boldsymbol{F}_B$, is 122 N at an angle of 72.0° relative to the horizontal. The force exerted by the humerus (the bone in the upper arm), $\boldsymbol{F}_H$, is 111 N at 70.1° relative to the horizontal. Define the $+x$ direction to be horizontal (either left or right), and the $+y$ direction to be vertical (either up or down). Using components in these directions, determine the magnitude of the resultant force on the forearm. (Be careful with significant digits.)
[Ans. 0 N (considering significant digits)]

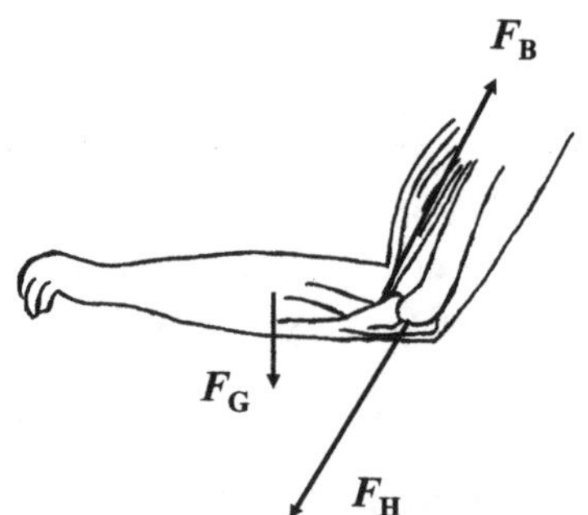

Figure 5-10 *Forces acting on the forearm in question 5-18. (Not to scale.)*

5.3 NEWTON'S SECOND LAW OF MOTION

In 1687, Sir Isaac Newton (1642-1727) published one of the greatest scientific works of all time, the *Philosophiae Naturalis Principia Mathematica (Mathematical Principles of Natural Philosophy)*, usually referred to simply as the *Principia*. In this book, the results of the work of Newton and other scientists (called natural philosophers at that time) were compiled, including Newton's famous three laws of motion and his law of universal gravitation. The *Principia* was the culmination of centuries of thought concerning the motion of objects, from earthly ones such as falling apples to astronomical ones such as orbiting planets, and represented a huge step forward in our understanding of the workings of the universe.

The remainder of this chapter deals with Newton's laws of motion. We discuss his second law first. It might seem odd that Newton's first law is not treated right away, but as will be seen in the next section, Newton's first law is just a special case of his second law.

Newton's second law of motion relates the resultant force exerted on an object to the acceleration of the object. This law states:

> **If the resultant force on an object is not zero, the object experiences an acceleration in the direction of the resultant force. The magnitude of the acceleration is proportional to the magnitude of the resultant force, and inversely proportional to the mass of the object.**

This law should make intuitive sense to you. For a given object, if a larger resultant force is applied, then a larger acceleration results. For example, if you push this book across a table, then the harder you push, the larger is the acceleration of the book. For a given resultant force applied to a variety of objects, then the larger the mass of an object, the smaller is its acceleration. A given resultant force applied to a box of books produces a smaller acceleration than the same resultant force applied to a single book. A truck needs a bigger engine than a small car to get the same (or less) acceleration. With the bigger engine, a larger force can be applied to accelerate the more massive truck.

To write this law mathematically, we start with the proportionalities stated in the law:

$$a \propto F_{\mathrm{R}} \quad \text{and} \quad a \propto \frac{1}{m}$$

Combining these two proportionalities, $\quad a \propto \dfrac{F_{\mathrm{R}}}{m}$

The constant of proportionality is conventionally chosen to be one, so that we can now write

$$a = \frac{F_{\mathrm{R}}}{m}$$

Including the directions of the vectors, that is, writing the symbols for force and acceleration in boldface type, we have

$$\boldsymbol{a} = \frac{\boldsymbol{F}_{\mathrm{R}}}{m}$$

This is usually arranged with the force on the left-hand side:

$$\boldsymbol{F}_{\mathrm{R}} = m\boldsymbol{a} \quad \text{or} \quad \Sigma\boldsymbol{F} = m\boldsymbol{a} \qquad \textbf{(5-1)}$$

which is the customary way in which Newton's second law is written. For problem-solving, this relationship is most useful in terms of components:

$$\Sigma F_{\mathrm{x}} = ma_{\mathrm{x}} \quad \text{and} \quad \Sigma F_{\mathrm{y}} = ma_{\mathrm{y}} \qquad \textbf{(5-2)}$$

This law governs the motion of all macroscopic objects with which you are familiar: airplanes, planets, rivers, people, etc. It also works at the microscopic level of biological cells and small organisms such as amoebas. (It generally does not work at the level of molecules, atoms, nuclei and subatomic particles — in this realm, a different set of rules called quantum mechanics is needed instead of the Newtonian mechanics that we are discussing.)

We are now in a position to define the SI unit of force – the newton. **A newton (N) is the magnitude of force that, if applied to an object of mass 1 kg, will produce an acceleration of magnitude 1 m/s^2.** By substituting units into both sides of $F_{\mathrm{R}} = ma$, we see that 1 N is the same as 1 kg·m/s^2.

Gravitational Acceleration and Force

If you drop a pencil, a comb, or any object near the surface of Earth, it falls with a downward acceleration of approximately 9.8 m/s^2 (if air resistance is neglected). This acceleration is due solely to the force of gravity acting on the object. If an apple of mass 0.10 kg is free-falling with an acceleration of 9.8 m/s^2 downward, then by Newton's second law, the force of gravity (in this case, the resultant force) on the apple is just:

$$\begin{aligned} \boldsymbol{F}_{\text{G}} = \boldsymbol{F}_{\text{R}} &= m\boldsymbol{a} \\ &= (0.10\ \text{kg})((9.8\ \text{m/s}^2\ \text{downward}) \\ &= 0.98\ \text{kg}\cdot\text{m/s}^2\ \text{downward} \\ &= 0.98\ \text{N downward} \end{aligned}$$

This force of gravity is the same whether the apple is falling or not. If the apple is hanging on a tree, the force of gravity on it is still 0.98 N downward. Newton's second law gives us a method for determining the force of gravity on an object no matter what the object is doing, as long as the object is near the surface of Earth. All we need to do is multiply the object's mass by the acceleration due to gravity, $\boldsymbol{g}$, and we have the force of gravity on the object:

$$\boldsymbol{F}_{\text{G}} = m\boldsymbol{g} \quad \text{(force of gravity)} \tag{5-3}$$

Notice that Eqn. 5-3 is a vector equation; the force of gravity is downward, in the same direction as the acceleration due to gravity. The magnitude of this force is simply mg.

For objects such as satellites or spaceships that are not near Earth's surface, the force of gravity cannot be calculated in this way. Gravity far from Earth's surface, and gravity due to other planets and the sun, are discussed in Chapter 9.

The magnitude of the acceleration due to gravity is not a constant value of 9.8 m/s^2 at all points on Earth's surface. (The variability is due to Earth's non-spherical shape and non-uniform density; more details are provided in Chapter 9.) Thus, the force of gravity on a given object is not quite constant over Earth's surface. However, when solving problems in this book, assume that the gravitational acceleration at Earth's surface has a constant magnitude of 9.80 m/s^2, unless indicated otherwise.

The gravitational force on an object is sometimes referred to as the object's **weight**. Unfortunately, the term "weight" is often used in everyday conversation in place of "mass." For example, some people might say that the weight of an apple is 0.10 kg, when in fact this is the apple's mass. In this book, we will normally use the unambiguous "force of gravity" or "gravitational force," instead of "weight."

Contrary to popular belief, it is easy to lose or gain weight. To lose weight, all you need to do is go to a place such as a mountain top, where the force of gravity is smaller, and your weight will be smaller! To gain weight, go to sea-level, where gravity is larger. Regrettably, these manoeuvres have no effect on your mass.

Practice

5-19 A horizontal force is applied to a hockey puck of mass 0.15 kg at rest on ice. (Neglect friction.) If the magnitude of the resulting acceleration of the puck is 32 m/s^2, what is the magnitude of the force? [Ans. 4.8 N]

5-20 Magnetic forces are used to alter the direction of motion of the electron beam(s) in TVs that have picture tubes. If a magnetic force of magnitude 3.20×10^{-15} N is exerted on an electron (mass $m_e = 9.11 \times 10^{-31}$ kg), what is the magnitude of the resulting acceleration? [Ans. 3.51×10^{15} m/s^2]

5-21 A ball is thrown vertically upward. Neglect air resistance. On the way up, after the ball has left the thrower's hand,
(a) what is the direction of the acceleration of the ball?
(b) what is the magnitude of this acceleration?
(c) what is the direction of the resultant force on the ball?
(d) Repeat parts (a) - (c) when the ball is at the top of its path.
(e) Repeat parts (a) - (c) when the ball is on the way down.

5-22 A baseball is thrown from an outfielder to an infielder. Neglect air resistance. (Therefore, the trajectory will be parabolic.) Before the ball has reached its maximum height,
(a) what is the direction of the acceleration of the ball?
(b) what is the magnitude of this acceleration?
(c) what is the direction of the resultant force on the ball?
(d) Repeat parts (a) - (c) when the ball is at its maximum height.
(e) Repeat parts (a) - (c) after the ball has reached its maximum height.

5-23 (a) A constant resultant force is applied to various masses. Sketch the shape of a graph of the magnitude of the resulting acceleration vs. mass.
(b) A variable resultant force is applied to a constant mass. Sketch the shape of the graph of the magnitude of the resulting acceleration vs. the magnitude of the resultant force.

5-24 What is the magnitude of the force of gravity on a book of mass 2.45 kg? [Ans. 24.0 N]

5-25 Determine the mass (in grams) of a pencil if the magnitude of the force of gravity on it is 0.118 N. [Ans. 12.0 g]

5-26 The molar mass of Infectious Pancreatic Necrosis Virus (IPNV), which is a trout virus, is 5.4×10^7 g/mol. Determine the magnitude of the force of gravity on one IPNV particle. Avogadro's number is 6.02×10^{23} mol^{-1}. [Ans. 8.8×10^{-19} N]

5-27 The force of gravity on a 3.5 kg rock on Mars is 13 N in magnitude. What is the magnitude of the gravitational acceleration on Mars? [Ans. 3.7 m/s^2]

5-28 On Venus, the magnitude of the acceleration due to gravity is 8.9 m/s^2. If you were to travel to Venus, by what percentage would the magnitude of the force of gravity on you change? [Ans. 9% (decrease)]

5.4 NEWTON'S FIRST LAW OF MOTION

In Section 5.3, Newton's second law of motion was presented: an object on which there is a resultant force experiences an acceleration in the direction of the resultant force. The magnitude of this acceleration is proportional to the magnitude of the resultant force and inversely proportional to the object's mass. What if the resultant force is zero? According to Newton's second law, the object's acceleration is zero. Hence, the object's velocity must be constant, that is, the object travels in a straight line at constant speed. (A special case of this situation is a constant speed of zero, in other words, the object is at rest.)

This particular circumstance of zero resultant force, zero acceleration, and constant velocity, discussed above using Newton's second law, is usually presented in a separate law, namely **Newton's first law of motion**, which deals with objects that experience no resultant force. It states:

> **If the resultant force on an object is zero, the object travels in a straight line at constant speed (which could be zero).**

At first glance, this law might seem surprising to you. You know that if you stop exerting a force on something, say a table that you have been pushing across the floor, it does *not* continue moving in a straight line at constant speed. It slows down and comes to rest. However, it comes to rest only because there has been a resultant force acting on it, namely the force of friction. If you push an object across a very smooth surface such as ice, and then stop pushing, it takes a long time for the object to come to rest because the force of friction is small. If you could reduce the force of friction to zero, so that the resultant force would be zero, then the object would continue traveling indefinitely in a straight line at constant speed. We are more accustomed to objects being at rest (that is, having a constant speed of zero), if they are subject to no resultant force. Being at rest is just a special case of the more general situation in which objects have a constant non-zero speed in a straight line.

You have experienced many examples of Newton's first law in your everyday life. For example, when you are standing on a moving bus or subway train and the brakes are suddenly applied, you lurch forward. The brakes slow down the bus or train, but your body tends to continue to move forward at constant speed. Normally this forward motion is soon stopped by the force of friction between your feet and the floor, or by a force exerted because you are holding on to a post or handle. Imagine what would happen if you wore roller skates on a bus! Because the skates provide very little friction, when the bus slows down, you would roll forward down the aisle until you collided with something (the windshield, for instance) that would stop you. In a car, seatbelts are used to stop your forward motion when the brakes are applied.

You can easily demonstrate Newton's first law yourself with a coin and playing card. If you place the coin on the card which is projecting somewhat over the edge of a table, and then flick the card horizontally with your finger, the card will move across the table and the coin will stay essentially in place. As the card moves, it exerts only a small force on the coin for a very short time. Thus the resultant force on the coin is virtually zero and it stays at rest. (However, if you measure the position of the coin carefully, you will find that it has indeed moved somewhat because of the force – friction – exerted by the card.) The old "magician's" trick of pulling a tablecloth out from under a set of dishes on a table is similar. The dishes remain essentially at rest because the force exerted by the tablecloth is small and acts for only a short time. By the way, this trick is best left to magicians; don't try it with family-heirloom dishes!

The fact that objects continue moving with constant velocity or stay at rest (if there is no resultant force) is sometimes described by assigning a property to matter called **inertia**. Thus we say that an object's inertia is what keeps it moving or at rest. Newton's first law is sometimes called **the law of inertia**. In a sense, this law should really be called Galileo's Law, because it was discovered by Galileo Galilei (1564-1642), who performed a number of experiments on the motion of objects. Galileo was the first true experimental scientist. He studied nature not by just thinking about it, as people had done before him, but rather by doing careful experiments and analyzing the results mathematically.

Sample Problem 5-4

A fish of mass 1.23 kg is swimming with a constant velocity of 0.56 m/s at an angle of 37° up from the horizontal. What is the resultant force on the fish?

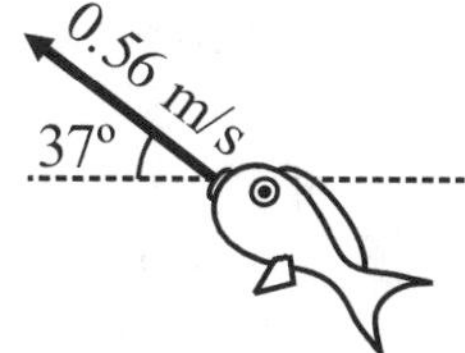

Figure 5-11 *The resultant force is zero on a fish swimming at constant velocity.*

Solution: The key phrase in this problem is "constant velocity." If the fish is swimming at constant velocity, then by Newton's first law the resultant force on the fish must be zero. This conclusion is true regardless of the detailed nature of the many forces acting on the fish: gravity, viscous friction, buoyant force, etc. The vector sum of all these forces must be zero in order for the fish to swim at constant velocity (Figure 5-11).

Sample Problem 5-5

A woman exerts a force of 7.5 N upward on her purse, and as a result it moves upward at constant velocity. What is the magnitude of the force of gravity on the purse?

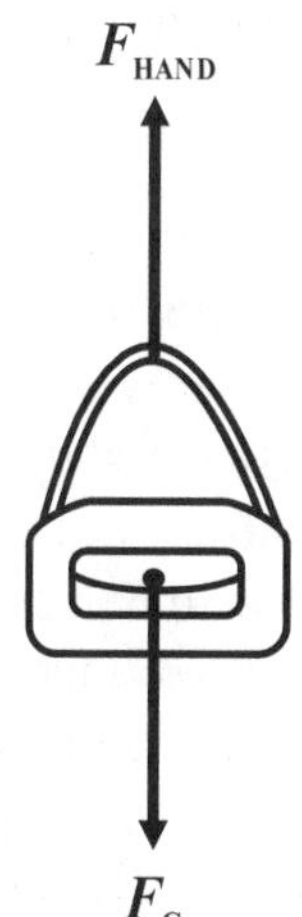

Figure 5-12 *The forces on the purse in Sample Problem 5-5.*

Solution: Figure 5-12 shows the two forces exerted on the purse: $\boldsymbol{F}_{HAND}$ exerted by the woman, and the downward force of gravity $\boldsymbol{F}_G$. Because we are told that the purse moves at constant velocity, we know that the resultant force must be zero. Therefore, the upward force and the downward force must have equal magnitudes. Since the upward force has a given magnitude of 7.5 N, then the downward force of gravity also has a magnitude of 7.5 N.

Practice

In questions 5-29 to 5-36 below, is the resultant force on object A zero?

5-29 A hamburger (A) is sitting on a table.

5-30 A red blood cell (A) is settling at a constant velocity of 4 mm/h downward in blood plasma.

5-31 An egg (A) is falling toward the ground, having fallen from a table.

5-32 A skydiver (A) is falling at "terminal speed," i.e., is falling downward at a constant speed.

5-33 A hawk (A) of mass 2.12 kg is diving with a constant velocity of 10.6 m/s at an angle of 25.3° below the horizontal.

5-34 A marble (A) tied to the end of a string swings back and forth as a pendulum.

5-35 Earth (A) travels at constant speed in a circular orbit around the sun. (In actual fact, the speed is not quite constant, and the orbit is not quite a circle, but they are close.)

5-36 A girl (A) is standing on a moving escalator that is half-way between the floors in a department store. The escalator is moving at constant velocity.

5-37 A man is trying to push a table across a carpeted floor. He is exerting a horizontal force of 35 N, but the table is not moving. What are the magnitude and direction of the friction force exerted by the floor on the table? [Ans. 35 N, opposite to boy's push]

5-38 A book of mass 1.3 kg is sitting on a table. What is the magnitude of the normal force exerted by the table on the book? [Ans. 13 N]

5-39 (a) A metal beam is hanging at rest from a vertical cable on a crane. If the magnitude of the tension in the cable is 2.57×10^4 N, what is the mass of the beam?
(b) If the same beam is being moved upward by the cable with a constant speed of 0.78 m/s, what is the magnitude of the tension in the cable?
[Ans. (a) 2.62×10^3 kg (b) 2.57×10^4 N]

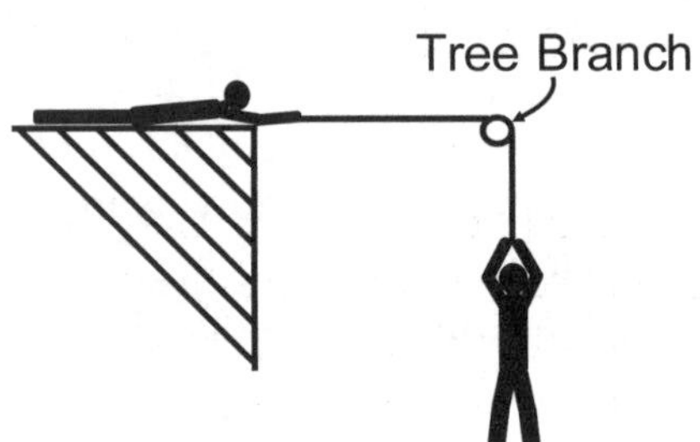

Figure 5-13 *Question 5-40.*

5-40 In Figure 5-13, one person is lying flat, holding a rope that passes horizontally to a tree branch, then over the branch and downward to a friend who is hanging onto the lower end of the rope. There is negligible friction on the tree branch, and hence the

branch only changes the direction of the rope, but does not affect the magnitude of its tension. The force of gravity on the hanging person has a magnitude of 108 N, and the people and rope are stationary. (a) Draw a FBD for the hanging person, and determine the magnitude of the tension in the rope.
(b) Draw a FBD for the other person, and determine the magnitude of the friction force acting on this person.
[Ans. (a) 108 N (b) 108 N]

5-41 Three spheres are hung by light threads to form a holiday decoration (Figure 5-14). The magnitudes of the force of gravity on spheres A, B, and C are 21 N, 15 N, and 11 N, respectively.
(a) Draw a FBD for sphere C, and determine the magnitude of the tension in the lowest thread.
(b) Repeat for sphere B and the tension in the middle thread.
(c) Repeat for A and the highest thread.
[Ans. (a) 11 N (b) 26 N (c) 47 N]

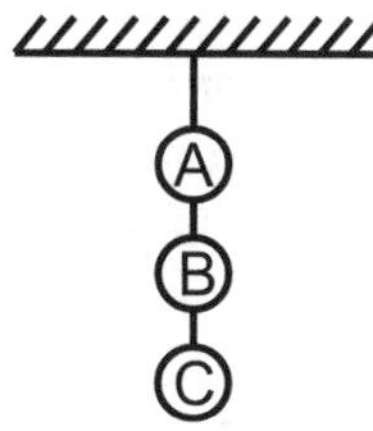

Figure 5-14
Question 5-41.

5-42 A large protein molecule having molar mass 4.1×10^{13} g/mol is sedimenting downward with constant velocity in water. In addition to the force of gravity acting on the molecule, there is an upward buoyant force of magnitude 5.13×10^{-13} N, and an upward fluid friction force. What is the magnitude of the fluid friction force? Avogadro's number is 6.02×10^{23} mol^{-1}.
[Ans. 1.5×10^{-13} N]

5.5 SOLVING PROBLEMS USING NEWTON'S FIRST AND SECOND LAWS

Newton's first and second laws of motion can be used in solving a wide variety of real-world problems in engineering, biomechanics, aerodynamics, astronomy, sports, space missions to other planets, etc. The simplest problems to deal with are those in which the forces are constant during the times of interest. Most of the problems that you will be asked to solve in this book are of the constant-force type. However, in research and industry today, many problems requiring Newton's second law involve complicated forces that are not constant over time. Computers are used to analyze these problems by considering the motion in a series of extremely short time intervals, during each of which the forces can be considered to be approximately constant. The motion of the object (spaceprobe, long-jumper, etc.) can then be determined for each interval and the complete motion worked out.

Because of the enormous variety of possible problems that can be solved using Newton's first and second laws, it is useful to employ a systematic approach that can be used to solve many problems in this area. By using the approach outlined below, you should be able to tackle new problems with confidence.

***Problem-Solving Approach*:**

1. Read the problem carefully. Check the definitions of words about which you are uncertain.
2. Make a diagram on which you include all relevant information, including any numerical values given.
3. Identify the object (or group of objects) whose motion is important.
4. Make a free-body diagram (FBD) for that object (or group). Be careful to use *only the forces acting on that object* (group). For simple problems, you can sometimes skip the diagram in step 2 and proceed directly to the FBD.
5. On your FBD, label an x-y co-ordinate system in which either the $+x$-direction or $+y$-direction is in the *direction that the object (group) is actually accelerating.* The other positive direction (if needed) is chosen at right angles to this direction. This choice of co-ordinate system means that the acceleration will have a positive component along one axis and a component of zero along the other axis, thus making the solution *much* easier.
6. Determine the x- and y-components of all known forces on your FBD.
7. Write down $\Sigma F_x = ma_x$ and/or $\Sigma F_y = ma_y$. On the next line of your solution, replace ΣF_x and/or ΣF_y with a list summing the appropriate x- and y-components of all the forces acting. On the right-hand side, replace m with the appropriate mass symbol for the problem (for example, m_1). If the object is not accelerating in the x (or y) direction, then write $a_x = 0$ (or $a_y = 0$), that is, use Newton's first law in this direction.
8. Repeat steps 3-7 for other objects (or groups) as necessary.
9. Use algebra to solve the resulting equations for the unknown(s). It is easier to do the algebra first and then substitute known numbers, rather than substituting numbers first, especially if you have to redo your work after making a mistake.
10. Substitute the known quantities and calculate the unknowns.
11. Check your answers. Are they reasonable? (For example, if you calculate the mass of a bird to be 757 kg, you know there must be a mistake somewhere.) Have you included the appropriate units in your answers?

Sample Problem 5-6

During the takeoff of a space shuttle, the acceleration is about 0.50 g upward. The mass of the shuttle (including fuel, etc.) is approximately 2.0×10^6 kg. Determine the approximate magnitude of the upward force on the shuttle, i.e., the thrust due to the rockets.

Solution: After reading the problem carefully, we draw a diagram such as Figure 5-15 (a), transposing all the information from the problem to the diagram. Since it is the motion of the shuttle that is important, we then draw a

Did You Know? *At takeoff, more than 85% of a space shuttle's mass consists of fuel. This means that the maximum acceleration does not occur at takeoff, when the mass is very large, but later when most of the fuel has been used and the mass is much smaller.*

FBD for the shuttle (Figure 5-15 (b)). At takeoff, since air resistance is negligible at low speeds, the only forces are the force of gravity and the upward rocket thrust.

The acceleration of the shuttle is upward; therefore, we choose the $+y$-direction to be upward. This is simply a convenience so that the acceleration of the shuttle will have a positive value. There is a smaller chance of mistakes if negative numbers can be avoided.

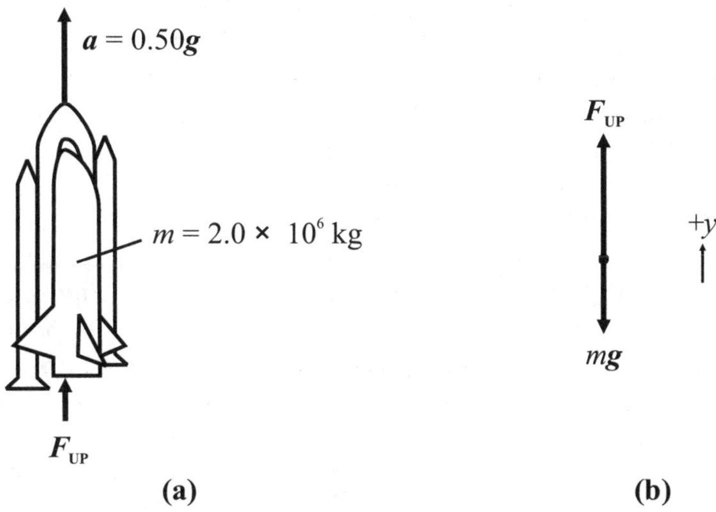

Figure 5-15 **(a)** *Diagram for Sample Problem 5-6.* **(b)** *FBD for shuttle.*

We now write Newton's second law in the y-direction: $\Sigma F_y = ma_y$

On the left-hand side of this equation, add all the forces: $F_{UP} + (-mg) = ma_y$

Re-arrange to solve for the unknown F_{UP} : $F_{UP} = mg + ma_y$

$$= m(g + a_y)$$

Substitute known values (recall that the upward acceleration is given: $a_y = 0.50\ g = 4.9\ \text{m/s}^2$):

$$F_{UP} = (2.0 \times 10^6\ \text{kg})\ ((9.80 + 4.9)\ \text{m/s}^2)$$
$$= 2.9 \times 10^7\ \text{N}$$

> ***Units Tip:*** *Mass in kg multiplied by acceleration in m/s^2 gives force in $kg{\cdot}m/s^2$, which is a newton (N).*

Thus, the upward thrust is approximately 2.9×10^7 N in magnitude.

Sample Problem 5-7

A box is being dragged at constant velocity across a horizontal floor by a person pulling on a horizontal rope. The magnitudes of the tension in the rope and the force of gravity on the box are 6.05 N and 21.3 N, respectively. Determine the magnitudes of: (a) the normal force on the box, and (b) the friction force on the box.

Solution: (a) Figure 5-16 (a) shows a sketch of the situation, and Figure 5-16 (b) presents a FBD for the box.

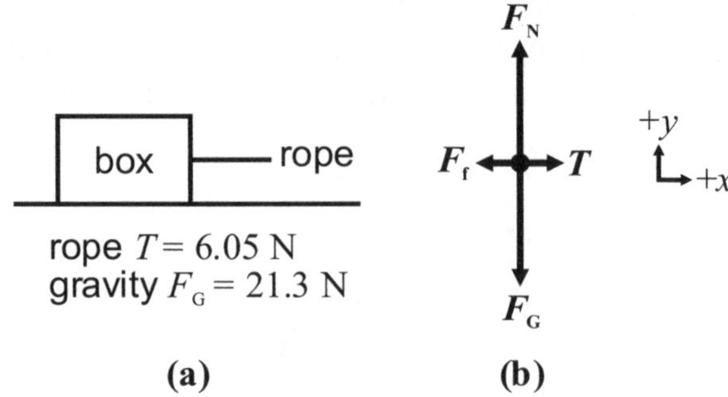

Figure 5-16
(a) *Diagram for Sample Problem 5-7.*
(b) *FBD for box.*

Since the box is moving at constant horizontal velocity, the horizontal acceleration and horizontal resultant force must be zero.

In the vertical direction, the box has no motion, that is, its vertical velocity is constant at zero, and hence the vertical acceleration and resultant force are both zero.

If we define an *x-y* co-ordinate system as shown in Figure 5-16 (b), we have:

$$\Sigma F_x = 0 \quad \text{and} \quad \Sigma F_y = 0$$

In order to use these equations, we need to resolve the forces in the problem into *x*- and *y*-components. In this particular problem, tension and friction each have only an *x*-component, and gravity and the normal force each have only a *y*-component.

In part (a), we are asked to find the magnitude of the normal force, which has only a *y*-component, so we use $\Sigma F_y = 0$.

> ***Notation Tip:***
> *Remember that F_G is the magnitude of the force $\mathbf{F_G}$ and therefore is positive. Since the +y direction is upward, then the y-component of the downward force $\mathbf{F_G}$ is negative and is written as $-F_G$.*

This gives $F_N + (-F_G) = 0$

Therefore, $F_N = F_G = 21.3$ N

Thus, the magnitude of the normal force is 21.3 N.

(b) Now use $\Sigma F_x = 0$ to find the friction force.

$$T + (-F_f) = 0$$

Thus, $F_f = T = 6.05$ N

Therefore, the magnitude of the friction force is 6.05 N.

Sample Problem 5-8

Two sleighs are connected by a horizontal rope, and the front sleigh is pulled by another horizontal rope with tension of magnitude 5.39 N. The sleigh masses are: front, 5.72 kg; rear, 6.89 kg. If the sleighs move on a horizontal frozen lake on which friction is negligible, determine the magnitudes of: (a) the acceleration of the sleighs, and (b) the tension in the connecting rope.

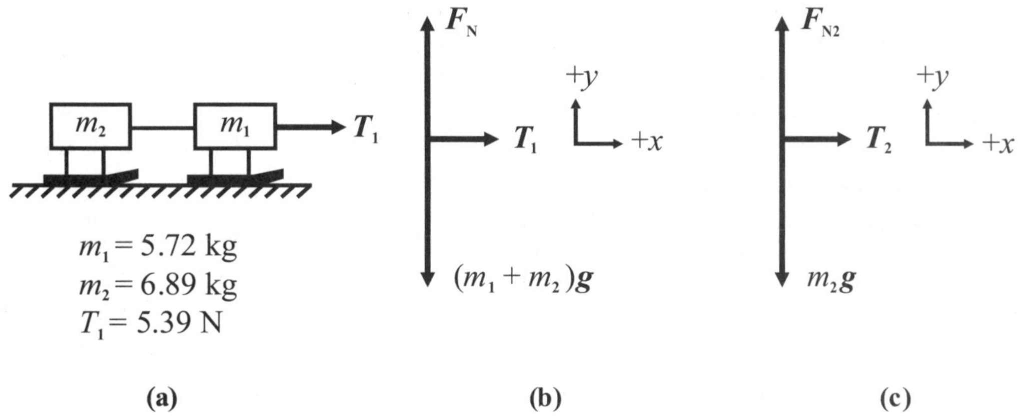

Figure 5-17 **(a)** *Diagram for Sample Problem 5-8.*
(b) *FBD for the two sleighs together.*
(c) *FBD for rear sleigh.*

Solution: (a) This problem illustrates how important the selection of object(s) for FBDs can be. Figure 5-17 (a) shows a diagram for the problem. Since we are asked first to determine the acceleration of the sleighs, we choose our FBD object to be the two sleighs together. The fact that the sleighs have the same acceleration (magnitude and direction) allows us to consider the sleighs as one object. The FBD is shown in Figure 5-17 (b). It shows the total gravitational force $(m_1 + m_2)\boldsymbol{g}$, the horizontal tension $\boldsymbol{T}_1$, and the total normal force $\boldsymbol{F}_N$ acting on the two sleighs.

Notice that the tension in the connecting rope is not shown. It pulls to the right on the rear sleigh and to the left on the front sleigh, and thus for the two sleighs considered together, there is no net contribution from this tension. Recall that tension pulls away from whatever object we are considering.

Since the sleighs accelerate to the right, the +*x*-direction is chosen to the right. We know that there will be no acceleration in the *y*-direction (the sleighs do not fly into the air, nor sink into the ground), and therefore we need to use only:

$$\Sigma F_x = ma_x$$

The only force with an *x*-component is $\boldsymbol{T}_1$, and the mass $m = m_1 + m_2$.

Therefore, $$T_1 = (m_1 + m_2)a_x$$

Solving for the unknown a_x :

$$a_x = \frac{T_1}{m_1 + m_2}$$

Substituting known values:

$$a_x = \frac{5.39\text{ N}}{(5.72 + 6.89)\text{ kg}} = 0.427\text{ m/s}^2$$

Thus, the magnitude of the acceleration of the sleighs is 0.427 m/s^2.

(b) In order to determine the tension in the connecting rope, we need to use Newton's second law for one of the sleighs by itself. The only horizontal force acting on the rear sleigh is the tension in the connecting rope to the right, which we designate as $\boldsymbol{T}_2$. For the front sleigh, there are two horizontal forces, $\boldsymbol{T}_1$ and $-\boldsymbol{T}_2$, and therefore it will be easier to choose the rear sleigh for our FBD (Figure 5-17 (c)). Use Newton's second law:

$$\Sigma F_x = ma_x$$

Since $\boldsymbol{T}_2$ is the only force with an x-component, and $m = m_2$:

$$T_2 = m_2 a_x = (6.89\text{ kg})(0.427\text{ m/s}^2) = 2.94\text{ N}$$

Therefore, the magnitude of the tension in the connecting rope is 2.94 N. You should check that you can also arrive at this answer by using a FBD for the front sleigh.

Sample Problem 5-9

Two children, of masses 35 kg and 45 kg, are hanging vertically from opposite ends of a rope that passes over a fixed horizontal metal rod in a playground. If friction between the rope and rod is neglected, what are the magnitudes of:
(a) the acceleration of the children?
(b) the tension in the rope?
(c) If the children start from rest, how far will each of them travel in 0.50 s?

Solution: (a) A general diagram is given in Figure 5-18 (a). The child having the larger mass will accelerate downward, and the other child will accelerate upward. The accelerations of the two masses have the same magnitude (since they are connected by a single rope), but opposite directions. Because of the opposite directions of the accelerations, it is not appropriate to consider the masses as one object, and we draw a FBD for each mass (Figures 5-18 (b) and (c)).

Since the smaller mass accelerates upward, we choose its $+y$-direction upward (Figure 5-18 (b)). For the larger mass, its acceleration is downward and hence the $+y$-direction is chosen downward for this mass (Figure 5-18 (c)). This approach might seem unusual to you, but it ensures that the *y*-component of acceleration of *each* child will be positive, and we will be able to set these *y*-components equal as the solution proceeds.

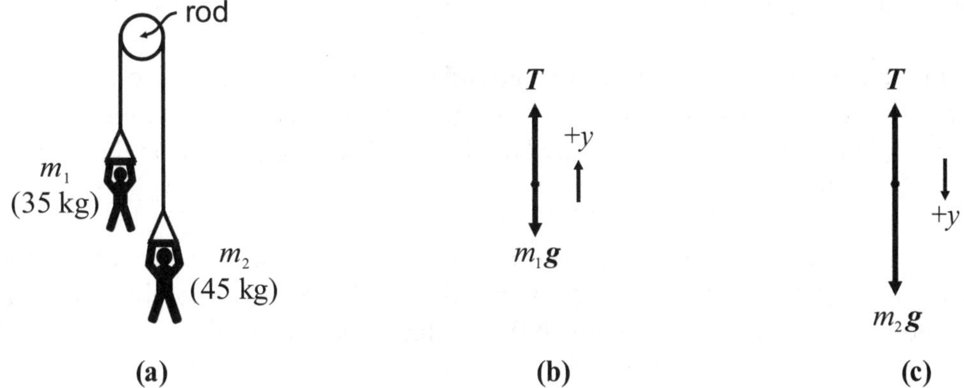

Figure 5-18 (a) *Diagram for Sample Problem 5-9.* **(b)** *FBD for smaller mass.* **(c)** *FBD for larger mass.*

We now use Newton's second law for the smaller child:

$$\Sigma F_y = ma_y$$

Thus,

$$T + (-m_1 g) = m_1 a_y$$

For the larger mass, using $\Sigma F_y = ma_y$ gives

$$m_2 g + (-T) = m_2 a_y$$

Since m_1 and m_2 are known, we now have two equations in two unknowns (a_y and T) that can be solved.

To solve the equations, first add them to eliminate T and then re-arrange to find a_y:

Adding and re-arranging,

$$m_2 g - m_1 g = m_1 a_y + m_2 a_y$$
$$(m_2 - m_1)g = (m_1 + m_2)a_y$$

This gives

$$a_y = \frac{(m_2 - m_1)g}{m_1 + m_2}$$

Substituting known values:

$$a_y = \frac{((45-35)\text{ kg})(9.8\text{ m/s}^2)}{(45+35)\text{ kg}} = 1.2\text{ m/s}^2$$

Thus, the acceleration has a magnitude of 1.2 m/s^2.

(b) The value of a_y can now be substituted back into either of the original equations to solve for T, which turns out to be 3.9×10^2 N.

Notice that the rope tension is not equal in magnitude to the force of gravity on either of the two masses (3.4×10^2 N and 4.4×10^2 N). The tension must be greater than the force of gravity on the smaller mass in order to accelerate it upward, and smaller than gravity on the larger mass for a downward acceleration.

(c) Since we know the acceleration, we can use one of the constant-acceleration equations of kinematics to find how far each child moves in 0.50 s. The appropriate equation is Eqn. 2-9, which we write with y-subscripts to designate the vertical motion:

$$y = y_0 + v_{0y}t + \tfrac{1}{2}a_y t^2$$

We are told that the children start from rest; hence, v_{0y} = 0 m/s. We choose y_0 = 0 m for either child. Thus,

$$y = \tfrac{1}{2}a_y t^2 = \tfrac{1}{2}(1.2\text{ m/s}^2)(0.50\text{ s})^2 = 0.15\text{ m}$$

Hence, each child moves 0.15 m in the first 0.50 s after being at rest.

 **Practice**

5-43 Soon after jumping out of an airplane, a skydiver of mass 67 kg experiences an upward air resistance force of 567 N. What is the acceleration (magnitude and direction) of the skydiver? [Ans. 1.3 m/s^2 downward]

5-44 A woman applies a force of 0.35 N upward to lift a spoon, and the resulting acceleration of the spoon is 0.15 m/s^2 upward. What is the mass of the spoon? [Ans. 0.035 kg]

5-45 A forklift truck is lifting a large crate of computer disk drives vertically upward at a constant speed of 0.12 m/s. The force of gravity on the crate is 2.07×10^3 N in magnitude.
(a) What are the magnitude and direction of the force exerted by the forklift on the crate?
(b) Would you call this a normal force, friction force, or tension?
[Ans. (a) 2.07×10^3 N upward]

5-46 A hot-air balloon has an acceleration of 0.24 m/s^2 downward. The total mass of the balloon, basket, and contents is 315 kg.
(a) Determine the magnitude of the upward buoyant force on the balloon, basket, and contents.
(b) The balloonists want to reduce the acceleration to zero, but there is no fuel left to heat the air in the balloon. How much ballast must be thrown overboard? Neglect air resistance.
[Ans. (a) 3.01×10^3 N (b) 8 kg]

5-47 When a karate expert breaks a brick, the velocity of his hand changes from (typically) 13 m/s downward to essentially 0 m/s in a time of only 3.0 ms.
(a) What is the acceleration (assumed constant) of the hand?
(b) If the mass of the hand is 0.65 kg, what are the magnitude and direction of the resultant force on it? What object exerts almost all of this force on the hand?
(c) Compare (make a ratio of) the magnitude of the force in (b) to the magnitude of the gravitational force on the entire man, if his mass is 65 kg.
[Ans. (a) 4.3×10^3 m/s^2 upward (b) 2.8×10^3 N upward; brick (c) 4.4]

5-48 A woman having mass 55.3 kg is standing in an elevator that has an upward acceleration of 1.08 m/s^2. What is the magnitude of the normal force exerted by the floor on the woman? (This force is sometimes called the "apparent weight" of the woman. See the following question.) [Ans. 602 N]

5-49 (a) If the woman in the previous question were standing on bathroom scales in the elevator, what would the scales read in newtons? (Bathroom scales show the magnitude of the upward force exerted by the scales.)
(b) Repeat (a) if the elevator has a downward acceleration of 1.08 m/s^2.
(c) Repeat (a) if the elevator and woman are in free fall as a result of a break in the elevator cable.
(d) A person in free-fall is sometimes said to be "weightless." Why is this term used? Is the force of gravity on such a person zero?
(e) Repeat (a) if the elevator has a constant velocity of 1.08 m/s downward; and finally, a constant velocity of 1.08 m/s upward.
[Ans. (a) 602 N (b) 482 N (c) 0 N (e) 542 N, 542 N]

5-50 A small particle of clay having a mass of 1.06×10^{-14} kg is settling downward in water. At a certain time the particle's speed is 1.2 mm/h. The upward buoyant force on the particle has a magnitude of 4.0×10^{-14} N. There is also an upward fluid friction force on the particle; this force is proportional to the particle's speed v, and therefore its magnitude can be written as fv, where f is a constant called the friction factor. The numerical value of this constant depends on the size and shape of the particle, and on the viscosity of water. For this particular clay particle, $f = 1.88 \times 10^{-8}$ N·s/m. Determine the acceleration (magnitude and direction) of the particle. [Ans. 5.4 m/s^2 downward]

5-51 The oriental rat flee, a major carrier of bubonic plague, can jump a vertical distance more than 100 times its body length. (Imagine if you could do that!) During the initial phase of the jump, the flea is in contact with the ground for a typical time of 1.2 ms, and has an average upward acceleration of 1.0×10^3 m/s^2 (about 100 g). The mass of an average oriental rat flea is 2.1×10^{-7} kg. Neglect air resistance.
(a) During the initial phase of the jump, what is the magnitude of the resultant force on the flea?

Did You Know? *The maximum acceleration during the oriental rat flea's takeoff has a magnitude of about 140 g which is roughly 50 times the peak acceleration of 2 to 3 g for a space shuttle. For a human doing a standing vertical jump, the maximum acceleration is about 1 to 2 g in magnitude.*

(b) Draw a FBD for the flea in (a). What object exerts the upward force on the flea?
(c) After the flea has lost contact with the ground, what is the resultant force (magnitude and direction) on it?
(d) How high does the flea jump?
[Ans. (a) 2.1×10^{-4} N (b) ground (c) 2.1×10^{-6} N downward (d) 0.073 m]

5-52 A treehouse has a vertical metal "firepole" for quick exits. A boy of mass 35.7 kg slides down the pole, starting from rest. The pole is 3.10 m high, and the boy wants to slide to the bottom in 2.00 s.
(a) What constant downward acceleration is required?
(b) What is the magnitude of the upward force of friction exerted on the boy by the pole?
[Ans. (a) 1.55 m/s^2 (b) 295 N]

5-53 When a resultant force is applied to a particular mass "*m*," an acceleration of magnitude "*a*" results. When the mass is increased by 2.0 kg, and the same resultant force is applied, the acceleration is halved. Determine mass *m*. [Ans. 2.0 kg]

5-54 Repeat the previous question, but use a value of 0.37 for the ratio of the new acceleration to the old acceleration, instead of 0.50. [Ans. 1.2 kg]

5-55 A woman is pushing a stove straight across a kitchen floor with a constant speed of 25 cm/s. She is exerting a horizontal force of 85 N, and the force of gravity on the stove has a magnitude of 447 N.
(a) What are the magnitudes of the friction force and normal force exerted by the floor on the stove?
(b) What are the magnitude and direction of the total force exerted by the floor on the stove?
[Ans. (a) 85 N, 447 N (b) 455 N at 79.2° above horizontal]

5-56 In Figure 5-19, two blocks are held in place by three ropes connected at point A, and by the force of friction (1.8 N) on block 2. The magnitudes of the force of gravity on blocks 1 and 2 are 2.5 N and 6.7 N, respectively.
(a) Draw a FBD for block 1, and determine the magnitude of the tension in the vertical rope.
(b) Draw a FBD for block 2, and determine the magnitudes of the tension in the horizontal rope and the normal force acting on block 2.
(c) Draw a FBD for point A, and determine the magnitude and the direction (angle θ) of tension T_3.
[Ans. (a) 2.5 N (b) 1.8 N, 6.7 N (c) 3.1 N at $\theta = 54°$]

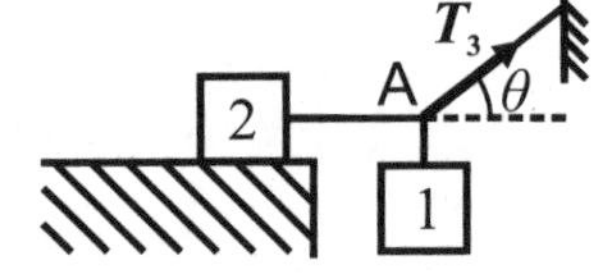

Figure 5-19 *Question 5-56.*

5-57 A sign outside a hair stylist's shop is suspended by two wires. The force of gravity on the sign has a magnitude of 55.7 N. If the angles between the wires and the horizontal are as shown in Figure 5-20, determine the magnitude of the tensions in the two wires.
[Ans. $T_1 = 49.9$ N; $T_2 = 40.8$ N]

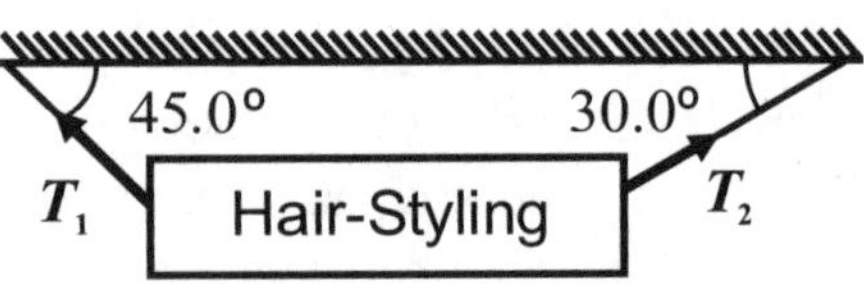

Figure 5-20 *Question 5-57.*

5-58 Two sleds are connected by a horizontal rope, and the front sled is pulled by another horizontal rope with tension of magnitude 29 N. The sled masses are: front, 6.7 kg; rear, 5.6 kg. The magnitude of the force of friction on the front sled is 9 N; on the rear sled, 8 N. Determine the magnitudes of: (a) the acceleration of the sleds (b) the tension in the connecting rope (c) the normal force on the front sled.
[Ans. (a) 0.98 m/s^2 (b) 13 N (c) 66 N]

5-59 A large family has solved its food-shopping problem by connecting three shopping carts together with two horizontal ropes (Figure 5-21). The masses of the loaded carts are: m_1 = 15.0 kg, m_2 = 13.2 kg, and m_3 = 16.1 kg, Neglect friction. A third rope, which pulls the first cart, makes an angle of θ = 21.0° above the horizontal and has a tension of magnitude 35.3 N. Determine the magnitudes of: (a) the acceleration of the carts (b) the tensions in the connecting ropes
[Ans. (a) 0.744 m/s^2 (b) 12.0 N (last rope), 21.8 N (middle rope)]

Figure 5-21 *Question 5-59.*

5-60 Two small boxes are attached to opposite ends of a string that passes over a fixed horizontal metal rod. The boxes hang vertically from the ends of the string. When released, the boxes have an acceleration of magnitude 0.38 m/s^2. The mass of the smaller box is 0.75 kg. What is the mass of the other box? Neglect friction between the rope and rod.
[Ans. 0.81 kg]

5-61 In the previous question, what is the magnitude of the tension in the string?
[Ans. 7.6 N]

5-62 Two blocks are connected by a string passing over a pulley (Figure 5-22). Neglect friction and the rotation of the pulley. If the masses are m_1 = 3.7 kg and m_2 = 2.7 kg, determine the magnitudes of: (a) the acceleration of the blocks (b) the tension in the string.
[Ans. (a) 5.7 m/s^2 (b) 15 N]

5-63 Repeat the previous question, but include a friction force of magnitude 5.7 N between block 2 and the surface beneath it.
[Ans. (a) 4.8 m/s^2 (b) 19 N]

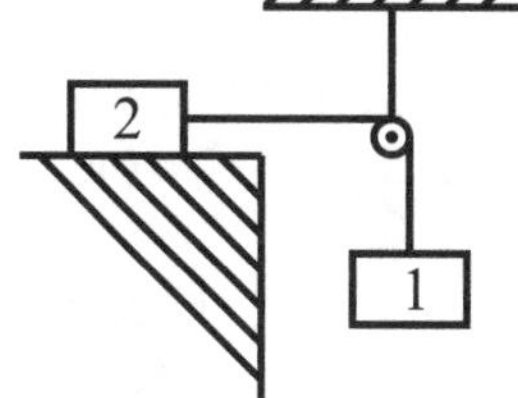

Figure 5-22 *Questions 5-62 and 5-63.*

5.6 MORE PROBLEM-SOLVING

Now that you have gained some experience in solving problems using Newton's second law, you have some idea of the wide variety of physical situations in which this fundamental law of nature is applicable – from launching a space shuttle to breaking a brick with a karate blow. You have solved many problems that involved a normal force, which was often equal in magnitude to the force of gravity on an object. In this section, we look at situations in which the normal force and the force of gravity do not have equal magnitudes.

Sample Problem 5-10

A girl pushes a lawnmower of mass 17.9 kg from rest across a horizontal lawn by exerting a force of 32.9 N straight along the handle, which is inclined at an angle of 35.1° above the horizontal. If the magnitude of the acceleration of the mower is 1.37 m/s^2, determine the magnitudes of:
(a) the normal force on the mower;
(b) the friction force on the mower.
If the acceleration lasts for only 0.58 s, and then the mower moves at constant velocity, find:
(c) the final speed of the mower;
(d) the magnitude of the force that the girl must then exert along the handle in order to maintain the constant speed.

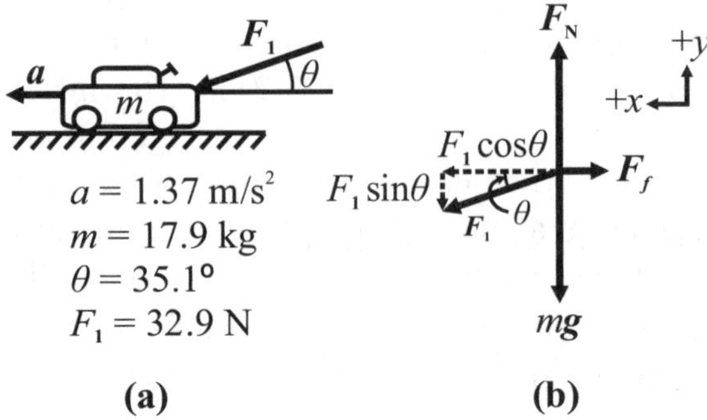

Figure 5-23
(a) *Diagram for Sample Problem 5-10.*
(b) *FBD for the lawnmower.*

Solution: (a) After reading the problem carefully, we draw the general diagram (Figure 5-23 (a)) and the FBD for the mower (Figure 5-23 (b)). Since the mower accelerates to the left, the $+x$-direction is chosen to the left. The $+y$-direction is at right angles to this, either upward or downward (upward in this example). The only force that has both x- and y-components is the force exerted by the girl ($\boldsymbol{F}_1$), and these components are shown on the FBD.

We are first asked to find the magnitude of the normal force, which acts vertically. Therefore, we use Newton's second law in the y-direction:

$$\Sigma F_y = ma_y$$

However, there is no vertical acceleration, that is, $a_y = 0$. Therefore, $\Sigma F_y = 0$. Writing the y-components of all the forces, and adding them to give zero:

$$F_N + (-mg) + (-F_1 \sin\theta) = 0$$

Hence,
$$\begin{aligned} F_N &= mg + F_1 \sin\theta \\ &= (17.9\text{ kg})(9.80\text{ m/s}^2) + (32.9\text{ N})(\sin 35.1°) \\ &= 194\text{ N} \end{aligned}$$

Therefore, the magnitude of the normal force is 194 N.

(b) To find the friction force, we use Newton's second law in the x-direction:

$$\Sigma F_x = ma_x$$

Hence,

$$F_1 \cos\theta + (-F_f) = ma_x$$

$$\begin{aligned} F_f &= F_1 \cos\theta - ma_x \\ &= (32.9\text{ N})(\cos 35.1°) - (17.9\text{ kg})(1.37\text{ m/s}^2) \\ &= (26.9 - 24.5)\text{ N} \\ &= 2.4\text{ N} \end{aligned}$$

The magnitude of the friction force is 2.4 N.

(c) In order to find the final speed of the mower, we can use one of the constant-acceleration equations of kinematics:

$$\begin{aligned} v_x &= v_{0x} + a_x t \\ &= 0 + (1.37\text{ m/s}^2)(0.58\text{ s}) \\ &= 0.79\text{ m/s} \end{aligned}$$

Thus, the final speed of the lawnmower is 0.79 m/s.

(d) We now need to find the magnitude of the force (call it $\boldsymbol{F}_2$) that the girl needs to exert in order to maintain the constant speed of the mower. Figure 5-24 shows the FBD in this case. Force $\boldsymbol{F}_2$ is not as large as the original $\boldsymbol{F}_1$, and the new FBD has been drawn so that $F_2 \cos\theta$ has the same magnitude as F_f, so that there will be zero acceleration. Since the normal force is no longer the same magnitude as in parts (a), (b), and (c) of this problem, it is now labeled as $\boldsymbol{F}_{N2}$ instead of $\boldsymbol{F}_N$. In the x-direction, we use Newton's second law (or first law, since $a_x = 0$):

$$\Sigma F_x = ma_x = 0$$

$$F_2 \cos\theta + (-F_f) = 0$$

This gives

$$F_2 \cos\theta = F_f$$

$$F_2 = \frac{F_f}{\cos\theta} = \frac{2.4\text{ N}}{\cos 35.1°} = 2.9\text{ N}$$

Therefore, the girl needs to exert a force of magnitude 2.9 N.

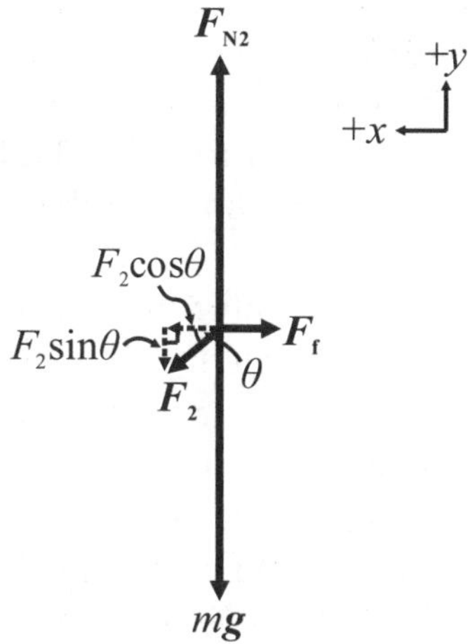

Figure 5-24
SampleProblem 5-10, part (d).

Sample Problem 5-11

A skier of mass 65 kg slides down a snow-covered hill inclined at 12° from the horizontal. If friction is neglected, what are the magnitudes of:
(a) the normal force on the skier? (b) the acceleration of the skier?

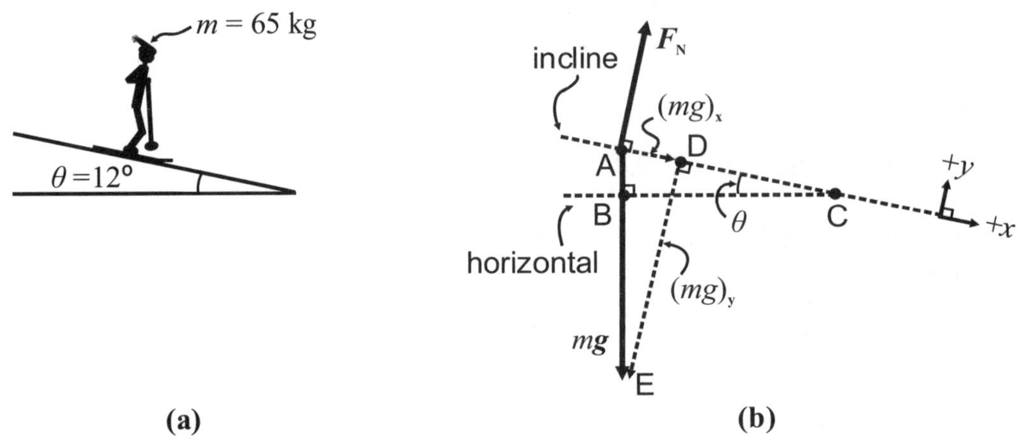

Figure 5-25 **(a)** *Diagram for Sample Problem 5-11.* **(b)** *FBD for the skier.*

Solution: This problem illustrates the use of an *x-y* co-ordinate system that is not horizontal-vertical. Figures 5-25 (a) and (b) show a general diagram and the FBD for the skier. Since the skier's acceleration is along the incline, we choose the +*x* axis in this direction. The +*y* axis is perpendicular to this. The force of gravity has both *x*- and *y*-components, shown in Figure 5-25 (b) as $(mg)_x$ and $(mg)_y$, but the normal force has only a *y*-component.

In order to solve this problem, we will need to express the components of the force of gravity in terms of angle θ, which is the angle (12°) between the incline and the horizontal. To do this, consider triangles ABC and ADE in Figure 5-25 (b). In triangle ABC, angle ABC is 90°, since it lies between a horizontal line and the vertical force *mg*. Angle ACB is θ. In order for the angles in triangle ABC to add up to 180°, angle BAC must be $(90° - \theta)$. In triangle ADE, side AE is the force *mg*, and sides AD and DE are its *x*- and *y*-components, respectively. Angle EAD is the same as angle BAC, that is, $(90° - \theta)$. Angle ADE is 90°, since it is the angle between the *x*- and *y*-components. Since the angles in triangle ADE must add up to 180°, angle AED must be equal to θ. We now can use the following information about triangle ADE:

- angle ADE is 90°
- angle AED is θ
- the hypotenuse has a magnitude of *mg*
- side AD represents the *x*-component of *mg*, that is, $(mg)_x$
- side DE represents the *y*-component of *mg*, that is, $(mg)_y$

Since triangle ADE has a right angle (ADE), the components of mg can be written in terms of $\sin\theta$ and $\cos\theta$:

$$(mg)_x = mg\sin\theta$$
$$(mg)_y = -mg\cos\theta$$

Notice the negative y-component of mg. (In Figure 5-25 (b), the y-component of mg and the $+y$ axis are in opposite directions.)

(a) To find the magnitude of the normal force, which is in the y-direction, we use Newton's second law:

$$\Sigma F_y = ma_y$$

The acceleration $a_y = 0$, because the skier does not accelerate perpendicular to the plane. (The skier does not sink into the plane, nor fly into the air.)

Thus,

$$\Sigma F_y = 0$$
$$F_N + (-mg\cos\theta) = 0$$
$$\begin{aligned} F_N &= mg\cos\theta \\ &= (65\text{ kg})(9.8\text{ m/s}^2)(\cos 12°) \\ &= 6.2\times10^2\text{ N} \end{aligned}$$

Therefore, the normal force is 6.2×10^2 N in magnitude. (Notice that the magnitude of the normal force in this problem is not equal to mg, but rather $mg\cos\theta$.)

(b) To find the acceleration in the x-direction:

$$\Sigma F_x = ma_x$$

The only force in the x-direction is the x-component of gravity.

> ***Problem-solving Tip:*** *When you first looked at this problem, you might have been tempted to choose a horizontal-vertical x-y co-ordinate system. If you had done this, both the normal force and the acceleration would have had x- and y-components, which would have made the solution much more difficult.* ***Remember always to choose the +x- or +y-axis in the direction of the acceleration of the object.*** *In particular, if a problem involves an object that moves up or down an incline, choose one co-ordinate axis parallel to the incline, and the other axis perpendicular to this.*

Therefore, $mg\sin\theta = ma_x$

Dividing both sides by mass m, and re-arranging with a_x on the left:

$$a_x = g\sin\theta = (9.8\text{ m/s}^2)(\sin 12°) = 2.0\text{ m/s}^2$$

Hence, the skier has an acceleration of 2.0 m/s^2 in magnitude. Notice that the skier's mass was not used in the final calculation of the acceleration. Therefore, an object of *any mass* will slide down a 12° incline with the same acceleration (neglecting friction).

Practice

Figure 5-26
Question 5-64.

5-64 A woman is leaning on a box (Figure 5-26). The box has a mass of 25 kg and is stationary. If the force exerted by the woman on the box is 35 N at 37° below the horizontal, determine the magnitudes of:
(a) the normal force exerted by the floor on the box
(b) the friction force exerted by the floor on the box.
[Ans. (a) 2.7×10^2 N (b) 28 N]

5-65 A newspaper delivery girl pulls her papers in a small sleigh during the winter. The rope with which she pulls the sleigh makes an angle of 25.0° above the horizontal, and the magnitude of the tension in the rope is 6.73 N. The force of gravity on the sleigh and papers has a magnitude of 35.6 N, and the sleigh is moving horizontally at constant velocity. Determine the magnitude and direction of the (a) normal force, and (b) friction force, exerted on the sleigh. [Ans. (a) 32.8 N upward (b) 6.10 N in opposite direction to sleigh's motion]

5-66 One day the rope used by the girl in the previous question broke, and she had to push her sleigh. She pushed slightly downward, with a force of 8.25 N at an angle of 15.2° below the horizontal. The force of gravity on the sleigh and papers was still 35.6 N in magnitude, and the sleigh still moved horizontally at constant velocity. Determine the magnitude and direction of: (a) the normal force; (b) the friction force; (c) the total force exerted on the sleigh by the ground. [Ans. (a) 37.8 N upward (b) 7.96 N in opposite direction to sleigh's motion
(c) 38.6 N at 11.9° from vertical]

Figure 5-27
Question 5-67.

5-67 A man starts to pull a large chair across a horizontal floor by pulling at an angle of 15° above the horizontal (Figure 5-27). The force that he exerts is 91 N in magnitude, and there is a normal force of 221 N upward on the chair. If the chair's horizontal acceleration is 0.076 m/s^2 in magnitude, what are: (a) the mass of the chair?
(b) the magnitude of the friction force on the chair?
[Ans. (a) 25.0 kg (b) 86 N]

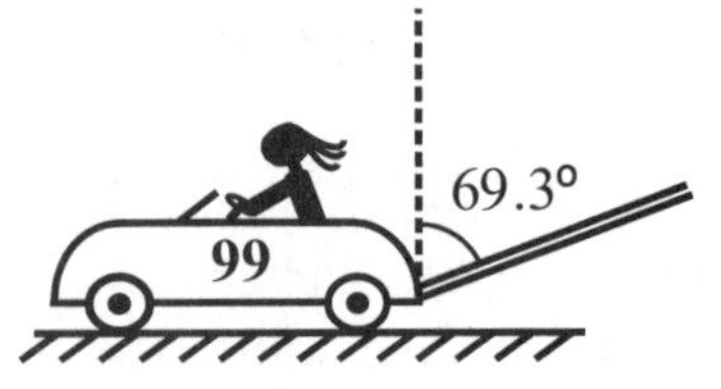

Figure 5-28 *Question 5-68.*

5-68 A girl's soapbox derby car is pushed with a broom handle (Figure 5-28). The total mass of the car and girl is 36.7 kg, and a force of 72.7 N is applied along the direction of the broom handle, making an angle of 69.3° with the vertical. There is a friction force of magnitude 12.7 N on the car. Determine the magnitudes of:
(a) the acceleration of the girl and car
(b) the normal force exerted by the ground on the girl and car
(c) the distance the car will travel in 1.50 s, assuming it started from rest.
[Ans. (a) 1.51 m/s^2 (b) 385 N (c) 1.70 m]

5-69 A box of mass m is pulled at constant velocity across a horizontal floor by a force of magnitude F applied at an angle of θ above the horizontal (Figure 5-29). In terms of given parameters and "g," determine expressions for the magnitudes of:
(a) the normal force on the box ; (b) the friction force on the box.
[Ans. (a) $mg - F\sin\theta$ (b) $F\cos\theta$]

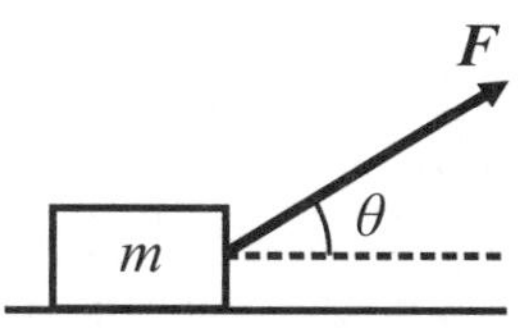

Figure 5-29
Question 5-69.

5-70 In a fish-canning plant a box of fresh fish slides down a slippery ramp inclined at 16° to the horizontal. Neglecting friction, what is the magnitude of the acceleration of the box? [Ans. 2.7 m/s^2]

5-71 A girl on a toboggan slides down a hill with an acceleration of magnitude 1.5 m/s^2. If friction is neglected, what is the angle between the hill and the horizontal? [Ans. 8.8°]

5-72 An object slides down an incline that makes an angle of ϕ with the horizontal. Determine an algebraic expression for the magnitude of the object's acceleration, in terms of ϕ and "g." Neglect friction. [Ans. $g\sin\phi$]

5-73 A man is pushing a baby carriage up a ramp in a shopping mall. The mass of the baby and carriage is 23 kg, and the maximum force that the man can exert (parallel to the ramp) is 88 N. What is the maximum angle that the ramp can make with the horizontal, if the carriage is not to roll down the ramp? Neglect friction between the carriage wheels and the ramp. [Ans. 23°]

5-74 Two blocks are connected by a string passing over a pulley (Fig. 5-30). The incline makes an angle of 35.7° with the horizontal, and the masses of the blocks are m_1 = 5.12 kg and m_2 = 3.22 kg. Neglect friction and the rotational motion of the pulley. (a) If the blocks start from rest, will block 1 slide up or down the incline?
What are the magnitudes of:
(b) the acceleration of the blocks? (c) the tension in the string?
[Ans. (a) up (b) 0.27 m/s^2 (c) 30.7 N]

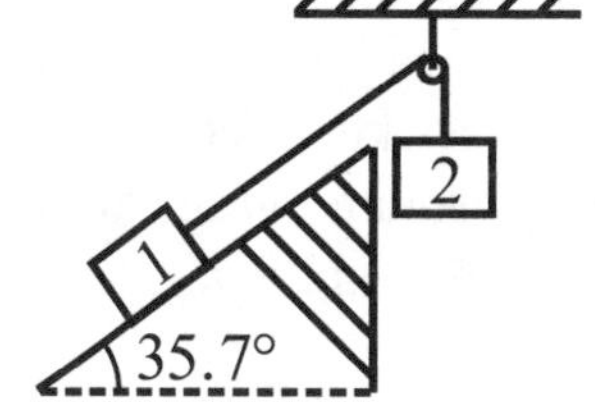

Figure 5-30
Question 5-74.

5.7 NEWTON'S THIRD LAW OF MOTION

What do you think happened to the lines painted on the road shown in Figure 5-1 on the first page of this chapter? Were the bends caused by an earthquake? Did the road-painters just decide to have some fun? The crooked lines are actually the result of **Newton's third law of motion**, which is his famous law of action and reaction. This law states that:

If object A exerts a force on object B,
B simultaneously exerts an equal but opposite force on A.

Another way of saying this is that for every action, there is an equal and opposite reaction.

Figure 5-31
A car accelerating over the lines.

The road lines in Figure 5-1 are at a busy intersection, where a large number of vehicles have to stop for traffic lights. When the light turns green, the vehicles accelerate over the lines on the road (Figure 5-31). In order for a vehicle to accelerate forward, its tires exert a backward force on the road (Figure 5-32). By Newton's third law, the road exerts a forward force on the tires, and hence on the vehicle. (This forward force that accelerates the vehicle is just the friction force between the road and the tires. Without friction, a car would simply sit and spin its wheels.) At the intersection shown in Figures 5-1 and 5-31, the backward force exerted by the vehicles on the road has caused the road surface to slip backward, carrying the painted lines with it. The upper layer of asphalt must have been poorly bonded to the underlying layers.

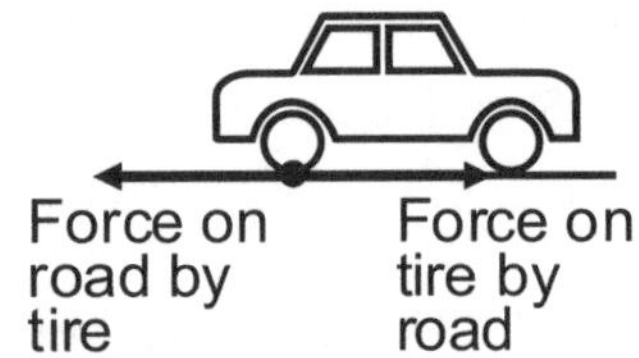

Figure 5-32
Forces when a car accelerates toward the right.

Newton's third law comes into play whenever a force is exerted on an object. To illustrate the importance of this law, we consider some other forms of transportation (Figure 5-33):

(a) When we walk, our feet push backward on the ground; the ground pushes forward on our feet, thus moving us forward.
(b) Boat propellers push backward on the water; the water pushes forward on the propellers.
(c) A rocket expels hot gases downward; the gases push upward on the rocket.
(d) Airplane wings are shaped so that they deflect air downward, that is, they exert a downward force on the air; the air pushes upward on the wings.

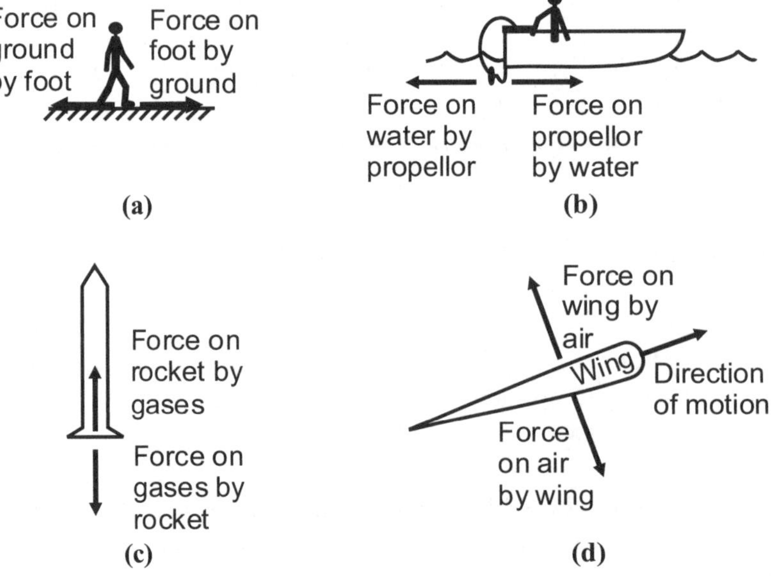

Figure 5-33 *Newton's third law in transportation.*

In each of the transportation examples, note that there are only two objects involved, and that we are considering only one force exerted on each object. People often become confused about Newton's third law because they try to include more than two objects at a time, or because they introduce additional forces.

For example, consider the situation of you standing on the ground. Earth exerts a downward force of gravity (the "action") on you. There is a common misconception that the "reaction" force in this instance is the upward normal force exerted by Earth on you. If this were so, the action-reaction pair would be two forces exerted on you, not one force exerted on you and one on Earth, as required in Newton's third law. The correct "reaction" force is the *upward force of gravity exerted by you on Earth* (Figure 5-34 (a)). It seems unusual to think of an *upward* force of gravity; however, because gravity is an attractive force between objects, the force of gravity exerted on Earth by you is indeed upward.

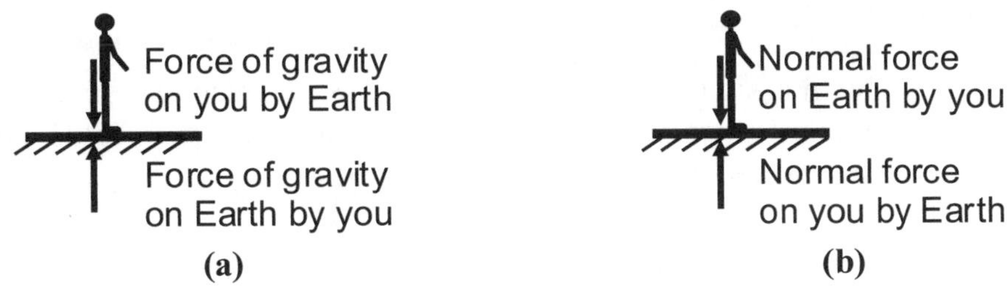

Figure 5-34 *Two action-reaction pairs.*

What about the upward normal force exerted by Earth on you? What action-reaction pair is it a part of? By Newton's third law, the other force in the pair must be a *downward* force *exerted by you on Earth* (Figure 5-34 (b)). This is the force exerted on Earth because you are in contact with it. This force is also a normal force because it is perpendicular to the surfaces in contact, namely the soles of your shoes and the ground. (Recall that "normal" means "perpendicular.") Note that this force is not the downward force of gravity, because that force is exerted downward on you, not on Earth. The downward force of gravity acts on you whether you are in contact with Earth or in mid-air during a jump, but the downward normal force that you exert on Earth acts only when you are touching it.

Notice that the two forces in an action-reaction pair are always the same type of force. They are both normal forces, or both gravitational forces, etc.

It does not matter which of the two forces you consider to be the "action", and which the "reaction." Cause and effect are not implied by these terms; the forces are applied at the same time.

Sample Problem 5-12

A baseball player sliding into second base experiences a frictional force. What is the other force in the action-reaction pair? (What is its name? What is its direction? What object exerts it? On what object is it exerted?)

Solution: Let us call the frictional force exerted by the ground on the player the "action." Its direction is opposite to the player's slide. By Newton's third law, the "reaction" is exerted by the player on the ground, in the same direction as the player's slide. It is also a frictional force.

Sample Problem 5-13

Two people of masses $m_1 = 55$ kg and $m_2 = 65$ kg are standing, one just in front of the other, on roller skates on a horizontal floor. A third person applies a horizontal force $\boldsymbol{F}$ of magnitude 84 N to the smaller skater (#1), who in turn pushes the other skater (#2), so that both skaters accelerate at the same rate. Determine the magnitudes of (a) their acceleration, and (b) the contact force $\boldsymbol{F}_C$ exerted by one skater on the other. Neglect friction.

Solution: (a) This problem is similar to sample problem 5-8 in which two sleighs connected by a rope were pulled by another rope. We first draw a diagram for the problem (Figure 5-35 (a)), and then a FBD for the two skaters together (Figure 5-35 (b)).

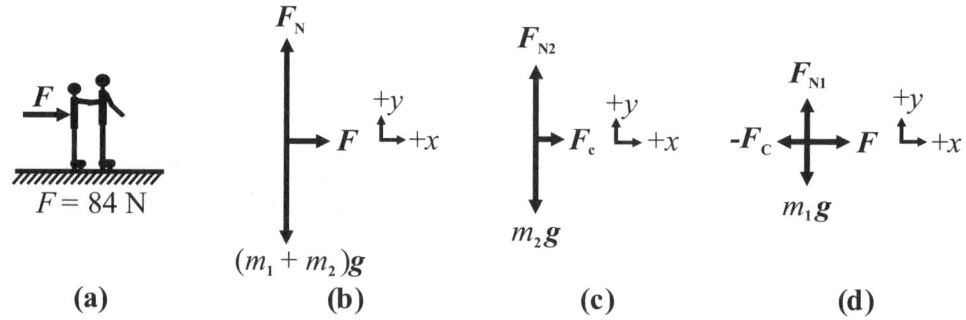

Figure 5-35 *Sample Problem 5-13.*
(a) *Diagram of the system.* **(b)** *FBD for the two skaters together.*
(c) *FBD for skater 2.* **(d)** *FBD for skater 1.*

We can solve for the acceleration by using Newton's second law in the x-direction:

$$\Sigma F_x = ma_x$$
$$F = (m_1 + m_2)a_x$$

Therefore, $$a_x = \frac{F}{m_1 + m_2} = \frac{84\ \text{N}}{(55 + 65)\ \text{kg}} = 0.70\ \text{m/s}^2$$

Thus, the acceleration has a magnitude of $0.70\ \text{m/s}^2$.

(b) In order to determine the force exerted between the two skaters, we need to draw a FBD for only one skater. The force $\boldsymbol{F}_C$ exerted on skater 2 by skater 1 is to the right; it is this force that accelerates skater 2. By Newton's third law, skater 2 exerts a force on skater 1, of equal magnitude but to the left, that is, $-\boldsymbol{F}_{\mathrm{C}}$.

Figure 5-35 (c) shows the FBD for skater 2. Using Newton's second law:

$$\Sigma F_{\mathrm{x}} = ma_{\mathrm{x}} \qquad \text{which gives} \qquad F_{\mathrm{C}} = m_2 a_{\mathrm{x}}$$

Substituting known values: $F_{\mathrm{C}} = (65\ \mathrm{kg})(0.70\ \mathrm{m/s^2})\ 46\ \mathrm{N}$

Hence, the force exerted by one skater on the other has a magnitude of 46 N.

Alternatively, we could use a FBD for skater 1 (Figure 5-35 (d)), and use Newton's second law:

$$\Sigma F_{\mathrm{x}} = ma_{\mathrm{x}} \qquad \text{giving} \qquad F + (-F_{\mathrm{C}}) = m_1 a_{\mathrm{x}}$$

Thus, $F_{\mathrm{C}} = F - m_1 a_{\mathrm{x}} = 84\ \mathrm{N} - (55\ \mathrm{kg})(0.70\ \mathrm{m/s^2}) = 46\ \mathrm{N}$

This is the same answer as we determined with the FBD for skater 2, but using the FBD for skater 2 required fewer steps.

PROFILE: Sir Isaac Newton (1642-1727)

> "Nature and Nature's laws lay hid in night;
> God said, *Let Newton Be!* and all was light."

These lines, written by the English poet Alexander Pope, appear as the epitaph on Newton's tomb in Westminster Abbey, where Newton is buried along with other great Britons. Although he was undoubtedly one of the greatest scientists ever known, he had psychological problems and was not an easy person to get along with. He was very solitary and became involved in a number of personal controversies with other distinguished people of his time.

Isaac Newton was born on December 25, 1642. His father had died three months before Isaac's birth, and when his mother remarried three years later, Isaac was sent to live with his grandmother. When he was eleven, his stepfather died and Isaac returned to his mother, half-brother, and two half-sisters. Some psychologists have suggested that these moves during his youth may have had negative effects on his personality.

In elementary school, Newton was a good, but not exceptional, student and his mother thought that perhaps he should become a farmer. However, a clergyman suggested that he should attend Cambridge University, which he entered in 1661. His academic talents were recognized at Cambridge by his mathematics professor, Isaac Barrow, and four years later, Newton received the degree of Bachelor of Arts. Soon after, the plague struck England, and the university was closed for two years to avoid the spread of the disease. Newton returned home to his mother, and in the quiet surroundings there, made a number of rapid and important advances in science and mathematics.

In a period of some 18 months, Newton invented calculus, discovered the law of universal gravitation, developed his three laws of motion, and made a number of discoveries in optics related to light, colour, and interference phenomena. His work in optics led him to build the first reflecting telescope. This list of achievements is enough to fill a normal person's lifetime; to accomplish all this in only 18 months is amazing! The famous story of an apple falling from a tree and hitting Newton on the head during this period, thus inspiring his development of the gravitation law, may or may not be true. However, the story is a reminder that his gravitation law is indeed universal, determining the motion of apples on Earth, and also the orbits of the moon, planets, and stars.

When the plague was over, Newton returned to Cambridge for further studies, and was named Lucasian professor of Mathematics in 1669. His first scientific paper, in 1672, was on light and colour, along with a description of his newly invented telescope. The paper was criticized by some other scientists, and Newton's reaction was withdrawal. He decided not to publish any more of his discoveries except when strongly encouraged by colleagues. As a result, he was later involved in a number of conflicts with other scientists and mathematicians concerning the credit for certain discoveries. Normally the first person to publish a result is acknowledged as the discoverer, but since Newton was publishing very little of his work, he wanted credit to be given to the person who first had the idea, even if it was kept secret.

Fortunately, Newton was persuaded by Edmund Halley (after whom Halley's comet is named) to publish his *Philosophiae Naturalis Principia Mathematica* in 1687, in which his laws of motion and universal gravitation were presented.

In 1692, Newton fell into a serious depression, with delusions of persecution. He recovered reasonably well, but having tired of the academic life of a professor, was made Warden of the Mint in London in 1691, where he busied himself with the development of new coinage. In 1699, he was promoted to Master of the Mint, a post he held until his death.

Newton became increasingly difficult to deal with in his later years. One of his most famous controversies was with the German philosopher and mathematician Gottfried Leibnitz over the discovery of calculus. Newton and Leibnitz had developed calculus independently, and initially there was a period of goodwill and mutual recognition. But by 1699 there was a great battle involving national pride and a number of supporters on both sides. The story is very complicated and the issue was never satisfactorily resolved to the satisfaction of the parties involved.

In 1703, Newton became President of the Royal Society, a group of distinguished British scientists, and he reigned over science in England with a firm hand until his death. He was ennobled in 1705 by Queen Anne, and thus became Sir Isaac Newton.

Newton spent only a small part of his adult life involved in physics and mathematics. He devoted a great deal of time to the study of theology, writing entire books on religious subjects, and he also worked on alchemy. He often professed disgust for his advances in physical science, an odd attitude for a man who had accomplished so much.

In 1727, Sir Isaac Newton died and was buried with state honours in Westminster Abbey.

Practice

5-75 In each case below, one force is given. What is the other force in the action-reaction pair? Give its name (if possible) and direction, and indicate which object exerts it, and on which object it is exerted. Answers are provided at the end of the chapter.
(a) The sun exerts a gravitational force on Jupiter.
(b) A book on a table is supported by an upward normal force.
(c) A chef exerts a force on a baking pan to pull it out of an oven.
(d) A canoeist uses a paddle to exert a backward force on the water.
(e) Earth exerts a gravitational force on a falling apple.
(f) The upward force of air resistance (a type of friction) is exerted on a falling hailstone.

5-76 A train consisting of an engine and two cars is speeding up with an acceleration of magnitude 0.33 m/s^2. Neglect friction. If each car has a mass of 3.1×10^4 kg, determine the magnitudes of: (a) the force exerted by the first car on the second
(b) the force exerted by the engine on the first car.
[Ans. (a) 1.0×10^4 N (b) 2.0×10^4 N]

5-77 Repeat the previous question if the train is slowing down with an acceleration of magnitude 0.33 m/s^2. [Ans. (a) 1.0×10^4 N (b) 2.0×10^4 N]

5-78 Two books are sitting side by side (touching each other) on a table. A horizontal applied force of magnitude 0.58 N causes the books to move together with an acceleration of 0.21 m/s^2 horizontally. The mass of the book to which the force is directly applied is 1.0 kg. Neglecting friction, determine: (a) the mass of the other book
(b) the magnitude of the force exerted by one book on the other.
[Ans. (a) 1.8 kg (b) 0.37 N]

5-79 A figure skater of mass 56 kg pushes horizontally against the boards at the side of a skating rink for 0.75 s. Having started at rest, she leaves the boards with a speed of 75 cm/s. Neglect friction. What were the magnitudes of: (a) her acceleration (assumed constant)?
(b) the force exerted on her by the boards?
(c) the force that she exerted on the boards?
[Ans. (a) 1.0 m/s^2 (b) 56 N (c) 56 N]

5-80 A boy sitting in a boat pushes horizontally against a dock with a paddle for 1.2 s. During the push, the boy and boat move 0.55 m east. Neglect friction.
(a) If the boat was initially at rest, what is its final speed? Assume constant acceleration.

(b) If the total mass of the boy and boat is 95 kg, determine the magnitude and direction of the force exerted by the dock on the paddle.
(c) What were the magnitude and direction of the force exerted by the paddle on the dock?
[Ans. (a) 0.92 m/s (b) 73 N east (c) 73 N west]

5-81 (a) A chocolate bar of mass 0.055 kg is suspended from a spring scale that reads in newtons (Figure 5-36 (a)). What is the reading on the scale?
(b) The same chocolate bar is suspended from the same scale in the orientation shown in Figure 5-36 (b). What is the reading?
(c) Two identical bars of mass 0.055 kg are suspended from the scale as in Figure 5-36 (c). What is the reading?
[Ans. (a) 0.54 N (b) 0.54 N (c) 0.54 N]

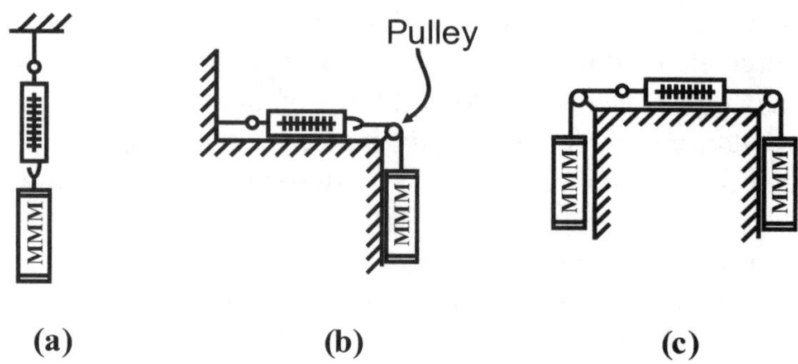

Figure 5-36 *Question 5-81.*

5.8 THE FUNDAMENTAL FORCES

There appears to be a wide variety of forces in the world around us – gravity, friction, normal force, air resistance, rope tension, muscle forces, and so on – but all forces can be traced to just four fundamental types. One of these is *gravity* (discussed earlier in this chapter), which is a force of attraction between all objects, and is responsible for the attraction of objects toward our own Earth. Gravity is the most important force at the astronomical level, and determines the motion of planets, stars, and galaxies.

Most of the other forces with which we are directly familiar are fundamentally **electrical forces**.[2] Electrical forces exist only between charged objects or particles, such as negatively charged electrons and positively charged nuclei in atoms. The forces holding together the atoms and molecules in all the objects around us — cars, tables, people, alligators — are electrical. If a book is sitting on a table, the upward normal force exerted by the table on the book is due to the electrical forces between the molecules in the table. Muscle forces, frictional forces, and forces exerted by objects (such as springs) which are being stretched or compressed are all

[2] Electrical forces are considered in detail in Chapter 10.

fundamentally electrical forces. Magnetic forces have been shown to be very closely related to electrical forces, and often electrical and magnetic forces are referred to together as the **electromagnetic interaction**.

The other two fundamental forces are less noticeable in everyday life, since they are both related to the tiny nuclei of atoms. The **nuclear strong force** is the attractive force that holds together the protons and neutrons in nuclei. The **nuclear weak force** is related to processes such as beta-decay, in which nuclei emit high-speed electrons called beta-particles. A recent theory has shown that the weak force is essentially the same as the electromagnetic interaction, and thus it is now more correct to say that there are three fundamental forces: *gravity*, *nuclear strong*, and *electroweak*. A number of physicists around the world are attempting to develop a theory in which the electroweak and nuclear strong forces are shown to be essentially the same force. Such a theory would be a "grand unified theory" (GUT). It might be possible eventually to show that all forces are simply different manifestations of the same single fundamental force, in a "theory of everything" (TOE).

Did You Know? *The 1979 Nobel Prize in Physics was awarded to Sheldon Glashow, Abdus Salam, and Steven Weinberg for their "unified model of the action of the weak and electro-magnetic forces."*

Practice

5-82 In each case below, identify the fundamental force that is responsible for the interaction given.
(a) The molecules in this book are bound to each other.
(b) A well-hit baseball returns toward the ground.
(c) Someone pushes you.
(d) Jupiter travels in an elliptical orbit around the sun.
(e) The floor supports you.
(f) A moving boat slows down because of water resistance after the engine has been turned off.
(g) There are 92 protons and 143 neutrons contained in a small volume in a nucleus of uranium-235.

CHAPTER FOCUS

In previous chapters, we discussed kinematics, that is, the study of motion described by quantities such as position, velocity, and acceleration. We paid little attention to what caused the motion.

In the present chapter, the main emphasis has been on force, the physical quantity responsible for motion. More correctly, *force* is the quantity responsible for *acceleration*. Considerable space has been devoted to Newton's three laws of motion, and in the second law, we have seen the relation between (resultant) force and the acceleration studied in kinematics. Newton's laws have been applied to a wide variety of physical situations, from pushing a lawn mower to launching a space shuttle. We have discussed how all forces can be traced to just three fundamental types: gravity, nuclear strong, and electroweak.

The next chapter will continue the focus on forces with a detailed discussion of friction, and forces involved in circular motion.

VOCABULARY REVIEW

You should be able to define or explain each of the following words or phrases.

dynamics
gravity
normal force
force of friction
tension
contact force
free-body diagram (FBD)
resultant force
Newton's second law of motion
newton (unit)
weight
Newton's first law of motion
inertia
law of inertia
Newton's third law of motion
electrical force
electromagnetic interaction
nuclear strong force
nuclear weak force

CHAPTER REVIEW

5-83 What is the approximate magnitude of the force of gravity (in newtons) on a typical adult person?
(a) 7 (b) 7×10^1 (c) 7×10^2 (d) 7×10^3 (e) 7×10^4

5-84 A ball is thrown vertically upward. As it travels upward after leaving the thrower's hand, which force(s) act(s) on it? Neglect air resistance.
(a) the downward force of gravity $\boldsymbol{F}_G$ only
(b) $\boldsymbol{F}_G$ and a decreasing upward force
(c) $\boldsymbol{F}_G$ and an increasing downward force
(d) $\boldsymbol{F}_G$ and a constant upward force
(e) $\boldsymbol{F}_G$ and the force due to the motion of the ball

5-85 A very large protein molecule is sedimenting downward in water at a constant velocity. There are three forces acting on the molecule: the force of gravity $\boldsymbol{F}_G$ downward, an upward buoyant force $\boldsymbol{F}_B$ and an upward fluid friction force $\boldsymbol{F}_{ff}$. Which of the following expresses the correct relation between the magnitudes of these three forces?
(a) $F_G > F_B + F_{ff}$ (b) $F_G = F_B + F_{ff}$ (c) $F_G < F_B + F_{ff}$

5-86 A soft-drink can is sitting on a table. If we consider the force of gravity on the soft-drink can to be the "action", then the "reaction" is:
(a) the upward normal force on the can by the table
(b) the downward force of gravity on the table
(c) the downward normal force on the table by the can
(d) the upward force of gravity on Earth by the can
(e) none of the above.

5-87 A small car has become stuck in deep snow, and the driver of a large truck offers to use his truck to push the car out of the snow. As the truck is pushing the car,
(a) the force exerted by the truck on the car is smaller than the force exerted by the car on the truck
(b) the force exerted by the truck on the car is larger than the force exerted by the car on the truck
(c) the force exerted by the truck on the car has the same magnitude as the force exerted by the car on the truck

5-88 A golf club is used to hit a golf ball. The mass of the golf club is much greater than that of the ball. During the collision between the golf club and the ball,
(a) the force exerted by the club on the ball is smaller than the force exerted by the ball on the club.
(b) the force exerted by the club on the ball has the same magnitude as the force exerted by the ball on the club.
(c) the force exerted by the club on the ball is larger than the force exerted by the ball on the club.

5-89 A canoe is being paddled across a windy lake. There is a 75.3 N force exerted forward (north) by the water on the paddles, and a 67.2 N force of water resistance backward. In addition, there is a force on the canoe due to the wind: 7.8 N, *from* a direction 25.7° west of north. Determine the magnitude and direction of the resultant force on the canoe.
[Ans. 3.5 N at 72° east of north]

5-90 The data below were obtained from an experiment in which a varying resultant force, $\boldsymbol{F}_R$, was applied to an object, and the resulting accelerations, $\boldsymbol{a}$, were measured. Using these data, plot a graph and determine the mass of the object. [Ans. 3.6 kg]

F_R (N)	0	1.0	2.0	3.0	4.0	5.0	6.0	7.0
a (m/s^2)	0	0.29	0.54	0.83	1.10	1.42	1.69	1.89

5-91 A certain fishing line can withstand a maximum tension of 63 N before breaking. A woman is using the line to hold a fish of mass 0.92 kg. What is the maximum upward acceleration that she can give to the fish without breaking the line? [Ans. 59 m/s^2]

5-92 Below are experimental data obtained by allowing a constant, but unknown, resultant force to act on a variety of masses (m). The magnitudes of the accelerations (a) of the masses were then determined. Use the data to plot graphs of:
(a) a vs. m
(b) a vs. $1/m$, and use this graph to determine the magnitude of the resultant force.
[Ans. (b) 2.8 N]

m (kg)	0.57	1.1	1.6	2.0	2.5	3.2
a (m/s^2)	5.0	2.4	1.9	1.3	1.2	0.9

5-93 In running a 100-m sprint in 10 s, a world-class runner accelerates to a speed of about 8.0 m/s in the first 2.0 s. Determine the magnitude of the average horizontal force on a 63-kg runner during this interval. [Ans. 2.5×10^2 N]

5-94 Three boxes are connected by two cables (Figure 5-37). The masses are m_1 = 26 kg, m_2 = 38 kg, and m_3 = 41 kg. Friction and the rotational motion of the pulleys are neglected. Determine the magnitudes of: (a) the acceleration of the blocks
(b) the tensions in the connecting cables.
[Ans. (a) 1.4 m/s^2 (b) $T_{12} = 2.9 \times 10^2$ N; $T_{23} = 3.4 \times 10^2$ N]

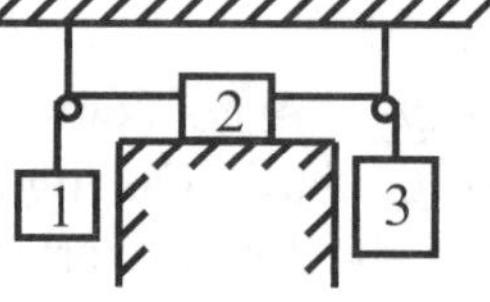

Figure 5-37
Question 5-94.

5-95 Three salamis, P, Q, and R, having masses 1.1 kg, 1.5 kg, and 1.3 kg, respectively, are hung in a "deli" by strings (Figure 5-38). Determine the magnitude of the tension in the string joining P and Q. [Ans. 27 N]

Figure 5-38
Question 5-95.

5-96 If you hang a stone from a string inside a car, you can use it as an accelerometer to determine the car's acceleration by measuring the angle between the string and the vertical. If the mass of the stone is 0.57 kg and the string is 45 cm long, making an angle of 5.1° with the vertical, what is the magnitude of the car's acceleration? What information given in this question is not necessary for the solution? [Ans. 0.87 m/s^2]

5-97 A delivery girl is running with constant velocity, carrying a pizza toward a house. The mass of the pizza is 0.42 kg, and the speed of the girl (and pizza) is 2.0 m/s. Determine the magnitude and direction of the resultant force on the pizza. [Ans. 0 N]

5-98 A mountain climber of mass 67.5 kg is using a rope to "stand" horizontally against a vertical cliff (Figure 5-39). The tension in the rope is 729 N at 27.0° from the horizontal. Determine: (a) the horizontal and vertical components of the force exerted by the cliff on the climber's feet
(b) the magnitude and direction of this force.
[Ans. (a) 650 N, 331 N (b) 729 N at 27.0° above horizontal]

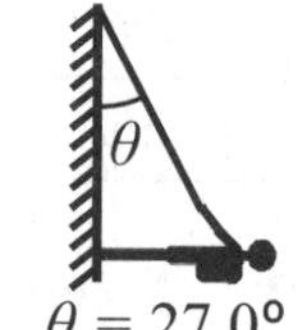

$\theta = 27.0°$

Figure 5-39
Question 5-98.

5-99 Figure 5-40 shows the femur, tibia, and knee cap (patella) in a person's leg. The quadriceps tendon connects the patella to the quadriceps muscle in the thigh. This tendon exerts a tension $\boldsymbol{T}_Q$ on the patella, and this tension makes an angle α = 23° relative to the *x*-axis, as shown. The patella is connected to the tibia by the patella tendon, which exerts a tension $\boldsymbol{T}_P$ on the patella. The direction of this tension relative to the *x*-direction is θ = 68°. If the magnitudes of the tensions are $T_Q = 1.5 \times 10^3$ N and $T_P = 1.3 \times 10^3$ N, determine the magnitude and direction of the total force exerted on the patella by these two tensions.
[Ans. 2.0×10^3 N at 63° below the +*x*-axis]

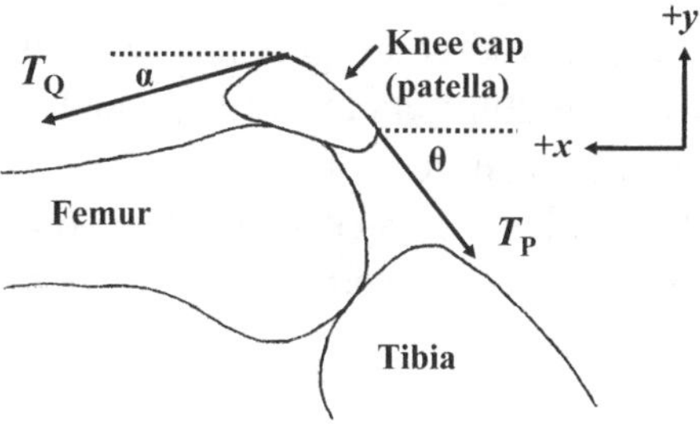

Figure 5-40 *Question 5-99.*

5-100 A man is pushing an upholstered chair of mass 22.3 kg by exerting a force of 157 N at 71.0° from the vertical (Figure 5-41). The force of friction on the chair is 128 N in magnitude. Determine the magnitude of the acceleration of the chair. [Ans. 0.92 m/s^2]

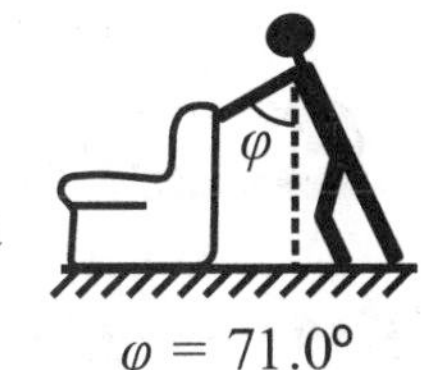

φ = 71.0°
Figure 5-41
Question 5-100.

5-101 In the amusement park ride shown in Figure 5-42, the cars and riders slide down the incline before going around loop-the-loops. The incline makes an angle of 36° with the horizontal (that's steep!). What is the magnitude of the acceleration of the cars down the incline?
[Ans. 5.8 m/s^2]

Figure 5-42 *Question 5-101.*

5-102 A skier of mass 79 kg is sliding at constant velocity down a slope inclined at 8.3° to the horizontal. Determine the magnitudes of:
(a) the normal force exerted on the skier
(b) the frictional force on the skier.
[Ans. (a) 7.7×10^2 N (b) 1.1×10^2 N]

5-103 A girl is pulling a wagon of mass 7.38 kg up a hill inclined at 75.7° to the *vertical* by applying a force parallel to the hill. If the acceleration of the wagon is 0.0645 m/s^2 up the hill, and if friction is neglected, determine the magnitudes of:
(a) the force applied by the girl, and (b) the normal force on the wagon.
[Ans. (a) 18.3 N (b) 70.1N]

5-104 Sometimes a little education can cause problems, as shown in the following classic story. A donkey is told by its owner to pull a cart, but it objects by citing Newton's third law: "If I pull on the cart, it pulls back on me with an equal but opposite force, and I will never be able to get going." Draw separate free-body diagrams for the donkey and cart, and explain why the donkey's argument is incorrect. Do not neglect friction.

5-105 Two hamburgers that are touching each other are being pushed across a grill. The masses of the hamburgers are 113 g and 139 g, and friction is negligible. If the applied horizontal force has a magnitude of 5.38×10^{-2} N and is exerted on the 139-g hamburger, determine the magnitudes of: (a) the acceleration of the hamburgers
(b) the force exerted by one hamburger on the other.
[Ans. 0.213 m/s^2 (b) 2.41×10^{-2} N]

<u>5-106</u> What is the fundamental force that is responsible for both the force of friction and the normal force?

APPLYING YOUR KNOWLEDGE

5-107 By using high-speed movies, it is possible to determine that the impact time during which a golf club is in contact with a golf ball is typically 1.0 ms, and that the speed of the ball when it leaves the club is about 65 m/s (2.3×10^2 km/h!). The mass of a golf ball is 0.045 kg. Determine the magnitude of the average force exerted by the club on the ball. (You can neglect the gravitational force on the ball because it is extremely small in comparison with the force from the club.) [Ans. 2.9×10^3 N]

5-108 Tiny Tompfind, a man of mass 72 kg, steps from a table 92 cm to the floor below. Assume that his velocity is zero as he leaves the table. As he lands, he bends his knees so that he decelerates over a distance of 35 cm.
(a) What is Tiny's speed just as he hits the floor?
(b) As he decelerates, what is the magnitude of the force exerted on him by the floor? Assume constant acceleration.
[Ans. (a) 4.2 m/s (b) 2.6×10^3 N]

5-109 A rocketship is coasting in space from A to B (Figure 5-43). Between A and B, no forces act on the ship. At B, the rockets fire as shown and provide a constant acceleration until the ship reaches a point C in space. Make a sketch of the rocket's path between B and C.

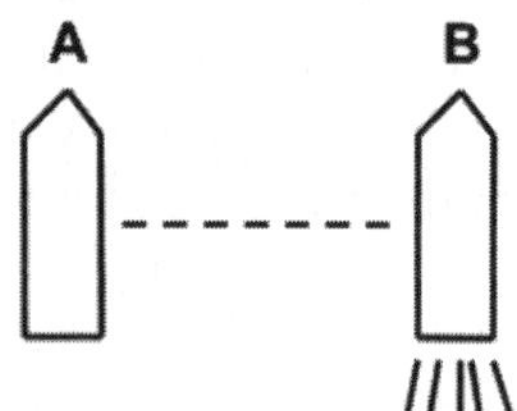

Figure 5-43
Question 5-109.

5-110 A girl on a toboggan slides down a hill inclined at 18° to the horizontal. Friction is negligible. If she starts from rest, what is her speed after sliding for 2.6 s? [Ans. 7.9 m/s]

5-111 A long jumper just after takeoff (Figure 5-44) experiences two forces: gravity and air resistance. The magnitude of the air resistance can be calculated from: $F_{AIR} = kv^2$, where v is the jumper's speed, and the quantity k depends on the air density and the jumper's shape and size. For a typical jumper, k is about 0.25 kg/m. Reasonable takeoff velocity components are: horizontal, 9.2 m/s; vertical, 3.5 m/s.
(a) Use the takeoff velocity components to determine v^2 at takeoff.

(b) Determine F_{AIR} at takeoff. By considering units of k and v, check that you are getting the correct SI units for F_{AIR} .
(c) The air resistance is in the opposite direction to the jumper's velocity. Calculate the horizontal and vertical components of the takeoff air resistance.
(d) Draw a free-body diagram for the jumper (mass 65 kg) just after leaving the ground, and determine the magnitude and direction of the net force on him.
[Ans. (a) 97 m^2/s^2 (b) 24 N (c) 23 N (horizontal), 8.6 N (downward)
(d) 6.5×10^2 N at 2.0° from vertical]

Figure 5-44 *Question 5-111.*

5-112 In an oscilloscope, an electron beam is deflected by an electric force produced by charged metal plates (AD and BC in Figure 5-45). In the region ABCD, there is a uniform downward electric force of 3.20×10^{-15} N on each electron. The electrons enter halfway between A and B with a velocity of 2.25×10^7 m/s parallel to the plates. Outside ABCD, the electric force is zero, and the gravitational force can be neglected during the short time that the electrons take to reach the fluorescent screen S. When an electron hits S, how far below the axis will it be? The electron mass is 9.11×10^{-31} kg.
[Ans. 3.02×10^{-2} m]

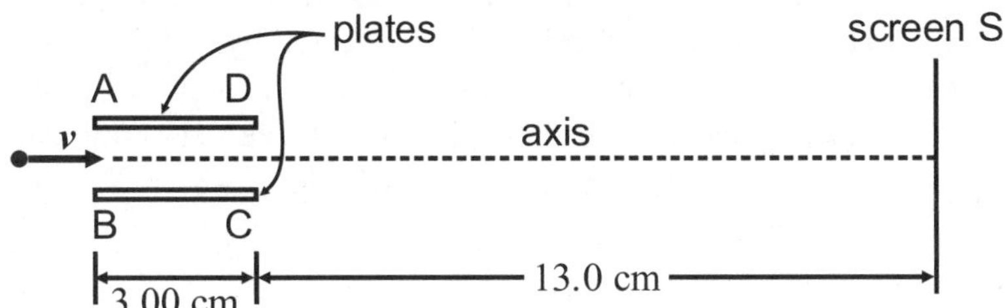

Figure 5-45 *Question 5-112.*

5-113 *Fermi Question:* Determine the magnitude of the force required to accelerate an automobile from rest to a typical in-city driving speed.
[Ans. approximately 5×10^3 N to 10×10^3 N]

KEY OBJECTIVES

Having completed this chapter, you should now be able to do the following:

1. Identify the forces acting on objects in a wide variety of physical situations.
2. Add forces as vectors.
3. State Newton's three laws of motion, and use them in solving problems in one and two dimensions.
4. Draw free-body diagrams for objects in various situations.
5. Define a newton.
6. Relate the gravitational force on an object to the gravitational acceleration.
7. Correctly identify action-reaction pairs of forces.
8. List the fundamental forces and state how other forces are related to them.

ANSWERS TO SELECTED QUESTIONS

5-10 (a) 0 N (b) 19 N downward
5-21 (a) downward (b) 9.8 m/s^2 (c) downward (d) downward, 9.8 m/s^2, downward
(e) downward, 9.8 m/s^2, downward
5-22 (a) downward (b) 9.8 m/s^2 (c) downward (d) downward, 9.8 m/s^2, downward
(e) downward, 9.8 m/s^2, downward
5-29 yes 5-30 yes 5-31 no 5-32 yes 5-33 yes 5-34 no 5-35 no 5-36 yes
5-75 (a) gravitational force toward Jupiter, exerted by Jupiter on the sun
(b) downward normal force, exerted by the book on the table
(c) force exerted by the pan on the chef, directed toward the oven
(d) forward force exerted by the water on the canoeist (and paddle)
(e) upward gravitational force exerted by the apple on Earth
(f) downward force (friction) exerted by the hailstone on the air
5-82 (a) electrical force (b) gravity (c) electrical force (d) gravity
(e) electrical force (f) electrical force (g) nuclear strong force
5-83 (c) 5-84 (a) 5-85 (b) 5-86 (d) 5-87 (b) 5-88 (c)
5-106 electrical force

CHAPTER 6

APPLYING NEWTON'S LAWS

Applications of Newton's laws are in evidence all around us, from the graceful movement of a flying bird, to the aerodynamic design of modern automobiles, to the motion of a skier coming down a hill. This chapter concentrates on applying Newton's laws in situations involving friction and circular motion. We will be exploring answers to questions such as: what is special about Teflon®? and how does a centrifuge work?

6.1 STATIC AND KINETIC FRICTION

Imagine how different our world would be without friction. Most modes of transportation would be impossible: walking, cars, trains, etc. We would be unable to hold a pen, or more importantly, a fork. Of course, since friction is due to attractive electrical forces between molecules, a lack of friction would imply that the electrical force does not exist. Without this force to hold atoms and molecules together, there would be no cars, trains, pens, forks, or even people to talk about these things.

Friction was discussed briefly in Chapter 5. Recall that if an object is moving, friction acts in the opposite direction to the motion. If an object is stationary, friction acts only if there is another force applied with a component parallel to the surfaces in contact. In this case, friction acts in the opposite direction to the motion that would occur if friction did not exist.

In this section, we will deal with friction more completely by introducing the concepts of static friction, kinetic friction, and coefficients of static and kinetic friction. Our discussion will apply to *rigid* objects that *slide* over each other. You know from everyday experience that *rolling* friction is considerably less than sliding friction — imagine trying to move an automobile by sliding it! — but we will not be dealing quantitatively with rolling friction in this book.

Figure 6-1 illustrates a demonstration that you can do yourself if you have a spring scale available. The scale is used to apply measurable

$F_{APPLIED} = 2$ N $F_S = 2$ N (b)

$F_{APPLIED} = 10$ N $F_S = 10$ N (c)

constant v $F_{APPLIED} = 9$ N $F_K = 9$ N (d)

Figure 6-1 **(a), (b),** *and* **(c)***: The book is stationary, as a horizontal applied force is increased from (a) 1 N, to (b) 2 N, to (c) 10 N. Static friction (F_S) matches the applied force up to a maximum value (10 N in this example).*
(d) *Once an object begins to move, friction usually decreases. In this example, an applied force of magnitude 9 N moves the book at constant velocity because the kinetic friction (F_K) is only 9 N.*

horizontal forces on an object such as a book. For small applied forces, the book does not move because the force of friction is equal to the applied force (in magnitude). Since the book is static (or stationary), we refer to friction in this case as **static friction** ($\boldsymbol{F}_S$). Static friction is the friction force between two objects at rest relative to each other. As the force applied to the book increases, the static friction force does not increase in size indefinitely. It has a maximum magnitude ($F_{S,MAX}$) that is dependent on the types of materials in contact. The maximum magnitude also depends on the size of the normal force between the objects. In the example shown in Figure 6-1, $F_{S,MAX} = 10$ N.

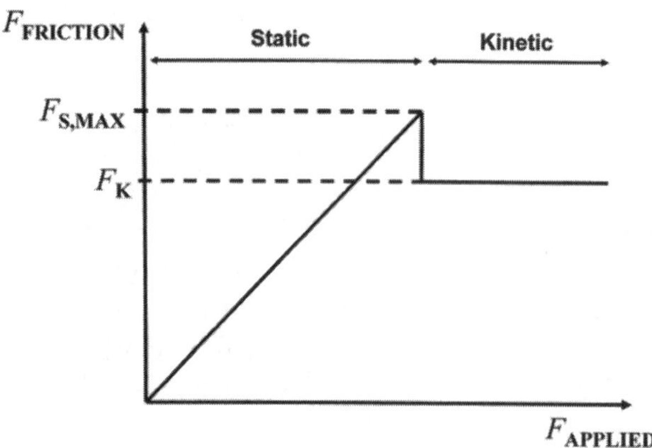

Figure 6-2 *A graph of friction force vs. applied force (magnitudes). The magnitude of kinetic friction (F_K) is usually less than the maximum magnitude of static friction ($F_{S,MAX}$).*

Once an object begins to slide, we refer to the friction as **kinetic friction** ($\boldsymbol{F}_K$), that is, moving friction. The kinetic friction force is usually smaller than the maximum value of static friction (Figures 6-1 (d) and 6-2). Al-though kinetic friction usually decreases somewhat as the speed of the sliding object increases, in this book we will treat kinetic friction as being independent of speed. As is the case with the maximum value of static friction, the kinetic friction force depends on the kinds of materials in contact and on the magnitude of the normal force between the objects.

Coefficients of Friction

It has been established experimentally that the maximum magnitude of static friction between two objects is proportional to the magnitude of the normal force between them, that is,

$$F_{S,MAX} \propto F_N \tag{6-1}$$

The constant of proportionality depends on the types of materials in contact. The constant is higher for rough or sticky materials than for slippery materials. It is called the **coefficient of static friction** and is represented by μ_S (μ is the lower case Greek letter mu.) Writing the relation between $F_{S,MAX}$ and F_N as an equation, we have:

$$F_{S,MAX} = \mu_S F_N \tag{6-2}$$

Remember that this equation deals only with the magnitudes of the forces. The directions of $\boldsymbol{F}_{S,MAX}$ and $\boldsymbol{F}_N$ are at right angles to each other. ($\boldsymbol{F}_{S,MAX}$ is parallel to the surfaces in contact, and $\boldsymbol{F}_N$ is perpendicular to the surfaces.) Values of μ_S range typically from 0.1 to 1 (Table 6.1). Notice that since μ_S is the ratio of the magnitudes of two forces, $F_{S,MAX}/F_N$, it has no units.

Equation 6-2 is sometimes expressed as an inequality involving F_S (not $F_{S,MAX}$) and F_N:

$$F_S \le \mu_S F_N \tag{6-3}$$

It has also been found experimentally that kinetic friction is proportional to the magnitude of the normal force. The proportionality constant is called the **coefficient of kinetic friction,** represented by μ_K. Hence,

$$F_K = \mu_K F_N \tag{6-4}$$

Since F_K is usually less than $F_{S,MAX}$, then $\mu_K < \mu_S$. Table 6.1 gives some representative values of the coefficients μ_S and μ_K. Note the low values of μ_S and μ_K for steel on Teflon®, Teflon is a compound of carbon and fluorine that experiences extremely weak electrical forces with virtually all other types of molecules. Since the strength of friction forces is determined by the strength of the intermolecular electrical forces, friction involving Teflon[1] is very small.

Table 6.1
Coefficients of Static (μ_S) and Kinetic (μ_K) Friction

Materials	μ_S	μ_K
copper on cast iron	1.05	0.29
oak on oak (parallel to grain)	0.62	0.48
hard steel on hard steel (dry)	0.78	0.42
hard steel on hard steel (greasy) (values depend on lubricant used)	0.11 – 0.23	0.03 – 0.11
steel on Teflon®	0.04	0.04
steel on ice	?	0.01

It must be emphasized here that coefficients of friction are poorly known, and poorly reproducible in experiments. They depend strongly on the state of the surfaces being used — the cleanliness, roughness, degree of oxidation, temperature, wear, etc. Therefore, in problems in this book, coefficients of friction will be given to two significant digits at most.

Figure 6-3 shows a highly magnified view of one object sliding over another. Even highly polished surfaces appear rough when magnified, and in regions where the molecules of the two surfaces come into close contact, electrical attractive forces cause the molecules to bind together, and we say that molecular bonds are formed. This is the cause of friction. In order to produce and maintain a sliding motion, a force must be applied to break these bonds. As the sliding continues, new bonds are being constantly formed and broken. The molecules, which are stretched somewhat just before the bonds are broken, "snap back" into place as the bonds break, and vibrate with

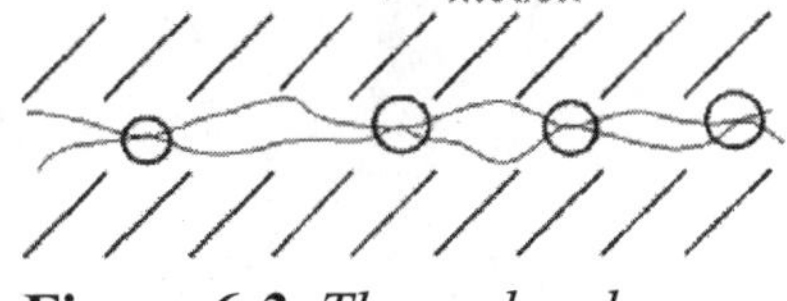

Figure 6-3 *The molecular cause of friction. As one object slides over another, molecules bind together at points of close contact (circled). A force must be applied to break the bonds and maintain the motion.*

[1] Teflon® is used as a coating on cookware because of its weak bonding to other materials (eggs, potatoes, etc.). As well, it is used in surgical implants because it does not interact with body fluids, and the space industry is also a large user of this inert material. Teflon was created by chance by two research chemists in 1938.

more energy than they had previously. We say that the thermal energy (or internal energy) of the objects increases, or that the objects get hotter. *Whenever kinetic friction is acting, thermal energy is produced.* You can show this yourself by rubbing the palms of your hands together vigorously; they get quite hot! Sometimes an increase in thermal energy due to friction can produce melting of a material. For example, the motion of skis on snow melts some of the snow to produce a thin layer of water, which aids the sliding of the skis.[2]

Did You Know? *The science and technology of friction and lubrication is known as "tribology." "Triboluminescence" refers to the production of light by friction; you can demonstrate it by crushing (or biting) certain types of hard candy in a darkened room. As you crush, the friction between the moving layers of candy causes a visible glow. "Nanotribology," which is the study of atomic friction, such as at a liquid-solid interface, may one day result in comfortable prosthetic joints and smoother-running machines.*

What happens if two extremely smooth surfaces are placed in contact? A large number of molecular bonds can be formed, and it is possible for the two surfaces to weld together. You might have encountered this phenomenon yourself with flat microscope slides, which can stick together if they come into close contact. Another example occurs in machine shops, where small steel blocks used for precision measurements can be temporarily bonded together by pushing the very flat edges of the blocks together. Thus a single block, say three units long, can be created from two blocks of lengths one unit and two units. The blocks can later be pulled apart by hand. These blocks are commonly known as "Jo blocks" (Figure 6-4), a short form for Johansson blocks, named after C.E. Johansson, a Swedish engineer.

Figure 6-4 *Two "Jo blocks," shown separated (left), and bonded together (right).*

[2] Frictional heating is not sufficient to explain the existence of a thin layer of water under skate blades gliding on ice. Without this water, it would be very difficult to skate. It is often stated in physics textbooks that the pressure due to the weight of the skater on the blades is so large that melting occurs, or that a combination of this pressure and frictional heating produces the melting. However, a detailed analysis shows that these mechanisms are not enough to generate the melting. Rather, the thin layer of water is due to a phenomenon known as *surface melting*, which means that some solids at a temperature *below* the melting point naturally have a thin liquid layer all over the surface, even without anything pressing or moving against the surface. This was first suggested by the physicist Michael Faraday in 1842, and has been well established for many solids by experiments in the past couple of decades. In the case of ice at −10°C, the surface water film has a thickness of only 2 nm, which is only about seven water molecules thick.

A *permanent* weld can be achieved, say between two metal surfaces, if the surfaces are carefully polished and cleaned, and placed together in a chamber with very little air. (Otherwise, surface oxide films interfere with the strong bonding.) With a permanent weld, friction becomes essentially infinite.

Sample Problem 6-1

A box of lettuce of mass 7.52 kg is at rest on a wooden floor. The coefficients of friction between the box and the floor are: static, 0.57; kinetic, 0.45. A horizontal force is applied to the box. What are the magnitudes of the friction force and the acceleration of the box, if the applied force has a magnitude of (a) 21 N? (b) 42 N? (c) 63 N?

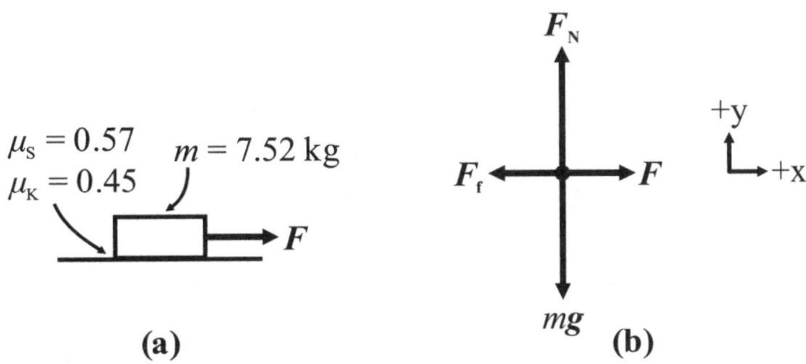

Figure 6-5 **(a)** *Diagram for Sample Problem 6-1.*
(b) *Free-body diagram for the box of lettuce.*

Solution: (a) Figure 6-5 shows a diagram for the problem and the FBD for the box. In order to determine whether the box will have any acceleration at all, we need to calculate the maximum magnitude of static friction:

$$F_{\text{S,MAX}} = \mu_{\text{S}} F_{\text{N}}$$

The coefficient μ_{S} is known, but F_{N} is unknown. We can use Newton's first (or second) law in the *y*-direction to determine F_{N}.

$$\Sigma F_{\text{y}} = ma_{\text{y}} = 0$$

This gives

$$F_{\text{N}} + (-mg) = 0$$

$$F_{\text{N}} = mg = (7.52\text{ kg})(9.80\text{ m/s}^2) = 73.7\text{ N}$$

Then

$$F_{\text{S,MAX}} = \mu_S F_{\text{N}} = (0.57)(73.7\text{ N}) = 42\text{ N}$$

Thus, the maximum static friction force possible is 42 N.

In the x-direction, the only forces acting are the applied force and the friction force. Since the applied force has a magnitude of 21 N, which is less than $F_{S,MAX}$, then the (static) friction force will also have a magnitude of 21 N, and the box will have an acceleration of zero.

(b) The magnitude of the applied force (F) is now 42 N, which is equal to $F_{S,MAX}$, and the box will be on the verge of slipping. The friction force will be at its maximum value of 42 N, and the box will still have an acceleration of zero.

(c) Now F = 63 N > $F_{S,MAX}$, and the box will accelerate in the direction of the applied force. The box will move almost instantaneously and therefore we need to consider the *kinetic* friction force:

$$F_K = \mu_K F_N = (0.45)(73.7\text{ N}) = 33\text{ N}$$

Hence, the friction force has a magnitude of 33 N in this case. To find the acceleration, we use Newton's second law:

$$\Sigma F_x = ma_x$$

Therefore,

$$F + (-F_K) = ma_x$$

$$a_x = \frac{F - F_K}{m} = \frac{(63 - 33)\text{ N}}{7.52\text{ kg}} = 4.0\text{ m/s}^2$$

Thus, when F = 63 N, the box has an acceleration of magnitude of 4.0 m/s^2.

Sample Problem 6-2

A roofer is working on a roof inclined at 34° to the horizontal. Friction between the worker's boots and the roof is sufficient to prevent him from sliding, but his metal tool case does slide. The coefficient of static friction between the roof and tool case is 0.48, and the mass of the tool case is 9.2 kg. What is the magnitude of the minimum force that the roofer can exert parallel to the slope of the roof to keep the case from sliding?

Solution: Figure 6-6 shows the general diagram and the FBD for the tool case. If the worker is exerting the minimum possible force $\boldsymbol{F}$ (Figure 6-6 (b)), the tool case must be on the verge of slipping, and static friction must be at its maximum possible value $F_{S,MAX}$. Since the tool case would slip down the roof if released, the direction of friction must be up parallel to the roof. As in problems in Chapter 5 involving motion along an incline, the x-y axes are chosen parallel and perpendicular to the incline. The x- and y-components of $\boldsymbol{mg}$ are shown on Figure 6-6 (b). Since the tool case is at rest and remains at rest, the x- and y-components of its acceleration are zero.

We need to determine F. Using Newton's first or second law in the x-direction:

$$\Sigma F_x = ma_x = 0$$

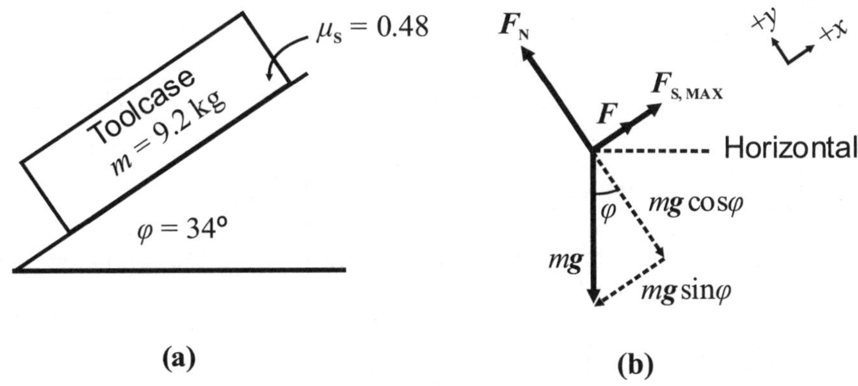

Figure 6-6 **(a)** *Diagram for Sample Problem 6-2.*
(b) *Free-body diagram for the tool case.*

Therefore, $$F + F_{S,MAX} + (-mg\sin\varphi) = 0$$

Hence, $$F = mg\sin\varphi - F_{S,MAX} \qquad \text{Eqn. [1]}$$

We know m, g, and φ, but $F_{S,MAX}$ is unknown. However, we can write $F_{S,MAX} = \mu_S F_N$ because the tool case is on the verge of slipping. We are given that $\mu_S = 0.48$, and we can get an expression for F_N from the y-direction:

> ***Problem-solving Tip:*** *Be careful when using the relation $F_{S,MAX} = \mu_S F_N$. It is valid only when an object is on the brink of slipping.*

$$\Sigma F_y = ma_y = 0$$

This gives
$$F_N + (-mg\cos\varphi) = 0$$
$$F_N = mg\cos\varphi$$

Now we can use
$$F_{S,MAX} = \mu_S F_N$$
$$= \mu_S\, mg\cos\varphi \qquad \text{Eqn. [2]}$$

Using Eqn. [1]:
$$F = mg\sin\varphi - F_{S,MAX}$$
$$= mg\sin\varphi - \mu_S\, mg\cos\varphi \qquad \text{from Eqn. [2]}$$
$$= mg(\sin\varphi - \mu_S\cos\varphi)$$

Now we can substitute known values: $F = (9.2\text{ kg})(9.8\text{ m/s}^2)(\sin 34° - 0.48\cos 34°) = 15\text{ N}$

Thus, the minimum force required to prevent sliding is 15 N in magnitude.

Practice

6-1 If friction did not exist, what would happen if you tried to walk?

<u>6-2</u> If a person slides a plate eastward across a table, in which direction is the force of friction on the plate? Is this friction static or kinetic?

6-3 A box of hamburger buns of mass 11 kg is at rest on a horizontal floor in a fast-food restaurant. The coefficients of friction between the box and the floor are: static, 0.55; kinetic, 0.47. A horizontal force is applied to the box. What are the magnitudes of the friction force and the acceleration of the box, if the applied force has a magnitude of (a) 55 N? (b) 61 N?
[Ans. (a) 55 N, 0 m/s^2 (b) 51 N, 0.94 m/s^2]

6-4 The coefficients of friction between a stove of mass 65 kg and the horizontal floor beneath it are: static, 0.71; kinetic, 0.64. (a) What is the minimum horizontal force that must be applied to the stove to set it in motion? (b) Once the stove is moving, what magnitude of horizontal force will keep it moving at constant velocity?
[Ans. (a) 4.5×10^2 N (b) 4.1×10^2 N]

6-5 A woman of mass 51 kg is standing on a wet floor. The coefficients of friction between her shoes and the floor are: static, 0.25; kinetic, 0.17. In order to open a large door, she exerts a horizontal force of 130 N. Does she slide? Explain, using calculations. [Ans. Yes]

6-6 A girl applies a horizontal force of magnitude 31 N to a chair of mass 5.8 kg. As a result, the chair slides across a horizontal floor with an acceleration of magnitude 0.32 m/s^2. What is the coefficient of kinetic friction between the chair and the floor? [Ans. 0.51]

6-7 A hockey puck travels 33 m along an ice rink before coming to rest. Its initial speed was 11 m/s. (a) What is the magnitude of the acceleration of the puck?
(b) What is the coefficient of kinetic friction between the puck and the ice?
[Ans. (a) 1.8 m/s^2 (b) 0.19]

<u>6-8</u> A small book is sitting on top of a large book, which is sitting on a horizontal tabletop. A student exerts a horizontal force on the large book and both books are accelerated together, that is, the small book does not slip on the large one.
(a) Draw a FBD for the small book when it is accelerating.
(b) What is the name of the force that produces the horizontal acceleration of the small book?
(c) If the acceleration of the books has a magnitude of 2.5 m/s^2, what is the smallest coefficient of static friction between the books that will prevent slipping? [Ans. (c) 0.26]

6-9 Draw a FBD for the large book in the previous question when the book is accelerating. (This is tricky – remember Newton's third law.)

6-10 A toboggan of mass 10.8 kg is pulled along a horizontal snow-covered field by a rope that makes an angle of 21° above the horizontal. The coefficients of friction between the toboggan and the snow beneath it are: static, 0.15; kinetic, 0.095. What magnitude of rope tension is required to keep the toboggan moving at constant velocity? (Hint: $F_N \neq mg$ in this problem.) [Ans. 1.0×10^1 N]

6-11 A child is sliding down a water slide inclined at 25° to the horizontal. The coefficient of kinetic friction between the child and the slide is 0.10. What is the magnitude of the acceleration of the child? (Hint: $F_N \neq mg$) [Ans. 3.3 m/s^2]

6-12 In an experiment to determine the coefficient of static friction μ_S between two materials, a small block of one material rests on an incline made of the other material. The angle between the incline and the horizontal is increased to a value ϕ where the block is on the verge of slipping. (a) Determine an expression for μ_S in terms of ϕ. (b) Describe a similar experiment to determine μ_K. [Ans. (a) $\mu_S = \tan \phi$]

6-13 James Bond is being dragged along a horizontal surface by a rope attached to a large container of diamonds that is falling vertically. The rope passes over a pulley as shown in Figure 6-7. James has a mass of 83 kg, and the container of diamonds has a mass of 45 kg. If the magnitude of the acceleration of James and the diamonds is 1.2 m/s^2, determine the coefficient of kinetic friction between James and the surface beneath him. Neglect the rotational motion of the pulley. [Ans. 0.35]

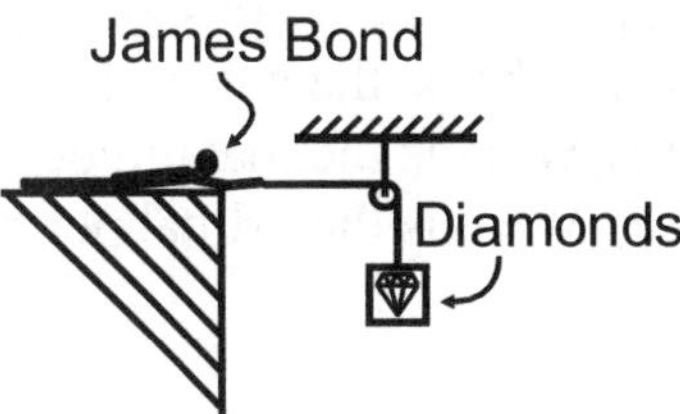

Figure 6-7 *Question 6-13.*

6.2 CENTRIPETAL FORCE

There are many examples of circular motion in nature and in human-made devices. Many planets follow orbits that are essentially circular, each point on Earth travels in a daily circle because of Earth's rotation, and rotating shafts (whether in CD-players, food processors, or drills) move in circles. We saw in Chapter 4 that an object traveling at constant speed in a circle, or on a path that is a portion of a circle, is undergoing an acceleration directed toward the centre of the circle. By Newton's second law, this acceleration must be the result of a resultant force acting toward the centre. For instance, in the case of a planet in a circular orbit about a star, the force acting on the planet toward the centre of the circle is the force of gravity exerted by the star.

The resultant force toward the centre of a circle is often called the **centripetal force**. Students sometimes get the mistaken impression that the centripetal force is a separate force of nature. In fact, it is just one of the forces that you know about already, such as the force of gravity acting on the planet mentioned in the previous paragraph. In other situations, the centripetal force might be a force such as tension, friction, etc., or a combination of forces. The sample problems in this section illustrate a number of different forces acting as the centripetal force.

In Chapter 4, the magnitude of the centripetal acceleration of an object in circular motion was expressed as v^2/r, where v is the object's speed and r is the circle's radius. In dealing with problems involving *forces* on objects in circular motion, Newton's second law, $\Sigma F = ma$, can be used along with $a = v^2/r$ to give $\Sigma F = mv^2/r$. Since the acceleration, v^2/r, is directed toward the centre of the circle, then the force represented by ΣF must be the (component of the) resultant force directed toward the centre; this (centripetal) force can normally be determined easily from a free-body diagram.

Sample Problem 6-3

The orbit of Uranus around the sun is approximately a circle of radius 2.9×10^{12} m. The (approximately constant) speed of Uranus is 6.8×10^3 m/s, and its mass is 8.73×10^{25} kg.
(a) What is the name of the force that constitutes the centripetal force in this case?
(b) What is the magnitude of this force?
(c) What is the orbital period of Uranus?

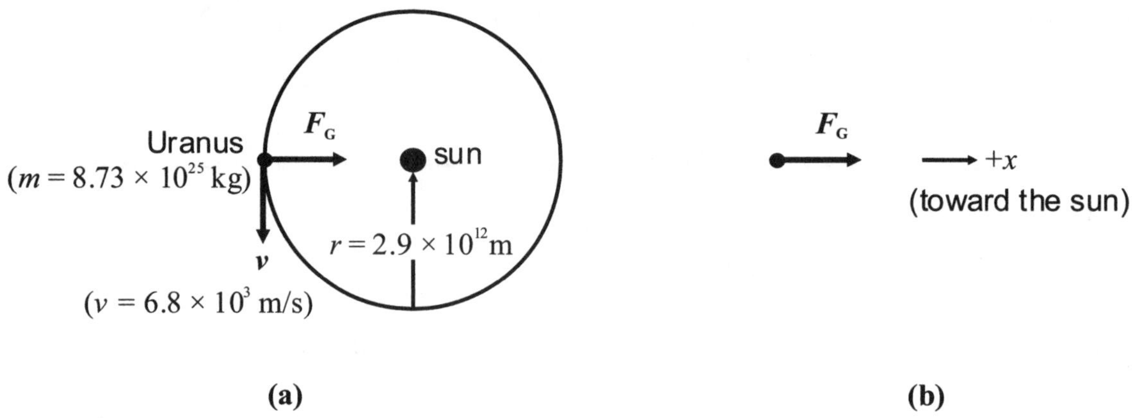

Figure 6-8 **(a)** *Sample Problem 6-3.* **(b)** *Free-body diagram for Uranus.*

Solution: (a) A diagram is given in Figure 6-8 (a). The only force that acts on Uranus is the gravitational force of attraction toward the sun. This is the centripetal force.

(b) A free-body diagram for Uranus is shown in Figure 6-8 (b). The acceleration is toward the sun, and the +x-axis has been chosen in this direction. Writing Newton's second law:

$$\Sigma F_{x} = ma_{x}$$

$$F_{G} = ma_{x}$$

Since a_x is the centripetal acceleration, we can write $a_x = v^2/r$, giving $F_G = mv^2/r$.

Substituting known values: $$F_G = (8.73\times10^{25}\text{ kg})\times\frac{(6.8\times10^3\text{ m/s})^2}{(2.9\times10^{12}\text{ m})} = 1.4\times10^{21}\text{ N}$$

Thus, the magnitude of the gravitational (centripetal) force is 1.4×10^{21} N.

(c) The orbital period is the time for one revolution, that is, the time to travel one circumference of the circle ($2\pi r$). Since the speed is constant, we can write: time = distance/speed.

Thus, $$t = \frac{2\pi r}{v} = \frac{2\pi(2.9\times10^{12}\text{ m})}{6.8\times10^3\text{ m/s}} = 2.7\times10^9\text{ s} \quad \text{(or 84 yr)}$$

Therefore, the orbital period of Uranus is 2.7×10^9 s.

Sample Problem 6-4

A bird of mass 0.211 kg pulls out of a dive, the bottom portion of which can be considered as a circular arc of radius 25.6 m. At the bottom of the arc,
(a) if the bird's speed is 21.7 m/s, what is the magnitude of the upward lift on the bird's wings?
(b) which force(s) constitute(s) the centripetal force?

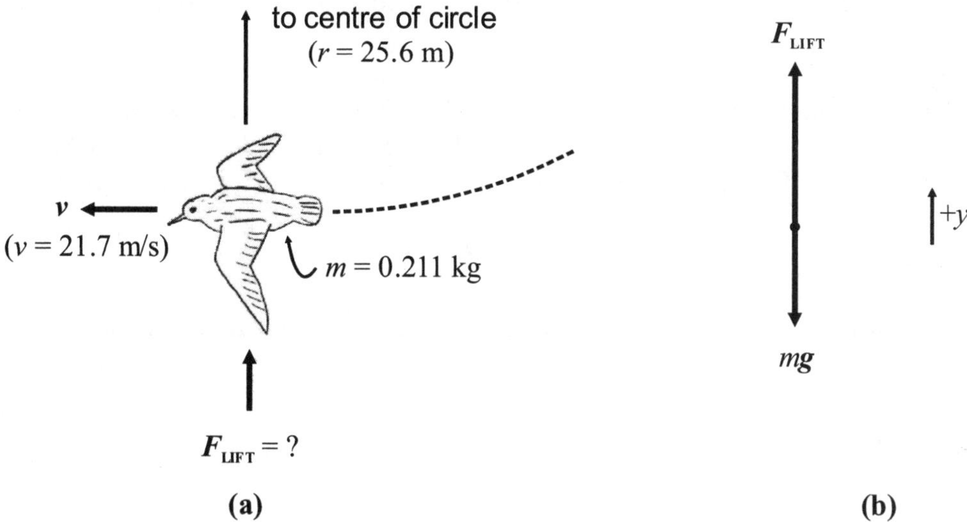

Figure 6-9 **(a)** *Sample Problem 6-4.* **(b)** *Free-body diagram for the bird.*

Solution: (a) Figure 6-9 shows a diagram of the problem, and a free-body diagram for the bird. The forces on the bird are an upward lift exerted by the air, and the downward force of gravity.

We have neglected the horizontal air-drag force. (Including it would not change the solution to this particular problem.) The centre of the circle is upward from the bird. Therefore, the centripetal acceleration is upward, and we choose the +*y*-axis in this direction. Writing Newton's second law:

$$\Sigma F_y = ma_y$$

$$F_{LIFT} + (-mg) = ma_y$$

Substituting $a_y = v^2/r$, and solving for F_{LIFT}:

$$F_{LIFT} = mg + m\frac{v^2}{r}$$

$$= m\left(g + \frac{v^2}{r}\right)$$

$$= (0.211\text{ kg})\left[9.80\text{ m/s}^2 + \frac{(21.7\text{ m/s})^2}{25.6\text{ m}}\right]$$

$$= 5.95\text{ N}$$

Did You Know? *For something such as a spinning fan, the centripetal force on each atom and molecule in the fan blades is an electrical force toward the centre of rotation, exerted by surrounding atoms and molecules. If the fan spins very rapidly, the electrical force might not be large enough to provide the required centripetal force, and the blades could fly apart, that is, the molecules would become separated. The strength of materials, which depends on the intermolecular electrical forces, is important in designing anything that spins rapidly, from food processors to jet engines.*

Therefore, the upward lift force has a magnitude of 5.95 N.

Note that the solution does not require that the bird travel at constant speed. The algebraic expression for F_{LIFT} is valid whether or not the speed v is changing. Of course, it was essential to substitute the correct numerical value for the bird's speed at the bottom of the dive.

(b) The centripetal force is always the resultant force acting toward the centre of the circle. In this problem, the centre is upward from the bird (Fig. 6-9 (a)). The upward lift acts toward the centre, and gravity acts away from the centre. Therefore, the resultant force toward the centre, that is, the centripetal force, is the difference between the upward lift and gravity. In terms of symbols:

$$F_{CENTRIPETAL} = \Sigma F_y = F_{LIFT} - mg$$

Sample Problem 6-5

Highway curves are banked so that even if the road is extremely slippery, cars will be able to negotiate the curve without sliding. (a) Which force(s) constitute(s) the centripetal force on the car? (b) What is the proper banking angle (φ in Figure 6-10 (a)) for a car travelling at 90 km/h around a curve of radius 500 m? (Assume two significant digits.)

Solution: (a) The free-body diagram for the car is shown in Figure 6-10 (b). The car is travelling along part of a horizontal circle, and therefore the direction from the car to the centre of the circle is horizontal. Hence, the (centripetal) acceleration is horizontal, and the $+x$-axis has been chosen in this direction (with the $+y$-axis at right angles to it). We assume that the road is very slippery (i.e., no friction), and thus there are only two forces acting on the car, gravity and the normal force. The only force acting horizontally, that is, toward the centre of the circle, is a component of the normal force. Hence, this horizontal component of the normal force is the centripetal force.

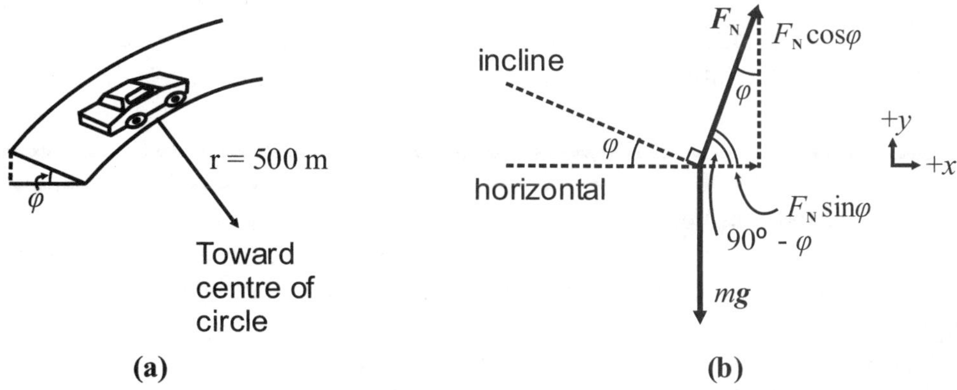

Figure 6-10 **(a)** *Sample Problem 6-5.* **(b)** *Free-body diagram for the car.*

(b) Writing Newton's second law in the x-direction:

$$\Sigma F_x = ma_x$$
$$F_N \sin\varphi = ma_x$$

Since a_x is the centripetal acceleration, $a_x = v^2/r$, giving:

$$F_N \sin\varphi = mv^2/r \qquad \text{Eqn. [1]}$$

Because F_N, φ, and m are unknown, we need another equation. In the y-direction, there is no acceleration (the car does not slide up or down the plane if the banking angle is correct). Hence, using Newton's first or second law:

$$\Sigma F_y = ma_y = 0$$
$$F_N \cos\varphi + (-mg) = 0$$
$$F_N \cos\varphi = mg \qquad \text{Eqn. [2]}$$

We can eliminate F_N and m in one step by dividing Eqn. [1] by Eqn. [2] :

$$\frac{\sin\varphi}{\cos\varphi} = \frac{v^2}{rg} \quad \text{giving} \quad \tan\varphi = \frac{v^2}{rg}$$

and therefore $\varphi = \tan^{-1}(v^2/rg)$

Did You Know? *Highway engineers must design roads with the proper banking angles. The next time you travel on a highway, notice that the banking angles for on- and off-ramps are larger than the angles for the more gradual curves on the main highway. Why is this so? Why is the posted speed for a ramp lower than the speed limit on the main highway?*

Before substituting known values, we need to convert the units of the speed to m/s.

$$90\frac{\text{km}}{\text{h}}\times\frac{1000\text{ m}}{1\text{ km}}\times\frac{1\text{ h}}{3600\text{ s}}=25\text{ m/s}$$

Substituting values: $$\varphi=\tan^{-1}\left(\frac{v^2}{rg}\right)=\tan^{-1}\left[\frac{(25\text{ m/s})^2}{(500\text{ m})((9.8\text{ m/s}^2)}\right]=7.3°$$

Thus, the correct banking angle is 7.3° (to two significant digits). Notice that the mass *m* "cancelled out" during the solution.

Determining the Centripetal Force

In the three sample problems above, note that the centripetal force has been
(i) gravity
(ii) the difference between aerodynamic lift and gravity, and
(iii) a component of the normal force.

When solving problems, remember that *centripetal force is not a separate additional force.* It is found automatically on the free-body diagram as the resultant force acting toward the centre of the circle.

Practice

<u>6-14</u> In each case below, draw a free-body diagram for object "A" and name the force(s) that constitute(s) the centripetal force.
(a) A communications satellite (A) is in a circular orbit around Earth.
(b) Earth (A) is in a circular orbit (approximately) around the sun.
(c) A skier (A) slides over the top of a hump that has the shape of a circular arc.
(d) A car (A) travels around an *unbanked* curve on a highway without sliding. (Hint: the phrase "without sliding" is important.)
(e) A car (A) travels around a *banked* curve at the correct speed for the banking angle (i.e., friction is not required for the car to go around the curve).
(f) An electron (A) travels in a circular orbit around a nucleus (in a simple model of the atom).

<u>6-15</u> A wet pair of jeans travels in a horizontal circle in the spin cycle of a washing machine.
(a) What object exerts the centripetal force on the jeans?
(b) What is the name of the force that is the centripetal force?
(c) The radius of the circle in which the jeans travel is 27 cm. If the machine has a frequency of 8.5 rev/s, how far do the jeans travel in 1.0 s?
(d) What is the speed of the jeans?

(e) The mass of the wet jeans is 1.7 kg. What is the magnitude of the centripetal force on the jeans?
[Ans. (c) 14 m (d) 14 m/s (e) 1.3×10^3 N]

6-16 Neptune follows an essentially circular orbit of radius 4.5×10^{12} m around the sun. The mass of Neptune is 1.0×10^{26} kg, and the gravitational force exerted on Neptune by the sun has a magnitude of 6.8×10^{20} N. (a) What is Neptune's speed? (b) How long does it take Neptune to complete one orbit around the sun? Express your answer in seconds and years.
[Ans. (a) 5.5×10^3 m/s (b) 5.1×10^9 s; 1.6×10^2 yr]

6-17 In a hydrogen atom, the electron (mass 9.11×10^{-31} kg) in its lowest energy state travels around the nucleus in a circle of radius 5.3×10^{-11} m. The speed of the electron is 2.2×10^6 m/s.
(a) What is the name of the force that is the centripetal force?
(b) What are the magnitude and direction of this force?
[Ans. (b) 8.3×10^{-8} N, toward nucleus]

6-18 A ball attached to the end of a string is whirled in a vertical circle (Figure 6-11). Neglect air resistance.
(a) Draw a free-body diagram for the ball at each of the points A, B, C, and D.
(b) In each free-body diagram, which force(s) constitute(s) the centripetal force?

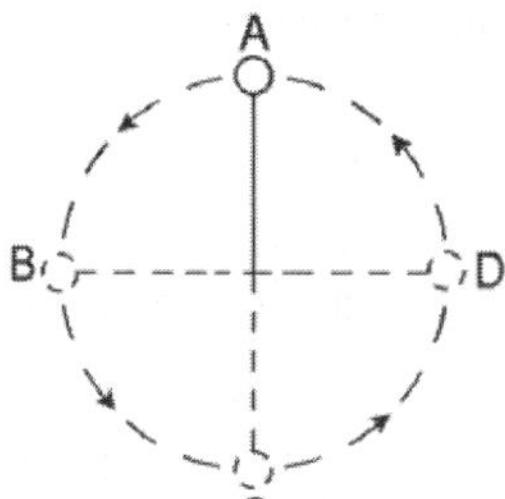

Figure 6-11
Question 6-18.

6-19 A rollercoaster car is sliding around a circular loop-the-loop (Figure 6-12). For each of the points A, B, C, D, and E, draw a free-body diagram for the car, and name the force(s) that constitute(s) the centripetal force. Neglect friction and air resistance.

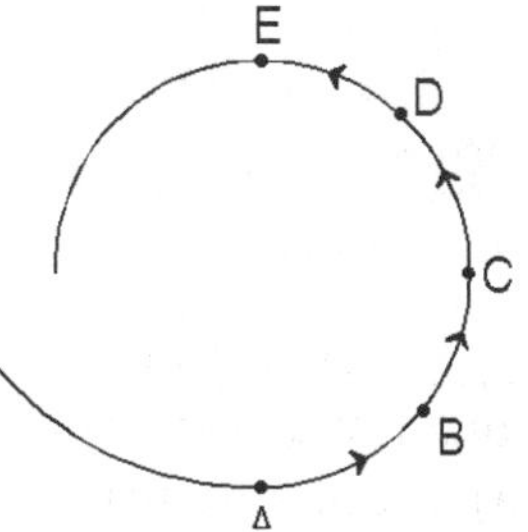

Figure 6-12
Question 6-19.

6-20 A girl of mass 45.7 kg is on a swing. The radius of the circular arc that she follows is 3.80 m. When the girl is at the lowest point, where her speed is 2.78 m/s, what is the magnitude of the tension in each of the two vertical supporting chains? [Ans. 2.70×10^2 N]

6-21 A car of mass 1.12×10^3 kg goes around an *unbanked* curve of radius 312 m at a speed of 28 m/s without sliding.
(a) What is the name of the force that is the centripetal force?
(b) What is the minimum coefficient of static friction between the tires and the road that will permit the car to go around the curve without sliding?
(c) If the radius of the curve were smaller, making the curve "sharper", would your answer to (b) increase or decrease? Explain.
(d) If the mass of the car were larger, how would your answer to (b) be affected?
[Ans. (b) 0.26]

6-22 Railroad tracks are banked at curves to reduce wear and stress on the wheel flanges and the rails, and to prevent the train from tipping over. If tracks are banked at an angle of 5.7° from the horizontal, and follow a curve of radius 5.5×10^2 m, what is the ideal speed for a train rounding the curve? [Ans. 23 m/s]

6-23 A child has tied a piece of wood of mass 0.47 kg to a string and is swinging it in a vertical circle of radius 83 cm. At the top of the circle:
(a) draw a free-body diagram for the wood
(b) determine the magnitude of the tension in the string, if the speed of the wood is 3.7 m/s.
[Ans. (b) 3.1 N]

6-24 In the previous problem, the wood will not "make it over the top" if its speed is too low. Determine the minimum speed of the wood at the top of its path if it is to follow a complete circle. Use the following steps:
(a) For a piece of wood of mass m traveling in a circle of radius r, and having speed v at the top, determine the magnitude of the string tension T (at the top) in terms of r, v, m, and g (similar to part (b) of the previous problem).
(b) According to your expression in (a), what happens to T as v decreases?
(c) If the wood has a speed at the top such that it just barely completes the circle, what happens to T? (Hint: the string will go slack momentarily.)
(d) Use your results from (a) and (c) to determine an expression for the minimum speed v_{MIN} at the top for the wood to complete the circle, in terms of g and r.
(e) Calculate v_{MIN} for r = 83 cm. Is the speed given in part (b) of the previous problem larger than v_{MIN}?
[Ans. (a) $T = m((v^2/r) - g)$ (d) $v_{MIN} = \sqrt{gr}$ (e) 2.9 m/s; yes]

6-25 On a loop-the-loop roller coaster (Figure 6-13), passengers at any instant follow a path that can be considered part of a circle, and have an acceleration with a component toward the centre of the circle. The passengers' safety is assured by seatbelts and/or shoulder braces. However, the coaster is designed so that it will normally be travelling fast enough that the passengers will be able to loop-the-loop without being secured in their seats. Follow the steps below to determine the minimum speed v_{MIN} of the coaster at the top, if the passengers just make it around the loop without being fastened in the seats.
(a) Draw a free-body diagram for an unsecured passenger at the top of the loop if the speed is larger than v_{MIN}.
(b) From (a), which forces constitute the centripetal force?
(c) If the coaster is traveling *just* fast enough at the top so that the passenger makes it around the loop, what happens to one of the forces given in the answer to (b)? (Hint: the passenger momentarily loses contact with the seat, and falls ever so slightly downward away from it.)
(d) Using your result from (c), determine an expression for v_{MIN} in terms of r (the loop's radius) and g.
(e) Use a typical value of r to determine an estimate of v_{MIN}.
[Ans. (d) $v_{MIN} = \sqrt{gr}$ (e) approx. 8 m/s]

Figure 6-13
Question 6-25.

6.3 CENTRIFUGAL "FORCE"

You have probably heard of centrifugal "force" and might be wondering what it is. Centrifugal "force" is not a true force in the way that gravity, tension, and friction are. It is often referred to as a fictitious force or a pseudoforce, and hence quotation marks have been placed around the word "force" in the previous lines. In order to explain centrifugal "force," we begin with a discussion of inertial and noninertial frames of reference.

Inertial and Noninertial Frames of Reference

Imagine that you are travelling in a bus at constant speed down a straight, smooth highway. If you place a ball on the floor of the bus, it stays at rest relative to you and the bus, just as it would if you placed it on the floor of your kitchen. The ball remains stationary because there is no resultant force acting on it. However, if the bus driver applies the brakes, then relative to the bus, the ball appears to accelerate toward the front, even though there is still no resultant force acting on it! (There is nothing actually pushing the ball forward.)

Relative to a bus travelling at constant velocity, the ball stays at rest if there is no resultant force; that is, the law of inertia (Newton's first law) is obeyed. Therefore, we call a constant-velocity bus an **inertial frame of reference**. A **frame of reference** is just an object such as a bus, room, or even a subatomic particle, relative to which the positions, velocities, etc., of other objects such as a ball can be measured.[3] In an inertial frame of reference, the law of inertia and other laws of physics are valid. Any frame moving at constant velocity relative to an inertial frame is also an inertial frame.

When the brakes are applied to a bus, it undergoes an acceleration. As we have seen, the law of inertia does not hold relative to the accelerating bus, which is a **noninertial frame of reference**. How can the ball accelerate toward the front of the braking bus if there is no resultant force on the ball? The answer is that we are looking at the motion of the ball from the "wrong" frame of reference, the noninertial frame of the accelerating bus. The situation is much simpler if we consider it from an inertial frame such as the ground. Relative to the ground, when the brakes are applied to the bus, the ball tends to continue moving forward at constant velocity[4] (by Newton's first law). Since the bus is slowing down, and the ball is not, the ball accelerates toward the front, relative to the bus (Figure 6-14).

If we try to analyze the motion of the ball in the noninertial frame of the accelerating bus, we have to invent a force toward the front of the bus. This **fictitious force**, also called a pseudoforce or inertial force, would explain the acceleration of the ball. The analysis of motion in any noninertial frame involves fictitious forces, but no such forces are necessary in inertial frames. If a noninertial frame such as the bus accelerates in a straight line relative to an inertial frame, the fictitious force (on the ball) is in the opposite direction to the acceleration of the noninertial frame itself.

---

[3] More formally, a frame of reference is defined as a co-ordinate system attached to an object such as a bus, room, etc. Without this co-ordinate system, it would be impossible to perform measurements of quantities such as position and velocity.

[4] The ball actually does not continue moving forward quite at constant velocity. However, if the floor of the bus had negligible friction, then any object sitting on the floor would indeed continue to slide forward at constant velocity relative to the ground as the bus is braking.

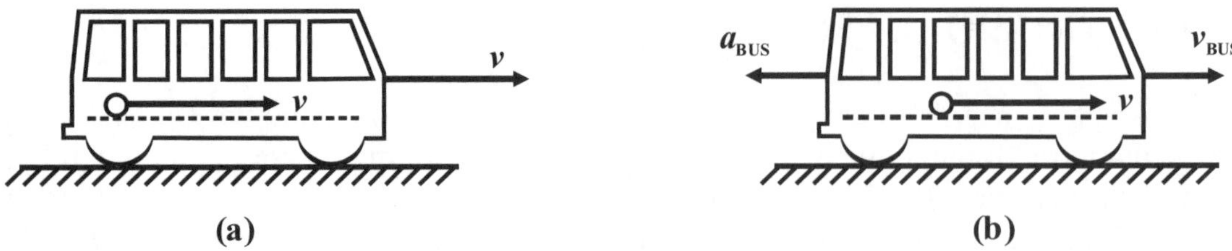

Figure 6-14 **(a)** *A bus and ball moving at constant velocity relative to the ground. Relative to the bus, the ball is at rest.*
(b) *When the brakes are applied to the bus, it slows down. However, the ball tends to continue moving forward at its former (constant) velocity, relative to the ground (see footnote 4 on the previous page). Thus, relative to the bus, the ball accelerates toward the front.*

If we try to analyze the motion of the ball in the noninertial frame of the accelerating bus, we have to invent a force toward the front of the bus. This fictitious force, also called a pseudoforce or inertial force, would explain the acceleration of the ball. The analysis of motion in any noninertial frame involves fictitious forces, but no such forces are necessary in inertial frames. If a noninertial frame such as the bus accelerates in a straight line relative to an inertial frame, the fictitious force (on the ball) is in the opposite direction to the acceleration of the noninertial frame itself.

We often assume that the surface of Earth is an inertial frame of reference. In actual fact, it is an accelerated (noninertial) frame. Because of Earth's daily rotation, the surface of Earth has a centripetal acceleration toward Earth's centre. In addition, Earth's annual motion around the sun, and the motion of the sun in the galaxy, etc., involve accelerations. However, because the accelerations involved in all these motions are small, Earth's surface is very close to being an inertial frame for everyday purposes.

All the laws of physics, such as Newton's three laws of motion, are valid in any inertial frame (bus, Earth, sun, galaxy, or galactic cluster), and therefore there is no inertial frame that is somehow preferred over the others. However, the velocity of any object is different relative to different inertial frames. For example, a ball having zero velocity relative to a moving bus has a non-zero velocity relative to Earth. Consequently, there is no such thing as an absolute velocity, relative to some special absolute inertial frame.

Centrifuges and Centrifugal "Force"

In the bus example above, the motions were linear. Rotating objects provide examples of more complicated noninertial frames. Each point on a rotating object travels in a circle, and therefore experiences a centripetal acceleration. Therefore, a rotating object is an accelerated, or noninertial, frame. One practical example is a centrifuge, which is a rapidly rotating device that separates substances in solution according to their densities. For example, if a sample of blood is allowed to stand in a test-tube, the red blood cells settle to the bottom of the less dense plasma. Without a centrifuge, this settling is very slow, at a rate of about 3 mm/h for blood from males, and 4 mm/h for females. Using a centrifuge can speed up the settling by a factor of almost a million.

Figure 6-15 shows how a centrifuge works. The test-tubes containing samples are rotated in a horizontal circle. (The rotation is very rapid — some centrifuges rotate with frequencies of millions of revolutions per minute.) A dense molecule or cell near the "top" of a tube at A tends to continue moving at constant speed in a straight line. This straight line motion carries it toward the "bottom" of the tube, as shown. Relative to the tube, the dense molecule is moving toward the bottom, and is settling out. Relative to Earth, the molecule is simply moving in a straight line, and the tube has an acceleration toward the centre of the centrifuge. The detailed motion of the molecule is affected by the viscous and buoyant forces exerted on it by the surrounding liquid, but the above discussion outlines the general principle involved in centrifugation.

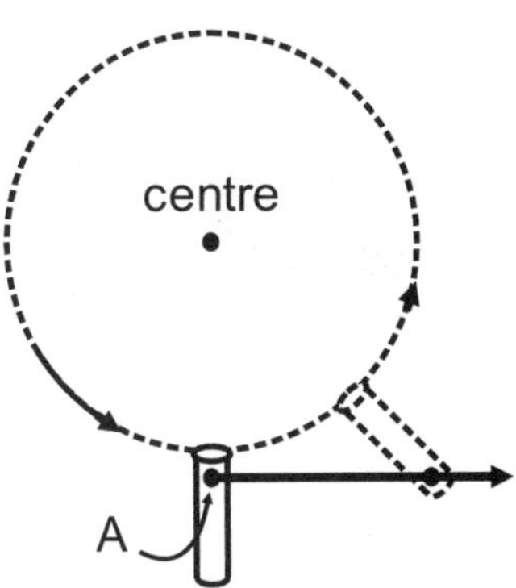

Figure 6-15 *Operation of a centrifuge. A dense molecule at A tends to continue in motion at constant velocity, and thus settles toward the bottom of the tube.*

If you could be stationary relative to the test-tube, that is, rotating with it relative to Earth, then in order to explain the motion of the molecule outward from the centre of the circle, you would have to invent a fictitious force called the **centrifugal "force."** ("Centrifugal" means "fleeing from the centre.") The centrifugal "force" is directed outward from the centre of rotation in a rotating noninertial frame of reference. To explain the motion of the molecule relative to Earth (an inertial frame), the centrifugal "force" is not needed.

A detailed analysis of the motion of the molecule relative to the test-tube or centrifuge would show that another fictitious force is also required, one that is perpendicular to the velocity of the molecule in the rotating frame. This force is called the **Coriolis "force,"** named after the French mathematician Gaspard Gustave de Coriolis (1792-1843). It is exerted on objects that are *moving* relative to rotating frames.

Sample Problem 6-6

A child is standing on a rotating playground merry-go-round. Draw a free-body diagram for the child and explain her motion in: (a) the (inertial) frame of Earth (b) the rotating frame of the merry-go-round.

Solution: (a) Figures 6-16 (a) and (b) show a diagram for the problem, and the free-body diagram in the frame of Earth. Since we are told that the child is *standing*, the only possible horizontal force is the force of static friction, $\boldsymbol{F}_S$. This is the centripetal force that maintains the child's circular motion.

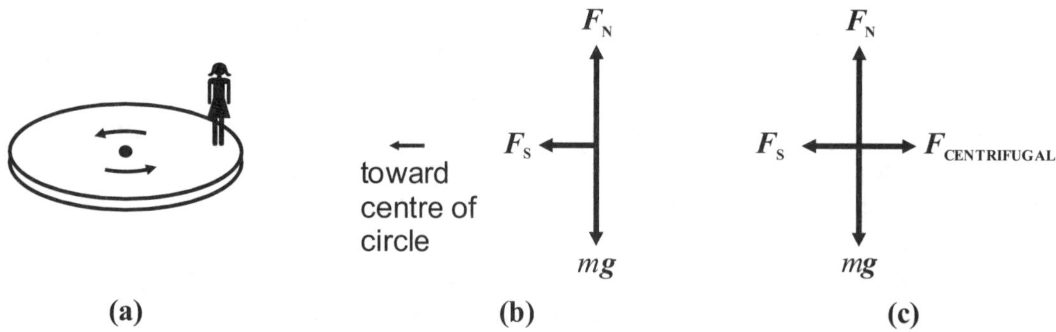

Figure 6-16 **(a)** *Sample Problem 6-6.* **(b)** *Free-body diagram for girl, relative to Earth.* **(c)** *Free-body diagram for girl, relative to merry-go-round.*

(b) In the rotating frame of the merry-go-round, the child is stationary. On the free-body diagram (Figure 6-16 (c)), we have the three forces found in the inertial frame, and also a centrifugal "force" outward from the centre. (There is no Coriolis "force," because the child is not moving relative to the merry-go-round.) The child is stationary in the frame of the merry-go-round because the static friction force and the centrifugal "force" are equal in magnitude, but opposite in direction.

Earth's Surface as a Noninertial Frame of Reference

Because Earth spins about its axis, it is a rotating noninertial frame of reference, although the effects due to the rotation are small. If you were to stand at the equator (Figure 6-17) and drop a ball, it falls toward the centre of Earth because of the force of gravity. However, relative to the rotating Earth, there is also a centrifugal "force" on the ball directed outward from the centre of Earth. Therefore, the resultant force in the frame of Earth is less than the gravitational force, and the measured acceleration of the ball relative to Earth is less than the acceleration due to gravity alone. This is a real effect, albeit a small one; at the equator, the magnitude of the acceleration relative to Earth (what we normally think of as g) is only 0.35% less than that due to gravity alone. This centrifugal decrease of acceleration depends on latitude; the effect is maximum at the equator, zero at the poles.

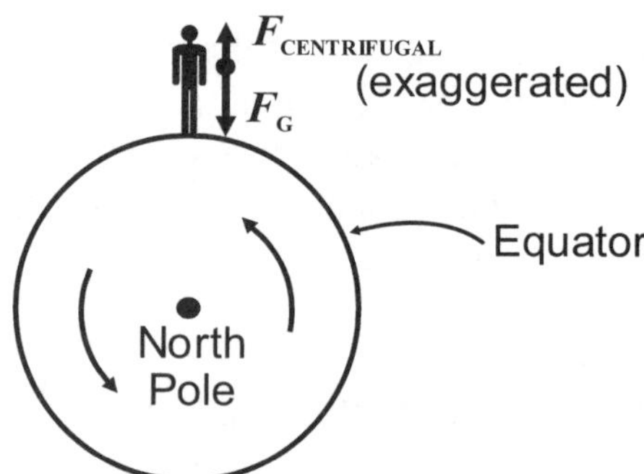

Figure 6-17 *Relative to the rotating Earth (a noninertial frame), both a gravitational force and a centrifugal "force" are exerted on a falling ball. Thus, the ball's acceleration relative to Earth is less than the acceleration due to gravity alone.*

The effect of the Coriolis "force" on an object moving relative to Earth is small unless the object is moving very fast or for a very long time. For example, unless a dropped ball falls for a long distance, the effect of the Coriolis "force" is negligible. However, the Coriolis "force" is responsible for the spiral shape of many weather patterns such as cyclones, and is important in the design of the sights of large military guns. During a naval battle near the Falkland Islands in World War I, British gunners were surprised to see their shells landing 100 m to the left of German ships. The gunsights had been adjusted for the Coriolis "force" at 50° N latitude, but the battle was in the southern hemisphere, where this "force" produces a deflection in the opposite direction.

Practice

6-26 Suppose that you are riding in a train moving at constant velocity relative to Earth, and that you place a ball on the floor in the centre of the aisle. The ball is initially at rest relative to the train.
(a) Relative to the train, what happens to the ball if the brakes are applied to the train?
(b) Relative to the frame of reference of the train, what is the direction of the acceleration of the ball as the brakes are applied?
(c) Is the force causing this acceleration a real one?

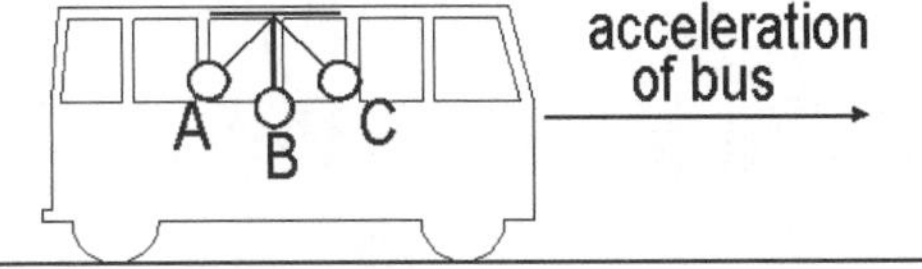

Figure 6-18 *Question 6-27.*

6-27 Imagine that you are in a bus that is speeding up, and that you suspend a small ball from a string (Figure 6-18).

(a) In which direction (A, B, C) does the string hang?
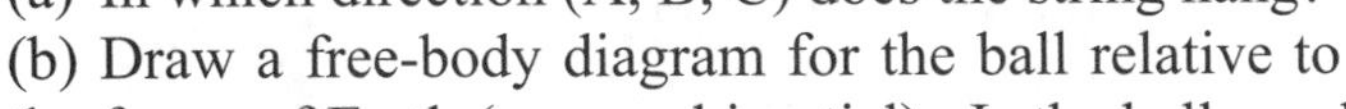
(b) Draw a free-body diagram for the ball relative to the frame of Earth (assumed inertial). Is the ball accelerating? If so, what force is providing the acceleration?
(c) Draw a free-body diagram for the ball relative to the noninertial frame of the accelerating bus. Is the ball accelerating relative to this frame? Use your diagram to explain the ball's motion, or lack of it, relative to the bus.

6-28 If you are sitting in a car that rounds a sharp curve to the right, you tend to move to the left, relative to the car. Explain your motion, first relative to Earth (assumed inertial), and then relative to the (noninertial) car. Diagrams will be helpful.

6-29 In an amusement park ride, people stand with their backs against the inside wall of a large cylindrical shell, that starts rotating in a horizontal circle (Figure 6-19).
(a) Relative to Earth (assumed inertial), each person is travelling in a circle. Draw a free-body diagram for one person, and identify the force that is the centripetal force. (Neglect friction between the person's feet and the floor.)
(b) Relative to the rotating noninertial frame of the ride, each person is stationary. Draw a free-body diagram for a person relative to this frame, and explain the lack of motion.

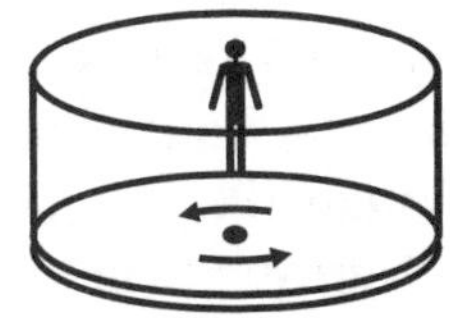
Figure 6-19 *Question 6-29.*

CHAPTER FOCUS

Thus far in the book, we have been considering mechanics — the study of motion and forces. We started by studying motion itself through quantities such as displacement, velocity, and acceleration, and then considered the connection between motion and forces by discussing Newton's famous three laws of motion.

The application of Newton's laws has been the focus of this chapter. We have discussed friction, forces involved in circular motion, and the fictitious forces that arise in noninertial frames of reference. The concepts that we developed have been illustrated through a variety of examples, such as "Jo blocks," the banking of highway curves, planetary motion, and centrifuges.

The next chapter will continue the development of mechanics by introducing work, energy, and power. A knowledge of these concepts is important in understanding many aspects of modern society — electrical power generation, automobile efficiency, etc.

VOCABULARY REVIEW

You should be able to define or explain each of the following words or phrases.

static friction
kinetic friction
coefficient of static friction
coefficient of kinetic friction
centripetal force
frame of reference
inertial frame of reference
noninertial frame of reference
fictitious force
centrifugal "force"
Coriolis "force"

CHAPTER REVIEW

6-30 The maximum magnitude of the static friction force acting on an object is usually
(a) less than the magnitude of the kinetic friction force
(b) equal to the magnitude of the kinetic friction force
(c) greater than the magnitude of the kinetic friction force.

6-31 A student is trying to push a large box of books across a carpeted floor in a university residence room. The student is exerting a horizontal force of magnitude 95 N, but the box is not moving. The magnitude of the friction force exerted by the carpeted floor on the box is
(a) 0 N (b) 95 N (c) less than 95 N (d) greater than 95 N.

6-32 A woman is standing on a moving walkway in an airport. The walkway is moving at constant velocity, and since the woman is standing (not walking) her velocity is the same as that of the walkway. In Figure 6-20 which drawing shows the correct free-body diagram for the woman? The symbols have their usual meanings. The direction of the woman's velocity is toward the right in the diagrams.

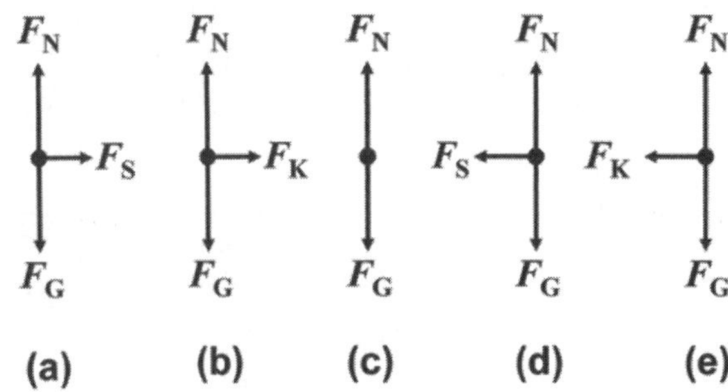

Figure 6-20 *Question 6-32.*

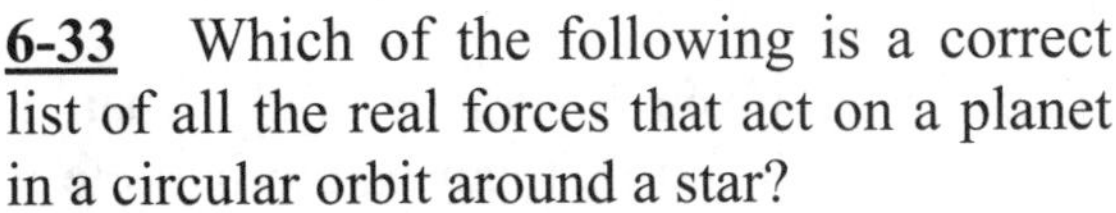

<u>6-33</u> Which of the following is a correct list of all the real forces that act on a planet in a circular orbit around a star?
(a) the gravitational attractive force $\boldsymbol{F}_{\mathrm{G}}$ toward the star, the centrifugal "force," and the force due to the motion of the planet
(b) $\boldsymbol{F}_{\mathrm{G}}$ and the force due to the motion of the planet
(c) $\boldsymbol{F}_{\mathrm{G}}$ and the centrifugal "force"
(d) $\boldsymbol{F}_{\mathrm{G}}$ and the centripetal force
(e) $\boldsymbol{F}_{\mathrm{G}}$, which is the centripetal force

6-34 A horizontal force is applied to an object sitting at rest on a horizontal surface. The force is gradually increased. Sketch the shape of the graph of (the magnitude of) the friction force on the object vs. (the magnitude of) the applied force.

<u>6-35</u> A woman exerts a horizontal force of magnitude 512 N on a stationary refrigerator of mass 117 kg that is sitting on a horizontal floor. The coefficients of friction between the refrigerator and the floor are: static, 0.69; kinetic, 0.60. What happens? Show your reasoning.

6-36 A man is pushing horizontally on a table of mass 16 kg to move it across a horizontal floor. The coefficient of kinetic friction between the table and floor is 0.61. What magnitude of applied force is necessary to keep the table moving at constant velocity? [Ans. 96 N]

6-37 If the actual applied force in the previous question has a magnitude of 109 N, and the table starts from rest, how long will it take to travel 0.75 m? [Ans. 1.3 s]

<u>6-38</u> A car is accelerating on a level road.
(a) Draw a free-body diagram for the car if the tires are not slipping. Neglect air resistance.
(b) What force provides the acceleration?
(c) If the coefficient of static friction between the tires and road is 0.60, what is the maximum acceleration the car can have without the tires slipping? [Ans. 5.9 m/s^2]

6-39 A boy is pushing horizontally on a Teflon® block to hold it against a vertical steel wall.
(a) If the block has a mass of 0.12 kg, what minimum magnitude of force must the boy apply if the block is not to slide? Use Table 6.1.
(b) Compare your answer in (a) with the magnitude of upward force required to simply hold the block in the boy's hand, i.e., determine the ratio of your answer in (a) to the upward force magnitude.
[Ans. (a) 3×10^1 N (b) approx. 25 to 1]

6-40 A bird of mass 78 g is making a *horizontal* banked turn of radius 9.7 m at a speed of 17 m/s. (a) What provides the centripetal force on the bird?
(b) What is the magnitude of this centripetal force?
[Ans. (b) 2.3 N]

6-41 When an electrically charged particle enters a uniform magnetic field that is perpendicular to the particle's velocity, a magnetic force is produced that causes the particle to move in a circle at constant speed.
(a) What is the radius of the resulting circle when an electron (mass 9.11×10^{-31} kg) travelling with speed 6.5×10^{6} m/s is acted on by a magnetic force that has a magnitude of 1.2×10^{-15} N?
(b) How long does it take the electron to make one revolution?
[Ans. (a) 3.2×10^{-2} m (b) 3.1×10^{-8} s]

6-42 A woman is standing without slipping in a subway car that is accelerating forward. Draw a free-body diagram for the woman in (a) the (inertial) frame of reference of Earth, and (b) the frame of reference of the subway car. (c) If the coefficient of static friction between the woman's shoes and the floor is 0.47, what is the maximum acceleration of the subway car if the woman is not to slip? [Ans. (c) 4.6 m/s^2]

6-43 A girl is standing on a rotating merry-go-round at a carnival. Her father makes the statement that in the (inertial) frame of reference of Earth, the girl remains at the same distance from the centre of the merry-go-round because there is no resultant force on her. Comment on his statement.

APPLYING YOUR KNOWLEDGE

6-44 A skier slides over a hump that has the shape of a circular arc of radius 5.72 m (Figure 6-21). Determine his speed at the top if his skis just barely lose contact with the snow.
[Ans. 7.49 m/s]

Figure 6-21 *Question 6-44.*

6-45 In a small factory near Las Vegas, dice travel around a vertical loop-the-loop. The dice do not lose contact with the top of the loop if they have a speed of at least 1.8 m/s at the top. What is the radius of the loop? [Ans. 0.33 m]

6-46 In the early 1900s, the first upside-down roller coasters had circular loops, which proved to be uncomfortable and dangerous. To make the rides smoother and safer, loops are now in the form of a Klothoid[5] curve, as shown in Figure 6-13. In this curve, the radius of the loop gradually gets smaller on the way up on each side and then is constant around the top of the loop. Discuss why the Klothoid loop provides a safer, smoother ride. (Hint: consider the centripetal acceleration required at various points around the loop, and which forces provide the centripetal force.)

[5] This is sometimes spelled Clothoid.

Hint for questions 6-47 to 6-52: $F_N \neq mg$.

6-47 A boy drags a huge garbage can of mass 27 kg along a horizontal driveway at a constant speed of 1.8 m/s. He exerts a force of 112 N at an angle of 27° above the horizontal. Determine the coefficient of kinetic friction between the can and the driveway. [Ans. 0.47]

6-48 A rope is used to exert a force of magnitude 21 N, at an angle of 31° above the horizontal, on a box at rest on a horizontal floor. The coefficients of friction between the box and the floor are: static, 0.55; kinetic, 0.50. Determine the smallest possible mass of the box, if it remains at rest. [Ans. 4.4 kg]

6-49 A girl on a toboggan slides down a hill inclined at 32° to the horizontal. Starting from rest, she travels 12 m in 2.5 s. (a) What is the magnitude of her acceleration?
(b) What is the coefficient of kinetic friction between the toboggan and the snow?
[Ans. (a) 3.8 m/s^2 (b) 0.16]

6-50 A skier is on a gradual slope inclined at 4.7° to the horizontal. She gives herself a push and starts down the slope with an initial speed of 2.7 m/s. If the coefficient of kinetic friction between her skis and the ground is 0.11, how far will she slide before coming to rest?
[Ans. 13 m]

6-51 Two boxes are connected by a rope that passes over a pulley (Figure 6-22). Box #1 is on a ramp inclined at 35° to the horizontal, and the coefficient of kinetic friction between the box and ramp is 0.54. The masses of the boxes are $m_1 = 2.5$ kg and $m_2 = 5.5$ kg. Neglecting the motion of the pulley, what is the magnitude of the acceleration of the boxes?
[Ans. 3.6 m/s^2]

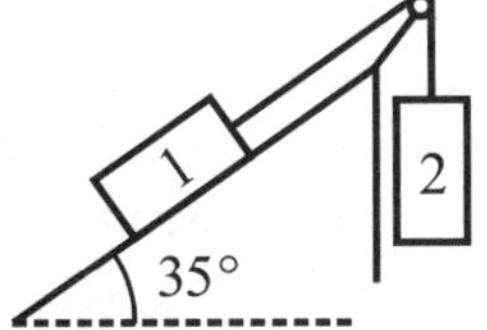

Figure 6-22
Question 6-51.

6-52 A box of canned pears of mass 22 kg is sitting on a ramp inclined at 45° to the horizontal. The coefficients of friction between the box and ramp are: static, 0.78; kinetic, 0.65.
(a) What is the magnitude of the *largest* force that can be applied upward, parallel to the ramp, if the box is to remain at rest?
(b) What is the magnitude of the *smallest* force that can be applied onto the top of the box, perpendicular to the ramp, if the box is to remain at rest?
[Ans. (a) 2.7×10^2 N (b) 43 N]

<u>6-53</u> A *conical* pendulum (Figure 6-23) consists of a mass m (the bob) on the end of a string. The top end of the string is held fixed, and as the bob travels in a horizontal circle at constant speed, the string traces out a *cone*. For the pendulum shown, mass $m = 1.95$ kg, length $\ell = 1.03$ m, and angle $\theta = 36.9°$.
(a) Draw a free-body diagram for the bob at the instant shown.
(b) What force constitutes the centripetal force?
(c) Determine the speed of the bob.
(d) How long does it take the bob to make one revolution?
[Ans. (c) 2.13 m/s (d) 1.82 s]

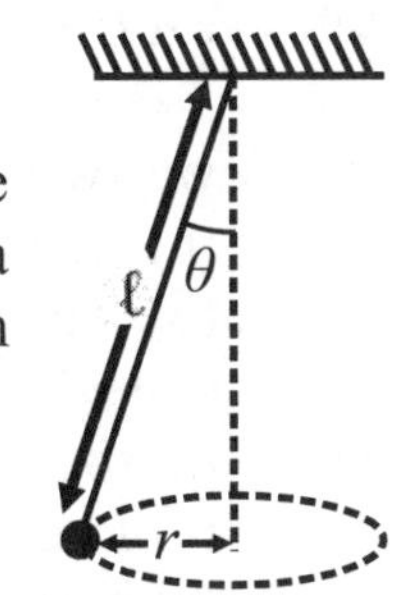

Figure 6-23
Question 6-53.

6-54 A car is heading toward a brick wall at a speed of 25 m/s (Figure 6-24). When the driver is 1.00×10^2 m from the wall, she decides that she has two choices: (i) apply the brakes and travel straight ahead, or (ii) steer without braking so that the car will travel on a circular arc just missing the wall. What is the minimum coefficient of static friction between the tires that will prevent a collision if she: (a) brakes without skidding? (b) steers on a circular arc of radius 1.00×10^2 m?
[Ans. (a) 0.32 (b) 0.64]

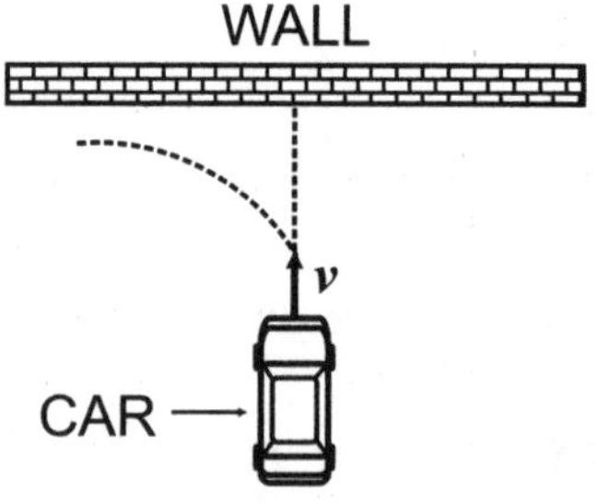

Figure 6-24 *Question 6-54.*

6-55 "Gravitropism" is the tendency of plants to align their stems and roots along the direction of the force of gravity. This tendency is caused by differential concentrations of auxins (plant hormones). If you had designed an experiment with seedlings placed in pots near the outer edge of a rotating platform that has a centre point C, in which direction would you expect to observe the stems to tilt: toward C, vertically upward, or away from C? Explain your answer.

KEY OBJECTIVES

Having completed this chapter, you should now be able to do the following.

1. Discuss the source of friction.
2. Distinguish between static and kinetic friction.
3. Define coefficients of static and kinetic friction.
4. List reasonable values of coefficients of friction between various materials.
5. Solve problems involving coefficients of friction.
6. State the meaning of centripetal force, and be able to identify the force(s) that constitute(s) the centripetal force in various examples of circular motion.
7. Solve force problems involving circular motion.
8. State the meaning of frame of reference, inertial and noninertial frames of reference, and the law of inertia.
9. Explain how fictitious forces arise in noninertial frames.
10. Discuss basic properties of the centrifugal and Coriolis "forces."
11. Draw free-body diagrams for objects in simple situations involving noninertial frames.

ANSWERS TO SELECTED QUESTIONS

6-2 westward; kinetic
6-8 (b) static friction
6-12 (b) Adjust the angle of the incline until the block, once it has been set in motion, will slide downward along the incline at constant velocity.
6-14 (a) force of gravity toward Earth (b) force of gravity toward the sun
(c) force of gravity minus the normal force (d) static friction exerted by the road
(e) horizontal component of the normal force (f) electrical force toward the nucleus
6-15 (a) the interior wall of the spinning chamber in the washing machine
(b) normal force

6-17 (a) electrical force
6-18 (b) A — tension plus gravity; B and D — tension; C — tension minus gravity
6-19 A — normal force minus the force of gravity
B — normal force minus the component of gravity away from the circle's centre
C — normal force
D — normal force plus the component of the force of gravity toward the circle's centre
E — normal force plus the force of gravity
6-21 (a) static friction
6-25 (b) sum of normal force (downward) and gravitational force (downward)
6-26 (a) The ball accelerates toward the front of the train as the brakes are applied.
(b) The direction of the acceleration is toward the front of the train.
(c) The force is not a real one; it is a fictitious force.
6-27 (a) A
(b) The ball is accelerating because of the horizontal component of the string tension.
(c) The ball is not accelerating relative to the bus. The horizontal component of the string tension is "balanced" by a fictitious force toward the rear of the bus.
6-30 (c) 6-31 (b) 6-32 (c) 6-33 (e)
6-35 The refrigerator does not move.
6-38 (b) the static friction force applied by the road on the tires
6-40 (a) the air
6-43 The statement is incorrect. In the (inertial) frame of reference of Earth, the velocity vector of the girl is continually changing in direction, and therefore the girl is undergoing an acceleration (toward the centre of the merry-go-round). The force providing this acceleration is the static friction force exerted on her feet by the platform of the merry-go-round.
6-53 (b) the horizontal component of the string tension
6-55 away from C

CHAPTER 7

WORK, ENERGY, AND POWER

Although energy is hard to define precisely, it is familiar to all of us, and is probably the single most important "resource" that the world has. Without a continuous input of energy from the sun, all life on Earth would cease to exist. Reliable sources of energy are required to operate most of the material objects associated with the high standard of living in North America — automobiles, televisions, computers, microwave ovens, airplanes, refrigerators, etc. — and large amounts of energy are used in their manufacture. An understanding of energy is necessary for a full appreciation of many major issues facing society today: use of finite resources (oil, gas, uranium), environmental pollution, climate change, and so on.

As we proceed through this chapter, we will see that there are various forms of energy, and that energy can be converted from one form into another. The most important concept in this chapter is the law of conservation of energy — a universal law that states that although energy can be converted into different forms, it cannot be created nor destroyed.

7.1 WORK DONE BY A CONSTANT FORCE

Many words have different meanings in different situations. For example, if a friend says to you, "Look at all the fans," the meaning of *fans* depends on whether you are in a baseball stadium or in an electrical appliance store. Similarly, the word *work* has a scientific meaning that is very different from its everyday meaning. If you hold a heavy box stationary for a long time, with your muscles aching and sweat dripping from your brow, most people would say that you are "working," but in the scientific sense you are going no work at all. Before we begin discussions of energy, we need to introduce the closely related concept of work.

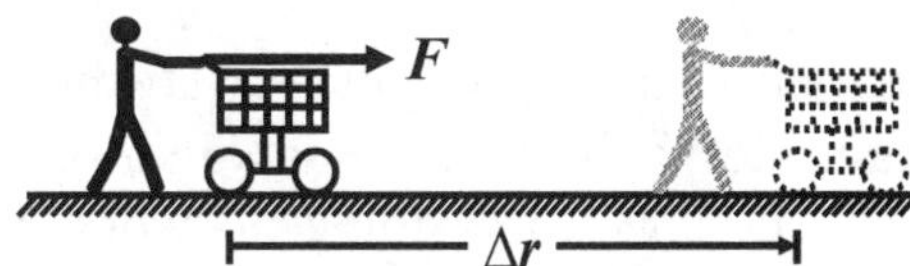

Figure 7-1 *The work (W) done on an object, when a force (**F**) is applied and the object's displacement (Δ **r**) is in the same direction as the force, is $W = F\Delta r$.*

Suppose that you apply a constant horizontal force to push a shopping cart along in a store (Figure 7-1). If the force has a magnitude F, and the displacement of the cart has a magnitude Δr, then the work (W) done by you on the cart is given by $W = F\,\Delta r$.

The force vector and the displacement vector are in the same direction in the above example. However, in general, the force and displacement can be in different directions. If you push a lawnmower across level ground by applying a constant non-horizontal force (Figure 7-2), the work done by you (or, we often say, by the force) on the lawnmower is:

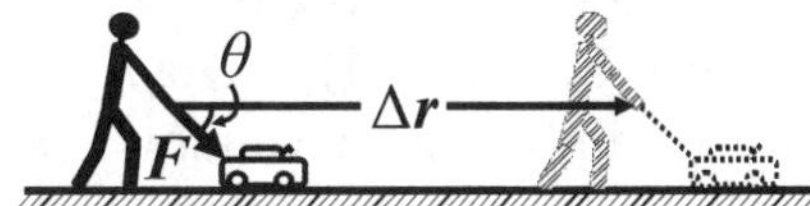

Figure 7-2 *The work done on the lawnmower is $W = F\,\Delta r\cos\theta$, where θ is the angle between the constant force (**F**) and the displacement (Δ**r**).*

$$W = F\,\Delta r \cos\theta \qquad \textbf{(7-1)}$$

where F = *magnitude* of the constant force (hence, $F \geq 0$)
Δr = *magnitude* of the displacement (hence, $\Delta r \geq 0$)
θ = angle between the vectors $\boldsymbol{F}$ and $\Delta\boldsymbol{r}$

Equation 7-1 *defines* the **work** done by a constant force. Note that work is a *scalar* quantity — it has a magnitude, but no direction.

If $\boldsymbol{F}$ and $\Delta\boldsymbol{r}$ are in the same direction, the angle (θ) between them is zero. Hence, $\cos\theta = 1$ and we have $W = F\,\Delta r$ as before.

In SI units, F is in newtons, Δr in metres, and $\cos\theta$ is unitless. Therefore, we would expect that the unit of work would be newton·metre (N·m). However, this is conventionally called a **joule** (J), named after James Prescott Joule (1818-1889), an outstanding British experimental physicist who was one of the leaders in the development of the law of conservation of energy (Section 7.4).

We can see from the equation $W = F\,\Delta r \cos\theta$ that in order for work to be done, three important conditions must be met:

1. A force must be applied to an object.
2. The object must undergo a displacement, that is, it must move.
3. The force and displacement must not be at right angles to each other. If they are, $\theta = 90°$, and hence $\cos\theta = 0$ and $W = 0$.

We discuss the second and third conditions in more detail below.

Figure 7-3 *No work is done on the lawnmower if it remains at rest. ($\Delta r = 0$)*

Suppose that you push a lawnmower against a tree. If you continue to push, with the lawnmower firmly at rest against the tree (Figure 7-3), you are doing no work on the lawnmower because its displacement is zero. Notice how the scientific and everyday concepts of work are different. In normal conversation we would say that someone exerting a force on a stationary lawnmower is working, or doing work. However, in the scientific sense, no work is being done on the lawnmower.

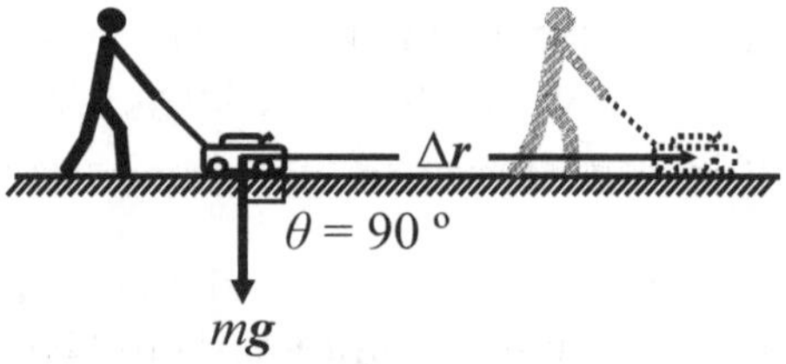

When the lawnmower is being pushed across level ground, the force of gravity is not doing work on the lawnmower (Figure 7-4). Gravity is acting vertically downward and the lawnmower's displacement is horizontal. Since the force and displacement are perpendicular to each other, $\cos\theta = \cos 90° = 0$ and the work done is zero. Can you think of another force that does no work on the lawnmower in this situation because the force is perpendicular to the displacement?

Figure 7-4 *As the lawnmower moves across the ground, the force of gravity does no work on the lawnmower, because $\theta = 90°$. Thus, $\cos\theta = 0$ and $W = 0$.*

In the equation $W = F\,\Delta r \cos\theta$ the quantities F and Δr represent magnitudes of vectors, and hence they are positive quantities (or possibly zero). However, $\cos\theta$ may be either positive or negative, depending on the value of θ. The angle θ may be chosen as either the larger or smaller angle between the vectors $\boldsymbol{F}$ and $\Delta\boldsymbol{r}$ (Figure 7-5), since $\cos(360° - \theta) = \cos\theta$. (You might like to use your calculator to confirm this for a few angles.) Normally the smaller angle is used.

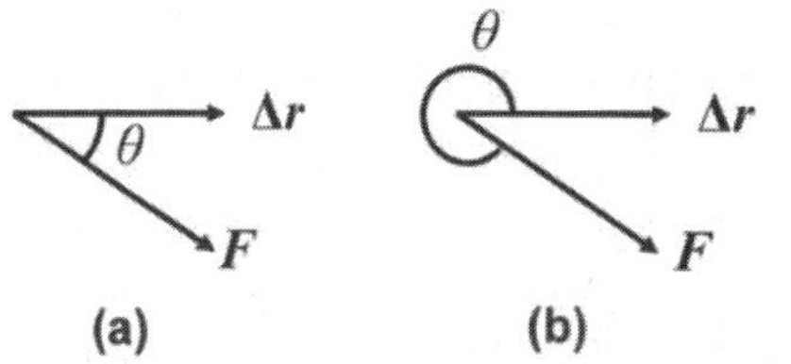

Figure 7-5 *Either* **(a)** *the smaller angle or* **(b)** *the larger angle between* ***F*** *and* ***Δr*** *can be used as angle θ in calculating work, using W = F Δr cosθ, but usually the smaller one is used.*

Depending on the sign of $\cos\theta$, the work done on an object can be either positive or negative. As discussed further in Section 7.2, positive work indicates that the force is tending to increase the speed of the object. Negative work means that the force is tending to decrease the speed of the object on which the work is being done.

Sample Problem 7-1

A pen of mass 0.020 kg falls from a desktop to the floor. If the desktop is 0.60 m above the floor, what is the work done on the pen by gravity during the fall?

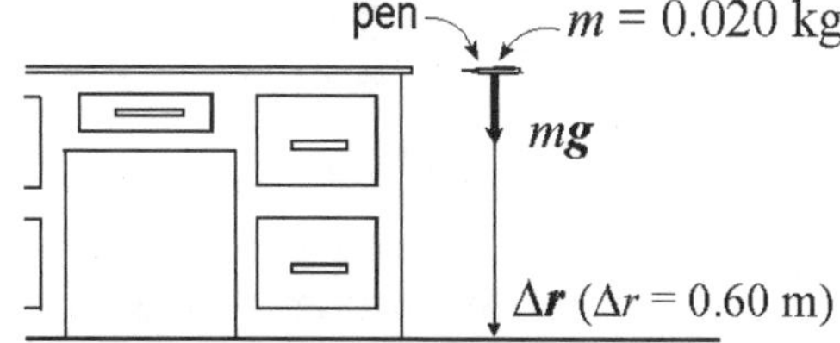

Figure 7-6 *Sample Problem 7-1.*

Solution: Figure 7-6 provides a diagram. Since the force of gravity ($m\boldsymbol{g}$) and the displacement ($\Delta\boldsymbol{r}$) are in the same direction, the angle (θ) between these two vectors is zero. To calculate the work done, we use Eqn. 7-1:

$$\begin{aligned} W &= F\,\Delta r \cos\theta \\ &= mg\,\Delta r \cos\theta \\ &= (0.020\text{ kg})(9.8\text{ m/s}^2)(0.60\text{ m})(\cos 0) \\ &= 0.12\text{ J} \end{aligned}$$

> ***Units Tip:*** *The units of mg are kg·m/s², which is a Newton (N). Multiplying this by the units of Δr (metres) gives N·m, equivalent to a joule (J). Since cosθ is unitless, multiplication by cosθ produces no change in units.*

Using Vector Components to Determine Work

There is an alternative way to define work (in two dimensions):

$$W = F_x \Delta x + F_y \Delta y \qquad \textbf{(7-2)}$$

where F_x, F_y, Δx, and Δy are the x- and y-components of the applied force and the displacement, respectively. Each of these four quantities can be either positive or negative. It is possible to show that $F_x\Delta x + F_y\Delta y = F\ \Delta r\cos\theta$, using trigonometry. (This is left as a problem for you in the "Applying Your Knowledge" section at the end of the chapter.) In Sample Problem 7-2 below, calculations of work are performed using both $W = F\ \Delta r\cos\theta$ and $W = F_x\Delta x + F_y\Delta y$.[1]

Sample Problem 7-2

A woman pushes a computer printer of mass 5.3 kg at constant velocity across a desk by exerting a force of 22 N at 25° below the horizontal. Determine the work done by each force acting on the printer, if its displacement is 0.25 m in magnitude.

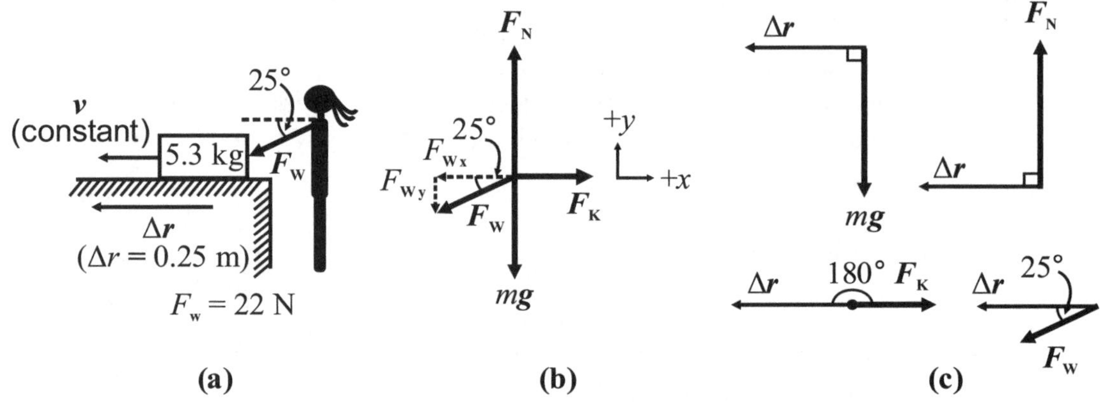

Figure 7-7 **(a)** *Sample Problem 7-2.* **(b)** *Free-body diagram for printer.* **(c)** *Angles between* $\Delta\boldsymbol{r}$ *and the forces.*

Solution (using $W = F\ \Delta r\cos\theta$): We need first to identify the forces. Figures 7-7 (a) and (b) show a diagram for the problem and a free-body diagram for the printer. The forces are gravity $m\boldsymbol{g}$, normal force $\boldsymbol{F}_N$, kinetic friction $\boldsymbol{F}_K$, and the force $\boldsymbol{F}_W$ exerted by the woman.

It is now useful to check if any of the forces are at right angles to the displacement; if so, the work done by these forces is zero (from $W = F\ \Delta r\cos\theta$, with $\theta = 90°$). Figure 7-7 (c) shows the relative directions of the various forces and the displacement $\Delta\boldsymbol{r}$. Since both gravity and the normal force make a 90° angle with $\Delta\boldsymbol{r}$, then the work done by each of these forces is zero:

work done by gravity: $W = mg\ \Delta r\cos 90° = 0\text{ J}$ (since $\cos 90° = 0$)

work done by normal force: $W = F_N\ \Delta r\cos 90° = 0\text{ J}$

We now calculate the work done by $\boldsymbol{F}_W$, which makes an angle of 25° with $\Delta\boldsymbol{r}$:

work done by force $\boldsymbol{F}_W$: $W = F_W\ \Delta r\cos\theta = (22\text{ N})(0.25\text{ m})\cos 25° = 5.0\text{ J}$

[1]If you have encountered the vector dot product in mathematics, you might recognize that the most compact way to write the work done by a constant force is to use the vector dot product notation, $W = \boldsymbol{F}\cdot\Delta\boldsymbol{r}$, but this notation will not be discussed further in this book. When solving problems, it is more convenient to use either $W = F\ \Delta r\cos\theta$ or $W = F_x\Delta x + F_y\Delta y$.

Before calculating the work done by friction, $\boldsymbol{F}_K$, we need to determine the magnitude of this force, which is not given in the problem. We can determine this unknown force magnitude by considering horizontal forces and using Newton's first law (since the printer is not accelerating horizontally):

$$\Sigma F_x = ma_x = 0$$

On the left-hand side of this equation, we need the x-components of all the forces. The normal force and gravity have zero x-components. From Fig. 7-7 (b), the x-component of $\boldsymbol{F}_K$ is just[2] F_K , and the x-component of $\boldsymbol{F}_W$ is

$$F_{Wx} = -F_W \cos 25° = -(22\text{ N}) \cos 25° = -20\text{ N}$$

Substituting x-components of forces into Newton's first law:

$$F_{Wx} + F_K = 0$$

Thus, $\quad (-20\text{ N}) + F_K = 0, \text{ which gives } F_K = 20\text{ N}$

We can now calculate the work done by the friction force $\boldsymbol{F}_K$, noting from Fig. 7-7 (c) that the angle between $\boldsymbol{F}_K$ and $\Delta\boldsymbol{r}$ is 180°:

work done by friction: $\quad W = F_K\ \Delta r \cos 180° = (20\text{ N})(0.25\text{ m})(-1) = -5.0\text{ J}$

(The negative work done by $\boldsymbol{F}_K$ indicates that friction, if acting alone, would decrease the printer's speed, and the positive work done by $\boldsymbol{F}_W$ shows that this force alone would increase the speed. The total work done by all the forces is zero, showing that the speed of the printer is not changing. These statements will be justified formally in Section 7.2.)

Alternative solution (using $W = F_x\Delta x + F_y\Delta y$): To use $W = F_x\Delta x + F_y\Delta y$, we need to determine the x- and y-components of the displacement and the forces. The x-y axes are shown in Figure 7-7 (b). The displacement vector $\Delta\boldsymbol{r}$ has components of $\Delta x = -0.25$ m and $\Delta y = 0$. Since Δy is zero, the product $F_y\Delta y$ will be zero for each force. Therefore, to calculate the work done by each force, we need to calculate only $F_x\Delta x$. The x-components of each force are:

$mg_x = 0$ N $\qquad\qquad F_{Nx} = 0$ N

$F_{Wx} = -20$ N $\qquad\qquad F_{Kx} = 20$ N

(To see how F_{Wx} and F_{Kx} were determined, look at the above solution using $W = F\ \Delta r \cos\ \theta$.)

---

[2]A reminder about notation in this book: a vector quantity is indicated in boldface type ($\boldsymbol{F}_K$, for example) and its magnitude is indicated in normal (non-boldface) type (F_K).

Calculating the work done by each force,

gravity: $W = mg_x \Delta x = (0\text{ N})(-0.25\text{ m}) = 0\text{ J}$

normal: $W = F_{Nx} \Delta x = (0\text{ N})(-0.25\text{ m}) = 0\text{ J}$

force $\boldsymbol{F}_W$: $W = F_{Wx} \Delta x = (-20\text{ N})(-0.25\text{ m}) = 5.0\text{ J}$

friction: $W = F_{Kx} \Delta x = (20\text{ N})(-0.25\text{ m}) = -5.0\text{ J}$

All the answers are of course the same as those calculated previously using $W = F\,\Delta r\cos\theta$.

Work Done by a Centripetal Force

An important special case to consider is the work done by a centripetal force. Recall that a centripetal force acts toward the centre of the circle on an object undergoing circular motion (or moving on a path that is a circular arc). Strictly speaking, the equation $W = F\,\Delta r\cos\theta$ is valid only if $\boldsymbol{F}$ is constant in both magnitude and direction. Nonetheless, we can use it to show that the work done by any centripetal force is zero, even though such a force is continually changing in direction.

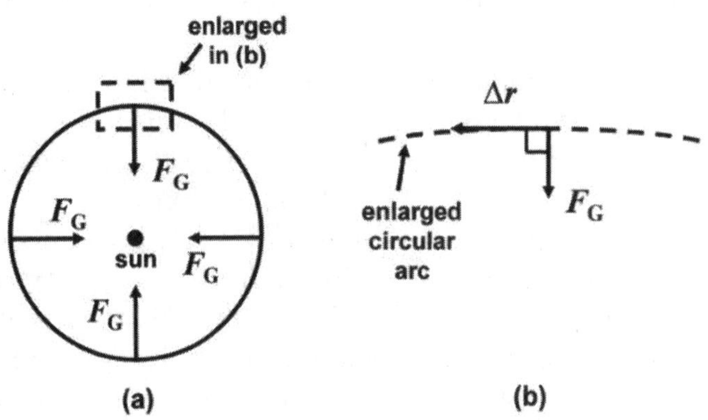

Figure 7-8
(a) *As Venus moves in its circular orbit, the gravitational force on it changes in direction.*
(b) *For any small portion of the orbit,* $\Delta\boldsymbol{r} \perp \boldsymbol{F}_G$. *Therefore,* $\theta = 90°$, *and* $W = F_G\,\Delta r\cos\theta = 0$.

As an example, we use the circular motion of Venus about the sun. The centripetal force in this situation is the gravitational force $\boldsymbol{F}_G$ on Venus; this force changes in direction as the planet moves (Figure 7-8 (a)). However, if we consider any small portion of the orbit, where $\Delta\boldsymbol{r}$ is very small (Figure 7-8 (b)), the force is essentially constant in magnitude and direction. Hence, the work done as Venus moves along this small portion can be determined using $W = F\,\Delta r\cos\theta$. The displacement $\Delta\boldsymbol{r}$ is perpendicular to the force, that is, $\theta = 90°$. Therefore, $\cos\theta = 0$, and the work $W = 0$. Since the work done is zero for any small piece of the orbit, then the work done is zero over the entire orbit (which can be considered to be a series of small pieces). This analysis can be applied to any centripetal force, and so we can state that *the work done by any centripetal force on an object in circular motion is zero.*

Practice

*In questions 7-1 to 7-9 below, is work being done on object A by force **F**? If so, is the work positive or negative?*

7-1 A forearm A is stationary in a horizontal orientation. The biceps muscle is exerting a force ***F*** vertically upward on the forearm.

7-2 A woman, walking at constant velocity, carries a golf bag A by exerting an upward force ***F*** on it. The golf bag is moving horizontally as the woman walks.

7-3 A woman exerts an upward force ***F*** on a briefcase A to lift it to her desk.

7-4 A man exerts a force ***F*** on a briefcase A as he lowers it at constant velocity toward the floor.

7-5 A quarterback A is pushed away from the line of scrimmage by a linebacker who exerts a horizontal force ***F***.

7-6 The force of gravity ***F*** acts on a baseball A moving vertically upward.

7-7 A normal force ***F*** is exerted by a road on a car A accelerating away from an intersection.

7-8 In a simple model of the atom, an electron A travels in a circular orbit as a result of the electrical force ***F*** toward the nucleus.

7-9 A string tension ***F*** acts on a ball A attached to the string. The ball is swinging as a pendulum.

7-10 A force is applied to an object, which is undergoing a displacement. If the work done on the object by the force is zero, what can you conclude?

7-11 A magnetic force on a moving charged particle is always perpendicular to the particle's velocity. What can you conclude about the work done on a charged particle by a magnetic force? (Hint: for a small time interval, how are the directions of the velocity and displacement related?)

7-12 The work done by a centripetal force is always ___________ .

7-13 Express a joule in terms of SI base units: kilogram (kg), metre (m), and second (s).

7-14 A soccer ball of mass 0.425 kg is kicked straight up. If it reaches a maximum height of 11.8 m, (a) what is the work done on the ball by gravity on the way up?
(b) on the way down?
(c) what is the total work done on the ball by gravity during the entire flight?
[Ans. (a) –49.1 J (b) 49.1 J (c) 0 J]

7-15 A soccer ball of mass 0.425 kg is kicked on a parabolic trajectory such that its maximum height is 11.8 m. What is the work done on the ball by gravity on the way up? on the way down? (Hint: use $W = F_x\Delta x + F_y\Delta y$) [Ans. –49.1 J; 49.1 J]

7-16 While pushing a shopping cart down the aisle in a store, a person exerted a constant horizontal force of magnitude 2.7 N and did 17.0 J or work on the cart. How far did the person push the cart? [Ans. 6.3 m]

7-17 As the shopping cart in the previous question was pushed down the aisle, what was the work done on the cart by (a) the normal force? (b) the force of gravity? [Ans. (a) 0 J (b) 0 J]

7-18 A boy carries a hamburger of mass 0.25 kg on a tray at a constant velocity of 0.45 m/s horizontally, for a horizontal displacement of magnitude 6.7 m. What is the total work done on the hamburger? [Ans. 0 J]

7-19 (a) What magnitude of force is required to lift a cooking pot of mass 0.58 kg at a constant velocity of 0.330 m/s upward?
(b) If the pot is lifted a distance of 0.64 m, what is the work done by the upward force? by gravity?
[Ans. (a) 5.7 N (b) 3.6 J; –3.6 J]

7-20 A woman pushes a lawnmower by exerting a constant force of magnitude 9.30 N. If she does 87 J of work on the lawnmower while pushing it 11 m across level ground, what is the angle between the horizontal and the force that she applies to the mower? [Ans. 32°]

7-21 A man is pulling a vacuum cleaner of mass 5.7 kg straight across a horizontal rug by exerting a force of 19 N at an angle of 42° above the horizontal. There is a friction force on the cleaner of magnitude 12 N. If the cleaner is pulled for 1.5 m, what is the work done on it by each force? Use $W = F\,\Delta r\cos\theta$.
[Ans. by gravity: 0 J; by normal force: 0 J; by friction: –18 J; by applied force: 21 J]

7-22 Solve the previous problem using $W = F_x\Delta x + F_y\Delta y$.

7-23 A girl pulls a toboggan of mass 4.81 kg up a hill inclined at 25.7° to the horizontal. The vertical height of the hill is 27.3 m. Neglecting friction between the toboggan and the snow, determine how much work the girl must do on the toboggan to pull it at constant velocity up the hill. [Ans. 1.29×10^3 J]

<u>7-24</u> Repeat the above question, if the vertical height is still 27.3 m, but the angle is 19.6°. What general conclusion can you state? [Ans. 1.29×10^3 J]

7-25 The girl in the previous two questions now slides down the hill on the toboggan. If the girl's mass is 25.6 kg, determine the total work done on the girl and toboggan during the slide. Neglect friction. [Ans. 8.14×10^3 J]

7.2 KINETIC ENERGY AND THE WORK-ENERGY THEOREM

Think about a golfer hitting a golf ball. The club exerts a force on the ball, and the ball moves parallel to the force; hence, the club does work on the ball. The speed of the ball increases, and we show in this section that there is a close connection between the total work done on an object (such as the golf ball) and a special quantity that depends on the object's mass and speed. This quantity is the object's **kinetic energy**.

What is kinetic energy? In words, we describe it as "energy of motion." We shall see that we write kinetic energy mathematically as $\frac{1}{2}mv^2$, where m and v represent an object's mass and speed, respectively. The connection between work and kinetic energy is known as the **work-energy theorem**, which states that the total work done on an object equals the change in the object's kinetic energy.

We first prove the work-energy theorem for a one-dimensional constant-force situation. Consider the total work done by all the (constant) forces acting on an object:

$$W_{\text{TOT}} = \Sigma(F_{\text{x}}\Delta x)$$

where the subscript "TOT" is an abbreviation for "total," and "Σ" indicates a sum including all the forces. Since the displacement Δx of an object in a given case is the same for all the forces, we can remove Δx from the summation:

$$W_{\text{TOT}} = (\Sigma F_{\text{x}})\Delta x$$

Now $\Sigma F_{\text{x}} = ma_{\text{x}}$ from Newton's second law. Thus, $W_{\text{TOT}} = ma_{\text{x}}\,\Delta x$.

For constant forces, the resulting a_{x} is constant, and we can relate Δx to the initial and final velocities by using one of the equations for constant-acceleration kinematics:

$$v_{\text{x}}^2 - v_{0\text{x}}^2 = 2a_{\text{x}}(x - x_0)$$

The difference between the final and initial positions, $x - x_0$, is just the displacement, Δx. Hence, the above equation can be written as

$$v_{\text{x}}^2 - v_{0\text{x}}^2 = 2a_{\text{x}}\Delta x$$

Thus, $$\Delta x = \frac{v_x^2 - v_{0x}^2}{2a_x}$$

Substituting for Δx in the expression for W_{TOT} gives:

$$\begin{aligned} W_{TOT} &= ma_x\left(\frac{v_x^2 - v_{0x}^2}{2a_x}\right) \\ &= \tfrac{1}{2}mv_x^2 - \tfrac{1}{2}mv_{0x}^2 \end{aligned}$$

The quantity $\frac{1}{2}mv_x^2$ is the kinetic energy of the object in this one-dimensional situation.

Thus, $\frac{1}{2}mv_x^2 - \frac{1}{2}mv_{0x}^2$ is the change in the object's kinetic energy.

We have just proven the work-energy theorem — **the total work done on an object equals the change in the object's kinetic energy.**

It is important to note that the change in kinetic energy equals the total work done by *all* the forces, or equivalently, the work done by the *resultant* force (ΣF_x). If we consider the work done by a single force (out of many acting), we can say that if the work done is positive, then the force is tending to increase the object's kinetic energy; if the work done is negative, the force tends to decrease the kinetic energy. Of course, an increase (decrease) in kinetic energy means also an increase (decrease) in speed.

Although the theorem has been proven only for one-dimensional constant forces, it is valid also in two and three dimensions, and for varying forces. Thus, we can write the theorem in a more general form without the x-subscripts:

$$W_{TOT} = \tfrac{1}{2}mv^2 - \tfrac{1}{2}mv_0^2 \quad \text{(work - energy theorem)} \qquad \textbf{(7-3)}$$

where v and v_0 represent the object's final and initial speeds, respectively.

In this book, we will represent the kinetic energy of an object by E_K:

$$E_K = \tfrac{1}{2}mv^2 \quad \text{(kinetic energy)} \qquad \textbf{(7-4)}$$

Thus, the work-energy theorem can be written most compactly as:

$$W_{TOT} = \Delta E_K \quad \text{(work - energy theorem)} \qquad \textbf{(7-5)}$$

Note that kinetic energy is a scalar quantity, as is work.

It is useful at this point to verify that the units of work are the same as the units of kinetic energy. To do this, we determine the units of work and kinetic energy in terms of SI base units: kilogram, metre, and second.

Units of work: The fundamental SI unit of work is the joule (J), which is equivalent to a newton·metre (N·m). By remembering Newton's second law ($\Sigma F = ma$), we can rewrite N as kg·m/s^2. Thus N·m is (kg·m/s^2) ·m, that is, kg·m^2/s^2.

Units of kinetic energy: Consider the expression $\frac{1}{2}mv^2$ for kinetic energy. The "½" is unitless; the unit for mass m is kg; for v^2, (m/s)^2. Therefore, the basic SI unit for kinetic energy is kg·m^2/s^2, the same as the unit that we determined for work. Neither kg·m^2/s^2 nor N·m is commonly used, being replaced by J (joule).

Notice that kinetic energy depends on the *square* of an object's speed. This means that relatively modest increases in the speed of an object can lead to rather large increases in its kinetic energy. Traffic accidents involving vehicles moving at high speeds are much more destructive than accidents at lower speeds because of the much higher kinetic energies involved. As an example, consider a car of mass 1.2×10^3 kg moving at a speed of 25 m/s (90 km/h). The car's kinetic energy is:

$$E_K = \tfrac{1}{2}mv^2 = \tfrac{1}{2}(1.2\times10^3 \text{ kg})(25 \text{ m/s})^2 = 3.8\times10^5 \text{ J}$$

Suppose now that the car increases its speed by 20%, to 30 m/s. Calculation of the new kinetic energy gives 5.4×10^5 J. This represents a 44% increase in the kinetic energy, from only a 20% increase in the speed! In an accident, all this energy must be dissipated somehow, much of it in deformation of the car and its occupants. You might have heard the phrase "Speed kills," but perhaps a better one would be "Kinetic energy kills."

Sample Problem 7-3

A baseball of mass 0.15 kg is travelling with a velocity of 36 m/s horizontally just before it is caught in a glove.
(a) What is the kinetic energy of the ball before being caught?
(b) During the catch, what is the change in the ball's kinetic energy?
(c) The ball moves 0.047 m horizontally during the catch. Use work and energy to determine the magnitude and direction of the force (assumed constant) exerted on the ball by the glove.

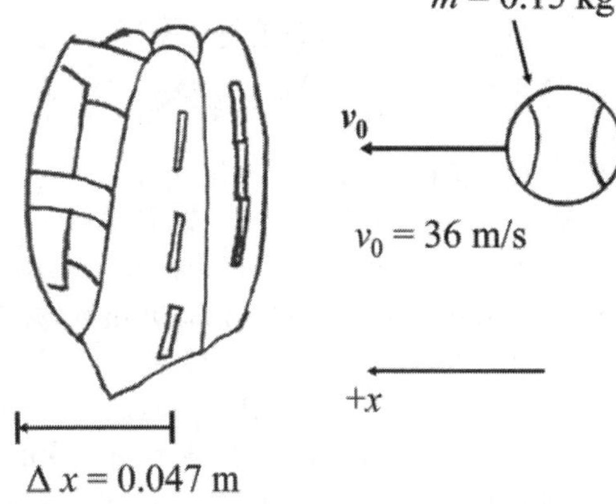

Figure 7-9 *Sample Problem 7-3.*

Solution: (a) Figure 7-9 shows a diagram for this problem. The (initial) kinetic energy of the ball is:

$$E_K = \tfrac{1}{2}mv_0^2 = \tfrac{1}{2}(0.15\text{ kg})(36\text{ m/s})^2 = 97\text{ J}$$

(b) As a result of the catch, the ball comes to rest and its kinetic energy decreases to 0 J. The change in kinetic energy is:

$$\Delta E_K = \tfrac{1}{2}mv^2 - \tfrac{1}{2}mv_0^2 = (0-97)\text{ J} = -97\text{ J}$$

Notice that ΔE_K is always the *final* kinetic energy minus the *initial* kinetic energy. The negative value for ΔE_K indicates that the kinetic energy has decreased (by 97 J in this problem).

(c) We can use the work-energy theorem to find the force exerted by the glove, which is the only horizontal force:

$$W_{TOT} = \Delta E_K$$

Thus,

$$F_x \Delta x = \Delta E_K$$

$$F_x = \frac{\Delta E_K}{\Delta x} = \frac{-97\text{ J}}{0.047\text{ m}} = -2.1\times 10^3\text{ N}$$

Notice that the +x direction has been chosen to be in the direction of the original velocity (Figure 7-9).

Hence, the force is 2.1×10^3 N in the $-x$ direction, that is, in the direction opposite to the ball's original velocity.

Practice

7-26 Is kinetic energy a scalar or vector?

7-27 (a) If the speed of a cyclist doubles, by what factor does the cyclist's kinetic energy increase? (b) Repeat, if the cyclist's speed triples. [Ans. (a) 4 (b) 9]

7-28 What is the kinetic energy of a car of mass 1.50×10^3 kg that is moving with a velocity of 18.0 m/s eastward? [Ans. 2.43×10^5 J]

7-29 (a) If the speed of the car in the previous question increases by 15.0%, what is the car's new kinetic energy?
(b) By what percentage has the car's kinetic energy increased?
(c) How much work was done on the car to increase its kinetic energy?
[Ans. (a) 3.21×10^5 J (b) 32% (c) 7.8×10^4 J]

7-30 A sprinter of mass 55 kg has a kinetic energy of 3.3×10^3 J. What is her speed? [Ans. 11 m/s]

7-31 A red blood cell moving with a speed of 3.2 cm/s in an artery has a kinetic energy of 6.1×10^{-17} J. What is the mass of the red blood cell? [Ans. 1.2×10^{-13} kg]

7-32 A plate of mass 0.353 kg falls (essentially from rest) from a table to the floor 89.3 cm below. (a) What is the work done by gravity on the plate during the fall?
(b) Use the work-energy theorem to determine the speed of the plate just before it hits the floor.
[Ans. (a) 3.09 J (b) 4.18 m/s]

7-33 An executive throws her pen straight up into the air after signing a lucrative contract. If the pen has a mass of 0.090 kg and has an initial upward velocity of 5.6 m/s,
(a) what is the work done by gravity on the pen as it travels 0.75 m upward?
(b) what is the pen's speed after traveling the 0.75 m? (Use the work-energy theorem.)
[Ans. (a) –0.66 J (b) 4.1 m/s]

7-34 A physician is injecting a child with 3.0×10^{-3} kg of vaccine. With what magnitude of force (assumed constant) must he push on the plunger of the syringe, if the speed of the vaccine coming out is 1.4 m/s and the length of the plunger's motion is 3.4 cm? Neglect friction.
[Ans. 8.6×10^{-2} N]

7-35 A girl pulls a large box of mass 20.8 kg across a horizontal floor. She is exerting a force on the box of 95.6 N, inclined at 35.0° above the horizontal. The kinetic friction force on the box has a magnitude of 75.5 N. Use the work-energy theorem to determine the speed of the box after being dragged 0.750 m, assuming that it starts from rest. [Ans. 0.45 m/s]

7-36 A snowboarder of mass 73 kg coasts up a hill inclined at 9.3° to the horizontal. Neglect friction. Use the work-energy theorem to determine how far along the hill he slides before stopping, if his initial speed at the bottom is 4.2 m/s. [Ans. 5.6 m]

7-37 An ice-skater of mass 55.2 kg falls and then slides along the ice, undergoing a horizontal displacement of magnitude 4.18 m before stopping. If the coefficient of kinetic friction between the skater and the ice is 0.27, what was her speed when she started to slide? Use the work-energy theorem. [Ans. 4.7 m/s]

7-38 What is the original speed of an object if its kinetic energy increases by 50% when its speed increases by 2.00 m/s? [Ans. 8.9 m/s]

7.3 GRAVITATIONAL POTENTIAL ENERGY

We have seen that an object has kinetic energy when it is moving. However, even when something is at rest, it can have energy. To illustrate this, suppose that you hold a ball in your hand and then drop it. Gravity pulls it down toward Earth's surface, increasing the ball's kinetic energy. When you were holding the ball in your hand, the ball had the *potential* to develop kinetic energy — the ball needed only to be released. We say that the ball had **gravitational potential energy**, which we define in words as energy due to elevation (above the surface of Earth). We develop a mathematical expression for gravitational potential energy below.

Figure 7-10 shows a ball falling from rest. Notice the vertical co-ordinate system, with $+y$ being upward. The initial position of the ball is represented by "y," and its final position by $y = 0$. We use the work-energy theorem to equate the work done by gravity to the increase in the ball's kinetic energy during the fall:

$$W_{\text{TOT}} = \Delta E_{\text{K}}$$

$$F_y \Delta y = \tfrac{1}{2}mv^2 - 0$$

Now, $F_y = -mg$, and $\Delta y = 0 - y = -y$. Therefore,

$$(-mg)(-y) = \tfrac{1}{2}mv^2$$

Thus,

$$mgy = \tfrac{1}{2}mv^2$$

Hence, the work done by gravity is mgy, and this equals the increase in the kinetic energy of the ball.

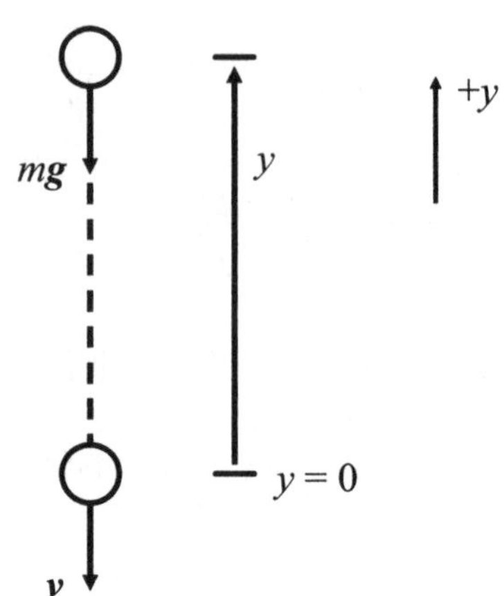

Figure 7-10
A ball falling from rest.

We now interpret the quantity mgy in another way. The gravitational potential energy of an object of mass m at an elevation y is *defined* to be mgy. This is the gravitational potential energy *relative* to the position where $y = 0$. (Sample problem 7-4 below will provide further clarification on this point.) We represent gravitational potential energy by E_p ("p" for potential).

$$E_{\text{p}} = mgy \qquad \text{(gravitational potential energy)} \qquad \textbf{(7-6)}$$

Notice that gravitational potential energy depends on vertical position (y), but has no dependence on horizontal position.

The equation that we developed above, $mgy = \frac{1}{2}mv^2$, can now be given the following interpretation. Prior to falling, the ball had gravitational potential energy (mgy) and no kinetic energy (since it was at rest). When the ball falls to $y = 0$, its gravitational potential energy is converted into an equal amount of kinetic energy ($\frac{1}{2}mv^2$). (More is found about this conversion in Section 7.4.)

Equation 7-6 for gravitational potential energy is valid only for small elevations (y) above the surface of Earth, that is, for elevations over which the magnitude of the gravitational acceleration (g) is approximately constant. In Chapter 9, a different expression for gravitational potential energy that has more general validity will be introduced.

Notice that gravitational potential energy depends on mass. Anyone who has ever tried to hammer a large nail or spike into a piece of wood knows that the job is easier if a large hammer is used. This is simply because a large hammer has more mass and thus more gravitational potential energy when lifted, and therefore is able to deliver more energy to the nail. Similarly, a heavy axe is much easier to use than a small hatchet for splitting wood.

The SI unit for gravitational potential energy (and for all types of energy) is the joule (J).

Sample Problem 7-4

A ruler of mass 0.12 kg falls from a table to the floor 0.60 m below.
(a) Relative to the floor, what is the ruler's gravitational potential energy when on the table? on the floor?
(b) Relative to the table, what is the ruler's gravitational potential energy when on the table? on the floor?
(c) What is the change in the ruler's gravitational potential energy during the fall, relative to the floor? relative to the table?

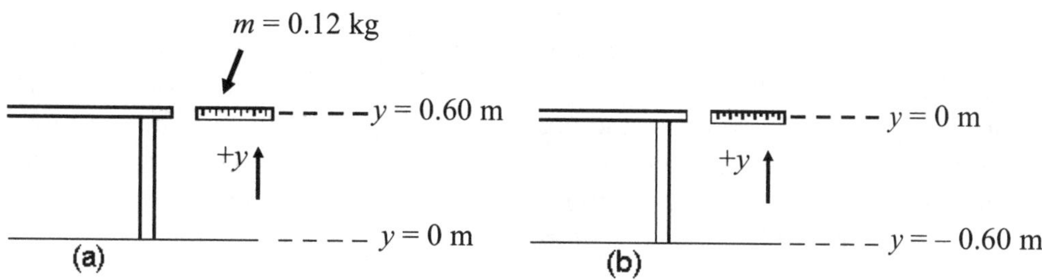

Figure 7-11 **(a)** *Sample Problem 7-4, part (a).* **(b)** *Sample Problem 7-4, part (b).*

Solution: (a) A diagram is given in Figure 7-11 (a). Since the question asks for gravitational potential energy relative to the floor, we have chosen the $y = 0$ position to be at the floor. *The +y direction is upward, as it must be whenever we use $E_p = mgy$.* When the ruler is on the table, it has an elevation of $y = 0.60$ m, and its gravitational potential energy is:

$$\begin{aligned} E_p &= mgy \\ &= (0.12\text{ kg})(9.8\text{ m/s}^2)(0.60\text{ m}) \\ &= 0.71\text{ J} \quad \text{(relative to the floor)} \end{aligned}$$

> ***Units Tip:*** *Notice the units in the calculation of mgy. We have (kg)(m/s²)(m) = kg·m²/s², which is equivalent to a joule (J).*

When the ruler is on the floor, $y = 0$, and therefore its gravitational potential energy is 0 J (relative to the floor).

(b) Since we are now asked for the gravitational potential energy relative to the table, we choose $y = 0$ to be at the level of the table (Figure 7-11 (b)). Therefore, when the ruler is on the table, its gravitational potential energy is 0 J (relative to the table). On the floor, since $+y$ must still be upward, $y = -0.60$ m. (Notice the negative sign.) Thus, the ruler's gravitational potential energy on the floor is:

$$E_p = mgy = (0.12\,\text{kg})(9.8\,\text{m/s}^2)(-0.60\,\text{m}) = -0.71\,\text{J} \quad \text{(relative to the table)}$$

(c) To determine the change in the ruler's gravitational potential energy, we subtract the initial value from the final value.

Relative to the *floor*, this change is: $\Delta E_p = (0 - 0.71)\,\text{J} = -0.71\,\text{J}$

Relative to the *table*, the change is: $\Delta E_p = (-0.71 - 0)\,\text{J} = -0.71\,\text{J}$

Thus, the change in gravitational potential energy does not depend on our choice of position for $y = 0$.

A few comments should be made here about the selection of the $y = 0$ position. Gravitational potential energy is a relative quantity, always measured with respect to some arbitrary position where $y = 0$. In the sample problem above, the wording of the questions essentially told us which positions to choose for $y = 0$, but as this chapter continues, you will often have to make your own choice of $y = 0$ position in problem solutions. In most cases, it does not matter where $y = 0$ is chosen, but *it is usually easiest to choose* $y = 0$ *at the lowest possible position in the diagram* (for example, at floor level in the preceding sample problem). This ensures that all y-values and all gravitational potential energies will be positive (or zero) and will be easy to work with. We shall see that what is usually important is the *change* in gravitational potential energy, which does not depend on where we have chosen $y = 0$.

Practice

7-39 Determine the SI unit of gravitational potential energy in terms of the base units of kilogram (kg), metre (m), and second (s). Similarly, determine the SI unit of kinetic energy. Are the units the same? What is the conventional SI unit used for all types of energy?

7-40 A girl of mass 55 kg climbs a set of stairs with a total vertical rise of 3.4 m. Relative to the bottom of the stairs, what is her gravitational potential energy at the top? [Ans. 1.8×10^3 J]

7-41 An orange of mass 125 g falls from a branch to the ground 3.50 m below.
(a) Relative to the ground, what is the gravitational potential energy of the orange on the branch? on the ground?
(b) Relative to the branch, what is the gravitational potential energy of the orange on the branch? on the ground?
(c) During the orange's fall, what is its change in gravitational potential energy relative to the ground? relative to the branch?
[Ans. (a) 4.29 J, 0 J (b) 0 J, –4.29 J (c) –4.29 J, –4.29 J]

7-42 After being hit by a bat, a baseball of mass 0.15 kg reaches a maximum height where its gravitational potential energy has increased by 22 J from the point where the ball was hit. What is the ball's maximum height (above the point where it was hit)? [Ans. 15 m]

7-43 In a biceps curl, a weightlifter lifts a mass of 15 kg a vertical distance of 66 cm.
(a) How much work is done by gravity on the mass?
(b) Neglecting any accelerations, how much work is done by the weightlifter on the mass?
(c) By how much does the gravitational potential energy of the mass increase?
[Ans. (a) −97 J (b) 97 J (c) 97 J]

7.4 LAW OF CONSERVATION OF ENERGY

What does a person who is running have in common with a television? What does the production of starlight have in common with waterfalls? They all involve the conversion of one form of energy into other forms, and therefore are all governed by an extremely important and pervasive law of nature – the **law of conservation of energy**. As far as we know, this law cannot be violated, and it is one of the fundamental principles at work in the universe. It states:

Energy can be converted into different forms, but it cannot be created nor destroyed.

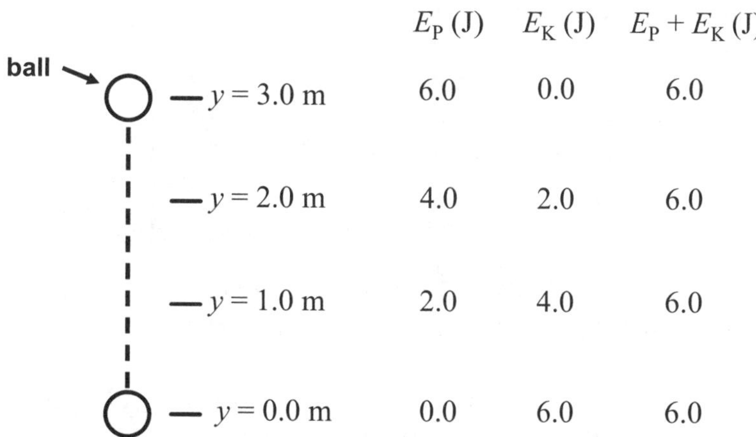

	E_P (J)	E_K (J)	$E_P + E_K$ (J)
$y = 3.0$ m	6.0	0.0	6.0
$y = 2.0$ m	4.0	2.0	6.0
$y = 1.0$ m	2.0	4.0	6.0
$y = 0.0$ m	0.0	6.0	6.0

Figure 7-12
Gravitational potential energy, kinetic energy, and total energy of a falling ball.

As an example, consider a falling ball. As already shown in Section 7.3, as the ball falls, its gravitational potential energy decreases and its kinetic energy increases by an equal amount. Thus, as the gravitational potential energy is converted into kinetic energy, the total amount of energy is unchanged. Figure 7-12 shows the various energies of a falling ball (of mass 0.204 kg) at a few points during its fall. Notice that, although both the ball's gravitational potential energy and kinetic energy change, the total energy (that is, the sum of gravitational potential energy and kinetic energy) remains constant.

So far we have discussed only two forms of energy (what are they?), but there are many other types — thermal energy, electrical energy, sound energy, and so on. In this book, we will be applying conservation of energy to many different physical situations involving various forms of energy. Conservation of energy applies to all processes involving energy — conversion of food energy into kinetic energy of your body, production of sunlight, commercial generation of electrical energy, conversion of chemical energy in gasoline to kinetic energy of an automobile, interactions of subatomic particles, etc.

Note that "conservation of energy" differs from "energy conservation," which refers to the careful use of energy resources. Conservation of energy is a law of nature; energy conservation is something that we should all practise.

Sample Problem 7-5

A basketball player makes a free-throw shot at the basket. The ball's speed is 7.2 m/s as it is released from the player's hand, and its height is 2.21 m above the floor. What is the ball's speed as it goes through the hoop, which is 3.05 m above the floor? Neglect air resistance.

Solution: A diagram is given in Figure 7-13. By the law of conservation of energy, the total energy of the ball is constant as it travels through the air. In this problem, the two forms of energy involved are kinetic energy and gravitational potential energy. Referring to the release point as position 1, and to the point where the ball goes through the hoop as position 2, we can write:

$$\text{Total energy at 1} = \text{Total energy at 2}$$

$$\tfrac{1}{2}mv_1^2 + mgy_1 = \tfrac{1}{2}mv_2^2 + mgy_2$$

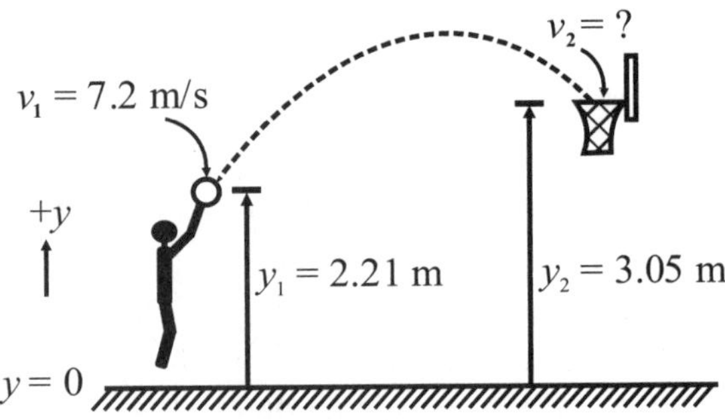

Figure 7-13 *Sample Problem 7-5.*

Notice that the details of the trajectory are unimportant in this energy-conservation equation. The direction of the initial velocity and the particular parabolic path that the ball follows do not affect the kinetic and potential energies, which are scalar quantities that do not depend on direction.

Note also in Figure 7-13 that we have chosen the y = 0 position to be at the lowest position of interest in the diagram, in this case the floor.

We need to solve for v_2. Dividing the above equation by m and moving the gy_2 term to the left-hand side:

$$\tfrac{1}{2}v_1^2 + g(y_1 - y_2) = \tfrac{1}{2}v_2^2$$

Multiplying by 2: $v_1^2 + 2g(y_1 - y_2) = v_2^2$

Therefore,

$$\begin{aligned} v_2 &= \sqrt{v_1^2 + 2g(y_1 - y_2)} \\ &= \sqrt{(7.2\text{ m/s})^2 + 2(9.80\text{ m/s}^2)(2.21\text{ m} - 3.05\text{ m})} \\ &= 5.9\text{ m/s} \end{aligned}$$

Thus, the speed of the ball as it passes through the hoop is 5.9 m/s. Notice that this is less than the speed when the ball was released — because the ball is at a higher elevation when it passes through the hoop, its gravitational potential energy is greater, meaning that its kinetic energy (and speed) must be less.

Mechanical Energy

Often the sum of kinetic energy and potential energy is called *mechanical energy*. Notice that we did not specify *gravitational* potential energy. Another kind of potential energy that can be included in mechanical energy is elastic potential energy, which is discussed later in this chapter.

 **Practice**

7-44 Why do rollercoaster rides always start by going up a hill?

7-45 An egg is cracked and the contents (mass 0.052 kg) are dropped from rest 11 cm above a frying pan. Relative to the frying pan ($y = 0$), determine:
(a) the initial gravitational potential energy of the egg contents;
(b) the final gravitational potential energy of the egg contents;
(c) the change in gravitational potential energy as the egg falls.
(d) What are the kinetic energy and speed of the egg contents just before hitting the pan?
[Ans. (a) 0.056 J (b) 0 J (c) –0.056 J (d) 0.056 J, 1.5 m/s]

7-46 A stone (mass 50 g) is dropped from rest from a roof. (a) Neglecting air resistance, what is the stone's speed when it has fallen 15 m? Use conservation of energy. (b) If air resistance is included, would your answer to (a) increase, decrease, or remain the same? [Ans. (a) 17 m/s]

7-47 A baseball having a mass of 0.149 kg is thrown vertically upward with an initial speed of 5.75 m/s. Neglecting air resistance, use conservation of energy to determine:
(a) its speed on the way up, 0.800 m above the release point
(b) its maximum height
(c) its speed on the way down, 0.800 m above the release point.
[Ans. (a) 4.17 m/s (b) 1.69 m (c) 4.17 m/s]

7-48 A woman throws a ball, which hits a vertical wall at a height of 1.2 m above the ball's release point. Just as it starts to hit the wall, the ball's speed is 9.9 m/s. What was the ball's initial speed? Use conservation of energy and neglect air resistance. [Ans. 11 m/s]

7-49 A river is flowing with a speed of 3.74 m/s just upstream from a waterfall of vertical height 8.74 m. During each second, 7.12×10^4 kg of water pass over the fall.
(a) Relative to the bottom of the fall, what is the gravitational potential energy of this mass of water?
(b) If there is complete conversion of gravitational potential energy to kinetic energy, what is the speed of the water at the bottom of the fall?
[Ans. (a) 6.10×10^6 J (b) 13.6 m/s]

7-50 A stick is thrown from a cliff 27 m high with an initial velocity of 18 m/s at 37° above the horizontal. (a) Use conservation of energy to determine the speed of the stick just before it hits the ground below the cliff. (b) Repeat, if the angle is 37° below the horizontal.
[Ans. (a) 29 m/s (b) 29 m/s]

7-51 A boy is playing with a rope tied to a tree near his favourite swimming hole (Figure 7-14). Initially the boy is stationary and the rope (of length 3.7 m) makes an angle of 48° with the vertical. He then lifts his feet slightly and starts to swing freely. If air resistance is neglected, use conservation of energy to determine:
(a) his speed at the bottom of the swing
(b) the maximum height, relative to his initial position, to which he can swing.
[Ans. (a) 4.9 m/s (b) back to original vertical level]

Figure 7-14 *Question 7-51.*

7-52 A skier slides down a slope of length 11.7 m inclined at an angle ϕ to the horizontal. If her initial speed is 65.7 cm/s, and her speed at the bottom of the slope is 7.19 m/s, determine ϕ. Use conservation of energy, neglecting friction and air resistance. [Ans. 12.9°]

<u>**7-53**</u> Two skiers start from rest at the same point at the top of a slope. They take different routes to the bottom, but end at the same point. Neglecting friction and air resistance, how do their final speeds compare? Does it make a difference if the slope has dips and rises, instead of being smooth?

7-54 A small ice-cube is released from rest at the top edge of a hemispherical bowl (Figure 7-15). When it reaches the bottom of the bowl, its speed is 1.5 m/s. Use conservation of energy to find the radius of the bowl. Neglect friction.
[Ans. 11 cm]

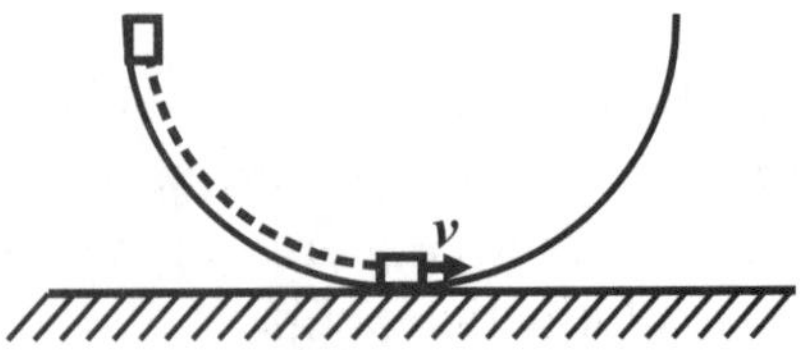

Figure 7-15 *Question 7-54.*

7.5 WORK DONE BY FRICTION

Think about a baseball player sliding into a base. As he starts the slide, he has kinetic energy, but when the slide is over, there is no kinetic energy left. Where did it go? While he was sliding, there was no change in elevation, so there has been no change in gravitational potential energy. We shall see in this section that the kinetic energy has been converted into a different form — thermal energy — and that the amount of thermal energy produced is closely related to the work done by friction.

During the baseball player's slide, there is a horizontal displacement $\Delta \boldsymbol{r}$ (Figure 7-16). The only force that does work on him is the kinetic friction force $\boldsymbol{F}_K$. (Gravity and the normal force are both perpendicular to the displacement, and hence do no work.) The kinetic friction force is in the opposite direction to the displacement, and hence the angle θ between this force and the displacement is 180°. The work done by friction is:

Figure 7-16 *The work done by kinetic friction on the sliding player is:* $W = F_K \, \Delta r \cos\theta = F_K \, \Delta r \cos 180° = -F_K \, \Delta r$.

$$W = F \, \Delta r \cos\theta = F_K \, \Delta r \cos 180° = -F_K \, \Delta r \quad \text{(since } \cos 180° = -1\text{)}$$

Since F_K and Δr are both positive (being magnitudes of vectors), the work done by friction is negative. This means that friction is removing kinetic energy from the player. Since energy is always conserved, this energy must be converted into another form — in this particular case, into **thermal energy** (also called **internal energy**) of the player and ground. As the player slides, the atoms in the player and ground vibrate with more energy, that is, the player and ground get hotter.

Whenever kinetic friction does negative work to slow something down, the magnitude of this work done equals the thermal energy produced. For example, if the work done by kinetic friction is –5 J, then the thermal energy produced is +5 J. Since kinetic friction is always opposite to the direction of the displacement, the work done by kinetic friction can always be written as $-F_K\Delta r$ (as above), and the magnitude of this work is just $F_K\Delta r$. Thus, we can write the thermal energy produced by kinetic friction as $F_K\Delta r$. In this book, we will use E_{th} as the symbol for thermal energy. Thus,

$$E_{th} = F_K\Delta r \qquad \text{(thermal energy produced by friction)} \qquad \textbf{(7-7)}$$

Thermal energy is associated with the motion of atoms and molecules, which are always moving in a haphazard way. As the thermal energy of an object increases, the atoms and molecules move more quickly. For a monatomic gas such as helium, the thermal energy is just the total kinetic energy of all the atoms. For more complicated molecules, or for atoms in solids, the thermal energy is partly kinetic and partly in a form called electric potential energy. The details of the production of thermal energy by kinetic friction were discussed in Section 6.1.

The terms "heat" and "thermal energy" are often confused. **Heat** refers to energy *transferred* between objects as a result of a difference in temperature between them, whereas thermal energy refers to the energy contained in the objects themselves. Thus, we say that heat flows from a cup of hot coffee, decreasing the thermal energy of the coffee and increasing the thermal energy of the air around it.

Sample Problem 7-6

A baseball player slides into home plate. (a) If she slides for 6.0 m before stopping, and the force of friction on the player has a constant magnitude of 3.3×10^2 N, how much thermal energy is produced during the slide? (b) If the player's mass is 55 kg, what was her speed before sliding?

Solution: (a) Figure 7-17 shows a diagram for the problem. We can write the thermal energy (E_{th}) as $F_K\Delta r$, and since we know F_K and Δr, we can easily calculate E_{th}:

$$\begin{aligned} E_{th} &= F_K \Delta r \\ &= (3.3 \times 10^2\ \text{N})(6.0\ \text{m}) \\ &= 2.0 \times 10^3\ \text{J} \end{aligned}$$

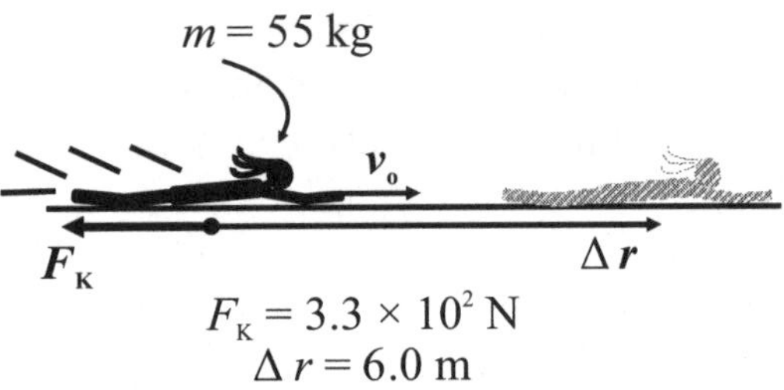

Figure 7-17 *Sample Problem 7-6.*

Thus, the thermal energy produced is 2.0×10^3 J.

(b) By the law of conservation of energy, the player's initial kinetic energy must equal the thermal energy produced during the slide, since there is no kinetic energy remaining at the end of the slide. Thus,

$$\tfrac{1}{2}mv_0^2 = E_{th}$$

Re-arranging to solve for the initial speed v_0:

$$\begin{aligned} v_0 &= \sqrt{\frac{2E_{th}}{m}} \\ &= \sqrt{\frac{2(2.0 \times 10^3\ \text{J})}{55\ \text{kg}}} \\ &= 8.5\ \text{m/s} \end{aligned}$$

Therefore, the player's initial speed was 8.5 m/s.

Sample Problem 7-7

A boy is pushing a large pot containing a plant across a floor by exerting a constant horizontal force. The pot and plant have a combined mass of 27 kg. The kinetic friction force on the pot has a magnitude of 93 N. If the pot starts from rest, and has a speed of 0.74 m/s after being pushed for 2.0 m, what is the magnitude of the force exerted by the boy?

Solution: There are many ways to solve this problem; we will use conservation of energy. Figure 7-18 shows a diagram.

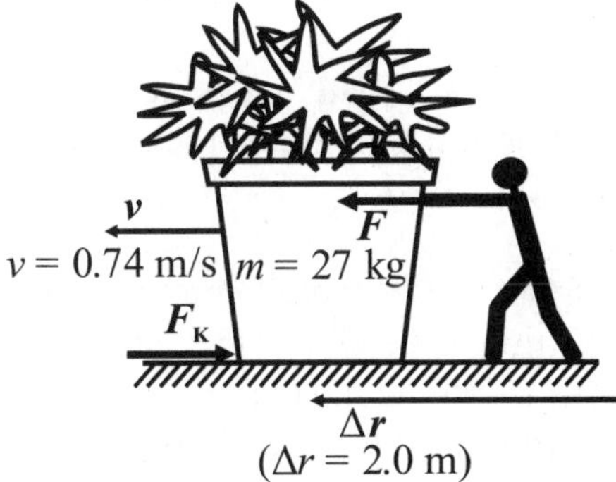

Figure 7-18 *Sample Problem 7-7.*

The boy provides the pot with energy, which equals the work done by him. If he pushes with a horizontal force of magnitude F, the energy supplied by him is just $F\Delta r$ (where Δr = 2.0 m), since $\boldsymbol{F}$ and $\Delta \boldsymbol{r}$ are in the same direction.

By conservation of energy, the energy provided ($F\Delta r$) equals the sum of the kinetic energy of the pot and the thermal energy produced in the floor and the bottom surface of the pot. The kinetic energy can be determined from the expression ½mv^2, since both m and v are known. The thermal energy is just $F_K\Delta r$, and both F_K and Δr are given.

$$\text{Energy provided} = \text{kinetic energy} + \text{thermal energy}$$

Thus,

$$F\Delta r = \tfrac{1}{2}mv^2 + F_K\Delta r$$

Solving for the unknown F:

$$F = \frac{mv^2}{2\Delta r} + F_K = \frac{(27\text{ kg})(0.74\text{ m/s})^2}{2(2.0\text{ m})} + 93\text{ N} = 97\text{ N}$$

Therefore, the boy exerts a force of magnitude 97 N.

Practice

7-55 What is the SI unit of thermal energy?

7-56 (a) Suppose that you push this book across a horizontal desk at *constant velocity*. You are supplying some energy to the book. Into what form(s) does this energy go?

(b) Suppose that you push the book with a larger force so that the book accelerates. Into what form(s) does the energy now go?

7-57 A kinetic friction force of magnitude 67 N acts on a box as it slides across the floor. If the displacement of the box along the floor is 3.5 m in magnitude,
(a) what is the work done by friction on the box?
(b) how much thermal energy is produced?
[Ans. (a) -2.3×10^2 J (b) 2.3×10^2 J]

7-58 As a plate slides across a table, 0.620 J of thermal energy is produced. If the kinetic friction force acting on the plate is 0.83 N in magnitude, how far did the plate slide?
[Ans. 0.75 m]

7-59 A chalkboard eraser of mass 55 g slides along the ledge at the bottom of a chalkboard. Its initial speed is 1.9 m/s, and, after sliding for 54 cm, it comes to rest.
(a) Determine the eraser's initial and final kinetic energies.
(b) Into what form of energy is the kinetic energy converted?
(c) Use conservation of energy to determine the magnitude of the friction force acting on the eraser. [Ans. (a) 0.099 J, 0 J (c) 0.18 N]

7-60 The brakes are applied to a car travelling at 85 km/h along a horizontal road. The wheels lock and the car skids to a halt in 47 m. The magnitude of the kinetic friction force between the skidding car and the road is 7.4×10^3 N.
(a) How much thermal energy is produced during the skid?
(b) In what form was this thermal energy before the skid?
(c) Use conservation of energy to determine the mass of the car.
[Ans. (a) 3.5×10^5 J (c) 1.2×10^3 kg]

7-61 In the previous question, determine the coefficient of kinetic friction between the tires and road. [Ans. 0.61]

7-62 A pen of mass 0.057 kg is sliding across a horizontal desk. In sliding 25 cm, its speed decreases to 5.7 cm/s. What was its initial speed if the force of kinetic friction exerted on the pen by the desk is 0.15 N in magnitude? Use conservation of energy. [Ans. 1.1 m/s]

7-63 A clerk pushes a file cabinet (mass 22.0 kg) across the floor by exerting a horizontal force of magnitude 98 N. The force of kinetic friction acting on the cabinet is 87 N in magnitude. Assuming that the cabinet starts from rest, what is its speed after moving 1.2 m? Use conservation of energy. [Ans. 1.1 m/s]

7-64 A large box of flower seeds (mass 18 kg) is pushed 1.6 m by a woman who is exerting a force of 1.5×10^2 N at 22° below the horizontal. The coefficient of kinetic friction between the box and the horizontal floor beneath it is 0.55.
(a) Use Newton's laws of motion to determine the magnitudes of the normal force and friction force on the box.
(b) Use conservation of energy to determine the final speed of the box if it starts from rest.

(c) How much thermal energy is produced?
[Ans. (a) 2.3×10^2 N, 1.3×10^2 N (b) 1.4 m/s (c) 2.0×10^2 J]

7-65 A box of apples (mass 22 kg) slides down a ramp inclined at 44° to the horizontal. The friction force on the box has a magnitude of 79 N. If the box starts from rest and slides 2.5 m along the ramp, determine:
(a) the work done by friction
(b) the box's final kinetic energy (using conservation of energy)
(c) the thermal energy produced
[Ans. (a) -2.0×10^2 J (b) 1.8×10^2 J (c) 2.0×10^2 J]

7.6 OTHER TYPES OF ENERGY

So far in this chapter we have discussed kinetic energy, gravitational potential energy, and thermal energy. But there are many forms of energy with which you are familiar that we have not yet introduced — chemical energy in gasoline, electrical energy, food energy, and so on. Although we do not have space to discuss all the possible forms of energy, the following provides a brief description of some of them.

LIGHT ENERGY — Light energy is carried by travelling oscillations called electromagnetic waves (or their particle equivalent, photons). *Visible* electromagnetic waves are referred to as light, but there are invisible kinds such as gamma rays, X rays, ultraviolet waves, infrared waves, microwaves, and radiowaves.

ELECTRICAL ENERGY — Electrical energy usually refers to the passage of electrons along wires, such as in appliances in your home.

ELECTRIC POTENTIAL ENERGY — Just as there is gravitational potential energy associated with the gravitational force, there is electric potential energy connected with the electric force. Gravitational potential energy changes as masses are moved relative to each other, and electric potential energy changes as charges are moved (more about this topic in Chapters 11 and 12).

CHEMICAL ENERGY — Chemical energy is a combination of kinetic energy of electrons in molecules and electric potential energy of the charged electrons and nuclei. For example, gasoline has chemical energy that is released as thermal energy when it is burned. During this burning, the electrons and nuclei are put into different arrangements with a resulting decrease in chemical energy and production of an equivalent amount of thermal energy.

FOOD ENERGY — This is a type of chemical energy.

NUCLEAR ENERGY — Nuclear energy is a potential energy associated with the nuclear strong force. It can be converted to other forms by re-arrangements of the particles inside a nucleus, by fusing certain small nuclei together, or by breaking some types of large nuclei apart.

SOUND ENERGY — Sound energy is associated with the movement of compression waves through materials such as air and water. It is a combination of electric potential energy and kinetic energy of molecules.

ELASTIC POTENTIAL ENERGY — This type of energy is stored in objects that are stretched (or compressed), such as elastic bands, springs, and various types of sports equipment (as discussed below).

Elastic Potential Energy in Sports

Elastic potential energy is important in many sports. For example, the poles used by pole-vaulters store elastic potential energy when bent. Pole-vaulting is essentially a conversion of the vaulter's initial kinetic energy into gravitational potential energy at the top of the vault, with an intermediate conversion into elastic potential energy. As the pole bends early in the vault, kinetic energy is converted into elastic potential energy. As it unbends, the elastic potential energy changes to gravitational potential energy.

We can use conservation of energy to calculate an estimate for the height attainable by pole-vaulters. We start by assuming that the initial kinetic energy is completely converted into gravitational potential energy, ignoring the small kinetic energy as the vaulter goes over the bar (Figure 7-19):

$$\tfrac{1}{2}mv^2 = mgy$$

Solving for height y: $$y = \frac{v^2}{2g}$$

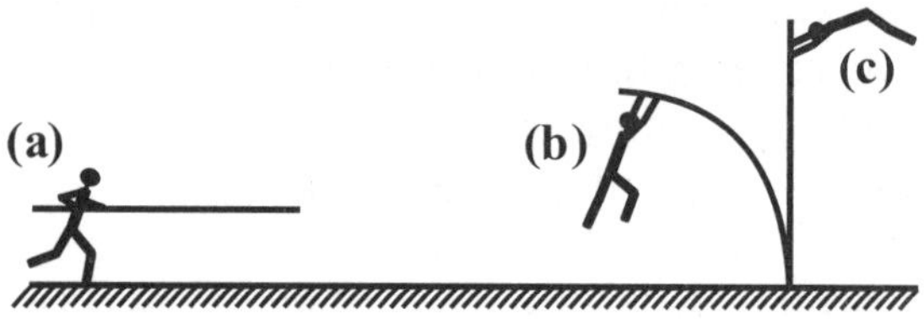

Figure 7-19 *In the pole-vault, the vaulter starts with* **(a)** *kinetic energy, and finishes with* **(c)** *gravitational potential energy.* **(b)** *In between, much of the energy is stored in the pole as elastic potential energy.*

A typical running speed (v) for a pole-vaulter is about 10 m/s. (People can run faster, up to roughly 12.5 m/s, but not carrying a pole.) Since we are making only an estimate, we will use 10 m/s^2 for g.

Thus, $$y \approx \frac{(10\text{ m/s})^2}{2(10\text{ m/s}^2)} \approx 5\text{ m}$$

However, some energy is lost when the pole hits the ground, and thermal energy is generated in the pole (and thus lost) when it is bent and unbent. With modern fibreglass poles, the energy lost is very small — roughly 10% of the total. A 10% decrease in the final gravitational potential energy means that the height should be decreased by 10%, to 4.5 m.

There are two refinements still to be made. When we use mgy for gravitational potential energy, y represents the height of the *centre of mass* (CM) of the object, in this case the vaulter. The CM of an object is the average position of the object's mass at any instant. Our y-value of 4.5 m indicates that the height of the vaulter's CM increases by 4.5 m during the vault. The CM of a typical vaulter is about 1 m from the ground when running, and just clears the bar (or can even go under it!) at the top of the vault. Therefore, in order to determine the height of the CM above the *ground* as the vaulter clears the bar, we need to add 1 m, giving a value of about 5.5 m.

The last correction is that, at the top of the vault, the athlete essentially does a handstand, thus providing more energy and increasing the height by about 0.3 m. We now have a final estimate of about 5.8 m, which corresponds closely to the heights attained by world-class athletes. (As of January 2007, the world record was 6.14 m.)

There are numerous other examples of storage and recovery of elastic potential energy in sports equipment:

- tennis rackets (frames and strings)
- many types of balls, which become compressed on impact (in golf, tennis, baseball, basketball, football, etc.)
- flexible shafts in golf clubs and hockey sticks.

A high-tech application of elastic potential energy in sports is the design of tuned running tracks. When a runner's foot strikes the track, the track is deformed as it absorbs energy from the runner. Some of this energy is stored as elastic potential energy in the track material, and partially returned to the runner during the rebound of the track as the runner's foot leaves the track. Running tracks can be designed with the right springiness for effective return of energy to the runner, with a 2% to 3% reduction in running times.

Energy Units

Although the SI unit of energy is the joule, there are a number of other units in common use. Some are used scientifically, and some in the everyday world. Table 7.1 lists the names, abbreviations, and joule equivalents of a number of these units.

Table 7.1
Non-SI Energy Units

Name	Abbreviation	Joule equivalent
electron-volt	eV	1.60×10^{-19} J
calorie	cal	4.184 J
kilocalorie	kcal	4184 J
Calorie	Cal	4184 J
food calorie	Cal	4184 J
British thermal unit	Btu	1055 J

The electron-volt (eV) and its common multiples, keV (10^3 eV), MeV (10^6 eV), etc., are used widely in atomic and subatomic physics. The various "calories" and the British thermal unit arose as units for heat and thermal energy in the 1700s and 1800s, when it was not apparent that what we now call thermal energy is indeed just another form of energy. Note that the food calorie, the kilocalorie, and the Calorie (with a capital "C") are all the same. In North America, food energy is still commonly measured in the archaic Calories, but civilization is proceeding at a more rapid pace in some other countries, where joules are being used (Figure 7-20).

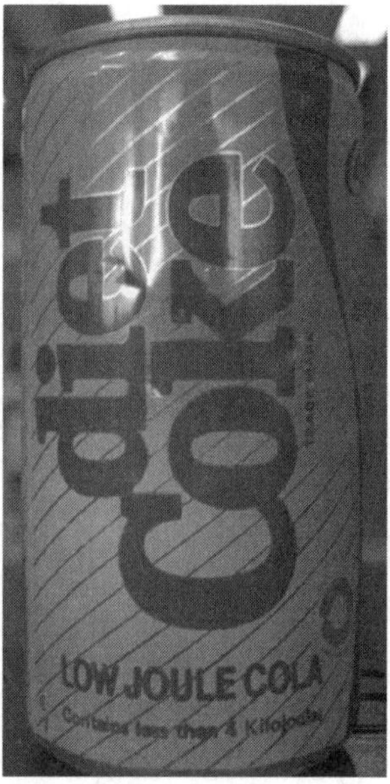

Figure 7-20 *SI units are taken seriously in Australia.*

Practice

7-66 When an insect such as a flea jumps, the energy is provided not by muscle alone, but also by an elastic protein that has been compressed like a spring. If a flea of mass 210 μg jumps vertically to a height of 65 mm, and 75% of the energy comes from elastic potential energy stored in the protein, determine the initial quantity of stored elastic potential energy. Neglect energy losses due to air resistance. [Ans. 1.0×10^{-7} J]

7-67 Use the conversion factors in Table 7.1 to perform the following unit conversions:
(a) 13.6 eV to J (b) 1.3 MeV to J (c) 2.3 cal to J
(d) 2.8 J to Cal (e) 3.7 J to Btu (f) 4.57 cal to Btu
[Ans. (a) 2.18×10^{-18} J (b) 2.1×10^{-13} J (c) 9.6 J
(d) 6.7×10^{-4} Cal (e) 3.5×10^{-3} Btu (f) 1.81×10^{-2} Btu]

7-68 A particular apple has an energy content of 87 Cal. Convert this value to kilojoules. [Ans. 3.6×10^{2} kJ]

7.7 EFFICIENCY OF ENERGY CONVERSIONS

Often we are interested in converting one form of energy into another. For instance, we use lightbulbs to convert electrical energy into light, and plants convert light energy into chemical energy via photosynthesis. Since energy is always conserved, the total energy before any conversion always equals the total energy after. However, the energy might not be going into forms that we consider useful. For example, only 5% of the electrical energy used in an incandescent lightbulb is converted into light. The remaining 95% goes into heat. Since the purpose of lightbulbs is the generation of light, we say that they are only 5% efficient. The **efficiency** of an energy conversion is the ratio of useful energy out to total energy in:

$$\text{efficiency} = \frac{\text{useful energy out}}{\text{total energy in}} \qquad \textbf{(7-8)}$$

By the law of conservation of energy, the useful energy out can never be greater than the total energy in, and thus efficiencies are always less than 1. Efficiency is often multiplied by 100% to express it as a percentage.

Table 7.2
Approximate efficiencies of energy conversions.

Device	Energy In (E_1)	Useful Energy Out (E_2)	Efficiency (E_2/E_1) × 100%
fluorescent light	electrical	light	20%
incandescent light	electrical	light	5%
automobile engine	chemical	kinetic	14%
steam locomotive	chemical	kinetic	8%
dry cell battery	chemical	electrical	90%
electrical generator	kinetic	electrical	98%
steam-electric power plant	chemical or nuclear	electrical	30-40%
hydroelectric plant	kinetic	electrical	95%
people	chemical	any useful energy	25%

Efficiencies for various energy conversions are listed in Table 7.2. Notice the low efficiencies of automobile engines and lights. If you want to get rich, invent a more efficient type of light or auto engine! Electrical generators have a very high efficiency (about 98%); these are the machines that spin in electrical generating plants and generate the electrical currents. However, most electrical plants have a much lower *overall* efficiency. In order to spin the generators, steam is often used that has been produced by burning a fossil fuel (coal, oil, or natural gas) or by using a nuclear reactor to provide heat. Only about 30% to 40% of the thermal energy in the steam can be converted into kinetic energy of the spinning generators; the rest is wasted and simply goes into heating the surrounding air (Figure 7-21) or water in a nearby lake or river. Hydroelectric plants use falling water to spin the generators and have a much higher efficiency (about 95%).

Figure 7-21 *Cooling towers at a nuclear electrical generating station in France.*

People have an efficiency of only about 25%. If you lift a 1.0-kg mass through a vertical distance of 1.0 m, you increase its gravitational potential energy by

$$mgy = (1.0\,\text{kg})(9.8\,\text{m/s}^2)(1.0\,\text{m}) = 9.8\,\text{J}$$

but the actual energy used by your body to do this is roughly four times as great (about 40 J). Approximately 30 J goes into thermal energy of your body. When you are producing a great deal of useful energy, such as when running, you generate a lot of wasted thermal energy and become very hot.

Sample Problem 7-8

A person of mass 70 kg (two significant digits) requires about 5.0×10^5 J of food energy to walk 2.0 km on level ground. How much *more* energy is required if the walk is done at 24° above the horizontal? Assume an efficiency of 25% in conversion of food energy to usable energy. Express the answer in joules and food calories.

Solution: In terms of energy, the only difference between the level walk and the inclined walk is that there is an increase in gravitational potential energy, *mgy*, in the inclined walk (Figure 7-22):

$$\begin{aligned} E_\mathrm{p} &= mgy \\ &= (70\ \mathrm{kg})(9.8\ \mathrm{m/s^2})(2.0\times10^3\ \mathrm{m})(\sin 24°) \\ &= 5.6\times10^5\ \mathrm{J} \end{aligned}$$

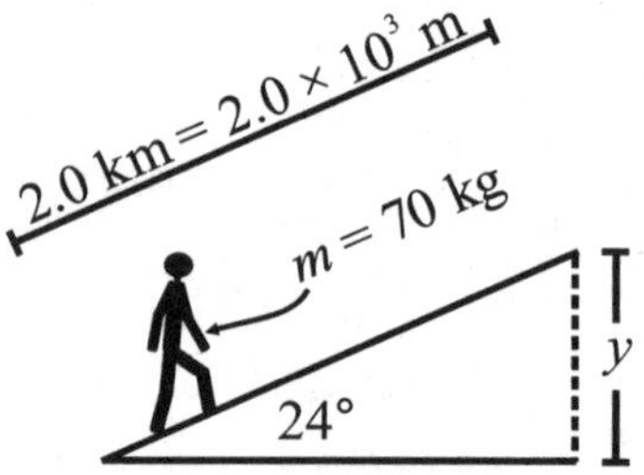

Figure 7-22
Sample Problem 7-8.
$y = (2.0 \times 10^3$ m) (sin 24°)

Then,
$$\text{efficiency} = \frac{\text{useful energy out}}{\text{total energy in}}$$

Therefore,
$$\text{total energy in} = \frac{\text{useful energy out}}{\text{efficiency}} = \frac{5.6\times10^5\ \mathrm{J}}{0.25} = 2.2\times10^6\ \mathrm{J}$$

Thus, the total (food) energy required is 2.2×10^6 J.

To convert to food calories, we use the conversion factor provided in Table 7.1 (1 food calorie = 1 Cal = 4184 J):

$$2.2\times10^6\ \mathrm{J}\times\frac{1\ \mathrm{Cal}}{4184\ \mathrm{J}} = 5.3\times10^2\ \mathrm{Cal}$$

Hence, the extra energy needed is 5.3×10^2 food calories (Cal or kcal).

Energy Conservation and Alternative Energy Sources

If energy is always conserved, why should we try to conserve it, that is, why should we use as little energy as possible in transportation, industry, etc.? Part of the answer is that in all conversions and uses of energy, there is generation of some thermal energy, which is a form of energy that is not very useful to us. It is impossible to convert thermal energy to other forms with 100% efficiency. Thus, for example, when thermal energy is produced in an automobile engine, most of it is essentially lost to us forever. Once we have burned the gasoline, its energy has been used and is not retrievable. As well, as shown in Figure 7-23, fossil fuels (oil, coal, and natural gas) account for 92% of annual world energy consumption. Since fossil-fuel reserves are finite, it makes sense to use these resources wisely if we can use them only once.

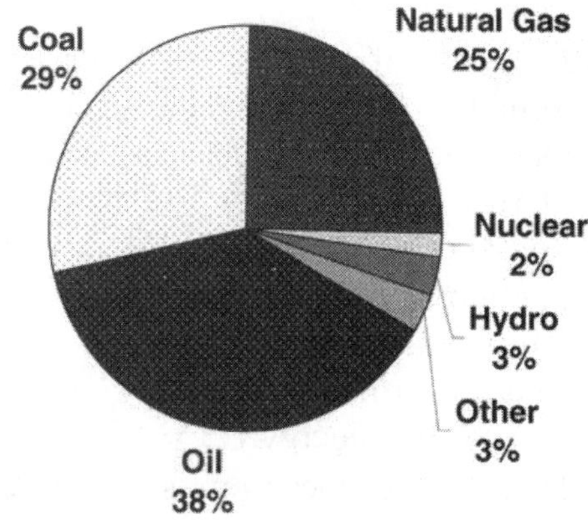

Figure 7-23 *World energy consumption by source in 2005.*

Using fossil fuels also creates environmental problems such as global warming due to the *greenhouse effect*. This refers to the warming of the atmosphere due to the absorption of radiation by atmospheric gases such as carbon dioxide produced by combustion of fossil fuels. As more carbon dioxide is put into the atmosphere, more infrared radiation emitted by Earth can be absorbed in the atmosphere. (Infrared radiation is a form of electromagnetic radiation — like light, but invisible.) The energy in this radiation is thus trapped in the atmosphere, which gets warmer.

Alternative energy sources such as the wind (Figure 7-24), sun, nuclear energy, tides, geothermal energy, and tides are being developed worldwide. The choice of energy sources in any country depends on many factors: local availability, cost, environmental impact, availability of qualified personnel to develop the technology, and so on.

Figure 7-24 *Wind turbines near Shelburne, Ontario.*

Practice

7-69 How much food energy is required for a boy of mass 47 kg to climb a 12-m high tree (over and above that required for him to rest for an equal time)? Assume an efficiency of 25% in conversion of food energy to usable energy. [Ans. 2.2×10^4 J]

7-70 How many food calories are required for a person to lift a box of books (mass 15 kg) through a vertical distance of 0.30 m? Assume an efficiency of 25% in conversion of food energy to usable energy. [Ans. 0.042 Cal]

7-71 A 52-kg woman is doing pushups. During each one, she raises the centre of mass of her body by 0.25 m. How many pushups must she do in order to use at least 1.0 Cal of food energy (over and above the energy required for her to rest for an equal time)? Neglect the energy used in lowering her body, and assume an efficiency of 25% in conversion of food energy to usable energy. [Ans. 9]

7-72 A car of mass 1.2×10^3 kg is driving up a hill 2.3 km long, inclined at 5.2° above the horizontal. How much more chemical energy (in megajoules) in the gasoline is required, in comparison with that used on a level road? Use the efficiency for automobiles provided in Table 7.2. [Ans. 18 MJ]

7-73 Suppose that the efficiency of conversion of wind energy into electrical energy in a particular wind turbine is 35%.
(a) In what form is wind energy? (Choose from kinetic energy, gravitational potential energy, or elastic potential energy.)
(b) If the wind energy passing through the turbine each second is 7.5×10^6 J, how much electrical energy is generated per second?
(c) If the turbine is producing 2.2×10^6 J of electrical energy each second, how much wind energy is passing through it per second?
[Ans. (b) 2.6×10^6 J (c) 6.3×10^6 J]

7-74 Electric heat is sometimes claimed to be a good way to heat homes because there is 100% conversion of electrical energy to thermal energy in electric heaters. While this statement is true, there are energy conversions in the *production* of the electrical energy that have efficiencies less than 100%. Assuming that the electrical energy is produced in a coal-fired plant, use the following efficiencies to calculate the *overall* efficiency of conversion of chemical energy in coal to thermal energy in your home.

extraction of coal — 96%
transportation of coal — 97%
generation of electricity — 33%
transmission of electricity — 90%
electrical heating — 100%

[Ans. 28%]

7-75 Calculate the overall efficiency of a fluorescent light powered by electricity from a coal-fired power plant. Use data from the previous question and from Table 7.2. [Ans. 6%]

7.8 POWER

In everyday speech, the terms force, energy, and power are often used interchangeably, but the scientific meanings of these words are different. We have already studied force and energy, and now turn our attention to power. The SI unit of power, the watt, is one with which you are undoubtedly familiar; for example, hairdryers and lightbulbs are labeled according to their power consumption in watts.

Power is the time rate of production or use of energy. For instance, if a car's kinetic energy increases, the power input to the car is the increase in the kinetic energy divided by the time taken. Mathematically, we write power (P) as:

$$P = \frac{E}{t} \qquad \text{(power)} \qquad \textbf{(7-9)}$$

where E is energy and t is time.

With energy in joules (J) and time in seconds (s), we get a unit of joule per second (J/s) for power. This unit is conventionally referred to as a **watt** (W), in honour of the Scottish physicist James Watt (1736 – 1819), who modified the steam engine to improve its efficiency greatly.

$$\text{W (watt)} = \frac{\text{J}}{\text{s}} \qquad \text{(SI unit of power)}$$

Watts and kilowatts (kW) are often used to indicate the power consumption of home appliances such as lightbulbs and electric heaters, and megawatts (MW) are used in describing power output of electrical plants. A 60-watt lightbulb uses 60 J of electrical energy each second (but as we saw in the previous section, only 5% of this energy is converted to light). A typical electrical generating station produces about 1000 MW of electrical power, enough for about 500 000 homes. As you sit reading this book, you generate about 100 W of thermal power, which is then radiated away. The solar power striking Earth's surface is approximately 178 000 TW, or 178 PW. (SI prefixes are given in Appendix 3.)

A unit of power that is often used for engines is the *horsepower* (hp), which is equivalent to 746 W.

Sample Problem 7-9

In a 100-m race, a particular sprinter has a power output of 1.12 kW for 10.3 s. (This includes all forms of energy.) Determine the energy output during this time.

Solution: We first convert the power to watts:

$$1.12\ \text{kW} \times \frac{1000\ \text{W}}{1\ \text{kW}} = 1.12 \times 10^3\ \text{W}$$

Since $P = \frac{E}{t}$, we have $\quad E = Pt = (1.12 \times 10^3\ \text{W})(10.3\,\text{s}) = 1.15 \times 10^4\ \text{J}$

Therefore, the sprinter uses 1.15×10^4 J of energy.

Units Tip: *Watts (W) multiplied by seconds (s) gives joules (J).*

Sample Problem 7-10

What mass of coal is required per year in an electric power plant that produces 1.0×10^3 MW of electrical power? The plant has an efficiency of 36% in converting the coal's chemical energy into electrical energy, and the energy content per unit mass of coal is 26 MJ/kg.

Solution: We first convert all units to base SI units:

Since 1 MW = 10^6 W, then 1.0×10^3 MW = 1.0×10^9 W.

Similarly, 1 MJ = 10^6 J, and hence 26 MJ/kg = 26×10^6 J/kg = 2.6×10^7 J/kg.

Our plan of attack will be to calculate the electrical energy produced by the plant in one year, then use the given efficiency to determine the chemical energy required, and finally to calculate the mass of coal based on its energy content per unit mass.

To get the annual electrical energy production, we first re-arrange $P = E/t$ to give $E = Pt$. The electrical power P is 1.0×10^9 W, or 1.0×10^9 J/s. The time t is the number of seconds in one year.

$$E = Pt = (1.0 \times 10^9\ \text{W})\left(365\ \text{d} \times 24\frac{\text{h}}{\text{d}} \times 60\frac{\text{min}}{\text{h}} \times 60\frac{\text{s}}{\text{min}}\right) = 3.2 \times 10^{16}\ \text{J}$$

Thus, the annual electrical energy produced by the plant is 3.2×10^{16} J.

Then,
$$\text{efficiency} = \frac{\text{useful energy out}}{\text{total energy in}} = \frac{E_{\text{ELECTRICAL}}}{E_{\text{COAL}}}$$

Therefore,
$$E_{\text{COAL}} == \frac{E_{\text{ELECTRICAL}}}{\text{efficiency}} = \frac{3.2 \times 10^{16}\ \text{J}}{0.36} = 8.8 \times 10^{16}\ \text{J}$$

Thus, 8.8×10^{16} J of energy must be provided by the coal. The mass of coal required is determined by dividing the required energy by the energy content per unit mass.

$$\text{mass } m = \frac{8.8 \times 10^{16}\ \text{J}}{2.6 \times 10^7\ \text{J/kg}} = 3.4 \times 10^9\ \text{kg}$$

The annual coal requirement is 3.4×10^9 kg (3.4 billion kg!). This represents about 100 railroad cars of coal per day.

Kilowatt·hour — An Energy Unit

One of the most confusing energy units is the kilowatt·hour (kW·h). Because part of the unit is kilowatt, which is a unit of power, many people believe that the kilowatt·hour is a power unit. However, since the kilowatt·hour involves multiplying a kilowatt by a time unit (hour), the kilowatt·hour is actually a unit of energy, as shown in more detail below.

Since power is energy divided by time ($P = E/t$), then we can write:

$$Pt = E$$

This equation indicates that the product of power and time is energy (regardless of the particular units used). If SI units are used, then power in watts multiplied by time in seconds gives energy in watt·seconds, but since a watt is defined as a joule per second, then a watt·second is just a joule. But we can express power and time in other units; if power has units of kilowatts and time has units of hours, then the product — still an energy — has units of kilowatt·hours (kW·h).

We can express 1 kW·h in terms of joules by performing a unit conversion, remembering that 1 kW = 10^3 W; 1 W = 1 J/s; and 1 h = 3600 s:

$$1\,\text{kW}\cdot\text{h} \times \frac{10^3\ \text{W}}{1\,\text{kW}} \times \frac{1\,\text{J/s}}{1\,\text{W}} \times \frac{3600\,\text{s}}{1\,\text{h}} = 3.6\times10^6\ \text{J} = 3.6\,\text{MJ}$$

Hence, 1 kW·h is equivalent to 3.6 MJ.

The kilowatt·hour is a handy unit of electrical energy consumption, since the total power requirement of a house is often in the range of kilowatts, and time can easily be measured in hours. Using joules for electrical energy would result in extremely large numbers — a typical home consumes 1000 to 3000 kW·h of electrical energy per month, which is of the order of 10^9 to 10^{10} J! For electrical energy consumption at national and world levels, gigawatt·hours (GW·h) and terawatt·hours (TW·h) are often used. For example, electrical energy production in Canada in 2004 was 599 TW·h.

Sample Problem 7-11

A 100-W lightbulb is turned on for 12 h. What is the energy consumption in kilowatt·hours?

Solution: To determine the energy in kilowatt·hours, we multiply the power in kilowatts by the time in hours. Since the power is given in watts, we first convert this to kilowatts:

$$100\ \text{W} \times \frac{1\,\text{kW}}{10^3\ \text{W}} = 0.10\,\text{kW} \qquad \text{(assuming 2 significant digits)}$$

Then, $E = Pt = (0.10 \text{ kW})(12 \text{ h}) = 1.2 \text{ kW·h}$

Thus, the electrical energy consumed is 1.2 kW·h.

Practice

7-76 Determine: (a) the power input to a ball if its kinetic energy increases from 0 J to 35 J in a time of 0.86 s
(b) the electrical energy (in joules) used by a 100-W lightbulb that is turned on for 65.0 min
(c) the electrical energy (in kilowatt·hours) consumed by a 1.10-kW hairdryer that is used for 25.7 min
(d) the power input (in kilowatts) to a woman of mass 66 kg standing in an elevator that lifts her through a vertical distance of 15 m in 2.4 s (without increasing her speed).
[Ans. (a) 41 W (b) 3.90×10^5 J (c) 0.471 kW·h (d) 4.0 kW]

7-77 The metabolic rate in humans is proportional to the volume of oxygen supplied by the blood. For each litre of oxygen supplied, the energy produced is 2.0×10^4 J. Determine the metabolic power generated by a person completely at rest who consumes 15 L of oxygen per hour. [Ans. 83 W]

7-78 If you eat a 250-Calorie candy bar, how long could you cycle from this energy input? Assume a power output of 400 W while cycling. [Ans. 44 min]

7-79 The sun's power output is about 4×10^{26} W. How much energy is released by the sun in 1 y? [Ans. 1×10^{34} J]

Did You Know? *A supernova (a massive exploding star) releases about 100 times as much energy in 1 s as does our sun in its entire lifetime.*

7-80 What is the cost of using a 100-W lightbulb for 24 h if the price of electrical energy is 9.4¢ per kilowatt·hour?
[Ans. 23¢]

7-81 A typical small car moving at 80 km/h can travel 14 km using 1.0 L of gasoline. What is the power consumption (in watts) of such a car? The energy content per unit volume for gasoline is about 35 MJ/L. [Ans. 5.6×10^4 W]

7-82 In a nuclear reactor, nuclear energy is converted to thermal energy by the fission (breakup) of nuclei of uranium-235. The energy content per unit mass of uranium-235 is 8.4×10^7 MJ/kg. What mass of uranium-235 is needed per year in a nuclear electrical generating plant that produces 1.0×10^3 MW of electrical power with 32% efficiency? [Ans. 1.2×10^3 kg]

7-83 A 2.65-kW motor is used to lift crates vertically upward in a factory. What is the maximum speed at which a crate of mass 147 kg can be lifted by this motor? Assume that all the motor's power goes into lifting. (Hint: determine the height that the crate can be lifted in 1.00 s.) [Ans. 1.84 m/s]

7-84 A car moving at 75 km/h ascends a hill inclined at 2.7° above the horizontal. The car's mass is 1.4×10^3 kg. What power is needed for the climb up the hill over and above the normal power used when moving horizontally? [Ans. 1.3×10^4 W]

7-85 A woman is pushing a box straight across a horizontal floor with a *constant* speed of 0.74 m/s. The mass of the box is 24 kg, and the magnitude of the friction force on it is 98 N.
(a) During a time of 2.5 s, how much work does the woman do on the box?
(b) What is the power output of the woman (for the pushing)?
(c) If the woman has an efficiency of 25% for conversion of food energy to useful work, what is the internal power requirement of the woman when pushing (over and above the power required when resting)?
[Ans. (a) 1.8×10^2 J (b) 73 W (c) 2.9×10^2 W]

7-86 Calculate the water flow-rate (in kg/s) over a waterfall producing electrical power of 97 MW from a turbine generator that is 93% efficient. The waterfall has a vertical height of 47 m. Neglect the kinetic energy of the water before it goes over the fall, and after it leaves the turbine. [Ans. 2.3×10^5 kg/s]

CHAPTER FOCUS

In earlier chapters, we concentrated on the motion of objects and on the forces causing the motion.

In this chapter, we have looked at motion from a different point of view by considering work and energy. We have seen how work and energy are related, and have introduced a number of types of energy in detail: kinetic energy, gravitational potential energy, and thermal energy. The important law of conservation of energy has been discussed and applied in situations from pole-vaulting to generation of electricity by burning coal. The efficiency of energy conversions has been illustrated with a number of real-world examples: lightbulbs, automobiles, etc. Finally, we have considered the concept of power and its relation to energy and time.

The next chapter deals with another important law of mechanics — the law of conservation of momentum, particularly in its application to collisions of objects such as cars, billiard balls, and subatomic particles.

VOCABULARY REVIEW

You should be able to define or explain each of the following words or phrases.

work
joule (unit)
thermal energy (internal energy)
heat

kinetic energy
work-energy theorem
gravitational potential energy
law of conservation of energy
efficiency
power
watt (unit)

CHAPTER REVIEW

7-87 A joule is equivalent to:
(a) kg·m/s^3 (b) kg·m^2/s^3 (c) kg^2·m^2/s^3 (d) kg·m/s (e) kg·m^2/s^2

7-88 A car of mass 1200 kg skids to a stop in a distance of 25 m along a horizontal road. During the skid how much work is done on the car by the normal force?
(a) 0 J (b) 2.9×10^5 J (c) 3.0×10^4 J (d) 1.2×10^4 J (e) -2.9×10^5 J

7-89 A hockey puck of mass 0.20 kg is sliding across a horizontal ice surface. The coefficient of kinetic friction between the puck and the ice is 0.070. As the puck slides 2.0 m, how much work is done by the friction force on the puck?
(a) 0 J (b) −0.27 J (c) 0.29 J (d) −4.0 J (e) 4.0 J

7-90 The planet Venus follows an orbit that is circular (or very nearly so) around the sun. If the radius of this orbit is r, and the gravitational attractive force exerted on Venus by the sun is $\boldsymbol{F}_G$, how much work is done on Venus by this gravitational force as Venus travels around half of its orbit?
(a) 0 (b) $2F_G\pi r$ (c) $F_G\pi r$ (d) $2F_Gr$ (e) $F_G\pi r/2$

7-91 During a portion of the movement in a biceps curl, you are lifting a weight vertically upward. During this upward movement, which of the following expresses the correct mathematical statement about the change in the gravitational potential energy E_p of the weight?
(a) $\Delta E_p = 0$ (b) $\Delta E_p > 0$ (c) $\Delta E_p < 0$

7-92 A pencil falls from a table to the floor. As the pencil falls, ΔE_p is the change in the pencil's gravitational potential energy, and ΔE_K is the change in its kinetic energy. Neglect air resistance. Which of the following is correct?
(a) $\Delta E_p > 0$ and $\Delta E_K > 0$ (b) $\Delta E_p > 0$ and $\Delta E_K < 0$ (c) $\Delta E_p < 0$ and $\Delta E_K < 0$
(d) $\Delta E_p < 0$ and $\Delta E_K > 0$ (e) $\Delta E_p > 0$ and $\Delta E_K = 0$

7-93 A skateboarder is initially at rest at the top of a ramp. He then slides down the ramp, and attains a speed v at the bottom. To achieve a speed $2v$ at the bottom, how many times as high must a new ramp be? Neglect friction and air resistance.
(a) 2 (b) 3 (c) 4 (d) 6 (e) 8

7-94 Two balls are dropped from the same height above the floor. One ball has twice the mass of the other one. If v_H represents the speed of the heavy ball just before it hits the floor, and v_L

represents the speed of the light ball just before it hits the floor, which of the following is true? Neglect air resistance.
(a) $v_H = v_L$ (b) $v_H > v_L$ (c) $v_H < v_L$

<u>7-95</u> A watt is equivalent to:
(a) kg·m/s^3 (b) kg·m^2/s^3 (c) kg^2·m^2/s^3 (d) kg·m/s (e) kg·m^2/s^2

<u>7-96</u> The kilowatt·hour is a unit of:
(a) power (b) force (c) energy (d) time (e) speed

<u>7-97</u> Identify each quantity below as a vector or scalar.
(a) work (b) kinetic energy (c) force (d) velocity (e) speed
(f) gravitational potential energy (g) distance (h) displacement (i) thermal energy

7-98 Work can be expressed as $W = F\,\Delta r\,\cos\theta$. For constant F and constant Δr, sketch the shape of the graph of W vs. θ for $0 \le \theta \le 360°$.

7-99 Biological muscle cells, which can be considered tiny nanomotors, transform chemical potential energy into mechanical work. If an active protein such as actin within a muscle cell produces a force of magnitude 7.2 pN over a displacement of 8.5 nm in the same direction as the force, how much work is done by the protein? [Ans. 6.1×10^{-20} J]

<u>7-100</u> What would happen to Earth's speed if the gravitational force toward the sun did positive work on Earth?

7-101 Sketch the shape of the graph of kinetic energy E_K vs. speed v for a given object.

7-102 A boy throws a stone vertically downward from a cliff with an initial speed of 4.03 m/s. Use the work-energy theorem to determine the height of the cliff if the speed of the stone at the bottom is 22.8 m/s. Neglect air resistance. [Ans. 25.7 m]

7-103 In throwing a 0.46-kg football (which is initially at rest), a woman applies a horizontal force over a horizontal displacement of 36 cm. The speed of the ball at release is 8.9 m/s. Use work and/or energy to determine the average magnitude of the force. [Ans. 51 N]

7-104 A child drops a fork from a tabletop. If the speed of the fork is 4.3 m/s just before it hits the floor, how high is the table? Use conservation of energy. [Ans. 0.94 m]

7-105 A girl constructs a simple pendulum by tying a stone to a string of length 1.15 m. The stone is lifted so that the string makes an angle of 33° with the vertical (Figure 7-25) and is released from rest so that the pendulum swings. Use conservation of energy to find the speed of the stone at the bottom of the swing. [Ans. 1.9 m/s]

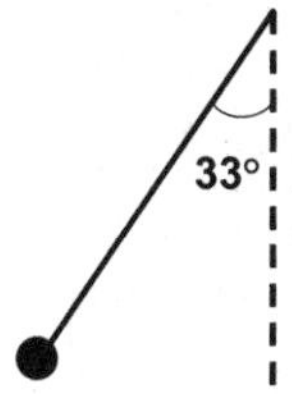

33°

Figure 7-25
Question 7-105.

7-106 A hockey puck of mass 0.17 kg is sliding across a horizontal sheet of ice. The coefficient of kinetic friction between the puck and ice is 0.13. The initial speed of the puck is 3.7 m/s.
(a) What is the initial kinetic energy of the puck?
(b) Use analysis of forces to determine the magnitude of the friction force on the puck.
(c) As the puck slides 0.75 m, what is the work done by friction on the puck, and how much thermal energy is generated?
(d) What is the speed of the puck after sliding 0.75 m? (Use energy methods.)
[Ans. (a) 1.12 J (b) 0.22 N (c) –0.16 J; 0.16 J (d) 3.4 m/s]

7-107 Two men are dragging a boat of mass 57 kg straight across a level beach. Together, they are exerting a force of 3.4×10^2 N at 21° above the horizontal. The magnitude of the friction force on the boat is 2.9×10^2 N. Use work and energy to determine the speed of the boat after it has been dragged 2.3 m if it starts from rest. [Ans. 1.5 m/s]

7-108 Two identical balls A and B are released from rest on inclines that have the same vertical drop and the same horizontal distance from one end to the other. However, the inclines are different in detail, as seen in Figure 7-26.
(a) Which ball arrives at the end first? Explain your answer. Note that rolling friction removes very little energy from the balls.
(b) How can racing cyclists use this result on inclined oval tracks?
[Ans. (a) B]

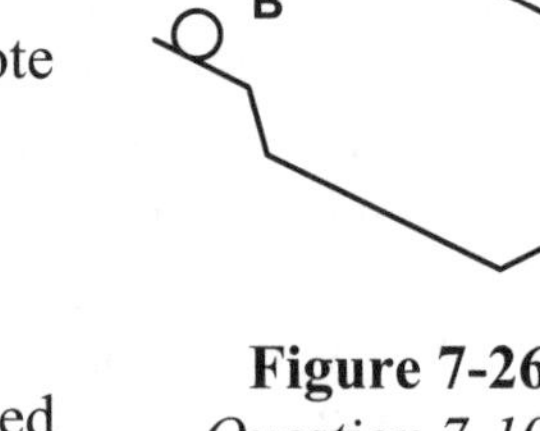

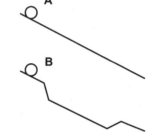

Figure 7-26
Question 7-108.

7-109 An otter slides down a hill of length 7.3 m. The hill is inclined at 15° to the horizontal, and the otter starts from rest. Use the work-energy theorem to determine the otter's speed at the bottom. Neglect friction. [Ans. 6.1 m/s]

7-110 Solve the previous problem using conservation of energy.

7-111 Use conservation of energy to solve the previous problem including friction. The coefficient of kinetic friction between the otter and the hill is 0.14. [Ans. 4.2 m/s]

7-112 Alpha particles (each of mass 6.6×10^{-27} kg) emitted by nuclei generally have kinetic energies in the range of 4 to 9 MeV. If an alpha particle has a kinetic energy of 4.0 MeV, what is its speed? [Ans. 1.4×10^7 m/s]

7-113 The energy required to produce a metric tonne (1000 kg) of aluminum from aluminum ore is about 83 MBtu. Convert this value to megajoules. (Refer to Table 7.1.) [Ans. 8.7×10^4 MJ]

Did You Know? *The energy required to recycle aluminum is only about 25% of that needed to produce it from the ore.*

7-114 Suppose that you use a 60-W incandescent lightbulb for 1.5 h. (a) How much electricity energy is used (in joules and kilowatt·hours)?
(b) How much of this energy (in joules) goes into light? (Use Table 7.2.)
[Ans. (a) 3.2×10^5 J; 0.090 kW·h (b) 2×10^4 J]

7-115 Table 7.3 shows the energy required per person·km for passenger transportation. Approximately how much energy is required for a person to:
(a) ride a bicycle for 17 km?
(b) take an urban bus for the same distance?
[Ans. (a) 2.2×10^6 J (b) 3.1×10^7 J]

Table 7.3
Approximate Energy Required Per Person·km (Passenger Transportation)

Mode of travel	Energy (in 10^5 J) per person·km
bicycle	1.3
walking	2.0
bus (intercity)	6.3
railroad	9.8 to 16
bus (urban)	18
automobile	23 to 40
airplane	40

7-116 Running at 16 km/h requires a total power output of about 0.56 kW. Determine the energy output for a person running 35 min at this speed.
[Ans. 1.2×10^6 J]

7-117 *Fermi Question:* Estimate the total power you produce in running as fast as you can up a flight of stairs. Show your reasoning. Assume an efficiency of 25% in conversion of food energy to usable energy. [Ans. approx. 2×10^3 W to 4×10^3 W]

7-118 A typical person (mass 70 kg) requires about 7.5×10^5 J of food energy to walk 3.0 km on level ground. How much more food energy is required if the walk is done at 21° above the horizontal? Use Tables 7.2 and 7.1, and express your answer in joules and Calories.
[Ans. 3.0×10^6 J; 7.0×10^2 Cal]

7-119 A colour television consumes about 145 W of electrical power. If the price of electrical energy is 9.7¢ per kilowatt·hour, how much does it cost to watch television for 2.5 h?
[Ans. 3.5¢]

7-120 Many appliances such as televisions have an "instant-on" feature, which means that the appliance is actually consuming electrical energy even when it is turned "off," in order than it will turn "on" immediately when needed. The typical power consumed by such devices when "off" ranges from about 0.5 W to 2.0 W. Suppose that a particular television consumes 2.0 W when "off," and that it is turned off during a 30-day month when the owners are on vacation.
(a) During the month, how much more electrical energy (in kilowatt·hours) does this television consume than one that consumes only 0.5 W when "off?"
(b) If the price of electrical energy is 9.4¢ per kilowatt·hour, how much more does it cost for the month to have the 2.0-W television than a 0.5-W television?
(c) Some countries have regulations that the maximum power allowed for appliances when turned "off" is 0.5 W. Do you think Canada should have a similar regulation?
[Ans. (a) 1.1 kW·h (b) 10¢]

7-121 The energy content per unit mass of oil is about 42 MJ/kg. Determine the daily mass of oil required to fuel a steam-electric generating plant that produces 8.3×10^2 MW of electrical power with an efficiency of 37%. [Ans. 4.6×10^6 kg]

APPLYING YOUR KNOWLEDGE

7-122 A baseball of mass 0.15 kg is thrown with an initial velocity of 29 m/s at an angle of 37° above the horizontal. Neglect air resistance.
(a) When it reaches its maximum height, how much work has been done on it during its flight?
(b) When it returns to its initial height, how much work has been done on it during its flight?
[Ans. (a) –23 J (b) 0 J]

7-123 Two people hang onto opposite ends of a rope that passes over a pulley (Figure 7-27). The masses are m_1 = 105 kg and m_2 = 67 kg. Initially the people are at rest, with one on the floor and the other supported 1.5 m above the floor. The support is then removed, and the people and rope are free to move. Use conservation of energy to determine the speed of the people just as person #1 hits the floor. [Ans. 2.5 m/s]

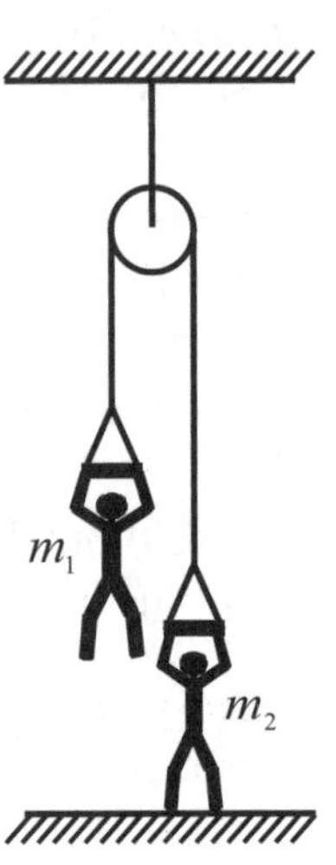

Figure 7-27
Question 7-123.

7-124 In a tidal power plant, the incoming tide fills up a catchment area enclosed by concrete walls, and then at low tide, this water is allowed to fall through openings in the concrete to spin turbines. In a particular tidal plant, the square catchment area has sides of 1.5 km, and the tide rises by 4.2 m. Assume that the process of emptying takes 1.0 h, and that all of the energy of the water is converted to energy of the turbines. Determine the power (assumed constant) available from the plant during emptying. The density of salt water is 1.03×10^3 kg/m^3. (Hint: when $E_p = mgy$ is used, "y" represents the elevation of the centre of mass.) [Ans. 56 MW]

7-125 *Fermi Question:* (a) Assuming your brain operates at a power of 20 W, estimate how much energy your brain has consumed since you were born.
(b) If your current average daily intake of energy is 10 MJ, how many days' worth of energy could make up for your brain's energy consumption that you determined in (a)?

7-126 The intensity of radiation from a distant source such as the sun varies inversely with the square of the distance from the source. At the top of Earth's atmosphere, the solar intensity (power per unit area) is 1.35 kW/m^2. If a spaceship is located halfway between the sun and Earth, and has a solar panel of area 1.00×10^2 m^2, determine the total solar energy incident on the panel in a day. [Ans. 4.67×10^{10} J]

7-127 A stretched elastic band of mass 0.55 g is released so that its initial velocity is horizontal and its initial position is 95 cm above the floor. What was the elastic potential energy stored in the stretched band, if when it lands it has a horizontal displacement of 3.7 m from the initial point? Neglect air resistance. [Ans. 0.019 J]

7-128 A waiter carrying a tray above his head accidentally inclines it at 19° to the horizontal, and a plate of mass 0.48 kg starts to slide. If the coefficient of kinetic friction between the plate and tray is 0.27, determine the total work done on the plate as it slides 41 cm along the tray. [Ans. 0.14 J]

7-129 Use trigonometry to show that $F\Delta r \cos\theta = F_x\Delta x + F_y\Delta y$.

KEY OBJECTIVES

Having completed this chapter, you should now be able to do the following:

1. Identify whether work is being done in various physical situations.
2. Define the work done by a constant force and use this definition in solving related problems.
3. Explain why the work done by any centripetal force is zero.
4. State the work-energy theorem and use it to solve problems.
5. Define kinetic energy.
6. State the SI unit for work and energy, and relate to the SI base units of kilogram, metre, and second.
7. Define gravitational potential energy and solve related problems.
8. State the law of conservation of energy and solve problems using this law.
9. Calculate the work done by friction in problems, and relate this work to the thermal energy produced.
10. Give a qualitative description of various types of energy such as light energy, electrical energy, etc.
11. Perform unit conversions involving energy units such as joules, electron-volts, Calories, etc.
12. Define efficiency of energy conversions and solve problems related to efficiency.
13. State approximate efficiencies for devices such as automobile engines and lightbulbs.
14. Discuss why energy conservation is important.
15. State the relation between power, energy, and time, and use this relation in problems.
16. Define a watt.
17. Use kilowatt·hour as an energy unit.
18. Do calculations involving energy, power, and efficiency in commercial production of electrical energy.

ANSWERS TO SELECTED QUESTIONS

7-1 no 7-2 no 7-3 yes, positive 7-4 yes, negative 7-5 yes, positive
7-6 yes, negative 7-7 no 7-8 no 7-9 no
7-10 The force and displacement are at right angles to each other.
7-11 The work done is zero.
7-12 zero
7-13 1 J = 1 kg·m^2/s^2
7-24 If friction is neglected, the work required to pull a given object up an incline is independent of the angle of the incline.
7-39 kg·m^2/s^2; kg·m^2/s^2; yes; joule (J)
7-53 same speeds, no difference
7-56 (a) thermal energy (b) thermal energy and kinetic energy
7-59 (b) thermal energy

7-87 (e) 7-88 (a) 7-89 (b) 7-90 (a) 7-91(b) 7-92 (d) 7-93 (c) 7-94 (a)
7-95 (b) 7-96 (c)
7-97 (a) scalar (b) scalar (c) vector (d) vector (e) scalar (f) scalar (g) scalar (h) vector (i) scalar
7-100 Earth's speed would increase.

CHAPTER 8

MOMENTUM AND COLLISIONS

Collisions are occurring around you all the time — molecules in the air are continually colliding with each other and with objects (such as you) near them. Balls collide with tennis rackets, baseball bats, and golf clubs. Automobiles collide. The diffusion of molecules across biological cell membranes is the result of random molecular collisions. Energetic particles from the sun undergo collisions with molecules in Earth's atmosphere to produce the northern and southern lights (*aurora borealis* and *aurora australis*). Even entire galaxies collide with each other. In order to understand collisions, and thereby the universe around us, we first need to study momentum and the law of conservation of momentum. We shall see that momentum is also useful in explaining processes such as rocket propulsion.

8.1 MOMENTUM

At some time, you have probably hit a baseball with a bat, or a tennis ball with a racket, or a golf ball with a club. In previous chapters, the motion of objects such as baseballs, tennis balls, and golf balls has been described in terms of quantities such as velocity, acceleration, and kinetic energy. In order to discuss what happens in a collision, it is useful to introduce the concept of momentum.

Did You Know? *When a baseball is hit by a bat, the collision occurs in about 1 ms (10^{-3} s).*

The **momentum** of an object is defined as the product of the object's mass and velocity, and is usually represented by the symbol $\boldsymbol{p}$. Writing mass as m and velocity as $\boldsymbol{v}$, we have:

$$\boldsymbol{p} = m\boldsymbol{v} \qquad \text{(momentum)} \qquad \textbf{(8-1a)}$$

Momentum depends on both the mass and velocity of an object. A large truck has more momentum than a small car travelling at the same speed. But it is possible for a rapidly moving small car to have the same momentum as a slow large truck.

Note that momentum is a vector, being the product of a scalar (mass) and a vector (velocity). We will often be working with components of momentum:

$$p_x = mv_x \quad \text{and} \quad p_y = mv_y \qquad \text{(components of momentum)} \qquad \textbf{(8-1b)}$$

Since the SI units of mass and velocity are kilogram and metre/second, respectively, the SI unit of momentum is kilogram·metre/second (kg·m/s). This unit does not have any special name (such as a newton or a joule) and is the standard unit of momentum.

Strictly speaking, what we are referring to as momentum is more correctly called **linear momentum**. However, the *linear* is often omitted, except when there could be confusion with another quantity called angular momentum (which is not discussed in this book).

Momentum, Force, and Time

In Chapter 7, we saw how change in kinetic energy is related to force and displacement. We now investigate how change in momentum is associated with force and time. We begin by considering a one-dimensional situation; our example is a collision between a baseball and bat to produce a line-drive, with the ball travelling horizontally just before and just after the collision.

Suppose that during the collision with the bat, the baseball undergoes an acceleration (a_x) in a time interval (Δt), and its velocity changes from v_{0x} to v_x (Figure 8-1). These quantities are related by Eqn. 2-7 for constant-acceleration kinematics:

$$v_x = v_{0x} + a_x \Delta t$$

(The original form of Eqn. 2-7 used t instead of Δt, assuming that $t_0 = 0$. However, in dealing with momentum, it is customary to use Δt.)

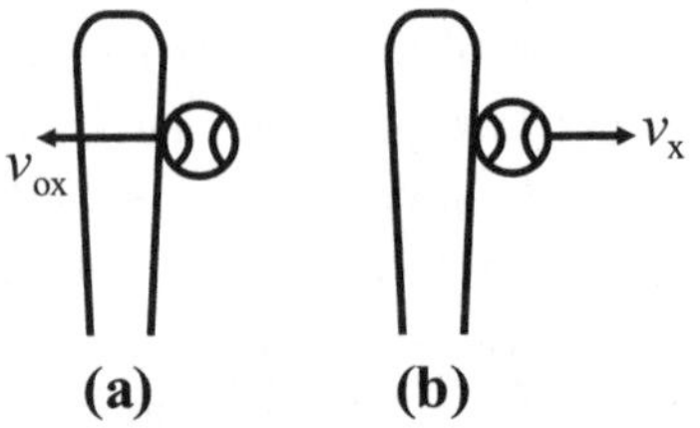

For now, we assume that a_x is constant. The more general case of variable a_x, as would be the situation in an actual collision of a ball with a bat, is discussed later.

v_{ox} v_x

(a) **(b)**

Figure 8-1
(a) *Initial contact of ball and bat.*
(b) *Final contact, after a time interval Δt.*

We now multiply the above equation by the mass (m) of the baseball and then re-arrange the equation slightly:

$$mv_x = mv_{0x} + ma_x \Delta t$$

$$mv_x - mv_{0x} = ma_x \Delta t$$

On the left-hand side of this equation, we now have the *change* in the baseball's momentum, that is, the final momentum (mv_x) minus the initial momentum (mv_{0x}). We can write this simply as Δp_x. Hence,

$$\Delta p_x = ma_x \Delta \mathrm{t}$$

On the right-hand side, Newton's second law can be used to replace ma_x with the resultant force (ΣF_x or F_{Rx}) exerted by the bat on the ball:

$$\Delta p_x = (\Sigma F_x)\Delta t \qquad \textbf{(8-2)}$$

This equation states that the *change in momentum equals the product of the resultant force and the time interval.* It is valid whenever any object's momentum changes. To change the momentum of, say, a car by a given amount, there is an infinite number of combinations of force and time intervals that could be used. For example, if we want to reduce a car's momentum (and thus its speed), we can apply the brakes strongly for a short time interval, or apply them gently for a longer time interval.

The relationship between momentum, force, and time interval could also be developed in the y- and z-directions:

$$\Delta p_y = (\Sigma F_y)\Delta t \qquad \text{and} \qquad \Delta p_z = (\Sigma F_z)\Delta t$$

Therefore, we can write a vector equation relating the change in the momentum vector to the (resultant) force vector and the time interval:

$$\Delta \boldsymbol{p} = (\Sigma \boldsymbol{F})\Delta t \qquad \text{or} \qquad \Delta \boldsymbol{p} = \boldsymbol{F}_R \Delta t \qquad \textbf{(8-3)}$$

This vector equation is very compact and shows that the change in momentum and the resultant force have the same direction. However, when solving problems, it is usually easiest to work with individual components.

Sometimes the change in momentum is called *impulse*. However, since impulse is just the same as change in momentum, this additional term will not be used further in this book.

You are accustomed to seeing Newton's second law of motion written as $\Sigma \boldsymbol{F} = m\boldsymbol{a}$, but by re-arranging $\Delta \boldsymbol{p} = (\Sigma \boldsymbol{F})\Delta t$, we can express the second law in a different way:

$$\Sigma \boldsymbol{F} = \frac{\Delta \boldsymbol{p}}{\Delta t} \qquad \text{(Newton's second law restated)} \qquad \textbf{(8-4a)}$$

Did You Know? *For sub-atomic particles moving at speeds close to that of light, Newton's second law written as* $\Sigma \boldsymbol{F} = m\boldsymbol{a}$ *is not valid. However,* $\Sigma \boldsymbol{F} = \Delta \boldsymbol{p}/\Delta t$ *is still applicable to these speedsters.*

In other words, the resultant force on an object equals the time rate of change of the object's momentum. This is actually the way in which Newton originally stated his second law, although he referred to momentum as "quantity of motion." In terms of components, we can write:

$$\Sigma F_x = \frac{\Delta p_x}{\Delta t} \qquad \Sigma F_y = \frac{\Delta p_y}{\Delta t} \qquad \Sigma F_z = \frac{\Delta p_z}{\Delta t} \qquad \textbf{(8-4b)}$$

Average Force

In the preceding derivation, we have assumed that the acceleration of the object being considered (a baseball) is constant; this implies, of course, that the resultant force on the object is constant. In reality, in many circumstances involving change of momentum, the resultant force and the acceleration are not constant. However, our conclusion — $\Delta \boldsymbol{p} = (\Sigma \boldsymbol{F})\Delta t$ — is still valid, as long as $\Sigma \boldsymbol{F}$ is interpreted as the *average* force acting on the object during the time interval Δt.

What exactly do we mean by average force? To answer this, consider Figure 8-2 (a), which shows the typical shape of a graph of (magnitude of) force as a function of time during a collision of duration Δt. It could represent, for instance, the force acting on a baseball being hit by a bat. The area under the graph has been shaded. The average force is *defined* as the constant force, which, if applied for the same time interval Δt, would give the same amount of shaded area (Figure 8-2 (b)).

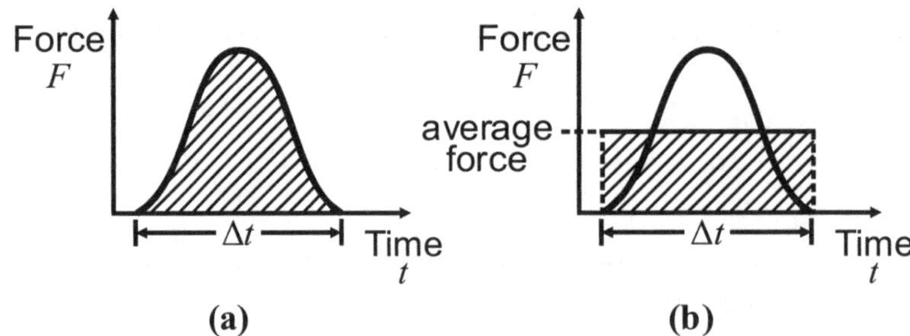

Figure 8-2 **(a)** *Magnitude of force acting on an object during a typical collision.* **(b)** *The average force, acting for* Δt*, gives the same shaded area as in (a).*

Integral calculus can be used to show that the shaded area under the curve in Figure 8-2 (a) is equal to the change in momentum of the object on which the force acts. Thus, it is indeed legitimate to define average force as the constant force that would give the same change in momentum as the actual variable force.

Sample Problem 8-1

A baseball of mass 0.15 kg, travelling horizontally with a speed of 38 m/s, hits a bat. Immediately after the collision, of duration 1.1 ms, the ball travels in the opposite direction horizontally with a speed of 51 m/s.
(a) What are the magnitude and direction of the initial momentum of the ball?
(b) What is the average force (magnitude and direction) exerted on the ball by the bat?
(c) What is the ratio of the magnitude of this force to the magnitude of the force of gravity on the ball?

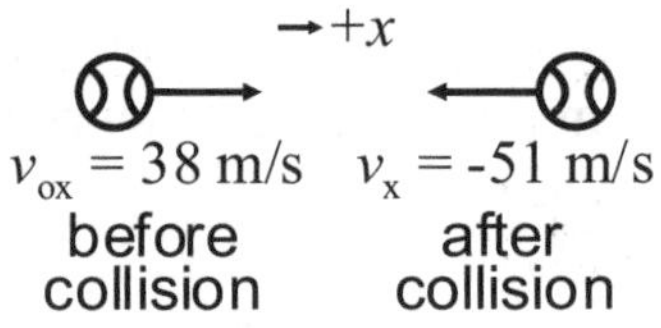

$\rightarrow +x$

v_{ox} = 38 m/s before collision

v_x = -51 m/s after collision

Figure 8-3
Sample Problem 8-1.

Solution: (a) We start by choosing a co-ordinate system. The problem is one-dimensional, and it matters little in this problem which direction we choose for $+x$. We choose it arbitrarily to be in the direction of the initial velocity of the ball (Figure 8-3). Thus, the initial velocity, v_{0x}, equals +38 m/s.

The initial momentum of the ball is:

$$mv_{0x} = (0.15 \text{ kg})(38 \text{ m/s}) = 5.7 \text{ kg·m/s}$$

Thus, the ball has an initial momentum of 5.7 kg·m/s in the same (horizontal) direction as the initial velocity.

Units Tip: *Note the SI unit of momentum – mass in kg multiplied by velocity in m/s gives momentum in kg·m/s.*

(b) In order to determine the average force on the ball, we use Eqn. 8-4b:

$$\Sigma F_x = \frac{\Delta p_x}{\Delta t} = \frac{m(v_x - v_{0x})}{\Delta t}$$

Before substituting known quantities, it is important to note that v_x is a *negative* quantity (–51 m/s) since the ball's velocity after the collision is in the $-x$ direction. As well, we must remember to express Δt in seconds ($\Delta t = 1.1\text{ ms} = 1.1 \times 10^{-3}\text{ s}$). Now we substitute numbers:

$$\Sigma F_x = \frac{(0.15\text{ kg})(-51\text{ m/s} - 38\text{ m/s})}{1.1 \times 10^{-3}\text{ s}} = -1.2 \times 10^4\text{ N}$$

The average force exerted by the bat on the ball (that is, the resultant force on the ball) has a magnitude of 1.2×10^4 N and a direction (indicated by the negative sign) opposite to the ball's initial velocity.

(c) The force of gravity on the ball has a magnitude of:

$$F_G = mg = (0.15\text{ kg})(9.8\text{ m/s}^2) = 1.5\text{ N}$$

Therefore, the required ratio of the force exerted by the bat to the force of gravity is:

$$\frac{1.2 \times 10^4\text{ N}}{1.5\text{ N}} = 8.3 \times 10^3$$

The average force exerted by the bat is more than eight thousand times larger than the force of gravity. *The forces between objects involved in collisions are often much larger than other forces such as gravity, and thus we typically can neglect other forces when analyzing collisions.*

Practice

8-1 (a) What is the SI unit of momentum?
(b) In the relation $\Delta \boldsymbol{p} = (\Sigma \boldsymbol{F})\Delta t$, what is the SI unit of $\Delta \boldsymbol{p}$ (from (a))? of $(\Sigma \boldsymbol{F})\Delta t$? Are these units the same?

8-2 What are the magnitude and direction of the momentum of:
(a) a sprinter of mass 65 kg running east at 9.8 m/s?
(b) a red blood cell of mass 1.2×10^{-13} kg moving downward at a speed of 4.2 cm/s in an artery?
[Ans. (a) 6.4×10^2 kg·m/s east (b) 5.0×10^{-15} kg·m/s downward]

8-3 An automobile speeds up as it leaves an intersection. Sketch the shape of the graph of the magnitude of the automobile's momentum as a function of its speed.

8-4 The momentum of a baseball of mass 0.15 kg has a magnitude of 4.8 kg·m/s. What is the ball's speed? [Ans. 32 m/s]

8-5 The momentum of a runner triples as her speed increases by 3.00 m/s. What is her initial speed? [Ans. 1.50 m/s]

8-6 What is impulse?

8-7 An egg of mass 59 g is dropped onto the floor where it breaks and comes to rest. Its speed just before hitting the floor is 4.3 m/s. What are the magnitudes and directions of:
(a) its momentum before hitting the floor?
(b) its momentum after hitting the floor?
(c) its change in momentum?
[Ans. (a) 0.25 kg·m/s downward (b) zero (c) 0.25 kg·m/s upward]

8-8 The magnitude of the momentum of a car is 2.5×10^4 kg·m/s. A force of magnitude 2.1×10^3 N increases the car's momentum for 3.6 s. What is the magnitude of the car's new momentum? [Ans. 3.3×10^4 kg·m/s]

8-9 A tennis ball of mass 59 g, having an initial velocity of 26 m/s horizontally, hits a net and comes to rest (then drops to the ground). If the force exerted on the ball by the net (the "net" force) is 1.3×10^2 N horizontally, how long is the ball in contact with the net during the collision? Express your answer in milliseconds. [Ans. 12 ms]

8-10 A rubber ball of mass 95 g is dropped onto the floor. Just before it hits the floor, its speed is 4.4 m/s. It then rebounds upward, having a speed of 3.9 m/s just as it leaves the floor. What are the magnitude and direction of:
(a) its momentum just before hitting the floor?
(b) its momentum just after hitting the floor?
(c) its change in momentum?
(d) the average force exerted on the ball by the floor, if they are in contact for a time interval of 4.2×10^{-3} s? Use momentum methods.
[Ans. (a) 0.42 kg·m/s downward (b) 0.37 kg·m/s upward (c) 0.79 kg·m/s upward
(d) 1.9×10^2 N upward]

8-11 In the previous question, why can the force of gravity be neglected during the collision between the ball and floor?

8-12 A bird of mass 9.87×10^{-2} kg is flying with a velocity of 25.7 m/s at 11.7° above the horizontal. Determine its horizontal and vertical components of momentum. [Ans. 2.48 kg·m/s; 0.514 kg·m/s]

8-13 A nitrogen molecule (mass 4.7×10^{-26} kg) in the air bounces off a wall (Figure 8-4). Its speed just before and after the collision is the same, 5.1×10^2 m/s.
(a) Draw a vector scale diagram, showing the initial momentum and final momentum of the nitrogen molecule.
(b) Use your diagram to perform a vector subtraction, thus giving the change in momentum (magnitude and direction) of the molecule.

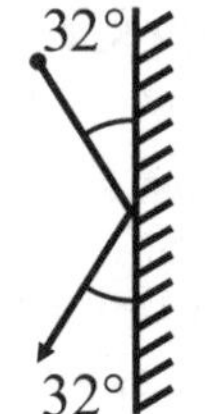

Figure 8-4
Question 8-13.

(c) Use your result in (b) to determine the average resultant force (magnitude and direction) on the molecule during the collision, if the molecule is in contact with the wall for 2.0×10^{-13} s.
[Ans. (b) 2.5×10^{-23} kg·m/s to left (c) 1.2×10^{-10} N to left]

8-14 A stationary golf ball of mass 0.045 kg is hit by a club and leaves with a velocity of 2.4×10^2 km/h at 19° above the horizontal. The ball and club are in contact for 0.97 ms.
(a) Use momentum to determine the magnitude and direction of the average force exerted by the club on the ball. (This is essentially a one-dimensional question. Just choose your $+x$ axis in the direction of the ball's final velocity.)
(b) What is the average force (magnitude and direction) exerted by the ball on the club?
[Ans. (a) 3.1×10^3 N at 19° above horizontal (b) 3.1×10^3 N at 19° below horizontal]

8.2 CONSERVATION OF MOMENTUM IN ONE DIMENSION

Have you ever had the experience of walking along in a small untethered boat toward a dock and having the boat moving backward under you? It can be awkward to discover that, when you reach the end of the boat, it is no longer close enough to the dock for you to get out. This phenomenon can be explained by Newton's third law (you exert a backward force on the boat, and it exerts a forward force on you), but it also can be explained by a closely related law of nature — the **law of conservation of momentum**. This law is applicable in a wide range of circumstances such as walking in a boat, positron emission tomography (PET) scans used in medical diagnosis, rocket propulsion, and in many collisions of objects.

To understand when the law of conservation of momentum applies, we start with Eqn. 8-3, which gives the relationship between change of momentum, resultant force, and time interval:

$$\Delta \boldsymbol{p} = \boldsymbol{F}_{\mathrm{R}} \Delta t$$

If the resultant force ($\boldsymbol{F}_{\mathrm{R}}$) acting on an object is zero, then the change in momentum ($\Delta \boldsymbol{p}$) of the object is zero. Therefore, the momentum is constant or conserved. (This is really just another way of phrasing Newton's first law, which states that, if the resultant force on an object is zero, its acceleration is zero, which means that its velocity is constant and therefore its momentum is also constant.) Conservation of momentum is equally valid for systems (collections) of objects — **if the resultant force acting on a system is zero, then the momentum of the system is conserved**. This is the law of conservation of momentum.

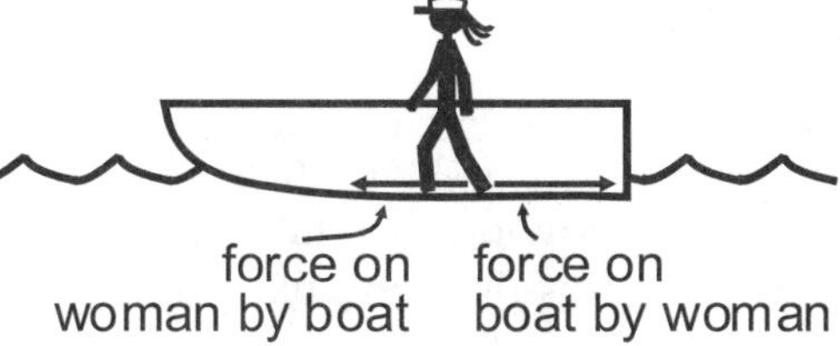

Figure 8-5 *As the woman walks in the boat, the force exerted on the boat is equal and opposite to the force exerted on the woman. Hence, the resultant force on the boat-woman system is zero, and the momentum of this system is conserved.*

To illustrate this law, we apply it to the case of a woman walking in a boat (Figure 8-5). In order to walk, the woman exerts a backward force on the boat, and by Newton's third law, the boat exerts an equal but opposite force on the woman. If we consider the *system of the boat and woman together*, these two forces will add to give a resultant force of zero. (We are neglecting the viscous friction between the boat and the water, and since there is no vertical acceleration, there must be a resultant force of zero vertically.) Therefore, the total momentum of the boat and woman is conserved.

Suppose that the boat and woman are both initially stationary. The momentum of each is zero, and the total momentum of the boat-woman system is therefore zero (Figure 8-6 (a)). If the woman now starts walking, the total momentum of the system is conserved, that is, it must remain zero (Figure 8-6 (b)). Mathematically:

$$m_1\boldsymbol{v}_1 + m_2\boldsymbol{v}_2 = 0$$

where "1" refers to the woman and "2" to the boat. The momentum of the woman in one direction is equal and opposite to the momentum of the boat in the other direction, and the total momentum is zero. (Remember that momentum is a *vector.*) Notice that the momentum of just the woman is *not* conserved; initially she has zero momentum, and when walking, she has non-zero momentum. Similarly, the momentum of just the boat is not conserved. When dealing with conservation of momentum, it is important to identify the system on which the resultant force is zero, and which therefore has its momentum conserved.

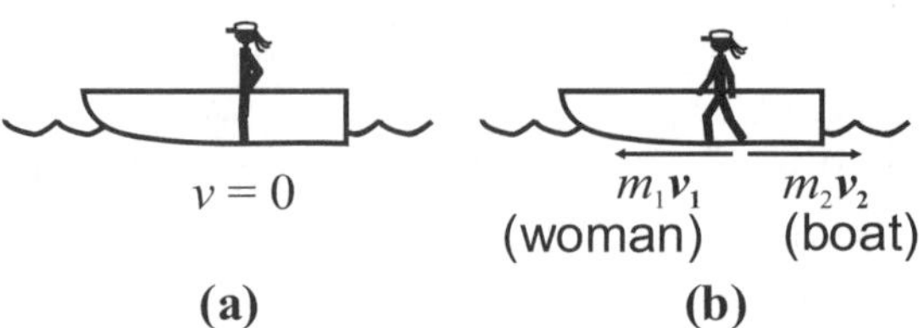

Figure 8-6 **(a)** *If the boat and woman are stationary, the total momentum of the system is zero.* **(b)** *If the woman now walks, the total momentum is still zero, that is,* $m_1\boldsymbol{v}_1 + m_2\boldsymbol{v}_2 = 0$.

Sample Problem 8-2

A man of mass 75 kg is standing in a stationary boat of mass 55 kg. He then walks toward one end of the boat at a speed of 2.3 m/s relative to the water. What is the resulting velocity (magnitude and direction) of the boat relative to the water? Neglect viscous friction between the boat and water.

Solution: In problems involving conservation of momentum, it is extremely useful to draw diagrams showing the initial and final situations (Figure 8-7). A co-ordinate system is then chosen; in this problem, we arbitrarily select the $+x$ direction to lie in the direction of the man's final velocity. By the law of conservation of momentum, we know that, in the boat-man system, the initial momentum equals the final momentum, since there is no resultant force acting on this system. Mathematically:

$$m_1 v_{1x} + m_2 v_{2x} = m_1 v'_{1x} + m_2 v'_{2x}$$

where subscripts "1" and "2" refer to the man and boat, respectively. The velocities on the left-hand side of the equation are the initial velocities, and the velocities on the right-hand side, with the primed superscript (′), are the final velocities. Since this is a one-dimensional problem, it is somewhat redundant and tedious to label all the velocities with x-subscripts and we now drop these subscripts:

$$m_1 v_1 + m_2 v_2 = m_1 v_1' + m_2 v_2'$$

However, *it is important to remember that the v's in the above equation represent velocity components and can have positive or negative values. They do not represent the magnitudes of the velocities, which must be positive.*

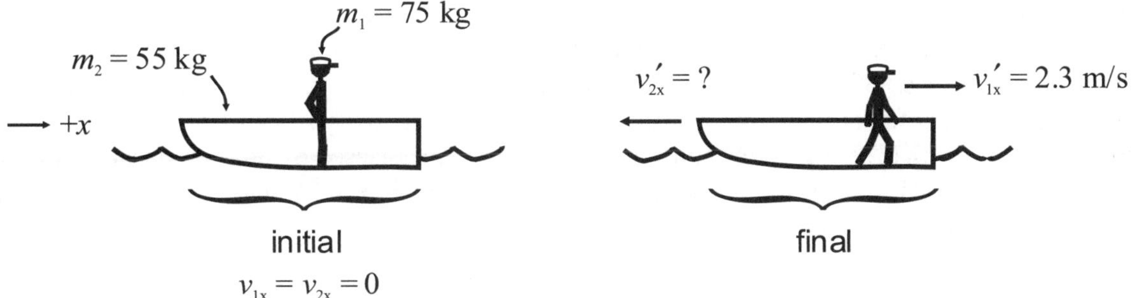

Figure 8-7 *Sample Problem 8-2.*

In this problem, $v_1 = v_2 = 0$, since the man and boat are initially stationary. Thus, we can write:

$$0 = m_1 v_1' + m_2 v_2'$$

Solving for the final velocity of the boat (v_2') and substituting numbers:

$$v_2' = \frac{-m_1 v_1'}{m_2} = \frac{-(75\text{ kg})(2.3\text{ m/s})}{55\text{ kg}} = -3.1\text{ m/s}$$

Therefore, the boat's final velocity is 3.1 m/s in the opposite direction (indicated by the negative sign) to the man's velocity.

Rocket Propulsion

Figure 8-8 **(a)** *Rocketship at rest; momentum equals zero.* **(b)** *Rocketship with engines firing; total momentum still equals zero.*

An interesting application of conservation of momentum is rocket propulsion. Imagine a rocketship at rest somewhere in space (Figure 8-8 (a)). It fires its engines — what this means is that hot gases are ejected from them. To eject these gases, the rocketship must exert a force on them, and the gases exert an equal but opposite force on the rocketship. The resultant force on the system of the rocketship and gases together is zero, and thus the momentum of the system consisting of the rocketship and gases together is conserved. Since the rocketship and its fuel (which provides the gases) are initially stationary, the momentum of the system is initially zero, and must remain zero. Thus, as the gases are ejected in one direction, the rocketship moves in the opposite direction (Figure 8-8 (b)).

Did You Know? *When rocket propulsion was first being discussed in the early 1900s, some scientists thought that rockets would never work outside Earth's atmosphere because they would have nothing to push against.*

As a rocketship continues to fire its engines, its fuel supply becomes smaller. Thus, there is a decrease in the mass of the rocketship and remaining fuel. As a consequence of this variable mass, the detailed mathematics of rocket propulsion, which we will not present here, is more complicated than that of a person walking in a boat. (The masses of the person and boat each remain constant.) However, the basic principle — conservation of momentum — is the same in the two situations.

Positron Emission Tomography (PET) Imaging

A very useful medical imaging technique that involves the conservation of momentum is positron emission tomography (PET). A positron is a subatomic particle that has the same properties (mass, for example) as an electron except that the positron has a positive electric charge. Positrons and electrons are antiparticles of each other, and if a positron and electron meet, they annihilate each other and emit two high-energy photons[1] called gamma (γ) rays.

To create a PET scan, a radioactive substance that emits positrons is injected into a patient and accumulates in the organ or region to be studied. For example, if a glucose solution is injected, it will accumulate preferentially at cancer sites because glucose is metabolized rapidly in cancerous tumours. Any positron that is emitted will encounter an electron in a surrounding molecule and annihilate with it. The γ rays that are produced have very high momentum, and in comparison the positron and electron have negligible momentum. Momentum is conserved in the annihilation process, and since the initial momentum of the positron-electron system is essentially zero, the total momentum of the two γ rays must also be zero. Therefore, the γ rays must move in opposite directions. The γ rays are detected in a ring-shaped detector (Fig. 8-9) surrounding the patient, and with the aid of a computer, the source of the γ rays can be pinpointed and an image is created

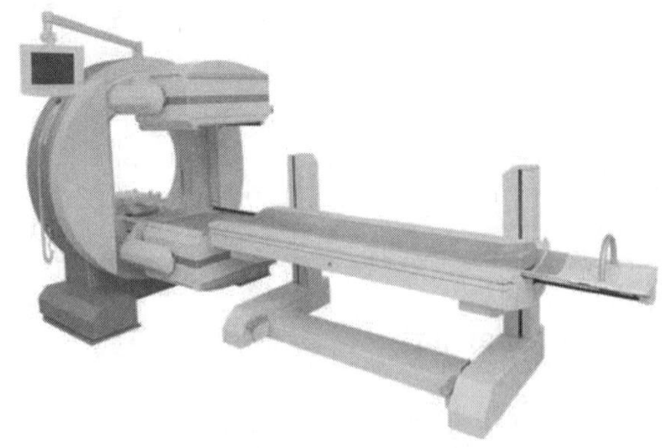

Figure 8-9 *A PET scanner. Photo courtesy of Bork/Shutterstock*

[1] The energy of electromagnetic radiation, such as light and γ rays, is quantized in packets called photons (discussed further in Chapter 15).

showing where the radioactive material has accumulated.

PET scans are commonly used to detect cancer and to create images after cancer therapy to determine if the therapy has been effective. They can also be used to scan the heart to look for indications of coronary artery disease, or to evaluate damage from a heart attack. PET scans of the brain are useful in examining patients who have memory problems that might be the result of Alzheimer's disease, brain tumours, or other disorders.

Conservation of Momentum in Collisions

Conservation of momentum can be applied to many collisions. For example, in the collision of two billiard balls on a table (Figure 8-10), the force exerted by one ball is equal but opposite to the force exerted by the other, and hence the resultant force exerted on the system of the two balls together is zero. Therefore, the momentum of the two-ball system is conserved, that is, the total momentum before the collision equals the total momentum after the collision. (We can safely neglect the friction between the balls and the table during the collision because it is very small compared to the forces exerted by the balls on each other. Vertically, there is no acceleration and thus there must be no resultant vertical force.)

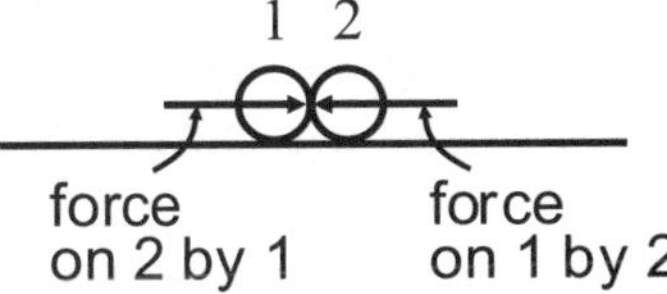

Figure 8-10 *Two billiard balls colliding. The total momentum of the two-ball system is conserved.*

Sample Problem 8-3

During a football game, a fullback of mass 108 kg, running at a speed of 9.1 m/s, is tackled head-on by a defensive back, having a mass of 91 kg and a speed of 6.3 m/s. What is the speed of this pair just after the collision?

Solution: The initial and final diagrams are given in Figure 8-11. The $+x$ axis has been chosen in the direction of the initial velocity of the fullback. Therefore, the initial velocity of the defensive back is negative.

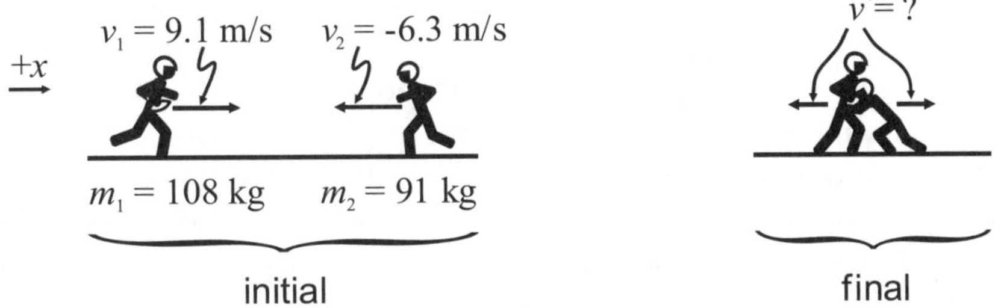

Figure 8-11 *Sample Problem 8-3.*

During the collision, there is no resultant force on the two-player system. (The horizontal forces exerted between the players are much larger than friction, which can therefore be neglected. In the vertical direction, there is no acceleration, which reflects no vertical resultant force.)

Therefore, the momentum of this system is conserved. As in the previous problem we write:

$$m_1 v_1 + m_2 v_2 = m_1 v_1' + m_2 v_2'$$

where "1" and "2" refer to the fullback and defensive back, respectively. The velocities before the collision have no superscript; those after the collision have a primed superscript. Remember that the v's represent velocity *components* and not velocity *magnitudes*. In this problem, the two players have the same final velocity, and so we write v_1' and v_2' each as v':

$$m_1 v_1 + m_2 v_2 = (m_1 + m_2)\, v'$$

Solving for the unknown v' and substituting known numbers:

$$\begin{aligned} v' &= \frac{m_1 v_1 + m_2 v_2}{m_1 + m_2} \\ &= \frac{(108\text{ kg})(9.1\text{ m/s}) + (91\text{ kg})(-6.3\text{ m/s})}{(108 + 91)\text{ kg}} \\ &= +\,2.1\text{ m/s} \end{aligned}$$

Therefore, the final velocity of the players is 2.1 m/s in the direction (indicated by the positive sign) of the initial velocity of the fullback.

Is Momentum Conserved in All Collisions?

Students often have the mistaken impression that momentum of a system is conserved in *all* collisions. However, there are many collisions in which the resultant force on the particular colliding objects being considered is not zero, and therefore the momentum is not conserved. For instance, when a person jumps from a ladder to a wooden deck, the momentum of the person-deck system is not conserved because there is a huge normal force exerted by the deck supports (and the ground) during the collision. Stated another way, the deck is not free to move and cannot take up the momentum of the person. However, if we were to consider the system of the person, the deck, and Earth, momentum is conserved, because Earth is free to take up the person's momentum. Because the mass of Earth is very large compared to that of the person, the change in Earth's velocity when the person lands is, of course, very small.

Another type of situation in which the momentum of a particular pair of colliding objects is not conserved occurs when one of the objects is constrained to rotate about hinges or an axle.

For example, suppose that a snowball is thrown against a gate (Figure 8-12), thus causing it to rotate. During the collision, there is a large force exerted on the gate by the hinges to prevent the gate from simply being forced backward by the ball without rotating; hence, the momentum of the ball-gate system is not conserved. However, if the system being considered is the snowball, gate, and Earth, then the momentum of this system *is* conserved. In other words, momentum is always conserved when a collision occurs, but the system has to be chosen to include all the relevant objects that have momentum before and after the collision.

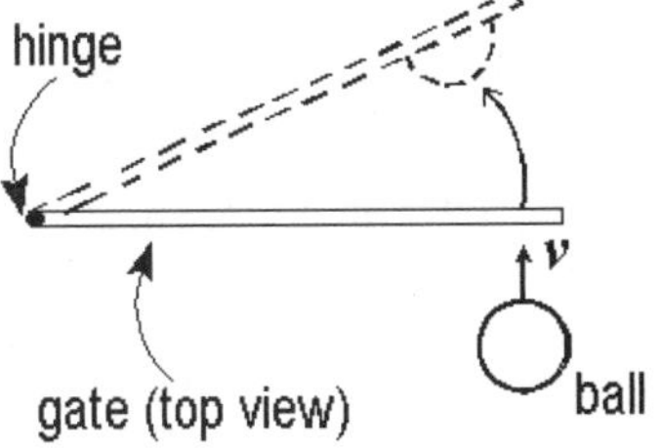

Figure 8-12 *During the collision between a snowball and a hinged gate, the momentum of the ball-gate system is not conserved because the hinges exert a non-negligible force on the gate.*

Conservation of Momentum in Sports

When a baseball player hits a ball, is the momentum of the ball-bat system conserved? The answer is not obvious. Perhaps the situation is similar to the snowball and gate described above; that is, the force exerted by the player's arms on the bat during the collision might not be negligible in comparison with the forces between the bat and ball. In this case, the momentum of the ball-bat system would not be conserved. We showed in Sample Problem 8-1, using realistic numbers, that the average force exerted by the bat on the ball is about 10^4 N. This is approximately the same magnitude as the force of gravity on an object having a mass of 10^3 kg. Could a baseball player use his arms to hold up a thousand-kilogram object? Obviously not. The player's arms can exert only a small force in comparison with the bat-ball force, and hence the momentum of the ball-bat system is indeed conserved. This result has been confirmed in experiments.

A similar conclusion would be reached for tennis, cricket, and golf — the momentum of the system of the ball and racket, bat, or club is conserved. In the case of golf, the head of the club is the important object that strikes the ball (because the head is massive relative to the club shaft), and the momentum of the head-ball system is conserved. Momentum is also conserved in collisions between players in sports such as hockey and football, as considered in Sample Problem 8-3.

Did You Know? *The law of conservation of momentum in collisions was discovered by the Dutch physicist Christian Huygens (1629-1695).*

Practice

8-15 In which of the following situations is the momentum conserved for the system consisting of objects A and B?

(a) A boy (A) stands in a stationary boat (B); the boy then walks in the boat. Neglect viscous friction.

(b) A bowling ball (A) collides with a bowling pin (B).

(c) A dart (A) is thrown against a door (B), which rotates as a result of the collision.

(d) A rocket (A) on a spaceship ejects hot gases (B) created by the burning of fuel.

(e) A moving billiard ball (A) strikes a stationary billiard ball (B).
(f) A woman uses a golf club (A) to strike a golf ball (B).
(g) A free-rolling railroad car (A) strikes a stationary railroad car (B).
(h) A hamburger (A), dropped vertically into a frying pan (B), comes to rest.

8-16 A boy of mass 45 kg stands on a stationary boat of mass 33 kg. He then walks with a speed of 1.9 m/s relative to the water. What is the resulting velocity (magnitude and direction) of the boat relative to the water? Neglect viscous friction.
[Ans. 2.6 m/s in opposite direction to boy's velocity]

8-17 Two ice-skaters, initially stationary, push each other so that they move in opposite directions. One skater (of mass 56.9 kg) has a speed of 3.28 m/s. What is the mass of the other skater if her speed is 3.69 m/s? Neglect friction. [Ans. 50.6 kg]

8-18 A stationary artillery shell of mass 35 kg accidentally explodes, sending two fragments of mass 11 kg and 24 kg in opposite directions. The speed of the 11-kg fragment is 95 m/s. What is the speed of the other fragment? [Ans. 44 m/s]

8-19 Suppose that you drop a hairbrush and it falls downward.
(a) What is the direction of the gravitational force exerted by Earth on the hairbrush?
(b) What is the direction of the gravitational force exerted by the hairbrush on Earth?
(c) How do the forces in (a) and (b) compare in magnitude?
(d) What is the resultant force on the system consisting of Earth and the hairbrush?
(e) What can you conclude about the momentum of this system?
(f) If we consider Earth and the hairbrush to be initially stationary, how does Earth move as the hairbrush falls down?

8-20 A factory worker of mass 57 kg takes a ride on a large freely-rolling cart having a mass of 26 kg. Initially the worker is standing on the cart and they both have a speed of 3.2 m/s relative to the floor. The worker then walks on the cart in the same direction as the cart is moving. Her speed is now 3.8 m/s relative to the floor. What is the new velocity (magnitude and direction) of the cart? [Ans. 1.9 m/s in original direction of cart's velocity]

8-21 A man of mass 65 kg is standing on a stationary boat of mass 35 kg. He is carrying a sack of potatoes of mass 19 kg. He then throws the potatoes horizontally. If the resulting velocity of the man and boat is 1.1 m/s relative to the water, what is the velocity (magnitude and direction) with which the man threw the potatoes, relative to the water?
[Ans. 5.8 m/s in opposite direction to velocity of man and boat]

8-22 Two automobiles collide. One has a mass of 1.13×10^3 kg and is initially travelling east with a speed of 25.7 m/s. The other (mass 1.25×10^3 kg) has an initial velocity of 13.8 m/s west. The autos attach together during the collision. What is their common velocity (magnitude and direction) immediately after the collision? [Ans. 4.95 m/s east]

8-23 (a) In the previous question, determine the change in momentum (magnitude and direction) for each automobile.

(b) How are these two quantities related?
(c) What is the total change in momentum of the two-automobile system?
[Ans. (a) 2.34×10^4 kg·m/s west; 2.34×10^4 kg·m/s east (c) zero]

8-24 A stationary quarterback is hit and tackled by a linebacker of mass 89 kg travelling with an initial speed of 5.2 m/s. As the pair of players move together in an embrace of sporting friendship immediately after the collision, they have a speed of 2.7 m/s. What is the mass of the quarterback? [Ans. 82 kg]

8-25 A railroad car of mass 1.37×10^4 kg rolling north at 20.0 km/h collides with another railroad car of mass 1.12×10^4 kg, also initially rolling north but more slowly. After the collision, the coupled cars have a speed of 18.3 km/h. What was the initial speed of the other car? [Ans. 16.2 km/h]

8-26 A golf ball (mass 0.045 kg) is hit with a driver. The head of the driver has a mass of 0.15 kg and a speed of 56 m/s before the collision. The ball has a speed of 67 m/s as it leaves the clubface. What is the speed of the head immediately after the collision? [Ans. 36 m/s]

8-27 Two balls are rolling directly toward each other. One, of mass 0.25 kg, has a speed of 1.7 m/s; the other has a mass of 0.18 kg and a speed of 2.5 m/s. After the collision, the 0.25-kg ball has reversed its direction and has a speed of 0.10 m/s. What is the velocity (magnitude and direction) of the other ball? [Ans. 0 m/s]

8.3 ELASTIC AND INELASTIC COLLISIONS

Imagine that two balls are thrown toward each other so that they collide: first two "superballs," then two tennis balls, and finally two balls made of soft putty. The collisions are very different. When the "superballs" collide, they bounce off each other with high speed; at the other extreme, the putty balls stick together and have only a small speed after the collision. The tennis-ball collision is intermediate between the other two — the tennis balls bounce off each other with moderate speed. In each of these collisions, momentum is conserved; in order to explain the differences between the collisions, we have to consider something other than momentum. That "something" is kinetic energy.

In the superball collision, the total kinetic energy of the two balls after the collision is equal to the total kinetic energy before the collision. Such a collision is called an **elastic collision**. When the tennis balls collide, the total kinetic energy after the collision is not equal to the total kinetic energy before. This is an **inelastic collision**. For a tennis ball collision, the total final kinetic energy is *less* than the total initial kinetic energy. However, there can be inelastic collisions in which kinetic energy is produced, such as a collision that initiates an explosion, giving a total final kinetic energy that is *greater* than the initial kinetic energy.

When two objects *stick together* during a collision, as in the case of the putty balls, we have a **completely inelastic collision**. The decrease in total kinetic energy in a completely inelastic collision is the maximum possible. You might think that, if there is a maximum decrease in kinetic energy, the objects must be at rest after the collision, but by the law of conservation of momentum, the objects usually must be moving. The three categories of collision are summarized below.

Types of Collisions

Elastic:	Total final kinetic energy = Total initial kinetic energy
Inelastic:	Total final kinetic energy ≠ Total initial kinetic energy
Completely Inelastic:	Total final kinetic energy < Total initial kinetic energy Objects stick together. Decrease in total kinetic energy is maximum possible.

Visually, there is a bounciness or springiness in an elastic collision, whereas a completely inelastic collision has no springiness to it at all.

Where does the kinetic energy go that is "lost" in inelastic and completely inelastic collisions? We know that energy is conserved, and so this lost kinetic energy must be transformed into other types of energy. For example, if two putty balls collide, they become warmer — kinetic energy has been converted into thermal energy. Depending on the objects that collide, kinetic energy could be converted into elastic potential energy, acoustical energy (sound), thermal energy, etc.

In practice, it is almost impossible to have a truly elastic collision between two macroscopic objects such as superballs. There is always some small amount of kinetic energy transformed into other forms. For instance, when superballs collide, thermal energy and acoustical energy are produced. (We can hear the collision.) Nonetheless, in this book, we include problems in which we treat certain collisions between macroscopic objects as being elastic, that is, we neglect the small kinetic energy that is lost. Collisions between molecules, atoms, and subatomic particles are often (but not always) perfectly elastic.

Figure 8-13 *Craters on the moon are the result of completely inelastic collisions with large rocks. (Photo courtesy of NASA.)*

In the early history of the solar system, there were many completely inelastic collisions between relatively large objects such as the moon (Figure 8-13) and smaller chunks of rock. Such collisions were the source of the craters on the moon. Most similar craters that were formed on Earth have been destroyed by erosion due to rain and wind. However, some relatively recent craters still exist, such as the famous Barringer Crater in Arizona, which is believed to be about 25 000 years old. This crater, with a diameter of 1.3 km and a depth of 180 m, resulted when a large meteorite collided with Earth.

Solving Collision Problems

When solving problems involving collisions, it is important to distinguish between inelastic, completely inelastic, and elastic collisions. Although we will point out differences below, all of these types of collisions share the common feature that momentum is conserved:

$$m_1v_1 + m_2v_2 = m_1v_1' + m_2v_2'$$

where m_1 and m_2 are the masses of the colliding objects, v_1 and v_2 are their velocities before the collision, and v_1' and v_2' are their velocities after the collision. If the collision is inelastic, this is the only equation that can be used. The last two practice questions in Section 8.2 illustrate examples of inelastic collisions. In the case of a completely inelastic collision, the objects stick together, and hence their final velocities are equal $(v_1' = v_2')$. Sample Problem 8-3 in Section 8.2 gave an example of a completely inelastic collision.

If a collision is known to be elastic (this is usually stated clearly in the problem), then the total kinetic energy before the collision equals the total kinetic energy after the collision:

$$\tfrac{1}{2}mv_1^2 + \tfrac{1}{2}mv_2^2 = \tfrac{1}{2}mv_1'^2 + \tfrac{1}{2}mv_2'^2$$

How to solve problems involving elastic collisions by using this equation, along with the equation for conservation of momentum, is shown in the following two sample problems.

Sample Problem 8-4

A billiard ball having mass *m* and initial speed *v* makes a head-on elastic collision with another billiard ball (initially stationary) having the same mass *m*. What are the final speeds of the two balls?

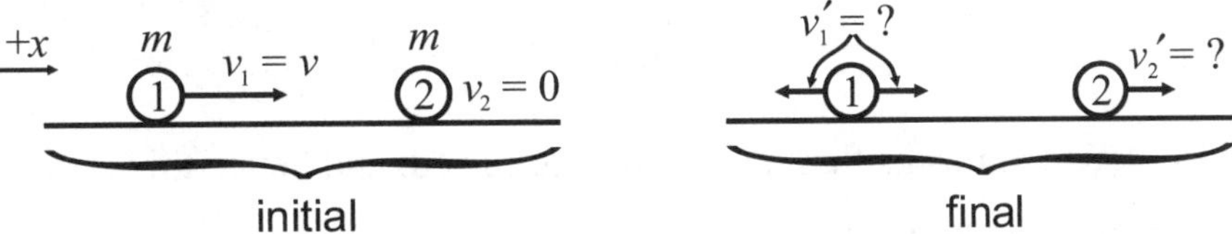

Figure 8-14 *Sample Problem 8-4.*

Solution: Initial and final diagrams are shown in Figure 8-14. The +*x* axis has been chosen in the direction of motion of the initially moving ball. Since we are told that the collision is *elastic*, we know that the total initial kinetic energy equals the total final kinetic energy. If the problem did not state that the collision is elastic, then we could not have made this assumption.

Momentum is also conserved in this collision. We can thus write two equations, one for kinetic energy and one for momentum.

$$\frac{1}{2}mv_1^2 + \frac{1}{2}mv_2^2 = \frac{1}{2}mv_1'^2 + \frac{1}{2}mv_2'^2$$

$$mv_1 + mv_2 = mv_1' + mv_2'$$

where "1" and "2" refer to the (initially) moving and stationary balls, respectively. The final velocities are primed, and the initial velocities are unprimed. Remember that the v's represent velocity components (not velocity magnitudes) and therefore can be positive or negative.

Since ball #2 is initially stationary, $v_2 = 0$. As well, we are given that $v_1 = v$ for the ball that is initially moving. Making these two substitutions in the equations above, multiplying the kinetic energy equation by two to eliminate the fractions, and dividing both equations by the mass m, we have:

$$v^2 = v_1'^2 + v_2'^2 \qquad \text{Eqn. [1]}$$

$$v = v_1' + v_2' \qquad \text{Eqn. [2]}$$

Since the speed v is a given quantity, we now have two equations in two unknowns, v_1' and v_2'. Our plan of attack will be to re-arrange Eqn. [2] to get v_1' in terms of v_2', substitute this expression for v_1' into Eqn. [1], and solve the resulting equation for the unknown v_2'. We then can use Eqn. [2] to determine the other unknown, v_1'.

First, re-arranging Eqn. [2]: $$v_1' = v - v_2'$$

Substituting for v_1' in Eqn. [1]: $$v^2 = (v - v_2')^2 + v_2'^2$$

Expanding and simplifying:

$$v^2 = v^2 - 2vv_2' + v_2'^2 + v_2'^2$$

$$0 = -2vv_2' + 2v_2'^2$$

$$0 = -v_2'(v - v_2')$$

Hence, either $v_2' = 0$ (which means that no collision occurred, and hence this is not an appropriate solution) or $v - v_2' = 0$, from which we conclude that $v_2' = v$.

Thus, $$v_2' = v$$

Substituting $v_2' = v$ in Eqn. [2] gives

$$v = v_1' + v$$

$$v_1' = 0$$

Therefore, the ball (#1) that is initially moving is at rest after the collision ($v_1' = 0$), and the ball (#2) that is initially stationary has the same speed after the collision that the other ball had before the collision ($v_2' = v$). If you have had any experience with billiard balls, you know that this result is correct for head-on collisions. However, this conclusion is not valid for all elastic collisions in which one object is initially stationary — the colliding objects must have the same mass. In the next sample problem, we investigate an elastic collision in which the objects have different masses.

Sample Problem 8-5

In the operation of a PET scanner, when a positron is emitted from a radioactive nucleus inside the patient, it typically travels a short distance (at most a few millimetres) before it undergoes annihilation. Suppose that while it is travelling, a positron undergoes an elastic head-on collision with a stationary proton (i.e., the nucleus of a hydrogen atom). If the speed of the positron just prior to the collision is 923 m/s, determine the velocity (magnitude and direction) of each particle after the collision. The mass of a positron is 9.109×10^{-31} kg, and the mass of a proton is 1.673×10^{-27} kg.

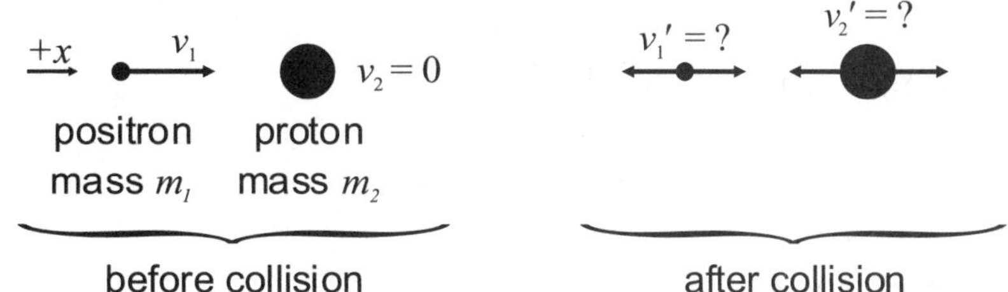

Figure 8-15 *Sample Problem 8-5.*

Solution: Figure 8-15 provides diagrams before and after the collision. The +*x* axis has been chosen in the direction of the initial velocity of the positron. The basic setup of the solution is similar to that of the previous sample problem, but the analysis is more complicated because the particles have different masses. Since the collision is elastic, both kinetic energy and momentum are conserved:

$$\frac{1}{2}m_1v_1^2 + \frac{1}{2}m_2v_2^2 = \frac{1}{2}m_1v_1'^2 + \frac{1}{2}m_2v_2'^2$$
$$m_1v_1 + m_2v_2 = m_1v_1' + m_2v_2'$$

where "1" and "2" refer to the positron and proton, respectively. Since the proton is initially stationary, $v_2 = 0$. Making this substitution into both equations, and multiplying the kinetic energy equation by two:

$$m_1v_1^2 = m_1v_1'^2 + m_2v_2'^2 \qquad \text{Eqn. [1]}$$

$$m_1 v_1 = m_1 v_1' + m_2 v_2' \qquad \text{Eqn. [2]}$$

Since we know m_1, m_2, and v_1, we now have two equations in two unknowns, v_1' and v_2'. As in the previous problem, our plan will be to re-arrange Eqn. [2] to get v_1' in terms of v_2', substitute the expression for v_1' into Eqn. [1], and solve the resulting equation for v_2'. We then can determine v_1'. Although we normally recommend doing all the algebra first and then substituting numbers, in this case it is easier to substitute numbers first. Substituting into Eqn. [2], omitting units for convenience, gives

$$(9.109 \times 10^{-31})(923) = (9.109 \times 10^{-31})v_1' + (1.673 \times 10^{-27})v_2'$$

We now divide by 9.109×10^{-31} to simplify the equation:

$$923 = v_1' + 1837 v_2'$$

Re-arrange to get v_1' in terms of v_2': $\quad v_1' = 923 - 1837 v_2' \qquad$ Eqn. [3]

Before substituting this expression into Eqn. [1], we substitute known numbers into [1]:

$$(9.109 \times 10^{-31})(923)^2 = (9.109 \times 10^{-31})v_1'^2 + (1.673 \times 10^{-27})v_2'^2$$

As before, divide by 9.109×10^{-31}, to give:

$$(923)^2 = v_1'^2 + 1837 v_2'^2 \qquad \text{Eqn. [4]}$$

Now substituting the expression for v_1' (Eqn. [3]) into [4]:

$$(923)^2 = (923 - 1837 v_2')^2 + 1837 v_2'^2$$

Expanding $(923 - 1837 v_2')^2$ on the right-hand side:

$$(923)^2 = (923)^2 - 2(923)(1837)v_2' + (1837)^2 v_2'^2 + 1837 v_2'^2$$

Subtracting $(923)^2$ from both sides of the equation, and then dividing all the remaining terms by 1837:

$$0 = -2(923)v_2' + 1837 v_2'^2 + v_2'^2$$

Adding the last two terms, and removing a common factor of v_2':

$$0 = [-2(923) + 1838 v_2']v_2'$$

Therefore, $-2(923)+1838v_2'=0$ or $v_2'=0$

Since the solution $v_2'=0$ corresponds to no collision, we must have:

$$-2(923)+1838v_2'=0$$
$$\text{which gives } v_2'=1.00\text{ m/s}$$
$$(\text{or } v_2'=1.004\text{ m/s, keeping one extra significant digit})$$

We now substitute $v_2'=1.004\text{ m/s}$ into Eqn. [3] to determine v_1':

$$\begin{aligned} v_1' &= 923-1837v_2' \\ &= 923-1837(1.004) \\ &= -921\text{ m/s} \end{aligned}$$

Calculation tip: *When calculating v_1', keeping one extra significant digit in the value of v_2' prevents round-off error.*

Thus, the final results are $v_2'=1.00\text{ m/s}$ and $v_1'=-921\text{ m/s}$.
These values indicate that, after the collision, the proton has a velocity of 1.00 m/s in the direction in which the positron was originally moving, and the positron has a velocity of 921 m/s in the opposite direction (indicated by the negative value for v_1'). This result should make physical sense to you — the low-mass positron rebounds from the heavy proton with very little reduction in speed, and the proton moves very slowly after the collision.

Practice

<u>**8-28**</u> What is the most appropriate word or phrase to complete the sentence?
(a) A collision in which the two objects stick together is a(n) __________________ collision.
(b) In an elastic collision, the total kinetic energy before the collision __________________ the total kinetic energy after the collision.
(c) A collision in which the decrease in kinetic energy is the maximum possible is referred to as a(n) __________________ collision.
(d) If the total kinetic energy before a collision is not equal to the total kinetic energy after, the collision is __________________.

8-29 During a snowball fight, two snowballs (each of mass 145 g) collide in mid-air in a completely inelastic collision. Just before the collision, both balls are travelling horizontally, one ball with a velocity of 22 m/s north, and the other, 22 m/s south. What is the velocity (magnitude and direction) of each ball after the collision? [Ans. 0 m/s]

8-30 A proton travelling with an initial speed of 815 m/s collides head-on elastically with a stationary proton. What is the velocity (magnitude and direction) of each proton after the collision? Show your work. [Ans. 0 m/s; 815 m/s in direction of initial velocity]

8-31 A truck of mass 1.3×10^4 kg travelling at 9.0×10^1 km/h north collides with a car of mass 1.1×10^3 kg travelling at 3.0×10^1 km/h north. If the collision is completely inelastic, what is the velocity (magnitude and direction) of the vehicles immediately after the collision?
[Ans. 85 km/h north]

8-32 In the previous question, calculate the total kinetic energy before and after the collision, and the decrease in kinetic energy during the collision. [Ans. 4.1×10^6 J; 4.0×10^6 J; 1×10^5 J]

8-33 A bullet of mass 3.5 g travelling at 6.2×10^2 m/s horizontally collides with a stationary block of wood on a table. The bullet passes through the wood, and emerges with a speed of 1.6×10^2 m/s. The wood has a speed of 6.6 m/s immediately after the collision. (a) What is the mass of the wood? (b) Is this collision elastic, inelastic, or completely inelastic?
[Ans. (a) 2.4×10^2 g]

8-34 A superball of mass 22 g rolls with a speed of 3.5 m/s toward another (stationary) superball of mass 27 g. If the balls have a head-on elastic collision, what are the velocities (magnitudes and direction) of the balls after the collision?
[Ans. 3.1 m/s forward, and 0.4 m/s backward]

8-35 A nitrogen molecule (mass 4.65×10^{-26} kg) in the air undergoes a head-on elastic collision with a stationary oxygen molecule (mass 5.31×10^{-26} kg). After the collision, the nitrogen molecule has reversed its direction and has a speed of 34.1 m/s, and the oxygen is travelling at 481 m/s in the original direction of motion of the nitrogen. What was the initial speed of the nitrogen molecule? [Ans. 515 m/s]

8-36 An object of mass *m* makes an elastic collision with another object initially at rest and continues to move in the original direction but with one-third its original speed. What is the mass of the other object in terms of *m*? [Ans. *m*/2]

8-37 A skier of mass 66 kg slides down a hill 25 m high and then makes a completely inelastic collision with a stationary skier of mass 72 kg. Immediately after the collision, what is the speed of each skier? Neglect friction. [Ans. 11 m/s]

8.4 CONSERVATION OF MOMENTUM IN TWO DIMENSIONS

Life would be rather dull if the universe were one-dimensional. (Stop and really contemplate that possibility for a moment.) Fortunately we live in a three-dimensional universe (four-dimensional if you consider time as another dimension). We now discuss how conservation of momentum applies in more than one dimension.

In this chapter, we have already applied conservation of momentum to a number of one-dimensional phenomena, such as the head-on tackle of a football player or the recoil of a boat when a person walks in it. Momentum is conserved because the forces exerted by the objects on each other are equal in magnitude but opposite in direction (by Newton's third law), and thus the resultant force on the system is zero (assuming that there are no other significant forces acting on the objects). If the resultant force on a system is zero, then the total momentum of the system is conserved (Section 8.2).

In two- and three-dimensional situations, the same reasoning applies. The forces exerted between parts of a system are equal but opposite, the resultant force is thus zero, and the total momentum of the system is conserved. Both the resultant force and momentum are vector quantities. Thus, when we say that momentum is conserved, we mean that both the magnitude and direction of the momentum vector are unchanging. Alternatively, we can state that the x- and y-components of the momentum are each unchanging (if we are dealing with a two-dimensional collision). When solving problems involving two-dimensional conservation of momentum, we usually write two equations, one involving x-components, and another involving y-components.

The great value of the law of conservation of momentum is its generality. It can be used in any situation in which a system is subject to a resultant force of zero. It applies to collisions between all sorts of objects: subatomic particles, tennis balls, and even galaxies consisting of billions of stars. It can be applied to systems that do not involve collisions. For example, in the Earth-sun system, the gravitational force exerted by Earth on the sun is equal but opposite to the force exerted by the sun on Earth, and hence the momentum of the system is conserved. As Earth travels in its orbit around the sun, the sun wobbles a bit (that is, it does not stay stationary) so that the momentum of the system is constant.

Sample Problem 8-6

A boy (mass 47 kg) is standing on a raft of mass 53 kg that is drifting with a velocity of 1.2 m/s north relative to the water. The boy then walks on the raft with a net velocity of 0.75 m/s east relative to the water. What is the resulting velocity (magnitude and direction) of the raft relative to the water? Neglect viscous friction between the raft and water.

Approximate solution (using a vector scale diagram): Figure 8-16 shows an approximate solution to this problem, using a vector scale diagram. Since the boy and raft have the same initial velocity, the initial momentum is the total mass (100 kg) multiplied by the velocity (1.2 m/s north), giving 1.2×10^2 kg·m/s north (Figure 8-16 (a)).

When the boy walks east, the force exerted by him on the raft is equal and opposite to the force exerted on him by the raft, and therefore the momentum of the boy-raft system is conserved. Thus, the total momentum must still be 1.2×10^2 kg·m/s north. Figure 8-16 (b) shows this total final momentum as the *vector* sum of the boy's momentum and the raft's momentum. The boy's momentum is the product of his mass (47 kg) and his velocity (0.75 m/s east), giving 3.5 kg·m/s east. The momentum of the raft can be determined by direct measurement with a ruler and protractor: 1.3×10^2 kg·m/s at 73° north of west. To determine the velocity of the raft, we divide its momentum by its mass. The result is 2.5 m/s at 73° north of west.

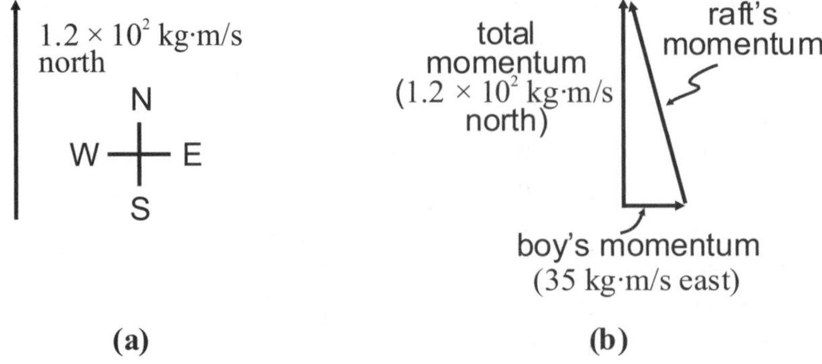

Figure 8-16 *Sample Problem 8-6 (vector scale diagram solution). Scale: 1 cm = 45 kg·m/s.* **(a)** *Initial momentum* **(b)** *Final momentum*

Probably the most difficult part of the solution is the drawing of Figure 8-16 (b). Look carefully at this diagram and think about how you would draw it, given only the total momentum northward and the boy's momentum eastward. Remember that the boy's momentum and the raft's momentum add as vectors to give the total momentum. Alternatively, you can draw the raft's momentum as the total momentum minus the boy's momentum.

Exact solution (using components): A more accurate solution can be obtained by using vector components (Figure 8-17). We write equations expressing conservation of momentum in the *x*- and *y*-directions:

$$m_1 v_{1x} + m_2 v_{2x} = m_1 v'_{1x} + m_2 v'_{2x} \qquad \text{Eqn. [1]}$$

$$m_1 v_{1y} + m_2 v_{2y} = m_1 v'_{1y} + m_2 v'_{2y} \qquad \text{Eqn. [2]}$$

where "1" represents the boy and "2" the raft. The final velocities have a primed superscript, and the initial velocities have no superscript. We define the +*x* and +*y* directions to be east and north, respectively. This simplifies the solution, since the boy and raft initially each have a zero *x*-component of velocity $(v_{1x} = v_{2x} = 0)$, and a common *y*-component $(v_{1y} = v_{2y} = 1.2\text{ m/s})$, as shown in Figure 8-17 (a).

In the final situation with the boy walking east (Figure 8-17 (b)), the boy's velocity has no *y*-component $(v'_{1y} = 0)$ and a positive *x*-component $(v'_{1x} = 0.75\text{ m/s})$. In order that the total momentum be conserved, notice that the raft's final velocity must have a positive *y*-component and a negative *x*-component. Since the masses are known (m_1 = 47 kg; m_2 = 53 kg), the only unknown quantities in Eqns. [1] and [2] are the components of the raft's final velocity v'_{2x} and v'_{2y}.

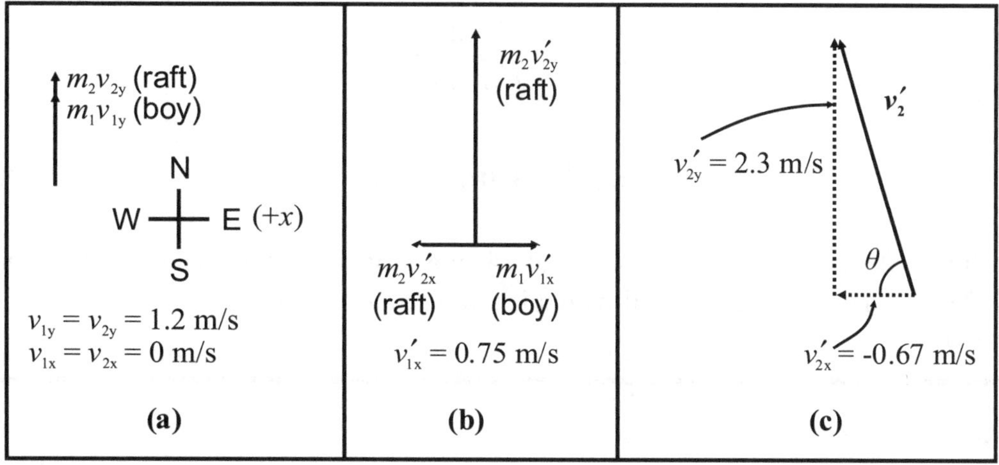

Figure 8-17 *Sample Problem 8-6 (solution using components).*
(a) *Initial momentum.* **(b)** *Final momentum.* **(c)** *Final velocity of raft.*

We start by substituting $v_{1x} = v_{2x} = 0$ into Eqn. [1]:

$$0 = m_1v'_{1x} + m_2v'_{2x}$$

Re-arranging and substituting other known values to solve for the unknown v'_{2x}:

$$v'_{2x} = \frac{-m_1v'_{1x}}{m_2} = \frac{-(47\text{ kg})(0.75\text{ m/s})}{53\text{ kg}} = -0.67\text{ m/s}$$

Similarly, substituting $v'_{1y} = 0$ into Eqn. [2], and then solving for v'_{2y}:

$$m_1v_{1y} + m_2v_{2y} = m_2v'_{2y}$$

$$v'_{2y} = \frac{m_1v_{1y} + m_2v_{2y}}{m_2}$$

$$= \frac{(47\text{ kg})(1.2\text{ m/s}) + (53\text{ kg})(1.2\text{ m/s})}{53\text{ kg}}$$

$$= 2.3\text{ m/s}$$

The magnitude and direction (θ) of the raft's velocity $\boldsymbol{v}'_2$ can now be determined from its components (Figure 8-17 (c)).

$$v'_2 = \sqrt{(v'_{2x})^2 + (v'_{2y})^2} = \sqrt{(-0.67\text{ m/s})^2 + (2.3\text{ m/s})^2} = 2.4\text{ m/s}$$

and $$\tan\theta = \frac{2.3\ \text{m/s}}{0.67\ \text{m/s}}$$

Hence, $$\theta = \tan^{-1}\left(2.3/0.67\right) = 74°$$

Thus, the final velocity of the raft is 2.4 m/s at 74° north of west. Our scale-diagram answer of 2.5 m/s at 73° north of west agrees well with this more accurate result.

Sample Problem 8-7

Two children are playing marbles; a collision occurs between two marbles of equal mass (m). One marble is initially at rest, and after the collision, this marble has a velocity of 1.10 m/s at an angle of 40.0° from the original direction of motion of the other marble, which has a speed of 1.36 m/s after the collision. What was the initial speed of the moving marble?

Solution: Momentum is conserved in the collision, and we write equations to express conservation of momentum in the x- and y-directions:

$$m_1 v_{1\text{x}} + m_2 v_{2\text{x}} = m_1 v'_{1\text{x}} + m_2 v'_{2\text{x}} \qquad \text{Eqn. [1]}$$

$$m_1 v_{1\text{y}} + m_2 v_{2\text{y}} = m_1 v'_{1\text{y}} + m_2 v'_{2\text{y}} \qquad \text{Eqn. [2]}$$

where "1" represents the marble that is initially moving, and "2" the one initially at rest. We define the $+x$ axis to be in the initial direction of motion and the $+y$ axis at right angles to it (Figure 8-18). This choice of axes will simplify our solution since there is no y-component of velocity (and momentum) initially.

Before the collision, marble 1 has velocity components $v_{1\text{x}} > 0$ and $v_{1\text{y}} = 0$, and the velocity components of marble 2 are $v_{2\text{x}} = v_{2\text{y}} = 0$. Notice that we are asked to find the magnitude of $v_{1\text{x}}$. After the collision, both marbles have non-zero x- and y-components of velocity, as shown. Substituting into equations [1] and [2] that $v_{1\text{y}} = v_{2\text{x}} = v_{2\text{y}} = 0$ and also that $m_1 = m_2 = m$:

$$m v_{1\text{x}} = m v'_{1\text{x}} + m v'_{2\text{x}} \qquad \text{Eqn. [3]}$$

$$0 = m v'_{1\text{y}} + m v'_{2\text{y}} \qquad \text{Eqn. [4]}$$

We can see from Eqns. [3] and [4] that the initial x-component of momentum of marble 1 is shared after the collision by both marbles, and that the two final y-components of momentum must add to zero. (In Figure 8-18, notice the directions of the y-components of the final velocities.) We simplify Eqns. [3] and [4] by dividing all terms by m:

$$v_{1x} = v'_{1x} + v'_{2x} \qquad \text{Eqn. [5]}$$

$$0 = v'_{1y} + v'_{2y} \qquad \text{Eqn. [6]}$$

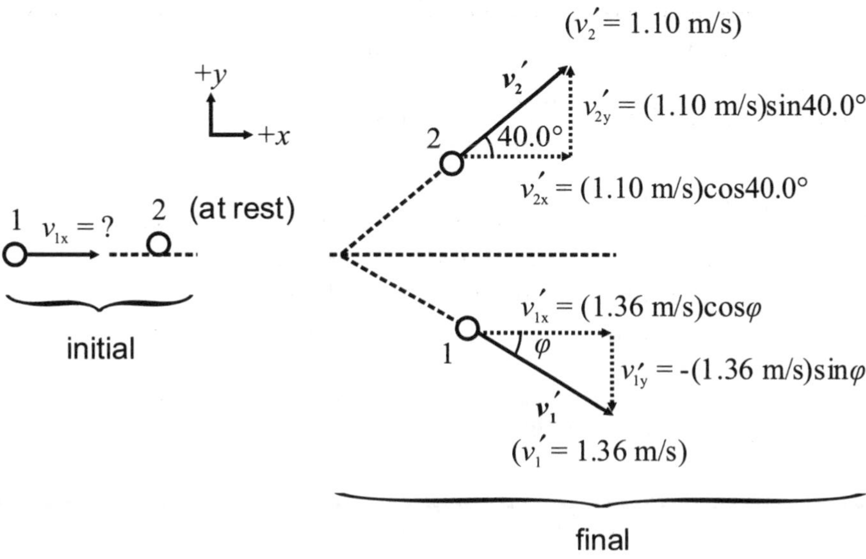

Figure 8-18 *Sample Problem 8-7.*

We now use the remaining numerical information given in the problem. After the collision, marble 2 has a velocity of 1.10 m/s at 40.0° to the $+x$ axis; this velocity has components of

$$v'_{2x} = (1.10 \text{ m/s}) \cos 40.0° \quad \text{and} \quad v'_{2y} = (1.10 \text{ m/s}) \sin 40.0°$$

(Notice the direction of the final velocity of marble 2 in Figure 8-18 — at "40.0° from the original direction of motion of the other marble," that is, at 40.0° from the $+x$ axis.)

The final velocity of marble 1 has a magnitude of 1.36 m/s, but an unknown direction (indicated by angle φ in Figure 8-18). Thus, its final velocity components are

$$v'_{1x} = (1.36 \text{ m/s}) \cos \varphi \quad \text{and} \quad v'_{1y} = -(1.36 \text{ m/s}) \sin \varphi$$

Notice that v'_{1y} must be negative so that the total final y-momentum is zero (equal to the initial value). Substituting the four final velocity components into Eqns. [5] and [6]:

$$v_{1x} = (1.36 \text{ m/s}) \cos \varphi + (1.10 \text{ m/s}) \cos 40.0° \qquad \text{Eqn. [7]}$$

$$0 = -(1.36 \text{ m/s}) \sin \varphi + (1.10 \text{ m/s}) \sin 40.0° \qquad \text{Eqn. [8]}$$

We are asked to determine the magnitude of v_{1x}, which appears in Eqn. [7]. However, the unknown angle φ also appears in [7]. Therefore, we will use Eqn. [8] to solve for φ, substitute for φ in [7], and hence find v_{1x}. From Eqn. [8]:

$$\sin \varphi = \frac{(1.10 \text{ m/s}) \sin 40.0°}{1.36 \text{ m/s}}$$

This gives $$\varphi = 31.3°$$

Substituting this value of φ in Eqn. [7]:

$$v_{1x} = (1.36 \text{ m/s}) \cos 31.3° + (1.10 \text{ m/s}) \cos 40.0°$$
$$= 2.00 \text{ m/s}$$

Therefore, the initial speed of the moving marble is 2.00 m/s.

Practice

8-38 A girl of mass 52 kg is standing on a cart of mass 26 kg that is free to move in any direction. Initially, the cart is moving with a velocity of 1.2 m/s south relative to the floor. The girl then walks on the cart, and has a net velocity of 1.0 m/s west relative to the floor. Use a vector scale diagram to determine the approximate final velocity (magnitude and direction) of the cart. [Ans. 4.1 m/s at 29° east of south]

8-39 Solve the previous problem using components.

8-40 Two automobiles collide at an intersection. One car (mass 1.4×10^3 kg) is travelling south at 45 km/h and the other (mass 1.3×10^3 kg) is going east at 39 km/h. If the cars have a completely inelastic collision, what is their velocity (magnitude and direction) just after the collision?
[Ans. 30 km/h at 51° south of east]

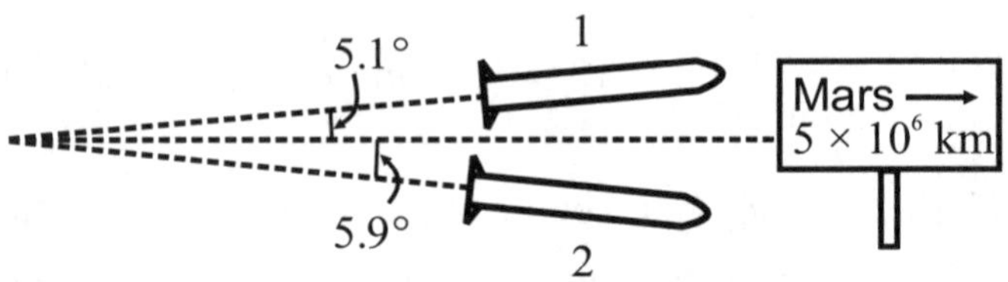

Figure 8-19 *Question 8-41.*

8-41 Two spaceships from different nations have linked up in space and are coasting with their engines off, heading directly toward Mars. The spaceships are then thrust apart by the use of large springs. Spaceship #1 (mass $m_1 = 1.9 \times 10^4$ kg) then has a velocity of 3.5×10^3 km/h at 5.1° to its original direction, and ship #2 ($m_2 = 1.7 \times 10^4$ kg) has a velocity of 3.4×10^3 km/h at 5.9° to its original direction (Figure 8-19). Use vector components to find the original speed of the ships when they were together. [Ans. 3.4×10^3 km/h]

8-42 Solve the previous problem approximately by using a vector scale diagram.

8-43 Two balls of equal mass *m* undergo a collision. One ball is initially stationary. After the collision, the velocities of the balls make angles of 31.1° and 48.9° relative to the original direction of motion of the moving ball.
(a) Draw a diagram showing the initial and final situations. If you are uncertain about the final directions of motion, remember that momentum is conserved.
(b) If the initial speed of the moving ball is 2.25 m/s, what are the speeds of the balls after the collision?
(c) Is this collision elastic? Justify your answer.
[Ans. (b) 1.18 m/s at 48.9°; 1.72 m/s at 31.1° (c) no]

8-44 Use a vector scale diagram to determine approximate answers for part (b) of the previous problem.

8-45 A neutron (mass 1.7×10^{-27} kg) travelling at 2.7 km/s hits a stationary lithium nucleus (mass 1.2×10^{-26} kg). Afterwards, the velocity of the lithium nucleus is 0.40 km/s at 54° to the original direction of motion of the neutron. If the speed of the neutron after the collision is 2.5 km/s, in what direction is it travelling?
[Ans. 66° from initial direction of neutron's velocity]

8-46 Two ice-skaters undergo a collision, after which their arms are intertwined and they have a common velocity of 0.85 m/s at 27° south of east. Before the collision, one skater (mass 71 kg) had a velocity of 2.3 m/s at 12° north of east, and the other skater's velocity was 1.9 m/s at 52° south of west. What is the mass of the second skater? [Ans. 55 kg]

CHAPTER FOCUS

Thus far in the book, we have considered various aspects of mechanics: kinematics, Newton's laws of motion, energy, and momentum.

In this chapter, we have defined (linear) momentum, and have seen that the change in an object's momentum equals the product of the resultant force on the object and the time interval during which the resultant force acts. In addition, the law of conservation of momentum has been explained and used in discussions of various physical phenomena, such as collisions and rocket propulsion. Various types of collisions have been considered — elastic, inelastic, and completely inelastic — depending on the relationship between the initial kinetic energy and the final kinetic energy. Collisions in one and two dimensions have been discussed in detail.

Gravitation is the topic of the next chapter, as we continue our study of mechanics. The force of gravity is responsible for many of the large-scale properties of the universe — for example, the existence and motion of planets, stars, galaxies, and black holes.

VOCABULARY REVIEW

You should be able to define or explain each of the following words or phrases.

momentum (linear)
law of conservation of momentum
elastic collision
inelastic collision
completely inelastic collision

CHAPTER REVIEW

8-47 The SI unit of momentum is
(a) newton (b) joule (c) watt (d) kg·m/s (e) kg·m^2/s

8-48 One way that an octopus propels itself is by ejecting a jet of water from its gill chamber. Suppose that an octopus of mass 3.8 kg is initially at rest and ejects 0.80 kg of water. The speed of the water is 1.2 m/s. What is the resulting speed of the octopus? Neglect fluid friction and assume that the 0.80 kg of water is not included in the 3.8-kg mass of the octopus.
(a) 0.30 m/s (b) 1.2 m/s (c) 5.7 m/s (d) 0.20 m/s (e) 0.25 m/s

8-49 The contact times in collisions between various balls used in sports and the objects (bats, rackets, etc.) used to hit them are typically a few
(a) nanoseconds (b) microseconds (c) milliseconds (d) picoseconds (e) kiloseconds

8-50 Which of the following statements describe properties of completely inelastic collisions between two objects?
1. The objects stick together.
2. There is a maximum loss of kinetic energy.
3. Both objects are at rest after the collision.
4. Momentum is conserved.
(a) 1, 2, and 3 (b) 1 and 4 (c) 1, 2, 3, and 4 (d) 1, 2, and 4 (e) 3 and 4

8-51 In a collision between a small car and a large truck, how does the magnitude of the momentum change of the car ($|\Delta \boldsymbol{p}_c|$) compare with the magnitude of magnitude of the momentum change of the truck ($|\Delta \boldsymbol{p}_t|$)?
(a) $|\Delta \boldsymbol{p}_c| = |\Delta \boldsymbol{p}_t|$ (b) $|\Delta \boldsymbol{p}_c| < |\Delta \boldsymbol{p}_t|$ (c) $|\Delta \boldsymbol{p}_c| > |\Delta \boldsymbol{p}_t|$
(d) impossible to say unless the masses and velocities are known

8-52 A billiard ball moving with speed v collides head-on with a stationary ball of the same mass. After the collision, the ball that was initially moving is at rest. What is the speed of the other ball after the collision?
(a) $v/2$ (b) 0 (c) v (d) 2 (e) $3v/4$

8-53 A helium atom in the air collides with a wall, as shown in Fig. 8-20. The speed of the atom is unchanged as a result of the collision. Which of the following diagrams shows the correct direction of the change of momentum of the helium atom?

(a) ← (b) ↗ (c) → (d) ↑ (e) ↓

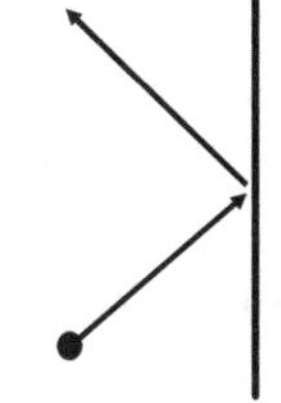

Figure 8-20
Question 8-53.

8-54 A number of objects of different masses have the same speed. Sketch the shape of the graph of the magnitude of momentum vs. mass for these objects.

8-55 A car of mass 1.1×10^3 kg is travelling in a direction 22° north of east. Its eastward component of momentum is 2.6×10^4 kg·m/s. What is the speed of the car? [Ans. 25 m/s]

8-56 A car of mass 1.2×10^3 kg travelling west at 53 km/h collides with a telephone pole and comes to rest. The duration of the collision is 55 ms. What are the magnitude and direction of the average force exerted on the car by the pole? [Ans. 3.2×10^5 N east]

8-57 A tennis ball of mass 59 g is thrown upward and then hit (served) just as it comes to rest at the top of its motion. It is in contact with the racket for 5.1 ms, and the average force exerted on the ball by the racket is 324 N horizontally. What is the velocity (magnitude and direction) of the ball just as it leaves the racket? [Ans. 28 m/s horizontally]

8-58 Each second, 1.3 kg of water leaves a hose with a speed of 24 m/s. The water, travelling horizontally, hits a vertical wall and is stopped. Neglecting any splash-back, what is the magnitude of the average force exerted by the water on the wall? [Ans. 31 N]

8-59 A girl of mass 38 kg is standing on a stationary wagon. She then walks forward on the wagon with a speed of 1.2 m/s, and the wagon moves backward with a speed of 3.0 m/s (both speeds relative to the ground). What is the mass of the wagon? Neglect friction. [Ans. 15 kg]

8-60 A boy places a spring of negligible mass between two toy cars (Figure 8-21) of masses 112 g and 154 g. He compresses the spring and ties the cars together with a string. He then cuts the string, thus releasing the spring, and the cars move in opposite directions. The 112-g car has a speed of 1.38 m/s. What is the speed of the other car? [Ans. 1.00 m/s]

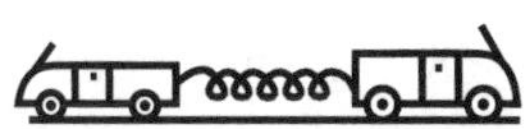

Figure 8-21
Question 8-60.

8-61 A space vehicle and its fuel tank are moving with a velocity of 3.50×10^2 m/s toward a space station. The fuel tank is then jettisoned to the rear, and the velocity of the tank is then only 2.50×10^2 m/s toward the station. What is the new speed of the space vehicle? The mass of the vehicle is 3.25 times that of the tank. [Ans. 381 m/s]

8-62 Give an example of a collision in which the momentum of the system of the colliding objects is not conserved. Explain why momentum is not conserved in this collision, but is conserved in many other collisions.

8-63 A proton (mass 1.67×10^{-27} kg), travelling with an initial speed of 1.57 km/s, collides head-on with a stationary alpha particle (mass 6.64×10^{-27} kg). The proton rebounds with a speed of 0.893 km/s. What is the speed of the alpha particle? [Ans. 0.619 km/s]

8-64 Two children each roll a marble on the ground so that there is a head-on collision. One marble has a mass of 2.5 g and a speed of 2.6 m/s before colliding, and the other has a mass of 2.9 g and a speed of 1.8 m/s. After the collision, the less massive marble has reversed direction and has a speed of 2.0 m/s. What is the velocity (magnitude and direction) of the other marble? [Ans. 2.2 m/s in opposite direction to its original velocity]

8-65 Two rocks in space undergo a collision. One has a mass of 2.67 kg and has an initial velocity of 1.70×10^2 m/s toward Jupiter; the other has a mass of 5.83 kg. After the collision, the rocks are both moving toward Jupiter, with speeds of 185 m/s and 183 m/s for the 2.67-kg and 5.83-kg rocks, respectively. What was the initial velocity (magnitude and direction) of the more massive rock? [Ans. 1.90×10^2 m/s toward Jupiter]

8-66 Two objects having masses $m_1 = 2.0$ kg and $m_2 = 4.0$ kg undergo head-on collisions. For the following initial ("i") and final ("f") velocities, identify the collisions as elastic, inelastic, or completely inelastic.

(a) $v_{1i} = 6.0$ m/s; $v_{2i} = 0$; $v_{1f} = v_{2f} = 2.0$ m/s

(b) $v_{1i} = 24$ m/s; $v_{2i} = 0$; $v_{1f} = -4.0$ m/s; $v_{2f} = 14$ m/s

(c) $v_{1i} = 12$ m/s; $v_{2i} = 0$; $v_{1f} = -4.0$ m/s; $v_{2f} = 8.0$ m/s

8-67 Imagine that you are standing still and someone is about to run into you, making a completely inelastic collision. In which situation would your speed after the collision be greater — if the runner has a large mass and small speed, or a small mass and large speed (but the same magnitude of momentum)? Show your work.

8-68 Two cars on an airtrack are equipped with spring bumpers and make an elastic collision. One car (mass 253 g) has an initial speed of 1.80 m/s. The other car has a mass of 232 g and is initially stationary. What is the velocity (magnitude and direction) of each car after the collision? [Ans. 0.08 m/s for 253-g car; 1.88 m/s for 232-g car; both cars move in same direction as initially moving car]

8-69 Two birds are flying horizontally and make a completely inelastic collision. Initially one bird (mass 2.3 kg) is flying east at 18 m/s, and the other is flying west at 19 m/s. Afterward, the two birds tumble together at 3.1 m/s east. What is the mass of the second bird? [Ans. 1.6 kg]

8-70 Two nuclei make a head-on elastic collision. One nucleus (mass m) is initially stationary. The other nucleus has an initial velocity $\mathbf{v}$, and a final velocity of $-\mathbf{v}/5$. What is the mass of this nucleus? [Ans. $2m/3$]

8-71 A girl is standing on a raft of mass 48 kg moving at 1.5 m/s west relative to the water. The girl then walks on the raft with a net velocity of 1.0 m/s at 30° north of west, relative to the water. As the girl walks, the velocity of the raft is 2.0 m/s at 10.5° south of west, relative to the water. Use a vector scale diagram to determine the approximate mass of the girl. Neglect viscous friction between the water and raft. [Ans. 35 kg]

8-72 Solve the previous problem using components.

8-73 Two hockey pucks of equal mass undergo a collision on a hockey rink. One puck is initially at rest, and the other is moving with a speed of 5.4 m/s. After the collision, the velocities of the pucks make angles of 33° and 46° relative to the original velocity of the moving puck.
(a) Make a diagram showing the initial and final situations. Make sure that the geometry of your diagram is such that momentum is conserved.
(b) Determine the speeds of the pucks after the collision.
[Ans. (b) 3.0 m/s; 4.0 m/s]

8-74 Solve the previous problem approximately by using a vector scale diagram.

8-75 Two trucks have a completely inelastic collision. After the collision, they have a velocity of 11 m/s at 35° south of west. Before the collision, one truck (mass 2.3×10^4 kg) has a velocity of 15 m/s at 51° south of west. Determine the initial velocity (magnitude and direction) of the other truck (mass 1.2×10^4 kg). [Ans. 9.1 m/s at 26° north of west]

8-76 In the previous problem, what percentage of the initial kinetic energy is "lost" in the collision? [Ans. 31%]

8-77 Two subatomic particles have a collision. Initially the more massive particle (A) is at rest and the less massive particle (B) is moving. After the collision, the velocities of A and B make angles of 67.8° and 30.0°, respectively, to the original direction of B's motion. The ratio of the final speeds of the particles (v_B/v_A) is 3.30. What is the ratio of the particle masses (m_B/m_A)? [Ans. 0.561]

APPLYING YOUR KNOWLEDGE

8-78 A variety of objects of different masses are moving at different speeds, but the momentum of each object has the same magnitude. Sketch the shape of the graph of speed vs. mass for these objects.

8-79 A piece of putty is dropped vertically onto a floor where it sticks. A rubber ball of the same mass is dropped from the same height onto the floor, and rebounds to almost its initial height. For which of these objects is the magnitude of the change of momentum greater during the collision with the floor? Explain your answer.

<u>8-80</u> Suppose that a small moving object hits a larger stationary object. In which situation is the force exerted by the small object (on the large object) of greater magnitude — if the small object bounces off the large object, or if it sticks to it? (Assume that the collision takes the same amount of time in either case.) Relate this to the use of rubber bullets by riot police.

8-81 *Fermi question:* A large cruise liner having a mass of 100 000 tonnes is arriving in a port. It is slowing down and is only 100 m from the dock. Estimate the magnitude of the liner's momentum and the force that is required to bring the liner to a halt just as it reaches the dock. [Ans. approx. 10^8 kg·m/s; 5×10^5 N]

8-82 A football of mass 0.41 kg is kicked from rest and given a velocity of 24 m/s at 29° above the horizontal. The ball is in contact with the kicker's foot for 8.2 ms. Determine:
(a) the horizontal and vertical components of the ball's momentum
(b) the horizontal and vertical components of the average force exerted by the foot on the ball (using momentum methods)
(c) the magnitude and direction of the force in (b)
[Ans. (a) 8.6 kg·m/s; 4.8 kg·m/s (b) 1.0×10^3 N; 5.8×10^2 N
(c) 1.2×10^3 N at 29° above horizontal]

8-83 Two rolling golf balls of the same mass make a collision. Initially, the velocity of one ball is 2.70 m/s east. After the collision, the velocities of the balls are 2.49 m/s at 62.8° north of west, and 2.37 m/s at 69.2° south of east. What is the unknown initial velocity (magnitude and direction)?
[Ans. 3.00 m/s west – Did you pay attention to significant digits in the north-south direction?]

8-84 A ball (mass 0.25 kg) is attached to a string of length 26 cm (Figure 8-22). The ball is raised so that the string is taut and horizontal, and the ball is released so that at the bottom of its swing it undergoes an elastic head-on collision with another ball (mass 0.21 kg) that is free to roll along a horizontal table.
(a) Just before the collision, what is the speed of the swinging ball?
(b) Just after the collision, what is the speed of the 0.21-kg ball?
[Ans. (a) 2.3 m/s (b) 2.5 m/s]

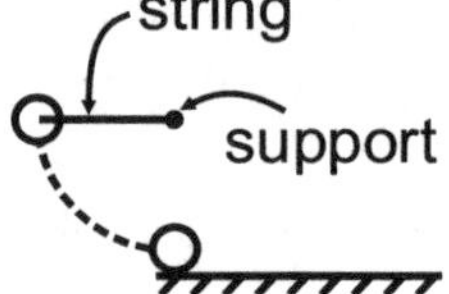

Figure 8-22
Question 8-84.

8-85 Figure 8-23 shows a device called a ballistic pendulum, which was used to determine speeds of bullets before the advent of modern electronic timing. A bullet is shot horizontally into a block of wood suspended by two strings. The bullet remains embedded in the wood, and the wood and bullet together swing upward.
(a) Explain why the *horizontal* momentum of the bullet-wood system is conserved during the collision, even though the strings exert tension forces on the wood.
(b) If the bullet and wood have masses m and M, respectively, and the bullet has an initial speed of v, determine an algebraic expression for the speed of the bullet

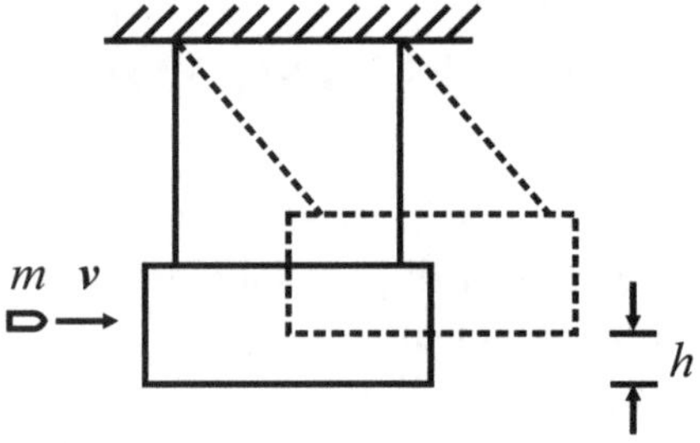

Figure 8-23
Question 8-85
(ballistic pendulum).

and wood immediately after the collision (before they swing upward) in terms of *m*, *M*, and *v*.
(c) As the bullet and wood swing up, what law of nature can be used to relate the maximum vertical height to the speed just after the collision?
(d) Use your answers from (b) and (c) to determine an expression for the maximum vertical height *h* in terms of *m*, *M*, *v*, and *g* (magnitude of gravitational acceleration).
(e) Now re-arrange your expression in (d) so that, if *h* is a known quantity, v can be calculated.
(f) If a bullet of mass 8.7 g hits a block of wood of mass 5.212 kg, and the bullet and wood swing up to a maximum height of 6.2 cm, what is the initial speed of the bullet?
[Ans. (b) $mv/(m+M)$ (d) $h = m^2v^2/\left(2g(m+M)^2\right)$
(e) $v = \left((m+M)/m\right)\sqrt{2gh}$ (f) 6.6×10^2 m/s]

8-86 A large ball of modeling clay (mass 4.5×10^2 g) is rolled on a tabletop so that it collides with a stationary small wooden box (mass 7.9×10^2 g). The collision is completely inelastic, and the ball and box then slide on the table for a distance of 5.1 cm. If the speed of the ball is 2.2 m/s just before the collision, determine: (a) the speed of the ball and box just after the collision
(b) the magnitude of the friction force acting on the ball and box
[Ans. (a) 0.80 m/s (b) 7.7 N]

8-87 Two linebackers simultaneously hit a stationary quarterback of mass 85 kg. Just before the completely inelastic collision, one linebacker (mass 82 kg) is running with a velocity of 8.3 m/s north, and the other (mass 95 kg) has a velocity of 6.7 m/s at 25° west of north. Just after the collision, what is the velocity (magnitude and direction) of the players?
[Ans. 4.9 m/s at 12° west of north]

8-88 Figure 8-24 shows a popular science toy called "Newton's cradle." It consists of a row of metallic spheres suspended by strings from a support. If one of the end spheres is lifted and allowed to swing down and collide with the line of spheres, the sphere at the other end rises up, and none of the other spheres moves appreciably. Why does this toy behave in this way? Try to find one of these toys and play with it. (Two spheres can also be lifted initially.)

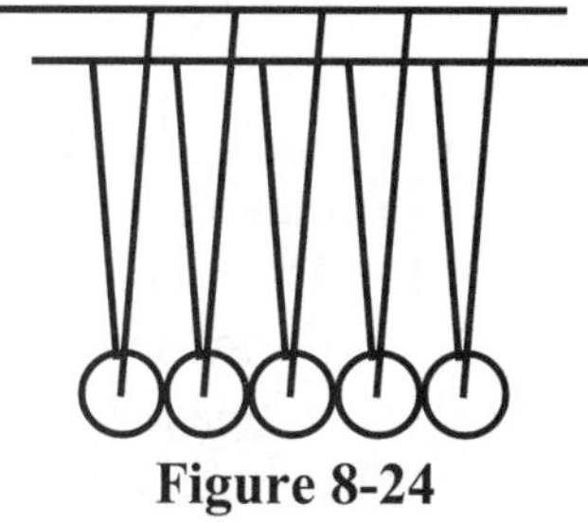
Figure 8-24
Question 8-88.

8-89 (a) *A ping pong ball as a deadly weapon.* Hold a ping pong ball above a "superball" and drop them together (touching) from waist height onto a hard floor. Watch out! Write down what you observe, and explain what happens. Assume that the collisions are elastic and that the mass of the ping pong ball is very much less than the mass of the "superball." Another pair of balls that works well is a baseball above a basketball, but safety precautions must *definitely* be taken in this case.
(b) Assuming elastic collisions, a very large mass difference between the balls, and negligible air resistance, show that the lighter ball in (a) will go upward to nine times its release height above the floor.

8-90 An object of mass m_1 and initial velocity v_{1i} undergoes a head-on elastic collision with a stationary object of mass m_2.
(a) In terms of m_1, m_2, and v_{1i}, determine the final velocity of each mass.

What do your answers in (a) become if:
(b) $m_1 = m_2$? (two billiard balls collide)
(c) $m_1 >> m_2$? (a bowling ball hits a superball)
(d) $m_1 << m_2$? (a superball hits a bowling ball)
[Ans. (a) $v_1' = (m_1 - m_2)v_{1i}/(m_1 + m_2)$; $v_2' = 2m_1v_{1i}/(m_1 + m_2)$ (b) $v_1' = 0$; $v_2' = v_{1i}$
(c) $v_1' \approx v_{1i}$; $v_2' \approx 2v_{1i}$ (d) $v_1' \approx -v_{1i}$; $v_2' \approx 2m_1v_{1i}/m_2$]

KEY OBJECTIVES

Having completed this chapter, you should now be able to do the following:

1. Define (linear) momentum.
2. State the relation between momentum, resultant force, and time interval, and use it in solving problems.
3. State the law of conservation of momentum.
4. Use conservation of momentum to solve problems (particularly involving collisions) in one and two dimensions using either vector scale diagrams or vector components.
5. Distinguish situations (such as collisions) in which momentum is not conserved from those in which momentum is conserved.
6. State the essential features of elastic, inelastic, and completely inelastic collisions.

ANSWERS TO SELECTED QUESTIONS

8-15 (a) yes (b) yes (c) no (d) yes (e) yes (f) yes (g) yes (h) no
8-19 (a) downward (b) upward (c) equal in magnitude (d) zero
(e) The momentum of the hairbrush-Earth system is conserved.
(f) Earth moves upward.
8-28 (a) completely inelastic (b) is equal to
(c) completely inelastic (d) inelastic
8-47 (d) 8-48 (e) 8-49 (c) 8-50 (d) 8-51 (a) 8-52 (c) 8-53 (a)
8-66 (a) completely inelastic (b) inelastic (c) elastic
8-67 small mass and large speed
8-79 rubber ball
8-80 larger force for bouncing off

CHAPTER 9

GRAVITATION

It is a wonderful experience to gaze up at the stars and planets on a warm summer night, away from bright city lights. People have been fascinated for millennia with the night sky, not only with its beauty, but also with its puzzles. Why do the moon and planets move relative to the background stars? Why are different regions of the sky visible at different times of the year? What keeps stars and planets together? And so on. Many of the dominant features of the universe are due to gravitation. The force of gravity is responsible for the very existence of planets and stars, as well as for the patterns of their motion. Even the intricate beauty of the rings of Saturn (Figure 9-1) can be explained through an understanding of gravitation.

Figure 9-1 *The rings of Saturn consist of particles in orbit around the planet, and the gaps in the rings are due to the gravitational effects of Saturn's moons, shown here in a photographic collage. Typical ring particles have diameters between 1 cm and 1 m, with a few as large as 20 m. Photo courtesy of NASA.*

9.1 LAW OF UNIVERSAL GRAVITATION

Many early peoples were interested in astronomy, especially in the movements of the sun, moon, and planets. The Chinese and the Babylonians kept careful records of astronomical events for several centuries before Christ. There is evidence of astronomical interest in the pre-Christian Assyrians and Egyptians, the Mayans in Central America, and Bronze Age people in northwestern Europe, especially in the British Isles.

In the Greek civilization from 600 BCE to 400 CE[1], there was a great deal of study in astronomy. In the second century CE, the Greco-Egyptian astronomer, Claudius Ptolemy, building on ideas of earlier Greeks, created a complex geometrical representation of the solar system that explained and predicted the motion of the planets very well. In this model, Earth was at the centre of the solar system; this geocentric (Earth-centred) hypothesis and Ptolemy's general representation were accepted throughout the Middle Ages, until the advent of the heliocentric (sun-centred) hypothesis of the Polish scientist, Nicholas Copernicus (1473-1543). The Greek

Figure 9-2 *This Greek stamp commemorates the heliocentric model of Aristarchus.*

[1]BCE: Before the Common (or Current or Christian) Era, sometimes written as BC (Before Christ). CE: Common (or Current or Christian) Era, sometimes written as AD (*Anno Domini*, i.e., "in the year of the Lord").

astronomer, Aristarchus, had proposed a heliocentric model (Figure 9-2) in the third century BCE, but it was not accepted.

In 1543, Copernicus published *De Revolutionibus Orbium Coelestium* ("On the Revolutions of the Heavenly Spheres"), in which planetary motion was described in terms of orbits around the sun. However, his ideas did not gain general acceptance for over a century, in part because the Roman Catholic Church upheld the Ptolemaic system. In the meantime, the German, Johannes Kepler (1571-1630), was studying the details of the planets' orbits and published his three laws of planetary motion early in the 1600s. His laws seemed to indicate that the sun occupied a special place in planetary orbits. Kepler's contemporary, Galileo Galilei[2] (1564-1642), accepted the Copernican hypothesis of the solar system, and his support of it resulted in a great deal of conflict between Galileo and the Church.

Did You Know? *The word "planet" is derived from the Greek word "planets" which means "wanderer." The planets wander in the sky relative to the stars, which appear essentially fixed relative to each other.*

Kepler recognized that a force pulled on the planets toward the sun, but he did not know the mathematical details of this force. It remained for Isaac Newton to unravel the force's secrets. (A short biography of Newton (1642-1727) is given in Section 5.7.) It is said that an apple falling from a tree triggered Newton's thought that the same fundamental force attracting the apple toward Earth also attracts the moon toward Earth, but this story might not in fact be true. His **law of universal gravitation** was published in the book called the *Principia* in 1687.

The law of universal gravitation states that **two particles are attracted to each other by a force directed along the line between them; the magnitude of the force is proportional to the product of the particles' masses, and inversely proportional to the square of the distance between the particles**. Mathematically, we write:

$$F \propto \frac{m_1 m_2}{r^2}$$

where F is the magnitude of the force, m_1 and m_2 are the two masses, and r is the distance between the particles (Figure 9-3). We can write this law as an equation by introducing a constant of proportionality, conventionally given the symbol G:

$$F = \frac{Gm_1 m_2}{r^2} \quad \textbf{(9-1)}$$

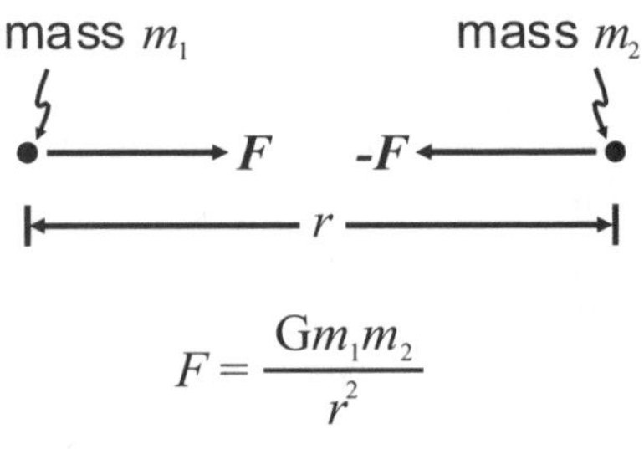

mass m_1 mass m_2

F $-F$

r

$$F = \frac{Gm_1 m_2}{r^2}$$

Figure 9-3 *Newton's law of universal gravitation.*

The constant, G, is known as the **universal gravitation constant**. In SI units, it has the numerical value of

$$G = 6.67 \times 10^{-11}\ \text{N·m}^2/\text{kg}^2$$

[2]A biographical profile of Galileo is given in Chapter 2.

Notice that the gravitational force is a mutual force between the two objects; each object feels an attractive force toward the other. This is in complete agreement with Newton's third law of motion, of course.

Newton was able to *derive* Kepler's laws of planetary motion from his law of universal gravitation, and thus was able to explain all the details of planetary orbits — shapes, periods, etc. — from one basic law. The voyage of discovery and explanation started by Ptolemy and other early Greeks had been completed by Newton.

In the following sample problem, we illustrate that the gravitational force is rather weak unless the masses are extremely large.

Sample Problem 9-1

Determine the magnitude of the gravitational force between:
(a) two 1.0-kg masses separated by a distance of 1.0 m
(b) Earth (mass 5.98×10^{24} kg) and the sun (mass 1.99×10^{30} kg) separated by 1.50×10^{8} km.

Solution: (a) This problem involves only straightforward substitution into Eqn. 9-1 for the gravitational force.

$$F = \frac{Gm_1m_2}{r^2} = \frac{\left(6.67\times10^{-11}\ \text{N}\cdot\text{m}^2/\text{kg}^2\right)\left(1.0\ \text{kg}\right)\left(1.0\ \text{kg}\right)}{\left(1.0\ \text{m}\right)^2} = 6.7\times10^{-11}\ \text{N}$$

Hence, the gravitational force between the 1.0-kg masses is only 6.7×10^{-11} N in magnitude.

(b) For the Earth-sun system[3], we first convert the separation from kilometres to metres:

$$1.50\times10^{8}\ \text{km}\times\frac{10^{3}\ \text{m}}{1\ \text{km}} = 1.50\times10^{11}\ \text{m}$$

Then, substituting numbers into Eqn. 9-1:

$$\begin{aligned} F &= \frac{Gm_1m_2}{r^2} \\ &= \frac{\left(6.67\times10^{-11}\ \text{N}\cdot\text{m}^2/\text{kg}^2\right)\left(5.98\times10^{24}\ \text{kg}\right)\left(1.99\times10^{30}\ \text{kg}\right)}{\left(1.50\times10^{11}\ \text{m}\right)^2} \\ &= 3.53\times10^{22}\ \text{N} \end{aligned}$$

[3]Notice that the law of universal gravitation refers to "particles," and Earth and the sun are obviously not particles. However, since the Earth-sun distance is very large compared to the size of the sun and Earth, they can be considered to be particles. Later in this section, we discuss how to apply the law of universal gravitation to extended objects that cannot be treated as particles.

Thus, the gravitational force between the sun and Earth and has a magnitude of 3.53×10^{22} N. This force is very large because of the huge masses involved, which more than compensate for the large Earth-sun distance (even though this distance is squared in Eqn. 9-1).

Sample Problem 9-2

Two objects separated by a distance, *d*, exert a mutual gravitational force. If the same objects are separated by a distance of *5d*, by what factor will the force have increased or decreased?

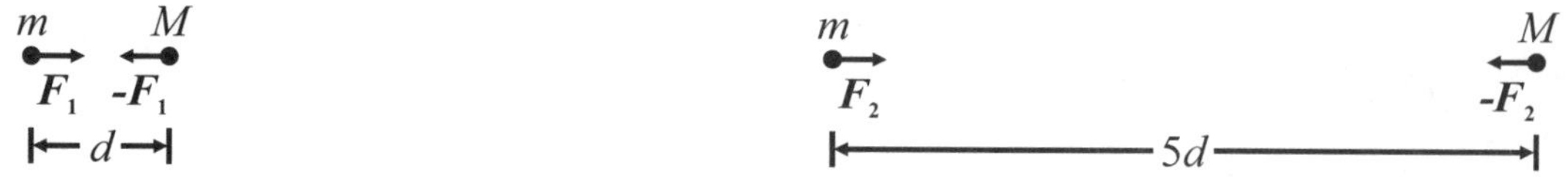

Figure 9-4 *Sample Problem 9-2.*

Solution: Let the two masses be m and M, and let the magnitude of the force be F_1 at separation d and F_2 at separation $5d$ (Figure 9-4). We are asked to find F_2 relative to F_1 . When the separation is d, we have:

$$F_1 = \frac{GmM}{d^2} \qquad \text{Eqn. [1]}$$

When the separation is $5d$:

$$F_2 = \frac{GmM}{(5d)^2} \qquad \text{Eqn. [2]}$$

Dividing Eqn. [2] by [1]:

$$\begin{aligned}\frac{F_2}{F_1} &= \frac{GmM}{(5d)^2} \div \frac{GmM}{d^2} \\ &= \frac{GmM}{25d^2} \times \frac{d^2}{GmM} \\ &= \frac{1}{25}\end{aligned}$$

Therefore, as the separation increases from d to $5d$, the force decreases by a factor of 25.

> ***Math Tip:*** *Note that when we say that a quantity increases or decreases by a factor, the factor is conventionally a number greater than 1. Thus, we normally would say that the force decreases by a factor of 25, not by a factor of 1/25.*

Determination of G

Because the gravitational force between non-astronomical objects (such as you and your best friend) is so small, the determination of the numerical value of the gravitation constant G is not easy. The first experiment that gave an accurate value of G was performed by the Englishman Henry Cavendish (1731-1810) in 1798, more than a century after Newton published his gravitation law.

Cavendish's torsional-balance apparatus is sketched in Figure 9-5. Two small lead spheres are fastened to the ends of a light horizontal rod, which is suspended at its centre by a fine fibre. Two larger lead spheres are positioned close to the small spheres and attract them gravitationally. The small spheres move slightly toward the large ones, causing the fibre to twist very slightly. If it has already been determined how much force is required to twist the fibre through various angles, then the gravitational attractive force of the spheres, and hence G, can be calculated.

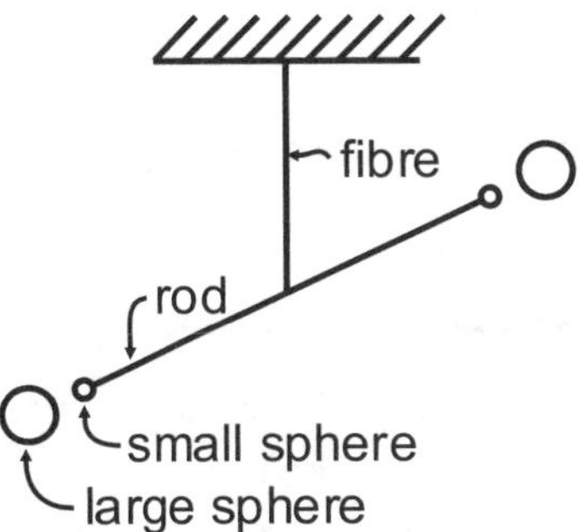

Figure 9-5 *The apparatus used by Henry Cavendish in 1798 to determine G.*

Because gravity is such a weak force, it is difficult to measure G precisely, and the experimental uncertainty in its value is rather large in comparison with uncertainties in other fundamental constants. As of February 2007, the best measured value of G was $(6.674 \pm 0.001) \times 10^{-11}$ N·m^2/kg^2 or 6.674×10^{-11} N·m^2/kg^2 ± 0.015%. While this percentage uncertainty might seem small to you, the uncertainty in the mass of an electron is much smaller, only 0.000 017%, and the charge on an electron is known to within 0.000 009%. If you are interested in the most recent values of any of the fundamental physical constants and their uncertainties, check out http://physics.nist.gov/cuu/Constants/.

Gravitational Force Between Extended Objects

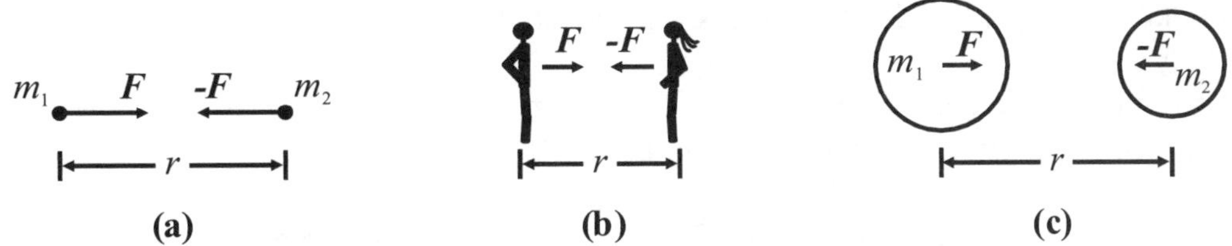

Figure 9-6 **(a)** *For particles, $F = Gm_1m_2/r^2$.*
(b) *For objects that are large compared to "r", $F = Gm_1m_2/r^2$ does not give an accurate value for F.*
(c) *Exception to (b): if the objects are spheres with spherical symmetry, $F = Gm_1m_2/r^2$.*

Notice that the law of universal gravitation refers to two "particles," that is, two objects small in size compared to the distance between them (Figure 9-6 (a)). If we want to determine the gravitational force between two objects that are large relative to the distance between them (for example, two people standing close together as shown in Figure 9-6 (b)), we cannot simply use the gravitation law. That is, we cannot just use $F = Gm_1m_2/r^2$ with r being the distance between the centres of the objects. We would have to use calculus to add up (vectorially) the gravitational forces (given by the gravitation law) between all the small particles that make up the objects — not an easy task!

There is one exception to this: if the objects are spheres that have spherical symmetry[4], then we can use the gravitation law no matter how close together the spheres might be. In this case, the distance r is the distance between the centres of the spheres (Figure 9-6 (c)). For a person standing on Earth, the gravitation law gives a very good value for the force of gravity because (i) Earth's shape is very close to being a sphere with spherical symmetry, and (ii) the size of the person is small relative to the distance from the person to the centre of Earth.

Practice

9-1 (a) What is the gravitational force (magnitude and direction) exerted by Earth (mass 5.98×10^{24} kg) on the moon (mass 7.35×10^{22} kg)? Their average separation distance (centre-to-centre) is 3.8×10^8 m. (b) What is the gravitational force (magnitude and direction) exerted by the moon on Earth?
[Ans. (a) 2.0×10^{20} N toward centre of Earth (b) 2.0×10^{20} N toward centre of moon]

9-2 Two objects are moved farther and farther apart. Sketch the shape of the graph of the magnitude of the gravitational force on each object vs. the distance between the objects.

<u>9-3</u> In which of the following situations could we determine the magnitude of the gravitational force between the objects A and B by straightforward substitution of numbers into $F = Gm_1m_2/r^2$ (assuming that values for m_A, m_B, and r were provided)?
(a) Jupiter (A) and Europa (B), one of Jupiter's moons
(b) a man (A) and a woman (B) hugging each other
(c) a baseball (A), travelling from a pitcher to a catcher, and Earth (B)
(d) two basketballs (A and B), sitting on a gym floor
(e) two books (A and B) beside each other on a bookshelf

9-4 As a meteor travels toward Earth, the Earth-meteor distance is halved. By what factor does the Earth-meteor gravitational force increase? [Ans. 4]

9-5 As a spaceship moves away from Earth, the gravitational force between them decreases by 75%. Be what factor has the spaceship-Earth distance increased? [Ans. 2]

9-6 At a certain distance above Earth's surface, the gravitational force on an object is 1/36 of its value at Earth's surface. What is this distance as a multiple of Earth's radius, r_E? [Ans. $5r_E$]

---

[4]Spherical symmetry means that at all points located the same distance from the centre of the sphere, there is the same composition, density, etc. These properties must not depend on the *direction* from the centre to a point, only on the *distance*. The following objects have spherical symmetry (or close to it): baseballs, planets, and gumballs. Any sphere with constant density also has spherical symmetry. If you were to form a sphere by gluing together half a baseball (simply sliced through the centre) and a hemispherical rock of the same radius, it would not have spherical symmetry because, at a given distance from the centre, you could find either rock or baseball "stuffing," depending on the direction from the centre.

9-7 What is the magnitude of the gravitational force between two baseballs, each having mass 145 g, whose centres are separated by 35.0 cm? [Ans. 1.14×10^{-11} N]

9-8 The orbit of Venus is almost a perfect circle around the sun. What is the acceleration (magnitude and direction) of Venus? The Venus-sun distance is 1.1×10^{8} km. The mass of Venus is 4.9×10^{24} kg; of the sun, 1.99×10^{30} kg.
[Ans. 1.1×10^{-2} m/s^2 toward centre of Sun]

9-9 Determine the resultant gravitational force (magnitude and direction) on the moon (mass 7.35×10^{22} kg) due to the attraction of the sun (mass 1.99×10^{30} kg) and Earth (mass 5.98×10^{24} kg). The Earth-moon and sun-moon separations are 3.84×10^{5} km and 1.50×10^{8} km, respectively. Assume that the Earth, moon, and sun have the positions shown in Figure 9-7. [Ans. 4.77×10^{20} N at 24.6° from line to sun]

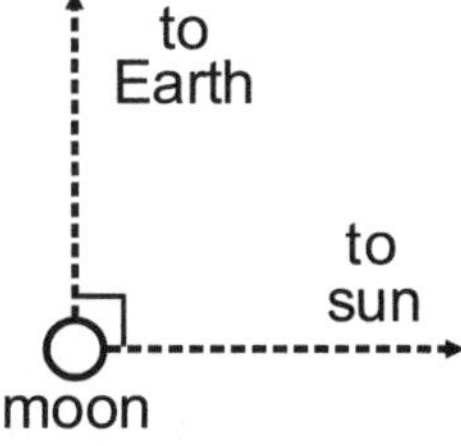

Figure 9-7 *Question 9-9.*

9.2 GRAVITY DUE TO PLANETS, STARS, ETC.

Imagine trying to "weigh the Earth" — we cannot just pick it up and place it on a balance (Figure 9-8). How *do* we know the mass of Earth? Cavendish's determination of the universal gravitation constant, G, in 1798 was important not only because it established a value for a fundamental constant of nature, but also because it permitted the measurement of the mass of Earth.

Figure 9-8 *How can we measure the mass of Earth?*

Figure 9-9 shows a person of mass m standing on Earth, having mass M and radius r. From the law of universal gravitation, the magnitude of the force of gravity on the person (and on the Earth) is:

$$F = \frac{GmM}{r^2}$$

In Section 5.3, we showed that this gravitational force is often written as $F = mg$, where g is the magnitude of the acceleration due to gravity. Hence:

$$mg = \frac{GmM}{r^2}$$

Dividing by m:

$$g = \frac{GM}{r^2} \qquad \textbf{(9-2)}$$

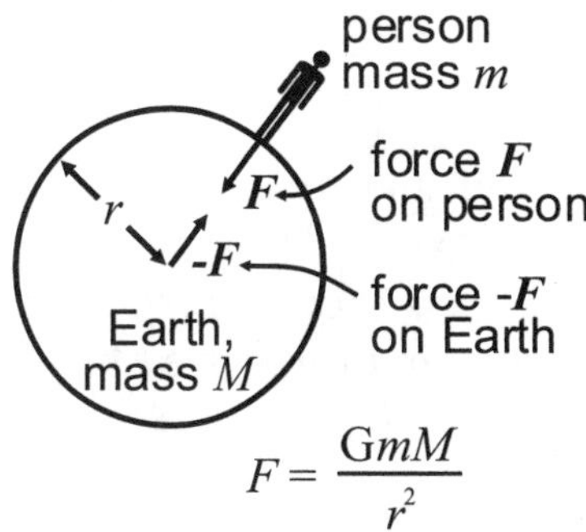

Figure 9-9 *The force of gravity on a person standing on Earth.*

Thus, the gravitational acceleration at the surface of Earth depends on the universal gravitation constant, and on the mass and radius of Earth; it does not depend on the mass (m) of the person (or any other object). If g, G, and r are known, then M can be determined. The acceleration g is easy to measure, G is known from Cavendish's experiment (and from more recent ones), and r has been known reasonably well since the time of the early Greeks. Re-arranging the above equation to solve for M, and substituting in values for g, G, and r:

$$M = \frac{gr^2}{\text{G}} = \frac{(9.80\ \text{m/s}^2)(6.37\times10^6\ \text{m})^2}{6.67\times10^{-11}\ \text{N}\cdot\text{m}^2/\text{kg}^2} = 5.96\times10^{24}\ \text{kg}$$

Our result for Earth's mass differs somewhat from the accepted value of 5.98×10^{24} kg because we assumed that Earth is a sphere and that g is constant at all points on Earth's surface. In actual fact, Earth is somewhat nonspherical and g is not constant, as discussed in more detail later in this section.

Notice that the relation $g = \text{G}M/r^2$ is valid not only for objects on Earth's surface, but also for objects *above* Earth's surface. In this case, r represents the distance from an object to Earth's centre, and g is not 9.80 m/s^2 (except very close to Earth's surface). The symbol g still represents the magnitude of the gravitational acceleration, which decreases with increasing distance r from the centre of Earth, according to $g = \text{G}M/r^2$. We can also use $g = \text{G}M/r^2$ for other planets, stars, etc., by simply substituting the appropriate mass M.

Sample Problem 9-3

For a satellite of mass 225 kg located 1.2×10^7 m above Earth's surface, determine the magnitudes and directions of (a) the gravitational force, and (b) the resulting acceleration.

Solution: (a) The magnitude of the force can be calculated from the law of universal gravitation:

$$F = \frac{\text{G}m_1m_2}{r^2}$$

Let m_1 and m_2 represent the mass of the satellite and Earth, respectively. The separation r is the distance from the satellite to the *centre* (not the surface) of Earth (Figure 9-10), and therefore is the sum of the given height above Earth's surface and Earth's radius (average value 6.37×10^6 m). Thus:

$$\begin{aligned} r &= (6.37\times10^6 + 1.2\times10^7)\ \text{m} \\ &= (0.637\times10^7 + 1.2\times10^7)\ \text{m} \\ &= 1.8\times10^7\ \text{m} \end{aligned}$$

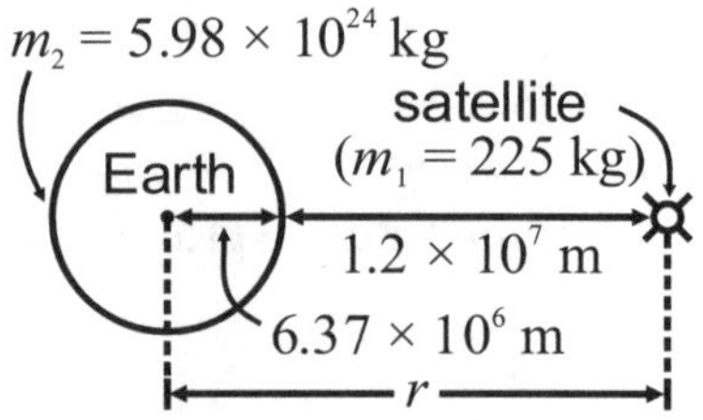

$m_2 = 5.98 \times 10^{24}$ kg
Earth
satellite ($m_1 = 225$ kg)
1.2×10^7 m
6.37×10^6 m
r

Figure 9-10
Sample Problem 9-3.

We can now substitute numbers to calculate F:

$$F = \frac{(6.67\times10^{-11}\ \text{N}\cdot\text{m}^2/\text{kg}^2)(225\ \text{kg})(5.98\times10^{24}\ \text{kg})}{(1.8\times10^{7}\ \text{m})^2}$$

$$= 2.7\times10^{2}\ \text{N}$$

Thus, the gravitational force on the satellite is 2.7×10^2 N toward the centre of Earth.

(b) To find the gravitational acceleration of the satellite, we will use two different, but equivalent, methods. First, we will use Newton's second law ($F_R = m_1a$), since we already know the resultant force magnitude, F_R , and the mass. Afterward, we will use the expression $g = GM/r^2$ that we derived above, where M is the mass of Earth and r is the distance from the satellite to Earth's centre. Using Newton's second law:

$$F_R = m_1 a$$

Hence:

$$a = \frac{F_R}{m_1} = \frac{2.7\times10^{2}\ \text{N}}{225\ \text{kg}} = 1.2\ \text{m/s}^2$$

Now using the other method:

$$g = \frac{GM}{r^2} = \frac{(6.67\times10^{-11}\ \text{N}\cdot\text{m}^2/\text{kg}^2)(5.98\times10^{24}\ \text{kg})}{(1.8\times10^{7}\ \text{m})^2} = 1.2\ \text{m/s}^2$$

Thus, the acceleration of the satellite is 1.2 m/s^2 toward the centre of Earth.

Sample Problem 9-4

Calculate the magnitude of the surface gravitational acceleration on Mars, which has a mass of 6.4×10^{23} kg and a radius of 3.4×10^6 m.

Solution: This problem involves only a simple substitution into Eqn. 9-2:

$$g = \frac{GM}{r^2}$$

$$= \frac{(6.67\times10^{-11}\ \text{N}\cdot\text{m}^2/\text{kg}^2)(6.4\times10^{23}\ \text{kg})}{(3.4\times10^{6}\ \text{m})^2}$$

$$= 3.7\ \text{m/s}^2$$

Thus, the surface gravitational acceleration on Mars has a magnitude of 3.7 m/s^2, roughly one-third of that on Earth. Table 9.1 gives the magnitudes of the surface gravitational accelerations (relative to that on Earth) for all the planets. Appendix 6 provides other planetary data, such as mass, radius, etc.

Table 9.1
Magnitudes of Surface Gravitational Accelerations (Relative to Earth $g = 1$)

Planet	Surface gravity (Earth $g = 1$)
Mercury	0.39
Venus	0.90
Earth	1.00
Mars	0.38
Jupiter	2.58
Saturn	1.11
Uranus	1.07
Neptune	1.40

Variations in *g* on Earth

Because Earth is rotating about its axis once per day, its shape is not perfectly spherical — it bulges slightly at the equator and is slightly "squashed" at the poles. The equatorial radius is 6378 km, the polar radius 6357 km. As a consequence, a person standing at the equator is farther away from the dense core near Earth's centre than is a person standing at a pole, and the gravitational force and acceleration are therefore less at the equator. Because of this nonsphericity, the difference between the equatorial and polar *g*-values is 0.18%, and *g*-values in general increase with increasing latitude (i.e., as one moves toward a pole). Note the phrase "dense core" above; if Earth were of uniform density, the 0.18% difference would be only 0.06%. Most other planets are also nonspherical, some such as Saturn visibly so (Figure 9-11).

Figure 9-11 *Notice the difference in the polar and equatorial radii of Saturn (shown here with its moons photographically superimposed.) Measure the radii on the photograph if you are not convinced. Photo courtesy of NASA.*

An additional effect due to Earth's rotation is a centrifugal decrease in the measured *g*-value relative to Earth (Section 6.3). This effect is maximum at the equator and zero at the poles, and produces an additional increase in *g*-values as latitude increases. The polar *g*-value is 0.35% larger than the equatorial value because of the centrifugal effect.

Gravitational force and acceleration on Earth's surface also depend on elevation. If you climb a mountain, you are moving farther from Earth's dense core and gravity becomes weaker. The decrease in *g* is roughly 2.0×10^{-3} m/s^2 for every kilometre of land elevation. Note that this is smaller than the "free-air" decrease of 3.1×10^{-3} m/s^2 for every kilometre that you go up in the *air*, say in an airplane. If you are climbing a mountain, the mountain beneath you exerts a downward gravitational force on you, and thus the *g*-value does not decrease as rapidly as if you went up in an airplane.

In addition to variations in g-value due to Earth's nonsphericity, the centrifugal effect, and elevation, there are also variations due to the local density of Earth. For example, mineral deposits have high densities that produce local increases in g. Geologists use local variations to assist them in searching for minerals, oil, and gas.

Table 9.2 gives the latitude, altitude, and g-values for a number of different locations on Earth. Notice that for the places close to sea level, the g-values increase as the latitude increases. The lowest g-value in the table is for Mexico City, which is close to the equator and also has a high altitude. As a result of low g and low air density at Mexico City, athletic performances there are improved in events such as the long jump and triple jump. For example, a world-class triple-jumper can jump about 13 cm farther at Mexico City than at Moscow. About 35% of the 13-cm increase is due to reduced gravity, and 65% to decreased air resistance. It is not surprising that a large number of world and Olympic records in track and field have been set at Mexico City.

Table 9.2
Values of g at Various Locations

Location	Latitude	Altitude (m)	g (m/s²)
Mexico City	19.3° N	2300	9.779
Los Angeles	34.0° N	50	9.796
Montreal	45.4° N	50	9.806
Moscow	55.5° N	150	9.816
North Pole	90.0° N	0	9.832

Practice

9-10 The mass of Earth is 5.98×10^{24} kg. Determine the magnitude and direction of the gravitational acceleration at a point in space located 7.4×10^{7} m from the centre of Earth. [Ans. 7.3×10^{-2} m/s^2]

9-11 If we represent the magnitude of Earth's surface gravitational acceleration as 1 g, then what are the magnitudes of the accelerations (as fractions or multiples of g) at the following distances above Earth's surface? (a) 1 Earth radius (b) 2 Earth radii (c) 9 Earth radii
[Ans. (a) $g/4$ (b) $g/9$ (c) $g/100$]

9-12 A satellite is in a circular orbit 655 km above the surface of Earth, which has an average radius of 6.37×10^{6} m and a mass of 5.98×10^{24} kg. Determine the magnitude of the gravitational acceleration at this height. [Ans. 8.06 m/s^2]

9-13 A satellite above Earth experiences a gravitational acceleration of 4.5 m/s^2 in magnitude. (a) How far above Earth's surface is the satellite? The average radius of Earth is 6.37×10^{6} m. Do not use the mass of Earth in your calculations, but *do* use surface $g = 9.8$ m/s^2. (b) If the mass of the satellite is 5.6×10^{2} kg, what is the magnitude of the gravitational force on the satellite? [Ans. (a) 3.0×10^{6} m (b) 2.5×10^{3} N]

9-14 If a planet of the same mass as Earth had a radius 0.50 times that of Earth, what would be the magnitude of the planet's surface gravitational acceleration, as a multiple of Earth's surface *g*? [Ans. 4.0 *g*]

9-15 What would be the magnitude of a planet's surface gravitational acceleration (as a multiple of Earth's surface *g*) if it had a mass 0.25 times that of Earth, and a radius 0.60 times that of Earth? [Ans. 0.70 *g*]

9-16 (a) Calculate the magnitude of Mercury's surface gravitational acceleration. Its mass is 3.3×10^{23} kg and its diameter is 4878 km.
(b) Compare your answer to the value given in Table 9.1.
[Ans. (a) 3.7 m/s^2]

9-17 The moon has a radius of 1.74×10^3 km, and a surface gravitational acceleration of magnitude 1.6 m/s^2. (a) What is the mass of the moon?
(b) What would be the magnitude of the gravitational force on *you* if you were on the moon?
[Ans. (a) 7.3×10^{22} kg]

<u>9-18</u> Does the gravitational acceleration on Earth's surface increase, decrease, or stay the same: (a) as latitude increases (at constant elevation)?
(b) as elevation increases (at constant latitude)?

9-19 A satellite of mass 367 kg in a circular orbit around Earth has a speed of 3.9 km/s and an elevation of 2.5×10^7 m from the centre of Earth. Using only the numbers provided, determine the magnitude and direction of:
(a) the acceleration of the satellite (b) the gravitational force on the satellite.
[Ans. (a) 0.61 m/s^2 toward the centre of Earth (b) 2.2×10^2 N toward the centre of Earth]

9-20 A small rock is heading toward Jupiter with a speed of 5.1 m/s. Its distance to the centre of Jupiter (mass 1.90×10^{27} kg) is 5.7×10^5 km. In a time of 3.0 s, (a) how far will the rock travel, and (b) what will be its new speed? (In such a short time, the rock will travel only a small fraction of the total distance to Jupiter, and thus the gravitational force on the rock will be essentially constant.) [Ans. (a) 17 m (b) 6.3 m/s]

9.3 GRAVITATIONAL FIELD

Physicists often like to think of forces in terms of quantities called fields. For example, there are gravitational fields, electric fields, and magnetic fields — you have probably heard of Earth's magnetic field. We will illustrate the way that fields "work" by first discussing Earth's gravitational field. Because Earth has mass, it creates in the space around it a gravitational field. If another object with mass (say the moon) encounters this field, it experiences a gravitational force. So the force is a two-step phenomenon: Earth creates the field, and the field interacts with the moon to produce the force. Fields are more than just abstract concepts; in advanced physics courses, students learn that fields are real physical entities that can carry energy and momentum.

To understand gravitational field in a quantitative way, consider first the gravitational force on a mass placed at a point P in space at a distance of 9×10^6 m from the centre of Earth. (This point is about 2600 km above Earth's surface.) The magnitude of the gravitational force on a mass at P can be calculated from Newton's law of universal gravitation: $F = \mathrm{G}m_1m_2/r^2$ where m_1 is the mass at P, m_2 is the mass of Earth, $r = 9 \times 10^6$ m, and G is the universal gravitational constant. For example, if a 1-kg mass is placed at P, the gravitational force turns out to be 5 N in magnitude. For a 2-kg mass, the force magnitude is 10 N; for a 3-kg mass, it is 15 N, and so on. (Notice that the magnitude of the force is proportional to the amount of mass placed at P, that is, $F \propto m_1$. This follows directly from $F = \mathrm{G}m_1m_2/r^2$ of course.)

Suppose that we now divide the force magnitudes determined above by the corresponding masses (m_1). For example, divide 15 N by 3 kg, giving 5 N/kg, or divide 10 N by 2 kg, again giving 5 N/kg. The result is a constant, 5 N/kg in this particular instance. This quantity (force magnitude per unit mass) is *defined* to be Earth's gravitational field magnitude at point P. It does not depend on how much mass is placed at P, but it does depend on the mass of Earth, and on the distance between P and Earth's centre. (Earth's mass and the distance were used in the original calculations of the force magnitudes.)

We now can deal with **gravitational field** in a more general way. Suppose that we want to determine the gravitational field at some point P which is at a distance r away from a mass M. We can imagine placing a "test mass" m at this position, and measuring the gravitational force $\boldsymbol{F}$ on this mass. The gravitational field is defined as the ratio of the force $\boldsymbol{F}$ to the mass m. In words, the **gravitational field created at a point P by an object is the gravitational force produced per unit mass of another object placed at P**. The gravitational field is a *vector* quantity, having a magnitude and direction. Since the gravitational force is attractive, the force vector $\boldsymbol{F}$ points toward the mass M; dividing this vector by mass m gives a vector, the gravitational field, which also points toward M. We think of the field existing at point P even when there is no actual mass (m) placed there; the field exists in the space around M.

Now a mathematical expression for the magnitude of gravitational field can be developed. The magnitude of force on a mass m at a distance r away from another mass M is $F = \mathrm{G}mM/r^2$. The magnitude of the gravitational field due to M is defined as F/m, which gives

$$\text{magnitude of gravitational field} = \frac{\mathrm{G}M}{r^2} \qquad \textbf{(9-3)}$$

As mentioned above, the direction of the gravitational field is toward the object (mass M) creating the field (Figure 9-12).

Notice that the magnitude of the gravitational field, $\mathrm{G}M/r^2$, is the same as the magnitude of the gravitational acceleration given in Section 9.2. The gravitational field and the gravitational acceleration have the same direction as well — since the field is force divided by mass (vector divided by scalar), the field has the same direction as the force, and this is the same direction as the acceleration (by Newton's second law, $\boldsymbol{a} = \boldsymbol{F}/m$). Hence, gravitational acceleration and gravitational field represent essentially the same vector, and the same symbol is used for both: $\boldsymbol{g}$. Hence, Eqn. 9-3 can be rewritten as:

$$g = \frac{GM}{r^2} \quad \text{(magnitude of gravitational field)} \qquad \textbf{(9-4)}$$

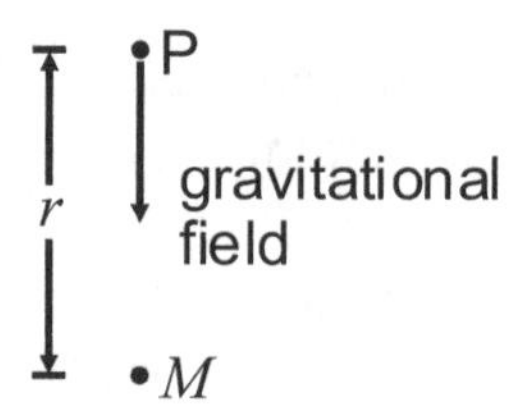

Figure 9-12
The gravitational field at point P, which is a distance r away from mass M, has a magnitude of GM/r^2. The direction of the field is toward M.

We now have two different interpretations for $g = GM/r^2$. The quantity g can represent the magnitude of either the gravitational acceleration or the gravitational field. To distinguish between the two concepts, the unit of newtons per kilogram (N/kg), i.e., force/mass, is customarily used for field, and metres per second squared (m/s^2) is used for acceleration. Thus, we say that at Earth's surface the gravitational field has a magnitude of 9.80 N/kg, and the gravitational acceleration has a magnitude of 9.80 m/s^2. These units are actually equivalent, of course; since $N = kg \cdot m/s^2$, then $N/kg = (N = kg \cdot m/s^2)/kg = m/s^2$.

Calculating Gravitational Force from Gravitational Field

If the gravitational field $\boldsymbol{g}$ at some position is known, then the gravitational force $\boldsymbol{F}$ exerted on an object of mass m placed at that position can easily be determined. Since field is force per unit mass, then the force is just the product of the mass and the field:

$$\boldsymbol{F} = m\boldsymbol{g} \quad \text{(gravitational force)} \qquad \textbf{(9-5)}$$

Sample Problem 9-5

(a) What is the gravitational field (magnitude and direction) due to Earth at a height of 2.00 Earth radii above Earth's surface? The average radius of Earth is 6.37×10^6 m and its mass is 5.98×10^{24} kg. (b) What is the gravitational force on a satellite of mass 178 kg at this height?

Solution: (a) The magnitude of the gravitational field is given by Eqn. 9-4:

$$g = \frac{GM}{r^2}$$

where M is the mass of Earth and r is the distance from the centre of Earth. In this particular problem, r = 3.00 Earth radii = 3.00 (6.37×10^6 m) = 1.91×10^7 m.

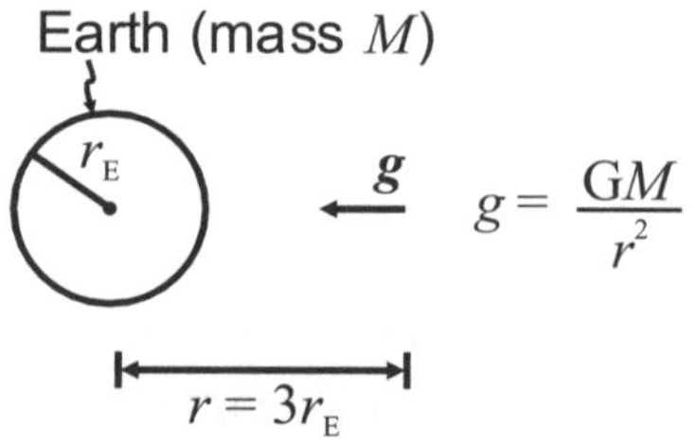

Earth (mass M)

r_E $\boldsymbol{g}$ $g = \frac{GM}{r^2}$

$r = 3r_E$

Figure 9-13
Sample Problem 9-5.

Substituting numbers:

$$g = \frac{\left(6.67 \times 10^{-11}\ \text{N} \cdot \text{m}^2/\text{kg}^2\right)\left(5.98 \times 10^{24}\ \text{kg}\right)}{\left(1.91 \times 10^7\ \text{m}\right)^2} = 1.09\ \text{N/kg}$$

The direction of the field is the same as the direction as the gravitational force exerted by Earth on any mass at this position, that is, toward the centre of Earth (Figure 9-13). Thus, the gravitational field is 1.09 N/kg toward the centre of Earth.

(b) The magnitude of the gravitational force on the satellite is the product of the satellite's mass and the magnitude of the gravitational field (Eqn. 9-5):

$$F = mg = (1.78 \text{ kg})(1.09 \text{ N/kg}) = 194 \text{ N}$$

Thus, the force on the satellite is 194 N toward the centre of Earth.

 **Practice**

9-21 What is the gravitational field (magnitude and direction) of the sun at the position of Earth? The mass of the sun is 1.99×10^{30} kg and the sun-Earth distance is 1.50×10^{11} m.
[Ans. 5.90×10^{-3} N/kg toward the centre of the sun]

9-22 If the total gravitational field at a point in interstellar space is 5.42×10^{-9} N/kg in magnitude, what is the magnitude of the gravitational force at this point on an object of mass: (a) 1.00 kg? (b) 2.00 kg? [Ans. (a) 5.42×10^{-9} N (b) 1.08×10^{-8} N]

9-23 (a) On the surface of Titan, a moon of Saturn, the gravitational field has a magnitude of 1.3 N/kg. Titan's mass is 1.3×10^{23} kg. What is its radius in kilometres?
(b) What is the magnitude of the force on gravity on a hamburger (mass 0.181 kg) on Titan?
[Ans. (a) 2.6×10^{3} km (b) 0.24 N]

9-24 What is the gravitational field (magnitude and direction) due to a golf ball of mass 0.045 kg at a distance of 15 cm from the ball?
[Ans. 1.3×10^{-10} N/kg toward the centre of the ball]

9-25 Given only that Earth's surface gravitational field has a magnitude of 9.80 N/kg, determine the distance (as a multiple of Earth's radius, r_E) above Earth's surface at which the field is 3.20 N/kg. [Ans. 0.75 r_E]

9-26 The moon and Earth have masses of 7.35×10^{22} kg and 5.98×10^{24} kg, respectively, and are separated by a centre-to-centre distance of 3.84×10^{8} m. At what distance from the centre of Earth, on the Earth-moon line, is the total gravitational field due to Earth and the moon zero?
[Ans. 3.46×10^{8} m]

9.4 ORBITS AND WEIGHTLESSNESS

Here are some common questions asked by students: If satellites are attracted gravitationally toward Earth, why do they not just fall into Earth? If planets are attracted toward the sun, why do they not plummet into the sun and meet a fiery end? What does "weightlessness" mean — is the force of gravity zero on astronauts in a space shuttle? These are good questions. We first deal with the case of satellites orbiting Earth.

Suppose that you drop a hamburger from rest. We can calculate how far it falls in 1.0 s by using one of the equations for constant-acceleration kinematics given in Chapter 4:

$$y = y_0 + v_{0y}\, t + \tfrac{1}{2} a_y\, t^2$$

The initial vertical velocity, v_{0y}, is zero, and assuming that the hamburger starts at $y_0 = 0$ m we have:

$$y = \tfrac{1}{2} a_y\, t^2$$

Choosing $+y$ to be downward means that $a_y = +9.80 \text{ m/s}^2$, and using the given time of 1.0 s:

$$y = \tfrac{1}{2} a_y\, t^2 = \tfrac{1}{2}\left(9.80 \text{ m/s}^2\right)(1.0 \text{ s})^2 = 4.9 \text{ m}$$

Thus, the hamburger falls 4.9 m in 1.0 s. Now suppose that instead of dropping the hamburger, you throw it horizontally. Since the initial motion is horizontal, the initial vertical component of velocity is zero, just as it was for the dropped hamburger. Therefore, the hamburger still falls 4.9 m vertically in 1.0 s, but in addition moves horizontally at constant velocity. If the initial horizontal velocity is, say, 2.0 m/s, then in 2.0 s, the hamburger moves 2.0 m horizontally as well as 4.9 m vertically. The vertical motion of the hamburger is unaffected by the horizontal motion, so it does not matter how fast you throw the hamburger — it still falls 4.9 m in 1.0 s (Figure 9-14). Increasing the initial horizontal velocity just increases how far the hamburger travels horizontally[5]. Air resistance has been neglected.

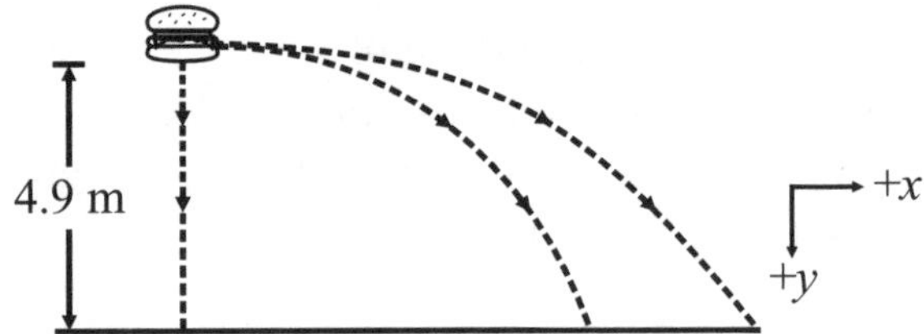

Figure 9-14 *In 1.0 s, an object falls 4.9 m regardless of its initial horizontal velocity*

What if you could throw the hamburger horizontally at 8 km/s? In 1.0 s, the hamburger would fall 4.9 m and move 8 km horizontally. However, Earth's curvature is such that, in 8 km, the surface of Earth drops 4.9 m (Figure 9-15), and thus the hamburger gets no closer to the surface of Earth. You have put the hamburger into a "close-Earth" orbit! It is "falling" toward Earth but Earth keeps curving away from it, and the hamburger just goes round and round in a circular orbit. Because the gravitational force is always perpendicular to the hamburger's

[5]Projectile motion is covered in detail in Section 4.3 in Chapter 4.

circular motion, this force does zero work on the hamburger, which therefore travels at constant speed.

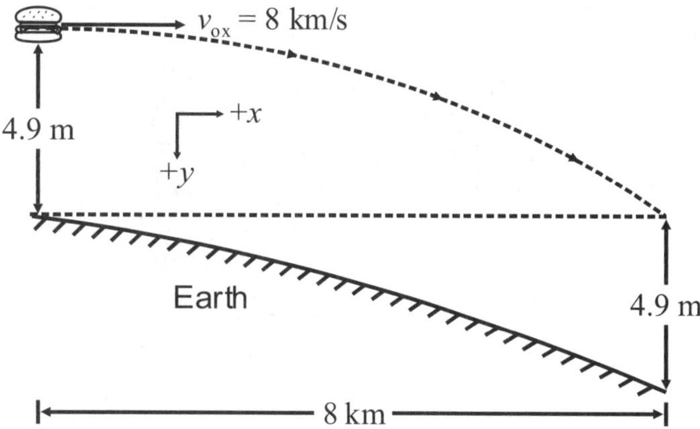

Figure 9-15 *If an object is projected horizontally with a speed of 8 km/s, then in 1.0 s, it falls 4.9 m and travels 8 km horizontally. But Earth has curved downward 4.9 m, and thus the object is no closer to Earth. (Horizontal and vertical distances are not to scale.)*

So the answer to the question "Why do satellites not fall into Earth?" is twofold: (i) the satellites go too fast, and (ii) Earth is curved. At higher altitudes, the speed required for a circular orbit decreases, as shown in Sample Problem 9-6 below.

Of course, in reality, the "close-Earth" orbit that we have described would be strongly affected by air resistance. Actual satellites must be at least 150 km above Earth's surface for a long-term orbit. Even at 150 km, which is relatively low for a satellite, air resistance is large enough that satellites eventually slow down and burn up as they enter lower (and thus denser) parts of the atmosphere.

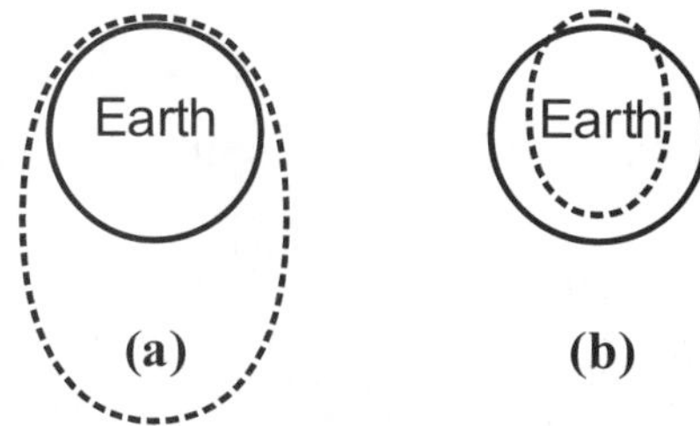

Figure 9-16 **(a)** *If the initial horizontal speed, v_{0x} , is somewhat greater than 8 km/s, the object follows an elliptical orbit.*
(b) *If $v_{0x} < 8$ km/s, the object tries to follow an elliptical orbit, but crashes into Earth.*

What would happen if a hamburger were thrown horizontally near Earth with a speed somewhat greater than 8 km/s? This speed is too large for a circular orbit, and the hamburger follows a curve called an ellipse, such as shown in Figure 9-16 (a). Similarly, if the initial speed is somewhat less than 8 km/s, the hamburger follows an ellipse but crashes into Earth before it travels very far (Figure 9-16 (b)). If the initial speed is 11.2 km/s, the hamburger follows a path that is half of a parabola, and never returns near Earth. For a speed greater than 11.2 km/s, the path is half of a hyperbola. Again, the hamburger escapes from Earth.

The above discussion can be applied to planetary motion around the sun, except that the numbers are different. Essentially, planets do not fall into the sun because they go too fast and because the sun is curved. Similarly, moons do not fall into planets.

Sample Problem 9-6

Determine the speeds of particles in Saturn's rings (a) for a particle at the innermost boundary, 6.7×10^7 m from the centre of Saturn, and (b) for a particle at the outer edge of the easily visible rings, 13.9×10^7 m from Saturn's centre. The mass of Saturn is 5.64×10^{26} kg.

Solution: (a) The particles in Saturn's rings are in circular orbits (Figure 9-17). The only appreciable force acting on an individual particle is the gravitational force toward Saturn, which is the centripetal force on the particle. The gravitational force (***F***) on a particle at the outer edge of the rings is shown; the $+x$ direction is toward Saturn, that is, in the direction of the centripetal acceleration of the particle. We use Newton's second law in the x-direction:

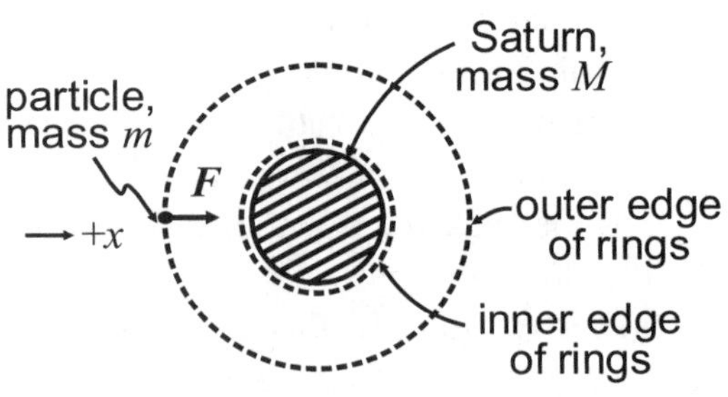

Figure 9-17 *Sample Problem 9-6; the rings of Saturn.*

$$F_x = ma_x$$

where F_x is the gravitational force and m is the mass of the particle. We can write F_x as GmM/r^2 (where M is Saturn's mass, and r is the distance from the particle to the centre of Saturn), and a_x can be written as v^2/r. (Recall from Chapter 4 that the magnitude of the centripetal acceleration of an object travelling with speed v in a circular path of radius r is v^2/r.)

Thus, we have: $$\frac{GmM}{r^2} = m\frac{v^2}{r}$$

Dividing by m, and multiplying by r: $$\frac{GM}{r} = v^2$$

Re-arranging for the speed v: $$v = \sqrt{\frac{GM}{r}}$$

Substituting numbers: $$v = \sqrt{\frac{(6.67\times10^{-11}\ \text{N}\cdot\text{m}^2/\text{kg}^2)(5.64\times10^{26}\ \text{kg})}{6.7\times10^{7}\ \text{m}}}$$
$$= 2.4\times10^{4}\ \text{m/s}$$

Thus, a particle at the innermost edge of Saturn's rings has a speed of 2.4×10^4 m/s.

(b) For a particle at $r = 13.9 \times 10^7$ m, we have:

$$v = \sqrt{\frac{GM}{r}}$$
$$= \sqrt{\frac{(6.67\times10^{-11}\ \text{N}\cdot\text{m}^2/\text{kg}^2)(5.64\times10^{26}\ \text{kg})}{13.9\times10^{7}\ \text{m}}}$$
$$= 1.65\times10^{4}\ \text{m/s}$$

Did You Know? *Saturn is not the only planet that has a ring system, but it is the only one that has rings visible from Earth. Jupiter and Uranus also have rings, and Neptune appears to have a series of arcs instead of continuous rings.*

The speed of a particle at the outer edge of the easily

visible rings is 1.65×10^4 m/s. Notice that the speed decreases as the distance from the planet's centre increases.

The relationship $v = \sqrt{GM/r}$ developed in the solution to the above sample problem is valid not just for the rings of Saturn — it works for any object travelling with speed v in a circular gravitational orbit of radius r about a central object having mass M.

Weightlessness

You have probably seen photographs and video images of astronauts who are weightless in orbiting space shuttles. What exactly does "weightless" mean? It cannot mean that the force of gravity on the astronauts is zero. The astronauts are close enough to Earth that the force of gravity is only a little smaller than gravity on Earth's surface (see practice question 9-34), and it is gravity that causes the astronauts and their ship to orbit Earth.

To understand weightlessness, we start with a down-to-earth example, a person standing in a moving elevator (Figure 9-18 (a)). We assume for the moment that the elevator has a downward acceleration of magnitude a. The only forces acting on the person are gravity ($m\mathbf{g}$) downward and the upward normal force ($\mathbf{F}_N$) exerted by the floor. We now use Newton's second law:

$$\Sigma F_y = ma_y$$

Choosing $+y$ to be downward, we have:

$$mg + (-F_N) = ma$$

Solving for F_N: $\quad F_N = mg - ma = m(g - a)$

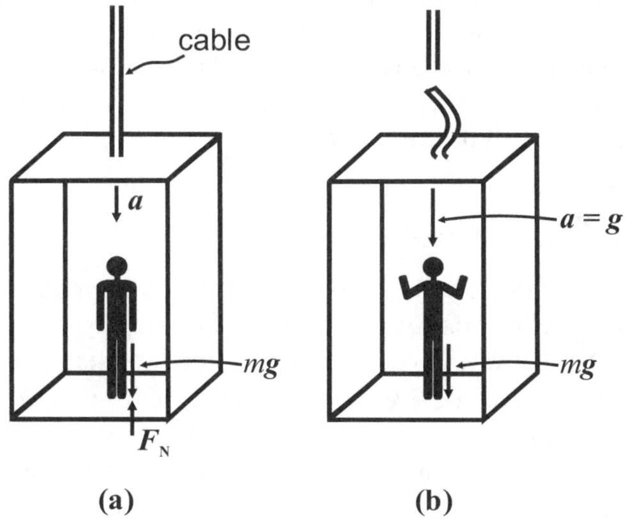

Figure 9-18 **(a)** *A person in an elevator accelerating downward.*
(b) *A person and elevator in free-fall.* $\mathbf{a} = \mathbf{g}$ *and* $\mathbf{F}_N = 0$. *The person is "weightless."*

Thus, the magnitude of the normal force depends on the downward acceleration. The larger the value of a, the smaller is F_N. If the person is standing on bathroom scales on the elevator floor, the scales provide the upward normal force and the scale reading gives the magnitude of this force.

What if the elevator cable is cut and the elevator and person go into free-fall (Figure 9-18 (b)), that is, they both have a downward acceleration of $\mathbf{a} = \mathbf{g}$? Then $F_N = m(g - g) = 0$; this means that the person, who is "floating" in the elevator, experiences no force from the elevator floor (or scales). It is the force F_N that gives the usual sensation of "weight," and in the absence of this force, the person feels "weightless." The bathroom scales would read zero.

Thus, what **weightlessness** really means is *being in free-fall*, that is, being in motion with only the force of gravity acting. There are no forces exerted by a person's surroundings such as floors, walls, etc. Astronauts are weightless, not because they are in space but because they are in free-fall (along with their ship). If you jump from a chair or table to the floor, you are weightless during your short period of free-fall. Some people have the misconception that weightlessness is somehow associated with the lack of air in space, but the foregoing discussion shows that this is not the case.

Weightlessness has advantages and disadvantages for astronauts. It is easy for them to move around the space cabin and easy to carry massive objects. However, an accidental bump from someone will send an astronaut to the other end of the cabin. Think about the problem of opening a sticky drawer in free-fall (remember Newton's third law). Weightless astronauts experience a number of physiological effects. They temporarily grow 2 to 3 cm in height because of the decompression of the spongy discs in their spines. Their faces become puffy because the body fluids are also in free-fall and can more easily be in the facial region; when the astronauts are on the ground, the fluids tend to be more concentrated in the lower parts of the body. The cardiovascular system becomes deconditioned — normally it is harder to pump the blood up toward the head than down toward the feet, but in a weightless environment it is easy to pump the blood anywhere in the body. If astronauts are in space for an extended period of time, they must exercise to keep the cardiovascular system in condition so that they will be able to adapt when they return to Earth.

Practice

9-27 (a) A ball is thrown horizontally with an initial speed of 3.0 m/s. After 2.0 s, how far has it travelled horizontally? vertically? Neglect air resistance.
(b) What would your answers be for an initial speed of 5.0 m/s?
[Ans. (a) 6.0 m; 2.0×10^1 m (b) 1.0×10^1 m; 2.0×10^1 m]

9-28 Earth is attracted by gravity toward the sun; why does it not fall into the sun?

9-29 Why does the gravitational force acting on a satellite in a circular orbit around Earth not change the speed of the satellite?

9-30 (a) What is the speed of a satellite in a circular orbit 525 km above the surface of Earth? Earth has an average radius of 6368 km and a mass of 5.98×10^{24} kg.
(b) How long does it take the satellite to complete one orbit?
(c) What is the name of the force that is the centripetal force on the satellite?
[Ans. (a) 7.61×10^3 m/s (b) 5.69×10^3 s (or 1.58 h)]

9-31 (a) If a satellite is to have a circular orbit about Earth (mass 5.98×10^{24} kg) with a period of 4.0 h, how far (in kilometres) above the centre of Earth must it be?
(b) What must be its speed?
[Ans. (a) 1.3×10^4 km (b) 5.6×10^3 m/s]

9-32 A satellite could be placed in a circular orbit very close to the surface of the moon because there would be no air resistance. What would be the required speed for such a satellite? The moon's mass and radius are 7.36×10^{22} kg and 1738 km. [Ans. 1.68×10^3 m/s]

9-33 A typical orbital height for a space shuttle is 4.00×10^2 km above Earth's surface.
(a) Determine the magnitude of the gravitational acceleration at this height. Earth's (average) radius is 6.37×10^6 m and its mass is 5.98×10^{24} kg.
(b) Express your answer to (a) as a percentage of surface-level g.
[Ans. 8.70 m/s^2 (b) 89% of g]

9-34 An astronaut is in a rocketship that is "blasting off." The ship is 10 km above the surface of Earth and the rockets are burning. Is the astronaut weightless? Explain your answer.

9-35 An astronaut in a space-cabin in orbit around Earth has been placed in the centre of the cabin by her astronaut "friends." She is stationary relative to the cabin and is not touching the walls, ceiling, or floor. (a) Why is this a problem for the astronaut?
(b) How could she solve this problem?

9-36 (a) Can weightless astronauts walk in the usual way?
(b) How do you think weightless astronauts drink?

9.5 GRAVITATIONAL POTENTIAL ENERGY IN GENERAL

What are black holes? Why does Earth's atmosphere not contain hydrogen or helium? Why does the moon have no atmosphere at all? How fast would a rocket have to be going in order to escape completely from Earth? from Mercury? In order to answer these questions, we need to know how to calculate gravitational potential energy for objects far from the surface of Earth (or another planet, the moon, etc.).

In Chapter 7, we saw that the gravitational potential energy (E_p) of a mass m near Earth's surface is mgy, where g is the magnitude of the gravitational acceleration (9.80 m/s^2), and y is the elevation of the mass relative to some arbitrary position ($y = 0$). The expression mgy is valid only near Earth's surface, that is, where g is approximately a constant value. As an object moves upward in the atmosphere, g changes, and the equation $E_p = mgy$ cannot be used to determine gravitational potential energy.

The expression for gravitational potential energy that is valid for an object, say a rocketship, of mass m far from Earth's surface is:

$$E_p = -\frac{GmM}{r} \qquad \textbf{(9-6)}$$

where G is the universal gravitation constant, M is the mass of Earth, and r is the distance from the centre of Earth to the rocketship. This expression is valid also near Earth's surface, as we shall see.

Notice that as $r \rightarrow \infty$, that is, as the rocketship moves very far from Earth, $E_p \rightarrow 0$. When using the equation $E_p = mgy$, we were free to choose the position where $E_p = 0$. However, for the equation $E_p = -GmM/r$, the position where $E_p = 0$ has been pre-selected at $r \rightarrow \infty$.

The equation $E_p = -GmM/r$ is valid not just for Earth and an object such as a rocketship; this expression gives the gravitational potential energy of any two objects of masses m and M, separated by a distance r. Notice that, strictly speaking, this is the potential energy *of the two-mass system*, but we will often say that it is the potential energy associated with only one of the objects. As was the case for the equation $F = Gm_1m_2/r^2$, the objects either have to be far enough apart that they can be considered to be particles, or they must have spherical symmetry.

> ***Math Tip:*** *If you know calculus, notice the relationship between gravitational force and gravitational potential energy:*
>
> *(i)* $F_y = -\frac{d}{dy}(mgy) = -mg$
>
> *(ii)* $F_r = -\frac{d}{dr}\left(-\frac{GmM}{r}\right) = -\frac{GmM}{r^2}$
>
> *The force, expressed as a component in the +y (upward) or +r (radial, also upward) direction, is the negative of the derivative of the potential energy.*

The negative sign in $-GmM/r$ often troubles students. Because G, m, M, and r are positive quantities, then gravitational potential energy is always negative (unless zero). However, as mentioned in Chapter 7, the important quantity is not potential energy itself but rather the *change* in potential energy from one position to another. We illustrate this in the following example, and show that the negative sign should not be a cause for concern.

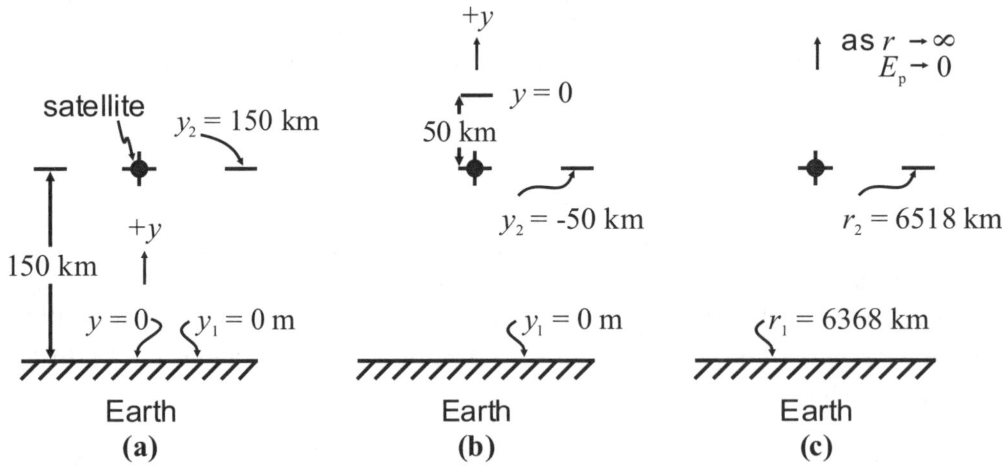

Figure 9-19 *Calculating the gravitational potential energy of a satellite relative to Earth's surface. For* **(a)** *and* **(b)**, $E_p = mgy$ *is used.*
In **(a)**, $y = 0$ *and* $E_p = 0$ *at Earth's surface.*
In **(b)**, $y = 0$ *and* $E_p = 0$ *at a height of 50 km above the satellite.*
For **(c)**, *the more accurate* $E_p = -GmM/r$ *is used;* $E_p \rightarrow 0$ *as* $r \rightarrow \infty$.

Figure 9-19 shows a satellite of mass 1.00×10^2 kg located 1.50×10^2 km above Earth's surface. The drawing is repeated three times: (a), (b), and (c). We will calculate in three different ways the gravitational potential energy of the satellite relative to Earth's surface, that is, the difference between its potential energy in its present position and its potential energy if it were at Earth's surface. If the satellite were dropped from rest from its height of 150 km, its potential energy would decrease by this amount as it falls to Earth, and its kinetic energy would increase equivalently (if we neglect air resistance).

In Figure 9-19 (a), we choose $y = 0$ at Earth's surface, and use $E_p \approx mgy$. This is only an approximation because g is not constant up to a height of 150 km. The $+y$ direction is upward, as always when we use $E_p = mgy$. The calculation of the required difference in potential energy (ΔE_p) gives:

$$\begin{aligned}\Delta E_p &\approx mgy_2 - mgy_1 \\ &\approx mg(y_2 - y_1) \\ &\approx (100\ \text{kg})(9.80\ \text{m/s}^2)(1.50 \times 10^5\ \text{m} - 0\ \text{m}) \\ &\approx 1.5 \times 10^8\ \text{J}\end{aligned}$$

Thus, the satellite has a gravitational potential energy of about 1.5×10^8 J relative to Earth's surface.

For Figure 9-19 (b), we again use $E_p \approx mgy$, but choose $y = 0$ at a height of 50 km above the satellite, that is, 200 km above Earth's surface. This is the position where $E_p = 0$. Therefore, the potential energy of the satellite 150 km above Earth is negative, and its potential energy at the surface would be even more negative. The difference in potential energy is:

$$\begin{aligned}\Delta E_p &\approx mgy_2 - mgy_1 \\ &\approx mg(y_2 - y_1) \\ &\approx (100\ \text{kg})(9.80\ \text{m/s}^2)(-5.0 \times 10^4\ \text{m} - (-2.00 \times 10^5\ \text{m})) \\ &\approx 1.5 \times 10^8\ \text{J}\end{aligned}$$

This change of potential energy is just the same as in (a). The fact that the two potential energies, mgy_2 and mgy_1 , are negative in this particular calculation is irrelevant; the potential energy of the satellite at a height of 150 km above the surface is still about 1.5×10^8 J larger than that at the surface.

Finally, for Figure 9-19 (c), we use the more correct expression $E_p = -GmM/r$. At an infinitely large distance from the centre of Earth ($r \rightarrow \infty$), $E_p \rightarrow 0$. The potential energy of the satellite 150 km above Earth is negative, and its potential energy at the surface is even more negative. At the surface, the distance from Earth's centre is $r_1 = 6368$ km (average value of Earth's radius), and at an elevation of 150 km, $r_2 = (6368 + 150)$ km = 6518 km. The calculation of ΔE_p gives:

$$\Delta E_p = -\frac{GmM}{r_2} - \left[-\frac{GmM}{r_1}\right]$$

$$= -GmM\left[\frac{1}{r_2} - \frac{1}{r_1}\right]$$

$$= -\left(6.67\times10^{-11}\ \text{N}\cdot\text{m}^2/\text{kg}^2\right)\left(100\ \text{kg}\right)\left(5.98\times10^{24}\ \text{kg}\right)\left[\frac{1}{6.518\times10^6\ \text{m}} - \frac{1}{6.368\times10^6\ \text{m}}\right]$$

$$= 1.44\times10^8\ \text{J}$$

Thus, the difference in gravitational potential energy is 1.44×10^8 J. Our approximate answers of 1.5×10^8 J in (a) and (b) were not too bad! (Why not?)

Again, it does not matter that both potential energies are negative; the satellite's potential energy at the higher elevation is 1.44×10^8 J larger than at the surface. As you can see from this example, how much the potential energy *changes* from one position to another is not affected by whether the potential energy at a particular point is positive or negative — so do not be bothered by the negative sign in $E_p = -GmM/r$.

Sample Problem 9-7

What is the gravitational potential energy of the Earth-moon system? The masses of Earth and the moon are 5.98×10^{24} kg and 7.36×10^{22} kg, respectively, and their centre-to-centre distance is 3.84×10^8 m.

Solution: This problem involves just a straightforward substitution into Eqn. 9-6:

$$E_p = -\frac{GmM}{r}$$

$$= -\frac{(6.67\times10^{-11}\ \text{N}\cdot\text{m}^2/\text{kg}^2)(7.36\times10^{22}\ \text{kg})(5.98\times10^{24}\ \text{kg})}{3.84\times10^8\ \text{m}}$$

$$= -7.64\times10^{28}\ \text{J}$$

Thus, the potential energy of Earth and moon is -7.64×10^{28} J. It is not uncommon to refer to this just as the potential energy of the moon, but it is more correct to say that it is the potential energy of the Earth-moon system.

In the answer to Sample Problem 9-7 above, what does the potential energy of -7.64×10^{28} J actually mean? Recall that as $r \to \infty$, $E_p \to 0$; in other words, if Earth and the moon were separated by a very large distance, their potential energy would be zero. Therefore, at their present separation, their potential energy is 7.64×10^{28} J *less* than the potential energy they would have at a very large (infinite) separation. This negative potential energy is also equal to the work that would be done by gravity if the moon were to be moved from its present position to a distance infinitely far away. This is similar to the situation of lifting an object that is close to the surface of Earth; as the object is lifted, the work done by gravity is negative.

Sample Problem 9-8

Suppose that an asteroid is moving directly toward Earth. If the asteroid's speed when it is 24 000 km from the centre of Earth is 4.2 km/s, what will its speed be when it is 12 000 km from Earth's centre? (Assume 2 significant digits in the given distances.) The mass of Earth is 5.98×10^{24} kg.

Did You Know? *There is strong evidence indicating that the extinction of the dinosaurs 65 million years ago was caused by a huge collision between an asteroid or comet and Earth.*

Solution: This problem involves using conservation of energy. The energies involved are the asteroid's kinetic energy and gravitational potential energy. Using subscript "1" for the energies when the asteroid is 24 000 km away, and "2" when it is 12 000 km away, we can express conservation of energy as:

$$E_{K1} + E_{p1} = E_{K2} + E_{p2} \qquad \text{Eqn. [1]}$$

Because the asteroid is not close to Earth's surface, $E_p = -GmM/r$ (not $E_p = mgy$) must be used, where m and M represent the masses of the asteroid and Earth, respectively. Substituting the expression for E_p into Eqn. [1], along with $E_K = ½mv^2$ gives:

$$\frac{1}{2}mv_1^2 - \frac{GmM}{r_1} = \frac{1}{2}mv_2^2 - \frac{GmM}{r_2} \qquad \text{Eqn. [2]}$$

We need to solve for the speed v_2. We first simplify Eqn. [2] by dividing all terms by m and multiplying by 2:

$$v_1^2 - \frac{2GM}{r_1} = v_2^2 - \frac{2GM}{r_2} \qquad \text{Eqn. [3]}$$

Notice that the mass of the asteroid has now been eliminated. This means that the asteroid's speed does not depend on its mass. Re-arranging Eqn. [3] to solve for v_2:

$$v_2^2 = v_1^2 + 2GM\left(\frac{1}{r_2} - \frac{1}{r_1}\right)$$

$$v_2 = \sqrt{v_1^2 + 2GM\left(\frac{1}{r_2} - \frac{1}{r_1}\right)}$$

Substituting known quantities, remembering first to convert kilometres to metres:

$$v_2 = \sqrt{(4.2\times10^3\ \text{m/s})^2 + 2(6.67\times10^{-11}\ \text{N}\cdot\text{m}^2/\text{kg}^2)(5.98\times10^{24}\ \text{kg})\left(\frac{1}{1.2\times10^7\ \text{m}} - \frac{1}{2.4\times10^7\ \text{m}}\right)}$$

$$= 7.1\times10^3\ \text{m/s}$$

$$= 7.1\ \text{km/s}$$

Thus, the speed of the asteroid when it is 12 000 km from Earth's centre will be 7.1 km/s. The asteroid is speeding up as it moves closer to Earth because of the gravitational force exerted on it by Earth.

Escape Speed

You know that if you throw something upward, it eventually falls back down. But if you could throw it fast enough, it would keep on going forever, gradually slowing down because of the pull of Earth's gravity on it but never returning. What goes up does not always come down! How fast does an object (space probe, satellite, gas molecule) have to be travelling near Earth's surface in order not to return? The minimum speed required to escape from Earth (or another planet or star) is called the **escape speed**. We will now determine this speed for Earth.

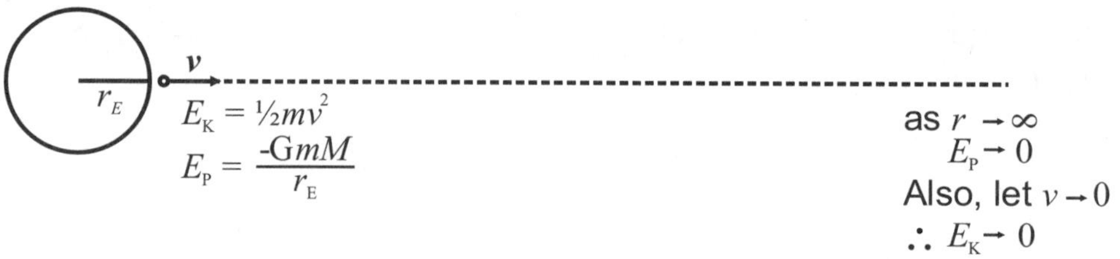

r_E — v

$E_K = \frac{1}{2}mv^2$

$E_P = \frac{-GmM}{r_E}$

as $r \to \infty$

$E_P \to 0$

Also, let $v \to 0$

$\therefore E_K \to 0$

Figure 9-20 *A space probe escaping from Earth.*

Figure 9-20 shows an object — say a space probe — travelling with speed v near Earth's surface. Initially, the distance r that separates the probe and the centre of Earth is Earth's radius, r_E. As the probe moves away from Earth, Earth's gravity slows it down, but when the probe is very far away (i.e., as the separation distance $r \to \infty$), the gravitational force is effectively zero. If we neglect other forces acting on the probe, it would then travel at constant velocity (by Newton's first law of motion). In order to determine the *minimum* speed required to escape from Earth, we let the probe approach a constant speed of zero as $r \to \infty$. That is, the probe eventually tends to come to rest, but, since the gravitational force is approaching zero, it stays at rest.

We now consider the energies involved. When the probe (mass m) is close to Earth (mass M), it has kinetic energy, $E_K = \frac{1}{2}mv^2$, and gravitational potential energy, $E_p = -GmM/r_E$. When the probe is very far away, its kinetic energy approaches zero (since we are letting $v \to 0$), and its potential energy also approaches zero (since $-GmM/r \to 0$ as $r \to \infty$). By the law of conservation of energy, the probe's total energy must remain constant, that is, the sum of kinetic and potential energies stays the same. Hence,

$$\text{total energy } (E_K + E_p) \text{ at Earth's surface} = \text{total energy } (E_K + E_p) \text{ as } r \rightarrow \infty$$

$$\text{Therefore,} \quad \tfrac{1}{2}mv^2 + \left(-\frac{GmM}{r_E}\right) = 0 + 0$$

We now solve for the speed v. Dividing by m (which disappears), multiplying by 2, and rearranging:

$$v^2 = \frac{2GM}{r_E} \quad \text{and thus,} \quad v = \sqrt{\frac{2GM}{r_E}}$$

Substituting numbers:

$$\begin{aligned} v &= \sqrt{\frac{2(6.67 \times 10^{-11}\ \text{N} \cdot \text{m}^2/\text{kg}^2)(5.98 \times 10^{24}\ \text{kg})}{6.37 \times 10^{6}\ \text{m}}} \\ &= 1.12 \times 10^{4}\ \text{m/s} \\ &= 11.2\ \text{km/s} \end{aligned}$$

Thus, the escape speed from Earth is 11.2 km/s. Note that the escape speed does not depend on the mass of the moving object — it is the same for space probes and gas molecules. You probably know that Earth's atmosphere consists mainly of nitrogen and oxygen. These molecules are much more massive than atoms of hydrogen and helium, which are also gases. The speeds of gas molecules and atoms depend on the gas temperature and on the masses of the individual molecules or atoms. For a given temperature, the more massive molecules and atoms move more slowly than lighter ones. Therefore, nitrogen and oxygen molecules in the atmosphere move more slowly than hydrogen and helium atoms. It is this difference in speed that accounts for the composition of our atmosphere. Hydrogen and helium atoms move so quickly that they can escape from Earth, whereas nitrogen and oxygen cannot escape because of their slower speeds (a lucky break for us oxygen-breathers).

The method that we used to find the escape speed from Earth can be applied to any planet, moon, or star. We simply use $v = \sqrt{2GM/r}$, where M and r represent the mass and radius of the object to be escaped. Table 9.3 gives escape speeds for various planets, etc. Note the low escape speed for the moon; even nitrogen and oxygen (and other heavy gases) can escape from the moon, which therefore has no atmosphere.

Table 9.3
Escape Speeds

Object	Mass (kg)	Radius (m)	Escape Speed (km/s)
Mercury	3.3×10^{23}	2.4×10^{6}	4.3
Earth	6.0×10^{24}	6.4×10^{6}	11.2
Moon	7.4×10^{22}	1.7×10^{6}	2.4
Mars	6.4×10^{23}	3.4×10^{6}	5.0
Jupiter	1.9×10^{27}	7.1×10^{7}	60
Sun	2.0×10^{30}	7.0×10^{8}	618

Black Holes

One of the most exotic objects believed to exist in the universe is the **black hole** — a region around a collapsed star where gravity is so strong that not even light can escape. When a massive star has had a long and energetic life its core implodes, releasing a great deal of energy and blowing off the outer layers of the star. This event is called a *supernova.* The star's brightness increases by roughly a factor of a billion (10^9) and then gradually decreases over a few months.

What the star turns into depends on what its original mass was. If the mass of its core was between about 1.5 and 3 solar masses[6], then it becomes a *neutron star* consisting almost entirely of neutrons and having a radius of only about 10 to 20 km. The density of a neutron star is huge: approximately 10^{17} kg/m^3. A spoonful of neutron-star material has about the same mass as 7×10^{12} people, about a thousand times the world's population. Objects have been observed in space that emit radiation in pulses; these *pulsars* are believed to be rotating neutron stars.

Did You Know? *In 1987, a supernova visible to the naked eye was discovered by a Canadian astronomer, Ian Shelton. It was the first naked-eye supernova in 383 years.*

If the core mass of a star is above 3 solar masses (approximately), then there is no known force that can stop gravity from continuing the implosion of the core indefinitely until all the core mass is concentrated at a single point in space that mathematicians call a singularity. In a fairly small region around the singularity, gravity is so strong that not even light can escape. It is this region that is called a black hole (Figure 9-21) because neither light nor material particles can be emitted. (A popular bumper sticker among physicists and astronomers says "Black holes are outa sight.") The outer limit of a black hole is called the *event horizon* — we can never learn anything of events that occur inside this "horizon." The radius of a black hole is often called the *Schwarzschild radius* in honour of the German astrophysicist Karl Schwarzschild (1873-1916) who first calculated this critical size.

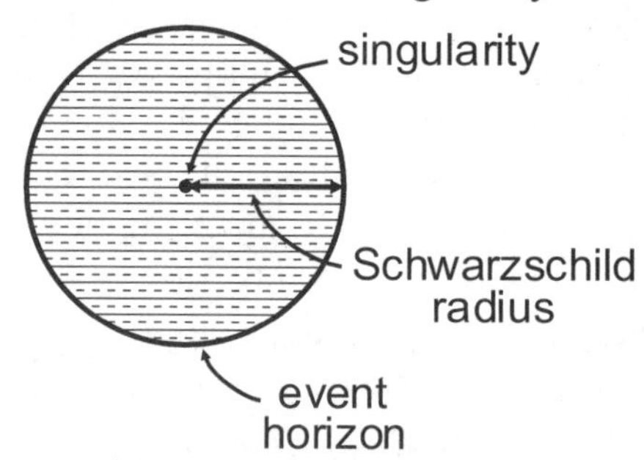

Figure 9-21 *A black hole.*

In order to calculate the Schwarzschild radius, we should use Einstein's general theory of relativity (which is *very* complicated). However, it turns out that the final answer is just the same as using Newtonian gravity. We can just use the equation for escape speed, $v = \sqrt{2GM/r}$, that we worked out earlier. At the Schwarzschild radius, the escape speed is the speed of light, 3.00×10^8 m/s. The mass M is the mass of the collapsed star — we will use 4 solar masses, that is, 7.96×10^{30} kg. We want to solve for the radius r. First squaring the equation and re-arranging for r:

---

[6]Masses of stars are often expressed in solar masses, that is, in terms of the mass of the sun. A star of 2 solar masses has a mass which is twice that of the sun (1 solar mass = 1.99×10^{30} kg).

$$v^2 = \frac{2GM}{r} \quad \text{and hence} \quad r = \frac{2GM}{v^2}$$

Substituting numbers:

$$r = \frac{2(6.67 \times 10^{-11}\ \text{N} \cdot \text{m}^2/\text{kg}^2)(7.96 \times 10^{30}\ \text{kg})}{(3.00 \times 10^8\ \text{m/s})^2}$$

$$= 1.18 \times 10^4\ \text{m}$$

$$= 11.8\ \text{km}$$

Thus, if a star with a core of 4 solar masses collapses to a singularity, then there is a black hole of radius 11.8 km around it. A star with a larger mass would have a larger Schwarzschild radius.

Have black holes been detected? Perhaps a better question is: how could we detect a black hole? They are invisible and rather small as far as astronomical sizes are concerned — hence, they are rather difficult to find, so we have to look for them indirectly. Outside the event horizon, the gravity due to the collapsed star is quite strong, and we can observe events in this region. Any material there will be accelerated by the strong gravitational force, and will heat up because of internal friction to such a high temperature that X rays will be emitted. There are a number of X-ray sources in space that astronomers are confident are associated with black holes. One of the most popular candidates is Cygnus X-1, a powerful source of X rays in the constellation Cygnus. There is also evidence of a supermassive black hole at the centre of our own galaxy — the speeds of stars near this area indicate the presence of a very massive, but unseen, object. To explain the observed stellar speeds, the mass of this black hole must be about 2.6 *million* solar masses.

Einstein's Theory of Gravity

Earlier in this chapter, we wrote that "the voyage of discovery and explanation started by Ptolemy and other early Greeks had been completed by Newton." Newton's law of universal gravitation explained the motion of the planets and other astronomical objects, as well as objects here on Earth. However, it turns out that Newton's gravitation law is not quite correct in all cases. For example, the details of the orbit of Mercury do not quite fit with Newtonian predictions. In 1916, Albert Einstein published his general theory of relativity, which is very complicated mathematically. His theory deals with gravity in a more complete way and is able to explain Mercury's orbit and other subtle gravitational effects. So far, Einstein's theory has been able to handle everything required of it, but perhaps in time a new theory will be required to explain newly discovered phenomena.

Practice

9-37 (a) Calculate the units of $-GmM/r$ in terms of kilograms, metres, and seconds.
(b) Calculate the units of $\frac{1}{2}mv^2$ in terms of kilograms, metres, and seconds.
(c) Are the units in (a) and (b) the same?

(d) What is the SI unit of energy, and how is it related to your answers above?

9-38 (a) Determine the gravitational potential energy of the Earth-sun system. The masses of Earth and the sun are 5.98×10^{24} kg and 1.99×10^{30} kg, respectively, and the Earth-sun separation is 1.50×10^{11} m.
(b) If Earth could be moved so that the Earth-sun distance were extremely large (essentially infinite), what would be the gravitational potential energy?
[Ans. (a) -5.29×10^{33} J (b) 0 J]

9-39 A satellite of mass 757 kg is in orbit 3.10×10^{2} km above Earth's surface. Earth's mass and radius are 5.98×10^{24} kg and 6368 km. Determine the difference between the satellite's gravitational potential energy at its present elevation and its potential energy at ground level (a) approximately by using $E_p = mgy$, and (b) exactly by using $E_p = -GmM/r$. (c) If the satellite could be brought to rest and allowed to fall toward Earth, what would be its kinetic energy just before it hit Earth? Neglect air resistance.
[Ans. (a) 2.30×10^{9} J (b) 2.2×10^{9} J (c) 2.2×10^{9} J]

9-40 If a rock of mass 1.50×10^{2} kg is released from rest 761 km above the surface of Mercury, determine its speed just before it hits the surface. Mercury's mass and radius are 3.3×10^{23} kg and 2439 km. [Ans. 2.07×10^{3} m/s]

<u>9-41</u> Craters on the moon (as shown in Fig. 8-13) are evidence of collisions with asteroids, comets, and other "rocks in space." Suppose that a large rock is travelling on a head-on collision course with the moon. When the rock is 8500 km from the centre of the moon, which has a radius of 1740 km, its speed is 6.3 km/s. The mass of the moon is 7.36×10^{22} kg.
(a) What will be the rock's speed when it is just about to hit the moon's surface?
(b) As the rock moves from 8500 km to 1740 km from the moon's centre, how is the change in its gravitational potential energy, ΔE_p, related to the change in its kinetic energy, ΔE_K?
[Ans. (a) 6.6 km/s]

9-42 An atmospheric probe is fired from Earth and reaches an elevation of 452 km, where it comes to rest momentarily. Determine the probe's speed near Earth's surface. Neglect air resistance. The mass and radius of Earth are 5.98×10^{24} kg and 6368 km, respectively.
[Ans. 2.88×10^{3} m/s]

9-43 Determine the escape speed from Uranus, which has a mass of 8.7×10^{25} kg and a diameter of 5.1×10^{4} km. [Ans. 2.1×10^{4} m/s]

9-44 (a) What is the escape speed from a neutron star of mass 3.2×10^{30} kg (1.6 solar masses) and radius 16 km?
(b) What percentage of the speed of light (3.00×10^{8} m/s) is this?
[Ans. (a) 1.6×10^{8} m/s (b) 54%]

9-45 Neptune has an escape speed of 24 km/s and a radius of 2.53×10^{4} km. What is its mass?
[Ans. 1.1×10^{26} kg]

9-46 Calculate the Schwarzschild radius (in kilometres) for a collapsed star having 3.5 solar masses (7.0×10^{30} kg). [Ans. 1.0×10^{1} km]

9-47 A black hole has a radius of 18 km. What is the mass of the object at its centre? Express your answer in (a) kilograms, and (b) solar masses. (1 solar mass = 1.99×10^{30} kg)
[Ans. (a) 1.2 10^{31} kg (b) 6.1 solar masses]

CHAPTER FOCUS

All the topics covered so far in this book have been related to mechanics: measurement, motion, forces, energy, and momentum.

In this chapter, we have concentrated on the dominant force at the astronomical level: gravitation. We have discussed Newton's law of universal gravitation and related it to the gravitational acceleration (and gravitational field) near planets and other astronomical objects. We have seen why satellites do not crash even though they are attracted by gravitation toward Earth, and have calculated speeds and radii of circular orbits around objects such as Saturn. A careful discussion has been given of the often-misunderstood concept of weightlessness. The topic of gravitational potential energy has led us to the idea of escape speed and into the exotic realm of black holes.

The next chapter begins a three-chapter sequence on the fundamentals of electricity. We start by discussing electric charges, the fields they produce, and the forces between charges.

VOCABULARY REVIEW

You should be able to define or explain each of the following words or phrases.

law of universal gravitation
universal gravitation constant
gravitational field
weightlessness
escape speed
black hole

CHAPTER REVIEW

<u>9-48</u> Two objects each of mass *m*, separated by a distance *d*, attract each other with a certain gravitational force. How many times larger is the gravitational force between two objects each of mass 2*m*, separated by *d*/2? (a) 16 (b) 8 (c) 4 (d) 2 (e) 32

__9-49__ If the distance between a spacecraft and Jupiter increases by a factor of 4, the magnitude of Jupiter's gravitational field at the position of the spacecraft:
(a) increases by a factor of 4 (b) decreases by a factor of 4 (c) increases by a factor of 16
(d) decreases by a factor of 16 (e) decreases by a factor of 2

__9-50__ A satellite is in a circular orbit, travelling at constant speed around Earth. Which of the following is a correct list of the forces acting on the satellite?
(a) the force of gravity toward Earth, and the force due to the motion of the satellite
(b) the force of gravity toward Earth, and the centripetal force
(c) the force of gravity toward Earth, which is the centripetal force
(d) the force of gravity toward Earth, and the rocket force that placed the satellite in orbit
(e) the force of gravity toward Earth, the centripetal force, and the force due to the motion of the satellite

__9-51__ A space probe is travelling outward from Earth. At a particular time, the probe is at a distance of 2 Earth radii ($2r_E$) from Earth's centre. At this position, the gravitational force exerted by Earth on the probe has a magnitude F_1 and the gravitational potential energy of the probe is $E_{p1.}$ A few hours later the probe is at a distance of $4r_E$ from Earth's centre, where the gravitational force has a magnitude F_2 and the gravitational potential energy of the probe is $E_{p2.}$ Which of the following is correct?
(a) $F_2 = \frac{1}{2}F_1$ and $E_{p2} = \frac{1}{2}E_{p1}$ (b) $F_2 = \frac{1}{2}F_1$ and $E_{p2} = \frac{1}{4}E_{p1}$ (c) $F_2 = \frac{1}{4}F_1$ and $E_{p2} = \frac{1}{4}E_{p1}$
(d) $F_2 = \frac{1}{8}F_1$ and $E_{p2} = \frac{1}{2}E_{p1}$ (e) $F_2 = \frac{1}{4}F_1$ and $E_{p2} = \frac{1}{2}E_{p1}$

__9-52__ (This question appeared in an international test of science achievement.) An aircraft flies in a vertical circular path of radius R at a constant speed. When the aircraft is at the top of the circular path the passengers feel "weightless." What is the speed of the aircraft? (g = magnitude of acceleration due to gravity)
(a) gR (b) $(gR)^{1/2}$ (c) g/R (d) $(g/R)^{1/2}$ (e) $2gR$

9-53 What is the magnitude of the gravitational force between the sun (mass 1.99×10^{30} kg) and Jupiter (mass 1.90×10^{27} kg) separated by 7.8×10^8 km? [Ans. 4.1×10^{23} N]

9-54 (a) What are the magnitude and direction of the gravitational acceleration 3.10×10^6 m above Earth's surface? Earth's mass and radius are 5.98×10^{24} kg and 6.37×10^6 m.
(b) Using your answer from (a), determine the gravitational force (magnitude and direction) on a spacecraft of mass 1.25×10^4 kg at the elevation given in (a).
[Ans. (a) 4.45 m/s^2 toward centre of Earth (b) 5.3×10^4 N toward centre of Earth]

9-55 Suppose that a man throws a golf ball straight up with a speed of 17.30 m/s. Using data from Table 9.2, determine how much higher the ball will travel in Mexico City than in Moscow. Neglect air resistance. [Ans. 0.25 m]

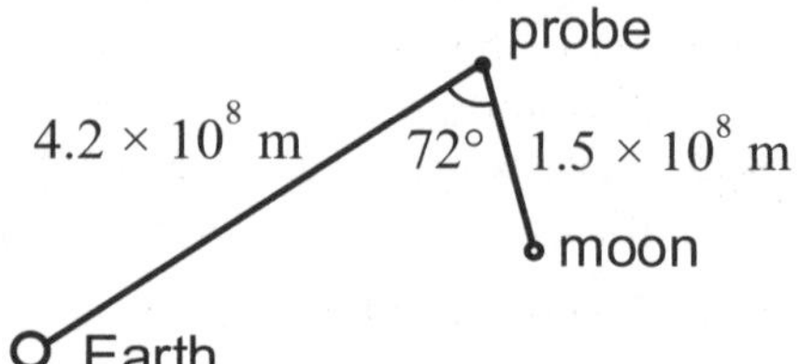

Figure 9-22. *Question 9-56.*

9-56 A space probe is at the position shown in Figure 9-22. Use components to determine the gravitational acceleration (magnitude and direction) of the probe due to the effects of Earth and the moon. The masses of Earth and the moon are 6.0×10^{24} kg and 7.4×10^{22} kg, respectively. [Ans. 2.3×10^{-3} m/s^2 at 5.1° from probe-Earth line]

9-57 Neptune has a surface gravity 1.18 times that of Earth. Its diameter is 5.05×10^4 km. What is the mass of Neptune? [Ans. 1.11×10^{26} kg]

9-58 The gravitational field at a certain height above Earth is 4.9 N/kg in magnitude. What is the gravitational force (magnitude and direction) on a spaceball of mass 0.14 kg at that height? (A spaceball is a baseball lost in space.) [Ans. 0.69 N toward centre of Earth]

9-59 What is the magnitude of Europa's gravitational field at a point in space 4.0×10^3 km from the centre of Europa? Europa, a moon of Jupiter, has a mass of 4.8×10^{22} kg.
[Ans. 2.0×10^{-3} N/kg]

9-60 At what elevation (in kilometres) above the surface of Uranus does its gravitational field have a magnitude of 1.0 N/kg? Its mass and radius are 8.73×10^{25} kg and 2.54×10^4 km.
[Ans. 5.1×10^4 km]

9-61 Since a satellite in orbit around Earth is attracted gravitationally toward Earth, why does it not fall into Earth?

9-62 Explain in a few sentences what weightlessness means.

9-63 A satellite in a circular orbit around Earth has a speed of 6.42×10^3 m/s. The mass of Earth is 5.98×10^{24} kg. (a) How far is the satellite from the centre of Earth?
(b) How long (in hours) does it take to complete one orbit?
(c) What force is the centripetal force on the satellite?
[Ans. (a) 9.68×10^6 m (b) 2.63 h]

9-64 Io (Figure 9-23), a moon of Jupiter first discovered by Galileo, completes one revolution around Jupiter in 1.77 days. Determine the mass of Jupiter, assuming that its orbit is circular with a radius of 4.22×10^5 km,.
[Ans. 1.90×10^{27} kg]

Figure 9-23 *Io (question 9-64), a moon of Jupiter, is the only moon in the solar system known to have active volcanoes, two of which can be seen in this photograph. Photo courtesy of NASA.*

9-65 Tethys is a moon of Saturn that has a circular orbit. Its speed is 1.1×10^4 m/s and the mass of Saturn is 5.6×10^{26} kg. Determine the radius and period of the orbit of Tethys.
[Ans. 3.1×10^8 m; 1.8×10^5 s]

9-66 The gravitational potential energy of the sun and Jupiter is -3.2×10^{35} J. Determine the distance between the sun and Jupiter. The masses of the sun and Jupiter are 1.99×10^{30} kg and 1.90×10^{27} kg, respectively. [Ans. 7.9×10^{11} m]

9-67 What speed is required to escape from Mimas, a moon of Saturn? The mass and diameter of Mimas are 3.7×10^{19} kg and 3.9×10^{2} km. [Ans. 1.6×10^{2} m/s]

9-68 If you are trying to escape from a planet, is the direction of your velocity important? For example, does it matter whether you move straight up or horizontally? Explain your answer. (Neglect atmospheric resistance.)

9-69 A probe is fired straight up from Earth with an initial speed of 9.0 km/s. How high above Earth's surface does it go? Earth's mass and radius are 5.98×10^{24} kg and 6368 km. Neglect air resistance. [Ans. 1.2×10^{7} m]

9-70 A proton (mass 1.67×10^{-27} kg) is moving away from the sun (mass 1.99×10^{30} kg). At a point in space 1.4×10^{9} m from the sun's centre, the proton's speed is 3.5×10^{2} km/s.
(a) What is the proton's speed when it is 2.8×10^{9} m from the sun's centre?
(b) Will the proton escape from the Sun?
[Ans. (a) 1.7×10^{2} km/s (b) no]

9-71 What is the radius (in kilometres) of a black hole surrounding a collapsed star of 4.5 solar masses (9.0×10^{30} kg)? [Ans. 13 km]

APPLYING YOUR KNOWLEDGE

9-72 Two baseballs are released in space so that they are at rest relative to each other. They then move toward each other as a result of their mutual gravitational attraction. As they move, what happens to the total momentum of the two-ball system?

9-73 Venus has a surface gravity 0.91 times that of Earth and a diameter 0.95 times that of Earth. Using no numbers other than these, what is the mass of Venus relative to the mass of Earth, that is, what is the ratio of m_{Venus} to m_{Earth}? [Ans. 0.82]

9-74 Assume that the horizontal and vertical velocity components of a long-jumper at take-off are 9.20 m/s and 3.50 m/s, respectively. Neglecting air resistance, determine the length of jump at (a) Moscow, and (b) Mexico City. Refer to Table 9.2 for appropriate *g*-values. Assume that the jumper is at the same horizontal level at takeoff and landing. (More detailed calculations taking air resistance into account show that a jumper can travel 5 cm farther at Mexico City than at Moscow.) [Ans. (a) 6.56 m (b) 6.59 m]

9-75 A piece of space-garbage is ejected from a spacecraft. It is at rest relative to the sun (mass 1.99×10^{30} kg) and is 1.25×10^{6} km from it. It starts to fall toward the sun. How long does it take to travel the first 1.00×10^{2} m? (Since 100 m $\ll$ 1.25×10^{6} km, the gravitational force and acceleration will be roughly constant over this short distance.) [Ans. 1.53 s]

9-76 Most telecommunications satellites are in *geosynchronous orbits* above Earth, that is, they have periods of 24 h. As a result, since Earth turns on its axis once in 24 h and each satellite goes around Earth once in 24 h, any individual satellite stays positioned above a particular point on Earth. (a) How far above Earth's surface must a geosynchronous satellite be? Earth's mass and average radius are 5.98×10^{24} kg and 6368. (b) What is the satellite's speed?
[Ans. (a) 3.6×10^7 m (b) 3.1×10^3 m/s]

9-77 Using the law of universal gravitation and the expression v^2/r for centripetal acceleration, show that for a planet in a circular orbit around a star, the orbital period T of the planet is related to the radius r of the orbit by $T^2 \propto r^3$.

9-78 When we say that the escape speed from Earth is 11.2 km/s, we mean the speed relative to the centre of Earth, not the surface. Any speed that a rocket has by virtue of starting on a rotating Earth can be used as part of the required 11.2 km/s for escape.
(a) Where on Earth is the speed due to rotation greatest?
(b) Determine this greatest speed in km/s. Use 6378 km for Earth's radius.
(c) In order to take best advantage of this starting speed, in what direction (east, south, north, west) should a rocket be launched? Explain your answer.
(d) Why is Cape Canaveral in Florida a good choice for rocket launches? You might wish to consult an atlas.
[Ans. (b) 0.464 km/s (c) east]

9-79 You can demonstrate weightlessness yourself (without jumping off a building). Make a hole in a styrofoam cup about 2 cm above the bottom, and fill the cup with water. Not surprisingly, the water will flow out of the hole. (Have a pail ready!) Now stand on a chair or table and fill the cup with water, keeping a finger over the hole. Drop the cup of water into a pail on the floor. Describe and explain what happens.

KEY OBJECTIVES

Having completed this chapter, you should now be able to do the following:

1. State the contributions of Ptolemy, Copernicus, Kepler, and Newton in the development of our understanding of planetary motion.
2. State Newton's law of universal gravitation and apply it in situations involving the force of gravity between masses.
3. Discuss the scientific significance of Cavendish's experiment.
4. Recognize situations in which $F = Gm_1m_2/r^2$ cannot be applied directly.
5. Relate the gravitational acceleration on (or near) a planet or other object to the law of universal gravitation.
6. Discuss reasons why gravitational acceleration is not constant over Earth's surface.
7. Define gravitational field and be able to calculate its magnitude (near a planet, for example).
8. Explain why satellites (and other objects in gravitational orbits) do not crash.
9. Use the law of universal gravitation and the expression v^2/r for centripetal acceleration to solve problems involving circular orbits.
10. Explain weightlessness.

11. State the general expression for gravitational potential energy.
12. Use gravitational potential energy in problems involving speeds (particularly escape speeds) of objects subject to gravitational forces.
13. Explain why different planets have different atmospheric compositions.
14. Discuss the origin of a black hole.

ANSWERS TO SELECTED QUESTIONS

9-3 (a) yes (b) no (c) yes (d) yes (e) no

9-18 (a) increase (b) decrease

9-34 The astronaut is not weightless because he/she is not in free fall.

9-35 (a) The astronaut cannot grab onto anything on the walls, ceiling, etc., to help her move around. (b) In order to move, she could throw something, for example, a glove or a pen, and she would recoil in the opposite direction (using Newton's third law of motion).

9-41 (b) $\Delta E_p = -\Delta E_K$

9-48 (a) 9-49 (d) 9-50 (c) 9-51 (e) 9-52 (b)

9-63 (c) gravitational force toward centre of Earth

9-72 The total momentum remains constant at zero.

9-78 (a) at the equator (c) east

CHAPTER 10

ELECTRIC CHARGE AND ELECTRIC FIELD

It is difficult to imagine life without electricity. Just stop and think of everything we use that is electrically powered — lights, CD players, hair dryers, televisions, toasters, and so on. In order to understand what electricity is and how it "works," we start with a discussion of electric charge and electric field.

10.1 ELECTRIC CHARGE AND ATOMS

When you comb your hair in dry weather, you often get "fly-away hair." You can achieve the same effect by removing a pullover sweater, and if you shuffle across a carpet, you can sometimes cause a spark to jump when you touch a doorknob. These all are examples of objects becoming electrically charged through rubbing, and experiencing a force as a result. Before describing how things become charged, we need to see where charges reside.

You probably know that matter consists of atoms. At the core of each atom is a small dense **nucleus** consisting of **protons** and **neutrons**. The protons are electrically charged, and by convention, they are said to have *positive* charge. A neutron is electrically neutral, and has about the same mass as a proton. Outside the nucleus is a cloud of *negatively* charged **electrons**. The charge on an electron has the same magnitude as that on a proton, and this size of charge is fundamental — *all* charges are integer multiples of this basic charge (or simple fractions of it, as has been recently discovered on particles called quarks). Electrons are much lighter than a nucleus — each electron has a mass of only about 1/2000 of that of a proton or neutron.

Did You Know? *A typical nucleus is only of the order of* 10^{-14} *m across, and has a volume of only about* 10^{-42} m^3*. The distance from the nucleus to the orbital electrons is about* 10^{-10} *m, which is 10,000 times the nuclear diameter. This means that an atom is mainly empty space!*

In 1913, the Danish physicist, Niels Bohr (1885-1962), proposed a model in which the electrons are pictured as moving in circular or elliptical orbits about the nucleus, much as the planets move around the sun. We now know that atomic electrons are better represented as spread-out distributions of charge, but the Bohr model (Figure 10-1) is still useful in thinking about atoms.

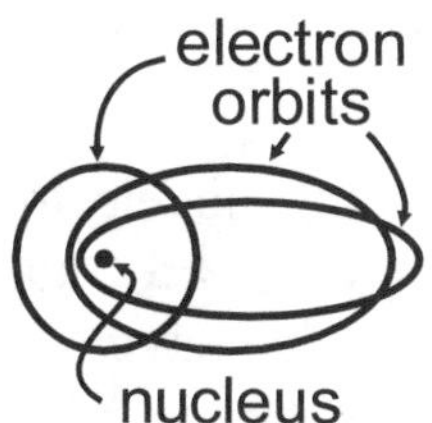

Figure 10-1
Bohr model of the atom.

In an electrically neutral atom, there are equal numbers of negatively charged electrons and positively charged protons, giving a total (or net) charge of zero. Most objects around you right now — this book, your clothes, your pet alligator — are electrically neutral (or nearly so) because the electrons and protons are equal in number. If one or more electrons are removed from a neutral atom, the net charge is then positive and the atom is referred to as a **positive ion**. If one or more electrons are added to a neutral atom, a **negative ion** results.

Practice

10-1 State the sign of the charge on: (a) an electron (b) a proton (c) a nucleus (d) an ion that has more electrons than protons (e) an ion that has more protons than electrons

10-2 Imagine that the nucleus of an atom is as large as an apple. Estimate the diameter of an apple and use data from the text to determine the distance from the nucleus (apple) to the electrons. [Ans. approx. 1 km]

10-3 Protons and neutrons are made of smaller particles called quarks, which have charges that are fractions of the charge on a single proton or electron. For example, the up quark and down quark have charges that are +2/3 and –1/3, respectively, of the proton charge.
(a) A single proton consists of three quarks, a combination of only up and down quarks. What combination must it be?
(b) Which three quarks (only ups and downs) make up a neutron?

10.2 TRANSFER OF ELECTRIC CHARGE

The ancient Greeks knew as early as 600 B.C. that when amber (fossilized tree resin) is rubbed with wool, it can pick up bits of straw and dust. If you pass a plastic comb through your hair, or rub a plastic ruler with a cloth, it will attract small bits of paper. What is happening is that electrons are being transferred from one object to the other during the rubbing. Thus, the objects become electrically charged — one positively and one negatively — and can exert electric forces on each other and on other objects.

Did You Know? *The word "electron" comes from the Greek "electron," which means amber. Electrons are transferred to amber when it is rubbed with wool (and most other materials).*

Why do electrons move from one object to another upon rubbing? Different atoms and molecules have different attractions (or *affinities*) for electrons. When amber is rubbed with wool, the molecules in the amber and wool come into close contact, and since the amber molecules have a greater affinity for electrons, they remove electrons from the wool. The amber becomes negatively charged and the wool positively charged. Only a tiny fraction of the total charge in an object is transferred during rubbing — the negatively charged amber has only a slight excess

Did You Know? *The terms "positive" and "negative" in reference to electric charge were introduced by Benjamin Franklin, the American scientist, statesman, and inventor. Although he made many contributions to the study of electricity, he is most often remembered for his dangerous experiment with a kite in a thunderstorm, which demonstrated the electric nature of lightning.*

of electrons over protons, and the positively charged wool has a slight deficiency of electrons.

Table 10.1
Static Electricity Series

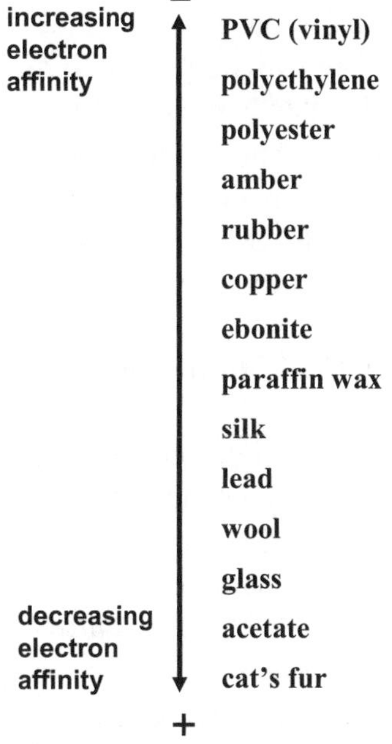

Materials can be placed in a list to show their relative attraction for electrons. In this *static electricity series* (Table 10.1), you can see that, for example, amber has a greater affinity for electrons than does wool. (*Static electricity*, or *electrostatics*, refers to electric charges at rest. Current electricity refers to charges in motion, such as in a wire in your home or in a spark.)

When objects are rubbed together, new charge is not created. **The net electric charge created in any process is zero**; in other words, electric charge is conserved. This is the **law of conservation of electric charge**, discovered in the mid-1700s by several people independently. This law is as fundamental in nature as the laws of conservation of energy and momentum.

Electric Force

Suppose that two glass rods are each charged positively by rubbing with silk, and that one rod is then suspended from a thread. If the other rod is brought nearby, the suspended rod twists away (Figure 10-2 (a)). This simple experiment shows that *like charges repel.* Rubbing a plastic[1] rod with fur will charge it negatively, and if it is held close to the suspended glass rod, the glass rod twists toward the plastic (Figure 10-2 (b)), showing that *unlike charges attract.*

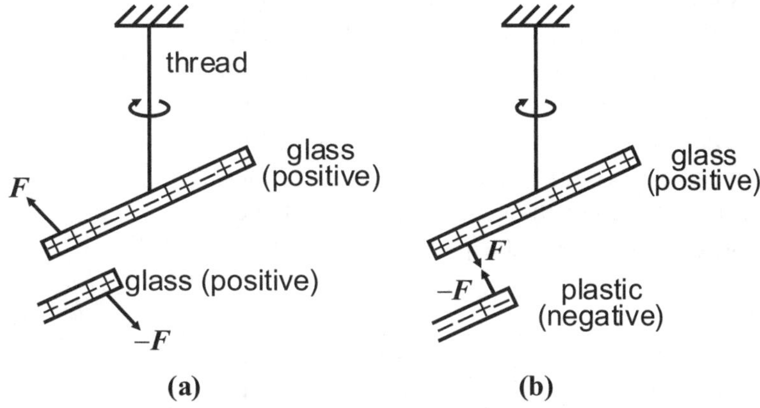

Figure 10-2 **(a)** *Like charges repel.* **(b)** *Unlike charges attract.*

The Frenchman, Charles Dufay (1698-1739), discovered the nature of the **electric force**, which is an attractive force between unlike charges and a repulsive force between like charges.

[1]You will not find "plastic" as a single entry in Table 10.1 because different types of plastic (vinyl, acetate, etc., in the table) have different electron affinities.

Dufay found also that there are only two kinds of charge. The electric force is what holds an atom together — there is an attraction between the negative electrons and the positive nucleus. Just as gravity is responsible for planetary orbits around the sun, the electric force is responsible for electron orbits around the nucleus (in the Bohr model). In addition, the electric force — in various guises called hydrogen bonds, ionic bonds, etc. — causes atoms and ions to form molecules, solids, and liquids. Relative to the gravitational force, the electric force is extremely strong. The magnitude of the electric force between an electron and proton is about 2×10^{39} times their gravitational attraction. Strong as the electric force is, it is no match for the nuclear strong force that holds the positively charged protons close together in the nucleus in spite of their electric repulsion.

Practical Static Electricity

You might have noticed that after combing your hair, the comb (which has become charged through rubbing with your hair) can attract something that is electrically *neutral*, such as a piece of paper. How is this possible? In each molecule in the paper, the electrons are repelled by the negative comb, and some of them move to the end of the molecule farthest from the comb (Figure 10-3). Thus, the ends of each molecule have opposite charges, one negative and the other positive. Such a molecule is said to be electrically polarized, or to have **electric polarization**. The negative comb is closer to the positive end of each molecule than to the negative end. The electric force depends on the distance between charges — the closer the charges, the stronger the force (Section 10.4). Thus, the attraction between the positive end of each molecule and the comb is greater than the repulsion between the negative end and the comb, and the paper moves toward the comb.

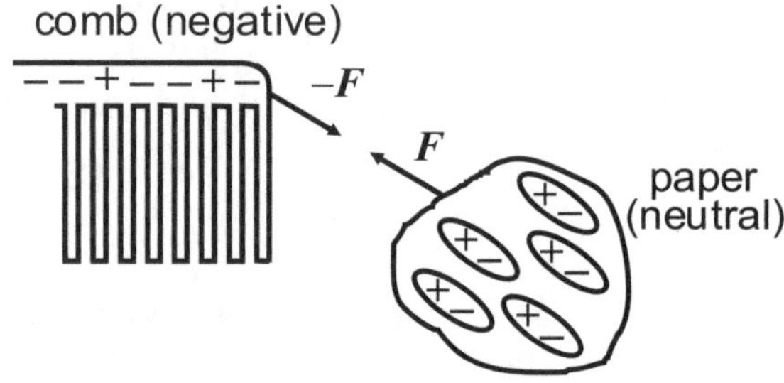

Figure 10-3 *Because of electric polarization, a charged comb can attract an electrically neutral piece of paper.*

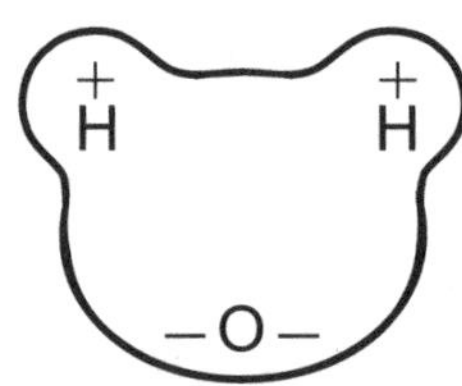

Figure 10-4 *Water molecules have a permanent electric polarization, and are important in dissipating the excess charge of charged objects.*

Once a comb or other object is charged, it does not stay charged forever. Charged ions in the air (formed by cosmic rays, etc.) can remove or add electrons from a charged object; airborne water molecules do this as well. Water molecules (Figure 10-4) have a permanent electric polarization, and hence are called *polar molecules*. The oxygen atom has a net negative charge and the hydrogen atoms a net positive charge. A negatively charged comb can lose electrons to hydrogen atoms in airborne water, and a positively charged glass rod can gain electrons from the oxygen atoms. On dry days, objects can retain a net charge much longer than on damp, humid days.

Static electricity is also responsible for clothes clinging to the body and lint sticking to clothing, especially in cold, dry climates. As well, it causes dust particles to adhere to newly polished tables. One way to overcome these problems is to use a humidifier to add more water molecules to the air so that the static charges can be neutralized more quickly. Another solution is to use an anti-static spray.

Static electricity can be dangerous because of small sparks that can occur. In hospital operating rooms, anaesthetics, which are explosive gases stored under pressure, are often used. A spark could have lethal consequences in this situation, especially for the patient. To prevent spark discharges, the floor and the shoes and socks worn by the medical team must be good electric conductors[2].

Shocks received on the outside of the body must be relatively large to cause permanent damage. However, even tiny shocks received directly by the heart can result in death. Therefore, hospital personnel must again be careful not to cause even the smallest spark near a patient when there are conducting tubes leading to the heart.

Did You Know? *Dangerous explosions have occurred when large oil tankers were washed by powerful jets of water. The explosions were caused by spark discharges from the water jets that had become charged as the water came out of the nozzle. Grounding the nozzle helps to prevent charges from building up on the water jets.*

Despite this catalogue of dangers, static electricity does have its benefits. One simple use is in the wrapping of food. Static electricity forces help plastic wrap to cling to food or containers, thus sealing the food from the surrounding air and maintaining its freshness.

An electronic air cleaner uses electric charging to purify the air circulating in a home with a central forced-air system. Millions of dust and pollen particles pass through the home's air ducts. The particles that are small enough to pass through a filter screen reach a cell where a large positive charge ionizes them positively. They are then attracted to negatively charged collectors, where they accumulate. The collectors must be washed periodically to maintain the air cleaner's efficiency.

Practice

10-4 If paraffin wax is rubbed with wool,
(a) what sign of charge results on each? (Refer to Table 10.1.)
(b) what type of particles move during the transfer of charge?
(c) do the particles named in (b) move onto, or off, the wool?

10-5 If a balloon is rubbed against a wall, it "sticks" there and can remain for several hours. Explain.

---

[2]Conductors are discussed in Section 10.3.

10-6 A positively charged glass rod attracts another object. What can you conclude about the charge on the other object?

10-7 If a plastic comb or ruler is charged by rubbing and then used to attract small bits of paper, often the paper will be attracted to the plastic, touch it, and then immediately fly away. Explain.

10.3 CONDUCTORS AND INSULATORS

You probably are aware that metals such as copper are used in electric wires, and that these wires are encased in plastic or rubber so that we cannot touch the metal and receive a shock. Why are metals good **electric conductors**, that is, why do they allow charge to move through them easily? Why are other materials such as plastic good **electric insulators**, which do not permit charge to flow easily?

In metals, there are electrons that are *very* loosely attached to the atoms. For example, in copper roughly one electron per atom is effectively free to roam about the copper as a whole. When electric current is flowing in a copper wire, what is happening is that these *conduction electrons* are moving. In insulators the electrons are tightly bound to atoms and molecules, and it is difficult to get charge to flow.

If one end of an insulator acquires a charge, say by being rubbed by another material, this charge tends to stay at that end of the insulator. In contrast, a charge acquired at one end of a conductor is free to move, and becomes distributed all along the conductor[3].

There are also *semiconductors* such as silicon and germanium, with current-conducting abilities between that of a good conductor and that of a good insulator. In the electronics industry, semiconductors are usually "doped" with selected impurity elements to acquire specific electric properties. *Superconductors* are materials having absolutely no resistance to the flow of electric current. Until the last few years, superconductors operated only at temperatures close to absolute zero, but new superconducting alloys work at temperatures well above this, and it is possible that room-temperature superconductors will eventually be made. If so, more efficient transmission of commercial electric energy from power plants might result. An understanding of semiconductors and superconductors requires a background in quantum physics beyond the scope of this book.

Charging by Contact (Conduction) and by Induction

Since electrons flow freely in conductors, it is possible to charge a conductor in a variety of ways. If a neutral conducting sphere on an insulated stand is touched with a positively charged object such as a glass rod (Figure 10-5), some negative electrons will be attracted from the sphere to the positive rod. If the rod is then removed, the sphere will have a net positive charge,

[3]In the absence of other nearby charged objects, any net charge in a conductor is found on the outside surface; for example, if a conductor is negatively charged, the excess electrons reside on the surface.

and the rod's positive charge will have been reduced somewhat. This method of charging a conductor is called **charging by contact** or **charging by conduction**. This technique works also for insulators to a small extent, but since electrons flow poorly in insulators, there is little transfer of charge. To charge an insulated conductor *negatively* by contact (conduction), we touch it with a negatively charged object. Some electrons are repelled from the negative object to the conductor, which acquires a net negative charge.

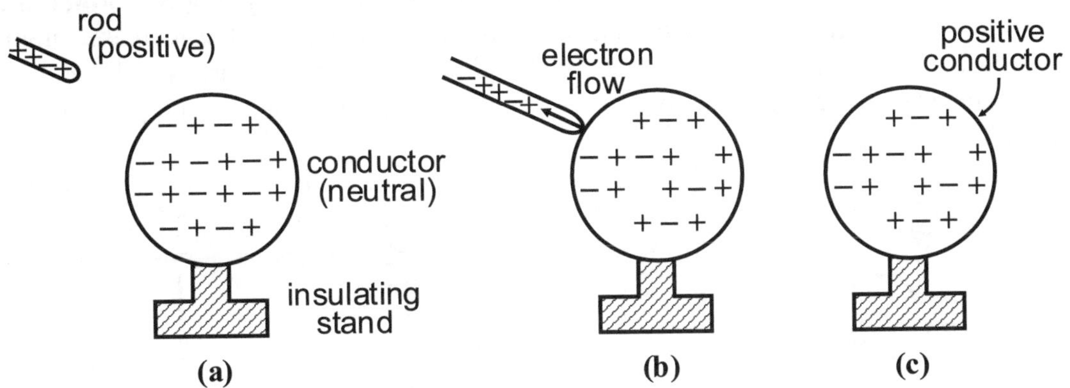

Figure 10-5 *Charging by contact (conduction).*
(a) *A charged rod and an insulated conductor.*
(b) *Rod in contact with conductor.*
(c) *Rod removed; conductor has net positive charge.*

Another method of charging a conductor does not involve direct contact with a charged object. If a negatively charged plastic rod is held near an insulated conductor, some electrons in the conductor move (still in the conductor) until they are far from the rod (Figure 10-6 (a)). Thus, the conductor has a net positive charge at one side, and a net negative charge at the other.

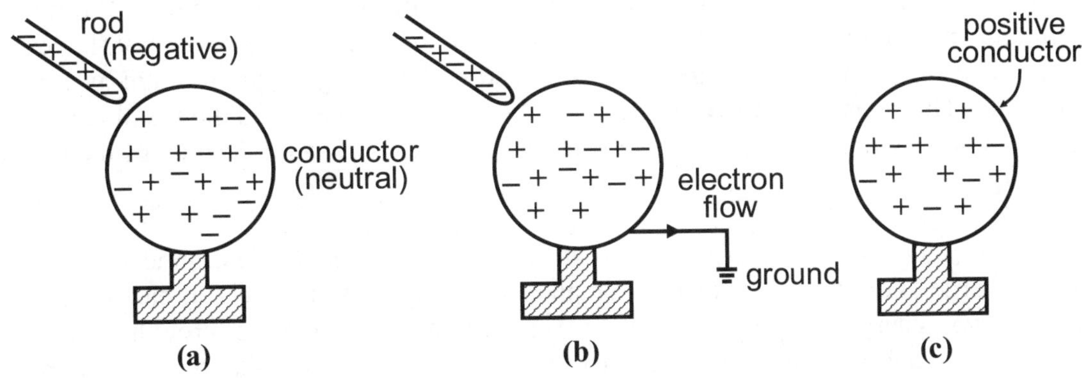

Figure 10-6 *Charging by induction.*
(a) *A negative rod near an insulated conductor.* **(b)** *Grounding the conductor.*
(c) *Grounding connection removed, then rod removed; conductor has net positive charge.*

The side opposite the rod is then connected by a wire to the ground, i.e., to Earth (Figure 10-6 (b)), or simply is touched by a person (thus allowing charge flow through the person to ground). The process of conducting a charge to or from the ground is called **grounding**. The electrical connection to the ground is indicated on diagrams by the symbol shown in Figure 10-6 (b). During grounding, the negative rod repels electrons from the negatively charged side of the sphere to the ground. If the grounding connection and *then* the rod are removed, the conductor is left with a net positive charge (Figure 10-6 (c)). This method is **charging by induction**; a net charge is *induced* in the conductor by the charged rod. What about the increased number of electrons in Earth as a result of this procedure? Adding electrons to Earth can be compared to pouring water from a glass into the ocean — it makes a big difference to the glass, but little to the ocean.

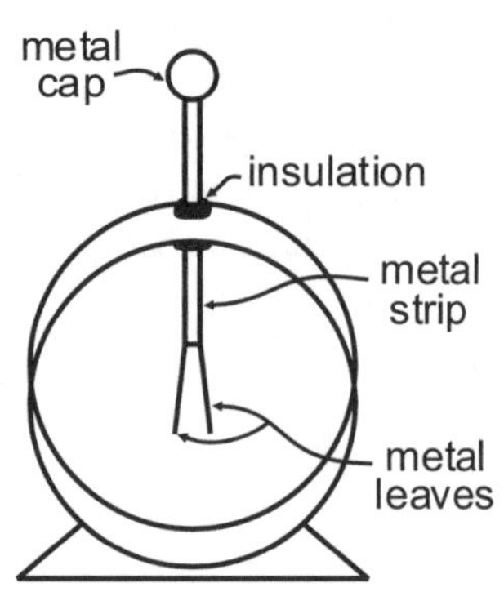

Figure 10-7
Leaf electroscope.

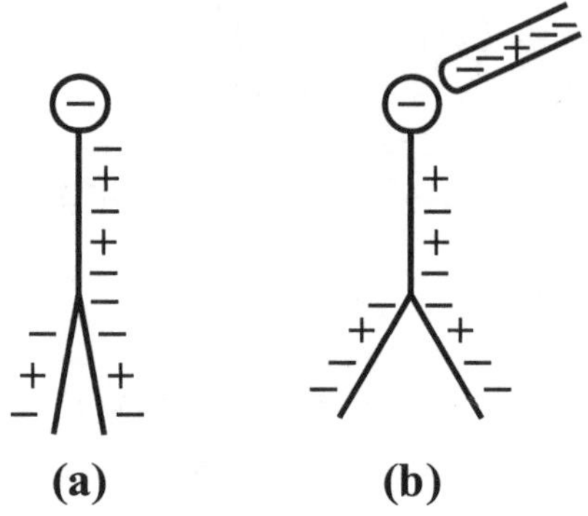

Figure 10-8
(a) *A negatively charged electroscope.*
(b) *A negatively charged rod repels more electrons into the leaves, thus increasing their separation.*

A *leaf electroscope* (Figure 10-7) is a sensitive instrument used to detect charge and to determine its sign. It consists of two thin metal leaves attached to the bottom of a metal strip supported in an insulating stand. On top of the strip is a metal cap. One or both of the leaves are movable. The cap of the electroscope can be charged with a charge of known sign by conduction or induction. The charge distributes itself along the conducting strip and the metal leaves, which repel each other (Figure 10-8 (a)). The separation of the leaves is an indication of the magnitude of the charge.

An electroscope with a charge of known sign can be used to determine the sign of an unknown charge. For example, suppose that an electroscope has an excess of electrons, and thus a net negative charge (Figure 10-8(a)). If an unknown charge is brought close to the electroscope cap and the leaves move farther apart (Figure 10-8(b)), what must be happening is that more electrons are moving into the leaves, thus increasing their mutual repulsion. This could happen only if the unknown charge is negative and is repelling electrons from the cap to the leaves. If the leaves move closer together, the unknown charge is positive. Stop and think about why this must be so. In either case, the amount of movement of the leaves is an indication of the magnitude of the unknown charge.

Practice

10-8 Silver is a slightly better electric conductor than copper, but copper is more widely used. Why?

10-9 In charging a conductor by contact, does the conductor acquire a charge of the same sign as the other charged object?

10-10 Repeat the previous question for charging by induction.

10-11 Using a series of diagrams, describe how to give an insulated conductor a negative charge by induction.

10-12 In charging by induction, what would happen if the rod were removed before the grounding connection was removed?

10-13 When a conductor is being charged by conduction, electrons flow briefly until the conductor and other object reach some equilibrium charge concentration. Why do the electrons stop flowing?

10-14 Use a series of diagrams to describe how you could charge a left electroscope positively by (a) conduction, and (b) induction.

10-15 A rod with an unknown charge is brought close to the cap of a positively charged electroscope and the leaves move farther apart. What is the sign of the unknown charge? Explain, using diagrams.

10-16 What happens if a negatively charged object is brought close to the cap of a neutral electroscope? Explain, using diagrams.

10-17 Repeat the previous question for a positively charged object.

10-18 Use your answers to the previous two questions to explain why an electroscope is more useful if it has a charge of known sign.

10-19 Static electricity generators such as the one shown in Figure 10-9 separate large quantities of charge.
(a) Why does the girl's hair stand on end?
(b) Why is she standing on an insulating platform (not shown)? What would happen if she did not?

Figure 10-9 *Getting charged up. Question 10-19.*

10.4 COULOMB'S LAW

Electrostatics experiments are tricky to perform. Charges leak from objects, a slight rubbing can charge something that should remain neutral, etc. As a result, the experimental foundations of static electricity proceeded more slowly than those of mechanics. In 1687, Newton published his law of universal gravitation, but it was not until 1788 that the corresponding force law between charges was established by Charles Augustin Coulomb (Figure 10-10) of France. Coulomb used a device called a torsion balance (Figure 10-11) to determine how electric force depends on charge and distance. Coulomb's torsion balance was similar to that used by Cavendish in 1798 for his determination of the universal gravitation constant (Section 9.1).

Figure 10-10 *Charles Augustin Coulomb (1736-1806). After a career as a military engineer, including several years in Martinique supervising construction of fortifications, he retired at age 53 to pursue scientific research full-time. Using a torsion balance (which he invented), he discovered the force law between electric charges. (Stamp courtesy of J.L. Hunt.)*

Coulomb's law of force between charges states that for charged objects that are much smaller than the distance between them, **the magnitude of the electric force is proportional to the (absolute value of the) product of the charges, and inversely proportional to the square of the distance between them**.

Mathematically, we write Coulomb's law as:

$$F = \frac{\mathrm{k}|q_1 q_2|}{r^2} \qquad \textbf{(10-1)}$$

where F is the magnitude of the force, q_1 and q_2 are the two charges, r is the distance between the charges (Figure 10-12), and k is a constant of proportionality. Note the similarity to the universal gravitation law, in which the force is proportional to the product of masses, and is inversely proportional to the square of the separation distance:

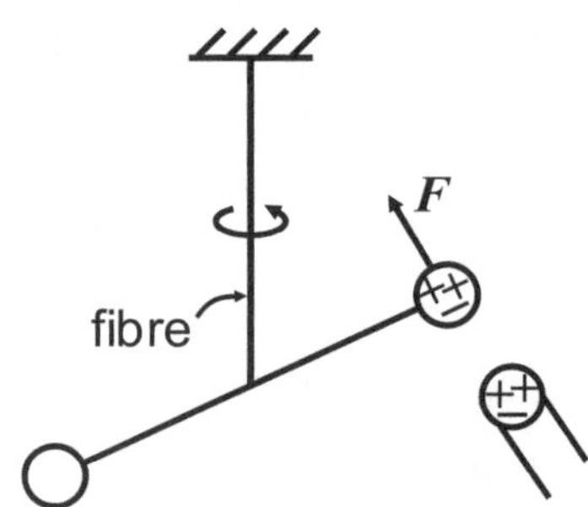

Figure 10-11 *Schematic diagram of Coulomb's apparatus. The forces between charges of various magnitudes, and separated by various distances, can be determined by measuring the twist of the fibre. The twist is proportional to the force.*

$$F \propto m_1 m_2 / r^2$$

However, whereas gravity only attracts, the electric force can either attract or repel.

The SI unit of charge is the coulomb (C). For practical reasons related to accuracy of measurements, the coulomb is defined in terms of electric current (Chapter 11). A net charge of 1 C is enormous; the net charge produced on an object by rubbing is typically of the order of a microcoulomb (μC = 10^{-6} C) or less. The absolute value of the charge on an electron (or proton) is a fundamental constant represented by "e," and has the value

$$e = 1.60 \times 10^{-19}\ \text{C} \qquad \textbf{(10-2)}$$

In SI units, the proportionality constant in Coulomb's law is

$$k = 8.99 \times 10^{9}\ \text{N·m}^2/\text{C}^2 \qquad \textbf{(10-3)}$$

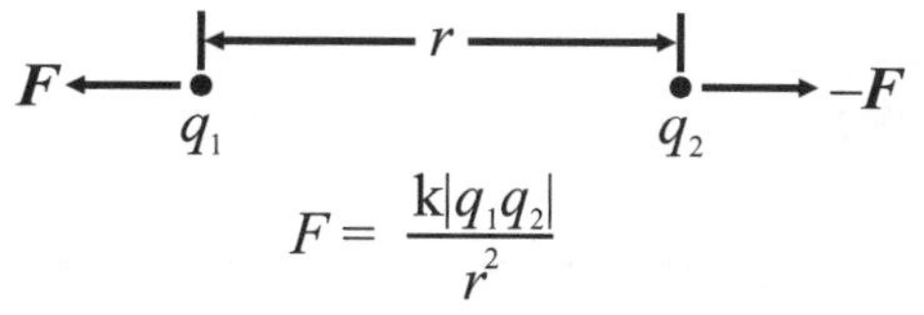

$$F = \frac{k|q_1 q_2|}{r^2}$$

Figure 10-12 *Coulomb's law. (The directions of the forces shown result from like charges.)*

> ***Did You Know?*** *The charge that flows in a lightning bolt is about 25 C. Your body contains about 4 × 10^9 C of positive charge, and the same amount of negative charge.*

for charges separated by vacuum. For charges separated by other materials, the electric force is reduced from its vacuum value because molecules in the materials "shield" the charges. For example, for charges in water, the electric force is reduced by a factor of 80 from the vacuum value. For charges in air (a poor shield), the value of k for vacuum is usually used; this introduces an error of only about one part in two thousand.

Sample Problem 10-1

What is the electric force (magnitude and direction) on the electron in a hydrogen atom, if the electron is in an "orbit" at an average distance of 5.3 × 10^{-11} m from the nucleus?

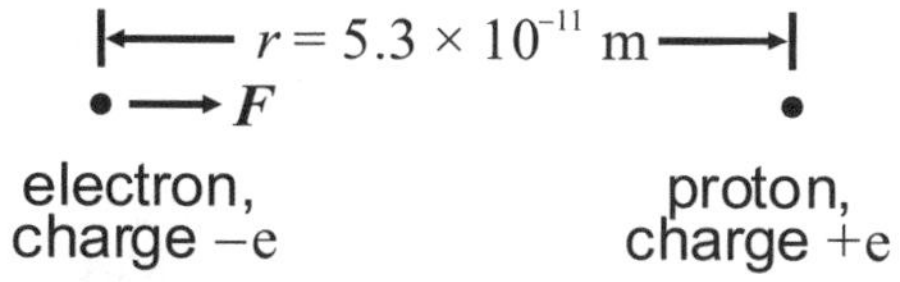

electron, charge −e — $r = 5.3 \times 10^{-11}$ m — proton, charge +e

Figure 10-13 *Sample Problem 10-1.*

Solution: A hydrogen nucleus (Fig. 10-13) is a proton, having a charge q_1 = e = 1.60 × 10^{-19} C, which also equals the absolute value of the charge on the electron (q_2). The magnitude of the force on the electron is given by Eqn. 10-1:

$$F = \frac{k|q_1 q_2|}{r^2}$$

Substituting values:

$$F = \frac{(8.99\times10^{9}\ \text{N}\cdot\text{m}^2/\text{C}^2)|(1.60\times10^{-19}\ \text{C})(-1.60\times10^{-19}\ \text{C})|}{(5.3\times10^{-11}\ \text{m})^2}$$

$$= 8.2\times10^{-8}\ \text{N}$$

Thus, the magnitude of the force is 8.2×10^{-8} N. Since the nucleus is positive and the electron is negative, the force on the electron is attractive, i.e., toward the nucleus.

Sample Problem 10-2

Two charges separated by a distance d exert an electric force on each other. If the same charges are separated by a distance of $d/4$, by what factor will the force increase or decrease?

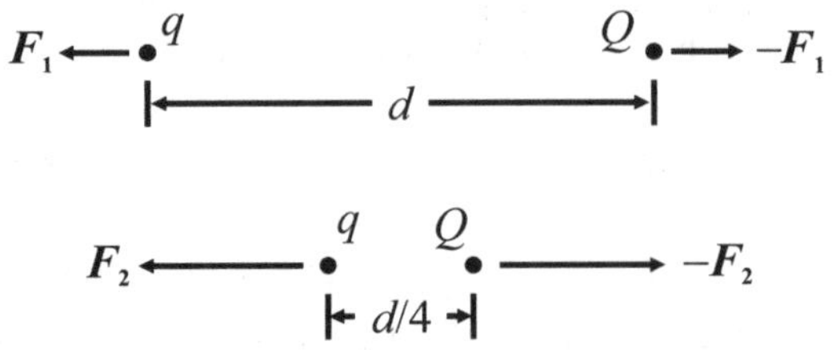

Figure 10-14 *Sample Problem 10-2.*

Solution: Let the two charges be q and Q, and the magnitude of the force be F_1 at separation d, and F_2 at separation $d/4$ (Figure 10-14). We are asked to find F_2 relative to F_1. When the separation is d, we have

$$F_1 = \frac{k|qQ|}{d^2} \qquad \text{Eqn. [1]}$$

When the separation is $d/4$,

$$F_2 = \frac{k|qQ|}{(d/4)^2} \qquad \text{Eqn. [2]}$$

Dividing Eqn. [2] by Eqn. [1]:

$$\frac{F_2}{F_1} = \frac{k|qQ|}{(d/4)^2} \div \frac{k|qQ|}{d^2} = \frac{k|qQ|}{d^2/16} \times \frac{d^2}{k|qQ|} = 16$$

Hence, as the separation decreases from d to $d/4$, the force increases by a factor of 16.

Sample Problem 10-3

An alpha (α) particle (i.e., a helium nucleus, having charge +2e) is passing near a hydrogen nucleus (charge +e) and a carbon nucleus (charge +6e), as shown in Figure 10-15(a). (Note the 77° and 36° angles.) The distances from the α particle to the hydrogen nucleus and carbon nucleus are 9.0×10^{-11} m and 1.5×10^{-10} m, respectively. What are the magnitude and direction of the resultant electric force on the α particle?

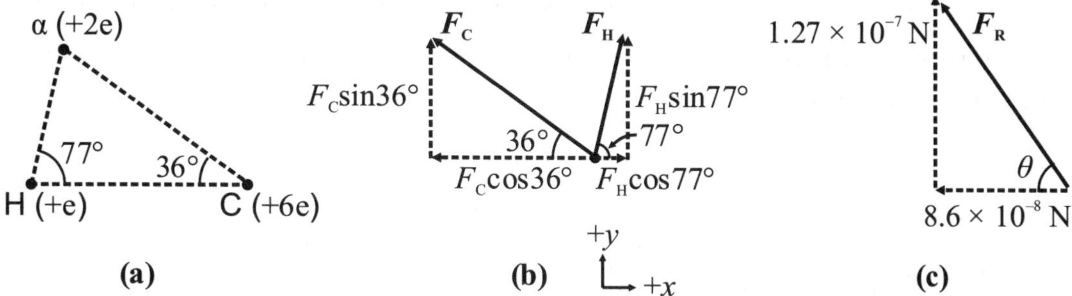

Figure 10-15 *Sample Problem 10-3.*
(a) *Positions of the charges.* **(b)** *Forces on α particle.* **(c)** *The resultant force.*

Solution: The resultant force on the α particle is the *vector* sum of the forces due to the other two nuclei. These forces are repulsive, since all the charges are positive. In Figure 10-15 (b), we label these forces $\boldsymbol{F}_C$ and $\boldsymbol{F}_H$ (due to the carbon and hydrogen nuclei, respectively), choose a convenient x-y co-ordinate system, and write x- and y-components of the forces in terms of given angles. We now determine the magnitude F_C:

$$F_C = \frac{k|q_1 q_2|}{r^2}$$

Since F_C is the force exerted on the α particle by the carbon nucleus, we use

$$q_1 = +2e = 3.20 \times 10^{-19}\ \text{C}$$
$$q_2 = +6e = 9.60 \times 10^{-19}\ \text{C}$$
$$r = 1.5 \times 10^{-10}\ \text{m}$$

Thus,
$$F_C = \frac{\left(8.99\times10^9\ \text{N}\cdot\text{m}^2/\text{C}^2\right)\left(3.2\times10^{-19}\ \text{C}\right)\left(9.60\times10^{-19}\ \text{C}\right)}{\left(1.5\times10^{-10}\ \text{m}\right)^2} = 1.2\times10^{-7}\ \text{N}$$

Similarly, $F_H = 5.7 \times 10^{-8}$ N. From Figure 10-15 (b), the x-component of the resultant force is

$$\begin{aligned}\Sigma F_x &= F_H \cos 77° - F_C \cos 36° \\ &= \left(5.7\times10^{-8}\ \text{N}\right)\cos 77° - \left(1.2\times10^{-7}\ \text{N}\right)\cos 36° \\ &= -8.6\times10^{-8}\ \text{N}\end{aligned}$$

Similarly, the y-component of the resultant force is

$$\Sigma F_y = F_H \sin 77° + F_C \sin 29° = 1.27 \times 10^{-7}\ \text{N}$$

These resultant x- and y-components are added in Figure 10-15 (c). The magnitude of the resultant force ($\boldsymbol{F}_R$) is given by

$$F_R = \sqrt{\left(-8.6 \times 10^{-8}\ \text{N}\right)^2 + \left(1.27 \times 10^{-7}\ \text{N}\right)^2} = 1.54 \times 10^{-7}\ \text{N}$$

The direction of $\boldsymbol{F}_R$ can be specified by angle θ in Figure 10-15 (c):

$$\tan\theta = \frac{1.27 \times 10^{-7}\ \text{N}}{8.6 \times 10^{-8}\ \text{N}} \qquad \text{which gives } \theta = 56°$$

Thus, the resultant force is 1.54×10^{-7} N at an angle $\theta = 56°$ as shown in Figure 10-15 (c).

Practice

10-20 An electron is 1.5×10^{-10} m from an oxygen nucleus (charge $+1.3 \times 10^{-18}$ C). What are the magnitude and direction of the force on (a) the electron? (b) the oxygen nucleus?
[Ans. (a) 8.3×10^{-8} N toward oxygen (b) 8.3×10^{-8} N toward electron]

10-21 If two charged objects are moved apart so that the separation distance increases by a factor of 3, does the force between them increase or decrease? By what factor?

10-22 If two charges move closer together so that the force between them increases by a factor of 2.0, by what factor has their separation distance decreased? (Such factors are usually quoted as numbers greater than 1.) [Ans. 1.4]

10-23 Sketch the shape of a graph of magnitude of electric force vs. separation distance.

10-24 How many electrons make up a charge of magnitude 1.00 C? [Ans. 6.25×10^{18}]

10-25 At what distance would the force between two protons have a magnitude of 1.00 N?
[Ans. 1.52×10^{-14} m]

Did You Know? *The speed of light (c), i.e., the speed of electromagnetic radiation, is closely related to the strength of electric and magnetic forces. Indeed, c is equal to* $(10^7\ k)^{1/2}$*, where k is the constant in Coulomb's law, and the "*10^7*" is a constant related to magnetic forces.*

10-26 What is the ratio of the magnitudes of the electric and gravitational forces between two electrons? (Refer to Appendix 4 for useful data.) [Ans. 4.16×10^{42}]

10-27 Three charges are in a straight line. Charge #1 (+4.5 μC) is separated by 4.3 cm from charge #2 (−3.7 μC), which is between #1 and #3. Charge #2 is 3.7 cm from #3 (−4.1 μC). What are the magnitude and direction of the force on (a) charge #2? (b) charge #1?
[Ans. (a) 181 N toward #1 (b) 107 N toward #2]

10-28 Three oxygen nuclei (charge on each = +8e) are arranged in an equilateral triangle of side 1.5×10^{-10} m. Calculate the magnitude and direction of the resultant force on each nucleus. [Ans. 1.1×10^{-6} N away from centre of triangle]

10-29 Solve the previous problem by using a vector scale diagram.

10-30 Four equal charges of the same sign are placed at the corners of a square. What is the direction of the resultant force on each charge?

10-31 Figure 10-16 shows the positions of two α particles (charge on each is +2e) and an electron. What are the magnitude and direction of
(a) the resultant force on the electron?
(Hint: choose the $+x$ axis along the line from the electron to the right-hand α particle.)
(b) the acceleration of the electron? (ref. Appendix 4)
[Ans. (a) 1.31×10^{-8} N at 13.3° to left of line from electron to right-hand α
(b) 1.43×10^{22} m/s^2, same direction as in (a)]

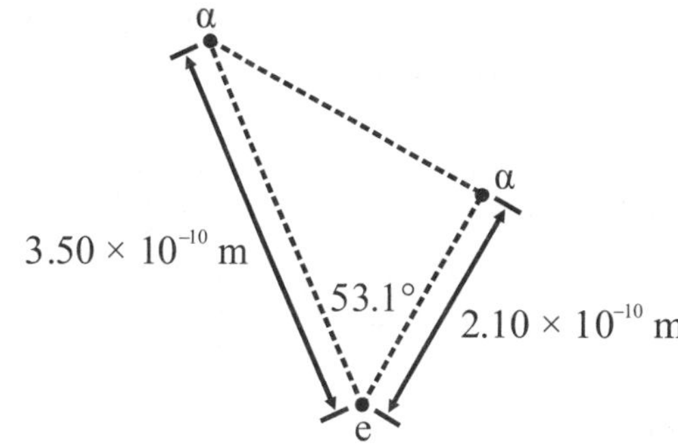

Figure 10-16 *Question 10-31.*

10-32 Two small spheres of equal mass $m = 3.2 \times 10^{-3}$ kg are suspended from a common point by threads each of length 31 cm (Figure 10-17). Equal positive charges are placed on the spheres, which move to equilibrium positions as shown.
(a) Draw a free-body diagram for either sphere at equilibrium.
(b) What is the charge on each sphere? [Ans. 1.6×10^{-7} C]

Figure 10-17 *Question 10-32.*

10.5 ELECTRIC FIELD

It is easy to understand how you can exert a force on this book when you are lifting it — you are touching it. But how does an electron in a hydrogen atom "know" that there is a proton in the nucleus exerting a force on it? Or how does Earth "know" that the sun is attracting it? This difficulty with forces acting at a distance, in contrast with contact forces, has led to the concept of fields. Physicists commonly refer to gravitational field (Chapter 9), electric field, and magnetic field.

The way that an electric field "works" is this: a charge sets up an electric field in the space around it, and when another charge encounters the field, this second charge experiences a force. The force is thus a two-step phenomenon — first the field is created, and then there is a force on any charge in the field. Electric field is more than just an abstraction; in advanced physics courses, students learn that the electric field can carry energy and momentum in electromagnetic waves. The concept of field has led to the development of radio, television, radar, and a wide variety of other devices such as electric motors, generators, etc.

Did You Know? *Sharks, as well as a variety of other creatures, can detect weak electric fields created by their prey. The duck-billed platypus can find food such as shrimp in extremely murky water because it can sense the electric field generated by tail flicks of the shrimp. In experiments investigating this phenomenon, a platypus attacked a small 1.5-V battery as if it were food.*

Imagine that you have charged a comb by passing it through your hair. An electric field exists in the space around the comb, and any charge (say q') in the vicinity will experience a force, $\boldsymbol{F}$. The **electric field**, $\boldsymbol{E}$, is defined as the ratio of this force to the charge.

$$\boldsymbol{E} = \frac{\boldsymbol{F}}{q'} \qquad \text{(electric field)} \qquad \textbf{(10-4)}$$

The SI unit of electric field is newton/coulomb (N/C).

Notice that the definition of electric field is similar to that of gravitational field (Chapter 9), which is the ratio of gravitational force to mass.

The charge q' is not part of the charge in the comb creating the field; it is a charge that we imagine to be in the field created by the comb. We assume that this charge does not alter the charge distribution on the comb significantly.

Electric field is a vector — its direction is the same as that of the force exerted on a positive charge. *The electric field due to a single positive charge points away from the charge; for a single negative charge, it points toward the charge.*

If the field due to a charge distribution is known, the force on a charge q' in the field is given by re-arranging $\boldsymbol{E} = \boldsymbol{F}/q'$ to give:

$$\boldsymbol{F} = q'\boldsymbol{E} \qquad \textbf{(10-5)}$$

Electric Field Due to a Single Charge

The magnitude of the electric field at a distance r away from a charge q is easy to determine. We start with the magnitude of the force on a charge q', using Eqn. 10-1:

$$F = \frac{k|qq'|}{r^2}$$

where r is the distance separating the charges.[4] To determine the magnitude of the field due to q, we simply divide F by q', which gives

$$E = \frac{k|q|}{r^2} \qquad \textbf{(10-6)}$$

Notice that the electric field due to a single charge has the same inverse-square dependence on distance as the electric force.

Sample Problem 10-4

What is the electric field (magnitude and direction) at a distance of 1.5×10^{-10} m from a proton?

Solution: Since a proton has a positive charge (+e), the electric field is directed away from the proton. (Recall that the electric field has the same direction as the force on a positive test charge.) Using Eqn. 10-6, the magnitude of the field is

$$E = \frac{k|q|}{r^2} = \frac{(8.99 \times 10^9 \text{ N}\cdot\text{m}^2/\text{C}^2)(1.60 \times 10^{-19} \text{ C})}{(1.5 \times 10^{-10} \text{ m})^2} = 6.4 \times 10^{10} \text{ N/C}$$

Thus, the field is 6.4×10^{10} N/C, directed away from the proton.

Electric Field Due to More than One Charge

The resultant electric field due to many charges is just the vector sum of the individual fields. Figure 10-18 (a) shows the separate fields due to two charges, and Figure 10-18 (b) shows the resultant field. As in any vector sum, each component of the resultant vector (Figure 10-18 (c)) is simply the sum of the corresponding components of the individual vectors:

$$E_{\text{Rx}} = E_{1\text{x}} + E_{2\text{x}} \qquad \text{and} \qquad E_{\text{Ry}} = E_{1\text{y}} + E_{2\text{y}}$$

[4]We assume here that the charges q and q' are distributed over regions of space that are small compared to the distance r (i.e., that the charges can be considered to be "point" charges), or that the charge distributions have spherical symmetry.

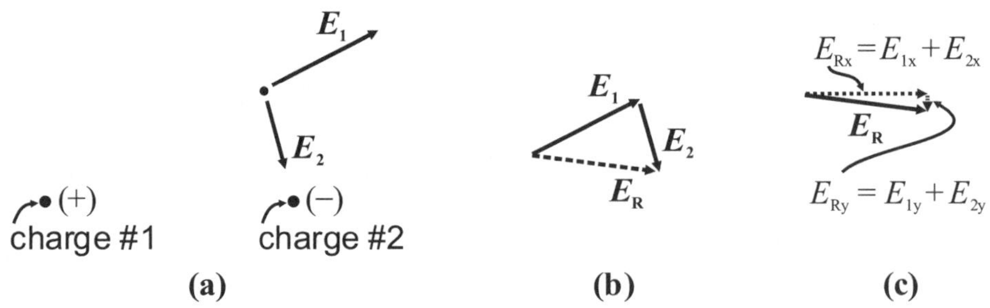

Figure 10-18 **(a)** *Electric fields (at point P) due to two charges.* **(b)** *Resultant field* $\boldsymbol{E}_R$. **(c)** *Components of* $\boldsymbol{E}_R$.

Adding the components of electric field vectors to give the resultant electric field is just the same as adding the components of any type of vector to give the resultant. You might wish to refer to Chapter 3 to review vector components, or to look again at Sample Problem 10-3 in which components were used to determine a resultant electric force.

Practice

10-33 What is the direction of the electric field at each of the following positions?
(a) near a proton (b) near an electron (c) near a carbon nucleus
(d) near a negatively charged chloride ion

10-34 The magnitude of the electric field at a point P is 2.3×10^7 N/C. What is the magnitude of the electric force that would be exerted at P on (a) an electron? (b) an oxygen nucleus (charge +8e)? [Ans. (a) 3.7×10^{-12} N (b) 2.9×10^{-11} N]

10-35 Determine the electric field (magnitude and direction) at a distance of 2.1×10^{-10} m from an α particle (charge +2e). [Ans. 6.5×10^{10} N/C away from α]

10-36 An electron experiences an acceleration of 1.3×10^6 m/s^2 northward because of an electric field. What are the magnitude and direction of the field?
[Ans. 7.4×10^{-6} N/C southward]

10-37 The magnitude of the electric field at a point P near an electron is 3.53×10^9 N/C.
(a) What is the distance between P and the electron?
(b) What is the direction of the electric field at P?
[Ans. (a) 6.38×10^{-10} m (b) toward electron]

10-38 Two charges have locations as shown in Figure 10–19. Charge q_1 is -3.6×10^{-8} C, and charge q_2 is -5.2×10^{-8} C. What is the electric field (magnitude and direction) at (a) point A? (b) point B?
[Ans. (a) 5.2×10^{13} N/C toward q_2
(b) 1.3×10^{14} N/C toward q_2 (and q_1)

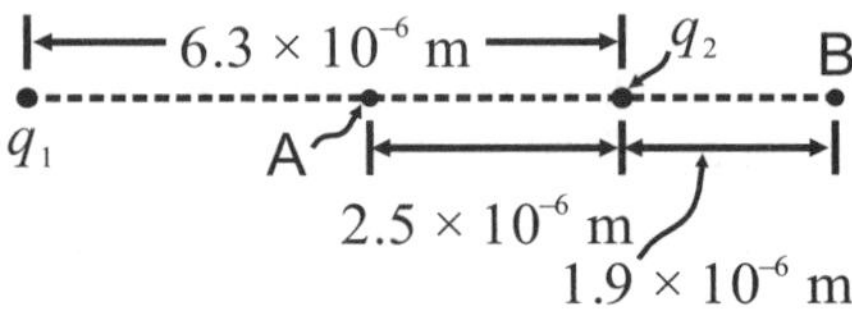

Figure 10-19 *Question 10-38.*

10-39 For the two charges in the previous question, where is the electric field zero?
[Ans. 2.9×10^{-6} m to right of q_1]

10-40 What is the electric field (magnitude and direction) at point D in Figure 10-20 due to the two charges? Charges q_1 and q_2 are −1.21 μC and +3.40 μC, respectively.
[Ans. 6.0×10^{14} N/C at −33° relative to +*x* axis]

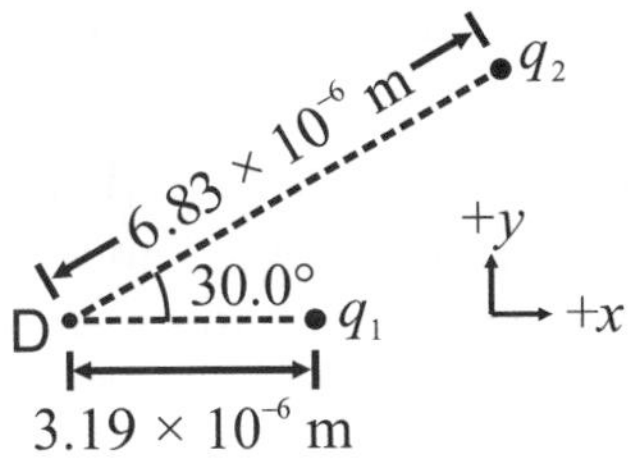

Figure 10-20 *Question 10-40.*

10-41 Solve the previous problem using a scale diagram.

10.6 ELECTRIC FIELD LINES

Have you ever seen an electric field? Of course not. But it is helpful to visualize electric fields through **electric field lines**, which are lines whose orientation and spacing indicate the direction and relative magnitude of the field. Figure 10-21 shows the electric field lines around a negative charge. The arrows on the lines point inward, showing the direction of the field. As the distance from the charge increases, the lines become farther apart, indicating a decrease in the magnitude of the field. The actual field lines form a *three-dimensional pattern*; we are looking at the lines only in a two-dimensional plane.

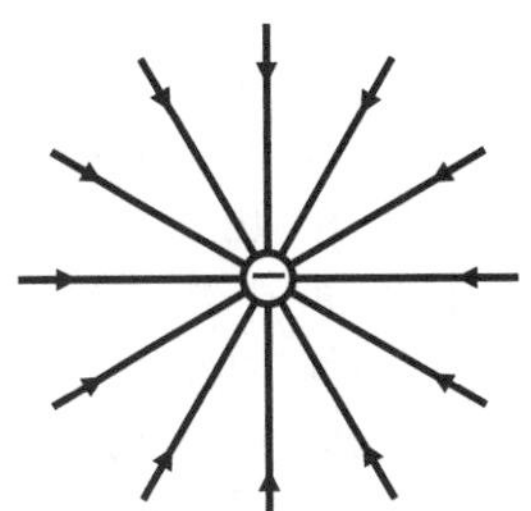

Figure 10-21
Electric field lines around a negative charge.

Figure 10-22 shows the electric field lines around a positive and negative charge of equal magnitude. This pattern illustrates three key points about field lines:

- The tangent to the field line at any point gives the direction of the resultant electric field at that point. For example, at point P, the resultant field, which is tangent to the field line, is the vector sum of the fields due to the two charges.

- The arrows on electric field lines point from positive charges toward negative charges, in other words, the direction of the field line at any point is in the direction of the force that would be exerted on a positive test charge placed at that point.

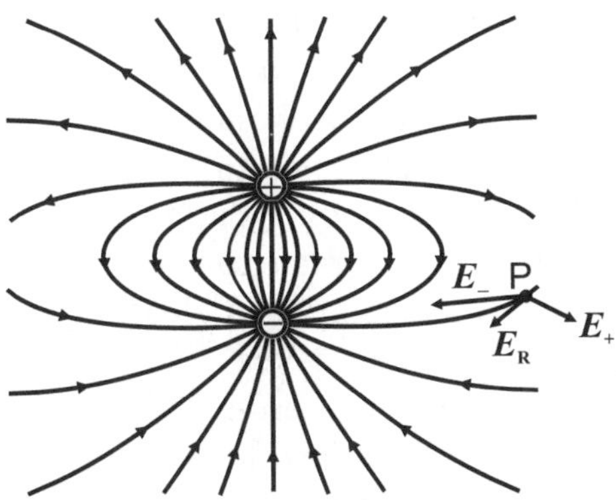

Figure 10-22 *Electric field lines around a positive and negative charge of equal magnitude. The resultant field (**E_R**) at P is the vector sum of the fields (**E_+** and **E_-**) due to the two charges.*

- Where field lines are close together, the field is large; where lines are far apart, the field is small. (At any point where there is no field line, it does not mean that there is zero field — the spaces between lines are there to indicate the relative magnitude of the field in different areas.)

Figure 10-23 shows the field lines around two equal positive charges. The field is weak between the charges, as shown by the small number of field lines there. In looking at this particular pattern, you can almost "see" the charges pushing themselves apart. How would the pattern change if the charges were both negative?

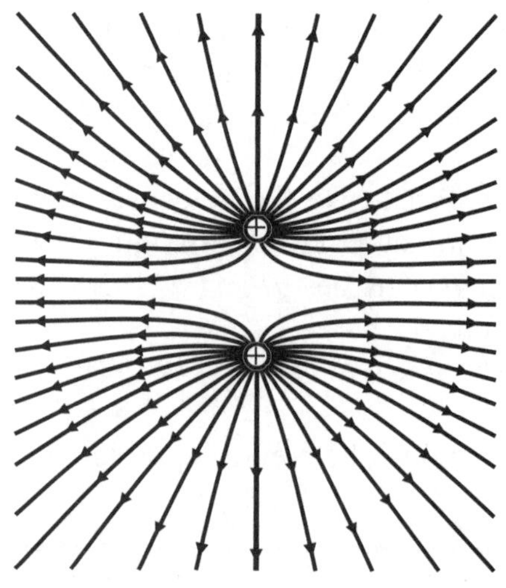

Figure 10-23 *Electric field lines around two equal positive charges.*

The electric field lines close to a section of a very large plate of uniformly distributed positive charge are shown in Figure 10-24 (a). The field is the vector sum of the fields due to all the positive charges, and is uniform, that is, constant in magnitude and direction. Notice that the field lines are equally spaced and neither converge nor diverge. The field is perpendicular to the plate; we can justify this by considering the field at a point P close to the plate (Figure 10-24 (b)). The charge at point A on the plate produces a field $\boldsymbol{E}_{\mathrm{A}}$ at P, and charge at point B produces a field $\boldsymbol{E}_{\mathrm{B}}$. Points A and B have been chosen to be symmetric relative to point P. Hence, when $\boldsymbol{E}_{\mathrm{A}}$ and $\boldsymbol{E}_{\mathrm{B}}$ are added to give the resultant field $\boldsymbol{E}_{\mathrm{R}}$, this field is perpendicular to the plate, as shown. Another way of thinking about this is that field components parallel to the plate "cancel out," and the resultant field $\boldsymbol{E}_{\mathrm{R}}$ is perpendicular to the plate. The field at point P due to *all* the charges on the plate can be determined by summing the fields due to charges taken in symmetrical pairs such as A and B. Since the field due to any symmetrical pair is perpendicular to the plate, the total field must be perpendicular to the plate.

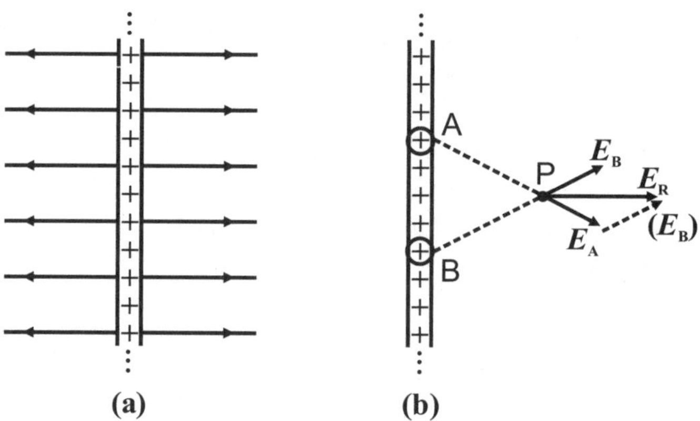

Figure 10-24 **(a)** *Electric field lines close to a section of a large plate of uniformly distributed positive charge.* **(b)** *Showing that the field is perpendicular to the plate (see text).*

You might be thinking that the above discussion makes sense if point P is close to the centre of the plate (so that for every point A "above" P there is another point B "below" it), but what if point P is closer to one end of the plate than the other? As we consider symmetrical pairs of charges progressively farther along the plate, will we not eventually run into a situation where all charges toward one end have been considered, leaving some charges at the other end that produce a non-perpendicular component at P? The answer is "no." Since the fields due to charges far away on the plate are extremely small compared to the fields of charges close to P (remember that $E \propto 1/r^2$), any such effects are negligible. (We are assuming that the distance between P and the plate is small enough that some charges on the plate are extremely close to P.)

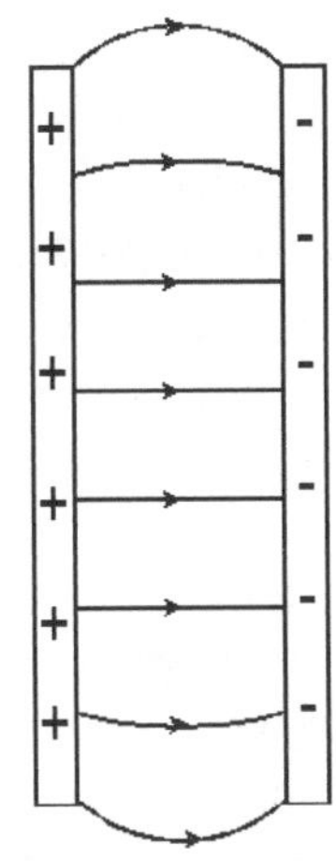

Figure 10-25
Electric field lines between oppositely charged plates.

Two parallel plates of uniform charge, one positive and the other of equal magnitude but negative, are often used to produce a region of uniform electric field (Figure 10-25). The total field is the sum of the fields due to the two plates. Since the field due to the positive plate points away from the positive plate and toward the negative plate, and the field due to the negative plate also points in this direction, the total field between the plates is twice the field due to one plate alone. Outside the plates, the fields due to the two plates point in opposite directions (think about this for a moment), and therefore, the resultant field is zero in this region. Note that the field is uniform near the middle of the plates, but non-uniform near the ends, where the cancellation of field components mentioned in the previous paragraphs does not apply. (Why not?) When solving problems, we usually assume that the field is uniform throughout the entire region between the plates.

Figure 10-26 *An oscilloscope uses oppositely charged plates to deflect the electron beam.*

Oppositely charged plates are used in a number of devices to deflect moving charged particles. Oscilloscopes (Figure 10-26) are commonly used to display voltage (Chapter 11) as a function of time. The pattern on the oscilloscope screen is produced by a moving beam of electrons whose path is deflected as it passes through charged plates in the oscilloscope. Both the sign and magnitude of charge on the plates can be changed quickly and automatically, thus allowing display of rapidly varying voltages. (As a matter of interest, televisions that have "old-fashioned" picture tubes — i.e., not plasma screen or LCD TVs — use magnetic deflection of the electron beam(s).)

Another device that uses deflecting plates is the ink-jet printer. In this type of printer, tiny drops of ink about 30 μm in diameter are given a computer-controlled charge and pass through a pair of deflecting plates on their way to the paper (Figure 10-27). The final position of a drop depends on its charge and on the electric field between the plates. In practice, the field is held constant and the charge is varied from drop to drop. It takes about 100 drops to make up a single printed character.

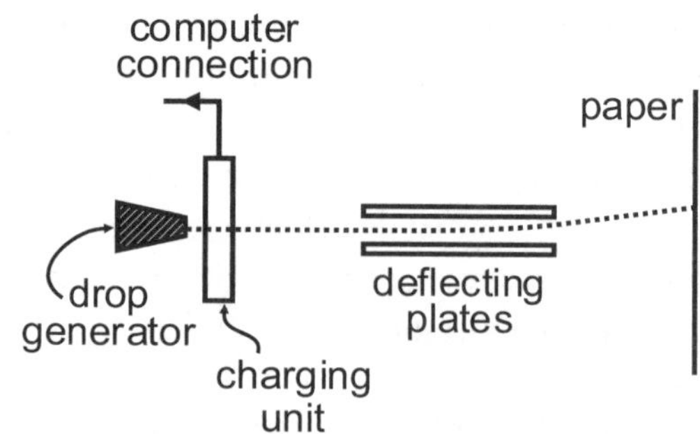

Figure 10-27 *An ink-jet printer. Ink drops are given computer-controlled charges and pass through deflecting plates to the paper.*

Charged metal surfaces (but not in the shape of flat plates) are used also in *electrostatic precipitators*, which remove smoke particles emitted from industrial chimneys. As smoke and dust particles move, they acquire electric charges by rubbing with each other. In electrostatic precipitators, the particles pass through a metal tube containing a central metal rod. The rod and tube are given opposite charges by an electric generator, and each charged particle is attracted to either the tube or rod, where the particle's charge is neutralized. As the particles collect, they agglomerate and become large enough to settle out.

Discovery of the Elementary Charge – The Millikan Experiment

During the years 1910-1913, the American physicist, Robert A. Millikan, performed experiments in which he was able to establish the value of the elementary charge, e. He sprayed tiny drops of oil from an atomizer into a chamber; in the process, the drops acquired small net charges. By observing an individual drop through a microscope (Figure 10-28), he was able to measure the terminal speed of the drop falling through the air under the influence of gravity downward and air friction upward. From this he was able to determine the radius and mass of the drop. Then, by applying a uniform electric field to the drop, he could cause the drop to move upward at a different terminal speed, with the electric force upward, and gravity and air friction downward. By measuring this speed and knowing the magnitude of the electric field, he could calculate the net charge on the drop.

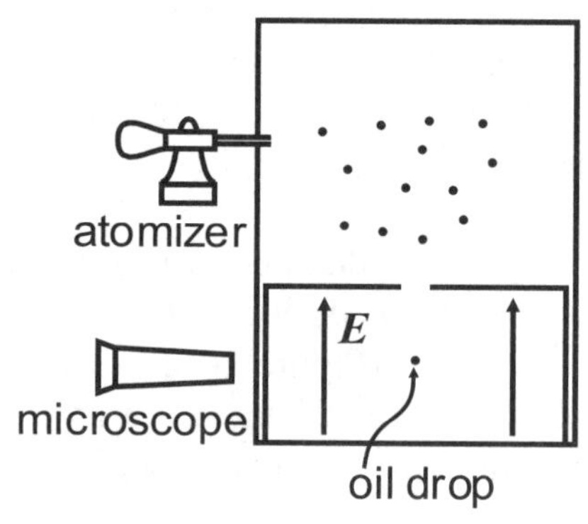

Figure 10-28
The Millikan apparatus.

Millikan and his colleagues measured the charges on thousands of drops, and found that they were always integral multiples of e, that is, charges such as 2e and –4e were found, but never ones such as 2.3e or –4.5e. He thus concluded that the charge e represented the elementary charge, and was awarded the 1923 Nobel Prize in Physics for his work.

Motion of a Charged Particle in a Uniform Electric Field

What does baseball have to do with ink-jet printing and oscilloscopes? Plenty, as it turns out. A pitched or hit baseball follows a parabolic trajectory as it moves in a uniform gravitational field, that is, as it experiences a constant acceleration due to gravity. The charged drops in an ink-jet printer and the electrons in an oscilloscope beam follow a parabolic trajectory between the deflecting plates as they move in a uniform electric field.

The acceleration of the baseball has a constant vertical component (9.80 m/s^2 downward) and no horizontal component. The acceleration of a positively charged particle in a uniform electric field has a constant component in the direction of the field, and no component perpendicular to the field. (A negatively charged particle has an acceleration opposite to the field direction.)

Sample Problem 10-5

An electron (mass 9.1×10^{-31} kg) is projected between the deflecting plates in an oscilloscope with an initial velocity of 1.8×10^7 m/s parallel to the plates (Figure 10-29). The uniform electric field between the plates is 2.0×10^4 N/C upward.

(a) What is the acceleration (magnitude and direction) of the electron while between the plates?

(b) How long does it take to go through the plates?

(c) How far has it dropped or risen (specify which) when it leaves the plates?

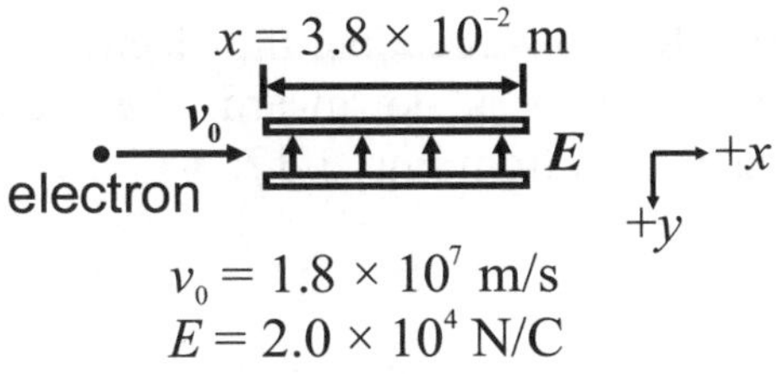

$x = 3.8 \times 10^{-2}$ m

v_0

E

electron

$+x$

$+y$

$v_0 = 1.8 \times 10^7$ m/s

$E = 2.0 \times 10^4$ N/C

Figure 10-29 *Sample Problem 10-5.*

Solution: (a) To determine the acceleration, we will use Newton's second law ($\Sigma \boldsymbol{F} = m\boldsymbol{a}$), and therefore need to know the force acting on the electron. The field is upward, and since the electron has a negative charge, the force on it is downward. The magnitude of the force is the product of the magnitude of the charge on the electron and the field:

$$F = eE = \left(1.60 \times 10^{-19}\ \text{C}\right)\left(2.0 \times 10^4\ \text{N/C}\right) = 3.2 \times 10^{-15}\ \text{N}$$

This force acts downward, which we define to be the $+y$ direction (Figure 10-29). We use

$$\Sigma F = ma_y$$

Hence,
$$a_y = \frac{\Sigma F_y}{m} = \frac{3.2 \times 10^{-15}\ \text{N}}{9.1 \times 10^{-31}\ \text{kg}} = 3.5 \times 10^{15}\ \text{m/s}^2$$

Thus, the acceleration is 3.5×10^{15} m/s^2 downward. (How does the gravitational acceleration of the electron compare to this electric acceleration?)

(b) To determine the time taken to pass through the plates, we consider motion in the x-direction. There is no force in this direction, and therefore the x-component of acceleration is zero ($a_x = 0$), giving a constant x-component of velocity. Just as we did in projectile-motion problems in Chapter 3, we use Eqn. 3-9b:

$$x = x_0 + v_{0x} t$$

Letting $x_0 = 0$ as the electron enters the region between the deflecting plates, we have

$$x = v_{0x} t$$

Therefore,

$$t = \frac{x}{v_{0x}} = \frac{3.8 \times 10^{-2}\ \text{m}}{1.8 \times 10^{7}\ \text{m/s}} = 2.1 \times 10^{-9}\ \text{s}$$

Thus, the electron takes 2.1×10^{-9} s to go through the plates.

(c) In the *y*-direction, the electron's initial velocity component is zero ($v_{0y} = 0$), and since the acceleration is downward, the electron will move downward. Its *y*-displacement can be calculated from Eqn. 3-12:

$$y = y_0 + v_{0y} t + \frac{1}{2} a_y t^2$$

Setting $y_0 = 0$ as the electron enters the space between the plates, and substituting $v_{0y} = 0$:

$$\begin{aligned} y &= \frac{1}{2} a_y t^2 \\ &= \frac{1}{2}\left(3.5 \times 10^{15}\ \text{m/s}^2\right)\left(2.1 \times 10^{-9}\ \text{s}\right)^2 \\ &= 7.8 \times 10^{-3}\ \text{m} \end{aligned}$$

Hence, the electron has dropped 7.8×10^{-3} m (or 7.8 mm) when it leaves the plates.

Notice that this solution is exactly analogous to the solution of projectile-motion problems in Chapter 3.

 **Practice**

10-42 Sketch the field line pattern around
(a) a single positive charge (b) two equal negative charges, separated in space.

10-43 A proton is moving from left to right. Describe its resulting motion if it enters a uniform electric field that is directed:
(a) from left to right (b) from right to left (c) downward (d) upward.
You might wish to use diagrams in your descriptions.

10-44 Answer the above question for an electron.

10-45 Suppose that, in the Millikan experiment, an electric field of magnitude 5.0×10^5 N/C is applied to a tiny oil drop of mass 2.45×10^{-14} kg, and that this electric field is just the right magnitude to hold the drop motionless against gravity. How many units of elementary charge are on the drop? [Ans. 3]

10-46 A proton having an initial speed of 3.4×10^5 m/s enters a uniform electric field of magnitude 6.2×10^9 N/C having the same direction as the proton's velocity. After a time interval of 1.2×10^{-12} s, (a) what is the proton's speed? (b) how far has it travelled?
[Ans. (a) 1.05×10^6 m/s (b) 8.4×10^{-7} m]

10-47 An electron with an initial speed of 5.5×10^6 m/s enters a uniform electric field that acts only to retard the motion of the electron. The field's magnitude is 3.7×10^6 N/C.
(a) Relative to the electron's velocity, in what direction is the field?
(b) How much time is required for the electron to come to rest (momentarily)?
(c) How far has the electron travelled? [Ans. (b) 8.5×10^{-12} s (c) 2.3×10^{-5} m]

10-48 A proton is released from rest at the surface of a positively charged plate, and travels to a parallel negatively charged plate 2.1 cm away in a time of 1.6×10^{-8} s. What is the electric field (magnitude and direction) between the plates?
[Ans. 1.7×10^6 N/C from positive to negative plate]

10-49 An electron in an oscilloscope beam travels between the deflecting plates with an initial velocity of 2.0×10^7 m/s parallel to the plates, which lie in a horizontal plane. The electric field is 2.2×10^4 N/C downward, and the plates have a length of 4.0 cm. When the electron leaves the plates, (a) how far has it dropped or risen? (Specify which.)
(b) what is its velocity (magnitude and direction)?
[Ans. (a) risen 7.7×10^{-3} m (b) 2.1×10^7 m/s at 21° above horizontal]

CHAPTER FOCUS

We have just begun our study of electricity. In this chapter, we have discussed basic atomic structure, paying particular attention to electric charges in atoms. We have described how charges can be transferred from one object to another by rubbing. The properties of conductors and insulators were introduced, and we showed how to charge conductors by contact and by induction. Coulomb's law, which is the basic law of electric forces, was presented in detail, as was the fundamental concept of electric field. The use of electric field lines was discussed as a means of visualizing electric fields. Finally, we showed how the motion of charged particles in a uniform electric field is analogous to projectile motion under the influence of gravity.

In the next chapter, we discuss some electrical concepts that you have almost certainly heard of in your daily activities — voltage and current. What exactly is a volt? an ampere? How is voltage (or electric potential difference) related to energy? Answers to these questions and more are coming up in Chapter 11.

VOCABULARY REVIEW

You should be able to define or explain each of the following words or phrases.

nucleus
proton
neutron
electron
positive ion
negative ion
law of conservation of electric charge
electric force
electric polarization
electric conductors
electric insulators
charging by contact (by conduction)
grounding
charging by induction
Coulomb's law
electric field
electric field lines

CHAPTER REVIEW

10-50 As two charges move apart, the force between them decreases by a factor of 27.0. By what factor has their separation distance increased?
(a) 27.0 (b) 729 (c) 5.20 (d) 3.00 (e) 2.28

10-51 Two charges $+q$ and $+2q$ experience a mutual force of magnitude F when separated by a distance d. What is the magnitude of the force between two charges $-2q$ and $-3q$ separated by $d/4$?
(a) 96 F (b) 12 F (c) 24 F (d) 32 F (e) 48 F

10-52 Four charges are placed at the corners of a square, one at each corner. The charges have the same magnitude, but not the same sign. Two of the charges are positive, and are at opposite corners of the square. The other two charges are negative, and are also at opposite corners. The resultant force on each charge
(a) is zero
(b) is directed toward the centre of the square
(c) is directed away from the centre of the square
(d) is directed along one side of the square
(e) has a direction not given in any of the previous answers.

10-53 Two small spheres of equal mass are suspended from a common point by threads of equal length. A charge $+q$ is placed on one sphere, and $+3q$ on the other. Which of the drawings in Figure 10-30 best shows the resulting equilibrium positions of the spheres?

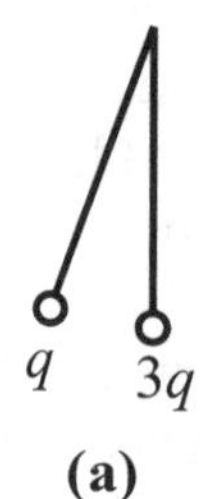

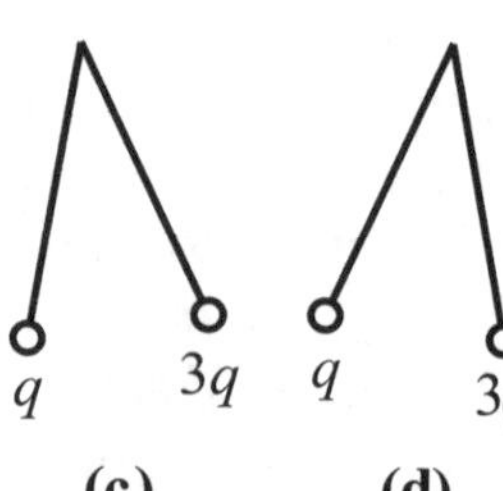

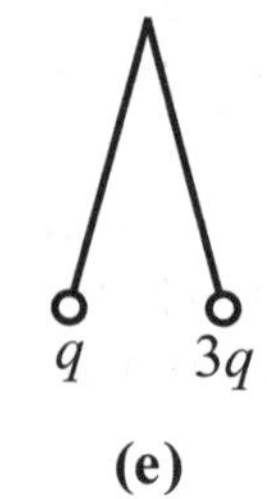

Figure 10-30 *Question 10-53.*

<u>10-54</u> Which of the drawings in Figure 10-31 best shows the total electric field at point P, which is equidistant from two equal but opposite charges $+q$ and $-q$?

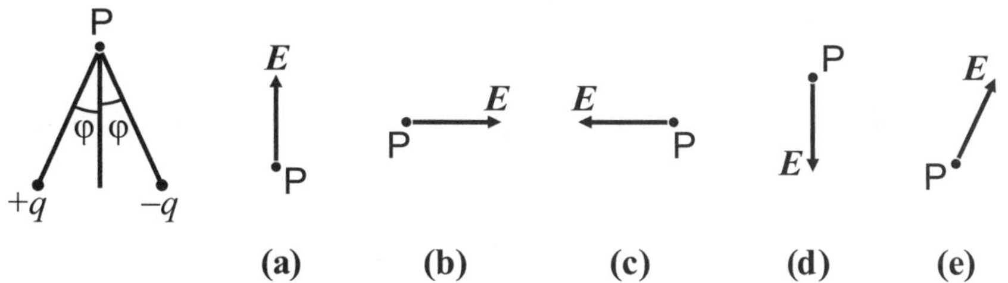

Figure 10-31 *Questions 10-54, 10-55.*

<u>10-55</u> Repeat the previous question if both charges are $+q$.

<u>10-56</u> An electron with an initial velocity eastward enters a uniform electric field and is deflected northward. What is the direction of the field?
(a) eastward (b) westward
(c) southward (d) northward
(e) northeastward

<u>10-57</u> Which of the drawings in Figure 10-32 best shows the resulting path of an electron (with initial velocity v) that enters a region containing a uniform electric field directed from left to right?

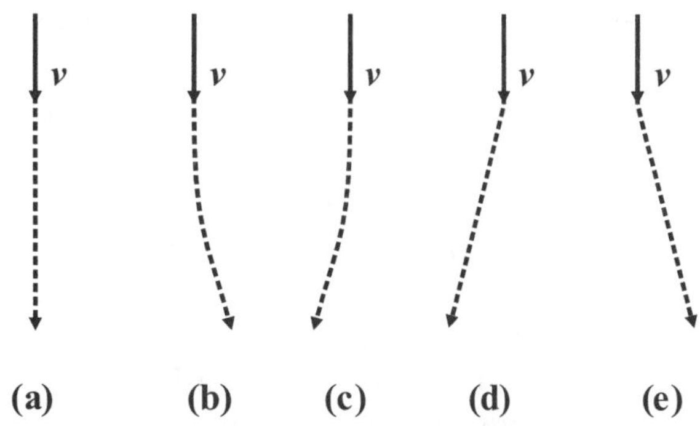

Figure 10-32 *Question 10-57.*

10-58 If you walk across a carpet, you can sometimes cause a spark when you touch a doorknob (or another person!). Explain why this happens and discuss how it could be prevented.

10-59 Explain how a charged object such as a comb can attract an electrically neutral object such as a piece of paper.

10-60 Why do static electricity experiments not work well on humid days?

<u>10-61</u> If you hold a conducting sphere in your hand, instead of placing it on an insulating stand, and attempt to charge it by contact, what happens? Explain.

10-62 (a) Use diagrams to describe how to charge a leaf electroscope negatively by induction.
(b) If a negatively charged plastic rod is brought close to the cap of the negatively charged electroscope, what happens? Explain, using diagrams.

10-63 A positively charged glass rod is brought close to the cap of a charged electroscope. The leaves move closer together.
(a) What is the sign of the charge on the electroscope? Explain, using diagrams.
(b) If the rod moves closer to the electroscope cap, the leaves start to move farther apart. Explain.

10-64 If r represents the distance separating two charges, and F represents the magnitude of the electric force between them, sketch the shape of a graph of F vs. $1/r^2$.

10-65 An α particle (charge +2e) experiences an electric force of magnitude 3.2×10^{-8} N near a proton. (a) What is the magnitude of the force on the proton? (b) Is the force repulsive or attractive? (c) How far apart are the α particle and the proton?
[Ans. (a) 3.2×10^{-8} N (b) 1.2×10^{-10} m]

10-66 Figure 10-33 shows the separations of a proton, electron, and α particle (charge +2e). What is the force (magnitude and direction) on the proton? [Ans. 3.67×10^{-8} N at 68.0° below $+x$ axis]

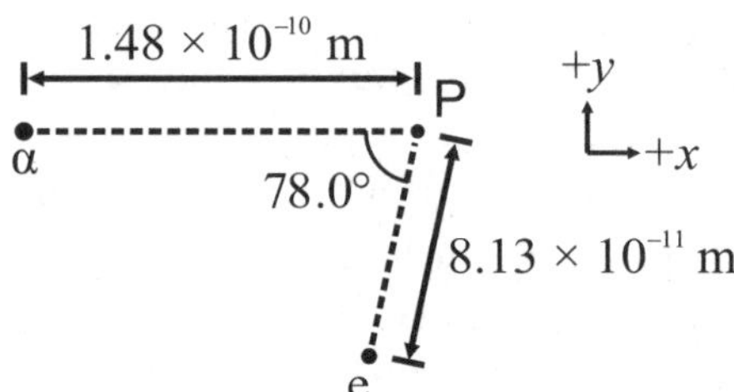

Figure 10-33 *Questions 10-66, 10-67.*

10-67 Use a scale diagram to answer the previous question.

10-68 Earth has an electric field pointing toward the centre of Earth and having an average magnitude of about 1.5×10^2 N/C.
(a) What is the sign of the charge on Earth?
(b) What is the charge on Earth, assuming that all the charge can be assumed to be concentrated at the centre? This assumption is valid for a sphere such as Earth with a surface charge. (Earth's radius = 6.37×10^6 m) [Ans. (b) -6.8×10^5 C]

Did You Know? *The charge on Earth is the result of lightning, which transfers charge from clouds to Earth. Earth's charge gradually leaks into the atmosphere, but is continually replenished by thunderstorms around the world.*

10-69 If the distance from a charge is increased by a factor of 6, does the magnitude of the electric field increase or decrease? by what factor?

10-70 What are the magnitude and direction of the electric field 5.5×10^{-10} m away from an electron? [Ans. 4.8×10^9 N/C toward electron]

10-71 What is the magnitude of the electric field at the surface of a uranium nucleus? The nucleus has a radius of 6.8 fm and a charge of +92e. Assume that the charge is distributed uniformly throughout the nucleus (assumed spherical); hence, the electric field is the same as if the charge is concentrated at the centre. [Ans. 2.9×10^{21} N/C]

10-72 If an electron is placed at each corner of an equilateral triangle of sides 1.2×10^{-10} m, what are the magnitude and direction of the electric field at the midpoint of one of the sides?
[Ans. 1.3×10^{11} N/C toward centre of triangle]

10-73 A charged water droplet of mass 1.41×10^{-11} kg and charge $+5.22 \times 10^{-15}$ C enters a uniform electric field of magnitude 1.30×10^2 N/C with an initial velocity of 7.30 cm/s opposite to the field direction.
(a) What is the acceleration (magnitude and direction) of the droplet?
(b) After 2.00 s, what is its velocity (magnitude and direction)?
(c) How far has it moved?
[Ans. (a) 4.81×10^{-2} m/s^2 opposite to initial velocity (b) 2.33 cm/s opposite to initial velocity (c) 4.97 cm]

APPLYING YOUR KNOWLEDGE

10-74 Many biological processes occur in an aqueous environment. Because water is a polar molecule, it shields the electric fields of charged particles such as ions that are in the water. Hence, the electric forces between charges in water are reduced relative to the forces if the charges were in air. Equation 10-6, which gives the magnitude of the electric field E at a distance r from a charge q, can be altered to account for the screening effect of water (or any other material) by including a dielectric constant, K, in the equation:

Table 10.2
Dielectric Constants

Substance	**Dielectric Constant *K***
Air	1.005
Palmitic acid*	2.3
Stearic acid*	2.3
Wood (approximate)	5.0
Ethanol	26.8
Water	80.4

*components of biological membranes

$$E = \frac{k|q|}{K r^2}$$

The dielectric constant, which is dimensionless, is a measure of the screening effect of the material — the larger the value of K, the larger the screening effect and the smaller the electric field due to a charge. Values of K for a few materials are given in Table 10.1. The large value of K for water indicates that it strongly screens electric fields. Consider a sodium ion Na^+ and a chloride ion Cl^- separated by 5.0 nm in aqueous solution.
(a) What is the electric field (magnitude and direction) due to the sodium ion, at the position of the chloride ion?
(b) Determine the electric force (magnitude and direction) on the chloride ion due to the sodium ion. [Ans. (a) 7.16×10^5 N/C away from sodium ion (b) 1.14×10^{-13} N toward sodium ion]

10-75 You are given two identical uncharged metal spheres on insulating stands. Explain how you could give them equal but opposite charges, using only a plastic rod rubbed with fur. You are not permitted to touch the rod to either sphere.

10-76 A charge of +2.0 μC is separated by 12 cm from a charge of −3.2 μC. Where can a third charge be placed so that it experiences no resultant force?
[Ans. 45 cm from positive charge, on side opposite negative charge]

10-77 Two particles of total charge 4.81×10^{-19} C experience a repulsive electric force of magnitude 3.80×10^{-8} N when they are 1.10×10^{-10} m apart. Determine the charge on each particle. [Ans. 3.22×10^{-19} C; 1.59×10^{-19} C]

10-78 Two spheres of equal mass 4.5 g are suspended from a common point by threads of equal length 25 cm. The spheres are given charges of like sign, with one sphere receiving a charge 4.5 times that on the other. The spheres move to equilibrium positions such that the angle between the threads is 41°. What is the magnitude of the charge on each sphere?
[Ans. 1.1×10^{-7} C; 5.0×10^{-7} C]

10-79 The electric field is zero at a point one-quarter of the way along the straight line joining two unknown point charges q_1 and q_2. What can you conclude about these charges?
[Ans. $q_1 = q_2/9$, if $\boldsymbol{E} = 0$ closer to q_1]

10-80 A proton has an acceleration of magnitude 1.1×10^{14} m/s^2 in a uniform electric field.
(a) What is the magnitude of the field?
(b) How long would it take the proton to reach a speed of 3.0×10^5 m/s (1/1000 of the speed of light) if it starts from rest?
(c) How far would it travel in this time?
[Ans. (a) 1.1×10^6 N/C (b) 2.7×10^{-9} s (c) 4.1×10^{-4} m]

10-81 An electron enters a uniform electric field with an initial speed of 7.8×10^6 m/s. The field acts only to increase the electron's speed. After 3.4×10^{-8} s, the kinetic energy of the electron has increased by 55%. What are the magnitude and direction of the electric field?
[Ans. 3.2×10^2 N/C opposite to electron's velocity]

10-82 Two parallel plates 4.50 cm apart are given equal but opposite charges so that an electric field of magnitude 5.41×10^4 N/C exists between them. An electron is released from rest at the negative plate at the same time that a proton is released from rest at the positive one. Neglecting the force exerted between the particles themselves,
(a) How far are they from the positive plate when they pass each other?
(b) What is the kinetic energy of each particle when it strikes the opposite plate?
[Ans. (a) 2.45×10^{-3} cm (b) 3.90×10^{-16} J for each particle]

10-83 An α particle (charge +2e, mass 6.6×10^{-27} kg) enters a uniform electric field as shown in Figure 10-34. The initial speed of the particle is 4.3×10^5 m/s, and the magnitude of the field is 3.0×10^5 N/C.
(a) Sketch the resulting path of the α particle.
(b Where on your sketch is the speed of the particle a minimum?
(c) What is this minimum speed?
(d) When the particle's y-component of displacement is zero, how much time has elapsed, and what is the total displacement?

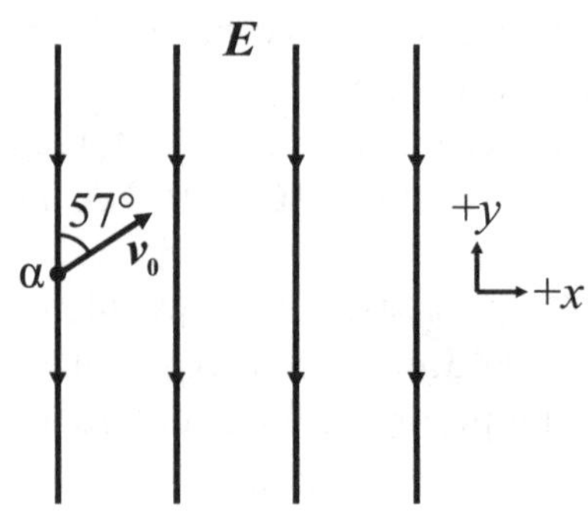

Figure 10-34 *Question 10-83.*

[Ans. (c) 3.6×10^5 m/s (d) 1.8×10^{-4} s; 65 m in the +x direction]

10-84 Determine an approximate value for the total amount of positive charge (or negative charge) in your body. Use an estimate of your body's mass and assume that your body is 100% water, which has a molar mass of 0.018 kg/mol. How does your answer compare to the value given in the "Did You Know?" in Section 10.4?

KEY OBJECTIVES

Having completed this chapter, you should now be able to do the following:

1. Describe the basic structure of atoms and nuclei.
2. Discuss how the electric force is responsible for the structure of atoms.
3. State the law of conservation of electric charge.
4. Describe how objects can be charged by rubbing.
5. Explain what is meant by the static electricity series.
6. Discuss how a charged object can attract an electrically neutral object.
7. Explain the term electric polarization.
8. Discuss how charged objects "leak" charge.
9. Explain the difference between electric conductors and insulators.
10. Describe how to charge an object by contact (conduction) and by induction.
11. Know how to use an electroscope to determine the sign and relative magnitude of an unknown charge.
12. State Coulomb's law and use it in solving problems.
13. Define electric field and explain how the electric force on a charge arises from the electric field.
14. Use electric field in solving related problems.
15. Discuss the basic properties of electric field lines, and draw field lines around simple distributions of charge.
16. Solve problems about the motion of charged particles in a uniform electric field.

ANSWERS TO SELECTED QUESTIONS

10-3 (a) up, up, and down (b) up, down, and down
10-4 (a) wax negative, wool positive (b) electrons (c) off the wool
10-6 The other object could have a negative charge, or it could be electrically neutral.
10-8 Silver is more expensive than copper.
10-9 yes
10-10 no
10-12 As the rod is removed, electrons would flow through the ground connection and the final charge on the insulated conductor would be neutral.
10-13 The electrons stop flowing because the concentrations of charge on the conductor and the other object have become equal.
10-15 positive
10-16 The leaves move apart.
10-17 The leaves move apart.

10-21 decrease by factor of 9
10-30 away from the centre of the square
10-33 (a) away from proton (b) toward electron (c) away from carbon nucleus
(d) toward negatively charged chloride ion
10-43 (a) The proton continues moving from left to right and speeds up.
(b) The proton continues moving from left to right, but slows down. If the field is not turned off, the proton will eventually stop and reverse direction, and will speed up in the opposite direction.
(c) The proton continues moving from left to right with a constant velocity, but also develops an ever-increasing downward component of velocity.
(d) The proton continues moving from left to right with a constant velocity, but also develops an ever-increasing upward component of velocity.
10-44 (a) The electron continues moving from left to right, but slows down. If the field is not turned off, the electron will eventually stop and reverse direction, and will speed up in the opposite direction.
(b) The electron continues moving from left to right and speeds up.
(c) The electron continues moving from left to right with a constant velocity, but also develops an ever-increasing upward component of velocity.
(d) The electron continues moving from left to right with a constant velocity, but also develops an ever-increasing downward component of velocity.
10-50 (c) 10-51 (e) 10-52 (b) 10-53 (e) 10-54 (b) 10-55 (a) 10-56 (c) 10-57 (c)
10-61 The sphere cannot be charged because any charge that is placed on it will immediately flow through your body to ground.
10-63 (a) negative
(b) Eventually enough positive charge is forced onto the leaves that they acquire a net positive charge and repel each other.
10-64 The graph will be linear.
10-69 decrease by a factor of 36

CHAPTER 11

ELECTRIC POTENTIAL ENERGY, POTENTIAL, AND CURRENT

We live in a permanently electrified environment. The most spectacular evidence of this electrification is lightning, which strikes Earth 50 to 100 times each second and kills thousands of people worldwide every year. Lightning causes forest fires, electric power interruptions, and damage to computers and communications equipment. However, it also contributes to the production of atmospheric fixed nitrogen, which is essential for the growth of plants. Even on a clear day, there is a downward electric field of about 100 to 200 N/C near Earth, resulting from a net negative charge on Earth. In order to understand more about lightning and many other electrical phenomena, including commercial electricity and nerve impulses in our own bodies, we need to discuss electrical potential energy, potential (voltage), and current.

11.1 ELECTRIC POTENTIAL ENERGY IN A UNIFORM ELECTRIC FIELD

Physicists are always looking for similarities in different areas of physics. General conclusions or concepts developed in one area can often be transferred to another similar field. Since both the gravitational force and electric force are inversely proportional to the square of a distance, it is not surprising that a concept such as gravitational potential energy will reappear in this chapter in the guise of electric potential energy.

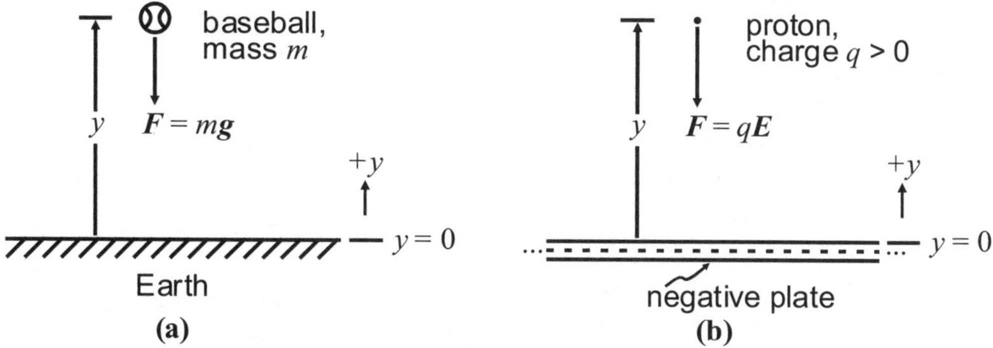

Figure 11-1 **(a)** *A baseball near Earth is analogous to* **(b)** *a proton near a large negatively charged plate. The baseball has gravitational potential energy, mgy, and the proton has electric potential energy, qEy.*

Figure 11-1 shows a baseball of mass m close to Earth, and a proton of positive charge q near a large negatively charged plate. Near Earth, the gravitational acceleration (or gravitational field) $\boldsymbol{g}$ is constant, and near the plate the electric field $\boldsymbol{E}$ is constant, or uniform. The force on the baseball is $m\boldsymbol{g}$; the force on the proton is $q\boldsymbol{E}$. If the baseball is moved from Earth ($y = 0$) to a position, y, above Earth, it gains gravitational potential energy, mgy. Similarly, if the proton is moved from the plate ($y = 0$) to position y (Figure 11-1 (b)), it gains electric potential energy, qEy. **Electric potential energy** is the energy of a charge due to its position in an electric field, and is often symbolized as U:

$$U = qEy \qquad \text{(electric potential energy, if } \boldsymbol{E} \text{ is uniform)} \qquad \textbf{(11-1)}$$

Another way to arrive at the same result is to consider the work done on each object. Suppose that the baseball is lifted at constant speed from $y = 0$ to some final position, y. Since the acceleration is zero, the resultant force must be zero, and the upward lifting force must be equal in magnitude to the force of gravity, $\boldsymbol{mg}$, on the ball. Hence, the work, W, done on the ball by the lifting force is

$$W = F_y \Delta y = (mg)(y - 0) = mgy$$

This work represents a transfer of energy (from whatever is lifting the ball) into gravitational potential energy, mgy. In a similar way, if the proton is "lifted" at constant speed from $y = 0$ to a position y, the work done by the lifting force is

$$W = F_y \Delta y = (qE)(y - 0) = qEy$$

The electric potential energy of the proton has been increased by an amount qEy.

If the baseball is dropped from rest, it loses gravitational potential energy as it falls and gains an equivalent amount of kinetic energy. If the proton is released, it moves toward the negative plate as a result of the attractive electrical force, losing electric potential energy and gaining an equal amount of kinetic energy. Notice that *a mass or charge released from rest always moves in the direction of decreasing potential energy.*

You can see that gravitational potential energy and electric potential energy are analogous to each other. However, there is one important difference — mass can only be positive, whereas charge can be either positive or negative. What if the charge q is negative? We can still use $U = qEy$ for electric potential energy, as it turns out. (See practice question 11-6 for a justification of this.) As shown in Figure 11-2, a negative charge located at the surface of the negatively charged plate ($y = 0$) has zero electric potential energy just as does a positive charge, but at a position $y > 0$, a negative charge has a negative electric potential energy (using $U = qEy$, where q is negative). A negative charge released from $y = 0$ is repelled by the negative plate and moves in the direction of decreasing potential energy, that is, it moves from zero potential energy at the plate to negative potential energy away from the plate. At the same time, the kinetic energy of the charge increases. A negative charge released from some position, y, away from the plate is repelled to even greater

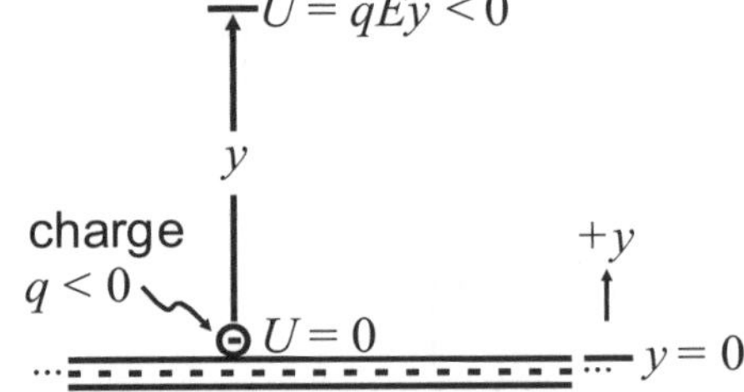

Figure 11-2 *A negative charge released at the surface of the negative plate is repelled. It moves in the direction of decreasing electric potential energy (U), from zero potential energy at the plate to negative potential energy (U = qEy, and q < 0) at position y. As the potential energy decreases, the kinetic energy increases by an equivalent amount.*

values of y, thus decreasing its potential energy even more.

When the equation $E_p = mgy$ is used for gravitational potential energy, the $+y$ direction must be upward, that is, opposite to the direction of the gravitational field and gravitational acceleration. Similarly, when using $U = qEy$ for electric potential energy, *the $+y$ direction must be opposite to the electric field direction.*

The equation $E_p = mgy$ gives the gravitational potential energy *relative* to the position $y = 0$. Correspondingly, $U = qEy$ gives the electric potential energy relative to $y = 0$. When solving problems, you are free to choose the position where $y = 0$. In problems involving gravitational potential energy, it was suggested in Chapter 7 that you choose $y = 0$ at the lowest possible position so that all potential energies would be positive. However, as pointed out in Chapter 7, what is really important is the *change* in potential energy as an object moves from one position to another, and this change does not depend on your choice of $y = 0$ position. In problems involving electric potential energy in a uniform field, charges can be positive or negative, and it is often impossible to choose a position for $y = 0$ so that all electric potential energies in the problem are positive. Hence, it is usually most convenient simply to choose the location for $y = 0$ so that all y-values in a problem are positive.

Sample Problem 11-1

A large positively charged plate produces an electric field of magnitude 1.3×10^3 N/C. An electron is released from a point 1.2×10^{-2} m from the plate. Use energy methods to determine its speed just as it strikes the plate.

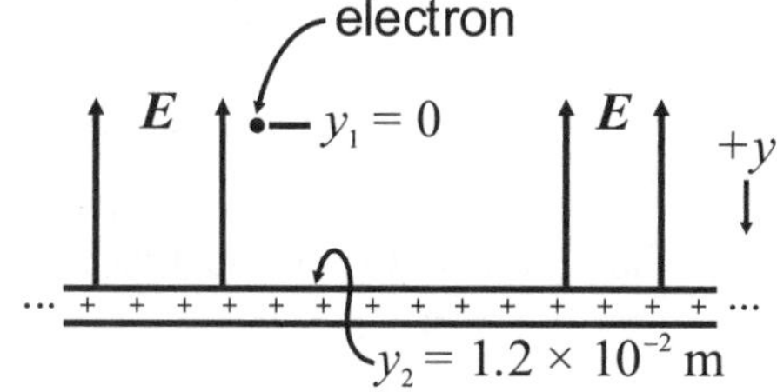

Figure 11-3 *Sample Problem 11-1.*

Solution: The field near a positively charged plate points away from the plate, and since the $+y$ direction must be opposite to this, $+y$ is toward the plate (Figure 11-3). We choose $y = 0$ at the initial position of the electron so that the electron's final position at the plate will be positive, and therefore slightly easier to deal with. (However, our final answer will not depend on our choice of $y = 0$ position.)

The initial electric potential energy ($U_1 = qEy_1$) of the electron is zero because $y_1 = 0$. Its final potential energy (U_2) at the surface of the plate is

$$\begin{aligned} U_2 &= qEy_2 \\ &= \left(-1.60 \times 10^{-19}\ \text{C}\right)\left(1.3 \times 10^3\ \text{N/C}\right)\left(1.2 \times 10^{-2}\ \text{m}\right) \\ &= -2.5 \times 10^{-18}\ \text{J} \end{aligned}$$

> ***Units Tip:** Notice the units in $U = qEy$:*
>
> *q (in C) times E (in N/C) times y (in m) gives*
>
> *C·(N/C) ·m = N·m = J*

Watch signs when substituting into $U = qEy$. The charge q for an electron is negative, E is the *magnitude* of the electric field and hence must be positive, and y (positive in this case) is determined by our choice of $y = 0$ position.

By the law of conservation of energy, the sum of the electron's initial potential energy and its initial kinetic energy (E_{K1}), both of which are zero, equals the sum of its final potential and kinetic energies:

$$U_1 + E_{K1} = U_2 + E_{K2}$$

$$\text{Therefore,}\quad 0 + 0 = U_2 + \tfrac{1}{2}mv^2$$

Solving for v:

$$v = \sqrt{\frac{-2U_2}{m}}$$

Do not be concerned by the negative sign inside the square root; remember that U_2 is also negative.

Substituting $m = 9.11 \times 10^{-31}$ kg for the mass of the electron, and $U_2 = -2.5 \times 10^{-18}$ J:

> ***Reference Tip:*** *When you need to know the mass of an electron or another physical constant, refer to Appendix 4.*

$$v = \sqrt{\frac{-2(-2.5 \times 10^{-18}\,\text{J})}{9.11 \times 10^{-31}\,\text{kg}}}$$

$$= 2.3 \times 10^{6}\,\text{m/s}$$

Thus, the electron's speed just as it hits the plate is 2.3×10^{6} m/s.

Practice

11-1 Sketch the shape of a graph of electric potential energy vs. height (y) for a proton above a large negatively charged plate. Choose $y = 0$ at the surface of the plate.

11-2 Repeat the above question for an electron above the plate.

11-3 A typical fair-weather electric field near Earth is 1.5×10^{2} N/C downward. Relative to the surface of Earth, what is the electrical potential energy of:
(a) an electron 2.0 m above the surface? (b) a proton 2.0 m above the surface?
[Ans. (a) -4.8×10^{-17} J (b) 4.8×10^{-17} J]

11-4 When thunderstorms occur, the electric field in the atmosphere near Earth is directed upward because of a large quantity of negative charge in the lower portions of the clouds. A typical electric field magnitude in this situation is 1.0×10^{4} N/C. Relative to the surface of

Earth, what are the electrical potential energies of the two particles in the previous question? (Hint: remember that the $+y$ direction must be opposite to the direction of the field.)
[Ans. (a) 3.2×10^{-15} J (b) -3.2×10^{-15} J]

11-5 What are the gravitational potential energies of the two particles in the previous question, relative to the surface of Earth? [Ans. (a) 1.8×10^{-29} J (b) 3.3×10^{-26} J]

11-6 A charge q is located near a large positively charged plate.
(a) Is the electric field due to the plate directed toward, or away from, the plate?
(b) Show that the work done by the electric force on the charge, as the charge moves from $y = 0$ (at the plate's surface) to any other position, y, is given by $-qEy$ for either positive or negative q. Thus, the electric potential energy is $U = qEy$ regardless of the sign of q. (The solution to this problem does not depend on whether the plate is horizontal or vertical, or on which side of the plate the charge is located.)

11-7 Each of the following objects is released from rest at point A. In which direction (toward B or away from B) will each object move?
(a) A proton has an electric potential energy of zero at A, $+3.5 \times 10^{-18}$ J at B.
(b) A baseball has a gravitational potential energy of 4.2 J at A, 2.1 J at B.
(c) A toboggan has a gravitational potential energy of -2×10^{4} J at A, -1×10^{4} J at B.
(d) A positive ion has an electric potential energy of -3.4×10^{-17} J at A, $+2.1 \times 10^{-17}$ J at B.

11-8 An α particle (charge +2e) is located 0.87 cm from a large negatively charged plate. The field due to the plate has a magnitude of 3.56×10^{3} N/C.
(a) What is the particle's electric potential energy relative to the surface of the plate?
(b) If the α particle is released from rest, what is its kinetic energy as it strikes the plate? Use energy methods.
[Ans. (a) 9.9×10^{-18} J (b) 9.9×10^{-18} J]

11-9 (a) If an electron is "boiled off" a wire located in a vertical evacuated tube, will it fall because of gravity, or rise because of Earth's downward electric field (average magnitude 1.5×10^{2} N/C)? (b) Use energy methods to determine the electron's speed after moving 0.25 m in the tube, assuming that it starts from rest. [Ans. (a) rise (b) 3.6×10^{6} m/s]

11-10 An electron is released from rest halfway between two parallel, oppositely charged plates. The field between the plates has a magnitude of 1.25×10^{3} N/C.
(a) What is the sign of the charge on the plate toward which the electron moves?
(b) Just before it hits the plate, the electron has a speed of 2.36×10^{6} m/s. Use energy methods to determine the separation of the plates. [Ans. (b) 2.54×10^{-2} m]

11-11 A proton traveling at 3.54×10^{5} m/s enters a region of uniform electric field of magnitude 2.18×10^{5} N/C in the same direction as the proton's velocity. What is the proton's speed after traveling 1.20 cm? Use energy methods. [Ans. 7.91×10^{5} m/s]

11.2 ELECTRIC POTENTIAL ENERGY OF POINT CHARGES

The electric field near the surface of Earth on a clear day is approximately constant, and the field near a large charged plate is also constant. However, any arbitrary distribution of charges gives rise to a non-constant field, and it is important to remember that the discussion of electric potential energy in Section 11.1 is applicable only in the special case of a uniform (i.e., constant) electric field.

We now consider the electric potential energy associated with point charges, that is, charges that are each distributed over a small enough volume that they can be considered to be concentrated at single points. Any charge distribution can be thought of as a collection of point charges, and thus our discussion here could be applied to very complicated charge distributions. However, we will limit ourselves to the electric potential energy of only two point charges.

Figure 11-4 shows two point charges q_1 and q_2 separated by a distance r. The electric potential energy, U, of the two-charge system is defined as

$$U = \frac{\mathrm{k}q_1q_2}{r} \quad \text{(electric potential energy)} \qquad \textbf{(11-2)}$$

where k is the constant in Coulomb's law (k = 8.99×10^9 N·m^2/C^2). Although this is the potential energy of the two-charge system, often we think of one charge as fixed and the other as moving, and refer to the potential energy of the moving charge (just as we did with the potential energy of a charge moving in a uniform field in Section 11.1).

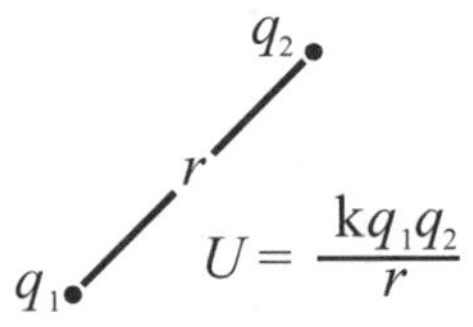

q_2, r, q_1, $U = \frac{\mathrm{k}q_1q_2}{r}$

Figure 11-4
Electric potential energy, U, of two point charges.

The expression kq_1q_2/r is analogous to $-GmM/r$ for gravitational potential energy (Chapter 9). The negative sign included in gravitational potential energy reflects the attractive nature of the gravitational force. If q_1 and q_2 are of opposite sign, that is, if the electrical force between them is attractive, the product q_1q_2 and the electric potential energy (U) are negative. When q_1 and q_2 have the same sign, U is positive.

Notice that as $r \to \infty, U \to 0$. Thus, we are not free to choose the position where electric potential energy is zero. It has been pre-selected that the electric potential energy of point charges approaches zero when the charges are separated by a very large distance.

Sample Problem 11-2

(a) What is the electric potential energy of two protons separated by 1.50×10^{-10} m?
(b) If the separation were to increase, would the electric potential energy increase or decrease?
(c) If the two particles were a proton and an electron, what would be the answer to (b)?
(d) If the protons (1.50×10^{-10} m apart) were released from rest, in which directions would they move?

(e) What would be the speed of the above protons after each one has moved 1.00×10^{-10} m?

Solution: (a) The electric potential energy of the protons can be determined by simple substitution into Eqn. 11-2:

$$
\begin{aligned}
U &= \frac{kq_1q_2}{r} \\
&= \frac{(8.99\times10^{9}\ \mathrm{N\cdot m^2/C^2})(1.60\times10^{-19}\ \mathrm{C})(1.60\times10^{-19}\ \mathrm{C})}{1.50\times10^{-10}\ \mathrm{m}} \\
&= 1.53\times10^{-18}\ \mathrm{J}
\end{aligned}
$$

> ***Units Tip:*** *Notice the units for kq_1q_2/r:*
>
> *$(N{\cdot}m^2/C^2){\cdot}C{\cdot}C/m$*
> *$= N{\cdot}m$*
> *$= J$*

Thus, the electric potential energy of the two-proton system is 1.53×10^{-18} J.

(b) Since the electric potential energy (U) of the protons is positive, and since $U \propto 1/r$, then, if the separation were to increase, the electric potential energy would decrease.

(c) If the two particles were a proton (positive charge) and electron (negative charge), then q_1q_2 would be negative and U would be negative. If the separation r were to increase, U would change from an initial negative value to a negative value closer to zero. In other words, the electric potential energy would *increase*, that is, become more positive. (The *absolute value* of the potential energy would decrease.)

(d) If the protons were released from rest, they would move in the direction of decreasing potential energy, that is, they would move away from each other.
or: Their mutual electrical repulsion would cause them to move away from each other.

(e) As the protons move apart (Figure 11-5), their electric potential energy decreases and their kinetic energy increases by an equal amount, by the law of conservation of energy. The initial sum of potential energy (U_1) and kinetic energy ($E_{K1} = 0$) equals the final sum, ($U_2 + E_{K2}$):

$$U_1 + E_{K1} = U_2 + E_{K2} \qquad \text{Eqn. [1]}$$

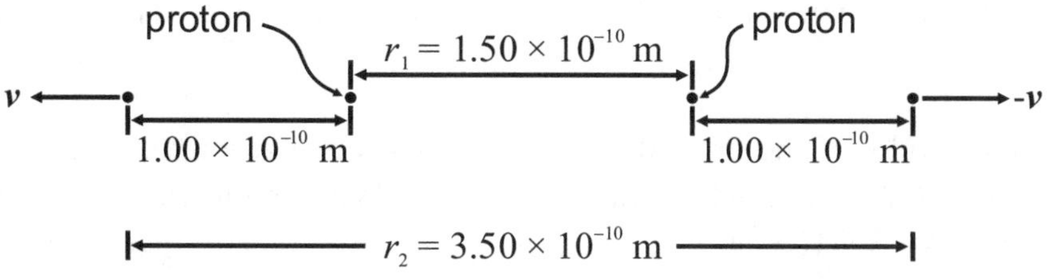

Figure 11-5 *Sample Problem 11-2, part (e).*

U_1 is known from part (a), and $E_{K1} = 0$. To determine U_2, we use the same method as in part (a); the protons are now 3.50×10^{-10} m apart, and we find that U_2 is 6.58×10^{-19} J. Since the protons are in identical situations, their speeds must be the same. (Physicists would say "Their speeds are the same by symmetry.") Thus, we can write E_{K2} as $2(\frac{1}{2}mv^2) = mv^2$, where m (the proton mass) is 1.67×10^{-27} kg (from Appendix 4). Hence, Eqn. [1] becomes

$$U_1 = U_2 + mv^2$$

Re-arranging for v:

$$v = \sqrt{\frac{U_1 - U_2}{m}}$$

Substituting numbers:

$$v = \sqrt{\frac{(1.53 \times 10^{-18} - 0.658 \times 10^{-18})\text{ J}}{1.67 \times 10^{-27}\text{ kg}}}$$

$$= 2.3 \times 10^4 \text{ m/s}$$

Thus, the speed of each proton is 2.3×10^4 m/s. (This answer has only two digits because the subtraction of the potential energies results in a number with only two significant digits.)

 **Practice**

11-12 Sketch the shape of a graph of electric potential energy vs. separation distance r for (a) two positive charges (b) two negative charges (c) one positive and one negative charge.

11-13 Repeat the above question, instead plotting electric potential energy vs. $1/r$.

<u>11-14</u> (a) What is the electric potential energy of two point charges separated by a very large distance?
(b) If the charges have different signs, does the electric potential energy increase or decrease as the separation decreases?
(c) Will the charges with different signs move toward each other or away from each other if released from rest? Explain, using electric potential energy.

11-15 Two protons are separated by 6.0×10^{-15} m in a uranium nucleus. What is their electric potential energy? [Ans. 3.8×10^{-14} J]

11-16 In the Bohr model of the ground state of the hydrogen atom, an electron has a circular orbit of radius 5.3×10^{-11} m around a proton (nucleus). What is the electric potential energy of such an atom? [Ans. -4.3×10^{-18} J]

<u>11-17</u> In the Bohr atom in the previous question, what is the name of the force that is the centripetal force on the electron?

11-18 The electric potential energy of an electron near a uranium nucleus (charge +92e) is -1.41×10^{-16} J. How far is the electron from the nucleus, considered to be a point charge?
[Ans. 1.50×10^{-10} m]

11-19 Two α particles (charge +2e, mass 6.6×10^{-27} kg each) are released from rest, separated by 3.40×10^{-12} m. (a) Will their separation increase or decrease? Use electric potential energy to explain your answer. (b) When the speed of each particle is 1.7×10^5 m/s, how far apart are they? [Ans. (b) 1.2×10^{-11} m]

11.3 ELECTRIC POTENTIAL

You have undoubtedly seen signs such as: "Danger. High Voltage! Keep out." You might already know that the voltage available from normal electrical outlets in North America is 120 V (volts), and you probably know that different batteries have different voltages: 1.5 volts, 6 volts, etc. What exactly is voltage?

To answer this question, we start by considering a charge placed at some point P where there is an electric field (Figure 11-6). This charge will have electric potential energy, which is proportional to the amount of charge. The larger the charge, the larger is the potential energy. The **electric potential** at point P is defined as the electric potential energy per unit charge. In other words, if the electric potential energy of a charge q placed at P is divided by that charge q, the result is the electric potential at P. Using the customary symbol V for electric potential:

$$V = \frac{\text{electric potential energy}}{q}$$

or $V = \dfrac{U}{q}$ (definition of electric potential, V) **(11-3)**

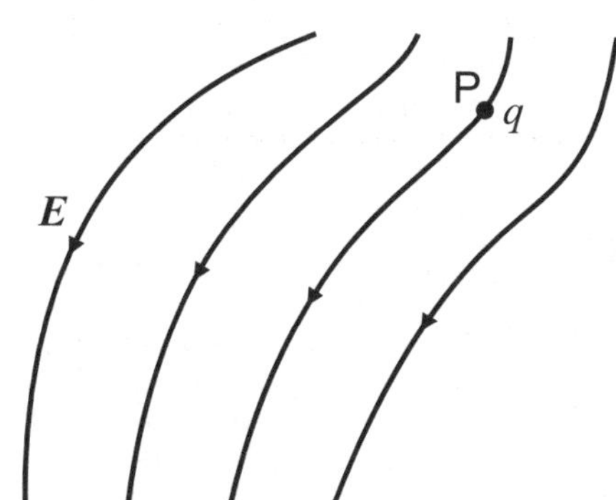

Figure 11-6 *The electric potential at a point P in an electric field is the electric potential energy per unit charge q placed at that point.*

Be careful not to confuse *electric potential energy* and *electric potential* (often just called potential, when "electric" is implied by the physical situation being considered). We have discussed electric potential *energy* in Sections 11.1 and 11.2, and now we have *electric potential, which is electric potential energy per unit charge.* Since both potential energy and charge are scalar quantities, electric potential is also a scalar.

Notice that we refer to the potential at a particular point in space. The electric potential is a result of the presence of nearby charges that produce the electric field at that point. The potential is not associated with any particular charge *at* that point. If a charge happens to be placed at a point of known potential V, the charge's potential energy can be determined by simply re-arranging Eqn. 11-3 to give

$$U = qV \text{ (electric potential energy, } U\text{)} \qquad \textbf{(11-4)}$$

Since potential is energy per unit charge, one possible SI unit is joule/coulomb (J/C), but this is given the special name of **volt**, abbreviated V:

volt (V) = joule/coulomb (J/C) **(11-5)**

This unit is named in honour of the Italian physicist, Alessandro Volta (Figure 11-7), who invented the electric battery, thus starting modern electricity. Notice that the symbol for potential is written as V, and that the unit is also V. There is some "potential" for confusion here, but it should be easy to understand what is intended in a given situation.

Figure 11-7 *Alessandro Volta (1745-1827), inventor of the battery. (Stamp courtesy of J.L. Hunt)*

Since the electric potential energy is always relative to some position, such as $y = 0$ for a uniform field, or infinite separation for two point charges, the electric potential is also relative to this position. As is the case with potential energy, what is important is not the actual value of potential but rather the *change* in potential, or **potential difference** ΔV, from one point to another. This potential difference is commonly called **voltage**. When we say that a car battery provides 12 V, this means that the potential difference between one terminal and the other is 12 V. The battery terminal with the higher potential is referred to as the *positive* terminal, the lower-potential terminal being *negative*.

Did You Know? *Most of the standard electrical units such as volt were adopted in 1881 at an International Congress in Paris.*

Very often, a quoted voltage is the potential difference between a point and Earth (or "ground"). For example, a 120-V electrical outlet provides a potential difference of 120 V between one of its wires and ground. If you read that the ionosphere[1] has a voltage of 3×10^5 V, it is implicitly assumed that this is the potential difference between the ionosphere and Earth.

The term "potential difference" is often used somewhat imprecisely. If a charge moves from a point where the potential is +5 V to a point where it is +12 V, the change in potential, that is, the

Did You Know? *An electrocardiogram (ECG or EKG) is a recording of electric potential differences (as a function of time) on the skin as a result of the electrical activity of the heart. The voltages detected are of the order of a few millivolts (mV). An electroencephalogram (EEG) is a recording of the electrical activity of the cerebral cortex, with voltages in the range of a few tens of microvolts (μV).*

[1]The ionosphere is a region of the atmosphere, from about 70 to 300 km above Earth, where there are many ions produced by solar ultraviolet radiation and by energetic particles from the sun.

potential difference, is +7 V. If the charge moves from +12 V to +5 V, the potential difference is now –7 V. However, it is common practice to say that the charge has moved through a potential difference of 7 V in either case. In other words, *potential difference often means the absolute value of the true potential difference.* As you will see, this should not cause you any difficulty when solving problems.

Since we know that the electric potential energy of a charge q, at a point where the potential is V, is given by $U = qV$ (Eqn. 11-4), then the *change* in the charge's potential energy as it moves is given by

$$\Delta U = q\Delta V \qquad \textbf{(11-6)}$$

$$\text{or} \qquad U_2 - U_1 = q(V_2 - V_1) \qquad \textbf{(11-6b)}$$

where "1" and "2" represent two points in space (Figure 11-8). Notice that Eqn. 11-6 is valid regardless of the particular path followed by the charge.

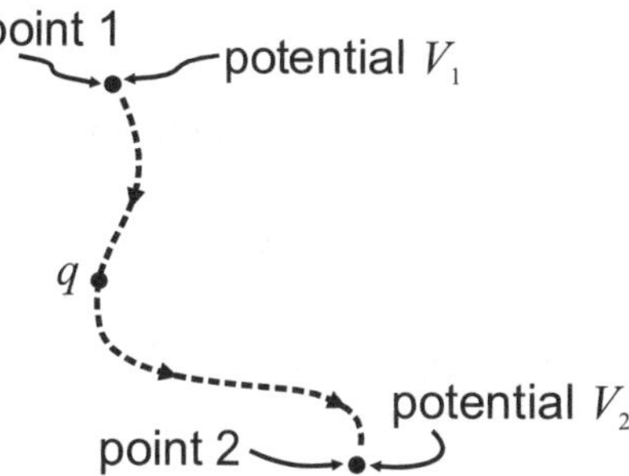

Figure 11-8 *As the charge q moves from point 1 to 2, its electric potential energy changes by: $\Delta U = q\Delta V$, that is, $U_2 - U_1 = q(V_2 - V_1)$.*

Sample Problem 11-3

(a) If the ionosphere has a potential of $+3.0 \times 10^5$ V relative to Earth, what is the electric potential energy of a proton in the ionosphere, relative to Earth (Figure 11-9)? (b) Repeat for an electron.

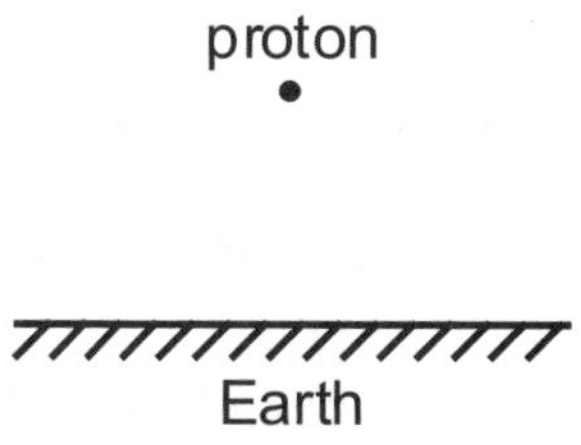

proton

Earth

Figure 11-9
Sample Problem 11-3.

Solution: (a) This problem is solved with a straightforward substitution into Eqn. 11-4:

$$U = qV = (1.60 \times 10^{-19}\text{ C})(3.0 \times 10^5\text{ V}) = 4.8 \times 10^{-14}\text{ J}$$

Therefore, the electric potential energy of the proton is 4.8×10^{-14} J, relative to Earth.

We could have also solved this problem by using Eqn. 11-6: $\Delta U = q\Delta V$. In this equation, ΔU is the required difference between the proton's potential energy in the ionosphere and its potential energy on Earth's surface. In other words, ΔU is the proton's potential energy in the ionosphere relative to Earth. ΔV is the difference between the ionospheric potential and the ground potential, that is, ΔV is the given ionospheric potential relative to Earth.

> ***Units Tip:*** *In problems involving voltage, it is often handy to remember that a volt is a joule per coulomb (V = J/C). For example, when using the equation $U = qV$, charge q in coulombs times voltage in volts (that is, joules per coulomb) gives electric potential energy in joules.*

(b) For an electron, the only change is that the charge is negative. Hence, the electric potential energy of the electron is -4.8×10^{-14} J.

Sample Problem 11-4

When a car horn is sounded, charge flows from one terminal of the car battery, through the horn, and back to the other battery terminal. If the battery has a voltage of 12 V, the charge has been moved through a potential difference of 12 V. (As mentioned earlier, this commonly means that the absolute value of the potential difference is 12 V.) The charge moves in the direction of decreasing electric potential energy, and hence the charge loses potential energy, which is converted into sound energy in the horn (and some thermal energy). How much energy is converted, if the magnitude of charge that flows is 8.0 C?

Solution: We are not told what sign of charge is flowing (to be discussed in Section 11.5), nor whether the change in potential is positive or negative. Therefore, we consider only the absolute value of quantities, using Eqn. 11-6:

$$|\Delta U| = |q\Delta V| = (8.0\text{ C})(12\text{ V}) = 96\text{ J}$$

Thus, 96 J of electric potential energy is converted to sound (and thermal energy).

The Electron-Volt – An Energy Unit

In atomic and subatomic physics, the joule is an enormous energy unit. Tiny particles such as electrons have very small energies when measured on the scale of joules. For example, the kinetic energy of an electron moving with a speed of 1×10^6 m/s (think about that — one million metres per second!) is only 5×10^{-19} J. A more common energy unit on these scales is the electron-volt (eV), and its multiples, keV (10^3 eV), MeV (10^6 eV), etc.

An **electron-volt** is defined as the **electric potential energy gained or lost by an *electron* in moving through a potential differences of one *volt*.** If an electron moves to a point where the potential has increased by 1 V, its electrical potential energy decreases by 1 eV (since $\Delta U = q\Delta V$, and $q < 0$ for an electron). If the electron moves so that the potential decreases by 1 V, it gains electrical potential energy of 1 eV. In either case, it is common to say that the electron has moved through a potential difference of 1 V.

We can find the joule equivalent of 1 eV from $|\Delta U| = |q\Delta V|$. Using $\Delta V = 1$ V and, for an electron, $q = -e = -1.60 \times 10^{-19}$ C:

$$|\Delta U| = |q\Delta V| = (1.60 \times 10^{-19}\text{ C})(1\text{ V}) = 1.60 \times 10^{-19}\text{ J}$$

Thus, $$1 \text{ eV} = 1.60 \times 10^{-19} \text{ J} \quad \textbf{(11-7)}$$

Converting the 5×10^{-19} J of kinetic energy of an electron moving at 1×10^6 m/s to electron-volts gives:

$$5 \times 10^{-19} \text{ J} \times \frac{1 \text{ eV}}{1.60 \times 10^{-19} \text{ J}} = 3 \text{ eV}$$

which is much more convenient to deal with than 5×10^{-19} J.

The electron-volt is particularly easy to use when dealing with particles that are moving through potential differences. The electric potential energy gained or lost by an electron moving through 1 V is 1 eV, by definition. From the equation $|\Delta U| = |q\Delta V|$, we see that the potential energy change is proportional to the charge, and also proportional to the potential difference. Thus, if an electron moves through 2 V, the energy gained or lost is simply 2 eV; through 10 V, the energy is 10 eV, etc. Since a proton has the same magnitude of charge as an electron, then the electrical potential energy it gains or loses in moving through a voltage of, say, 5 V is also 5 eV. An α particle has a charge of +2e; if it moves through 1 V, its energy gained or lost is 2 eV. If it moves through 3 V, it gains or loses 6 eV.

Sample Problem 11-5

An electron is accelerated from rest through 3.1×10^6 V in a particle accelerator.
(a) As the electron is accelerated, does it move toward higher, or lower, potential?
(b) What is its final kinetic energy in electron-volts?

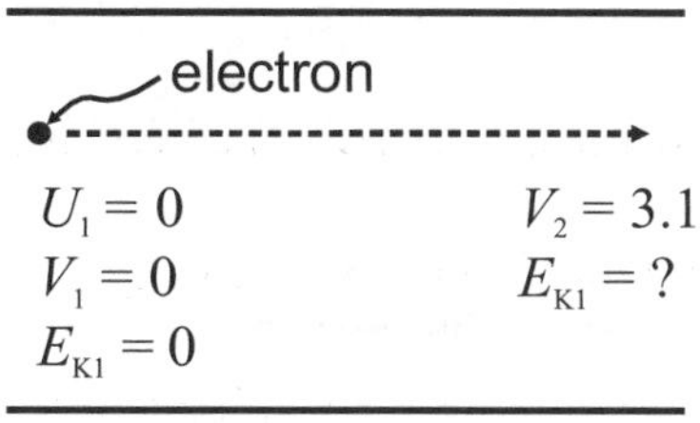

electron

$U_1 = 0$ $\quad V_2 = 3.1 \times 10^6$ V
$V_1 = 0$ $\quad E_{K1} = ?$
$E_{K1} = 0$

Figure 11-10 *Sample Problem 11-5.*

Solution: (a) We know that particles move toward decreasing potential energy if released from rest. Let us arbitrarily define the electron's initial potential energy (U_1) as zero (Figure 11-10), which means that the initial potential (V_1) is zero (since $V_1 = U_1/q$ from Eqn. 11-3). The electron will then move toward negative potential energy, which will become more and more negative as the electron moves. Since the electron has a negative charge ($q < 0$), then as U becomes more negative, V becomes more positive (from $V = U/q$). In other words, the electron is moving toward *higher* potential; $\Delta V > 0$. (Therefore, if the potential at the initial position is zero, the final potential, V_2, must be $+3.1 \times 10^6$ V, as shown in Figure 11-10.)

> ***Learning Tip:*** *In general, if negative particles are released from rest, they move toward higher or increasing potential; thus, $\Delta V > 0$. Positive particles move toward lower or decreasing potential; hence, $\Delta V < 0$. In either case, the particles are moving toward decreasing electric potential energy.*

(b) By the law of conservation of energy, the sum of the electron's potential energy and kinetic energy must remain constant:

$$U_1 + E_{K1} = U_2 + E_{K2}$$

or
$$E_{K2} - E_{K1} = U_1 - U_2$$

The left-hand side is the change in the kinetic energy; remember that the change in a quantity is always the final value minus the initial value. The right-hand side (RHS) is the negative of the change in the potential energy, that is, $-\Delta U$. Substituting $-\Delta U$ for the RHS, and also noting that $E_{K1} = 0$ (since the electron starts from rest):

$$E_{K2} = -\Delta U$$

But, $\Delta U = q\Delta V$ (Eqn. 11-6). Hence, $E_{K2} = -q\Delta V$.

To arrive at an answer in electron-volts, the charge q must be expressed in terms of e (the absolute value of the elementary electric charge). For the electron, $q = -\text{e}$. ΔV must be expressed in volts; $\Delta V = 3.1 \times 10^6$ V.

Thus, $E_{K2} = -(-\text{e})(3.1 \times 10^6 \text{ V}) = 3.1 \times 10^6 \text{ eV}$ (or 3.1 MeV)

Hence, the electron's final kinetic energy is 3.1×10^6 eV. As it accelerates through 3.1×10^6 V, the electron loses 3.1×10^6 eV of electric potential energy, and gains 3.1×10^6 eV of kinetic energy.

Practice

11-20 A chloride ion with a single net negative charge (Cl^-) has an electric potential energy of -4.2×10^{-19} J. What is the potential at the position of the ion? [Ans. 2.6 V]

11-21 The membranes of nerve cells (or neurons) in their normal resting state have an electric potential difference across them. The potential in a cell's interior is typically –85 mV relative to the cell's exterior. If a sodium ion (Na^+) diffuses across a cell membrane from the exterior to the interior, what is the change in electric potential energy of the ion? [Ans. -1.4×10^{-20} J]

11-22 On a particular day, two points (A) 1.00 m and (B) 1.50 m above Earth have potentials of 152 V and 228 V, respectively (both potentials relative to ground).
(a) What would be the potential energy in electron-volts of an α particle (charge +2e) at each point, relative to ground? (b) If the particle moves from B to A, is ΔV positive, or negative?
[Ans. (a) 304 eV; 456 eV (b) negative]

11-23 A flashlight is powered by two 1.5-V batteries, providing a total potential difference of 3.0 V. When the flashlight is turned on for 4.0 s, the total charge that flows through the bulb is 12 C. What amount of energy has been provided by the batteries? [Ans. 36 J]

11-24 (a) How much energy is dissipated by a lightning bolt that transfers –22 C of charge to Earth through a potential difference of 3.2×10^7 V? Express the answer in megajoules.
(b) As the negative charge goes from the cloud to Earth, is it moving toward higher, or lower, potential? [Ans. (a) 7.0×10^2 MJ (b) higher]

11-25 Perform the following unit conversions:
(a) 3.74×10^{-18} J to electron-volts (b) 511 keV to joules
(c) 2.98×10^{-13} J to mega-electron-volts
[Ans. (a) 23.4 eV (b) 8.18×10^{-14} J (c) 1.86 MeV]

11-26 A proton is accelerated by a voltage of 4.2×10^6 V in a particle accelerator.
(a) What is the change in the proton's electrical potential energy (in electron-volts)?
(b) What is the change in the proton's kinetic energy (in electron-volts)?
(c) Do your answers depend on whether or not the proton starts from rest?
[Ans. (a) -4.2×10^6 eV (b) $+4.2 \times 10^6$ eV (c) no]

11-27 What potential difference is required to give a helium nucleus (charge +2e) an increase in kinetic energy of 8 MeV? [Ans. 4×10^6 V, or 4 MV]

11-28 An electron having a speed of 1.43×10^6 m/s is at a point where the potential is +2.53 V (Figure 11-11). It then moves freely in a straight line to a point where the potential is +1.35 V. What is the electron's speed at this point? [Ans. 1.28×10^6 m/s]

Figure 11-11 *Question 11-28.*

11.4 ELECTRIC POTENTIAL IN VARIOUS SITUATIONS

In this section, we investigate the electric potential in a uniform electric field and the electric potential due to point charges. In the case of a uniform electric field, we will find a useful relationship between the potential and the field, which will lead us to an electric-field unit more commonly used than newton per coulomb (N/C).

Electric Potential in a Uniform Electric Field

A number of situations in which a uniform electric field exists have been described: near Earth's surface, near a large charged plate, and between oppositely charged plates. A uniform electric field can also exist across the membrane of a biological cell, as a result of charges on both the exterior and interior surfaces. Figure 11-12 shows a large negatively charged plate that produces a uniform electric field $\boldsymbol{E}$ close to the plate. We will investigate how the electric potential, V, at a distance d away from the plate is related to E and d.

We start by considering the electric potential energies of a positive charge q as it is "lifted" against the electric field, starting at position 1 at the surface of the plate and ending at position 2 at a distance d away from the plate (Figure 11-12). Equation 11-1 ($U = qEy$) for electric potential energy in a uniform field can be used to calculate the electric potential energies in this situation. As shown, the $y = 0$ position is defined to be at the plate, and the $+y$ direction is opposite to the field direction. At position 2, $y = d$, and hence the electric potential energy of the charge is

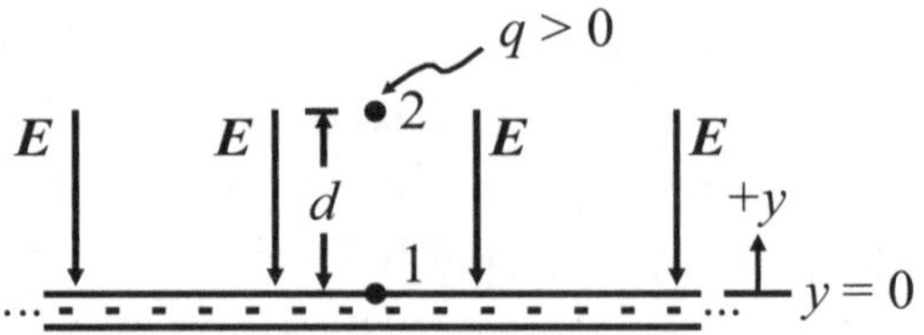

Figure 11-12 *In a uniform electric field, $E = (V_2 - V_1)/d = \Delta V/d$.*

$$U_2 = qEd$$

At position 1, $y = 0$, and hence the electric potential energy is zero:

$$U_1 = 0$$

The electric potential at positions 2 and 1 can be determined by using the defining equation for potential: $V = U/q$ (Eqn. 11-3). At position 2,

$$V_2 = \frac{U_2}{q} = \frac{qEd}{q} = Ed$$

At position 1,

$$V_1 = \frac{U_1}{q} = 0$$

We now subtract V_1 from V_2 to give the change in electric potential, ΔV from position 1 to position 2:

$$\Delta V = V_2 - V_1 = Ed - 0$$

Thus, $$\Delta V = Ed$$

or $$E = \frac{\Delta V}{d} \quad \text{(for uniform } \boldsymbol{E}\text{)} \qquad \textbf{(11-8)}$$

Equation 11-8 relating E and ΔV is valid in any uniform electric field: the magnitude (E) of a uniform electric field is equal to the potential difference (ΔV) between two points in the field divided by the distance (d) between the points. Note that d must be measured parallel to the field direction.

Notice the unit of electric field implied by $E = (\Delta V)/d$. With ΔV in volts and d in metres, *E is in volts per metre (V/m).* This is a more common unit for E than is newtons per coulomb (N/C), but the two are completely equivalent SI units:

$$1 \text{ V/m} = 1 \text{ N/C} \qquad \textbf{(11-9)}$$

The unit of volts per metre has a very useful physical interpretation — it tells us how much the potential changes with distance. If the uniform electric field near Earth is 150 V/m (read as volts per metre) downward, then for every metre moved downward the potential drops by 150 V. (Remember that the field points from high to low potential.) Equivalently, the potential increases by 150 V for every metre moved upward.

Dry air can withstand a maximum electric field of approximately 3×10^6 V/m. If exposed to an electric field of about this magnitude, the air molecules become ionized and form a conducting path for the charges creating the field. The charges flow rapidly along this path, generating light and thermal energy in what we call a *spark*. You can easily calculate the potential difference for any sparks that you see. Suppose that you shuffle across a rug in dry weather and generate a spark 2 cm (0.02 m) long when you touch a doorknob. As indicated above, the field magnitude required for a spark is 3×10^6 V/m. Re-arranging $E = (\Delta V)/d$ as $\Delta V = Ed$, and substituting numbers:

$$\Delta V = Ed = (3 \times 10^6 \text{ V/m})(0.02 \text{ m}) = 6 \times 10^4 \text{ V}$$

Hence, a 2-cm spark results from a potential difference of about 6×10^4 V. Lightning, which is essentially a very large spark, is discussed in Section 11.5.

Electric Potential Due to Point Charges

Figure 11-13 shows two point charges: q, which we will consider to be the "source charge" producing an electric field in space, and q', a "test charge" at point P. The electric potential energy of the two-charge system is $U = \text{k}qq'/r$. Recalling that potential is electric potential energy per unit charge, we can easily determine the potential at point P by dividing U by q':

Figure 11-13 *At point P, the electric potential, V, due to q is V = kq/r.*

$$V = \frac{U}{q'} = \frac{\text{k}qq'}{r} \times \frac{1}{q'} = \frac{\text{k}q}{r}$$

In summary, $$V = \frac{\text{k}q}{r} \qquad \text{(potential due to point charge } q) \qquad \textbf{(11-10)}$$

Equation 11-10 gives the electric potential at a distance r from a point charge q. Since the electric potential energy ($\text{k}qq'/r$) is relative to a point infinitely far away, then the potential is also relative to this point.

Sample Problem 11-6

(a) What is the potential at point A in Figure 11-14 due to the electron (e) and proton (p)?
(b) Determine the potential difference ($V_A - V_B$) between points A and B.
(c) If another electron is introduced into this system and moves from B to A, how much does its electric potential energy change?

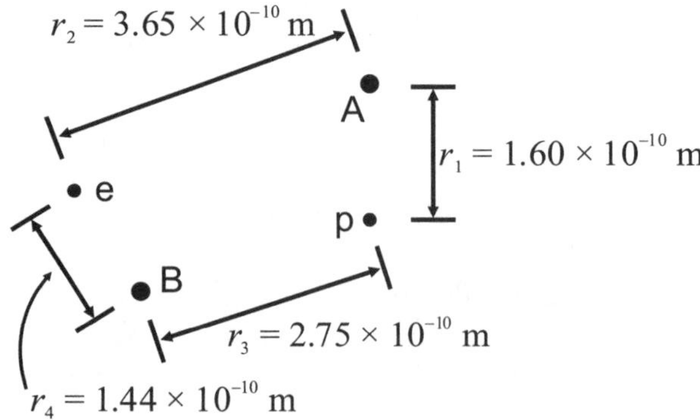

Figure 11-14 *Sample Problem 11-6.*

Solution: (a) The potential at A due to the electron and proton is just the sum of the separate potentials due to these two particles. Since potential is a scalar quantity, we do not consider components in the sum. Thus, using Eqn. 11-10, the potential at A is:

$$V_A = \frac{kq_p}{r_1} + \frac{kq_e}{r_2}$$

$$= k\left[\frac{q_p}{r_1} + \frac{q_e}{r_2}\right]$$

where q_p and q_e represent the charges on the proton and electron, respectively. Substituting numbers:

$$V_A = 8.99 \times 10^9 \text{ N}\cdot\text{m}^2/\text{C}^2 \left[\frac{1.60 \times 10^{-19}\text{ C}}{1.60 \times 10^{-10}\text{ m}} + \frac{-1.60 \times 10^{-19}\text{ C}}{3.65 \times 10^{-10}\text{ m}}\right]$$

$$= 5.0 \text{ V}$$

Thus, the potential at point A is 5.0 V.

> ***Units Tip:*** *When electric potential is calculated using $V = kq/r$, the SI units on the right-hand side are:*
>
> *N·m²/C² for k*
> *C for q*
> *m for r*
>
> *This gives a unit for V of (N·m²/C²)·C/m, which is N·m/C. The product N·m is equivalent to a joule (J), and so the unit for V is J/C, which is a volt (V).*

(b) The potential at point B can be calculated in a similar way.

$$V_B = k\left[\frac{q_p}{r_3} + \frac{q_e}{r_4}\right]$$

$$= 8.99 \times 10^9 \text{ N}\cdot\text{m}^2/\text{C}^2 \left[\frac{1.60 \times 10^{-19}\text{ C}}{2.75 \times 10^{-10}\text{ m}} + \frac{-1.60 \times 10^{-19}\text{ C}}{1.44 \times 10^{-10}\text{ m}}\right]$$

$$= -4.8 \text{ V}$$

Therefore, $V_A - V_B = (5.0 - (-4.8)\ \text{V} = 9.8\ \text{V}$.

Hence, the required potential difference is 9.8 V.

(c) If an electron moves from B to A, its change in electric potential energy can be determined from Eqn. 11-6:

$$\Delta U = q\Delta V$$

that is, $$U_A - U_B = q(V_A - V_B)$$

Remember that when we are considering the change in a quantity, we subtract the initial value from the final value. Since $q = -e = -1.60 \times 10^{-19}$ C for an electron, and $\Delta V = V_A - V_B = 9.8$ V in this problem:

$$\Delta U = (-1.60 \times 10^{-19}\ \text{C})(9.8\ \text{V}) = -1.6 \times 10^{-18}\ \text{J}$$

Thus, the electric potential energy of the electron *decreases* by 1.6×10^{-18} J (or 9.8 eV).

 **Practice**

11-29 Points A and B in a uniform electric field have potentials of 5 V and 7 V, respectively. The line joining A and B is parallel to the field direction. In which direction does the field point?

11-30 On a particular day, the uniform electric field near Earth is 232 V/m downward. If we define the ground potential to be zero, what is the potential 25 m above the ground?
[Ans. 5.8×10^3 V]

11-31 After walking on a rug on a dry day, you "zapped" a friend with a spark 1.0 cm long. What was the approximate potential difference between you and your friend?
[Ans. 3×10^4 V]

11-32 A uniform electric field exists across the membrane of a neuron cell. For a neuron having a membrane thickness of 7.2 nm, and a potential difference of 87 mV across the membrane, what is the magnitude of the electric field? [Ans. 1.2×10^7 V/m]

11-33 Figure 11-15 shows two parallel, oppositely charged plates with a potential difference of 6.0 V between them. The plates are separated by 1.1 cm. If we define the potential of the negative plate to be zero,
(a) what is the potential of the positive plate?
(b) what is the potential half-way between the plates?
(c) what is the potential at point A, which is 0.28 cm above the positive plate?
(d) what is the electric field (magnitude and direction) between the plates?
[Ans. (a) +6.0 V (b) +3.0 V (c) +4.5 V (d) 5.5×10^2 V/m, from positive plate to negative plate]

Figure 11-15
Question 11-33.

11-34 If the uniform electric field near Earth is 125 V/m downward, what is the electric potential energy (relative to Earth) of a dust particle having a charge of −84e, floating in the air 3.40 m above Earth? [Ans. -5.71×10^{-15} J]

11-35 A proton is accelerated from rest from a positively charged plate to a parallel negatively charged plate. The separation of the plates is 8.9 mm. If the potential difference between the plates is 75.3 V, what is the speed of the proton just as it hits the negative plate? The mass of a proton is given in Appendix 4. [Ans. 1.2×10^{5} m/s]

11-36 What is the electric potential 1.25×10^{-19} m from (a) an electron? (b) a sodium ion Na^{+}? [Ans. (a) −1.15 V (b) +1.15 V]

11-37 At what distance from a chlorine nucleus (charge +17e) is the electric potential 1.0 V? Assume that the nucleus acts as a point charge. [Ans. 2.4×10^{-8} m]

11-38 What is the electric potential at point "X" in Figure 11-16? [Ans. 16.9 V]

11-39 (a) If a chloride ion Cl^{-} were at point "X" in the previous question, what would its electric potential energy be?
(b) Relative to which point is this electric potential energy?
[Ans. (a) -2.70×10^{-18} J]

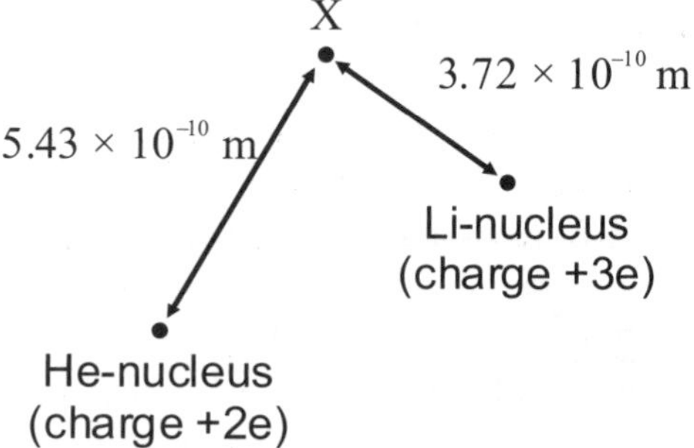

Figure 11-16
Questions 11-38 & 11-39.

11-40 Two point charges are positioned as shown in Figure 11-17. The potential difference ($V_T - V_R$) between points T and R on the line joining the charges is 1.86 MV. How far is T from the 350-μC charge?
[Ans. 2.4 cm]

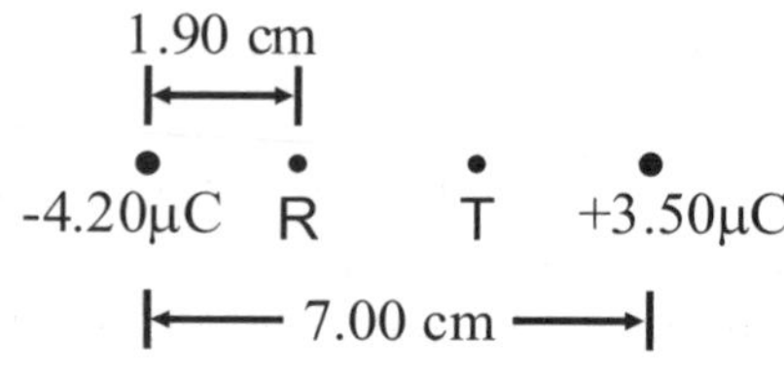

Figure 11-17 *Question 11-40.*

11.5 ELECTRIC CURRENT

You probably know that the voltage available from standard electrical outlets in North America is 120 V. Since electric potential (or voltage) is electric potential energy per unit charge, this means that for every coulomb of charge that flows, 120 J of electric potential energy is converted into other forms of energy. For example, in a toaster the electric potential energy is converted into thermal energy and some light. You are probably also aware that household circuits are protected by fuses or circuit breakers, which stop the flow of charge when the electric current exceeds a certain number of amperes. What *is* current, and what is an ampere?

Electric current is a measure of how much charge flows per unit time. It is defined as the charge that flows divided by the time taken, and is usually given the symbol *I*. Writing charge as *q* and time as *t*:

$$I = \frac{q}{t} \quad \text{(electric current, } I\text{)} \qquad \textbf{(11-11)}$$

From Eqn. 11-11, we see that one possible SI unit for current is coulomb/second (C/s), but this is given the name of **ampere** (A) in honour of André Marie Ampère (Figure 11-18). If one coulomb of charge flows per second, the current is one ampere. In a typical household circuit, a fuse or circuit breaker limits the current to 15 A.

Figure 11-18 *André Marie Ampère (1775-1836), French physicist and mathematician. Ampère showed that currents flowing in two parallel wires exert magnetic forces on each other, and studied the relationship between current and magnetic field. (Stamp courtesy of J.L. Hunt.)*

In a metal wire, only electrons, which have negative charges, are free to flow. However, when the concept of current was being established over a century ago, the atomic nature of matter was not well understood, and a principle was established that *conventional current is in the direction of the flow of positive charge.* This convention is still used today. A flow of electrons from left to right in a wire (Figure 11-19) is equivalent to a current (that is, a flow of positive charge) in the opposite direction, from right to left. Although current has this conventional direction associated with it, nonetheless current is considered to be a *scalar* quantity, not a vector.

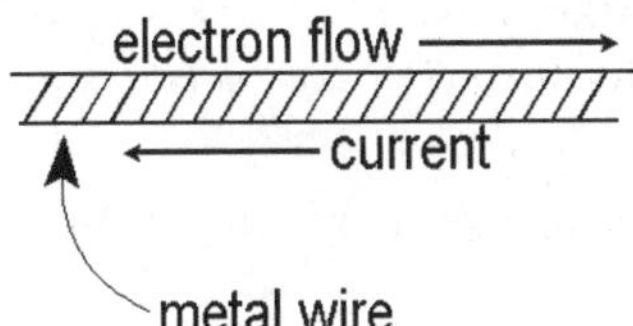

Figure 11-19 *A flow of negative electrons from left to right is equivalent to a current (flow of positive charge) from right to left.*

This standard current direction is not as anachronistic as it might appear. In ionized gases, both positive and negative ions can contribute to the flow of charge, and in some semiconductors, electron vacancies known as "holes" act effectively as positive charges that can move.

Electricity as a Hazard

Which is more dangerous — high voltage or high current? If harmless sparks between your finger and a doorknob result from a potential difference of about 10^4 V, then why is 120 V from a household outlet considered to be dangerous? In response, it is often said that "it is the current that kills." When you generate a spark between a finger and a doorknob, the potential difference and the instantaneous current are high. However, the current is extremely short-lived and affects only a small part of your body. If you were to allow the continuing voltage from a standard 120-V outlet to produce a current through your body, it would probably be lethal.

The current produced depends on the voltage, and on the electric resistance (Chapter 12) of the body; this resistance in turn depends on the points of contact on the body and on the skin condition (moist or dry). A current of from 3 to 8 mA through the body produces a mild tingling sensation. Above 10 mA, pain is felt, and 50 mA produces a severe shock. A current of about 100 to 200 mA (0.1 to 0.2 A) results in death. Above 200 mA, the resulting muscular contractions are so severe that the heart is effectively clamped during the shock, and the victim's chances for survival are actually better than for currents between 100 and 200 mA.

Did You Know? *Ampère was a classic case of an absent-minded professor. On one occasion, he erased a chalkboard with his handkerchief, and then immediately used the same handkerchief to wipe his face.*

In science centres and museums, a common demonstration involves a volunteer from the audience getting "fly-away hair" (as shown in Fig. 10-9) when touching a high-voltage static electricity generator. Although the person has a high potential relative to the ground, very little current travels through the person (standing on an insulating platform) and there is essentially no danger. However, if the insulating platform were not present, current could flow through the person to the ground with deadly results.

Sample Problem 11-7

During a time interval of 5.0 s, 15 C of charge flows through a lightbulb.
(a) How much current flows?
(b) If the potential difference between the ends of the wires leading into the lightbulb is 6.0 V, how much energy is dissipated in the lightbulb in 5.0 s?

Solution: (a) Using Eqn. 11-11, current is charge divided by time:

$$I = \frac{q}{t} = \frac{15\text{ C}}{5.0\text{ s}} = 3.0\text{ A}$$

Thus, the current is 3.0 A.

(b) This is similar to Sample Problem 11-4. The absolute value of the change in the electric potential energy is given by Eqn. 11-6:

$$|\Delta U| = |q\Delta V|$$

In 5.0 s, the charge q that flows is 15 C.

Thus, $$|\Delta U| = |q\Delta V| = (15\text{ C})(6.0\text{ V}) = 90\text{ J}$$

Therefore, as the charge flows through the lightbulb, 90 J of energy is dissipated. (This means that 90 J of electric potential energy is converted into 90 J of thermal energy and light energy.)

Useful Electricity

Electricity is used in so many ways that it is difficult to imagine life without it. Most people tend to take for granted the common uses in which electrical energy is converted into some other form of energy. Light energy is produced in lightbulbs; thermal energy in ovens, toasters, and hair dryers; mechanical energy (or energy of motion) in electric mixers, drills, and other tools; and sound energy in telephones in radios. Chemical energy is involved in such processes as the eletroplating of silver onto less expensive nickel to make jewellery and silverware. There are hundreds of other common uses of electricity for domestic, commercial, and industrial applications, as well as for transportation and leisure activities.

Beside the common uses, however, there are numerous unique and exciting uses that scientists and technologists have discovered or designed. Consider first some of the applications of electricity that relate to the human body. Because the body has its own electrical system, many medical uses of electrical energy exists. Tiny currents of 1 nA to 3 nA (n = nano = 10^{-9}) promote the healing of broken bones and burned areas. Pacemakers stimulate the heart electrically and allow people with certain heart problems to lead normal lives. Defibrillators send a large current through the body for a small fraction of a second to restore a normal heartbeat if the heart has been beating irregularly or to shock it back into beating if it has stopped. Other medical applications of electricity include the operation of heart and lung machines, the use of thermographs (temperature-sensitive photographs) to locate cancerous tumours near the skin surface, and the use of electrodes attached to the body to locate tumours beneath the surface

Did You Know? *Since the body's nervous system runs on electric impulses, electricity can be used to relieve pain as well as promote healing. The ancient Egyptians applied this principle when the electric charges generated by torpedo fish to ease pain. The Romans evidently used electric eels to treat headaches and arthritis. Today, physicians use electrical nerve stimulation to treat certain types of pain. A 9-V battery supplies a weak electric current across the patient's skin into the nerve cells beneath the skin's surface. The current stimulates the body's natural ability to fight pain.*

Computers require electrical energy to function, of course. Computers are found in control systems in airplanes, cars, and spacecraft. They are used to help design automobiles and architectural structures, to operate mechanical robots that help handicapped people function independently, and to operate devices that let blind people read. Without computers, the instant banking systems that offer 24-hour access to your money as well as daily-interest accounts would not be possible. Computers are also used in education and in the fields of art and music. Archaeologists are able to put together thousands of broken clay tablets in the proper order and decipher their ancient inscriptions with the help of computers. And astronomers study photographs of outer space that consist of millions of faint images combined by computers.

Of course, there are countless other applications of electricity, and many more to be discovered in the future.

Lightning

Now that you have learned about voltage and current, we can discuss one of nature's most fascinating displays — lightning. It was Benjamin Franklin who first established the electrical nature of lightning in 1752 by flying a kite during a thunderstorm. He was able to collect charge on a key on the lower end of the kite string and observed that this lightning charge performed just the same as earthly charge in static electricity experiments. Franklin was lucky he was not killed! Georg Richmann was not so fortunate — Richmann (1711-1753), a scientist of German origin, was killed in Russia when he approached a lightning rod during a storm. His assistant was knocked unconscious.

There are roughly 2000 active thunderstorms around the world at any one time. Lightning bolts carry negative charge from clouds to Earth, with the result that Earth has a permanent charge of about -5×10^5 C, and the upper atmosphere has an equivalent positive charge. In the absence of thunderstorms, these charges would gradually "leak" into each other, and Earth and the atmosphere would become electrically neutral. However, the constant activity of thunderstorms maintains the charge separation.

A thundercloud is predominantly negatively charged at the bottom and positively charged at the top. The details of the charging mechanisms are still not well understood; different charging theories involve updrafts and downdrafts, collisions, friction, and melting and freezing. Most theories attribute the charge distribution to a difference in size between the positive and negative charge carriers (such as raindrops, ice crystals, ions, and hail). According to these theories, the positively charged particles are smaller and rise to the top of the cloud; the negatively charged particles are larger and settle to the bottom.

In the absence of a thunderstorm, the electric field near Earth is downward because of Earth's negative charge; its magnitude is about 100 to 200 V/m. However, because of the large negative charge at the base of a thundercloud, the field between Earth and the cloud is upward, and has a typical magnitude of 10 000 V/m.

A lightning bolt is simply the flow of electrons from the bottom of the cloud to the ground. (There is often lightning within the cloud as well.) Because of the large electric field between the ground and the cloud, the air molecules become ionized and form a conducting path. An electric field of about 3×10^6 V/m is needed to ionize dry air at atmospheric pressure, but the moist air and lower pressure associated with a thunderstorm produces ionization at lower electric fields. The electric field has to reach the ionizing value in only a small region near the cloud. Once the electron flow begins, the large concentration of negative charge in the leading edge of the lightning bolt creates a large field nearby that causes the ionization and flow to continue. Usually the initial ionization near the cloud is accompanied by ionization and charge flow near the ground as well. Thus, there are two channels of charge flow, one starting at the cloud and one at the ground; these flows of charge come together, typically about 50 m above the ground, to form a lightning stroke.

A typical flash of lightning consists of three to five current pulses, separated by times of about 40 ms. The peak current in the pulses is roughly 2×10^4 A, and the temperature in the current channel can reach 30 000°C. The total charge transferred from the cloud to Earth is about –25 C (with wide variability), and since the potential difference between the cloud and ground is typically 5×10^8 V, the total energy released is of the order of 10^{10} V. (How was this number determined?) Most of this energy goes into thermal energy, but some goes into light, sound, and radio waves.

Lightning tends to strike high objects such as tall buildings and trees. Every year, golfers die because they stand under tall trees to try to keep dry during thunderstorms. Lightning rods are commonly used on buildings to provide a conducting path along which lightning can travel instead of passing through the building itself and causing damage. During a thunderstorm you should not stand near a tall tree or any other solitary object. If you are standing up or lying down and lightning strikes, the hazard is far greater than if you are squatting. The best choice is to seek shelter, for example in a car. If someone has been struck by lightning, it is worthwhile to administer proper first-aid revival techniques, even if the person appears lifeless. Reported cases verify that revival is possible.

We see lightning almost as soon as it strikes because the light travels at 3×10^8 m/s. However, the sound (thunder) travels at only about 340 m/s (or $^1/_3$ km/s), and so we hear the thunder a few seconds afterward. You can estimate the distance (in kilometres) to a lightning strike by counting the number of seconds between seeing the lightning and hearing the thunder, and then simply dividing by three.

Practice

11-41 If there is a flow of 3.4 C of charge in 1.7 s, what is the current? [Ans. 2.0 A]

11-42 The current through a flashlight bulb is 0.350 A. If it is used for 23 s, how much charge flows? [Ans. 8.1 C]

11-43 When a nerve cell is stimulated electrically, mechanically, or chemically, the permeability of the cell membrane changes and sodium ions (Na^+) can diffuse more readily into the cell. If 1.5×10^6 Na^+ ions move through the membrane in 5.0 ms, what is the corresponding electrical current? [Ans. 4.8×10^{-11} A]

11-44 In a lightning bolt, negative charge moves from a cloud to the ground. What is the direction of the current?

11-45 A current of 2.35 A flows in a wire. (a) How many coulombs of charge cross any cross-section of the wire per second? (b) How many electrons cross any cross-section per second? [Ans. (a) 2.35 C (b) 1.47×10^{19}]

11-46 In a particular lightning bolt, –24 C of charge are transferred in 0.21 s through a potential difference of 5.5×10^8 V. (a) What is the average current? (b) How much electric potential energy is dissipated? [Ans. (a) 1.1×10^2 A (b) 1.3×10^{10} J]

11-47 Suppose that, after seeing a lightning flash, you count six seconds until you hear the thunder. Approximately how far away was the flash? [Ans. 2 km]

11-48 When a large potential difference is applied to the terminals of a hydrogen gas-discharge tube, the hydrogen gas ionizes, producing free electrons and protons. The electrons move toward the positive terminal, and the protons toward the negative terminal. The resulting current is the sum of the currents due to the electrons and protons.
(a) What is the direction of the total current?
(b) What is the total current if, in 1.00 s, 3.50×10^{18} electrons and 1.35×10^{18} protons move in opposite directions past any cross-section in the tube? [Ans. (b) 0.776 A]

CHAPTER FOCUS

In the previous chapter, we discussed electric charges, Coulomb's law, and electric field.

The focus of this chapter has been on other important concepts in electricity: electric potential energy, potential, and current. Electric potential energy and potential have been presented for the cases of uniform electric fields and point charges, and the electron-volt has been introduced as a useful unit of energy. Electric current has been defined, and the natural phenomenon of lightning has been used to illustrate electric field, potential, charge, and current.

In the next chapter, we explore a fundamental relationship between voltage, current, and a new concept — electric resistance. We use this relationship, known as Ohm's law, to study direct-current (DC) circuits.

VOCABULARY REVIEW

You should be able to define or explain each of the following words or phrases.

electric potential energy
electric potential
volt
potential difference
voltage
electron-volt
electric current
ampere

CHAPTER REVIEW

11-49 An electron is released from rest in an electric field. In which direction will it move?
(a) toward decreasing potential, which for an electron is toward decreasing potential energy
(b) toward increasing potential, which for an electron is toward decreasing potential energy
(c) toward increasing potential, which for an electron is toward increasing potential energy
(d) toward decreasing potential, which for an electron is toward increasing potential energy
(e) none of the above

11-50 A potassium ion (K^+) is at rest at the surface of the membrane of a neuron, where there is an electric field. In which direction will it move?
(a) toward decreasing potential, which for a K^+ ion is toward decreasing potential energy
(b) toward increasing potential, which for a K^+ ion is toward decreasing potential energy
(c) toward increasing potential, which for a K^+ ion is toward increasing potential energy
(d) toward decreasing potential, which for a K^+ ion is toward increasing potential energy
(e) none of the above

11-51 Electric potential is
(a) equal to electric potential energy.
(b) the absolute value of electric potential energy.
(c) the negative of electric potential energy.
(d) electric potential energy per unit distance.
(e) electric potential energy per unit charge.

11-52 A charge q is placed at a distance of r from a charge Q. A charge $2q$ is placed at a distance of $2r$ from another charge Q (far away from the first charge Q). All the charges are positive. The electric potential of the first charge q is
(a) the same as that of the second charge q
(b) twice that of the second charge q
(c) one half of that of the second charge q
(d) four times that of the second charge q
(e) one quarter of that of the second charge q

11-53 Car batteries are often rated in ampere·hours (A·h). An ampere·hour is a quantity of:
(a) current (b) time (c) potential (d) charge (e) energy

11-54 A uniform electric field between two parallel, oppositely charged plates is directed from west to east.
(a) In which direction does an electron move if its electric potential energy is decreasing?
(b) If the electron's potential energy changes by 1.2×10^{-17} J as it moves 3.5 cm, what is the magnitude of the electric field? [Ans. (b) 2.1×10^3 V/m]

11-55 Under a particular thundercloud, there is a uniform electric field of 9.3×10^3 V/m upward. An electron in the field, initially at rest, travels freely for 3.5×10^{-6} m before undergoing a collision with a gas molecule. Just before it hits the molecule, what is its speed? Use energy methods. [Ans. 1.1×10^5 m/s]

11-56 What is the electric potential energy of an electron and an α particle (charge +2e) separated by 6.9×10^{-12} m? [Ans. -6.7×10^{-17} J]

11-57 When a stimulus is applied to a nerve cell, sodium ions (Na^+) rush through the cell's membrane. If a Na^+ ion moves through a potential difference of 42 mV in a time of 1.2 ms, what is the change, in electron-volts, in the electric potential energy of the ion?
[Ans. 4.2×10^{-3} eV]

11-58 An electron in the picture tube of a television is accelerated from rest through a potential difference of 25 kV.
(a) Does the electron move toward higher, or lower, potential?
(b) What is the change in the electron's electric potential energy? Express your answer in kilo-electron-volts and in joules.
(c) What is the change in the electron's kinetic energy?
[Ans. (b) -25 keV = -4.0×10^{-15} J (c) $+4.0 \times 10^{-15}$ J]

11-59 In a wire in which charge is flowing, the electric field in the wire is approximately uniform and its direction is along the wire. If the potential difference between the ends of a wire that is 1.50 m long is 5.3×10^{-2} V, what is the magnitude of the field in the wire?
[Ans. 3.5×10^{-2} V/m]

11-60 (a) If the potential increases from 101 V to 313 V in a vertical distance of 1.50 m near Earth, what is the magnitude of the uniform vertical electric field?
(b) If the potential increases with elevation, is the direction of this field upward or downward?
[Ans. (a) 141 V/m]

11-61 A pair of oppositely charged parallel plates is separated by 7.8 mm. If the resulting electric field between the plates has a magnitude of 6.41×10^{3} V/m, what is the electric potential difference across the plates? [Ans. 5.0×10^{1} V]

11-62 If an electron moves from the negative plate to the positive plate in the previous question, what is the change in its (a) kinetic energy (in electron-volts)? (b) electric potential energy (in electron-volts)? [Ans. (a) 5.0×10^{1} eV (b) -5.0×10^{1} eV]

11-63 Sketch the shape of a graph of electric potential vs. distance from (a) a positive point charge (b) a negative point charge.

11-64 Repeat the above question, plotting potential vs. $1/r$, where r is the distance from the charge.

11-65 What is the electric potential 1.5×10^{-10} m from a carbon nucleus ($q = +6e$)?
[Ans. 58 V]

11-66 The electric potential at a point 3.43×10^{-12} m from an electron and at a distance d from an α particle (charge +2e) is zero. Determine d. [Ans. 6.86×10^{-12} m]

11-67 In 15.4 s, 13.5 C of charge flow through a flashlight bulb. What is the current?
[Ans. 0.877 A]

11-68 In the previous question, if the potential difference across the bulb is 3.0 V, how much energy is dissipated in the bulb? [Ans. 41 J]

<u>11-69</u> In an oscilloscope, a beam of electrons is accelerated at the back of the main tube, passes through the deflecting plates, and hits the screen. What is the direction of the current in the beam?

11-70 Car batteries are often rated in ampere·hours (A·h). If a particular battery has a rating of 2.0 A·h, convert this rating to the equivalent amount of coulombs. [Ans. 7.2×10^3 C]

APPLYING YOUR KNOWLEDGE

11-71 A particular proton in space experiences two fields: a gravitational field (1.30×10^5 N/kg toward planet X), and an electric field (2.47×10^{-4} N/C away from planet X).
(a) If the proton is released from rest, in which direction will it move?
(b) After moving 1.50 m, what will be its speed? Use energy methods and assume uniform fields.
[Ans. (a) toward planet X (b) 565 m/s]

11-72 Solve the previous problem using Newton's second law and constant-acceleration kinematics.

<u>11-73</u> A proton is at rest 1.42×10^{-10} m from a uranium nucleus (charge +92e), which can be treated as a point charge since its size is much smaller than the proton-uranium distance. Assume that the uranium nucleus remains at rest.
(a) What is the electric potential energy of the proton?
(b) In which direction does the proton move?
(c) How far is the proton from the nucleus when its speed is 1.30×10^5 m/s?
[Ans. (a) 1.49×10^{-16} J (b) 1.57×10^{-10} m]

11-74 A proton and a carbon nucleus (considered as a point charge +6e, mass 1.9×10^{-26} kg) are separated by 3.2×10^{-12} m, and both are initially at rest. What is the speed of the carbon nucleus when the proton's speed is 9.5×10^3 m/s? Hint: remember conservation of momentum.
[Ans. 8.4×10^2 m/s]

11-75 A lithium nucleus (q = 3e) accelerates from rest through a potential difference of 4.6 kV.
(a) What is the final kinetic energy of the nucleus (in kilo-electron-volts)?
(b) What is the work done (in joules) on the nucleus by the electrical force during the acceleration? (Hint: remember the work-energy theorem.)
[Ans. (a) 13.8 keV (b) 2.21×10^{-15} J]

11-76 A potassium ion (K^+) and a calcium ion (Ca^{++}) are separated by 1.50×10^{-11} m At what point on the line joining them is (a) the electric field zero? (b) the electric potential zero?
[Ans. (a) 6.21×10^{-12} m (b) nowhere]

11-77 In an oscilloscope, an electron is accelerated from rest through a voltage of 1.14×10^3 V. It then passes through deflecting plates 2.00 cm apart, across which there is a voltage of 412 V

(Figure 11-20). Its velocity when it enters the plates is perpendicular to the electric field of the plates. When the electron leaves the plates, what distance will it have moved toward the positive plate?
[Ans. 7.23×10^{-3} m]

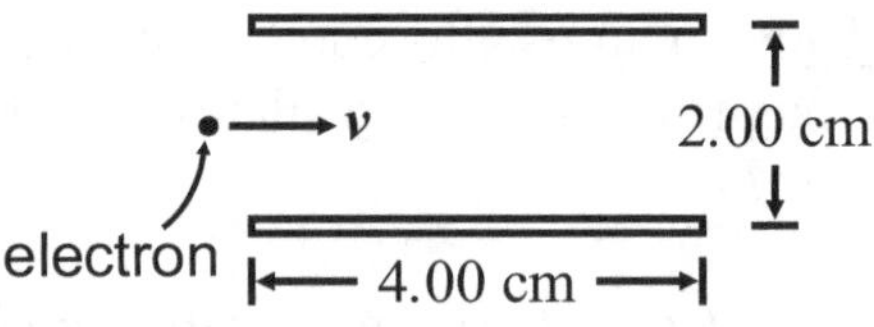

Figure 11-20 *Question 11-77.*

11-78 The current through a car radio is 0.753 A, and the potential difference across it is 12 V.
(a) How much charge flows through the radio in 30.0 s?
(b) How much energy is dissipated in the radio in this time?
(c) What is the power used by the radio?
[Ans. (a) 22.6 C (b) 2.7×10^2 J (c) 9.0 W]

11-79 By looking at the main fusebox or breakerbox at home, determine the maximum current allowed in each circuit. Also determine the maximum total current permitted in the supply wires leading into your home.

KEY OBJECTIVES

Having completed this chapter, you should now be able to do the following:

1. Define electric potential energy.
2. Use electric potential energy in problems involving uniform electric fields or point charges.
3. State the direction (in terms of increasing or decreasing potential energy) in which a mass or charge moves when released from rest.
4. Define electric potential and state its SI unit.
5. State the relation between volt, joule, and coulomb.
6. Define potential difference (voltage).
7. Solve problems involving electric potential energy, potential, and potential difference.
8. Define an electron-volt, and use it in determining changes in energy when charged particles are accelerated through potential differences.
9. State the relation between the magnitude of a uniform electric field, voltage, and distance.
10. Use the relation in the previous objective to solve problems.
11. State a common SI unit for electric field other than N/C.
12. State the expression for the electric potential due to a point charge, and use it in problems.
13. Define electric current and its SI unit, and solve related problems.
14. State the direction of electric current and its relation to the direction of electron flow.
15. Discuss the dangers associated with electric current and voltage.

ANSWERS TO SELECTED QUESTIONS

11-7 (a) away from B (b) toward B (c) away from B (d) away from B
11-14 (a) zero (b) decrease (c) toward each other
11-17 electric force
11-29 from B toward A
11-39 (b) relative to a point infinitely far away

11-44 The direction of the current is from the ground to the cloud.
11-48 The direction of the total current is toward the negative terminal.
11-49 (b) 11-50 (a) 11-51 (e) 11-52 (b) 11-53 (d)
11-54 (a) from east to west
11-58 (a) toward higher potential
11-60 (b) The field is downward.
11-69 The direction of the current is from the screen toward the back of the main tube.
11-73 (b) The proton moves away from the uranium nucleus.

CHAPTER 12

ELECTRIC RESISTANCE AND CIRCUITS

Many convenient devices that are part of our modern civilization — automobiles, televisions, lights, computers, etc. — involve the flow of electric current around specific loops called circuits. The amount of current flowing in a circuit depends on the applied voltage and also on the circuit's resistance to the flow of current. This chapter deals with the relationship between voltage, resistance, and current, and also considers another important quantity in electric circuits: the power consumed.

12.1 ELECTRIC RESISTANCE AND OHM'S LAW

If you connect a garden hose to a faucet and turn it on, the amount of water passing through the hose per second depends on a number of factors: the water pressure at the faucet, and the hose's size, shape, and interior roughness. Similarly, when you turn on a flashlight, the amount of electric charge that flows per second (that is, the current) depends on the battery voltage (analogous to the water pressure), and on various properties of the bulb filament, connecting wires, and contact points. These properties include materials, sizes, and (for contacts) degree of oxidation. All these non-voltage aspects are taken into account in a single property: electric resistance.

Suppose that we apply a voltage, that is, a potential difference (ΔV), across the ends of an object (such as a lightbulb, wire, or nerve fibre) and measure the resulting current (I). The **electric resistance** (R) of the object is *defined* as the ratio of voltage to current:

$$R = \frac{\Delta V}{I} \quad \text{(electric resistance)} \qquad \textbf{(12-1)}$$

The ratio $(\Delta V)/I$ has units of volt/ampere (V/A), but this is given the special name of **ohm** — the SI unit of resistance — in honour of the German physicist Georg Simon Ohm (1787-1854). It is represented by the uppercase Greek letter omega (Ω). The resistance of an object in ohms tells us the voltage required to produce a current of one ampere in the object.

$$\text{ohm}\,(\Omega) = \text{volt/ampere}\,(\text{V/A}) \qquad \textbf{(12-2)}$$

The relation $R = (\Delta V)/I$ is often written in the form

$$\Delta V = IR \qquad \textbf{(12-3)}$$

and is referred to as **Ohm's law**. This is not really a law of nature in the same sense as Newton's laws; rather, it is just a re-arrangement of the definition of resistance.

If an object such as a metal wire is said to *obey Ohm's law*, or is said to be *ohmic*, this means that the relation $\Delta V = IR$ is valid (at constant temperature) regardless of the size of the applied voltage. In other words, the resistance of the wire is constant at a given temperature. If various voltages (ΔV) are applied to the wire, and a graph of the resulting current (I) is plotted vs. ΔV, a straight line of slope $1/R$ results (Figure 12-1 (a)).

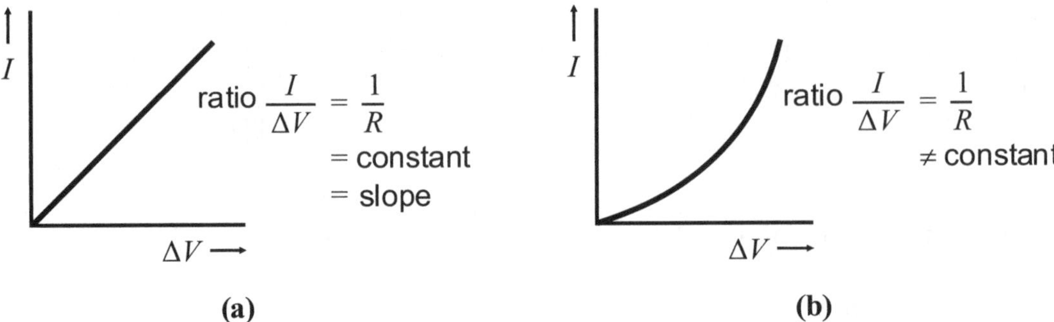

(a) **(b)**

Figure 12-1 **(a)** *Graph of I vs. ΔV for a device (a metallic wire, for example) that obeys Ohm's law.*
(b) *Representative graph of I vs. ΔV for a device that does not obey Ohm's law.*

There are many devices that do not have constant resistance at constant temperature; their resistance depends on the applied voltage. Examples include semiconductors and transistors, and we say that these devices *do not obey Ohm's law* or that they are *non-ohmic*. A graph of I vs. ΔV for such a device is non-linear (Figure 12-1 (b)). Nonetheless, we can still define the resistance of such a device as the ratio of $(\Delta V)/I$ in any given situation, but if the voltage changes, this ratio (i.e., the resistance) also changes. In the remainder of this chapter, we assume that all devices are ohmic unless stated otherwise.

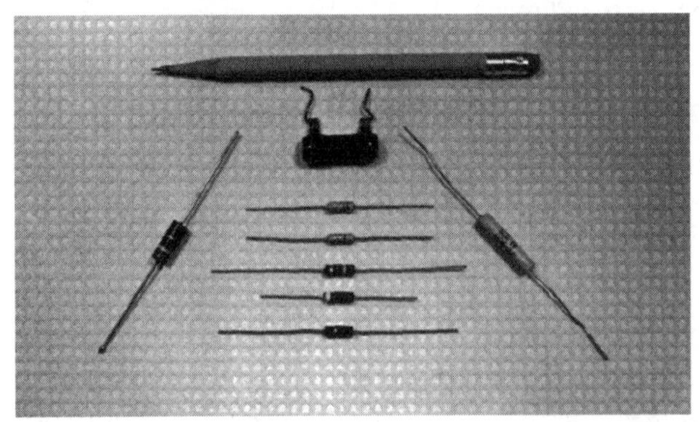

Figure 12-2 *A variety of resistors.*

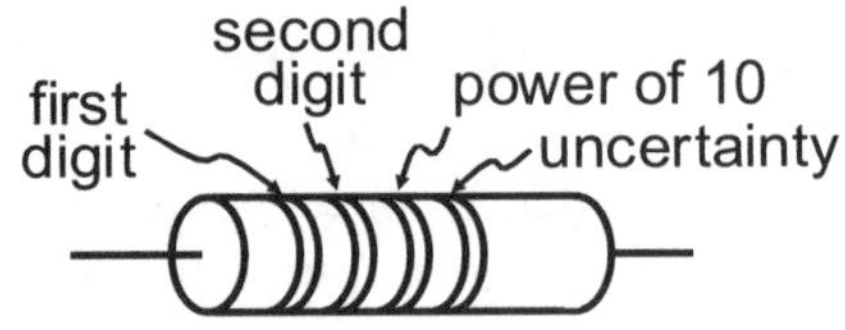

Figure 12-3 *The coloured bands indicate the resistance*

All conductors have some electric resistance, but for normal electrical wiring, it is rather small. For example, a 30-cm length of copper wire of diameter 1.0 mm has a resistance of only 0.0065 Ω. In order to control the current in electronic devices such as radios, standardized resistors (Figure 12-2) are used. These resistors come in a wide range of resistances, and are usually made of the semi-conductor carbon or a thin metal wire, surrounded by a plastic insulating casing. The resistance value is colour-coded on the outside of the plastic (Figure 12-3 and Table 12.1). For example, from Table 12.1, coloured bands in the order green-red-brown-silver form the code for 5,2,1, and ± 10%. The first two digits in this case give the number 52, the next digit indicates the power of ten, 10^1, and the last band gives the uncertainty in the resistance (± 10%). Therefore, the resistance is $52 \times 10^1\ \Omega \pm 10\%$ or $5.2 \times 10^2\ \Omega \pm 10\%$.

Table 12.1
The Resistor Colour Code

Colour	First or Second Digit	Power of Ten	Uncertainty
black	0	$10^0 = 1$	
brown	1	10^1	
red	2	10^2	
orange	3	10^3	
yellow	4	10^4	
green	5	10^5	
blue	6	10^6	
violet	7	10^7	
gray	8	10^8	
white	9	10^9	
gold		10^{-1}	± 5%
silver		10^{-2}	± 10%
no colour			± 20%

Sample Problem 12-1

A voltage is applied across the ends of a 150-Ω resistor, and a current of 0.12 A results. What is the applied voltage?

Solution: Ohm's law (Eqn. 12-3) is used:

$$\Delta V = IR = (0.12\ \text{A})(150\ \Omega) = 18\ \text{V}$$

Thus, the applied voltage is 18 V.

Electric resistivity

The electric resistance of a copper wire is less than that of an aluminum wire of the same size. Why? The ability of a material to conduct current depends on the number of conduction electrons (Section 10.3) per unit volume, and on the interaction (bumping) of these moving electrons with the atoms of the material. Different materials have different numbers of conduction electrons and different degrees of electron-atom interaction. We say that different materials have different **electric resistivities**, as defined below.

The electric resistance (R) of, say, a wire depends not only on the material of which it is made, but also on its size. The resistance is proportional to the wire's length (L) and inversely proportional to its cross-sectional area (A):

$$R \propto \frac{L}{A}$$

This relation is not surprising. We expect that a long wire will have a higher resistance than a short one because there are more obstacles to electron flow. A larger cross-sectional area means that there is more area across which the electrons can flow, and hence there is a lower resistance. The constant of proportionality in this relation is defined to be the electric resistivity of the material, which is a measure of its intrinsic "reluctance" to conduct current. The lower-case Greek letter rho (ρ) is used to represent electric resistivity (Figure 12-4). Hence,

Did You Know? *The fluids and tissues of the human body conduct electricity extremely well. The conduction in this case is due to the motion of ions. If the nerves in an area have been damaged, or if they are being compressed by a tumour, the resistance increases. This increase can be very significant in the case of lung cancer, and a measurement of electrical resistance in the chest is a quick and simple way to detect this disease.*

$$R = \rho\frac{L}{A} \qquad \textbf{(12-4)}$$

To determine the SI unit of ρ, we re-arrange Eqn. 12-4 to give $\rho = RA/L$. Substituting units on the right-hand side, we have: $\Omega{\cdot}m^2/m = \Omega{\cdot}m$. Thus, the SI unit of resistivity is $\Omega{\cdot}m$ (ohm·metre).

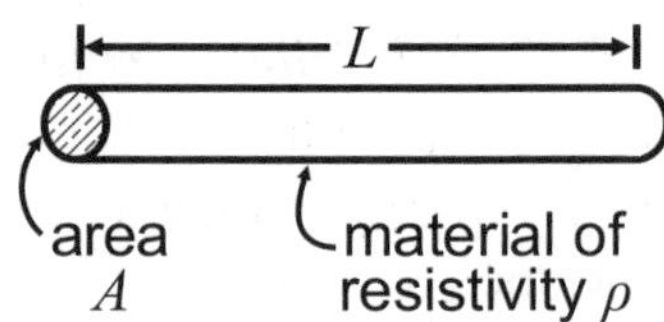

Figure 12-4
The electric resistance, R, of this wire is given by $R = \rho L / A$.

Table 12.2 gives approximate resistivities of some common materials at 20°C. The values depend to some extent on purity, heat treatment, and other factors. Copper is widely used in wiring because of its low resistivity and reasonable price. Notice that the resistivities of insulators are much, much larger than that of typical conductors.

The resistivity of any *metallic conductor* increases as temperature increases. At higher temperatures, the increased thermal vibration of the atoms in the conductor impedes the flow of electrons more strongly. Over a moderate range of temperatures, a conductor's resistivity at a temperature T can be written as

$$\rho = \rho_0\,[1 + \alpha(T - T_0)] \qquad \textbf{(12-5)}$$

where ρ_0 is the resistivity at some reference temperature T_0 (typically 20°C), and α is the **temperature coefficient of resistivity**. Some values of α are given in Table 12.2. The value of α indicates how much the resistivity increases with temperature; for example, the value of 3.8×10^{-3} (°C)$^{-1}$ for silver means that the resistivity of silver increases by 0.38% for each °C of temperature rise.

As temperature decreases, a conductor's resistivity gradually decreases. However, the resistivity of a superconductor (Section 10.3) drops precipitously to zero below a certain critical temperature.

Table 12.2
Approximate Resistivities and Temperature Coefficients of Some Materials at 20°C

Material	Resistivity (Ω·m)	Temperature Coefficient α (°C)$^{-1}$
Conductors		
Silver	1.6×10^{-8}	3.8×10^{-3}
Copper	1.7×10^{-8}	3.9×10^{-3}
Gold	2.4×10^{-8}	8.3×10^{-3}
Aluminum	2.8×10^{-8}	3.9×10^{-3}
Tungsten	5.5×10^{-8}	4.5×10^{-3}
Iron	9.7×10^{-8}	6.5×10^{-3}
Mercury	96×10^{-8}	9×10^{-4}
Semiconductors		
Carbon	3.5×10^{-5}	-5×10^{-4}
Axoplasm	1.1×10^{0}	
Silicon (pure)	2.5×10^{3}	-7×10^{-2}
Nerve membrane	1.6×10^{7}	
Insulators		
Glass	10^{10} to 10^{14}	
Wood	10^{8} to 10^{11}	

Sample Problem 12-2

(a) What is the electric resistance of 1.0 km of copper wire of diameter 2.2 mm?
(b) If the temperature increases by 20°C, what is the new resistance?

Solution: (a) To determine the resistance of the wire, we need only to substitute values into Eqn. 12-4 ($R = \rho L/A$), being careful that L and A have units of metres and metre^2, respectively. The resistivity (ρ) of copper is 1.7×10^{-8} Ω·m from Table 12.2, and the length (L) is 1.0 km, which equals 1.0×10^3 m. We must calculate the area (A) from the given diameter (2.2 mm). Since a diameter is given, we assume that the wire has a circular cross-section of area $A = \pi r^2$, where r is the radius (1.1 mm or 1.1×10^{-3} m). Hence,

$$R = \rho\frac{L}{A} = \rho\frac{L}{\pi r^2} = \left(1.7\times10^{-8}\ \Omega\cdot\text{m}\right)\frac{1.0\times10^{3}\ \text{m}}{\pi\left(1.1\times10^{-3}\ \text{m}\right)^2} = 4.5\ \Omega$$

Thus, the wire's resistance is 4.5 Ω.

(b) As the temperature increases, the wire's resistivity increases according to Eqn. 12-5:

$$\rho = \rho_0\,[1 + \alpha(T - T_0)]$$

Substituting values for ρ_0 and α from Table 12.2, and given that $T - T_0 = 20°\text{C}$:

$$\rho = (1.7 \times 10^{-8}\ \Omega\cdot\text{m})[1 + (3.9 \times 10^{-3}\ (°\text{C})^{-1}(20°\text{C})] = 1.8 \times 10^{-8}\ \Omega\cdot\text{m}$$

Substituting this new value of ρ into $R = \rho L/A$, with L and A as in part (a), gives $R = 4.8\ \Omega$.

Therefore, the resistance at the higher temperature is 4.8 Ω.

 **Practice**

12-1 If a current of 2.5 A results when a voltage of 23 V is applied to a resistor, what is the resistance? [Ans. 9.2 Ω]

12-2 (a) The resistance between two well-separated points on the human body is about $1.5 \times 10^3\ \Omega$. If a voltage of 120 V is applied across these points, how much current flows?
(b) If the skin is wet, the resistance drops to $5.0 \times 10^2\ \Omega$. What will the current be in this case for an applied voltage of 120 V?
[Ans. (a) 0.080 A (b) 0.24 A]

12-3 What does it mean if a circuit device obeys Ohm's law? if it does not obey Ohm's law?

12-4 What is the resistance (including uncertainty) of each of the following resistors?
(a) orange-orange-brown-silver (b) red-yellow-silver-gold (c) orange-white-yellow
[Ans. (a) $3.3 \times 10^2\ \Omega \pm 10\%$ (b) $0.24\ \Omega \pm 5\%$ (c) $3.9 \times 10^5\ \Omega \pm 20\%$]

12-5 A number of copper wires have the same length, but different cross-sectional areas, A. Sketch the shape of a graph of the resistances, R, of the wires (a) vs. A (b) vs. $1/A$.

12-6 What is the resistance of an aluminum wire of length 16 m and diameter 1.7 mm?
[Ans. 0.20 Ω]

12-7 The resistivity of axoplasm in a squid axon is 0.30 Ω·m. What is the length of a squid axon having a resistance of 1.5×10^5 Ω and a radius of 0.025 cm? (An axon, which is a long projection of a neuron cell, carries nerve impulses.) [Ans. 0.098 m]

12-8 An iron wire and a copper wire of the same length have the same voltage applied to them. If the currents are the same, what is the ratio of (a) the resistances of the wires? (b) the cross-sectional areas of the wires? (c) the radii of the wires? (d) the diameters of the wires?
[Ans. (a) $R_C/R_I = 1.0$ (b) $A_C/A_I = 0.18$ (c) $r_C/r_I = 0.42$ (d) $d_C/d_I = 0.42$]

12-9 As temperature increases, does the resistivity of a metallic conductor increase or decrease?

12-10 What is the resistivity of gold at 41°C? [Ans. 2.8×10^{-8} Ω·m]

12-11 A particular metal has a temperature coefficient of resistivity of 6.8×10^{-3} $(°C)^{-1}$. By what percentage does the resistivity of the metal change if the temperature increases by 5.0°C? [Ans. 3.4%]

12.2 BATTERIES AND ELECTRIC CIRCUITS

Everyone has used a battery — to provide energy for a flashlight, camera, cell phone, etc. But how do batteries work? How is the potential difference generated between the battery terminals? Who discovered batteries?

In the 1780s, Luigi Galvani (1737-1798), an anatomy professor in Italy, carried out a series of experiments involving the contraction of frogs' leg muscles due to electrical stimulation. In doing so, he was opening two separate areas of science — neurophysiology and current electricity. He was surprised to find that two dissimilar metals in contact with each other could induce the required stimulation. Galvani believed that the source of electricity was in the frog itself, and that the metals merely provided a conducting path. Galvani and others wondered if this electricity was associated with the "life force" in which people believed at that time. Alessandro Volta extended Galvani's experiments, and was able to show that the frog was acting merely as a detector of a potential difference created by the contact of the two metals. He found that some pairs of metals worked better than others, and he listed the metals in an *electrochemical series* showing their effectiveness. Metals far apart in the series provide a large potential difference.

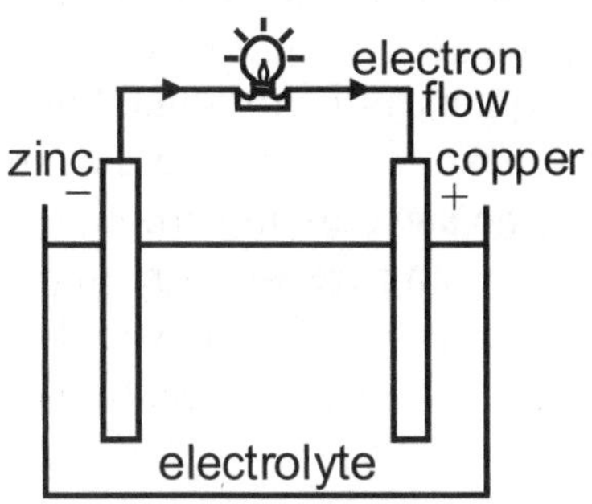

Figure 12-5
An elementary electric cell.

This potential difference between two metals in contact led Volta to his greatest contribution to science: the invention of the electric (or voltaic) cell and the battery. An electric cell (Figure 12-5) consists essentially of two different metals (carbon can also be used) in electrical contact via a conducting liquid such as a dilute acid. This conducting liquid is called an **electrolyte**. A

battery is a combination of several electric cells connected together. However, the term "battery" is commonly used even when there is only one cell.

The electric cell shown in Figure 12-5 operates in the following way. Some of the atoms in the zinc electrode dissolve in the electrolyte; they enter the solution as positive zinc ions, leaving behind electrons in the electrode. Thus, the zinc electrode becomes negatively charged. The same process occurs at the copper electrode but much more slowly, so that the zinc becomes negatively charged with respect to the copper. A potential difference is thus established between the electrodes. (Consult a chemistry textbook if you want more details.) If the electrodes are then connected, say, to a flashlight bulb, electrons flow from the zinc, through the bulb, to the copper. An electric circuit has been established. Eventually, one of the electrodes becomes so dissolved that a current cannot be maintained — the battery is "dead."

"Dry cell" batteries used in flashlights, etc., consist of two different metals (e.g., zinc and carbon) separated by an electrolytic paste. Car batteries use lead as one electrode and lead dioxide as the other, with a sulfuric acid solution as the electrolyte.

In electronics diagrams, a battery is indicated by the symbol shown at the top left of Figure 12-6. The two "vertical" lines having unequal lengths represent the battery terminals, and the two lines leading to the left and right from the terminals represent connecting wires. *The longer of the two terminal lines represents the positive (high potential) terminal, and the shorter terminal line indicates the negative (low potential) terminal.* Strictly speaking, the symbol indicates only one electric cell, but it is commonly used to denote a battery. The proper symbol for a battery is a series of several alternating short and long lines to represent a number of cells connected together.

Electric Circuits

You have undoubtedly heard of electric circuits — in your home, in computers, in automobiles, etc. An **electric circuit** is simply a conducting path that returns to its "starting point," i.e., that closes on itself. For example, when you turn on a car headlight, current[1] flows from the positive terminal of the car battery, through the light, into the chassis of the car, to the negative terminal of the battery, and through the battery back to the starting point, the positive terminal. Any point in the circuit can be chosen as the starting point, since the current starts to flow almost instantly in all parts of the circuit.

Current is not something that flows from a battery and gets smaller or becomes "used up" as it makes its way around a circuit. In a simple circuit such as the car headlight circuit, the current is the same in all parts of the circuit. This follows from the law of conservation of charge. For every ampere of current entering, say, a resistor, an ampere of current leaves the other end. Otherwise, a charge would build up on the resistor (and this does not happen).

[1]Recall from Chapter 11 that conventional current is in the direction of positive charge flow, which is opposite to the direction of the flow of negatively charged electrons, which are the actual moving charge carriers in metals.

If current is not flowing in a circuit (because a wire has been broken or a switch has not been closed, for example), the circuit is an **open circuit**. If current is flowing, we have a **closed circuit**.

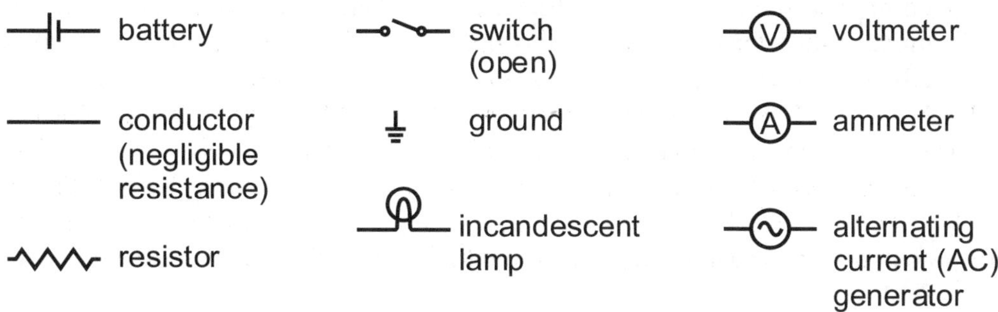

Figure 12-6 *Conventional symbols used in circuit diagrams. In the symbol representing a battery, the longer of the two vertical lines indicates the positive terminal, and the shorter vertical line indicates the negative terminal.*

Circuits are represented on paper by circuit diagrams, on which the various circuit elements or devices have specific symbols. Some common symbols are shown in Figure 12-6. A resistor is symbolized by a zigzag line, as shown. Connecting wires are normally considered to be conductors having negligible resistance (effectively, $R = 0$), and are shown by straight lines.

Since the potential difference (ΔV) across an object can be written as $\Delta V = IR$, and since $R = 0$ for connecting wires, then *the potential difference across a connecting wire must be zero.* In other words, the electric potential along a connecting wire is constant.

Sample Problem 12-3

In the circuit represented in Figure 12-7,
(a) what is the current direction?
(b) what are the following potential differences:
$V_B - V_C$? $V_A - V_D$? $V_B - V_A$? $V_C - V_D$?
(c) if we define the potential at the negative terminal of the battery to be zero, what are the potentials at points A, B, C, and D?
(d) what is the potential difference across the resistor?
(e) what is the current in the circuit (assuming that the resistance is known to two significant digits)?

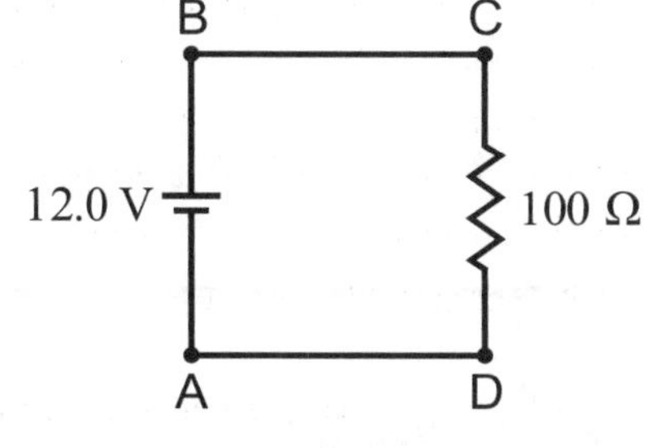

Figure 12-7
Sample Problem 12-3.

Solution: (a) The current is in the direction of positive charge flow. The positive terminal of the battery is indicated by the longer line (at the top of the battery symbol in Fig. 12-7). Therefore, the current flows from this terminal to B, to C, through the resistor to D, to A, and back to the battery via the negative terminal. In short, the current is *clockwise* around the circuit.

(b) Points B and C are on a connecting wire of negligible resistance. Hence, $V_B - V_C = 0$ V. Similarly, $V_A - V_D = 0$ V.

Point B is at the same potential as the positive battery terminal, since the resistance of the wire connecting point B to this terminal is negligible. Similarly, A is at the same potential as the negative terminal. Therefore, $V_B - V_A$ equals the potential difference across the battery, that is, $V_B - V_A = 12.0$ V.

Point C has the same potential as B, and D has the same potential as A.
Therefore, $V_C - V_D = V_B - V_A = 12.0$ V.

(c) If the potential at the negative terminal of the battery is defined as zero, then $V_A = 0$ V.

Since $V_B - V_A = 12.0$ V (from (b)), then $V_B = 12.0$ V.

Because B and C are at the same potential, $V_C = 12.0$ V.

Points A and D are at the same potential, and hence $V_D = 0$ V.

(d) The potential difference across the resistor is $V_C - V_D = 12.0$ V.

(e) We can calculate the current from Ohm's law (Eqn. 12-3):

$$\Delta V = IR \quad \text{and hence} \quad I = \frac{\Delta V}{R}$$

The potential difference (ΔV) across the 100-Ω resistor is 12.0 V, and thus

$$I = \frac{\Delta V}{R} = \frac{12.0\ V}{100\ \Omega} = 0.12\ A$$

Thus, the current through the resistor and through the entire circuit is 0.12 A.

Practice

12-12 Draw a circuit diagram consisting only of a 330-Ω resistor, a 15-V battery, and some wires, connected so that current will flow. How large is the current? [Ans. 0.045 A]

12-13 For the circuit in Figure 12-8,
(a) what is the direction of the current?
(b) what are the following potential differences?
$V_W - V_Z$? $V_X - V_W$? $V_X - V_Y$? $V_Y - V_Z$? $V_W - V_Y$?

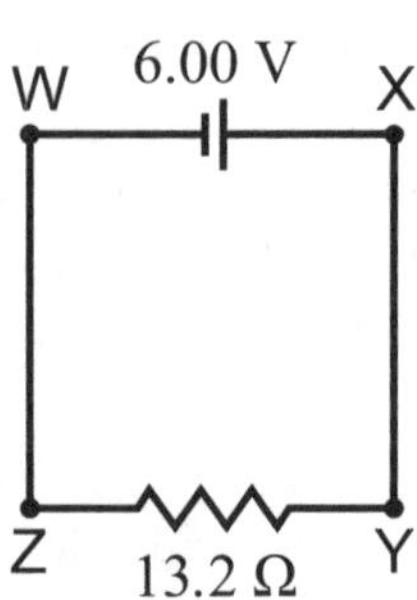

Figure 12-8
Question 12-13.

(c) if we define the potential at the negative terminal of the battery to be zero, what are the potentials at points W, X, Y, and Z?
(d) what is the current through the resistor? through wire XY? through the battery?
[Ans. (a) clockwise (b) 0 V; 6 V; 0 V; 6 V; −6 V (c) 0 V; 6 V; 6 V; 0 V (d) 0.455 A in each case]

12-14 In the circuit in Figure 12-9, the current is 2.38 A. What are
(a) the resistance R?
(b) the direction of the current through the resistor?
(c) the potential difference $V_A - V_C$?
[Ans. (a) 1.36 Ω (b) toward top of diagram (c) 3.24 V]

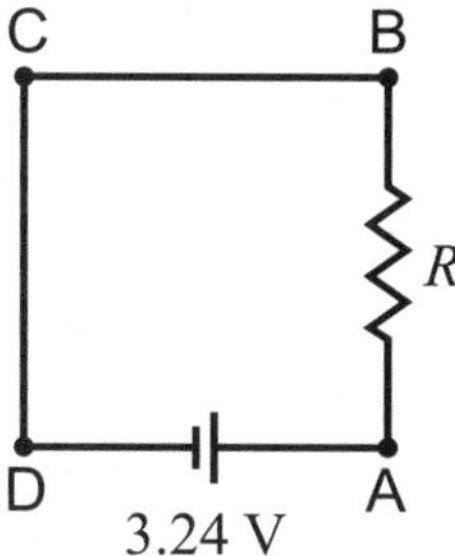

Figure 12-9
Questions 12-14 and 12-15.

12-15 In the previous question, if 9.7 C of charge flows through the battery, how much energy does the battery supply? [Ans. 31 J]

12.3 RESISTORS IN SERIES AND PARALLEL

Commercial resistors commonly used in electronic devices have only certain values of resistance. However, resistors can be connected together in various ways so that the total resistance of the combination can be virtually any resistance that might be required.

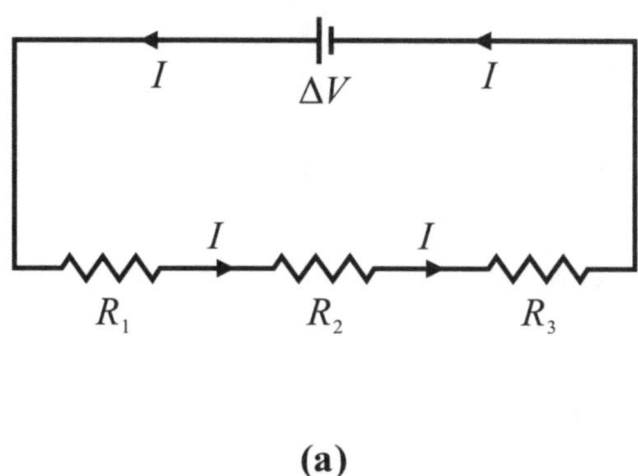

(a)

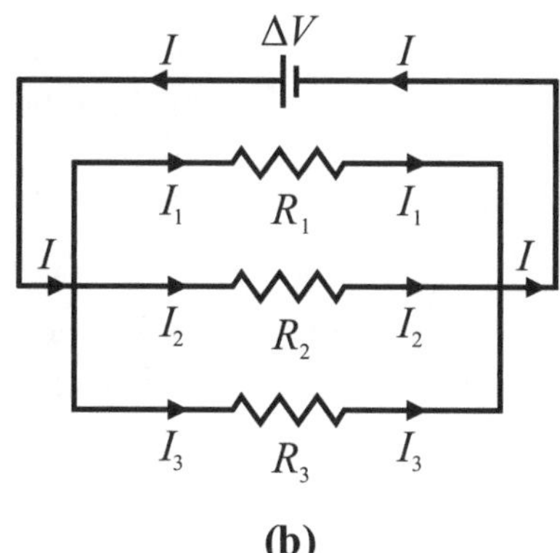

(b)

Figure 12-10 (a) *Resistors in series. The current is the same through each resistor.* **(b)** *Resistors in parallel. The potential difference across each resistor is the same, and the total current provided by the battery is split among the resistors.*

If resistors are connected so that the same current flows through each one in turn (Figure 12-10 (a)), they are said to be connected in **series**. If they are connected so that the current splits into separate branches (Figure 12-10 (b)), *so that the same potential difference exists across each resistor*, the resistors are said to be connected in **parallel**. The terms "series" and "parallel" are not restricted only to resistors; they apply to similar connections of any circuit components.

Equivalent Resistance of Resistors in Series

For resistors in series, we can determine an equivalent resistance, that is, a single resistance value for all the resistors together. We start with two resistors in series (Figure 12-11 (a)). In Figure 12-11 (b), the two resistors have been replaced by a single resistor having resistance R. If this resistor is "equivalent" to the two original resistors, this means that the current flowing in the circuit is the same in the two situations shown in Figure 12-11 (a) and (b). The equivalent resistance can be determined straightforwardly as indicated below.

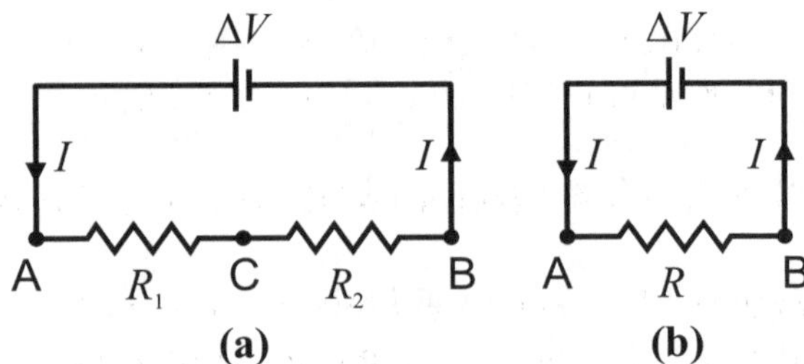

Figure 12-11 **(a)** *Two resistors in series.* **(b)** *The equivalent resistance, R.* $R = R_1 + R_2$

In Figure 12-11 (b), the battery voltage, ΔV, is applied across the single resistor, and hence, we can use Ohm's law:

$$\Delta V = IR \qquad \text{Eqn. [1]}$$

where I is the current in the circuit.

Turning our attention now to Figure 12-11 (a), we can write the potential difference between A and B (i.e., the battery voltage, ΔV) as the sum of two parts: across ΔV_1 across R_1, and ΔV_2 across R_2.

$$\Delta V = \Delta V_1 + \Delta V_2 \qquad \text{Eqn. [2]}$$

If this troubles you, go through the following steps:

$$\Delta V_1 + \Delta V_2 = (V_A - V_C) + (V_C - V_B) = V_A - V_B = \Delta V$$

The current through both R_1 and R_2 is I. Hence, we can write $\Delta V_1 = IR_1$, and $\Delta V_2 = IR_2$, using Ohm's law. Thus, Eqn. [2] becomes

$$\Delta V = IR_1 + IR_2$$

or $$\Delta V = I(R_1 + R_2) \qquad \text{Eqn. [3]}$$

We now compare Eqns. [1] and [3]. In order for the current I to be the same in the two situations, the single resistance R that is equivalent to the series combination of R_1 and R_2 must be

$$R = R_1 + R_2 \quad \text{(two resistors in series)}$$

For more than two resistors in series, we could use the same approach to show that the equivalent resistance is just the sum of all the single resistances:

$$R = R_1 + R_2 + R_3 + R_4 + \ldots \quad \text{(resistors in series)} \qquad \textbf{(12-6)}$$

Thus, for example, if we have three resistors in series — 100 Ω, 200 Ω, and 300 Ω — the total resistance is just the sum, 600 Ω.

Equivalent Resistance of Resistors in Parallel

Figure 12-12 shows (a) two resistors in parallel and (b) the single equivalent resistance. As was the case with resistors in series, if this single resistor is "equivalent" to the two original resistors, this means that the total current flowing in the circuit is the same in the two situations shown in Figure 12-12.

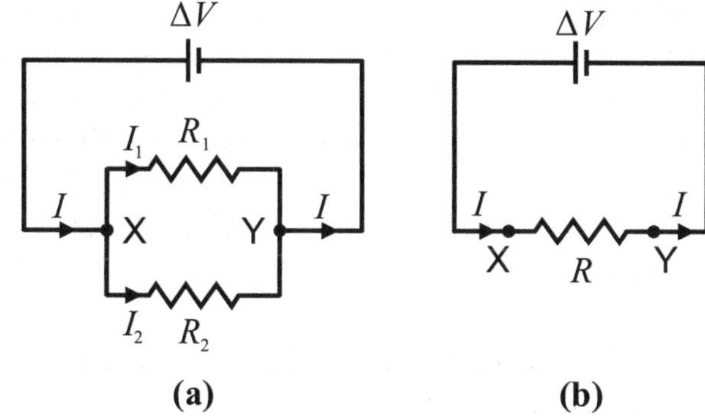

Figure 12-12 **(a)** *Two resistors in parallel.* **(b)** *The equivalent resistance, R.*

$$\frac{1}{R} = \frac{1}{R_1} + \frac{1}{R_2}$$

Applying Ohm's law to the circuit in Figure 12-12 (b), the current due to the voltage being applied across the equivalent resistance R is

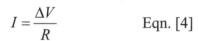

$$I = \frac{\Delta V}{R} \qquad \text{Eqn. [4]}$$

Considering now Figure 12-12 (a), we see that the total current I splits at point X into two parts, I_1 and I_2. Since charge is conserved, the sum of these two currents must equal I; otherwise, charge would accumulate at the junction point X. *At any junction point in a circuit, the total current flowing in must equal the total current flowing out.*

$$I = I_1 + I_2 \qquad \text{Eqn. [5]}$$

The potential difference across *each* of the two resistors (R_1 and R_2) is the battery voltage ΔV (or $V_X - V_Y$). Thus, for resistor 1, we can write the current as $I_1 = \Delta V/R_1$, and for resistor 2, $I_2 = \Delta V/R_2$. Substituting these expressions for I_1 and I_2 in Eqn. [5]:

$$I = \frac{\Delta V}{R_1} + \frac{\Delta V}{R_2} \qquad \text{Eqn. [6]}$$

Now, whether there are two resistors in parallel as in Figure 12-12 (a), or the single *equivalent* resistor (Figure 12-12 (b)), the current, I, from the battery must be the same. Hence, we can replace I in Eqn. [6] with $(\Delta V)/R$ from Eqn. [4]:

$$\frac{\Delta V}{R} = \frac{\Delta V}{R_1} + \frac{\Delta V}{R_2}$$

Dividing each term by ΔV, we get the expression for the equivalent resistance R:

$$\frac{1}{R} = \frac{1}{R_1} + \frac{1}{R_2} \quad \text{(two resistors in parallel)}$$

For more than two resistors in parallel, we just add more terms on the right-hand side:

$$\frac{1}{R} = \frac{1}{R_1} + \frac{1}{R_2} + \frac{1}{R_3} + \ldots \quad \text{(resistors in parallel)} \qquad \textbf{(12-7)}$$

If we have three resistors in parallel — say, 100 Ω, 200 Ω, and 300 Ω (Figure 12-13) — we can calculate the equivalent resistance from Eqn. 12-7:

$$\frac{1}{R} = \frac{1}{R_1} + \frac{1}{R_2} + \frac{1}{R_3}$$

$$= \frac{1}{100\ \Omega} + \frac{1}{200\ \Omega} + \frac{1}{300\ \Omega}$$

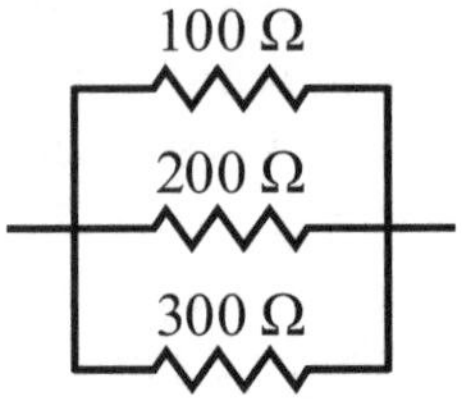

100 Ω

200 Ω

300 Ω

Figure 12-13 *Three resistors in parallel. The equivalent resistance (54.5 Ω) is less than any of the single resistances.*

We use a common denominator of 600 Ω to add the fractions:

$$\frac{1}{R} = \frac{6}{600\ \Omega} + \frac{3}{600\ \Omega} + \frac{2}{600\ \Omega} = \frac{11}{600\ \Omega}$$

Therefore, $R = \dfrac{600\ \Omega}{11} = 54.5\ \Omega$ (assuming three significant digits)

Notice that *the equivalent resistance of resistors in parallel is less than any of the single resistances.*

Sample Problem 12-4

In the circuit in Figure 12-14, what are
(a) the current in the circuit?
(b) the voltage across resistor 1?
(c) the current in resistor 2?
(Assume three significant figures for all the resistances.)

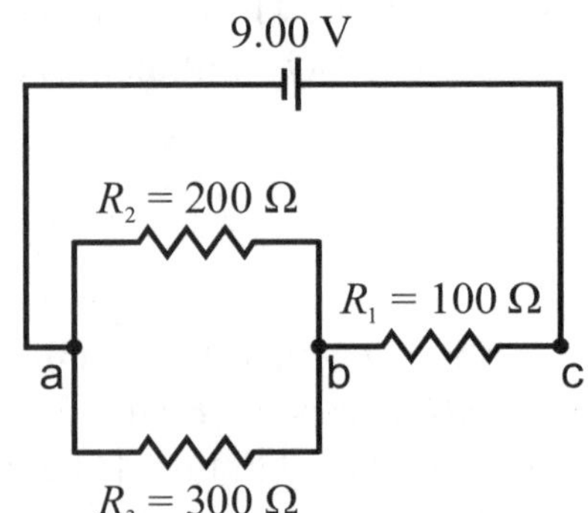

Figure 12-14
Sample Problem 12-4.

Solution: (a) To find the current in the circuit, that is, the total current through the battery, we need first to determine the equivalent resistance of the three resistors. Then Ohm's law can be used. Resistors 2 and 3 are in parallel with each other, and this two-resistor combination is in series with resistor 1. For the parallel combination, the equivalent resistance, which we will denote as R_{23}, can be calculated from Eqn. 12-7:

$$\frac{1}{R_{23}} = \frac{1}{R_2} + \frac{1}{R_3} = \frac{1}{200\ \Omega} + \frac{1}{300\ \Omega}$$

Re-arranging and solving for R_{23}, we get: $R_{23} = 120\ \Omega$

This 120-Ω resistance is in series with the 100-Ω resistor. Therefore, to determine the total resistance (R) of all the resistors, all we need to do is add these two series resistances:

$$R = R_{23} + R_1 = 120\ \Omega + 100\ \Omega = 220\ \Omega$$

The current in the circuit can now be easily determined from Ohm's law, $\Delta V = IR$, since we know the voltage and the resistance (Figure 12-15):

$$I = \frac{\Delta V}{R} = \frac{9.00\ \text{V}}{220\ \Omega} = 4.09 \times 10^{-2}\ \text{A}$$

Thus, the current is 4.09×10^{-2} A (or 40.9 mA).

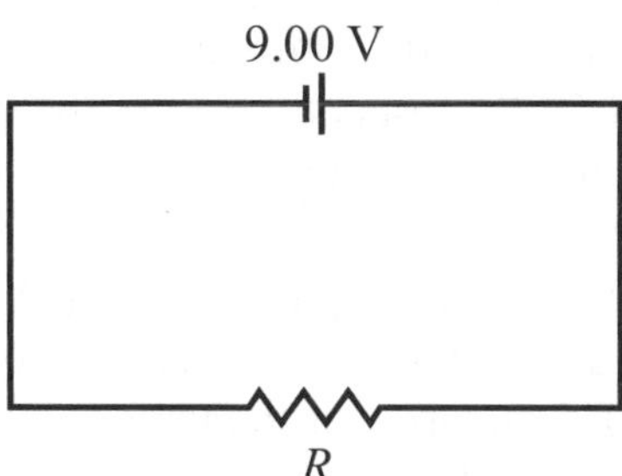

Figure 12-15
R is the equivalent resistance of R_1, R_2, and R_3 shown in Figure 12-14.

(b) To calculate the voltage (ΔV_1) across resistor 1, we again use Ohm's law. The current is the same as that calculated in part (a), since the entire current flows through resistor 1.

$$\Delta V_1 = IR_1 = (4.09 \times 10^{-2}\ \text{A})(100\ \Omega) = 4.09\ \text{V}$$

Hence, the voltage across resistor 1 is 4.09 V.

(c) The current through resistor 2 is not the total current calculated in (a). In Figure 12-14, the total current passes through resistor 1 from c to b, and then branches into two parts from b to a, through resistors 2 and 3.

The easiest way to determine the current in resistor 2 is through Ohm's law, $\Delta V_2 = I_2 R_2$. We know R_2, but do not know ΔV_2 nor I_2. Therefore, to find I_2, we need first to calculate ΔV_2. The total voltage from c to a is 9.00 V, and in part (b), we determined the voltage from c to b to be 4.09 V. Thus, the voltage from b to a, that is, the voltage across each of resistors 2 and 3, is[2]

$$\Delta V_2 = \Delta V_3 = (9.00 - 4.09)\ \text{V} = 4.91\ \text{V}$$

Did You Know? *Physicists in research laboratories are sometimes concerned about unauthorized people entering the labs. On more than one occasion, a sign has appeared on the door of a physics lab saying something such as: "KEEP OUT! TEN MILLION OHMS!" Think about it.*

[2]Recall that for resistors in parallel, the potential difference (i.e., the voltage) is the same across each of the resistors.

Now, from Ohm's law: $$I_2 = \frac{\Delta V_2}{R_2} = \frac{4.91\ \text{V}}{200\ \Omega} = 2.45 \times 10^{-2}\ \text{A}$$

Thus, the current through resistor 2 is 2.45×10^{-2} A (or 24.5 mA).

Sample Problem 12-5

In Figure 12-16 (a), the currents at M, N, and P, are 7.0 A, 4.0 A, and 1.0 A, respectively. What is the current through R_2?

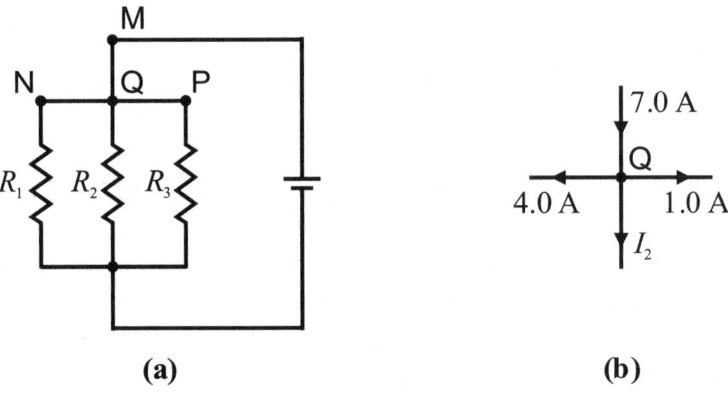

Figure 12-16 **(a)** *Sample Problem 12-5.* **(b)** *Currents at junction point Q.*

Solution: Figure 12-16 (b) shows the currents at junction point Q. The polarity of the battery produces a counterclockwise current in the circuit. Therefore, the 7.0-A current flows from M into Q, the 4.0-A current flows from Q to N (and then through R_1), and the 1.0-A current flows from Q to P (and through R_3). We know that at Q, the total current flowing in must equal the total current out. Therefore, labelling the current through R_2 as I_2,

$$7.0\ \text{A} = 4.0\ \text{A} + I_2 + 1.0\ \text{A}$$

Solving for I_2: $$I_2 = (7.0 - 4.0 - 1.0)\ \text{A} = 2.0\ \text{A}$$

Hence, the current through R_2 is 2.0 A.

Sample Problem 12-6

Figure 12-17 shows a 9.0-V battery providing current to three resistors in parallel. Switch S is closed.

(a) What is the voltage across each resistor?
(b) What is the current through each resistor?
(c) What is the current from B to C? from A to B?
(d) What is the current through the battery?
(e) If switch S is now opened, what are the answers to the above questions?

Solution: (a) Points A, B, and C are each connected by wires of negligible resistance to the positive terminal of the battery, and hence are at the same electric potential as this terminal. Similarly, points D, E, and F are at the same potential as the negative terminal of the battery. Therefore, the voltage from A to D, from B to E, and from C to F is just the voltage across the battery terminals, 9.0 V. Thus, the voltage across each resistor is 9.0 V.

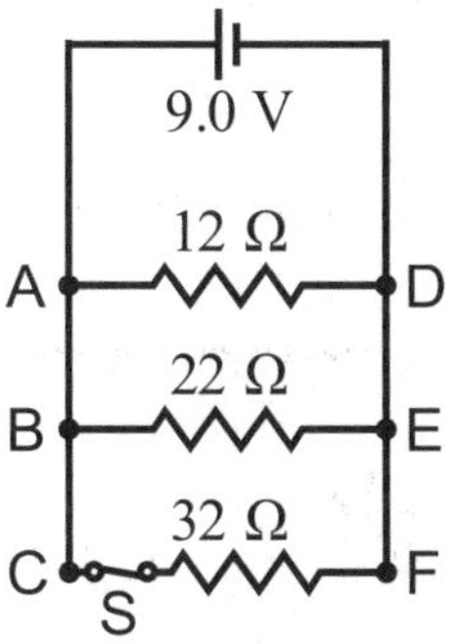

Figure 12-17 *Sample Problem 12-6.*

(b) Ohm's law can be used to determine the current through each resistor. Each resistance is known and the voltage is 9.0 V across each resistor. As an example, for the 12-Ω resistor:

$$\Delta V = IR \quad \text{gives} \quad I = \frac{\Delta V}{R} = \frac{9.0\ \text{V}}{12\ \Omega} = 0.75\ \text{A}$$

Similarly, the currents through the 22-Ω and 32-Ω resistors are 0.41 A and 0.28 A, respectively.

(c) The current that flows from B to C also flows through the 32-Ω resistor (and then from F to E). Hence, this current is the same as the current through the 32-Ω resistor, which we determined in part (b) to be 0.28 A.

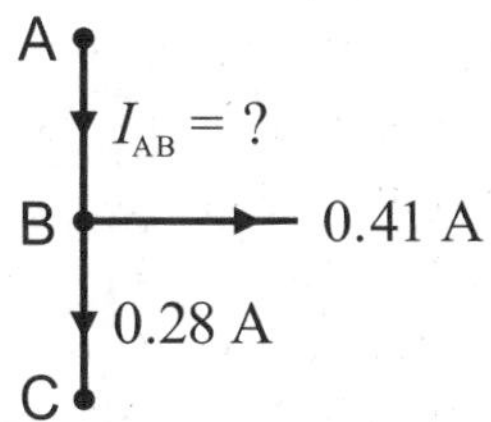

Figure 12-18 *Currents flowing into, and out of, point B.*

To determine the current from A to B, consider Figure 12-18, which shows the currents flowing into, and out of, point B. We are asked to find current I_{AB}. The current from B to C is 0.28 A, and the 0.41-A current flowing to the right is the current through the 22-Ω resistor (calculated in part (b)). Since current in equals current out at junction point B:

$$I_{AB} = 0.28\ \text{A} + 0.41\ \text{A} = 0.69\ \text{A}$$

Thus, the current from B to C is 0.28 A, and the current from A to B is 0.69 A.

(d) The current through the battery can be found from Figure 12-19, showing the various currents in the circuit. Notice how the total current, I_{TOT}, from the battery splits at point A and then splits further at B. The currents recombine at E and D to give a current of I_{TOT} returning to the battery. We can find I_{TOT} by considering either point A or D; we will use A. The current flowing into this point must equal the current flowing out:

$$I_{TOT} = 0.69\ \text{A} + 0.75\ \text{A} = 1.44\ \text{A}$$

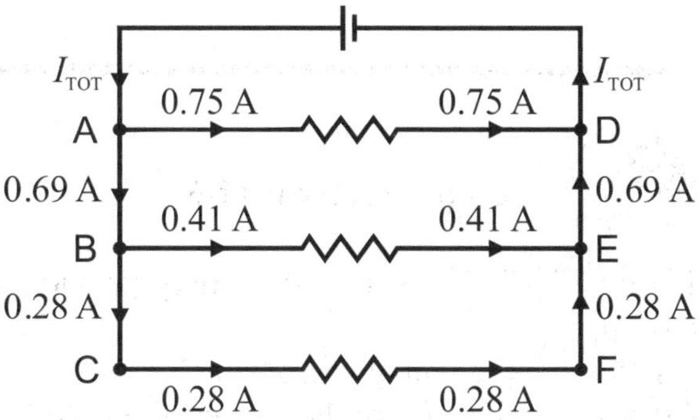

Figure 12-19 *The currents in the circuit.*

Hence, there is a current of 1.44 A through the battery.

(e) The circuit with switch S open (between C and F) is shown in Figure 12-20. The open switch prevents any flow of current through the bottom resistor, and hence, no current flows from B to C, nor from F to E. Since no current flows through this resistor, then, from Ohm's law, there is no voltage across it ($\Delta V = IR$). Thus, the voltage across the bottom resistor is 0 V. There is still a potential difference of 9.0 V across each of the other two resistors (think about this for a moment), and therefore, the currents through these resistors are unchanged by the opening of the switch. (Compare the currents through these resistors in Figures 12-19 and 12-20.)

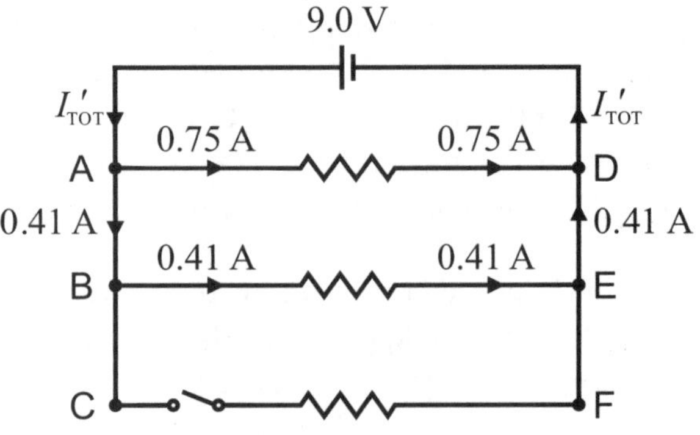

Figure 12-20
The circuit with the switch open between C and F.

The current from A to B is now just the current through the middle resistor, that is, 0.41 A. The total current provided by the battery can be determined by noting that the current flowing into point A must equal the sum of the currents flowing out of point A. Designating the total current provided by the battery as I'_{TOT} , we have:

$$I'_{TOT} = 0.75\text{ A} + 0.41\text{ A} = 1.16\text{ A}$$

Thus, because the switch is open, the current through the battery has been reduced from 1.44 A to 1.16 A.

Redrawing Circuit Diagrams

In the circuit diagrams that have been shown so far, resistors in series have been drawn in the same straight-line portion of the circuit. However, the two resistors shown in Figure 12-21 (a) are also in series, since the same current flows through each of them. Figure 12-21 (b) illustrates the same circuit with the resistors in a straight line. When solving problems, it is often helpful to redraw the circuit to show series resistors in a straight line.

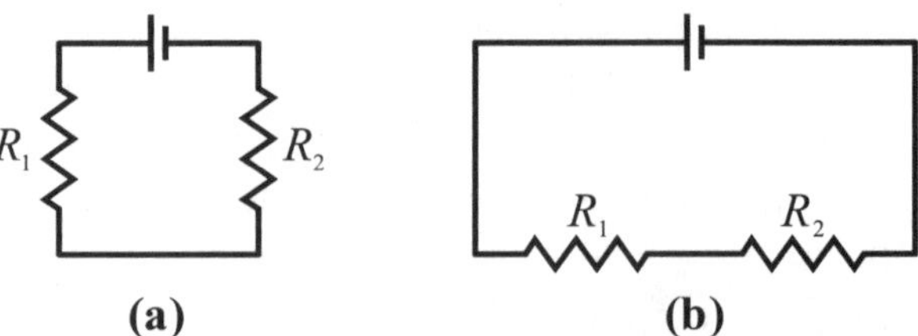

Figure 12-21 **(a)** *The two resistors are in series, since the same current flows through each one.* **(b)** *The same circuit, redrawn to show clearly that the resistors are in series.*

Similarly, if the same potential difference is applied across two or more resistors, the resistors are said to be in parallel, although they might not be drawn in portions of the circuit that are geometrically parallel (Figure 12-22 (a)). It is useful to redraw circuit diagrams to show parallel resistors in geometrically parallel sections of the circuit (Figure 12-22 (b)).

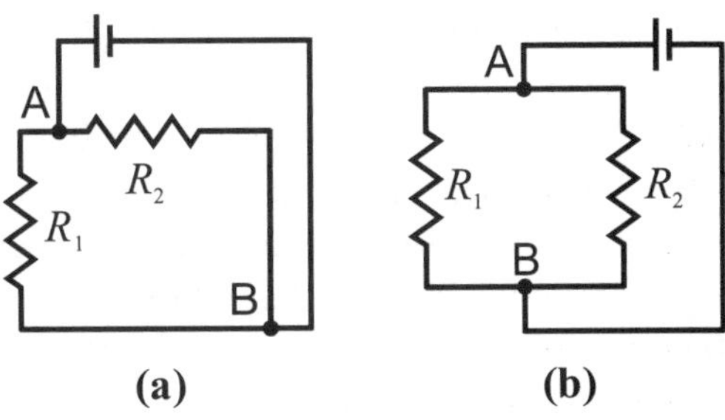

Figure 12-22 **(a)** *The same potential difference is being applied across the two resistors, which are therefore in parallel.* **(b)** *The diagram has been redrawn to show clearly that the resistors are in parallel.*

Measuring Voltage and Current

In order to measure voltage and current in laboratories, electronics workshops, or in your home, *voltmeters* and *ammeters* are used. These are commonly of two general types: galvanometer-based, and digital (Figure 12-23). A **galvanometer** consists of a coil of fine wire that is free to rotate between the poles of a magnet. When an electric current flows through the coil, the magnetic field exerts a torque (twist) on the coil, which therefore rotates. A pointer attached to the coil indicates the amount of rotation on a scale, which is calibrated in current or voltage units. In digital meters, electronic circuits provide a digital readout of voltage or current.

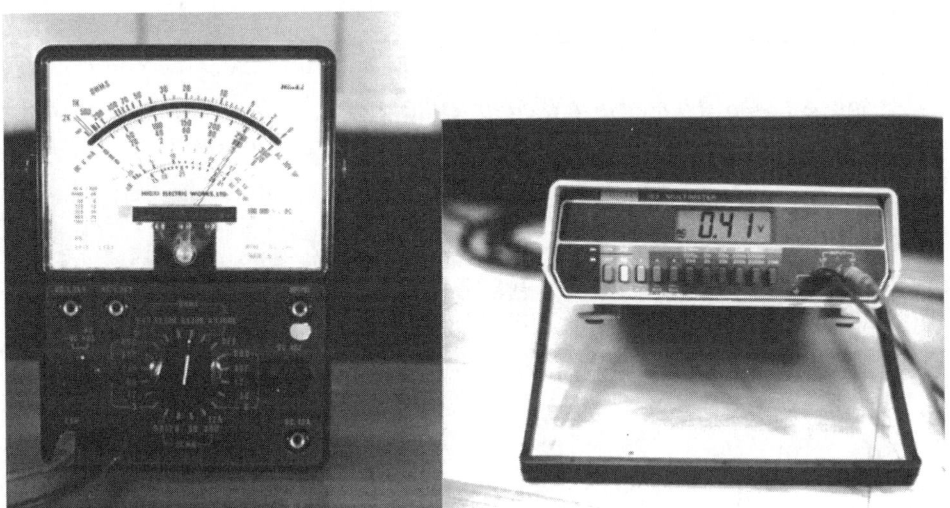

Figure 12-23 *Galvanometer-based meter (left) and digital meter.*

Many meters are multimeters, that is, multi-purpose meters that can measure a wide range of voltages and currents (and also resistances). Dials or push-buttons on a multimeter allow the user to change easily from one function to another.

A voltmeter measures the potential difference (or voltage) *between* two points in a circuit. For example, Figure 12-24 illustrates the use of a voltmeter (indicated by a "V" inside a circle) to determine the potential difference between A and B, that is, the voltage across resistor R_1. The two connecting wires from the meter are placed at points A and B at opposite ends of the resistor, thus placing the meter in *parallel* with the resistor. When a meter is used as a voltmeter, it has a large internal resistance, which results in only a small current flowing through the meter. Thus, using the meter has a negligible effect on the rest of the circuit. The current through the meter is proportional to the voltage being applied, and the meter has been calibrated at the factory so that this voltage can be read.

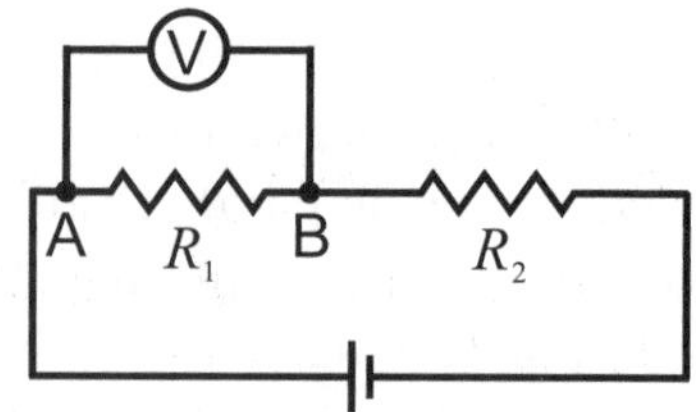

Figure 12-24 *A voltmeter is placed in parallel with a resistor (R_1) to measure the potential difference across it.*

An ammeter measures the current *at* a particular point in a circuit. The circuit is opened at that point and the meter is inserted, so that the current must flow through the meter. Thus, the meter is placed in *series* in the circuit. In Figure 12-25, an ammeter (indicated by an "A" inside a circle) has been inserted to measure the current flowing through point X. When a meter is used as an ammeter, it has a very small internal resistance, so that the current in the circuit is essentially unaffected by the insertion of the meter. Again, the meter has been pre-calibrated, in this case, so that current can be read.

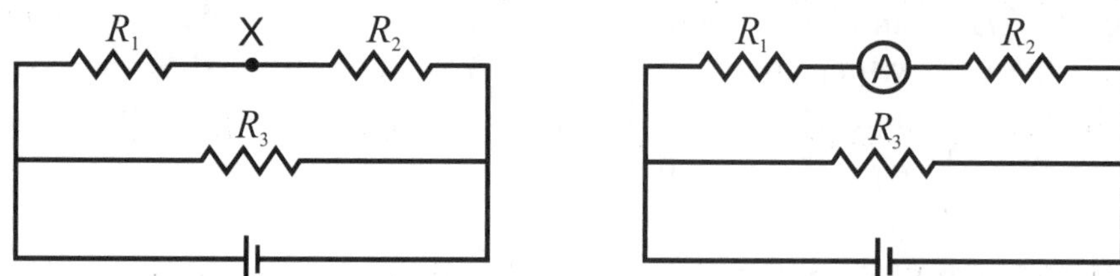

Figure 12-25 *To measure the current at point X, that is, the current through R_1 and R_2, an ammeter is inserted in series.*

Batteries in Series and Parallel

If two or more batteries are connected together in series (Figure 12-26), the total potential difference provided by the batteries is the sum of the individual potential differences. Thus, two 1.5-V batteries in a flashlight provide a total voltage of 3.0 V.

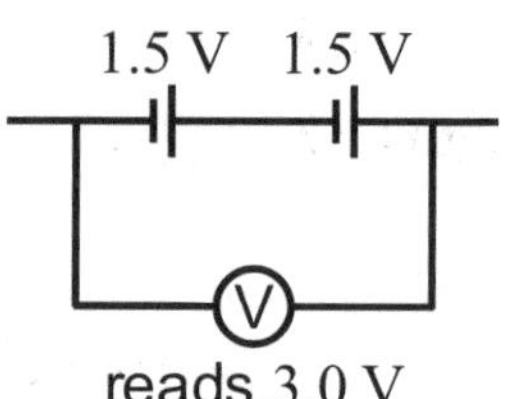

Figure 12-26 *Batteries in series. The total potential difference is the sum of the individual potential differences.*

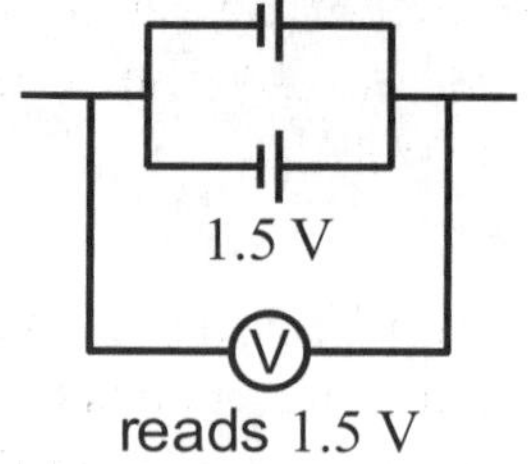

Figure 12-27 *Batteries in parallel. The total potential difference equals that of any one battery.*

If two or more identical batteries are connected in parallel, as shown in Figure 12-27, the total potential difference equals that of any one battery. The advantage of the parallel arrangement is that each battery provides only a fraction of the total current and will last longer than if used alone.

Practice

12-16 What is the equivalent resistance of two 15-Ω resistors connected (a) in series? (b) in parallel?
[Ans. (a) 3.0×10^1 Ω (b) 7.5 Ω]

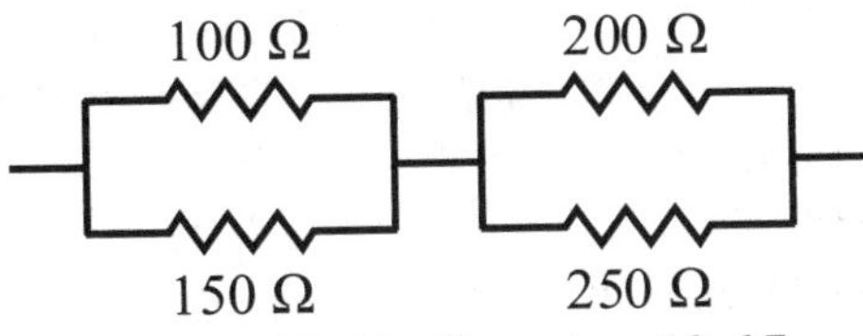

Figure 12-28 *Question 12-17.*

12-17 What is the equivalent resistance of the resistor network in Figure 12-28? (Assume three significant digits.)
[Ans. 171 Ω]

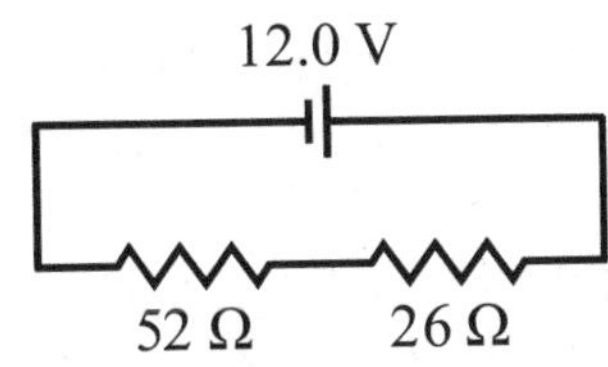

Figure 12-29 *Questions 12-19 and 12-20.*

12-18 You are given a box of 100-Ω resistors. Draw diagrams to show how to connect these resistors to give a total resistance of (a) 300 Ω (b) 50 Ω (c) 25 Ω (d) 250 Ω.

12-19 In Figure 12-29, what is the current in the circuit?
[Ans. 0.15 A]

12-20 Repeat the above question if the two resistors are connected in parallel.
[Ans. 0.71 A]

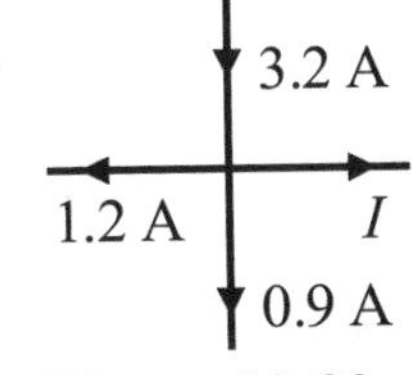

Figure 12-30 *Question 12-21.*

12-21 Figure 12-30 shows a portion of a circuit. What is the unknown current? [Ans. 1.1 A]

12-22 In Figure 12-31, what are
(a) the current through the 47-Ω resistor?
(b) the direction of the current through the 47-Ω resistor?
(c) the potential difference $V_A - V_B$? $V_B - V_A$?
(d) the voltage across the 84-Ω resistor?
(e) the potential at point C, if we define the potential at the negative terminal of the battery to be zero?
[Ans. (a) 0.046 A (b) from A to B (c) +2.2 V; –2.2 V
(d) 3.8 V (e) +3.8 V]

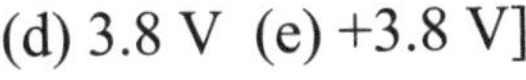

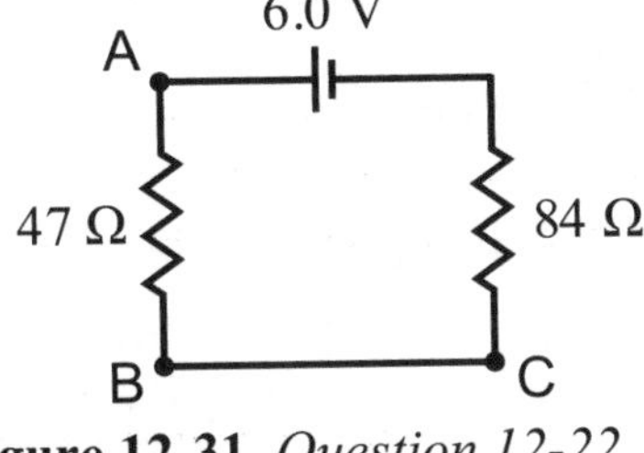

Figure 12-31 *Question 12-22.*

12-23 In Figure 12-32, what are
(a) the potential difference across each resistor?
(b) the current through each of the 150-Ω resistors?
(c) the current through the battery?
(d) the current flowing into point A through the 250-Ω resistor?
(e) the current flowing from point A toward the negative terminal of the battery?
(f) the current at point B?
[Ans. (a) 15 V for each resistor (b) 0.10 A for each 150-Ω resistor (c) 0.26 A (d) 0.060 A (e) 0.26 A (f) 0.20 A]

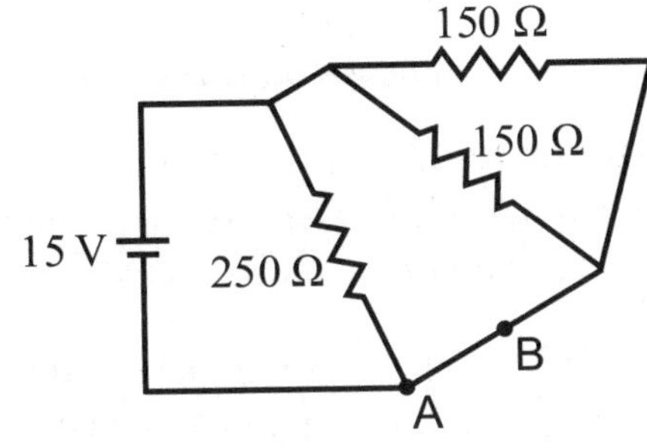

Figure 12-32 *Question 12-23.*

12-24 A circuit is constructed consisting of a 6.0-V battery, two resistors (75 Ω, 50 Ω) connected in series with the battery, and three resistors (200 Ω, 150 Ω, 170 Ω) connected in parallel with each other. This three-resistor combination is in series with the first two resistors and the battery.
(a) Draw a diagram of the circuit.
(b) What is the total current in the circuit? (Assume two significant digits in each resistance value.)
(c) What is the current through the 150-Ω resistor?
(d) What is the voltage across the 50-Ω resistor?
[Ans. (b) 0.033 A (c) 0.013 A (d) 1.6 V]

12-25 (a) For the circuit shown in Figure 12-33, what is the voltage across each resistor? What is the current through each resistor? Switches S_1 and S_2 are closed.
(b) Repeat if switch S_2 is open, and S_1 is closed.
(c) Repeat if both switches are open
[Ans. (a) 15 V and 3 A for each resistor
(b) 0 V and 0 A for the middle resistor; 15 V and 3 A for the other resistors
(c) 0 V and 0 A for each resistor]

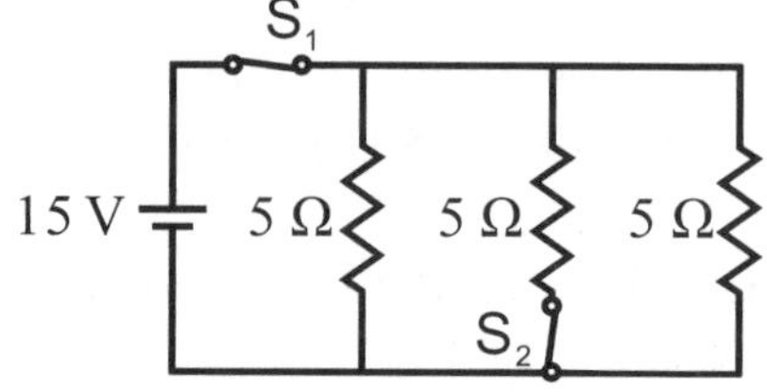

Figure 12-33 *Question 12-25.*

12-26 What are the readings of the voltmeters and ammeters in Figure 12-34 (a) and (b)? Assume two significant digits in the resistance values.
[Ans. (a) 1.0×10^1 V; 0.050 A
(b) 8.4 V; 0.028 A]

12-27 You are provided with three 1.5-V batteries. Draw diagrams to show how to use all three batteries to provide a voltage of:
(a) 4.5 V (b) 1.5 V (c) 3.0 V.

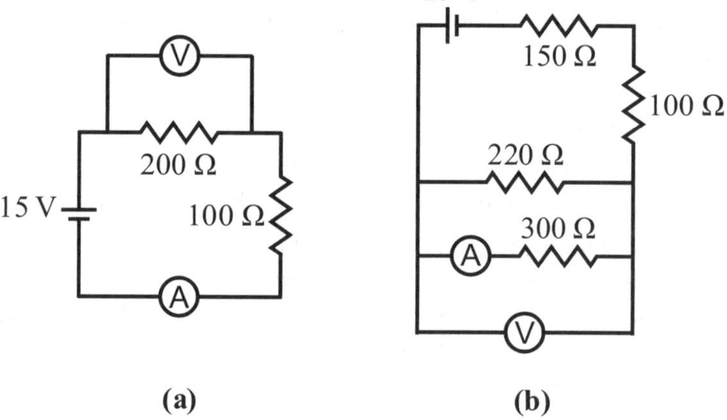

Figure 12-34 *Question 12-26.*

12.4 ELECTRIC ENERGY AND POWER

If you look at almost any electric appliance carefully, you will see a power rating in watts. For example, a hairdryer might be labelled as 1200 W, a radio as 12 W, and a television as 115 W (Figure 12-35). Since a watt is equivalent to a joule per second, this electric power of an appliance is the amount of electric potential energy converted per second into other forms of energy. For instance, a 750-W toaster converts 750 J of electric potential energy into thermal energy each second. But how is electric power related to voltage? to current? to resistance?

Figure 12-35 *This label on a television indicates that it uses a maximum of 115 W of power.*

To answer these questions, we consider a simple circuit consisting only of a 100-Ω resistor and a 10-V battery (Figure 12-36). We can calculate the current in the circuit from Ohm's law:

$$I = \frac{\Delta V}{R} = \frac{10\,V}{100\,\Omega} = 0.1\,A$$

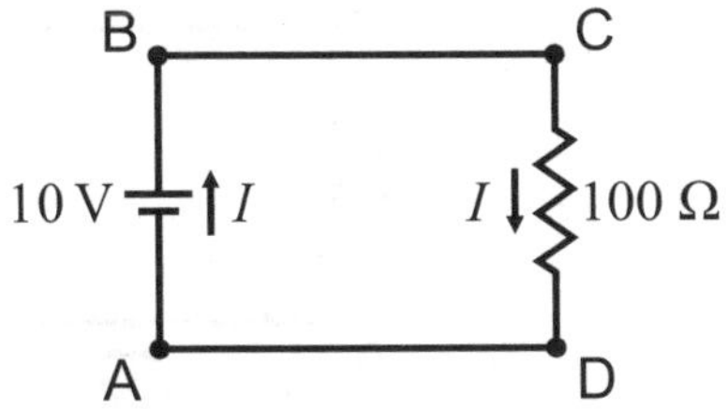

B C
10 V I I 100 Ω
A D

Figure 12-36 *As (positive) charge flows from A to B through the battery, it gains electric potential energy. In flowing from C to D through the resistor, it loses electric potential energy, which is converted to thermal energy in the resistor.*

Therefore, 0.1 C of charge flows past any point in the circuit every second. Since current I is defined as the charge q divided by the time t, then the charge q that flows during a time t is just the product of I and t:

$$q = It$$

If we think of positive charge as flowing (that is, considering conventional current), then in moving from A to B across the battery, the charge moves to higher potential and its electric potential energy increases by

$$\Delta U = q\Delta V \qquad \text{(Eqn. 11-6)}$$

To determine the power P provided by the battery, we divide the energy by the time:

$$P = \frac{E}{t} = \frac{\Delta U}{t} = \frac{q\Delta V}{t}$$

Now, q/t is the current I, and thus,

$$P = (\Delta V)I \qquad \text{(electric power)} \qquad \textbf{(12-8)}$$

This important and simple relationship, $P = (\Delta V)I$, tells us how much power is provided or consumed by an electric device, across which is a potential difference (voltage) ΔV and through which flows a current I. In the battery-resistor circuit shown in Figure 12-36, the battery provides an electric power of P = (10 V)(0.1 A) = 1 W. As (positive) charge flows through the resistor, it moves to lower potential, thus losing electric potential energy, which is converted into thermal energy in the resistor. (Resistors get hot as current flows through them.) The electric power removed or dissipated by the resistor, or the thermal power generated in it, is also 1 W, since the potential difference across the resistor is 10 V and the current through it is 0.1 A.

It is useful to consider the gravitational analogue of this simple circuit. As the electric charges move from A to B (Figure 12-37 (a)), their electric potential energy is increased by the battery. A similar situation occurs if a person lifts baseballs (Figure 12-37 (b)) from A′ to B′, thus increasing their gravitational potential energy. As the current flows from B to C, there is no change in potential, and thus no change in energy. As the balls roll from B′ to C′, there is no energy change. As the current flows from C to D, electric potential energy is converted into thermal energy. As the balls roll down the soft rubber baffles from C′ to D′, gravitational potential energy is converted into thermal energy. (We assume that the baffles are designed so that the kinetic energy of the balls at entrance and exit is the same.) Finally, there is no change in energy as the current flows from D to A, or as the balls from roll from D′ to A′.

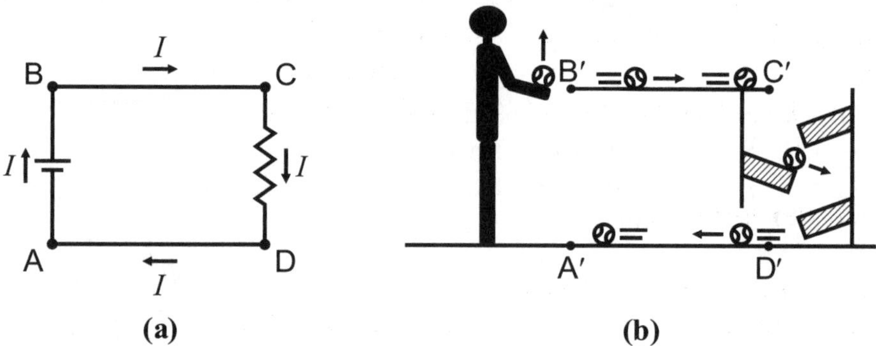

Figure 12-37 (a) *The flow of current through a battery and a resistor is analogous to* **(b)** *baseballs being lifted by a person, and then falling through soft rubber baffles.*

Power Dissipated in a Resistor

The relation $P = (\Delta V)I$ can be written in two other ways for the case where P represents the power dissipated in a resistor. We can substitute $\Delta V = IR$ (Ohm's law) into $P = (\Delta V)I$ to get

$$P = (IR)(I) = I^2R$$

Thus, $P = I^2R$ (power dissipated in a resistor) **(12-9)**

which is an equation that does not involve voltage. We can get a relation that does not include current by substituting $I = (\Delta V)/R$ (from Ohn's law) into $P = (\Delta V)I$:

$$P = \Delta V\left[\frac{\Delta V}{R}\right] = \frac{(\Delta V)^2}{R}$$

Hence, $P = \dfrac{(\Delta V)^2}{R}$ (power dissipated in a resistor) **(12-10)**

Thus, there are three ways to calculate the power consumed by a resistor: Eqns. 12-8, 12-9, and 12-10. Which one is most convenient to use in a given situation depends on which quantities are known.

The relationships $P = (\Delta V)I$, $P = I^2R$, and $P = (\Delta V)^2/R$ can be a source of confusion. For example, from $P = (\Delta V)I$, it appears that $P \propto \Delta V$. However, from $P = (\Delta V)^2/R$, it seems instead that $P \propto (\Delta V)^2$. How can P be proportional to both ΔV and $(\Delta V)^2$? The answer lies in how the other quantities, I and R, are changing (or not changing). In saying that the equation $P = (\Delta V)I$ implies $P \propto \Delta V$, we are assuming that I is constant; in other words, the constant of proportionality is I. Suppose that ΔV doubles, but with no change in I; P must double, that is, P is proportional to ΔV. How is it possible for ΔV to double without changing I? The resistance R must be changing. If ΔV doubles, and we double R at the same time, I will remain constant. Thus, to say that $P \propto \Delta V$ means that I is constant and R is changing. In saying that $P \propto (\Delta V)^2$ (from $P = (\Delta V)^2/R$), what assumptions are implicitly being made about R and I?

Sample Problem 12-7

In the circuit in Figure 12-38, determine the power
(a) dissipated by R_1 (assuming two significant digits in the value for R_1)
(b) dissipated by R_2
(c) provided by the battery.

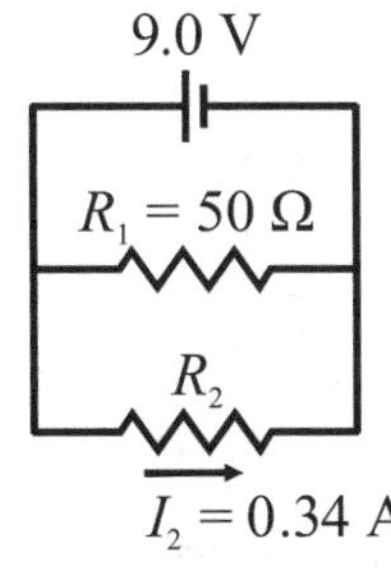

Figure 12-38
Sample Problem 12-7.

Solution: (a) The voltage across each resistor is 9.0 V since the resistors are in parallel. For resistor 1, we know the resistance R_1 (50 Ω) and the voltage (9.0 V). Therefore, the easiest way to calculate the power (P_1) dissipated is to use Eqn. 12-10:

$$P_1 = \frac{(\Delta V)^2}{R_1} = \frac{(9.0\ \text{V})^2}{50\ \Omega} = 1.6\ \text{W}$$

Thus, the power dissipated by R_1 is 1.6 W.

(b) For resistor 2, we know the voltage and the current, but not the resistance. Therefore, to find the power, we use Eqn. 12-8:

$$P_2 = (\Delta V)I_2 = (9.0\ \text{V})(0.34\ \text{A}) = 3.1\ \text{W}$$

Hence, the power dissipated by R_2 is 3.1 W.

(c) There are a number of ways to find the power provided by the battery. For example, we could determine the current through R_1 using Ohm's law, add this to the current through R_2 to find the total current through the battery, and then use $P = (\Delta V)I$ to find the battery power.

However, the easiest way is simply to use conservation of energy. The energy provided by the battery equals the thermal energy produced in both resistors together. Since power is the rate of energy production or consumption, it is also true that the power provided by the battery equals the thermal power dissipated in both resistors. Thus, the battery power (P_B) is just the sum of the powers calculated in (a) and (b):

$$P_B = P_1 + P_2 = 1.6\ \text{W} + 3.1\ \text{W} = 4.7\ \text{W}$$

Hence, the battery provides 4.7 W of power.

Practice

12-28 (a) For the relation $P = (\Delta V)^2/R$, sketch the shape of the graph of P vs. ΔV, assuming constant R. (b) Repeat, plotting P vs. $(\Delta V)^2$.

12-29 (a) For the relation $P = (\Delta V)^2/R$, sketch the shape of the graph of P vs. R, assuming constant ΔV. (b) Repeat, plotting P vs. $1/R$.

12-30 What is the electric power provided by a 6.0-V battery that is supplying a current of 1.25 A? [Ans. 7.5 W]

12-31 Suppose that a person receives an electric shock as a result of touching a "live" wire in a household circuit. Assume that the person's skin is dry, and hence the body's resistance is $1.5 \times 10^3\ \Omega$. (The resistance would be less if the skin were wet.) What is the thermal power dissipated in the person's body if the flowing during the shock is 0.24 A? [Ans. 86 W]

12-32 A 12.0-V battery and a 150-Ω (two significant digits) resistor are connected to form a closed circuit. Determine: (a) the electrical power provided by the battery (b) the thermal power dissipated in the resistor. [Ans. (a) 0.96 W (b) 0.96 W]

12-33 Three small lightbulbs are connected in series with a 6.0-V battery. If the power dissipated in each bulb is 5.4 W, what are the (a) current through each bulb? (b) voltage across each bulb? (c) resistance of each bulb's filament?
[Ans. (a) 2.7 A through each bulb (b) 2.0 V across each bulb (c) 0.74 Ω]

12-34 In the circuit in Figure 12-39,
(a) How much does the electric potential energy of 2.0 C of charge increase or decrease (specify which) as the charge flows from A to B?
(b) Repeat, but as the charge flows from C to D.
[Ans. (a) increases by 36 J (b) decreases by 36 J]

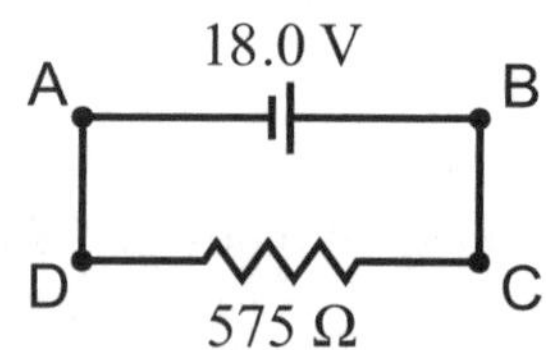

Figure 12-39
Question 12-34.

12-35 (Assume two significant digits in the resistance values in this problem.) In the circuit in Figure 12-40, the current through the 300-Ω resistor is 194 mA.
(a) How much thermal power is dissipated in this resistor?
(b) What is the battery voltage?

(c) How much thermal power is dissipated in each of the other resistors?
(d) How much electric power is provided by the battery?
[Ans. (a) 11 W (b) 58 V
(c) P_{100} = 34 W; P_{200} = 17 W (d) 62 W]

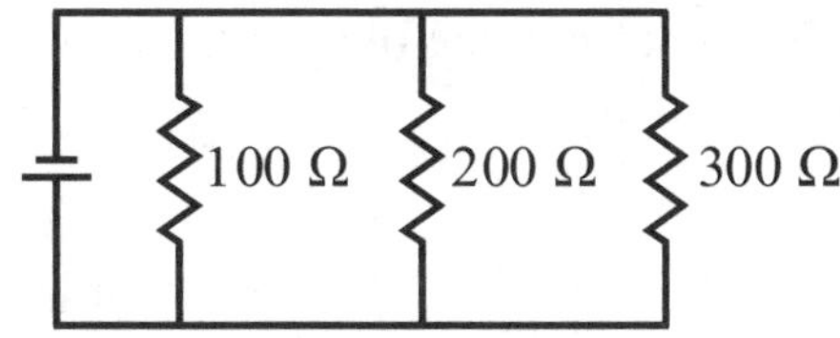

Figure 12-40 *Question 12-35.*

12.5 AC CIRCUITS

You might have noticed that all the circuits that we have considered so far have involved batteries as an energy source. What about standard electric circuits in your home? The energy is provided by falling water, nuclear fission, wind turbines, the burning of coal, oil, or gas, etc., then converted to electric energy and carried to your home through transmission lines.

There is a fundamental difference between a battery-powered circuit and a household circuit. In a battery circuit, the current flows in only one direction, and is called **direct current (DC)**. In the circuits that power your lights, television, refrigerator, etc., at home, the current changes direction 120 times each second, and is called **alternating current (AC)**.[3]

The alternating current is driven by a voltage that changes sign 120 times per second. In a two-prong electric outlet, one connector is said to be "neutral," that is, at ground potential. The other connector is at a higher potential than the neutral one for 1/120 s, then at a lower potential for the next 1/120 s, and so on.

A graph of this voltage is shown in Figure 12-41. You probably recognize it as a sine curve. Figure 12-42 shows the current that results when this voltage is applied to a 100-W lightbulb.

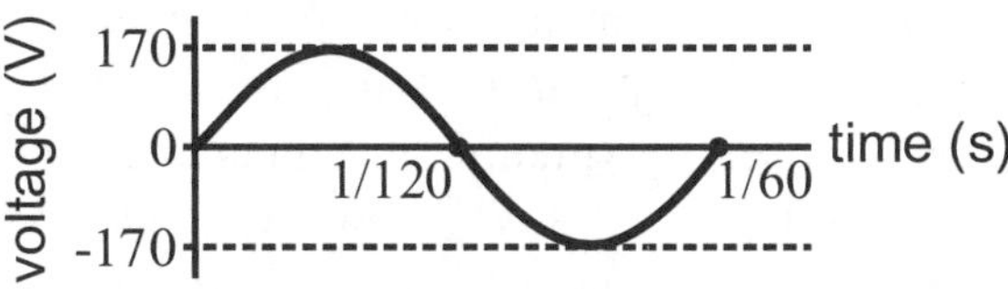

Figure 12-41 *Standard alternating voltage.*

You might know that the standard voltage in North America is referred to as "120 V, 60 Hz." It is easy to see where the 60 Hz comes from — the voltage goes through a complete cycle 60 times per second. But why is it 120 V, when the peak voltage is clearly 170 V? The 120-V value is the effective voltage, ΔV_{eff} , averaged over a complete cycle. It would be inappropriate to assign 170 V as the effective voltage because this peak value is reached only twice per cycle (counting both +170 V and −170 V). There is a mathematical relation between the peak voltage

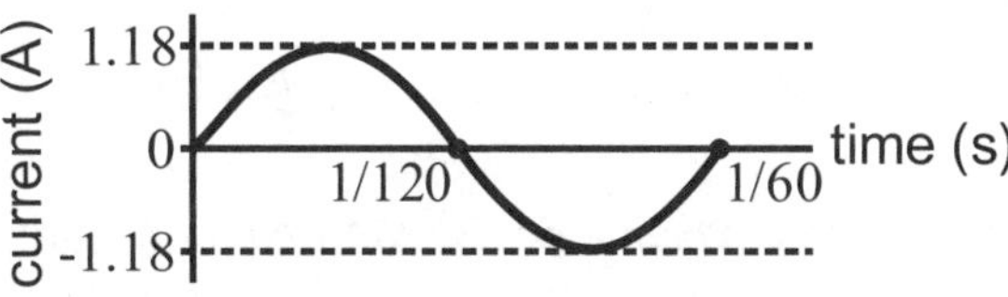

Figure 12-42 *The alternating current that results when the voltage in Fig. 12-41 is applied to a 100-W lightbulb.*

[3]Alternating current is used for commercial electricity because it can be transmitted at high voltage more easily than direct current, producing less thermal energy loss in the transmission lines themselves.

and the effective voltage:

$$\Delta V_{\text{peak}} = \sqrt{2}\,\Delta V_{\text{eff}} \qquad \textbf{(12-11)}$$

$$\text{that is,} \quad 170\text{ V} = \sqrt{2}\,(120\text{ V})$$

Similarly, when we say that an AC current is, say 3 A, this is the effective current. The peak current is larger by a factor of $\sqrt{2}$. More formally, what we are calling the effective voltage or current is the *root-mean-square (rms)* value, that is, the square *root* of the *mean* (average) of the *square* of the voltage (or current).

Notice that we have not said that the average voltage is 120 V. Because the voltage is continually changing sign, the average voltage is zero (over an integral number of cycles). However, its average effect is not zero. Consider a lightbulb operating on AC. When the voltage is positive, current flows in one direction through the bulb's filament, and electric potential energy is converted to light and thermal energy. When the voltage is negative, current flows in the other direction, and light and thermal energy are again generated. Thus, even through the average voltage is zero, energy is, nonetheless, delivered.

As is the case with DC circuits, the electric power consumed is the product of voltage and current. However, since the voltage and current are varying, the (instantaneous) power also varies (Figure 12-43). This power goes from a value of zero (when $\Delta V = I = 0$), to a positive maximum (when $\Delta V > 0$ and $I > 0$), back to zero, to a positive maximum (when $\Delta V < 0$ and $I < 0$, but the product $(\Delta V)I$ is positive), etc. In Figure 12-43, the maximum instantaneous power consumption is 200 W; however, the average power consumption over a cycle is 100 W.

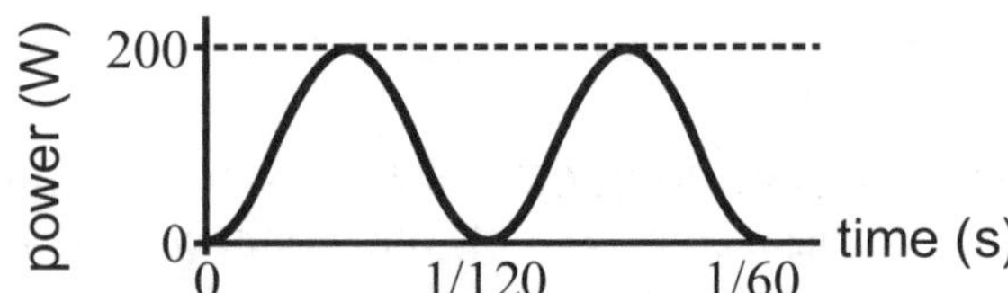

Figure 12-43 *The product of voltage and current gives the (instantaneous) power consumption of a 100-W lightbulb. The maximum power is 200 W; the average, 100 W.*

This average power consumption is what is of interest to the electrical consumer. When we speak of power in an AC circuit, we do not usually mean the instantaneous power, but rather the average power. The average power is related in a straightforward way to the effective voltage and current:

$$P = (\Delta V)I \quad \text{(average AC power)} \qquad \textbf{(12-12)}$$

where P is *average* power, and ΔV and I are *effective* (rms) voltage and current, respectively.

Notice that Eqn. 12-12 conveniently has the same form as Eqn. 12-8 that we developed for DC power earlier in this section. In Eqn. 12-12, the quantities P, ΔV, and I are usually referred to simply as the power, voltage, and current without the adjectives average, effective, or rms. The relations $P = (\Delta V)^2/R$ and $P = I^2R$ that we derived for DC can also be used for AC. In these equations, P is once again *average* power, and ΔV and I are *effective* voltage and current. The resistance R for an ohmic resistor is the same whether DC or AC is used.

$$P = \frac{(\Delta V)^2}{R} \quad \text{(average AC power dissipated in a resistor)} \qquad \textbf{(12-13)}$$

$$P = I^2 R \quad \text{(average AC power dissipated in a resistor)} \qquad \textbf{(12-14)}$$

Sample Problem 12-8

A toaster's power rating is 750 W.
(a) How much current does it draw when connected to a 120-V supply?
(b) What is the peak current?
(c) What is the resistance of the toaster's filament?

Solution: (a) The "current" refers to the effective or rms current, which can be calculated by re-arranging Eqn. 12-12 $(P = (\Delta V)I)$:

$$I = \frac{P}{\Delta V} = \frac{750 \text{ W}}{120 \text{ V}} = 6.3 \text{ A}$$

Thus, the current is 6.3 A.

(b) The peak current is $\sqrt{2}$ times the effective (or rms) current:

$$I_{\text{peak}} = \sqrt{2}\, I = \sqrt{2}\,(6.3 \text{ A}) = 8.8 \text{ A}$$

Hence, the peak current is 8.8 A.

(c) To determine the resistance of the toaster's filament, we can re-arrange Eqn. 12-13 ($P = (\Delta V)^2 / R$), which gives:

$$R = \frac{(\Delta V)^2}{P} = \frac{(120 \text{ V})^2}{750 \text{ W}} = 19\,\Omega$$

(Because we know the current from part (b), we could also have used Eqn. 12-14, $P = I^2 R$, to calculate the resistance.)

Thus, the resistance of the filament is 19 Ω.

Practical AC Electricity

In a typical house circuit, the outlets, lights, etc., are connected in *parallel*. To understand why this is done, consider Figure 12-44, which shows a 120-V AC supply connected to three lightbulbs in parallel. In this way, the potential difference across each bulb is 120 V, regardless of how many of the bulbs are turned on. If one bulb is turned off, unscrewed, or burns out, the current through this bulb becomes zero, but this does not affect the current through the rest of the bulbs, each of which is still supplied with 120 V. In contrast, if the bulbs were connected in series, as shown in Figure 12-45, then, if one bulb were to burn out, the current to the entire circuit is eliminated. Household circuits themselves are also connected in parallel with each other, so that, if current to one circuit is eliminated, other circuits are unaffected.

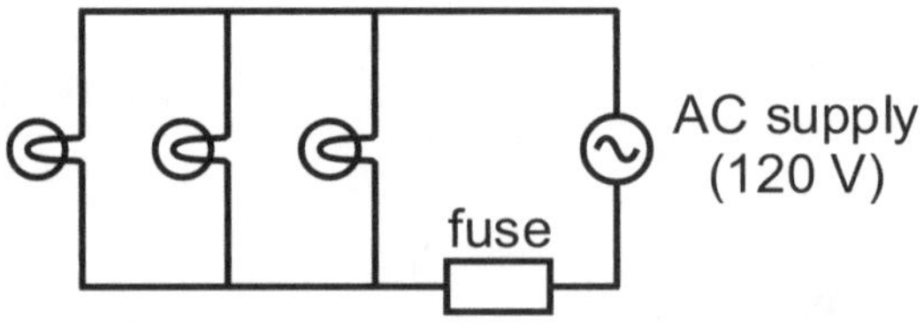

AC supply (120 V)
fuse

Figure 12-44 *If one of the bulbs connected in parallel burns out, the currents through the others are unaffected.*

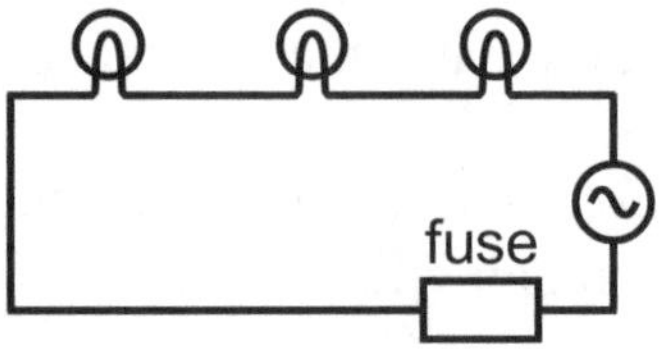

fuse

Figure 12-45 *If a bulb in a series circuit burns out, current is cut off to all the bulbs.*

Christmas-tree lights in common use a few decades ago were often wired in series — if one bulb burned out, the entire string of lights went out, and it was a time-consuming exercise to discover which bulb heeded replacement. Some modern Christmas mini-lights are connected in series, but when one bulb burns out, the rest of the lights continue to function. The bulbs have been cleverly designed so that, when the standard voltage is applied to a string containing a burned-out bulb, a small spark is produced inside this bulb.[4] The spark melts the insulation off a tiny jumper wire in the bulb, resulting in an electric connection across the interior of the bulb. This allows current to flow through the rest of the circuit and bypass the filament of the burned-out bulb.

Notice the fuse in Figure 12-44; each household circuit has a fuse (or circuit breaker) as a safety device. The fuse is in series with the AC source so that the total current in the circuit flows through the fuse. If too many appliances are turned on in a circuit, thus producing a very large total current, or if an appliance malfunctions and draws too much current, the fuse melts (or the circuit breaker "trips"), and no current can flow through the circuit. A typical household circuit has a fuse or breaker rated at 15 A; larger currents overheat the wires and constitute a fire hazard.

Figure 12-46 *The third prong in this outlet is connected to ground for safety.*

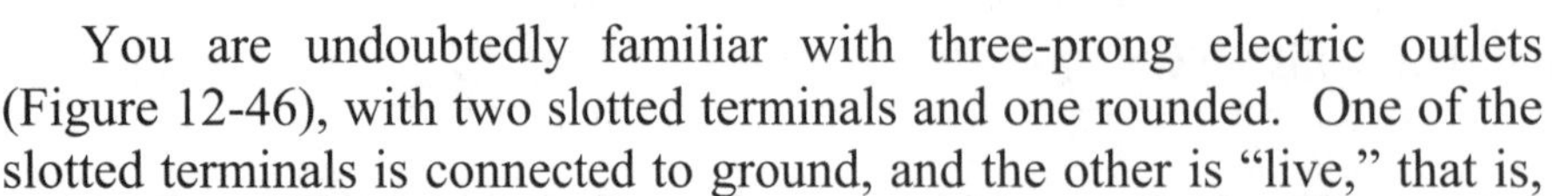

You are undoubtedly familiar with three-prong electric outlets (Figure 12-46), with two slotted terminals and one rounded. One of the slotted terminals is connected to ground, and the other is "live," that is,

[4]No current initially flows in the string because there is no conducting path through the burned-out bulb, and therefore, the entire 120 V is applied across this bulb, producing a spark. When the string is functioning properly, the voltage is divided equally across all the bulbs, and the small voltage across any one bulb is not large enough to create a spark.

it provides the alternating voltage relative to ground. The rounded terminal is connected to ground and functions as a safety device. An appliance such as a power saw with a three-prong plug has its third wire connected to the casing of the saw. If the "live wire" inside the saw becomes loose and makes contact with the casing, a large current flows through the third wire to ground and the circuit fuse "blows." In the absence of the third wire, the body of anyone touching the casing of the saw could provide an electrical path to ground and the person could be electrocuted.

Some appliances such as clothes dryers and stoves are connected to 240-V circuits. These devices need a large amount of power, and the larger voltage permits a smaller current. (Considering $I = P/\Delta V$, if ΔV is doubled then the same power P will be consumed using half the current I). If the power were delivered at 120 V, the current would be so large that the wires would become hot enough to be a fire hazard. The resistance of wires is small, but not zero, and for a given wire of resistance R, a current I produces a thermal power $P = I^2R$. Hence, reducing the current in a wire by a factor of two decreases the heating effect by a factor of four.

In order to provide 240 V, two 120-V alternating voltages that are out of phase with each other are supplied in separate wires. When one voltage is at its peak, at +170 V relative to ground, the other is −170 V relative to ground. Thus, the peak potential difference between the wires is 340 V, and the effective (rms) potential difference is 240 V.

A common unit used to express electric *energy* consumption is the kilowatt·hour (kW·h), discussed in Chapter 7. The product of power in kilowatts and time in hours gives energy in kilowatt·hours. Beware — although kilowatt·hour contains "watt," it is an energy unit, not a power unit. (1 kW·h = 3.60×10^6 J)

Practice

12-36 Sketch the shape of the graph of voltage vs. time for the DC voltage from a 12-V battery supplying current to a resistor.

12-37 Some old-fashioned Christmas-tree lights are connected in series. What are two disadvantages of this arrangement?

12-38 A 60-W lightbulb is in a lamp plugged into a standard 120-V outlet. Determine:
(a) the current through the bulb (assuming two significant digits in the given data)
(b) the peak current (c) the resistance of the bulb's filament.
[Ans. (a) 0.50 A (b) 0.71 A (c) $2.4 \times 10^2\ \Omega$]

12-39 A girl accidentally sticks a metal paperclip into the "live" connector of a 120-V outlet. If the resulting current that flows between her hand and her feet is 92 mA, what is the resistance between her hand and feet? [Ans. $1.3 \times 10^3\ \Omega$]

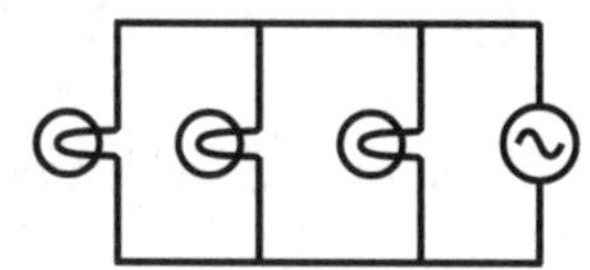

Figure 12-47
Question 12-40.

12-40 Figure 12-47 shows three 100-W lightbulbs connected to an AC source that provides 120 V. (a) If the bulbs are "on," what is the current

through each bulb? (Assume two significant digits in the given data.)
(b) If the middle bulb is unscrewed, what is the current through the other two bulbs?
[Ans. (a) 0.83 A through each bulb (b) 0.83 A through each of the other two bulbs]

12-41 A colour television uses 105 W of electric power. If it is turned on for 3.00 h, what is its energy consumption in (a) kilowatt·hours? (b) joules? (c) What is the cost of this energy, if electric energy costs 11¢/(kW·h)? [Ans. (a) 0.315 kw·h (b) 1.13×10^6 J (c) 3.5¢]

12-42 A 1.10-kW hairdryer and a 60.0-W lightbulb are turned on in the same 120-V AC parallel circuit. Assuming three significant digits in the given voltage, determine the current in the (a) hairdryer (b) lightbulb (c) fuse in the circuit. (d) If the fuse is rated at 15 A, will it blow?
[Ans. (a) 9.17 A (b) 0.500 A (c) 9.67 A (d) no]

12-43 The 60-Hz frequency of AC voltage remains almost constant, but the voltage does fluctuate, depending on demand and on equipment problems. (A "brownout" occurs when the voltage drops so much that lights become noticeably dimmer.) If an electric baseboard heater uses a power of 1.20 kW when the voltage is 120 V (three significant digits), what power will it use if the voltage drops to 105 V? Assume that the resistance of the heater does not change at the different power (and temperature) levels. [Ans. 919 W]

CHAPTER FOCUS

In the previous two chapters on electricity, we discussed the basic concepts of electric charge, field, potential energy, potential, and current.

This chapter has focused on resistance and circuits, both DC and AC. Electric resistance has been defined and its relation to the resistivity and size of a conductor has been presented. We have discussed Ohm's law, that is, the relation between voltage, current, and resistance, and have used it in calculating these quantities in simple circuits. The equivalent resistance of resistors in series and parallel has been determined, and we have seen how to calculate electric energy and power in circuits.

This chapter concludes our discussion of electricity. The next chapter is an introduction to vibrations and waves, which are important in an understanding of sound, music, light, optical instruments, lasers, etc.

VOCABULARY REVIEW

You should be able to define or explain each of the following words or phrases.

electric resistance
ohm
Ohm's law
open circuit
closed circuit
series (electrical connection)

electric resistivity
temperature coefficient of resistivity
electrolyte
battery
electric circuit
parallel (electrical connection)
galvanometer
direct current (DC)
alternating current (AC)

CHAPTER REVIEW

12-44 At a given temperature, which piece of copper wire has the highest resistance?
(a) 2.0 m length, 1.0×10^{-6} m^2 cross-sectional area
(b) 4.0 m length, 1.0×10^{-6} m^2 cross-sectional area
(c) 2.0 m length, 3.0×10^{-6} m^2 cross-sectional area
(d) 4.0 m length, 3.0×10^{-6} m^2 cross-sectional area
(e) 1.0 m length, 3.0×10^{-6} m^2 cross-sectional area

12-45 In the circuit of Figure 12-48, which switch(es) must be closed to produce a current in conductor FG?
(a) 1 and 4, only
(b) 2 and 3, only
(c) 1, 2, and 3, only
(d) 4, only
(e) 1, only

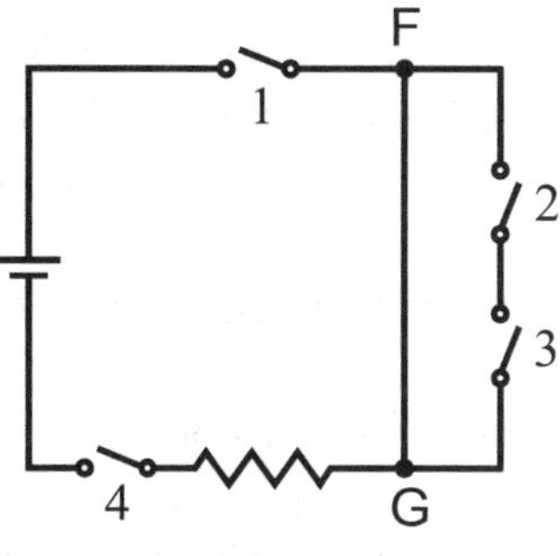

Figure 12-48
Question 12-45.

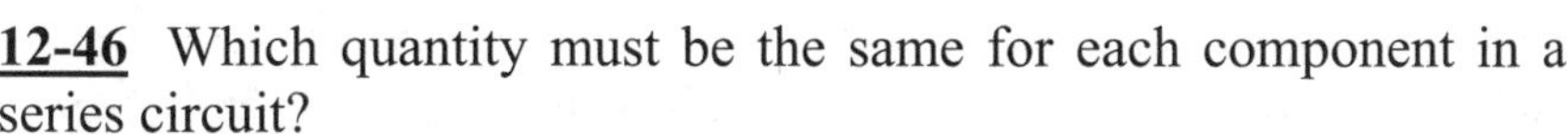

12-46 Which quantity must be the same for each component in a series circuit?
(a) voltage (b) power (c) current (d) resistance (e) energy

12-47 Repeat the previous question for a parallel circuit.

12-48 Two resistors are connected in a circuit with a battery as shown in Figure 12-49. If resistor R_1 is then removed from the circuit, leaving a gap where it used to be, but leaving the connecting wires and resistor R_2 intact, which of the following is true?
(a) The voltage across R_2 increases, and the current through R_2 increases.
(b) The voltage across R_2 decreases, and the current through R_2 decreases.
(c) The voltage across R_2 increases, and the current through R_2 decreases.
(d) The voltage across R_2 remains the same, and the current through R_2 increases.
(e) The voltage across R_2 remains the same, and the current through R_2 remains the same.

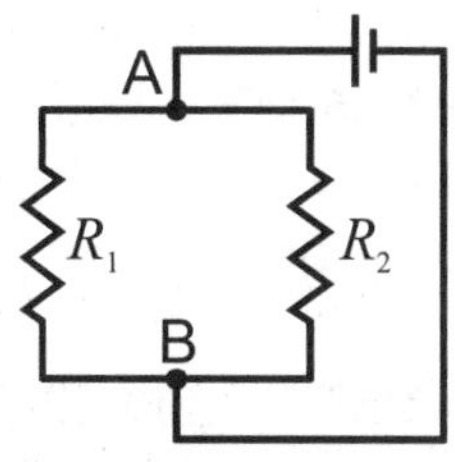

Figure 12-49
Question 12-48.

12-49 A current of only about 25 μA may cause ventricular fibrillation during open-heart surgery. Determine the voltage that would produce this current, if the resistance of the heart is 240 Ω. [Ans. 6.0×10^{-3} V = 6.0 mV]

12-50 A number of copper wires of the same diameter have different lengths (L). Sketch the shape of a graph of the resistances of the wires vs. L.

12-51 What is the diameter (in millimetres) of a 35-cm aluminum wire if its resistance is 1.0 Ω? [Ans. 0.11 mm]

12-52 An aluminum wire and a copper wire of the same length have the same voltage applied to them. If the currents are the same, what is the ratio of the diameters of the wires?
[Ans. $d_C/d_A = 0.78$]

12-53 As the temperature of a conductor is increased by 7.5°C, its resistivity increases by 3.2%. What is its temperature coefficient of resistivity? [Ans. 4.3×10^{-3} (°C)$^{-1}$]

12-54 Is the resistance of the filament of a lightbulb greater when the bulb is on, or off?

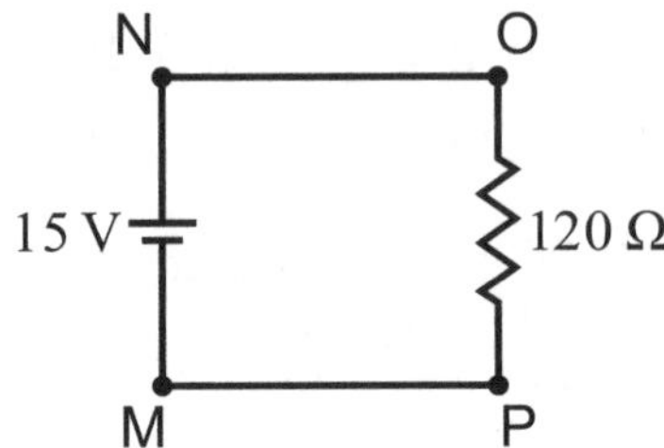

Figure 12-50
Question 12-55.

12-55 In Figure 12-50, follow the changes in potential as a positive charge moves around the circuit in the order M → N → O → P → M (that is, following the conventional current direction). Assume that the potential at the negative battery terminal is defined to be zero. Specifically, what are the following changes in potential?
(a) $V_N - V_M$ (b) $V_O - V_N$ (c) $V_P - V_O$ (d) $V_M - V_P$
(e) Use your results to calculate the total change in potential in going around the circuit, starting and finishing at point M.
(f) What would be your answer to (e) if the path started and finished at N?
[Ans. (a) 15 V (b) 0 V (c) −15 V (d) 0 V
(e) 0 V (f) 0 V]

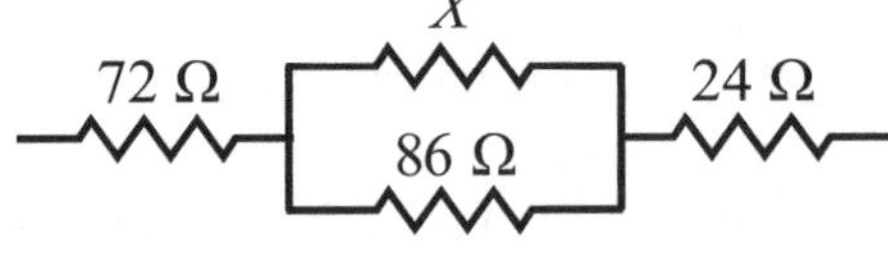

Figure 12-51 *Question 12-56.*

12-56 The equivalent resistance of the network shown in Figure 12-51 is 139 Ω. What is the resistance "X?"
[Ans. 86 Ω]

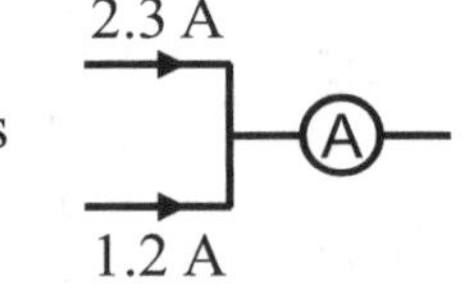

Figure 12-52
Question 12-57.

12-57 Figure 12-52 shows a portion of a circuit. What is the reading on the ammeter? [Ans. 3.5 A]

12-58 In Figure 12-53, what are the
(a) current through the 150-Ω resistor?
(b) potential difference across the 250-Ω resistor?
(c) current through the 350-Ω resistor?
(d) potential at point A (assuming zero potential at the negative terminal of the battery).
[Ans. (a) 0.057 A (b) 14 V (c) 0.035 A (d) 21 V]

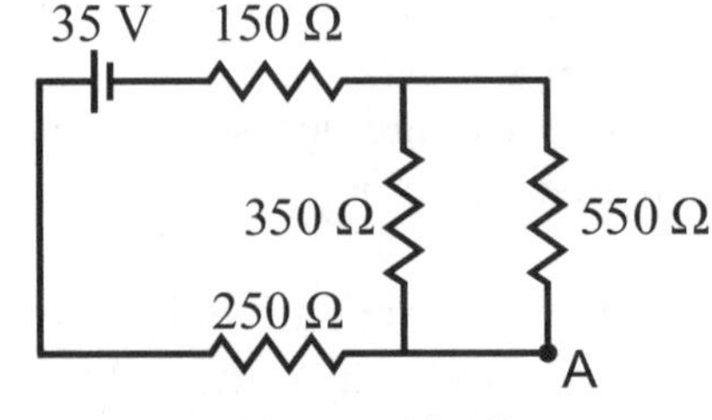

Figure 12-53
Questions 12-58 and 12-59.

<u>**12-59**</u> In Figure 12-53, what would be the correct location of (a) a voltmeter to measure the potential difference across the 250-Ω resistor? (b) an ammeter to measure the current flowing in the 350-Ω resistor?

12-60 Three resistors (1 Ω, 2 Ω, and 3 Ω) are connected together in series with a 6-V battery to form a closed circuit. What are the voltages across the resistors? [Ans. $\Delta V_1 = 1$ V; $\Delta V_2 = 2$ V; $\Delta V_3 = 3$ V]

<u>**12-61**</u> (a) As current flows through a resistor, does it flow from high to low, or low to high, potential? (b) Repeat, for electron flow.

<u>**12-62**</u> A lightbulb is powered by a battery (of negligible internal resistance).
(a) A second identical bulb is then connected in series in the circuit. How do the brightnesses of the two bulbs compare with each other, and how do they compare with the brightness of the original single bulb? Explain.
(b) Repeat, if the second bulb is connected in parallel.

<u>**12-63**</u> In the circuit shown in Figure 12-54, the battery maintains a constant potential difference across its terminals. The bulbs are all identical and are initially lit.
(a) Compare the brightnesses of the bulbs. Explain your answer.
In the parts that follow, in response to "What happens…?", indicate whether the quantity increases, decreases, or is unchanged. Explain each answer briefly.
(b) If bulb C is now unscrewed from its socket, what happens simultaneously to the brightnesses of the three bulbs? (Answer for each bulb individually.) What happens simultaneously to the currents at points 1, 2, and 3?

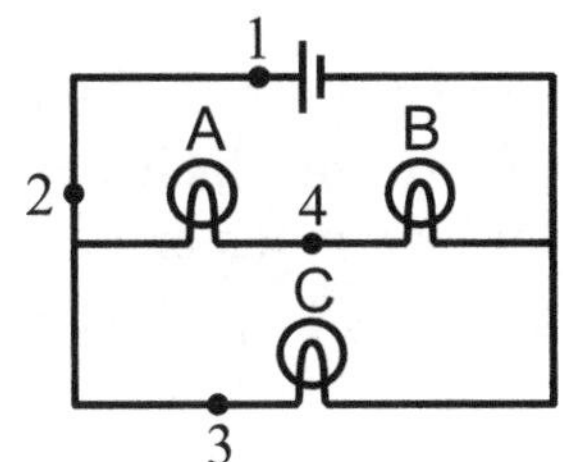

Figure 12-54
Question 12-63.

(c) Bulb A is now unscrewed from its socket. (Bulb C remains unscrewed.) What happens simultaneously to the brightnesses of the bulbs, and to the currents at points 1, 2, and 3?
(d) With all three bulbs inserted in their sockets and lit, a jumper wire of negligible resistance is connected from point 1 at the positive terminal of the battery to point 4. What happens simultaneously to the potential difference across bulb A? What happens simultaneously to the brightnesses of the three bulbs, and to the currents at points 1, 2, and 3?

<u>**12-64**</u> Why are electric circuits in automobiles connected together in parallel?

12-65 Using the relation $P = I^2R$, sketch the shape of a graph of (a) P vs. I (b) P vs. I^2. Assume that R is constant.

<u>**12-66**</u> If a number of extension cords are connected together to form an ultra-long cord, the voltage available to an appliance plugged into the end is less than 120 V. Why?

<u>**12-67**</u> As a lightbulb "grows old," its filament becomes thinner. How does this affect its (a) resistance? (b) power? (Assume that the voltage is constant.)

12-68 How long must a 100-W lightbulb be turned on to use 1.0 J of energy? (Assume two significant digits in the power rating.) [Ans. 1.0×10^{-2} s]

12-69 If the AC voltage available from an outlet changes from 120 V to 110 V (three significant digits), what is the new peak voltage? [Ans. 156 V]

12-70 High-voltage DC power supplies are devices that plug into a standard AC outlet and produce a large DC voltage between two terminals as output. They are often designed to have a large internal resistance in series with the output terminals. Why is this safer than having a small internal resistance and the same output voltage?

12-71 In the circuit in Figure 12-55, what is the power (a) dissipated in each resistor? (b) supplied by the battery? [Ans. (a) P_{16} = 4.0 W; P_{32} = 2.0 W each (b) 8.0 W]

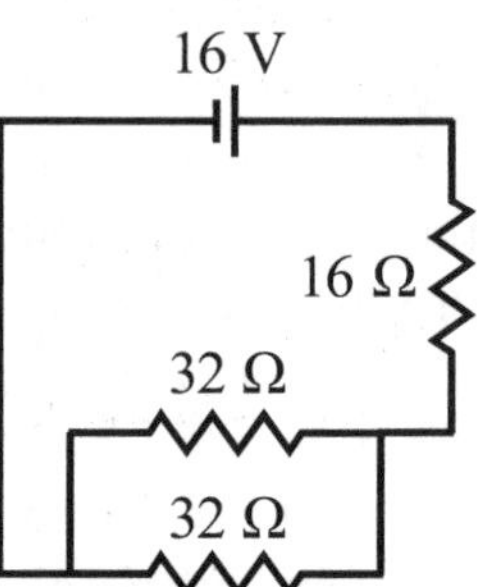

Figure 12-55
Question 12-71.

12-72 A heart defibrillator provides a voltage of 8.0×10^3 V through a patient's torso to re-establish normal beating of the heart. If the pathway of the current through the person has a resistance of 7.0×10^2 Ω, and the current flows for 3.0 ms, (a) how large is the current?
(b) how much charge flows?
(c) how much energy is deposited by the current?
[Ans. (a) 11 A (b) 0.034 C (c) 2.7×10^2 J]

12-73 An electric clothes-dryer consumes 2.5 kW of power.
(a) What is the current if the power is provided at 120 V?
(b) What is the current if the power is provided at 240 V?
(c) What is the advantage of using 240 V for the dryer?
[Ans. (a) 21 A (b) 1.0×10^1 A]

APPLYING YOUR KNOWLEDGE

12-74 In a single-loop circuit, the current is 1.50 A. When another resistor (1.2 kΩ) is added in series, the current is 1.30 A. What was the original resistance in the circuit? [Ans. 7.8 kΩ]

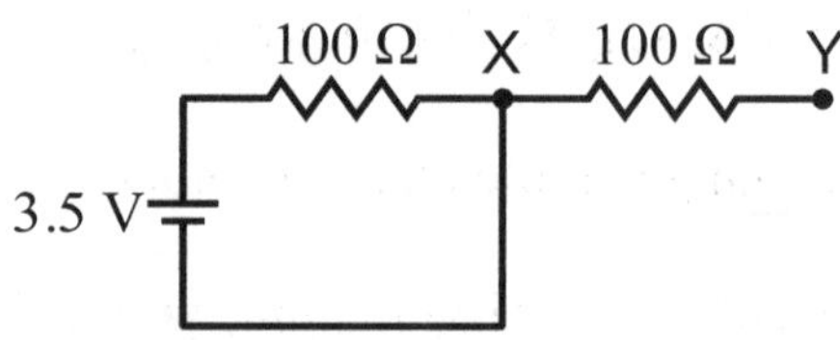

Figure 12-56 *Question 12-75.*

12-75 In Figure 12-56, if we define the potential at the negative terminal of the battery to be zero, what is the potential at X? at Y? [Ans. 0 V; 0 V]

12-76 A piece of copper wire of resistance 3.2×10^{-2} Ω is melted and reformed so that its length increases by a factor of 4.0. What is its new resistance? [Ans. 0.51 Ω]

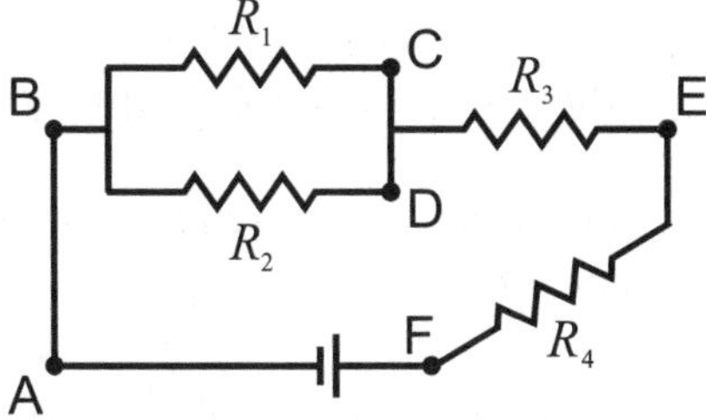

Figure 12-57 *Question 12-77.*

12-77 In Figure 12-57, if I_1 and I_2 represent the currents through resistors R_1 and R_2, respectively, at which lettered point(s) could an ammeter be connected to measure the sum $I_1 + I_2$?

12-78 For two resistors R_1 and R_2 connected in parallel, show that the ratio of the currents through them is given by $I_1/I_2 = R_2/R_1$.

12-79 In Figure 12-58, what is the current through (a) the 200-Ω resistor? (b) the battery? Assume three significant digits in given data. [Ans. (a) 0.0360 A (b) 0.248 A]

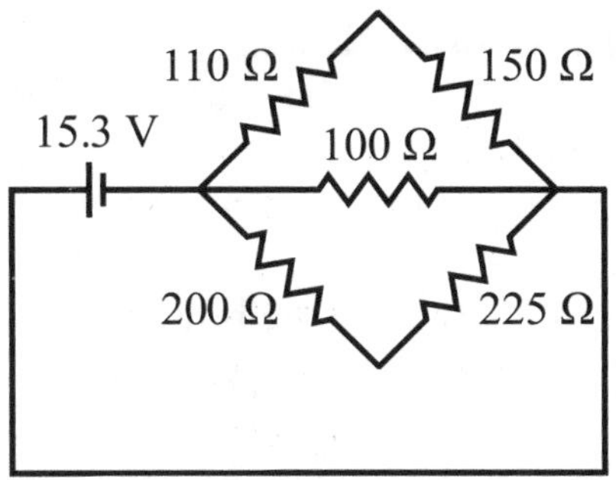

Figure 12-58 *Question 12-79.*

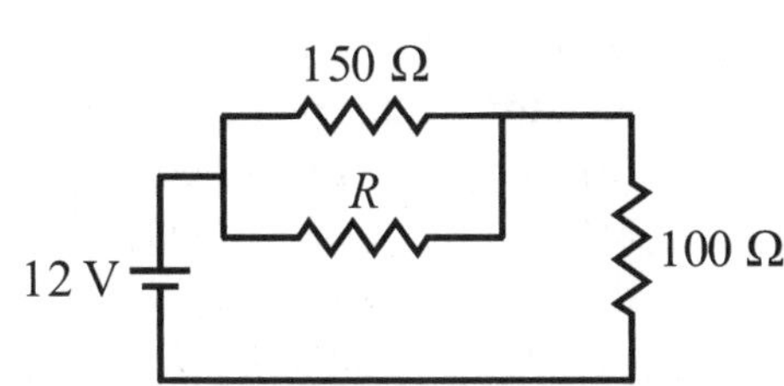

Figure 12-59 *Question 12-80.*

12-80 In Figure 12-59, a current of 59.5 mA flows through the 100-Ω resistor. What is the unknown resistance R? Assume three significant digits in the given resistances. [Ans. 316 Ω]

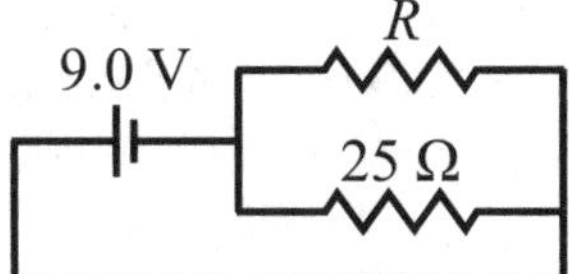

Figure 12-60 *Question 12-81.*

12-81 In Figure 12-60, the battery is providing 5.4 W of power. What is the resistance R? [Ans. 38 Ω]

KEY OBJECTIVES

Having completed this chapter, you should now be able to do the following:

1. Define resistance and state its SI unit.
2. State Ohm's law and use it in determining voltage, current, and resistance in simple circuits.
3. State the difference between electric resistivity and electric resistance, and use electric resistivities in related problems.
4 State how the resistivity of a metallic conductor changes with temperature, and use temperature coefficients of resistivity in problems.
5. Describe the basic construction of a battery.
6. Draw and use electric circuit diagrams.
7. Calculate the equivalent resistance of resistors in series and/or parallel.

8. Solve circuit problems involving resistors in series and/or parallel.
9. State how voltmeters and ammeters are inserted in circuits to measure voltage and current.
10. State the relation between electric power, voltage, and current, and use this relation (and similar ones involving resistance) in problems concerning electric power.
11. State the difference between DC and AC.
12. Discuss what is meant by peak and effective (rms) voltage and current.
13. Solve problems related to simple AC circuits.

ANSWERS TO SELECTED QUESTIONS

12-9 increase

12-44 (b) 12-45 (a) 12-46 (c) 12-47 (a) 12-48 (e)

12-54 on

12-59 (a) The voltmeter would be in parallel with the 250-Ω resistor, with one lead of the voltmeter connected just to the left of the resistor and the other lead connected just to the right of the resistor. (b) The ammeter would be connected in series with the 350-Ω resistor, either just above the resistor on the circuit diagram, or just below it.

12-61 (a) from high to low potential (b) from low to high potential

12-62 (a) The two bulbs are equal in brightness, and this brightness is less than the brightness of the original single bulb. When the second bulb is added in series, the total resistance in the circuit is increased, and the current decreases (from Ohm's Law, $I = \Delta V/R$). Since the current has decreased, the brightness is less than in the case of the single bulb. Since the two resistors have the same (reduced) current through them, the brightness of each is equal.

(b) The two bulbs are equal in brightness, and this brightness is equal to the brightness of the original single bulb. When the second bulb is added in parallel, the same voltage (i.e., the battery voltage) is applied to each bulb, and the same amount of current passes through each bulb, giving equal brightness. Since the battery voltage is applied to each bulb, the current through each bulb is the same as if the other bulb didn't even exist. Hence, the brightness of each bulb is the same as the brightness of the original single bulb.

12-63 (a) In brightness, C > A = B. The battery voltage is being applied across bulb C, and also across the series combination of A & B. The resistance of A & B together is greater than that of C alone; hence, the current through A & B is less than that through C, and A & B are not as bright as C.

(b) The brightness of C decreases to zero; A & B are unchanged (since the battery voltage is still applied across A & B together). Current at 3 has decreased to zero; current at 1 and 2 has decreased since the battery is no longer providing current to bulb C.

(c) No current now flows anywhere in the circuit; none of the bulbs is lit.

(d) The left side of bulb A and the right side of bulb A are now at the same electric potential, and hence the potential difference across A is zero. Therefore, no current flows through A, and its brightness decreases to zero. The battery voltage is now being applied across bulbs B and C in parallel. The brightness of C remains unchanged, and the brightness of B increases until it is the same as C. The current at point 3, that is, the current through C, is unchanged. The current at point 2 decreases — it is now only the current through C, whereas previously it was the sum of the current through C and the current through A & B. The current at point 1 is the total current in the circuit; the current through C is unchanged, but the current through B has increased, and therefore the current at 1 increases.

12-64 — so that all the circuits will be provided with the same voltage (typically 12 V) regardless of how many circuits are being used

12-66 Although the resistance of an extension cord is small, it is not zero. Since resistance is proportional to length (Eqn. 11-4), the resistance of an ultra-long extension cord can be large enough that there is an appreciable potential drop across it. Therefore, the voltage available to an appliance plugged into the end of it will be less than 120 V.

12-67 (a) Resistance is inversely proportional to cross-sectional area (Eqn. 11-4), and therefore a thinner filament has a higher resistance. (b) Since the voltage ΔV is constant and the resistance R is inreasing, the power P must be decreasing, from the relation $P = (\Delta V)^2/R$.

12-70 If a person were to accidentally touch the high-voltage terminals, the large internal resistance would prevent a large current from flowing and causing serious injury to the person.

12-77 A, or B, or E, or F

CHAPTER 13

VIBRATIONS AND WAVES

Waves are important in physics because certain types of energy, such as sound and light, travel from one place to another by some sort of wave action. Since waves are caused by vibrations, this chapter begins with a study of various types of vibrations. Then, several properties of waves we can see, such as waves on ropes, coiled springs, and water, are presented. Many examples of wave properties, especially those related to sound, will already be familiar to you. This chapter leads directly to the next chapter, which deals with the wave characteristics of light.

13.1 INTRODUCING VIBRATIONS AND WAVES

A **vibration** is the periodic motion of a particle or mechanical system. The word periodic means that the motion is repeated at regular intervals of time.

Three common types of vibration are called longitudinal, transverse, and torsional, all shown in Figure 13-1. A **longitudinal vibration** is one in which the motion is parallel to the axis of equilibrium. Examples are a vertical coil spring on which a mass is bouncing and the springs on vehicles used to help provide a smooth ride. A **transverse vibration** is one in which the basic motion is perpendicular to the axis of equilibrium. Examples are a simple pendulum and a child on a swing. A **torsional vibration** is a twisting around the axis of equilibrium. An example is the mechanism of a spring watch as it twists around and back. Besides illustrating these three types of vibration, Figure 13-1 shows that a **cycle** is one complete vibration.

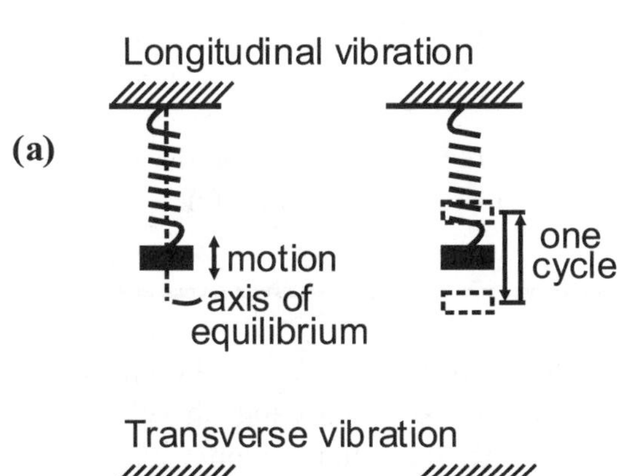

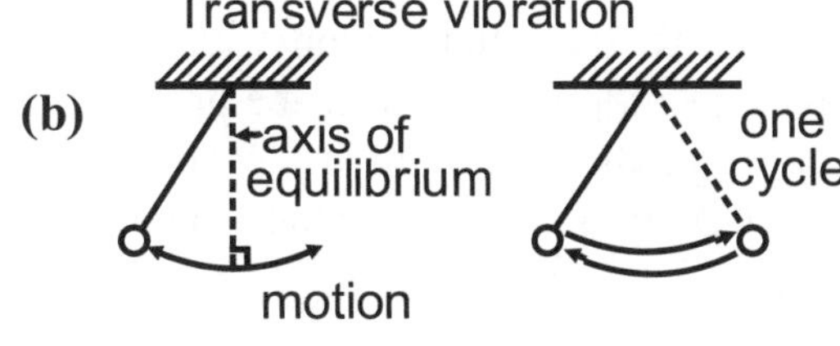

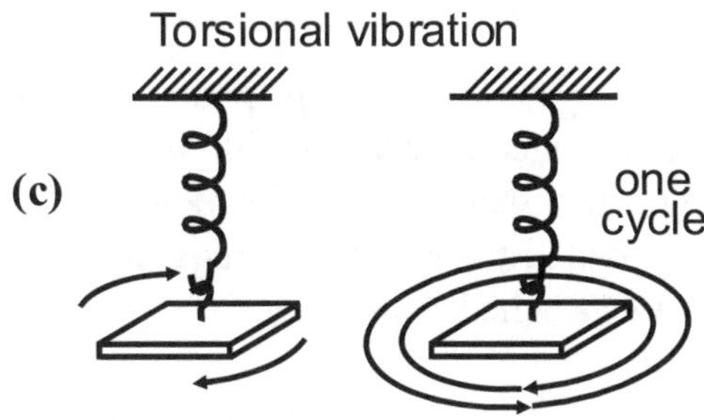

Figure 13-1 *Three common types of vibration, with a cycle shown for each.*

Period, Frequency, and Phase

Period and frequency were introduced in the topic of circular motion (Section 4.5). The same definitions and equations apply to vibrating objects, although in this case, the motion is generally linear. To review, *period* is the amount of time for one complete cycle; it is measured in seconds (or seconds per cycle). *Frequency* is the number of cycles per second; thus, it is the reciprocal of period. The official SI unit of frequency is the hertz (Hz), although it is sometimes expressed in cycles per second or simply s^{-1}. Since period and frequency are reciprocals, the following equations can be used:

$$f = \frac{1}{T} \quad \text{and} \quad T = \frac{1}{f} \qquad \textbf{(13-1)}$$

Sample Problem 13-1

Immediately after vigorous exercise, a person's heart beats 132 times in one minute. Calculate the (a) period and (b) frequency of the heartbeat to two significant digits.

Solution: (a) By definition, $\text{period} = \dfrac{\text{time}}{\#\text{ of cycles}} = \dfrac{60\text{ s}}{132\text{ cycles}} = 0.45\text{ s}$

Thus, the period is 0.45 s.

(b) Using Eqn. 13-1, $f = \dfrac{1}{T} = \dfrac{1}{0.45\text{ s}} = 2.2\text{ Hz}$

Thus, the frequency is 2.2 Hz. This could have been found by applying the definition of frequency as number of cycles per unit time.

The term *phase* refers to the part of a cycle an object with periodic motion is at. There are various ways of expressing phase, but for now, we will simply use fractions of a cycle. For example, if the pendulum in Figure 13-1 (b) starts vibrating from the position of maximum displacement to the left, then at a phase of ¼ cycle the pendulum is at the equilibrium position, at ½ cycle it is at the maximum displacement to the right, at 1 cycle it is back where it started, and so on. If two vibrating bodies have the same frequency, and start off at the same position, they will remain in phase with each other.

Resonance

Vibrating systems, such as pendulums and masses on springs, will vibrate at their natural frequencies once they are set into motion. For example, the natural frequency of a short pendulum is higher than that of a long pendulum. The natural frequency at which the vibration occurs most easily is called the **resonant frequency**, and a natural vibration that results in a large build-up of amplitude is called **resonance**.

Because the motion of most vibrating systems tends to dampen or decrease, energy must be given to the system to sustain the vibration. Imagine, for example, pushing a child on a swing. To build up a large amplitude, you must exert a force on the child, in other words impart energy, with the same frequency as the resonant frequency of the system. Thus, the energy transferred is maximum when the driving frequency equals the resonant frequency. If the driving frequency is different from the resonant frequency, the resulting vibration is forced to occur at the driving frequency, and is thus called a *forced vibration.* In this case, the vibrational energy that is developed is less than maximum and a small amplitude is achieved.

> ***Did You Know?*** *"Damp" in the context used here means to check or deaden something. A tragedy will dampen one's spirits; unwanted guests may dampen a party; highrise buildings must display damping characteristics in strong winds; a fireplace damper controls air motion through a chimney; a saxophone player's lips exercise controlled damping of the reed's vibrations; electronic synthesizers control the damping of sounds; and the damper pedal on a piano controls the time the sound remains audible. To illustrate this last example, try playing some notes on a piano without the damper pedal (the one on the right) suppressed. Then try pressing the pedal and again playing some notes. This time the dampers are removed from the keys and the sounds last much longer.*

A spectacular example of resonance of a mechanical system occurred in the collapse of a large suspension bridge in the State of Washington in 1940. The Tacoma Narrows Bridge was suspended by large cables across a valley. Shortly after its completion, the bridge was observed to be unstable, especially in windy conditions. One windy day, about four months after its official opening, the bridge began vibrating with a resonant frequency. At first, it vibrated in the transverse mode, then one of the suspension cables came loose at a tower, and the entire 850-m centre span of the bridge began to vibrate in the torsional mode. The vibration built up to such a large amplitude that the bridge collapsed. Nowadays, engineers test models of bridges and other structures in wind tunnels before beginning construction.

Resonance is important in more than just mechanical systems. Musical instruments produce sounds at resonant frequencies; the waves in microwave ovens have the resonant frequency of water molecules; and laser light is produced at specific resonant frequencies. Also, modern research into molecular structure is performed using a technique known as nuclear magnetic resonance. For example, hydrogen nuclei have a resonant frequency at which they will absorb electromagnetic radiation, so they can be detected in cancerous cells, brain matter, and other tissues in humans that have a large portion of hydrogen (in the form of water). Resonance is also important in the sending and receiving of radio and television signals.

> ***Did You Know?*** *Parts of the human body have certain resonant frequencies. Research has shown that the eyes have resonant frequencies between 35 Hz and 75 Hz, the head between about 13 Hz and 30 Hz, and the entire body about 6 Hz. Large amplitude vibrations at any of these frequencies could irritate or even damage parts of the body. In occupations such as road construction, efforts have been made to reduce the effects of mechanical vibrations on the human body.*

Energy Transfer with Waves

You have seen various ways of transferring energy. One way is to do work on an object by applying a force to it — this is the way in which a driving force helps maintain the swinging of a child on a playground swing. Other ways involve such techniques as conduction, convection, and radiation, three ways of transferring heat. The last method, radiation, is unlike the others because no particles are required for this form of energy transmission. Rather, it involves a type of wave.

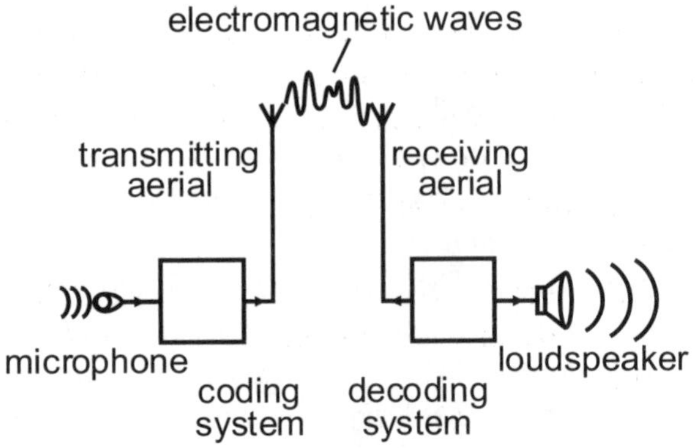

electromagnetic waves
transmitting aerial
receiving aerial
microphone
coding system
decoding system
loudspeaker

Figure 13-2 *A simplified illustration of the operation of a radio: Sound energy is transformed into electrical energy, which is then transformed into electromagnetic waves. These waves carry the information to the receiving aerial where the reverse transformations occur.*

A **wave** is a disturbance that transmits energy and/or information, but does not transfer matter. The source of energy of a wave is a vibration or oscillation. The energy may be transmitted by the wave to an object that changes the wave energy into some other form of energy. The operation of a radio is an example of transferring energy by waves called electromagnetic waves (Figure 13-2).

Transverse and Longitudinal Waves

Waves in a material medium are usually classified as either transverse or longitudinal, or a combination of these, depending on how the particles of the medium move relative to the direction of wave propagation. These motions correspond to the definitions of transverse and longitudinal vibrations. Thus, a **longitudinal wave** is one in which the particles of the medium move parallel to the direction of wave propagation. Longitudinal waves can propagate in all types of matter: solids, liquids, and gases. Figure 13-3 shows a longitudinal wave travelling along a stretched spring. The part of the spring where the coils are pressed together is called a **compression**, and a longitudinal wave is sometimes called a *compression wave*. Following the compression is part of the medium where the particles are spread out, called a **rarefaction**.

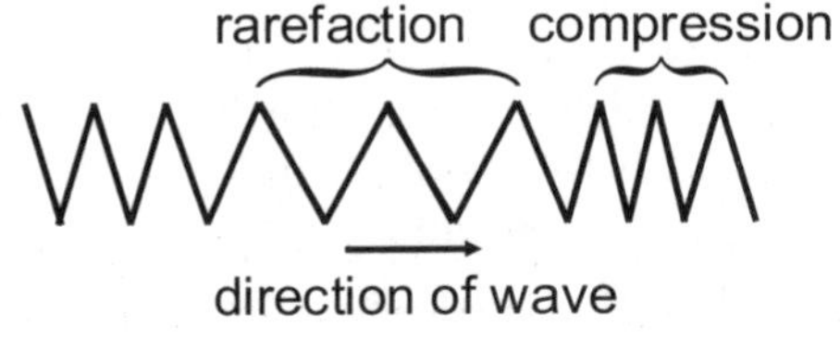

Figure 13-3 *A longitudinal or compression wave, shown travelling along a stretched spring, consists of a compression and a rarefaction.*

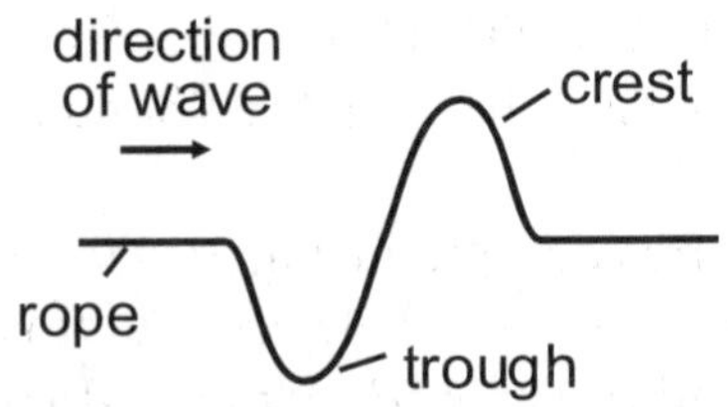

Figure 13-4 *A transverse wave, shown travelling along a rope, consists of a crest and a trough.*

A **transverse wave** is one in which the particles of the medium move perpendicular to the direction of wave propagation. Figure 13-4 shows that a transverse wave travelling along a rope has two main parts called a **crest**, the upper part of the wave, and a **trough**, the lower part of the wave.

Notice that these descriptions of longitudinal and transverse waves involve particle motion in materials. Waves that do not require a material in which to travel, namely electromagnetic waves such as light, have different properties. (Electromagnetic waves will be discussed in Chapter 14.)

Oceanic and Seismic Waves

You have often observed waves on oceans or lakes, which are known as surface waves. Waves can also occur beneath the surface of the water as well as through the solid and molten parts of Earth's interior.

The original source of energy of surface waves on oceans and lakes is the sun. Solar energy heats air particles in the atmosphere, causing convection currents (wind) to be set up. The wind gives energy to the surface of the water, causing waves. The water waves transmit energy, but they do not transmit water molecules, at least not very far. For example, consider the situation in which a small fishing boat is at rest in the middle of a wavy lake. The boat and the water molecules near it bob up and down as the waves (energy) travel beneath them, but the boat and the water molecules do not travel along with the waves to the shore. Figure 13-5 (a) illustrates the action of the boat and (b) shows the almost circular path of the water molecules in a surface wave. This path is actually a combination of longitudinal and transverse wave action.

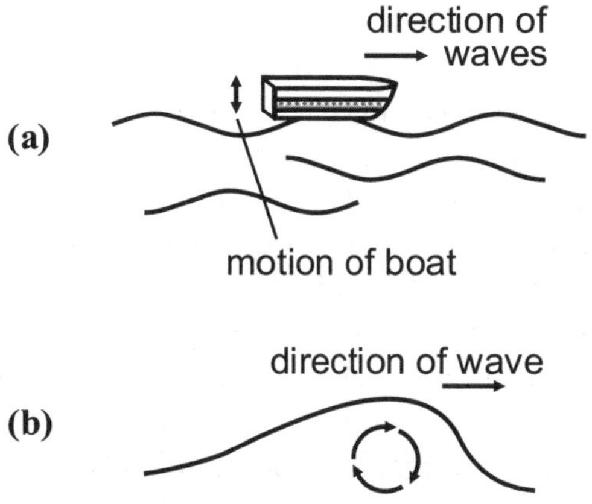

(a) direction of waves; motion of boat

(b) direction of wave

Figure 13-5 *Surface waves on water: In (a), a small boat on a wavy lake bobs up and down but does not advance with the waves. In (b), the path of an individual water molecule of a surface wave is nearly circular.*

An underwater earthquake or volcanic eruption can be the source of energy of a fast moving surface wave called a *tsunami*, which is set up on an ocean. In the deep part of the ocean, the tsunami may have a length of over 250 km, a height of about 5 m, and a speed of up to 800 km/h. Such a wave may pass unnoticed beneath a ship, despite the huge volume of water involved. However, when a tsunami approaches a shoreline where the normal water depth is low and the wave meets with resistance, the height can build up to perhaps 30 m, causing great damage along the shore.[1]

Besides producing surface waves (tsunamis), the energy of earthquakes can produce *body waves* or *seismic waves* that move through the depths of Earth. The two types of body waves are called *primary (P) waves* and *secondary (S) waves*. The differences between P and S waves help seismologists around the world determine the location of the origin of an earthquake as well as

[1] Some people mistakenly call a tsunami a "tidal wave." As its name suggests, a tidal wave relates to tides that are caused by the gravitational forces of the moon and sun on water on Earth.

other information about the structure of Earth's core. P waves are longitudinal (compression waves) so they travel through both solids and liquids. S waves are transverse and they travel only through solids. Also, P waves travel at a speed of about 8.0 km/s, while S waves travel more slowly, at about 4.5 km/s. (The name "primary" is used because such waves arrive at a destination before the secondary waves.) Following an earthquake, vibrations are observed at seismological stations around the world, revealing the location of the earthquakes as well as information about Earth's core. Figure 13-6 shows that only P waves are observed where Earth's liquid outer core is located between the earthquake and the seismological station. Studying the waves has helped scientists realize how Earth's interior is undergoing changes.

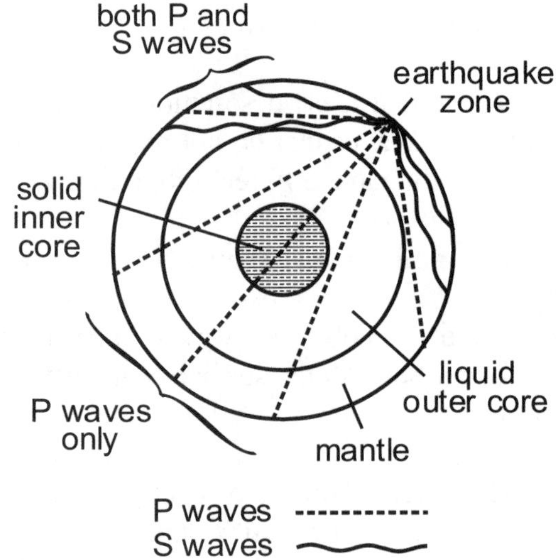

Figure 13-6 *Earthquakes produce body waves (also called seismic waves) that travel through Earth as P and S waves.*

Practice

13-1 State the type of vibration in each case.
(a) A daffodil vibrates back and forth in the wind.
(b) A child bounces up and down on a jumping stick or a "pogo" stick.
(c) A pile driver pounds a metal post into the ground.

13-2 Calculate the period of vibration in each case.
(a) A gymnast bounces 6 times on a trampoline in 8.0 s.
(b) During part of its motion a compact disk rotates at a rate of 210 times per minute.
(c) The range of audible frequencies heard by a young, healthy human is 25 Hz to 20 kHz.
[Ans. (a) 1.3 s (b) 0.29 s (c) 4.0×10^{-2} s to 5.0×10^{-5} s]

13-3 Calculate the frequency of vibration in each case.
(a) A person's eye blinks 15 times in 60 s.
(b) The needle of a sewing machine vibrates up and down 720 times per minute.
(c) The period of vibration of a metronome is 0.66 s.
[Ans. (a) 0.25 Hz (b) 12 Hz (c) 1.5 Hz]

13-4 What happens to the resonant frequency of a simple pendulum as the length decreases? Use your answer to explain why you walk with your arms stretched out but you run with your arms bent at the elbow.

13-5 Summarize the differences between longitudinal and transverse waves in a material medium by comparing:
(a) the motion of the individual particles.

(b) the type(s) of material they can travel in.
(c) the two main parts of each type of wave.

13-6 Why should a tsunami *not* be called a tidal wave?

13-7 How long in minutes would it take a P wave to travel through the entire Earth, assuming the speed is constant? (Earth's radius is about 6.4×10^3 km.) [Ans. 27 min]

13.2 PERIODIC WAVES

A **periodic wave** is a travelling wave produced by a source vibrating at some constant frequency. To study periodic waves and learn the related terminology, consider the transverse wave on the rope shown in Figure 13-7 (a), where A represents the **amplitude** or maximum displacement from the equilibrium position of the wave. The transverse wave consists of a series of crests and troughs above and below the equilibrium position. The hand at the left is the source of energy of the wave. In this case, the hand starts at the equilibrium position then moves down, all the way up, and then back down to the starting position. The hand continues vibrating up and down with (we assume) a constant amplitude, A, and a constant frequency, f. Of course, if the frequency is constant, the period, T, is also constant because $T = 1/f$. An observer at any position along the wave will see the wave passing by with the same frequency, f. In an "ideal" situation in which no energy is absorbed by the medium, the amplitude also remains constant.

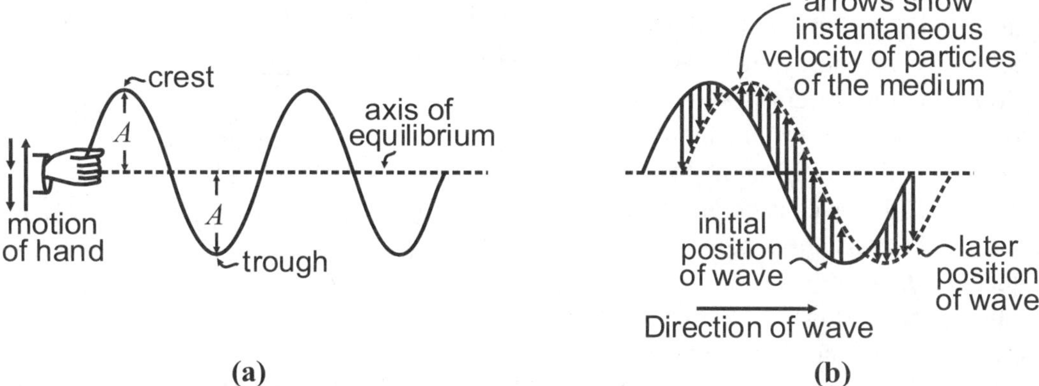

Figure 13-7 **(a)** *Transverse periodic wave: The hand acts as a source of energy of the wave. It vibrates perpendicular to the axis of equilibrium at a frequency f and period T = 1/f, and with an amplitude A.* **(b)** *Illustrating the motion of the individual particles of a medium, in this case a rope, as a transverse periodic wave travels along it. The short vertical arrows represent velocities.*

Remember that the particles of the medium do not move along with the wave. In the case of the transverse wave shown, the motion of the individual particles of the medium is perpendicular to the propagation of the wave. To help visualize this, we simply draw a second wave that would occur a short time after the first wave, as seen in Figure 13-7 (b). The velocities of the individual particles of the medium are illustrated with the vertical arrows. Thus, the energy is moving to the right but the particles of the medium are moving up and down.

Two positions on a wave are said to be **in phase** if they are at the same part of the wave. In Figure 13-8, the points B, E, and G are in phase with each other. They all occur on the crest of a wave in a part of the medium that is rising. B and D are not in phase with each other, even though they have the same displacement from the equilibrium position, because D is falling when B is rising. Can you see two other points that are in phase with each other?

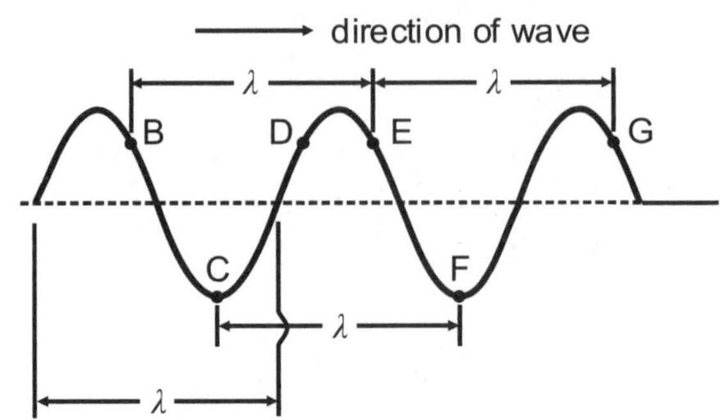

Figure 13-8 *Illustrating in-phase positions and wavelength (λ) for a transverse periodic wave. (See the text for explanations.)*

The shortest distance between any two in-phase points on a wave is called the **wavelength** of the wave. The wavelength is symbolized by lambda (λ), which is the lower case *L* in the Greek alphabet. Examples of wavelength are shown in Figure 13-8.

Similar terminology applies to a longitudinal wave. A mechanical longitudinal wave can be set up on a stretched coil or spring, such as a "Slinky" toy (Figure 13-9). Again, the hand at the left is the source of energy of the wave. Starting from an equilibrium position, the hand moves forward then all the way back, and then forward again to the starting position. It moves back and forth with motion at a constant amplitude, A, and frequency, f. An observer at any position along the spring will observe a wave passing by with the same frequency and amplitude as the source. The longitudinal wave consists of compressions where the particles are pressed close together and rarefactions where the particles are spread out.

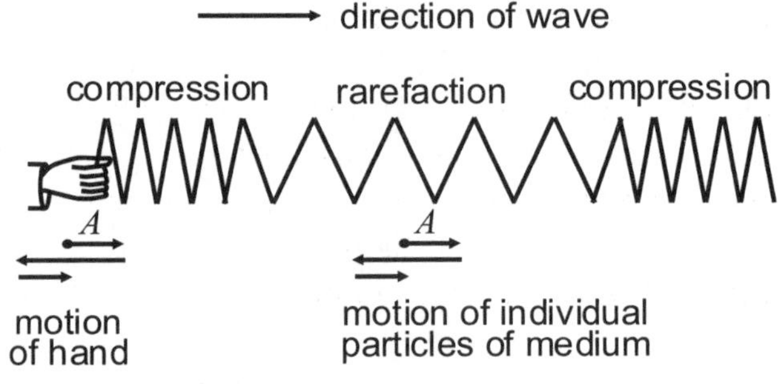

Figure 13-9 *Longitudinal periodic wave: The hand is the source of energy. It vibrates parallel to the direction of motion of the wave at a frequency f and with an amplitude A.*

With a longitudinal wave, the particles of the medium (in this case, the spring) move back and forth parallel to the direction of wave propagation. Again, the wavelength, λ, is the shortest distance between two in-phase points on the wave. In Figure 13-10 (a), points B, D, and F are all in phase, and C and E are in phase with each other. One wavelength is shown as the distance from B to D, from D to F, and from C to E. Figures 13-10 (b) and (c) show alternate ways of representing the longitudinal wave in (a).

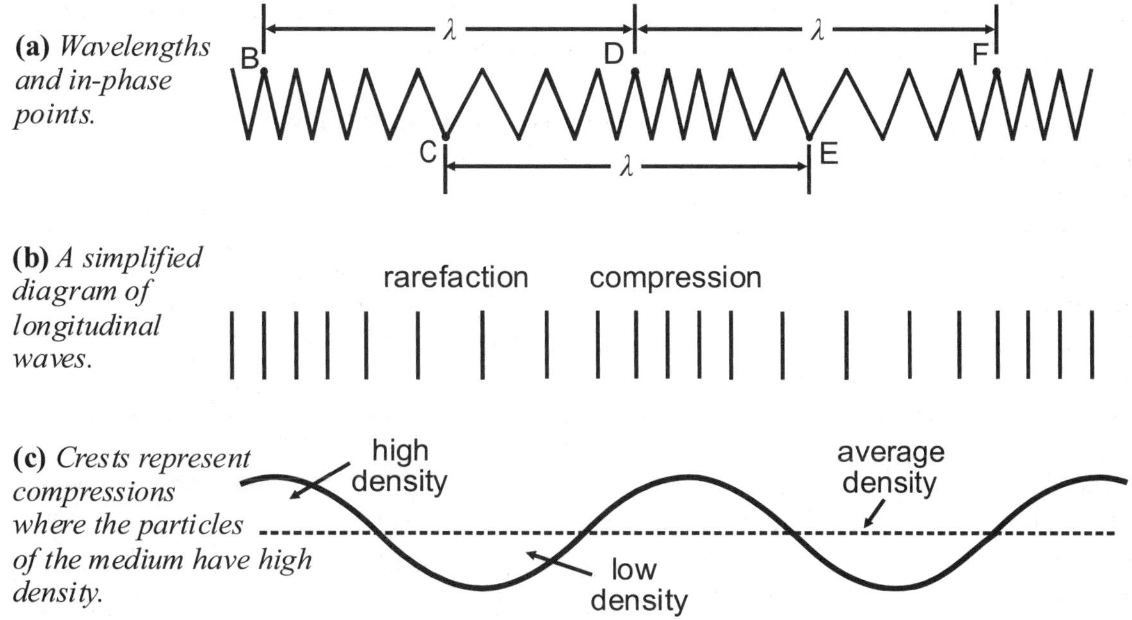
(a) Wavelengths and in-phase points.
B
D
F
C
E
λ
λ
λ
(b) A simplified diagram of longitudinal waves.
rarefaction
compression
(c) Crests represent compressions where the particles of the medium have high density.
high density
average density
low density

Figure 13-10 *Details about longitudinal periodic waves: (See the text for explanations.)*

The Universal Wave Equation

As a wave performs its function of transferring energy from one place to another, it does so at a certain speed. One way to find that speed is to determine how long the wave takes to travel a known distance, then apply the equation speed = distance/time. Another way is to relate this equation to the properties of a periodic wave. Each wavelength, λ, of the wave train passes by a specific position in a length of time equal to the period, T, of the wave. Thus,

$$\text{since speed} = \frac{\text{distance}}{\text{time}}, \quad \text{speed} = \frac{\text{wavelength}}{\text{period}} \quad \text{or} \quad v = \frac{\lambda}{T}$$

Now, since $f = 1/T$, the equation $v = \lambda / T$ can be written: $$v = f\lambda \qquad \textbf{(13-2)}$$

This equation, called the **universal wave equation**, indicates the speed of a periodic wave in terms of the frequency and wavelength of the wave.

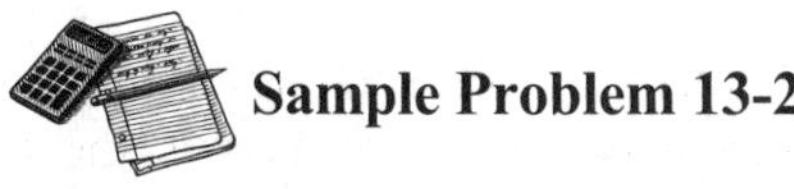

Sample Problem 13-2

A machine in a wavepool vibrates with a frequency of 1.4 Hz, producing periodic waves that are 6.5 m from crest to crest. What is the speed of the waves in the pool?

Solution: Using Eqn. 13-2,

$$\begin{aligned} v &= f\lambda \\ &= 1.4\ \text{Hz} \times 6.5\ \text{m} \\ &= 1.4\,\frac{\text{cycles}}{\text{s}} \times 6.5\,\frac{\text{m}}{\text{cycle}} \quad \text{(See the note below.)} \\ &= 9.1\ \text{m/s} \end{aligned}$$

Thus, the speed is 9.1 m/s. Note that the unit of frequency, hertz or Hz, was changed to the equivalent cycles/s and the unit of wavelength, metre or m, was changed to m/cycle to show how the cycles cancel, leaving metres per second, or m/s, the correct unit of speed.

The speed of a periodic wave in a material medium depends on the medium through which the wave is travelling and the condition of that medium. For example, the speed of a transverse wave along a rope is faster than the speed along a stretched coil under the same tension. Also, the speed of a wave along a coil with high tension is greater than the speed along the same coil with low tension.

Reflection and Transmission of Waves in One Dimension

You have studied the characteristics of waves travelling in one medium at a time. What happens when a travelling wave encounters the end of that medium? Let us look at how the answer depends on what, if anything, the medium is attached to. Consider a transverse pulse (a short portion of a wave) moving along a rope attached to a rigid barrier, such as a wall (Figure 13-11 (a)). When the pulse reaches the barrier, it exerts an upward force on the barrier, and, according to Newton's third

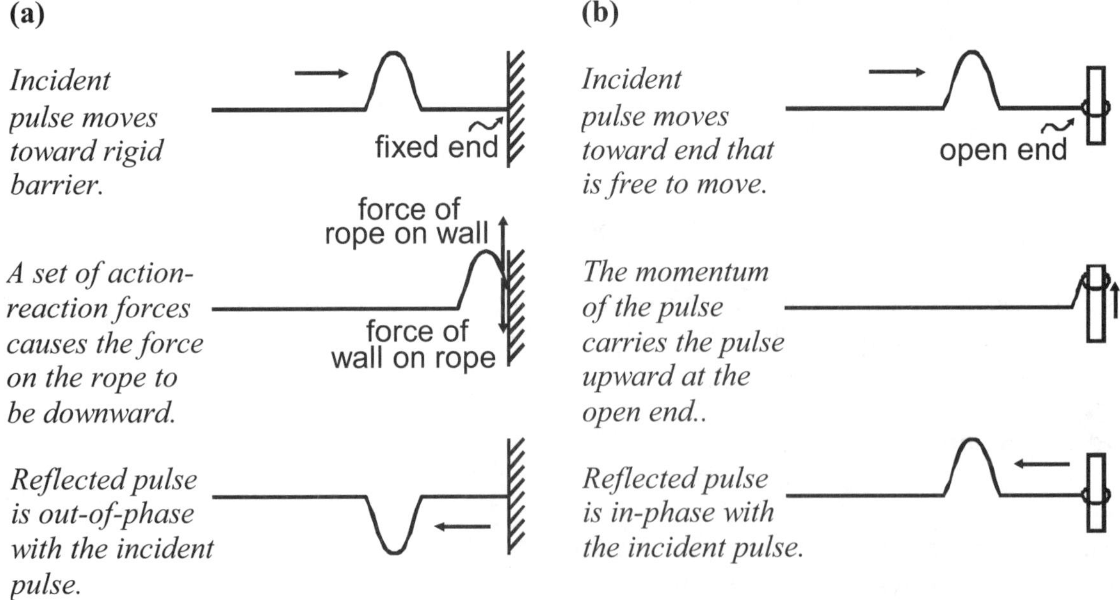

(a)
Incident pulse moves toward rigid barrier.
fixed end
force of rope on wall
A set of action-reaction forces causes the force on the rope to be downward.
force of wall on rope
Reflected pulse is out-of-phase with the incident pulse.
(b)
Incident pulse moves toward end that is free to move.
open end
The momentum of the pulse carries the pulse upward at the open end..
Reflected pulse is in-phase with the incident pulse.

Figure 13-11 *Reflection of pulses:* **(a)** *Fixed-end reflection.* **(b)** *Open-end reflection.*

law of motion, the wall exerts an equal force downward on the rope. This downward force causes the reflected pulse to be on the opposite side of the rope. The reflection is called *negative*; in other words, the reflected pulse is out-of-phase with the incident pulse. A similar argument could be used to prove that an incident trough would reflect as a crest. Thus, we conclude that:

When a pulse or wave undergoes fixed-end reflection, the reflected pulse or wave is out-of-phase with the incident one.

Next consider a transverse pulse reaching the end of a medium that is free to move. In Figure 13-11 (b) the free end for a rope is shown as a loop that can easily move up and down. When the pulse reaches the free end or "open end," it has nothing else to exert a force on, so its momentum keeps it rising above its original amplitude. This produces a return or reflected pulse on the same side of the equilibrium location. This reflection is called *positive*; in other words, the reflected pulse is in-phase. A wave acts in a similar manner. Thus, we conclude that:

When a pulse or wave undergoes open-end reflection, the reflected pulse or wave is in-phase with the incident one.

Rather than striking a completely rigid or completely free end, a pulse[2] might strike another medium in which the speed of wave propagation is different. In this situation, some of the pulse is transmitted and some is reflected. The transmitted pulse is always positive or in-phase. However, the phase of the reflected pulse depends on the two media involved. For a pulse trying to go from a "lighter" medium to a "heavier" one, the situation resembles fixed-end reflection, so the reflected pulse is negative or out-of-phase, and the speed and wavelength of the transmitted pulse are reduced (Figure 13-12(a)). For a pulse trying to travel from a "heavier" medium to a "lighter" one, the reflected pulse acts as if it has struck a free or open end, so the reflected pulse is positive or in-

(a) *A pulse in a lighter medium undergoes in-phase transmission and out-of-phase reflection when it reaches a heavier medium.*

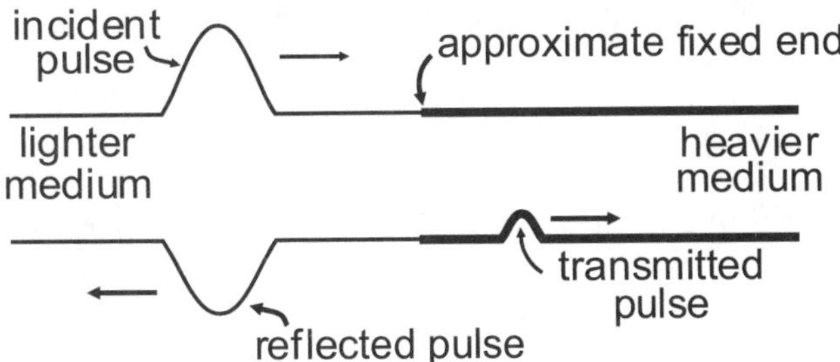

(b) *When a pulse in a heavier medium reaches a lighter medium, both the transmitted and reflected pulses remain in phase.*

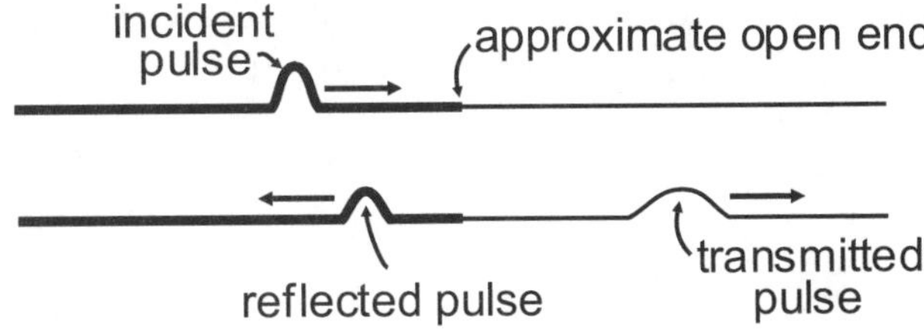

Figure 13-12 *Reflection and transmission at the interference between two media.*

[2] Although the discussion here uses pulses, the same arguments apply to waves.

phase and the speed and wavelength of the transmitted pulse are increased (Figure 13-12(b)). Fixed-end and open-end reflection are important in various aspects of light, as you will learn later.

Reflection of Waves in Two Dimensions

Water waves travelling in a swimming pool, on a lake, or in a water tank used in a physics laboratory are examples of waves in two dimensions. A two-dimensional wave displays characteristics similar to a wave in one dimension, such as a wave on a coil, or in three dimensions, such as a sound wave in air. Water waves can be demonstrated and studied in a device called a ripple tank. It is a raised shallow tank with a transparent bottom. The tank must be level, and water is added to a depth of about 10 mm. A light source mounted above the water allows transverse water waves to be viewed on a screen beneath the tank. Each crest acts like a magnifying glass (a converging lens) focusing the light to produce a bright region on the screen. Each trough spreads the light out, producing a dark region on the screen. See Figure 13-13.

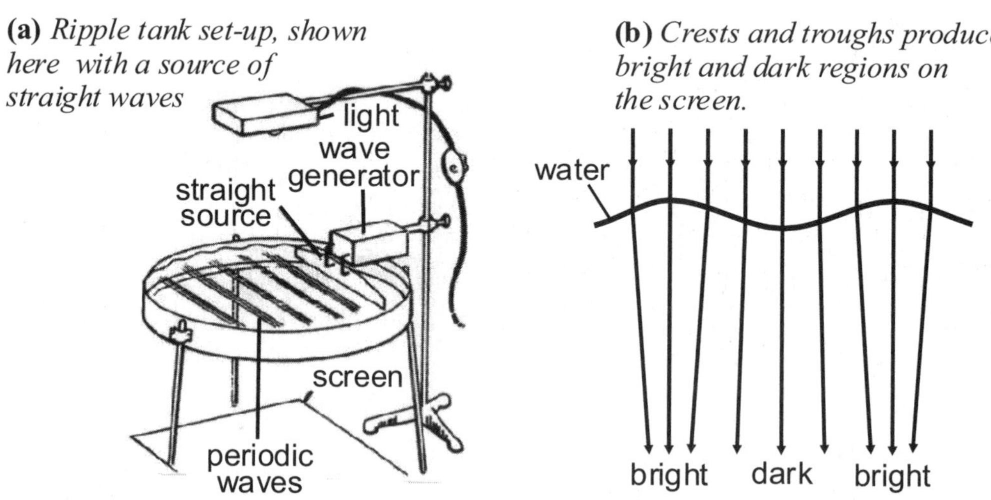

(a) *Ripple tank set-up, shown here with a source of straight waves*

(b) *Crests and troughs produce bright and dark regions on the screen.*

Figure 13-13 *Using a ripple tank to study periodic waves in two dimensions.*

Waves commonly generated in a ripple tank to study wave characteristics are periodic plane waves (straight waves) and circular waves, shown in Figure 13-14. In these diagrams, a **wavefront** is the entire crest or trough of a wave. A line drawn perpendicular to the wavefront is called a **ray**, and it indicates the direction of propagation of the waves. The wavelength, λ, of each set of waves is also shown in the diagrams.

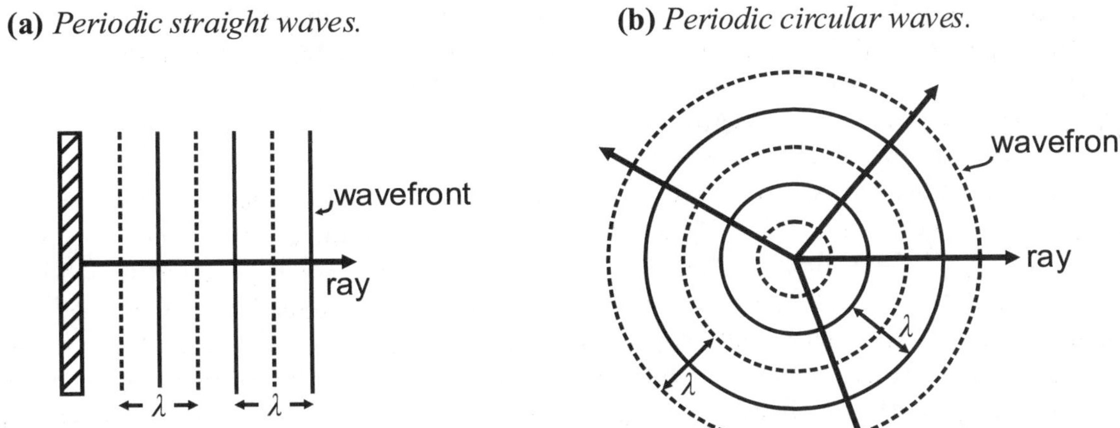

Figure 13-14 *Periodic waves in water showing crests (solid lines) and troughs (broken lines).*

When a wavefront reaches a barrier, most of the energy is reflected, as you have no doubt observed when water waves strike the side of a pool or ocean waves strike a breakwater. If the reflecting surface is smooth and regular, the wavefronts will reflect with the same angle as the incoming or incident wavefronts. In order to communicate information about wave reflections, we use a line called a **normal** which is perpendicular to the reflecting surface. (Recall from the study of forces that normal means perpendicular.) Then, the **angle of incidence** is the angle between the incident ray and the normal, and the **angle of reflection** is the angle between the reflected ray and the normal. Thus, for smooth reflection of waves, the angle of reflection equals the angle of incidence. This is illustrated for plane waves striking a straight barrier in Figure 13-15 (a).

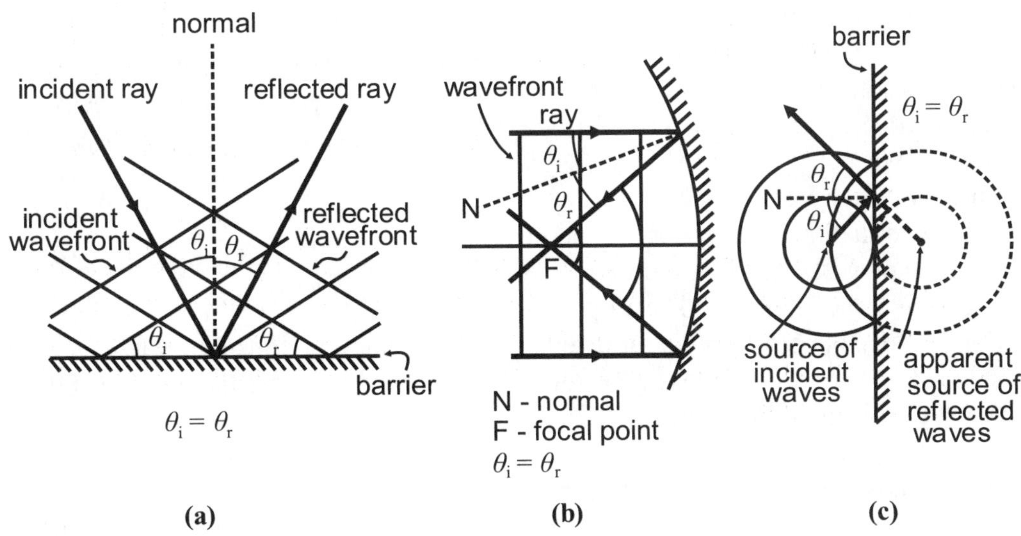

Figure 13-15 *Wave reflection off various solid barriers:* **(a)** *Plane waves; straight barrier* **(b)** *Plane waves; concave barrier.* **(c)** *Circular waves; straight barrier.*

Figure 13-15 illustrates two other sets of wavefronts striking reflecting surfaces. In both cases, the angle of reflection equals the angle of incidence for each part of the wavefront. In (b), the plane waves reflect off the curved surface and travel toward a common meeting place, called the focus or focal point. In Figure 13-15 (c), periodic circular waves from a point source travel toward a flat barrier and reflect off, causing circular waves whose origin *appears* to be as far from the barrier as the original source of the waves.

Wave reflection in two dimensions has characteristics similar to wave reflection in one dimension. For example, when the wave strikes a rigid barrier, most of the energy is reflected, but some of it is absorbed by the barrier and may change into some other form of energy such as sound and thermal energy. A small amount of energy may be transmitted through the barrier. If the wave strikes a less rigid barrier, more energy will be absorbed or transmitted by the barrier and less will be reflected. Let us now see what happens to the transmitted energy.

Refraction of Waves in Two Dimensions

When a travelling wave in one medium meets a second medium, some reflection, some absorption, and some transmission may occur. If the wavefronts are at any angle other than parallel to the interface between the two media, any transmitted wavefronts will undergo a change in direction. This change in direction as a wave travels from one medium into another is called **refraction**. It occurs because the speed of the wave in the second medium differs from that in the first medium. Figure 13-16 shows refraction of water waves from deeper water (region 1), where the speed of the waves is faster, to shallow water (region 2), where the speed of the waves is slower due to friction between the water and the solid surface beneath the water. A normal is drawn perpendicular to the interface and the angle of incidence is shown as the angle between the incident ray and the normal. The **angle of refraction** is the angle between the refracted ray and the normal. Since the wave has slowed down in the shallower water, the ray has bent toward the normal, causing the angle of refraction to be smaller than the angle of incidence.

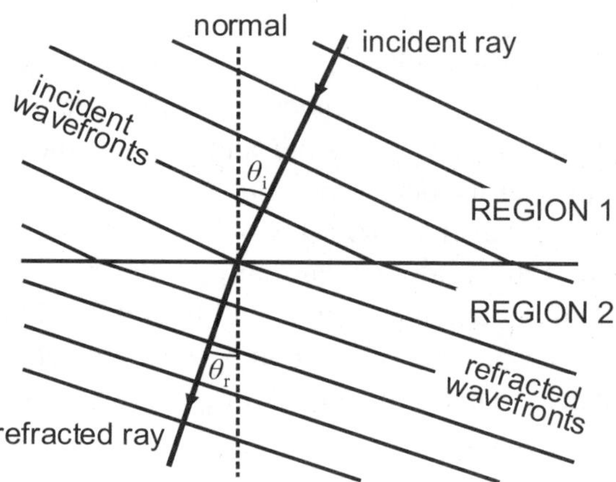

Figure 13-16 *The refraction or bending of water waves occurs as waves travel from one region to another where the speed is different. In this case, the speed in the second region is slower than in the first, and the wave direction, as indicated by the ray, refracts* toward *the normal.*

What happens as the difference between the speeds of the waves in the two media increases? It is logical to assume that the amount of refraction increases. This can be analyzed mathematically using the information in Figure 13-17. The wavefronts in medium 1 are produced with a period of T seconds and are travelling with a wavelength, λ_1, and at a speed of $v_1 = \lambda_1/T$. For the wavefronts that transfer into medium 2, the period of time between wavefronts remains constant at T seconds, so the new speed is $v_2 = \lambda_2/T$. If we divide the first equation by the second, we obtain

$$\frac{v_1}{v_2} = \frac{\lambda_1}{\lambda_2}$$

The ratio of speeds or wavelengths in two different media is called the **index of refraction**, symbol *n*. For waves travelling from medium 1 into medium 2, we indicate the direction of transmission with the symbol $n_{1\to 2}$. Thus:

$$n_{1\to 2} = \frac{v_1}{v_2} \qquad \textbf{(13-3)}$$

or

$$n_{1\to 2} = \frac{\lambda_1}{\lambda_2} \qquad \textbf{(13-4)}$$

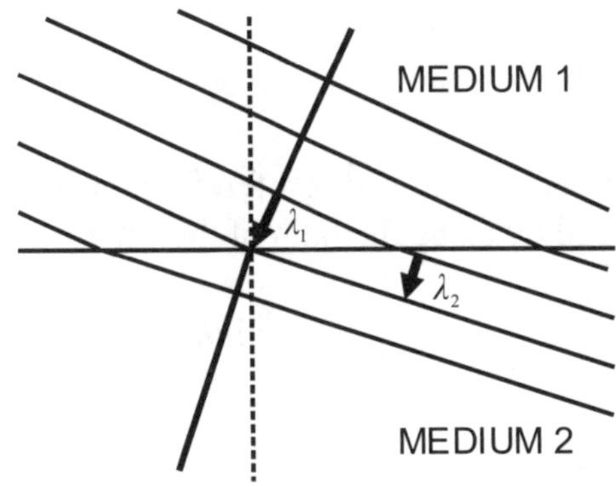

Figure 13-17 *Defining index of refraction in terms of speeds and wavelengths.*

where "$n_{1\to 2}$" is read "the index of refraction for waves travelling from medium 1 to medium 2." Since the index of refraction is a ratio of speeds or a ratio of wavelengths, it has no units.

Sample Problem 13-3

A 1.5-Hz source produces plane waves that travel at 0.66 m/s in water. When these waves reach shallow water, their wavelength becomes 0.31 m. What is the index of refraction for waves travelling from the deeper to the shallower water?

Solution: Since the index of refraction is equal to the ratio of speeds or the ratio of wavelengths, we need to find either the speed in the shallow water or the wavelength in the deep water. Let's use the second method. From $v = f\lambda$ (Eqn. 13-2), we have the following relation:

$$\lambda_1 = \frac{v_1}{f_1} = \frac{0.66 \text{ m/s}}{1.5 \text{ Hz}} = 0.44 \text{ m}$$

Now

$$n_{1\to 2} = \frac{\lambda_1}{\lambda_2} = \frac{0.44 \text{ m}}{0.31 \text{ m}} = 1.4$$

Thus, the index of refraction is 1.4.

The angles of incidence and refraction can also be used to determine the index of refraction. Refer to Figure 13-18, which shows the same situation described In Figures 13-16 and 13-17 but with the angles of incidence and refraction shown. In the diagram, $\sin\theta_1 = \lambda_1 / x$ and $\sin\theta_2 = \lambda_2 / x$. Thus, the ratio of $\sin\theta_1 / \sin\theta_2$ can be found.

$$\frac{\sin\,\theta_1}{\sin\,\theta_2} = \frac{\lambda_1/x}{\lambda_2/x} = \frac{\lambda_1}{\lambda_2} = n_{1\to 2}$$

Therefore, the index of refraction can also be found by using the ratio of the sines of angles.

$$n_{1\to 2} = \frac{\sin\,\theta_1}{\sin\,\theta_2} \qquad \textbf{(13-5)}$$

where θ_1 is the angle of incidence in medium 1 and θ_2 is the angle of refraction in medium 2.

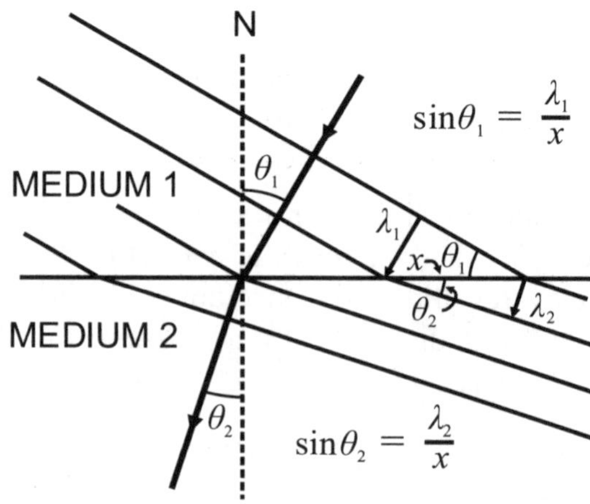

Figure 13-18 *Determining the index of refraction in terms of angles.*

Sample Problem 13-4

Ultrasonic waves, which have frequencies above the range of human hearing, can be used medically for diagnostic, therapeutic, and destructive purposes. Assume that for medical diagnosis, a transducer emits pulses of ultrasound that travel at 344 m/s before entering the human body. If the angle of incidence is 12.6°, and the index of refraction for ultrasound travelling from air into the body is 0.225, (a) what is the angle of refraction and (b) what is the speed of ultrasound in the body?

Solution:

(a)

$$n_{1\to 2} = \frac{\sin\,\theta_1}{\sin\,\theta_2} \quad \therefore \quad \sin\,\theta_2 = \frac{\sin\,\theta_1}{n_{1\to 2}} = \frac{\sin 12.6°}{0.225}$$

$$\therefore \quad \theta_2 = 75.8°$$

Thus, the angle of refraction is 75.8°.

(b)

$$n_{1\to 2} = \frac{v_1}{v_2} \quad \therefore \quad v_2 = \frac{v_1}{n_{1\to 2}} = \frac{344 \text{ m/s}}{0.225} = 1.53 \times 10^3 \text{ m/s}$$

Thus, the speed of the ultrasound is 1.53×10^3 m/s.

Practice

13-8 Describe the motion of the individual particles relative to the equilibrium position for a medium in which a periodic wave is (a) transverse and (b) longitudinal.

13-9 Repeat #13-8 for the direction of propagation of the energy transmitted by the wave.

13-10 A guitar string is producing sound waves that have a wavelength of 0.391 m and a speed in air of 344 m/s. Determine the frequency of the string producing the sound. [Ans. 8.80×10^2 Hz]

13-11 The wave in Figure 13-19 is travelling to the left in a medium. State the direction of the velocity of the particles of the medium at points B, C, D, and E.

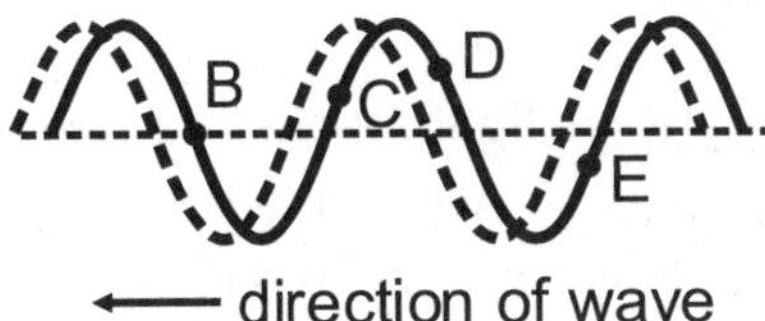

Figure 13-19 *Question 13-11.*

13-12 The scale used to draw the periodic waves in Figure 13-20 is 1.0 cm = 1.0 dm. Both waves are being generated at a frequency of 4.5 Hz. Determine the approximate:
(a) amplitude of the transverse wave.
(b) wavelength of the transverse wave.
(c) wavelength of the longitudinal wave.
(d) speed of the transverse wave.
(e) speed of the longitudinal wave.
[Ans. (a) 0.70 dm (b) 3.0 dm (c) 3.2 dm (d) 14 dm/s (e) 14 dm/s]

Figure 13-20 *Question 13-12.*

13-13 A buoy is anchored offshore to warn boaters in a lake of a shallow area. The buoy bobs up and down 6 times in 20 s as waves travel beneath it at a speed of 5.4 m/s. Assuming two significant digits, calculate the:
(a) frequency of oscillation of the buoy (b) wavelength of the water waves
[Ans. (a) 0.30 Hz (b) 18 m]

13-14 Sound waves used to determine the depth of water in a lake are emitted from a boat with a regular period of 2.5×10^{-5} s. If the wavelength of the waves in the water is 3.8×10^{-2} m, what is the speed of the sound in the water? [Ans. 1.5×10^3 m/s]

13-15 A bat searches for prey by emitting ultrasound with a wavelength of 3.73×10^{-3} m. If the ultrasound travels in air at 336 m/s, what is the period of the ultrasound waves?
[Ans. 1.11×10^{-5} s]

13-16 In the therapeutic application of ultrasound, called *ultrasound diathermy*, high-intensity ultrasound waves are converted into thermal energy for deep heat treatments. If a transducer emits ultrasound waves with a period of 1.05 μs that travel at 1530 m/s in the body, determine:
(a) the frequency of the ultrasound waves in megahertz
(b) the wavelength of the ultrasound waves in the body [Ans. (a) 0.800 MHz (b) 1.91×10^{-3} m]

13-17 Is reflection positive or negative for (a) fixed-end reflection and (b) open-end reflection?

13-18 A light rope is attached to a heavy rope, as illustrated in Figure 13-21 (a). Assume that the speed of a pulse or wave in the light rope is 2.0 cm/s and in the heavy rope it is 1.0 cm/s. An irregularly-shaped trough is travelling from left to right, as shown. Draw a diagram showing what is happening 4.0 s after the instant shown.

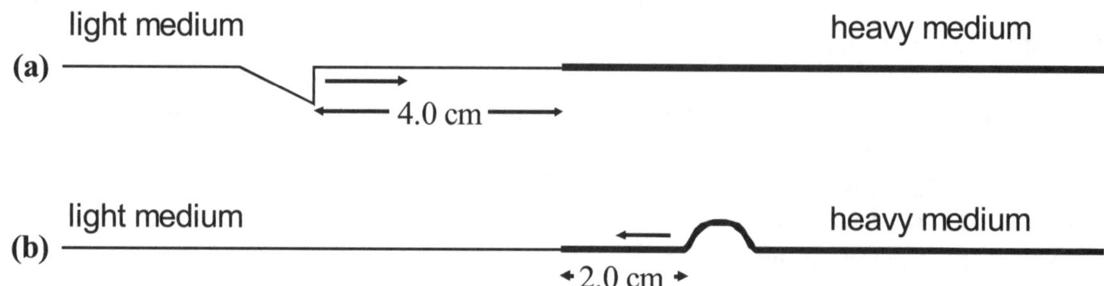

Figure 13-21 **(a)** *Question 13-18.* **(b)** *Question 13-19. (Diagrams are not to scale.)*

13-19 Repeat #13-18 for a crest travelling from right to left, as shown in Figure 13-21 (b).

13-20 The speed of a wave in medium A is 3.2 m/s and the measured wavelength of a set of periodic waves is 0.24 m. The waves refract into medium B where their wavelength becomes 0.18 m. What is the speed of the waves in B? [Ans. 2.4 m/s]

13-21 Plane waves of wavelength 1.5 cm are striking a solid barrier at an angle of incidence of 20°. Draw a diagram showing these waves and the corresponding reflected waves. Label the angles of incidence and reflection.

13-22 Plane periodic waves of wavelength 1.7 cm are striking an interface between two media at an angle of incidence of 35° and transferring into the second medium at an angle of refraction of 20°. (a) Determine the wavelength in the second medium. [Ans. 1.0 cm]
(b) Draw a diagram showing three incident waves and three refracted waves for this situation.

13-23 Periodic water waves, whose crests are separated by 16 cm, are travelling at 84 cm/s in a water tank. They reach a shallower region where their speed is 63 cm/s.
(a) What is the wavelength of the waves in the shallower region?
(b) What is the index of refraction for the waves travelling from the deeper to the shallower water?
(c) What is the index of refraction for waves travelling from the shallower to the deeper water?
(d) If the angle of incidence is 0°, what is the angle of refraction? What does this situation look like?
(e) If the angle of incidence is 32°, what is the angle of refraction?
[Ans. (a) 12 cm (b) 1.3 (c) 0.75 (d) 0° (e) 24°]

13-24 The primary (P) waves caused by an earthquake travel from one type of rock, where the speed is 7.8 km/s, into a different type of rock, where the speed is 6.4 km/s. The waves strike the interface between the two types of rock at an angle of incidence of 34°.
(a) What is the angle of refraction in the second type of rock?

(b) What is the index of refraction for this situation? [Ans. (a) 27° (b) 1.2]

13.3 INTERFERENCE OF WAVES

We have observed the characteristics of waves when they travel in a single medium, when they reflect off a barrier, and when they travel into a second medium. But what happens when two waves in the same medium meet each other? They interfere with each other in one of two basic ways. When waves meet and the resulting displacement is larger than the individual displacements, the type of interference is called **constructive interference**. If the resulting displacement of the interfering waves decreases, the interference is called **destructive interference**. In this section, we will study both types of interference and related phenomena in both one and two dimensions. The effects of interference are important in both sound and light, the latter presented in Chapter 14.

Interference in One Dimension

Constructive and destructive interference can occur for transverse, longitudinal, and torsional pulses and waves, but it is most easily demonstrated with transverse pulses or waves in one dimension, that is, on a rope or coil. Consider Figure 13-22, which shows both constructive and destructive interference of transverse pulses in one dimension. For transverse pulses, constructive interference occurs when a crest meets a crest causing a *supercrest* (a), or a trough meets a trough causing a *supertrough* (not shown). Destructive interference of transverse pulses occurs when a crest meets a trough (b). If the crest and trough have equal amplitude and shape, their displacements cancel each other for an instant, producing a position of zero amplitude, called a **node**. Then the crest and trough continue travelling in their original directions.

(a) *Constructive interference.*

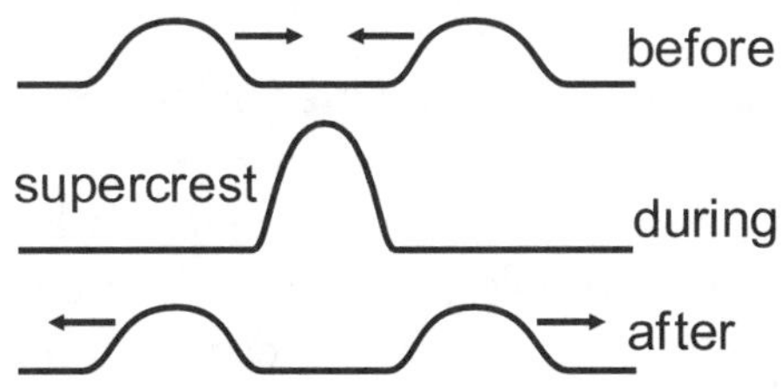

(b) *Destructive interference.*

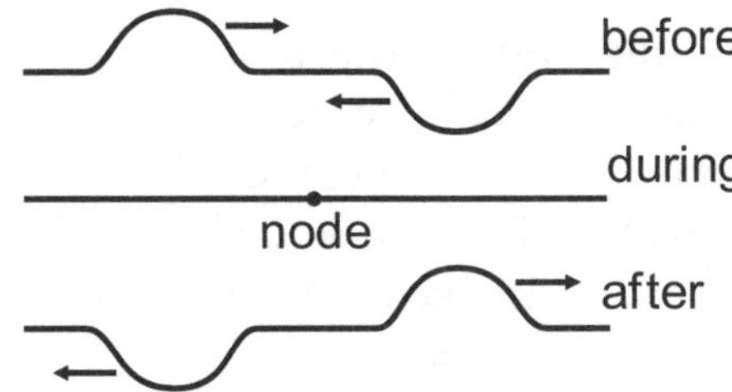

Figure 13-22 *Interference of transverse pulses in one dimension.*

If we observe any particular point in the medium where the pulses are interfering, the displacement that results is simply the algebraic addition of the displacements of the individual interfering pulses. The displacements are either positive or negative, depending on whether they are above or below the equilibrium position, respectively. Thus, for example, a displacement of +8.4 mm added to a displacement of –6.1 mm produces a displacement of +2.3 mm. The concept of displacement addition is summarized in the **principle of superposition**, which states:

The resulting displacement of two interfering pulses at a point is the algebraic sum of the displacements of the individual pulses at that point.

(The word "superposition" stems from the verbs superimpose or superpose, both of which mean "to put on top of something else.")

The principle of superposition is useful for finding the resultant wave pattern when pulses or waves of unequal size or shape interfere with one another. It applies only to displacements that are reasonable in size because overly large pulses may cause distortion of the medium through which they are travelling.

This principle can be applied in diagrams, as shown for one-dimensional pulses in Figure 13-23. The arrows show the displacements of the individual pulses in the first two diagrams, then the resulting displacement in the third diagram.

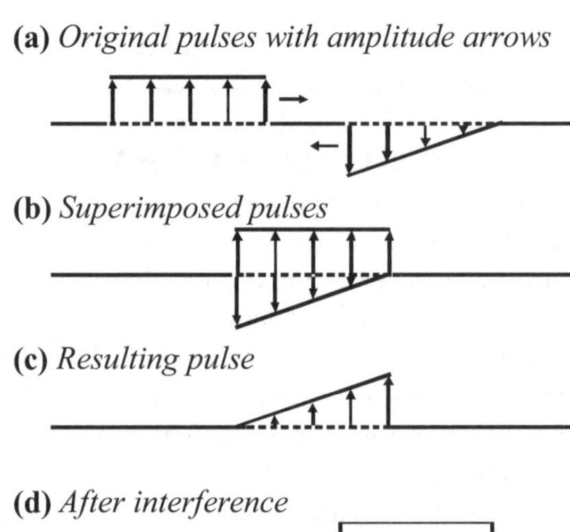

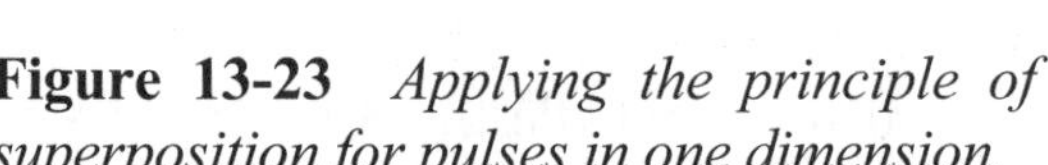

Figure 13-23 *Applying the principle of superposition for pulses in one dimension.*

Standing Waves in One Dimension

The principle of superposition can be applied not only to pulses, but also to periodic waves travelling in opposite directions. If periodic waves of equal wavelength and amplitude travel in opposite directions in the same medium, an interference pattern called a **standing wave pattern** is set up. It has positions of zero displacement, or *nodes*, and positions of maximum displacement called **antinodes**. These nodes and antinodes remain in the same locations, which explains why the formation is called "standing."

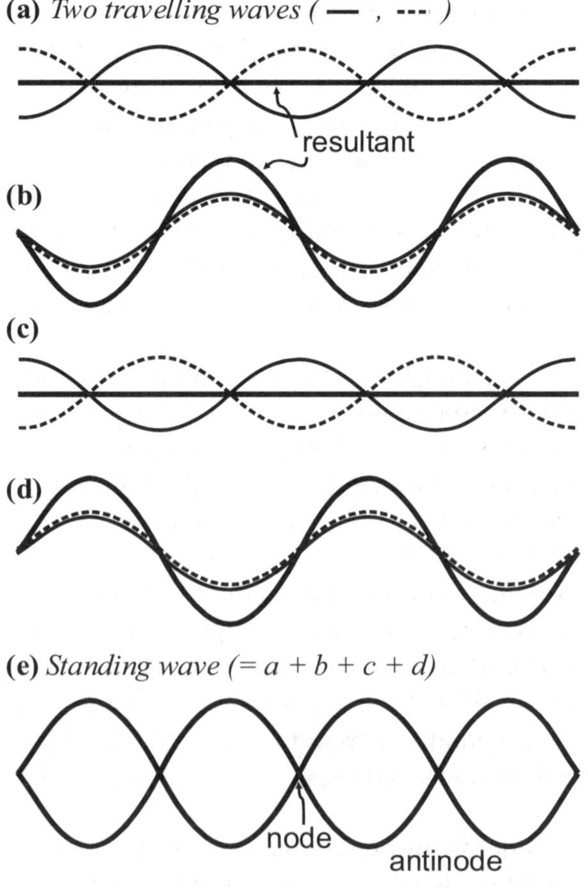

Figure 13-24 *A standing wave pattern on a rope: See the text for the explanation.*

To learn how a standing wave pattern is set up on a rope, consider Figure 13-24. In each of (a) to (e), one wave is travelling to the right, the other wave is travelling to the left, and the thickest line is the resultant wave found by applying the principle of superposition. In (a), the waves are seen at an instant when destructive interference occurs, leaving zero displacement. Then (b) is ¼ period later, producing constructive interference; (c) is ½ period after (a), producing destructive interference; and (d) is ¾ period after (a), again producing constructive interference. The resulting standing wave pattern is seen in (e). Notice that the lines representing the antinodes show only the envelope or limit of the pattern. In fact, the particles of the medium vibrate between these limits.

If two people were asked to produce a standing wave pattern on a rope, they would stretch the rope and generate periodic waves starting at the two ends. To produce a good standing wave pattern, the waves would have to have the same amplitude (a somewhat difficult task) and the same wavelength, which means the same frequency or period (a very difficult task, especially at higher frequencies). To overcome this problem, one end of the rope can be tied to a support, and one person can send waves toward the fixed end where the waves will reflect to give waves travelling in both directions with the same amplitude and wavelength. (Fixed-end reflection was described in Section 13.2.) Let us now use this set-up to describe various modes of vibration of a standing wave.

Our discussion is based on the assumption that a node can occur at both ends of a rope or string. This is certainly true of strings on stringed instruments, such as a guitar, where various modes of vibration can be set up. It is also true of the fixed end of a rope on which a person is

Did You Know? *Tidal action in the world's oceans and seas can set up standing wave patterns with very long wavelengths. A few places on Earth, including Tahiti in the South Pacific Ocean, have no noticeable tide because they lie on a tidal node. In contrast, some places, such as the Bay of Fundy in Eastern Canada, have very high tides due in part to the antinodes of standing waves.*

demonstrating a standing wave pattern, although at the end where the waves are generated, the displacement is slightly greater than zero. However, a rope is easier to observe than a guitar string, so we will consider it here.

Whenever a standing wave can be set up, the **fundamental mode** is the one with the longest wavelength. It can also be called the first mode or the first harmonic. On a rope or a string, the fundamental mode occurs when there is one antinode between the ends, as illustrated in Figure 13-25. In this case, the length of the rope is half the wavelength of the waves produced. To produce this pattern, the waves must be generated at the natural or resonant frequency which is the lowest frequency for the rope. The lowest resonant frequency is called the **fundamental frequency**, corresponding to the fundamental mode.

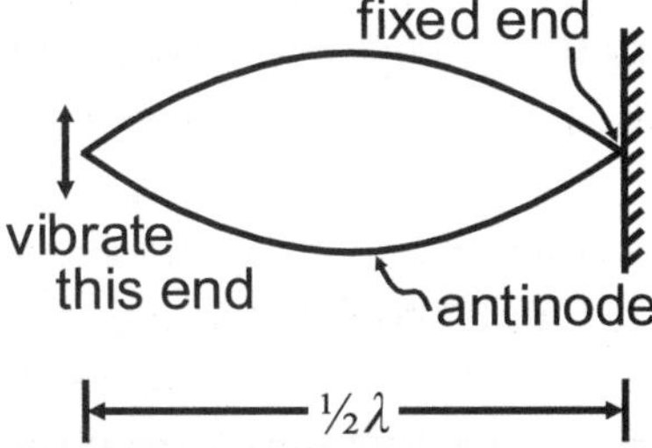

Figure 13-25 *The fundamental mode of a transverse standing wave. This may also be called the first mode or first harmonic.*

If the frequency of the generated wave is now doubled, a new resonance is developed and the second mode of vibration or second harmonic occurs (Figure 13-26 (a)). In this case, the length of the rope is one wavelength and there is one node between the two ends. The third and fourth modes or harmonics occur at higher resonant frequencies, producing two nodes then three nodes between the ends, as shown in Figures 13-26(b) and (c). If you try producing these modes yourself, you will appreciate why a standing wave pattern is possible only at specific resonant frequencies.

In observing all of the standing waves presented in this section, we can draw the following important conclusion:

The distance between adjacent nodes in a standing wave pattern is half the wavelength (½ λ) of the waves that produce the pattern.

The same relationship applies to the distance between adjacent antinodes.

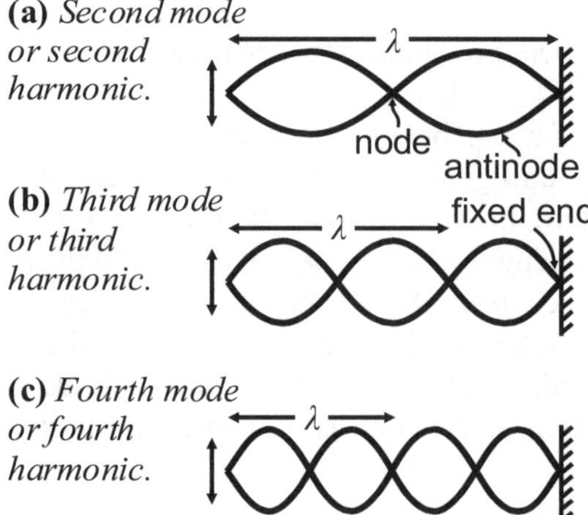

Figure 13-26 *Modes of vibration above the fundamental.*

Sample Problem 13-5

A 6.4-Hz source produces a standing wave pattern in the second mode on an 8.0 m rope.
(a) What is the fundamental frequency of the rope?
(b) What is the speed of the waves producing the pattern?

Solution: (a) The fundamental frequency is the lowest frequency that will produce the fundamental mode. In this case, it is half of 6.4 Hz, or 3.2 Hz.

(b) In the second mode, the length of the rope equals the wavelength, so $\lambda = 8.0$ m.

$$v = f\lambda = 6.4 \text{ Hz} \times 8.0 \text{ m} = 51 \text{ m/s}$$

Thus, the speed of the waves is 51 m/s.

We have considered standing waves on ropes and strings only, i.e., with transverse waves in one dimension. Standing waves can also be longitudinal and they can occur in two and three dimensions in a variety of media. For example, they can occur in air and in solid metal rods. In many cases, the modes may not be as simple as those on a string. For instance, instead of the modes occurring at 1*f*, 2*f*, 3*f*, etc., they may occur at 1*f*, 3*f*, 5*f*, etc. Standing waves are important in music and in atomic or quantum theory discussed later in the text.

Interference in Two Dimensions

Under certain circumstances, the interference of waves travelling in two dimensions can produce a pattern that is easily observed and analyzed. An example of an interference pattern in water is shown in Figure 13-27. The conditions used to produce this pattern are that two point sources of waves are vibrating up and down with the same frequency and amplitude, and they are in phase with each other. Notice the dull grey regions that spread out from the two sources; these tend to look as if they remain stationary when the pattern is observed in a ripple tank. Notice also the sets of very bright and very dark regions; these move away from the sources of the waves.

Figure 13-27 *Photograph of a two-dimensional interference pattern in water caused by two in-phase point sources.*

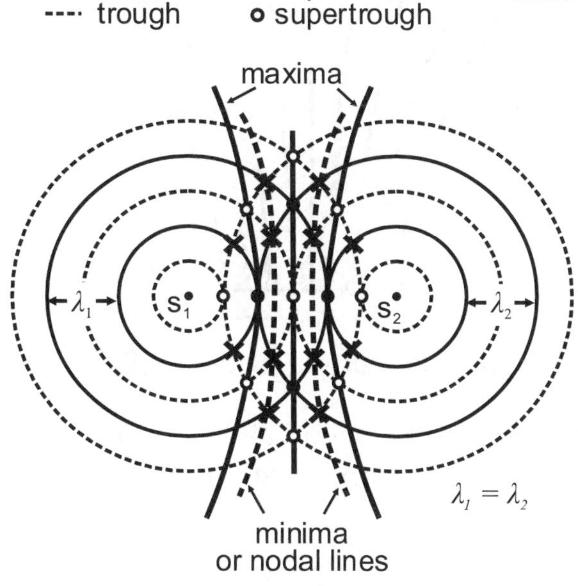

Figure 13-28 *Examining how a two-source interference pattern in water is created.*

To study how destructive and constructive interference occur in a two-source interference pattern, we draw a diagram of the pattern, as shown in Figure 13-28. The solid circles represent crests and the broken circles represent troughs, both of which are travelling away from the sources, S_1 and S_2. The wavelengths, λ_1 and λ_2, are equal because the frequencies of the sources are equal. Whenever a crest from S_1 meets a trough from S_2, destructive interference occurs and a *minimum* amplitude results. In this case, the minimum is a node because the amplitudes of the waves from the two sources are equal. A line of adjacent nodes in an interference pattern is called a **nodal line**. It is represented by the dashed lines in Figure 13-28. Although nodal lines appear to be straight far away from the sources of waves, they are actually in the shape of a curve called a hyperbola.

Again, in Figure 13-28, whenever a crest from one source meets a crest from the other source, a supercrest occurs; in a ripple tank pattern, this type of maximum appears as a very bright spot. Whenever a trough from one source meets a trough from the other source, a supertrough occurs; in water, this type of maximum is a very dark spot. The maxima appear to travel away from the sources.

The mathematical analysis of a two-source interference pattern can be useful for finding unknown quantities, such as the wavelength of a wave. We begin this analysis by numbering the minimum lines or nodal lines $N_1, N_2, N_3, \ldots$ on both sides of the perpendicular to an imaginary line joining the two sources (Figure 13-29). Similarly, the maximum lines are numbered $M_0, M_1, M_2, \ldots$, starting at the perpendicular bisector, which is also called the central maximum.

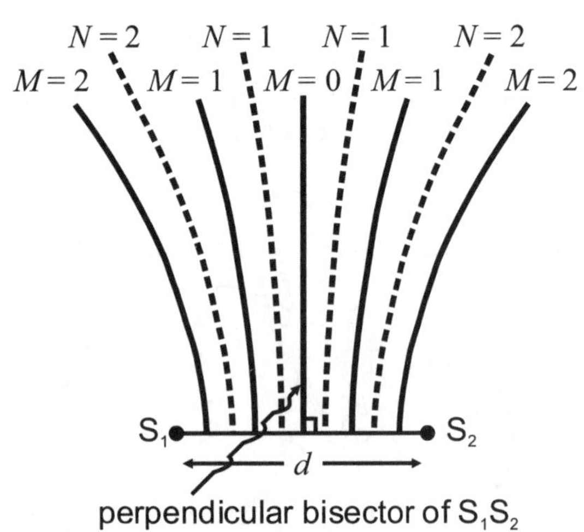

Figure 13-29 *Minima and maxima in a two-source interference pattern.*

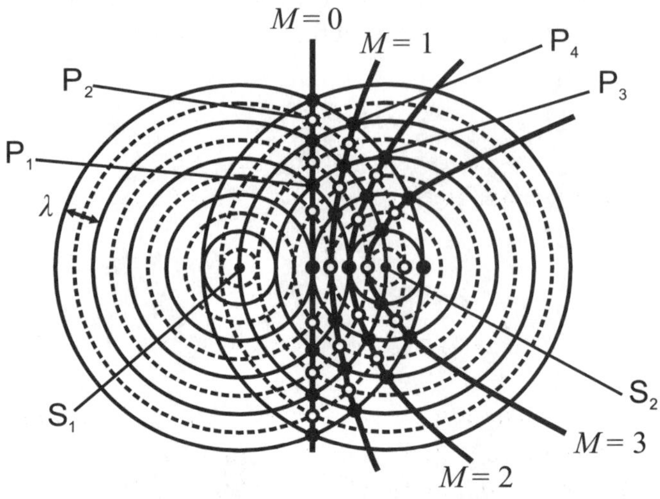

Figure 13-30 *Path length and path difference in a two-source interference pattern.*

Consider the distance travelled by individual waves in order to produce destructive or constructive interference. The distance between the source and a position of interference is called the **path length**. At any position of interference, there are two path lengths, one from each source, and the magnitude of the difference between these path lengths is called, simply, the **path difference** (symbol P.D.). To discover the path difference along the various maximum and minimum lines, refer to Figure 13-30. Along the central maximum ($M = 0$), P_1 is a supercrest with a path difference of

$$\text{P.D.} = |P_1S_1 - P_1S_2| = |3\lambda - 3\lambda| = 0$$

Also, P_2 is a supertrough with $\text{P.D.} = |P_2S_1 - P_2S_2| = |4.5\,\lambda - 4.5\,\lambda| = 0$

In fact, for any position along the central maximum, the path difference is zero. Now, consider the next maximum line, $M = 1$, on both sides of the central maximum. At P_3, the path difference is

$$\text{P.D.} = |P_3S_1 - P_3S_2| = |4\lambda - 3\lambda| = 1\lambda$$

and at P_4, $\text{P.D.} = |P_4S_1 - P_4S_2| = |5\lambda - 4\lambda| = 1\lambda$

Thus, along $M = 1$, the path difference is 1λ. Looking carefully at Figure 13-30, you should be able to prove to yourself that the following pattern exists.

Maximum Line Number	Path Difference
$M = 0$	0
$M = 1$	1λ
$M = 2$	2λ
$M = 3$	3λ
.	.
.	.
$M = M$	$M\lambda$

Thus, we conclude that, **for lines of constructive interference (maxima) in a two-source interference pattern, the path difference is:**

$$\text{P.D.} = M\lambda \text{ where } M = 0, 1, 2, 3, \ldots \qquad \textbf{(13-6)}$$

and λ is the wavelength of the waves producing the pattern.

Similar arguments can be used to determine the path difference along any of the lines of interference called minima, or nodal lines, $N = 1$, $N = 2$, etc. It is left as an exercise to prove that, **for lines of destructive interference (nodal lines or minima) in a two-source interference pattern, the path difference is:**

$$\text{P.D.} = (N - ½)\lambda \text{ where } N = 1, 2, 3, \ldots \qquad \textbf{(13-7)}$$

 **Sample Problem 13-6**

Point X is a nodal point along the second nodal line in a two-source interference pattern in a ripple tank. The path lengths from X to the sources are 28.5 cm and 31.3 cm. What is the wavelength of the water waves producing the pattern?

Solution: For a nodal line (Eqn. 13-7), $\text{P.D.} = \left(N - \frac{1}{2}\right)\lambda$

$$\therefore \quad \lambda = \frac{\text{P.D.}}{\left(N - \frac{1}{2}\right)} = \frac{\left|28.5 \text{ cm} - 31.3 \text{ cm}\right|}{2 - \frac{1}{2}} = 1.9 \text{ cm}$$

Thus, the wavelength is 1.9 cm.

Two-Source Interference Far from the Sources

For an interference pattern in water, the path difference equations can be used to find the wavelength fairly accurately. However, the equations become less useful when studying other types of waves, such as light, where the separation of the sources becomes very small and the distance to the maximum or minimum points becomes relatively large. Then, the path difference equations are used to derive equations involving other quantities besides *M*, *N*, and λ, as shown below.

Consider sources S_1 and S_2 separated by a distance *d*, and an interference point P at a distance much greater than *d* from the sources (Figure 13-31). If we draw point A on the path line PS_1 so that $PA = PS_2$, then the path difference of the two paths is $|PS_1 - PS_2| = AS_1$, as seen in the diagram. Now, if PS_1 and $PS_2 \gg d$, then figure AS_1S_2 is essentially a right-angled triangle that contains the angle $\theta' = AS_2S_1$ such that $\sin\theta' = AS_1/S_1S_2$ or

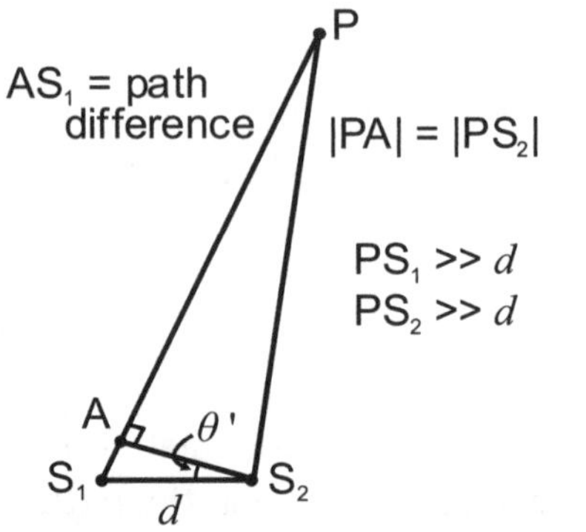

$$\sin\theta' = \frac{\text{path difference}}{d}$$

Figure 13-31 *Another look at path difference in a two-source interference pattern.*

Substituting the path difference equations (Eqns. 13-6 and 13-7) into this last equation, we get:

For maxima: $$\sin\theta' = \frac{M\lambda}{d} \quad \text{where } M = 0, 1, 2, 3, \ldots \tag{13-8}$$

For minima: $$\sin\theta' = \frac{(N - \tfrac{1}{2})\lambda}{d} \quad \text{where } N = 1, 2, 3, \ldots \tag{13-9}$$

Let us look at the physical meaning of the equation $\sin\theta' = M\lambda/d$ by rearranging the equation to obtain $M = d\sin\theta'/\lambda$. This equation obviously is true when $\theta' = 0°$, in which case $\sin\theta' = 0$ and $M = 0$, so the maximum line is the central maximum. The maximum value of $\sin\theta'$ is 1 (when $\theta' = 90°$), in which case the value of *M* varies directly as the source separation *d* and inversely as the wavelength λ. This can be verified by observing a two-source interference pattern while varying *d* and λ, one at a time.

For large distances from the sources, the angle θ' in Figure 13-31 is so small that it would be impossible to measure it directly. Thus, to apply the equations involving $\sin\theta'$, we must find another expression for it that can be measured easily. Another diagram is drawn, this time with point P as far away as possible on the page (Figure 13-32). The perpendicular distance from P to the central maximum line is given the symbol *x*, and the distance from P to the midpoint of the line joining the sources is given the symbol *L*. The information in Figure 13-32 (a) proves that, for large *L* and small *d* values, the angle θ very closely equals the angle θ'. Now, since $\sin\theta = x/L$, we can write two important equations involving measurable quantities in a two-source interference pattern. Thus, for maxima, since $\sin\theta = x/L$, $\theta = \theta'$, and $\sin\theta' = M\lambda/d$,

$$\frac{x}{L} = \frac{M\lambda}{d} \qquad \text{where } M = 0, 1, 2, 3, \ldots \qquad \textbf{(13-10)}$$

and for minima or nodal lines,

$$\frac{x}{L} = \frac{(N - \frac{1}{2})\lambda}{d} \qquad \text{where } N = 1, 2, 3, \ldots \qquad \textbf{(13-11)}$$

Figure 13-32 (b) shows a more realistic diagram involving these equations, and the next sample problem reveals how the equations are applied to find the wavelength of the waves producing an interference pattern.

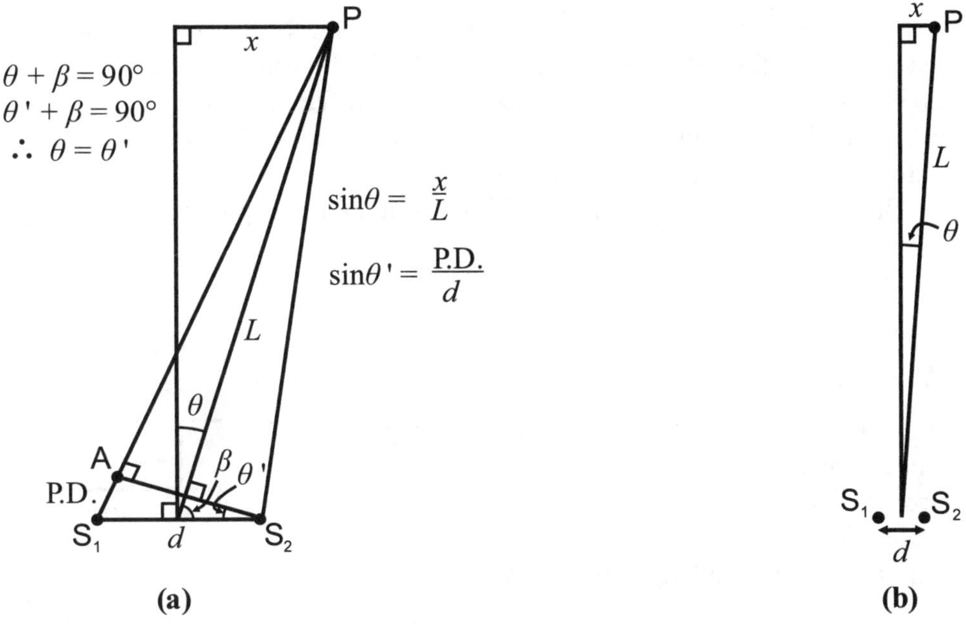

Figure 13-32 **(a)** *Developing equations for a two-source interference pattern.* **(b)** *More realistic dimensions for the equations.*

Sample Problem 13-7

Two in-phase sources of water waves, separated by 6.2 cm, produce an interference pattern. A student measures the distance from the point halfway between the sources to a position on the second maximum to be 34 cm. If the perpendicular distance from the same position to the central maximum line is 11 cm, what is the wavelength of the waves producing the pattern?

Solution: We are given that $d = 6.2$ cm, $L = 34$ cm, $x = 11$ cm, and $M = 2$.

From $\frac{x}{L} = \frac{M\lambda}{d}$, $\qquad \lambda = \frac{xd}{ML}$

$$= \frac{(11\text{ cm})(6.2\text{ cm})}{(2)(34\text{ cm})}$$
$$= 1.0\text{ cm}$$

Thus, the wavelength is 1.0 cm. Notice that the answer has two significant digits, even though the M value has only one digit. Recall that M is a whole number and thus is not considered in our final determination of significant digits.

Remember that the diagrams and equations for the two-source interference patterns discussed in this section have been for the special circumstance when the sources have been in phase. Both the pattern and the equations change if the frequencies are different or the sources are not vibrating in phase. For example, if the two sources have identical frequencies but are exactly opposite in phase, the perpendicular bisector of the line joining the sources is a minimum, *not* a maximum. (See Practice Question 13-42.) Furthermore, if the sources have quite different frequencies, no distinguishable pattern is noticeable.

Practice

13-25 State whether the type of interference is constructive or destructive in each case.
(a) A large trough meets a small trough.
(b) A supertrough is formed.
(c) A small rarefaction meets a large rarefaction.

13-26 What two conditions are necessary for two waves travelling in opposite directions on a rope to produce a complete node for an instant?

13-27 Apply the principle of superposition to draw the resulting pulses when the pulses shown in Figure 13-33 interfere. The point of superposition should be at the horizontal midpoints of the pulses.

(a)

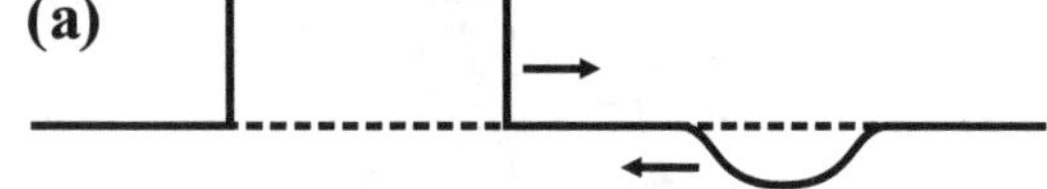

(b)

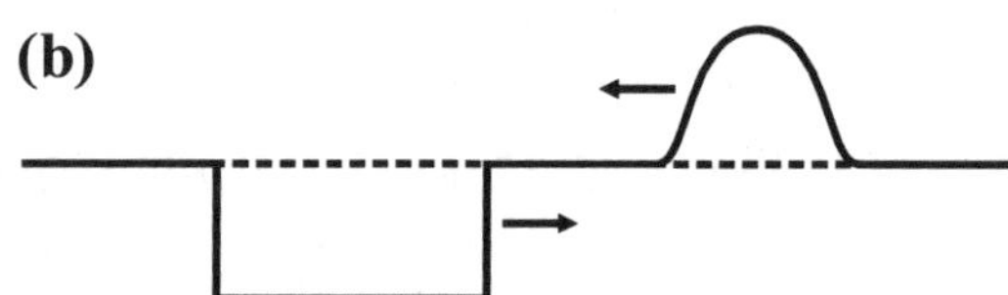

(c)

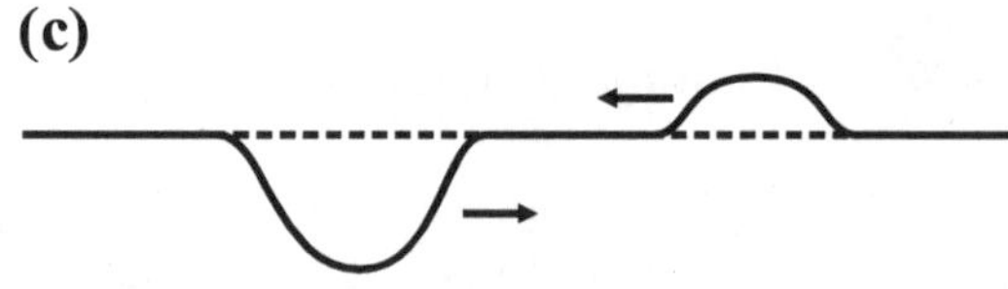

Figure 13-33 *Question 13-27.*

13-28 For a rope of fixed length attached rigidly at one end and vibrated at the other end, can a standing wave be set up at any arbitrary frequency? Why or why not?

13-29 Draw a scale diagram of a standing wave pattern that has four antinodes between the ends of a rope that is 6.0 m long. What is the wavelength of the waves producing this pattern?
[Ans. 3.0 m]

13-30 The speed of a wave on a 6.2-m long rope is 7.6 m/s. Determine the frequency of vibration required to produce a standing wave pattern having (a) 1 antinode, (b) 2 antinodes, and (c) 3 antinodes. [Ans. (a) 0.61 Hz (b) 1.2 Hz (c) 1.8 Hz]

13-31 The fundamental frequency of a certain rope of length 3.8 m is 1.2 Hz.
(a) Determine the wavelength in the fundamental mode *and* the speed of the wave on the rope.
(b) Determine the frequency of the fourth and fifth modes or harmonics.
[Ans. (a) 7.6 m; 9.1 m/s (b) 4.8 Hz; 6.0 Hz]

13-32 The distance between nodes on a standing wave pattern on a certain string is 16 cm and there are 5 nodes between the ends of the string. A single wave takes 1.2 s to travel to one end of the rope and back again.
(a) What is the wavelength of the waves producing the pattern?
(b) How long is the rope?
(c) What is the speed of the waves?
(d) What is the frequency of the waves?
(e) What mode of vibration is occurring (i.e., which harmonic)?
[Ans. (a) 32 cm (b) 96 cm (c) 1.6 m/s (d) 5.0 Hz (e) 6th]

13-33 Use a two-source interference pattern diagram similar to Figure 13-30 to prove that the path difference for minima (nodal lines) is P.D. = $(N - ½)\lambda$, where $N = 1, 2, 3$, etc.

13-34 Two sources of circular waves in a ripple tank are producing waves with a wavelength of 2.8 cm. (a) Determine on which maximum line the path difference is 8.4 cm.
(b) Determine on which nodal line the path difference is 7.0 cm. [Ans. (a) 3rd (b) 3rd]

13-35 Place two dots 6.0 cm apart in the middle of a blank page and label them S_1 and S_2. Using a wavelength of 2.0 cm, which means there will be new circles every 1.0 cm, draw a series of crests (solid lines) and troughs (broken lines) from each dot until the page is filled up. (The more accurately the circles representing the crests and troughs are drawn, the better the pattern will look.) Place small circles at all destructive interference locations and solid dots at all constructive interference locations. Draw the nodal lines and the maximum lines, then extend them straight back to the line joining S_1 and S_2. Do these lines pass through the midpoint of S_1S_2?

<u>13-36</u> State what happens to the number of nodal lines in a two-source interference pattern if:
(a) only the source separation is decreased.
(b) only the wavelength of the sources is decreased.
(c) only the amplitude of vibration of the sources is decreased.

13-37 Determine the wavelength of the waves producing a two-source interference pattern in each case. (a) On the fourth nodal line, the path difference is 14 cm.
(b) On the third maximum (from the central maximum), the path difference is 66 mm.
(c) With a source separation of 3.2 cm, the second nodal line makes an angle of 2.8° with the central maximum. [Ans. (a) 4.0 cm (b) 22 mm (c) 0.10 cm]

13-38 Determine the greatest number of maximum lines in a two-source interference pattern when the ratio of the source separation to the wavelength is 4:1. [Ans. 9]

13-39 In each case, one variable of a possible five is unknown. Solve for it.
(a) $M = 3$; $d = 4.2$ cm; $x = 16$ cm; $L = 86$ cm; $\lambda = ?$
(b) $M = 2$; $d = 2.0$ mm; $x = 4.2$ mm; $\lambda = 5.5 \times 10^{-7}$ m; $L = ?$
(c) $N = 3$; $\lambda = 2.0 \times 10^{-4}$ m; $x = 8.6 \times 10^{-2}$ m; $L = 2.2$ m; $d = ?$
[Ans. (a) 0.26 cm (b) 7.6 m (c) 1.3 cm]

13-40 A two-source interference pattern is set up using waves with a wavelength that is ¼ of the source separation. At what angles from the central maximum are the first three nodal lines?
[Ans. 7.2°; 22°; 39°]

13-41 In a two-source interference pattern, the maximum line $M = 1$ makes an angle of 12° to the central maximum. If the source separation is 6.6 mm, what is the wavelength of the waves?
[Ans. 1.4 mm]

13-42 Draw a two-source interference pattern with $d = 6.0$ cm and $\lambda = 2.0$ cm and with the two sources exactly out of phase. Include nodal lines, maximum lines, and a legend explaining the parts of the diagram.

13.4 DIFFRACTION OF WAVES

It is commonly known that we can hear around corners. The property of waves that allows this to occur is called diffraction. **Diffraction** is the bending of a wave as it passes by a barrier or through an opening. (Do not confuse diffraction, which occurs in one medium, with refraction, which occurs when waves enter a second medium.)

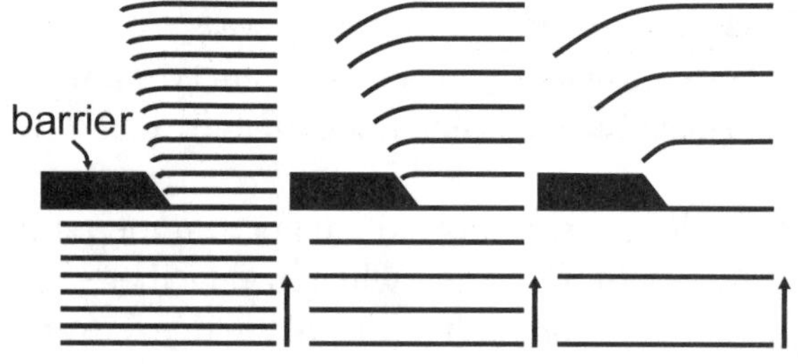

Figure 13-34 *Diffraction of water waves around the edge of a barrier: As the wavelength increases, the amount of diffraction increases.*

Diffraction of water waves can be observed on lakes and oceans as well as in ripple tanks. If straight periodic water waves meet the edge of a long straight barrier, they bend around the edge of it. The amount of bending, or diffraction, depends on the wavelength of the waves. At short wavelengths, the amount of diffraction is slight, but as the wavelength increases, so does the amount of diffraction (Figure 13-34).

If straight periodic waves strike a straight barrier that is approximately the same size as the wavelength, diffraction occurs around both edges of the barrier. Behind the barrier, a sort of "shadow" is observed, then the waves meet and continue travelling in the medium. With short wavelengths, the shadow is relatively long; as the wavelength increases, the shadow decreases because the waves diffract more. Using the symbol w for the width of the barrier and λ for the wavelength, the amount of diffraction does not depend on w by itself or λ by itself; rather, it depends on the ratio of λ to w. If $\lambda/w \ll 1$, then little diffraction is noticed, whereas, if $\lambda/w \geq 1$, the amount of diffraction is maximum (Fig. 13-35).

Diffraction can also occur through a narrow opening or aperture. In fact, this situation is quite important, especially in the study of the wave nature of light (Chapter 14). If the width of the aperture, w, is much larger than the wavelength, which is comparable to saying $\lambda/w \ll 1$, little diffraction occurs (Figure 13-36 (a)). As the size of the aperture approaches the wavelength, the ratio λ/w approaches 1 and the amount of diffraction becomes greater (Figure 13-36 (b)). By now, you should be able to predict the situation required for maximum diffraction through an aperture. It occurs when $\lambda/w \approx 1$, in other words, when the aperture width equals, or nearly equals, the wavelength of the waves in the medium. In this case, the emerging waves appear almost as if they had come from a single source of circular waves (c). (Notice the faded regions in Figure 13-37(c). The theoretical explanation and mathematical analysis of this will be dealt with in the study of the diffraction of light, Section 14.3.)

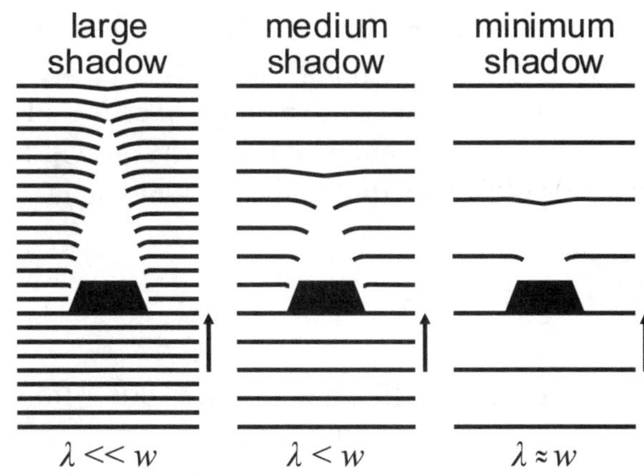

Figure 13-35 *Diffraction around a small barrier: As the wavelength approaches the width of the barrier, the diffraction increases to a maximum.*

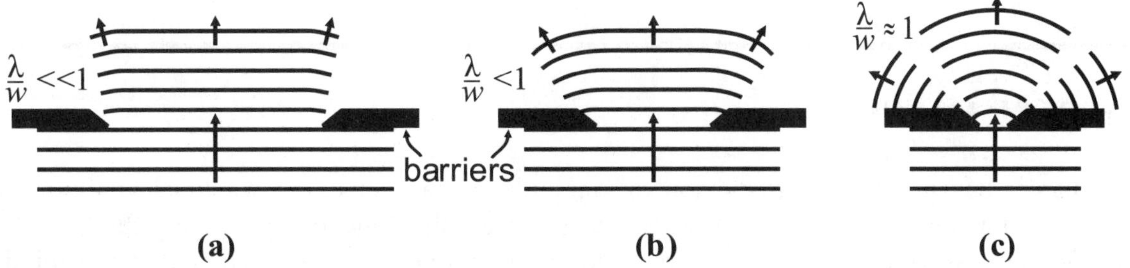

Figure 13-36 *Diffraction through apertures: As the aperture width approaches the size of the wavelength, the diffraction increases.*

Now, imagine straight periodic waves striking not one but two narrow apertures, separated by a small barrier. In this case, each aperture acts like a source of circular waves, causing an interference pattern that closely resembles the two-source interference pattern (Section 13.3). This pattern is most distinct when the width of each aperture is about the same as the wavelength (Figure 13-37).

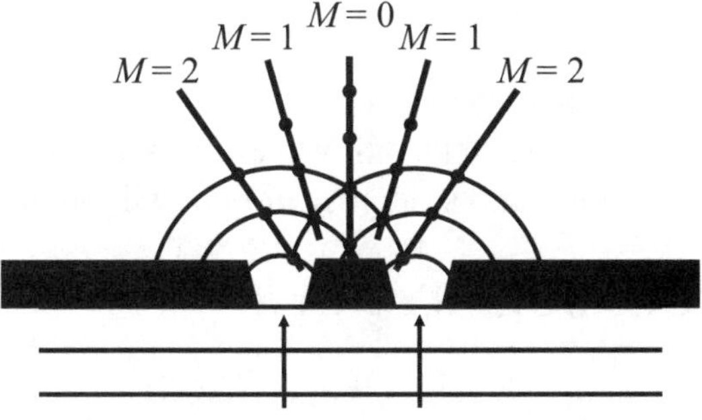

Figure 13-37 *Diffraction through a set of two apertures: Each aperture acts like a source of circular waves, resulting in a pattern that resembles a two-source interference pattern. Only the maxima are shown here because only the wavefronts (crests) are drawn.*

Although we have looked at diffraction for two-dimensional transverse water waves only, diffraction can occur in three dimensions for both transverse waves and longitudinal waves. In fact, the diffraction of sound waves explains why we can hear around corners. You will learn why we cannot *see* around corners in Chapter 14. (Try hypothesizing why the diffraction of light does not allow us to see around corners.) You will also learn what happens when three, four, or even thousands of tiny apertures are used rather than just two.

Practice

13-43 How does diffraction of waves differ from refraction of waves?

13-44 What condition is necessary for maximum diffraction of waves of wavelength λ travelling around a sharp-edged barrier of width w?

13-45 Repeat # 13-44 if the waves are travelling through an aperture of width w.

13-46 Speculate on the reason why the diffraction of light waves is something we usually do not observe.

CHAPTER FOCUS

This chapter began with an introduction to longitudinal, transverse, and torsional vibrations and their characteristics. The study of waves began with the function of waves, the types and characteristics of waves, and wave terminology for periodic waves. Then the transmission, reflection, refraction, interference (including the principle of superposition and standing waves), and diffraction were presented in detail. Where appropriate, both one- and two-dimensional waves were included.

The characteristics of waves presented in this chapter will be studied specifically for light in the next chapter. Not all wave characteristics were presented in Chapter 13. For example, the polarization and scattering of light will be described in Chapter 14.

VOCABULARY REVIEW

You should be able to define each of the following words or phrases.

longitudinal vibration
transverse vibration
torsional vibration
cycle
resonant frequency
resonance
wave
longitudinal (or compression) wave

wavefront
ray
normal
angle of incidence
angle of reflection
refraction
angle of refraction
index of refraction

compression
rarefaction
transverse wave
crest
trough
periodic wave
amplitude
in phase; out of phase
wavelength
universal wave equation
fixed-end reflection
open-end reflection
constructive interference
destructive interference
node
principle of superposition
standing wave pattern
antinodes
fundamental mode
fundamental frequency
nodal line
path length
path difference
diffraction

CHAPTER REVIEW

13-47 Of the properties of a wave listed, the one that does not depend on the others is:
(a) speed (b) wavelength (c) amplitude (d) frequency

13-48 In a longitudinal wave, the individual particles of the medium:
(a) move parallel to the direction of the wave's motion
(b) move perpendicular to the direction of the wave's motion
(c) move in ellipses
(d) move in circles

13-49 As the period of a periodic wave increases:
(a) the frequency remains constant and the wavelength increases
(b) the speed increases and the wavelength decreases
(c) the amplitude increases
(d) the frequency decreases and the wavelength increases
(e) none of the above is true

13-50 The superposition of two waves results in a standing wave if the waves have:
(a) the same amplitude, different frequencies, and opposite directions of motion
(b) the same amplitude and direction of motion, but different frequencies
(c) the same frequency and amplitude but opposite directions of motion
(d) the same frequency, amplitude, and direction of motion

13-51 A source of periodic waves, vibrating at an initial frequency f_1, results in waves of wavelength λ_1 travelling at a speed v_1 in a certain medium. If the frequency of the source changes to $2f_1$, then the wavelength and speed in the same medium become, respectively:
(a) $2\lambda_1$ and $2v_1$ (b) $2\lambda_1$ and v_1 (c) $0.5\lambda_1$ and $0.5v_1$ (d) $0.5\lambda_1$ and $2v_1$ (e) $0.5\lambda_1$ and v_1

13-52 Periodic waves travel at an angle from a medium in which the speed is low to one in which the speed is higher. If n is the index of refraction from the first medium to the second medium, R is

the angle of refraction, and i is the angle of incidence, choose the correct statement:
(a) $n > 1.0;\ R > i$ (b) $n < 1.0;\ R > i$ (c) $n > 1.0;\ R < i$ (d) $n < 1.0;\ R < i$ (e) $n = 1.0;\ R = i$

13-53 State the relationship, if any exists, between the sets of variables listed below. Where possible, write a mathematical variation (proportionality) statement based on the appropriate equation.
(a) period and frequency
(b) hertz and cycles per second
(c) the wavelength of a periodic wave and the frequency of the source causing the wave (in a medium where the speed of the wave is constant)
(d) the angle of reflection and the angle of incidence for a straight wave that reflects off a straight barrier
(e) the angle of reflection and the angle of incidence for a straight wave that reflects off a curved barrier
(f) the index of refraction and the ratio of the wavelengths for waves travelling from one medium into another
(g) the distance between adjacent nodes on a standing wave pattern and the wavelength of the waves producing the pattern
(h) the number of nodal lines in a 2-source interference pattern and the distance separating the sources
(i) the number of maximum lines in a 2-source interference pattern and the wavelength of the waves producing the pattern
(j) the amount of diffraction of waves passing through an aperture and the ratio of the wavelength of the waves to the aperture width

13-54 A centrifuge rotates 7.0×10^4 times per minute. Determine the period and frequency of this motion. [Ans. 8.6×10^{-4} s; 1.2×10^3 Hz]

13-55 How could the concept of resonance be applied to try to free a car that is stuck in snow or mud?

13-56 If the resonant frequency of a child on a swing is f, at which, if any, of the following frequencies would it be possible to push the child to maintain a large amplitude of vibration: $2f$; $3f$; $4f$; $\frac{1}{2}f$; f; $\frac{1}{4}f$?

13-57 A chef breaks two raw eggs, puts the contents into a hemispherical bowl, and proceeds to beat the eggs with a fork at a frequency *other* than the resonant frequency of the eggs in the bowl. Why "other"?

13-58 What is the main function of a wave?

13-59 Imagine a long, thin, solid metal rod suspended so it rests horizontally. (This imaginary rod may be 100 m long or more.) One end of the rod is struck, first parallel to the rod, then later perpendicular to the rod, as illustrated in Fig. 13-38.

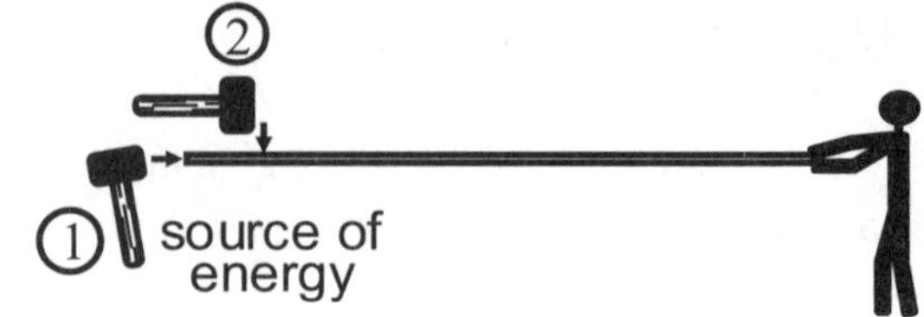

Figure 13-38 *Question 13-59.*

(a) Would energy from the blows travel at the same speed or at different speeds? Explain.
(b) Relate your answer in (a) to the speeds with which P and S waves travel through Earth.

13-60 An earthquake occurs 7.2×10^3 km from a seismological station. How long after receiving the initial primary wave does the station receive the initial secondary wave? (The approximate speeds of these waves were given in Section 13.1.) [Ans. 7.0×10^2 s later]

13-61 Ultrasonic waves used to shatter a brain tumour operate at a frequency of 23.0 kHz; the speed of the waves in the body is 1.53 km/s. What is the wavelength of the ultrasound?
[Ans. 0.0665 m]

Did You Know? *The ultrasonic device used for destructive purposes is called a cavitron ultrasonic surgical aspirator (CUSA). After the tumour is shattered, the fragments are removed by using a saline solution.*

13-62 Determine the range of frequencies of FM radio stations in megahertz (MHz) if their range of wavelengths is from 2.78 m to 3.43 m. The speed of the waves is 3.00×10^8 m/s. [Ans. 108 MHz to 87.5 MHz]

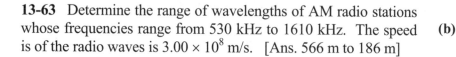

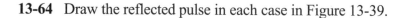

13-63 Determine the range of wavelengths of AM radio stations whose frequencies range from 530 kHz to 1610 kHz. The speed is of the radio waves is 3.00×10^8 m/s. [Ans. 566 m to 186 m]

13-64 Draw the reflected pulse in each case in Figure 13-39.

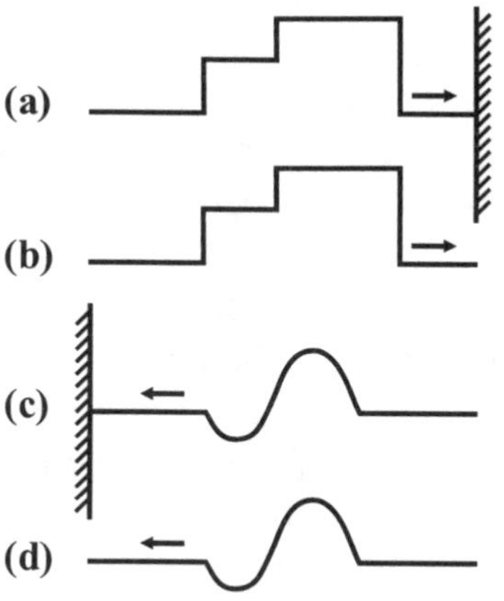

13-65 Two ropes, X and Y, are attached. The speed of waves in X is v and the speed in Y is $2v$. A wave of wavelength λ is travelling in X toward Y.
(a) For the wave that enters Y, what is the wavelength?
(b) Is the transmission from X to Y positive or negative?
(c) Is the reflection off the interface between X and Y positive or negative? How do the wavelength and amplitude of the reflected wave compare to the initial waves?

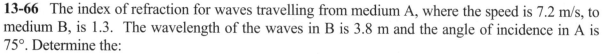

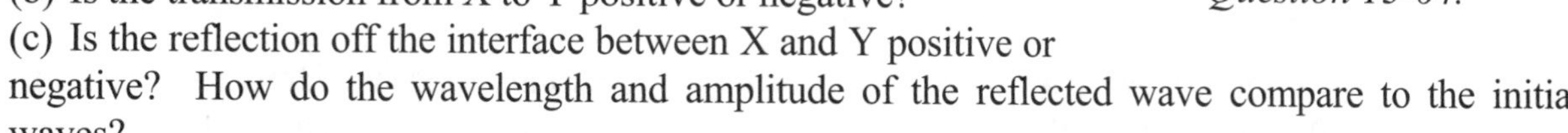

(a) (b) (c) (d)

Figure 13-39 *Question 13-64.*

13-66 The index of refraction for waves travelling from medium A, where the speed is 7.2 m/s, to medium B, is 1.3. The wavelength of the waves in B is 3.8 m and the angle of incidence in A is 75°. Determine the:
(a) speed of the waves in B.
(b) wavelength of the waves in A.
(c) angle of refraction in B. [Ans. (a) 5.5 m/s (b) 4.9 m (c) 48°]

<u>**13-67**</u> For longitudinal waves travelling in the same medium, under what condition(s) will (a) constructive interference and (b) destructive interference occur?

13-68 Two troughs, C and D, are travelling on a rope toward end E (Figure 13-40). Each trough is 10 mm wide, C is 7.0 mm deep, and D is 9.0 mm

Figure 13-40 *Question 13-68.*

deep. After D reflects from E, it meets C and interferes for an instant.
(a) At maximum interference, what are the width and height of the resulting pulse if E is a fixed end?
(b) Repeat (a) if E is an open end.
[Ans. (a) 10 mm; 2 mm (b) 10 mm; 16 mm]

13-69 A standing wave pattern is set up on a string of length 54 cm fixed at both ends. The wavelength of the waves is 36 cm, the amplitude is 8.0 cm, and the speed is 25 m/s.
(a) What is the distance between adjacent nodes on the string?
(b) What is the frequency of vibration of the source of the waves?
(c) Draw a scale diagram of this standing wave pattern. [Ans. (a) 18 cm (b) 69 Hz]

13-70 The frequency of vibration of the third mode or harmonic of a string with nodes at both ends is 660 Hz. What is the frequency of the fundamental mode? the fourth harmonic?
[Ans. 220 Hz; 880 Hz]

13-71 An interference pattern is produced in water by two in-phase sources 4.5 cm apart. The distance between crests from each source is 2.1 cm. Which nodal line of this pattern is at an angle of 44.4° to the perpendicular bisector of a line joining the two sources? [Ans. 2nd]

13-72 An interference pattern using microwaves of wavelength 3.0 cm is set up in a physics laboratory. (Microwaves are part of the electromagnetic spectrum; they travel at a speed of 3.0×10^8 m/s in air.) Two sources of in-phase waves are placed 18 cm apart and a receiver is located 4.8 m away from the midpoint between the sources.
(a) What is the frequency of the microwaves? Express your answer in megahertz (MHz) and gigahertz (GHz).
(b) As the receiver is moved across the pattern parallel to an imaginary line joining the sources, what is the distance between adjacent maxima? between adjacent minima? between a maximum and an adjacent minimum? [Ans. (a) 1.0×10^4 MHz; 1.0×10^1 GHz (b) 0.80 m; 0.80 m; 0.40 m]

13-73 A set of water waves of wavelength 1.0 cm is approaching a barrier. Draw two diagrams that show the diffraction pattern that results if the width of the barrier is (a) 5.0 cm (b) 1.0 cm.

APPLYING YOUR KNOWLEDGE

13-74 During flight, a sparrow's heart beats 800 times per minute and a pigeon respires (breathes) 400 times per minute.
(a) Determine the frequencies of each of these activities.
(b) Determine a reasonable estimate of the maximum frequency of your own heartbeat and respiring during or just after vigorous exercise.
(c) Speculate, with reasons, whether or not humans will ever be able to compete in the flying world with these high-revving "engines."

13-75 Describe how an athlete on a trampoline would apply the concept of resonance to:
(a) try to jump as high as possible.

(b) reduce the vibration amplitude to a minimum before getting off the trampoline .

13-76 In 1831 in England, an army was marching in-step across a bridge suspended over a river. Unfortunately, the frequency of the steps matched a resonant frequency of the bridge, and the bridge collapsed. What could have been done to march the troops across the bridge at the same speed without causing the collapse? Explain your answer.

13-77 The Bay of Fundy on Canada's Atlantic Coast has among the highest tides in the world, up to a maximum of about 15 m. Such high tides result not only from the general shape of the bay, but also because of the resonance effects. The length of the bay is such that the water in it oscillates back and forth with a period of about 13 h. This is just slightly more than the period of time between successive high tides or successive low tides, which is 12 h and 25 min.
(a) Why does "resonance" help increase the size of the tides in the Bay of Fundy?
(b) Proposals have been made to put a large dam across the mouth of the bay to harness tidal energy. Such a dam would reduce somewhat the effective length of the bay. How would this affect the resonant frequency of the water in the bay? Would this result in higher or lower maximum tides? Explain why you think so.

KEY OBJECTIVES

Having completed this chapter, you should now be able to do the following:

1. Describe and give examples of the three main types of vibration.
2. Describe and give examples of mechanical resonance.
3. State the main function of a wave.
4. Describe the motion and parts of longitudinal and transverse waves, including the wavelength and points that are in phase.
5. Distinguish between surface waves, such as tsunamis, and body waves, such as primary and secondary seismic waves.
6. Apply the universal wave equation to find any one of the speed, frequency, period, or wavelength of a periodic wave.
7. Describe the reflection of pulses or waves off fixed and open ends.
8. Recognize wavefronts and rays of waves travelling in two dimensions.
9. Draw and label diagrams of wavefronts reflecting off barriers or refracting into a second medium, including the normal as well as any angles of incidence, reflection, or refraction.
10. Define the index of refraction for waves travelling from one medium into another, and calculate it in terms of the speeds, the wavelengths, or the angles in the two media.
11. Recognize and describe constructive and destructive interference in one and two dimensions.
12. Apply the principle of superposition to determine the results of the interference of pulses or waves.
13. Recognize a standing wave pattern and describe how it is set up by transverse waves.
14. Recognize how different modes of vibration of standing waves are produced, and determine the wavelengths of the waves that produce them.
15. Recognize and draw an interference pattern in two dimensions, and analyze the variables of the pattern mathematically.
16. Define diffraction of waves in two dimensions, and state how diffraction through apertures or

around barriers depends on the wavelength of the waves and the width of the aperture of barrier.

17. Appreciate that the properties of vibrations and waves can be applied to describe and understand many properties of light (presented in Chapter 14) as well as sound.

ANSWERS TO SELECTED QUESTIONS

13-1 (a) transverse (b) longitudinal (c) longitudinal

13-4 The resonant frequency increases as the length decreases. When walking, the frequency of your pace is low and your extended arms tend to swing at or near that low frequency. When running, your pace frequency increases, making it more natural to vibrate your arms at a higher frequency. This occurs with your arms bent at the elbow, which is equivalent to a shorter length of pendulum.

13-6 A tsunami is caused by an underwater earthquake or a volcanic eruption, not by tidal forces.

13-11 B–down; C–up; D–down; E–up

13-17 (a) negative (b) positive

13-18 The leading edge of the transmitted pulse is 2.0 cm beyond the interface; it is the same shape and phase as the incident pulse, but only half as long and smaller in amplitude. The leading edge of the reflected pulse, which is travelling to the left from the interface, is negative (i.e., below the axis of equilibrium) and it is 4.0 cm from the interface, with the same wavelength and smaller amplitude because some energy went into the transmitted pulse.

13-19 The transmitted pulse is positive (i.e., on the same side of the axis of equilibrium), twice as long in wavelength, and a little smaller in amplitude. Its leading edge is 4.0 cm beyond the interface. The reflected pulse is positive with the leading edge 2.0 cm from the interface, the same wavelength as the incident pulse, but smaller amplitude.

13-25 (a) constructive (b) constructive (c) constructive

13-26 The two waves must have the same size (i.e., wavelength and amplitude) and as they approach each other their corresponding components must be opposite in phase.

13-28 No, a standing wave can be set up only at specific frequencies such that there are n antinodes between the ends of the rope, where $n = 1, 2, 3, \ldots$

13-36 You can use Eqn. 13-10 to determine the relationships among the variables of a two-source interference pattern. (N is directly proportional to x and d and inversely proportional to L and λ.)
(a) N decreases. (b) N increases. (c) N remains constant.

13-46 Light waves have a very small wavelength, so diffraction would be observed only under very special circumstances.

13-47 (c) 13-48 (a) 13-49 (d) 13-50 (c) 13-51 (e) 13-52 (b)

13-56 $\frac{1}{2}f$; f; $\frac{1}{4}f$

13-57 Stirring at the resonant frequency of the eggs in the bowl would cause a build-up of amplitude, possibly spilling the contents over the edge, so stirring at a different frequency is advised.

13-59 (a) The energy would travel faster when the rod is struck with a blow parallel to the rod, causing a longitudinal wave. A transverse wave, caused when the blow is perpendicular to the rod, travels more slowly than the longitudinal wave.
(b) P waves are longitudinal and travel more quickly that S waves, which are transverse.

13-65 (a) 2λ

(b) positive

(c) As the wave goes from X (a denser material) to Y, the reflected wave is positive because the reflection is an open-end reflection. The wavelength of the reflected wave in X is the same as that of the incident wave in X, but the amplitude is smaller because some of the energy is transferred to Y.

13-67 (a) Constructive interference occurs when a compression meets a compression or a rarefaction meets a rarefaction.

(b) Destructive interference occurs when a compression meets a rarefaction.

CHAPTER 14

WAVE OPTICS

If you had been at the scene shown in the photograph in Figure 14-1, your eyes would have observed normal, round light sources. The apparent streams of light emanating in various directions from each source occurred only after the light passed through a special filter on the camera that took the photo. This is just one of many wave phenomena of light found in this chapter. Other effects include the colours of soap bubbles and oil slicks, and the polarization of light.

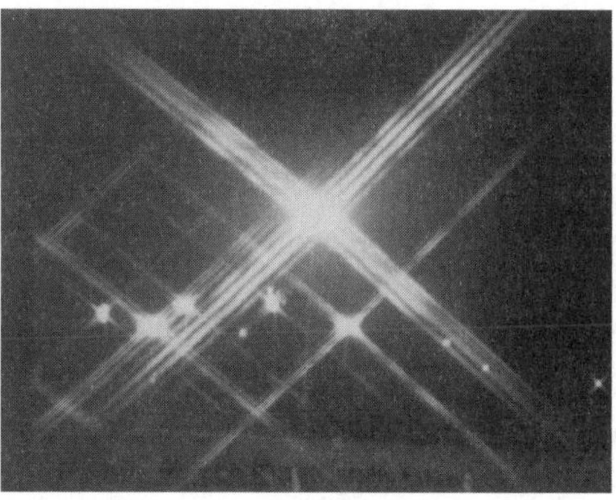

Figure 14-1 *The spreading out of light in this photograph can be explained by wave optics.*

It is obvious from the title of this chapter that we will explore concepts regarding the wave nature of light. If light acts like a wave, what are the period, frequency, and wavelength of the waves? Does the universal wave equation apply to light? What evidence do we have that light undergoes diffraction and interference? Many of the concepts related to these questions were presented in Chapter 13, where properties of mechanical vibrations and waves were described.

14.1 DIFFRACTION OF LIGHT AND HUYGENS' PRINCIPLE

Diffraction is the bending of a wave around an obstacle or through an aperture. It was shown to occur for water waves in Section 13.4. Does diffraction also occur for light? (Remember that diffraction occurs in a single medium; it differs greatly from refraction, which occurs from one medium to another.)

Under most circumstances, we do not observe the diffraction of light. However, if you look at a distant street light through a narrow gap between your fingers, or through the fibres of a curtain or other piece of cloth, you will notice bright and dark regions. These regions are caused by a rather complicated effect of diffraction. Typical diffraction patterns of light around a sharp edge and through a very fine aperture are shown in Figure 14-2 on page 14-2.

To explain how light diffracts around a sharp edge or though a small aperture, let us look at an old but useful theory about waves. The diffraction of light was first observed by an Italian university professor named Francesco Grimaldi (1618-1663), whose book describing his observation was published in 1665. That same year, the English scientist, Robert Hooke, began to describe his version of a wave model of light. Shortly after, in 1678, a Dutch physicist named Christian Huygens, (1629-1695), proposed an idea regarding wave properties that is still used in simple ways today. Huygens' idea is that the present shape and location of a wavefront can be used to predict the future shape and location of the wavefront. This idea, now called **Huygens' principle**, states:

> **Every point on a wavefront acts as a source of a new wavelet and the new wavefront is the forward envelope of the set of new wavelets.**

Figure 14-3 shows Huygens' principle applied to wavefronts moving outward from a point source and travelling at a constant speed in all directions. In three dimensions, the wavefronts would be spherical, but in the two-dimensional diagram shown here, the wavefronts are circular. Consider several points along the wavefront AB. Each point acts as if it is the source of a new wavelet, and each wavelet advances the same distance in the same time. The wavelets overlap and, for the most part, cancel each other out except along the leading edge. Thus, the leading edges of all the new wavelets join together to form an envelope, which is tangent to the wavelets. This envelope is the new wavefront, CD. Similarly, points on CD act as sources of new wavelets, causing the next new wavefront, EF, and so on. Far away from the point source of waves, the wavefronts become relatively flat, producing plane or straight wavefronts.

(a) *This type of diffraction pattern is produced when light passes by the sharp edge of a razor blade.*

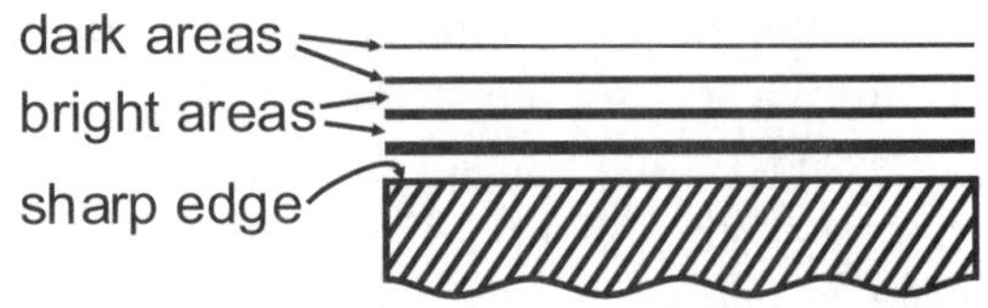

(b) *This pattern is produced when light passes through a tiny aperture.*

Figure 14-2 *Diffraction patterns.*

Did You Know? *Christian Huygens (pronounced hoi' guns) lived at a time when emperors and kings hired scientists to enhance the image of their court. Huygens worked in the French court of King Louis XIV, and his career was noted for several inventions and discoveries. Based on Galileo's discovery of the regular period of a pendulum, Huygens was first to build an accurate pendulum clock. In 1673, he proposed that a standard unit of length be based on the length of a pendulum that has a period of exactly 2.0 s. (This length is about the same as 1.0 m.) He was first to define centrifugal force, and, using telescopes of his own design, he discovered the rings of Saturn. Today he is remembered mostly for his work on wave optics.*

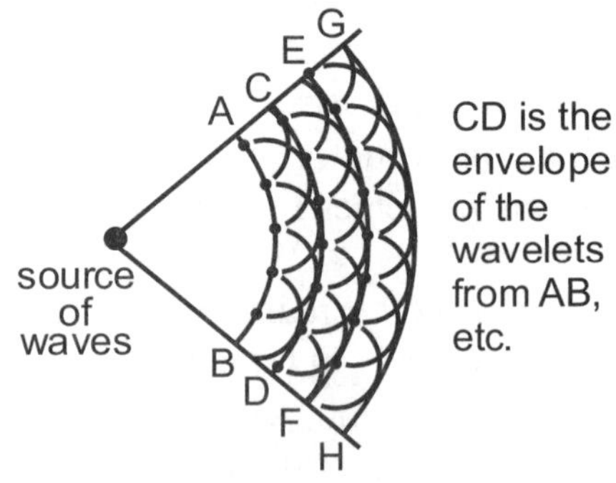

Figure 14-3 *Applying Huygens' principle to wavefronts from a point source.*

Let us now apply Huygens' principle to plane waves passing by the sharp edge of a barrier. As shown in Figure 14-4, the wavelets right at the edge do not have other wavelets to cancel them out, so the result is a bending effect around the edge of the barrier. This bending effect is what we observe as diffraction.

In order to explain the light and dark regions in the diffraction patterns shown in Figure 14-2, we must look more closely at how the wavelets in Figure 14-4 interfere to cause the more complex pattern. This will be explored further in the quantitative analysis of the diffraction of light through a narrow aperture (Section 14.3).

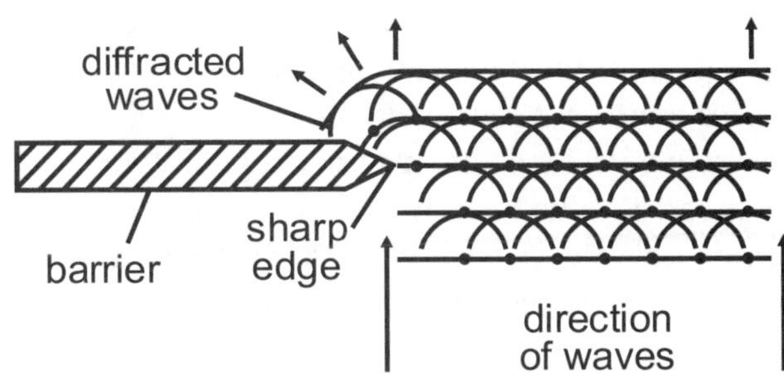

Figure 14-4 *Applying Huygens' principle to plane waves passing a sharp edge.*

Huygens' principle is helpful in trying to find an explanation for the diffraction and interference of light. It can also be applied to the reflection, refraction, and dispersion of light, although we will omit the details here. Huygens was a contemporary of Isaac Newton, but Newton had difficulty accepting the theory of wavelets, especially in trying to explain the straight line motion of light. Newton was aware of Grimaldi's discovery of diffraction, but suggested that if light acted truly like a wave, it would diffract much more than was observed, something like sound waves around corners or through open windows. Neither Newton nor Huygens realized just how small the wavelengths of visible light were. Thus, Newton favoured the particle model of light, and his followers stubbornly adhered to this model, until a very important discovery, discussed in the next section, was made.

Practice

<u>**14-1**</u> Under what condition(s) will the diffraction of Huygens' wavelets be maximum as the waves pass (a) around a barrier and (b) through an aperture? (Note: These concepts were presented for water waves in Section 13.4.)

<u>**14-2**</u> Why do we not observe the diffraction of light through a window?

<u>**14-3**</u> Like visible light, radio waves are part of the electromagnetic spectrum, which means they should display wave properties. Speculate on why radio waves diffract easily around most objects in our daily experience.

14-4 Draw a diagram applying Huygens' principle in each case.
(a) Waves of wavelength 1.5 cm are passing by a thin barrier that is 1.5 cm wide.
(b) Waves of wavelength 1.0 cm are passing through an aperture that is 1.0 cm wide.

14.2 DOUBLE-SLIT INTERFERENCE OF LIGHT

Interference is an important wave property, so if light has a wave nature, we should expect it to display interference patterns. (Interference of waves was described in Section 13.3.) However, if you look around yourself, the chances are extremely slight that you will notice any interference of light. For example, imagine that you and a friend are looking at two different light sources in a room such that light from the sources must cross in order to reach your eyes. As illustrated in Figure 14-5, the paths of light may cross, but, as you know from experience, there is no observed interference; the light reaches your eyes completely undisturbed.

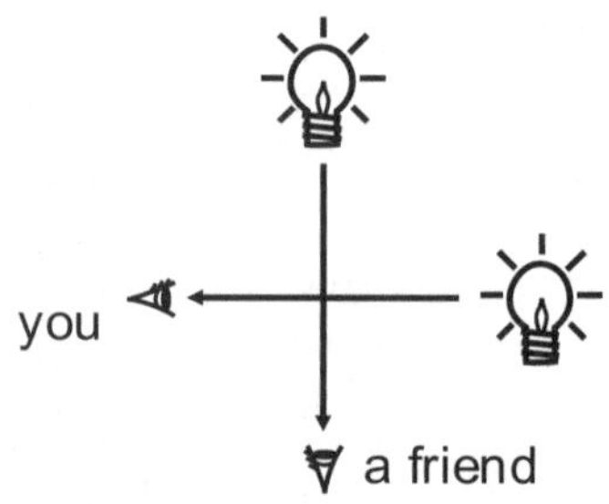

Figure 14-5 *Although the paths of light cross, the observers see no effects of interference.*

Despite this, it is very simple nowadays to set up a demonstration of light interference. One way is to pass a laser beam through a set of two narrow slits separated by a tiny distance and observe the resulting interference pattern on a screen. The set-up to view this "double-slit interference pattern" is illustrated in Figure 14-6 (a), and the resulting pattern of bright and dark regions, called fringes, is shown in (b).

Another technique for observing a double-slit interference pattern is to hold an opaque plate with two fine slits etched on it in front of one eye, and look at an incandescent light source that has a straight filament. The slits and the filament should be parallel for maximum effect, as shown in Figure 14-7 on page 14-5. This time, the pattern has a bright fringe in the centre and to the sides bright fringes of spectral colours separated by dark fringes. The bright fringes are called maxima and the dark fringes are called minima.

The pattern described here is called *Young's double-slit interference pattern,* named after Thomas Young (1773-1829), an English physician and physicist who first observed the pattern. Young discovered the interference of light more than 70 years before the incandescent light bulb was invented, so how did he set up his experiment? The answer provides an important clue about why the pattern can be observed only under very special circumstances.

(a) *A laser beam passing through two close narrow slits produces an interference pattern on a screen.*

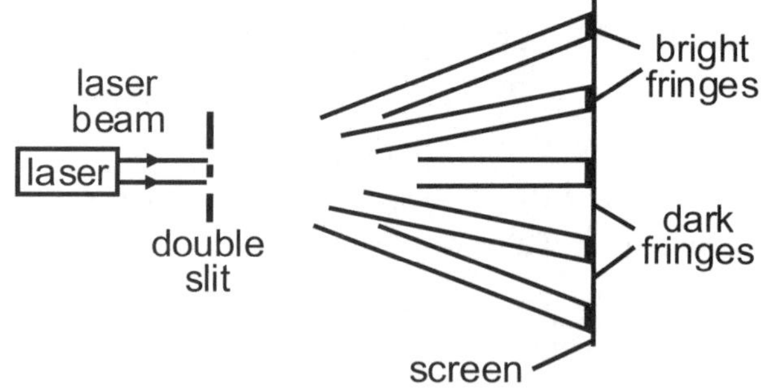

(b) *The double-slit interference pattern using laser light, as seen on the screen.*

Figure 14-6 *Viewing a double-slit interference pattern.*

Young's Experiment

Between the years 1801 and 1807, Young performed and reported on experiments in which he allowed sunlight to pass through a tiny pinhole that was in line with a set of two other pinholes that were extremely close together. Behind the double pinhole, he placed a screen on which he observed what occurred. If the light had been able to pass through the pinholes and continue in a straight line the way particles would be assumed to travel, the pattern on the screen would have been simply two bright spots. However, the pattern he observed was an interference pattern, as illustrated in Figure 14-8. As you can see, this pattern closely resembles the one observed when two parallel slits are used, although the fringes created by holes are curved rather than straight.

(a) *The set-up.*

(b) *This pattern has a white central maximum and other fringes with spectral colours.*

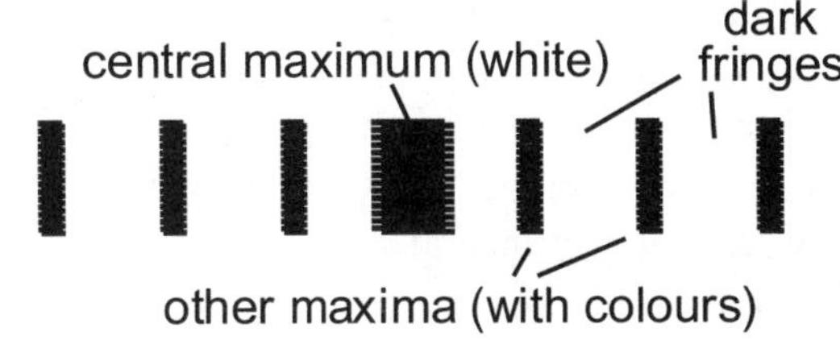

Figure 14-7 *Using a straight filament to view a double-slit interference pattern.*

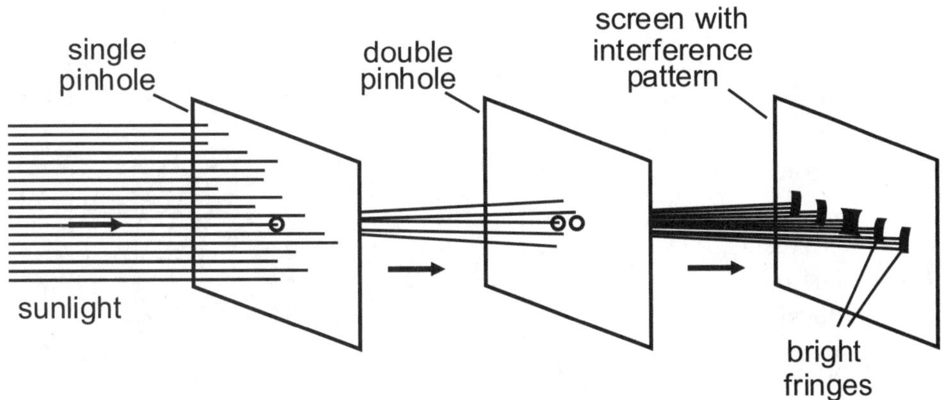

Figure 14-8 *Young's double-pinhole interference experiment.*

PROFILE: Thomas Young (1773-1829)

From the start of his life, Thomas Young's achievements were most impressive. At age 2, he was able to read, and by 4, he had read the Bible cover to cover twice. By age 14, he had learned eight languages, including the classical Latin and Greek, as well as Turkish, Hebrew, Persian, and Arabic. In university, he studied medicine, but he was able to devote much of his life to scientific research thanks to the financial security provided by an inheritance from an uncle.

Among his many scientific achievements are discoveries related to human vision. He discovered how the eye is able to focus on objects at different distances, the process called accommodation; he discovered the cause of the visual defect called astigmatism; and he proposed the theory of colour vision based on three types of receptors sensitive to red, green, and blue light. It was his study of human vision combined with his interest in the human voice that led to his experiment with the interference of light.

Young also researched the topics of heat, fluids, and mechanics. His discoveries regarding the elastic properties of materials are still recognized in the constant called Young's modulus, which is a characteristic property of materials, also known as the elastic modulus.

Young's interests went much beyond pure scientific research. He also found time to study Egyptian history, and he was among the first to decipher Egyptian hieroglyphics.

Young's discovery of the wave property of light, known as interference, was not immediately accepted in England, the country where Newton and his followers preferred the particle model. However, in continental Europe, especially in France, his work was soon hailed as an important turning point in the theory of light.

To explain the creation of a double-slit interference pattern in terms of waves, consider Figure 14-9 (a). Light from a distant source (the sun, for example) passes through the first slit, and Huygens' wavelets spread out from that slit toward the next slits. When these wavelets arrive at the two slits, they have a phase that will be maintained as they pass through the slits. Thus, beyond the slits, there are now two new sets of Huygens' wavelets that have the same phase relationship and thus can interfere with each other. From here on, the pattern resembles the two-source interference pattern observed in water (Section 13.3, especially Figure 13-27), with maxima (the bright fringes) and minima or nodal lines (the dark fringes). Figure 14-9 (b) shows the pattern observed on the screen with the same labels for maxima (M = 0, 1, 2, 3, . . .) and minima (N = 1, 2, 3, . . .) used in the two-source interference pattern.

(a) *Circular wavelets originate at each slit. After the double slit, the wavelets interfere to produce maxima where the crests from one slit meet the crests from the other slit (the dots) and minima between the maxima. The pattern resembles a two-source interference pattern of waves.*

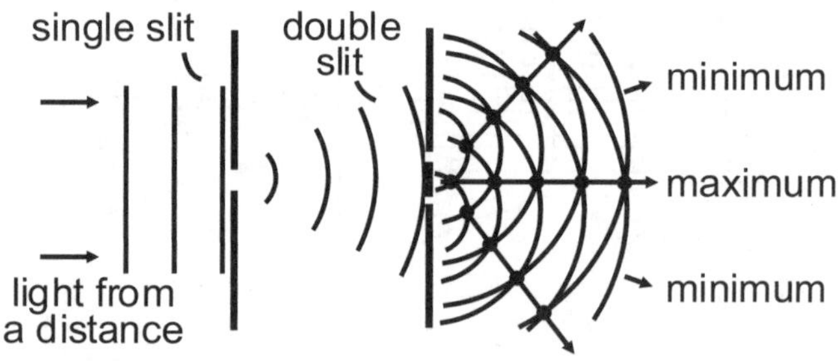

(b) *The interference pattern observed on a screen with maxima (M) and minima (N) labelled.*

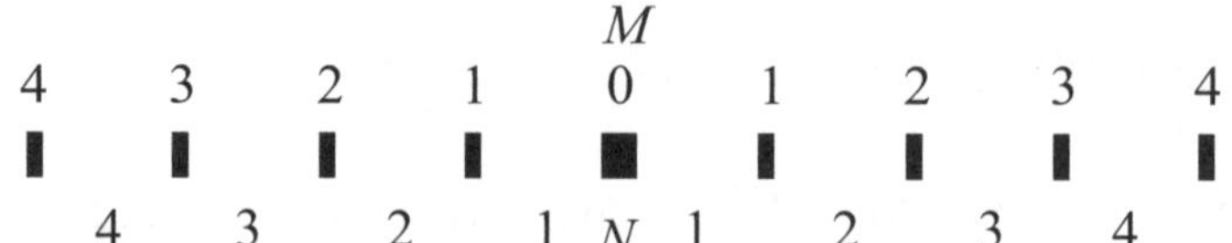

Figure 14-9 *Using Huygens' wavelets to explain a double-slit interference pattern.*

Coherence of Light

We are now able to explain why the interference of light is normally not observed. When a two-source interference pattern is set up in water in a ripple tank, the two sources have the same frequency and thus the same wavelength. Furthermore, they maintain the same phase relationship, which means that if they start out in phase they remain in phase, or if they start out 180° out of phase they remain that way. Waves that maintain their phase relationship and have the same wavelength are called **coherent waves**. All other waves are incoherent, and if incoherent waves are observed in water, there will be no distinguishable or constant pattern (Figure 14-10).

(a) *Sources S_1 and S_2 are producing coherent light.*

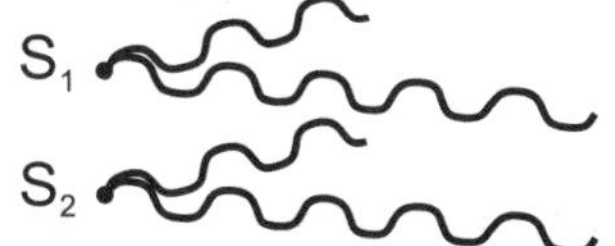

(b) *Sources S_3 and S_4 are producing incoherent light.*

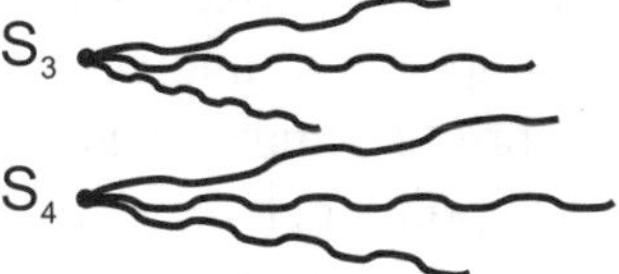

Figure 14-10 *Comparing coherent and incoherent light sources.*

All of the interference patterns described in this section result from coherent light sources. Thomas Young achieved coherent light by passing light through a single pinhole. A double slit parallel to the straight filament of an incandescent lamp achieves the same results. And the unique light from a laser is coherent, a feature that makes laser light extremely useful.

Light from ordinary sources, such as flames or light bulbs, is produced by the trillions of atoms and/or molecules that make up the source. The emission of light waves from such sources lasts for tiny fractions of a second and there are so many millions of emissions per second that there is no way such light could be coherent. Thus, we normally do not observe the interference effects of light.

Measuring the Wavelengths of Visible Light

Quantitative analysis of a two-source interference pattern of water waves applies to light waves in a double-slit interference pattern. Thus, equations 13-6 and 13-7 derived in Section 13.3 can be used to determine the wavelength(s) of the light causing the interference pattern. Let us review the interference pattern equations and the meanings of the symbols as they apply to light. Sources S_1 and S_2 are replaced by slits S_1 and S_2, separated by a distance d, and the waves passing through the slits have a wavelength λ. If the waves are in phase as they pass through the slits, the path difference that results in a *maximum* interference where a crest meets a crest or a trough meets a trough is given by:

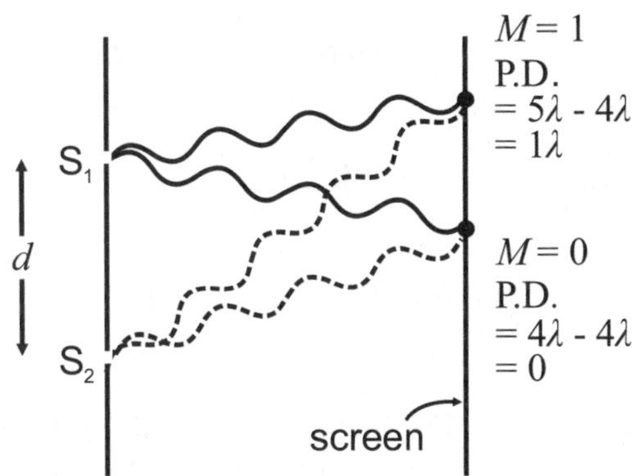

Figure 14-11 *For in-phase waves passing through S_1 and S_2 the path difference that produces a maximum is $M\lambda$.*

$$\text{P.D.} = M\lambda \quad \text{where } M = 0, 1, 2, 3, \ldots \qquad \textbf{(14-1)}$$

The maximum $M = 0$ is the central maximum, and it occurs along a line that is perpendicular to the line joining S_1 and S_2. Examples of maximum interference are illustrated in Figure 14-11.

Similarly, it could be shown that a *minimum* or *node* occurs when the path difference is:

$$\text{P.D.} = \left(N - \tfrac{1}{2}\right)\lambda \quad \text{where } N = 1, 2, 3, \ldots \qquad \textbf{(14-2)}$$

Next, consider Figure 14-12, which reviews the other variables involving a double-slit interference pattern. The distance x is the perpendicular distance from the central maximum to either a minimum or another maximum (a dark fringe or a bright fringe), and L is the distance from the midpoint between S_1 and S_2 and the same minimum or maximum. In actual experiments, L is essentially equal to L' in the diagram, where L' is simply the distance from the slits to the screen. This approximation is valid because L' and L are greater than d by a factor of at least 10 000 times and angle θ is very small. The approximations used in deriving the two-source interference pattern equations (in Section 13.3) are insignificant because of this large ratio. For example, the angles θ and θ' are essentially equal. Thus, the following equations apply to a double-slit interference pattern with in-phase light waves.[1]

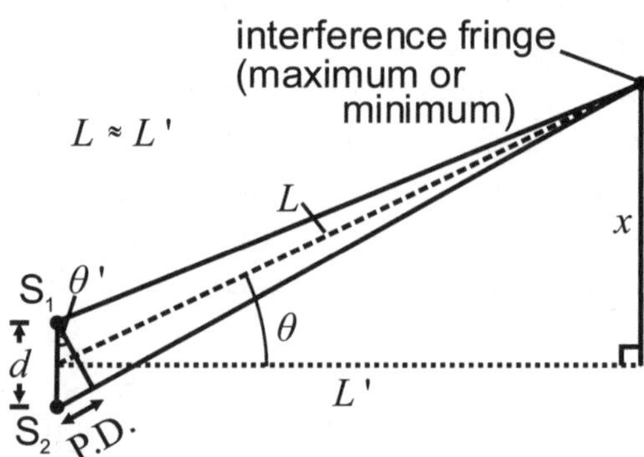

Figure 14-12 *Variables in a double-slit interference pattern. (In an actual experiment, θ is much smaller than is shown here.)*

For maxima or bright fringes:

$$\sin\theta = \frac{M\lambda}{d}; \ \sin\theta = \frac{x}{L}; \ \frac{x}{L} = \frac{M\lambda}{d} \quad \text{where } M = 0, 1, 2, \ldots \qquad \textbf{(14-3a,b,c)}$$

For minima or dark fringes:

$$\sin\theta = \frac{\left(N - \tfrac{1}{2}\right)\lambda}{d}; \quad \sin\theta = \frac{x}{L}; \ \frac{x}{L} = \frac{\left(N - \tfrac{1}{2}\right)\lambda}{d} \quad \text{where } N = 1, 2, 3, \ldots \qquad \textbf{(14-4a,b,c)}$$

In Sample Problem 14-1, we apply these concepts to see how Thomas Young succeeded in being the first person to measure the wavelengths of visible light. As you will discover, the wavelengths of visible light range from approximately 4×10^{-7} m to about 7×10^{-7} m. In most cases, we will convert these wavelengths to nanometres (1.0 nm = 1.0×10^{-9} m), so the range of wavelengths is from approximately 400 nm to about 700 nm.

---

[1] These equations are simply equations 13-8, 13-9, 13-10, and 13-11, but now applied to light waves.

Sample Problem 14-1

Light passing through a double slit produces an interference pattern on a screen located 1.80 m from the slits. The slits are separated by a distance of 0.20 mm, and the distance from the middle of the central maximum to the middle of the first bright fringe is 5.1 mm (Figure 14-13). Determine the wavelength of the waves producing this part of the fringe. (This wavelength is the average wavelength of white light, as found originally by Young.)

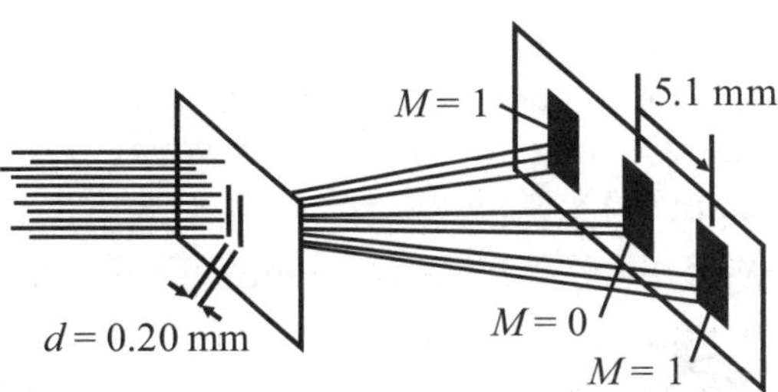

Figure 14-13 *Sample Problem 14-1.*

Solution:

From $\frac{x}{L} = \frac{M\lambda}{d}$, $\lambda = \frac{xd}{ML}$

$$= \frac{5.1\text{ mm} \times 0.20\text{ mm}}{1 \times 1.80\text{ m}}$$

$$= \frac{5.1 \times 10^{-3}\text{ m} \times 2.0 \times 10^{-4}\text{ m}}{1.80\text{ m}}$$

$$= 5.7 \times 10^{-7}\text{ m}$$

Therefore, the average wavelength of the white light is 5.7×10^{-7} m or 570 nm.

Young's value of 570 nm for the average wavelength of white light is relatively close to the currently accepted value of 555 nm. From the observations found in the double-slit interference pattern, it is obvious that different colours of light have different wavelengths. Since x is directly proportional to λ and x is smaller for colours at the violet end of the spectrum, we conclude that violet light has short wavelengths (in the region of 400 nm) and red light has longer wavelengths (in the region of 700 nm). The wavelength ranges of the colours of the visible spectrum are given in Table 14.1.

Table 14.1 Wavelengths of the Colours of the Visible Spectrum

Colour	Range of Wavelengths (nm)	
violet	400 to 450	all values are approximate
blue	450 to 500	
green	500 to 570	
yellow	570 to 590	
orange	590 to 610	
red	610 to 700	

It would take about 100 waves of visible light to equal the thickness of a human hair. Considering such short wavelengths, it is little wonder that early scientists had difficulty in finding evidence of the wave nature of light. Shortly after Young's discovery of the interference effects of light and his measurements of the wavelengths of light, however, scientists who had favoured the particle model of light began to agree with scientists who favoured the wave model. But Young's discovery did not provide all the answers. Like so many other discoveries, it presented more questions: for example, if light is a wave, does it require a medium through which to travel, and is it a transverse or longitudinal wave? We will explore these questions later in the chapter. Then in Chapter 15 we will explore the particle nature of light, which was discovered approximately 100 years after the double-slit experiments were first performed.

Practice

14-5 State how the first variable depends on the second variable:
(a) the *spacing* of the minima and maxima of a double-slit interference pattern and the *wavelength* of the waves producing the pattern.
(b) the *spacing* of the minima and maxima and the *distance* from the slits to the screen
(c) the *angle of separation* of the minima and maxima and the *slit separation*

14-6 Determine the unknown quantity in each case:
(a) P.D. = 2.43×10^{-6} m; $N = 5$; $\lambda = ?$
(b) $L = 2.9$ m; $M = 4$; $\lambda = 5.65 \times 10^{-7}$ m; $d = 2.1 \times 10^{-4}$ m; $x = ?$
(c) $L = 4.55$ m; $N = 3$; $\lambda = 475$ nm; $d = 1.90 \times 10^{-4}$ m; $x = ?$
(d) $L = 3.50$ m; $M = 7$; $d = 2.00 \times 10^{-4}$ m; $x = 5.64$ cm; $\lambda = ?$
(e) $L = 3.85$ m; $x = 3.43$ cm; $\lambda = 547$ nm; $d = 0.215$ mm; $N = ?$
[Ans. (a) 5.4×10^{-7} m (b) 3.1×10^{-2} m (c) 2.84×10^{-2} m (d) 4.60×10^{-7} m (e) 4]

14-7 Light from a sodium lamp is used to produce a double-slit interference pattern on a screen 2.45 m from the slits. The fifth bright line of a certain part of the sodium spectrum is located 3.00 cm to one side of the central maximum. The slit separation is 2.40×10^{-4} m. Determine:
(a) the angle of separation between the central maximum and the bright line
(b) the wavelength of the light
(c) the colour of the light (Reference: Table 14-1) [Ans. (a) 0.702° (b) 588 nm]

14-8 White light passing through two slits separated by 0.180 mm produces an interference pattern on a screen 4.00 m away. Determine the width of the spectrum from violet (400 nm) to red (700 nm) for the third maximum to one side of the central maximum. [Ans. 2.00 cm]

14-9 (a) Derive an equation for the distance between maxima (Δx) in a double-slit interference pattern in terms of L, d, and λ.
(b) In an interference pattern produced by light of wavelength 660 nm passing through a double-slit of separation 0.21 mm, there are 6 maxima in 9.5 cm. Determine the distance between the double slit and the screen. [Ans. 6.0 m]

14-10 A laser beam with light of wavelength 638.2 nm is used to check a manufacturer's claim that a double slit has a separation of 0.200 mm. The distance to the screen is 3.00 m and the measured distance from the central maximum to the middle of the fourth minimum is 33.2 mm. What is the measured slit separation? [Ans. 0.202 mm]

14.3 SINGLE-SLIT DIFFRACTION AND RESOLUTION

In the double-slit interference of light, each slit causes waves to diffract outward as if originating from a point source of circular waves. In order to have a large amount of diffraction, the width of each slit, w, must be approximately equal to or less than the wavelength of the diffracting waves. Another way of saying this is $\lambda/w \geq 1$ or $\lambda \geq w$. In this section, we consider a different example of diffraction, namely, the diffraction that occurs when light passes through a single slit whose width is much larger than the wavelength of the light; i.e., $\lambda/w << 1$ or $\lambda << w$. Although the width is much larger than the wavelength, it is still very small in terms of everyday measurements. For example, a slit of width 0.025 mm, which is less than the diameter of a human hair, is still about 50 times larger than the average wavelength of visible light.

A Qualitative Look at Single-Slit Diffraction

Figure 14-14 shows several features related to single-slit diffraction. In (a), the pattern on the

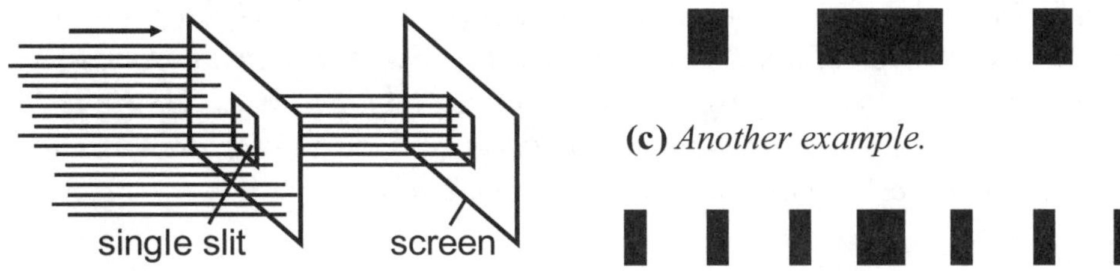

(a) Without diffraction, the image on the screen would look like the slit.
(b) One example of a single-slit diffraction pattern.
(c) Another example.
single slit
screen

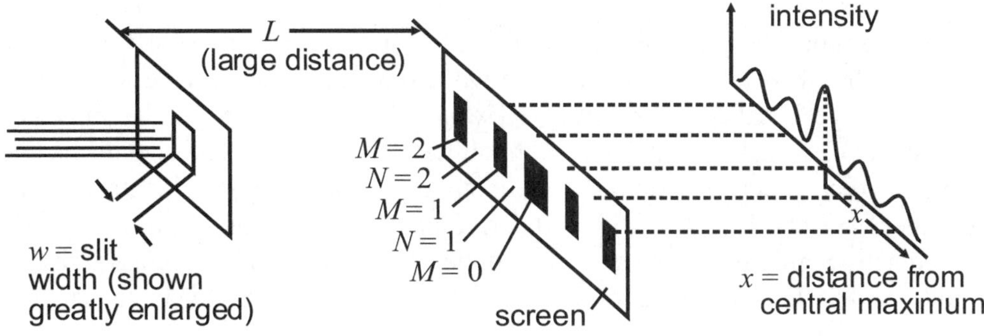

Figure 14-14 *Single-slit diffraction patterns.*

screen shows what we would expect to see if light travelled in a straight line through the slit, without experiencing diffraction. The illustrations in (b) and (c) show what actually happens when monochromatic (single colour) light diffracts through a single slit. A bright central maximum is surrounded by dark fringes, followed by alternating bright and dark fringes. Can you judge which of these two patterns was produced by the narrower slit? The diagram in (d) shows how the pattern corresponds to a graph of the intensity of the pattern as a function of the distance from the middle of the central maximum. It also illustrates some of the terminology associated with single-slit diffraction. Refer also to Figure 13-36, which shows the diffraction of water waves through a single aperture. By comparing the illustrations of diffraction through a single slit, it is evident that diffraction supports the wave theory of fight.

Notice in Figure 14-14 (d) that the distance between the single slit and the screen is large. This means that the paths of the light wavelets that produce the central maximum are parallel (or nearly parallel) to each other. This parallelism can also be achieved by using a converging lens between the slit and the screen if the screen is closer. In either case, the type of diffraction in which the paths of the light wavelets are parallel is called *Fraunhofer diffraction.* It is named after the first person who explained the pattern, Josef Fraunhofer (1787-1826), a German optician. It is this type of diffraction that we will analyze mathematically. (The other common type of diffraction, called *Fresnel diffraction*, occurs when the path of the light wavelets between the lens or slit and the screen or observer are not parallel. Fresnel diffraction is named after Augustin Fresnel, 1788-1827, a French physicist. Fresnel diffraction is much more complex mathematically than Fraunhofer diffraction.)

Did You Know? *Have you ever inspected the flat surface of an overhead projector? In many such projectors is a type of flat lens known as a Fresnel lens, which is composed of a transparent material with concentric stepped zones molded into it. The same type of lens is available commercially at low prices, and is sometimes seen on side or back windows of vans. The operation of a Fresnel lens is based on Fresnel diffraction.*

Quantitative Analysis of a Single-Slit Diffraction Pattern

A convenient way to analyze a single-slit diffraction pattern is to apply Huygens' principle to the light striking the slit. Consider a wavefront of monochromatic light just entering a slit of width w, as shown in Figure 14-15 (a) on page 14-13. The wavefront can be replaced with a series of sources of new wavelets, all of which are in phase, as in (b). We will number these "Huygens' sources" from 1 to 8 (although any convenient number of sources may be used). If we follow the wavelets near the middle of the slit, we see that the wavefronts at the screen are at a maximum. The resulting bright fringe is called the *central maximum.* Next, consider the diagram in (c) in which a path of the wavelets makes an angle θ to the initial path of light. The size of the angle is such that the path difference between source 4 and source 8 is half the wavelength of the light. This means that the wavelets from 4 and 8 will arrive at the screen out of phase, resulting in destructive interference. Similarly, wavelets 3 and 7 undergo destructive interference at the screen, as do 2 and 6, and 1 and 5. In this way, all of the wavelets from one half of the slit cancel all of the wavelets from the other half, producing a node or minimum fringe at the location shown.

Now the angles labelled θ in the diagram (c) are equal, and from the small triangle near the slit,

$$\sin\theta = \frac{\text{P.D.}}{w/2}$$

But P.D. $= \lambda/2$, so

$$\sin\theta = \frac{\lambda/2}{w/2}$$

or $\sin\theta = \lambda/w$ for the first minimum fringe (for which $N = 1$) in a single-slit diffraction pattern.

From this equation, we can see that $\sin\theta$, and thus θ, increases as the wavelength increases and increases as the width decreases. Therefore, as the wavelength becomes longer or the slit becomes narrower, the diffraction pattern spreads out more.

(a) *Monochromatic light enters a single slit.*

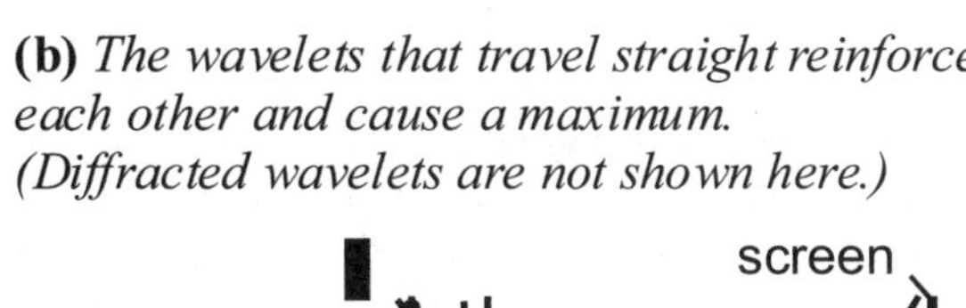

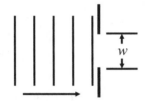

(c) *The first minimum fringe, N = 1, occurs when pairs of wavelet sources separated by w/2 have a path difference of λ/2 and thus cancel. In actual situations, L is much larger than x or w.*

(b) *The wavelets that travel straight reinforce each other and cause a maximum. (Diffracted wavelets are not shown here.)*

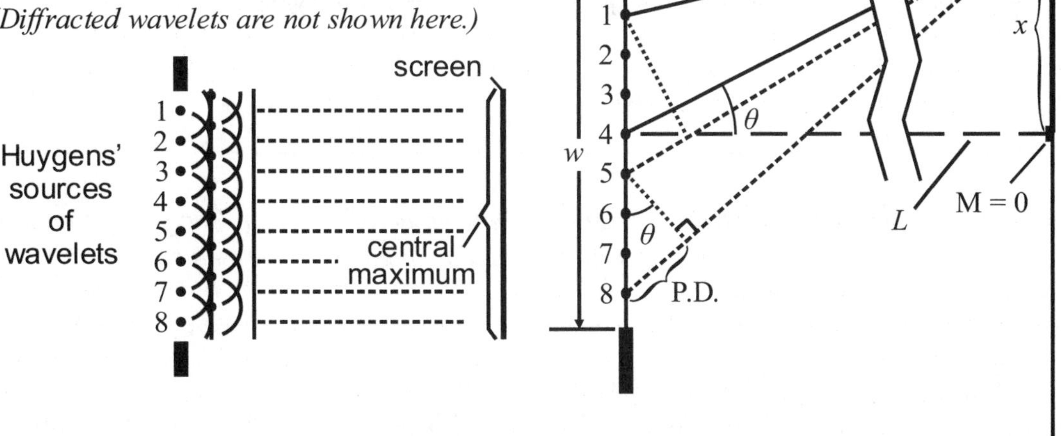

Figure 14-15 *Using Huygens' wavelets to explain single-slit diffraction.*

To locate the next node or minimum fringe in terms of the angle θ, let us split the eight Huygens' sources into four sets of two. As illustrated in Figure 14-16, 1 and 3 have a path difference of $\lambda/2$ and thus cancel; likewise, cancellation occurs for sources 2 and 4, 5 and 7, and 6 and 8. Thus,

$$\sin\theta = \frac{\text{P.D.}}{w/4}$$

$$\sin\theta = \frac{\lambda/2}{w/4}$$

$$\text{or}\quad \sin\theta = \frac{2\lambda}{w} \quad \textit{for}\ \text{N} = 2$$

The second minimum fringe, N = 2, occurs when pairs of wavelet souces separated by w/4 have a path difference of λ/2 and thus cancel. Again, L should be much larger than the diagram shows.

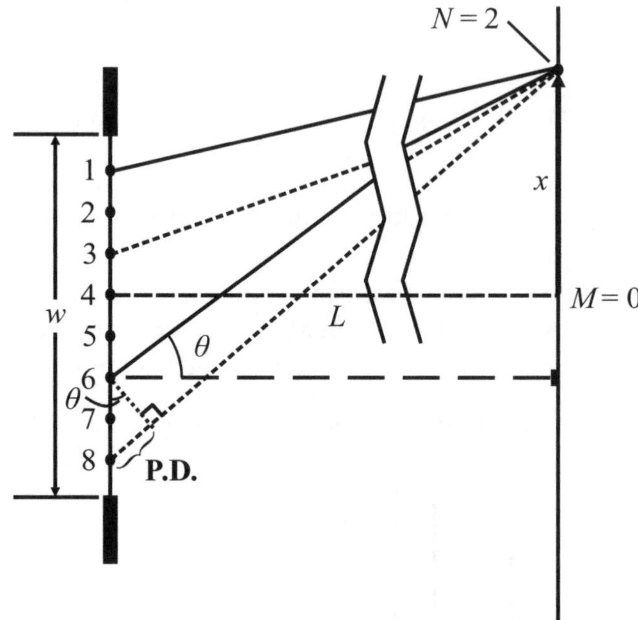

Figure 14-16 *Locating the second node or minimum fringe.*

To locate the node $N = 3$, we can divide the wavefront at the slit into six sets of sources such that the destructive interference occurs at the screen. In this case, $\sin\theta = 3\lambda/w$. Thus, in general, the minimum fringes of a single-slit diffraction pattern occur when

$$\sin\theta = \frac{N\lambda}{w} \qquad \textbf{(14-5)}$$

where $N = 1, 2, 3, \ldots$

Finally, in Figure 14-16, we see that if x is the distance from the middle of the central maximum to a minimum fringe and L is the distance from the slit to the screen, then $\tan\theta = x/L$. But $L >> x$, so $\tan\theta = \sin\theta$. Thus, the following relationship applies to the *minimum fringes* in a single-slit diffraction pattern.

$$\frac{x}{L} = \frac{N\lambda}{w} \quad \text{where } N = 1, 2, 3, \ldots \qquad \textbf{(14-6)}$$

Math Tip *For very small angles, tan θ and sin θ are essentially equal. Use your calculator to verify this fact, then draw a sketch of a right-angled triangle with one small angle to help you visualize why the equality exists.*

Notice that we have derived an equation (14-6) for minima but not for maxima in a single-slit diffraction pattern. Experimentally, the minima are dark, narrow bands that are quite obvious. However, the maxima are relatively bright and wide. In each of these wide regions there is a point where the intensity is maximum, but it is not in the centre of the region, and the mathematics to determine the position of each maximum is complicated.

Sample Problem 14-2

Monochromatic light of wavelength 570 nm is aimed at a single slit that is 0.15 mm wide.

(a) Determine the width of the central maximum on a screen located 3.2 m away from the slit.
(b) Determine the angle at which the third minimum fringe occurs.

Solution: (a) The width of the central maximum can be determined by calculating twice the position of the first minimum. From $\frac{x}{L} = \frac{N\lambda}{w}$,

$$x = \frac{LN\lambda}{w} = \frac{(3.2\text{ m})(1)(5.7\times10^{-7}\text{ m})}{1.5\times10^{-4}\text{ m}} = 1.2\times10^{-2}\text{ m}$$

But the width is double this value, or 2.4 cm.

(b)
$$\sin\theta = \frac{N\lambda}{w} = \frac{(3)(5.7\times10^{-7}\text{ m})}{1.5\times10^{-4}\text{ m}} = 0.0114$$
$$\therefore\quad \theta = \sin^{-1}(0.0114) = 0.65^\circ$$

Thus, the third minimum fringe occurs at an angle of 0.65°.

In the derivation of the equations involving single-slit diffraction, it was observed that the wavelets of light experienced interference. Diffraction and interference both result from the superposition of waves, but they are somewhat different properties of waves. However, when waves pass through apertures or around obstacles, both interference and diffraction occur simultaneously. In fact, a discussion of the *double-slit* interference pattern is more complete if it includes diffraction effects through each of the two slits. Figure 14-17 illustrates how diffraction affects the pattern observed in double-slit interference of monochromatic light.

(a) *Without diffraction the intensity of each maximum in the double-slit pattern would remain constant.*

(b) *Each slit produces a diffraction pattern with this intensity.*

(c) *The actual double-slit pattern is a combination of interference and diffraction.*

Figure 14-17 *The intensity of the maxima in a double-slit interference pattern is affected by the diffraction of light through the individual slits.*

Resolution

Imagine seeing a car with its headlights on approaching from a long distance away on an otherwise dark highway. From a far distance, the two headlights appear to be a single light source; they do not appear as separate or "resolved" objects. At some much closer distance, they begin to appear to be separate light sources, and at closer distances, the sources are totally resolved. **Resolution** is the ability to distinguish two or more objects as separate entities (Figure 14-18).

Resolution refers not only to emitted light from sources, but also reflected light from opaque objects. Consider, for example, some of the paintings of the French Impressionist movement. An artist brushed dabs of paint onto a canvas so that, from a close distance, the dabs appeared separate from each other; in other words, they were resolved. However, from a few metres or more away, depending on the separation of the dabs of paint, the dabs are not resolved, and an impression of a continuous colour pattern is seen.

It is evident from the examples of the headlights and art that resolution decreases as the distance to the objects increases, and increases as the separation of the objects increases. However, resolution also depends on the diffraction of light. To see why, consider two identical monochromatic light sources, S_1 and S_2, whose light passes through a single slit and produces a diffraction pattern on a screen. As shown in Figure 14-19 (a), the diffraction pattern of one source slightly overlaps the diffraction pattern of the other source, making it just barely possible to resolve the sources. Then, as the slit width decreases, the pattern spreads out more and the resolution decreases. Thus, as diffraction increases, resolution decreases. (Resolution also depends on the wavelength of the light. Can you tell how?)

(a) *At a large distance, the two lights are unresolved, so they appear as one.*

(b) *At some closer distance, the two lights are just resolved.*

(c) *At an even closer distance, the two lights are distinctly separate.*

Figure 14-18 *Resolving two headlights.*

(a) *S_1 and S_2 can just be reolved at the screen where the central maxima barely meet.*

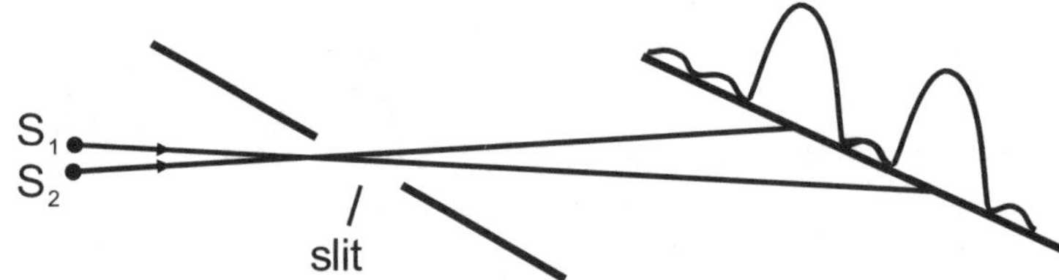

(b) *With a narrower slit, the diffraction is greater and S_1 and S_2 cannot be resolved at the screen because the central maxima overlap.*

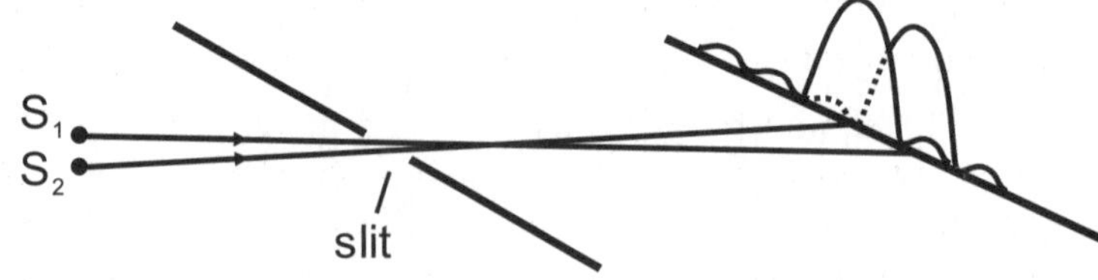

Figure 14-19 *Observing how resolution depends on diffraction: The diagrams illustrate the intensity of the diffraction patterns.*

Any two observers may find it difficult to decide when two sources appear to be resolved. To overcome this problem, a formal rule has been defined for determining resolution through a single slit. This rule, known as *Rayleigh's criterion*, states:

For light passing through a single slit, two sources are just resolved if the first minimum of the diffraction pattern of one source is in line with the middle of the central maximum of the other source.

For monochromatic light of wavelength λ, the minimum angular separation of the central maxima that allows resolution of the sources is equal to the angle that the two sources subtend with the slit, as shown in Figure 14-20. Thus,

$$\sin\theta = \frac{\lambda}{w} = \frac{x'}{L'} = \frac{x}{L} \qquad \textbf{(14-7)}$$

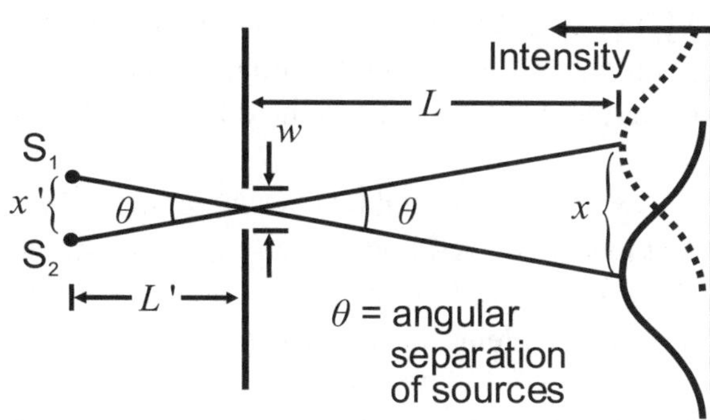

Figure 14-20 *Rayleigh's criterion and angular separation: S_1 and S_2 are just resolved if the first minimum of one source coincides with the middle of the central maximum of the other source. Therefore, $\sin\theta = \lambda/w$.*

Sample Problem 14-3

Two laser beams, both having a wavelength of 620 nm, are aimed toward a single slit that is 3.2 m away. If the laser beams are 4.4 cm apart at the sources, how wide must the slit be to just resolve the beams?

Solution: The criterion is $\sin\theta = \dfrac{\lambda}{w} = \dfrac{x'}{L'}$

$$\therefore \quad w = \frac{L'\lambda}{x'} = \frac{(3.2\ \text{m})(6.2\times10^{-7}\ \text{m})}{4.4\times10^{-2}\ \text{m}} = 4.5\times10^{-5}\ \text{m} \quad \text{or} \quad 0.045\ \text{m}$$

Thus, the slit must be 0.045 mm wide.

The diffraction of light is an important factor in determining how well our eyes can resolve objects as well as the limitations of such devices as microscopes and telescopes. These optical devices have circular apertures, and the criterion for the minimum angular separation of two sources to allow resolution is somewhat different than for a single slit.

Did You Know? *Rayleigh's criterion is named in honour of Lord J.W.S. Rayleigh, an English physicist (1842-1919), who was one of the first people to be awarded the Nobel Prize in physics. The year of the prize was 1904.*

Practice

14-11 Why is it said that a single-slit pattern results from both diffraction and interference?

14-12 A single narrow slit is obtained by supporting two razor blades so their edges are close and parallel. A laser beam is aimed through the slit, and the width of the slit is slowly made smaller. Describe what happens to the diffraction pattern observed.

14-13 For violet light of wavelength 420 nm, what is the angle between the initial path of light and the first nodal line of a single-slit diffraction pattern when the slit width is 350 times as large as the wavelength? Would your answer change if the only changes in the question were the colour and its wavelength? [Ans. 0.16°]

14-14 Monochromatic light passes through a single slit of width 0.085 mm, and produces a diffraction pattern on a screen located 2.4 m from the slit. Determine the distance between the $N = 2$ minima if the wavelength of the light is (a) 650 nm (b) 450 nm. [Ans. 7.3 cm; 5.1 cm]

14-15 The slit in the previous question is adjustable. How wide must it become to have a central maximum that is 22 mm wide with light of wavelength 450 nm? (Assume all other quantities remain constant.) [Ans. 0.098 mm]

14-16 State the relationship, if any, that exists between the resolution of two objects seen through a single slit and (a) the separation of the objects, (b) the distance from the objects, (c) the slit width, and (d) the wavelength of the light.

14-17 Two red light point sources (λ = 670 nm) subtend an angle of 0.32° with the centre of a single slit. The sources are 6.4 cm apart and the screen is 1.8 m from the slit.
(a) How wide is the slit?
(b) How far are the light sources from the slit?
(c) What is the distance between the two maxima on the screen caused by the two light sources?
[Ans. (a) 0.12 mm (b) 11 m (c) 1.0 cm]

14.4 DIFFRACTION GRATINGS AND SPECTROSCOPY

We have seen that, when coherent light passes through a double slit, it undergoes both interference and diffraction. When coherent light passes through many closely-spaced slits, all parallel to each other, again it undergoes interference and diffraction. The resulting pattern has similarities to a double-slit pattern, but, as you will soon see, it is more distinct and more useful.

An optical device made of many uniformly-spaced, parallel slits is called a **diffraction grating**. (Such a device could also be called an interference grating, but the traditional name will be used here.) Diffraction gratings are of three main types, depending on how they are made. A *transmission grating* is made by ruling fine parallel grooves on a smooth glass surface with a diamond-tipped tool. The grooves are opaque to light while the spaces between the grooves act as transparent slits. A *reflection grating* is made by ruling fine parallel grooves on a smooth metal surface. As its name implies, this type of grating causes the interference of reflected light rather than transmitted light. Both the transmission and reflection gratings require precision equipment and a relatively long time to manufacture, so they are expensive. An inexpensive type of grating, called a *replica grating*, is made by pouring molten plastic over a master grating. When the plastic solidifies, it is peeled off the master and fastened to a flat piece of glass or stiff plastic for support. Typical diffraction gratings may have between 2000 and 10 000 lines per centimetre.

The description of how an interference pattern is created in a double-slit can be applied and extended to a diffraction grating. Only the transmission grating will be analyzed mathematically here.

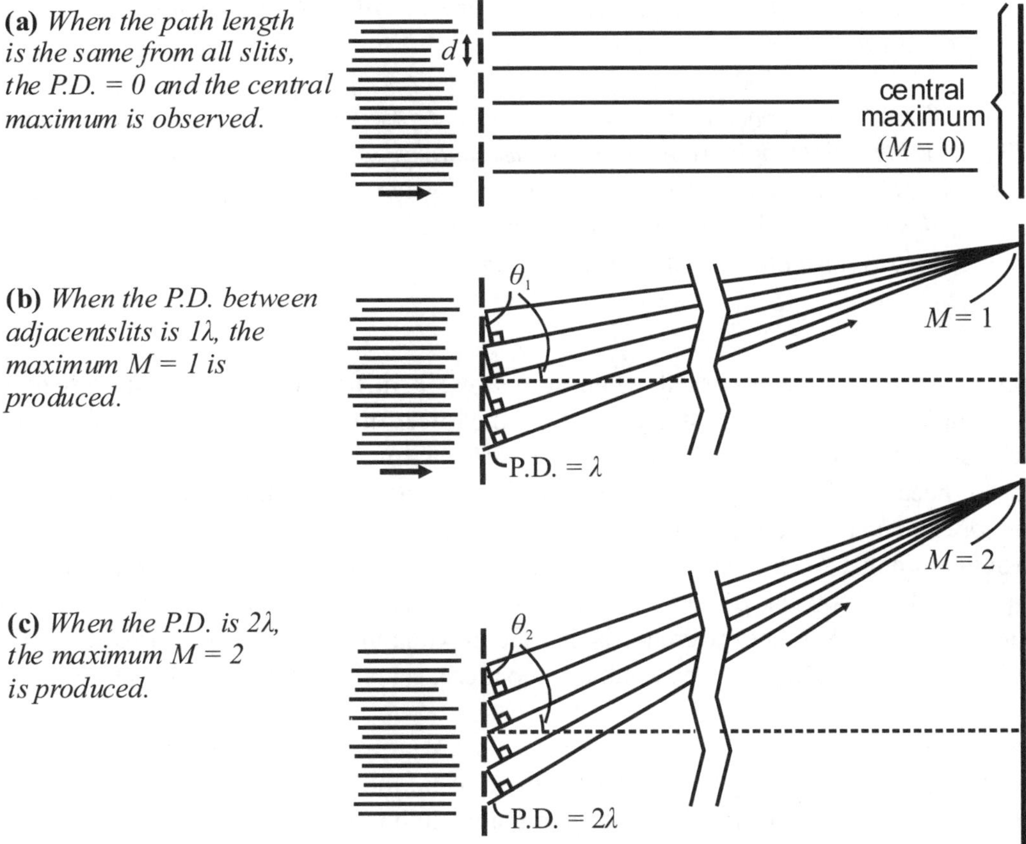

(a) When the path length is the same from all slits, the P.D. = 0 and the central maximum is observed.
d
central maximum (M = 0)
(b) When the P.D. between adjacentslits is 1λ, the maximum M = 1 is produced.
θ1
M = 1
P.D. = λ
(c) When the P.D. is 2λ, the maximum M = 2 is produced.
θ2
M = 2
P.D. = 2λ

Figure 14-21 *Deriving an equation for a diffraction grating.*

Consider Figure 14-21, which shows wavefronts of monochromatic light passing through a set of five slits. Just as with the double-slit pattern, the distance from the slits to the screen is large, so the wavefront directions, shown as rays, are parallel. In (a), the light coming through each slit is coherent, and the Huygens' wavelets that travel straight ahead interfere constructively, producing a maximum interference, or *central maximum* or zero-order maximum, labelled $M = 0$ in the diagram. In (b), we consider wavelets whose direction deviates by an angle θ with the original direction. At the screen, the path difference between each set of two slits is λ, so once again, constructive interference occurs, causing the first-order maximum $M = 1$. In (c), the second-order maximum, $M = 2$, is found when the path difference from each set of adjacent slits is $2\ \lambda$. These maxima occur on both sides of the central maximum. Thus, in general, a maximum in a multiple-slit diffraction pattern occurs when the path difference, P.D., is $M\lambda$, where $M = 0, 1, 2, 3, \ldots$

Just as with the double-slit pattern, sin θ = P.D./d, so, in general,

$$\sin\theta = M\lambda / d \quad \text{where } M = 0, 1, 2, 3, \ldots \qquad \textbf{(14-8)}$$

Did You Know? *A modern way of making diffraction gratings is to use an extremely narrow spacing to form an interference pattern on photographic film. This type of grating is called a holographic grating.*

Did You Know? *Compact discs, video discs, and phonograph records act as reflection gratings. When white light reflecting off the grooves of a disc or record is observed at certain angles, the interference seen is a coloured spectrum. This spectrum is more easily seen with discs than with records because the discs have approximately 5000 grooves/cm while the records have only about 100 grooves/cm.*

Several differences are observed when comparing a diffraction pattern experimentally to a double-slit interference patter. First, the angles of the lower-order maxima in the diffraction pattern are much larger than the angles of the lower-order maxima in a double-slit pattern. The large angles occur because of the very small values of slit separation. This means that the grating pattern is much more spread out than the double-slit pattern, and the total number of maxima is less. Also, the approximation that sin θ = tan θ, used in the double-slit pattern, cannot be used here, and if the equation $x/L = M\lambda/d$ is used, L must be measured from the grating to the maximum, not from the grating to the screen. Another difference is that the maxima in the grating pattern are much sharper and brighter than the maxima in the double-slit pattern, which in turn means that the minima are wide.

The advantages provided by the spread-out pattern and the sharp maxima in diffraction patterns are applied in viewing and analyzing light spectra and studying the structure of matter using X-ray diffraction. Details of these applications are described after the next sample problem.

Sample Problem 14-4

Light from a monochromatic source passes through a diffraction grating with 5000 lines/cm, and the second-order maxima (i.e., $M = 2$) on either side of the central maximum make an angle of 36.1° with the central maximum (Figure 14-22). What is the wavelength of the light from the source?

Solution: First, we find the slit separation, d, which is the reciprocal of 5000 lines/cm:

$$(1/5000)\text{ cm} = 2.00 \times 10^{-4}\text{ cm}$$
$$= 2.00 \times 10^{-6}\text{ m}$$

Now from $\sin\theta = \dfrac{M\lambda}{d}$,

$$\lambda = \frac{d\sin\theta}{M}$$
$$= \frac{(2.00 \times 10^{-6}\text{ m})(\sin 36.1°)}{2}$$
$$= 5.89 \times 10^{-7}\text{ m}$$

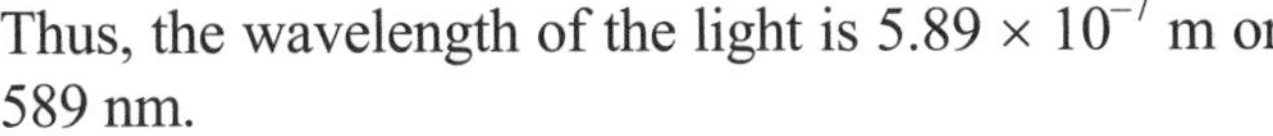

Thus, the wavelength of the light is 5.89×10^{-7} m or 589 nm.

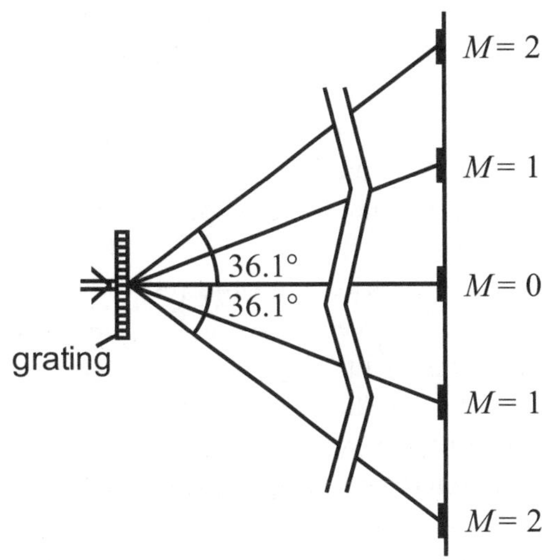

Figure 14-22 *Sample Problem 14-4.*

Spectroscopy

A *spectrum* is a band of colours observed when light consisting of more than one colour is split up. The study of spectra (the plural of spectrum) is called **spectroscopy**. White light from a hot solid or liquid, such as an incandescent light bulb or white molten iron, produces an unbroken band of colours ranging from red to violet, called a *continuous spectrum*. A continuous spectrum can be produced when white light disperses as it travels through a triangular prism. Continuous spectra are also observed when white light passes through a grating producing maximum fringes (other than the white central maximum). Gases that emit light, however, produce spectra of specific wavelengths that appear as bright lines separated by dark spaces. These spectra are called *bright line spectra*, or simply *line spectra*. Both continuous spectra and line spectra are **emission spectra**.

> ***Did You Know?*** *Colour vision helps our eyes act as crude spectroscopes when we try to identify light sources by their colour. Neon lights used in advertising appear red; sodium lamps used in highway tunnels, on bridges, and in some parking lots are orangish-yellow; and mercury lamps often used on city streets are bluish. However, spectrometers and spectroscopes can be used to determine exactly what colours are emitted by such sources.*

Gases can emit light when they are stimulated with heat or electricity. Each element or compound in the gaseous state emits its own unique set of wavelengths, just as each person has his or her own unique fingerprints. Various methods can be used to observe the spectra of such light sources. For example, a *spectrograph* is a photograph of a spectrum; a *spectrometer* is a device that uses electrical means to observe spectra; and a *spectroscope* is a device that uses either a prism or a diffraction grating to obtain a spectrum that can be viewed by a person's eye. We will consider the grating spectroscope here.

Figure 14-23 illustrates a typical student grating spectroscope using, in this instance, the light emitted by hydrogen in a transparent tube called a discharge tube. The hydrogen is stimulated by electricity to emit light. The light becomes parallel when it passes through a set of lenses in the collimator. The parallel rays strike a diffraction grating, and the resulting interference pattern is viewed through a microscope. The microscope can be moved to various angular positions, and the measured angles can be used to determine the wavelengths of the light emitted from the hydrogen gas (using $\sin\theta = M\lambda/d$).

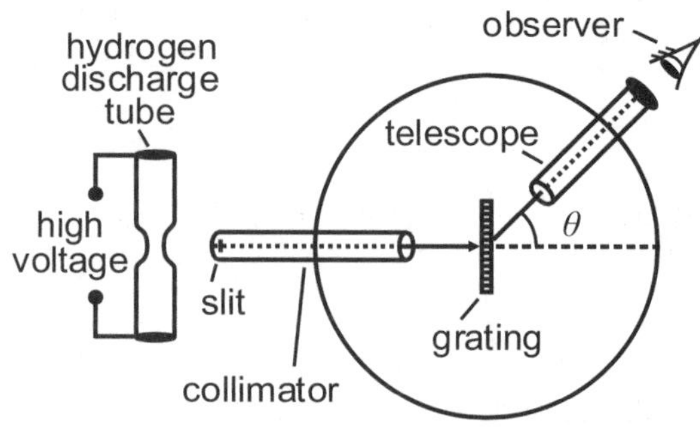

Figure 14-23 *A typical student grating spectroscope.*

The line spectrum of the light emitted by stimulated hydrogen atoms consists of a red line, a blue line, and various violet lines, as shown in Figure 14-24. Through a diffraction grating, the bright central maximum is the same colour as the light from the hydrogen in the tube. On either side of the central maximum, however, are spectra of the colours emitted by the hydrogen, with the first-order spectrum ($M = 1$) being the brightest. The equation $\sin\theta = M\lambda/d$ can be applied to determine the wavelengths of the different colours of light of the hydrogen. (See Practice Question 14-26.)

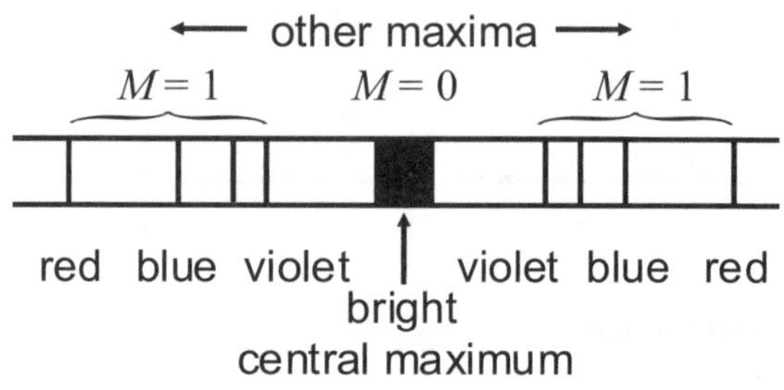

Figure 14-24 *The spectra of atomic hydrogen produced by a diffraction grating.*

If the discharge tube with hydrogen is replaced with a discharge tube containing a different element or compound in the gaseous state, a completely different spectrum is observed. Thus, the spectrum of light emitted by substances can be used to determine the composition of the substance. Astronomers have applied this principle to discover the composition of stars and the atmosphere of distant planets, as well as the gases (mainly hydrogen) that exist in interstellar space.

An element or compound that emits light of specific wavelengths also absorbs light of the same wavelengths. When a continuous spectrum is interrupted by elements or compounds that absorb some of the light, the resulting **absorption spectrum** has dark bands spaced throughout. For example, the white light emitted from the sun must pass through the cooler gases at the outer surface of the sun. These gases absorb some of the sun's light, causing the spectrum of the sun to be an absorption spectrum. By analyzing this absorption spectrum, astronomers have found that approximately two-thirds of the known elements are present in the solar atmosphere. Absorption spectra can also be used to analyze pollutants in Earth's atmosphere and identify the composition of unknown substances. To accomplish this latter

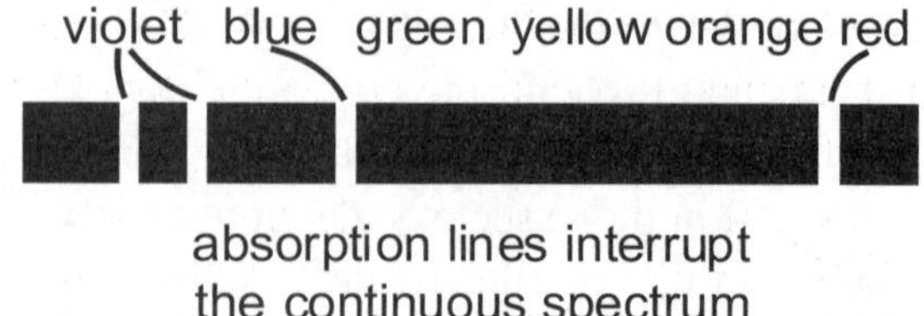

Figure 14-25 *Absorption spectrum of atomic hydrogen.*

task, light with a known spectrum is passed through a solution of the unknown substance and then through a diffraction grating. The wavelengths of the resulting absorption spectrum can be used to determine the elements or compounds present in the substance, and the intensity of the maxima in the pattern reveals the concentration of these elements or compounds (Figure 14-25).

Diffraction in Two and Three Dimensions

Our discussion of diffraction of light through single slits, double slits, and gratings has been restricted to one dimension only. What pattern do we observe for a two-dimensional array of slits? The photograph on the first page of this chapter shows an example of such a pattern. As you would expect, the maximum fringes form a two-dimensional pattern. The photograph was taken with a two-dimensional diffraction filter placed over the lens. Evidently the slits in the filter were nearly perpendicular because the light sources in the photograph produce a central maximum and a set of nearly perpendicular fringes. Similar patterns can be seen by viewing a distant light source, such as a street lamp, through a piece of sheer cloth. (Of course, the diffraction pattern through a circular aperture and the corresponding discussion of resolution were in two dimensions.)

Nature has provided us with three-dimensional diffraction gratings, namely the regular crystals of solids, such as sodium chloride, that have regular arrays of atoms. The spacing of these atoms is so tiny, however, that visible light cannot create a diffraction pattern through them. The atomic spacing is typically about 0.1 nm, which is thousands of times smaller than the wavelengths of visible light. Are there any waves that have a wavelength in the 0.1 nm range? In 1912, a German physicist named Max von Laue predicted that X rays, which are part of the same electromagnetic spectrum that visible light belongs to, could be used to create a diffraction pattern in solid crystals. This brilliant prediction turned out to be true. When X rays are passed through three-dimensional crystals, a diffraction pattern is formed due to the regular array of atoms in the crystal.

Did You Know? *Max von Laue won the Nobel prize in physics in 1914 for his discovery of X-ray diffraction through solid crystals. Even today, the maximum fringes that occur when X rays reflect from crystals are called Laue spots. In 1915, the father and son team of William and Lawrence Bragg, two English physicists, won the Nobel prize in physics for studying the structure of crystals using X-ray diffraction.*

The study of X-ray diffraction patterns, called *X-ray crystallography*, is a branch of physics with applications that extend to other sciences. Crystals with known atomic spacings can be used to determine unknown wavelengths of X rays. Conversely, X rays of known wavelength can be used to determine the atomic structure of unknown crystals. In fact, X-ray diffraction was instrumental in the discovery of the double-helical structure of DNA molecules, the carriers of the genetic code.

Practice

14-18 Two gratings are labelled 2500 lines/cm and 10000 lines/cm, respectively. Compare the diffraction patterns produced when monochromatic light is passed through each of these gratings.

14-19 The maxima in a diffraction grating pattern are brighter and sharper than the maxima in a double-slit interference pattern. Assuming equal intensities of light are incident upon both the grating and the double slit, is the grating giving us something for nothing? Explain.

14-20 Light near the opposite ends of the visible spectrum, having wavelengths of 420 nm and 680 nm, strike a diffraction grating with 5000 lines/cm. Determine the angular deflection of both wavelengths to the first and second order maxima. [Ans. 12.1°; 24.8°; 19.8°; 42.8°]

14-21 White light, with wavelengths between 400 nm and 700 nm, strikes a grating with 4000 lines/cm. Determine whether the $M = 2$ and $M = 3$ fringes overlap. Show your reasoning.

14-22 Monochromatic light of wavelength 515 nm is used to determine the spacing of the lines on a diffraction grating. The second order maximum is located at an angle of 32.8° to the original direction of the light. Determine the spacing of the lines *and* the number of lines per centimetre of the grating. [Ans. 1.90×10^{-4} cm; 5.26×10^{3} lines/cm]

14-23 What is the maximum number of bright fringes, including the central maximum, that can be obtained when light of wavelength 600 nm passes through a diffraction grating with 8000 lines/cm? [Ans. 5]

14-24 Monochromatic light is incident upon a grating with 2500 lines/cm, and the diffraction pattern is viewed on a screen located 3.80 m from the grating. The first bright fringe is located 64.5 cm from the middle of the central maximum. What is the wavelength of the light? (Remember that for a diffraction grating, $\sin \theta$ does not equal $\tan \theta$.) [Ans. 6.79×10^{-7} m]

14-25 A photographer without a diffraction filter improvises with a fine piece of sheer cloth placed over the camera lens. The cloth is placed so the threads that run horizontally have double the spacing of the threads that run vertically. The photographer takes a picture of a single bright street light. Draw a diagram of the resulting pattern.

14-26 A student uses a spectroscope to view the spectrum of hydrogen gas in a discharge tube. The spectroscope grating has 8000 lines/cm. The angles of deviation of three of the bright lines in the first order maximum are found to be 20.3°, 22.9°, and 31.7°, respectively. Calculate the wavelengths that produce these bright lines, and state what colour each wavelength is likely to be. [Ans. 434 nm; 486 nm; 657 nm]

14.5 REFRACTION OF LIGHT

Magnifying glasses, binoculars, cameras, eyeglasses, and even our sense of sight, all rely on the bending of light as it travels from one medium to another. Other effects of the bending of light you have probably noticed are the apparent twinkling of stars and the shortened view of your legs as you walk through clear, waist-deep water. The bending of light as it travels from one transparent medium to another at an angle is called the **refraction of light**.

Consider a beam of light travelling through air and striking the surface of a glass block at an angle of incidence different from 0°, as depicted in Figure 14-26. At the interface between the two media, some of the light is reflected such that the angle of reflection equals the angle of incidence. Some of the light enters the glass, whereupon it refracts toward the normal then travels in a straight line in the glass. The angle between the refracted ray and the normal is called the **angle of refraction**.

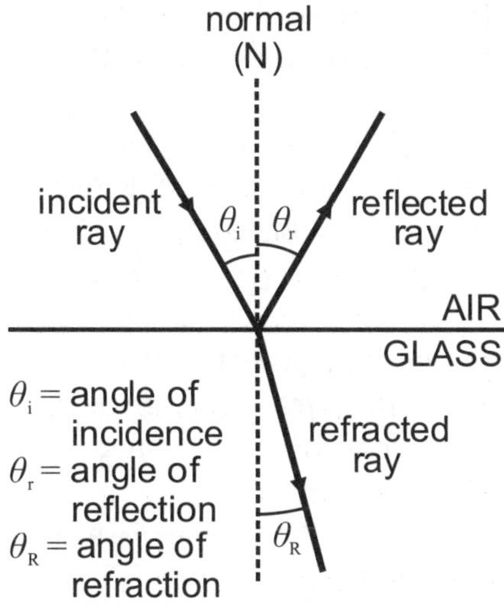

Figure 14-26 *A ray of light in air striking glass undergoes partial reflection and partial refraction.*

If we compare the refraction of light to the refraction of waves in two dimensions, described in Section 13.2, we might predict that, if light acts like a wave, the reason the refraction occurs is that the speed of the light waves in the glass is less than the speed of the light waves in air. It was discovered by Jean Foucault over 100 years ago that light does, in fact, travel more slowly in glass than it does in air. Another example of how a change in speed causes a change in direction is shown in Figure 14-27. A set of wheels travelling at a high speed on pavement reaches sand at an angle. The first wheel to reach the sand slows down first and the other wheels momentarily continue travelling at a greater speed on the pavement, causing the set of wheels to change its direction of motion.

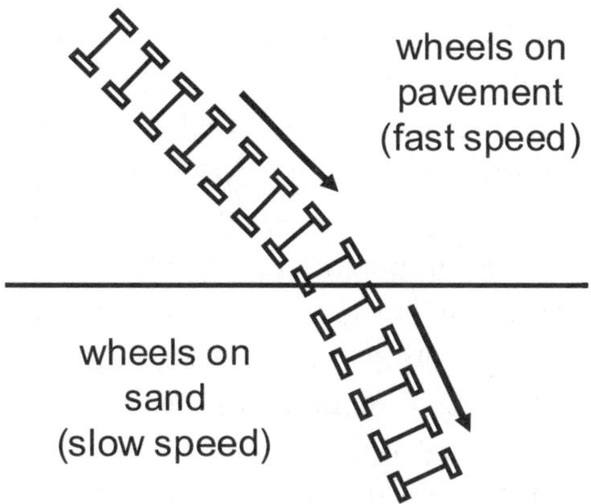

Figure 14-27 *Illustrating how a change of speed causes refraction.*

Although the wave model of light can be used in trying to explain why refraction occurs, we will analyze refraction mathematically, mainly by using rays of light, which are more convenient than waves.

What happens when the light travels from the glass back into the air, again at an angle of incidence other than 0°? Some of the light reflects at the surface between the media, and some light refracts as it emerges into the air, but this time, it refracts away from the normal. Evidently, the speed of light increases when it emerges back into the air from the glass. The angle between the emergent ray and the normal is called the **angle of emergence**. Furthermore, it can be easily verified experimentally that the path of the light in the reverse direction is exactly the same as the initial path. This provides another example of the reversibility of light (Fig. 14-28 on page 14-26).

Light travels at different speeds in different transparent media. When light is refracted upon entering one medium from another, the amount of refraction depends on the relative speed of light in the two media. For example, light is refracted more when entering glass from air at a given angle than when entering water from air at the same angle. We therefore say that glass has a greater optical density than water; light travels more slowly in the glass. Thus, **optical density** is a measure of the amount by which the speed of light is reduced in a medium. (Optical density has no relation to physical density.) In general, then, we can state the following conclusions:

1) When light travels at an angle from a medium of lower optical density to one of higher optical density, it is refracted toward the normal.

2) When light travels at an angle from a medium of higher optical density to one of lower optical density, it is refracted away from the normal. (At an angle of 0° the speed of light still changes in the second medium, but no refraction occurs.)

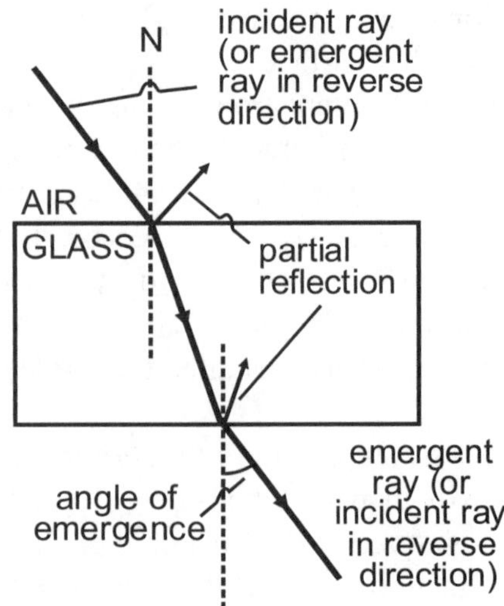

Figure 14-28 *The emergence and reversibility of light.*

Index of Refraction

In Section 13.2, you learned that the index of refraction, symbol n, is the ratio of the speed of a wave in one medium to the speed of a wave in a second medium. For light, we define the **index of refraction** of a medium as the ratio of the speed of light in a vacuum to the speed of light in the medium. Thus,

$$n = \frac{c}{v} \qquad \textbf{(14-9)}$$

where n is the index of refraction for light travelling from a vacuum where the speed of light is c into a medium where the speed of light is v. The units for this ratio of speeds cancel out, so index of refraction has no units.[2]

Since the speed of light in a vacuum is greater than the speed of light in any other medium, the index of refraction of a material medium is always greater than one. Table 14-2 (page 14-27) lists the speed of light and the index of refraction for several media; most data are given to three significant digits.

The speed of light in a vacuum, to six significant digits, is $2.997\ 92 \times 10^8$ m/s, and in air (at 0°C and atmospheric pressure) it is $2.997\ 05 \times 10^8$ m/s. These speeds are so close that, to three significant digits, they are equal. Thus, for most instances referred to in this text,

$$v_{air} = c = 3.00 \times 10^8 \text{ m/s} \quad \text{(to three significant digits)}$$

Also, for the accuracy required in most calculations involving light refraction, we will use the index of refraction of air (and other gases) to be 1.00 to three significant digits. Thus,

$$n_{vacuum} = n_{air} = 1.00 \quad \text{(to three significant digits)}$$

---

[2] Recall from page 13-15 that n is also equal to the ratio of the wavelengths in the two media. As light travels from one medium into another, the frequency remains constant but the wavelength changes.

Table 14.2 Indexes of Refraction for Various Media

(Note: The index of refraction of a material depends on the wavelength of the light. The data listed here are based on a wavelength of 600 nm.)

Medium	Speed of Light in Medium ($\times 10^8$ m/s)	Index of Refraction, n
air	2.997 05	1.000 29
carbon dioxide	2.996 57	1.000 45
ice	2.31	1.30
water	2.25	1.33
ethyl alcohol	2.21	1.36
carbon tetrachloride	2.05	1.46
oleic acid	2.05	1.46
glycerine	2.04	1.47
olive oil	2.04	1.47
benzene	2.00	1.50
ruby	1.95	1.54
glass		
fused quartz	2.05	1.46
crown glass	1.97	1.52
light flint	1.90	1.58
heavy flint	1.82	1.65
carbon disulfide	1.84	1.63
zircon	1.58	1.90
diamond	1.24	2.42

Sample Problem 14-5

The index of refraction of a substance is 1.72. What is the speed of light in the substance?

Solution: From $n = c/v$,

$$v = \frac{c}{n} = \frac{3.00 \times 10^8 \text{ m/s}}{1.72} = 1.74 \times 10^8 \text{ m/s}$$

Thus, the speed of light in the substance is 1.74×10^8 m/s.

Snell's Law of Refraction

As early as the second century A.D., some scientists studied the refraction of light. A Greco-

Egyptian scientist named Claudius Ptolemy predicted that the amount of refraction that occurs when light travels from air into another medium could be determined by assuming that the ratio of the angle of incidence ($\angle i$) to the angle of refraction ($\angle r$) remained constant for that medium. This ratio of ($\angle i/\angle r$) applies reasonably well to small angles, but it does not apply to all angles. More than eight centuries after Ptolemy, when the Arabs were leaders in world science, the Arabian mathematician Alhazen (965-1038) studied refraction in detail, but failed to find an acceptable mathematical analysis of it.

Still later, around 1621, a Dutch mathematician named Willebrord Snell (1591-1626) discovered by experiment what is now called **Snell's law of refraction**:

The ratio of the sine of the angle of incidence to the sine of the angle of refraction remains constant for light travelling from air into another transparent medium.

In simplified form, the law is written: $$\frac{\sin \angle i}{\sin \angle r} = \text{constant}$$

Snell did not relate the ratio of the sines of the angles to the ratio of the speeds in the two media, but later it was discovered that these ratios are equal. Thus, when light travels from a vacuum into a transparent medium at an angle, the index of refraction can be given by:

$$n = \frac{\sin \theta_{\text{vacuum}}}{\sin \theta_{\text{medium}}}$$

This is one way of stating Snell's law of refraction in equation form. A more common way can be derived as follows: For two media, 1 and 2,

$$n_1 = \frac{\sin \theta_v}{\sin \theta_1} \quad \text{and} \quad n_2 = \frac{\sin \theta_v}{\sin \theta_2} \qquad \text{where "v" stands for vacuum}$$

$$\therefore \quad n_1 \sin \theta_1 = \sin \theta_v \quad \text{and} \quad n_2 \sin \theta_2 = \sin \theta_v$$

Hence, $$n_1 \sin \theta_1 = n_2 \sin \theta_2 \qquad \textbf{(14-10)}$$

This is the most common and probably the most useful way of writing Snell's law in equation form. When applying this equation, it is customary to use medium 1 as the medium in which the incident light is travelling. If the medium is air or a vacuum, then the index of refraction, to three significant digits, is 1.00.

The equation $n = \sin \theta_1/\sin \theta_2$ was derived in Section 13.2 for waves travelling from medium 1 to medium 2. This provides evidence of the wave nature of light.

Sample Problem 14-6

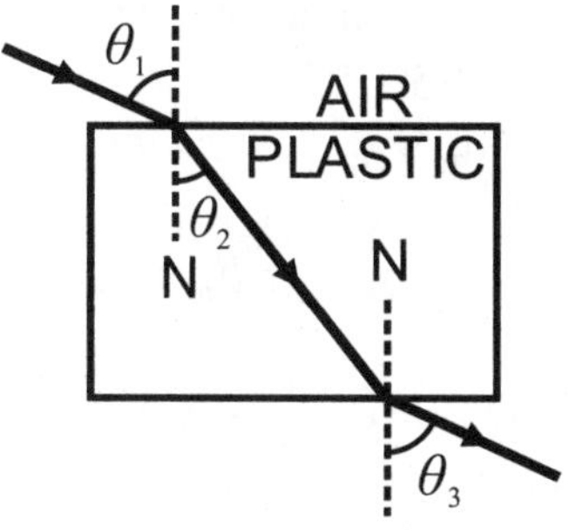

Figure 14-29
Sample Problem 14-6.

Light strikes a transparent plastic block (Figure 14-29) at an angle, θ_1, of 65.4° and refracts at an angle, θ_2, of 37.9° in the block.
(a) Determine the speed of light in the block.
(b) Calculate the angle, θ_3, at which the light emerges from the block.

Solution: (a) From Snell's law ($n_1 \sin\theta_1 = n_2 \sin\theta_2$), the index of refraction of the plastic is given by

$$n_2 = \frac{n_1 \sin\theta_1}{\sin\theta_2} = \frac{1.00 \sin 65.4°}{\sin 37.9°} = 1.48$$

From $n = \dfrac{c}{v}$,

$$v_2 = \frac{c}{n_2} = \frac{3.00 \times 10^8 \text{ m/s}}{1.48} = 2.03 \times 10^8 \text{ m/s}$$

Thus, the speed is 2.03×10^8 m/s.

(b) From $n_2 \sin\theta_2 = n_3 \sin\theta_3$,

$$\sin\theta_3 = \frac{n_2 \sin\theta_2}{n_3} \qquad \text{where } n_3 = 1.00 \text{ for air}$$

$$\therefore \quad \sin\theta_3 = 1.48 \sin 37.9° \qquad \text{which gives} \qquad \theta_3 = 65.4°$$

Thus, the angle at which the light emerges is 65.4° which is the same as the original angle of incidence in the air.

Practice

14-27 When window shopping, have you ever noticed that some store windows are not vertical but are slanted to reduce glare from the sun or street lights? To be effective, should such a window be slanted inward or outward at the top? Explain. (A diagram would help.)

14-28 Find the index of refraction of a liquid in which the speed of light is 2.22×10^8 m/s.
[Ans. 1.35]

14-29 What is the speed of light in a clear soup that has an index of refraction is 1.37?
[Ans. 2.19×10^8 m/s]

14-30 How long does it take light to travel 10.0 cm in water? (Note: $n_{\text{water}} = 1.33$.)
[Ans. 4.43×10^{-10} s]

14-31 Assume the index of refraction for radio waves in ice is the same as for light, that is, $n_{\text{ice}} = 1.30$. Radio waves are sent through a layer of ice in the Arctic, and a signal that reflects from the bottom of the layer is received back at the source in 1.80×10^{-5} s.
(a) What is the speed of the radio waves in the ice?
(b) How thick is the layer of ice? [Ans. (a) 2.31×10^{8} m/s (b) 2.08×10^{3} m]

14-32 In each situation described below, light travels from medium A into medium B. State whether the light bends toward or away from the normal as it enters B.
(a) A has a higher optical density than B.
(b) The speed of light in A is greater than the speed of light in B.
(c) The angle of incidence in A is greater than the angle of refraction in B.
(d) $n_{\text{A}} > n_{\text{B}}$

14-33 At what angle of incidence in air would a ray of light have to enter diamond (index of refraction = 2.42) in order to have an angle of refraction of 21.8°? [Ans. 64.0°]

14-34 A ray of light is used to determine if a certain crystal is made of the gemstone, zircon. The angle of incidence in air is 48.5° and the angle of refraction in the crystal is 27.0°. What is the composition of the crystal? (Indexes of refraction are found in Table 14-2.)

14-35 Assume you are given a sample of an unknown transparent liquid. How would you determine the speed of light in the liquid?

14-36 A ray of light in air is aimed toward the surface of carbon tetrachloride (n = 1.46) at an angle of incidence of 71.5°. Determine the angle between the refracted ray in the liquid and the reflected ray in the air. [Ans. 68.0°]

14-37 A red laser beam enters a crown glass prism in the shape of an equilateral triangle. The angle of incidence is 60.0° and the index of refraction for the red light in the prism is 1.51. Determine the angle of refraction in the glass and the angle of emergence in the air. (Hint: A diagram will help, especially in finding the angle of emergence.)
[Ans. 35.0°; 39.7°]

14-38 For a ray of light in air striking the surface of a glass block (n = 1.50), what is the maximum angle of refraction? [Ans. 41.8°]

N
30.0°
AIR
$n_1 = 1.00$
$n_2 = 1.20$
$n_3 = 1.40$
$n_4 = 1.60$
$n_5 = 1.80$
$n_6 = 2.00$

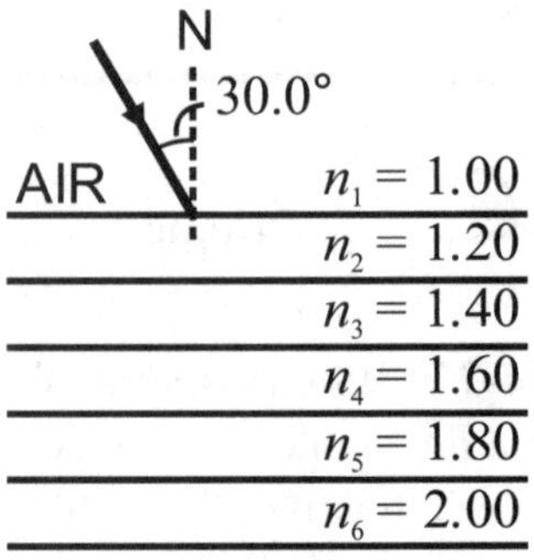

Figure 14-30
Question 14-39

14-39 Light from air enters a set of transparent materials at an angle of incidence of 30.0°, as shown in Figure 14-30.
(a) Determine the angle of refraction in the sixth medium ($n_6 = 2.00$).

(b) What pattern have you observed in solving this problem?
[Ans. (a) 14.5°]

14-40 Light from one last olive in a container of olive oil (n = 1.47) leaves the surface of the oil in the middle of the container and just passes over the edge of the container, as shown in Figure 14-31. Determine:
(a) the angle of incidence in the oil.
(b) the angle of refraction in the air.
(c) the height of the container.
[Ans. (a) 33.7° (b) 54.6° (c) 8.84 cm]

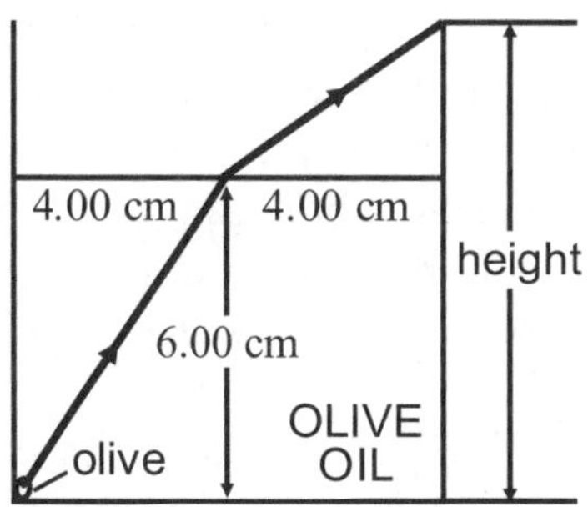

Figure 14-31 *Question 14-40.*

14.6 THIN-FILM INTERFERENCE

Oil and gasoline have rather drab colours, but under special conditions, they display beautiful colour fringes that appear to change when viewed from different angles. This occurs when white light strikes an extremely thin film of oil or gasoline that is spread out over a surface of water. Likely you have seen these coloured fringes in automobile service stations or truck stops. The colours of the light reflected from the thin film are an example of *iridescence*, which means the changing of colours. Other examples are the colours seen in soap films, on fish scales and insect wings, and in the plumage of some birds, such as the tail feather of a peacock, the head feathers of a male Mallard duck, and some hummingbirds.

Did You Know? *Iridescence comes from the Greek words iris and iridis, which mean rainbow. In Greek mythology, Iris was the goddess of the rainbow.*

Did You Know? *Some birds have feathers that produce iridescence caused by the diffraction of reflected light rather than by thin-film interference. Diffraction is what gives pigeon necks the appearance of changing colours as their heads jerk back and forth when they walk.*

The fringes in thin films are produced by the interference effects of light. The fringes are most easily observed when the light reflects from the thin film, but it can also be observed when the light is transmitted through the film. In white light, the interference fringes have various colours, but in monochromatic light, the fringes are bright and dark where constructive and destructive interference occur.

To explain how the interference of light can cause the fringes observed in thin films, we shall begin by reviewing what occurs when a wave travelling in one medium reaches a second medium. What was described for mechanical waves in Section 13.2 is assumed to apply to light waves as well. The following statements summarize the three possible situations when light strikes a different medium.

1) Any light that is transmitted from one medium to another undergoes no phase change.

2) Light reflected from the surface of an optically more dense medium where the speed is slower undergoes a complete phase change. (For example, a crest becomes a trough.) This is called fixed-end reflection, or negative reflection.
3) Light reflected from an optically less dense medium where the speed of light is faster undergoes no phase change. This approximates an open-end reflection, or positive reflection.

Consider, for example, a coherent beam of monochromatic light striking a thin film of oil resting on water. The indexes of refraction of the three media are $n_{\text{air}} = 1.00$, $n_{\text{oil}} = 1.48$, and $n_{\text{water}} = 1.33$. Assume the beam strikes at a small angle of incidence, as shown in Figure 14-32. Part of the beam reflects off the air-oil interface and undergoes a phase change because the oil has a greater optical density than the air. (A higher index of refraction corresponds to a greater optical density and a lower speed of light.) Another part of the beam transfers positively into the oil and reflects off the oil-water interface, this time without a phase change because the water has a lower optical density than the oil. This reflected light transfers positively back into the air and interferes with the first reflected light. In (a), the thickness, *t*, of the oil film is much less than the wavelength of the light, so the two reflected beams are opposite in phase and cancel. This causes a dark fringe to occur, as can be seen in the magnified view.

(a) *When $t << \lambda_{\text{film}}/4$, the reflected beams are out-of-phase, causing destrutive interference and thus a dark fringe.*

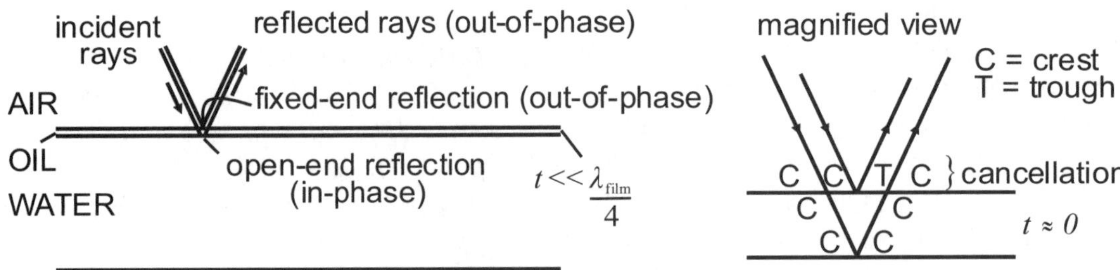

(b) *When $t = \lambda_{\text{film}}/4$, the beam that reflects off the water travels an extra $\lambda_{\text{film}}/2$, so the two reflected beams are now in-phase.*

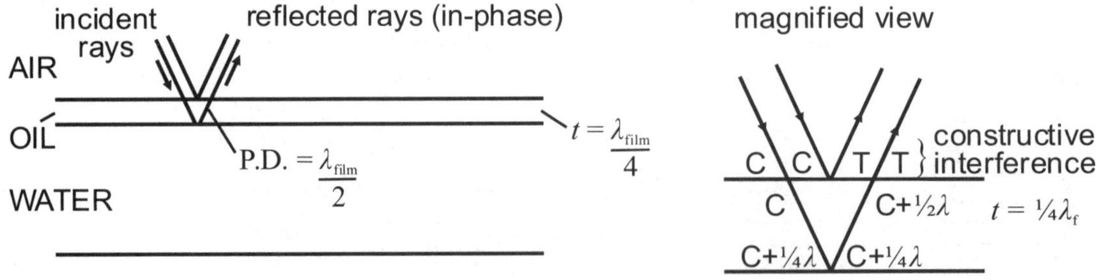

Figure 14-32 *Thin-film interference of reflected light.*

In (b), the thickness of the oil film is $\lambda_{\text{film}}/4$, where λ_{film} is the wavelength of the light in the oil film. Thus, the path difference of the two beams is $\lambda_{\text{film}}/2$. These two reflected beams are now in phase, causing constructive interference or a bright fringe. Again, the magnified view shows this more clearly. Using similar arguments for increasing thicknesses of the oil film, we find that destructive interference occurs when the path difference is $0\,\lambda, 1\,\lambda, 2\,\lambda, 3\,\lambda, \ldots,$ and constructive interference occurs when the path difference is $0.5\,\lambda, 1.5\,\lambda, 2.5\,\lambda,$ and so on. Since the path difference is approximately $2t$ (when the incident light is approximately normal to the film), we can write the following relationships:

$$2t = N\lambda_{\text{film}} \quad \text{where } N = 0, 1, 2, 3, \ldots \text{ represents the nodes or minimum fringes} \qquad \textbf{(14-11)}$$

$$2t = \left(M + \tfrac{1}{2}\right)\lambda_{\text{film}} \quad \text{where } M = 0, 1, 2, 3, \ldots \text{ represents the maximum fringes} \qquad \textbf{(14-12)}$$

It is important to remember that these equations apply *only* if the thin film has a higher optical density than the surrounding media. Thus, it applies not only to oil between air and water but also to a soap film surrounded by air. It is also important to remember that the wavelength is the wavelength of the light in the film. This can be found by knowing the wavelength of the light in air and applying the relation:

$$n = \frac{\lambda_{\text{air}}}{\lambda_{\text{film}}} \quad \text{or} \quad \lambda_{\text{film}} = \frac{\lambda_{\text{air}}}{n}$$

Sample Problem 14-7

A wire loop is dipped into soapy water and is then held vertically so the force of gravity causes the soap film to be thicker as it nears the bottom of the loop (Figure 14-33). The thin film of soap (with $n = 1.33$) reflects white light to an observer.

(a) At what least thickness of the film will the observer see blue reflected light having a wavelength 474 nm in air?

(b) At the thickness found in (a), what would an observer on the transmitted side of the film expect to see?

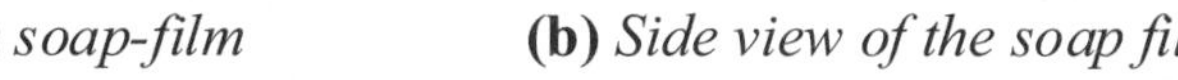

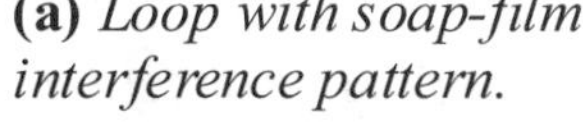

(a) *Loop with soap-film interference pattern.*

(b) *Side view of the soap film.*

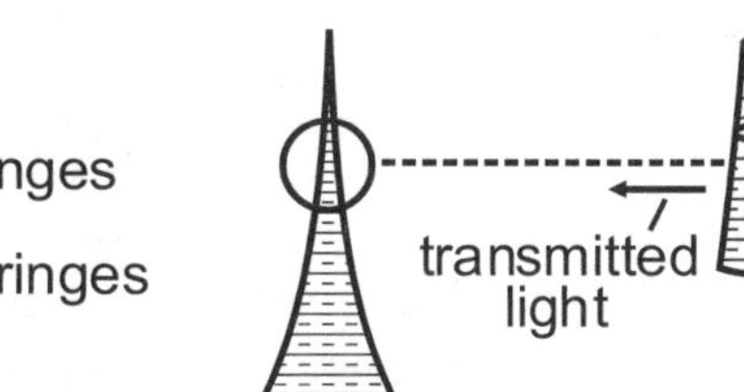

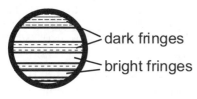

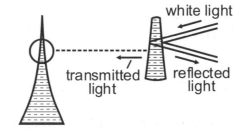

Figure 14-33 *Sample Problem 14-5.*

Solution: (a) The first maximum is $M = 0$. This corresponds to the minimum thickness (from Eqn. 14-12).

$$2t = (M + \tfrac{1}{2})\lambda_{\text{film}} \qquad \text{where} \qquad \lambda_{\text{film}} = \lambda_{\text{air}}/n$$

$$2t = \frac{(0 + \tfrac{1}{2})\lambda_{\text{air}}}{n}$$

$$\therefore \quad t = \frac{\tfrac{1}{2}\lambda_{\text{air}}}{2n} = \frac{\lambda_{\text{air}}}{4n} = \frac{4.74 \times 10^{-7}\ \text{m}}{(4)(1.33)} = 8.91 \times 10^{-6}\ \text{m} \quad \text{or} \quad 89.1\ \text{nm}$$

Thus, the thickness is 89.1 nm.

(b) Some light will be transmitted through the thin film, but since the thickness is such that blue light undergoes maximum reflection, blue must undergo minimum transmission. Thus, a colour different from blue will be observed on the transmitted side of the film. (See Applying Your Knowledge question 14-116 for a detailed description of this situation.)

It is evident from the above sample problem that each component wavelength will reflect at a different thickness of the thin film. Thus, in white light, a film of gradually changing thickness causes spectral colours to be reflected.

We have considered only incident light that is normal or nearly normal to the thin film. Interference can also occur at much larger angles of incidence, but the path difference of the interfering light beams is more difficult to find (Figure 14-34).

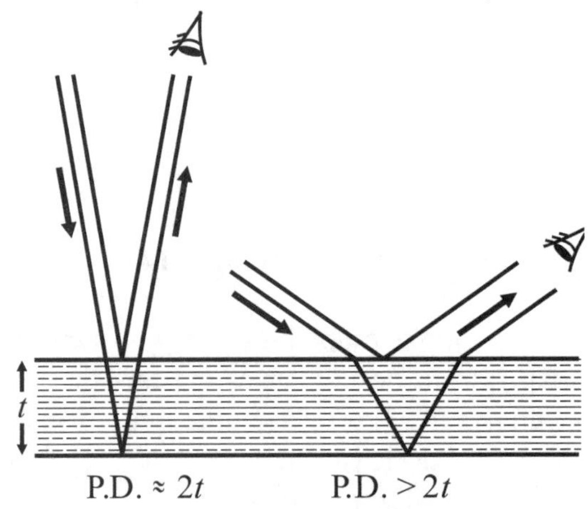

Figure 14-34 *Thin-film interference of light at an angle much greater than 0°.*

We have seen that constructive interference of reflected light occurs at a thickness of $\lambda_{\text{film}}/4$ if the film has an optical density greater than the surrounding media. What happens if the film of thickness $\lambda_{\text{film}}/4$ has an optical density between the densities of the surrounding media? This can occur if a soap film remains on a transparent glass, and it has important applications in the manufacture of lenses and solar cells.

Usually when light strikes a glass lens, about 96% of the light is transmitted. Most of the other 4% is reflected. Since most expensive cameras and microscopes have between 6 and 8 lenses, a high portion of the incident light will be reflected, resulting in a dull image. Moreover, double reflection within each lens can cause a blurred image. To overcome these problems, each lens is coated with a thin film that will cause minimum reflection and, thus, maximum transmission of light. For glass lenses, this film is usually made of magnesium fluoride (MgF_2), which has an index of refraction of 1.38. It can be shown (as you will be asked to do in Practice Question 14-43) that, when magnesium fluoride is located between air (n = 1.00) and glass ($n \geq 1.50$), destructive interference of the reflected rays will occur when $\lambda_{\text{film}}/4$. Such a film is called a *quarter-wavelength film*. In general,

$$2t = \left(N + \tfrac{1}{2}\right)\lambda_{\text{film}} \quad \text{where } N = 0, 1, 2, 3, \ldots \text{ for nodes or minimum fringes} \qquad \textbf{(14-13)}$$

$$2t = M\lambda_{\text{film}} \quad \text{where } M = 0, 1, 2, 3, \ldots \text{ for maximum fringes} \qquad \textbf{(14-14)}$$

These equations apply *only* if the thin film has an optical density between the optical densities of its surroundings.

Sample Problem 14-8

A quarter-wavelength film of magnesium fluoride (n = 1.38) is applied on a glass camera lens (n = 1.56). The film is 99.6 nm thick. Assuming this is the least thickness possible for minimum reflection, what are the wavelength and the colour of the light that undergoes minimum reflection?

Solution: The least thickness occurs when $N = 0$ in the equation $2t = \left(N + \tfrac{1}{2}\right)\lambda_{\text{film}}$.

Thus,
$$\lambda_{\text{film}} = \frac{2t}{\left(N + \tfrac{1}{2}\right)} = \frac{2 \times 9.96 \times 10^{-8}\ \text{m}}{\tfrac{1}{2}} = 3.98 \times 10^{-7}\ \text{m}$$

Now, from $\lambda_{\text{film}} = \lambda_{\text{air}}/n$, $\quad \lambda_{\text{air}} = n\lambda_{\text{film}} = 1.38\left(3.98 \times 10^{-7}\ \text{m}\right) = 5.49 \times 10^{-7}\ \text{m}$

Thus, the wavelength of the light that undergoes minimum reflection is 5.49×10^{-7} m or about 550 nm, which is at the middle of the visible spectrum. The colour is green.

A lens with a coating that reflects little green or yellow light must reflect most of the light at the red and violet ends of the spectrum. Red and violet combine to produce a purple hue, and that is exactly what you will observe if you look at most lenses in cameras, binoculars, telescopes, and other optical devices. Precision lenses may be coated with two, three, or more layers of material of different optical densities to maximize the transmission of most parts of the visible spectrum.

Some cars have an interior rear-view mirror that applies thin-film technology to reduce the reflective glare from bright lights of a following vehicle. The mirror has a thin coating of gel that is electrically conductive. Sensors reacting to bright light change the gel's density, causing it to go from clear and reflective to opaque and non-reflective.

Air-Wedge Interference

Another example of thin-film interference occurs when air is located between two glass surfaces. In this case, the air is the film and the interference is called *air-wedge interference*. As seen in Figure 14-35, destructive interference of reflected light occurs when the path difference is approximately 0λ, $\lambda/2$, 1λ, $3/2\lambda$ ... Similarly, constructive interference of reflected light occurs when the path difference is $\lambda/4$, $3/4\lambda$, $5/4\lambda$, ... Thus, the minima and maxima can be found using the same equations developed for a film between two media of lower optical density. Therefore, for air-wedge interference:

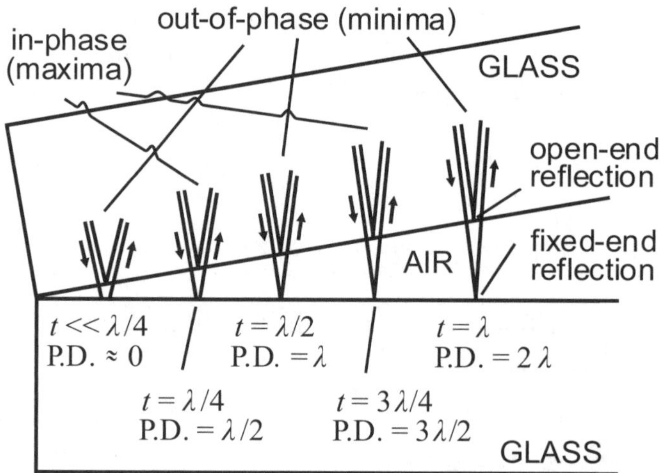

Figure 14-35 *Interference of reflected light in an air wedge. (In a real situation, the thickness of the air wedge is extremely small and the light comes through the glass to the observer.)*

$$2t = N\lambda_{\text{film}} \text{ where } N = 0, 1, 2, 3, \ldots \quad \text{for minima} \qquad \textbf{(14-15)}$$

$$2t = \left(M + \tfrac{1}{2}\right)\lambda_{\text{film}} \text{ where } M = 0, 1, 2, 3, \ldots \text{ for maxima} \qquad \textbf{(14-16)}$$

Air-wedge interference can be used to determine the precision with which a lens or glass plate has been made. For example, if a convex lens resting on an extremely flat glass plate is viewed in reflected monochromatic light, a series of circular bright and dark fringes is seen as the air wedge thickness increases. These fringes are called Newton's rings, because Isaac Newton first described them. If the lens is poorly ground, the rings will not be circular. Likewise, flat glass plates can be tested on a well-made plate called an optical flat. The surface of such a flat varies in height no more than about 1/100 of the wavelength of light. A glass plate resting on an optical flat will produce parallel fringes if the plate is well made.

So far in this chapter, we have observed several instances in which light acts like a wave. But we have not discussed whether light waves are transverse or longitudinal. And we have not learned how the light waves are created or propagated. These topics will be explored in the remainder of the chapter.

Practice

<u>**14-41**</u> Light travelling in medium A strikes the surface of medium B. In each case, state whether the portion of the light that reflects is in phase or out of phase with the incident light.
(a) $n_A > n_B$ where n is the index of refraction
(b) $v_A > v_B$ where v is the speed of light

(c) O.D.$_A$ > O.D.$_B$ where O.D. is the optical density

14-42 Monochromatic yellow light (λ = 583 nm in air) is directed vertically downward and strikes a horizontal oil film (n = 1.48) on water (n = 1.33). Determine the three least possible thicknesses of the oil film that would cause maximum reflection of this light.
[Ans. 98.5 nm; 295 nm; 492 nm]

14-43 Use the theory of fixed-end and open-end reflection to prove that a quarter-wavelength coating of magnesium fluoride (n = 1.38) over glass ($n \geq 1.50$) causes minimum reflection of light of a specific wavelength.

14-44 In order to maximize the transmission of incident light, a silicon solar cell is manufactured with a thin layer of silicon monoxide (n = 1.45) over the actual silicon (n = 3.50). Determine the minimum thickness of silicon monoxide that will allow maximum transmission of light of wavelength 5.50×10^{-7} m. [Ans. 94.8 nm]

14-45 A soap film has a uniformly increasing thickness that ranges from 200 nm to 900 nm. Determine how many red fringes (λ_{air} = 650 nm) will be observed in the interference pattern of reflected light from this film. Show your reasoning. [Ans. 3]

<u>14-46</u> A soap film (n = 1.33) has a thickness of ¾ λ_{film} for a certain monochromatic light. Is the reflected light maximum or minimum if the soap film is:
(a) surrounded by air? (b) between air and glass?

<u>14-47</u> A soap film is viewed in white light. At a certain location on the film, red light is reflected as a maximum. What can you say for sure about the colour of transmitted light at that same location?

<u>14-48</u> Photographs of Newton's rings show a dark circle in the middle of the pattern. This circle, produced when a convex glass surface sits on a flat glass surface, persists even if the convex surface is pressed tightly against the flat surface. Why is the reflected light a minimum at the centre? If the transmitted light is viewed, will a minimum also be observed? Explain.

<u>14-49</u> Monochromatic light strikes a convex lens resting on (a) an optical flat and (b) another convex lens, as illustrated in Figure 14-36. Compare the interference patterns viewed by reflected light. Assume all surfaces are well made.

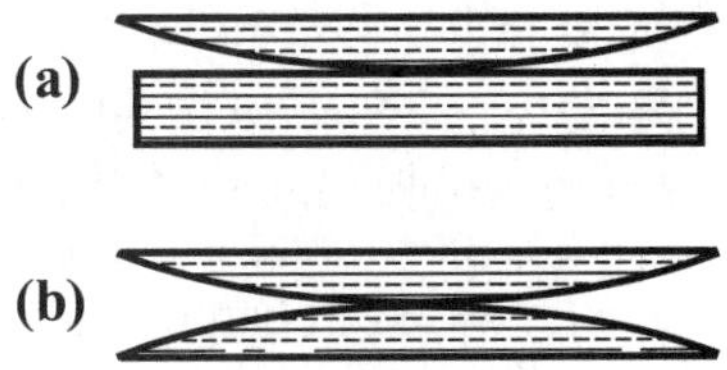

(a)

(b)

Figure 14-36
Question 14-49.

14-50 Two glass plates 8.0 cm long are touching at one end and are separated by a fine fibre at the other end. The air wedge between the plates is viewed in reflected monochromatic light (λ_{air} = 500 nm) and parallel bright fringes are seen every 0.50 mm.
(a) By how much does the thickness of the air wedge increase with every new fringe?
(b) What is the thickness of the fibre? [Ans. (a) 250 nm (b) 4.0×10^{-5} m]

14.7 LIGHT THEORIES AND THE ELECTROMAGNETIC SPECTRUM

Having observed several situations in which light displays properties of waves, we are now ready to review and extend our notions of the theories of light. After Thomas Young's double-slit experiment and measurement of the wavelengths of visible light at the beginning of the 19th century, an increasing portion of scientists supported the wave theory of light. By the middle of that century, the speed of light in water had been determined, further strengthening the wave theory and weakening the particle theory.

During the same period of time, several discoveries were made about electricity and magnetism. When current electricity was first discovered, it seemed to be separate from magnetism, and electricity and magnetism seemed to have nothing to do with light. But scientists later discovered that electricity creates magnetism and magnetism can create electricity. The discovery that is important for our discussion here is that **a changing magnetic field causes a changing electric field, and a changing electric field causes a changing magnetic field**. Let us see how this relates to the topic of light.

A Scottish mathematician and physicist named James Clerk Maxwell (1831-1879) was working on a mathematical analysis of the relationship between electricity and magnetism. In his calculations, he discovered that energy moving outward from a source of a changing electric field travels as a wave with a speed of 3.00×10^8 m/s. He knew that this was the speed of light in a vacuum, so he hypothesized (correctly) that light must be a wave with electric and magnetic components. Such a wave is called an **electromagnetic wave**. Thus, in 1864, Maxwell proposed that **light travels through space as an electromagnetic wave**.

Maxwell summarized his discoveries in a set of equations, called Maxwell's equations. These are far beyond the scope of this book, but the consequences of his discoveries are what are important to our understanding of light. We will look at these consequences in terms of what is now known about the creation and propagation of light.

Electromagnetic waves, including visible light, can be created by the acceleration of electrically charged particles. The charged particles are often electrons, although other types of accelerated charged particles also produce electromagnetic waves. Radio waves are produced by the oscillations of electrons in the antennas of the radio stations; as the electrons oscillate, they undergo acceleration and radiate electromagnetic waves (or e.m. waves). In order to explain the detail the radiation of e.m. waves from atoms, molecules, and nuclei, quantum physics (Chapter 16) must be used, and it is not appropriate in these cases to consider the waves to be produced by the acceleration of charged particles.

Light is transferred by means of electromagnetic waves. Such a wave consists of two perpendicular components, an electric field and a magnetic field (thus the word "electro-magnetic"). These fields are constantly changing and, thus, they continue to create each other. This is the miracle of light — it can travel without any material medium because the electric and magnetic fields help each other along as the wave travels. The electric and magnetic fields are both perpendicular to the direction of propagation of the e.m. wave. This is illustrated in Figure 14-37. (Be sure you understand this diagram before you read on.)

Electromagnetic waves are transverse. This is evident in Figure 14-37 which shows that the electric and magnetic components drop to zero amplitude at the same time, and rise to maximum amplitude at the same time, and so on. Furthermore, each component faces alternately one way and then the other way as the wave travels along. The distance from one wave peak to the next is one wavelength, λ. (You will discover further evidence of the transverse nature of light in the final section of this chapter.)

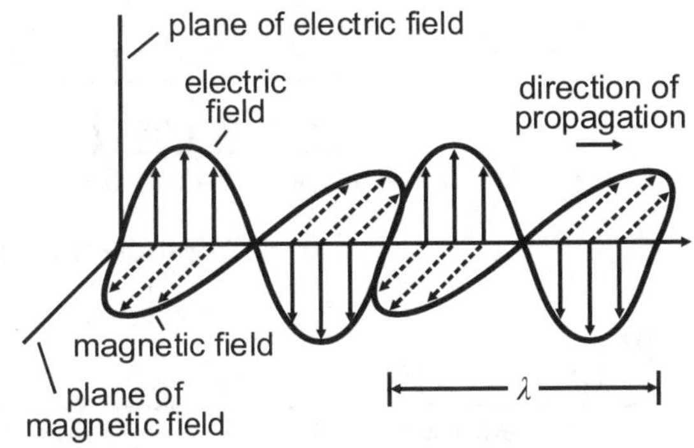

Figure 14-37 *The propagation of an electro-magnetic (e.m.) wave.*

Electromagnetic waves produced by charged particles with regular periodic accelerations have the same frequency as the accelerations causing them. Since an e.m. wave has a frequency and a wavelength and travels at a constant speed in a vacuum, it must obey the universal wave equation, $c = f\lambda$, where c is the speed of the wave, f is the frequency of the wave, and λ is the wavelength. (If an electromagnetic wave is travelling in a vacuum, its speed is 3.00×10^8 m/s, and this speed is given the symbol c rather than v.)

Now, let us relate the consequences of Maxwell's discoveries to the wavelengths of visible light, discovered by Thomas Young. The visible colours range from red, with long wavelengths, to violet, with short wavelengths. The human eye receives the different wavelengths and interprets them as different colours.

Sample Problem 14-9

What is the range of frequencies of visible light, assuming the range of wavelengths in a vacuum is from 400 nm to 700 nm? (Use three significant digits.)

Solution: From $c = f\lambda$,

$$f_1 = \frac{c}{\lambda_1} = \frac{3.00 \times 10^8 \text{ m/s}}{4.00 \times 10^{-7} \text{ m}} = 7.50 \times 10^{14} \text{ Hz}$$

$$f_2 = \frac{c}{\lambda_2} = \frac{3.00 \times 10^8 \text{ m/s}}{7.00 \times 10^{-7} \text{ m}} = 4.29 \times 10^{14} \text{ Hz}$$

Thus, the range of frequencies is from 4.29×10^{14} Hz to 7.50×10^{14} Hz.

The range of frequencies and wavelengths of the visible spectrum are illustrated in part of Figure 14-38. Notice that the visible spectrum forms only a small portion of the entire set of e.m. waves, called the **electromagnetic spectrum** (or e.m. spectrum). The waves in this spectrum all have common properties that the speed is constant (in a vacuum) and they obey the relation $c = f\lambda$.

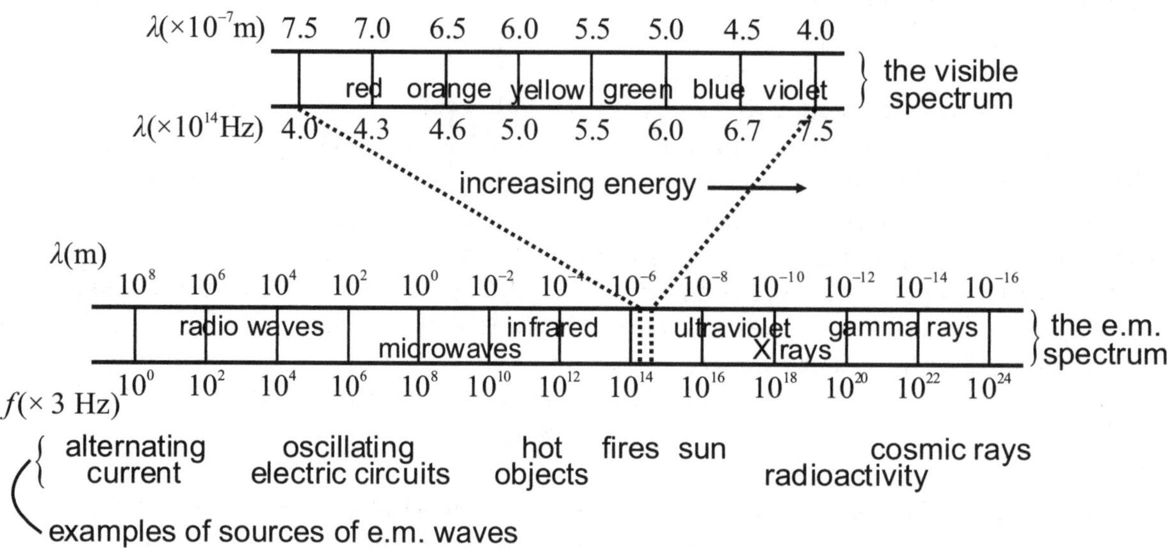

Figure 14-38 *The visible spectrum and the electromagnetic spectrum.*

However, the waves have different energies associated with them. As shown in the diagram, the higher-frequency waves have higher energies than the lower-frequency waves. The relationship between frequency and energy is discussed in detail in Chapter 15. Infrared waves, which are often used for heat treatment, have lower frequencies and energies than visible light. (*Infra* means lower than.) Ultraviolet waves, the type that can cause sunburns and can also lead to skin cancer, have higher frequencies and energies than visible light. (*Ultra* means higher than.) X rays and gamma rays have still higher frequencies and energies. Notice that, in many cases, the classifications of waves overlap each other. For example, radio waves overlap with microwaves, etc.

Did You Know? *James Clerk Maxwell was a brilliant mathematician whose theories of e.m. waves were based on the solutions to mathematical equations rather than on experimental results. Although he was a theoretical physicist and mathematician, he was given the position of professor of experimental physics at Cambridge University, England, in 1871 where he used a fund given to the university to set up the Cavendish Laboratory, a famous science laboratory that he directed until his death in 1879. Approximately eight years after his death, his prediction that accelerating charged particles cause e.m. waves was proven experimentally. This led to numerous applications, such as the transmission of telegraph, radio, and television signals.*

The different energies associated with the different parts of the e.m. spectrum stem from the energies used in producing the waves. Naturally, if an electron loses more energy when it accelerates, the e.m. wave it emits will have a higher energy. The bottom part of Figure 14-38 lists some of the ways in which charged particles are made to accelerate to produce e.m. waves. Once the e.m. waves are produced, they can be used for a wide variety of applications. For example, a modern surgical device called a "Gamma Knife Machine" uses radioactive cobalt-60 to produce gamma rays. These high-energy rays can bombard brain tumours in a precise way without scalpels or incisions.

Like many other scientific theories and proposals, Maxwell's theory of e.m. waves opened the door to many more questions and discoveries. As the 20th century approached, the search for a greater understanding of the nature of light involved the question of what medium, if any, was required for the propagation of e.m. waves. The answers to this question and others led to the photon theory of light, in which light is believed to consist of photons with specific amounts of energy, called quanta. Photons were found to display properties of particles in certain circumstances, and properties of waves in other circumstances. Details of the photon nature of light are left for later in the text (Chapter 15).

Practice

14-51 Why can light energy travel in a vacuum whereas sound energy requires a medium?

14-52 A laser beam is travelling eastward and the magnetic component of one of the laser waves is in the horizontal plane. In what plane is the electric component?

14-53 In each case, which type of wave is associated with the higher energy?
(a) microwaves; X rays
(b) infrared light; ultraviolet light
(c) green light; blue light

14-54 A hydrogen gas emission tube emits light with a wavelength of 411 nm. What are the frequency and colour of this light? [Ans. 7.30×10^{14} Hz]

14-55 Determine the wavelength of each of the following:
(a) an electromagnetic wave with a frequency of 60.0 Hz.
(b) a microwave with a frequency of 99.9 MHz.
(c) a gamma ray with a frequency of 4.17×10^{22} Hz.
[Ans. (a) 5.00×10^6 m (b) 3.00 m (c) 7.19×10^{-15} m]

14-56 For your favourite AM and FM radio stations, calculate:
(a) the frequency in hertz
(b) the wavelength of the emitted waves (The speed of light in air is 3.00×10^8 m/s.)

14.8 POLARIZATION OF LIGHT

Have you ever compared polarizing (or "Polaroid") sunglasses with regular sunglasses by looking through them? Both types of sunglasses reduce the brightness of the light, but only the polarizing glasses reduce the glare off roads or water. How do polarizing sunglasses reduce glare? In what ways can light be polarized? What applications are made of the polarization of light? These and other questions are explored in this section.

Polarization of Transverse Waves

In Sections 14.1 to 14.6, we investigated several instances in which light displayed wave properties, and, in Section 14.7, we learned of the theory that light travels as a transverse electromagnetic (e.m.) wave. Evidence that light waves are transverse rather than longitudinal is found in the polarization of light.

Imagine transverse waves being generated on a rope in the vertical plane, as shown in Figure 14-39 (a). Such a wave is said to be **plane polarized**, which means the wave is oriented in one plane only, in this case, the vertical plane. Diagram (b) shows a convenient symbol indicating plane polarization in the vertical plane; it resembles a view of the rope with the wave travelling toward the observer.

(a) *The hand is vibrating in the vertical plane producing waves on the rope that are polarized vertically.*

direction of waves

(b) *Symbol for a vertically polarized wave.*

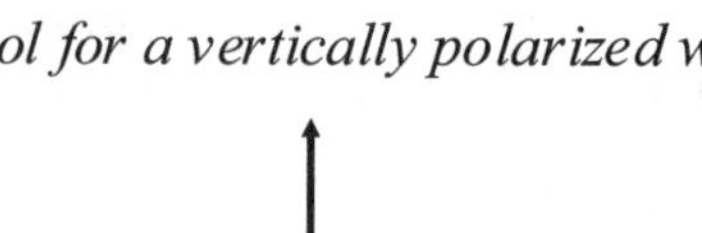

Figure 14-39
A plane polarized wave.

Transverse waves on a rope can be polarized in any plane that is perpendicular to the direction of propagation of the wave. Figure 14-40 shows a horizontally polarized wave with its symbol, as well as a randomly polarized set of waves, again with a convenient symbol. (Besides plane polarization, transverse waves can undergo circular polarization or elliptical polarization. We will restrict our discussion to plane polarization.)

(a) *A horizontally polarized wave and its symbol.*

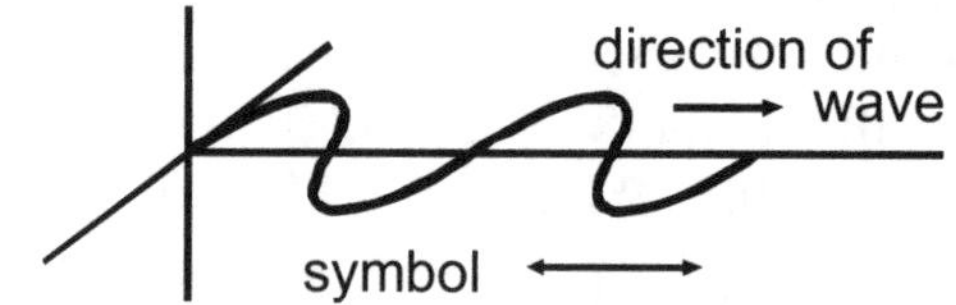

(b) *Randomly polarized waves, with symbol.*

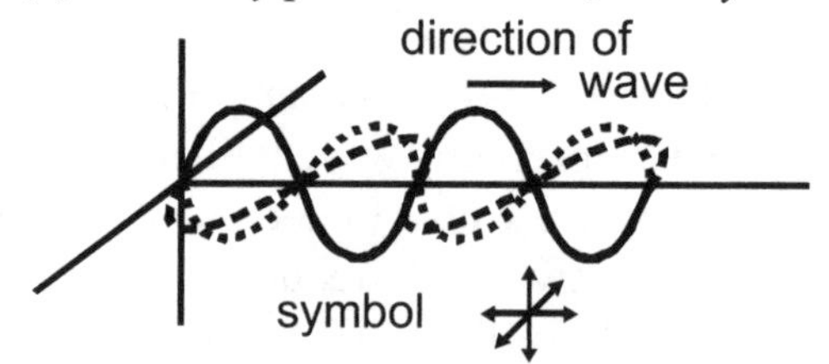

Figure 14-40
Other examples of plane polarized waves.

Longitudinal waves cannot be polarized because they transfer by vibrations that are parallel to their direction of travel, so they have only one possible orientation. Thus, if light waves can be polarized those waves must be transverse.

Ordinary light from such sources as the sun or an incandescent light bulb is not polarized. A source of light, such as the filament of a light bulb, has millions of atoms, each of which can emit light in any direction. Thus, the light emitted has millions upon millions of waves that are oriented randomly.

If ordinary light is unpolarized, how can it become polarized? The four main methods, called selective absorption, reflection, scattering, and double refraction, are described next.

Light Polarization by Selective Absorption

Certain crystals found in nature absorb the transverse light waves in all planes except one; in other words, many of the e.m. waves have been selectively absorbed. Thus, the light transmitted through these crystals is plane polarized. Crystals or other materials that transmit light in one plane and absorb it in the other planes are called *dichroic*. The semi-precious stone called tourmaline has transparent varieties that are dichroic (Figure 14-41).

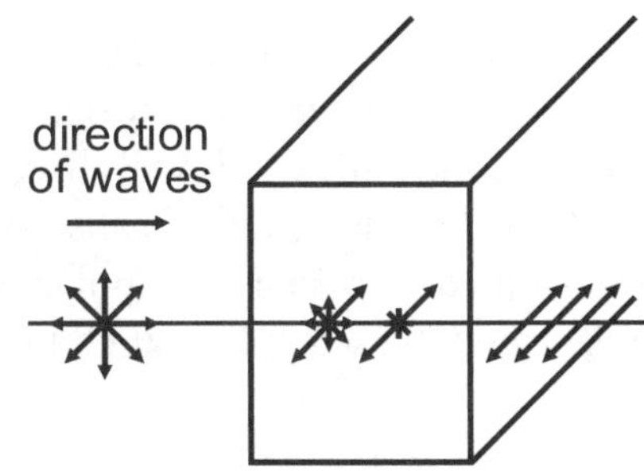

Figure 14-41
An example of a dichroic material. In this case, the material transmits light in the horizontal plane.

The most common polarizing material in use today is called *Polaroid*, which is a plastic absorbing filter containing a dichroic substance; it was invented by an American scientist, Edwin Land. In one technique of manufacturing Polaroid, thin sheets of a substance composed of long-chain molecules of some hydrocarbon, such as polyvinyl alcohol, are stretched so the molecules become parallel. Then the stretched sheets are dipped in iodine which attaches to the long molecules and causes them to become electric conductors. When light interacts with these conducting molecules, it is absorbed.

(a) *Set-up for viewing unpolarized light: If the polarizer and analyzer are perpendicular, the light is absorbed.*

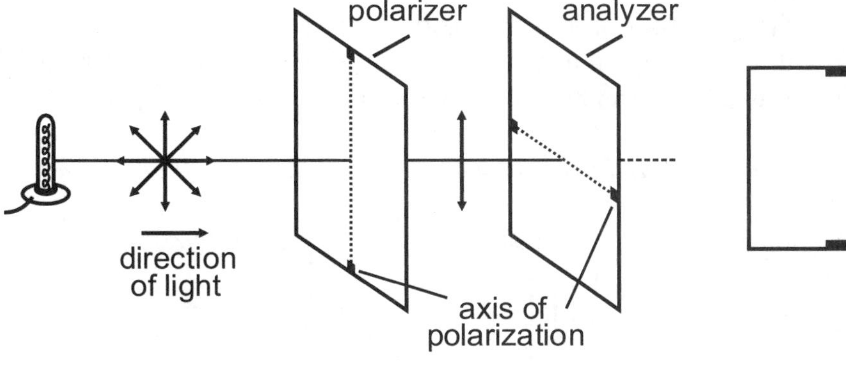

(b) *When two polarizing filters are crossed at 90°, no light is transmitted.*

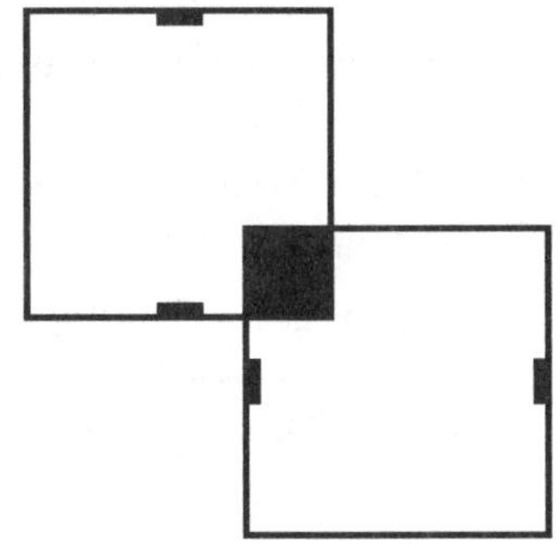

Figure 14-42 *Polarizing filters.*

If unpolarized light from a source, such as a light bulb, strikes a Polaroid filter, the transmitted light is plane polarized in a direction that is parallel to what is called the *axis of polarization* of the filter. (The note[3] at the bottom of the page explains why the polarization axis is perpendicular to the long-chain molecules in the filter.) Often, a little mark on the filter indicates the direction of

[3]The explanation of how long-chain conducting molecules absorb light in all but one plane is based on electromagnetic wave theory, described briefly in the previous section. Like other electromagnetic waves, light waves consist of an electric component and a magnetic component that are perpendicular to each other. The electric component is important in polarization because, when it is parallel to the stretched electrically conducting molecules, it sets up an electric current in the molecules and becomes absorbed. Electric components of the light wave perpendicular to the molecules do not interact with the molecules, and are thus transmitted. Waves with electric components at angles between these extremes are partially absorbed and partially transmitted. We conclude that the axis of polarization is perpendicular to the alignment of the molecules of the type of polarizing filter described.

this axis (Figure 14-42). If you look through such a filter at a light bulb, you will not detect any polarization. However, if you place a second Polaroid filter between the first one and your eyes and rotate either filter, you will discover that, when the two axes of polarization are perpendicular, all or almost all of the light is absorbed. (A small amount of very short wavelength light may still be transmitted.) When two polarizing filters are used to observe light, the first is called the **polarizer** and the second is called the **analyzer**.

> ***Did You Know?*** *The dates given in reference books for Edwin Land's contribution of Polaroid filters vary from about 1928 to 1938. Land was born in 1909, and some books say he discovered the process of making polarizing filters at 19 years of age and developed the technology of mass production later. Of the over 500 inventions that he patented, one of the most famous is the instant camera, which he conceived when he took a photo of his three-year-old daughter and she asked why she could not see the photo right away. The instant camera was manufactured by the Polaroid-Land Corporation, so it is also called a Polaroid camera, after the company name. However, this name has nothing to do with the polarization of light.*

To help visualize polarization, consider vertically polarized waves on a rope travelling toward a set of barriers, each with a slit (Figure 14-43). The first barrier is the polarizer and the second is the analyzer. When the slits of the polarizer and analyzer are both parallel to the plane in which the waves are vibrating, the waves will be transmitted. If, however, the analyzer slit is perpendicular to

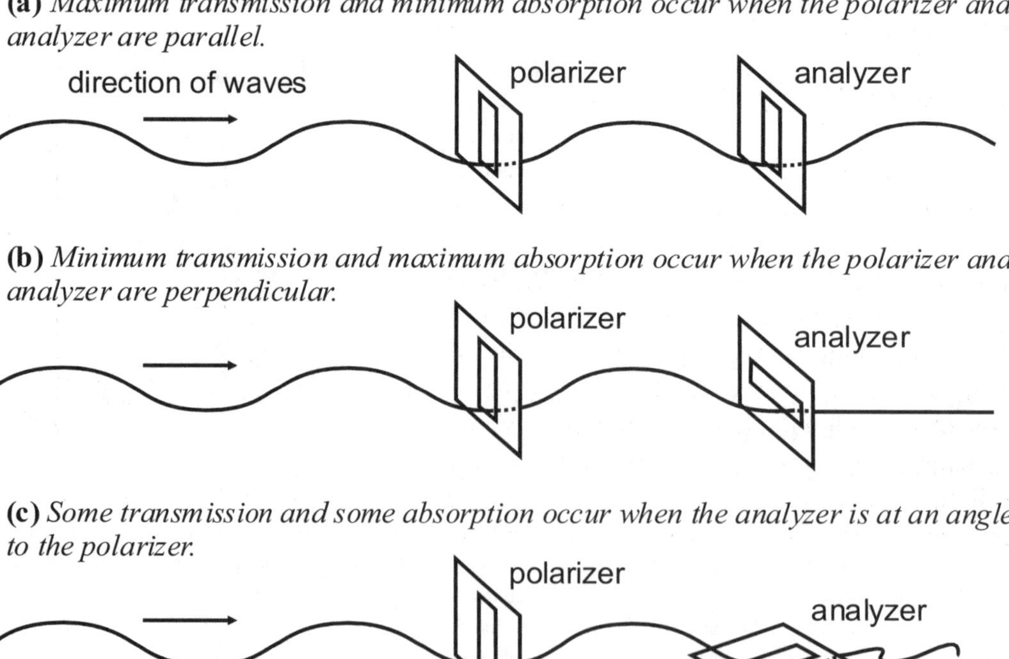
(a) Maximum transmission and minimum absorption occur when the polarizer and analyzer are parallel.
direction of waves
polarizer
analyzer
(b) Minimum transmission and maximum absorption occur when the polarizer and analyzer are perpendicular.
polarizer
analyzer
(c) Some transmission and some absorption occur when the analyzer is at an angle to the polarizer.
polarizer
analyzer

Figure 14-43 *The transmission and absorption of polarized waves on a rope.*

the polarizer slit, the wave energy will be absorbed. (This analogy is helpful to understand why the axes of the polarizer and analyzer must be perpendicular to absorb all the light, but it is opposite to the "physics" of what occurs when light interacts with the long-chain molecules in the polarizing material.)

To determine the amount of light transmitted through a polarizing material, consider a transverse wave striking a polarizer with a vertical polarizing axis at an angle θ to the wave. As shown in Figure 14-44, the amplitude of the transmitted light is the vertical component of the amplitude of the original wave. Thus,

$$A = A_0 \cos\theta \qquad \textbf{(14-17)}$$

where A_0 is the original amplitude and A is the amplitude of the transmitted wave.

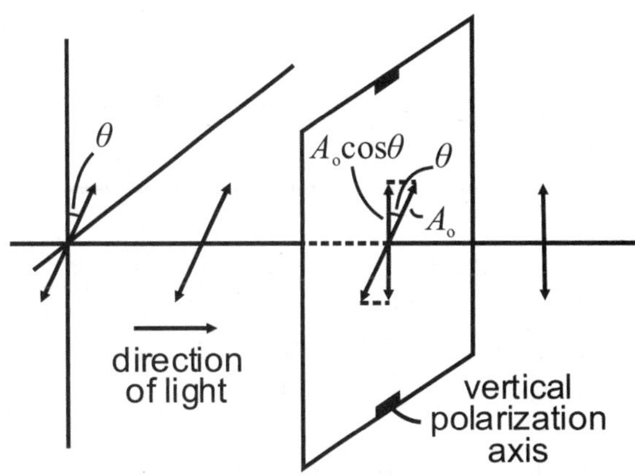

Figure 14-44 *When a wave is at an angle θ to the polarization axis, the amplitude of the transmitted wave is $A_0 \cos\theta$.*

It is known that the intensity of light is proportional to the square of the amplitude, so we can write:

$$I = I_0 \cos^2\theta \qquad \textbf{(14-18)}$$

where I_0 is the intensity of the incident light and I is the intensity of the transmitted light.

Let us extend the situation of a wave in a single plane to unpolarized light, which has waves in all planes perpendicular to the direction of propagation. Figure 14-45 uses a small number of waves to represent all the possible number of waves striking a polarizing filter with a vertical polarizing axis. To determine the total intensity of the transmitted light, we add the components of the individual waves. It should be obvious that 100% of the light in the vertical plane will be transmitted, none of the light in the horizontal plane will be transmitted, and 50% of the light in the plane at 45° will be transmitted (because $\cos 45^\circ = 0.707$ and $\cos^2 45^\circ = 0.5$). Considering these and the remaining components, the average transmitted intensity is 50% of the incident light. This value is a maximum because some of the energy is absorbed even without polarization.

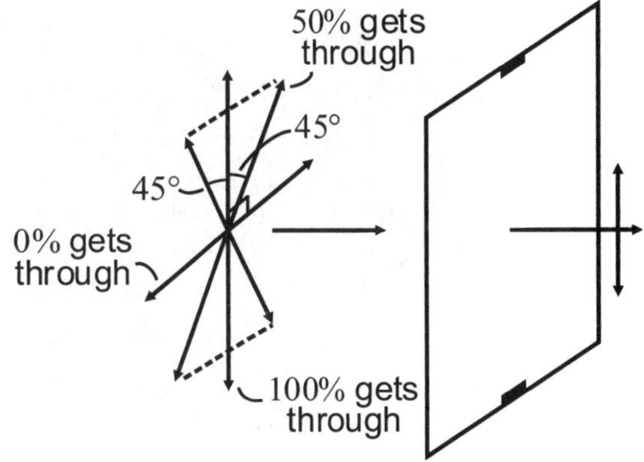

Figure 14-45 *Proof that a maximum of 50% of the intensity of the original unpolarized light is transmitted through a polarizing filter.*

Sample Problem 14-10

Unpolarized light strikes a set of two polarizing filters whose axes are at 45° to each other. What fraction of the intensity of the unpolarized light is observed after the second filter?

Solution: As was just shown, the maximum intensity transmitted through the first filter is 50%, or 1/2 of the intensity of the unpolarized light, I_o. From Eqn. 14-18, the intensity transmitted through the second filter is

$$I_2 = I_1 \cos^2\theta = \left(\tfrac{1}{2} I_o\right)\cos^2 45° = \left(\tfrac{1}{2} I_o\right)\left(\tfrac{1}{2}\right) = \tfrac{1}{4} I_o$$

Thus, ¼ of the initial intensity is transmitted.

An interesting consequence of the transmission of polarized light is that two polarizing sheets can be crossed so no light is transmitted, but when a third sheet is placed between the other two at an angle of 45° to both of them, a fraction of the light gets through. You will be asked to prove this in Practice Question 14-62.

Light Polarization by Reflection

When light strikes flat, non-metallic surfaces such as glass, water, pavement, or paint, it is partially reflected and partially absorbed or transmitted. At most angles of incidence, the reflected portion is partially polarized. The direction of this polarization is parallel to the surface, so reflection from a

Figure 14-46 *Using a polarization filter to reduce glare: These two photos were taken at the same location. The one at the left shows the glare off a restaurant window (a vertically polarized reflection) , allowing you to see trees on the other side of a river. The other photo shows how the polarized light can be absorbed by using a polarization filter, allowing you to see through the restaurant window and beyond another set of windows.*

horizontal surface produces light polarized horizontally. This polarized light is seen as a bright glare that can be eliminated by placing a polarizing filter (the "analyzer") between the reflecting surface and the observer. Polarizing sunglasses are worn with their axis of polarization in the vertical plane, which means they will absorb light waves in the horizontal plane. Polarizing sunglasses do not eliminate the glare from vertical surfaces such a glass windows because such glare is caused by vertically polarized light. Polarizing filters used on cameras can be oriented in any direction to eliminate glare in any one plane at a time. (See Figure 14-46.)

The amount of polarization from a reflecting surface depends on the material as well as the angle of incidence of the light. The maximum polarization of reflected light occurs at an angle of incidence or reflection called the **polarization angle**, θ_p. In 1812, a Scottish physicist named David Brewster discovered that the polarization angle for light travelling from one medium (n_1) into a second medium (n_2), is given by

$$\tan\theta_p = n_2/n_1 \qquad \textbf{(14-19)}$$

where n_1 is the index of refraction of the first medium and n_2 is the index of refraction of the second medium (Figure 14-47).

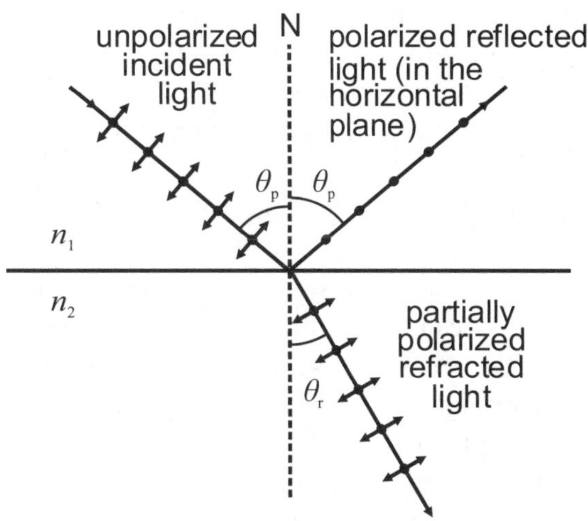

Figure 14-47 *The polarization angle is the angle at which maximum polarization of reflected light occurs.*

Sample Problem 14-11

(a) Determine the polarization angle for light striking water ($n = 1.33$) from air.
(b) What is the angle between the reflected ray in the air and the refracted ray in the water?

Solution: (a) $\tan\theta_p = n_2/n_1 = 1.33/1.00$

$$\therefore \quad \theta_p = 53.06° \quad \text{or} \quad 53.1°$$

(b) Figure 14-48 illustrates the situation. Using Snell's law,

$$n_1 \sin\theta_p = n_2 \sin\theta_r$$

$$\sin\theta_r = \frac{n_1 \sin\theta_p}{n_2} = \frac{1.00 \sin 53.06°}{1.33}$$

$$\therefore \quad \theta_r = 36.9°$$

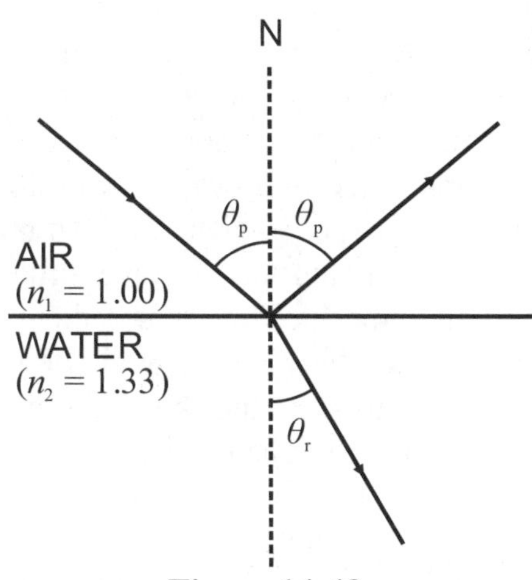

Figure 14-48
Sample Problem 14-11.

Thus the angle of refraction is 36.9°. Notice that 36.9° + 53.1° = 90°

The final line in the solution in the sample problem above leads to a simple conclusion that the **sum of the polarization angle and the angle of refraction is 90°**; i.e., $\theta_p + \theta_r = 90°$.

Did You Know? *The polarization angle is also known as Brewster's angle. David Brewster (1781-1868) was the person who invented the kaleidoscope.*

An application of the polarization angle is that the end windows of certain lasers are attached at this angle so the maximum amount of light coming from the laser is transmitted through the glass window. (Remember that minimum reflection occurs with maximum polarization, and results in maximum transmission.)

Light Polarization by Scattering

When light strikes a system of atoms and molecules, such as a gas, the electrons in the atoms and molecules can absorb the light and re-radiate part of it. The absorption and re-radiation of light by a substance is called **scattering**. A common example of the scattering of light occurs in the sky when sunlight is incident upon air molecules. The amount of scattering depends on the size of the wavelength of the light relative to the particles doing the scattering. White light from the sun consists of many different wavelengths, but it is the blue waves that are scattered the most in Earth's atmosphere, so the sky appears to be blue. The longer wavelengths, from yellow to red, are transmitted through the atmosphere more readily, so the sun appears to be yellow when it is viewed more directly and reddish when the light passes through more atmosphere (at sunrise and sunset).

Scattered light is polarized. To see why, refer to Figure 14-49, which shows unpolarized light from the sun striking air molecules in Earth's atmosphere. The sun, the observer, and the molecules observed form a plane. To simplify our discussion, we will consider only the transverse light waves from the sun that are parallel and perpendicular to that plane[4]. Waves that are parallel to the plane strike electrons in the air molecules and cause them to accelerate parallel to the plane. Any light re-radiated by these electrons cannot be in the direction of the acceleration, so the observer will not see any of this light. However, waves perpendicular to the plane strike electrons in the molecules and cause them to accelerate perpendicular to the plane. The re-radiated light in this case can be observed. Thus, if the plane is horizontal, the scattered light is vertical, a situation that can be observed at sunrise and sunset. Other polarization planes occur at other times of the day, and the direction of the planes depends on where the observer looks in the sky. (The best way to observe scattered light in the sky is to view the sky away from the sun through an analyzer. Never look directly toward the sun, even through a filter.)

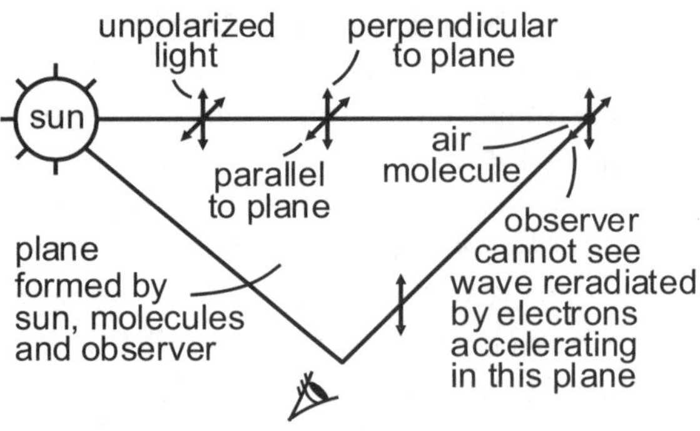

Figure 14-49
The polarization of scattered light in the sky.

[4]To be more precise, what we are talking about is the electric component of the transverse e.m. waves.

The scattering of light has many applications. Photographers take into consideration the scattering of light in the sky. Some insects, such as bees, and other animals, such as the horseshoe crab, have eyes that are sensitive to polarized light. Thus, they can navigate using the scattered light in the sky. Biologists study internal cell structure using light scattering; the process is non-destructive and does not interfere with normal cell functions. In the field of medicine, for example, the scattering of laser light is used to analyze cancerous cells. Chemists use light scattering to analyze the structure of molecules of such substances as nylon, rubber, and compounds found in living organisms. Atmospheric scientists study regions high in the atmosphere by using the scattering of radar waves, which are electromagnetic waves with longer wavelengths than light. These waves scatter off rain droplets, hailstones, and snowflakes. And astronomers use starlight scattered off particles in the far corners of the universe to learn more about the evolution of stars and galaxies.

Light Polarization by Double Refraction

When light travels from air into another transparent medium, its speed changes and it refracts (except if the incident light is normal to the surface). In many substances, such as glass and water, the speed of light is the same in all directions, so the amount of refraction can be found by applying Snell's law $\left(n_1 \sin \theta_1 = n_2 \sin \theta_2\right)$. In some crystalline substances, however, the speed of light may be different in different directions, and light that enters can be split so that two portions refract different amounts. The double refraction that occurs in a transparent crystalline substance in which the speed of light can differ in different directions is called **birefringence**. Calcite (also called Iceland spar) and quartz are examples of birefringent media.

If a prism made of birefringent material is used to view an object, a double image of the object is seen. This observation has been known for hundreds of years because calcite was found in its natural state in Iceland by sailors who took samples of the crystal to other parts of the world.

How does light entering a birefringent medium "know" which portion should travel at which speed? The answer depends on the plane in which the transverse light waves are vibrating. This explains why double refraction causes polarization of light. Figure 14-50 shows an unpolarized light beam incident upon a birefringent medium. Waves parallel to the surface slow down more and thus refract more, as shown by the dots. Think of these dots as waves vibrating into and out of the page. Waves perpendicular to the surface slow down less and thus refract less, as shown by the arrows. Light emerging on the far side of the medium remains split into two plane-polarized beams. Thus, double refraction provides the fourth means of polarizing light.

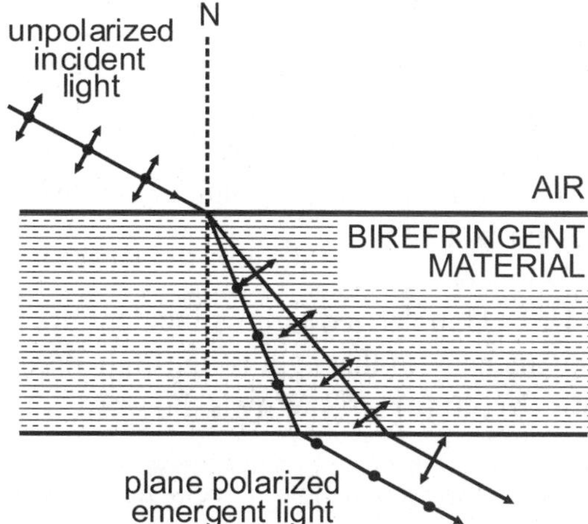

Figure 14-50 *Polarization by double refraction.*

Did You Know? *There is evidence that the Vikings, who sailed the northern seas more than 1000 years ago, used a dichroic mineral called cordierite to help them navigate. Near the Arctic Circle in the summer the sun dips below the horizon, so it cannot be used directly for navigation, but the sky remains bright so the stars commonly used for navigation cannot be seen. The Vikings could look at the scattered light of the sky through cordierite and use their observations to determine directions.*

Another form of birefringence, called *stress birefringence*, occurs when light passes through a transparent medium that is undergoing various amounts of stress. A typical example of such a material is plexiglass. Light interacts differently with molecules under high stress than those under low stress. This causes the light to travel at different speeds through the material. When the material is placed between two polarizing sheets and viewed in white light, beautiful colour patterns are seen and regions of high stress can be identified by the closeness of the colour bands. A similar method is applied to plexiglass models of bridges, tools, and machine parts to determine regions of high stress during the designing stages.

Practice

14-57 Name two sources of unpolarized light. How is this light different from plane polarized light?

14-58 Can sound waves be polarized? Explain.

14-59 What is the difference between a polarizer and an analyzer?

14-60 An unpolarized flashlight beam is aimed directly upward. Can any of the waves be oriented in a plane that is:
(a) vertical in the east-west direction?
(b) vertical in the north-south direction?
(c) horizontal?

14-61 Unpolarized light is incident upon a pair of polarizing sheets. What maximum fraction of the intensity of this light is transmitted through the sheets if their axes are oriented at an angle of (a) 30° (b) 60° (c) 90°? Why is the word "maximum" used here? [Ans. 3/8; 1/8; 0]

14-62 Two polarizing sheets are placed with their axes crossed, then a third sheet is placed between them at an angle of 45° to both of them. What fraction of the initial intensity of the light is transmitted through this set of sheets? [Ans. ¼]

14-63 A store has several pairs of sunglasses that are labelled "Polaroid." Describe how you would check to be sure the glasses are indeed polarizing using:
(a) two pairs of sunglasses (b) a single pair of sunglasses.

14-64 You are given a Polaroid plate that has not had its polarizing axis marked. How would you determine the orientation of the polarization axis of the plate?

14-65 (a) What is the polarization angle (the angle of maximum polarization) for light striking glass (n = 1.52)?
(b) What is the angle of refraction in the glass for the situation in (a) above?
[Ans. (a) 56.7° (b) 33.3°]

14-66 Determine the polarization angle for light that is travelling in water (n = 1.33) toward glass (n = 1.56). [Ans. 50.0°]

14-67 A person is facing toward the sun while fishing in a calm lake (n = 1.33).
(a) In what plane is the light reflected from the lake polarized?
(b) The person puts on a pair of polarizing sunglasses. In what plane should the polarization axis of the glasses be to reduce glare from the water?
(c) If the reflected light from the lake is most strongly polarized, at what angle is the sun above the horizon? [Ans. (c) 36.9°]

14-68 What colour does the sky appear to be on the moon where there is no atmosphere? Explain why.

14-69 When clouds are not in a dark shadow, they appear to be white in daylight. Explain why the clouds are white while the surrounding sky is blue. (Hint: Water droplets are different in size from air molecules.)

14-70 A prism made of calcite or some other birefringent material is placed on a printed page and a double image is seen. Predict what you would observe if you viewed the double image through an analyzer and rotated the analyzer through 360°. (If possible, try this.)

CHAPTER FOCUS

In this chapter, we observed many light phenomena that can be explained if we consider light to be a wave. We compared the characteristics of light waves to the characteristics of mechanical waves (Chapter 13). Light undergoes diffraction and interference when it interacts with objects whose size is approximately the same as the wavelength of the light. Equations derived for single- and double-slit interference patterns were used to determine the wavelengths of visible light. The ability to resolve two objects depends on the diffraction of light (as well as on other factors). The concepts and equations for double-slit interference extend to multiple-slit diffraction gratings. These gratings provide one means of studying various kinds of spectra. Refraction of light occurs when light travels (at an angle) from one medium to another of different optical density.

Fringes observed when light reflects off (or is transmitted through) thin films or air wedges are also interference phenomena. These fringe patterns can be analyzed mathematically and the interference can be applied in practical ways.

Light is an electromagnetic (e.m.) wave that can be produced by a charged particle undergoing acceleration. Such a wave can propagate through space as the electric and magnetic components continually create each other as the wave travels along at a constant speed of 3.00×10^8 m/s (in a vacuum). The visible spectrum is only a small part of the set of e.m. waves called the e.m. spectrum. The waves have different frequencies, wavelengths, and energies, as well as many different uses.

The transverse nature of e.m. waves is verified by the ability of light to be plane polarized. The four ways of polarizing light are by selective absorption, reflection, scattering, and double refraction. Polarization has several applications.

In the next chapter, we will see that certain discoveries near the beginning of the 20th century revealed a particle nature of light that forced another rethinking of the theories of light. This will lead to an understanding of the photon theory of light.

VOCABULARY REVIEW

You should be able to define or explain each of the following words or phrases.

Huygens' principle
coherent waves
resolution
diffraction grating
spectroscopy
emission spectrum
absorption spectrum
refraction of light
angle of refraction
angle of emergence
optical density
index of refraction
Snell's law of refraction
electromagnetic (e.m.) waves
electromagnetic (e.m.) spectrum
plane polarized waves
polarizer
analyzer
polarization angle
scattering (of light)
birefringence

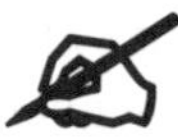

CHAPTER REVIEW

14-71 For incident light of wavelength λ in a double-slit experiment, the path difference from the two slits to the middle of the second-order maximum is:
(a) $\lambda/4$ (b) $\lambda/2$ (c) λ (d) 2λ (e) 0

14-72 In a single-slit interference pattern, the light source is changed from red light to blue light. The corresponding interference pattern:
(a) spreads out more because the wavelength increases
(b) becomes narrower because the frequency decreases
(c) spreads out more because the frequency increases

(d) becomes narrower because the wavelength decreases
(e) remains the same width because as the wavelength decreases the frequency increases

14-73 A diffraction grating diffracts violet light through an angle that is:
(a) independent of the frequency of the light
(b) the same as the angle for red light
(c) less than the angle for red light
(d) greater than the angle for red light
(e) none of these

14-74 When a beam of light travels from air into water at an angle of incidence greater than 0°, it undergoes a change in:
(a) speed and direction only
(b) speed, direction, and wavelength only
(c) speed, direction, wavelength, and frequency
(d) wavelength and frequency only
(e) direction, speed, and frequency only

14-75 Which statement is false?
(a) Both transverse and longitudinal waves can be polarized.
(b) Both transverse and longitudinal waves can diffract.
(c) Both transverse and longitudinal waves can interfere.
(d) Both transverse and longitudinal waves can be reflected.
(e) Both transverse and longitudinal waves can be refracted.

14-76 The polarization angle for light striking a transparent medium is 49°. If unpolarized light strikes the medium at an angle of incidence of 49°, the:
(a) maximum transmission of the light occurs
(b) any light that refracts does so at an angle of 49°
(c) any light that refracts does so at an angle of 41°
(d) both (a) and (b) are true
(e) both (a) and (c) are true

14-77 What is monochromatic light?

14-78 Under what conditions do Huygens' wavelets produce (a) a maximum and (b) a minimum?

14-79 Could Huygens' principle be used to explain the diffraction of sound around an obstacle? Why or why not?

14-80 Do the lines in Figure 14-51 appear to be resolved? At what distance can you just resolve the lines using (a) both eyes (b) your left eye only (c) your right eye only? If you wear eyeglasses or contact lenses, repeat the experiment without them.

Figure 14-51
Question 14-80.

14-81 Monochromatic light passes through a double slit and creates an interference pattern on a screen 2.84 m from the slits. The slit separation is 0.160 mm and the distance between the first maxima on either side of the central maximum is 2.12 cm.
(a) What is the wavelength of the light?
(b) What is the angular separation between the central maximum and the adjacent bright fringes?
(c) Compare the sine and tangent of the angle found in (b) above. What is the significance of your answer in terms of the derivation of the double-slit interference equations?
[Ans. (a) 597 nm (b) 0.214°]

14-82 Light of wavelength 444 nm is used to compare a double-slit pattern and a single-slit pattern. The double slits are separated by 0.150 mm and the single slit is 0.150 mm wide. In both cases, the distance from the slit(s) to the screen is 3.65 m. Compare the distance from the middle of the central maximum to the first dark fringe for each pattern. [Ans. 5.40 mm; 10.8 mm]

14-83 A point source emits light of wavelength 520 nm toward a single slit of width 0.085 mm. The light creates an interference pattern on a screen located 2.2 m from the screen.
(a) What is the width of the central maximum?
(b) What angle do the first-order fringes subtend with the slit? [Ans. (a) 2.7 cm (b) 0.70°]

14-84 The situation in the previous question is altered by adding a second point source of the same wavelength, with both sources located 3.6 m from the slit.
(a) Determine the distance between the sources so they are just resolved on the screen.
(b) What angle do the sources subtend with the slit? [Ans. (a) 2.2 cm (b) 0.35°]

14-85 How does the resolution of two point sources of light depend on (a) the wavelength of the light and (b) the width of the aperture through which the point sources are viewed?

14-86 Which colour filter, red or blue, would allow for better resolution of distant stars viewed through a telescope? Why?

14-87 How does the spacing of the maxima in a diffraction grating pattern depend on (a) the number of lines per centimetre of the grating and (b) the wavelength of the light?

14-88 Monochromatic light is incident upon a diffraction grating with 4500 lines/cm. At a distance of 1.60 m from the grating, the diffraction pattern is observed on a screen, and the distance between maxima is found to be 38 cm. Determine the wavelength of the light.
[Ans. 5.1×10^2 nm]

14-89 White light incident upon a diffraction grating with 5000 lines/cm produces a pattern on a screen 1.8 m from the grating. The first blue and red maxima are located at distances from the central maximum of 25 cm and 35 cm, respectively. What is the ratio of the red wavelength to the blue wavelength? [Ans. 1.4:1.0]

14-90 The speed of light in carbon disulfide is 1.84×10^8 m/s. A ray of light in air strikes the surface of the carbon disulfide at an angle of incidence of 37.1°.
(a) What is the index of refraction of this medium?

(b) What is the angle of refraction in the carbon disulfide? [Ans. (a) 1.63 (b) 21.7°]

14-91 The index of refraction of carbon tetrachloride is 1.46. Determine:
(a) the speed of light in this medium.
(b) the angle of emergence in air for a light ray in the carbon tetrachloride (CCl_4) to air, having an angle of incidence of 22.8° at the CCl_4-air interference. [Ans. (a) 2.05×10^8 m/s (b) 34.5°]

14-92 State how the first variable depends on the second variable:
(a) the *speed of light* in a medium and the *index of refraction* of the medium
(b) the *amount of refraction* of a light ray entering a medium from air and the *index of refraction* of the medium

14-93 Estimate how many wavelengths of yellow light would fit into a cross-section of a pane of window glass. Why is even thin glass not considered to be a "thin film?"

14-94 A thin film of plastic (n = 1.52) is placed over another material (n = 1.36) and light with a wavelength in air of 555 nm reflects from the plastic.
(a) What minimum thickness of plastic will cause a maximum reflection? [Ans. 91.3 nm]
(b) When the film is the thickness found in (a), is the transmission maximum or minimum?
(c) If the film were three times as thick as found in (a) above, would the reflected light be maximum or minimum? Explain.

14-95 A quarter-wavelength coating of magnesium fluoride (n = 1.38) covers a lens (n = 1.56). The coating is 86.5 nm thick. What are the wavelength and colour of the light undergoing maximum transmission through the lens? [Ans. 477 nm]

14-96 Do the equations for air-wedge interference correspond to an air-oil-water situation or a quarter-wavelength film of magnesium fluoride over glass? Explain.

14-97 Monochromatic light of wavelength 430 nm reflects off two parallel glass plates, each 12.0 cm long, separated by an air wedge. Assuming the plates touch at one end and are separated by a hair of diameter 0.064 mm at the other end, determine the number of bright fringes per centimetre observed in the pattern. [Ans. 23 fringes/cm]

14-98 What does X-ray diffraction through crystals reveal about the structure of matter?

14-99 Estimate or determine the diameter of a hair from your head, then state what waves in the e.m. spectrum would diffract most easily around the hair.

14-100 An electron is forced to accelerate back and forth in a radio transmission tower at a frequency of 1.12 MHz. Determine the frequency and wavelength of the e.m. waves emitted during these accelerations. [Ans. 1.12 MHz; 2.68×10^2 m]

14-101 State how light waves are (a) produced and (b) transmitted through a vacuum.

14-102 (a) What properties does visible light have in common with other parts of the e.m. spectrum? (b) What properties are different?

14-103 One example of wave interference described in Chapter 13 and not discussed for e.m. waves is a standing wave. Assume that e.m. waves reflect off a barrier so that a standing wave pattern is set up with 65 cm between the nodes.
(a) What is the frequency of these waves? [Ans. 2.3×10^8 Hz]
(b) To what part of the e.m. spectrum do these waves belong?

14-104 Compare the methods used for manufacturing polarizing filters and diffraction gratings.

14-105 What experimental evidence strongly suggests that light waves are transverse?

<u>14-106</u> In certain types of Polaroid filter, the stretched molecules absorb light waves having their electric field parallel to the molecules. Compare the direction of the magnetic field of those waves with the axis of transmission of the filter.

14-107 Unpolarized light passes through a polarizer and an analyser. What should be the angle between the polarizing axes if the transmitted intensity is (a) 1/4 and (b) 1/2 of the original intensity? [Ans. (a) 60° (b) 45°]

14-108 The angle between the axes of a polarizer and an analyzer is 52°. What percentage of the initial intensity of unpolarized light is absorbed? [Ans. 81%]

14-109 Light in air strikes a transparent medium at an angle of incidence equal to the polarization angle of the medium. For the light that enters the medium, the angle of refraction is 31.5°.
(a) Draw a diagram of this situation, showing the angles of incidence, reflection, and refraction.
(b) Determine the index of refraction of the medium. [Ans. 1.63]

APPLYING YOUR KNOWLEDGE

<u>14-110</u> What would happen to the spacing of the maxima in a double-slit interference pattern if the entire set-up were viewed under water? Why?

14-111 Determine the maximum number of bright fringes, including the central maximum, that can be observed in a double-slit interference pattern using 685 nm light passing through slits separated by 6.20×10^{-6} m. [Ans. 19]

<u>14-112</u> A single slit of adjustable width is used to view a diffraction pattern of 628 nm light.
(a) Assuming the slit width starts at about 6300 nm, what happens to the pattern as the slit width decreases?
(b) As the slit width decreases, at what width will there no longer be any dark fringes observed?

14-113 What are the advantages of a diffraction grating over a prism for use in a spectroscope?

14-114 Snell's law ($n_1 \sin \theta_1 = n_2 \sin \theta_2$) applies if the angles are measured from the normal. Would it also apply if the angles were measured from the interface between the two media? If so, verify that it does with an example. If not, offer a new form of the law.

14-115 Derive two equations for light transmitted through a thin film of soap surrounded by air. One equation is for maxima and the other for minima. These equations will resemble equations 14-11 and 14-12 but will be for transmitted light rather than reflected light. (Hint: Consider two rays of light, one being transmitted straight through the film and the other being reflected twice off the interior surface of the film.)

14-116 A faint bright and dark fringe pattern is observed on the *transmitted* side of a vertical soap film in light of wavelength 544 nm. Determine the thickness of the film at the:
(a) third minimum from the top of the film.
(b) fourth maximum from the top of the film. [Ans. (a) 716 nm (b) 818 nm]

14-117 Unpolarized light is incident upon a set of four polarizing filters, each at an angle of 30° to the previous one. What portion of the intensity of the original light is transmitted through the filters? [Ans. 27/128, or 21%]

14-118 Prove that the sum of the polarization angle of a medium of index of refraction n_2 and the angle of refraction in the medium is 90°. (Hint: Consider Snell's law of refraction as well as the equation for the polarization angle.)

KEY OBJECTIVES

Having completed this chapter you should now be able to do the following.

1. Recognize a diffraction pattern of light around a sharp edge or through a single aperture.
2. Apply Huygens' principle in a diagram to illustrate why diffraction of light occurs.
3. Recognize a double-slit interference pattern and describe how various factors affect the pattern.
4. Define coherent waves and describe why light must be coherent to produce a double-slit interference pattern.
5. Manipulate the equations involving double-slit interference variables (θ, λ, x, L, d, N, or M) to determine unknown quantities.
6. Describe the conditions under which a single-slit diffraction pattern is produced.
7. Manipulate the equations involving single-slit interference variables (θ, λ, x, L, w, N, or M) to determine unknown quantities.
8. State what factors affect the resolution of two objects and describe how they do so.
9. Apply Rayleigh's criterion to determine the angular separation for resolution through a single slit.
10. Compare the interference pattern produced by a diffraction grating with that produced by a double slit.
11. Manipulate the equations involving diffraction grating variables (θ, λ, x, L, d, and M) to determine unknown quantities.
12. Distinguish between a continuous spectrum and a line spectrum, and between an emission spectrum and an absorption spectrum.

13. Describe applications of spectroscopy.
14. Describe examples of diffraction patterns in two and three dimensions.
15. Define refraction of light, and describe how it relates to optical density and the speed of light in different media.
16. Define and calculate the index of refraction in terms of the speed of light in different media.
17. Apply Snell's law of refraction to determine any of the index of refraction, the angle of incidence, or the angle of refraction for light travelling from air into another medium.
18. Draw ray diagrams of the refraction of light through prisms.
19. Recognize whether or not light will undergo a phase change when it reaches the interface between two media, and apply this knowledge to explain how a thin-film or an air-wedge interference pattern is created.
20. Explain the conditions required to observe spectral colours in a thin-film or air-wedge interference pattern.
21. Manipulate the equations involving thin-film and air-wedge interference variables (t, λ_{film}, λ_{air}, n, N, and M) to determine unknown quantities.
22. Describe applications of both thin-film and air-wedge interference.
23. Describe how an electromagnetic (e.m.) wave is produced and propagated through space.
24. Recognize the various parts of the electromagnetic spectrum.
25. Apply the universal wave equation to determine any one of the speed, frequency, or wavelength of an e.m. wave given the other two quantities.
26. Appreciate why the search for an explanation of light is a good example of the process of science.
27. Describe how light can become plane polarized by selective absorption, reflection, scattering, and double refraction.
28. Determine the portion of the intensity of light transmitted through a single polarizing filter, or through a set of two or more filters, knowing the angle between the axes of polarization of the filters.
29. Determine the polarization angle for light reflecting off the surface of a medium of known index of refraction.
30. Describe applications of the polarization of light.

ANSWERS TO SELECTED QUESTIONS

14-1 The diffraction of the wavelets will be maximum when the wavelength of the wavelets is approximately the same as the width of (a) the barrier and (b) the aperture.

14-2 Diffraction of light can be observed through very small apertures because of the very short wavelengths of visible light, but not through large openings, such as windows.

14-3 Radio waves diffract easily around regularly sized objects because they have a much longer wavelength than the waves of visible light.

14-5 (a) The spacing is directly proportional to the wavelength.
(b) The spacing is directly proportional to the distance from the slits to the screen.
(c) The sine of the angle of separation is inversely proportional to the slit separation, and since θ is small, $\sin\theta$ is approximately equal to θ (if θ is measured in radians) and therefore, the angle is also inversely proportional the slit separation.

14-12 As the slit width decreases, the diffraction pattern spreads out more. (As Eqn. 14-6 shows, x is inversely proportional to w.)

14-13 By applying Eqn. 14-5 with $N = 1$, you can see that the answer would be the same because sin θ will remain 1/350 even if the wavelength changes.

14-16 (a) The resolution increases as the separation of the objects increases.
(b) The resolution decreases as the distance from the objects increases.
(c) The resolution increases as the as the slit width increases.
(d) The resolution decreases as the as the wavelength on the light increases.

14-18 The grating labelled 10 000 lines/cm has smaller spacings than the other grating, so the pattern will be more spread out and will have a fewer number of maxima. (Referring to Eqn. 14-8, we see that sin θ is inversely proportional to the spacing of the lines on the grating.)

14-19 Nature never gives us something for nothing. The brighter, sharper maxima are a result of a greater concentration of light at the maxima. This contrasts with a double-slit pattern in which the maxima are more spread out.

14-21 By applying Eqn. 14-8 (sin $\theta = M\,\lambda\,/d$) to the given data to two significant digits, we see that the $M = 2$ spectrum is spread out from 19° to 34°, while the $M = 3$ spectrum is spread out from 29° to 57°. Thus, the patterns overlap between 29° (the violet end of the $M = 3$ spectrum) and 34° (the red end of the $M = 2$ spectrum).

14-25 Your diagram should show two overlapping diffraction patterns, one vertical and one horizontal, with the vertical pattern spread out farther than horizontal one because the vertical spacing is smaller and sin θ is inversely proportional to the spacing.

14-32 (a) away from the normal (b) toward the normal
(c) toward the normal (d) away from the normal

14-34 The crystal is heavy flint glass (with an index of refraction of 1.65).

14-41 (a) in phase (open-end reflection) (b) out of phase (fixed-end reflection) (c) in phase

14-46 (a) maximum (b) minimum

14-47 The colour of the transmitted light cannot be red.

14-48 The minimum occurs because the light reflecting off the inside surface of the convex surface undergoes open-end reflection while the light that reflects nearby off the flat surface undergoes fixed-end reflection, causing the two reflections to be out-of-phase. If the reflected light is a minimum then the transmitted light must be a maximum.

14-49 When the reflected light is viewed, concentric circular patterns of minima and maxima will be observed in both cases, with the very centre of each pattern dark (a minimum). However, the pattern in (a) will be more spread out than that in (b). (Recall that adjacent maxima (or minima) are created when the air-wedge thickness changes by one-half the wavelength of the light.)

14-52 the vertical plane

14-53 (a) X rays (b) ultraviolet light (c) blue light

14-58 Sound waves cannot be polarized because they are longitudinal.

14-60 (a) yes (b) yes (c) no

14-63 (a) Cross one lens of a pair of sunglasses with one lens of the second pair, and if no light is transmitted through the crossed lenses, they must be polarizing lenses.
(b) Find an example in the room of glare off a horizontal surface, such as the floor, then view the glare though the sunglasses; if the glare is eliminated (or at least substantially reduced), the glasses must have polarizing lenses.

14-64 One way is to view the polarized light reflected off a non-metallic surface through the Polaroid plate. If the surface is horizontal, the reflected light is polarized horizontally, so if you orient the Polaroid plate so the glare is removed from the reflection, you can conclude that you are holding it such that the polarization axis is vertical.

14-68 The sky appears black on the moon because there are no atmospheric particles to scatter the light.

14-70 Assume for this description that the double image consists of two letter *a*'s, one of which is slightly above and to the left of the other. If you view the double image through an analyser such that you see only the upper-left *a*, as you rotate the analyser through 90° that *a* will disappear and the lower-right *a* will appear. Rotating the analyser a further 90° will produce the first *a*, then through another 90° (a total rotation so far of 270°) will produce the second *a*.

14-71 (d); 14-72 (d); 14-73 (c); 14-74 (b); 14-75 (a); 14-76 (e)

14-86 Resolution of light sources such as stars becomes poorer as the wavelength of the light increases because diffraction is greater with longer wavelengths. Thus, a blue filter would provide better resolution because blue light has a shorter wavelength than red light.

14-93 You can use ballpark numbers to determine that a window pane's thickness is in the order of 10^4 wavelengths of yellow light. This is huge compared to thin films, which are generally less than one wavelength in thickness.

14-94 (b) The transmission is minimum.

(c) The reflected light would again be a maximum. In (a), the plastic film is $1/4\lambda_{\text{film}}$ thick. So in (c) it is $3/4\lambda_{\text{film}}$ thick. In the latter case, the path length of the reflected light is one wavelength longer than in (a), so the phase of the reflected wave is same when it emerges from the thin film.

14-96 The reflected light from a one-quarter wavelength air wedge is maximum, which would also be the case with an air-oil-water situation. (This can be shown using basic theory of fixed-end and open-end reflections combined with path length of the waves.) The quarter wavelength film of magnesium fluoride over glass produces a minimum reflection, not a maximum.

14-106 The direction of the magnetic field is parallel to the axis of transmission.

14-110 The spacing (Δx) of the maxima in a double-slit interference pattern is directly proportional to the wavelength of the light, and under water the wavelength of the light is lower than that in air, so the spacing is closer.

14-112 (a) At the beginning, the slit width is about 10 times the wavelength, so the pattern would be spread out slightly, like that in Figure 14-14(c). Then as the width decreases, the pattern spreads out more and more, like the pattern illustrated in Figure 14-14(b).

(b) When the slit width decreases to about the size of the wavelength (628 nm), the diffraction pattern spreads to its maximum amount, so there will no longer be any dark fringes.

CHAPTER 15

WAVE-PARTICLE DUALITY

We know that light has wave properties (Chapter 14), but we shall see in this chapter that light has particle properties as well, often exhibited when light interacts with matter. So what does light consist of? Particles or waves? This question puzzled the best scientific minds early in the 20th century; the answer is in this chapter. We shall also see that particles have wave properties, which we shall use in Chapter 16 in describing the quantum nature of atoms. It seems bizarre to think of particles as waves, but this approach is unavoidable if we are to explain certain experimental results.

15.1 THE PHOTOELECTRIC EFFECT

In the late 1800s, the wave nature of light was firmly established. The interference and diffraction of light could be explained readily in terms of waves, and the description of light as waves of oscillating electric and magnetic fields seemed to present a complete picture of light. This period was a rather smug one for physicists because *classical physics* (pre-1900 mechanics, electricity and magnetism, and thermodynamics) was extremely well understood. Many physicists believed that all that remained to be done was to measure various fundamental quantities to a few more decimal places.

Then some experimental puzzles began to emerge, which led the way to the new 20th-century physics: quantum mechanics, special and general relativity, etc. This is physics that scientists in the 1700s and 1800s never dreamed of. The physics of atoms, molecules, nuclei, and elementary particles involves radical new approaches to the way we think about the universe.

One of the puzzling experiments resulted from work done by Heinrich Hertz in 1887. While investigating the propagation of electromagnetic waves, he noticed that sparks would jump more readily between two charged metal spheres if their surfaces were illuminated by the light from another spark. The light seemed to facilitate the release of charges from the surfaces. This in itself was not too surprising — since light has energy, we might expect that the energy could be transferred to electrons in the spheres, with the resulting release of the electrons. Hertz did not pursue this experiment, but other researchers did, and they came up with some strange results.

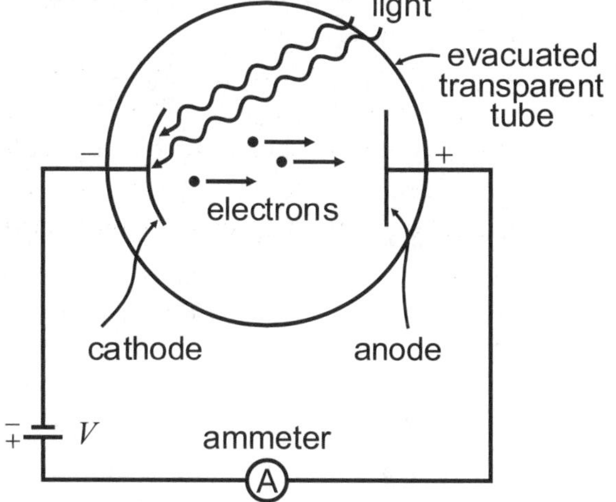

Figure 15-1 *A photocell circuit. Light causes electrons to be emitted from the cathode and flow through the circuit.*

Before discussing these results, we describe a modern version of the apparatus. Figure 15-1 shows light striking a metal plate connected to the negative terminal of a voltage source. Some electrons in the metal absorb energy from the light and are released from the metal surface. This liberation of electrons from the surface of a metal by the absorption of light is referred to as the

photoelectric effect. These electrons are then electrically attracted to the metal plate attached to the positive terminal. This movement of electrons constitutes an electric current[1], which flows through the circuit. **Cathode** is the name given to the metal plate from which electrons are liberated, and the plate toward which they then flow is the **anode**. The evacuated transparent tube with its cathode, anode, and terminals is a *phototube* or *photocell.* Sometimes the cathode in a photocell is called a *photocathode*, and the released electrons, *photoelectrons*.

Current flows in the circuit only when light shines on the cathode. As we shall discuss later in more detail, the external voltage source is not required for a current flow. Even with no battery in the circuit, some electrons emitted from the cathode will find their way to the anode, thus creating a current.

The first surprise from this apparatus is that, with a given material such as copper, silver, etc., as cathode, no electrons at all are emitted (and thus there is no current) unless the wavelength of the light is *smaller* than some critical value. Equivalently, the frequency of the light must be *larger* than some value to produce a current. If the frequency is too small, increasing the intensity (brightness) of the light, even enormously, has no effect on the current; it remains zero. This is quite bizarre. Since increasing the intensity means that more energy is falling on the cathode, one might think that eventually some current would flow, but it does not.

The minimum frequency to produce a current due to the photoelectric effect is called the **threshold frequency**. This frequency varies with the cathode material, and usually corresponds to light in the ultraviolet region of the electromagnetic spectrum. For some materials, the threshold is in the visible region.

A second surprise is that, if electrons are being liberated from the cathode, the *maximum* kinetic energy of these electrons does not depend on the light *intensity*, but does depend on the light's *wavelength* or *frequency*. It would seem reasonable to think that, if the light intensity were increased, thus increasing the total amount of light energy available, then some electrons would pick up larger amounts of energy, but this does not happen. Increasing the intensity does produce a larger current because a larger number of electrons are emitted, but the maximum kinetic energy of the electrons does not change. However, increasing the frequency (or decreasing the wavelength) of the light does increase the maximum kinetic energy of the photoelectrons.

The wave theory of light cannot explain the details of the photoelectric effect. According to the wave theory, if the frequency is below the threshold frequency, then increasing the light intensity should eventually cause current to flow. As well, increased intensity should lead to increased maximum kinetic energy of photoelectrons. In order to understand the photoelectric effect, we need a new model of light, given in 1905 by Albert Einstein. (A short biography of Einstein is presented at the end of this section.)

Einstein postulated that light consists of small particle-like bundles or packets of energy called **photons** or **light quanta** (singular: quantum). Because light energy comes in separate quanta, the energy is said to be *quantized.* The concept of quantization should not surprise you — electric

[1]Recall from Chapter 11 that any flow of charge, whether positive or negative, constitutes a current. The conventional direction of current is in the direction of flow of positive charge, which is opposite to the flow of negatively charged electrons.

charge, for example, is also *quantized*. The energy, E, of a single photon is proportional to the frequency, f, of the light, that is, E is equal to f multiplied by a constant:

$$E = \mathrm{h}f \quad \text{(energy of a photon)} \qquad \textbf{(15-1)}$$

where h is a universal constant called **Planck's constant**, which has a numerical value of

$$\mathrm{h} = 6.63 \times 10^{-34}\ \mathrm{J \cdot s} \quad \text{(Planck's constant)} \qquad \textbf{(15-2)}$$

Did You Know? *It was primarily for his explanation of the photoelectric effect that Einstein received the Nobel Prize in Physics in 1921.*

The German physicist Max Planck (Figure 15-2) introduced this constant in 1900 in explaining the electromagnetic radiation given off and absorbed by "blackbodies" — objects that absorb all electromagnetic radiation incident on them. Such an object at room temperature appears black. However, at much higher temperatures, blackbodies — the sun, for example — glow.

Figure 15-2
Max Planck (1858-1947). Planck received the Nobel Prize in Physics in 1918 for his explanation of black-body radiation. (Stamp courtesy of J.L. Hunt.)

Equation 15-1 is often expressed in terms of wavelength, λ, instead of frequency, by using the universal wave equation introduced in Chapter 13. Since we are now dealing with light, the wave equation is not written as $v = f\lambda$, but rather as $\mathrm{c} = f\lambda$, where c is the conventional symbol for the speed of light in a vacuum:

$$\mathrm{c} = f\lambda \quad \text{which gives} \quad f = \mathrm{c}/\lambda$$

Substituting this latter relation into Eqn. 15-1:

$$E = \frac{\mathrm{hc}}{\lambda} \quad \text{(energy of a photon)} \qquad \textbf{(15-3)}$$

In Einstein's explanation of the photoelectric effect, still accepted today, a single photon transfers all its energy to a conduction electron in the metal cathode, and the electron leaves the metal (Figure 15-3). The photon disappears. A certain minimum energy is required to liberate an electron from a metal — the amount depending on the type of metal — and if a photon does not have at least this energy, no electron is liberated. The light, in its interaction with the conduction electrons, is behaving as if it consists of particles. We can now see why, if light of a certain frequency produces no photocurrent, increasing the intensity of the light still results in no current. The number of photons increases with the intensity, but the energy of any single photon remains the same ($E = \mathrm{h}f$) and is still insufficient to free an electron from the metal.

Figure 15-3 *The photoelectric effect: a photon liberates a conduction electron from a metal.*

As well, we can understand why the maximum kinetic energy of the liberated electrons depends on the light frequency, but not on the light intensity. The photon energy absorbed by a conduction electron does two things: it frees the electron from the metal, and it provides kinetic energy for the electron (assuming that there is energy "left over" after liberation of the electron). For a given metal, the *minimum* energy required to free an electron is known as the **work function**, W (Table 15.1).[2] Suppose that a photon of energy E (or hf) strikes an electron and is able to free it by providing this minimum energy W (Figure 15-4). By conservation of energy, the photon energy equals the sum of the work function W and the electron's kinetic energy. Since W represents the minimum energy for liberation, the resulting kinetic energy must represent the maximum kinetic energy ($E_{K,MAX}$) possible for a freed electron. In equation form:

Table 15.1
Approximate Work Functions for Various Metals

Metal	Work Function (eV)
aluminium	4.3
calcium	3.2
cesium	1.9
copper	4.5
lithium	2.5
silver	4.7
sodium	2.3

$$\mathrm{h}f = W + E_{K,MAX}$$

$$\text{or} \quad E_{K,MAX} = \mathrm{h}f - W \qquad \textbf{(15-4)}$$

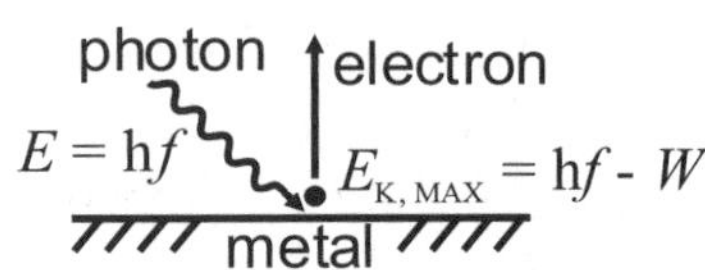

Figure 15-4
By conservation of energy, the maximum kinetic energy of a photoelectron is hf − W.

Equation 15-4 is known as **Einstein's photoelectric equation.** Using it, we see how the maximum electron kinetic energy depends on the frequency, f, of the light. Increasing (decreasing) the frequency increases (decreases) the maximum kinetic energy. Changing the light intensity has no effect on f, and thus no effect on $E_{K,MAX}$.

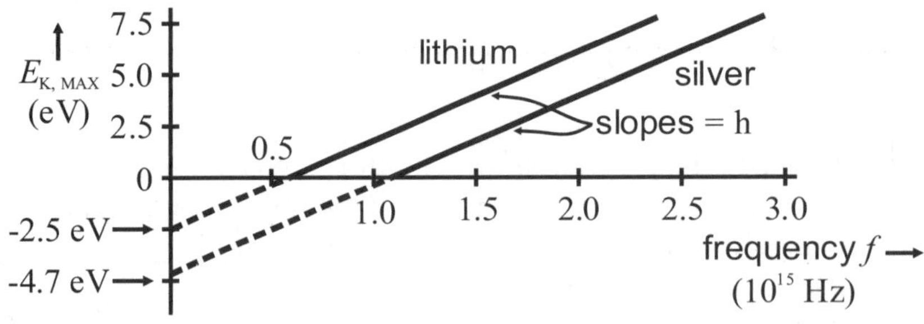

Figure 15-5 *$E_{K,MAX}$ vs. f for lithium and silver.*

If the frequency of the light is varied, and the resulting maximum kinetic energies are measured (how to do this is discussed after the sample problems below), then plotting a graph of $E_{K,MAX}$ vs. f (Figure 15-5) provides a method of measuring Planck's constant and determining the work function of the metal. Equation 15-4 has the form $y = mx + b$, which is the equation of a straight line. The y-variable is $E_{K,MAX}$, the x-variable is f, the slope "m" is h, and the y-intercept "b" is $-W$. Hence, a graph of $E_{K,MAX}$ vs. f gives a straight line that has slope h and a y-intercept (that is, $E_{K,MAX}$-intercept)

[2]Actual values depend on metal purity, surface cleanliness, etc. Freeing a conduction electron from a metal surface takes about half as much energy as freeing a bound electron from an isolated atom of the same metal.

of $-W$. Notice in Figure 15-5 that the slopes of the lines for the two metals are the same, being equal to Planck's constant, and that the y-intercepts correspond to the work functions listed in Table 15.1. The portions of the lines that correspond to actual data are indicated as solid lines; the dashed lines represent extrapolations to determine the y-intercepts.

Sample Problem 15-1

What is the energy of a photon from a common helium-neon laser, which generates red light of wavelength 633 nm?

Solution: To determine photon energy, given the wavelength of light, we simply use Eqn. 15-3:

$$E = \frac{\text{hc}}{\lambda}$$

Before substituting numbers, we convert the wavelength from nanometres to metres:

$$633\text{ nm} \times \frac{10^{-9}\text{ m}}{1\text{ nm}} = 6.33 \times 10^{-7}\text{ m}$$

Then, $$E = \frac{\left(6.63 \times 10^{-34}\text{ J}\cdot\text{s}\right)\left(3.00 \times 10^{8}\text{ m/s}\right)}{6.33 \times 10^{-7}\text{ m}}$$

> ***Reference Tip:*** *The SI value of the speed of light, 3.00 × 10⁸ m/s, can be found (along with other physical constants), in Appendix 4.*

Hence, the photon energy is 3.14×10^{-19} J.

Sample Problem 15-2

From Figure 15-6, determine
(a) Planck's constant in SI units
(b) the work function of zinc
(c) the threshold frequency for zinc.

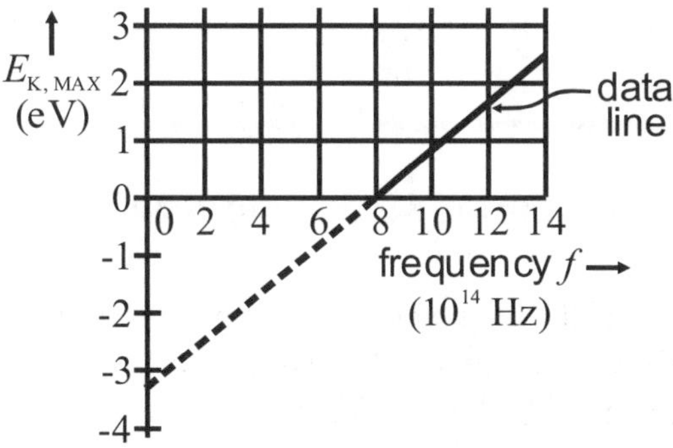

Figure 15-6 *Sample Problem 15-2. $E_{K,MAX}$ vs. f for zinc.*

Solution: (a) As discussed in the paragraph prior to Sample Problem 15-1, the slope of the data line on the graph is Planck's constant, h. To calculate the slope, we use two well-separated points on the line and determine the ratio of rise/run. We will use the following two points, *estimated* from the graph:

Frequency (Hz)	$E_{K,MAX}$ (eV)
8.0×10^{14}	0.0
14.0×10^{14}	2.5

First we determine the rise: $(2.5 - 0.0)\ \text{eV} = 2.5\ \text{eV}$

Because we want Planck's constant in SI units, we convert this to joules:

$$2.5\ \text{eV} \times \frac{1.60 \times 10^{-19}\ \text{J}}{1\ \text{eV}} = 4.0 \times 10^{-19}\ \text{J}$$

> ***Units Tip:*** *Recall from Chapter 11 that 1 eV = 1.60 × 10^{-19} J.*

The run is: $(14.0 - 8.0) \times 10^{14}\ \text{Hz} = 6.0 \times 10^{14}\ \text{Hz}$

Hence, the slope is:

$$m = \frac{\text{rise}}{\text{run}} = \frac{4.0 \times 10^{-19}\ \text{J}}{6.0 \times 10^{14}\ \text{Hz}} = 6.7 \times 10^{-34}\ \text{J/Hz}$$

Since 1 Hz = 1 s^{-1}, we can write J/Hz as J/ s^{-1} = J·s.

Thus, Planck's constant, as *estimated* from this graph, is 6.7 × 10^{-34} J·s, which is very close to the accepted value of 6.63 × 10^{-34} J·s.

(b) If the line on the graph is extrapolated back (as shown by the dashed line) to $f = 0$, the intercept on the $E_{K,MAX}$-axis is $-W$. Therefore, from Figure 15-6, we *estimate* the work function of zinc to be 3.3 eV.

(c) The threshold frequency is the lowest frequency of light for which electrons are emitted. We see from the graph that 8.0 × 10^{14} Hz is the (approximate) threshold frequency for zinc, since no electrons are emitted below this frequency. A photon of light of the threshold frequency has energy equal to the work function. Do you understand why this must be so?

Measuring the Maximum Kinetic Energy of Photoelectrons

It is possible to measure the maximum kinetic energy of photoelectrons by using a variation (Figure 15-7) of the photocell circuit described earlier. Notice the *reversed battery connections* — the positive terminal is connected to the cathode, and the negative terminal (through a variable resistor) to the anode. By changing the variable resistance, the potential difference (voltage) applied between the cathode and the anode can be varied.

Since the anode is now at a negative electric potential relative to the cathode, electrons emitted from the cathode are repelled by the anode and slow down as they travel toward it. Hence, this potential difference between the cathode and anode is often referred to as the *retarding potential*. If an electron is emitted with sufficiently high kinetic energy, it still can travel all the way to the anode. However, electrons that start with low kinetic energy reverse their direction before reaching the anode. If the voltage between the cathode and anode is increased, eventually a voltage is reached such that even the electrons released from the cathode with maximum kinetic energy are turned back, and no current flows in the circuit. The minimum voltage at which the current ceases to flow is termed the **stopping potential**, or the *cut-off potential*, symbolized by V_0. A typical graph of current vs. retarding potential is shown in Figure 15-8; the stopping potential is indicated.

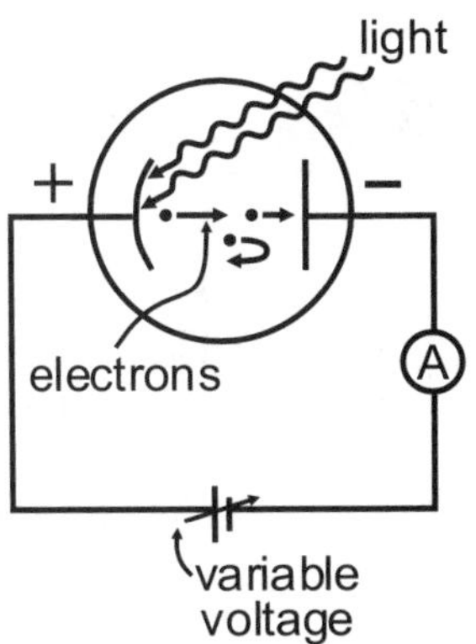

Figure 15-7
A photocell in a circuit with a variable retarding potential.

If the stopping potential is measured experimentally, it is easy to calculate the maximum kinetic energy of the electrons by using conservation of energy. Figure 15-9 shows an electron that has been emitted with maximum kinetic energy from the cathode. In order to just barely prevent this electron from reaching the anode, the stopping potential V_0 must be applied between the cathode and anode. Let us define the electric potential at the cathode to be zero; then the potential at the anode is $-V_0$. At position 1, essentially at the cathode, the electron has kinetic energy $E_{K,MAX}$. Since the potential is zero at the cathode, $V_1 = 0$, and the electron's electric potential energy is zero at this point. (Recall from Chapter 11 that electric potential energy, U, is related to electric potential, V, by $U = qV$.) At position 2 at the anode, the electron has slowed down to zero speed, and its kinetic energy is zero. Its electric potential energy at this point is:

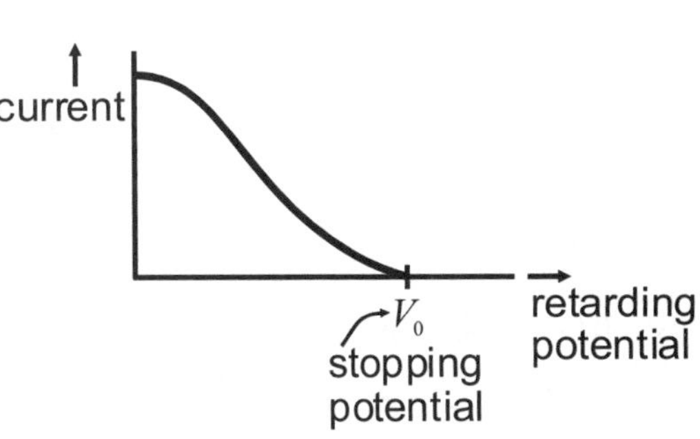

Figure 15-8 *Current vs. retarding potential for a photocell.*

$$U_2 = qV_2 = (-e)(-V_0) = eV_0$$

By conservation of energy: $$E_{K1} + U_1 = E_{K2} + U_2$$

Thus, $$E_{K,MAX} + 0 = 0 + eV_0$$

or $$E_{K,MAX} = eV_0 \quad \textbf{(15-5)}$$

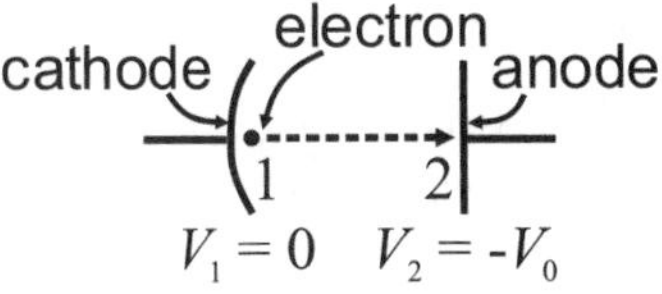

Figure 15-9 *As the electron moves from position 1 to 2, kinetic energy is converted to electric potential energy.*

Thus, the maximum kinetic energy of the photoelectrons is the product of the magnitude of the charge on the electron and the stopping potential.

Sample Problem 15-3

For a particular type of cathode in a photoelectric experiment, a stopping potential of 1.90 V is required when light of wavelength 4.00 × 10^2 nm is used. Determine the work function of the material in the cathode in joules and electron-volts.

Solution: We start with Einstein's photoelectric equation (Eqn. 15-4):

$$E_{\text{K,MAX}} = \text{h}f - W$$

Since we are given the stopping potential, we use Eqn. 15-5 to replace $E_{\text{K,MAX}}$ with $\text{e}V_0$:

$$\text{e}V_0 = \text{h}f - W$$

The wavelength, λ, instead of the frequency, f, of the light is given, and therefore we now write the photon energy not as hf, but rather as hc/λ (Eqn. 15-3):

$$\text{e}V_0 = \frac{\text{hc}}{\lambda} - W$$

Re-arranging to solve for W:

$$W = \frac{\text{hc}}{\lambda} - \text{e}V_0$$

Substituting numbers (having first converted 4.00 × 10^2 nm to 4.00 × 10^{-7} m):

$$W = \frac{(6.63 \times 10^{-34}\ \text{J}\cdot\text{s})(3.00 \times 10^{8}\ \text{m/s})}{4.00 \times 10^{-7}\ \text{m}} - (1.60 \times 10^{-19}\ \text{C})(1.90\ \text{V})$$
$$= 1.93 \times 10^{-19}\ \text{J}$$

> ***Units Tip:*** *Recall that a volt is a joule per coulomb. Hence, the quantity* eV_0 *has units of:*
> $C \cdot V = C \cdot (J/C) = J$

Converting to eV:

$$1.93 \times 10^{-19}\ \text{J} \times \frac{1\ \text{eV}}{1.60 \times 10^{-19}\ \text{J}} = 1.21\ \text{eV}$$

Thus, the work function is 1.93 × 10^{-19} J or 1.21 eV.

The Photoelectric Effect — More Generally

Thus far, we have been defining the photoelectric effect as the liberation of electrons from the *surface* of a *metal* by the absorption of light. Although the photoelectric effect was first discovered in the freeing of electrons from metals, it now has a broader definition. **The photoelectric effect refers to the process, in any material, in which a photon unbinds an electron. After the process, there is no photon.**

The word "unbinds" here has different meanings in different situations. In the case of a metal surface, to "unbind" a conduction electron means that the electron is removed from the metal completely. In most other situations, to "unbind" an electron means removing it from its orbital in an atom or molecule. The electron becomes free to move around the material of which the atom or molecule is a part (Figure 15-10), and often moves only a short distance before recombining with another atom or molecule. If the photoelectric effect happens to occur near the surface of a material, the electron might escape from the material altogether.

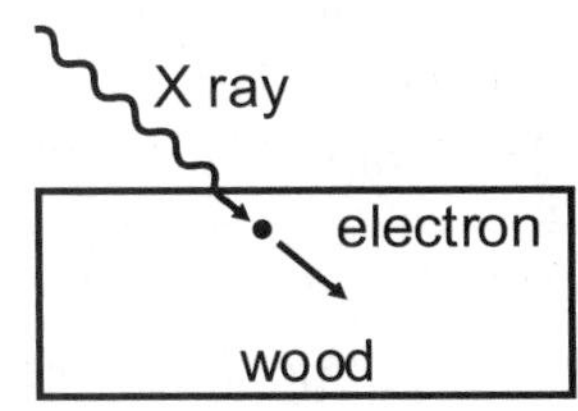

Figure 15-10 *Another example of the photoelectric effect: an X-ray photon removes an electron from a molecule in a piece of wood.*

The condition that there is no photon after the photoelectric process is important. In Section 15.2, we discuss a similar phenomenon, called the Compton effect, in which a photon of lower energy exists after the interaction.

Many types of electromagnetic radiation can produce the photoelectric effect: high-energy gamma (γ) rays and X rays, lower-energy ultraviolet and visible light, and even lower-energy infrared light. Whether or not the photoelectric effect can be produced in a particular material by photons of a given energy depends on how tightly bound the electrons are and how energetic the photons are. Photons with lower energy than infrared photons do not have enough energy to liberate electrons in most materials. Therefore, radiowaves and microwaves are normally not involved in the photoelectric effect. Indeed, even infrared light produces the photoelectric effect only in specialized semiconductor materials with electrons that are very loosely bound.

Applications of the Photoelectric Effect

You are probably unaware of the many ways that the photoelectric effect is used in the everyday world. Nevertheless, during the past 24 hours, you have probably witnessed at least one application of the photoelectric effect, such as:

- automatic turning on and off of streetlights
- door-openers and burglar alarms (a person, passing through a beam of light — often invisible infrared light — prevents the light from hitting a photoelectric device; as the current from the device ceases, a door opens or an alarm sounds, etc.)
- solar cells for calculators (the current that is produced actually provides the energy to run the calculator)
- photographic light meters

- remote-control devices for televisions, DVD-players, etc. (discussed in more detail in the following subsection)

Regardless of the specific construction of a photoelectric device, the basic operation is the same: photons produce an electric current via the photoelectric effect[3], and this current can be used to initiate some operation, such as turning something on or off. In devices such as photographic light meters, the amount of photocurrent is monitored so that a measure of the light intensity can be determined.

One important scientific application of the photoelectric effect has been the development of photomultiplier tubes. In these tubes, designed to detect light of extremely low intensity, light produces a small photocurrent from a metal cathode. This current is amplified to a much larger measurable one with a magnitude that depends on the initial light intensity.

Remote Controls for Televisions, etc.

Hand-held remote controls for TVs, DVD-players, etc., are common everyday devices. When a button on a remote control is pressed, a coded sequence of pulses of infrared (IR) light is sent out from a light-emitting diode (LED) in the remote control. When the IR pulses are received by the TV, etc., the IR photons produce an electric current as a result of the photoelectric effect in a semiconductor material in the TV's receiving unit.

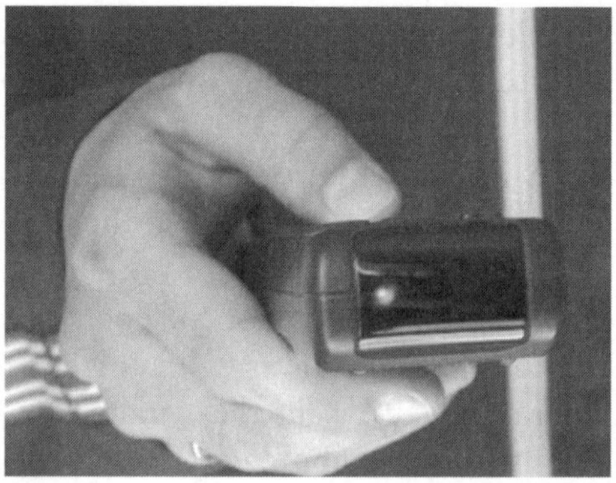

Figure 15-11 *Pressing a button on a remote control sends a pulse of IR light, visible in this photo (taken using a digital camera) as a small patch of white light on the end of the remote control.*

Figure 15-11 shows a photograph of someone pressing a button on a remote control. The photograph was taken using a digital camera, and since most digital cameras are sensitive to IR light as well as visible light, the IR light being emitted from the remote control appears in the photo as a patch of white light on the end of the remote control.

If a remote control is pointed at an IR-sensitive solar cell, and the output from the solar cell is connected directly to an oscilloscope, then the coded signals produced by pressing the various buttons on the remote control can be viewed easily on the oscilloscope display. Shown in Figure 15-12 is the display produced when the "play" button is pushed on a Sony VCR remote control. The display is a graph of voltage generated by the solar cell as a function of time in milliseconds. The voltage is a measure of the brightness of the IR signal.

---

[3]The material in which the photons liberate the electrons is nowadays usually a semiconductor (often in a component referred to as a photodiode or phototransistor). In these devices, the current is carried not only by electrons, but also by positively charged "holes," which are spots where electrons could be, but aren't. The detailed operation of these devices will not be discussed in this book.

As seen in Figure 15-12, the signal consists of 13 pulses; the first is a 2.4-ms header pulse that activates the VCR. The remaining 12 pulses constitute a binary code (1s and 0s), with a "1" having a longer duration (1.2 ms) than a "0" (0.6 ms). The 1s and 0s are separated by time intervals of 0.6 ms, during which the IR burst is off. The code after the header pulse in Figure 15-12 is 010110001000. Of course, when different buttons are pressed, different codes result. As well, there are various codes used by different manufacturers.

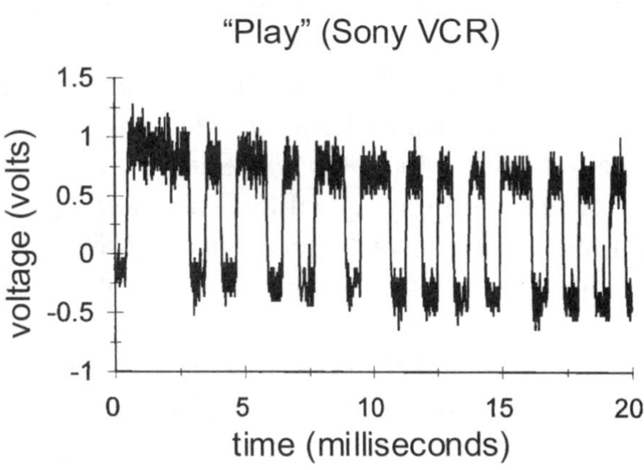

Figure 15-12 *The voltage from a solar cell receiving the coded IR pulse when the "play" button on a Sony VCR remote control is pressed.*

PROFILE: Albert Einstein (1879-1955)

"Einstein" — the very name is now virtually synonymous with "genius." But Einstein was not only a brilliant theoretical physicist; he was also an outspoken critic of militarism, and a lover of sailing and music. He showed great independence of thought not only in his scientific work, but also in his personal life — he wore no socks, for example.

Albert Einstein (Figure 15-13) was born on March 14, 1879, into a Jewish family in Germany. Early in his life, there were two events that aroused his curiosity a great deal: at the age of four or five, his father showed him a magnetic compass, and when he was twelve, he read a book on Euclidian geometry. He learned to play the violin at the age of six, and music was a constant joy to him.

Figure 15-13 *Albert Einstein (1879-1955), shown during a trip to Bermuda in 1935. (Photo courtesy of J.L. Hunt.)*

His early schooling was in Germany, but, at the age of seventeen, he began studies at the Swiss Federal Polytechnic School in Zurich, in a four-year program for science and mathematics teachers. He preferred not to attend many of the lectures, and spent a lot of time reading works by physicists such as Maxwell and Hertz.

After graduation in 1900, he had some part-time work in teaching and private tutoring in Zurich. He became a Swiss citizen in 1901, and, in 1902, obtained a job as a clerk in the Swiss Patent Office in Bern. His job was not particularly demanding, and he found that he had plenty of time to think about physics. Many evenings were spent with friends in discussions of physics, philosophy, and other fields. He was married in 1903 and had two sons, in 1904 and 1910.

From 1901 to 1904, he wrote and published one or two scientific papers each year. In 1905, he published three amazing works, one of them being his famous paper on special relativity. In his first 1905 paper, Einstein explained the photoelectric effect on the basis of the existence of light quanta. For this work, he received the 1921 Nobel Prize in Physics. In his second paper, Einstein explained Brownian motion as being the result of collisions between visible particles and molecules that are continually in motion. Einstein's third paper, *On the Electrodynamics of Moving Bodies*, was on special relativity, which deals with how quantities such as displacement, speed, time, and energy are affected by rapid motion at constant speed. In just a few months, Einstein had made major contributions to three different fields of physics, an incredible accomplishment!

Einstein soon became known internationally, and held academic posts in Zurich, Prague, Zurich again, and then Berlin, beginning in 1914. When the First World War began, his wife and children moved back to Zurich. This was effectively the end of his first marriage, although there was not a formal divorce until 1919, after which he married again.

During the early years of World War I, he was working a great deal on the *general* theory of relativity, which deals with gravitation and how physical quantities are affected by accelerated motion. This theory was published in 1916, and is viewed as a major intellectual triumph. Special relativity might well have been developed by someone else if Einstein had not come along, but general relativity would have waited for a long time. Even without relativity, Einstein would have been recognized as a great physicist for his work on quantum theory. Einstein's name became a public word in 1919 when his general relativity theory was confirmed by an experiment measuring the deflection of starlight by the sun during a solar eclipse.

After the War, he remained in Berlin, although he was often criticized there for being a Jew and a pacifist — his chief concern outside physics was world peace. In 1933, because of increasing German militarism and the persecution of Jews, he moved to the U.S.A. Einstein's post was at the Institute for Advanced Studies at Princeton, where he remained until his death in 1955, although he officially "retired" in 1945. From the 1920s onward, his scientific work increasingly was focused on developing a unified theory of gravitation and electromagnetism, but he was unsuccessful in this quest.

In 1939, Einstein signed a famous letter to American President F.D. Roosevelt, urging research on nuclear bombs in light of similar work being done already by Germany. Although he did not write the letter, signing it added the prestige of his name, and undoubtedly had some effect in increasing nuclear weapons research. In 1945, when it was clear that the bomb would work, he wrote another letter to Roosevelt on behalf of a number of scientists, arguing that the bomb was now not needed. Roosevelt died three weeks later, and the decision concerning bombing was passed on to other people.

There is a common perception that Einstein was a frail person, but, in fact, he was physically strong, with a booming laugh that contrasted with his soft speech. Although his command of English was excellent, he was more at home speaking his native German. He was friendly, particularly with children, but developed few deep friendships; he seemed to be in a world somewhat apart both personally and scientifically. He was not a worldly person, and showed none of the ruthless competitiveness displayed by some other great scientists.

When Einstein died, the world lost not only a great physicist, but also a humanitarian who worked for world peace.

Practice

15-1 Draw a photocell, and label all its important parts.

15-2 A light is shone on a photocathode in a photocell circuit, but no current results. If the intensity of the light is increased, what happens? Explain briefly.

15-3 A light is shone on a photocathode in a photocell circuit, and a current results. If the intensity of the light is increased, what happens to (a) the current? (b) the maximum kinetic energy of the photoelectrons?

15-4 In the photoelectric effect, what is meant by the threshold frequency?

15-5 The threshold frequency for the photoelectric effect in silver is 1.14×10^{15} Hz. What is the corresponding wavelength of the light? [Ans. 2.63×10^{-7} m]

15-6 The photoelectric effect is just barely produced in a particular material by light of a certain wavelength. What happens if light of a longer wavelength is used? Explain briefly.

15-7 What is the energy of a photon having a frequency of 6.57×10^{14} Hz?
[Ans. 4.36×10^{-19} J]

15-8 A γ-ray photon has an energy of 1.57 MeV. What is its frequency?
[Ans. 3.79×10^{20} Hz]

15-9 The solar spectrum has its peak intensity at a wavelength of about 5.0×10^2 nm. What is the energy of a photon with this wavelength? [Ans. 4.0×10^{-19} J]

15-10 Determine the missing entries in the table below. The values are typical for the spectral regions indicated.

Spectral Region	*Photon Energy*	*Wavelength*	*Frequency*
γ ray	2.0 MeV	0.62 pm	?
X ray	? keV	50 pm	6.0×10^{18} Hz
Ultraviolet	10 eV	? nm	2.9×10^{15} Hz
Visible	2.5 eV	500 nm	?
Infrared	? eV	10 μm	3.0×10^{13} Hz
Microwave	0.1 meV	? cm	2.4×10^{10} Hz
Radiowave	4.1 neV	300 m	?

[Ans. 4.8×10^{20} Hz; 25 keV; 1.0×10^2 nm; 6.0×10^{14} Hz; 0.12 eV; 1.3 cm; 1.0×10^6 Hz]

15-11 Sketch the shape of a graph of photon energy vs. frequency. What is the significance of the slope of the graph?

15-12 How many photons of wavelength 505 nm (in the green region of the visible spectrum) are required to make up a total energy of 1.00 J? [Ans. 2.54×10^{18}]

15-13 The work function for platinum is 5.6 eV. Determine the threshold frequency of light for the photoelectric effect in platinum. [Ans. 1.4×10^{15} Hz]

15-14 What would happen to conduction electrons in a metal if the work function were zero?

15-15 Figure 15-14 shows a graph of maximum kinetic energy of photoelectrons vs. photon frequency. The cathode used was tungsten. From this graph, determine:
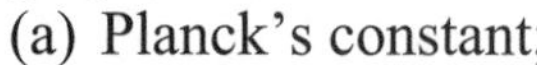
(a) Planck's constant;
(b) the work function of tungsten;
(c) the threshold frequency for tungsten.
[Ans. (b) approx. 4.5 eV
(c) approx. 1.1×10^{15} Hz]

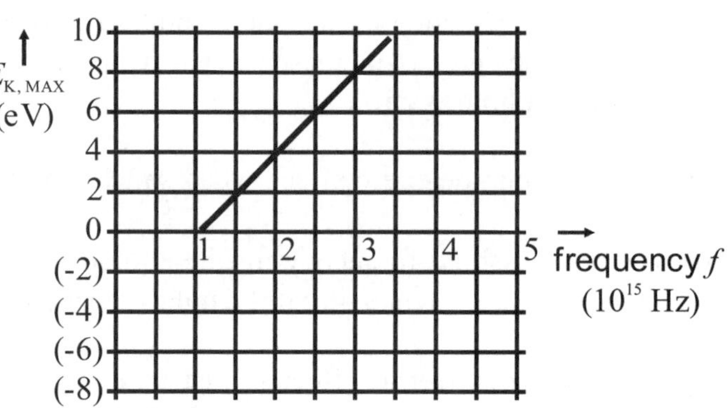

Figure 15-14 *Question 15-15.*

15-16 How are your answers to parts (b) and (c) of the previous question related?

15-17 Using the data from Table 15.1, plot (on one piece of graph paper) a graph of maximum kinetic energy of photoelectrons vs. photon frequency for cesium and calcium.

15-18 The work function of nickel is 5.0 eV. (a) Convert this to joules. (b) What minimum or maximum wavelength (choose which) of light produces the photoelectric effect in nickel?
[Ans. (a) 8.0×10^{-19} J (b) maximum wavelength of 2.5×10^{-7} m]

15-19 True or false? If false, explain why. A photocell can produce a current only if the positive terminal of a battery is connected to the anode, and the negative terminal to the cathode.

15-20 If the stopping potential in a photoelectric experiment is 5.3 V, what is the maximum kinetic energy of the photoelectrons? [Ans. 8.5×10^{-19} J]

15-21 What is the maximum speed of the photoelectrons in the previous question?
[Ans. 1.4×10^{6} m/s]

15-22 For a particular cathode in a photoelectric experiment, a stopping potential of 1.75 V is required when light of wavelength 367 nm is used. Determine the work function of the material in the cathode in joules and electron-volts. [Ans. 2.62×10^{-19} J; 1.64 eV]

15-23 Define the photoelectric effect (generally).

15-24 List five applications of the photoelectric effect.

15.2 THE COMPTON EFFECT

The early decades of the 20th century were exciting times for physicists. They were struggling with models of the atom (Chapter 16), relativity, and the nature of light. Einstein's description of light in terms of photons did not receive instant acceptance. (New scientific theories rarely do.) However, experiments by Arthur Holly Compton (1892-1962) in 1923 at Washington University in St. Louis presented experimental evidence that photons have not only energy but also momentum, and support for the photon theory of light became widespread.

Compton was investigating the scattering of X rays from a graphite target. The incident X rays were monochromatic, that is, they had a single wavelength (or frequency), but the scattered X rays had two different wavelengths. Some had the same wavelength as the original X rays; this was not surprising, and was exactly what the wave model of light predicted. However, other X rays had a *longer* wavelength (smaller frequency) than the original rays. This could not be explained at all by a wave theory, but it could be understood by considering light to consist of photons that have energy and momentum.

***Did You Know?** The word "photon" was coined by Compton.*

Compton explained his results by treating the scattering of X rays as being due to billiard-ball-like collisions between photons and electrons in the graphite. The **Compton effect** or **Compton scattering** refers to this scattering of a photon by an electron, with the production of a longer wavelength photon. The photons act essentially like particles in the collisions. The electrons can be considered as free, that is, not bound to atoms in the graphite, because the energy required to liberate an electron from graphite (carbon) is very small compared to the total energy provided by an X ray photon. In other words, the fact that the electron must be freed from an atom has very little effect in terms of energy. In the collisions, both energy and momentum are conserved. We show below how the conservation of these quantities explains the production of longer-wavelength scattered X rays, although we will not go through all the mathematical details.

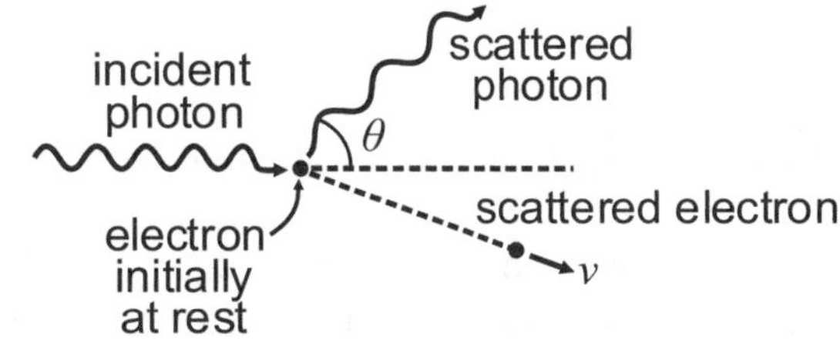

Figure 15-15 *A photon-electron collision (the Compton effect). Conservation of energy and momentum apply.*

Figure 15-15 shows a photon-electron collision in which the electron is treated as free and at rest[4] before the collision. The incident photon strikes the electron and is scattered at an

[4]This assumption is reasonable since any initial kinetic energy that the electron might have is much smaller than the huge amount of energy imparted to it by an X-ray photon.

angle (θ) relative to the initial photon direction. By conservation of energy, the energy of the incident photon before the collision equals the sum of the energy of the scattered photon and the kinetic energy of the electron after the collision:

energy of incident photon = energy of scattered photon + kinetic energy of electron

In symbols: $hf = hf' + E_K$

Momentum is also conserved in the collision:

initial photon momentum = final photon momentum + final electron momentum

This is the first time that we have encountered photon momentum. The magnitude of the momentum, p, of a photon is given by

$$p = \frac{E}{c} \quad \text{(magnitude of momentum of a photon)} \qquad \textbf{(15-6)}$$

where E is the photon energy, and c is the speed of light.

Did You Know? *Compton's discovery of the Compton effect earned him the Nobel Prize in Physics in 1927. He later studied cosmic rays and helped show that they consist of charged particles, primarily protons.*

Notice that we have been careful to specify that this relation gives the *magnitude* of the photon momentum. The *direction* of the momentum vector is the direction of motion of the photon. Momentum is conserved in both magnitude and direction in the photon-electron collision. The magnitude of photon momentum can be expressed in terms of frequency, f, or wavelength, λ, instead of energy, E. Since photon energy $E = hf$, then magnitude of photon momentum can be written as:

$$p = \frac{hf}{c} \quad \text{(magnitude of momentum of a photon)} \qquad \textbf{(15-7)}$$

and since $f = c/\lambda$,

$$p = \frac{h}{\lambda} \quad \text{(magnitude of momentum of a photon)} \qquad \textbf{(15-8)}$$

Of the three relations that we now have for the magnitude of the momentum of a photon, $p = E/c$ and $p = h/\lambda$ are the most useful to remember.

Assuming conservation of energy and momentum[5] in a photon-electron collision, Compton was able to derive an expression for the change in photon wavelength, that is, final wavelength λ' minus initial wavelength λ:

---

[5]Energy and momentum are always conserved in a collision between a photon and an electron. However, if the photon is a high-energy X ray or γ ray, the speed of the scattered electron is so high that the usual expressions for kinetic energy ($\frac{1}{2}mv^2$) and momentum (mv) are no longer applicable and must be replaced with expressions from Einstein's special theory of relativity. When Compton analyzed his scattering results, he used the relativistic expressions, although the energy of the X rays that he used was small enough that the low-speed expressions would have been adequate. Equation 15-9 was derived using the results of special relativity, and hence is valid whether the speed of the scattered electron is large or small.

$$\lambda' - \lambda = \frac{h}{mc}(1 - \cos\theta) \qquad \textbf{(15-9)}$$

where m is the mass of the electron, and θ is the *scattering angle* as shown in Fig. 15-15. Notice that the change in wavelength depends on the scattering angle. Compton used this equation to calculate the theoretical change in wavelength that should result in his experiments, and was delighted to find agreement with his experimental results. The existence of photons could no longer be denied.

Did You Know? *The Compton effect results in an "electromagnetic pulse" from atmospheric nuclear weapons explosions. The X rays and γ rays produced by such an explosion collide with electrons in the atmosphere and give them large amounts of energy. This tremendous surge of charge produces the electromagnetic pulse (similar to an electromagnetic wave but of short duration), which can disrupt unshielded electric circuits. This phenomenon was first noticed when power and communications circuits failed in Hawaii because of a nuclear test 4 000 km away.*

To complete the story, we should mention how it is that some photons in Compton's experiments were scattered with no change in wavelength. These photons are scattered from the electrons closest to the atomic nuclei. These electrons cannot be considered to be free, but are tightly bound to the nuclei. When a photon scatters from such an electron, which does not become liberated from the atom, it effectively scatters from the entire atom. Thus, in the expression for $\lambda' - \lambda$ above, the mass (m) of a single electron should be replaced by the mass of an entire atom, which is many thousands of times larger. Hence, $\lambda' - \lambda$ is much smaller, essentially zero, and the scattered photon has the same wavelength as the incident photon. This type of scattering, in which there is no change in photon wavelength or energy, is referred to as *elastic scattering*.

Sample Problem 15-4

What is the magnitude of the momentum of (a) an X-ray photon with energy 389 keV? (b) a visible photon of wavelength 451 nm?

Solution: (a) We can use Eqn. 15-6, $p = E/c$, but first we must convert the given energy to joules:

$$378\ \text{keV} \times \frac{10^3\ \text{eV}}{1\ \text{keV}} \times \frac{1.60 \times 10^{-19}\ \text{J}}{1\ \text{eV}} = 6.05 \times 10^{-14}\ \text{J}$$

Then,

$$p = \frac{E}{c} = \frac{6.05 \times 10^{-14}\ \text{J}}{3.00 \times 10^{8}\ \text{m/s}}$$

$$= 2.02 \times 10^{-22}\ \text{kg} \cdot \text{m/s}$$

Thus, the magnitude of the momentum of the photon is 2.02×10^{-22} kg·m/s.

Units Tip: *Recall that 1 J = 1 kg·m²/s². Hence, the quantity E/c has units of*

$$\frac{kg \cdot m^2/s^2}{m/s} = kg \cdot m/s$$

(b) Since we are given wavelength and are asked for photon momentum, we use Eqn. 15-8, $p = \mathrm{h}/\lambda$. The wavelength, 451 nm, must be converted to metres, giving 451×10^{-9} m, or 4.51×10^{-7} m.

$$p = \frac{\mathrm{h}}{\lambda} = \frac{6.63 \times 10^{-34}\ \mathrm{J \cdot s}}{4.51 \times 10^{-7}\ \mathrm{m}} = 1.47 \times 10^{-27}\ \mathrm{kg \cdot m/s}$$

Therefore, the photon has momentum of magnitude 1.47×10^{-27} kg·m/s.

Sample Problem 15-5

A γ ray of energy 1.38 MeV undergoes Compton scattering through a scattering angle of 38.7°.
(a) What is the energy (in MeV) of the scattered γ ray?
(b) What is the kinetic energy of the scattered electron?

Solution: (a) The change in wavelength of the γ ray is given by Eqn. 15-9:

$$\lambda' - \lambda = \frac{\mathrm{h}}{mc}(1 - \cos\theta)$$

In this problem, we are given (and asked for) energy instead of wavelength. The easiest approach is to use the incident γ-ray photon energy (E) to calculate the incident wavelength (λ), substitute numbers into the above equation to determine the scattered wavelength (λ'), and then use this wavelength to determine the scattered photon energy (E').

The relation between photon energy and wavelength is just Eqn. 15-3:

$$E = \frac{\mathrm{hc}}{\lambda} \qquad \text{which gives} \qquad \lambda = \frac{\mathrm{hc}}{E}$$

Before calculating the incident wavelength from this equation, we must convert the incident photon energy units from mega-electron-volts to joules:

$$1.38\ \mathrm{MeV} \times \frac{10^{6}\ \mathrm{eV}}{1\ \mathrm{MeV}} \times \frac{1.60 \times 10^{-19}\ \mathrm{J}}{1\ \mathrm{eV}} = 2.21 \times 10^{-13}\ \mathrm{J}$$

Then, $$\lambda = \frac{\mathrm{hc}}{E} = \frac{(6.63 \times 10^{-34}\ \mathrm{J \cdot s})(3.00 \times 10^{8}\ \mathrm{m/s})}{2.21 \times 10^{-13}\ \mathrm{J}} = 9.01 \times 10^{-13}\ \mathrm{m}$$

Hence, from Eqn. 15-9:

$$\lambda' = \lambda + \frac{\mathrm{h}}{mc}(1 - \cos\theta)$$

$$= \left(9.01 \times 10^{-13}\ \mathrm{m}\right) + \frac{6.63 \times 10^{-34}\ \mathrm{J \cdot s}}{\left(9.11 \times 10^{-31}\ \mathrm{kg}\right)\left(3.00 \times 10^{8}\ \mathrm{m/s}\right)}\left(1 - \cos 38.7°\right)$$

$$= 1.43 \times 10^{-12}\ \mathrm{m}$$

Therefore, the scattered photon energy is:

$$E' = \frac{\mathrm{hc}}{\lambda'} = \frac{\left(6.63 \times 10^{-34}\ \mathrm{J \cdot s}\right)\left(3.00 \times 10^{8}\ \mathrm{m/s}\right)}{1.43 \times 10^{-12}\ \mathrm{m}} = 1.39 \times 10^{-13}\ \mathrm{J}$$

Converting to MeV:

$$1.39 \times 10^{-13}\ \mathrm{J} \times \frac{1\ \mathrm{eV}}{1.60 \times 10^{-19}\ \mathrm{J}} \times \frac{1\ \mathrm{MeV}}{10^{6}\ \mathrm{eV}} = 0.867\ \mathrm{MeV}$$

Thus, the scattered photon has an energy of 0.867 MeV (or 867 keV).

(b) To determine the kinetic energy of the scattered electron, we use conservation of energy. The initial photon energy, E, equals the sum of the energy of the scattered photon, E', and the kinetic energy of the electron, E_K:

$$E = E' + E_{\mathrm{K}}$$

Thus,

$$E_{\mathrm{K}} = E - E' = (1.38 - 0.867)\,\mathrm{MeV} = 0.51\,\mathrm{MeV}$$

Hence, the kinetic energy of the scattered electron[6] is 0.51 MeV.

Other Interactions of Photons with Matter

When photons interact with matter, there are many types of interesting processes that can occur, although some of them are so rare that we will not describe them here. We have discussed in detail two types of interaction so far: the photoelectric effect and the Compton effect. The photoelectric effect is an example of an *absorption* process, that is, one in which no photon exists after the interaction. The Compton effect is a scattering process, in which a photon does exist afterward. We have also mentioned elastic scattering, in which the scattered photons have the same energy as the incident photons.

[6]Notice that this procedure for determining the kinetic energy is correct whether the electron is moving slowly or at relativistic speeds (that is, speeds close to that of light). However, having found the kinetic energy, if we then had to determine the speed of the electron, the equation $E_K = \frac{1}{2}mv^2$ could be used only if the electron's speed was not close to that of light.

Another common type of absorption is an *excitation* in which a photon gives all its energy to an electron, which remains bound in an atom or molecule. (If it were to become unbound, we would have the photoelectric effect.) Other types of excitations involve a photon giving its energy to a molecule with a resulting increase in the molecule's vibrational and/or rotational energy. A *single* visible photon can produce excitations by donating its energy to (1) an electron in a molecule, and/or (2) molecular vibrations, and/or (3) molecular rotations (Figure 15-16). Absorption of visible light by everyday objects (clothing, people, houses, etc.) involves these sorts of excitations, as well as the photoelectric effect. A red car appears red because red photons are reflected (elastically scattered) from the car's paint, whereas photons corresponding to other colours are absorbed.

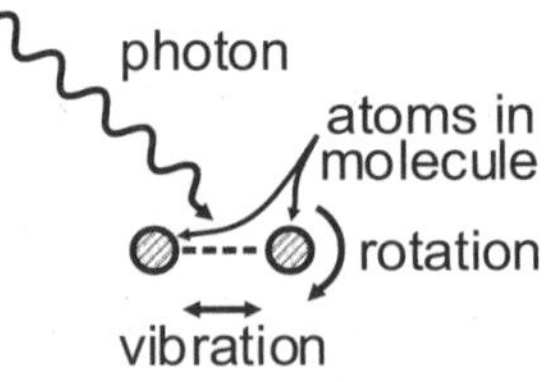

Figure 15-16 *When a visible photon is absorbed by a molecule, it can cause not only an excitation of an electron, but also increased vibration and/or rotation of the molecule.*

A fascinating absorption process involving *high-energy* X-ray or γ- ray photons is **electron-positron pair production**, often called just **pair production**. In this process, a photon disappears and two particles, an electron and positron, are produced from the photon's energy (Figure 15-17). (A positron is similar to an electron — it has the same mass, but a *positive* electric charge.) Pair production is a marvellous example of the equivalence of energy and mass, as expressed through Einstein's famous equation $E = mc^2$. In order to produce an electron-positron pair, the photon energy, E, must be at least large enough to be equivalent to the combined masses, m, of an electron and positron. Pair production always occurs near a nucleus — in order for both energy and momentum to be conserved in the process, there must be another object (the nucleus) to receive some energy and momentum.

Did You Know? *The process of vision is initiated by excitations of molecules as a result of the absorption of light.*

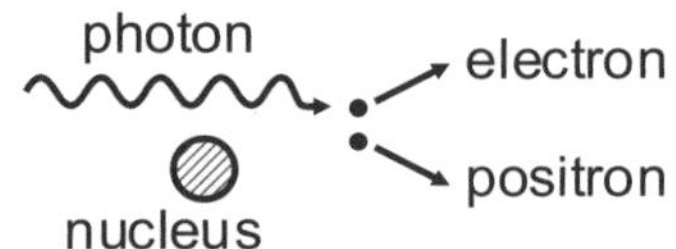

Figure 15-17 *In electron-positron pair production, a photon disappears and an electron and positron are created.*

Although pair production is somewhat an exotic process, nonetheless it is occurring around (and in) you all the time. Everything in your environment, including you yourself, has some natural radioactive materials from which γ rays are emitted. These γ rays are absorbed in matter via pair production (if the γ- ray energy is large enough), the photoelectric effect, and the Compton effect. The probability of γ-ray absorption by a given effect depends on the γ-ray energy and on the types of atoms in the absorbing material.

Did You Know? *A positron is the antiparticle of an electron. If a positron and electron meet, they annihilate each other in a burst of subatomic passion, and two γ-ray photons are produced. The positron and electron disappear.*

The Nature of Light

Well, what *is* light? This question has puzzled people for centuries. According to experiments such as Young's double slit interference, light consists of waves. But in order to understand the photoelectric effect and the Compton effect, we have to think of light as photons — particle-like bundles of energy and momentum. Does light consist of waves, or photons? The answer is "yes."

If we are to explain all the phenomena related to light, we have to consider light to have *both* wave-like properties and particle-like properties. This **wave-particle duality** of light was difficult for physicists in the early part of the 20th century to accept, and might well be hard for you to accept. However, as we shall see in Section 15.3, wave-particle duality applies not only to light, but also to particles such as electrons. In other words, electrons have wave properties as well as particle properties. For a complete description of light or electrons, we must consider both the wave aspects and the particle aspects. Because we are used to dealing with macroscopic objects such as automobiles ("particles") and water waves ("waves") for which the particle and wave aspects are clearly distinct, it is admittedly difficult to have to think about wave-particle duality at the submicroscopic level. Nonetheless, in order to explain all the experimental evidence, wave-particle duality is a necessity.

Practice

15-25 How are the photoelectric effect and the Compton effect similar? different?

<u>15-26</u> The Compton effect involves the collision of (a) a ____________________ and (b) an ____________________. In this collision, both (c) ____________________ and (d) ____________________ are conserved.

15-27 The energy of an infrared photon is 0.63 eV. What is the magnitude of its momentum? [Ans. 3.4×10^{-28} kg·m/s]

15-28 A photon has a momentum of magnitude 4.78×10^{-25} kg·m/s. What is its frequency? [Ans. 2.16×10^{17} Hz]

15-29 What is the magnitude of the momentum of an X-ray photon that has a wavelength of 1.50×10^{-10} m? [Ans. 4.42×10^{-24} kg·m/s]

15-30 In a Compton-scattering event, a photon of energy 1.12 MeV scatters from an electron, which acquires a kinetic energy of 0.38 MeV. What is the energy of the scattered photon? [Ans. 0.74 MeV]

15-31 A γ-ray photon of wavelength 2.36×10^{-12} m undergoes Compton scattering through a scattering angle of 55.7°. What is the wavelength of the scattered photon? [Ans. 3.42×10^{-12} m]

15-32 Through what angle must an incident photon of energy 778 keV be scattered in the Compton effect, if the scattered photon has an energy of 389 keV? [Ans. 70.0°]

15-33 Sketch the shape of the graph of change in wavelength ($\Delta\lambda = \lambda' - \lambda$) vs. scattering angle ($\theta$) for the Compton effect for $0 \leq \theta \leq 180°$.

15-34 Distinguish between absorption and scattering of light.

15-35 List four ways in which visible light can be absorbed by matter.

15-36 Why does pair production not occur for low-energy γ rays?

15.3 MATTER WAVES

The idea that light consists of photons came about as the result of strong evidence in experiments involving the photoelectric and Compton effects. It is hard to imagine proposing such a radically new idea without having first some experimental proof. But this is essentially what Louis de Broglie (1892-1987) did in 1924 when he suggested, on the basis of no experimental evidence whatsoever, that particles such as electrons exhibit wave properties.

De Broglie was a student in Paris working toward his doctorate in physics. He was thinking about the dual nature of light, and wondering if particles might also have a wave-particle duality. After all, both light and particles have energy, so perhaps they could have other common properties as well. In his doctoral thesis, de Broglie proposed that, just as there is a relation $p = h/\lambda$ between the magnitude of momentum, p, and wavelength, λ, of a photon, there is also the same relation between the momentum and wavelength of a particle. In other words, he suggested that a particle has wave-like properties, with the wavelength given by:

Did You Know? *De Broglie's proposal that particles have wave properties earned him the Nobel Prize in Physics in 1929.*

$$\lambda = \frac{h}{p} \qquad \textbf{(15-10)}$$

where h is Planck's constant, the same as in the photon relation. The wavelength of a particle given by the above relation has come to be known as the **de Broglie wavelength**.

Experimental confirmation of de Broglie's proposal came quickly. In 1927, Clinton Davisson and Lester Germer in the U.S.A., and George Thomson independently in Britain, showed that a beam of electrons can exhibit *diffraction*, which, of course, is a property of waves. It had been known since about 1913 that X rays can be diffracted by solids, and it was now shown that electrons show the same type of diffraction. Figure 15-18 illustrates a typical diffraction pattern produced by X rays or electrons incident on powdered aluminum.

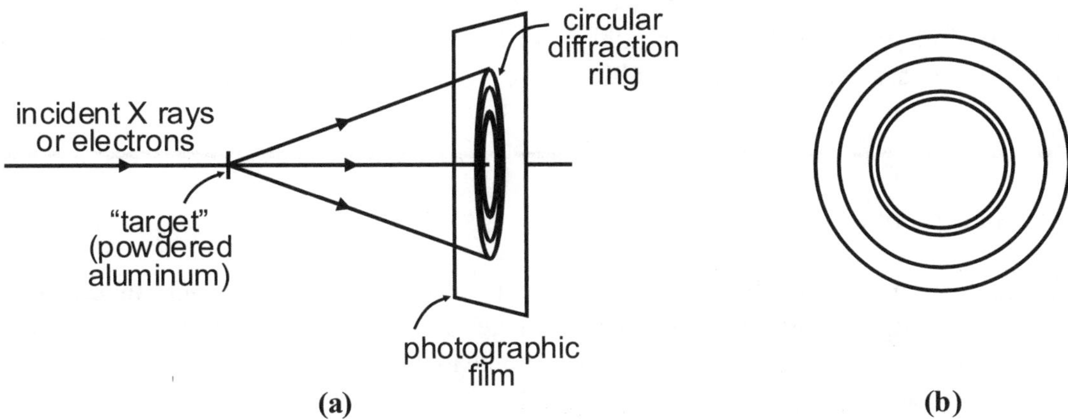

Figure 15-18 **(a)** *Experimental arrangement to show diffraction of X rays or electrons by powdered aluminum.* **(b)** *Diffraction pattern produced by X rays or electrons having the same wavelength.*

If particles have wave properties, why is it that these aspects were not noticed before de Broglie's suggestion? As shown in the sample problem that follows, the wavelength of a normal macroscopic object such as a baseball is immeasurably small, and thus its wave properties are impossible to detect. The wave aspects of a particle are measurable only if its mass is very small, such as for an electron or neutron, and even then the wavelength is rather small, often about the same size as an atom. We shall see in Chapter 16 how the waves associated with particles — **matter waves** — are important in our understanding of atoms and molecules.

So what is an object such as an electron? Is it a particle, or a wave? Although you are accustomed to thinking of an electron as a particle, it also has undeniable wave properties. Thus, a complete description of an electron is that it is both a particle and a wave, just as a complete description of light involves both waves and photons.

Sample Problem 15-6

Determine the de Broglie wavelength of (a) an electron that has a speed of 5.0×10^6 m/s (b) a baseball (mass 0.15 kg) travelling at 25 m/s.

Solution: (a) The de Broglie wavelength is given by Eqn. 15-10, $\lambda = \mathrm{h}/p$, and since $p = mv$, where m is mass and v is speed, we have:

$$\lambda = \frac{\mathrm{h}}{mv} = \frac{6.63 \times 10^{-34}\ \mathrm{J \cdot s}}{(9.11 \times 10^{-31}\ \mathrm{kg})(5.0 \times 10^{6}\ \mathrm{m/s})} = 1.5 \times 10^{-10}\ \mathrm{m}$$

This distance is about the size of an atom. Hence, we see that the wave properties of electrons manifest themselves at atomic dimensions.

The calculation for the baseball is similar to that for the electron, and the result is a de Broglie wavelength of 1.8×10^{-34} m. This is an incredibly small distance, even compared with the size of an atom (10^{-10} m) or a nucleus (10^{-14} m). In other words, the wave properties associated with a baseball are not measurable.

Electron Microscopes

A useful application that involves the wave aspects of electrons is the **electron microscope**. Instead of using light to form a magnified image of an object, as in a standard *optical microscope*, an electron microscope uses an electron beam.

The reason for using electrons lies in the size of their de Broglie wavelength, which can be made much smaller than the wavelength of visible light. The amount of fine detail that can be shown by a microscope is fundamentally limited by diffraction effects. These effects depend on the wavelength of the light or particle being used. A microscope using typical visible light of wavelength 500 nm cannot show detail in objects smaller than a few hundred nanometres, regardless of how well its lenses are crafted. However, if a beam of electrons is used instead, with a wavelength thousands of times smaller than that of visible light, then objects thousands of times smaller can be "seen." Electron microscopes are used extensively in biology, and blurred images of actual atoms have been obtained.

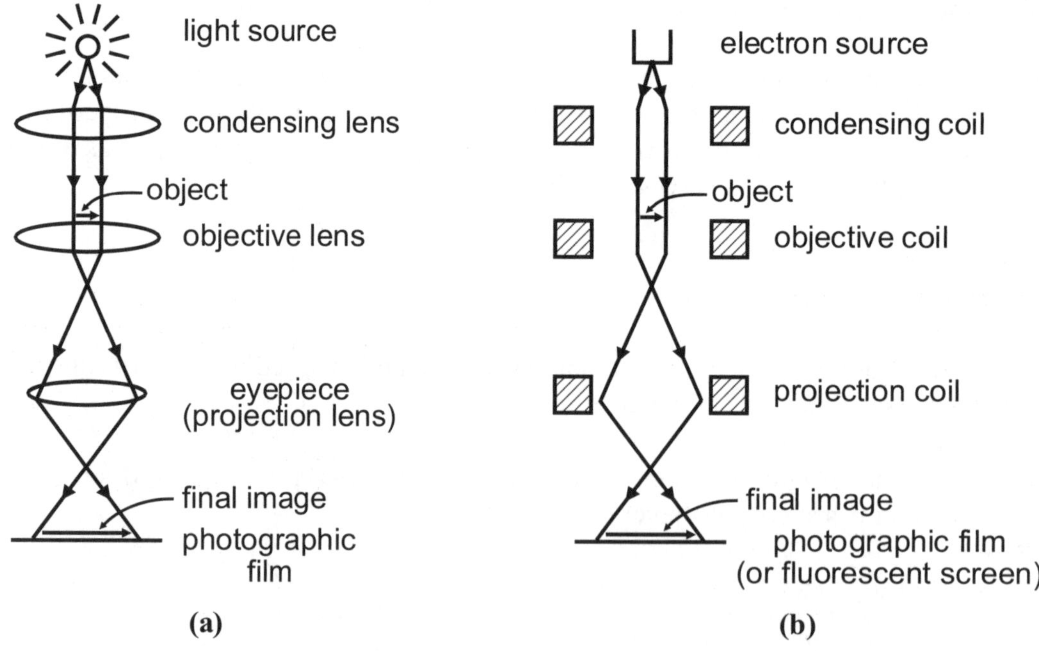

Figure 15-19 **(a)** *Optical microscope.* **(b)** *Transmission electron microscope.*

Two common styles of electron microscopes are *transmission electron microscopes*, which produce two-dimensional images, and *scanning electron microscopes*, which give images with a three-dimensional quality. With either of these styles, the optical lenses in a standard optical microscope are replaced by coils of wire, through which electric current flows to produce magnetic fields. These coils act as magnetic "lenses" to focus an electron beam.

Did You Know? *The first crude electron microscope was constructed in Germany in 1931. The first electron microscope with a commercially practical design was developed in 1937-38 by Albert Prebus and James Hillier, two graduate students at the University of Toronto.*

Figure 15-19 shows a comparison of an optical microscope and a transmission electron microscope. Cross-sections of the coils of wire in the electron microscope are shown as squares. The electron source consists of a hot wire filament, from which electrons are "boiled off," then accelerated through a potential difference of 10^4 to 10^5 V. The object in a transmission electron microscope must be very thin (about 10 nm to 100 nm). Otherwise, the electrons will be scattered somewhat as they pass through, thus producing a blurry image. The electron wavelength, which depends on the accelerating voltage, is usually about 0.005 nm to 0.01 nm. Hence, we might expect that objects of about this size could be imaged. However, the magnetic lenses have aberrations (that is, they are not perfect) and details smaller than approximately 0.5 nm are blurred. This distance is about 10^3 times smaller than that attainable using optical microscopes.

In a scanning electron microscope (Figure 15-20), a narrow electron beam scans the object in much the same way as electrons in an old-style television tube move across the screen. As the beam strikes the object, electrons are ejected from the object and travel to an electron collector maintained at a positive electric potential relative to the object. The varying current that results in the collector controls the details displayed in the image shown on a cathode ray tube (CRT) or a liquid crystal display (LCD) screen. A scanning microscope cannot produce the fine details possible with the transmission type, with objects smaller than about 10 nm appearing fuzzy. However, the three-dimensional character of the image is very useful in picturing the shape of microscopic objects.

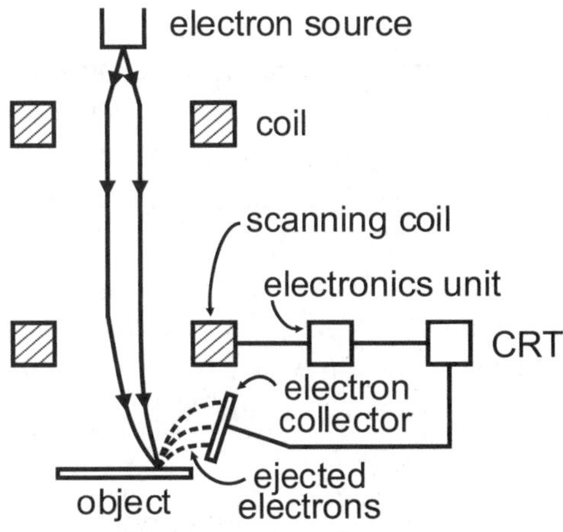

Figure 15-20
Scanning electron microscope.

It is important to realize that the *image-producing capability* of an electron microscope does not depend on the wave properties of electrons. The trajectories of the electrons can be determined by treating electrons as charged particles and considering the action of the magnetic forces exerted on them by the various coils. However, the wave properties are important in determining the degree of *detail* that can be shown by the microscope.

Scanning Tunnelling Microscope and Atomic Force Microscope

Another type of non-optical microscope, developed in the 1980s, is the **scanning tunnelling microscope** (STM). Although this instrument involves the flow of electrons, it is not usually considered to be an electron microscope.

The STM works in a similar way to that of an old-fashioned record player. A small sharp metal tip is used to explore the surface of a material, normally a conductor of some sort (Figure 15-21). A voltage (in the millivolt to volt range) is applied between the tip and the conductor, and as a result, electrons can jump from the tip to the conductor, or vice-versa. The distance between the conductor and the tip is extremely small, only about 0.5 to 1.0 nm, or 2 to 4 atomic diameters. The jumping of the electrons is a quantum mechanical process known as tunnelling, and this gives the "tunnelling" part of the name of this microscope.

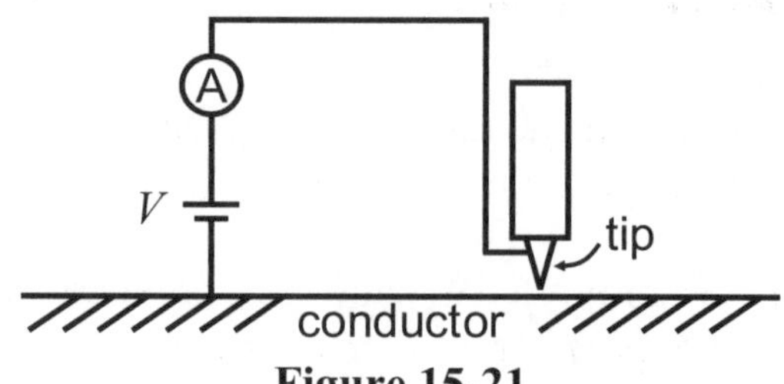

Figure 15-21
Scanning tunnelling microscope.

The tunnelling current depends very strongly on the distance between the tip and the nearest atom in the surface. For every atomic diameter added to the distance, the current decreases by a factor of about 1000. As the tip is moved to scan the surface, the tip-to-surface distance changes and the current changes accordingly. When the tip is directly above an atom, the distance is small, and when the tip is above a point between two atoms, the distance is larger.

In practice, as the tip is scanning, it is continually moved up and down in order to maintain a constant current, usually between a few nanoamperes (10^{-9} A) and a few picoamperes (10^{-12} A). The up-and-down movements are monitored to create an image of the atoms that make up the surface. Individual atoms can actually be imaged.

Another type of microscope, developed soon after the STM, is the **atomic force microscope** (AFM).[7] In an AFM, the tip actually touches the surface instead of being kept a short distance away from it (Figure 15-22). It does not measure the tunnelling current but instead the small force between the tip and the surface. This force measurement is accomplished by having the tip attached to an extremely small leaf spring, which bends up and down as the tip moves over the atoms along the surface. A laser beam is reflected from the spring to record its motion. The forces that are detected can be as small as a few piconewtons, and as with the STM, actual atoms can be imaged.

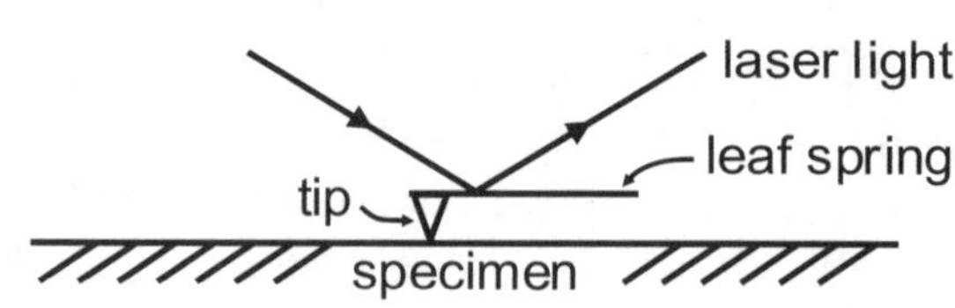

Figure 15-22
Atomic force microscope.

---

[7]STMs and AFMs are both included in a broader category: Scanning Probe Microscopes (SPMs).

One advantage of the AFM is that because current is not being measured, this microscope can be used on non-conducting materials, including macromolecules and biological specimens. AFMs have been employed in studies of muscle proteins, DNA, plant cell walls, and bacterial flagellae, as well as integrated circuits, data storage media, ceramics, and silicon wafers.

Practice

15-37 An electron is travelling with a speed of 8.38×10^5 m/s. What is its de Broglie wavelength? [Ans. 8.68×10^{-10} m]

15-38 What is the magnitude of the momentum of a neutron that has a de Broglie wavelength of 13.6 fm? [Ans. 4.88×10^{-20} kg·m/s]

15-39 Determine the speed of a proton that has a de Broglie wavelength of 10.6 nm.
[Ans. 37.5 m/s]

15-40 Sketch the shape of a graph of de Broglie wavelength vs. speed of a particle.

15-41 What kinetic energy (in joules) does an electron have if its de Broglie wavelength is 0.385 nm? [Ans. 1.63×10^{-18} J]

15-42 An electron is accelerated from rest in an electron microscope through a potential difference of 1.3×10^3 V. What is its de Broglie wavelength? [Ans. 3.4×10^{-11} m]

15-43 (a) Suppose that the kinetic energies of an electron and proton are equal. Determine, in terms of electron mass, m_e, and proton mass, m_p, an algebraic expression for the ratio of the de Broglie wavelength of the electron to that of the proton.
(b) Determine the numerical value of your answer.
[Ans. (a) $(m_p/m_e)^{1/2}$ (b) 42.8]

CHAPTER FOCUS

This chapter is the first in a two-chapter sequence devoted to the new ideas of physics that were advanced in the 1900s and whose development continues today.

The topic of the present chapter has been the advancements made toward a more complete understanding of the nature of light and particles. We have shown how the discoveries of the photoelectric effect and the Compton effect resulted in the photon concept of light, which seemed at odds with the wave theory of light that had been firmly established in the 1800s. We have discussed how these apparently contradictory aspects of light — photons and waves — are interwoven in wave-particle duality. As well, the wave nature of particles, first suggested by de Broglie, has been introduced. Practical applications have been presented, such as automatic control of streetlights (photoelectric effect), and electron microscopes (de Broglie wavelength of electrons).

In the next chapter, our exploration of modern physics continues. We see how models of atomic structure evolved during the first few decades of the 20th century, and how our present understanding of atoms has led to exciting and useful developments such as lasers.

VOCABULARY REVIEW

You should be able to define or explain each of the following words or phrases.

photoelectric effect
cathode
anode
threshold frequency
photons
light quanta
Planck's constant
work function
Einstein's photoelectric equation
stopping potential
Compton effect
Compton scattering
electron-positron pair production
pair production
wave-particle duality
de Broglie wavelength
matter waves
electron microscope
scanning tunnelling microscope
atomic force microscope

CHAPTER REVIEW

15-44 If the frequency of the light shining on a photocathode is increased, which one of the following also increases?
(a) the maximum kinetic energy of the photoelectrons
(b) the wavelength of the light
(c) the threshold frequency
(d) the work function
(e) none of the above

15-45 As the frequency of photons decreases, which of the following is true?
(a) Their energy increases and the magnitude of their momentum increases.
(b) Their energy increases and the magnitude of their momentum decreases.
(c) Their energy remains constant and the magnitude of their momentum decreases.
(d) Their energy remains constant and the magnitude of their momentum increases.
(e) Their energy decreases and the magnitude of their momentum decreases.

15-46 In the Compton effect,
(a) the probabilistic nature of quantum waves is demonstrated.
(b) the particle nature of light is demonstrated.
(c) the ejection of an electron from an irradiated metal surface is demonstrated.
(d) the wave nature of light is demonstrated.
(e) none of the above is correct.

<u>15-47</u> All of the following objects have the same speed. Which has the greatest de Broglie wavelength?
(a) proton (b) neutron (c) electron (d) yourself (e) an automobile

<u>15-48</u> An electron (mass m_e) and a proton (mass 1836 m_e) have the same magnitude of momentum. What is the ratio of the de Broglie wavelength of the proton to that of the electron?
(a) 1 (b) 1836 (c) 1/1836 (d) 1.22×10^{-30} (e) 3.61×10^{-37}

15-49 What are photoelectrons? How, if at all, do they differ from "normal" electrons?

15-50 Sketch the shape of a graph of photon energy vs. wavelength.

15-51 The energy of an X-ray photon is 127 keV. What are its speed (in a vacuum), frequency, and wavelength? [Ans. 3.00×10^8 m/s; 3.06×10^{19} Hz; 9.79×10^{-12} m]

15-52 The threshold frequency of light for the photoelectric effect in barium is 6.0×10^{14} Hz. What is the work function of barium in joules and electron-volts? [Ans. 4.0×10^{-19} J; 2.5 eV]

<u>15-53</u> Einstein's photoelectric equation is a consequence of the law of conservation of ____________.

15-54 Plot a graph of maximum kinetic energy of photoelectrons vs. photon frequency for aluminium. Use Table 15.1.

15-55 The maximum kinetic energy of photoelectrons in an experiment is 5.31×10^{-19} J. What is the stopping potential in this experiment? [Ans. 3.32 V]

15-56 A photon has momentum of magnitude 4.19×10^{-21} kg·m/s. What are its energy, frequency, and wavelength? [Ans. 1.26×10^{-12} J; 1.90×10^{21} Hz; 1.58×10^{-13} m]

15-57 A γ-ray photon scatters via the Compton effect, producing a scattered electron of kinetic energy 118 keV and a scattered photon of energy 653 keV. What was the energy of the initial photon? [Ans. 771 keV]

15-58 A photon, in undergoing Compton scattering, has a wavelength increase of 827 fm. What is the scattering angle? [Ans. 48.8°]

15-59 What is meant by elastic scattering of a photon?

15-60 What is wave-particle duality?

15-61 An electron has a momentum of magnitude 9.18×10^{-26} kg·m/s. Determine its de Broglie wavelength. [Ans. 7.22×10^{-9} m]

15-62 Sketch the shape of a graph of a graph of de Broglie wavelength vs. $1/v$, where v is the speed of a particle.

15-63 Determine the speed of a neutron that has a de Broglie wavelength of 3.87 pm. [Ans. 1.03×10^5 m/s]

APPLYING YOUR KNOWLEDGE

15-64 Make a list of (a) phenomena that can be explained by the wave theory of light (b) phenomena explainable via the photon theory.

15-65 The intensity of sunlight at the top of Earth's atmosphere is 1.37×10^3 W/m^2. How many photons per square metre per second does this represent? Assume that the average wavelength of the light is 550 nm. [Ans. 3.79×10^{21}]

15-66 One way to propel a spacecraft would be through the use of a "photon sail." Photons from the sun would hit the sail, thus imparting momentum to the spacecraft. Which would be better — a shiny sail that reflects photons, or a black sail that absorbs photons? Explain your answer.

15-67 The threshold frequency for the photoelectric effect in mercury is 1.09×10^{15} Hz. If light of wavelength 225 nm illuminates mercury, what is the maximum kinetic energy of the emitted photoelectrons? [Ans. 1.6×10^{-19} J]

15-68 Light of frequency 8.1×10^{14} Hz shines on a photocathode that has a work function of 1.2 eV. What is the maximum speed with which an electron leaves the photocathode? [Ans. 8.7×10^5 m/s]

15-69 A retarding potential of 1.4 V is applied to a photocell. When the photocathode is illuminated by ultraviolet light of frequency 2.3×10^{15} Hz, the maximum speed with which photoelectrons strike the anode is 1.50×10^6 m/s. What is the work function of the photocathode? [Ans. 1.7 eV]

15-70 An incident photon of energy 1.54 MeV undergoes Compton scattering through an angle of 45.0°, and then the resulting scattered photon also undergoes Compton scattering, through an angle of 37.1°. What is the energy of the final photon in keV? [Ans. 619 keV]

15-71 In a Compton scattering event, an X-ray photon of energy 16.7 keV results in a scattered photon of energy 15.3 keV. What is the speed of the scattered electron? (The energies are small enough that nonrelativistic mechanics may be used.) [Ans. 2.2×10^7 m/s]

15-72 What is the kinetic energy (in electron-volts) of a proton that has a de Broglie wavelength of 37.5 pm? [Ans. 0.585 eV]

15-73 If electrons in an electron microscope are to have de Broglie wavelengths of 0.036 nm, through what voltage must they be accelerated from rest? [Ans. 1.2×10^3 V]

15-74 If the de Broglie wavelengths of a proton and an electron are equal, determine an algebraic expression for the ratio of the electron kinetic energy to the proton kinetic energy in terms of the electron mass, m_e, and the proton mass, m_p. [Ans. m_p/m_e]

15-75 In the Bohr model of the hydrogen atom (Chapter 16), an electron in the lowest energy state has a speed of 2.19×10^6 m/s, and travels in a circular orbit of radius 5.29×10^{-11} m.
(a) Determine the de Broglie wavelength of the electron.
(b) How does your answer compare with the circumference of the orbit?
[Ans. (a) 3.32×10^{-10} m]

KEY OBJECTIVES

Having completed this chapter, you should now be able to do the following:

1. Describe the photoelectric effect.
2. Explain how the photon model of light can be used to explain experimental results in the photoelectric effect.
3. Solve numerical problems related to energy, wavelength, and frequency of photons, maximum kinetic energy of photoelectrons, threshold frequency, and work function.
4. List practical applications of the photoelectric effect.
5. Describe the Compton effect.
6. State the conservation laws that apply in the Compton effect.
7. Discuss the importance of Compton's experiments in the acceptance of the photon theory of light.
8. Describe the basic scattering and absorption processes that light undergoes when it interacts with matter.
9. State the meaning of wave-particle duality.
10. Discuss the theoretical and experimental development of the concept of matter waves.
11. Solve numerical questions related to de Broglie wavelength.
12. Describe the operation of transmission electron microscopes and scanning electron microscopes.
13. Discuss why electron microscopes can show finer detail than optical microscopes.

ANSWERS TO SELECTED QUESTIONS

15-2 Still no current will result. Increasing the intensity means that there are more photons, but the energy of each individual photon is still not enough to liberate a photoelectron.

15-3 (a) The current increases. (b) The maximum kinetic energy of the photoelectrons does not change.

15-6 The photoelectric effect will not occur if light of a longer wavelength is used because the longer-wavelength photons have less energy ($E = hc/\lambda$).

15-11 The slope is equal to Planck's constant.

15-14 The electrons would not be bound to the metal at all, and would be free to "escape" from the metal without any external stimulus.

15-16 Work function (*W*) = Planck's constant (h) times threshold frequency.

15-19 False. A battery is not required in order for a photocell to produce a current. If a photon of sufficient energy is absorbed, an electron can be liberated from the photocell material and thus a current can be produced.

15-26 (a) photon (b) electron (c) energy (d) momentum

15-44 (a) 15-45 (e) 15-46 (b) 15-47 (c) 15-48 (a)

15-53 energy

15-66 A shiny sail that would be better. The *change* in a photon's momentum *vector* is greater if it reflects than if it absorbed. For example, if the photon's momentum has a magnitude of 1 unit in the $+x$ direction before reflection, and a momentum of magnitude 1 unit in the $-x$ direction after reflection, then the change (final momentum – initial momentum) is 2 units in the $-x$ direction. If the photon is absorbed, it will have a final momentum still in the $+x$ direction, and the change in its momentum will be somewhat less than 1 unit in the $-x$ direction. Since the total momentum of the photon and sail together is conserved, the change in the sail's momentum vector must be the negative of the change in the photon's momentum vector (to give a total change of zero), and therefore the sail's momentum will have a greater change if the sail is shiny.

CHAPTER 16

THE QUANTUM NATURE OF ATOMS

The year 1900 seems a long time ago, but in the history of civilization, it is not so far in the past. The twentieth-century developments in science, technology, transportation, medicine, etc., have been truly amazing, especially when viewed against the long, slow rate of progress in previous centuries. In 1900, the nature of atoms was not at all well understood — indeed, some established scientists did not even believe in atoms — but the first few decades of the twentieth century saw a rapid improvement in our "picture" of atoms. In this chapter, we explore the evolution of ideas about the structure of atoms, and also see that our present knowledge has led to the development of a fascinating and useful device: the laser.

16.1 MODELS OF ATOMS

The idea that matter consists of tiny "particles" — atoms — is not a recent one. The Greek philosopher, Democritus (Figure 16-1), postulated the existence of atoms about 400 B.C., although his suggestion was based solely on philosophical reasoning, not on experimental evidence. The notion that matter is made of atoms did not receive serious support until the eighteenth and nineteenth centuries, when laboratory experiments involving chemical reactions gave results that led the British chemist, John Dalton (1766-1844), to suggest that matter consists of atoms, like tiny balls, which could combine to produce various compounds.

Figure 16-1 *A Greek postage stamp in honour of Democritus (circa 460-370 B.C.).*

In 1897, an English physicist, Sir Joseph John Thomson (1856-1940), measured the charge-to-mass ratio of the particles that we now call electrons, and hypothesized that these particles were constituents of atoms. Because of this measurement and hypothesis, he is generally credited with "discovering the electron." He proposed that the positive charge in atoms was spread out over the entire volume of the atom, and that the negative electrons were embedded in this sphere. This is the so-called "plum pudding" model of the atom, with the electrons being the "plums" and the positive charge the "pudding." This model, in vogue at the beginning of the twentieth century, did not last long — the stage had been set for the development of some dramatically new models of atoms.

Did You Know? *The word "atom" is derived from the Greek "atomos," which means "indivisible." (However, we now know that atoms are not indivisible.)*

The Rutherford Model

In 1910, Sir Ernest Rutherford (Figure 16-2) and his associates performed crucial experiments showing that the positive charge in atoms was concentrated in a small volume at the centre.

Positively charged particles called alpha (α) particles were used to bombard thin foils of gold and silver. Most of the α particles passed through the foils undeflected, but a few were deflected almost backward. Such a huge deflection (Figure 16-3) indicated that an α particle had encountered a massive concentration of positive charge. The fact that most α particles experienced no deflection showed that much of the metal foil must consist of empty space. In other words, an atom must contain largely empty space, and at an atom's centre, there is a small, dense, positively charged object, called the **nucleus** of the atom.

Figure 16-2 *Sir Ernest Rutherford (1871-1937). This postage stamp illustrates Rutherford's α-particle scattering experiments. Rutherford was born in New Zealand, but did most of his research in Canada and England. (Stamp courtesy of J.L. Hunt.)*

Rutherford theorized that an atom is like a tiny solar system (Figure 16-4). Most of the atom's mass is concentrated in the small, positively charged nucleus, and the negatively charged electrons move in orbits around the nucleus, much as the planets move around the Sun. Rutherford's α-particle data indicated that nuclei have diameters of about 10^{-14} m. Albert Einstein in 1905 had estimated the radius of atoms to be about 10^{-10} m, which would correspond to the radii of the electron orbits. Thus, Rutherford's model suggested that an atom was roughly 10^4 times larger than a nucleus. The **Rutherford model** of the atom was an important step forward in our understanding of atoms, but, as we shall see, it was incomplete.

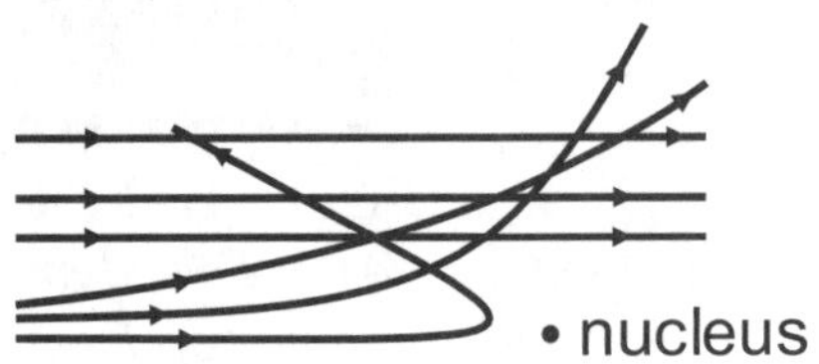

Figure 16-3 *Alpha-particle trajectories (hyperbolae). An α-particle that comes close to a nucleus experiences a large electric repulsion and is deflected almost backward.*

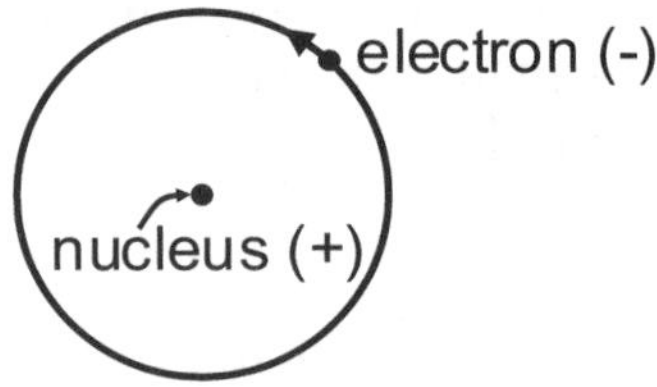

Figure 16-4 *The Rutherford planetary model of the atom (not to scale). Electrons orbit the nucleus, and most of the atom is empty space.*

Atomic Spectra[1]

The next major contribution to the knowledge of atomic structure was made by a Danish physicist, Niels Bohr. But before we can discuss his work, a brief digression about *spectra* (singular: *spectrum*) is in order.

Well before Rutherford's time, it was known that, if light passes through a prism or a diffraction grating, it is separated into a spectrum showing various colours, corresponding to different wavelengths of light. If the object emitting the light is a hot solid, such as the tungsten

[1] See also Section 14.4.

filament in an incandescent lightbulb, the spectrum is a continuous band of colours, ranging from red at one end, through orange, yellow, and green, to blue and violet at the other end. Hot dense gases (such as the sun) and hot liquids emit continuous spectra as well. You have undoubtedly observed continuous spectra in rainbows or from white light bouncing off a CD.

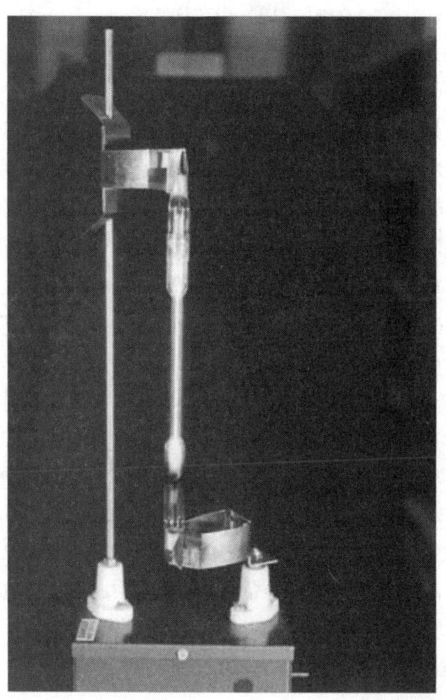

Figure 16-5 *A high-voltage gas discharge tube. A large potential difference applied across the ends of the tube causes excitation and ionization of the gas in the tube, with the resulting emission of light.*

A low-pressure (not dense) gas can also emit light — either through heating, or, more commonly, as a result of exciting it with a high-voltage electric discharge (Figure 16-5) — but the spectrum is not continuous. Rather, the light consists only of a few discrete wavelengths. Since the light usually passes through a linear slit in the production of a spectrum (Figure 16-6), the spectrum from a low-pressure gas appears as a number of separated lines. As an example, low-pressure hydrogen gas emits visible light of only four wavelengths: 656 nm, 486 nm, 434 nm, and 410 nm. Thus, its visible spectrum has only four lines, one for each of these wavelengths; the corresponding colours are red, blue, blue-green, and violet. The details of line spectra differ for different types of gases, and hence the spectra can be used to identify gases. The gas helium was actually discovered via its line spectrum from the sun before it was found (in 1895) here on Earth. (The name *helium* is derived from *helios*, the Greek word for "sun.") Spectra are routinely used to detect elements in stars, interstellar space, and planetary atmospheres.

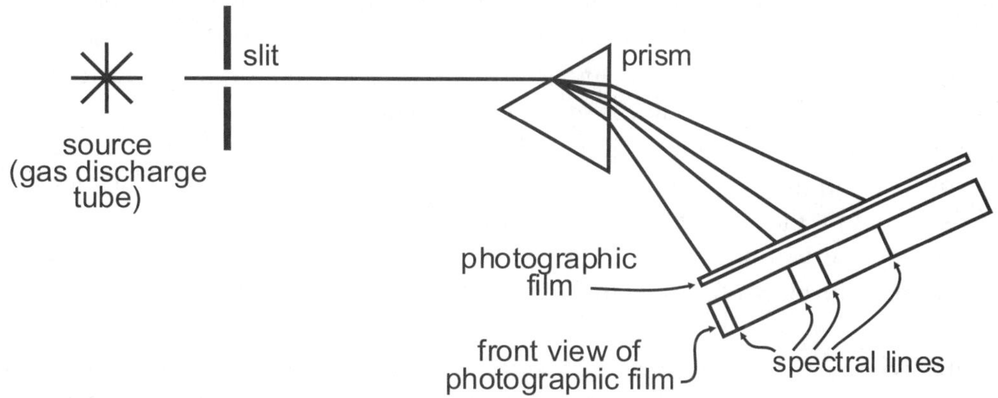

Figure 16-6 *Production of a line spectrum.*

Thus far, we have been discussing emission spectra, that is, spectra *emitted* by objects. Another type of spectrum is an absorption spectrum, which is the spectrum of light transmitted through a material such as a low-pressure gas, when white light containing all possible wavelengths is shone on it.

Did You Know? *Neon signs are just high-voltage discharge tubes containing the gas neon.*

The spectrum of the incident white light is just a continuous spectrum, but the spectrum of the transmitted light contains black (or missing) lines. These lines indicate that the gas is *absorbing* light of certain wavelengths; light of these wavelengths is then not present in the spectrum. Interestingly, the *wavelengths of light absorbed by a gas exactly match the wavelengths that it emits* (Figure 16-7). The solar spectrum, when looked at in detail, is not, in fact, a continuous spectrum. Rather, it shows a number of dark absorption lines produced by absorption of the sun's light by atoms and molecules in the outer layers of the sun's atmosphere and in the Earth's own atmosphere.

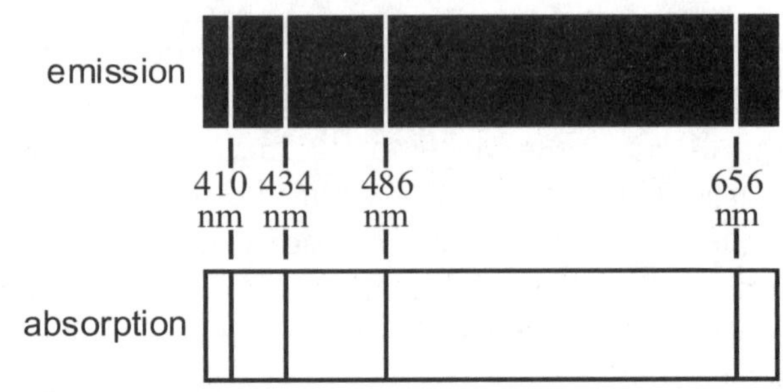

Figure 16-7 *Emission and absorption spectra of hydrogen (in the visible region of the spectrum), showing also the wavelengths of the spectral lines.*

In low-pressure gases, the atoms are far enough apart that they interact infrequently, and hence, line spectra (emission or absorption) must be due to processes within single atoms. Therefore, any theory of atoms must be able to explain why low-pressure gases have line spectra, and also predict the particular wavelengths of light that are emitted and absorbed by various gases.

Rutherford's model of the atom could not explain line spectra. In Rutherford's theory, electrons follow curved paths in their orbits around the nucleus, and must therefore be undergoing an acceleration. (Recall that a change in either the magnitude or *direction* of a velocity vector implies an acceleration.) According to classical electromagnetic theory, an accelerating charge produces electromagnetic radiation. Thus, the orbiting electrons should be constantly emitting radiation, and, in doing so, losing energy. As the electrons lose energy, they should spiral in toward the nucleus, gradually increasing their revolution frequency and the frequency of the emitted radiation until the electrons collide with the nucleus. Hence, Rutherford's model predicts a continuous spectrum of electromagnetic radiation from atoms, in contrast with the observed line spectra, and also predicts that atoms are unstable because of the spiraling motion of the electrons. In actual fact, of course, atoms are stable.

The Bohr Model

We can now turn to the developments made by Niels Bohr (Figure 16-8). In 1911 and 1912, Bohr had been thinking about the structure of atoms, and, in 1913, a friend suggested that he have a look at *Balmer's equation.* Soon after Bohr saw this equation, he found a solution to the problems of Rutherford's model. What is Balmer's equation, and how was it useful as a key in unlocking the problems of atomic structure?

Johann Jakob Balmer (1825-1898), a Swiss high school teacher, had noticed in 1885 a fascinating regularity in the wavelengths of visible light emitted and absorbed by hydrogen. These wavelengths (λ) are given by his equation:

$$\frac{1}{\lambda} = R\left[\frac{1}{2^2} - \frac{1}{n^2}\right] \qquad \textbf{(16-1)}$$

Figure 16-8 *Niels Bohr (1995-1962). This postage stamp from Greenland commemorates the 50th anniversary of Bohr's atomic theory. (Stamp courtesy of J.L. Hunt.)*

where R is the *Rydberg constant* ($R = 1.097 \times 10^7\ m^{-1}$), and $n = 3, 4, 5, \ldots, \infty$. For values of n between 3 and 6 (inclusive), the wavelengths are in the visible region of the spectrum (thus giving the four visible spectral lines of hydrogen). For $n > 6$, the lines are in the (invisible) ultraviolet region. The spectral lines corresponding to this formula are known as the *Balmer series* of hydrogen. There are other similar series in the infrared and ultraviolet spectrum of hydrogen. Their wavelengths are given by:

$$\frac{1}{\lambda} = R\left[\frac{1}{n_1^2} - \frac{1}{n_2^2}\right] \qquad \textbf{(16-2)}$$

where R is the Rydberg constant, n_1 is a *constant* positive integer (1 or 2 or 3, etc.) for a given series, and n_2 is any integer greater than n_1. For example, with $n_1 = 1$, we have the *Lyman series* (in the ultraviolet); possible values of n_2 in this series are 2, 3, 4, …, ∞. For $n_1 = 3$, 4, and 5, we have the *Paschen, Brackett, and Pfund series*, respectively, all in the infrared.

The regularity and mathematical form of Balmer's formula was the final clue that Bohr needed to develop the **Bohr model** of the atom in 1913. He postulated that electrons in an atom travel in circular orbits, but that orbits of certain sizes only are allowed. An electron can move in any one of these orbits, called **stationary states**, without radiating energy. Each stationary state corresponds to a particular electron energy, and orbits with other energies are not permitted. In other words, the *energy of electrons in atoms is quantized* — it can have only certain values. Electrons can move from one stationary state to a lower energy one by emitting a photon. The photon energy equals the difference in electron energy in the two states. As well, electrons can move to a state of higher energy by absorption of a photon of the right energy.[2]

Bohr was able to calculate the energies of electrons in stationary states in hydrogen atoms, and, from these, determine the energies, frequencies, and wavelengths of photons that could be emitted when electrons changed states. These photon wavelengths agreed extremely well with those actually observed in the various series (Balmer, etc.) of spectral lines in hydrogen.

Did You Know? *Bohr received the Nobel Prize in Physics in 1922 for his model of atoms.*

[2]What determines the sizes of the permitted orbits? Bohr suggested that, in the stationary states, a quantity called the angular momentum (L) of an electron equals a positive integer (n) multiplied by $h/2\pi$, where h is Planck's constant. (Thus, $L = nh/2\pi$.) In short, the angular momentum of electrons in atoms is also quantized. This condition leads to the quantization of the electron energy.

The details of Bohr's work are presented in Section 16.2.

Although Bohr's paper was another important step forward in our understanding of atomic structure, the journey was by no means complete. The atomic story continues to unfold as this chapter proceeds.

Sample Problem 16-1

(a) For the first spectral line in the Balmer series in hydrogen, what is the wavelength in nanometres?
(b) What is the corresponding photon energy (in electron-volts)?

Solution: (a) The wavelengths in the Balmer series of hydrogen are given by Eqn. 16-1:

$$\frac{1}{\lambda} = \mathrm{R}\left[\frac{1}{2^2} - \frac{1}{n^2}\right]$$

For the "first" spectral line, we have the lowest possible value of n, which is 3. This corresponds to the largest value of λ. Substituting numbers:

$$\frac{1}{\lambda} = \left(1.097 \times 10^7 \text{ m}^{-1}\right)\left[\frac{1}{2^2} - \frac{1}{3^2}\right]$$

Thus, $$\frac{1}{\lambda} = 1.52 \times 10^6 \text{ m}^{-1}$$

Hence, $$\lambda = \frac{1}{1.52 \times 10^6 \text{ m}^{-1}} = 6.56 \times 10^{-7} \text{ m}$$

> ***Units Tip:*** *Since the given value for the Rydberg constant (R) has units of metre^{-1}, and the 2^2 and 3^2 are unitless, the units for $1/\lambda$ are metre^{-1}.*

Converting this to nanometres: $$6.56 \times 10^{-7} \text{ m} \times \frac{1 \text{ nm}}{10^{-9} \text{ m}} = 656 \text{ nm}$$

Thus, the wavelength is 656 nm.

(b) From Chapter 15, we know that photon energy, E, is given by $E = \mathrm{h}f = \mathrm{hc}/\lambda$, where h is Planck's constant, f is the light frequency, and c is the speed of light. Since we know the wavelength λ, we use

$$E = \frac{\mathrm{hc}}{\lambda} = \frac{\left(6.63 \times 10^{-34} \text{ J}\cdot\text{s}\right)\left(3.00 \times 10^8 \text{ m/s}\right)}{6.56 \times 10^{-7} \text{ m}} = 3.03 \times 10^{-19} \text{ J}$$

Converting to electron-volts: $$3.03 \times 10^{-19} \text{ J} \times \frac{1 \text{ eV}}{1.60 \times 10^{-19} \text{ J}} = 1.89 \text{ eV}$$

Thus, the photon energy is 1.89 eV.

 **Practice**

16-1 In Rutherford's experiments, which observations indicated that
(a) an atom is mostly empty space?
(b) the positive charge in an atom is concentrated in a small volume?

16-2 Complete the following. In a typical atom, the nucleus is about $10^?$ m in diameter and the electron orbits are roughly $10^?$ m from the nucleus.

16-3 Convert your first answer in the previous question to femtometres, and your second answer to nanometers. [Ans. 10 fm; 0.2 nm]

16-4 Low-pressure helium gas in an electric discharge tube produces a (an) ______________ spectrum.

16-5 Give one example of an object that emits a continuous spectrum of light.

16-6 What were the deficiencies of Rutherford's model of the atom?

16-7 Why do you suppose that the Balmer series in hydrogen was discovered before the other series (Lyman, Paschen, etc.)?

16-8 (a) What is the second longest wavelength in the Balmer series in hydrogen?
(b) What is the photon energy (in joules and electron-volts) corresponding to your answer in (a)?
[Ans. (a) 4.86×10^{-7} m (b) 4.09×10^{-19} J; 2.56 eV]

16-9 Determine the smallest frequency of light in the Lyman series in hydrogen.
[Ans. 2.47×10^{15} Hz]

16-10 What are the major differences between the Rutherford and Bohr models of the atom?

16-11 In the Bohr model of the atom, what is meant by a stationary state?

16.2 THE BOHR MODEL IN DETAIL

We present here the mathematical details and results of the Bohr model, which is a lovely blend of classical and quantum ideas. Be careful in all the mathematics not to lose sight of the main features of Bohr's model:

1. Electrons in atoms can have only certain circular orbits[3] (stationary states) with well-defined energies.
2. Electrons can move from one orbit to another by releasing (or gaining) energy through emission (or absorption) of a photon.

Did You Know? *The word "electron" was coined by the Irish physicist G. Johnstone Stoney.*

Since a nucleus is positively charged and an electron is negatively charged, an electron orbiting a nucleus experiences an attractive electric force, $\boldsymbol{F}$, toward the nucleus (Figure 16-9). By Newton's second law, this force equals the product of the electron's mass and its acceleration:

$$F = ma \qquad \text{Eqn. [1]}$$

We can write the magnitude of the electric force as k $|q_1q_2|/r^2$ (Coulomb's law – Chapter 10), where k is the usual Coulomb constant, q_1 and q_2 are the charges on the nucleus and electron, respectively, and r is the distance between the nucleus and electron. For a circular orbit, the magnitude of the acceleration is v^2/r, where v is the electron speed, and thus Eqn. [1] becomes (in terms of vector magnitudes):

$$\frac{\mathrm{k}|q_1q_2|}{r^2} = m\frac{v^2}{r}$$

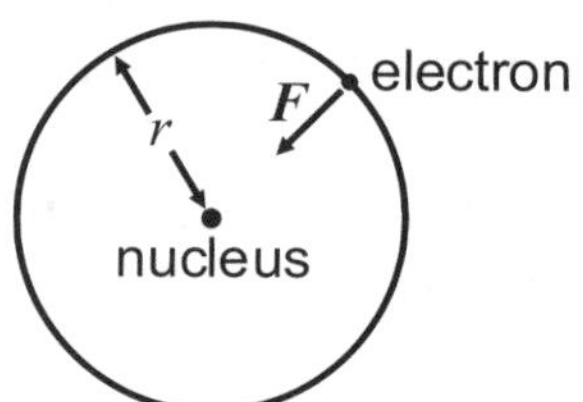

Figure 16-9 *The electric force (**F**) exerted on an electron in a circular orbit around a nucleus.*

Multiplying both sides by r, and writing $q_2 = -\mathrm{e}$ (the charge on an electron) and $q_1 = +\mathrm{e}$ (the charge on a hydrogen nucleus, which is just a proton):

$$\frac{\mathrm{ke}^2}{r} = mv^2 \qquad \text{Eqn. [2]}$$

So much for the classical physics part. Now some quantum physics is applied. Bohr's quantization condition for the angular momentum, L, of the electron was mentioned in Section 16.1:

$$L = \frac{n\mathrm{h}}{2\pi}$$

where $n = 1, 2, 3, \ldots$, and h is Planck's constant. The angular momentum of an object of mass m moving with speed v in a circle of radius r is given by

$$L = mvr$$

Therefore, Bohr's statement of quantization of angular momentum becomes:

[3]Bohr's model was later refined to include elliptical orbits.

$$mvr = \frac{nh}{2\pi} \qquad \text{Eqn. [3]}$$

We can now solve Eqns. [2] and [3] for the allowed radii of electron orbits in terms of fundamental quantities such as electron mass, Planck's constant, etc. To do so, we eliminate a quantity that is not fundamental: the speed v. From Eqn. [3],

$$v = \frac{nh}{2\pi mr} \qquad \text{Eqn. [4]}$$

Substituting this into Eqn. [2]:

$$\frac{ke^2}{r} = m\left[\frac{nh}{2\pi mr}\right]^2$$

Thus,

$$\frac{ke^2}{r} = \frac{mn^2h^2}{4\pi^2m^2r^2}$$

Cancelling m's, cancelling r's, and solving for the remaining r, we have:

$$r = \frac{n^2h^2}{4\pi^2mke^2} \qquad \textbf{(16-3)}$$

This equation gives the desired radii. The smallest orbit in hydrogen has $n = 1$. Evaluating the radius of this orbit:

$$r = \frac{(1)^2\left(6.63\times10^{-34}\ \text{J}\cdot\text{s}\right)^2}{4\pi^2\left(9.11\times10^{-31}\ \text{kg}\right)\left(8.99\times10^{9}\ \text{N}\cdot\text{m}^2/\text{C}^2\right)\left(1.60\times10^{-19}\ \text{C}\right)^2}$$
$$= 5.3\times10^{-11}\ \text{m}$$

This value is known as the **Bohr radius**, and is often used as a representative atomic distance. It is commonly written as 0.53×10^{-10} m.

Choosing different values of n gives different radii, corresponding to different allowed orbits. Since r is proportional to n^2, the radius for $n = 2$ is four times the Bohr radius; for $n = 3$, nine times the Bohr radius, etc. The value of n is referred to as the **quantum number** of the orbit. Figure 16-10 shows the first three orbits; orbits in between are not permitted. Table 16.1 lists the orbital radii for $1 \le n \le 5$.

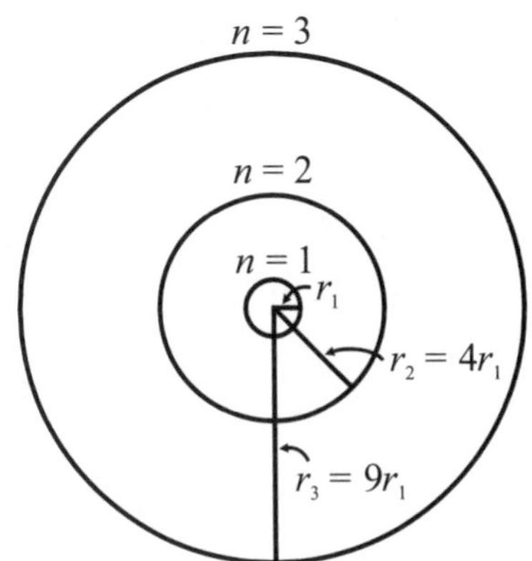

Figure 16-10 *The first three Bohr orbits in hydrogen. The smallest radius, corresponding to n = 1, is 0.53 × 10⁻¹⁰ m.*

We now calculate the energy of an electron in an allowed orbit. This energy is the sum of its kinetic energy ($E_K = ½\, mv^2$, from Chapter 7), and its electric potential energy ($U = k\, q_1 q_2 / r$, from Chapter 11). For $q_1 = +e$ and $q_2 = -e$, the electric potential energy is: $U = -ke^2/r$. (Notice that this potential energy is negative. Recall from Chapter 11 that the electric potential energy of two point charges is defined to be zero when the charges are infinitely far from each other ($r \rightarrow \infty$). The negative potential energy of the electron means only that its potential energy is less than that if it were very far away from the nucleus.) The total energy, E, is

Table 16.1
Orbital Radii in the Bohr Model of the Hydrogen Atom

Quantum Number n	Orbit Radius (m)	
1	0.53×10^{-10}	(r_1)
2	2.12×10^{-10}	$(4\, r_1)$
3	4.76×10^{-10}	$(9\, r_1)$
4	8.47×10^{-10}	$(16\, r_1)$
5	13.23×10^{-10}	$(25\, r_1)$

$$E = E_K + U = \tfrac{1}{2} mv^2 - \frac{ke^2}{r}$$

If we substitute the expression for v from Eqn. [4], and also the expression for r from Eqn. 16-3 into this equation for energy, and do a little algebra, we obtain

$$E = -\frac{2\pi^2 e^4 m k^2}{n^2 h^2} \qquad \textbf{(16-4)}$$

Substituting numerical values (except for n) into this equation, we have

$$E = \frac{-2.17 \times 10^{-18}\ \text{J}}{n^2}$$

Since energies in atomic physics are commonly given in electron-volts (1 eV = 1.60×10^{-19} J), we convert the numerator of this equation to electron-volts, obtaining −13.6 eV:

$$E = \frac{-13.6\ \text{eV}}{n^2} \qquad \textbf{(16-5)}$$

For the first Bohr orbit of hydrogen, the quantum number n is 1, and from Eqn. 16-5, the energy of the electron in this orbit is simply:

$$E = -13.6\ \text{eV} \qquad (\text{for } n = 1)$$

For larger orbits in hydrogen, $n = 2, 3, 4$, etc. Since the energy, E, is inversely proportional to n^2, the energy for $n = 2$ is 1/4 of that for $n = 1$; for $n = 3$, it is 1/9, etc. Actual numerical values are presented in Table 16.2. Notice that the energy values for $n = 2, 3, 4, \ldots$, are more positive than the −13.6 eV for $n = 1$. Thus, the energy of an electron in, say, the $n = 2$ orbit is greater (more positive) than that in the $n = 1$ orbit. Similarly, an electron with $n = 3$ has a greater energy than one with $n = 2$. If an electron moves from the $n = 3$ orbit to the $n = 2$ orbit, it is going to an orbit with lower energy, and emits energy in the form of a photon. The photon energy equals the energy lost by the electron: $-1.51-(-3.40)=1.89\ \text{eV}$.

Table 16.2
Electron Energies in the Bohr Model of the Hydrogen Atom

Quantum Number n	Electron Energy (eV)	Electron Energy Above the $n = 1$ Energy (eV)
1	−13.6	0
2	−3.40	10.2
3	−1.51	12.1
4	−0.85	12.8
5	−0.54	13.1
$\rightarrow\infty$	0	13.6

Now we can show where the Balmer, Lyman, and other series in the hydrogen spectrum come from. Suppose that an electron, initially in an orbit with quantum number n_2, moves to an orbit of lower energy and quantum number n_1. When an electron moves to a different orbit (stationary state), it is said to undergo a **transition**. The energy of the photon emitted in the transition is just the difference in the electron energies:

$$E_{\text{photon}}=-\frac{2\pi^2 e^4 mk^2}{n_2^2 h^2}-\left[-\frac{2\pi^2 e^4 mk^2}{n_1^2 h^2}\right]$$

Writing the photon energy as hc/λ, and collecting a common factor on the right-hand side:

$$\frac{hc}{\lambda}=-\left[\frac{2\pi^2 e^4 mk^2}{h^2}\right]\left[\frac{1}{n_1^2}-\frac{1}{n_2^2}\right]$$

Finally, dividing both sides by hc, we arrive at something that should look familiar to you:

$$\frac{1}{\lambda}=-\left[\frac{2\pi^2 e^4 mk^2}{h^3 c}\right]\left[\frac{1}{n_1^2}-\frac{1}{n_2^2}\right] \qquad \textbf{(16-6)}$$

Here at last is the equation that gives the wavelengths of spectral lines emitted by hydrogen. The collection of constants in the first set of brackets on the right-hand side is equivalent to the Rydberg constant, R. Imagine Bohr's thrill when the wavelengths calculated from this formula agreed with experimental ones. Atoms were finally starting to yield their secrets.

We are now in a position to understand the physical meaning of Eqn. 16-6 above. Photons are produced by hydrogen atoms when electrons move from a higher energy state to a lower one. The photon wavelength depends on the energy difference between the states. How does, say, the

Balmer series arise? For this series, $n_1 = 2$, that is, the final state in the transition is the state with quantum number 2. The different photon energies and the different spectral lines in the Balmer series correspond to transitions of electrons from *initial* states with $n_2 = 3, 4, 5, \ldots$, to a *final* state with $n_1 = 2$. Other series result from transitions to $n_1 = 1$ (Lyman series), $n_1 = 3$ (Paschen series), etc.

Did You Know? *The northern and southern lights, "aurora borealis" (Figure 16-11) and "aurora australis" consist of photons produced when electrons in molecules (primarily oxygen and nitrogen) in the upper atmosphere make transitions to lower energy levels. The molecules are excited by collisions with protons and electrons emitted by the sun. Electron energies in molecules, as well as in atoms, are quantized.*

It is convenient to show the various energies and transitions on an *energy-level diagram* (Figure 16-12). The "vertical" axis corresponds to energy, which increases toward the top of the diagram; the various possible energies are represented as "horizontal" lines called *energy levels*. The arrows represent transitions. You can see how the many spectral series in hydrogen arise from the various transitions. When the electron in a hydrogen atom is in the lowest possible energy level ($n = 1$), the atom is said to be in its **ground state**.

Figure 16-11
The northern lights, "aurora borealis."

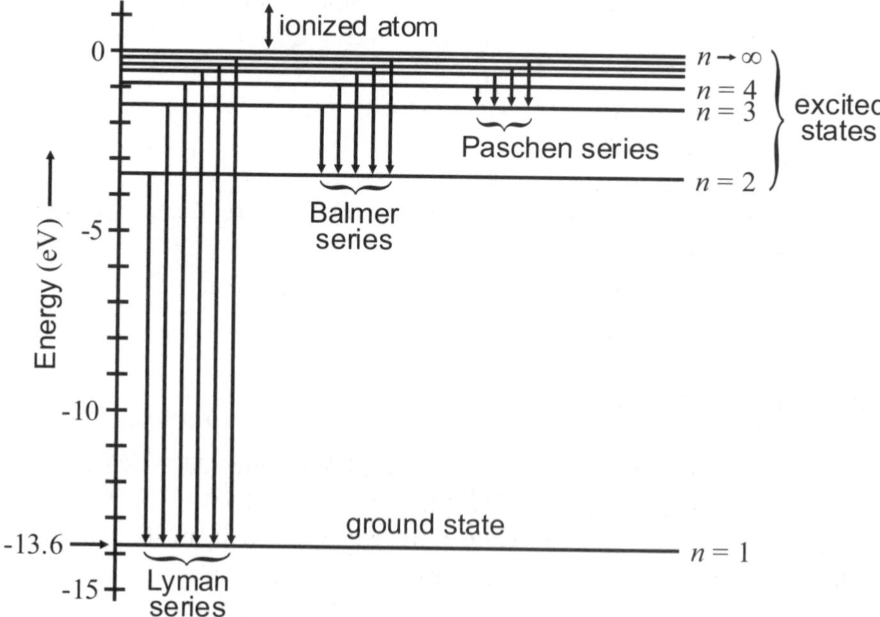

Figure 16-12 *Energy-level diagram for the hydrogen atom.*

(More generally, an atom that has many electrons is in its ground state when all the electrons have the lowest possible energies. There are rules restricting the number of electrons that can have each energy.) At room temperature, most hydrogen atoms are in the ground state.

Upward transitions in the energy-level diagram are possible. An electron in an atom can gain enough energy to move from one energy level to a higher one by a number of means, for example, by absorbing a photon, or by being exposed to an electric discharge (in which there are many collisions of free electrons and atoms). If the electron in a hydrogen atom is in an energy level other than $n = 1$, the atom is in an **excited state**. (A multi-electron atom is in an excited state if at least one of its electrons has received energy and made a transition to a higher energy level.)

Notice that, as the quantum number n gets larger, the energy levels get closer together and the total energy E approaches zero. A total energy of zero (or greater) corresponds to ionization of the atom. This means that if an electron in the $n = 1$ level (energy −13.6 eV) receives an energy of 13.6 eV or more, it escapes from the hydrogen atom, becoming a free electron. The atom becomes a hydrogen ion (H^+ — a "naked" proton). Electron energies for free electrons are continuous, that is, not quantized.

Bohr's theory of atoms was an enormous breakthrough. You can see from the analysis above how it explained the spectral series in hydrogen. However, he had made radical assumptions that took some getting used to: quantization of angular momentum (which produced quantization of energy), and the existence of stationary states in which electrons emit no radiation even through they are undergoing acceleration. He was able to make his suggestions more believable by showing that, for large quantum numbers, his quantum theory gave the same results as classical theory. For example, if an electron in a hydrogen atom makes a transition from the $n = 10\ 001$ level to the $n = 10\ 000$ level, the wavelength of the photon produced is the same as that predicted by classical electrodynamics. This equivalence of results from classical theory and quantum theory when quantum numbers are large was called by Bohr the **correspondence principle**.

Although Bohr's results solved a number of problems, nonetheless, there was still work to be done. Bohr's theory worked well for hydrogen, but it gave poor quantitative results for atoms with many electrons. In addition, as spectroscopic techniques improved, it became apparent that each spectral line actually consisted of two or more closely spaced lines, and Bohr's model could not explain this *fine structure*. As well, it could not account for the relative brightness of various spectral lines. We continue the story of atomic models in Section 16.4.

Sample Problem 16-2

(a) Determine the energy (in electron-volts) of the photon emitted when an electron makes a transition from the $n = 2$ level to the $n = 1$ level in a hydrogen atom.
(b) What photon energy is required to excite a hydrogen atom from its ground state to its first excited state (the state that requires the least energy for excitation)?

Solution: (a) To determine the photon energy, we first note that the photon wavelength is given by Eqn. 16-2:

$$\frac{1}{\lambda} = \mathrm{R}\left[\frac{1}{n_1^2} - \frac{1}{n_2^2}\right]$$

where $n_1 = 1$ and $n_2 = 2$.

Then, recalling that photon energy is given by $E = \mathrm{h}f = \mathrm{hc}/\lambda$, we have

$$E = \frac{\mathrm{hc}}{\lambda} = \mathrm{hcR}\left[\frac{1}{n_1^2} - \frac{1}{n_2^2}\right]$$

Substituting numbers (all in SI units, of course):

$$E = \left(6.63 \times 10^{-34}\ \mathrm{J \cdot s}\right)\left(3.00 \times 10^{8}\ \mathrm{m/s}\right)\left(1.097 \times 10^{7}\ \mathrm{m^{-1}}\right)\left[\frac{1}{1^2} - \frac{1}{2^2}\right]$$
$$= 1.64 \times 10^{-18}\ \mathrm{J}$$

Converting to electron-volts: $1.64 \times 10^{-18}\ \mathrm{J} \times \dfrac{1\ \mathrm{eV}}{1.60 \times 10^{-19}\ \mathrm{J}} = 10.2\ \mathrm{eV}$

Thus, the photon energy is 10.2 eV.

Alternate Solution to Sample Problem 16-2 (a):
Since Table 16.2 happens to list the energies of the $n = 1$ and $n = 2$ energy levels, we can simply subtract these energies to give the photon energy:

$$E = -3.40\ \mathrm{eV} - (-13.6\ \mathrm{eV}) = 10.2\ \mathrm{eV}$$

(b) In order for a hydrogen atom to be excited from its ground state to its first excited state, the electron must make a transition from the $n = 1$ level to the $n = 2$ level. In part (a), we determined the energy difference between these levels to be 10.2 eV, and this energy must be provided by the photon. Hence, the photon energy is 10.2 eV.

The Franck-Hertz Experiment

According to Bohr's theory, the energy of electrons in atoms is quantized. For one-electron atoms, we have seen that his theory can be used to calculate transition energies that agree very well with experimental values. But what about multi-electron atoms? These atoms have line spectra, and we might expect that electron energies in these atoms are quantized. We have mentioned that Bohr's theory did a poor *quantitative* job with atoms having more than one electron, that is, it could not predict energies, etc., very accurately. Does this poor agreement mean that electron energies in multi-electron atoms are not quantized, or that these atoms are just more complicated and Bohr's model is not sophisticated enough? In 1914, less than one year after Bohr developed his theory, the German physicists, James Franck and Gustav Hertz, performed an experiment that confirmed quantization of energy for atoms containing many electrons.

Did You Know? *Gustav Hertz was a nephew of Heinrich Hertz (after whom the SI unit of frequency was named).*

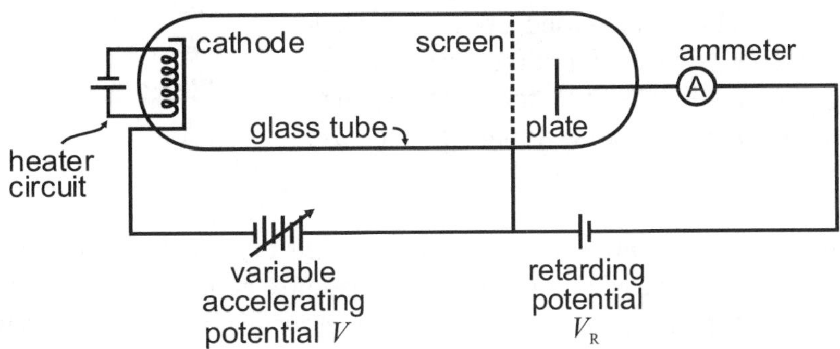

Figure 16-13 *Apparatus of the Franck-Hertz experiment.*

Figure 16-13 shows the apparatus (somewhat simplified) of the Franck-Hertz experiment. Electrons are "boiled off" the heated cathode and are accelerated by the potential difference, V, to the wire screen. Most of the electrons pass through the screen and reach the metal plate, assuming that their kinetic energy is large enough to overcome a small retarding potential, V_R, between the screen and the plate. Any electrons collected by the plate constitute a current measured by the ammeter, A. Franck and Hertz were conducting experiments to measure how this current varied with the applied voltage, V, when various vapours were in the glass tube.

Their first experiment was performed with mercury vapour; Figure 16-14 shows a portion of their results. As the voltage is increased through low values, the current increases steadily. However, at one particular voltage — 4.9 V — the current drops precipitously, and then gradually increases as the voltage increases further. What is happening at 4.9 V? At this voltage, some process must be being initiated that prevents electrons from reaching the plate. The interpretation is that electrons accelerated by this voltage have just enough energy to cause excitation of mercury atoms to their first excited states. Since an electron accelerated through 4.9 V has a kinetic energy of 4.9 eV, the minimum energy required to excite a mercury atom must be 4.9 eV. An electron with a kinetic energy of 4.9 eV can lose all of this energy by

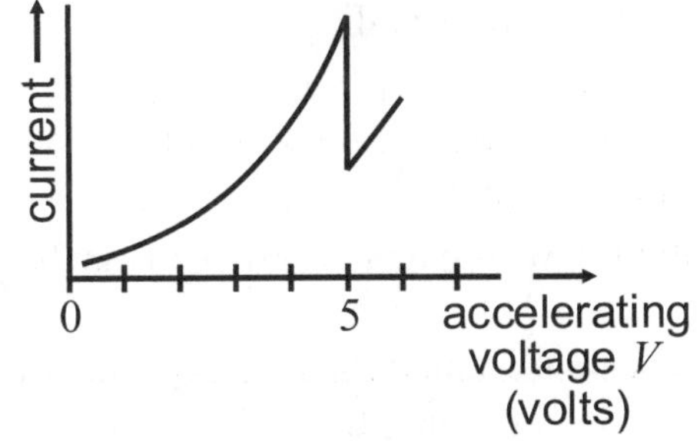

Figure 16-14 *Current measured in the Franck-Hertz experiment.*

colliding with a mercury atom and exciting it. Hence, the electron speed drops to zero, and the electron becomes unavailable to contribute to the current.

If the voltage is less than 4.9 V, the electrons have kinetic energies less than 4.9 eV and are unable to transfer any energy to mercury atoms. These electrons undergo only *elastic* collisions with the atoms, that is, there is no loss of kinetic energy as a result of the collision. In contrast, electrons with kinetic energies of 4.9 eV or more undergo *inelastic* collisions in which kinetic energy is "lost." When the voltage is increased above 4.9 V, an electron can lose 4.9 eV of energy to a mercury atom and still have enough energy left over to travel to the plate. Thus, the current increases as the voltage is increased beyond 4.9 V.

Did You Know? *An electron can be captured briefly into an orbit around a positron (the electron's antiparticle), thus forming a hydrogen-like "atom" called "positronium" until the electron and positron annihilate each other.*

To check this explanation, Franck and Hertz analyzed the spectrum emitted by the mercury vapour as the current was passing through it, and, sure enough, there was a spectral line corresponding to a photon energy of 4.9 eV. This line corresponded to photons being released by the excited mercury atoms as they made the transition back to the ground state. The Franck-Hertz experiment was very elegant — the mercury atoms were being excited by electrons, whose energy could be determined by a simple voltage measurement. Then the energy could be confirmed by a measurement of photon energy upon de-excitation of the atoms.

As the voltage was increased well above 4.9 V, there were other drops in the current. These resulted from excitations to other states and also from multiple inelastic collisions of electrons with atoms. For example, there was a decrease in current at 9.8 V, corresponding to an electron colliding with two mercury atoms, giving up 4.9 eV per collision.

Strange as quantization of energy seemed to physicists at the time, the success of the Bohr theory and the experimental confirmation by Franck and Hertz indicated that quantization was the way to understanding the nature of atoms.

Practice

16-12 Draw a scale diagram of Bohr's electron orbits in a hydrogen atom for $1 \leq n \leq 5$.

16-13 Sketch the shape of a graph of electron orbit radius in a hydrogen atom vs. quantum number n, according to the Bohr theory. (Note that n is not a continuous variable. How will this affect your graph?)

16-14 Explain what is meant by *ground state* and *excited state* of an atom.

16-15 Substitute numerical values into Eqn. 16-4 to calculate directly the energy of the electron in a hydrogen atom if $n = 4$. [Ans. -1.35×10^{-19} J]

16-16 Sketch the shape of a graph of electron energy vs. quantum number n (according to the Bohr theory). Notice that n is not a continuous variable.

16-17 In Eqn. 16-6, substitute numerical values to show that the collection of constants in the first set of brackets on the right-hand side is equal to the Rydberg constant given in Section 16.1.

16-18 What are the wavelength and energy of the photon produced when the electron in a hydrogen atom makes a transition from the $n = 4$ level to the $n = 3$ level?
[Ans. 1.88×10^{-6} m; 1.06×10^{-19} J or 0.663 eV]

16-19 In the previous question, what is the name of the spectral series to which the photon belongs?

16-20 What photon energy is required to excite a hydrogen atom from its ground state to its second excited state? [Ans. 2.1 eV]

16-21 How much energy is needed to ionize a hydrogen atom in the $n = 2$ state? [Ans. 3.4 eV]

16-22 What is the (total) energy of an electron in a hydrogen atom as the quantum number n becomes infinitely large? [Ans. 0 eV]

16-23 What were the deficiencies of Bohr's model?

16-24 Determine the electric potential energy of an $n = 3$ electron in a hydrogen atom. Use Table 16.1 for the radius of the orbit. [Ans. -4.83×10^{-19} J or -3.02 eV]

16-25 What is the angular momentum of an $n = 2$ electron in a hydrogen atom, according to the Bohr theory? [Ans. 2.11×10^{-34} J·s]

16-26 Imagine a collision between a moving electron and a stationary ground-state hydrogen atom. For what range of electron kinetic energy is the collision certain to be elastic?
[Ans. $0 < E_K < 10.2$ eV]

16.3 DE BROGLIE ELECTRON WAVES IN ATOMS

Bohr's model of the hydrogen atom was published in 1913, and, about a decade later, Louis de Broglie postulated the existence of matter waves (Section 15.3). There is an interesting connection between the matter waves of electrons in a hydrogen atom and quantization of energy. Indeed, one of de Broglie's arguments for the existence of matter waves was that they provided an explanation for Bohr's theory of the atom. We shall see that each allowed Bohr orbit contains a whole number of de Broglie wavelengths of an electron in the orbit.

We begin with an analogy involving sound waves. When a guitar string is plucked, waves of many different wavelengths are produced. As discussed in Section 13.3, most of them die out quickly because of destructive interference, leaving only resonant standing waves for which a half-integral number (½ , 1, 1½ , etc.) of wavelengths fits exactly into the length of the string (Figure 16-15). For a circular wire loop (Figure 16-16 (a)), the requirement is that an integral number (1, 2, 3, etc.) of wavelengths exactly fits around the circumference, so that a wave will mesh with itself constructively after travelling once around the loop. For a non-integral number of wavelengths on a loop, a wave undergoes destructive interference with itself (Figure 16-16 (b)), and quickly is dissipated.

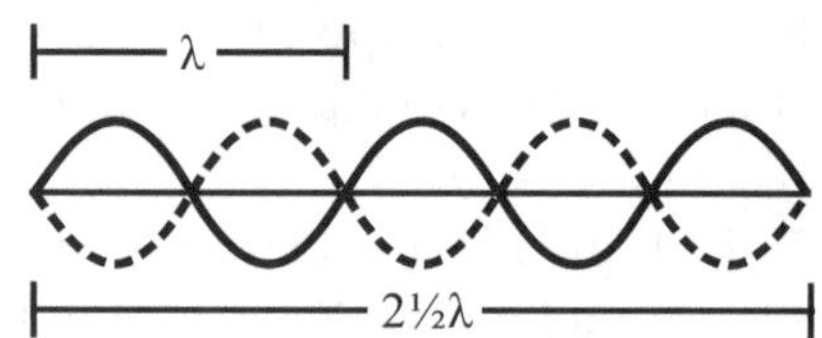

Figure 16-15 *Waves on a guitar string. Resonance occurs when a half-integral number of wavelengths equals the length of the string.*

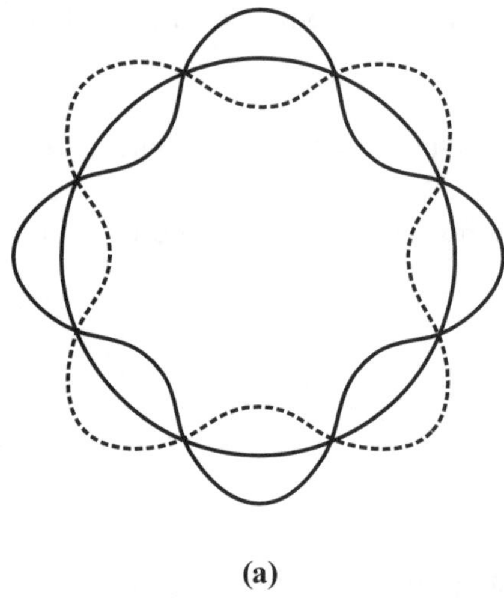

(a)

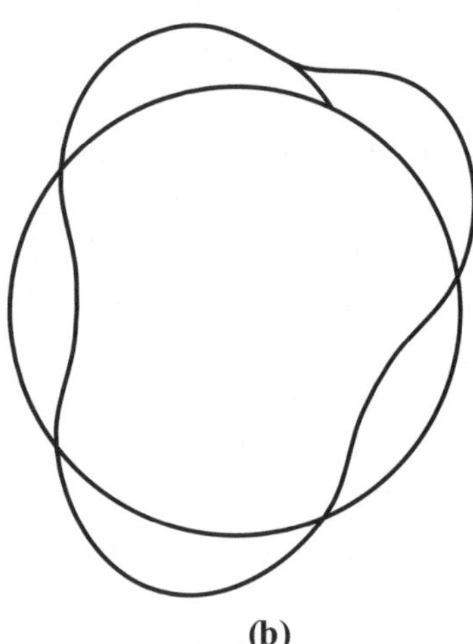

(b)

Figure 16-16 **(a)** *Resonance on a circular wire loop. An integral number of wavelengths equals the loop's circumference.* **(b)** *If an integral number of wavelengths does not fit the circumference, destructive interference occurs and the wave quickly dies out.*

De Broglie pointed out that, if an electron's matter wave is to interfere constructively with itself in a circular orbit in a hydrogen atom, then a whole number of de Broglie wavelengths must fit exactly around the orbit's circumference. Since the circumference of a circle of radius r is $2\pi r$, then we must have

$$n\lambda = 2\pi r$$

where $n = 1, 2, 3$, etc. Writing the de Broglie wavelength as $\lambda = \mathrm{h}/mv$ (from Section 15.3):

$$\frac{n\mathrm{h}}{mv} = 2\pi r$$

Re-arranging, we have:

$$mvr = \frac{n\mathrm{h}}{2\pi}$$

This is just Bohr's condition for quantization of angular momentum (Eqn. 3 in Section 16.2), which leads to quantization of energy in the hydrogen atom! In other words, quantization of energy can be considered to be the result of a requirement that the de Broglie wave of an electron in an atom must interfere constructively with itself. Bohr's quantum number, n, is just the number of electron wavelengths contained in the circumference of the orbit. Wave-particle duality obviously plays an important role in atomic structure.

Figure 16-17 shows de Broglie standing waves that are allowed for an electron in various orbits in a hydrogen atom. (Note that, from our earlier discussion of Bohr orbits, the higher n-value corresponds to an orbit of larger radius.) It is important to understand that an electron, considered as a particle in Bohr's theory, does not follow the undulating pattern of the waves. Each electron follows a circular orbit. The oscillating wave shows the wavelength associated with the electron.

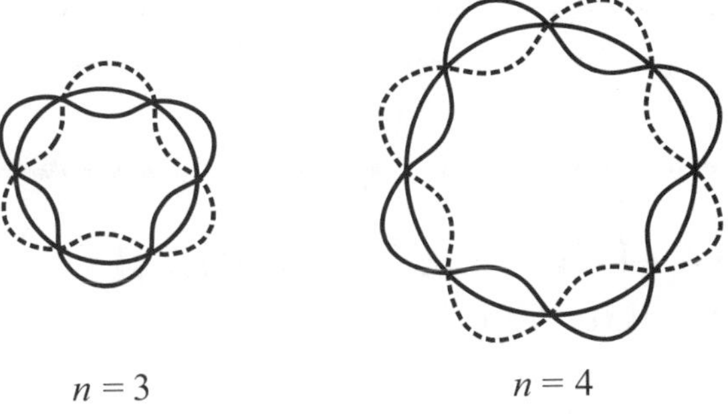

Figure 16-17 *De Broglie waves for an electron in a hydrogen atom.*

Sample Problem 16-3

Determine the de Broglie wavelength for an electron in a hydrogen atom in
(a) the $n = 3$ energy level (b) the $n = 4$ energy level.

Solution: (a) An electron with quantum number $n = 3$ travels in an orbit with a circumference equal to 3 times the de Broglie wavelength of the electron (Figure 16-17 (a)). Thus, the de Broglie wavelength is 1/3 of the circumference ($2\pi r$). The radius r (4.76×10^{-10} m) is given in Table 16.1. Hence, for the de Broglie wavelength, we have

$$\lambda = \frac{2\pi r}{3} = \frac{2\pi\left(4.76 \times 10^{-10}\ \text{m}\right)}{3} = 9.97 \times 10^{-10}\ \text{m}$$

Thus, the de Broglie wavelength for an $n = 3$ electron is 9.97×10^{-10} m.

(b) The de Broglie wavelength for an electron in the $n = 4$ energy level is 1/4 of the orbit's circumference. As in part (a), the radius of the orbit is available in Table 16.1. Therefore, the de Broglie wavelength is

$$\lambda = \frac{2\pi r}{4} = \frac{2\pi\left(8.47 \times 10^{-10}\ \text{m}\right)}{4} = 1.33 \times 10^{-9}\ \text{m}$$

Notice that this wavelength is larger than that for $n = 3$. This is consistent with what we would expect from an inspection of the waves shown for $n = 3$ and $n = 4$ in Figure 16-17.

Practice

16-27 Sketch the electron waves in a hydrogen atom, according to the Bohr theory, for quantum number $n = 1, 2, 3$, and 4. (Draw the orbital radii to scale.)

16-28 Determine the de Broglie wavelength of an $n = 2$ electron in a hydrogen atom. Use Table 16.1 for the orbital radius. [Ans. 6.66×10^{-10} m]

16.4 THE QUANTUM-MECHANICAL (ELECTRON "CLOUD") MODEL OF ATOMS

Did You Know? ***For their work in laying the foundations of quantum mechanics, Erwin Schrödinger and Werner Heisenberg won the Nobel Prize in Physics (Heisenberg in 1932, and Schrödinger in 1933).***

Bohr's atomic theory was an important and useful step toward a deeper understanding of atoms. However, as mentioned in Section 16.2, it was far from complete — his model did not work well for multi-electron atoms, for example. A new theory — quantum mechanics — was developed in 1925-1926 by Erwin Schrödinger (1887-1961), Werner Heisenberg (1901-1976), and others. Schrödinger was an Austrian working at the University of Zurich, Switzerland, and Heisenberg was a German physicist. Within a few years, quantum mechanics was applied to a number of problems involving atoms, molecules, nuclei, and light, and showed itself to be amazingly versatile and successful in this submicroscopic world. We will not go into all the details of quantum mechanics here — entire books are devoted to the subject, and the mathematics is very complex. However, we will discuss some of its important features related to the structure of atoms.

Some of the results of quantum mechanics are similar to aspects of Bohr's theory. For instance, in both theories, the energy of electrons in atoms is quantized. However, many of the ideas of quantum mechanics are completely new. One of its radical features is its view of the motion and properties of particles such as electrons. In Bohr's theory of the hydrogen atom, an electron has a well-defined orbit around the nucleus; the radius of the orbit and the speed of the electron are accurately known. In contrast, in quantum mechanics, the orbit is not well-defined, and we speak of the *probability* of finding the electron at a particular distance from the nucleus, or the *probability* of the electron having a certain speed. In Bohr's model, the radius of the electron orbit in the ground-state hydrogen atom is the Bohr radius, 0.53×10^{-10} m. In quantum mechanics, the equivalent statement is that the most probable distance between the electron and the nucleus is 0.53×10^{-10} m.

Imagine an experiment in which the electron-nucleus distance in a ground-state hydrogen atom is measured repeatedly. It turns out that the distance is sometimes larger than the Bohr radius, sometimes smaller, and sometimes equal to it. If a graph is drawn showing the relative number of times the electron is found at certain distances from the nucleus, we have a plot as in Figure 16-18, called a *probability distribution*. You can see that the graph peaks at a distance of one Bohr radius, indicating that the electron spends most of its time at about this distance from the nucleus. However, there is a significant probability of finding the electron at two, or even three, Bohr radii from the nucleus.

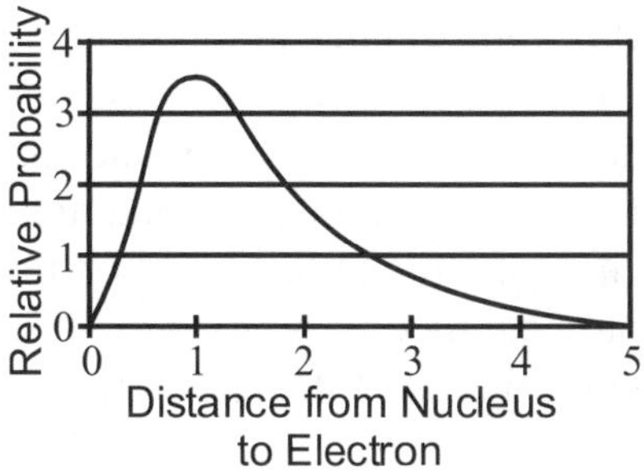

Figure 16-18 *Relative probability of finding the electron in a ground-state hydrogen atom as a function of distance from the nucleus. The distance is expressed in units of the Bohr radius, and the relative probability is in arbitrary units.*

We can illustrate this probability distribution in another way, as indicated in Figure 16-19, which shows a "slice" through the centre of a ground-state hydrogen atom. The probability of finding an electron at various points is indicated by shading, with deep shading corresponding to high probability. Instead of thinking of an electron as having a definite orbit as in the Bohr theory, in quantum mechanics, we consider the electron to be spread out in space, forming an *electron cloud.* Figure 16-19 gives you a feeling of the "cloud" corresponding to the electron.

The probability distribution of electrons in atoms is closely related to the wave nature of the electrons. We tend to think of a particle as localized in a small volume, but a wave is spread out in space. Thus, it is not surprising to consider an electron that is spread out in an electron "cloud" as having wave properties. Indeed, in quantum mechanics, an electron (or any other particle) is described by a mathematical expression known as a *wave function.* The square of the wave function at any point in space is directly related to the probability of finding the electron at that point.

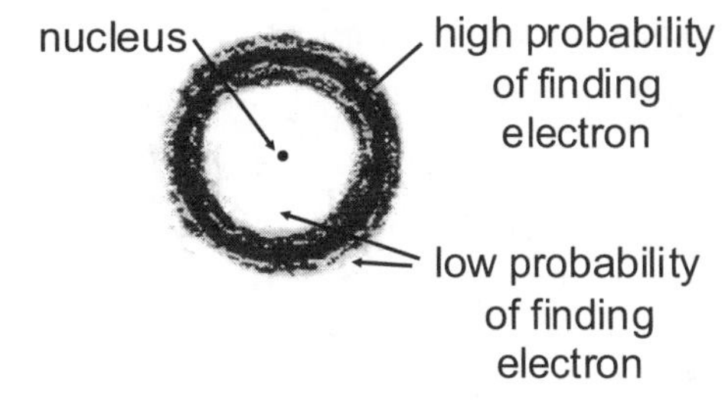

Figure 16-19 *The electron "cloud," or probability distribution of the electron, in a ground-state hydrogen atom.*

There are many other aspects of the quantum-mechanical model of atoms that differ from the Bohr theory. Instead of one quantum number, n, there are four. The electron clouds are not always spherical in shape (corresponding to circular orbits in Bohr's model), but are distorted for certain quantum numbers. We leave such details for later courses in physics or chemistry.

You might feel somewhat uncomfortable with the notion of electron "clouds" and the uncertain nature of electron orbits in atoms. This reaction is quite natural — in our daily activities, we are used to dealing with relatively large objects such as automobiles and hair dryers, and their positions do not appear to be uncertain. When asked where an automobile is, you can reply with confidence that it is in the driveway — none of this fuzzy business of a probability that it will actually be found in the bathtub. But, in order to explain what is going on at the submicroscopic scale of atoms and nuclei, we have to use quantum mechanics; it is our best model yet. To deal with the macroscopic world, we can use the classical physics of Newton and Maxwell. Interestingly, if quantum mechanics is applied to macroscopic objects, it actually yields the old classical laws. This is just Bohr's correspondence principle — the equivalence of results from classical theory and quantum theory when quantum numbers are large (that is, in macroscopic situations). Quantum mechanics is a more complete theory than any of the classical ones; it holds true in the world of atoms and in the world of cars, and, hence, it is very powerful. The classical theories work only in special cases, but quantum mechanics, strange as it may seem is more universal in its applications.

The Heisenberg Uncertainty Principle

One of the most fascinating results in quantum mechanics was developed by Werner Heisenberg in 1927. Known as the **Heisenberg uncertainty principle**, it states that **it is impossible to know the exact location and momentum of a particle at the same time**. This principle is not the result of a lack of sufficient accuracy in measuring devices; rather, it is a fundamental limitation in nature.

There is always some uncertainty in any measurement. For example, if you measure the width a page in this book, there might be an uncertainty of ± 0.5 mm. Heisenberg's uncertainty principle relates the uncertainty (Δx) in the measurement of the position (x) of an object and the uncertainty (Δp) in a simultaneous measurement of the momentum (p) of the object:

$$\Delta x \, \Delta p \geq \frac{\mathrm{h}}{2\pi} \qquad \textbf{(16-7)}$$

where h is Planck's constant. This is a mathematical statement of Heisenberg's uncertainty principle. (Note that what we are referring to as position and momentum here are, strictly speaking, magnitudes of position and momentum.) Notice that Heisenberg's uncertainty principle states that the product of Δx and Δp must be at least as large as h/2π. Sample Problem 16-4 below illustrates how to use this relation.

The combination of quantities, h/2π, appears frequently in quantum mechanics, and is often written as ħ (spoken as "h-bar"). Hence, we have

$$\Delta x \, \Delta p \geq \hbar \qquad \textbf{(16-8)}$$

Numerically,

$$\hbar = 1.05 \times 10^{-34} \text{ J} \cdot \text{s} \qquad \textbf{(16-9)}$$

Sample Problem 16-4

(a) If the position of an electron is measured with an uncertainty of $\pm\, 10^{-10}$ m (about the size of atom), what is the minimum possible uncertainty in a simultaneous measurement of its momentum? What uncertainty in electron speed does this correspond to?
(b) Repeat, for an automobile of mass 1.50×10^{3} kg, for which the position is measured with an uncertainty of ± 0.5 mm.

Solution: (a) We start with the Heisenberg uncertainty principle, Eqn. 16-8:

$$\Delta x \, \Delta p \geq \hbar$$

where Δx is given as $\pm\ 10^{-10}$ m. Then the uncertainty in the momentum is

$$\begin{aligned} \Delta p &\geq \frac{\hbar}{\Delta x} \\ &\geq \frac{1.05 \times 10^{-34}\ \text{J} \cdot \text{s}}{10^{-10}\ \text{m}} \\ &\geq 1 \times 10^{-24}\ \text{kg} \cdot \text{m/s} \end{aligned}$$

> ***Units Tip:*** *Notice the units for $\hbar/\Delta x$: J·s/m. But joule (J) is equivalent to kg·m²/s², and hence, J·s/m is the same as (kg·m²/s²)·s/m or kg·m/s, which is the SI unit for momentum.*

Hence, the *minimum* uncertainty in the momentum of the electron is $\pm\ 1 \times 10^{-24}$ kg·m/s, or simply $\pm\ 10^{-24}$ kg·m/s. (In performing the calculation, we ignore the ± sign in the uncertainties Δx and Δp.)

From the definition of momentum as the product of mass and velocity, $p = mv$, we can write the uncertainty in the momentum as $\Delta p = m\Delta v$. Solving for the minimum uncertainty in speed, Δv:

$$\Delta v = \frac{\Delta p}{m} = \frac{10^{-24}\ \text{kg} \cdot \text{m/s}}{9 \times 10^{-31}\ \text{kg}} = 1 \times 10^{6}\ \text{m/s}$$

Hence, the minimum uncertainty in the electron speed is $\pm\ 10^{6}$ m/s. This uncertainty in the speed is huge because the uncertainty in the electron's position is small.

(b) When we repeat the calculation for an automobile, the uncertainty in momentum turns out to be $\pm\ 2 \times 10^{-31}$ kg·m/s, and the uncertainty in speed is $\pm\ 1 \times 10^{-34}$ m/s, a negligibly small value. Thus, for all practical purposes, the position and momentum of a macroscopic object can be measured with as small an uncertainty as we wish. However, as shown in part (a), for subatomic particles such as electrons, the uncertainty principle puts severe constraints on the precision of measurements.

Probability vs. Determinism

In Newtonian mechanics, we can determine the path of an object such as a baseball to any desired accuracy if we know the forces acting on the ball and its initial position and velocity. Newtonian mechanics is a *deterministic* theory. In contrast, quantum mechanics deals with *probabilities*. A particle such as an electron has to be thought of a spread out in space because of its inherent wave properties. Its present position and velocity cannot both be measured to any desired accuracy, and we cannot determine where it will be in the future, except in terms of probabilities. In the realm of atoms, nuclei, and molecules, nature has a built-in unpredictability that is not evident in our day-to-day macroscopic world.

Prior to the development of quantum mechanics, scientists believed that the workings of the universe were completely deterministic. However, in order for the world of atoms to be understood, uncertainty and unpredictability have had to be accepted as a basic part of natural phenomena. Scientists continue to search for more complete understandings of the physical universe, and there will undoubtedly be new theories that will be developed as new experimental evidence comes to light.

Did You Know? *There is another form of the uncertainty principle that relates energy, E, and time, t:* $\Delta E\, \Delta t \geq \hbar$. *E represents a particle's energy, and t the time taken to perform a measurement of the energy. This relation indicates that energy can be uncertain, or even not conserved, by an amount* ΔE *for a time interval given by* $\Delta t \approx \hbar / \Delta E$.

Practice

16-29 How is the quantum-mechanical model of the atom similar to Bohr's model? How are these models different?

16-30 State Heisenberg's uncertainty principle, both in words and in the form of a mathematical relation.

16-31 (a) If a proton's position is measured with an uncertainty of $\pm\ 10^{-14}$ m (about the diameter of a nucleus), what is the minimum possible uncertainty in a simultaneous measurement of its momentum?
(b) What is the resulting minimum uncertainty in the proton's speed?
[Ans. (a) $\pm\, 10^{-20}$ kg·m/s (b) $\pm\, 6 \times 10^{6}$ m/s]

16-32 The speed of a baseball of mass 0.15 kg is measured with an uncertainty of ± 0.1 m/s. Determine the minimum possible uncertainty in a simultaneous measurement of the ball's position. [Ans. $\pm\, 7 \times 10^{-33}$ m]

16-33 An electron in an oscilloscope beam has a measured speed of $(3.0 \pm 0.1) \times 10^{7}$ m/s. What is the minimum possible uncertainty in a simultaneous measurement of the position of the electron? [Ans. $\pm\, 1 \times 10^{-10}$ m]

16.5 LASERS

Laser. The word itself sounds a bit mysterious. What is a laser? – a death ray? a medical tool? a fun "toy" in a light show? or all of these? How does a laser work? When was the laser invented? Why was the laser once called "a solution looking for a problem?" Lots of questions — now for some answers.

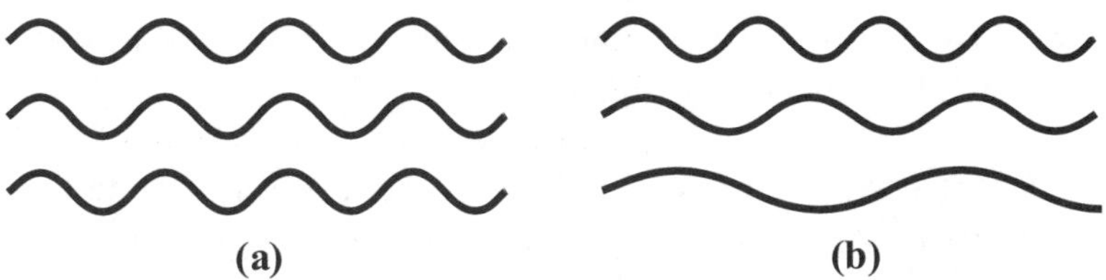

Figure 16-20 **(a)** *Laser light: coherent and monochromatic.*
(b) *Ordinary white light: incoherent and polychromatic.*

The word **laser** stands for *l*ight *a*mplification by *s*timulated *e*mission of *r*adiation. In a laser, one photon stimulates an excited atom to emit another photon of the same energy. (This process is discussed in more detail below.) Now there are two photons, of the same energy and wavelength, and they are in phase and travelling in the same direction. Each of these photons can stimulate another atom to emit a photon, resulting in a total of four photons, which can then stimulate the emission of more photons, and so on. Thus, the original photon is amplified into many, many photons in a strong, unidirectional beam of light (Figure 16-20 (a)). The beam is said to be *monochromatic* (literally, "one colour), because there is only one wavelength and frequency. The beam is also coherent, which means that the waves are in phase and unidirectional. These properties are in contrast with the incoherent, polychromatic nature of ordinary white light (Figure 16-20 (b)).

The physical principles involved in laser operation were first applied to microwaves in the development of *masers* (the *m* standing for microwave) in 1953, by the American physicist, Charles H. Townes (1915-). The first working laser (in the visible region of the spectrum) was developed in 1960 by Theodore Maiman at Hughes Research Laboratories. In 1964, Townes received the Nobel Prize in Physics, along with two Soviet laser pioneers, Aleksander Prokhorov and Nikolai Basov.

Did You Know? *Albert Einstein played an early role in the theoretical work that eventually led to the development of lasers.*

In order for a laser to work, the atoms must first be "set up" so that they are ready to emit photons when stimulated. Atoms can emit photons by two processes: **spontaneous emission** and **stimulated emission**. Spontaneous emission is the emission of photons that has been discussed already in this chapter — after an atom is excited by absorption of a photon or by collision with a particle such as an electron, it then emits a photon when it de-excites to a lower energy level. This spontaneous emission occurs very quickly after the original excitation — within about 10^{-8} s. For stimulated emission to occur, the atom must first be excited into what is called a **metastable state**, an excited state in which the atom can remain without undergoing spontaneous emission for a long time (on the atomic scale, about 10^{-4} to 10^{-3} s). When in this metastable state, an atom will de-excite and emit a photon if stimulated by another photon of the "right" energy that happens by. This "right" energy has to correspond to the energy difference between the excited metastable state and a lower-energy state in the atom. If atoms are not excited to metastable states, they de-excite quickly via spontaneous emission, and stimulated emission occurs infrequently. For a laser to operate, there must be more atoms exicted into metastable states than there are in the ground state, a situation called **population inversion**. The excitation is often done with an electric discharge.

There are many different types of lasers. The first successful laser used a ruby rod, which emitted red light. Now there are liquids, gases, semiconductors, glasses, and crystals employed in lasers. Some lasers produce visible light, and others work in the invisible ultraviolet or infrared regions of the spectrum. Some lasers can be "tuned" to give monochromatic light over a wide range of possible wavelengths, while others operate at only one wavelength.

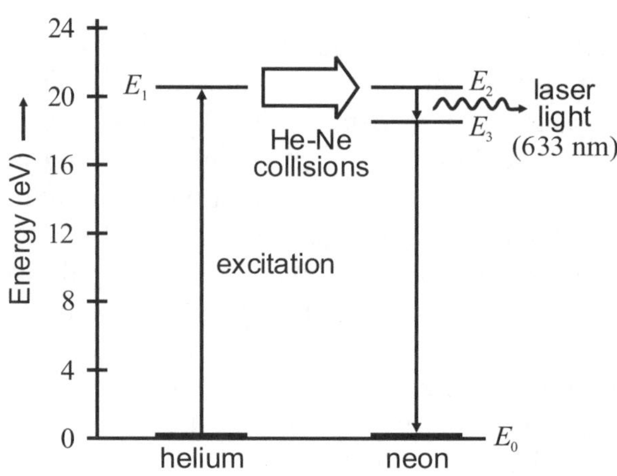

Figure 16-21
Important energy levels in a He-Ne laser.

One of the most common inexpensive lasers has a gas mixture, about 85% helium and 15% neon, as the lasing material. You have probably seen helium-neon (He-Ne) lasers — they emit red light — at supermarket checkout counters. The operation of this type of laser depends on a lucky coincidence: one excited metastable state of helium, 20.61 eV above the ground state, has almost the same excitation energy (20.66 eV) as another metastable state in neon. An electric discharge excites helium atoms into the metastable state (E_1 in Figure 16-21). When an excited helium atom and a ground-state neon atom collide, the helium atom can de-excite and provide energy directly to excite the neon atom to its metastable state E_2 (Figure 16-21). (The additional 0.05 eV of energy is provided from the kinetic energy of the atoms prior to the collision.) A neon atom in this state can readily participate in stimulated photon emission if a photon of energy 1.96 eV passes nearby. When stimulated, the neon atom drops to level E_3, emitting a visible "red" photon of energy 1.96 eV (wavelength 633 nm). The atom, still excited, then moves quickly to the ground state (E_0) via transitions that are not part of the laser action. You might wonder why the helium is used at all; why not just use the electric discharge to excite the neon atoms directly to their metastable states? Since neon has ten electrons and many different energy levels, the probability of exciting a neon atom to the right energy level for laser action is small. It is much easier to excite the helium, and then have helium collide with neon.

One of the useful features of laser light is that it is unidirectional. We mentioned that a photon emitted via stimulated emission has the same direction as the stimulating photon, and this property leads to the directionality. However, when a laser is turned on, the first few photons emitted come from spontaneous emission from the metastable states, and have random directions. These photons then act as the stimulators, so why does a laser not have beams in a number of different directions? The answer lies in the construction of a laser (Figure 16-22), which is normally a long, narrow tube with mirrors at each end. Photons that are emitted in any direction other than along the tube are absorbed by the tube walls. Photons emitted along the tube direction are reflected back and forth by the mirrors, stimulating the emission of many photons in this direction, and a strong beam builds up parallel to the length of the tube. One of the mirrors is essentially 100% reflecting, and the other reflects most, but not all, of the light. The light transmitted through this "leaky" mirror forms the external laser beam.

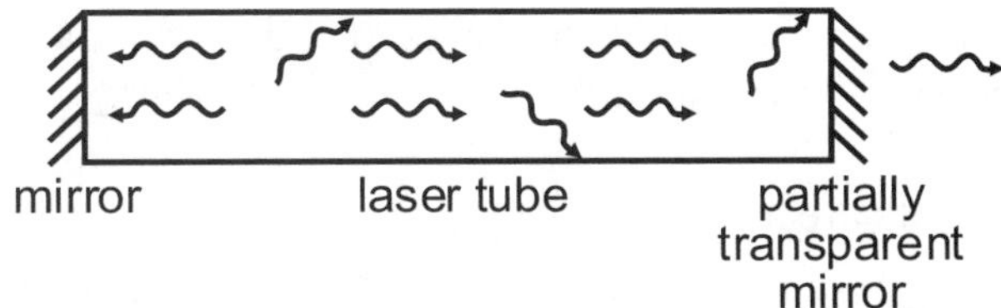

Figure 16-22 *Mirrors at the ends of the laser tube ensure that only photons emitted along the direction of the tube contribute to the laser beam.*

Using Lasers

When lasers were first invented, people wondered what to do with them. What uses could there be for a bright, coherent, linear beam of light? Although lasers appeared initially to be a "solution looking for a problem," applications were not long in coming, and lasers are now used in medicine, industry, commerce, communications, forensic science, etc.

The helium-neon laser already described has found a number of applications. For example, it is used in supermarket checkout scanners, in which the reflected laser beam carries the product-identification information contained in the black and white stripes of the Universal Product Code (UPC). This information is relayed to a computer that retrieves the current price of the product. Because a laser beam travels in a straight line, He-Ne lasers are used in guiding saws in lumber mills, in controlling machines that drill tunnels for railroads and highways, and in surveying.

Did You Know? *Infrared lasers with widths of only ¼ mm are now routinely used in telecommunications to send telephone calls along fibre-optics cables. One laser and one optical fibre can handle up to 32 000 calls simultaneously.*

Other types of lasers are in use in medicine, particularly in eye surgery. Because lasers concentrate a large amount of light energy onto a small area, they can be used to seal bleeding ulcers and blood vessels, vaporise tumors, and "weld" breaks in the retina. Lasers can be focused so finely that nearby cells are unaffected. By using optical fibers to carry the laser light, physicians can perform procedures in areas of the body — the stomach, for example — unreachable by other means except major surgery.

For applications requiring large amounts of energy, such as cutting steel saw blades, the carbon dioxide laser (which emits infrared light) is most often used. Lasers are proliferating in jobs such as welding, drilling, and heat treating, where precision and a large quantity of heat go hand in hand.

Semiconductor lasers are small and inexpensive, and the infrared light emitted is used in the operation of compact disk (CD) players and in fibre-optics communication systems. On CDs, the audio or video information is encoded in a pattern of tiny pits on the disk, and retrieved by reflection of the laser light.

Lasers are also used in:

- monitoring small movements of Earth to give advance warning of earthquakes
- missile guidance systems
- high-precision fabrication in the semiconductor industry
- fusion research — it is hoped that intense laser beams can create the high temperatures and pressures required for nuclear fusion to occur
- detecting fingerprints many years old on materials (such as leather) not suitable for standard fingerprint-detection techniques.

Holography

Who would have thought when the laser was developed in the 1960s that one of its most fascinating uses would be the production of three-dimensional images called **holograms**? A decade or two ago, most people had not seen a hologram, but they are now quite common, having appeared in magazines, on clothing, etc.

In an ordinary photograph, the light from a particular point on the object is focused to one point on the film, but, in holography, light from many points on the object travels to each point on the film. Figure 16-23 shows how a hologram is produced. Light from a laser is split into two parts by a half-silvered mirror. One part travels directly to the film, and the other part reaches the film only by reflection from the object. On the film, the light from the two paths interferes constructively in some places and destructively in others, thus producing a speckled pattern of light and dark points.

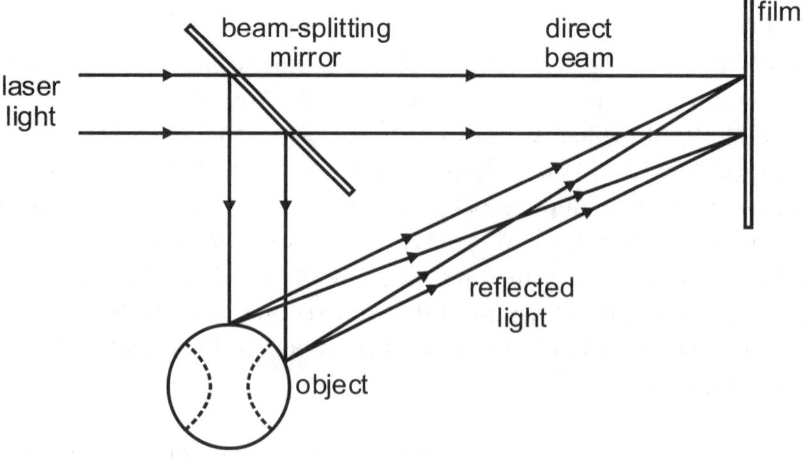

Figure 16-23 *Making a hologram.*

After the film is developed, if it is then illuminated with a laser (Figure 16-24), a three-dimensional image of the object is produced. If the viewer's head moves from side to side or up and down, different views of the object result, just as if the original object were present. The production of a hologram depends on the fact that laser light is coherent. Because the rays in the original laser light are all in phase, they have specific phase differences when they combine on the film to produce the interference pattern. When the film is illuminated with coherent laser light, the transmitted light essentially picks up the phase difference information from the film and appears just as if it originated from the object itself. Cylindrical holograms can be made such that the viewer can walk completely around them and see a 360° image of the original object.

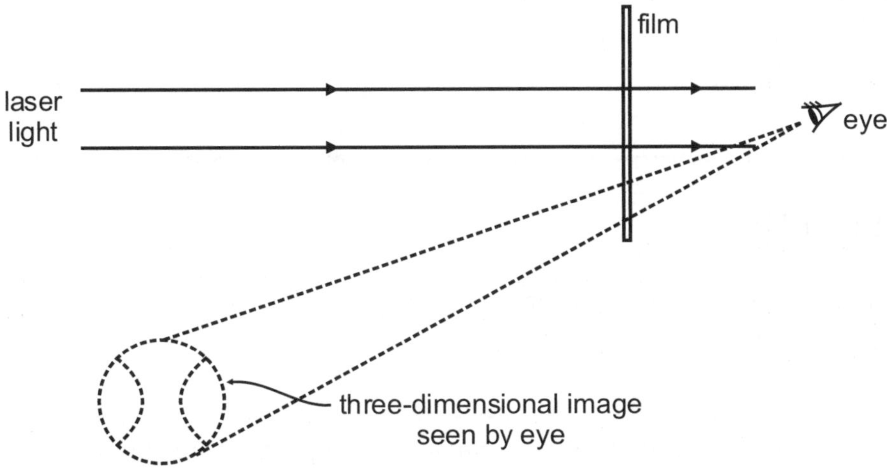

Figure 16-24 *Viewing a hologram.*

Some holograms can be viewed by reflection in white light. These are the common holograms that you have seen on credit cards, in magazines, etc. These *white-light holograms* normally give the impression of a three-dimensional image when viewed from side to side, but *not* up and down. This type of hologram is created with laser light in the same way as described in the previous paragraph, then the resulting hologram is "masked" in a certain way to remove the up-and-down information and produce a second hologram that can be viewed in white light.

Figures 16-23 and 16-24 illustrate what is referred to as the *geometric model* of holograms, that is, a model in which light travels in geometrically straight lines. However, holograms have properties that cannot be understood by using this geometric model — *diffraction* effects must also be included. When a hologram is illuminated by a laser beam as in Figure 16-24, the beam diffracts around the various light and dark regions on the hologram to produce diffraction patterns which, superimposed, make up the three-dimensional image. We will not delve into the details of diffraction in holography, but you should be aware that diffraction is important for a complete understanding of this field.

Holography has a wide range of uses other than simply producing three-dimensional images. For example, it can be used in pattern recognition, such as fingerprint-matching or searching for occurrences of a particular word in a book. Microwave (radar) holography is applied in *side-looking radar* in airplanes to produce finely detailed images used in geological surveying, cartography, and military surveillance. Holography is also employed in detecting stresses in manufactured materials, and in a variety of other applications.

Practice

16-34 List three ways in which laser light differs from the light emitted by a normal light bulb.

16-35 Why is laser light dangerous?

16-36 What is the frequency of light emitted by a He-Ne laser? Its wavelength is 633 nm.
[Ans. 4.73×10^{14} Hz]

16-37 List four uses of lasers.

CHAPTER FOCUS

This chapter is the second in a two-chapter sequence on introductory quantum physics. The previous chapter dealt with wave-particle duality.

In the present chapter, the focus has been on the evolution of our understanding of the structure of atoms. We have presented the Rutherford model of atoms, the Bohr model, and the quantum mechanical (electron "cloud") model. The importance of experimental results in the development and support of the various models has been emphasized. We have seen that the best model of atoms, that is, the quantum mechanical model, includes uncertainties that seem to be an unavoidable part of nature. These uncertainties have been described both in terms of Heisenberg's uncertainty principle, and in terms of the probabilities associated with the position of an electron in an atom. Finally, we have used the quntum nature of atoms to discuss the operation of lasers, and have presented a number of applications of these fascinating devices.

VOCABULARY REVIEW

You should be able to define or explain each of the following words or phrases.

nucleus
Rutherford model (of the atom)
Bohr model (of the atom)
stationary states
Bohr radius
quantum number (in the Bohr model)
transition (of an electron)
ground state (of an atom)
excited state (of an atom)
correspondence principle
Heisenberg uncertainty principle
laser
spontaneous emission
stimulated emission
metastable state (of an atom)
population inversion
hologram

CHAPTER REVIEW

16-38 Which of the following can emit line spectra?
(a) only solids (b) only liquids (c) only gases
(d) solids, liquids, and gases (e) only liquids and gases

16-39 Which of the following can emit continuous spectra?
(a) only solids (b) only liquids (c) only gases
(d) solids, liquids, and gases (e) only liquids and gases

16-40 In the Bohr model of the hydrogen atom, what is the ratio of the radius of the $n = 3$ orbit to the radius of the $n = 3$ orbit?
(a) 9/4 (b) 3/2 (c) 4/9 (d) 2/3 (e) none of these

16-41 An electron is in the $n = 5$ orbit (Bohr theory) around a hydrogen nucleus. The ratio of the circumference of the orbit to the de Broglie wavelength of the electron is
(a) 1/5 (b) 5 (c) 1/25 (d) 25 (e) $\sqrt{5}$

16-42 The position of a neutron is measured with an uncertainty of $\pm 3 \times 10^{-12}$ m. What is the minimum possible uncertainty in a simultaneous measurement of the neutron's speed?
(a) $\pm 2 \times 10^4$ m/s (b) $\pm 1 \times 10^5$ m/s (c) $\pm 2 \times 10^7$ m/s (d) $\pm 1 \times 10^7$ m/s (e) $\pm 3 \times 10^6$ m/s

16-43 What was the significance of Rutherford's α-particle scattering experiments?

16-44 In Rutherford's model of the atom, what prevents the electrons from flying off into space?

16-45 What is the longest wavelength of light in the Brackett spectral series in hydrogen? (As mentioned in Section 16.1, $n_l = 4$ for the Brackett series.) Express your answer in metres and micrometres. [Ans. 4.05×10^{-6} m = 4.05 μm]

16-46 In principle, the orbital radius of the electron in an excited hydrogen atom could have a macroscopic value, say 1.0 cm. Using the Bohr model, what would be the quantum number n for this orbit? [Ans. 1.4×10^4]

16-47 (a) How much energy is require to cause the electron in a hydrogen atom to make a transition from $n = 1$ to $n = 4$?
(b) When the electron makes the reverse transition from $n = 4$ to $n = 1$, what is the energy of the photon produced?
[Ans. (a) 12.8 eV (b) 12.8 eV]

16-48 When light consisting of visible, infrared, and ultraviolet light is passed through hydrogen gas at room temperature, black absorption lines appear in the spectrum of the transmitted light. These lines are in the Lyman series only. Why?

16-49 What is the correspondence principle?

16-50 What was the importance of the Franck-Hertz experiment?

16-51 Does Heisenberg's uncertainty principle apply only to small particles such as electrons, or also to macroscopic objects such as cars and baseballs?

16-52 What does the acronym *laser* stand for?

16-53 What is meant by a metastable state in an atom?

16-54 (a) A lightbulb emits light in _____ directions; however, a laser emits light in ___________.

(b) The light waves from a lightbulb are out of phase with each other, but the light from a laser is ___________.

(c) The light from a lightbulb has many wavelengths; in contrast, laser light is ___________.

16-55 A laser amplifies light. Does this mean that it violates conservation of energy? Explain briefly.

APPLYING YOUR KNOWLEDGE

16-56 Determine the second smallest frequency of light in the Pfund series in hydrogen. (As mentioned in Section 16.1, $n_l = 5$ for the Pfund series.) [Ans. 6.45×10^{13} Hz]

16-57 Suppose that an α particle (charge +2e, mass 6.64×10^{-27} kg) in an experiment similar to Rutherford's scattering experiments makes a "head-on" collision with a gold nucleus (charge +79e). Use conservation of energy to determine the closest distance of approach between the α particle and the nucleus, if the α particle has a kinetic energy of 4.8 MeV far from the nucleus. Neglect recoil of the gold nucleus. [Ans. 4.7×10^{-14} m]

16-58 What is the longest wavelength of light that can ionize a hydrogen atom in the ground state? [Ans. 9.14×10^{-8} m]

16-59 What is the magnitude of the electric force between the orbiting electron ($n = 1$) and the nucleus in a hydrogen atom, using the Bohr theory? Use Table 16.1 for the radius of the orbit. [Ans. 8.2×10^{-8} N]

16-60 What is the speed of the electron in the previous question? [Ans. 2.2×10^{6} m/s]

16-61 Determine the ratio of the electric force to the gravitational force between the electron and nucleus in a ground-state hydrogen atom. Is the gravitational force significant, compared to the electric force? [Ans. 2.27×10^{39}]

16-62 A laser beam from, say, a He-Ne laser is normally not visible as it travels, but is visible where it strikes an object. How then is it possible to produce photographs that clearly show the paths of laser beams? (Hint: How could you make the beam from, say, a flashlight visible?)

16-63 A small He-Ne laser (wavelength 633 nm) has a power output of about 1 mW. How many photons are emitted per second? [Ans. 3×10^{15}]

KEY OBJECTIVES

Having completed this chapter, you should now be able to do the following:

1. Discuss the importance of Rutherford's α-particle scattering experiments.
2. Describe Rutherford's atomic model.
3. Define various types of spectra: continuous, line, emission, and absorption.
4. Discuss the deficiencies of Rutherford's model of atoms.
5. Solve numerical problems based on the Balmer (and other) spectral series of hydrogen.
6. Describe Bohr's atomic model.
7. Do problems related to Bohr's model, involving orbit radii, electron and photon energies, photon wavelengths, etc.
8. Use an energy-level diagram to show the source of the various spectral series in hydrogen.
9. Explain the importance of the Franck-Hertz experiment.
10. Discuss the connection between de Broglie wavelength and electron orbits in the Bohr model of the hydrogen atom.
11. State deficiencies of Bohr's atom model.
12. Describe, in general terms, the quantum-mechanical (electron "cloud") model of atoms.
13. State the Heisenberg uncertainty principle, both in words and in terms of a mathematical relation.
14. Solve numerical problems related to the Heisenberg uncertainty principle.
15. Describe how a laser produces its light.
16. State important properties of laser light.
17. List a number of applications of lasers.
18. Describe how a hologram is produced.

ANSWERS TO SELECTED QUESTIONS

16-4 line
16-38 (c) 16-39 (d) 16-40 (a) 16-41 (b) 16-42 (a)
16-48 At room temperature, virtually all the hydrogen atoms are in the ground state, and hence the only transitions that can happen are from the $n = 1$ level. All these transitions are in the Lyman series.
16-54 (a) all; one direction (b) coherent (c) monochromatic

APPENDIX 1

SI BASE UNITS

There are seven SI base units, one for each of length, mass, time, electric current, temperature, amount of substance, and luminous intensity. The following definitions of the base units were adopted by the Conférence Générale des Poids et Mesures in the years indicated.

Metre (m): "The metre is the length of the path travelled by light in a vacuum during a time interval of 1/(299 792 458) of a second" (adopted in 1983).

Kilogram (kg): "The kilogram is…the mass of the international prototype of the kilogram" (adopted in 1889 and 1901).

Second (s): "The second is the duration of 9 192 631 770 periods of the radiation corresponding to the transition between the two hyperfine levels of the ground state of the cesium-133 atom" (adopted in 1967).

Ampere (A): "The ampere is that constant current which, if maintained in two straight parallel conductors of infinite length, of negligible circular cross section, and placed one metre apart in vacuum, would produce between these conductors a force equal to 2×10^{-7} N/m (newtons per metre of length)" (adopted in 1948).

Kelvin (K): "The kelvin…is the fraction 1/273.16 of the thermodynamic temperature of the triple point of water" (adopted in 1967).

Mole (mol): "The mole is the amount of substance of a system which contains as many elementary entities as there are atoms in 0.012 kg of carbon-12" (adopted in 1967).

Candela (cd): "The candela is the luminous intensity, in a given direction, of a source that emits monochromatic radiation of frequency 5.40×10^{14} Hz and that has a radiant intensity in that direction of 1/683 watt per steradian" (adopted in 1979).

APPENDIX 2

SOME SI DERIVED UNITS

Derived units are formed from products and ratios of the base units. Some derived units are given special names, such as the newton or joule, to honour certain scientists.

Quantity	Derived Unit	Name	Symbol
area	m^2		
volume	m^3		
speed	m/s or $m \cdot s^{-1}$		
density	kg/m^3		
acceleration	m/s^2		
force	$kg \cdot m/s^2$	newton	N
energy	$kg \cdot m^2/s^2$ or $N \cdot m$	joule	J
power	J/s	watt	W
frequency	1/s or s^{-1}	hertz	Hz
pressure	N/m^2	pascal	Pa
electric charge	$A \cdot s$	coulomb	C
electric potential	J/C	volt	V
electric resistance	V/A	ohm	Ω
electric capacitance	C/V	farad	F
magnetic field	$N \cdot A^{-1} \cdot m^{-1}$	tesla	T
(radio)activity	1/s or s^{-1}	becquerel	Bq

APPENDIX 3

SI PREFIXES

Factor	Prefix	Symbol	Origin
10^{24}	yotta	Y	Italian *ott(o)* — eight (3 × 8 = 24)
10^{21}	zetta	Z	Italian *etta* — seven (3 × 7 = 21)
10^{18}	exa	E	Greek *exa* — out of
10^{15}	peta	P	Greek *peta* — spread out
10^{12}	tera	T	Greek *teratos* — monster
10^{9}	giga	G	Greek *gigas* — giant
10^{6}	mega	M	Greek *mega* — great
10^{3}	kilo	k	Greek *khilioi* — thousand
10^{2}	hecto	h	Greek *hekaton* — hundred
10^{1}	deca[1]	da	Greek *deka* — ten
10^{-1}	deci	d	Latin *decimus* — tenth
10^{-2}	centi	c	Latin *centum* — hundred
10^{-3}	milli	m	Latin *mille* — thousand
10^{-6}	micro	µ	Greek *micros* — very small
10^{-9}	nano	n	Greek *nanos* — dwarf
10^{-12}	pico	p	Italian *piccolo* — small
10^{-15}	femto	f	Greek *femten* — fifteen
10^{-18}	atto	a	Danish *atten* — eighteen
10^{-21}	zepto	z	Greek *(h)epto* — seven (-3 × 7 = -21)
10^{-24}	yocto	y	Greek *octo* — eight (-3 × 8 = -24)

[1] Alternative spelling: deka.

APPENDIX 4

NUMERICAL CONSTANTS

FUNDAMENTAL PHYSICAL CONSTANTS

Name	Symbol	Value
| Charge of electron |	e	1.602×10^{-19} C
Avogadro's number	N_A	6.022×10^{23} mol^{-1}
Planck's constant	h	6.626×10^{-34} J·s
Atomic mass unit	u	1.661×10^{-27} kg
Speed of light in vacuum	c	2.998×10^{8} m/s
Mass of electron	m_e	$9.109\,382 \times 10^{-31}$ kg
Mass of proton	m_p	$1.672\,621 \times 10^{-27}$ kg
Mass of neutron	m_n	$1.674\,927 \times 10^{-27}$ kg
Boltzmann's constant	k	1.381×10^{-23} J/K
Rydberg constant	R	1.097×10^{7} m^{-1}

OTHER USEFUL CONSTANTS

Name	Value
Density of water (at 4.0°C)	1.00×10^{3} kg/m^3
Specific heat of water	4186 J·kg^{-1}·K^{-1}
Latent heat of vaporization of water	2.26×10^{6} J/kg
Latent heat of fusion of water	3.33×10^{5} J/kg
Average radius of Earth	6.37×10^{6} m
Average sun-Earth distance	1.50×10^{11} m

APPENDIX 5

TRIGONOMETRIC RELATIONS

SINE, COSINE, AND TANGENT

The trigonometric functions, such as sine (sin), cosine (cos), and tangent (tan), are defined in terms of the right-angled triangle shown in Figure A5-1. In that triangle, the sides are labelled relative to the angle theta (θ): o for opposite side, a for adjacent side, and h for hypotenuse. Then the defining equations of sin θ, cos θ, and tan θ are:

$$\sin\theta = \frac{\text{opposite side}}{\text{hypotenuse}} = \frac{o}{h} \qquad \textbf{(A5-1)}$$

$$\cos\theta = \frac{\text{adjacent side}}{\text{hypotenuse}} = \frac{a}{h} \qquad \textbf{(A5-2)}$$

$$\tan\theta = \frac{\text{opposite side}}{\text{adjacent side}} = \frac{o}{a} \qquad \textbf{(A5-3)}$$

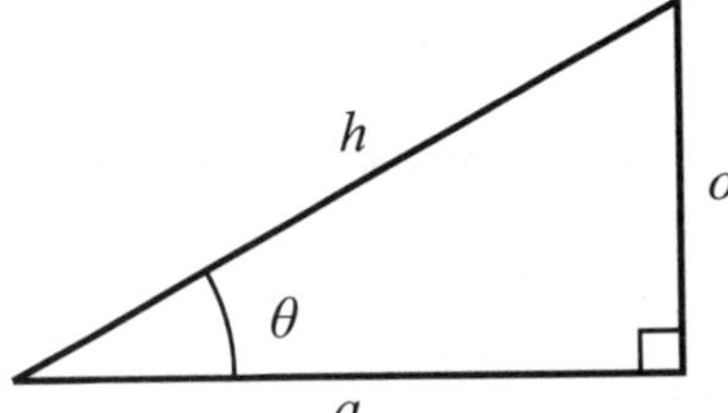

Figure A5-1 *The right-angled triangle used to define sin θ, cos θ, and tan θ.*

Based on these defining equations, you should be able to prove that tan θ = sin θ / cos θ.

If θ is a very small angle, sin $\theta \approx$ tan θ, as you can verify in Figure A5-2. (You can also verify this on your calculator by comparing, for example, sin 0.5° with tan 0.5°.)

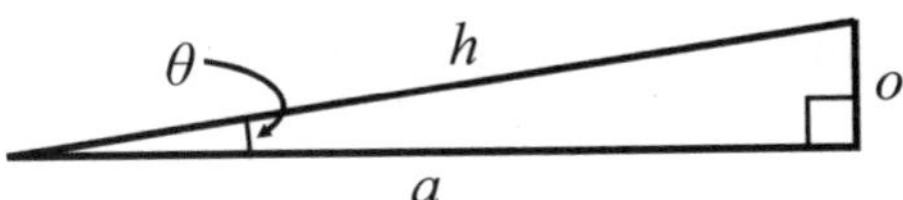

Figure A5-2 *For very small values of θ, sin θ is approximately equal to tan θ.*

Sample Problem A5-1

In Figure A5-1, if o is 3.50 cm and a is 4.20 cm, apply trigonometry to determine θ and h.

Solution: We begin by rearranging Eqn. A5-3, $\tan\theta = \frac{o}{a}$, to find θ.

$$\begin{aligned}\theta &= \tan^{-1}\frac{o}{a}\\ &= \tan^{-1}\frac{3.50\text{ cm}}{4.20\text{ cm}}\\ &= 39.8°\end{aligned}$$

Next we rearrange Eqn. A5-1, $\sin\theta = \frac{o}{h}$, to find h, although Eqn. A5-2 works equally well.

$$\begin{aligned} h &= \frac{o}{\sin\theta} \\ &= \frac{3.50\text{ cm}}{\sin 39.8°} \\ &= 5.47\text{ cm} \end{aligned}$$

Thus, the length of h is 5.47 cm. (In this example, the solution can also be found by using the law of Pythagoras, $h^2 = o^2 + a^2$, which applies to right-angled triangles.)

SINE LAW

For any triangle, such as the one in Figure A5-3, the sine law applies:

$$\frac{\sin A}{a} = \frac{\sin B}{b} = \frac{\sin C}{c} \qquad \textbf{(A5-4)}$$

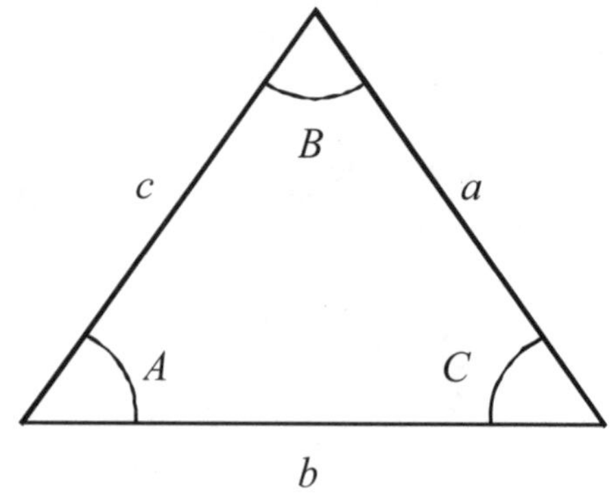

Figure A5-3 *In this triangle, side a is opposite angle A, etc.*

Sample Problem A5-2

In Figure A5-3, if $A = 31.5°$, $C = 40.2°$, and $c = 13.2$ cm, find the length of a.

Solution: Rearranging the equation $\frac{\sin A}{a} = \frac{\sin C}{c}$ to determine a, we have:

$$\begin{aligned} a &= \frac{c\sin A}{\sin C} \\ &= \frac{(13.2\text{ cm})(\sin 31.5°)}{\sin 40.2°} \\ &= 10.7\text{ cm} \end{aligned}$$

Thus, the length of a is 10.7 cm.

COSINE LAW

For any triangle, such as the one in Figure A5-3, the cosine law applies:

$$a^2 = b^2 + c^2 - 2bc\cos A \quad \textbf{(A5-5)}$$

Depending on what is given and what is required to find, other useful forms of the cosine law are:

$$b^2 = a^2 + c^2 - 2ac\cos B \quad \textbf{(A5-6)}$$

$$c^2 = a^2 + b^2 - 2ab\cos C \quad \textbf{(A5-7)}$$

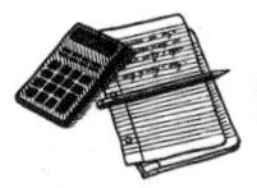

Sample Problem A5-3

In Figure A5-3, if $a = 4.5$, $b = 5.5$, and $c = 6.5$, find angle A.

Solution: From Eqn. A5-5,

$$2bc\cos A = b^2 + c^2 - a^2$$

$$\cos A = \frac{b^2 + c^2 - a^2}{2bc}$$

$$A = \cos^{-1}\left(\frac{b^2 + c^2 - a^2}{2bc}\right)$$

$$= \cos^{-1}\left(\frac{5.5^2 + 6.5^2 - 4.5^2}{2(5.5)(6.5)}\right)$$

$$= 43°$$

Thus, angle A is 43°.

TRIGONOMETRIC IDENTITIES

The definitions of sine and cosine can be applied to any angles, whether they are in triangles or not. The following relationships or trigonometric identities are useful in some circumstances in this text.

$$\sin 2\theta = 2\sin\theta\cos\theta \quad \textbf{(A5-8)}$$

$$\sin^2\theta + \cos^2\theta = 1 \quad \textbf{(A5-9)}$$

$$\cos(360° - \theta) = \cos\theta \quad \textbf{(A5-10)}$$

 **Practice**

A5-1 Refer to Figure A5-1 to determine the unknown quantities:
(a) If $\theta = 36°$ and $a = 1.4$ m, find h.
(b) If $\theta = 28.5°$ and $h = 65.8$ mm, find a.
(c) If $h = 0.85$ km and $a = 0.39$ km, apply trigonometry to find o.
(d) If $h = 55.8$ cm and $o = 17.1$ cm, find a. (Apply trigonometry, and then check your answer by applying the law of Pythagoras.)
[Ans. (a) 1.7 m (b) 57.8 mm (c) 0.76 km (d) 53.1 cm]

A5-2 Refer to Figure A5-3 to determine the unknown quantities:
(a) If $B = 41°$, $C = 17°$, and $b = 12$ cm, find c.
(b) If $A = 106°$, $a = 28.5$ mm, $c = 10.2$ mm, find angle C.
(c) If $a = 8.2$ cm, $b = 7.1$ cm, and c = 6.0 cm, find angle B.
(d) If $C = 33.3°$, $a = 18.5$ m, and $b = 26.5$ m, find c.
[Ans. (a) 5.3 cm (b) 20.1° (c) 58° (d) 15.0 m]

A5-3 An athlete's arm is injured and is placed in a sling such that the angle between the upper arm and the forearm is 62°. The distance from the tip of the shoulder (*S*) to the tip of the elbow (*E*) is *SE* = 37 cm. The distance from the tip of the shoulder to the tip of the end of the open hand (*H*) is *SH* = 44 cm. Determine the length (*EH*) of the forearm. [Ans. 47 cm]

A5-4 A roofer places a box of nails on a roof that is at an angle of 22.5° to the horizontal. The force of gravity acting on the box is 49.0 N vertically downward. Determine the component of the force on the box that is (a) parallel to the roof and (b) perpendicular to the roof. (Note: Figure 5-25 on page 5-28 will help you visualize the forces in this situation.)
[Ans. (a) 18.8 N (b) 45.3 N]

APPENDIX 6

DATA FOR THE SUN, MOON, AND PLANETS

Object	Mass (kg)	Radius (m)	Mean density (kg/m^3)	Surface gravity (m/s^2)	Period of rotation (days)	Mean distance from Earth (m)
Moon	7.35×10^{22}	1.74×10^{6}	3340	1.62	27.3	3.84×10^{8}
Sun	1.99×10^{30}	6.96×10^{8}	1410	274	≈ 26	1.50×10^{11}

Planet	Mean distance from sun (10^6 km)	Period of revolution (years)	Mass (kg)	Equatorial radius (km)	Surface gravity (Earth $g = 1$)	Period of rotation[2] (days)
Mercury	58	0.241	3.30×10^{23}	2 439	0.39	58.6
Venus	108	0.615	4.87×10^{24}	6 052	0.90	243
Earth	150	1.00	5.98×10^{24}	6 378	1.00	0.997
Mars	228	1.88	6.42×10^{23}	3 397	0.38	1.026
Jupiter	778	11.9	1.90×10^{27}	71 398	2.58	0.41
Saturn	1430	29.5	5.67×10^{26}	60 000	1.11	0.43
Uranus	2870	84.0	8.70×10^{25}	25 400	1.07	0.65
Neptune	4500	165	1.03×10^{26}	24 300	1.40	0.77
Pluto[3]	5910	248	6.6×10^{23}	2 500	0.02	6.39

[2] relative to the stars

[3] In late 2006, Pluto was demoted from a planet to a pseudoplanet. Astronomers argued that Pluto's orbit is quite flat (oval), and if Pluto is a planet then there are other satellites orbiting the sun even farther away that could be classified as planets. To prevent having to add several more planets, astronomers decided to call Pluto something other than a planet, thus the name "pseudoplanet." The authors of this text sincerely hope that this demotion does not take away from the amazing story of how Pluto was discovered after painstaking research by a 24-year-old lab assistant, Clyde W. Tombaugh, working in the Lowell Observatory in Flagstaff, Arizona, in 1930.

INDEX

SPECIAL FEATURES

Calculation Tip: 8-21
Learning Tip: 11-13
Math Tip: 1-7, 2-11, 2-26, 2-34, 3-2, 3-9, 4-4, 9-5, 9-22, 14-14
Nobel Prize: 5-39, 10-22, 14-23, 15-3, 15-14, 16-5, 16-20, 16-25
Notation Tip: 2-6, 2-33, 3-6, 5-6, 5-18
Problem-solving Tip: 2-23, 5-16, 5-29, 6-7
Profile: 2-29, 5-35, 14-5, 15-11
Reference Tip: 11-4, 15-5
Units Tip: 5-17, 7-3, 7-15, 7-33, 8-4, 11-3, 11-7, 11-11, 11-18, 15-6, 15-8, 15-17, 16-6, 16-23

A

absorption spectrum 14-22
acceleration
  and graphing 2-16, 2-17
  and equations for constant acceleration 2-20 to 2-24
  average (in 1-D) 2-14
  average (in 2-D) 4-8
  centripetal 4-25
  defined 2-14
  due to gravity 2-28, 2-31, 5-9, 5-10
  due to gravity on Earth 2-32
  equations for constant (1-D) 2-22
  instantaneous (in 1-D) 2-18
  instantaneous (in 2-D) 4-9
  in two dimensions 4-8, 4-9
  of electrically charged particles
  variable 2-18
action-reaction 5-32, 5-33
air-wedge interference 14-36
Alhazen (965 – 1038) 14-28
alternating current (AC) 12-27
ammeter 12-19
ampere 11-21
  defined A-1
Ampère, André Marie (1775-1836) 11-21
amplitude of a periodic wave 13-7
angle
  banking 6-13
  Brewster's 14-48
  of emergence 14-25
  of incidence 13-13
  of reflection 13-13
  of refraction 13-14
  of refraction of light 14-25
  polarization 14-47
analyzer 14-43
anode 15-2
antinode 13-20
antiparticle 15-20
Aristarchus 9-1
Aristotle (384 B.C. to 322 B.C.) 2-28
assumed uncertainty (in measurement) 1-13
atom 10-1
  Bohr model of 16-5
  excited state of 16-13
  ground state of 16-12
  ionization of 16-13
  metastable state of 16-25
  origin of word 16-1
  Rutherford model of 16-2
atomic force microscope 15-26
atomic spectra 16-2 to 16-4
aurora
  australis 16-12
  borealis 16-12
average
  acceleration 2-14, 4-7
  speed 2-1
axis of polarization 14-43

B

Bacon, Francis 2-29
balance
  torsion: electric force 10-9
  torsion: gravitational force 9-5
Balmer, J.J. (1825-1898) 16-5
Balmer's equation 16-4, 16,5
Balmer series 16-5
banking angle 6-13
Barringer Crater 8-17
base unit
  defined 1-4
  length 1-5
  mass 1-5
  time 1-5
Basov, N. 16-25
battery
  defined 12-8
  parallel connection 12-20
  series connection 12-20
becquerel A-2
birefringence 14-49
  and stress 14-50
black hole
  defined 9-28
body wave 13-5
Bohr, Niels (1885-1962) 10-1, 16-2, 16-5
Bohr
  model 16-5
  model and electron energies 16-11
  model in detail 16-7 to 16-13
  orbit radii (table) 16-10
  radius 16-9
bold-face type (for vectors) 3-1
Brackett series 16-5
Bragg, William and Lawrence 14-23
Brewster, David (1781-1868)) 14-47, 14-48
Brewster's angle 14-48
bright line spectrum 14-21
British thermal unit 7-27
Brownian motion 15-12

C

calcite 14-47
calorie, Calorie 7-27
candela **defined A-1**
Cavendish, Henry (1731-1810) 9-5, 10-10
cathode 15-2
cell (electric) 12-7
centre of mass 7-26
centrifugal force
  and Earth 6-19
  defined 6-19
centrifuge 6-19
centripetal acceleration
  defined 4-25
  direction of 4-25
  magnitude of 4-26, 4-27
centripetal force
  defined 6-9
  summary 6-14
  work done by 7-6
cesium clock 1-5
charge (electric)
  elementary 10-22
  law of conservation of 10-3
  like 10-3
  negative 10-1
  net 10-1, 10-3
  neutral 10-1, 10-4
  positive 10-1
  transfer of 10-2
  unlike 10-3
charging
  by conduction 10-7
  by contact 10-7
  by induction 10-8
circuit
  alternating current 12-27
  closed 12-9
  diagrams 12-9, 12-18
  electric 12-8
  open 12-9
circular motion
  and work 7-6
  uniform 4-24
classical physics 15-1
closed circuit 12-9
cloud, electron 16-21
coefficient
  of kinetic friction 6-3
  of resistivity (temperature) 12-4
  of static friction 6-2, 6-3
coherent light 16-25, 14-7
coherent waves 14-7

collisions
  completely inelastic 8-16
  elastic 8-15
  inelastic 8-15
  solving problems 8-17
  types of 8-16
colours
  of the visible spectrum 14-9
completely inelastic collision 8-16
components (of a vector) 3-5, 3-6
compression 13-4
compression wave: see wave, longitudinal
Compton, Arthur (1892-1962) 15-15
  Nobel prize 15-16
Compton
  effect 15-15
  scattering 15-15
conduction
  charging by 10-6, 10-7
conductor
  electric 10-6, 12-3
  metallic 12-4
  semi 10-6
  super 10-6
conservation of energy (law of) 7-17
conservation of momentum
  in collisions 8-11, 8-12, 8-15, 8-16
  in one dimension 8-7 to 8-13
  in two dimensions 8-22, 8-23
  law of 8-7
constant
  numerical constants A-4
constructive interference 13-19, 13-25
contact, charging by 10-7
contact force 5-2
continuous spectrum 14-21
conversion of energy 7-28
conventional current 11-21
Copernicus, Nicholas (1473-1543) 9-2
Coriolis force
  and Earth 6-20
  defined 6-19
correspondence principle 16-13
cosine law A-6, A-7
Coulomb, Charles Augustin (1736-1806) 10-10
Coulomb's law 10-10
coulomb (unit of electric charge) 10-11
crest 13-24
criterion, Rayleigh's 14-16
crystallography, X-ray 14-23
current, electric
  alternating (AC) 12-27
  defined 11-21
  direct (DC) 12-26
  measuring electric 12-19
cut-off potential: see stopping potential
cycle
  of vibration 13-1
  phase of 13-2

D

Dalton, John (1766-1844) 16-1
Davisson, Clinton 15-22
de Broglie electron waves 16-17, 16-18
de Broglie, Louis (1892-1987) 15-22, 16-17
  Nobel prize 15-22
de Broglie wavelength 15-22
Democritus 16-1
density
  physical 1-11
  optical 14-24
derived unit 1-8
description
  qualitative 1-1
  quantitative 1-1
destructive interference 13-19, 13-25
deterministic theory 16-23
dichroic crystals 14-43
difference
  electric potential 11-9
  path 13-24
diffraction
  and Huygen's principle 14-1
  Fraunhofer 14-11
  Fresnel 14-11
  grating 14-18
  in two and three dimensions 14-23
  of light 14-1
  of waves 13-30, 13-31
  single-slit 14-11 to 14-14
  X-ray 14-23, 15-22, 15-23
dimensional analysis 1-11
  defined 1-12
direct current (DC) 12-26
displacement
  defined 2-4
  in two dimensions 3-3, 4-2
  maximum horizontal range 4-22, 4-23
  resultant 4-3
distance 2-1, 3-3
  and speed 2-1
distribution, probability 16-20
double-slit interference of light 14-4
dry cell 12-8
duality, wave-particle 15-21
Dufay, Charles (1698-1739) 10-3, 10-4
dynamics 5-1

E

efficiency
  defined 7-28
  table 7-29
effect
  Compton 15-13
  photoelectric 15-1, 15-2
Einstein, Albert (1879-1955)
  and atomic sizes 16-2
  and the photoelectric effect 15-2
  Nobel Prize 15-3
  profile 15-11
Einstein (continued)
  theory of gravity 9-29
Einstein's photoelectric equation 15-4
elastic collision 8-15
electric
  cell 12-7
  charge 10-1
  charge, law of conservation of 10-3
  charge, transfer of 10-2
  circuit 12-8
  conductor 10-6, 12-3
  current 11-21
  dry cell 12-8
  field 10-16
  field and e.m. waves 14-38
  field due to a single charge 10-16, 10-17
  field due to more than one charge 10-17, 10-18
  field lines 10-19, 10-20
  force 5-39, 10-3, 10-14
  grounding 10-8, 12-30
  insulator 10-6
  polarization 10-4
  potential 11-9, 11-11 to 11-17
  potential difference 11-10
  potential energy 11-1, 11-2, 11-6
  power 12-24, 12-25
  resistance 12-1
  resistivity 12-4
  voltage 11-10
electrocardiogram 11-10
electroencephalogram 11-10
electrolyte 12-8
electromagnetic
  spectrum 14-40
  waves 14-38, 14-39
electron 10-1
  and electromagnetic waves 14-38
  and the electron-volt 11-12
  charge on 10-11
  cloud 16-21
  conduction 10-6
  microscopes 15-24 to 15-26
  origin of word 16-8
  transition 16-11
electron (Greek) 10-2
electron-positron pair production 15-20
electron-volt 7-27, 11-12
electrostatic precipitator 10-22
electrostatics: see static electricity
electroscope, leaf 10-8
electroweak force 5-39
elementary charge 10-22
emergence, angle of 14-25
emission
  spectra 14-21
  spontaneous 16-25
  stimulated 16-25
energy
  and collisions 8-14, 8-15
  and power 7-33
  and the electron-volt 11-12

energy (continued)
chemical 7-25
conservation 7-18, 7-30
conversions 7-28, 7-29
elastic potential 7-25
elastic potential in sports 7-26, 7-27
electrical 7-25
electrical potential 7-25
electric potential 11-1, 11-2
electric potential of point charges 11-6
food 7-25
gravitational potential 7-13
gravitational potential in general 9-21, 9-22
internal 7-21
kinetic 7-9
law of conservation of 7-17
level diagram 16-12, 16-13
levels 16-12, 16-13
light 7-25
mechanical 7-19
nuclear 7-25
of a photon 15-3
of electrons 16-11, 16-12
see also kilowatt·hour
sound 7-26
sources 7-30, 7-31
thermal 6-4, 7-21
transferred (heat) 7-22
units 7-27
equation
Balmer's 16-5
kinematics (1-D) 2-22
Einstein's photoelectric 15-4
universal wave 13-9
error
percent 1-14
round-off 1-16
escape speed
defined 9-26
table for planets 9-27
estimation
Fermi question 1-18
order-of-magnitude 1-17
event horizon 9-28
excitation (of electrons) 15-20
excited state 16-13
experiment, Franck-Hertz 16-15
experiment, Millikan 10-22

F

farad A-2
FBD: see free-body diagram
Fermi, Enrico (1901-1954) 1-18
Fermi question 1-18
fictitious force
defined 6-17
see also centrifugal force and Coriolis force
field
electric 10-15 to 10-17, 14-38
field (continued)
gravitational 9-12, 9-13
lines, electric 10-19, 10-20
magnetic 14-38
first law of motion 5-12
solving problems 5-15 to 5-22
fixed-end reflection 13-11
force
action 5-32, 5-33
addition 5-5
and momentum 8-2, 8-7
average and change of momentum 8-3
centrifugal 6-17 to 6-19
centripetal 6-9, 7-6
contact 5-2
Coriolis 6-19 to 6-20
diagram: see free-body diagram
electric 10-3
electrical 5-39
electromagnetic interaction 5-39
electroweak 5-39
fictitious 6-17
friction 5-2, 6-1 to 6-6
fundamental 5-38, 5-39
gravity 5-1
microscope (atomic) 15-26
normal 5-1, 6-2
nuclear strong 5-39
nuclear weak 5-39
of gravity 5-10, 9-2, 9-5, 9-7, 9-10, 9-11
reaction 5-32, 5-33
resultant 5-5
tension 5-2
work done by a constant force 7-1
Foucault, Jean 14-25
frame of reference 6-17
inertial 6-17
noninertial 6-17
Franck-Hertz experiment 16-15
Franck, James 16-15
Franklin, Benjamin 10-2, 11-24
Fraunhofer diffraction 14-12
Fraunhofer, Josef (1787-1826) 14-12
free-body diagram 5-16
defined 5-3
free-fall 9-19, 9-20
calculations involving 2-32
defined 2-28
frequency
fundamental 13-21
of revolution 4-27
of vibration 13-1, 13-2
resonant of a periodic wave 13-7
threshold 15-2
Fresnel, Augustin (1788-1827) 14-12
Fresnel diffraction 14-12
friction
coefficient of kinetic 6-2
coefficient of static 6-2
force 5-2
kinetic 6-2
rolling 6-1
friction (continued)
static 6-2
work done by 7-21
function
wave 16-21
work 15-4
work, table of 15-4
fundamental
frequency 13-21
mode 13-21

G

g **defined 2-31**
see also acceleration due to gravity
Galileo Galilei (1564-1643) 2-29, 5-13, 9-2
and the pendulum clock 14-2
profile 2-29 to 2-31
Galilei: see Galileo
Galvani, Luigi 12-7
galvanometer 12-19
geocentric hypothesis 9-1
Germer, Lester 15-22
grand unified theory (GUT) 5-38
graph
and tangents 2-9, 2-10
constant acceleration motion 2-16
current vs. voltage 12-2
non-uniform motion 2-9
slope of line 2-7
terminal speed 2-36
uniform motion 2-7
grating
diffraction 14-18
holographic 14-20
reflection 14-18
replica 14-19
transmission 14-18
gravitation
acceleration on planets (table) 9-10
between extended objects 9-5
constant of 9-2, 9-5
due to planets, etc., 9-7
field 9-12
force and field 9-14
law of universal 9-2
on Earth's surface 9-10, 9-11, A-9
potential energy in general 9-21, 9-22
gravitational field
and gravitational force 9-14
defined 9-13
gravitational potential energy
defined 7-13
in general 9-21 to 9-24
gravity
acceleration due to 2-28, 5-9, 5-10
defined 5-1
due to planets, etc., 9-10, A-9
force of 5-9, 9-14
g values on Earth 2-32, 9-10, 9-11
measuring acceleration due to 2-31

greenhouse effect 7-31
Grimaldi, Francesco (1618-1663) 14-1
ground state 16-12
grounding 10-8, 12-30
GUT: see theory

H

harmonic, first 13-21
harmonics 13-21
heat 7-22
Heisenberg uncertainty principle 16-22
Heisenberg, Werner (1901-1976) 16-20
heliocentric hypothesis 9-1
helium-neon laser 16-26
Hertz, Gustav 16-15, 16-16
Hertz, Heinrich 15-1, 16-15
hertz A-2
Hillier, James 15-25
hologram
  applications of 16-29
  cylindrical 16-29
  defined 16-28
  white-light 16-29
holographic grating 14-20
holography 16-28
Hooke, Robert 14-1
horizon, event 9-28
horsepower 7-33
Huygens, Christiaan (1629-1695) 8-12, 14-1, 14-2
Huygens'
  principle 14-2
  wavelets 14-6, 14-13, 14-14

I

Iceland spar 14-49
impulse 8-3
incidence, angle of 13-13
index of refraction 13-14, 14-26
induction, charging by 10-8
inelastic collision 8-15
inertia
  defined 5-13
  law of (Newton's first law) 5-13
inertial frame of reference 6-17
infrared waves 14-40
ink-jet printer 10-22
instantaneous acceleration
  defined 2-18
  equation 2-18
instantaneous speed
  defined 2-3
instantaneous velocity
  and graphing 2-9, 2-10
  defined 2-6
  equation 2-10
insulator, electric 10-6
interference
  air wedge 14-36
  constructive 13-19
interference (continued)
  destructive 13-19
  in one dimension 13-19
  in two dimensions 13-23 to 13-27
  thin-film 14-31 to 14-33
internal energy: see thermal energy
inversion, population 16-26
ion
  negative 10-1
  positive 10-1
ionization 16-12
iridescence 14-31

J

Jo blocks 6-4
Johansson, C.E. 6-4
joule 7-2, 7-15, 7-33, A-2
Joule, James Prescott (1818-1889) 7-2

K

kelvin A-1
Kepler, Johannes (1571-1630) 9-2
kilocalorie 7-25
kilogram 1-5, 5-9, A-1
kilowatt·hour 7-39
kinematics
  defined 2-1
  quantities in 2-23
  two-dimensional 4-1
kinetic energy
  and collisions 8-16, 8-17
  and work 7-9
  defined 7-9
  units 7-11
kinetic friction
  coefficient of 6-2
  defined 6-3

L

Land, Edwin 14-44
laser
  and holography 16-27
  defined 16-25
  helium-neon 16-27, 16-28
  uses of 16-26
Laue spots 14-23
law
  cosine A-6, A-7
  Coulomb's 10-10
  of conservation of electric charge 10-3
  of conservation of energy 7-17
  of conservation of energy in collisions 8-16, 8-17
  of conservation of momentum 8-7
  of conservation of momentum in collisions 8-11, 8-12, 8-15, 8-16
  of exponents 1-7
  of inertia: see Newton's first law
  of universal gravitation 9-2
law (continued)
  inverse square 9-2, 10-10, 10-17
  Newton's first (of inertia) 5-12
  Newton's second 5-8
  Newton's third 5-32
  Ohm's 12-1
  sine A-6
  Snell's, of refraction 14-28
leaf electroscope 10-8
length
  of a wave 13-8
  path 13-24
light
  amplification 16-24
  and air-wedge interference 14-36
  and electromagnetic waves 14-38, 14-39
  and resolution 14-15
  and the electromagnetic spectrum 14-38, 14-39, 14-40
  and thin-film interference 14-31 to 14-35
  coherence of 14-7, 14-8
  coherent 16-25
  diffraction of 14-1
  double refraction 14-49
  interference of 14-4
  line spectrum 14-21
  measuring wavelengths of 14-7
  monochromatic 16-25
  plane polarized 14-42
  polarization of 14-41 to 14-50
  quanta 15-2
  refraction of 14-24 to 14-27
  resolution 14-15, 14-16
  scattering 14-48
  single-slit diffraction 14-11 to 14-15
  spectrum 14-21
  speed of 14-26, 14-38
  visible 14-9, 14-40
lights
  northern 16-12
  southern 16-12
lightning 11-24, 11-25
line, nodal 13-39
linear momentum 8-1
lines, electric field 10-19 to 10-21
line spectrum 14-21
longitudinal
  vibration 13-1
  wave 13-4

M

magnetic field and e.m. waves 14-38
Maiman, Theodore 16-25
maser 16-25
mass 5-10
  centre of 7-26
  unit of 1-5
matter waves 15-23
Maxwell, James Clerk (1831-1879) 14-38, 14-40
maximum interference 14-7

measurement
and calculations 1-14, 1-15
and estimations 1-17
and percent error 1-14
and round-off error 1-16
and significant digits 1-14
and types of quantities 1-19
and uncertainty 1-13
defined 1-1
in our daily lives 1-2
in physics 1-3
in the past 1-2
metric 1-4, A-1
of force 5-9
of weight 5-10
see also units of measurement
mechanical energy 7-19
mechanics, quantum 16-20
metastable state 16-25
meter, electric
ammeter 12-19
galvanometer 12-19
multimeter 12-19
voltmeter 12-19
metre 1-5, A-1
metric system 1-4, A-1
conversions 1-8, 1-9
derived units A-2
prefixes 1-8, A-3
microscope
electron 15-24
optical 15-24
atomic force (AFM) 15-26
scanning electron 15-25
scanning tunnelling (STM) 15-26
transmission electron 15-25
Millikan, Robert 10-22
Millikan experiment 10-22
minimum interference 14-8
mode
first harmonic 13-21
fundamental 13-21
model
Bohr 16-5, 16-7 to 16-13
Rutherford 16-2
Thomson 16-1
mole A-1
molecules, polar 10-4
momentum
and collisions 8-11, 8-12, 8-15, 8-16
and positron emission tomography (PET) imaging 8-10
and rocket propulsion 8-9
and sports 8-13
change in 8-2
components of 8-1
defined 8-1
equation 8-1
in two dimensions 8-22, 8-23
law of conservation of 8-7
linear 8-1
of a photon 15-16, 15-17
monochromatic light 16-25
motion
and graphing 2-7
circular 4-24
circular (and work) 7-6
Newton's laws of 5-12 (first), 5-8 (second), 5-32 (third)
non-uniform 2-9
one-dimensional Chapter 2
projectile 4-12, 10-23 (see also projectile motion)
two-dimensional 4-1 (and Chapter 4)
uniform 2-3
uniform circular 4-24

N

nanotechnology 1-3
negative ion 10-1
net force: see resultant force
net vector: see resultant
neutral charge 10-4
neutron 10-1
neutron star 9-28
Newton, Sir Isaac (1642-1727)
and diffraction of light 14-3
first law 5-12
law of universal gravitation 9-2
profile 5-8, 5-35 to 5-37
second law 5-8, 5-9, 8-3
third law 5-32
newton (unit of force) 5-9, A-2
Newton's rings 14-37
nodal line 13-25
node 13-19
in a standing wave 13-20, 13-21
noninertial frame of reference
and Earth 6-18, 6-20
defined 6-17
non-ohmic resistance 12-2
non-uniform motion 2-9
normal 13-13
normal force 5-1, 6-2
northern lights 16-12
nuclear strong force 5-39
nuclear weak force 5-39
nucleus (of an atom) 10-1, 16-2
number, quantum 16-9

O

oceanic waves 13-5
ohm 12-1, A-2
Ohm, Georg Simon (1787-1854) 12-1
ohm·metre 12-4
ohmic resistance 12-2
Ohm's law 12-1
open circuit 12-9
open-end reflection 13-11
optical
density 14-25, 14-26
microscope 15-24
orbits 9-16, 9-17
order-of-magnitude estimation
defined 1-17
see also Fermi question
oscilloscope 10-21

P

pair production (electron-positron) 15-20
parallel connection (electric) 12-13
particle-wave duality: see wave-particle duality
pascal A-2
Paschen series 16-5
path
difference 13-24
length 13-24
pendulum, simple 13-1
percent error 1-14
period
of a periodic wave 13-7
of revolution 4-27
of vibration 13-1
periodic wave, 13-7
amplitude 13-7
speed of 13-9
wavelength 13-8
PET scans 8-10, 8-11
Pfund series 16-5
phase, 13-2, 13-8
in 13-8
photocathode 15-2
photocell 15-1, 15-2
photoelectric effect, 15-1, 15-2
applications of 15-9, 15-10
in general 15-9
photoelectric equation (Einstein's) 15-4
photoelectrons 15-2
photon 15-2
energy of 15-3
interactions with matter 15-19, 15-20
momentum of 15-16
origin of name 15-15
phototube 15-2
plane polarized light 14-42
Planck's constant 15-3
Planck, Max (1958-1947) 15-3
planetary data A-9
physics, classical 15-1
polarization
angle 14-47
axis of 14-43
by reflection 14-46, 14-47
by double refraction 14-49
by scattering 14-48
by selective absorption 14-43
filters 14-43
of light 14-41
electric 10-4
of transverse waves 14-42
polarizer 14-43
polar molecules 10-4

Polaroid (filter) 14-43
population inversion 16-26
position 2-4
  and velocity 2-5
positive ion 10-1
positron 15-20
positron emission tomography (PET)
  imaging 8-10
positronium 16-16
potential
  cut-off 15-7
  retarding 15-7
  stopping 15-7
potential difference, electric 11-10
potential, electric
  defined 11-9
  due to point charges 11-17
  in a uniform electric filed 11-16
potential energy
  electric 11-1
  electric, of point charges 11-6
  gravitational 7-13
power
  electric, average AC 12-28
  defined 7-32
  dissipated in a resistor 12-24
  electric 12-23
  electric average 12-28
  horsepower 7-33
  unit of 7-33
Prebus, Albert 15-25
precipitator, electrostatic 10-22
prefixes (metric) 1-8, A-3
primary (P) wave 13-5
principle
  correspondence 16-13
  Heisenberg uncertainty 16-21
  Huygens' 14-2
  of superposition 13-19
printer, ink-jet 10-22
probability 16-23
probability distribution 16-20
projectile
  defined 4-11
  maximum range 4-20
projectile motion 4-11 to 4-23, 10-24
  conclusions about 4-12
  defined 4-12
  equations for 4-13
  maximum range 4-22, 4-23
  Sections 4.3 and 4.4
Prokhorov, A. 16-25
propulsion, rocket 8-9, 8-10
proton 10-1
  charge on 10-11
pulsar 9-28
pulse 13-10; see also wave
Ptolemy, Claudius 9-1, 14-28

Q

qualitative descriptions 1-1
quanta (light) 15-2
quantitative descriptions 1-1
quantity
  scalar 1-19
  vector 1-19
quantization 15-2
  of electrons 16-5
quantum: see quanta
quantum mechanics 16-20
quantum number 16-9
quark 10-1
quintessence 2-29

R

radius,
  Bohr 16-9
  Schwartzchild 9-28
range (horizontal) 4-22, 4-23
rarefaction 13-4
ray 13-12
Rayleigh, J. (1942-1919) 14-17
  Nobel prize 14-16
Rayleigh's criterion 14-15, 14-16
reaction (and action) forces 5-32
reference, frame of 6-20
reflection
  and polarization 14-46, 14-47
  angle of 13-13
  fixed-end 13-11
  of waves in one dimension 13-10, 13-11
  of waves in two dimensions 13-12, 13-13
  open-end 13-11
reflection grating 14-18
refraction
  angle of 13-14
  angle of (light) 14-25
  defined 13-14
  double 14-49
  index of 13-15, 14-26, 14-27
  of light 14-24
  Snell's law of 14-27, 14-28
relativity, theory of 9-29
remote control 15-10
replica grating 14-17
resistance
  electric 12-1
  equivalent, in series 12-12
  equivalent, in parallel 12-13, 12-14
  non-ohmic 12-2
  ohmic 12-2
resistivity, electric 12-4
  temperature coefficient of 12-5, 12-6
resistor 12-2
  colour code 12-3
  electric power dissipated in 12-24
resistors
  in parallel 12-11, 12-13, 12-14
  in series 12-11, 12-12
resonance 13-2
  of electron waves 16-18
resonant frequency 13-2
resolution 14-16
resultant
  displacement 4-3
  force 5-5
  force and momentum 8-7
  vector 3-3
revolution
  frequency of 4-27
  period of 4-27
Richmann, Georg 11-24
rocket propulsion 8-9, 8-10
root-mean-square (rms)
  voltage 12-28
  current 12-28
round-off error 1-16
Rutherford, Ernest (1871-1937) 16-1, 16-2
Rutherford model 16-2
Rydberg constant 16-5

S

scalar: see scalar quantity
scalar quantity 1-19, 1-20
scanning electron microscope 15-25
scanning tunnelling microscope (STM) 15-26
scattering
  angle 15-17
  Compton 15-17
  of light 14-48
Schrödinger, Erwin (1887-1961) 16-20
Schwartzchild, Karl (1873-1916) 9-28
Schwartzchild radius 9-28
scientific notation
  defined 1-6
  examples 1-7
second 1-5, A-1
secondary (S) wave 13-5
second law of motion (Newton's) 5-8
  solving problems 5-15 to 5-22, 8-3
seismic wave 13-5
selective absorption (of light) 14-42 to 14-46
semiconductor 10-6
series
  Balmer 16-5
  Brackett 16-5
  connection (electric) 12-12
  electrochemical 12-7
  Paschen 16-5
  Pfund 16-5
  static electricity 10-3
Shelton, Ian 9-28
SI : see Système International d'Unités
significant digits
  defined 1-14
  rules of 1-14
simple pendulum 13-1
sine law A-6
single-slit diffraction 14-11 to 14-15
singularity 9-28
Snell, Willebrord (1591-1626) 14-28
Snell's law of refraction 14-28
solar mass 9-28

southern lights 16-12
spectra: see spectrum
spectrograph 14-21
spectrometer 14-21
spectroscope 14-21, 14-22
spectroscopy 14-21
spectrum 14-21
  absorption 14-22, 16-4
  bright line 14-21
  continuous 14-21, 16-2
  electromagnetic 14-38, 14-39
  emission 16-3
  hydrogen 14-22
  line 14-22, 16-3
  visible 14-9, 14-39
spontaneous emission 16-25
speed
  and distance 2-1
  average 2-1
  defined 2-1
  escape 9-26, 9-27
  instantaneous 2-3
  of a periodic wave 13-9
  of light 14-26, 14-27, 14-38
  terminal 2-36
spontaneous emission 16-25
standard form: see scientific notation
standard unit 1-4
standing wave
  and electrons 16-19
  pattern 13-20
star, neutron 9-28
state
  excited 16-13
  ground 16-12
  metastable 16-25
states, stationary 16-5
static electricity 10-3
  series 10-3
static friction
  coefficient of 6-2
  defined 6-2
stimulated emission 16-25
stopping potential 15-7
Stoney, Johnstone 16-8
stress birefringence 14-50
strong force: see nuclear strong force
superconductor 10-6
supercrest 13-19
supernova 9-28
superposition, principle of 13-19
supertrough 13-19
surface wave (tsunami) 13-5
Système International d'Unités (SI) 1-4
    base units A-1
    derived units A-2
    prefixes A-3

T

Tacoma Narrows Bridge 13-3
Tahiti 13-21
tangent to a curve 2-9
Teflon 6-3
temperature coefficient of resistivity 12-5
tension (force) 5-2
terminal speed
  defined 2-36
  graph 2-36
terminal velocity: see terminal speed
tesla A-2
theorem, work-energy 7-9, 7-10
theory
  deterministic 16-23
  grand unified (GUT) 5-39
  Einstein's, of relativity 9-29
  of everything (TOE) 5-39
  probabilistic 16-23
thermal energy 6-4, 7-21
thin-film interference 14-31 to 14-33
Thomson, George 15-22
Thomson, J.J. (1856-1940) 16-1
third law of motion 5-31
threshold frequency 15-2
time, unit of 1-5, A-1
TOE: see theory
torsional vibration 13-1
torsion balance, electric force 10-10
Townes, C.H. 16-25
transition 16-11
transmission grating 14-18
transverse
  electromagnetic wave 14-38, 14-39
  vibration 13-1
  wave 13-4
tribology 6-4
triboluminescence 6-4
trigonometric
  functions A-5
  relations A5 to A-8
trough 13-24
tsunami 13-5
tunneling microscope, scanning (STM) 15-26
two-source interference pattern 13-23 . . .

U

ultraviolet waves 14-40
uncertainty (in measurement) 1-13
uncertainty principle 16-22
uniform circular motion 4-24
uniform motion
  defined 2-3
  graphing 2-7
unit
  base 1-4
  British thermal 7-27
  derived 1-8
  electron·volt (eV) 11-12, 15-6, 15-8
  joule 7-2, 7-15, 7-33, A-2
  kilowatt·hour 7-35
  newton 5-9, A-2
  non-SI (for energy) 7-27
  standard 1-4
unit (continued)
  watt 7-33, A-2
  of Coulomb's constant 10-11
  of distance 1-5, A-1
  of electric charge 10-11
  of electric current 11-21, A-1
  of electric energy consumption 12-31
  of electric field 10-16
  of electric potential 11-10, 11-17
  of electric potential energy 11-3, 11-7
  of electric power 12-24, A-2
  of electric resistance 12-1, A-2
  of electric resistivity 12-4, A-2
  of energy 11-11, 11-12, A-2
  of gravitational constant 9-2
  in Heisenberg's uncertainty principle
    16-22
  of kinetic energy 7-11
  of length 1-5, A-1
  of mass 1-5, A-1
  of momentum 8-1
  of Rydberg constant 16-6
  of speed 1-8, A-2
  of time 1-5, A-1
  of work 7-11
units of measurement
  base 1-4, A-1
  derived 1-8, A-2
universal gravitation
  constant of 9-2, 9-5
  law of 9-2
universal wave equation 13-9

V

vector
  addition 3-3, 3-4
  addition, using components 3-7
  components and work 7-3
  components of 3-5, 3-6
  directions 3-2
  multiplying by a scalar 3-2
  properties of 3-1 to 3-3
  properties of vector addition 3-4
  resultant 3-3
  subtraction 3-5
  subtraction, for acceleration 4-8
  subtraction, using components 3-9
  sum: see resultant
  symbols 3-1
vector quantity 1-19; see also vector
velocity
  average 2-5, 4-5
  defined 2-5
  instantaneous 2-6 to 2-10, 4-6
  in two dimensions 4-6
vibration
  cycle of 13-1
  frequency of 13-1, 13-2
  longitudinal 13-1
  period of 13-1, 13-2
  torsional 13-1

transverse 13-1
visible spectrum 14-9
volt 11-10, A-2
and the electron·volt 11-12, 11-13
Volta, Alessandro 11-10, 12-7
voltage
electric 11-10
root-mean-square (rms) 12-28
voltmeter 12-19
von Laue, Max 14-23
Nobel prize 14-23

W

watt 7-33, A-2
Watt, James (1736-1819) 7-33
wave
body 13-5
compression 13-4
defined 13-4
diffraction of 13-30, 13-31
electromagnetic 14-38, 14-39
equation, universal 13-9
front 13-13
function of 16-21
infrared 14-40
interference 13-19
length 13-8
longitudinal 13-4
periodic 13-7
primary (P) 13-5
reflection of 13-11, 13-12
refraction of 13-14
secondary (S) 13-5
seismic 13-5
standing 13-20
standing, electron 16-19
surface 13-5
transmission of 13-11, 13-12
transverse 13-4
transverse, polarization of 14-42
tsunami (surface wave) 13-5
ultraviolet 14-40
universal equation 13-9
waves
and matter 15-23
coherent light 14-7
wavefront 13-29
wavelength 13-25
of visible light 14-7 to 14-9
wavelength, de Broglie 15-22
wave-particle duality 15-21
weak force: see nuclear weak force
weight 5-10
weightlessness 9-19
defined 9-20
work
and energy 7-9
defined 7-2
done by a constant force 7-1, 7-2
done by centripetal force 7-6
done by friction 7-21
unit of 7-2, 7-11
work-energy theorem 7-9, 7-10
work function 15-4

X

X ray
crystallography 14-23
diffraction 14-23
X rays
and the Compton effect 15-15

Y

Young, Thomas (1773-1829) 14-4, 14-6
Profile 14-5, 14-6
Young's double-slit experiment 14-5